THE BIG BASICS BOOK OF PCs

by Joe Kraynak, Lisa Bucki,
Gordon McComb, and Paul McFedries

QUE®

A Division of Macmillan Computer Publishing
201 West 103rd Street, Indianapolis, Indiana 46290 USA

International Standard Book Number:0-56761-624-0
Library of Congress Catalog Card Number: 95-69579

97 96 95 8 7 6 5 4 3 2 1

Interpretation of the printing code: the rightmost number of the first series of numbers is the year of the book's printing; the rightmost number of the second series of numbers is the number of the book's printing. For example, a printing code of 95-1 shows that the first printing of the book occurred in 1995.

Screen reproductions in this book were created by means of the program Collage Complete from Inner Media, Inc., Hollis, NH.

Printed in the United States of America

President
Roland Elgey

Vice President and Publisher
Marie Butler-Knight

Editorial Services Director
Elizabeth Keaffaber

Publishing Manager
Barry Pruett

Managing Editor
Michael Cunningham

Senior Development Editor
Seta Frantz

Production Editor
Kelly Oliver

Copy Editor
Barry Childs-Helton

Cover Designer
Jay Corpus

Book Designer
Barbara Kordesh

Indexer
Carol Sheehan

Production Team
Steve Adams
Angela D. Bannan
Claudia Bell
Anne Dickerson
Chad Dressler
Jennifer Eberhardt
Bill Hartman
Daryl Kessler
Bob LaRoche
Kaylene Riemen
Bobbi Satterfield
Scott Tullis
Suzanne Tully
Kelly Warner

Special thanks to C. Herbert Feltner and Discovery Computing, Inc. for ensuring the technical accuracy of this book.

Contents

Part 1 How To...

Buy and Set Up a Computer 3

- Decide What You Want to Use the Computer For 4
- Look at Software Requirements 7
- Decide What Kind of Computer You Want 10
- Decide on a Multimedia and MPC2 Computer 16
- Decide Where to Buy It 17
- Decide Where to Put a New Computer 20
- Unpack and Check a New Computer 22
- Plug the Components Together 23

Operate Your Computer 27

- Start Up Your Computer 28
  - Fix Startup Problems 28
- Shut Down at the End of the Day 30
- Insert and Remove Floppy Disks 31
- Understand Floppy Disk Capacity 33
  - Take Care of Your Floppy Disks 33
- Insert and Remove CD-ROMs 34
  - Use a Program's Controls to Open and Close the CD-ROM Drive 34
- Adjust a Monitor for Viewing Comfort 36
  - A Few Quick Exercises to Help Your Eyes 36
- Operate a Mouse 38
  - Master Common Mouse Techniques 38
- Reset (Warm-Boot) a Locked-Up Computer 41
- Cold-Boot Your System 43

Understand How the Computer Stores Files 45

- Understand Disks and Drives 46
  - Working by Bits and Bytes 46
  - Tracks, Sectors, and Formatting 47
- Understand How the Drive Reads and Writes 48
  - Name That Drive 48
- Understand Files 51
  - What's a FAT? 51
  - Where Files Go When You Delete Them 52
- Name Files and Decode File Names 53
- Understand Directories 55

Get Around in Windows 3.11 Programs 57

Start Windows ... 58
Check Your Mode ... 58
Load Windows Automatically When You Start Your Computer ... 60
Understand Program Manager ... 62
Open and Close a Windows Program Group ... 64
Find Wayward Groups ... 64
Create and Modify Program Groups ... 65
Start a Windows Program ... 68
Start a Program Without an Icon ... 68
Switch Between Open Programs ... 70
Select Commands from Menus ... 71
Skip the Menu ... 71
Speak in Command Code ... 71
Valuable Menu Command Secrets ... 72
Display the Control Menu for a Window ... 74
Display an Icon's Menu ... 74
Use a Dialog Box ... 75
Work with Directory Lists in Dialog Boxes ... 78
Work with Scroll Bars in Dialog Boxes ... 79
Size and Arrange Windows ... 80
Select a Window ... 80
Get Help in Windows ... 84
Use Other Help Window Buttons ... 84
Start a New File in a Windows Program ... 87
Jump-Start a File ... 87
Open a File in a Windows Program ... 89
Open a File ofAnother Type ... 89
Understand Wild Card Characters ... 90
Save Your Work in a Windows Program ... 92
Close Your FileAfter Saving ... 92
Save Your File Under a New Name ... 94
Save Your Files Automatically ... 95
Print in a Windows Program ... 96
Preview the Printed Document ... 96
Exit a Windows Program ... 98

Organize Files and Directories with Windows 3.11 99

Start and Exit File Manager ... 100
View Different Disks (Drives) ... 102
View Different Directories ... 104
Use the Tree Menu ... 104
Change the Tree Icons ... 104
Change the Directory Window View ... 107
Change the Split View ... 107

Open More Directory (Drive) Windows 109
Select an Open Directory Window 109
Open a Second Window for a Disk 109
Arrange and Close Directory Windows 110
Select Files 112
Associate Files with an Application 112
Open or Start Files 113
Copy Files to Different Locations 117
Move Files 122
Move Directories 122
Delete Files 128
Rename Files and Directories 130
Rename a Group of Files Using Wild Cards 130
Create Directories 132
Delete Directories 134

Find and Show Files and More with Windows 3.11 137

Rearrange the List of Files 138
Show Only Certain Files 140
Show File Details 142
Search for Files 144
Use Your Search Results 144
Format Disks 146
Label, System, and Quick Format Options 146
Name That Capacity 147

Work in Windows 95 149

Start and Shut Down Windows 95 150
Start Windows 95 in Safe Mode 150
Understand the New Look of Windows 154
Start Programs with the Start Button 157
Resize Program Windows 157
Switch Between Running Programs 159
Other Taskbar Tricks 159
Enter Commands in Windows 95 161
Get Help in Dialog Boxes 161
Get On-Screen Help 163
Install New Programs 168
Go to the DOS Prompt 172
Manage Disks, Folders, and Files 173
Arrange Icons in a Window 173
Icons: What They Stand for 173
Select Files and Folders 177
Copy or Move Files and Folders 179

Displaying the Destination for Copied or Moved Files 179
Delete and Restore Files and Folders 182
Rename Files or Folders 185
Create New Folders 187
Save Time with Shortcuts 188
Change an Object's Properties 190
Use Built-in Windows Programs 192
A List of the Windows 95 Programs 192
Control Your Printer 195
How Windows 95 Prints 195
Change Print Quality and Other Settings 195
Change the Video Display Properties 201
Take Control of Your Keyboard and Mouse 207

Work with DOS 211

Enter Commands in DOS 212
Identify Commands, Switches, and Parameters 213
Change Your DOS Prompt 213
Change Which Drive Is Active 215
Do This In Case of Error 215
When You Don't Need to Log On to a Drive 216
Change Which Directory Is Active 217
Moving Among Directory Levels 217
Create and Remove a Directory 219
Remove a Directory 219
List Directory Contents 221
Change the List Display 221
List Selected Files 221
Use DOS to Format Disks 224
Start a DOS Program from the DOS Prompt 225
Find the Startup Command 225
Find the Switches 226
Work with Menus in a DOS Program 227
Choose a Command from a Menu in a DOS Program 227
Work in a Dialog Box 229
Open a New or Existing File in a DOS Program 231
Save a File in a DOS Program 232
Exit a DOS Program 233
Shell Out to DOS Instead of Exiting 233

Connect with the Outside World Using Online Services 235

Understand Online Communication 236
Connect to PRODIGY 239
Jump to Your Next Destination 239
Send Mail on PRODIGY 243
The Name Game 243

Find and Read Information on PRODIGY 247
Post on PRODIGY Bulletin Boards 250
Connect to America Online 255
Use a Keyword to Move Around 256
Send Mail on America Online 258
E-Mail Recipient Names 258
Read Articles on America Online 262
Print or Save the Current Article 262
Post in America Online Message Boards 266
Download Files from America Online 269
Connect to CompuServe 271
Use a Go Command to Move Around 272
Send CompuServe Mail 274
E-Mail to Other Services 274
Work Offline 275
Use the Filing Cabinet 275
Read Articles on CompuServe 278
File or Save the Current Article 278
Post Messages in CompuServe Forums 282
Join and Leave a Forum 282
Download Files from CompuServe 285
Connect to The Microsoft Network with Windows 95 288
Get Up and Running on The Microsoft Network 293
Browse The Microsoft Network 295
Exchange E-Mail on The Microsoft Network 299
Converse with Other Microsoft Network Members 303

Connect with the Outside World Using BBSs and the Internet 309

Connect to a BBS with Windows 3.11 Terminal 310
Download and Upload Files with Terminal 313
Connect to the Internet: An Overview 316
Find an Internet Service Provider 316
Connect to an Internet Server Through Windows 3.11 Terminal 318
Get Wired with Windows 95 Dial-Up Networking 322

Part 2 Do It Yourself...

Keep Your Computer Clean and Healthy 327

Clean Your Computer 328
Clean the Monitor 331
Clean Your Printer 333
Clean the Keyboard 336

Clean the Mouse 338
Clean the Disk Drives 341
Clean a CD-ROM Drive 344
Clean a Tape Backup Drive 347
Clean Inside Your Computer 349
Select and Install a Surge Protector 353
First Aid: Spilled Liquid on Keyboard or Mouse 355
First Aid: Unstick a Jammed Disk 360

Install New Programs **363**

Install a DOS Program That Has a Setup Utility 364
Install a Windows 3.11 Program That Has a Setup Utility 366
Install a Windows 3.11 Program That Has No Installation Utility 369
Install a Program in Windows 95 372
Install a Program from a "ZIP" File 374
Uninstall a DOS Program 378
Uninstall a Windows 3.11 Program 381
Uninstall a Program in Windows 95 384

Make Your Computer Work Faster and Better **387**

Delete Old Files to Make More Room 388
Copy Old Files to a Disk 391
Make a "Startup" Disk 394
Optimize a Disk with Defrag 398
Increase Available Memory with MemMaker 402
Compress a Drive with DriveSpace 406
Modify Your Startup Files in Windows 3.11 and DOS 412

Install New Hardware **415**

Install a Printer 416
Install a Joystick 420
Install a Mouse 421
Install an External Modem 425
Attach Speakers to a Sound Card 430
Install an Adapter Card Inside Your Computer 432
Install a CD-ROM Drive 435
Install Hardware in Windows 95 439
Plug-and-Play Hardware in Windows 95 439

Keep Your Data Safe **443**

Make a Backup of Important System Files 444
Restore an Accidentally Deleted File with Undelete 448
Set Up Undelete to Maximize Your Undeletion Success 452

Check a Disk for Errors with ScanDisk 454
Back Up the Contents of Your Hard Disk Drive with Microsoft Backup 458
Restore the Contents of Your Hard Disk with Microsoft Backup 464
Check for Viruses with Microsoft AntiVirus 469

Part 3 101 Quick Fixes

Quick Finder Table 473
Startup Problems 485
1: I have no lights, no sounds, nothing. 485
2: I see the lights and hear the sounds, but there's still no display. 485
3: Why is my computer beeping? 486
4: My monitor displays "Non-system disk or disk error." 486
5: My monitor displays "CMOS RAM error." 487
6: What is a bad or missing command interpreter? 487
7: Can I slow down the startup to see what's happening? 487
Disk Problems 488
8: My computer says it cannot write to the disk. 488
9: I get error messages saying "Error writing to or reading from disk in drive." 488
10: What d'ya mean my drive's not valid?! 489
11: I get an error message saying that my disk is full. 489
12: What does "Sector not found" mean? 489
13: My disk seems slower than usual. 490
14: I've had trouble ever since I installed DoubleSpace (or DriveSpace). 490
File Problems 491
15: Oops! I deleted a file; can I get it back? 491
16: I know the file's here, but where is it? 492
17: The file I was working on is gone! 493
18: Why can't I insert this graphic in my document? 493
19: I just downloaded a file—how do I use it? 493
Memory Problems 495
20: I keep getting "Out of memory" messages in DOS. 495
21: Can I make the "Insufficient memory" messages in Windows go away? .. 496
22: I ran MemMaker, and now I can't run anything! 497
Video Problems 498
23: My monitor is dead! 498
24: Can I stop the high-pitched whining noise? 498
25: Why are the pictures so fuzzy? 499
26: I changed my Windows display driver, and now Windows won't display anything! 499
27: That flickering is driving me crazy! 500
28: My screen has all sorts of weird patterns. 500
29: Why are the pictures so tiny?! 501
30: My monitor gives me headaches. 501

Sound Card Problems ... 502
31: I just installed the sound card, and it doesn't work. ... 502
32: How do I turn it down (or up)? ... 503
33: The sound card worked before, but then I installed ________. ... 503
34 I run a DOS application from Windows, and when I return, my Windows applications won't play sounds. ... 504
35: The sound card upgrade *degraded* my system. ... 504
36: I can't get my sound card to work in Windows. ... 504
37: It's supposed to be in stereo! ... 505
38: My microphone doesn't work. ... 505
CD-ROM Problems ... 506
39: The CD-ROM drive doesn't work. ... 506
40: The drive seems to work all right, but I can't get at the files on the disc. ... 506
41: The CD-ROM drive locks up my system. ... 507
42: Where's the sound supposed to come from? ... 507
43: What about music CDs? ... 508
44: The movie clips are s-l-o-w. ... 509
45: I stood my system unit on end, and now the CD-ROM drive is slow. ... 509
Printing Problems ... 510
46: My printer won't print. ... 510
47: I tried three times to print this thing, and I haven't gotten even one copy! ... 511
48: It prints all right, but the print looks like garbage. ... 512
49: It prints only half of a page! ... 512
50: I can't get the type lined up right. ... 513
51: The print on-screen doesn't match the page. ... 513
52: I hate these paper jams. ... 514
53: Is it always this slow? ... 514
Mouse Problems ... 515
54: My mouse doesn't work, period. ... 515
55: My mouse pointer is jumping all over the screen. ... 516
56: I installed a modem, and now the mouse doesn't work! ... 517
57: My mouse won't do Windows. ... 518
58: My mouse won't do DOS applications from Windows. ... 518
59: My mouse pointer moves too fast or too slow. ... 520
Keyboard Problems ... 520
60: My keyboard doesn't work at all. ... 520
61: I get a "Keyboard not found" message. ... 521
62: When I type, everything is in UPPERCASE LETTERS. ... 521
63: Everything I type replaces existing text. ... 522
64: I press one key and it acts like a different one. ... 522
65: Each key I press beeps at me. ... 522
Modem Problems ... 522
66: There's no sign of life—no dialing, no lights, no modem. ... 522
67: My modem dials, but never connects. ... 523

68: I keep getting a busy signal. 524
69: I hear voices from the modem. 524
70: My modem dials and then immediately disconnects or displays a NO CARRIER message. 524
71: I have call waiting; whenever I get a call, I lose my modem. 525
72: Do I *have to* listen while my modem dials? 525
73: I'm typing, but I don't see anything. 526
74: Everything I type comes up double. 526
Problems with DOS 526
75: My screen displays "Abort, Retry, Fail?". Which should I pick? 526
76: I try to run my program, and I keep getting a "Bad command or file name" message. 526
77: When I try to copy a file, DOS tells me that the file cannot be copied onto itself. 527
78: When I try to copy or delete a file, DOS displays the "File not found" message. 527
79: What does "Not ready reading drive A" mean? 527
80: Is DOS always this s-l-o-w? 528
81: I know most of the basic DOS commands, but how can I learn more about them? 528
Problems with DOS Applications 529
82: When I install applications, my computer tells me to close any antivirus programs that are running. 529
83: I entered the command, but the program won't run. 529
84: The program runs and then crashes. 529
85: The display doesn't look quite right. 530
Microsoft Windows Woes 530
86: I entered the WIN command, but Windows won't start. 530
87: I can't get out of Windows. 532
88: Is Windows always this s-l-o-w? 532
89: I installed a fax program, and now I can't print. 534
90: I just deleted a program group, and I want it back! 534
91: I double-clicked on a file icon in Windows, but it won't run. 534
92: I got a General Protection Fault error—what does it mean? 535
93: I don't use many of my fonts and some of my Windows files; can I get rid of them? 537
94: Can I run a DOS application from Windows? 539
Problems with Windows Applications 540
95: I installed the application, now where is it? 540
96: My application locks up Windows. 540
97: When I try to run the application, it says I'm missing a file. 540
98: Why can't I run DOS utilities from Windows? 541
99: The documentation says I have to edit my system files; how do I do that? 541

Miscellaneous Problems 542
100: My computer loses time. 542
101: I just installed DOS 6.22 (or later), and when I try to run MS-Backup, I get a message saying I have the incorrect DOS version. 543

Software Buyers' Guide

What Software Categories Are Covered? 545
Communications 546
Databases 546
Desktop Publishing 546
Education 546
Games 547
Graphics and Drawing 547
Integrated Packages 547
Personal Finance and Accounting 547
Personal Organizers 547
Spreadsheets 547
Software Suites 548
Word Processing 548
What's in the Tables? 548
Communications Programs 550
Database Programs 552
Desktop Publishing Programs 554
Educational Programs—Adult 556
Educational Programs—Kids 558
Educational Programs—Reference 564
Games 566
Graphics and Drawing 570
Integrated Packages 570
Personal Finance and Accounting 572
Personal Organizer Programs 574
Spreadsheet Programs 576
Software Suites 578
Word Processing 578

Index 580

Introduction

You've avoided it whenever you could. You've dreaded it and tried to fake it. You've pretended that your kids and acquaintances aren't a little bit ahead of you. But you've finally accepted it. The computer age is here, and it's knocking at your door.

Welcome to *The Big Basics Book of PCs*. This book gives a gentle, thorough introduction to personal computers (PCs). It doesn't try to teach you a little bit about a lot of topics. It doesn't try to make you an expert in the span of 200 pages. It doesn't try to teach about things you'll use once in a computing lifetime, such as how to create a spreadsheet program for calculating the circumference of a circle.

Instead, *The Big Basics Book of PCs* provides complete information on all the features and tasks that you need and want to know. It zeroes in on the tasks that are essential for your computer survival, and teaches each one in simple, picture-by-picture steps. Like the visual books you've used to learn how to cook or how to add a deck to your house, this book offers concise, informal steps highlighted by clear illustrations that show you exactly what to do next.

- Learn how to buy the computer that's right for you, and how to set it up. You'll conquer your anxiety about dealing with the hardware, and your computer will enjoy a long, useful life, because you'll clean it like a pro and add new upgrades whenever they hit the market.
- Conquer Windows, the best thing to ever happen to PCs. Although the little pictures in Windows may seem obscure and confusing, you'll soon be navigating Windows (3.11 and 95) with no problem.
- Make peace with DOS, your computer's Disk Operating System. Even though you may not have to use it often, you'll benefit by knowing the tricks of the trade for communicating in DOS's secret code.
- Communicate with the outside world. Send and receive mail electronically. Get the latest news and stock quotes. Search for facts or shop. Take advantage of popular online services like CompuServe, PRODIGY, and America Online. And, jump onto the biggest part of the Information Superhighway, commonly called the Internet.
- Choose the programs you need, and see how to get them up and running on your system.
- Find out the best way to fix common problems when they crop up.

How Can I Find What I Need in This Book?

To make it easy to use, we've divided *The Big Basics Book of PCs* into four distinct parts. Each part keys in on a particular type of information and presents that information in the best format for beginners. You don't need to read the book from cover to cover if you don't want to. You can just skip to whichever section you need.

Part 1: How To covers all the skills that a new or casual computer user needs. It only takes a few pages to explain each operation, but you get all the facts and advice you need. A clear illustration accompanies almost every step, and you're told when another part of the book offers even more information about a topic.

Part 2: Do It Yourself also offers illustrated steps for particular operations. This part, however, covers practical projects you can use to hone your skills and get more productive with your computer.

Part 3: Quick Fixes anticipates the inevitable, identifying the problems every computer user will encounter and offering the simplest and most durable solutions for those problems. Scan the Quick Finder Table to find your problem quickly.

Software Buyers' Guide highlights a sampling of the thousands of computer programs that are now available. This part focuses in on the most popular and useful programs, giving you the lowdown on each so you can see if it's for you—before spending any money for it.

Conventions, Conventions, Conventions

This book was specially designed to make it easy to use. Each task has a title that tells you what you'll be doing. Immediately following the title is a *Guided Tour*, which shows you step-by-step how to perform the task. There is also additional text that tells you why you might want to perform the task and provides additional details on what to do. The following figure shows you the format of the book.

The following special conventions were used to make the book easier to use:

Text you are supposed to type appears bold. For example, if the step says, type **win** and press **Enter**, type the command "win" and press the Enter key on your keyboard.

Keys you are supposed to press are bold, too, to make them easier to spot.

Key+Key combinations are used when you have to press two or more keys to enter a command. When you encounter one of these combinations, hold down the first key and press the second key.

Menu names and **commands** you need to choose are also bold. When you're told to open a menu and select a command, move the mouse pointer over it, and press and release the left mouse button.

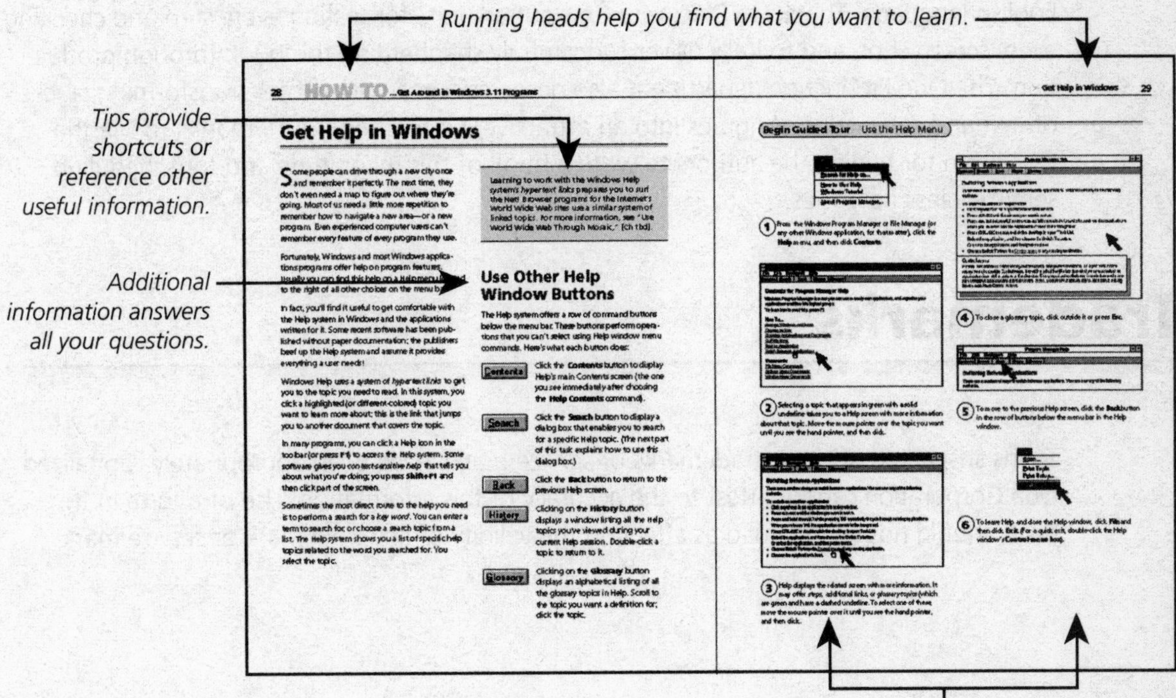

Look for these sidebars for tips, hints, and shortcuts.

In Conclusion...

Even if you think using a computer is as fun as having your toenails pulled out, you can learn something from this book. It makes the computer learning curve as painless as possible, so you can become as confident as the next person (or your kid) when you use your computer. And so, on to the action!

Acknowledgments

No book is an individual project. Special thanks to Marie Butler-Knight for developing the concept of the *Big Basics Book* series, and to Barry Pruett for his support. Thanks to Seta Frantz for her guiding questions and valuable input on the content of this book, and to Barry Childs-Helton for ensuring that the text followed all the proper conventions of the English language. Thanks to Discovery Computing, Inc., for testing every step and checking every screen shot, and to Kelly Oliver for carefully shepherding this book through production. The Que Production department also deserves a hearty cheer for transforming stacks of text and mountains of figures into an attractive, bound book. And thanks to Martha O'Sullivan for finding the authors to write a book of this magnitude and for scheduling semi-painless deadlines.

Trademarks

PART 1

How To...

Have you ever tried to pound in a nail with a screwdriver? If you have, you know that it usually doesn't work out very well. (And you know that screwdriver handles are not shatterproof.) You have to choose the right tool and use it correctly to get the job done.

This part of *The Big Basics Book of PCs* introduces you to what could become one of the most important tools in your life: your computer. You'll learn how to buy the computer that's right for your needs and how to set it up. After that, this part explains how to take command of your computer, from handling the hardware to developing good computing habits (like saving your work so you can change it later or use it again). Finally, you can take a crack at exploring the Information Superhighway. You'll see how you can connect with other computers all over the world.

Even if you've never been able to pound in a nail without bending it, the computer's one tool you'll soon master. With this part of the book (and a little practice to build your confidence), you'll be ready to tackle any computing project.

What You Will Find in This Part

Buy and Set Up a Computer 3

Operate Your Computer 27

Understand How the Computer Stores Files 45

Get Around in Windows 3.11 Programs 57

Organize Files and Directories with Windows 3.11 99

Find and Show Files and More with Windows 3.11 137

Work in Windows 95 149

Work with DOS 211

Connect with the Outside World Using Online Services 235

Connect with the Outside World Using BBSs and the Internet 309

HOW TO...

Buy and Set Up a Computer

These days, it's as convenient to buy a computer as it is to buy a pair of jeans. You can walk into any one of hundreds of office, computer, appliance, and department stores; plunk down a credit card; and walk out with several boxes of computer equipment.

Even though it's convenient, buying and setting up a computer isn't always easy. You may not know what size you need or what to do to make your computer as comfortable as a second skin.

The next few tasks in this book will help you with the process. You'll learn what you can do with a computer, how to select a computer that meets your needs, and how to set it up so it not only works correctly but is also convenient and comfortable to use.

What You Will Find in This Section

Decide What You Want to Use the Computer For 4

Look at Software Requirements 7

Decide What Kind of Computer You Want 10

Decide on a Multimedia and MPC2 Computer 16

Decide Where to Buy It 17

Decide Where to Put a New Computer 20

Unpack and Check a New Computer 22

Plug the Components Together 23

Decide What You Want to Use the Computer For

Before you buy a computer, you need to ask yourself the same kinds of basic questions you'd ask before buying a car or house. Consider this question first: "What am I going to use it for?"

If you're buying a computer for your home and family, you can use it for entertainment, education, keeping track of personal finances, and more. You can also use your computer to work at home, write letters, do your taxes, or run a small business.

When you're thinking about what you want to do with the computer you're about to buy, take a look at different *software programs*. Each program gives your computer the instructions to get a particular job done. You'll find programs you want to start using right away and others you may want to experiment with in a few months or when the need arises. Either way, knowing what programs you want to use will help you decide what kind of computer to buy. Each piece of software requires particular pieces of computer hardware (*components*). Deciding on the software first can help you make a list of just which components you'll need, and how powerful they need to be.

If you want to check out some different programs without schlepping to your local computer store, see, the "Software Buyers' Guide" beginning on page 545.

Begin Guided Tour Types of Programs

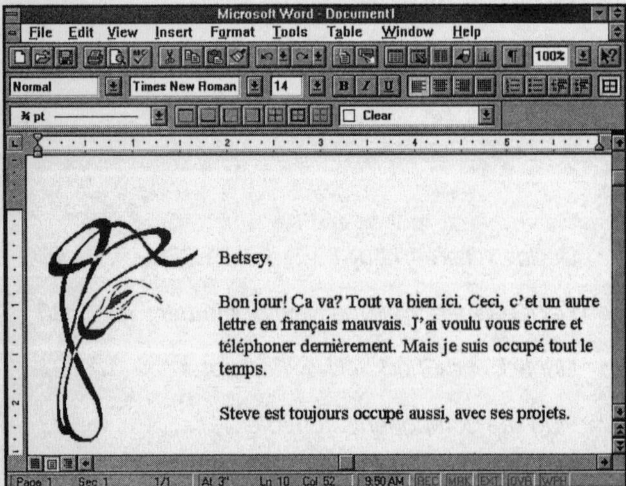

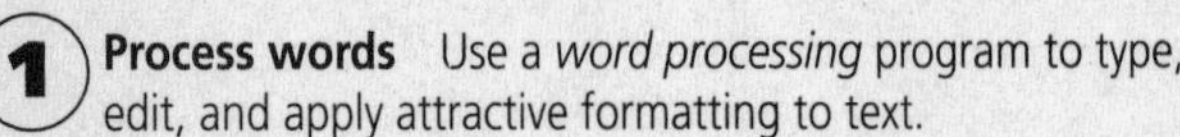

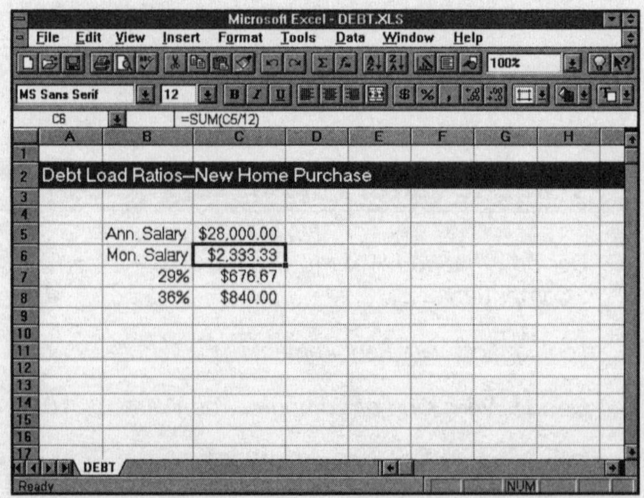

1 **Process words** Use a *word processing* program to type, edit, and apply attractive formatting to text.

2 **Crunch numbers** Use a *spreadsheet* program to organize numbers in a grid and use formulas to perform calculations.

Guided Tour Types of Programs

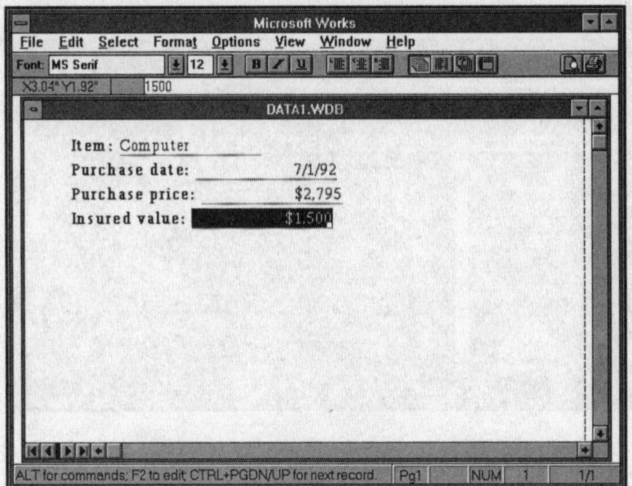

3 **Manage data** Use a *database* to store and sort lists of information, such as phone lists and home inventories.

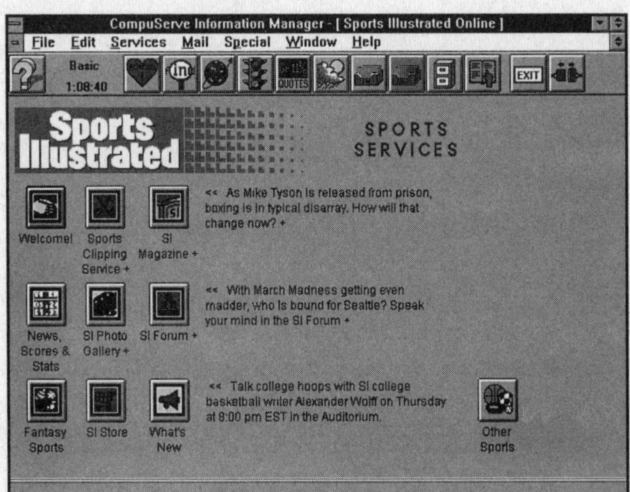

4 **Communicate** Use a piece of hardware called a *modem* with your computer to transmit data over phone lines. You can send and receive faxes and electronic mail (*e-mail*), chat with other users, or access a wealth of data available through online services.

5 **Educate and entertain** Have fun (mindless or otherwise) searching for treasure, learning from an illustrated online encyclopedia, and more. Today's more powerful computers have led to elaborate computer games, educational programs, and entertainment resources that use pictures, animation, and sound.

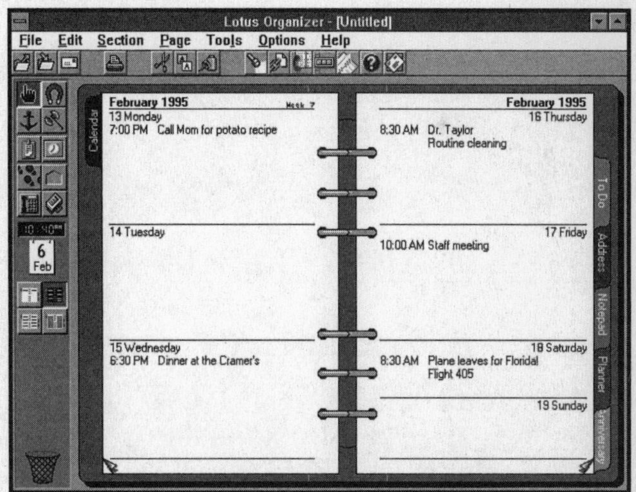

6 **Manage time, money, and more** Use computer programs to organize your time, manage your contact with others, or even write checks and budget your money. Specialized programs can help you track your diet, fitness level, or your progress toward goals.

(continues)

Guided Tour Types of Programs

(continued)

7 Present and publish information Use a *presentation graphics* program to create slides and presentations that convey a message with style or grab attention. Use a *desktop publishing* program to create newsletters, flyers, and other publications. Other programs let you create and work with drawings and *fonts* (fancy lettering).

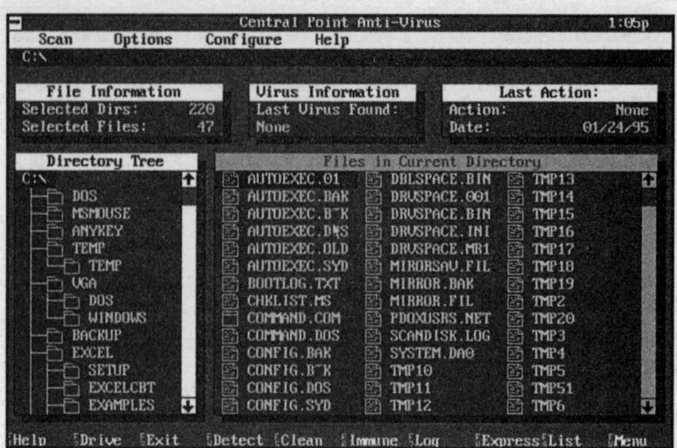

8 Maintain your computer and its files Use utility programs to back up files, check for viruses (data-destroying programs that can infect your computer anonymously), compress files so they take up less disk space, and perform more disk-management activities to keep your computer healthy.

Look at Software Requirements

After you've chosen the software programs you want to use, you'll need to figure out how powerful your computer has to be to run them. The program you want to run may also require you to have certain other kinds of software on your computer. Fortunately, software publishers give you a hand with figuring out what your program needs.

Check the software product box for a section called something like "Recommended Hardware and Software Requirements." This section usually appears on a side panel of the box; it tells you several important things (for example, whether the program requires Microsoft Windows or the latest version of DOS). Don't worry if you don't understand some of the techie terms you find on the box (or, for that matter, in this task). You'll learn more about DOS and Windows later in this part of the book. You'll learn more about *hardware*, the actual computer components, in the next task, "Decide What Kind of Computer You Want."

The system you buy should be able to run the software you choose—and meet its most demanding minimum requirements for hardware and software. You can't take the requirements for all the software programs and somehow "average" them.

Here are the requirements you need to consider; they're outlined on the package for each software program you purchase.

What type of computer do you need?

To run software created for a Macintosh computer, you must have a Macintosh. To run software created for an IBM-compatible computer, you need that kind of computer.

How powerful must the computer be?

Usually the box will tell you what kind of *central processing unit* (the *CPU* or "brain") your computer needs to have. This is designated by a number for the CPU such as "386" or "486"; a higher number indicates a more powerful processor. Yours must be as powerful as the one required—*or better*. A number such as "33MHz" or "90MHz" indicates how fast the processor is. Higher numbers designate faster processors. Most PCs have the processor type and speed stamped on the front.

Which operating system does it use?

Most of you will be buying computers that run under the operating system called *MS-DOS*. This *Disk Operating System* from Microsoft provides basic control of your computer. If your computer uses DOS, don't buy programs made for the OS/2, UNIX, or System 7 (Macintosh) operating systems. Also, make sure you have the right version of DOS to run the program. For example, if a program requires MS-DOS 5.0 to run, you must have MS-DOS with version number 5.0 *or higher*.

Does the computer need Windows?

Many newer programs need to be run under Microsoft Windows. That is, to work with the program, you need to first run the Windows program. Windows is a *graphical user interface* (*GUI*) that runs "on top" of DOS; you need to have DOS for Windows to work. Windows is called a GUI because you use a mouse and on-screen *graphics* (pictures) called *icons* to control your computer.

How much memory and storage should the computer have?

Random-Access Memory, or *RAM*, holds the instructions and data you're working with while your computer is turned on. When you install a program and *save* your work, it's stored on the computer's *hard drive*, a semipermanent storage area that lets you access the program or data later. Programs require a minimum amount of RAM to run correctly. They also take up a certain amount of storage space on the hard drive; make sure you have enough hard drive space available to install the program.

What kind of mouse and monitor are needed?

Some programs require a mouse, others don't; the software box will say which is the case. Monitors (and the internal *video cards* they connect to) come in several flavors, depending on the *resolution* each provides. The four available types of monitor, from lowest to highest resolution, are: CGA (Color Graphics Adapter), EGA (Enhanced Graphics Adapter), VGA (Video Graphics Array), and SVGA (Super VGA). Programs with generous graphics generally require better-resolution monitors such as Super VGA.

Are there optional programs or equipment that can or should be used?

Some programs may require a CD-ROM drive for playing CD-ROMs. For others, you may need a sound card and speakers to take full advantage of the program's features. Most communications programs require a modem or fax/modem; if any special equipment is required or recommended, usually the software box will say so.

If your computer doesn't meet the minimum software requirements, the software may run unreliably or may not run at all. Even if your computer meets the minimum, the program may not run to your satisfaction. Often the system that runs the program best has requirements that exceed those on the software box. The next task, "Decide What Kind of Computer You Want," gives guidelines for selecting a system that will run most software—and run it well.

Begin Guided Tour How to Read a Software Product Box

System Requirements
- IBM-compatible personal computer with 386 33MHz processor or above

1. What type of computer do you need?

2. How powerful must the computer be?

- DOS 5.0 or above
- Windows 3.1 or above

3. Which operating system does it use?

4. Does the computer need Windows?

- 8M RAM
- 28M hard disk space (13M for minimum install)

5. How much memory and storage should the computer have?

- VGA display or better
- Mouse

6. What kind of mouse and monitor are needed?

Optional Equipment
- TWAIN-compliant scanner
- Windows-supported multimedia devices

7. Are there optional programs or equipment that can or should be used?

Decide What Kind of Computer You Want

Once you've chosen the software you want to use (and know its hardware and software requirements), you should have a good starting point for choosing a computer. Before you go shopping, make a list of the features you want your computer system to have.

You need to decide which components you need now and which you would prefer to add later. For example, if you want to view *multimedia* CD-ROMs (that is, programs incorporating sound and motion video), you'll need a computer that's equipped with a CD-ROM drive, sound card, and speakers. Many computer sellers offer these as *multimedia-ready* systems. They are a good bet because you won't have to learn how to add the hardware on your own.

Your budget also has an impact on your computer purchase decisions. Obviously, if you're only planning to use your computer for word processing, there's no need to mortgage your house to buy a top-of-the-line setup. On the other hand, you don't want to buy a system that'll be obsolete as soon as you bring it home. Imagine how disappointed you'd be if an update to your favorite program came out and your year-old computer couldn't run it at all! Allow yourself room to grow with your computer. As a rule of thumb, decide what system you need now, add $500 to your budget, and then buy a system that's faster than the one you need now and has more memory and storage space.

This task reviews the components you need to make decisions about selecting the computer system you want. Any *Recommendations* you find here are designed to give you a system that will serve you well through the next few years.

If you travel for business, consider a computer that travels with you—that is, a *notebook* (sometimes called *laptop*) computer that's compact and folds open like a notebook. Convenience comes at a price, though. Notebooks cost about $1,000 more than comparable desktop systems.

System unit: All instructions flow through the components in this box. The system unit of a traditional desktop PC has a fairly large *footprint*, taking up a lot of desk space. *Slimline* system units are smaller (which might make them more appropriate for a home office). *Tower* units stand vertically and can be tucked away under a desk.

Central processing unit (CPU): This chip executes commands and controls the flow of data. A two-part number like "80486 DX/2, 50MHz" identifies most CPUs; the first part ("80486 DX/2") indicates processing power; a higher number means you have more ("Pentium" chips offer the most). "DX" processors—or those with no designation—have *math co-processors* to help handle number-crunching ("SX" means "no math co-processor"). "DX/2" chips are about twice as fast (and "DX/4" chips are about four times as fast) as their DX cousins. The second number in the processor's name (such as "50MHz") indicates speed; higher is better. *Recommendation:* Pentium 66MHz

Random-access memory (RAM): A computer's RAM consists of a bank of chips that act as "working memory," holding program instructions and data only while your computer's on. Unless the instructions and data are saved to a disk, RAM forgets them when you turn your computer off. RAM is measured in *megabytes* (*M*). Each M represents over one million characters of data. Most computers come with 8M of RAM. *Recommendation:* 16M

Hard drive: Your computer stores information semipermanently on the *hard drive*—several metal disks in an airtight case. You can save programs and data on the hard drive and then later delete them to reuse the space they occupied. Hard drive capacities are measured in megabytes (1,000M equals a *gigabyte*). A too-small hard drive limits the number of programs you can install; these days the minimum is 200M. You also want to consider a hard drive's *access time*. A slow hard drive can slow your whole system down, no matter how fast the processor is. Smaller access times indicate a faster drive (12ms is faster than 16ms). *Recommendation:* 540M or 720M, with 12ms access time or better

Floppy disk drive: Like a hard drive, this drive lets you store data and program instructions semipermanently. The difference: floppy drives store data on portable *floppy disks* you can slide in and out of a slot in the system unit. Older floppy drives used flexible 5.25-inch disks, which are now almost obsolete. Most recent floppy drives use 3.5-inch HD (high-density) disks that hold 1.44M of data; these have hard plastic shells and protect your data better. *Recommendation:* one 3.5-inch high-capacity drive

CD-ROM drive: This drive uses lasers to read a *CD-ROM* (*Compact Disc Read-Only Memory*). Like audio CDs, CD-ROMs are 4.5-inch metallic-looking platters. Each disc can hold more than 650M of data. Most CD-ROM drives are internal; you can pay more to get an external unit. The effectiveness of a CD-ROM drive depends on its *access time* and *transfer rate*—how fast it can get and deliver information. Look for a high transfer rate (in kilobytes per second) and a small access time (in milliseconds). *Double-speed* CD-ROM drives are common now, but faster quad-speed drives are better for multimedia. Make sure your CD-ROM drive is compatible with your sound card. *Recommendation:* Quad-speed (4X) or internal CD-ROM drive (600kps or better transfer rate, 200ms or lower access time)

Monitor: The monitor displays your program and data visually (like a TV screen) and connects to a graphics card inside your computer. The monitor's *resolution* must match that of the card; available resolutions, from worst to best, are: CGA (Color Graphics Adapter), EGA (Enhanced Graphics Adapter), VGA (Video Graphics Array), and SVGA (Super VGA). Also consider some basic numbers: *dots-per-inch* (*dpi*) should be at least 640 x 480; *dot pitch* (the distance between dots) should be as small as possible. Also, the graphics card contains its own RAM (*video RAM* or *VRAM*); make sure you have enough. Other available features include low-glare and flat screens. *Recommendation:* 15-inch color SVGA (1024 x 768 dpi), flat screen, .28mm dot pitch, non-interlaced, 1M VRAM

Keyboard/mouse/joystick: These devices let you control the computer by giving your input. Enter characters with the keyboard; use the mouse to point to things on-screen, click to make selections, and drag items from place to place; use a joystick to control computer games. With any of these, "try before you buy." Choose a device that operates smoothly and feels comfortable. *Recommendation:* Keyboard with numeric keypad, Microsoft-compatible mouse, joystick only for game use

Expansion slots: These slots within the system unit enable you to plug in additional circuit boards (expansion boards or expansion cards) for new devices, such as a scanner, that you add to your computer. You'll need these to add components to or upgrade your computer, especially if you don't buy a computer that's multimedia-equipped. *Recommendation:* at least 5 expansion slots (2 ISA slots for older expansion boards and 3 PCI slots for current and future technology)

Ports: Use these receptacles (on the back of your system unit) to plug in equipment like printers. Most computers now come with separate mouse, keyboard, and monitor ports. *Parallel* ports are usually for plugging in printers; *serial* ports connect to a mouse, external modem, or a printer designed to be used with them. Some computers also provide special game ports for plugging in joysticks. *Recommendation:* 1 port each for keyboard, mouse, and monitor, plus 1 parallel and 1 serial

Bus type: Data travels in a computer along circuits called *buses* on the computer's main circuit board (the *motherboard*). Although three main buses (data bus, address bus, and control bus) manage the computer's operation, often these are collectively called *the bus*. An *ISA bus* (for Industry Standard Architecture) carries data along 16 lines, that is, 16 bits at a time. The more powerful *EISA bus* (for Enhanced Industry Standard Architecture) carries 32 bits of data. Recent *local bus* computer designs add more buses so the system can communicate directly with components like the monitor, resulting in much better performance. Under a new standard, "PCI Local Bus," system components work almost seamlessly. *Recommendation:* EISA bus, with PCI Local Bus for graphics (monitor) and IDE interface (often used for the hard drive)

Printers: Printers make *hard copies* (printouts) of your work in black and white or color. *Dot-matrix* printers do it by pressing patterns of pins against an inked ribbon. These printers can be noisy, but are inexpensive to operate; they use continuous-feed paper. *Inkjet* or *bubblejet* printers blow liquid ink at the page in precise patterns, creating characters on single sheets of paper. You can operate these for 3 to 10 cents per page. *Laser* printers, generally more expensive, use an electrically charged drum to transfer *toner* (dry ink) onto paper at 3 to 7 cents per page. Dot-matrix printers offer the worst resolution (dpi), and laser printers the best (up to 1000 dpi). *Recommendation:* Laser printer with 600 dpi and 1M of printer memory

Modems: These devices let computers communicate and transfer data over phone lines. With a modem, you can exchange electronic mail and files with other computer users, send and receive faxes (if you have a fax/modem), and connect to online services or the Internet to gather information. Modems can be *internal* (on a card inside the system unit) or *external* (a box connecting to an expansion card). Modems transfer data at a rate measured in *bits per second* (*bps*); higher numbers mean a faster modem. Features that help a modem work faster include data compression and error correction (indicated with "V." plus a number, and perhaps "*bis*"). Modems that have *data compression* make the data more compact before sending it (so they can send more of it), and *decompress* it when they receive it. *Error correction* means your modem automatically senses mistakes in data and retransmits it as needed. *Recommendation:* (optional) 14,400-bps, Hayes-compatible, V.32*bis* internal fax/modem, supporting Class 1 and 2 Group III fax machines

Sound cards, speakers, and microphones: These enable your computer to play and record sound. The *sound card* plugs into a slot in the system unit; it runs speakers, a microphone, and even specialized music equipment that uses MIDI (Musical Instrument Digital Interface). Like the amount of data a bus can carry, sound quality is measured in bits; higher numbers are better. (High-end, 32-bit sound cards provide a fancy kind of output called *wavetable*.) In addition to a MIDI/game port, the card may offer a connection that lets you run a CD-ROM drive through the same port as the sound card. Sound cards that have a special *Digital Signal Processor* (*DSP*) chip work better; your card should be compatible with the popular Sound Blaster card. *Recommendation:* (optional) 16-bit or better,

CD-quality, Sound-Blaster-compatible sound card with MIDI/game port and CD connection; 10-watt speakers

Scanners: Scanners use light to convert an optical image to a digital image you can view or save using your computer. You can choose either a *hand-held* scanner (which you drag over the image much like a mouse), or a *flatbed* model that looks and works much like a photocopier. Color and *grayscale* (black-and-white) models are available; higher resolution (more dots per inch—higher dpi) produces crisper images. *Recommendation:* (optional) Small newsletter publishers can get away with a hand-held 400-dpi color scanner; professional publishers should choose color flatbed units with 1000-dpi resolution.

Surge suppressors and UPSs: *Surge suppressors* protect against sudden spikes in power, which can zap your computer and data. They also give you a strip of additional plugs for your computer's components. (Be careful—*not all* plug-in strips are surge suppressors.) A *UPS* (*uninterruptible power supply*) feeds electrical current to your computer in the event of a power loss (commonly called a *brownout*) that could cause data in RAM to be lost. *Recommendation:* surge suppressor

Begin Guided Tour Computer Components

1 **System unit:** All instructions flow through the components in this box.

2 **Central processing unit (CPU):** This chip executes commands and controls the flow of data.

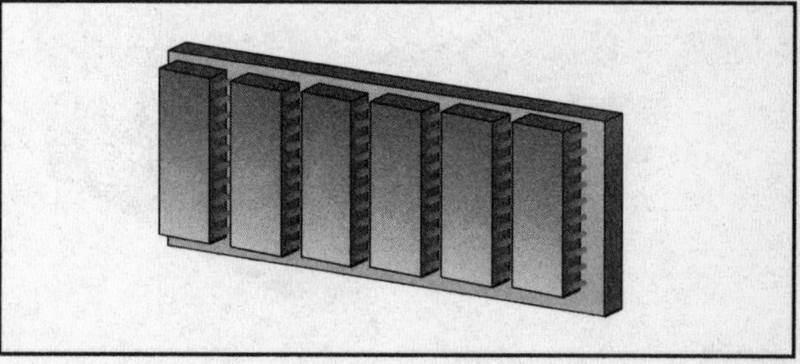

3 **Random-access memory (RAM):** A computer's RAM consists of a bank of chips that act as "working memory," holding program instructions and data only while your computer's on.

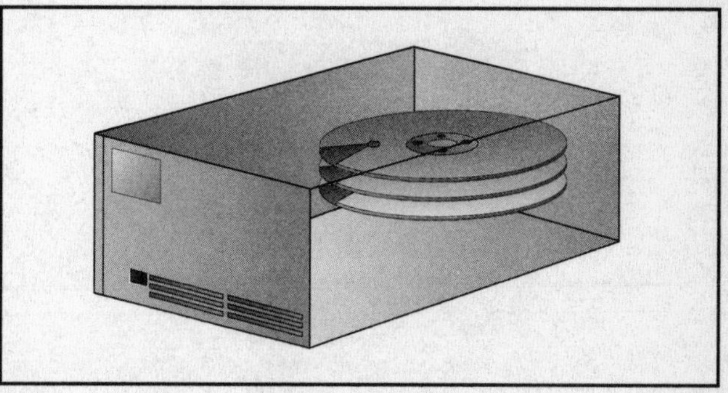

4 **Hard drive:** Your computer stores information semipermanently on the *hard drive*—several metal disks in an airtight case.

(continues)

Guided Tour Computer Components

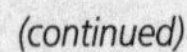
(continued)

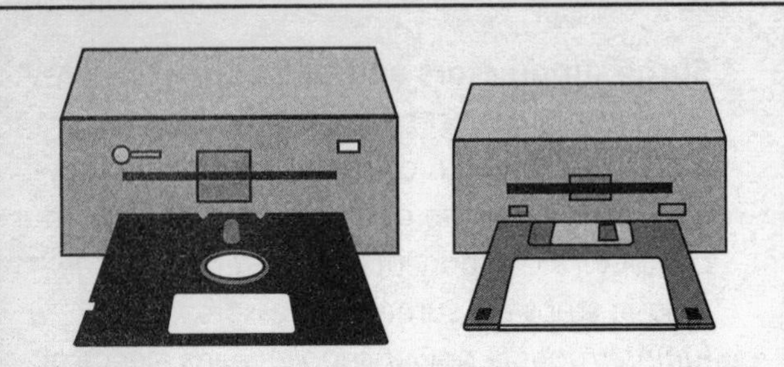

5 **Floppy disk drive:** Like a hard drive, this drive lets you store data and program instructions semipermanently. The difference: floppy drives store data on portable *floppy disks* you can slide in and out of a slot in the system unit.

6 **CD-ROM drive:** This drive uses lasers to read a *CD-ROM* (*Compact Disc Read-Only Memory*). Each disc can hold more than 650M of data.

7 **Monitor:** The monitor displays your program and data visually (like a TV screen) and connects to a graphics card inside your computer.

8 **Keyboard/mouse/joystick:** These devices let you control the computer by giving your input.

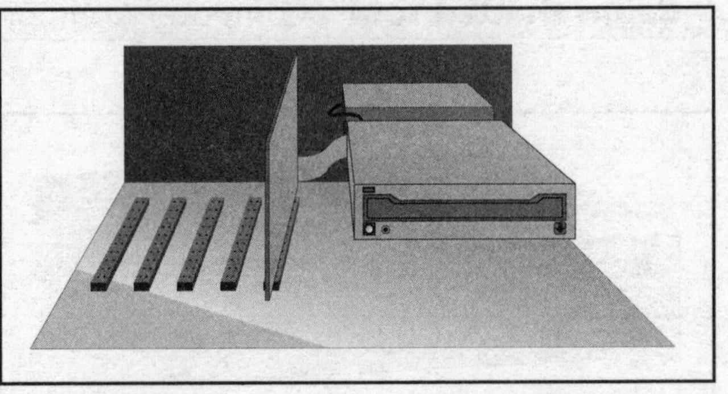

9 **Expansion slots:** These slots within the system unit enable you to plug in additional circuit boards (expansion boards or expansion cards) for new devices, such as a scanner, that you add to your computer.

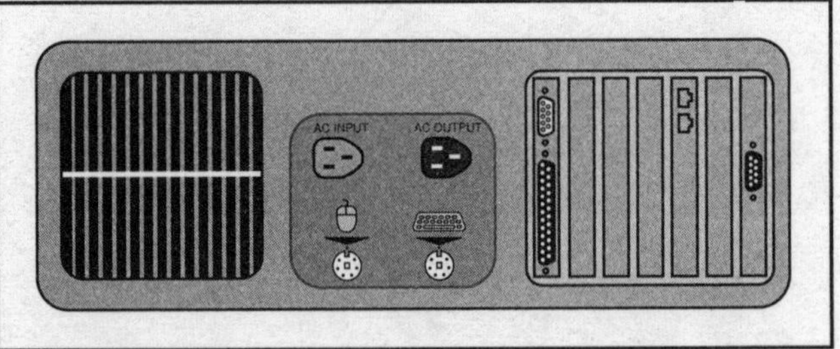

10 **Ports:** Use these receptacles (on the back of your system unit) to plug in equipment like printers.

11 **Bus type:** Data travels in a computer along circuits called *buses* on the computer's main circuit board (the *motherboard*).

Guided Tour Computer Components

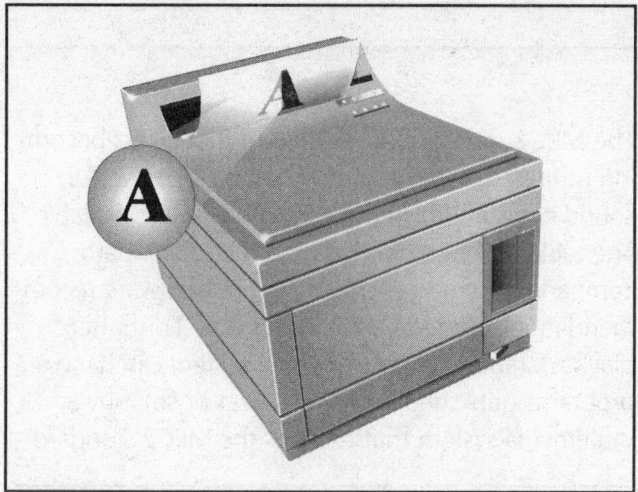

12 **Printers:** Printers make *hard copies* (printouts) of your work in black and white or color.

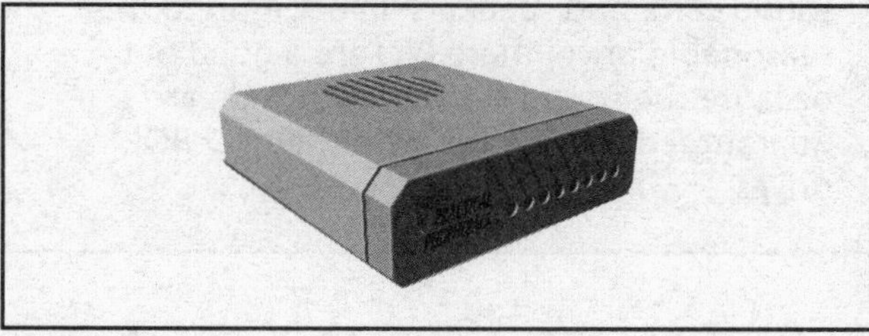

13 **Modems:** These devices let computers communicate and transfer data over phone lines.

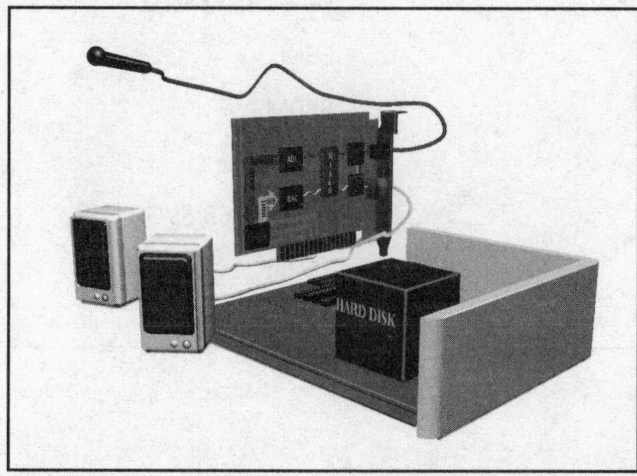

14 **Sound cards, speakers, and microphones:** These enable your computer to play and record sound.

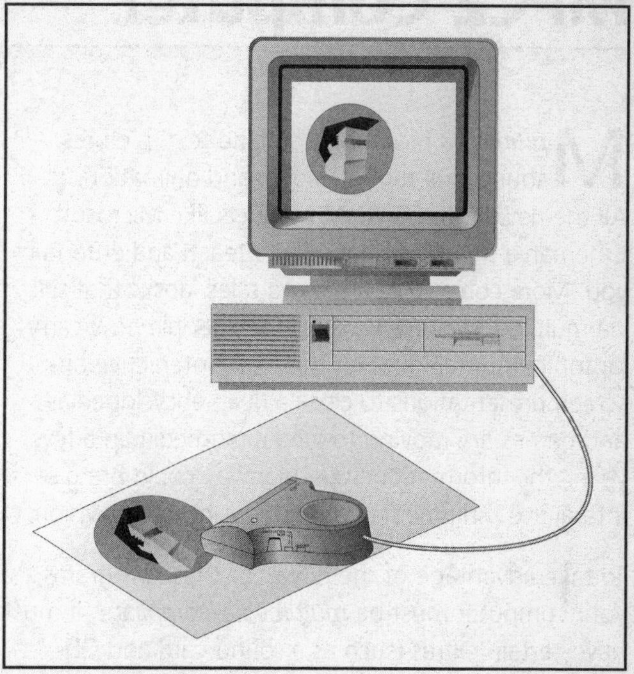

15 **Scanners:** Scanners use light to convert an optical image to a digital image you can view or save using your computer.

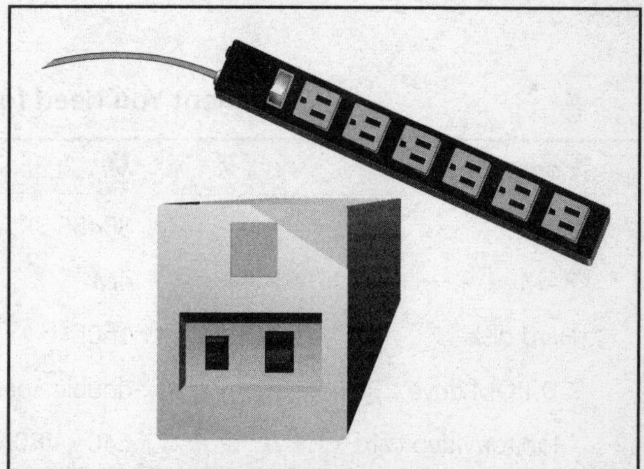

16 **Surge suppressors and UPSs:** Surge suppressors protect against sudden spikes in power, which can zap your computer and data. They also give you a strip of additional plugs for your computer's components. A UPS (uninterruptible power supply) is a battery that provides a current flow of electricity to your computer, even when there's a power outage.

Decide on a Multimedia and MPC2 Computer

Multimedia programs combine text, pictures, sound, full-motion video, and animation. All the new, cool CD-ROM products like Microsoft Cinemania 95 use multimedia to teach and entertain you. More companies are using sales kiosks that sell via multimedia presentations. Salespeople now carry laptop computers that let them use interactive on-screen presentations to close a deal; encyclopedias and games are moving toward multimedia. In a few years, the Information Superhighway could bring interactive multimedia right to your home television.

To take advantage of the power of these programs, your computer must be *multimedia-compliant*; it must have certain extras (such as a sound card and CD-ROM drive) and meet certain standards. The industry has set such a standard: *Multimedia PC 2*, abbreviated MPC2. Computer systems that meet this standard carry a special MPC2 logo—look for it when you shop.

The MPC2 standard is a minimum that is fast becoming outdated, especially now that more powerful sound cards and faster CD-ROM drives are available. The table included here lists the MPC2 standards, comparing them with the minimum hardware recommendations offered earlier in this task. For better playback (and to make sure your system can handle programs published in the next year or so), buy a multimedia system that *exceeds* the MPC2 standard.

You can buy a kit to upgrade your existing computer to multimedia, as long as your CPU, RAM, and hard disk space are already the ones you need. These kits include the CD-ROM drive, sound card, and speakers. In addition to their reasonable price, these kits are a good bet because the sound cards they include are guaranteed compatible with their CD-ROM drives.

Equipment You Need for Multimedia Applications

Component	*MPC2 Standard*	*Our Recommendation*
CPU	80486 SX, 25MHz	Pentium, 66MHz
RAM	4M	16M
Hard disk	160M	540M
CD-ROM drive	double-speed	quad-speed
Monitor/video card	640 x 480 VGA	1024 x 768 SVGA
Sound card	8-bit	16-bit
Floppy drive	3.5-inch HD	3.5-inch HD

Decide Where to Buy It

One final decision awaits you before you take the plunge and buy your new computer. You have to choose where to buy it, and this decision isn't as straightforward as it may seem. In the last few years, dozens of manufacturers and sellers have jumped into the fray, offering a variety of computer components through retail and mail outlets.

Where you decide to buy your computer depends not only on the kind of computer you want to buy, but also on your computing confidence and what you expect to happen after the sale. Computer magazines and your local newspaper offer advertisements for a variety of computer sellers. While the ads may look the same, there are great differences in what you get from various computer sellers.

When you choose where to buy your computer, compare factors like price, service, and warranty. Be sure you're comparing apples to apples where possible—compare prices on systems from the same manufacturer with the same features, or on comparable services. Here are the primary factors to consider.

Manufacturer and Packages

Make sure you're buying a computer from a reputable manufacturer. Go to the library and check computer magazines such as *PC Novice* and *PC World* to find the top brands that offer the most reliable products. Most sellers offer *pre-configured* systems with everything you need (such as a fully equipped multimedia package). Not only are these packages competitively priced, but they're also easier to set up than a system that requires you to add (for example) a sound card and CD-ROM drive. Also look for free software with a

Where You Can Buy Your Computer

Seller	*Description*
Mail/phone order companies	Sell equipment and software from a variety of manufacturers at very low prices. Offer convenience but minimum of service. Let you purchase with credit card. For highly experienced users.
Manufacturer direct	Manufacturer sells its own equipment only by phone or mail. Convenient, with competitive pricing and warranty. Purchase with credit card. Knowledgeable sales staff. For experienced users or those who want to purchase a particular brand.

(continues)

Where You Can Buy Your Computer Continued

Seller	*Description*
Appliance/department store	Your neighborhood appliance or department stores now offer computers alongside other electronic equipment. Typically, selection, service, and the salesperson's knowledge are limited, although financing may be offered. For moderately experienced users.
Computer discount stores	These computer superstores offer the broadest selection and best pricing available from retailers. Knowledgeable sales force and financing help smooth the sale. Most offer carry-in repair and upgrade service. Inexperienced users can comfortably buy a computer here.
Value-added resellers (VARs)	These sellers include small retail computer stores and companies that sell computers direct to businesses. Typically their salespeople are most knowledgeable, and they offer the highest level of after-sale service. Many perform warranty work for computer manufacturers. All this service costs more, though. For very inexperienced users, businesses, or those who want to purchase a high level of after-sale support.

system. Many manufacturers and dealers include hundreds of dollars' worth of software with every new system.

Pricing

Generally, you can get the best prices when you buy through mail order—direct from the manufacturer or from a computer discount store. Compare prices from a few sources and make sure you're getting the best deal. Check whether certain extras and necessities are included in the price; sometimes shipping or printer cables (for example) will cost extra.

Financing

Department stores, appliance stores, and computer discount stores frequently offer financing or special deals like "six months same as cash." Be careful with store financing; interest rates can be as high as credit card rates—or higher. Mail-order companies, manufacturers, and VARs typically let you use a credit card to purchase your computer.

Warranty

Most manufacturers offer a warranty (one year minimum) on parts and labor; the maximum is three years. Generally, the first year of any warranty is *on-site*—a repair representative will come to you to fix your system. After that, most warranties offer *carry-in* service—you must transport the system to the store where you purchased it (or to an authorized dealer) for repair. Appliance and department stores, computer superstores, and VARs all let you upgrade your warranty for a price. If you purchase your system via mail order, typically you need to ship it in at your own expense for repairs, even warranty repairs. Most warranties require that repairs or upgrades be performed by an authorized dealer; using any other repair service (or doing it yourself) voids the warranty.

Service

You can purchase additional computer services (for example, upgrading your system) from computer superstores and VARs. In general, a computer superstore's fees will be much lower than a VAR's.

The superstore requires you to carry your system in, however, while a VAR will come to you (for a fee, of course). Superstores offer some services (such as adding a modem to your system) at a flat rate rather than an hourly fee; if the technician encounters a problem while performing the service, you don't have to pay for extra time used to fix the problem. Be sure to have an authorized dealer perform repairs and upgrades to your system if it's still under warranty.

Begin Guided Tour Things to Look For When Buying a Computer

1 **Manufacturer and packages:** Make sure you're buying a computer from a reputable manufacturer.

2 **Pricing:** Compare prices from a few sources; make sure you're getting the best deal.

3 **Financing:** Be careful with store financing; interest rates can be as high as credit card rates—or higher.

✓ One year on-site warranty on parts and service
✓ We repair and upgrade computers

4 **Warranty:** Most manufacturers offer a warranty (one year minimum) on parts and labor; the maximum is three years.

5 **Service:** You can purchase additional computer services (for example, upgrading your system) from computer superstores and VARs.

Decide Where to Put a New Computer

Like any tool, your computer requires that you observe a few guidelines to use it comfortably and safely. Following these rules will prolong the life of your computer by protecting it from damage.

You should be particularly careful about where you place a computer within your home. Let common sense guide you. If the computer is for your whole family, put it in a room where you can easily supervise the kids while they use it. Make sure the kids can seat themselves at it comfortably without grabbing or leaning on any of the components. If you'll be using your home computer for business, put it in a more secluded spot (such as a den or home office) where you can have solitude while you work.

Likewise, you should use common sense with regard to what you place on and around your computer. Avoid bringing beverages around your computer; a spilled drink can fry a keyboard or burn up a CPU. You don't want to pile a ton of books on your system unit or get crumbs in a disk drive. You should also avoid smoking around your computer; smoke residue can clog and gunk up your disk drives.

Following are the common-sense guidelines you need to follow in deciding where to put your computer:

Use a computer desk and comfy chair. You need a wide, stable surface for your system unit, monitor, and printer; make sure you have a comfortable chair with good support and adjustable height. Computer desks can be an economical solution (prices range from around a hundred dollars to a couple thousand for decorator-style units).

Keep it cool and dry. Excessive heat can damage your computer, particularly the hard drive. Likewise, humidity (or worse, dripping water) can zap your computer or make it behave erratically. Avoid placing your computer in damp areas like basements, hot rooms like attics, or other areas that aren't air-conditioned. Also, make sure there are several inches of clearance behind the system unit, so its exhaust fan can draw in fresh air to cool the computer when it runs.

Avoid dust and pet hair. The system unit's fan tends to suck in dust along with fresh air; sliding a disk into a drive can push in dirt and hair, as well. Keep the area around your computer free from dust, hair, or equipment that attracts either of these (like a clothes dryer). If you can't avoid dust, consider buying plastic dust covers for your system components.

Provide proper lighting. Place your computer so the room's light source is above and slightly behind the monitor. Improper lighting that falls on the monitor from the front or sides causes glare and reflections on the monitor, which can strain your eyes and make the screen hard to read.

Use a stable electrical outlet. Never plug your computer into an outlet that's on a household circuit used by other appliances—even small ones like a toaster or blow-dryer. These can suck current away from the computer, causing power drops that will make the system lose data.

Put a modem-equipped computer near a phone line. If your computer system has a modem, be sure to put the system near a phone jack or a location where one can be installed.

Keep it away from family traffic. Use common sense. Don't place the computer where anyone can trip over the power or mouse cords, put the groceries down on the keyboard accidentally, throw things at the monitor, or the like.

Begin Guided Tour Set Up Your Work Environment

1 **Use a computer desk and comfy chair.** Keep the computer cool and dry, and avoid dust and pet hair.

2 **Keep it cool and dry.** Excessive heat can damage your computer, particularly the hard drive. Likewise, humidity (or worse, dripping water) can zap your computer or make it behave erratically.

3 **Avoid dust and pet hair.** The system unit's fan tends to suck in dust along with fresh air; sliding a disk into a drive can push in dirt and hair, as well.

4 **Provide proper lighting.** Place your computer so the room's light source is above and slightly behind the monitor.

5 **Use a stable electrical outlet.** Never plug your computer into an outlet that's on a household circuit used by other appliances.

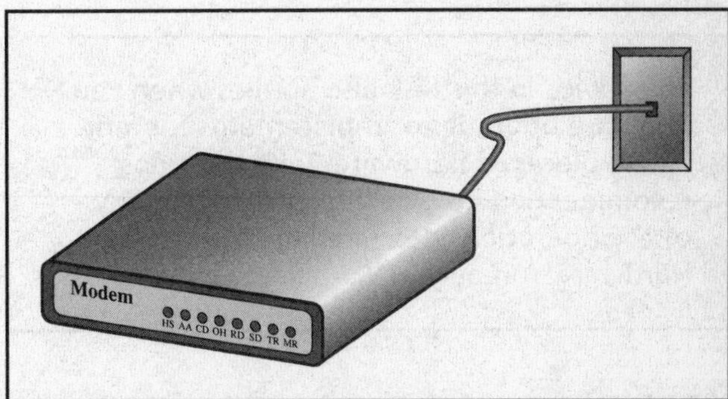

6 **Put a modem-equipped computer near a phone line.**

7 **Keep it away from family traffic.** Use common sense. You know where your home's traffic areas are.

Because computers use a lot of electricity, they tend to attract a lot of dust and pet hair. These can cause wear on your computer's parts—or even errors—if they get sucked into a disk drive. For information on keeping your computer happy and dust-free, see "Keep Your Computer Clean and Healthy" on page 327.

Unpack and Check a New Computer

Bringing home a new computer can be like getting a much-anticipated gift. You're tempted to just rip into the package and whoop it up. While there's no need to be a total party-pooper, resist the temptation to rip into your computer packages and burn the refuse.

Use a reasonable amount of care when unpacking your system to avoid damaging any of the components. Also, take the time to do things that will ensure you can take advantage of your computer's warranty—register the system and (horrors) keep a few things you would normally throw out. The *Guided Tour* explains the process.

The advice in this task also applies when you purchase upgrades or replacements for individual pieces of hardware. Take the steps recommended here before performing any of the operations described in "Install New Hardware" on page 415.

1. Carefully open the boxes containing the computer components by pulling the outside tape. Avoid slitting the box with scissors or a knife, which can scratch the components.
2. Remove each component from its box, placing it carefully on a computer desk or other flat, secure surface. Place any paperwork from the boxes in a handy location nearby. Also remove any cardboard protectors from the floppy disk drives.
3. Return all cardboard, Styrofoam, and plastic packing materials to the boxes, including the floppy disk protectors. Store the boxes in a safe, dry place. You'll use these if you ever need to transport the computer. (Also, some companies will not allow returns unless the computer is packed in its original boxes.)

Chet's Computers

Packing Slip

Order #	Order Date	Ship Date	P.O. Number
123-777	4/3/95	4/5/95	784-335

Quantity	Description	Price
1	486 DX/4 100mhz system w/540M hard drive, 8M memory, 15" .28mm SVGA display	$1,599.00
1	Multimedia upgrade kit, includes 2x CD-ROM drive, SoundBlaster-compatible sound card, and Altec 10-watt speakers; Installed	239.00
1	LaserJet Printer	499.00
Totals:		$2,337.00

4. Take the packing slip or receipt from the pile of papers you put aside, and check it to ensure you've received all the pieces you paid for. Review the setup instructions quickly; have you received all the connectors you need? If something's missing, contact the seller immediately.
5. Inspect all components for damage. If you find problems, call the seller immediately.

Chet's Computers

12 E. 10th, Illseeya, Wyoming 55555

Customer Registration

Complete this form within 30 days of your computer purchase and mail it to the above address to activate your warranty and make you eligible to receive free information about new products and product upgrades.

Name: __________

Street: __________

City: __________

State and ZIP: __________

System/components purchased: __________

Purchase date: __________

Purchase price: __________

Purchased from: __________

How did you learn about us? __________

6. Fill out and mail your Registration Card. If you want to get technical support from the manufacturer or seller, you must follow its registration process.
7. Take all the paperwork that came with your computer—packing slip, invoices, receipts, and warranty information—and file it with your other important personal papers.

Plug the Components Together

If you can plug in an electrical cord, you can connect a computer system's components. It's all a matter of plugging the right connector into the right socket. The sockets and connectors have similar shapes (and corresponding numbers of holes and pins), so matching them up is easy. Some computer manufacturers even label the various sockets on the back of the system unit for you.

Just remember—if you feel you're having to force a connector into position, back off. You may be trying to plug it into the wrong socket, and you may risk breaking pins off the connector if you force it. One more tip: avoid bringing magnetic or electrical fields too close to the computer (don't even use magnetic-head screwdrivers), and *don't turn on any component until you have the whole system assembled and you have plugged the system into a surge protector.*

You may need a few tools to assemble your computer. These are primarily used to tighten connectors into place. So, before you start, gather up a medium-sized Phillips-head screwdriver, a medium-sized flat-head screwdriver, and a small flat-head screwdriver. Also grab a small envelope or plastic baggie for leftover screws and the like; file these away with the paperwork that came with your computer.

One last thing before you follow the *Guided Tour* for assembling your system: take the time to lay out all the parts where you want them so that you won't have to untangle cables after you've connected components. For example, if you want to place the mouse to the right of the keyboard and the printer somewhere to the left, arrange them that way before making the connections.

1. **Connect the keyboard.** Find a round socket on the back of the computer that accommodates a connector with five or six pins and a square. The socket also will have a slot at the top or bottom. Align the keyboard plug's pins with the holes in the socket; this should also line up the ridge on the keyboard plug with the slot in the socket. Press the plug gently into place.

2. **Connect the mouse.** The connector will look like the round keyboard plug or will be an oblong shape (with 15 or fewer pins). Align the mouse plug's pins with the holes in the socket; press the plug gently into place. If you have an oblong connector with screws, gently tighten the screws.

3. **Connect the monitor.** It has two cords: one has an oblong plug with 15 or fewer pins; the other plugs into a source of power (on the back of the system unit or on a surge suppressor). Plug in the oblong connector and the power cord; *do not* turn on the monitor yet.

4. **Connect the printer.** Most likely, its cord will have a *parallel* connector with 25 pins that plugs into a socket with 25 holes on the system unit. Printers using serial ports have 9- or 25-pin connections; in this case, the system unit has the pins and the connecting end of the cable has the holes. Check your printer's cable: Which connection do you have? Ease the plug into place, tightening the screws or clicking the metal clips. Plug your printer's power cord into the surge suppressor, but *do not* turn on the printer yet.

5. **Set up your external modem.** You need to make several connections. Using a cord that ends in plastic clips like those on a phone cord (*RJ-11 connections*), plug one end into the Line jack on the back of the modem; plug the other end into your home's phone-line jack. Take the serial cable that comes with the modem. Plug one end into the serial port on the back of the modem, and plug the other into the corresponding 25-pin socket on the back of your computer. Finally, plug the modem power cord (if any) into the surge suppressor. (For internal modems, use

an RJ-11 cord to connect the Line jack on the back of the system unit to the wall phone jack. If your modem has an extra jack labeled "Phone," you can plug your phone into it.)

6. **Plug in the speakers and microphone (multimedia systems only).** Connect them to the sound card at the back of the system unit. Plug the microphone into the "Mic In" jack, and plug the speakers into the "Spk Out" jack. If you're not using batteries for the speakers, you'll need a DC adapter unit; plug one end into the DC jack on the back of one of the speakers and the other end into the surge suppressor (*don't* turn on the speakers yet)!
7. **Finally, plug the system unit itself into your surge-suppressor power source.** The cable for the system unit has one end with prongs and one with slots. Plug the end with slots into the receptacle with prongs (sometimes labeled "AC Input"). Plug the normal end of the cable into the surge suppressor.
8. See "Start Up Your Computer" on page 28 to learn how to power up your system.

Most computer manufacturers now provide documentation identifying the various sockets and connectors on the back of the system unit. If you have any doubts about where things go for your computer, specifically, check the documentation.

Begin Guided Tour Plug It All In

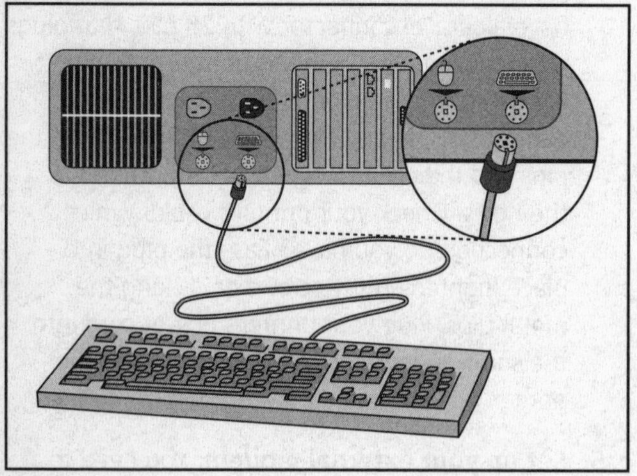

1 Connect the keyboard.

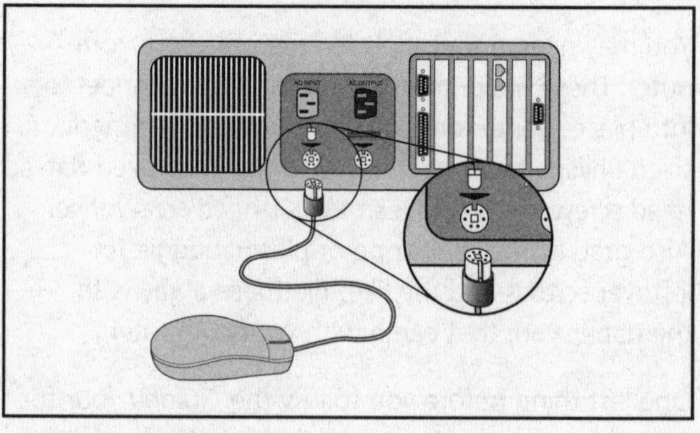

2 Connect the mouse.

Guided Tour Plug It All In

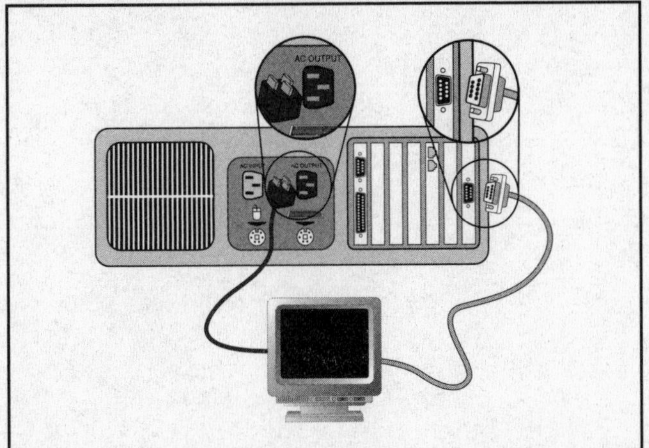

3 Connect the monitor.

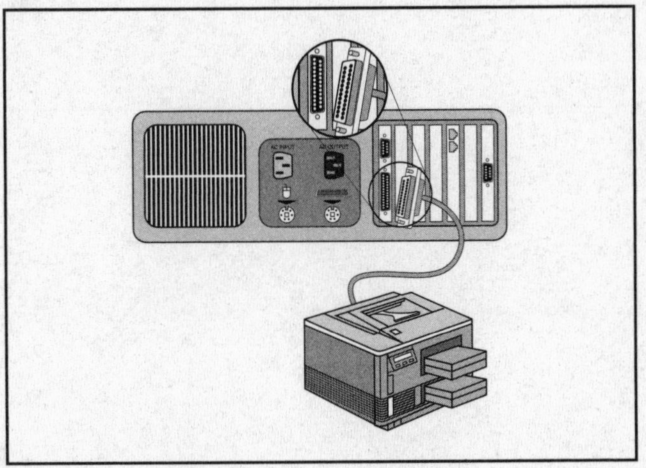

4 Connect the printer.

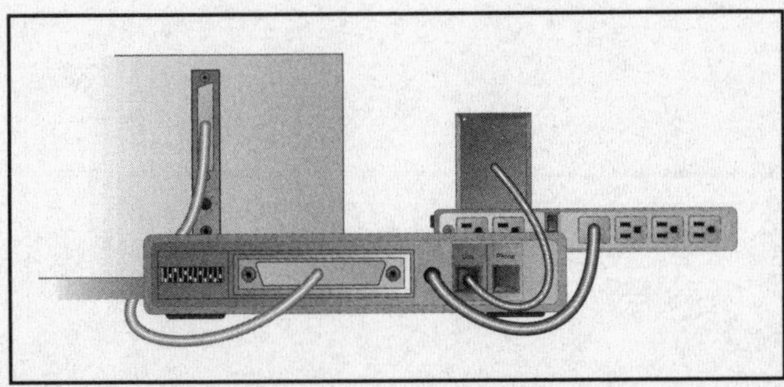

5 Set up your external modem.

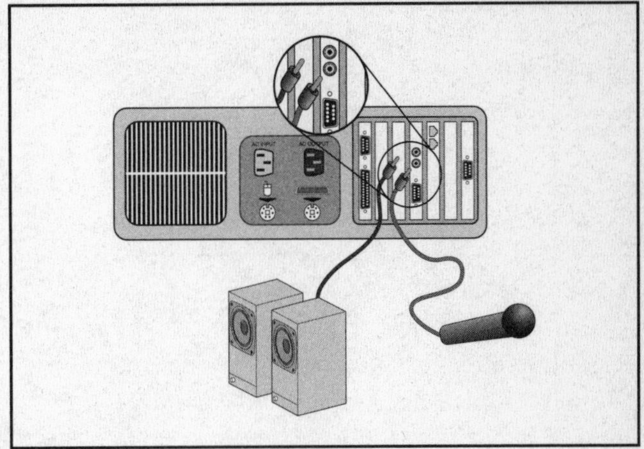

6 Plug in the speakers and microphone (multimedia systems only).

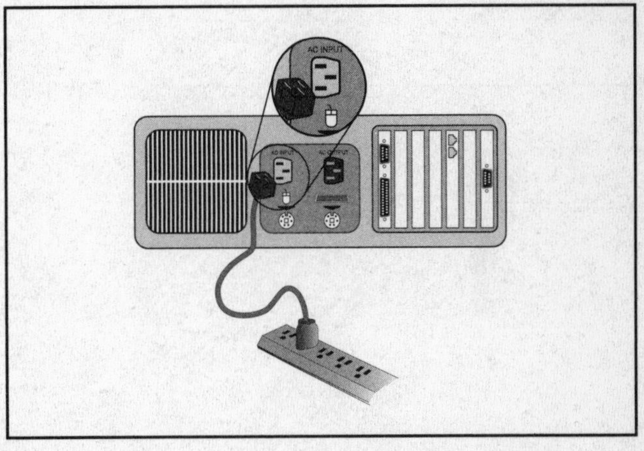

7 Finally, plug the system unit itself into your surge-suppressor power source.

HOW TO...

Operate Your Computer

Remember the footage of NASA from the late '60s and early '70s showing rows of people with monitors and huge, beastly computers that filled entire rooms? Back then, you literally had to be a rocket scientist to operate a computer.

Today's computers not only pack much more power into much smaller spaces, but also offer features to make them easier and more natural to use. Anyone can sit down and operate a computer by flipping a few switches and pecking at a keyboard or mouse.

This section takes you quickly through the basics of using your computer hardware. (The software's another story, and you'll learn about that soon.) Complete all these tasks, and you'll have earned your computing Ph.D.—but you still won't be a rocket scientist!

What You Will Find in This Section

Start Up Your Computer 28

Shut Down at the End of the Day 30

Insert and Remove Floppy Disks 31

Understand Floppy Disk Capacity 33

Insert and Remove CD-ROMs 34

Adjust a Monitor for Viewing Comfort 36

Operate a Mouse 38

Reset (Warm-Boot) a Locked-Up Computer 41

Cold-Boot Your System 43

Start Up Your Computer

As with any electronic device, you have to turn on your computer to get it to work. This simple process involves several steps you should use religiously. Although you might not damage your computer if you do it differently, turning on the system components in the right order can help prolong the life of your system.

Starting your computer is also called *booting up* (your system "pulls itself up by its bootstraps"). The computer reads built-in startup instructions from the operating system and some special chips; then it performs a Power-On Self-Test (POST) to check its ability to "talk" to the system components.

Many users debate when you should turn your computer on and off. Some insist that we all should conserve energy, turning a computer off every time we've finished using it. At the other extreme, some people think computers should never be shut down; they think all this powering up and down wears out the computer's components faster.

Most computer manufacturers recommend that you start your computer up at the beginning of the day and shut it down at the end of the day. However, most experts recommend the opposite; they say turning the system on and off frequently is a bad idea, especially because most failures occur during power-up. For best results, use the following *Guided Tour* to start off your computing day.

Depending on how your system is set up, you may see the DOS prompt, the Windows Program Manager screen if you have Windows 3.11, or the Windows Desktop if you have Windows 95. For more about DOS, see "Work with DOS" on page 211. To get started with Windows 3.11, see "Get Around in Windows 3.11 Programs" on page 57. For help with using Windows 95, see "Work in Windows 95" on page 149. Other systems may display a special menu or screen.

Some users like to plug all their computer components into the surge suppressor and leave all the power switches on. This lets them turn on the whole system just by flipping the switch on the surge suppressor. This is a BAD IDEA, because it sends a power surge into the individual components, zapping them slightly and causing excess wear. For safety, follow the steps here for powering up.

Fix Startup Problems

If you use the steps for starting your computer system and nothing happens—or you get an error—don't worry! Here's how you can fix common startup problems. If none of these solutions work, see the "101 Quick Fixes" section on page 471.

- If the monitor is completely dark, try turning up its brightness or contrast settings. For more about this, see "Adjust a Monitor for Viewing Comfort" later in this section, on page 36.
- If the monitor is dark or you don't hear a particular component whir to life, something isn't plugged together properly. Turn off the power for all the components and the surge suppressor. Make sure all the computer cables are firmly connected, and make sure all the pieces are plugged into the surge suppressor. Then retry the startup process.
- If you see a message on-screen saying **Non-system disk or disk error**, you probably have a disk in the floppy drive. Remove the disk, and press any key to continue the startup process.

Begin Guided Tour Start Your Computer

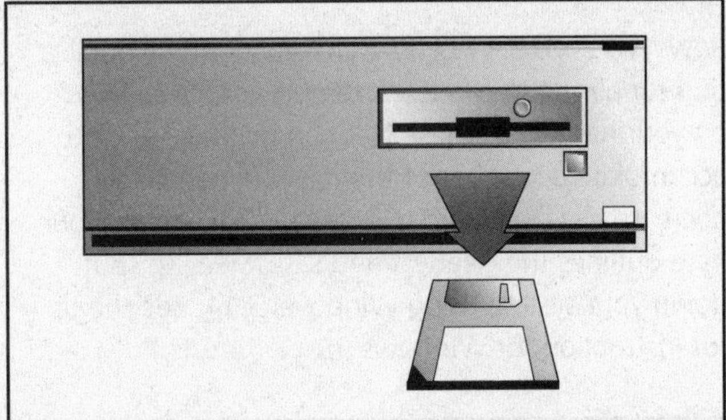

1 Make sure the floppy disk drives are empty. Otherwise, the computer will try to start itself from any floppy disk it finds in drive A (most will not have any system-startup instructions).

2 Make sure the surge-suppressor strip is plugged into the wall socket and that all system components are plugged into the surge suppressor. Turn on the surge suppressor.

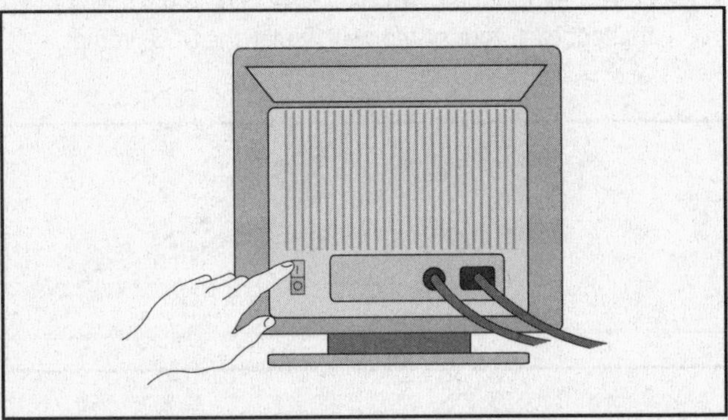

3 Turn on the monitor's power next. The power switch usually has a **I** (vertical hash mark) on the top half and a **O** (circle) on the bottom half. To turn the monitor on, press down the half with the **I** mark.

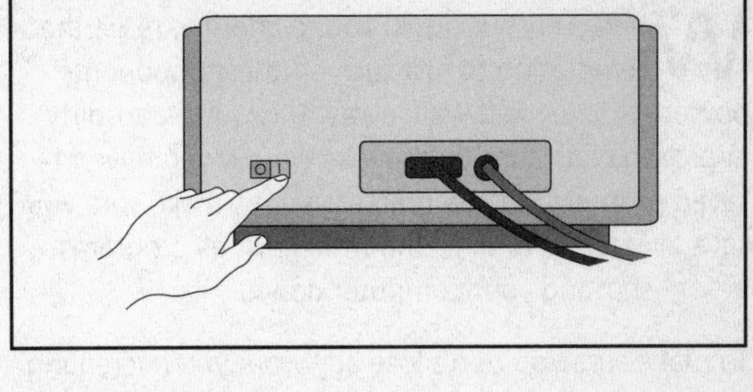

4 If you have a printer, turn it on next; the power switch is usually on the back or right side. The **Online** indicator for the printer should light up, indicating that it's ready to go.

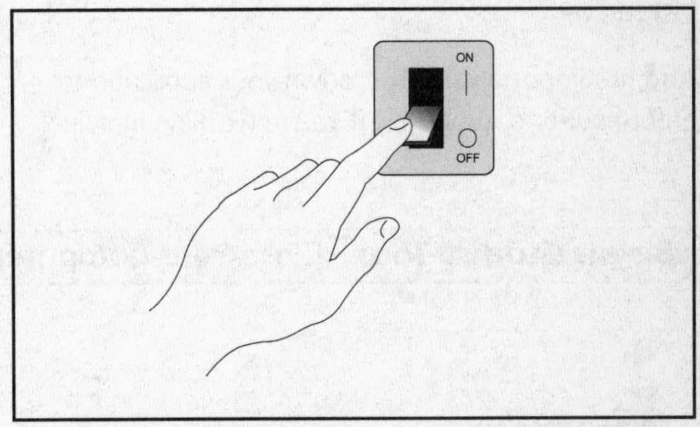

5 Time to turn on the system unit. Find the On/Off switch on the back, right, or front side of the system unit; turn it to **On** or depress it to the "on" position.

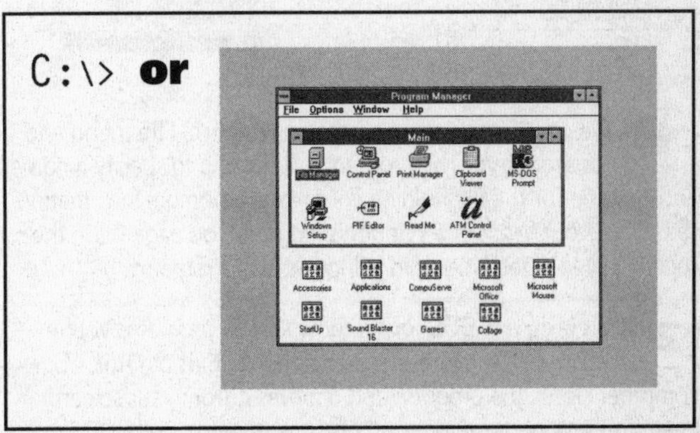

6 Watch the monitor; you'll see several self-test messages flash on the screen. When the computer finishes its self-test, you'll see the prompt for the system's Disk Operating System (DOS) or you'll see Windows. In any case, you're ready.

Shut Down at the End of the Day

When you shut down your computer, resist the temptation to just turn off the components' power switches and walk away. This quick-and-dirty approach can cause you to lose work if you haven't saved properly. For the greatest safety, make sure you save all your work first—and then exit all programs—before shutting your computer down.

To make sure you don't lose any work you're creating with a particular software application, *save* it to a file on the hard disk so you can work with it later. Otherwise, when you shut the system down, your work will be cleared out of Random-Access Memory (RAM) and lost forever.

Also, it's important to shut down your applications before quitting, especially if you're working in Windows (versions 3.11 or 95). Quitting with an application running also can leave temporary (.tmp) files on your hard disk. These files can be large—if you accumulate a number of them, you'll needlessly decrease available hard disk space. The *Guided Tour* here outlines the cleanest and safest way to shut down your system using Windows 3.11. See the tip for instruction for Windows 95.

To exit Windows 95, click the **Start** button in the lower left corner of the screen, and then click **Shut Down**. A dialog box appears, asking you to confirm. Click the **Yes** button. For more information about starting, exiting, and restarting Windows 95, see "Start and Shut Down Windows 95" on page 150.

Begin Guided Tour Close Your Computer Down

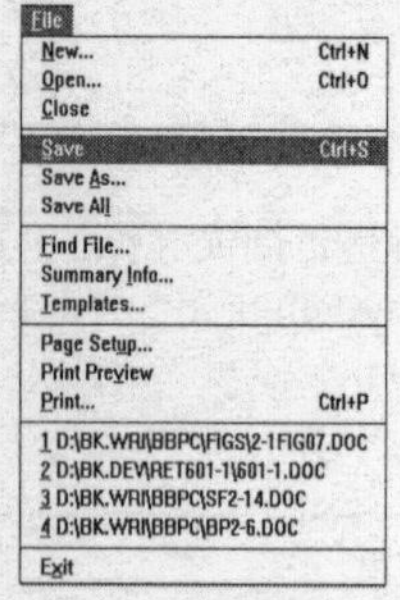

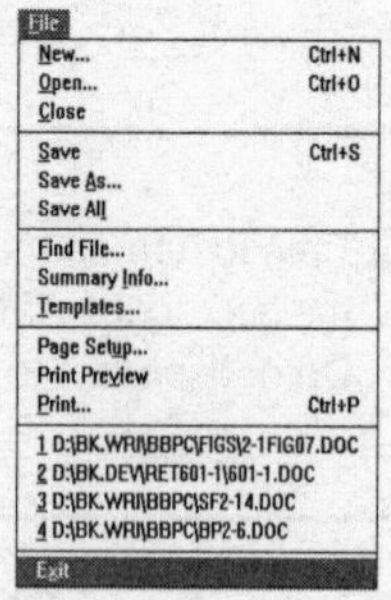

1 Save your files by opening the application's **File** menu and choosing **Save**. The program will ask you to specify a name and location for the file holding your work. (For more information, see "Save Your Work in a Windows Program" on page 92 in the section called "Get Around in Windows 3.11 Programs.")

2 Quit (exit) any DOS- or Windows-based programs you're using: open the **File** menu and choose **Exit** or **Quit**. Your computer closes the program and removes it from your screen. (See "Exit a Windows Program" on page 98 and "Exit a DOS Program" on page 233.)

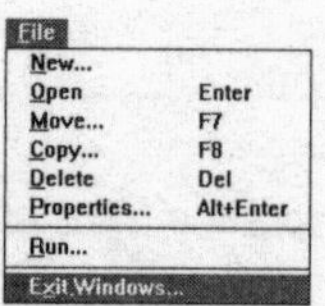

3 Exit Windows if it's running: open the **File** menu and choose **Exit** (or press **Alt+F4**). Select **OK** in the dialog box that appears; your system will display the DOS prompt.

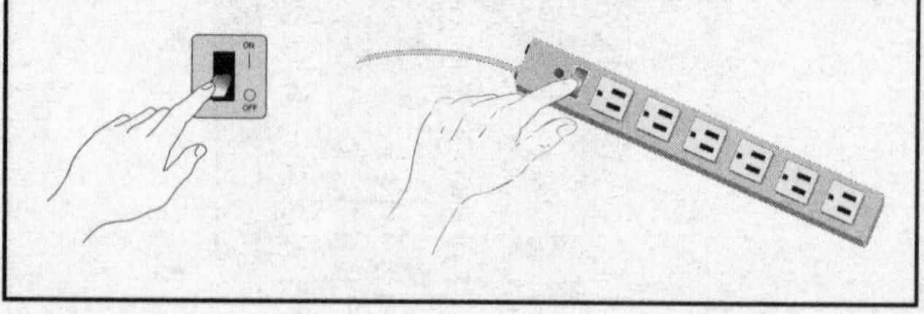

4 Turn off the power switch on the system unit first. Then turn off the power switches on the monitor and printer.

5 Turn off the surge suppressor's power switch.

Insert and Remove Floppy Disks

Computers let you work smarter because you can share information between them. If two similar computers have the same program installed, you can create work on one of the computers, save the work, transport it to the other computer, and then resume your work. In fact, your reason for buying a home computer might be to bring work home from the office so you can complete it at home in privacy and comfort (or to meet a looming deadline).

When you think of floppy disks, you may imagine the older type that has a flexible square plastic skin. This 5.25-inch floppy disk was the most common size used for IBM-compatible PCs in the early to mid-'80s. A drive for this kind of floppy has a 5.25-inch-wide slot, usually a lever that flips down over the slot, and a small indicator light.

Today, floppy disks come in two sizes: 5.25-inch and 3.5-inch (a newer design). Don't be fooled by the size. The smaller disk holds more data than the larger 5.25-inch disk.

Most newer PCs do not have a floppy drive for this size disk, and most software publishers no longer package their software on 5.25-inch disks. If you have an older machine with the larger floppy drive, you'll have to send a special request to the publisher of your software to get disks that fit.

The most common kind of floppy disk used today isn't floppy at all! Smaller, 3.5-inch floppy disks have a hard plastic shell encasing the magnetic storage material—better physical protection for your valuable magnetic data. You might think these smaller disks don't hold as much data as their larger 5.25-inch cousins, but actually the reverse is true (more about that soon). Their smaller size makes these floppies easier to store and more convenient to carry. Note that these floppy drives are so small that they might be positioned vertically in the system unit; this means you should hold a floppy disk vertically when inserting it into the drive.

Your computer can help you be an organizational genius and can help save space that used to be occupied by mountains of paper. For more about the way computers store data on hard and floppy disks, see "Understand How the Computer Stores Files" on page 45.

Begin Guided Tour Insert and Remove 3.5-Inch Disks

1 Turn your 3.5-inch disk label-side-up. Grip the edge *opposite* the edge covered by the sliding door.

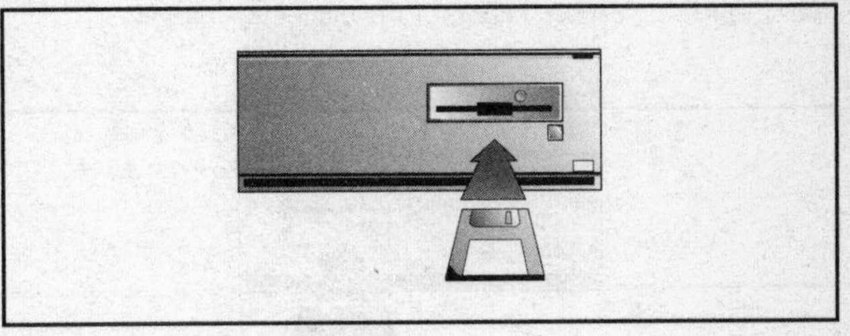

2 Insert the edge covered by the sliding door into the drive slot. Push it (gently) all the way into the drive. When the disk seats, the drive's eject button pops out.

(continues)

Guided Tour Insert and Remove 3.5-Inch Disks

(continued)

3 When you're finished using the disk, save your work on it. Once the drive's indicator light goes out, you're ready to remove the disk (which you should do before you use another one or shut down your computer).

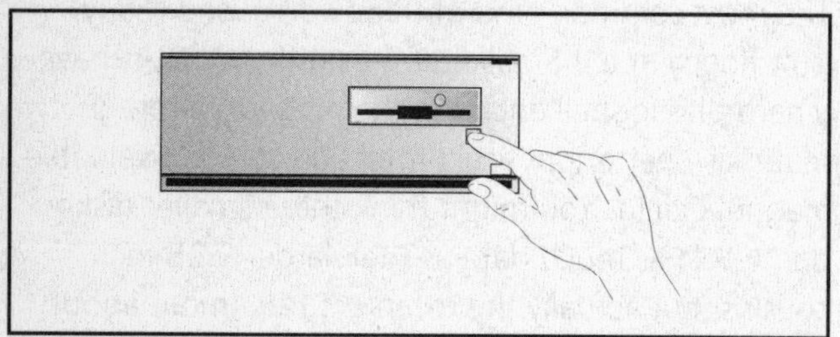

4 Press the drive's eject button; the disk pops partway out.

5 Pull the disk the rest of the way out.

Begin Guided Tour Insert and Remove 5.25-Inch Disks

1 With the drive lever clear of the slot, turn your 5.25-inch disk label-side-up with the rectangular notch on the right. Grip the disk at its top edge, and remove it from its envelope (don't touch the exposed areas of the magnetic disk).

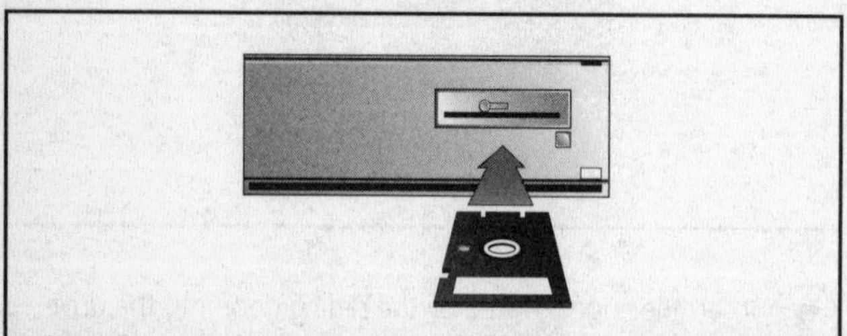

2 One edge of the disk has *two* small notches; this is the one you insert into the drive slot. Push it (very gently) all the way into the drive until it clicks.

3 Press down gently on the drive lever until it clicks into place across the drive slot. (If you have any trouble pressing the lever down, don't force it; pull out the disk and try again.)

4 When you're finished using the disk, save your work on it. Once the drive's indicator light goes out, you're ready to remove the disk (which you should do before you use another one or shut down your computer).

5 Gently flip the drive lever back up. The floppy disk should pop partway out of the drive.

6 Grip the disk by its labeled end, and pull it gently out of the drive.

Understand Floppy Disk Capacity

You may have noticed that your floppy disks or disk labels have "HD" or something similar on them. These hieroglyphics refer to the disk's *density* or *capacity*, which is as important as the floppy's size. Both affect how much data a floppy disk can hold.

Manufacturers indicate this amount in *kilobytes* (each K is just over 1,000 characters) and *megabytes* (each M is more than one million characters). All floppy disks sold today are *double-sided* (DS); they store data on both sides (many early floppies were single-sided).

The disk's capacity depends on how efficient its magnetic storage material is. The newer *high-density* (HD) disks hold more data than *double-density* (DD) disks of the same size.

Take Care of Your Floppy Disks

While floppy disks aren't as fragile as they used to be, they aren't indestructible, either. Use a reasonable amount of care and caution when handling floppy disks. Here are some guidelines:

- Avoid touching the magnetic disk surface where it's exposed, especially on 5.25-inch disks. Skin oil and other substances can damage the disk's magnetic properties.
- Avoid placing the disk anywhere near dust, dirt, or liquid; these can damage magnetic material. If you insert a dirty disk into a disk drive, the gunk on the disk can damage the drive.
- Keep the disk well away from magnets, electrical wires, electronic appliances, computer components, or anything that might be magnetized—like paper clips. That's right—never clip a disk to your paperwork. Electric power generates a magnetic field that can affect the disk's magnetic material.
- Keep disks away from heat sources (like photocopiers) that can warp them.
- For 5.25-inch disks, make sure you write on the label *before* sticking it on the disk. A sharp pencil or ballpoint could dent a disk's magnetic surface. (To be extra safe, always use a felt-tip pen.)
- *Write-protect* your disks to preserve data. This procedure lets the disk drive read what's on a disk, but prevents the drive from altering the data in any way. To write-protect a 5.25-inch disk, bend a piece of tape (or a write-protect tab) over the rectangular notch near one corner of the disk. Write-protect a 3.5-inch disk by moving a small tab (you'll see this if you look at the back of the disk) to open the little tab window.

Floppy Disk Capacities

Size	*Type*	*Capacity*
5.25-inch	DSDD, double-sided double-density	360K
5.25-inch	DSHD, double-sided high-density	1.2M
3.5-inch	DSDD, double-sided double-density	720K
3.5-inch	DSHD, double-sided high-density	1.44M

Insert and Remove CD-ROMs

Many computer users experience a thrill the first time they play an audio CD—or a multimedia CD-ROM computer program—from their PC's CD-ROM drive. The CD-ROM drive revolutionized personal computers, giving them the capability of handling text, graphics, video, animation, and sound—making the PC a true multimedia machine. The CD-ROM drive reads the data on the disc by spinning it and bouncing a laser off the surface.

Previously, multimedia escaped the reach of most computers because video, animation, and sound take huge amounts of storage space. Each reflective CD-ROM holds over 650M of information—more than the average hard drive held a year or so ago! In the next few years, CD-ROM drives that can write as well as read data will become widely available and affordable.

Some CD-ROM drives use a *disk caddy*; you have to put the disc in a caddy before you put it in the drive. Drives without a caddy have a drawer that slides in and out for the disc.

> **CD-ROM drives spin the disc so fast that your computer can grab data from any spot on the disc almost immediately. Data CDs organize information in drives and directories, just like hard and floppy disks. For more information, see "Understand How the Computer Stores Files" on page 45.**

Use a Program's Controls to Open and Close the CD-ROM Drive

In life, you can count on the fact that mechanical parts wear out and break. Your CD-ROM drive has several mechanical parts, especially if it uses a drawer rather than a caddy. For example, buttons like the eject button on audio equipment and computers are notorious for wearing out. Similarly, too much downward pressure on a drive drawer can move it out of alignment or break it.

To prevent such disasters, some publishers of software for use with CDs provide ways to use the software to open and close the drive door.

1. If the program requires it, insert the CD manually into the drive. If you try to run the program and there's no disc in the drive, you'll see an error message.
2. Make sure you're finished using the disc. If it's an audio CD, stop playing it. If it has a program, use the **Exit** command on the **File** menu to close it.

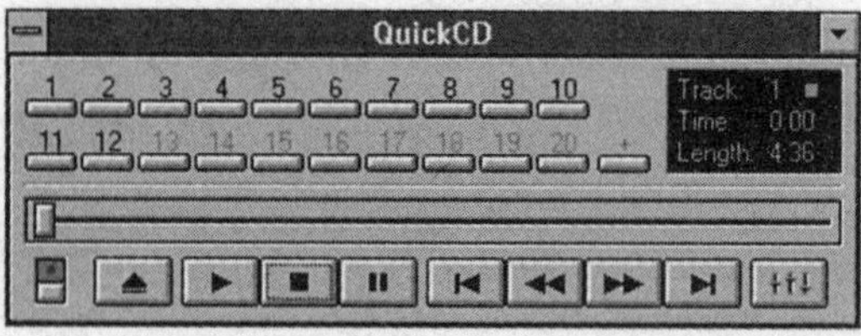

3. Open the drive or eject the caddy by clicking in the appropriate place or by choosing the appropriate menu command. For example, you may have to click an **eject icon** (symbol or picture), as shown here.

Begin Guided Tour Working with CD-ROMs

1 Check the shiny side of the CD for fingerprints, clinging hairs, or other debris. If you find any, wipe the CD gently with a soft cloth. Wipe from the center hole to the outside edges; do not wipe in a circular motion.

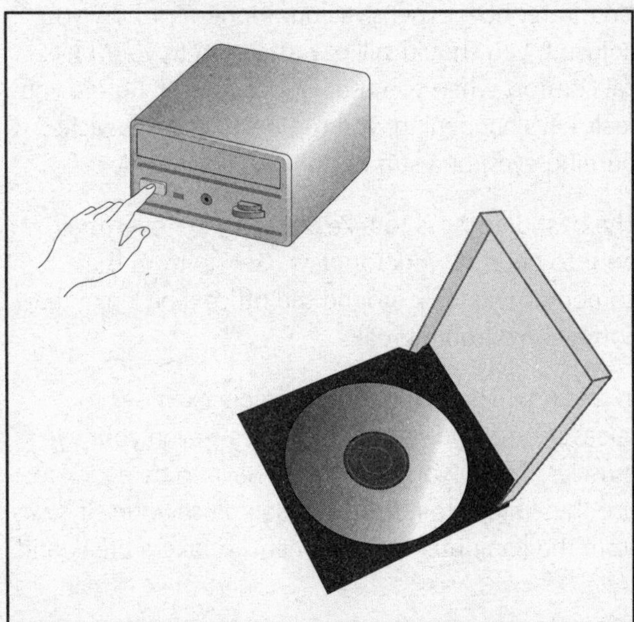

2 Open the CD-ROM drive by pressing its eject button; if your drive uses a caddy, flip open the CD-ROM caddy.

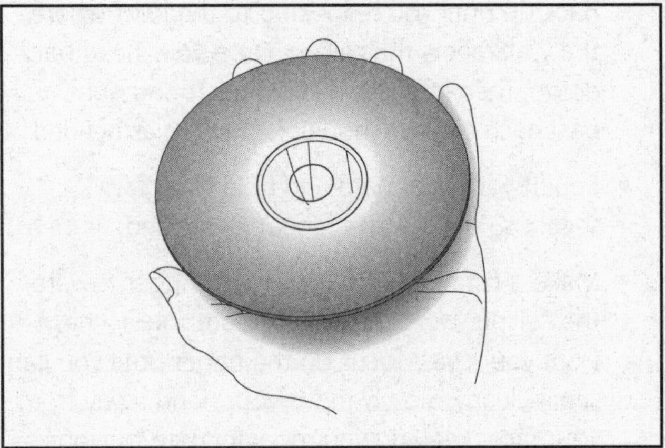

3 Grip the CD lightly (with your fingertips around its edge) and pick it up; the printed side should face your palm.

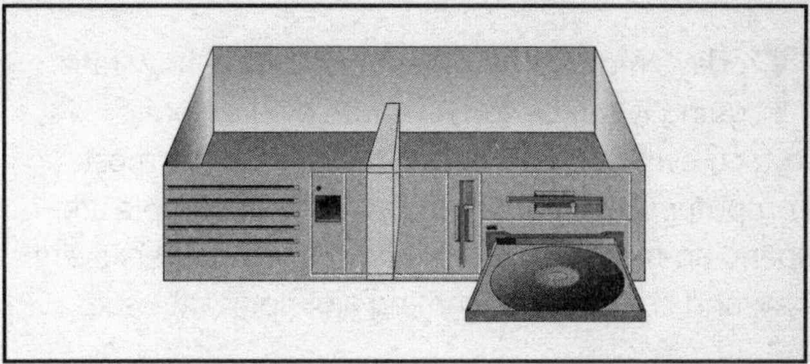

4 Carefully center the CD and place it in the drive drawer or the CD caddy. If you're using a caddy, close its lid and insert it into the slot in the drive.

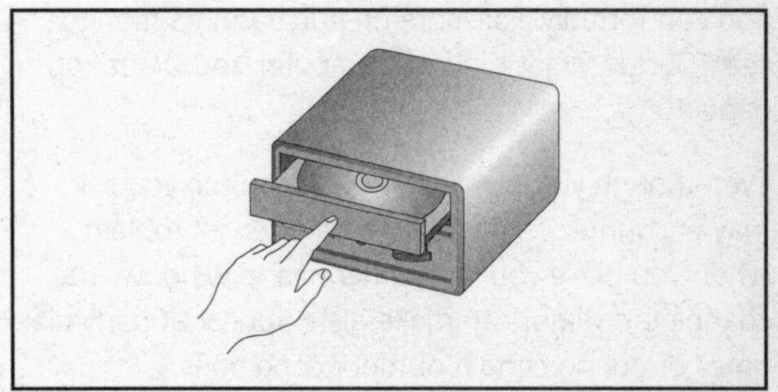

5 Gently push the drive drawer closed, or push the caddy into the drive slot. (Alternatively, you can press the eject button again.) The drive will close and the disc will be ready to use.

6 When you're finished using the CD-ROM, make sure you close any files from it that are open on-screen, or stop the disc if an audio CD is playing. Wait for the drive indicator light to go out; that means the CD's stopped spinning.

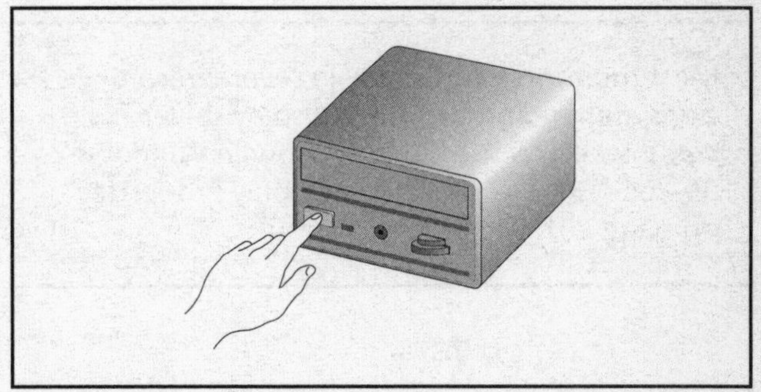

7 Press the CD-ROM drive's eject button. The drawer or caddy will slide out. Remove the CD or caddy from the drive. If the CD has a drawer, press it gently so it retracts into the drive, or press the eject button again to close it.

Adjust a Monitor for Viewing Comfort

Today's monitor manufacturers realize how fatiguing it can be to work with a bad monitor. In fact, eyestrain and neck strain still bother most computer users at one time or another; people are spending more and more time with computers every day, and comfort is becoming an important issue.

Buy a quality monitor that's *non-interlaced* (interlaced monitors flash in subtle ways that cause eye discomfort); it should also have a small dot pitch (about .28mm) for a sharp image. In addition, your monitor's controls can help you use your monitor more safely and comfortably. For more on purchasing a monitor, see "Decide What Kind of Computer You Want" on page 10.

Even though you can adjust your monitor, you still may encounter screen glare—it's often a problem when you place your computer near a window. The changing daylight can make glare appear at particular times or during certain outdoor conditions.

Of course, you can do the obvious: close the curtains or blinds to adjust the daylight coming in. Most people, however, find natural daylight restful—especially if the interior's lighted by fluorescent fixtures.

Don't worry. You can try a couple of tricks to get the best of both worlds.

Most monitors can display in several resolutions, depending on which display driver file you install and use. To learn how in Windows 95, see "Change the Video Display Properties" on page 201.

A Few Quick Exercises to Help Your Eyes

No matter how expensive your monitor or how you adjust it, you should still pay attention to your physical comfort when you use your computer. Before you realize it's happening, you can develop a headache, burning eyes, or a stiff neck.

The best defense is to take a break after every half-hour to hour of work (or play). Get up from the computer and walk around the office a bit. Take that coffee or restroom break.

In addition, you can do some simple exercises to release stress and rest your muscles—even your eye muscles. Don't worry, you don't have to be a jock to use these steps to refresh yourself. Push yourself away from the computer for a moment to take a break and try it.

- Release the tension in your neck by moving your head gently. In a seated position, place your hands in your lap and relax your shoulders. Slowly drop your chin to your chest, then raise it back up until you're looking to the joint where the wall meets the ceiling. Drop your head back down, then look slowly to the left and right, past each of your shoulders. Repeat as needed.
- Squint your eyes hard and hold for a few seconds. Release and repeat as needed.
- Make a fist and point your index finger toward the ceiling. Hold the finger about four inches from your eyes; focus on the finger until you can see it clearly. Slowly move your hand away from your face, keeping your eyes focused on your finger, until you've fully extended your arm. Then slowly bring your hand back to its original position, keeping your eyes focused on your finger. Repeat as needed.

Begin Guided Tour Adjust Your Monitor

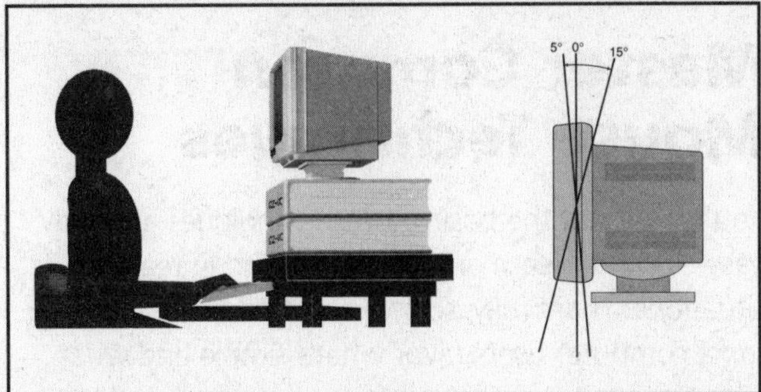

1 Place the monitor at the appropriate height and distance in relation to where you sit. The monitor should be about two feet from your eyes, at eye level or slightly below. If necessary, use a monitor stand or a few books to raise the monitor to eye level.

2 Most monitors have a tilt-and-swivel base that lets you adjust the screen even if you can't place it exactly at eye level.

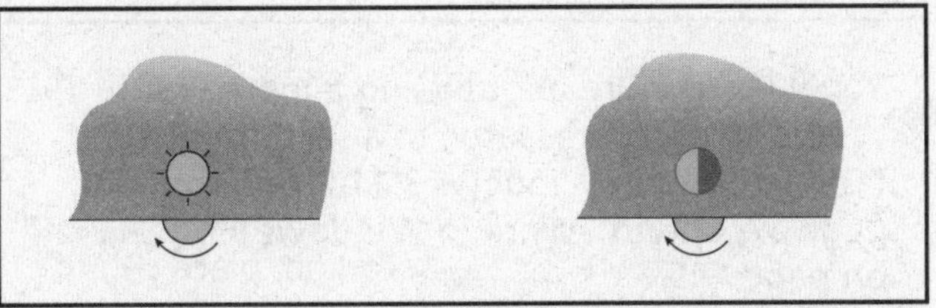

3 To adjust the brightness, look for the knob labeled **Bright** or indicated with a "sun" icon.

4 To adjust the contrast (the difference between light and dark), look for the knob labeled **Contrast** or indicated with a half-dark and half-light icon.

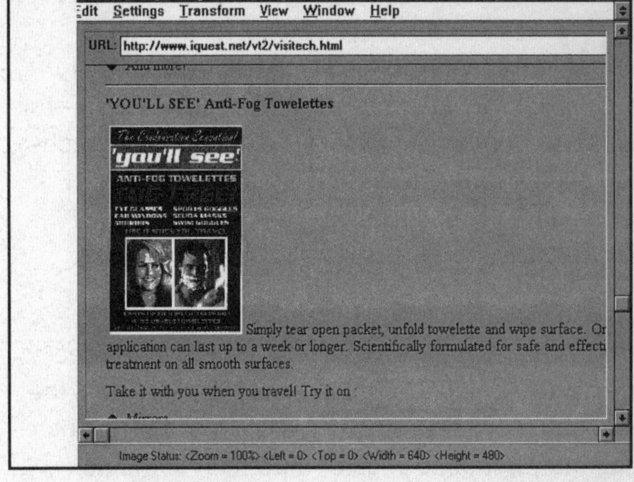

5 If the screen image is cut off or fuzzy on one side, you need to adjust the *H-phase* (horizontal control). Look for a knob and turn it to center the image on-screen.

6 If the screen image appears smashed or stretched vertically, you need to adjust the *V-size* (vertical control). Look for a knob and turn it to adjust the height of the image on-screen.

Begin Guided Tour Reduce Screen Glare

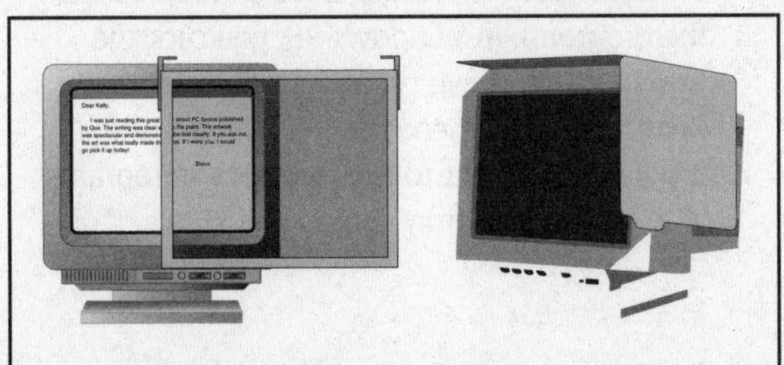

1 For around $30, you can buy an anti-glare screen that you can affix to the front of your monitor. More expensive filters also offer radiation protection and privacy protection (making it impossible to read your screen unless you're facing it head-on).

2 For a more down-and-dirty solution, you can use an ordinary manila file folder to cut glare. Simply put it on top of the monitor and fold it down both sides, and then tape it in place so it protrudes a few inches past the front of the monitor, shading glare.

Operate a Mouse

When you think of a computer, you might imagine a glorified typewriter you'd use to type a letter to your mother. Well, that was then—this is NOW! Computers do so much more now—graphics, games, music, and so on—that the keyboard alone doesn't cut it as the only input device. The *mouse* makes it easier to work in most programs.

As you move the mouse around on your desk, a smooth ball within it rolls and transmits your movements to a pointer on-screen; the pointer mirrors the way you move the mouse. You can move the pointer smoothly from one edge of the screen to the other, instead of wearing out your finger pressing the arrow keys. Depending on the program you're using, the pointer can take various shapes, including an arrow, a box, a vertical hash mark, or a *crosshair* (crossed lines resembling a plus sign).

A few years ago, computer users had to remember arcane command names or type in weird letter combinations to choose a program command. Now you can control most commercial software programs with the mouse—making easy procedures effortless—and doing in minutes some tasks that used to take hours of programming, especially in the graphics area.

For best results, you should have a *mouse pad* (purchased separately) under your mouse. The mouse's roller ball easily grips the pad's rubberized surface, which helps keep mouse movement smooth and even.

Master Common Mouse Techniques

You'll find that the basic mouse techniques are fairly easy—both to learn and to get used to in real-life situations. Thankfully, software publishers realize that most computer users favor what's simple and what works.

It's no accident, then, that software publishers (especially for Windows programs) design their products to let you use the mouse in a consistent way. If one publisher develops a new way of using the mouse, other publishers tend to use it in their programs as well. The result: once you learn a new technique, you can use it over and over.

You'll learn more about using a mouse with Windows programs later, in a section called "Get Around in Windows 3.11 Programs" on page 57, and in "Work in Windows 95" on page 149.

1. **Choosing menus, commands, and dialog box options.** Rather than using awkward or mysterious keystrokes, you can click or double-click to tell the computer what to do.

2. **Starting and exiting programs in Windows.** To start a program in Windows 3.11 with the mouse, you generally double-click the program's on-screen *icon* (a small picture that represents the program). In Windows 95, you click the **Start** button, move the mouse pointer over **Programs**, and then click the name of the program you want to run (see "Start Programs with the Start Button" on page 157).

3. **Making selections to edit, copy, move, or cut.** With the mouse, you can select a drawn object or block of text, and then quickly perform a command on the entire selection. Drag over text or click an on-screen object to select it. To move the selected text, open the **Edit** menu and select **Cut**; reposition the insertion point by clicking, open the **Edit** menu, and select **Copy**. To insert the selected text, open the **Edit** menu and select **Copy**; reposition the insertion point by clicking, open the **Edit** menu, and select **Copy**.
4. **Drawing and painting.** With your mouse and one of today's drawing or painting programs, you can create realistic, attractive drawings on-screen. Using a mouse to generate computer art takes some practice, just like learning to use a pencil or paintbrush.
5. **Dragging to manage files in Windows.** To copy files at the DOS prompt, you have to remember the exact file name to copy, and the exact name of the directory to copy it to—and then type everything in correctly. Now, you can use your mouse to move and copy files in Windows by dragging the file icons. You'll learn more about this in the section called "Organize Files and Directories with Windows 3.11" on page 99.
6. **Moving and copying data with drag-and-drop.** Most newer Windows programs offer this capability. Rather than selecting commands to move or copy what you've selected on-screen, you can simply drag it to a new location (which moves it), or press the **Ctrl** key while dragging to copy it to another spot.
7. Right-click to display shortcut menus. In some Windows 3.11 applications and in Windows 95, you can right-click on a selected object (a file icon, text, graphic, the desktop, etc.) to display a shortcut menu that contains options only for that object. You can then select an option from the menu.

Begin Guided Tour Work with a Mouse

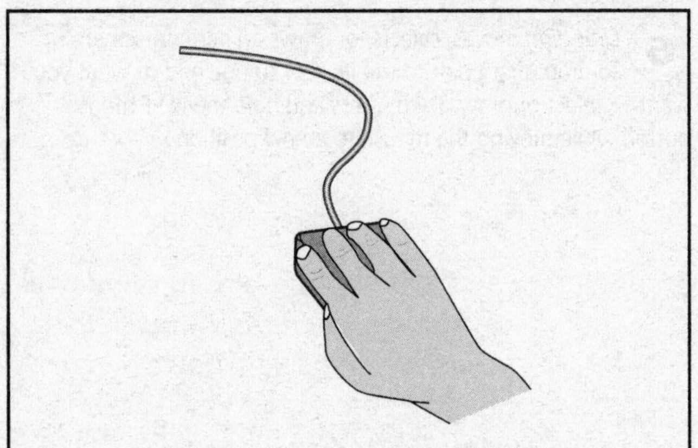

1 To use the mouse, rest the tip of your index finger on or near the left mouse button, and your palm should cup gently over the body of the mouse.

2 Move the mouse by pushing and pulling it around on the mouse pad making the mouse pointer on-screen move in the same direction. Lifting the mouse prevents its roller ball from moving.

(continues)

Guided Tour Work with a Mouse

(continued)

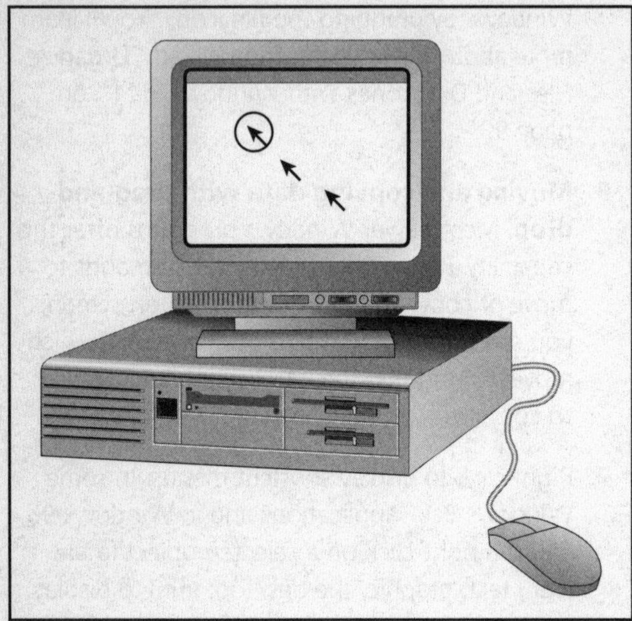

3 *Pointing* is the basic mouse movement. To point at something on-screen, move the mouse until the pointer rests on it.

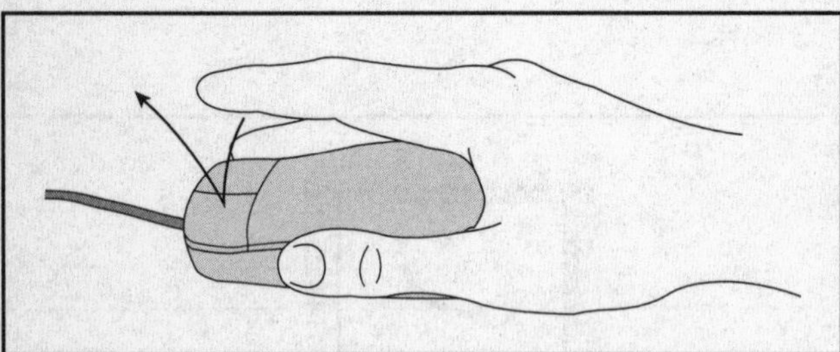

4 *Clicking* selects whatever the mouse pointer rests on. To click an item on-screen, first you point to it. Then you press and release the LEFT mouse button once. To *right-click*, point with the mouse, and then press and release the RIGHT mouse button once.

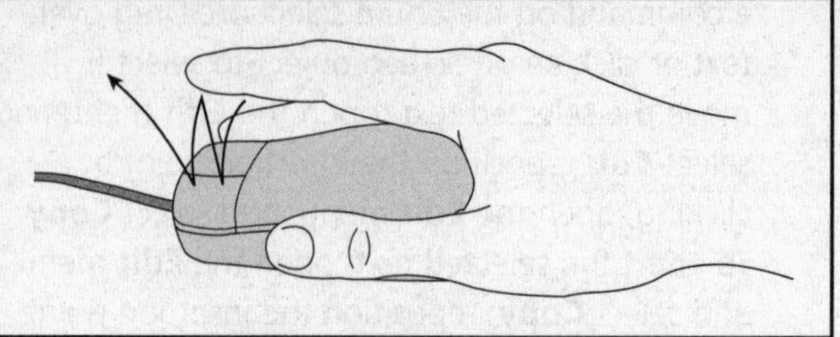

5 *Double-clicking* enters the command or activates the item the pointer rests on. To double-click an on-screen item, first point to it with the mouse. Then, without moving the mouse, quickly press and release the LEFT mouse button *twice*.

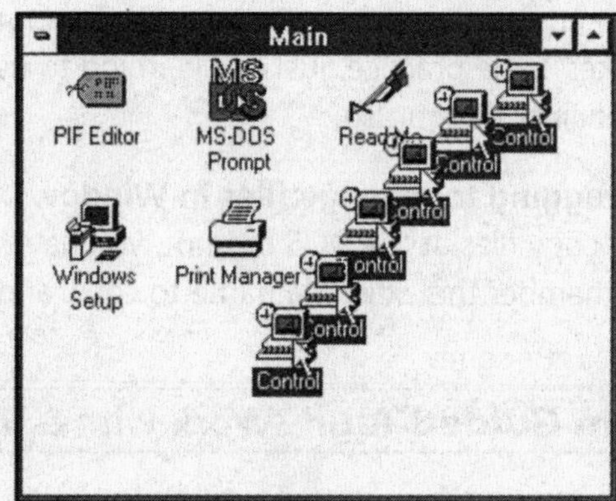

6 *Dragging* moves, selects, or draws an item on-screen. To drag, first point to the item or to one end of what you want to select or draw. Then, press and *hold* the LEFT mouse button while moving the mouse to a new position.

Reset (Warm-Boot) a Locked-Up Computer

Just about everyone knows that if you try to run a car when there's no oil or coolant in the engine, it'll lock up and stop dead in its tracks. What you may not know is that you can be working happily along on your computer system, and it can lock up or suddenly stop working.

Your computer can lock up for a variety of reasons. It usually happens because software instructions conflict and your computer can't decide what to do—or because too many instructions come flying at your computer at once, and it just gets paralyzed.

When your computer locks up, your only option is to *reset* or *reboot* it. Resetting or rebooting the system clears out whatever was jamming the computer, and takes the computer back through the Disk Operating System (DOS) and other startup instructions. Unfortunately, if your computer locks up and you haven't saved what you're working on, that work is lost. Therefore, save your work often—most experienced users save every 10 minutes, or after making any major addition to an important piece of work.

Most often, you will reboot by *warm-booting* your system. It's called a warm-boot because the computer's already warmed up; you use some keystrokes to reset the system without cutting the power flow to the computer. If this process doesn't work, jump to the *Guided Tour* for "cold-booting" later in this task. You should warm-boot rather than cold-boot whenever possible. Before you reboot your system, however, you should try a few tests to find out whether the computer's really locked up:

- Wait about 15 seconds and try resuming your work. You might be typing or entering commands faster than your computer can interpret them; if so, wait for it to catch up. You also need to make sure the computer isn't saving data while you reboot. Waiting a bit, and checking to make sure none of the drive lights are on, is a good safety measure.
- Press **F1** for Help. If you're trying to perform an operation that's impossible, Help will explain what's going on.
- Sometimes you can select something with the mouse without realizing it, which will keep you from performing a later operation. Try clicking in various places on-screen.
- Press the **Spacebar** or try some other keystrokes to see whether the keyboard simply has a stuck key.

Several things can cause your computer to lock up, including problems with the computer's memory, video, or with DOS or Windows. To help diagnose some of these problems, check out Part 3, "101 Quick Fixes" starting on page 471.

In Windows 95, you can press **Ctrl+Alt+Del** to cancel a program that's giving you trouble. Click the program's name in the list that appears, and then click **End Task**. To warm boot from Windows 95, click the **Start** button and click **Shut Down**. In the dialog box that appears, click **Restart the computer?** and click **Yes**.

Begin Guided Tour Warm-Booting from DOS

1 Remove any disks that are in floppy disk drives. Otherwise your computer will try to read from the floppy instead of your hard drive when it restarts.

2 Press and hold the **Ctrl** key, press and hold the **Alt** key, and then press the **Delete** key. Whatever was on-screen will be wiped off. The computer will go through its startup process all over.

3 Restart any programs you had opened before you warm-booted. If the system locks up every time you perform a particular operation, it has some kind of conflict. See "101 Quick Fixes" (starting on page 471) for clues to the problem.

Begin Guided Tour Warm-Booting from Windows 3.11

1 Press and hold the **Ctrl** key, the **Alt** key, and the **Delete** key simultaneously.

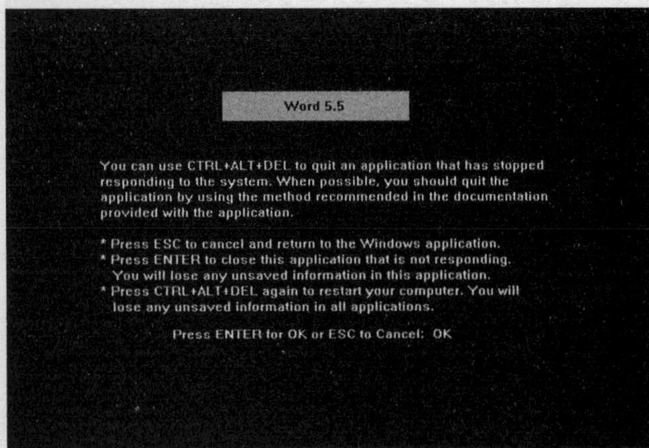

2 Your computer displays a screen naming the application that's locked up in Windows. Read this screen carefully to know exactly which program has locked up, and what your options are.

3 To shut down only the application program that's locked up (but leave Windows running), press the **Enter** key. The application closes, and Windows reappears on-screen. You should save your work in any other applications you're running; Windows still may be unstable.

4 If you want to do more than just shut down the locked-up application, you can continue the process and reboot the whole system. (WARNING: This is dangerous to do, because it can cause you to lose data and mess up your programs.) Start by removing any disks from the floppy disk drives.

5 Press and hold the **Ctrl** key, the **Alt** key, and the **Delete** key simultaneously.

6 You'll need to restart Windows and restart any programs you had opened before you warm-booted. For more information about doing this, see "Start Windows" on page 58.

Cold-Boot Your System

Sometimes warm-booting your system doesn't work. You press **Ctrl+Alt+Delete** and nothing happens. This usually means your computer has locked up in such a way that it can't accept keyboard and mouse commands.

When warm-booting doesn't work, you have to *cold-boot* your system. Cold-booting means you use the hardware to reset the computer, depriving it of power or making it "cold." There are two different ways to cold-boot. One involves your system's Reset button. The second method greatly resembles restarting your system, which was described in an earlier task ("Start Up Your Computer" on page 28). Don't use the second method unless the Reset button doesn't work, or your system doesn't have a Reset button.

Begin Guided Tour Cold-Boot with the Reset Button

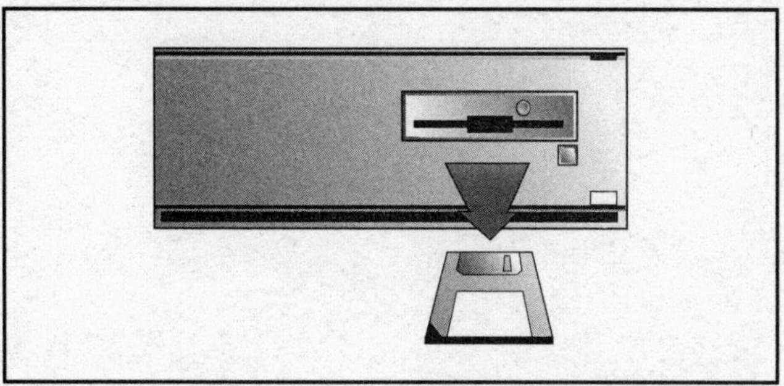

1 Remove any disks that are in floppy disk drives. Otherwise your computer will try to read from the floppy instead of your hard drive when it restarts.

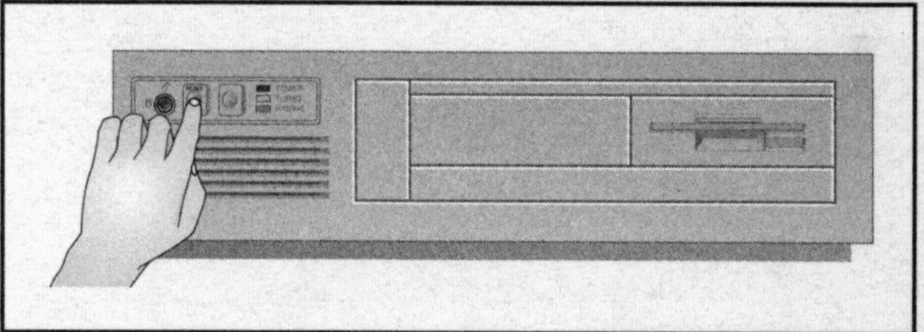

2 Press the **Reset** button on the front or side of the computer. Your computer will beep at you, and whatever was on-screen will be wiped off. The computer will go through its startup process all over.

Begin Guided Tour Cold-Boot with the Power Switch

1 Remove any disks that are in floppy disk drives. Otherwise your computer will try to read from the floppy instead of your hard drive when it restarts.

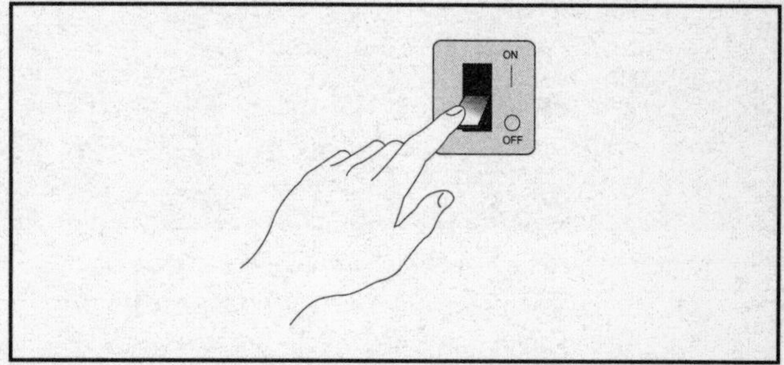

2 Turn the system unit's power switch to the **Off** position. Listen to your computer, so you can hear it power down. When it's silent (the power-down process has finished), wait about two minutes and turn the power switch back to the **On** position.

HOW TO...

Understand How the Computer Stores Files

Imagine your home or business office. You've got a nice, orderly desk. Your favorite framed lithograph hangs just above your desk. Sunlight streams in through the window. And you've got 50,000 pages of information stacked all around.

"Hey," you might think, "that last part doesn't sound so great." And it wouldn't be, because the average office isn't designed to hold 50,000 pages of information. But the average computer can hold that much and more!

The way the computer converts characters, sound, and pictures to an electrical state fascinates new and experienced users alike. But the computer's capability of condensing great mounds of information and storing it on a few magnetic disks not only fascinates—it serves an important purpose: it enables your office to absorb some of today's information overload.

The next few tasks explain how a computer stores and organizes files so you can make the best use of this resource. You'll also find tips here to help you make smarter use of the disk space you've got.

What You Will Find in This Section

Understand Disks and Drives *46*

Understand How the Drive Reads and Writes *48*

Understand Files *51*

Name Files and Decode File Names *53*

Understand Directories *55*

Understand Disks and Drives

A task earlier in this book explained the basics for working with floppy disks, but it didn't give you the lowdown on how the disks store information, or how your computer can work with that information. When you're working with your computer and it's powered up, your data exists only in the computer's *Random-Access Memory* (*RAM*). RAM holds the data and program instructions your computer is working with while the computer's turned on. Turn the computer off, and RAM's contents are lost.

To store that data so you can work with it again, you need to save the data in a more permanent way, or put it in *storage*. Disks are your computer's storage area. They hold your data for you until you delete it or move it. When you save information, your computer takes what's in RAM and writes it onto a disk. To use stored data again, your computer will look at that data on the hard drive, and read a copy of it back into RAM. If you change your data, you'll need to save it to the hard drive again to preserve your changes, and so on.

New users frequently use the terms "floppy disk" and "hard drive" to refer to the two main storage tools of the computer. A "disk" and a "drive," however, are not the same thing.

The *disk* is the spinning platter of magnetic material holding the stored data. The hard "disk" within your computer is actually a stack of these magnetic platters—that's how it holds so much data.

The actual collection of mechanisms that spins the disk, writes information on the disk, and reads information from the disk is the *disk drive*. The hard disk drive in your computer has a sealed case that holds both the drive and the stack of disks. As you've seen, you can insert and remove disks from floppy disk drives through a slot on the front of the drive.

To learn how to save your work (store it on a disk), see "Save Your Work in a Windows Program" on page 92.

Working by Bits and Bytes

Your computer isn't as smart as it might first seem. At its most basic level, it can only understand two digits: 0 and 1. The computer combines 0s and 1s to create unique characters, characters are combined to form words, values, commands, and so on.

Whether hard or floppy, your disks are coated with tiny magnetic particles, each of which can be magnetized by an electrical charge. Each of these particles is known as a *bit*—short for *BInary digiT*. The binary language a computer uses has only two characters: 0 and 1. When a bit has a high charge or is magnetized (the "on" state), the computer reads it as a 1. When a bit has a low charge or is not magnetized (the "off" state), the computer reads it as a 0.

A combination of eight bits forms a *byte*, which is one character of data. There is a unique set of bits for each letter of the alphabet, every single-digit number, and for many special characters (like $). For example, these two *bytes* (combinations of eight on/off bits) represent the number 53:

0	0	1	1	0	1	0	1

The capacity of every disk and memory chip can be measured in bytes. A *kilobyte* is just over 1,000 bytes. A *megabyte* is just over 1,000,000 bytes, and a *gigabyte* is roughly a thousand megabytes (a billion bytes).

To translate the capacity of any disk into real-world terms, think of each byte as a character. A 3.5-inch HD (high-density) diskette holds 1.44 megabytes, which is roughly 1.4 million characters. So, if the average page of data has 35 lines of 65 characters each (2,275 characters), a single 1.44-megabyte disk can hold over 600 pages of data (2,275 characters times 600 pages equals 1,365,000 characters)—about as many pages as there are in this book.

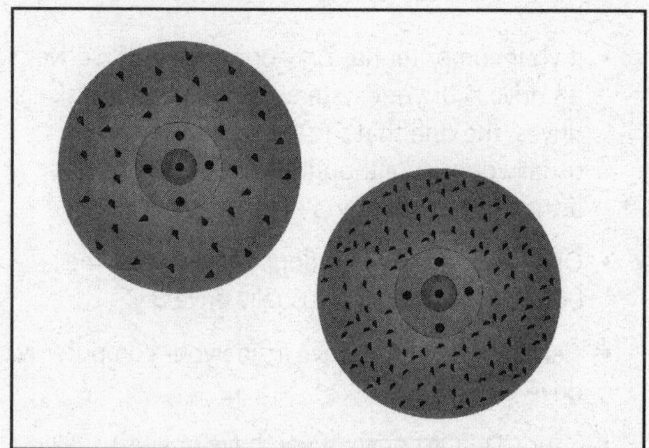

Tracks, Sectors, and Formatting

These magnetic bits aren't just floating around on the disk's surface. They're actually arranged in a very specific pattern to make it easy for the disk drive to store and find data. Each disk has concentric rings called *tracks* dividing it. To further organize the data, the disk has *sectors*, pie-shaped wedges separated by imaginary lines radiating from the center of the disk, like this:

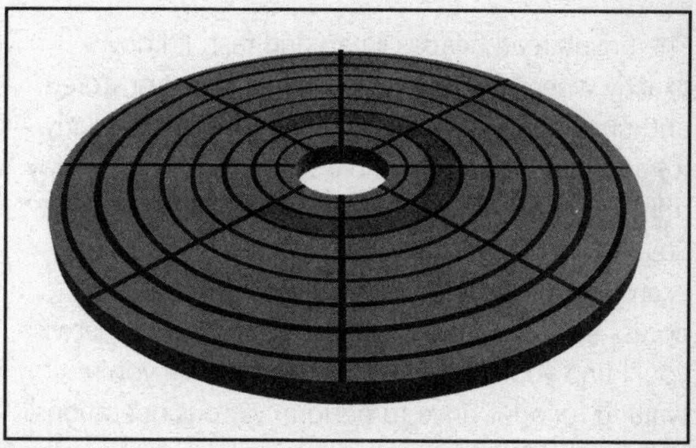

Tiny magnetic codes on the disk identify the tracks and sectors that store every group of bits.

Before your computer can write any information on a disk, the disk must be *formatted*—that is, the data must be arranged into tracks and sectors. Usually your hard drive is already formatted when you get your computer. On the other hand, you may need to format a floppy disk before using it. To learn how to do this, see "Format Disks" on page 146.

Understand How the Drive Reads and Writes

When a drive *writes to* a disk, it's actually magnetizing selected bits to create bytes, or characters. When the drive *reads from* a disk, it reads the bits comprising each byte, and places a copy of that information in RAM. A mechanical part called the *read/write head* floats over the disk surface, magnetizing bits or reading their magnetic charge.

The drive's read head is smart and fast. It knows exactly where the different parts of a file are stored, and finds them all to load them into RAM. Similarly, it's adept at finding available space on a disk to copy a file to. A disk drive's speed is called its *access time*. Smaller access times indicate a faster drive. For example, you should look for hard drives with an access time of 12 ms (milliseconds) or less. Otherwise, you'll find yourself tapping your toe while you're waiting for your drive to perform various operations.

The *Guided Tour* that follows will explain how the drive works with the disk.

You've got to keep dust out of your disk drive to keep it in good working order. To learn more about disk drive care and feeding, see "Clean the Disk Drives" on page 341.

Name That Drive

As you've already noticed, your computer probably has at least two drives. Your computer uses a simple system to tell them apart: the ABCs. You'll need to know this when you want to save, retrieve, or otherwise work with data—operations covered in the sections called "Get Around in Windows Programs," "Organize Files with Windows," and "Work with DOS."

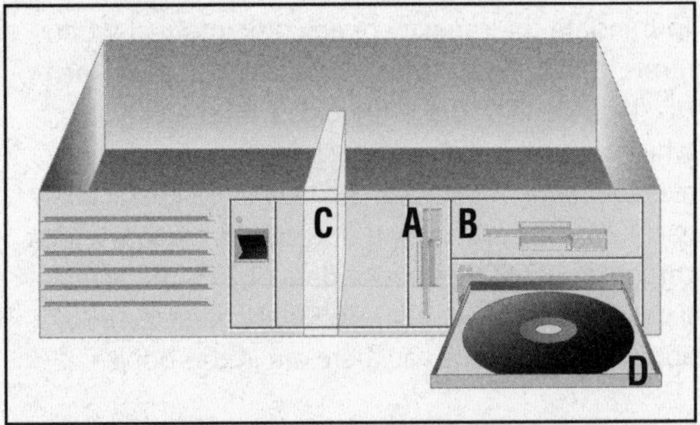

- If your computer has only one floppy disk drive, it's drive *A*. If your system has two floppy disk drives, the one that's to the left or on top is usually drive *A* (although this may not be true if the leftmost floppy is oriented vertically).
- On a system with two floppy disk drives, the bottom or right one is usually drive *B*.
- Generally, the hard drive inside your computer is drive *C*.
- Your CD-ROM drive, if you have one, is usually drive *D*.

Begin Guided Tour Write to a Disk

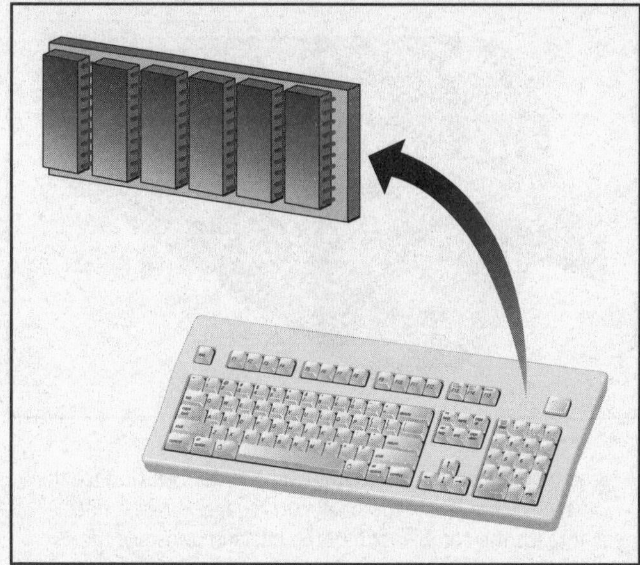

1 As you enter data or work with your computer, the computer holds that data with its RAM chips.

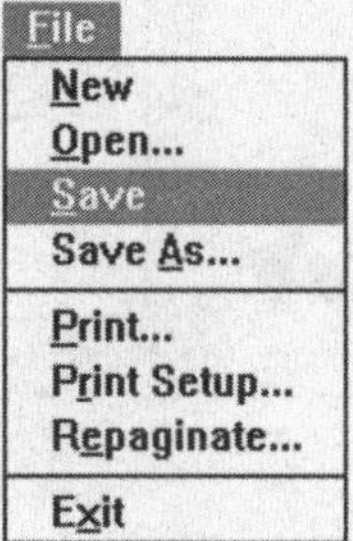

2 You issue a **Save** command from the program you're working in. You tell the computer what drive holds the disk you want to save the information to, and give a name for that data.

3 The disk drive motor starts spinning the disk. The disk drive indicator light comes on.

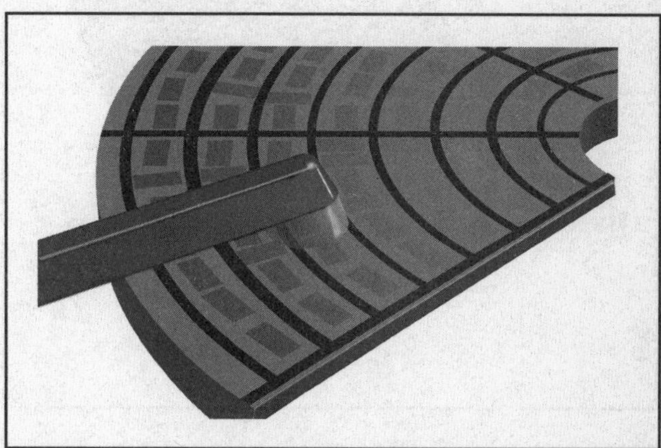

4 The read/write head moves over the disk, looking for tracks and sectors that are empty. When it finds an available byte, it magnetizes the appropriate bits to form a combination of eight bits to form a character, or byte, on the disk.

5 The read/write head continues moving over the disk and writing new bytes until it's written all the data from RAM on the disk. When the drive head finishes writing, the drive motor stops and the drive indicator light goes off.

Begin Guided Tour Read from a Disk

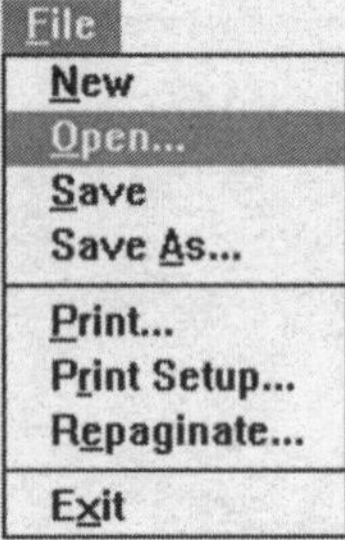

1 Choose the **Open** command in the application program you're using. A dialog box will appear and let you choose the file you want to open. (You'll find more on files in the next Task, and more on opening files in "Open a File in a Windows Program" on page 89.)

2 The disk drive motor starts spinning the disk. The disk drive indicator light comes on.

3 The read/write head moves over the disk, looking for the bytes (characters) that make up the file. When it finds a byte, it reads the combination of the bits and transmits the combination to RAM.

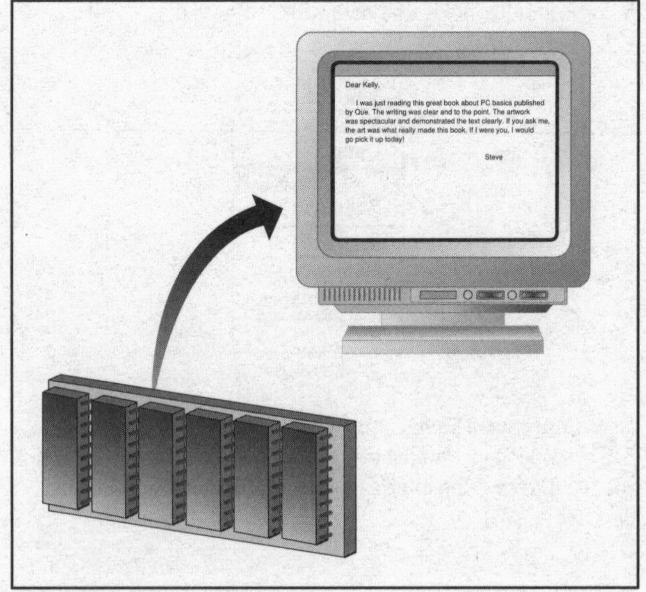

4 The RAM interprets each byte and displays the character it represents on-screen.

5 The read/write head continues moving over the disk and reading until it's read all the file's data from the disk to RAM.

6 When the drive head finishes reading, the drive motor stops and the drive indicator light goes off.

Understand Files

When you're working with a pile of papers that are all part of a single project, you generally don't just leave them lying around randomly. Instead, you put them all in a manila file folder, and write a name for that collection of papers on the tab of the folder.

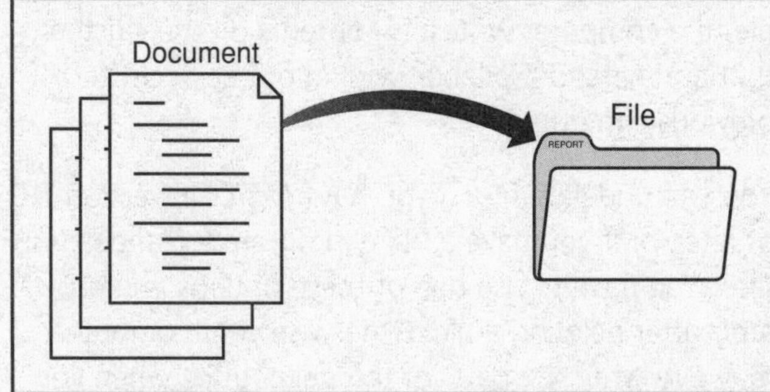

In the same way, your computer programs let you collect data that goes together—such as all the words that make up a document, or all the instructions for a program—and save them in a file with a unique name. When you create and name a file, simultaneously you tell your computer what disk to store it on. In general, computers have two kinds of files. *Program files*, which you usually purchase from a software publisher, hold program instructions that you install on your computer. *Data files* hold the work you create on your computer when you use the various programs.

When you want to work with a program, you *activate* or start the program file. When you want to work again with the information in a data file, you use your program to open the file, or read it into RAM. The mechanical steps for how this process works are basically the same as the writing-and-reading steps listed in the last task, "Understand Disks and Drives." The one exception, however, occurs because of the FAT.

See "Save Your Work in a Windows Program" on page 92 for more about this process, called *saving*.

What's a FAT?

FAT stands for *File Allocation Table*. Every formatted disk has specialized, hidden files holding the FAT. So what does the FAT do, you ask? The FAT keeps track of where all the bytes for each file are physically stored on the disk. Let's look at this in more detail.

As you learned in the task titled "Understand Disks and Drives," the surface of a disk is divided into *tracks* (concentric circles) and *sectors* (each of these, shaped like a wedge of pie, is the smallest space a file can occupy). Adjacent sectors on a track form a *cluster*. The smallest space that a file can occupy is a sector. Depending on the size of the file, it can take up one cluster or many clusters. The FAT keeps track of the clusters that hold the contents of each file.

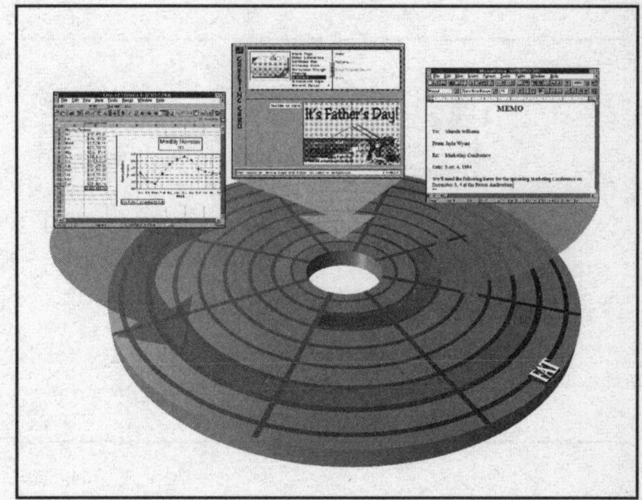

To make the situation even more complicated, suppose there's no empty group of clusters large enough to hold a particular file. Then the file has to be split up and stored on non-adjacent clusters (clusters that aren't *contiguous*). When this happens, the file is *fragmented*. In fact, this is the most typical situation, especially on hard disks. As you save and delete files on the disk, clusters break up into smaller and smaller groups. When a file is fragmented, the FAT becomes even more important if you're going to keep track of the file's pieces.

The *Guided Tour* that follows will give you an example of how the FAT helps work with the clusters of a file stored on a disk.

A disk with fragmented files takes more time to use, because the drive's read/write head has to skip around a lot to find information. For instructions on helping this problem, see "Optimize a Disk with Defrag" on page 398.

Where Files Go When You Delete Them

Deleting a file means you erase its contents so you can't use them any more, which sounds like it wipes the data from the disk immediately. Well, that's not completely true. When you delete a file, its contents remain on the disk. In the FAT, the file's *location* is deleted, so that the FAT *thinks* there isn't anything in that spot on the disk. Later, when you save another file, the computer writes its contents on the clusters that are marked available, wiping out each cluster's previous contents.

You can undelete files if you have MS-DOS version 5.0 or later, or if you have a utility program for undeleting files. You have to use one of these options *immediately* after deleting a file. Otherwise your computer may overwrite the parts of the deleted file when you save new files.

See "Delete Files" on page 128 for the steps for removing files to free up disk space.

Begin Guided Tour How the FAT Tracks Files

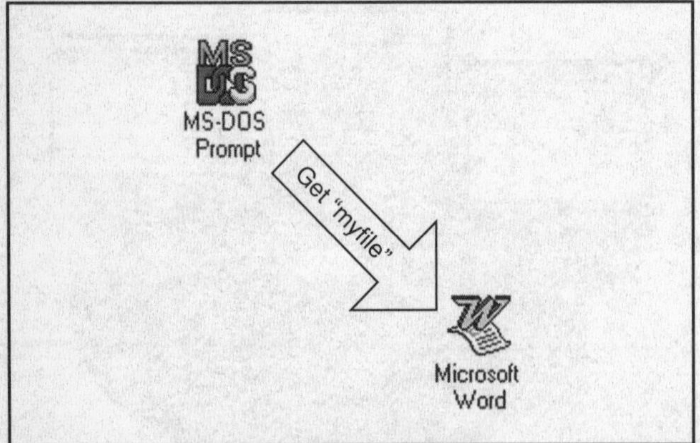

1 Let's say you're working with a program and you use its **Open** command to open a file. The program will start by talking with the Disk Operating System (DOS), telling DOS to get the file.

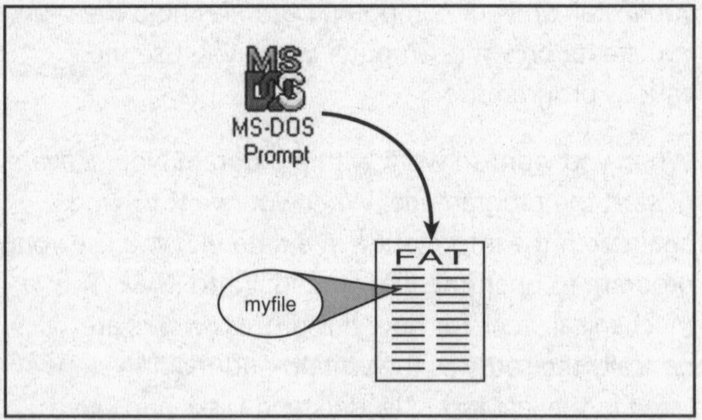

2 DOS looks at the FAT file, and looks up the locations of all the clusters that make up the file.

3 The program starts to read the file; a signal tells the read/write head of the drive where to find the first cluster. The drive reads the cluster's contents into RAM; a signal then directs the head to the next cluster, and so on, until the entire file is in RAM.

Name Files and Decode File Names

Although file names must be unique for your computer to be able to tell them apart, you can't go hog-wild and just name them anything you want. Certain *conventions* govern file naming; these conventions originated when DOS was created.

When you name a file, you give it a *base name* of up to eight characters and an optional *extension* (which tells what kind of file it is) of three characters. Some characters, however, you can't use in a file name's base name or extension; they're reserved for the system and commands. They are these:

" . / \ [ ] : * < > | + ; . ? space

The file name extension can give you a clue about what a file is used for, or what program it comes from. This table lists a few of the common file extensions.

With Windows 95, you can ignore most of the old file name rules. Windows 95 lets you use long file names (up to 255 characters). You can also use spaces, but you can't use any of the following characters: \ ? : * " < > |. With long file names, you can save a file using names like **Letter to Mortgage Company 09/05/96** and **Phone List for Little League**.

File Name Extensions for Common File Types

Extension	*File Type/Program It Comes From*
.BAK	Backup file
.BAT	Batch file (a collection of commands)
.COM	Program command file
.DAT	Data file
.DBF	Database file from the dBASE program
.DOC	Document file from Microsoft Word or another word processor
.EXE	Executable program file
.GIF	Graphics file from CompuServe
.HLP	Help file
.PCX	PC Paintbrush or Windows Paintbrush file
.TXT	Plain text (ASCII) file
.WKS, .WK1, .WK2, or .WK3	Lotus 1-2-3 files
.WP or .WPF	Document file from WordPerfect
.XLS	Spreadsheet file from Microsoft Excel
.ZIP	A file containing one or more files compressed with the PKZIP file-compression program

The file name may also include the *path* for the file. The path includes the letter for the drive where a file is stored, followed by a colon, followed by the directories (and subdirectories) leading to the one holding the file. Directory and subdirectory names are separated with backslashes (\). If, for example, a file is on drive C: in the \TEMP subdirectory within the \WINDOWS directory, the full path would be **C:\WINDOWS\TEMP**.

> When you save a file, most programs add the correct extension automatically. When you open a file, most programs filter the list of files in a directory to show only those files that have extensions indicating a kind of file the program can use.

Begin Guided Tour Parts of a File Name

```
C:\work\memos\maysales.doc
```

1 A *file name* consists of several parts; you will need to specify each of these parts when you name a file, and when you open it; they tell your system how to find the file. From left to right, a file name goes from general to specific as it identifies the file.

```
C:
```

2 First, you indicate the drive letter for the drive holding the disk you want to use for storing the file (or where the file is already stored).

```
C:\work\memos
```

3 The next part of the file name is the rest of its *path*: the route to the directory you want to store the file in (or retrieve it from; more on directories in the next task). Many programs let you choose the directory from a list rather than type it in.

```
C:\work\memos\maysales
```

4 Next comes the *base name* for the file. Specify up to eight characters. Make it unique, and choose a name that reflects what's in the file.

```
C:\work\memos\maysales.doc
```

5 A *period* ends the base name; follow it with the file's three-letter *extension* (which typically identifies the file type).

Understand Directories

You learned in an earlier task that even a small, hard disk can hold 50,000 pages of data. If each of these pages were stored in a separate file, you'd have 50,000 names to keep track of on that drive. Even Einstein couldn't remember all that!

Think of how you would solve this problem with paper files: get a file cabinet with drawers, and put files relating to the same project (or same client) in the same drawer. This technique cuts down drastically on the number of names you have to remember.

You can use a similar technique to organize files on the hard and floppy disks you use with your computer. For example, you would want to store all the files running the Excel spreadsheet program in the same "file drawer."

In computing, these electronic file drawers are called *directories*. When you install a program, the process creates directories for its program files. In addition, you can create a nearly-unlimited number of directories on any disk—hard or floppy. In file names, you separate directories with the backslash character (\), which is often located just to the left of the Backspace key, or at the right end of your keyboard's second row of keys.

You arrange directories according to a hierarchical structure that has a root and branches; it's usually called the *directory tree*. For many programs (such as the Windows File Manager), the directory resembles a tree of file folders when you put it on-screen. Other programs let you choose from directory lists. With DOS, you have to be able to remember and type in directory names.

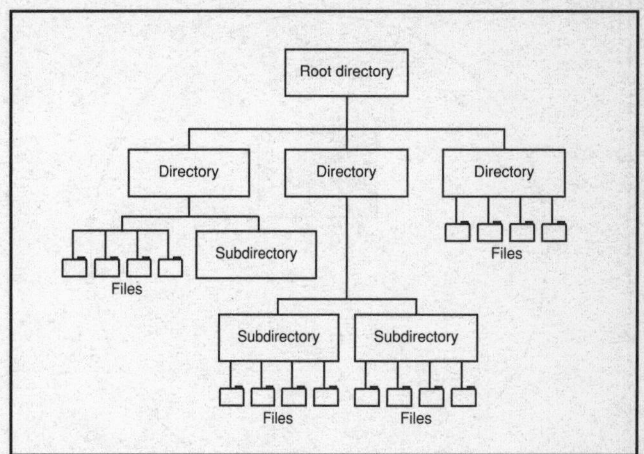

The main directory for every disk is called the *root directory*. All the remaining directories on the disk branch out from the root. When you store a file in the root directory, you use a single backslash to identify the root directory. You can have a virtually unlimited number of directories and subdirectories. Adding too many is overkill, and could slow you down if you have to search through a lot of directories to find what you need. As always, use moderation and common sense when you create directories.

Windows 95 takes a more logical approach to directories by treating them as folders. The root directory is the main folder, and it contains all the folders. Each folder can store additional subfolders and files.

Creating directories is as easy as picking a name and location. To learn how to do it, read "Create Directories" on page 132.

Begin Guided Tour Understanding Directories

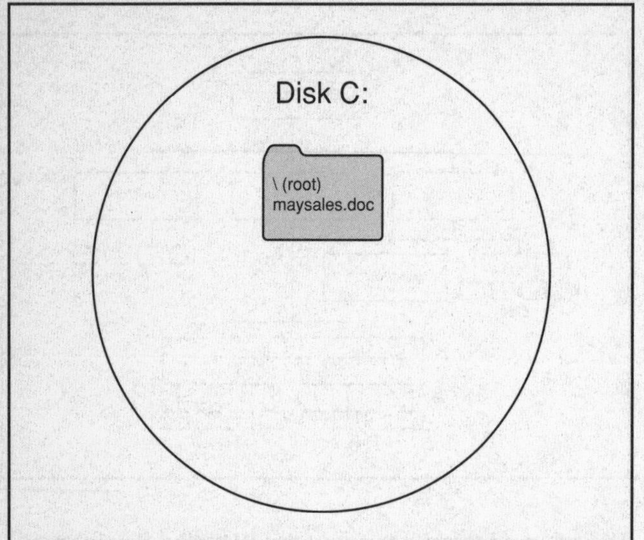

1 For example, the file name **c:\maysales.doc** signifies a file stored in the root directory, because there's only a backslash between the drive letter (**c:**) and the file name—the base name plus the extension (**maysales.doc**).

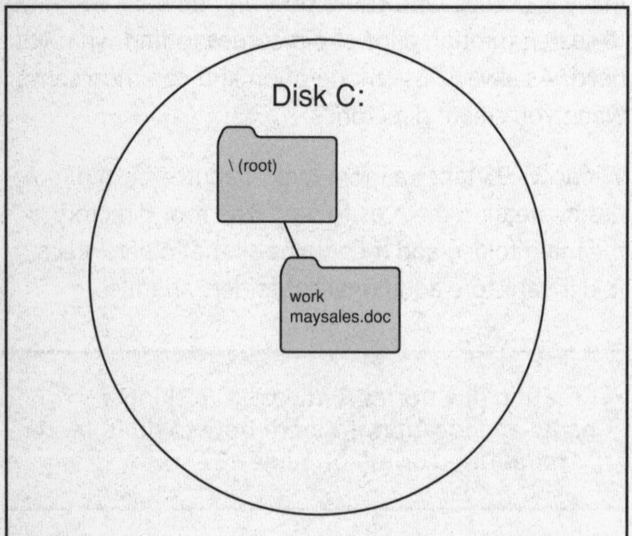

2 Any directory that branches directly from the root is just called a *directory*, or *first-level directory*. For example, in the file name **c:\work\maysales.doc**, **work** is a directory; it follows the first **** for the root directory (meaning that it branches off the root directory). The file **maysales.doc** is in the **\work** directory.

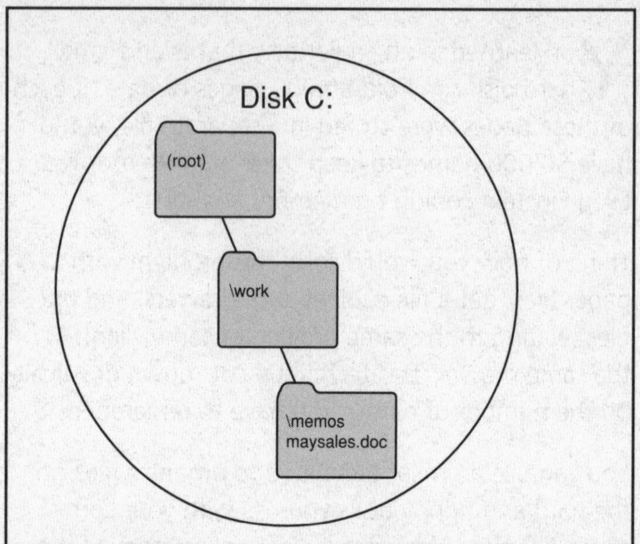

3 A *subdirectory* branches from a directory. In the file name **c:\work\memos\maysales.doc**, **memos** is a subdirectory within the **\work** directory.

HOW TO...

Get Around in Windows 3.11 Programs

Windows provides a graphical user interface (GUI) that lets you control your computer through icons (pictures) on-screen. Each application or document you open on-screen appears in its own window—hence the name of the product.

This section helps you get over the major hurdle—learning your way around Windows. Although most of the information in this section covers both Windows 3.*x* (3.1 and 3.11) and Windows 95 programs, see "Work in Windows 95" for specific information about running programs in Windows 95.

What You Will Find in This Section

Start Windows 58

Load Windows Automatically When You Start Your Computer 60

Understand Program Manager 62

Open and Close a Windows Program Group 64

Create and Modify Program Groups 65

Start a Windows Program 68

Switch Between Open Programs 70

Select Commands from Menus 71

Display the Control Menu for a Window 74

Use a Dialog Box 75

Work with Directory Lists in Dialog Boxes 78

Work with Scroll Bars in Dialog Boxes 79

Size and Arrange Windows 80

Get Help in Windows 84

Start a New File in a Windows Program 87

Open a File in a Windows Program 89

Save Your Work in a Windows Program 92

Save Your File Under a New Name 94

Save Your Files Automatically 95

Print in a Windows Program 96

Exit a Windows Program 98

Start Windows

As with any other program, you have to start up Windows to use it. If your computer manufacturer installed Windows for you, and it starts automatically when you start your system, you can skip this task altogether!

If you do have to start Windows manually, you do so by typing a command at the DOS prompt. Once Windows has started, the Windows Program Manager appears on your screen.

Windows can run in two different modes, depending on how capable your hardware is. Normally, Windows senses what kind of system you have and chooses the appropriate startup mode:

- *Standard mode* is for 80286 computers or 80386 computers with 2M of RAM or less.
- *386 Enhanced mode* lets 80386 or better computers with more than 2M of RAM take better advantage of Windows' ability to run more than one program at a time.

You can override Windows and choose a mode yourself when you type in the Windows startup command. You simply add a *switch* (extra characters that modify a DOS command). The **/s** switch specifies Standard mode; the **/3** switch specifies 386 Enhanced mode. For example, you would type **WIN /s**. You might want to choose a mode for Windows in these situations:

- You have an 80386 system with between 2M and 3M of RAM, and *all* your applications are designed to run with Windows. Choosing Standard mode in this case may make Windows run better.
- You get a lot of error messages, or have problems getting certain pieces of hardware (like a sound card) to work correctly in 386 Enhanced mode. Again, starting Windows in the Standard mode will help.
- You have an 80386 system with 4M of memory, and you want to run several Windows applications at once. Choosing 386 Enhanced mode may enable you to start more applications (though your computer may run more slowly than it would in Standard mode).

For more on using switches with DOS commands, see "Enter Commands in DOS" on page 212.

Check Your Mode

Once Windows is running, it can tell you what mode it's running in. Knowing how to display this information can come in handy if you're trying to diagnose a Windows problem. As a bonus, you'll also see what version of Windows you have (as if you didn't already know), and how much memory's available on your system.

1. Click the **Help** menu at the far right end of the menu bar in Program Manager. Then click **About Program Manager**.
2. Look near the bottom of the About Program Manager dialog box. You'll see the mode Windows is running in. Click the **OK** button in the upper right corner of the dialog box to put it away.

Begin Guided Tour Start Up Windows

```
C:\>cd windows
```

1 Type **cd windows** and press **Enter**. If the directory that holds your Windows files is named something other than **windows**, type in that directory name. Skip this step if you let Setup add Windows to your PATH statement when you installed Windows.

```
C:\WINDOWS>win
```

2 Type **win** at the **c:\windows>** prompt.

```
C:\WINDOWS>win /3
```

3 (Optional) Press the **Spacebar**, and then add the **/s** or **/3** switch to choose Standard or 386 Enhanced mode, respectively.

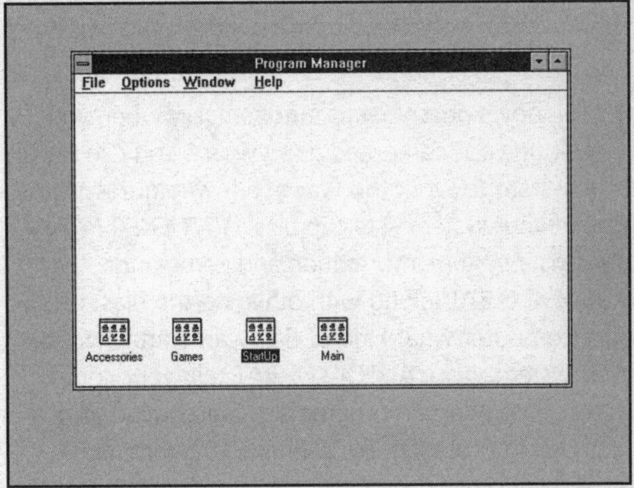

4 Press **Enter** to load Windows. After an introductory screen flashes on-screen briefly, the Windows Program Manager window appears on the *desktop* (the background area on which all open windows sit).

Load Windows Automatically When You Start Your Computer

If Windows doesn't start automatically when you boot up your computer, don't worry. You can set up your system to work this way in a few minutes or less. One of your system's startup files, *AUTOEXEC.BAT*, gives your system information and commands. AUTOEXEC.BAT (along with other startup files) tells your computer what kind of hardware's attached to your system. Also, AUTOEXEC.BAT tells your computer to load certain programs to help it work correctly, or to protect it. For example, a command in AUTOEXEC.BAT might start a virus-checking program automatically on your system.

Having AUTOEXEC.BAT load Windows automatically is as easy as adding the Windows startup command into the AUTOEXEC.BAT file. You can use a Windows program called the System Configuration Editor to edit AUTOEXEC.BAT to load a program, such as Windows, on startup.

Begin Guided Tour Automatically Start Windows

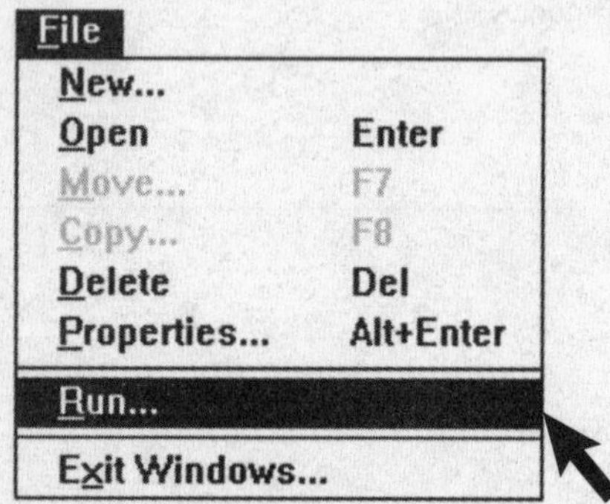

1 Click the **File** menu at the top of the screen (this area is called the *menu bar*) on the far left end, and then click the **Run** command. The Run dialog box appears, with a blinking insertion cursor in the **Command Line** text box.

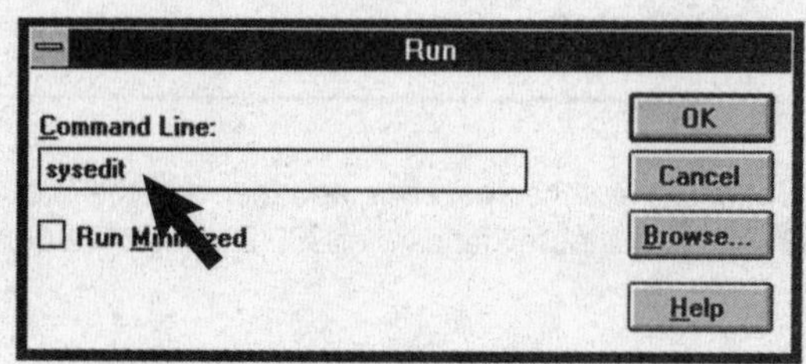

2 Type **sysedit**, and then click the **OK** button in the upper right corner of the dialog box. (For more on working with dialog boxes, see "Use a Dialog Box" on page 75.)

Guided Tour Automatically Start Windows

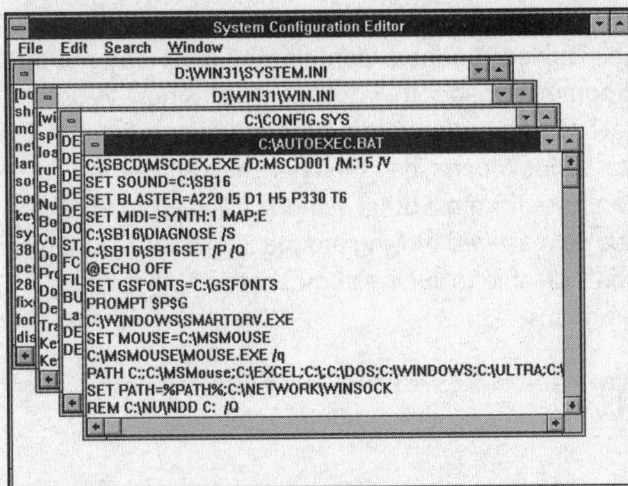

3 The System Configuration Editor screen appears and displays the contents of several key startup files. The window for AUTOEXEC.BAT appears in front; the blinking insertion cursor is in the work area of that window. Press and hold the **down arrow key** until you have placed the insertion cursor after all the other lines in the file.

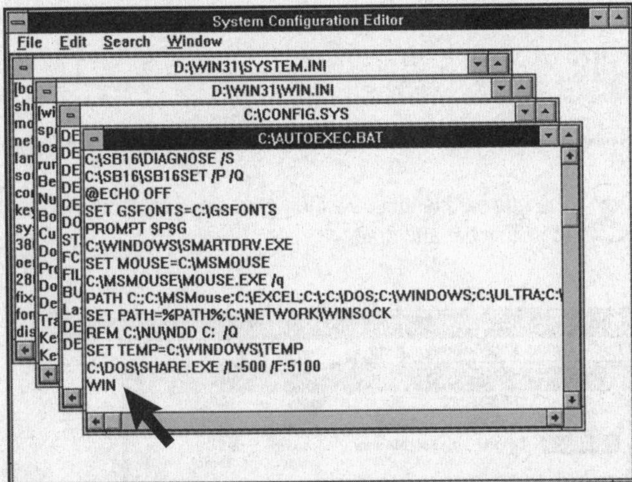

4 Type **WIN**, plus a startup switch if you want to choose a mode for Windows. (If the Windows directory isn't in your computer's path statement, enter **C:\WINDOWS\WIN** instead.)

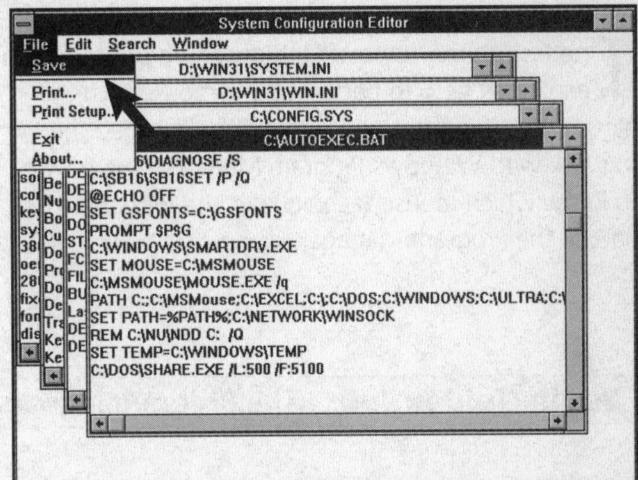

5 Click the **File** menu at the top of the window, and then click **Save** to preserve your changes.

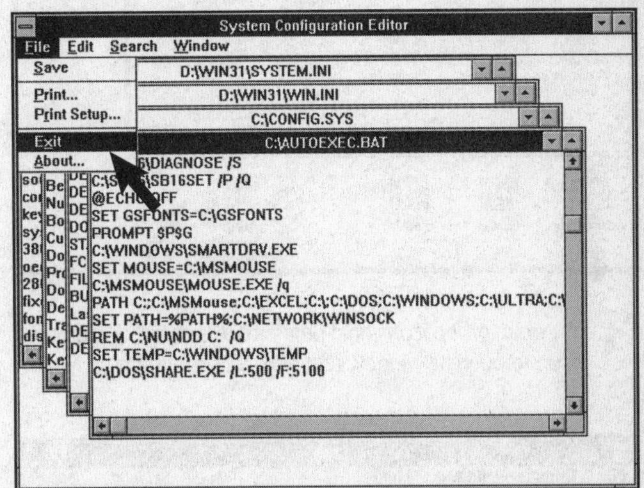

6 Click the **File** menu again, and then click **Exit** to close the System Configuration Editor program. The next time you start your system, Windows will load automatically.

Understand Program Manager

The task called "Operate a Mouse" on page 38 explained how to perform basic mouse techniques. You use the same techniques described there to work with Windows Program Manager. The trick is to know which mouse technique to use with which part of the Program Manager screen.

The Guided Tour here identifies the different parts of Program Manager for you and explains how to use each one to perform particular operations. Most of the window parts identified here also appear in windows for most other Windows applications. Once you've mastered moving around in Program Manager, you'll be able to survive in most other Windows programs.

Begin Guided Tour The Program Manager

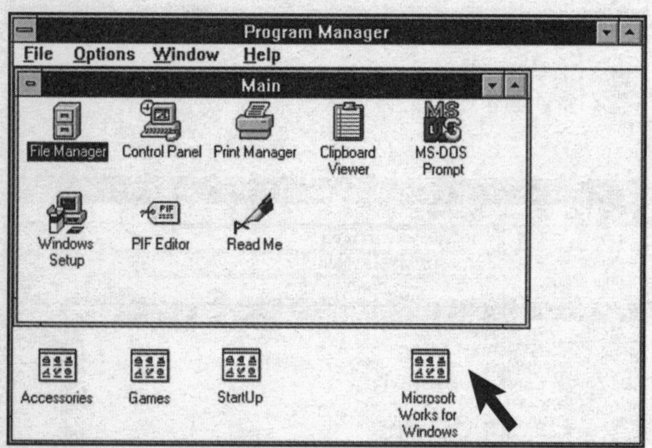

1 *Program group icons* hold programs. Double-click a group icon to open its window and display its programs.

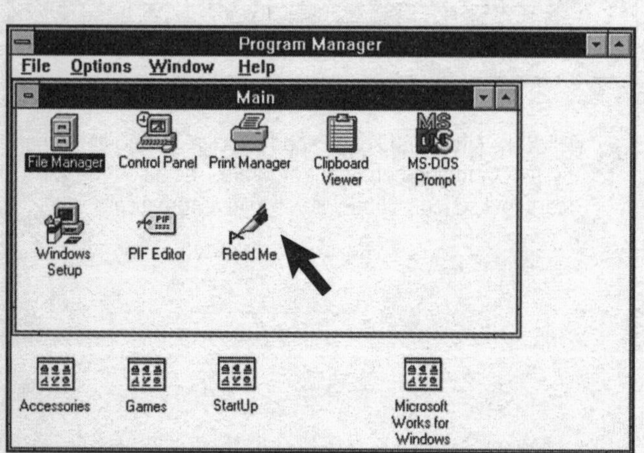

2 *Program-item icons* represent application programs. Double-click a program-item icon to open it (start the application in its own window).

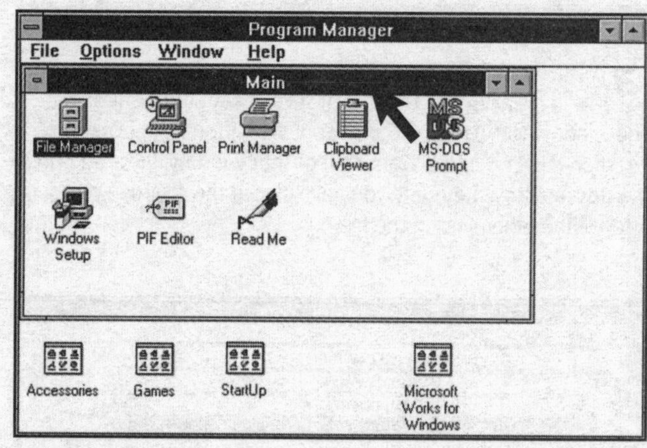

3 The *title bar* identifies a window. To move a window, point to its title bar and drag.

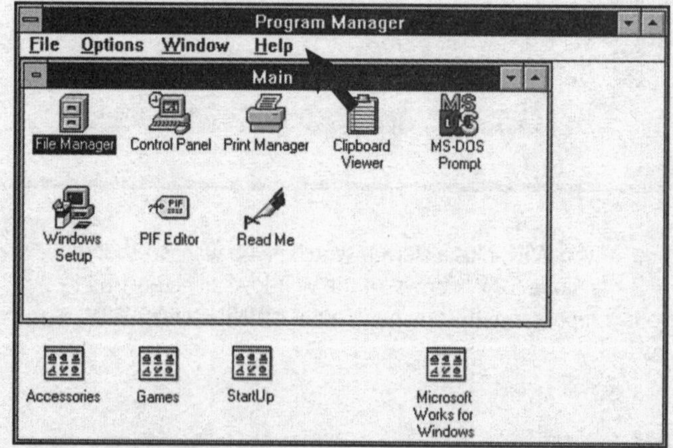

4 The *menu bar* lists the menus available in Program Manager (or your application program.) Click a menu name to open it and list its commands.

Guided Tour The Program Manager

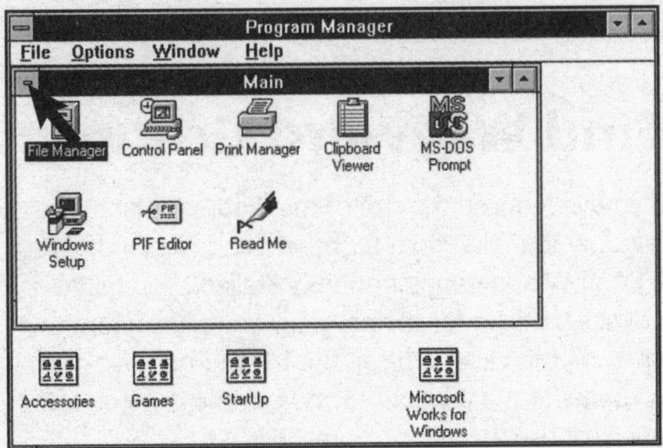

5 Click the *Control-menu box* to display a list of commands you can perform on a window. Double-click a Control-menu box to close an application.

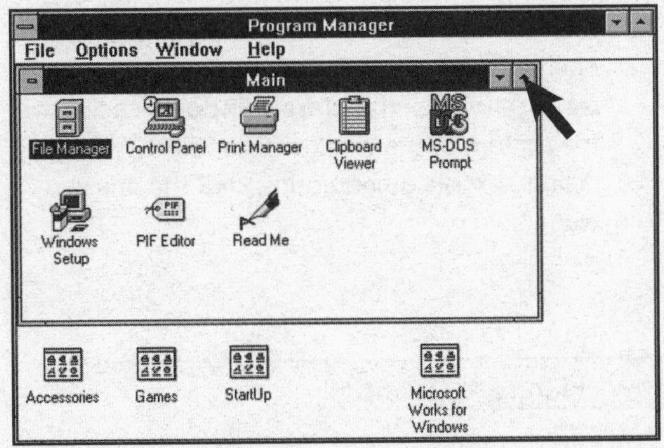

6 Click the *Maximize button*, when it appears on a window, to enlarge the window to full-screen size.

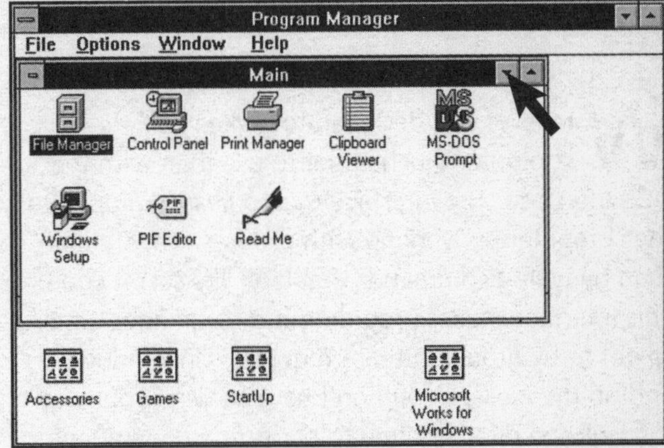

7 Click the *Minimize button* to shrink a window to an icon. Double-click the icon for the minimized window to open it back up.

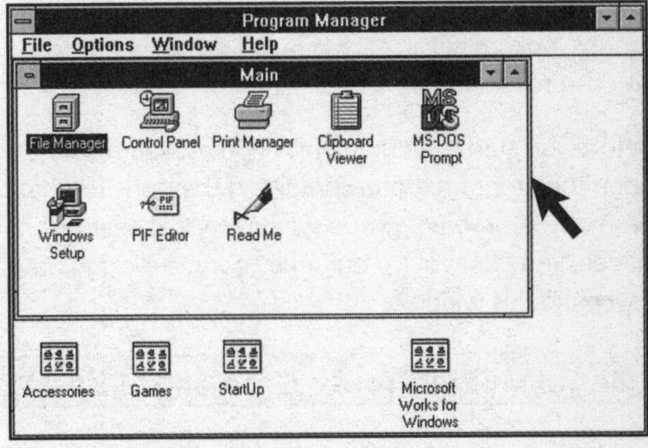

8 Drag a *window border* to resize the window.

Open and Close a Windows Program Group

Windows was designed to make your computer much easier to use than with the DOS interface. The interface is *graphical*; you operate the computer by working with pictures (icons) rather than by typing commands that look like secret code. This interface makes programs and commands easier to get to by grouping them together—in windows and on menus—so you don't have to wind your way through the directory tree to perform an operation.

A *program group* in the Windows Program Manager holds icons that represent all the program files and data files for every application. In the Program Manager window, a *program-group icon* represents each program group. Although the icons for program groups look identical, each one has its own label so you can tell them apart.

Before you start a program in Windows, you must open the program group containing the icons for that program. A *program-group window* will appear onscreen; you start your program by double-clicking on its icon in this window.

Find Wayward Groups

If you've reduced the size of the Program Manager window to make room for other windows (and have a lot of Windows applications installed), you might not see the icon for the program group you want to open. In this case, you can use the mouse to scroll the contents of the window so you can see the icon to open, or use the Windows menu.

- Click and hold on an arrow at one end of a vertical or horizontal scroll bar, until the group icon becomes visible.
- Click the **Window** menu in the menu bar, and then click the name of the group you want to open. If you have more groups than the menu can display, click the **More Windows** choice at the bottom of the window. The Select Window dialog box lists other groups; click the one you want.

Begin Guided Tour Open and Close a Windows Program Group

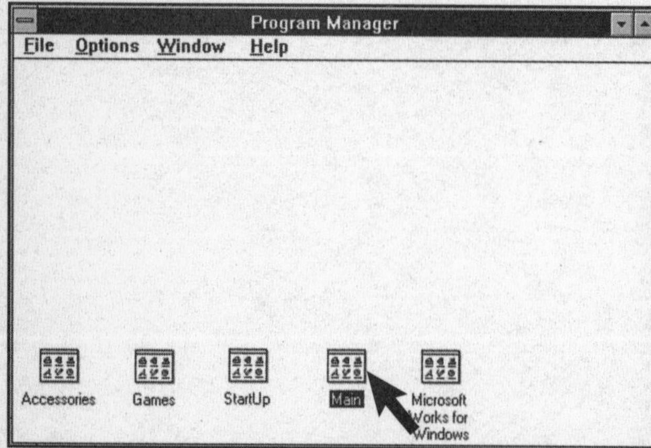

1 The simplest way to open a group is to move the mouse pointer over (that is, *point* it at) the **group icon**. When the mouse pointer is in position, double-click the icon.

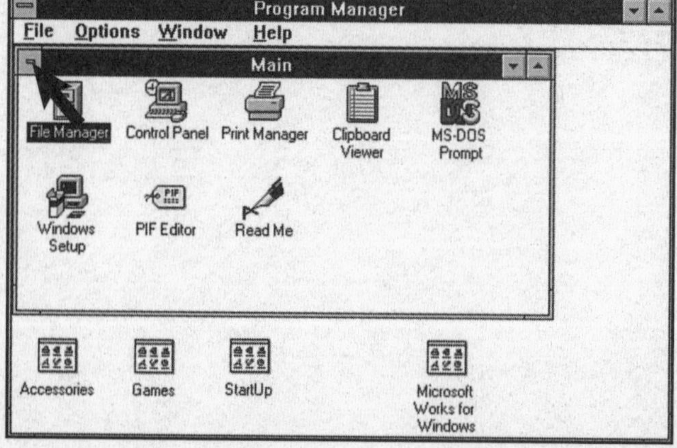

2 To close the group window, move (point) the mouse pointer over the **Control-menu box** (upper left corner of the window) and double-click.

Create and Modify Program Groups

When you install new Windows applications, the setup program generally creates a program group for you and adds the icons that start the programs (these are sometimes called *program-item icons* or just *icons*).

There may be times when you may have to create a group manually for a program, or combine programs from several groups into a single, customized group. For example, you may want to create a program group called "My Applications" to contain the icons for your word processor, spreadsheet, and game programs. You can customize the program groups in your Program Manager nearly any way you want.

Begin Guided Tour Work with Groups

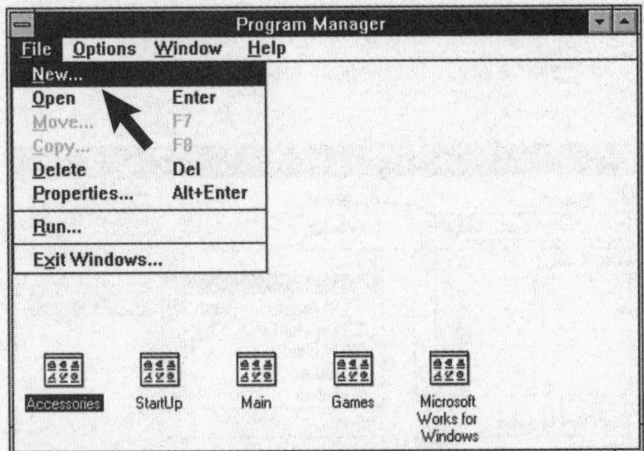

1 Click the **File** menu and then the **New** command.

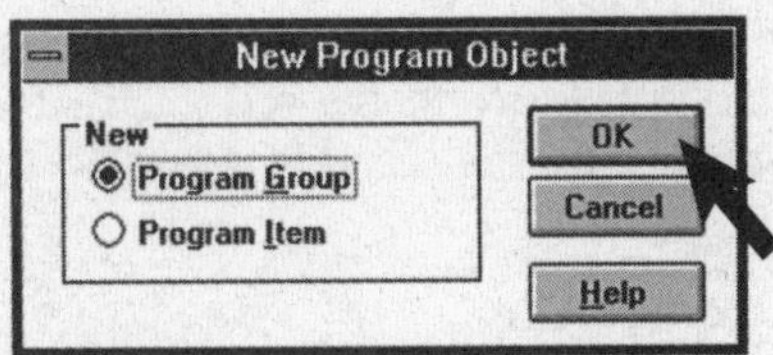

2 The New Program Object dialog box appears. Click the **Program Group** option button if it's not selected. Then just click the **OK** button.

3 The Program Group Properties dialog box appears. Type a name for your group in the **Description** text box. Then click the **OK** button. (There's no need to enter a Group File name when you're creating a new group.)

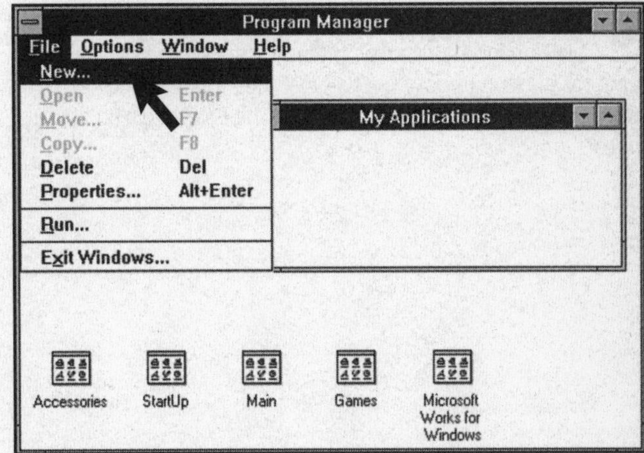

4 To add an icon for a program to any group, even a new group, open the group window by double-clicking on the icon. Then click the **File** menu, and click the **New** command.

(continues)

Guided Tour Work with Groups

(continued)

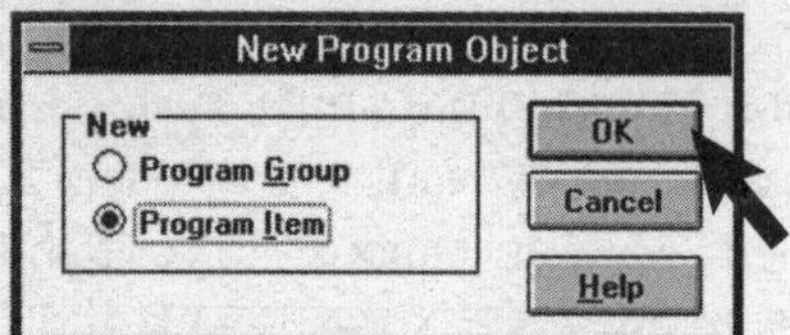

5 The New Program Object dialog box appears, with the **Program Item** choice selected because you have a group window selected. Just click the **OK** button.

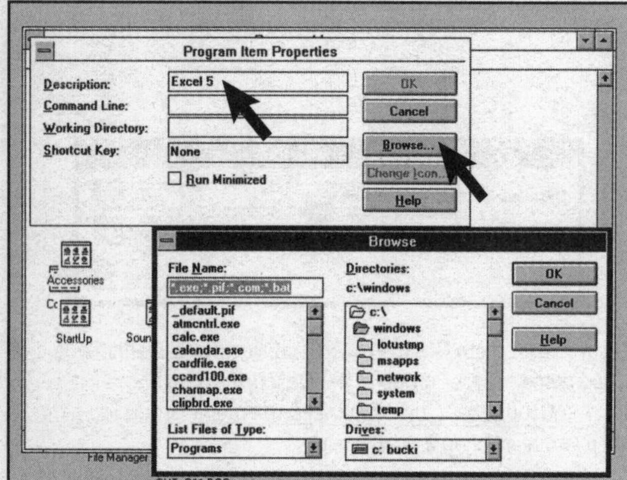

6 The Program Item Properties dialog box appears, with a blinking insertion cursor in the Description line. Type a name for the icon (usually the name of the program), such as **Excel 5**. Then click the **Browse** button. The Browse dialog box appears.

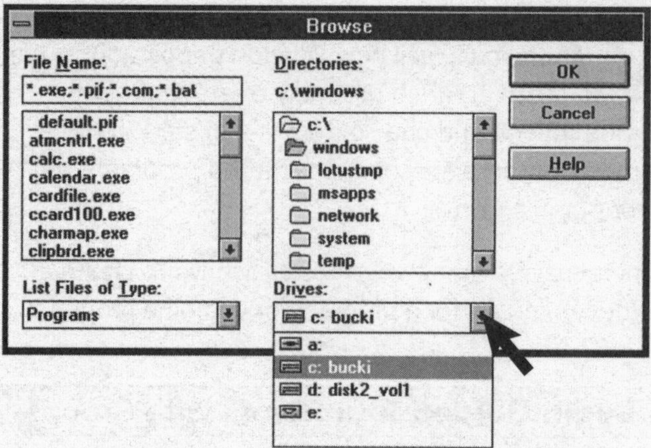

7 Click the **down arrow** beside the **Drives** list at the lower right corner of the dialog box, and then click the letter for the drive where the program file appears.

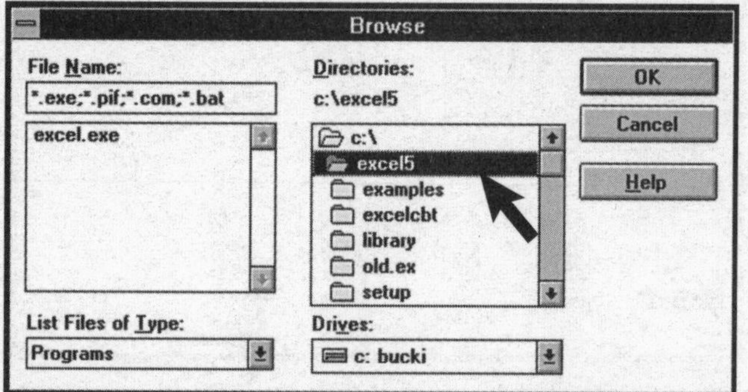

8 Click and hold on a scroll bar arrow on the **Directories** list to scroll to display the name of the directory that holds your program files. (If you need to move up one directory level first, double-click the file icon for the level you want to jump to.) Then double-click the directory name to select it.

Guided Tour Work with Groups

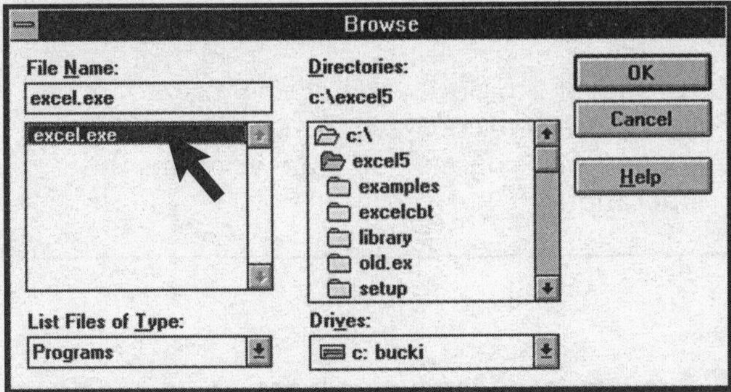

9 Click the name of the program startup file in the **File Name** list, and then click the **OK** button or press **Enter**.

10 Click the **OK** button to close the Program Item Properties dialog box and finish creating the program icon.

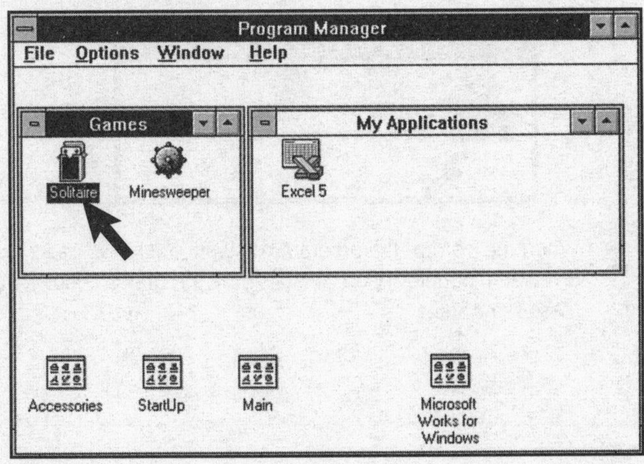

11 To move a program icon from one group to another, start by opening both group windows—the one you're moving the icon from, and the one you're moving the icon to.

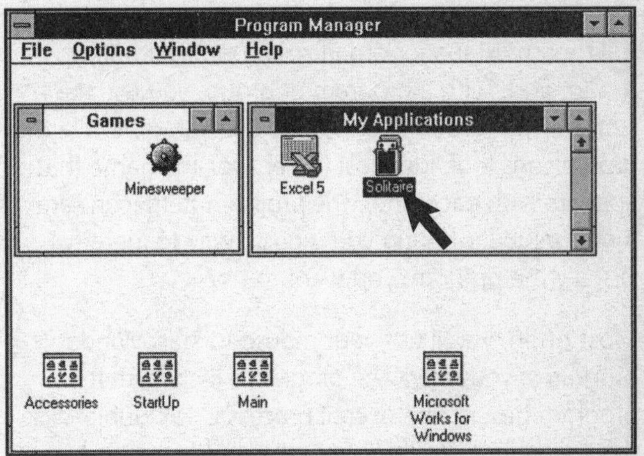

12 Move the mouse pointer over the program icon you want to move. Press and hold down the left mouse button. Then drag the mouse to move the icon to the new group. When it's in position, release the mouse button.

13 To delete a program item icon from a group (or a group icon, for that matter), click the icon to select it. Then press the **Delete** key on your keyboard.

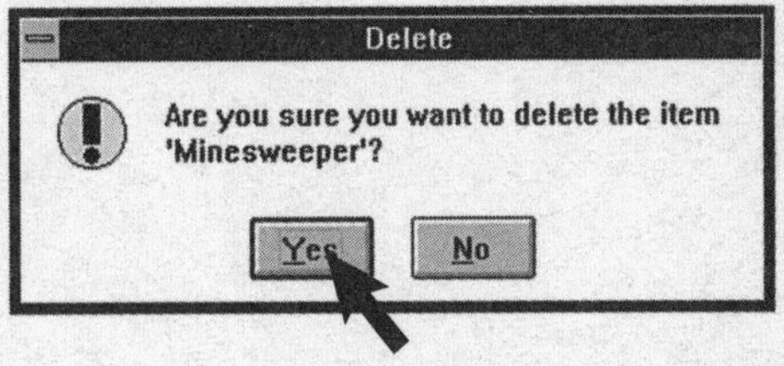

14 Click the **Yes** button to complete the deletion.

Start a Windows Program

Program Manager organizes programs in groups. To work with a program or group, you use the icon for that group and individual program. While the group icons look identical (except for the name that appears with each one), the program-item icons are more unique, offering you a quick way to identify visually the program you want to use.

Most often, you'll use your mouse to start Windows programs; you select the program's icon from its program group. The overall process is to double-click the group icon for the group that holds the program, then double-click to select a program.

If a program doesn't have an icon, don't worry, you can still run it. In fact, you can set up a Windows program to start at the same time you start Windows. You'll learn all these techniques in this task.

If you want to close a Windows program you've started, you have to exit from it. "Exit a Windows Program" on page 98 covers this operation.

Start a Program Without an Icon

You may use certain application programs so infrequently that you haven't set up an icon for them—or you might want to run a program from a floppy drive (in which case, you won't need to create an icon first). You don't always have to create a program item icon in Windows to run a program; you can run it from the Program Manager or File Manager instead (more on File Manager in the next section).

Begin Guided Tour Start a Program with an Icon

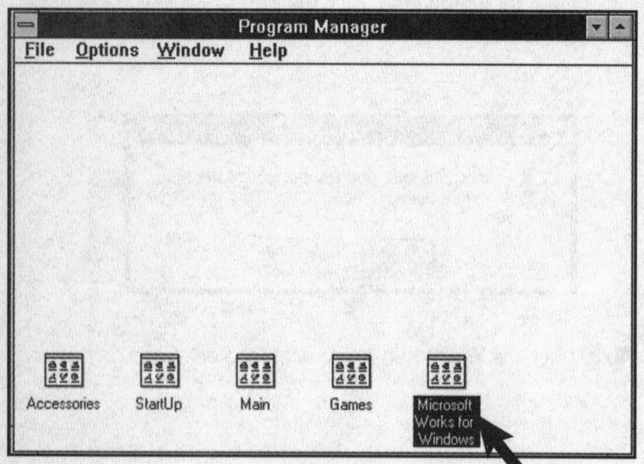

1 Double-click the icon for the program group that holds the program you want to start.

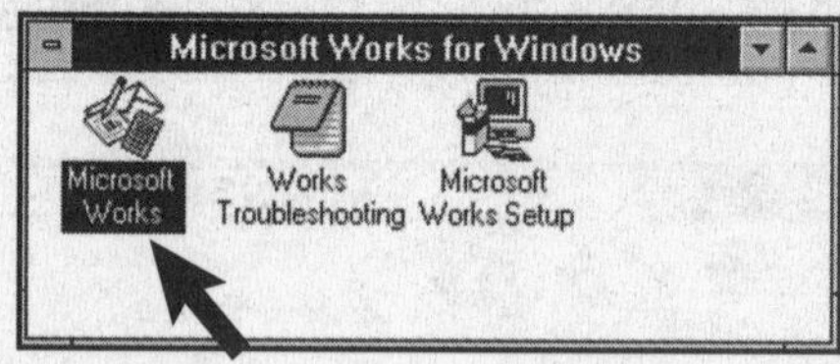

2 When the icon for the program you want to start appears on-screen, double-click it. To start other programs, follow these same steps.

Begin Guided Tour Start a Program Without an Icon

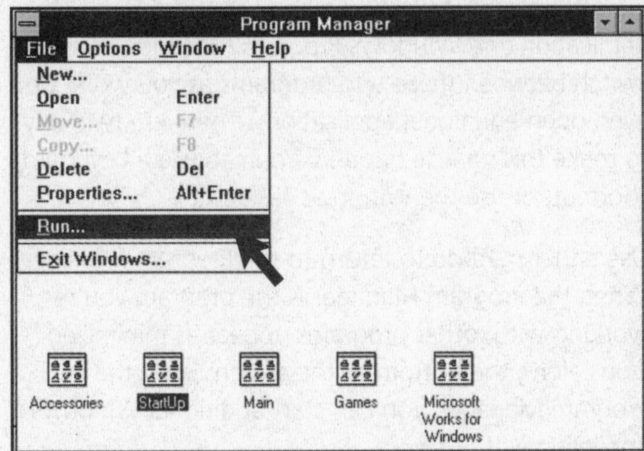

1 Click the **File** menu in either Program Manager or File Manager, and then click the **Run** command.

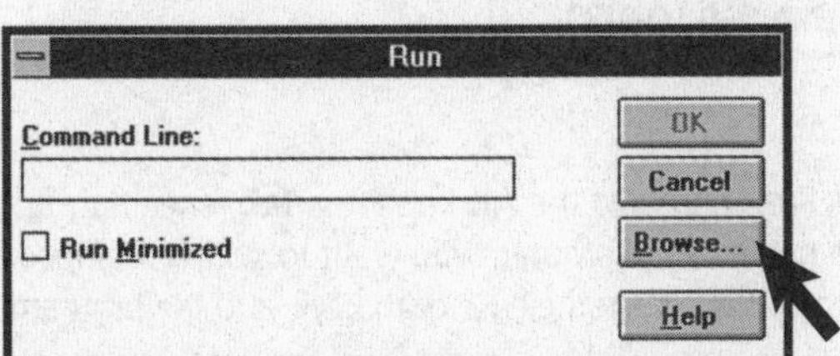

2 The Run dialog box appears, with a blinking insertion cursor in the Command Line text box. Click the **Browse** button.

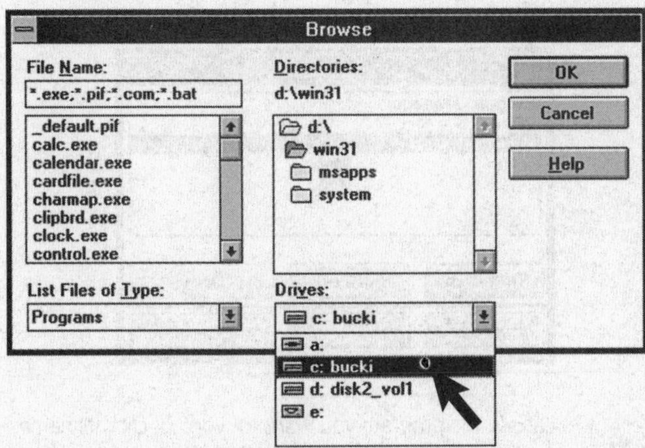

3 Click the **down arrow** beside the **Drives** list at the lower right corner of the dialog box, and then click the letter for the drive where the program file appears.

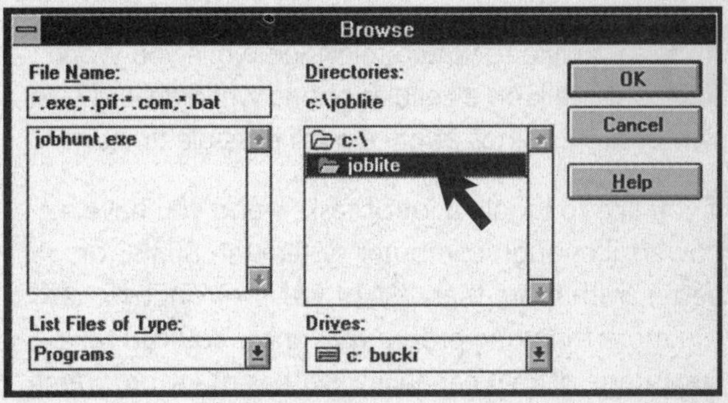

4 Click and hold on a scroll bar arrow on the **Directories** list; scroll until you display the name of the directory that holds your program files. (If you need to move up one directory level first, double-click the file icon for the level you want to jump to.) Then double-click the directory name to select it.

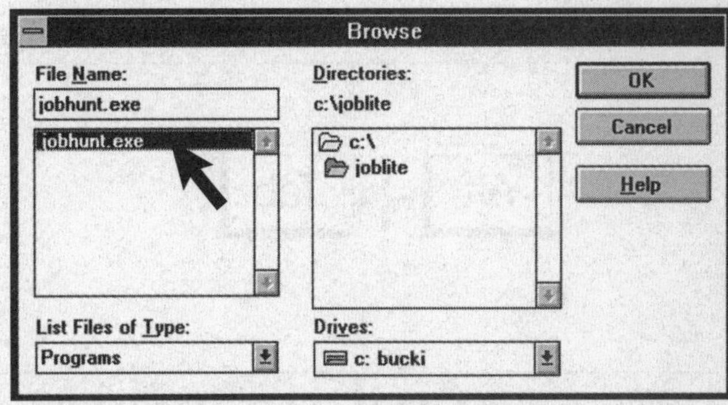

5 Click the name of the program startup file in the **File Name** list, and then click the **OK** button.

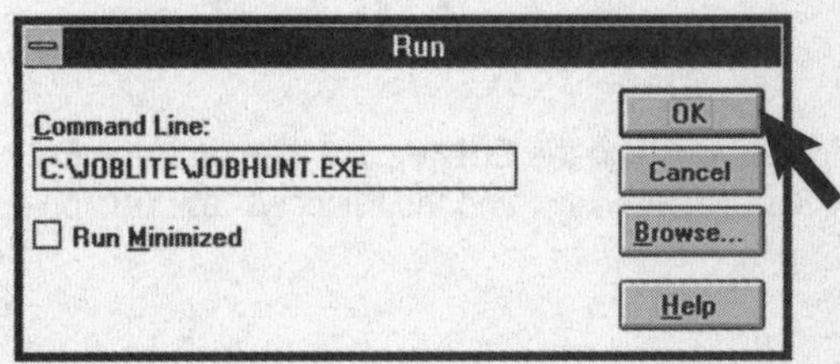

6 Click the **OK** button to close the Run dialog box and run the application program. The application appears onscreen.

Switch Between Open Programs

Do you like to watch television while you work out? Talk on a cellular phone while driving? Do two or more things at once at all possible times?

If you like to juggle a lot of tasks—and you have a powerful enough computer system (an 80386 or better, with more than 4M of RAM)—Windows can run more than one program at once. You can take advantage of that capability, start as many programs as your computer can handle, and switch between them to perform various operations.

Once you've started one Windows application, Windows is really running two programs: the application *and* Windows Program Manager. You can switch between these two programs as you work, or even open additional applications. There are two ways to make this miracle happen. You can use a keyboard shortcut, or use the Windows Task List.

Use either method to return to the Program Manager. When the Program Manager is the program you're working with, other programs appear as minimized icons along the bottom of the screen. From the Program Manager, you can start additional Windows applications.

Begin Guided Tour Switch Programs Using the Keyboard

1 Press and hold the **Alt** key. Press **Tab** repeatedly until the name of the program you want to switch to appears at the top of the screen. Release both keys, and the program appears.

Begin Guided Tour Switch Programs Using Task List

1 Press and hold the **Ctrl** key, and then press the **Esc** key. Release both keys, and the Windows Task List appears.

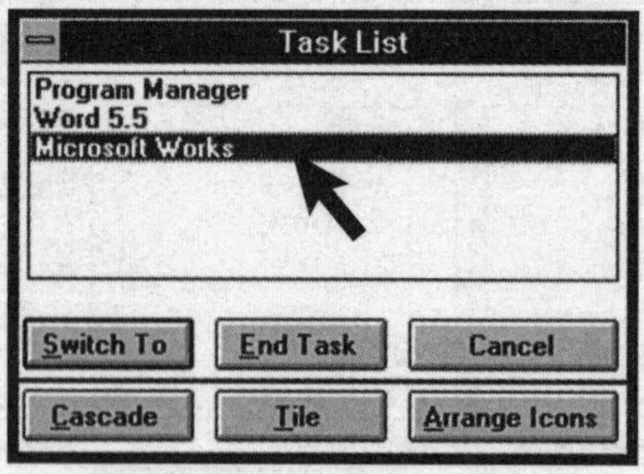

2 To choose the program you want to work in, click its name in the list, and then click the **Switch To** button. (Another method: simply double-click the program's name in the list, and the program appears on-screen.)

Select Commands from Menus

You may remember how Ali Baba said "Open sesame!" and a secret passageway opened magically before him. He gave a command, and the secret door performed an action; you issue a command to Windows (or a Windows application), and the program performs an action.

Near the top of the screen in the Windows Program Manager, the File Manager, and every Windows application, you'll find a *menu bar*. It lists the available *pull-down menus*, each of which offers a group of related commands.

To tell Windows or your application what to do, you open a pull-down menu, and then choose a command from that menu. To close a menu without selecting a command from it, press **Esc** or click outside the menu.

> You have to choose commands in DOS applications, too. For more on working in a DOS application, see "Enter Commands in DOS" on page 212.

Skip the Menu

Consistent with the promise that Windows programs are easier to use, many programs offer *icons* you can click instead of choosing a command from a menu; often you'll find these in a row called a *toolbar*. The icon performs exactly the same action as a typed command or a menu selection; it's just simpler and faster to use. Some icons even let you skip a few steps (dialog boxes, for example). Each icon has a picture that suggests what its command does; the icon for printing shows (surprise) a printer. Here are some common icons you might see in Microsoft applications; toolbar icons from other software publishers will look and act much like these.

Saves the current document to disk.

Prints the current document.

Lets you preview what the current document will look like when you print it.

Cuts out the text or data you've selected and puts it in the Windows Clipboard (temporary storage).

Copies the selected text or data you've selected; puts the copy in the Windows Clipboard.

Pastes what's in the Clipboard onto the screen at the insertion point.

Applies bold, italic, or underline formatting to the text you've selected.

Changes the alignment of the paragraph you've selected to left-, center-, or right-alignment.

Speak in Command Code

You may encounter books and tech-support people who use what sounds like a secret code when they discuss choosing a menu and a command. For example, you may read or hear something like "Select File, Exit."

Breaking the code is easy. The first word after "Select" is usually a menu name. The next word is the name of a command on that menu. So, "Select **File**, **Exit**" translates to "Open the **File** menu and choose the **Exit** command."

Valuable Menu Command Secrets

Most software publishing companies have agreed to use *common user access* standards; they design their Windows applications to be easy to use, and to work like other Windows applications. All Windows applications offer a *graphical user interface* (GUI) just like Windows; familiar visual cues help you get around in the program.

Whenever possible, Windows applications put their menus in much the same place on-screen, and offer similar commands. The File menu tends to be first on the menu bar, for example, and it usually offers New, Open, Save, and Exit commands—no matter what Windows application you're using. Normally you'll also find a Window menu that lists the names of open documents; to switch to the document you want to work on, choose it. Most applications also provide a Help menu at the far right end of the menu bar. Once you're familiar with where commands are in one program, it'll be easier to find them in another program.

Similarly, when you find symbols such as an ellipsis (**...**) next to command names on menus, they will mean the same thing from program to program: what will happen after you choose a command. Menus will provide *shortcut key combinations* next to some commands. Pressing such a combination runs the command it appears next to.

Begin Guided Tour Choose a Menu Command

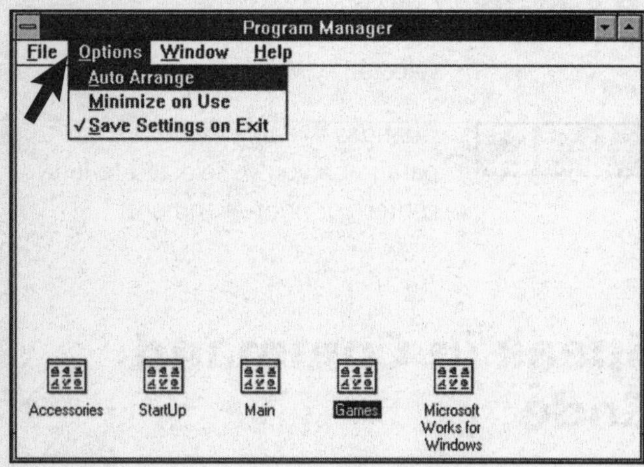

1 To open the pull-down menu, click its name in the menu bar (or press and hold the **Alt** key while you press the underlined *selection letter* in the menu's name; for example, press **Alt+O** to open the **Options** menu as shown).

2 If you want to close a menu without choosing a command from it, click another menu name, click outside the menu, or press **Esc**.

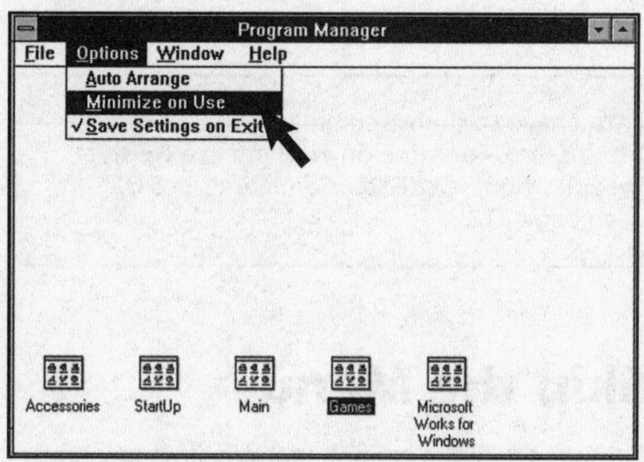

3 To choose a command from a menu, click it (to use keys, press the **down arrow** till you highlight the command name and then press **Enter**, or simply press the selection letter).

Begin Guided Tour The Parts of a Menu

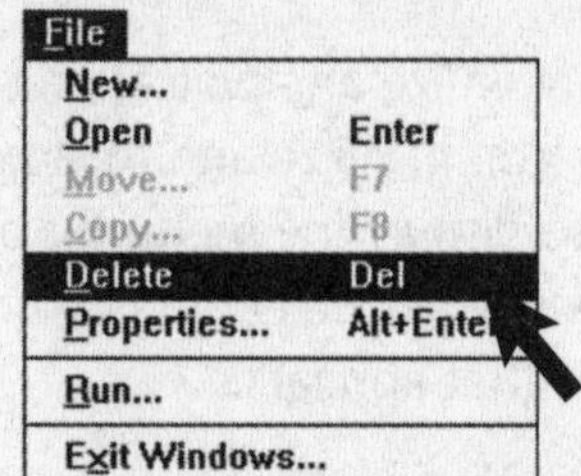

1 When a command doesn't have any symbol beside it, it simply runs when you choose it. For example, this **Delete** command would delete any icon, file, or text you've selected.

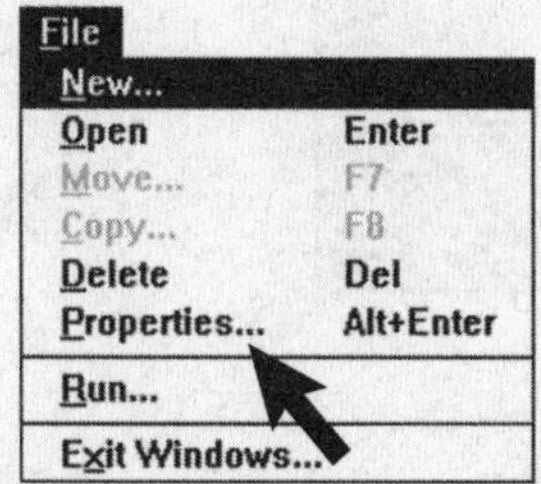

2 Commands that have an ellipsis (**...**) beside them open a dialog box that requests more information from you so the command can run. (See the task, "Use a Dialog Box" on page 75.)

3 Some commands *toggle* on and off (turn on or off) when selected. When a command like this is toggled on, a check mark appears to the left of it. Choosing the command again toggles it off and removes the check mark.

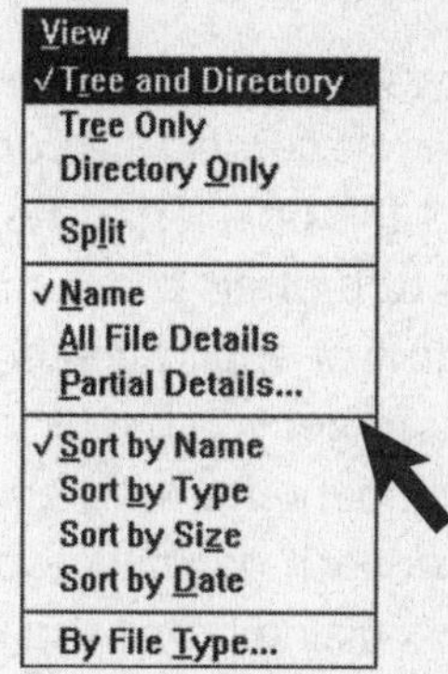

4 Sometimes (as for this File Manager menu) horizontal divider lines group commands. Only one command in the group can be selected (toggled on). A check mark appears to the left of the currently selected group command, as for the **Tree** and **Directory** command here.

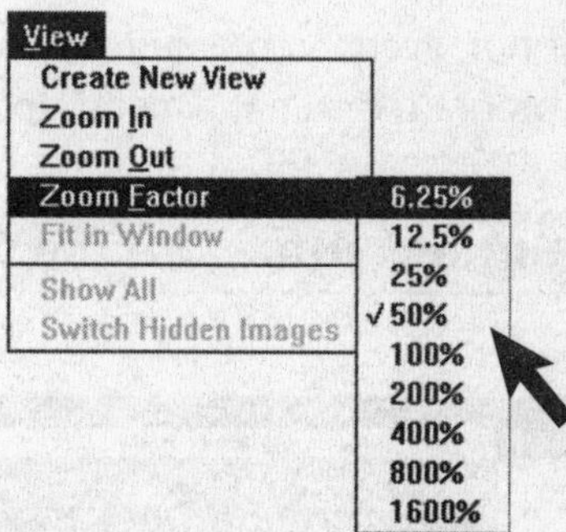

5 When a command has a triangle to the right of it, choosing that command displays a *submenu* (sometimes called a *cascading* menu) that offers more options; click the option you want.

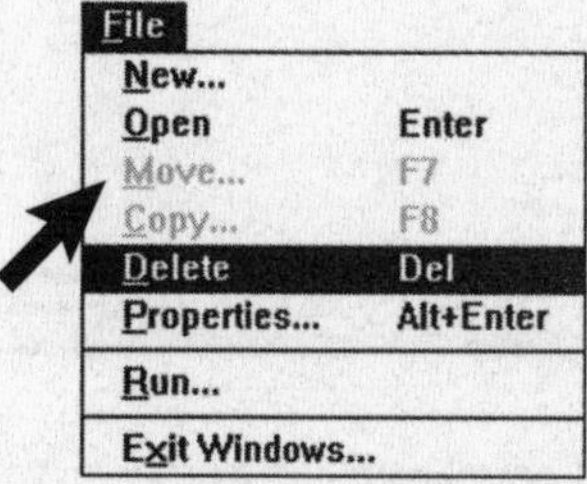

6 You can't choose commands that appear dim or *grayed out*, like the Move command on this File menu. Dimmed commands are unavailable.

Display the Control Menu for a Window

Every window has a square box with a hyphen in it in the upper left corner: the *Control-menu box*. When you select this box, it displays the *Control menu*, which in turn offers commands you can use within the window or application (for example, a Close command to get you out of the application). There's a Control menu for every application window, as well as one for each document you open in an application. Most dialog boxes also have a Control menu. Once you've displayed a Control menu, select commands from it as you would from any other menu.

Display an Icon's Menu

Believe it or not, every program-group icon and minimized program icon has a menu, too. (You'll learn how to minimize an application program window to an icon in "Size and Arrange Windows" on page 80.) To display the menu for one of these icons, just click it. Then select the command you want from the menu that appears.

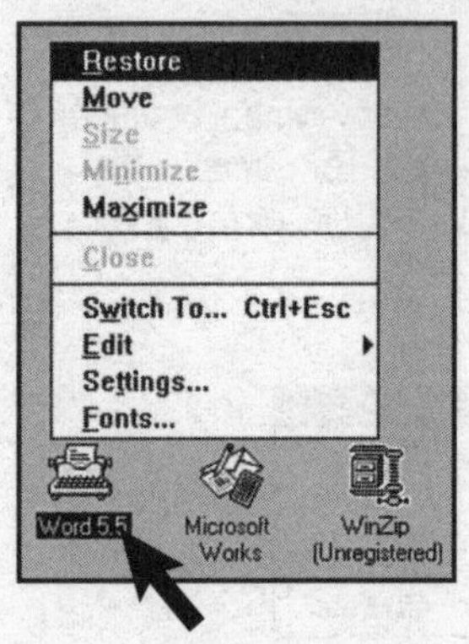

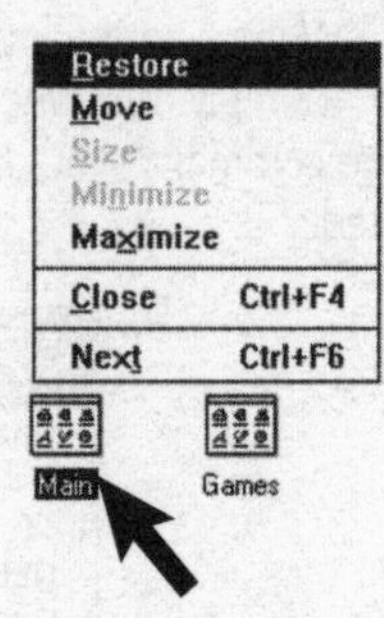

Begin Guided Tour Use the Control Menu

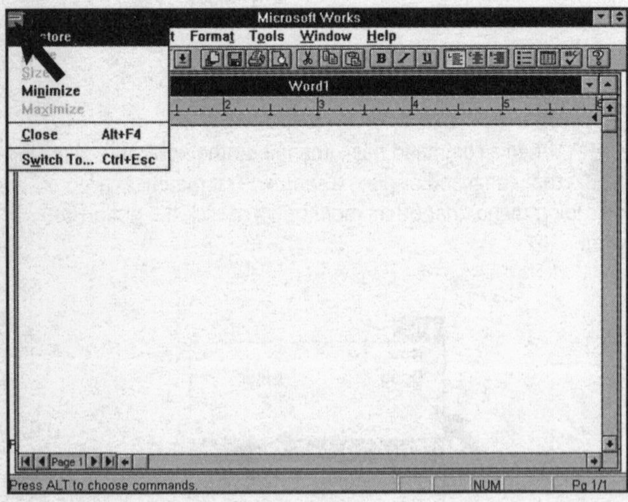

1. To open the Control menu for a program window or dialog box, click the **Control-menu box** or press **Alt+Shift+Spacebar**.

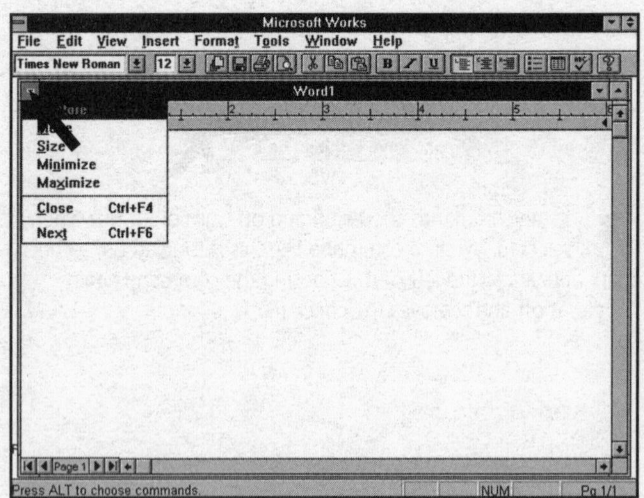

2. To open the Control menu for a document within an application, click the **Control-menu box** or press **Alt+-** (Alt plus the hyphen key).

Use a Dialog Box

In novels and short stories, any interaction between characters that has them talk to each other is called *dialog*. When you interact with Windows (or a Windows application), the program may "ask" you to provide information or a choice so it can do what you want. It "asks" you by displaying a *dialog box*, a special window that lets you tell it exactly what to do. When you tell the program to proceed, it does what you told it to do when you filled in the dialog box.

Dialog boxes appear after you choose a menu command that's followed by an *ellipsis* (**...**). The box may ask you to perform precise actions like these:

- Choose which file to open from a particular drive and directory.
- Specify whether you want your text to appear in bold, italicized, or underlined characters.
- Select a particular clip art (picture) file to insert into a document.
- Tell an application whether to ignore or change a word during a spelling check.

Dialog boxes offer different *controls* for choosing options. In some cases, you simply choose all the options that apply. In other cases, you have to select a single option from a group of several. Dialog boxes usually group related options in a *text box* with a title. In a dialog box you use to format text, for example, you may find effects like bold, italic, and underline grouped in an area called **Style**. Many dialog boxes offer preview areas to show you what the options you selected would do if you approved them. This task presents the different kinds of controls, and explains how to use each one.

> *Command buttons* run a command or display another dialog box when the button name is followed by an ellipsis (**...**). Simply click a command button with the mouse to select it. Most dialog boxes have the buttons described here.

Choosing **OK** accepts the options you selected, and then closes the dialog box. Choosing **Cancel** closes the dialog box without running a command. Choosing **Help** displays a *Help window* that offers more information about the command and dialog box choices.

Check boxes toggle an option on and off (an **X** appears in the box when it's turned on). To select or deselect a check box, click it. Even though check boxes may be grouped as shown here, you can select all the options in the group, none of them, or any combination of them.

Option buttons always appear in groups because they are mutually exclusive—you can select only one button at a time from each group. To select the one you want, click it.

When you have to enter a *value* (such as the number of copies you want to print of a document), or a *name* (like a new file name), the place you enter it is a *text box*. To use one, click it to place the *insertion point* (a vertical cursor) in it, and then type in your selection.

List boxes let you choose from a list of choices for an option. To make a choice, click it. In many cases, double-clicking on a choice in the list selects that choice and closes the dialog box, accepting any other options you've selected. (Sometimes a text box appears above the list box, giving you the option of typing a choice or choosing it from the list.)

Drop-down lists hide all but the currently selected option until you display the list. Click the **down arrow** beside the list to display the choices, and then click the new choice.

Tabs enable a dialog box to hold multiple groups of options. To select a tab to see the options it holds, click the tab.

Increment or *spinner buttons* let you increase or decrease a value. Click and hold on the **up arrow** to increase the value. Click and hold on the **down arrow** to decrease the value.

For some dialog box options (such as the line choices shown here), the dialog box displays an *icon* for each choice. Simply click the choice you want.

> To move between various dialog box controls with the keyboard, you can press the **Tab** key repeatedly until a dotted-line highlight surrounds the option. If the option has a *selection letter* (underlined letter), move to it by pressing and holding the **Alt** key, and then pressing the selection letter.

Begin Guided Tour Parts of a Dialog Box

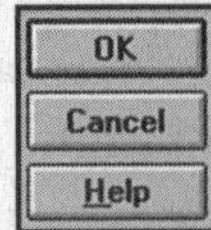

1 *Command buttons* run a command or display another dialog box when the button name is followed by an ellipsis (**...**).

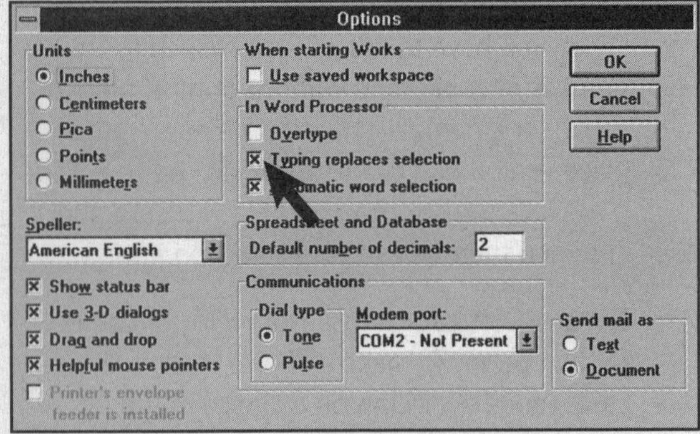

2 *Check boxes* toggle an option on and off (an **X** appears in the box when it's turned on).

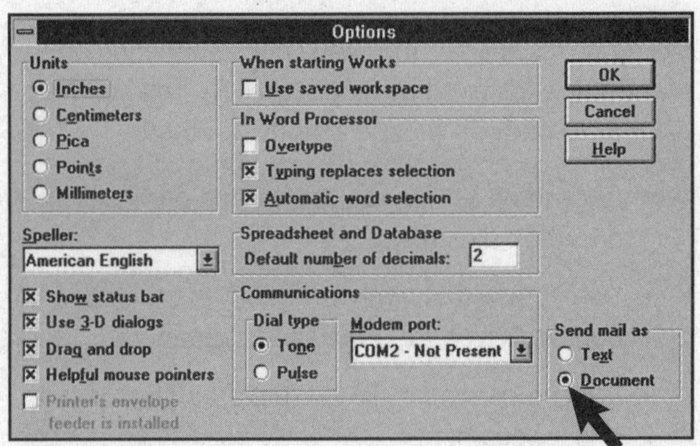

3 *Option buttons* always appear in groups. To select the one you want, click it.

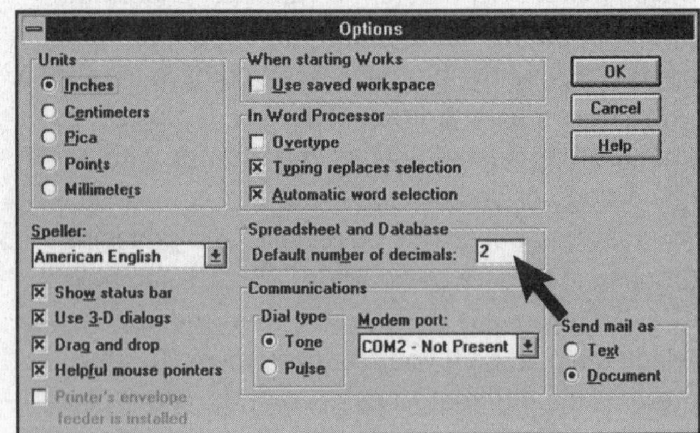

4 You enter a *value* or a *name* (like a new file name) in a *text box*.

Guided Tour Parts of a Dialog Box

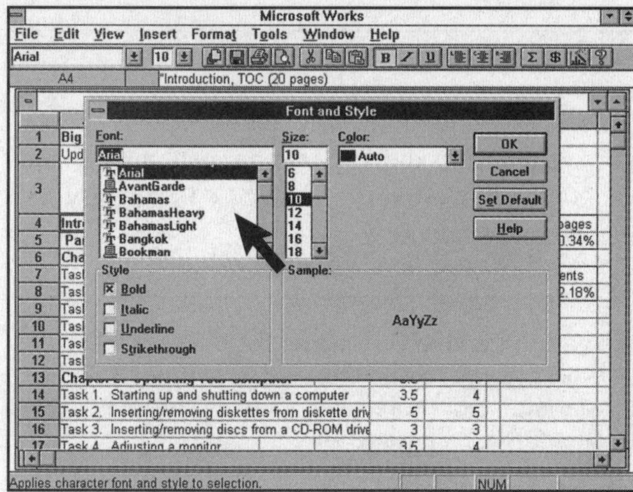

5 *List boxes* let you choose from a list of choices for an option.

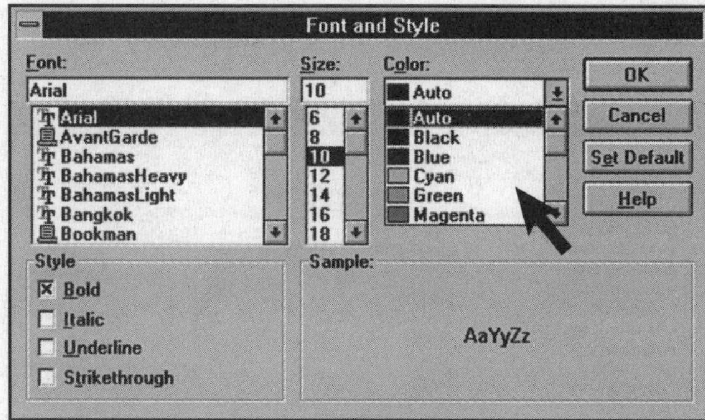

6 *Drop-down lists* open to display a list of choices. Click the **down arrow** beside the list to display the choices, and then click the new choice.

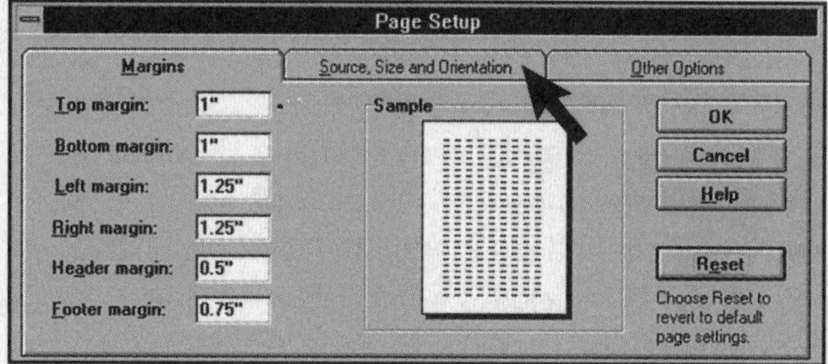

7 *Tabs* enable a dialog box to hold multiple groups of options. Click a tab to choose it.

8 *Increment* or *spinner buttons* let you increase or decrease a value. Click and hold an arrow to change a value.

9 For some dialog box options (such as the line choices shown here), the dialog box displays an *icon* for each choice. Simply click the choice you want.

Work with Directory Lists in Dialog Boxes

Whenever you issue a command to perform a *file operation* (such as the Open or Save commands on the File menu), the dialog box that appears usually includes a Directories list box.

This box displays the directory tree for the disk drive you're currently working in. Small icons to the left of each directory or subdirectory indicate whether you're viewing what's in that directory (an open-file icon) or what's in the directory one level above it (a closed-file icon). The files in the currently selected directory generally appear in a Files list to the left of the Directories list.

To work efficiently in virtually every Windows application, you need to know how to navigate through the various levels of a Directories list box. Fortunately, it's easy: use your mouse.

Working with a Directories list box is just like working with directories in the Windows File Manager. For more, see "View Different Directories" on page 104.

Begin Guided Tour Use a Directory List

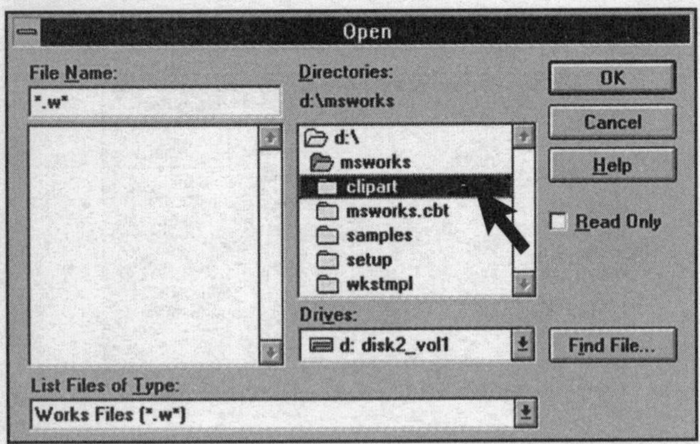

1. To move "down" one level in the tree (display the files in a subdirectory of a level that has an open-file icon beside it), double-click the lower directory, which should be indented slightly to the right.

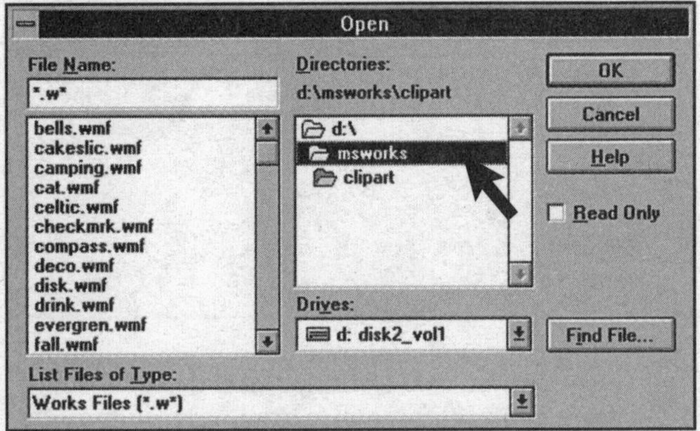

2. To move "up" one level in the tree, double-click the upper directory; it should have an open file icon beside it, and be indented to the left of the current directory.

3. To go to the root directory of the current drive, click its folder icon at the top of the tree.

Work with Scroll Bars in Dialog Boxes

When its list is particularly long, a dialog box may not be able to show all the list's contents at once. This problem also can occur when a program-group window in Program Manager is too small to display icons for all the programs it holds.

Whenever a dialog box or program can't display all the available choices in a list or window, it displays one or more *scroll bars*; you use these to move through the list or window to see the rest of the choices. *Vertical scroll bars* run down the right side of a list or window; *horizontal scroll bars* run along the bottom edge.

To work with scroll bars, use a mouse. You can choose from several techniques:

Begin Guided Tour Use Scroll Bars

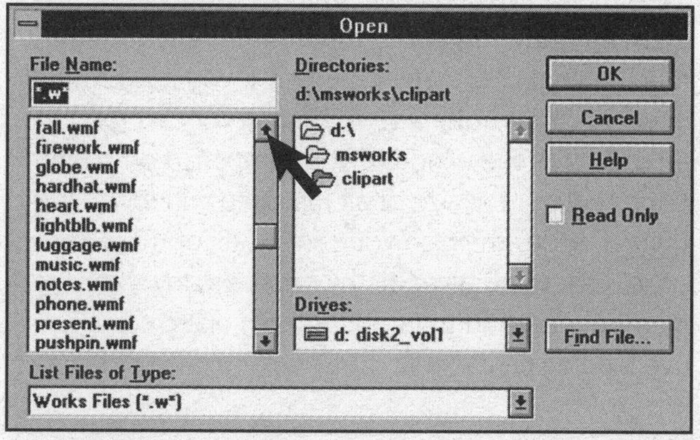

1 To display one more item at the top or bottom of the list (or to move through a window by a small increment), click the arrow at either end of the scroll bar. Click and hold on the arrow to scroll steadily; release the mouse button to stop.

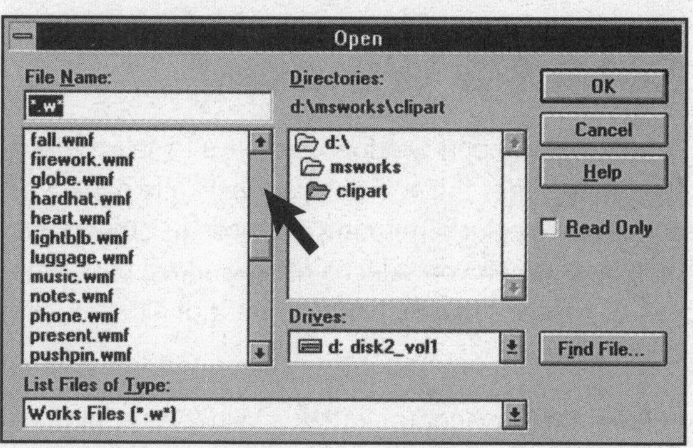

2 To move in larger increments, click the scroll bar itself. Click toward the arrow that indicates the direction you want to move in.

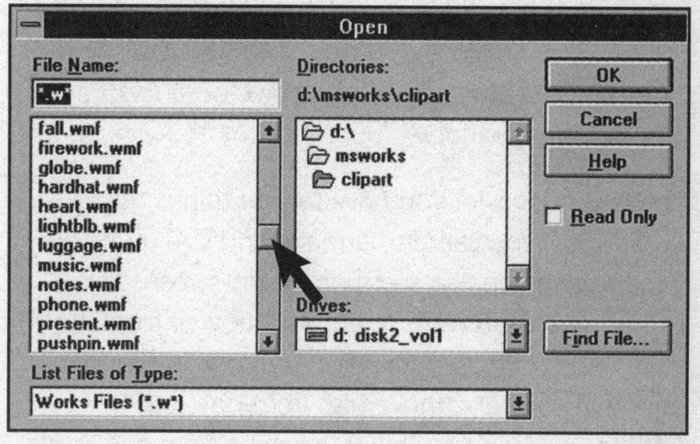

3 To move really fast, drag the scroll box along the scroll bar.

Size and Arrange Windows

Windows is called Windows for a couple of reasons. First, "Cool Interface with Little Pictures and Boxes" was just too long. Second, Windows uses *windows* on-screen to organize information and commands:

- Program-group icons open to windows that hold groups of program-item icons.
- Dialog boxes are windows you can move around on-screen.
- A window contains the Program Manager, File Manager, and every other application you start from Windows.
- The File Manager displays the contents of each disk in a window.

These windows let you have several things going on at once; you can also arrange and size multiple windows so you can see them all on-screen. This is useful when you want to copy or move information from window to window. For example, in File Manager you copy and move files from one disk to another by dragging their file names from one disk's window to another.

You can make a window any size you want—or move it anywhere on-screen—by dragging with the mouse. You also need to be familiar with two particular parts of the window to perform these operations. The window's *title bar* is the colored bar along the top that displays the name of the window's contents—whether it holds an application, document file, or dialog box options. The window *border* is the narrow, shaded area that surrounds the window. You can use several mouse shortcuts to change the size of a window.

Minimizing reduces an open window to an icon to save space.

Maximizing expands a window to full-screen size (if it's a program-group window, it simply fills the Program Manager window) to give you more workspace.

Restoring a window returns it to the size it was before you maximized it.

Closing a window puts it away, or removes its contents from the screen. Closing a program-group window turns it into a minimized icon in the Program Manager window.

Microsoft Windows offers you a great deal of flexibility. Although you can open many windows and size them any way you want, you may not want to spend much time doing that—especially if you have several open. Windows offers two shortcut options for arranging all the windows you've opened on-screen. *Tiling* reduces the size of all the open windows, and then arranges them so you can see all of them at once. *Cascading* gives all the open windows an identical size, and then stacks them on-screen like overlapping cards.

For more on working in the Windows in File Manager, see "Organize Files and Directories with Windows 3.11" on page 99.

Select a Window

To work in an open window, you have to select it first; then it becomes the *active window*; its title bar always appears in a color different from those of other open windows. When you select a new window, the one you've chosen typically jumps in front of all other open windows.

In Program Manager (or within a Windows application), click the window you want to select if it's visible. To move from one open application window to another, click the window you want (if you can see it on-screen).

As another method, most programs (and Windows itself) offer a Window menu. The names of open menus typically appear at the bottom of this menu. Click the **Window** menu to display it, and then click the name of the window you want to open.

Begin Guided Tour Move and Resize a Window

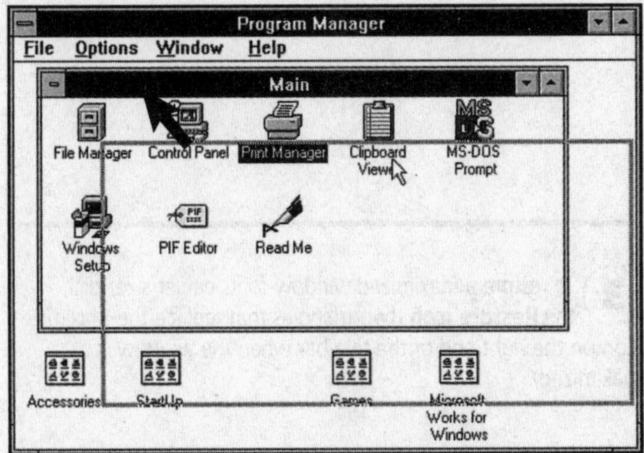

1 To move a window, click the window's title bar and drag it in the direction you want. When the gray shadow outline of the window is where you want it, release the mouse button.

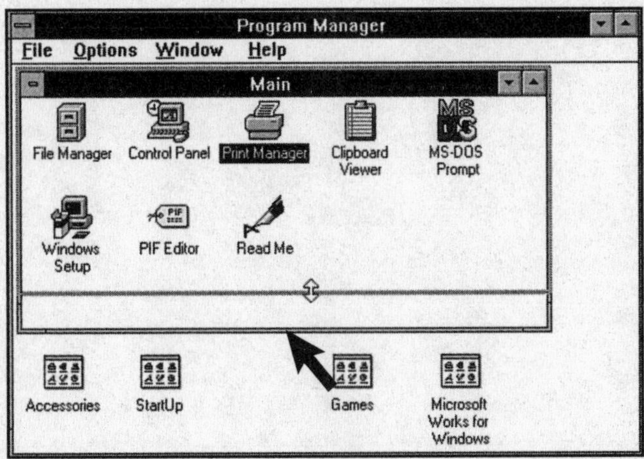

2 To resize a window's height or width, click and hold the mouse pointer over the side, top, or bottom border until it turns into a double-headed arrow. Drag the window's border outward or inward until it's the size you want (indicated with a gray shadow outline).

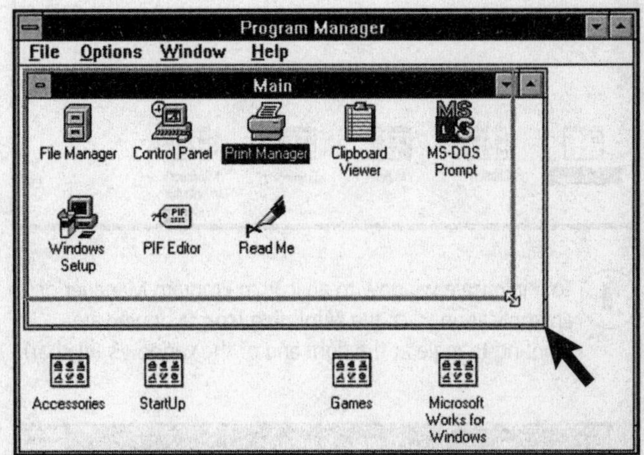

3 To resize a window's height and width at the same time, click and hold the mouse pointer on the corner of a border until the pointer turns into a double-headed arrow. Drag the border outward or inward until it's the size you want (indicated with a gray shadow outline).

Begin Guided Tour Minimize, Maximize, and Restore Windows

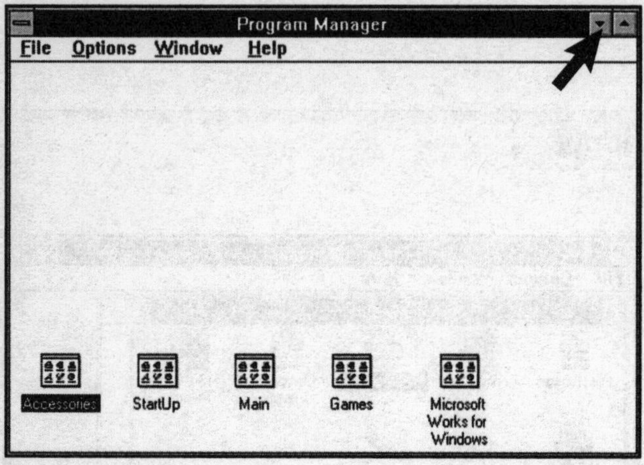

1 To minimize a window to an icon in Program Manager or an application, click the **Minimize icon** (a downward-pointing triangle at the right end of the window's title bar).

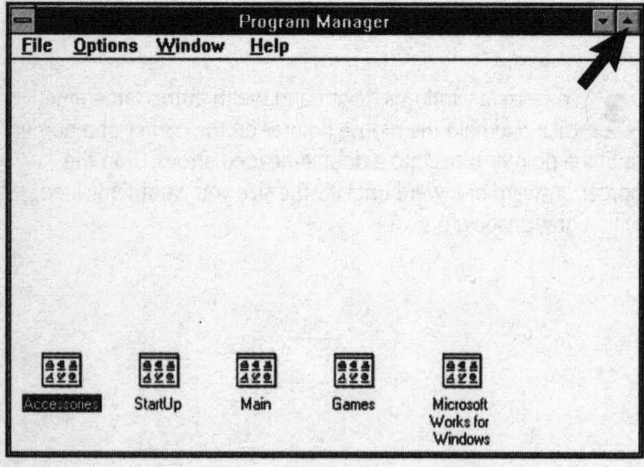

2 To maximize a window, click the **Maximize icon** (an upward-pointing triangle at the right end of the window's title bar).

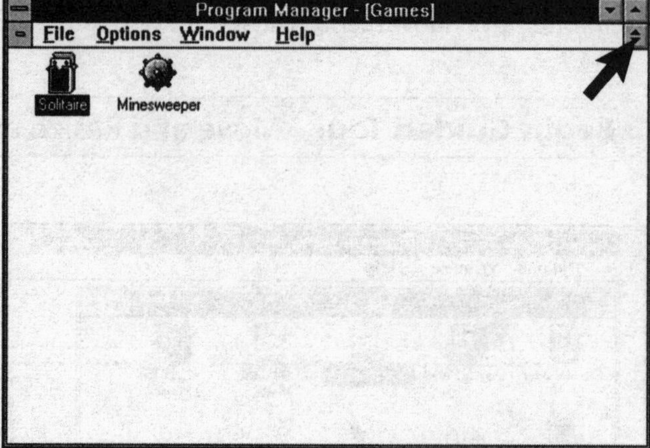

3 To restore a maximized window to its earlier size, click the **Restore icon** (two triangles that replace the Maximize icon on the right end of the title bar when the window is maximized).

Begin Guided Tour Close Windows

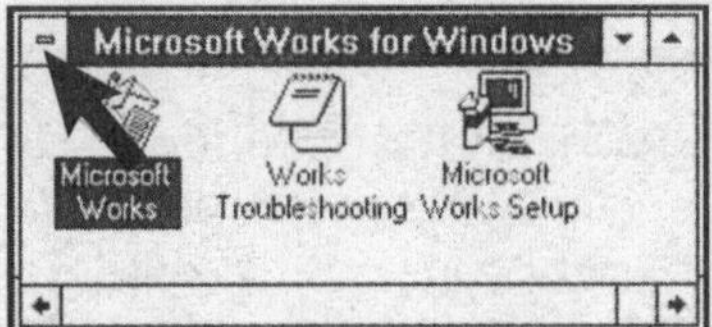

1 To close any window, double-click the **Control-menu box** at the left end of the window's title bar. Press **Ctrl+F4** to close a document window or program-group window. Press **Alt+F4** to close an application window.

Begin Guided Tour Tile and Cascade Windows

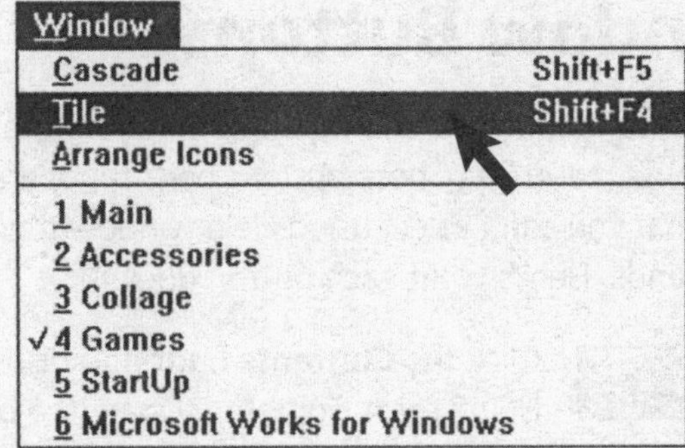

1 To *tile* windows (arrange them side by side), click the **Window** menu and then click **Tile** (or press **Shift+F4**).

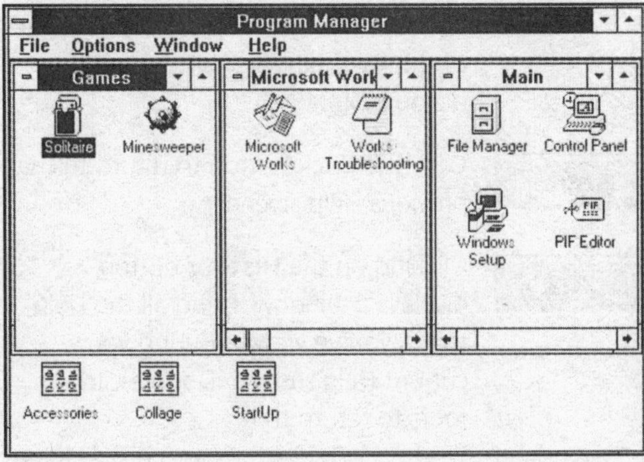

2 Windows resizes all the open windows, and then arranges them so you can see them all (and some of their contents) on-screen.

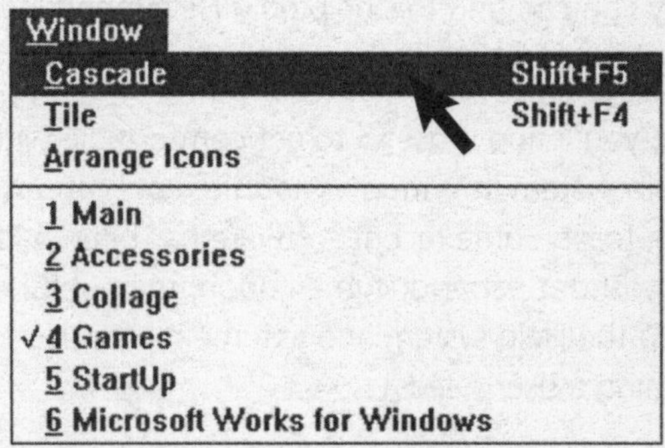

3 To *cascade* windows (overlap them in order), click the **Window** menu and then click **Cascade** (or press **Shift+F5**).

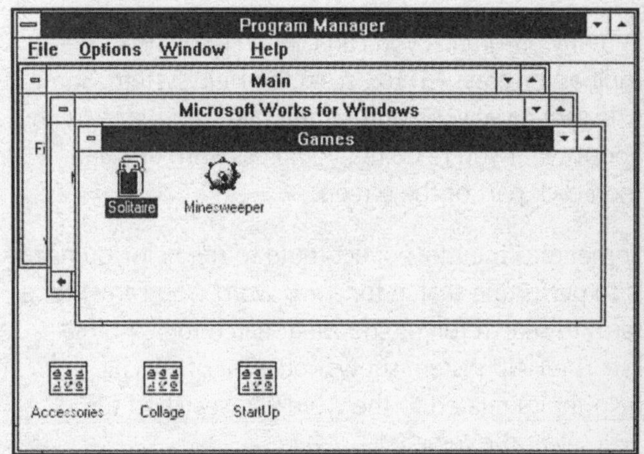

4 Windows resizes all the open windows, and then arranges them so they overlap in a neat stack on-screen. Only the contents of the top window are visible on-screen.

Get Help in Windows

Some people can drive through a new city once and remember it perfectly. The next time, they don't even need a map to figure out where they're going. Most of us need a little more repetition to remember how to navigate a new area—or a new program. Even experienced computer users can't remember every feature of every program they use.

Fortunately, Windows and most Windows applications programs offer help on program features. Usually you can find this help on a Help menu located to the right of all other choices on the menu bar.

In fact, you'll find it useful to get comfortable with the Help system in Windows and the applications written for it. Some recent software has been published without paper documentation; the publishers beef up the Help system and assume it provides everything a user needs!

Windows Help uses a system of *hypertext links* to get you to the topic you need to read. In this system, you click a highlighted (or different-colored) topic you want to learn more about; this is the link that jumps you to another document that covers the topic.

In many programs, you can click a Help icon in the toolbar (or press **F1**) to access the Help system. Some software gives you *context-sensitive help* that tells you about what you're doing; you press **Shift+F1** and then click part of the screen.

Sometimes the most direct route to the help you need is to perform a search for a *key word*. You can enter a term to search for, or choose a search topic from a list. The Help system shows you a list of specific help topics related to the word you searched for. You select the topic.

> Learning to work with the Windows Help system's *hypertext links* prepares you to surf the Net! Browser programs for the Internet's World Wide Web sites use a similar system of linked topics.

Use Other Help Window Buttons

The Help system offers a row of command buttons below the menu bar. These buttons perform operations that you can't select using Help window menu commands. Here's what each button does:

Contents — Click the **Contents** button to display Help's main Contents screen (the one you see immediately after choosing the **Help Contents** command).

Search — Click the **Search** button to display a dialog box that enables you to search for a specific Help topic. (The next part of this task explains how to use this dialog box.)

Back — Click the **Back** button to return to the previous Help screen.

History — Clicking on the **History** button displays a window listing all the Help topics you've viewed during your current Help session. Double-click a topic to return to it.

Glossary — Clicking on the **Glossary** button displays an alphabetical listing of all the glossary topics in Help. Scroll to the topic you want a definition for; click the topic.

Begin Guided Tour Use the Help Menu

1 From the Windows Program Manager or File Manager (or any other Windows application, for that matter), click the **Help** menu, and then click **Contents**.

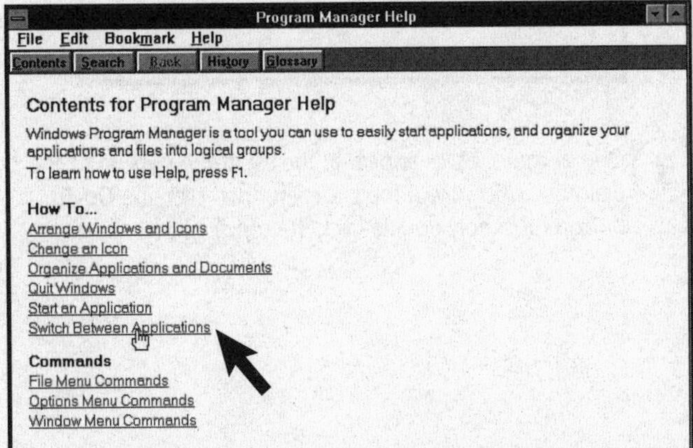

2 Selecting a topic that appears in green with a solid underline takes you to a Help screen with more information about that topic. Move the mouse pointer over the topic you want until you see the hand pointer, and then click.

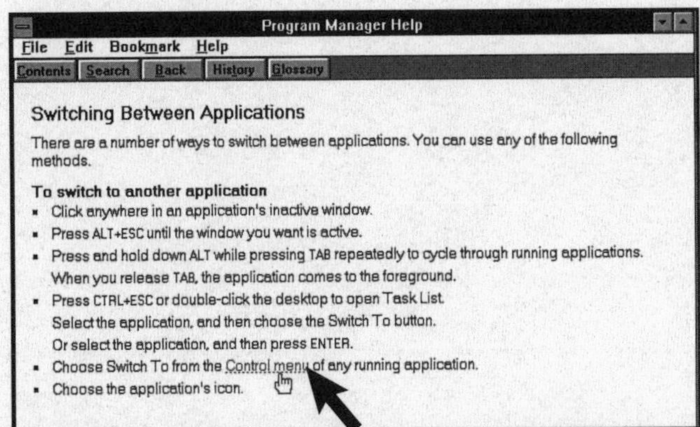

3 Help displays the related screen with more information. It may offer steps, additional links, or *glossary topics* (which are green and have a dashed underline. To select one of these, move the mouse pointer over it until you see the hand pointer, and then click.

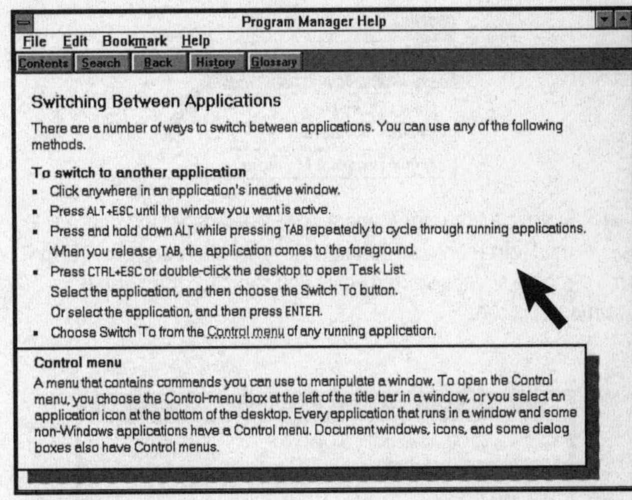

4 To close a glossary topic, click outside it or press **Esc**.

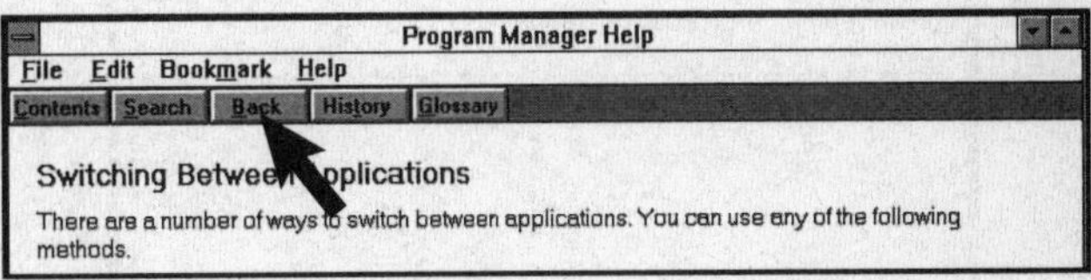

5 To move to the previous Help screen, click the **Back** button in the row of buttons below the menu bar in the Help window.

6 To leave Help and close the Help window, click **File** and then click **Exit**. (For a quick exit, double-click the Help window's **Control-menu box**).

Begin Guided Tour Search for Help About a Specific Topic

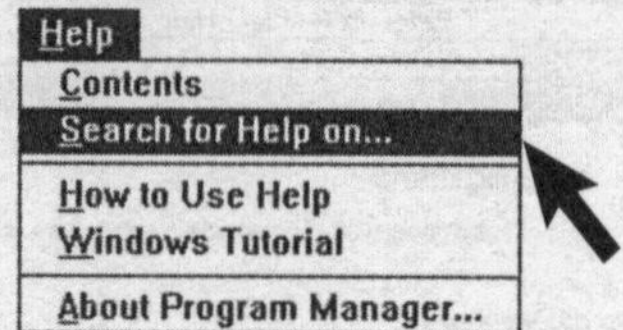

1 From the Program Manager or File Manager window, click the **Help** menu, and then click to select **Search for Help on**. (If you've already started Help, you can click the **Search** command button.)

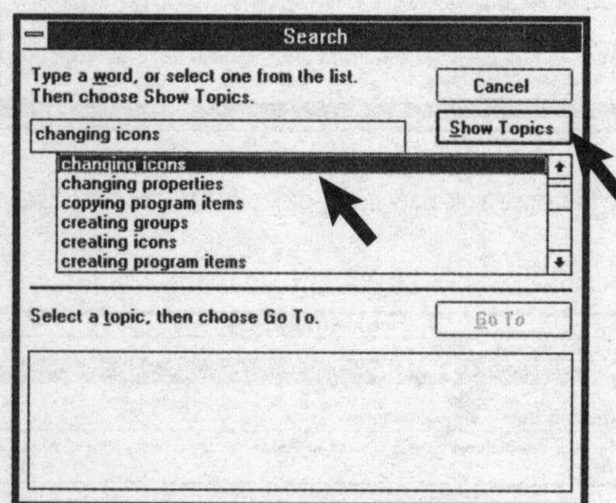

2 In the text box at the top of the dialog box, type the word you want to search for; the most similar topic will be highlighted in the list automatically. Another way: scroll down through the list and click a search word. Click the **Show Topics** button to display related topics (or double-click a word from the search list to see its topics).

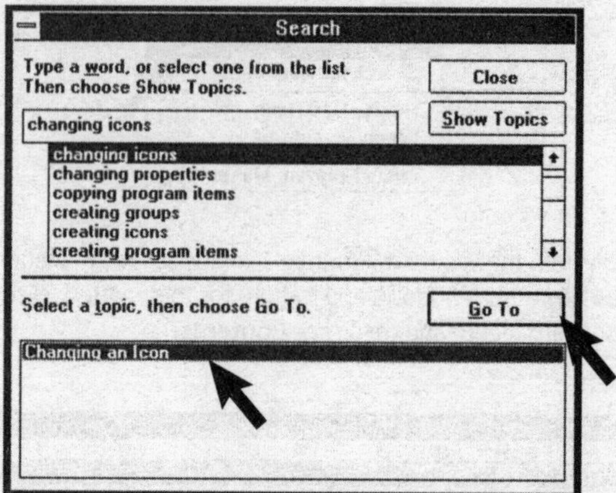

3 One or more topics appear in the list at the bottom of the dialog box. To view a topic, click it, then click the **Go To** button (or simply double-click the topic).

Start a New File in a Windows Program

When you start a Windows application, usually it will open a new, blank document on the screen. You can work with this document, or open a different file and work with that one instead. Chances are, however, that you will create more than one new document per work session. You might write a letter, create a report, and then put together a to-do list. Every time you want to start another document, you'll need to open a new file in the program.

In most programs, starting a new file takes no more than a simple menu command or the clicking of an icon. You issue the command, and a new document window appears on-screen. (In *integrated software* programs that combine several applications—for example, Microsoft Works for Windows—you have to tell the program what *kind* of file to open.)

Be aware that some programs can have only one document open at a time. (When you start a new document in the Windows Write accessory program, for example, it closes any document that's open on-screen.) Make sure you save your work in the open document before you start a new file (see "Save Your Work in a Windows Program"on page 92).

A *document* is a file you create in any Windows program. Documents can be (for example) spreadsheet, plain text, word processing, graphics, or database files.

Jump-Start a File

Many programs offer automated features that help you develop new files. These helpers display dialog boxes that ask you for information and give you choices for putting a document together. In a presentation graphics (slide show) program, for example, you could choose a look for your slide show, screen colors, and topic; the program would set the whole thing up and suggest an outline for you.

In Microsoft products, these automated helpers are called *Wizards*. In Novell/WordPerfect products, they're called *Experts*. Look for the command to start these helpers on the **File** menu in your application; some applications offer the startup command in a New File dialog box. Then you would follow the on-screen prompts to set up your document.

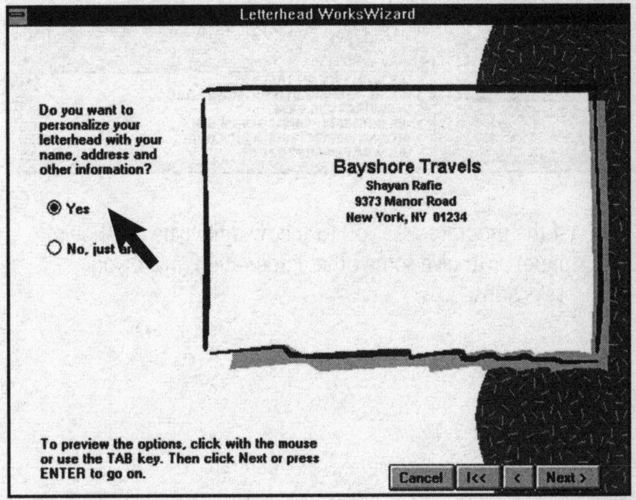

Begin Guided Tour Start a New File

1 Open the **File** menu, and then click the **New** command. In some applications, the command name may vary (for example, "Create New File"). If your program offers a toolbar, it may have a **New File** icon you can click to start a new file.

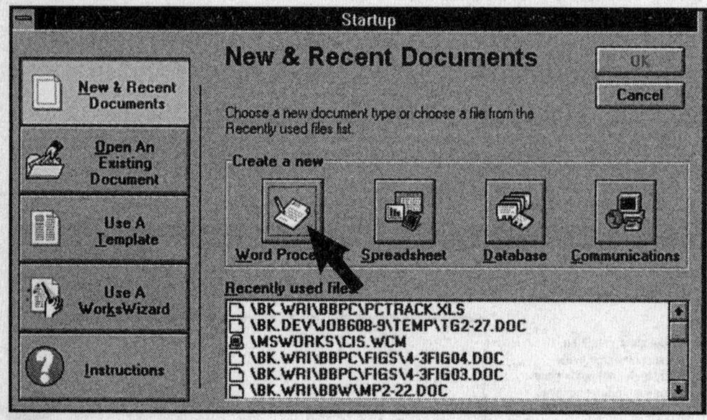

2 If the program asks you to specify a file type (as shown here) or to give some other information, make your selections.

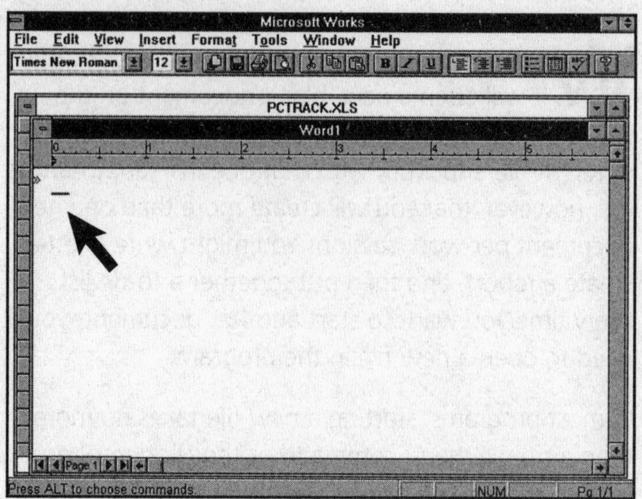

3 The new (blank) document window appears on-screen.

Open a File in a Windows Program

Going to the movie theater gives you a one-time thrill. You watch the movie once in sequence, and that's it. Renting a movie and watching it on a VCR is a different story. Once you load it into the VCR, you can watch it over and over, pause it, watch parts in slow motion, and otherwise have more fun.

Opening a file in a Windows application program is similar. To work on a file you previously saved to disk (more on that in the next task), first you need to open it. This procedure loads the file from the disk where it's stored into your computer's RAM (random-access memory). With the file in RAM, you can print it, add to it, change or delete the information in it, or update it in any way you see fit.

To open a particular file, you have to know which disk and directory it's stored on, and what the file's name is.

To learn how to save a file, see "Save Your Work in a Windows Program" on page 92.

Open a File of Another Type

Often you may have to take a file you've created in one program and open it in a different program. For example, let's say you use one word processing program at work. You create a file and you want to bring it home to finish it up, but you use a different word processing program on your home computer.

Many Windows applications enable you to open files that were created in various formats. In Microsoft Works for Windows (for example) you can open files from several different word processors: Microsoft Word for Windows, WordPerfect for DOS and Windows, Windows Write, and even Works and Word files for the Macintosh.

This *file exchange* capability makes it easy for many users to share work. The quality of the file exchange varies, depending on how sophisticated the program is. Some exchanges let you open only the file's basic data. Other programs preserve graphics and formatting when you open a file from another application.

If the Open dialog box in your application has a **List Files of Type** or similar option, that means you can open files in other formats. If your program doesn't have this option in the Open dialog box, look for an Import command on the File menu; it will do the same thing. The example in the steps is from Microsoft Works for Windows.

1. If your program closes the currently open file when you open a new file (as in Windows Write), be sure to save your work.

2. If the file you want to open is on a floppy disk, insert the floppy disk in the appropriate floppy disk drive.

3. Click the **File** menu, and then click the **Open** command or **Open Existing File** command. (If your program offers a toolbar, it may have an **Open File** icon you can click.)

4. Click the **down arrow** beside the **List Files of Type** list to display its choices. Use the scroll bar to display the type of file you want to open. Click that file type.

5. Finish opening the file by choosing a drive, directory, and file name. Then click the **OK** button.

6. If the program displays a dialog box that asks you to confirm that you're opening a file and transferring formats, click the **Yes** button or **OK** button to continue.

Understand Wild Card Characters

You may have noticed that the Open dialog box doesn't always spell out the full file name or file name extension. (For more on file names and extensions, see "Understand Files" on page 51 earlier in this book.) The dialog box replaces part of the file name with an asterisk *wild card character*.

You use wild card characters to search for groups of files with similar names. The ***** (asterisk) wild card takes the place of a group of *contiguous* characters, such as the three-letter extension in a file name. The **?** (question-mark) wild card stands for a single character. Suppose, for example, you entered a file name in the File Name text box of the Open dialog box and included a wild card character in the file name. You would see the File Name list display all the files in the current directory that matched what you typed.

Here are some examples of how wild card characters work:

client?.doc	Matching files have names with **client**, and then one more characters, and then **.doc**.
cl*.doc	Matching files have names with **cl**, and then a group of up to six more characters, and then **.doc**.
***.xls**	Matching files have any base name of up to eight characters, plus the **.xls** extension; all files of the type indicated by the extension match.
.	Indicates all files in the current directory of the current disk.

Begin Guided Tour Open a File

1 If the file you want to open is on a floppy disk, insert the floppy disk in the appropriate floppy disk drive.

2 Click the **File** menu, and then on the **Open** command. (In some programs, the command might be different; like **Open Existing File**). If your program offers a toolbar, it may have an Open File icon you can click to start a new file.

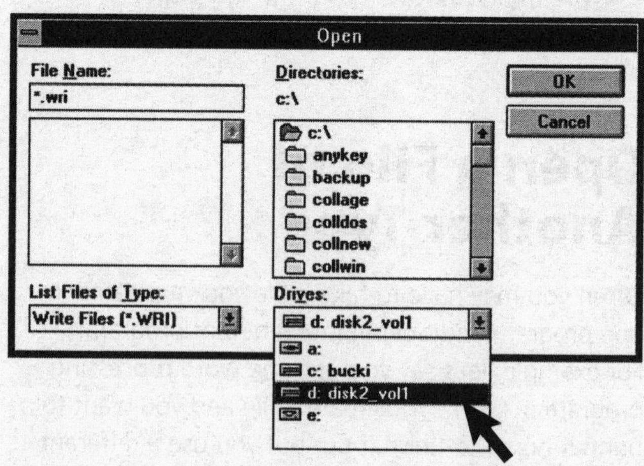

3 In the Open dialog box, click the **down arrow** beside the **Drives** list to display the list, and then click the drive letter for the disk that has the file you want to open.

Guided Tour Open a File

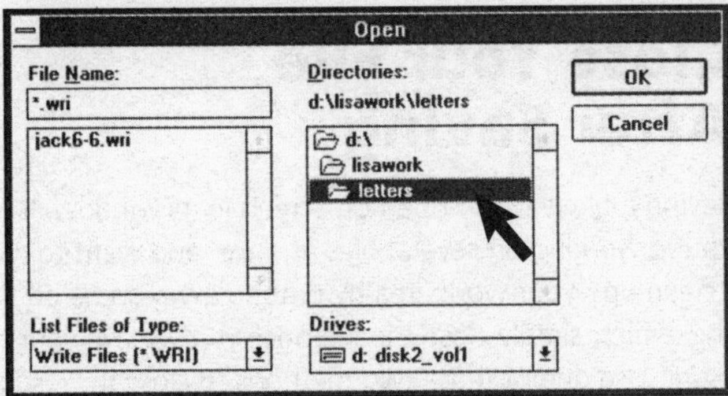

4 Click and hold on a scroll bar arrow on the **Directories** list to scroll to display the name of the directory that holds your program files. Then double-click the directory name to select it.

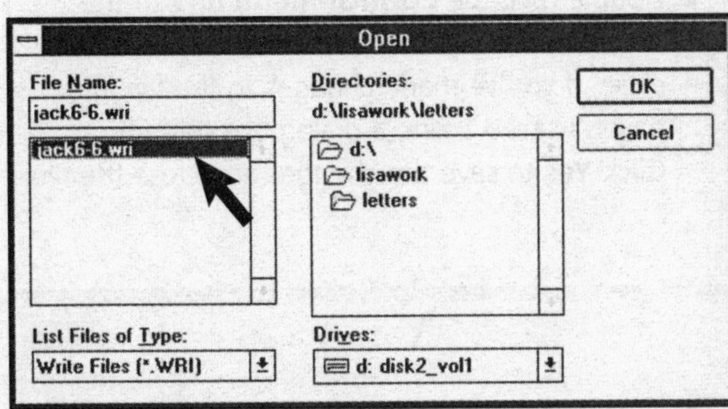

5 Click the name of the file you want to open in the **File Name** list or **Files** list. Then click the **OK** button. (To open a file quickly, simply double-click it.)

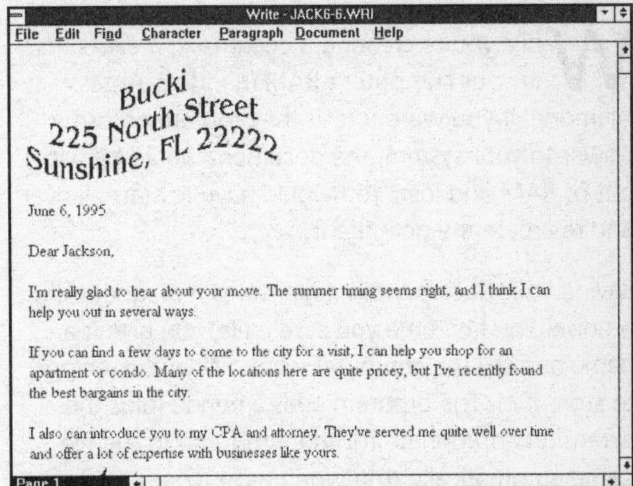

6 The file opens on-screen so you can work with it.

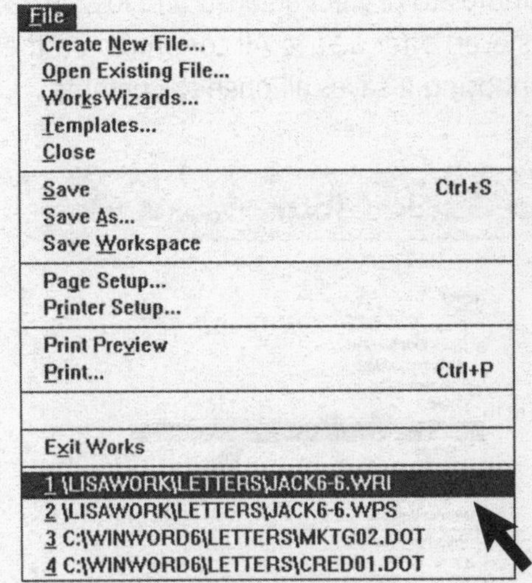

7 Some programs offer a shortcut for opening files you've worked with recently. These files appear at the bottom of the File menu. Simply open the menu, and then click the name of the file you want to open.

Save Your Work in a Windows Program

While you're creating a document, it exists first in your computer's RAM (Random-Access Memory). If you were to exit the program or lose power to your system, the document would be wiped out of RAM and lost. You would have to start all over and re-create the document.

Saving your document in a file stores it magnetically on disk. The first time you save a file, you give it a name and tell the computer what disk and directory to store it in. The program adds a period (plus the extension appropriate for that program) to the file name automatically. You won't have to specify the file's name again to save it; subsequent saves update the file on disk.

As a rule, you should try to save your work every five to ten minutes to protect against data loss. Some programs even offer a Save All command on the File menu. Choosing it saves all open documents.

Close Your File After Saving

Saving a file leaves it open on-screen in its window. If you're working on several files at once, and want to "clean up" your work area by putting away some of those files, simply close the file once you've save your work. Use one of these two methods to close it:

- Click the **File** menu to open it, and then click **Close**. If you've made changes to the file that haven't been saved, a dialog box will tell you so. Click **Yes** to save the changes and close the file.
- Double-click the **Control-menu box** of the window holding the document you want to close. If you've made changes to the file and haven't saved them, a dialog box tells you so. Click **Yes** to save the changes and close the file.

Begin Guided Tour Save a File

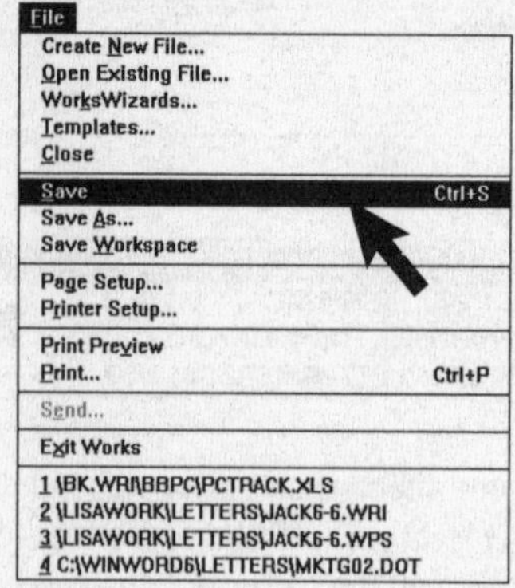

1 Click the **File** menu to open it, and then click the **Save** command (or simply press **Ctrl+S**). If your program offers a **Save File** icon on a toolbar, click it to save the file.

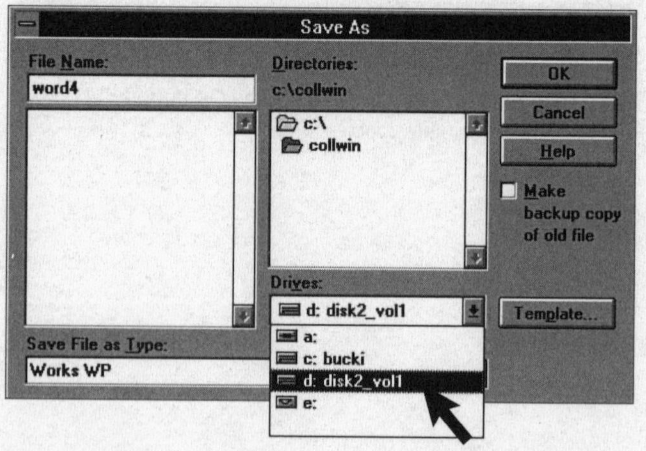

2 In the Save As dialog box, click the **down arrow** beside the **Drives** list to display the list, and then click the drive letter of the disk where you want to save the file.

Guided Tour Save a File

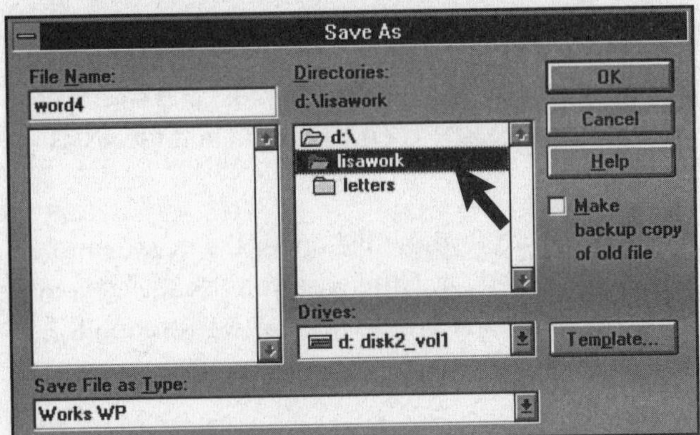

3 Click and hold on a **scroll bar arrow** on the **Directories** list to scroll to display the name of the directory you want to save to. Then double-click the directory name to select it.

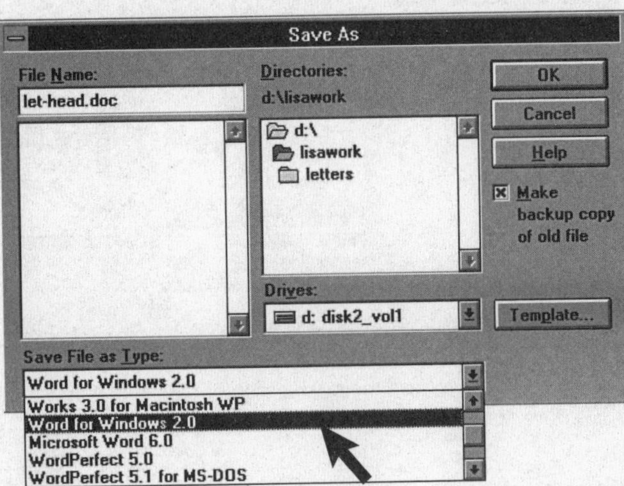

4 To save your file in another format, click the **down arrow** beside the **Save File as Type** list to display its choices. Scroll to the format you want, and then click your choice.

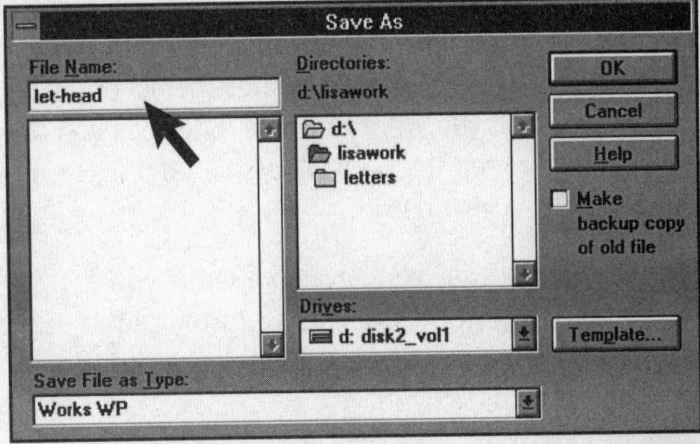

5 Double-click in the **File Name** box to highlight its contents. Type a name of up to eight characters for the new file. You don't have to add the file name extension.

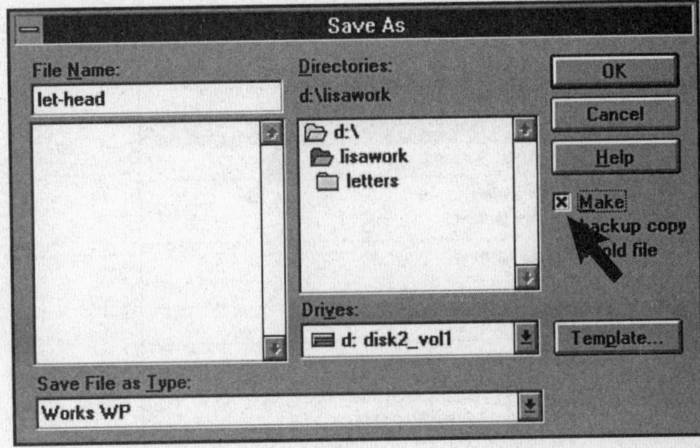

6 If the application offers an *automatic backup* option (which will create a backup file during subsequent saves), click to select that option. Then click the **OK** button.

7 If you continue working on the file, be sure to save it again before you close it or exit the program. Open the **File** menu and click **Save** again.

Save Your File Under a New Name

After you save a file the first time, using the Save command again simply updates the file under its existing name. If you want to create a new version of a file, and still keep the original version on disk, save the file under a new name.

For example, let's say you develop a January sales report that's really effective. You want to use the same format for February, but you still need to keep the January report on disk. You would open the January file (let's say it's called **jan.xls**) and save it as another file, **feb.xls**. Then you could edit feb.xls as needed.

It's important to save the file under the new name first, and *then* edit it. Otherwise you risk saving your new changes in the original file, where you don't want them to be.

Begin Guided Tour Save with a New Name

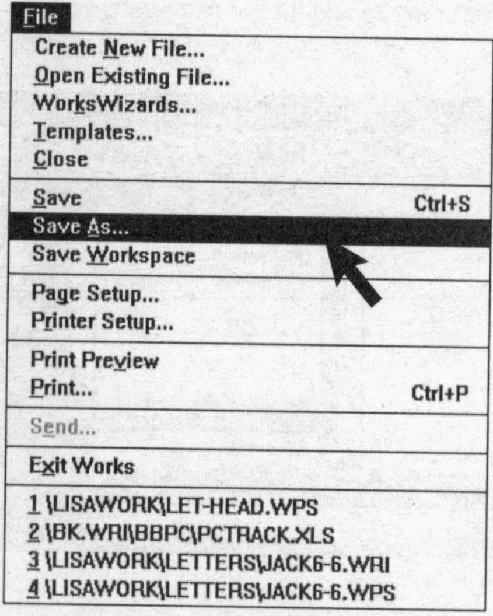

1 Click the **File** menu to open it, and then click the **Save As** command. (You can't click the Save File icon in this case.)

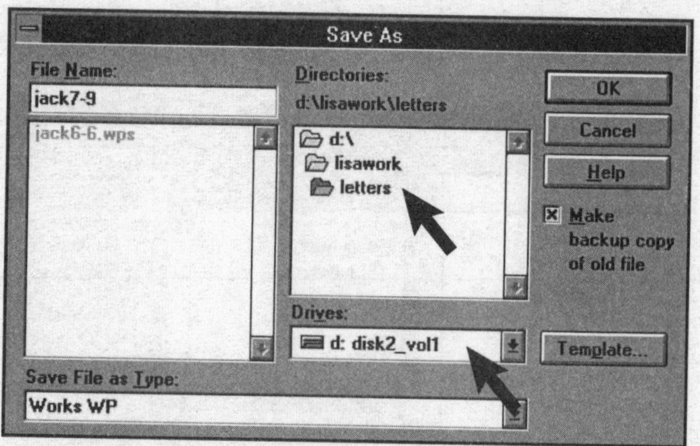

2 If you want to save the new version of the file to a new drive and directory, specify them.

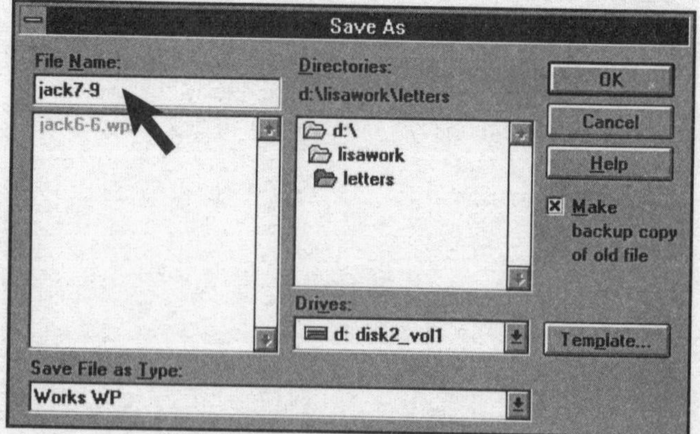

3 Double-click in the **File Name** text box to select its contents. Type a new name of up to eight characters for the file. You don't have to add the file name extension. Click **OK** to finish the Save As process.

Save Your Files Automatically

For safety's sake, you should save your files every five to ten minutes. This will prevent you from losing your changes if your computer loses power or locks up, forcing you to reboot. Some programs offer *autosave* protection; when you turn on this feature, the program saves all open files at an interval you specify. The *Guided Tour* here shows how to turn on the AutoSave feature in version 3.0 of Lotus Ami Pro for Windows. (The steps may be different for you, depending on the program you are working in.)

Begin Guided Tour Save Files Automatically

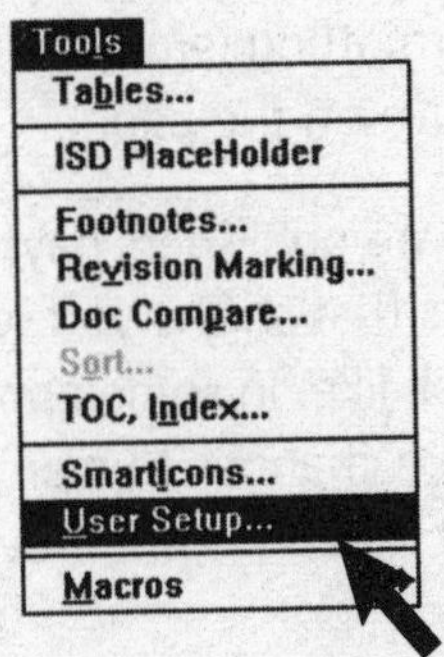

1 Click the **Tools** menu, and then click the **User Setup** command.

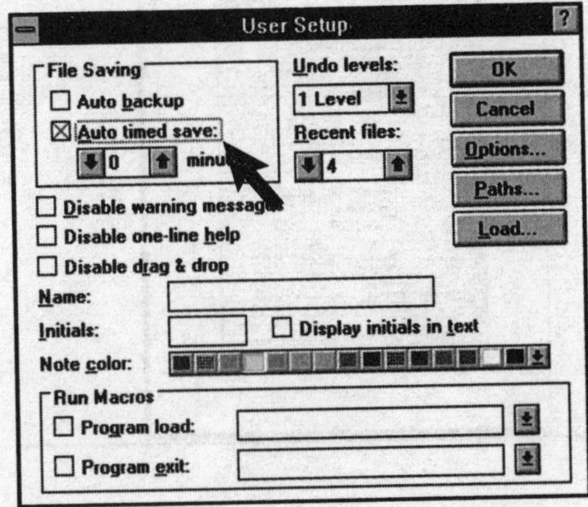

2 In the **File Saving** section of the User Setup dialog box, click to select the check box beside the **Auto timed save** option.

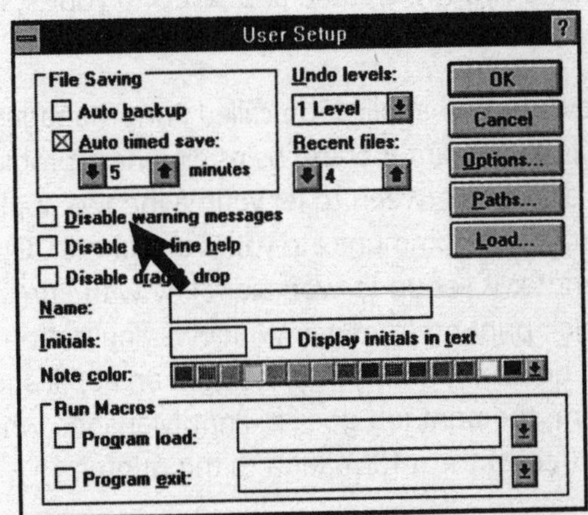

3 Double-click the **0** in the **Minutes** text box and type a new value (or you can click the **down** and **up arrows** beside the text box to adjust the value).

4 Click the **OK** button to close the dialog box and start autosaving. When the interval you've set has passed, the program will pause and save your file (and may tell you about it at the bottom of the screen).

Print in a Windows Program

Documents exist to be looked at. They carry a message from you to a friend, colleague, boss, client, student, teacher—anyone you want to communicate with or persuade. The reality is that you can't call every one of these people to come look at your computer screen.

Instead, you'll need to print out your document. This process means telling your computer to send the information you've created and saved to your system's printer so it can be put on paper.

Windows has an application called Print Manager that controls every print job and helps eliminate problems. It acts as a go-between to let your Windows application programs communicate with your printer. Once your printer is set up to work correctly with Print Manager, printing from any Windows application should be easy. When you print from an application program, the print job goes to Print Manager, which *spools* (feeds) the information to the printer.

The *Guided Tour* here shows how to print from Works for Windows. The available options vary from one application to the next (depending on your application's features), but generally you can specify how many copies to print, and whether you want to print all or part of a document.

A lot of problems can crop up when you try to print a document. If you run into trouble, see "Printing Problems" on page 510 in the "101 Quick Fixes" part of the book.

Preview the Printed Document

If you create a document, often you do a lot of *formatting*—which can include adjusting major settings like the page margins and page breaks; at some point you could lose sight of what the final document will look like. In the old days, you had to print out a preliminary copy of the file, and then go back to fix the formatting (either to fit the page or to look more attractive on the page).

Today most software publishers have built a feature into their products that shows you what the printed document will look like. In some applications, you can even print (or make changes to margins and the like) while a document is in this *Print Preview mode*.

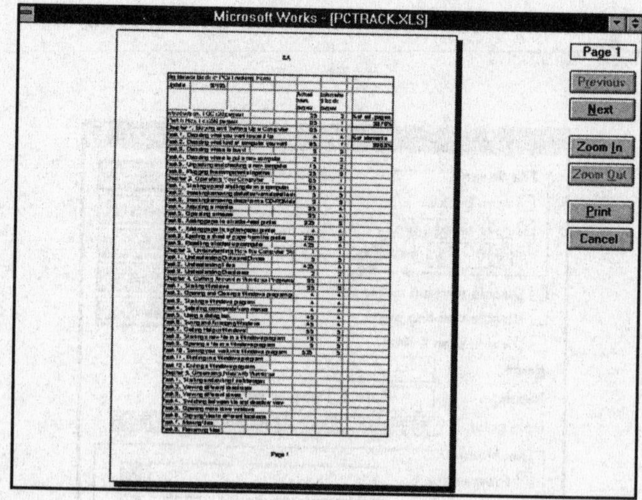

The command for entering Print Preview mode depends on your application. Look for the **Preview** or **Print Preview** command on the **File** menu or in the **Print** dialog box. (Some applications put a Print Preview icon on the toolbar.) Click **Cancel** to leave Print Preview mode.

Begin Guided Tour Print a File

1 Open the file you want to print; once it's open, click the **File** menu and then **Print**. (You can click the **Print** icon in the application's on-screen toolbar, if it has one, but this may bypass the dialog box that lets you set printing options).

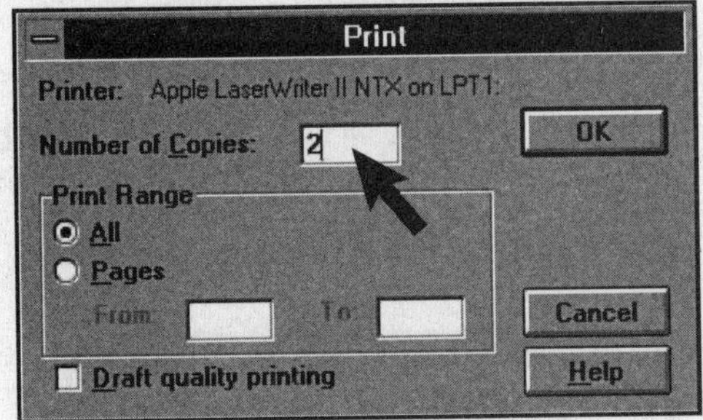

2 (Optional) Double-click in the **Number of Copies** text box to select it; type a new value.

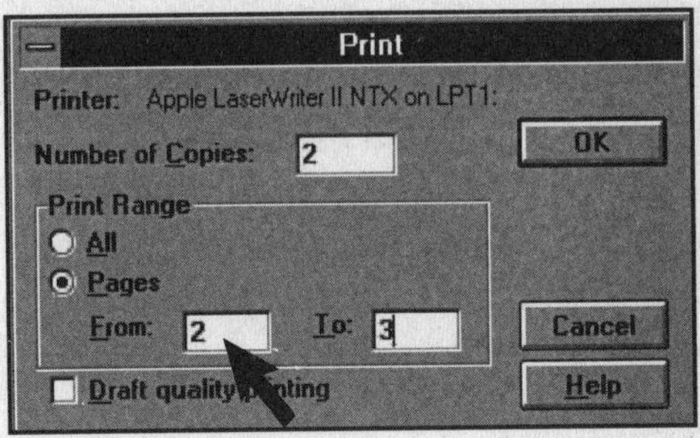

3 (Optional) To print part of the document, click to select the **Pages** option in the **Print Range** area. Double-click in the **From** box; type the number of the first page you want to print. Double-click in the **To** box; type the number of the last page you want to print.

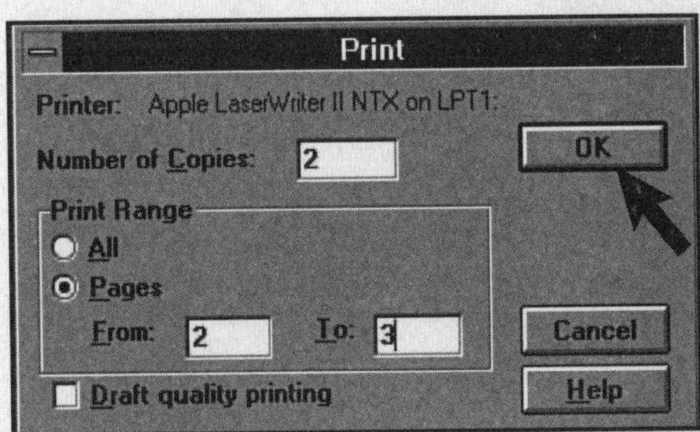

4 Specify any other available options you want to choose. Click the **OK** button to start the print job. A dialog box may appear, giving you the option of canceling the print job. This dialog box disappears once the application sends the whole print job to Windows Print Manager.

Exit a Windows Program

Exiting a program closes any open files in the program and removes them from RAM (random-access memory). Then the program itself closes (is removed from RAM); its application window is minimized back to an icon in the program group where it resides.

Before you exit from any program, you should save your work. This prevents data loss and gets you out of there faster. If you haven't saved your work, the program will prompt you to do so. Click **Yes** to save if you've saved an open file before. If you haven't saved the open file, the Save As dialog box will appear; name the file and specify a location for it. You have several ways to exit a file; they follow here.

Begin Guided Tour Exit a Program

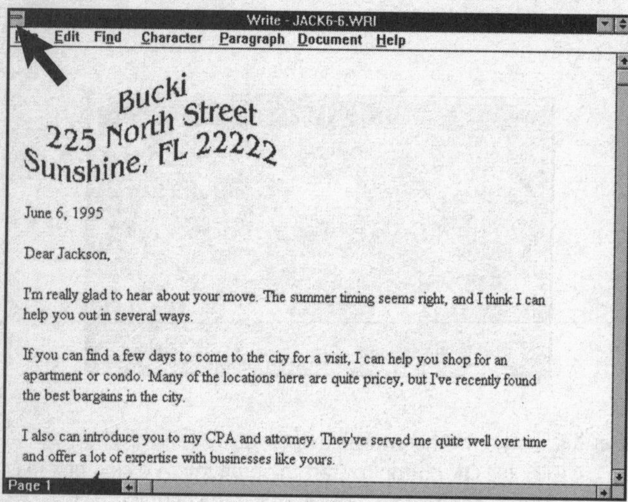

• Double-click the application window's **Control-menu box**.

• Click the **File** menu to open it, and then click the program's **Exit** command.

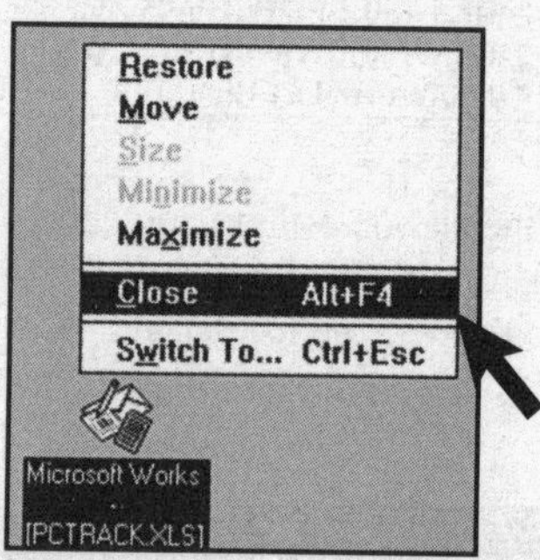

• If the program is minimized to an icon on the desktop, click the icon to display its menu, and then click the **Close** command.

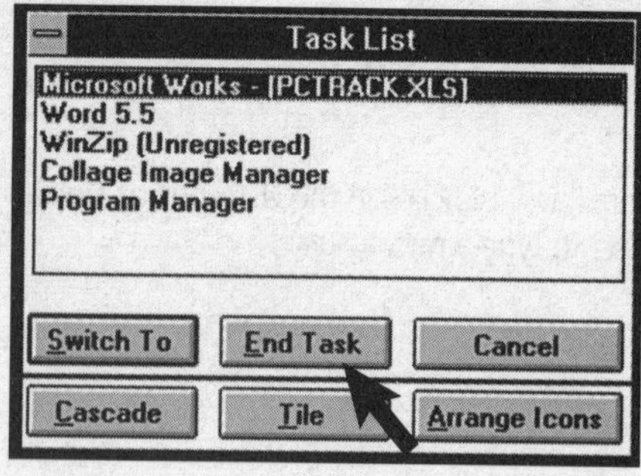

• If the application you want to exit from isn't currently active, press **Ctrl+Esc** to display the Windows Task List. Click the name of the application you want to exit, and then click the **End Task** button.

HOW TO...

Organize Files and Directories with Windows 3.11

The Windows 3.11 File Manager provides easy tools for managing your files and directories. It provides a graphical view of the directory tree and the files in a directory, so you can move around or select a file with a simple mouse click. This approach not only offers common-sense menu commands to get the job done, but also enables you to handle some operations with the mouse alone!

This section covers the File Manager basics, and some tricks to make you more effective! Although most of the file management techniques in Windows 3.x (3.1 and 3.11) are similar to those in Windows 95, there are some major differences. To learn about file management in Windows 95, see the section called "Work in Windows 95" on page 147.

What You Will Find in This Section

Start and Exit File Manager 100

View Different Disks (Drives) 102

View Different Directories 104

Change the Directory Window View 107

Open More Directory (Drive) Windows 109

Select Files 112

Copy Files to Different Locations 117

Move Files 122

Delete Files 128

Rename Files and Directories 130

Create Directories 132

Delete Directories 134

Start and Exit File Manager

Managing your files through DOS can give you a headache. You have to remember exactly what you named a file—and the full path to where you saved it—before you can do anything with it. Even worse, you have to remember another full path name if you want to copy a file somewhere. DOS just wasn't made to save you time and effort.

Luckily, Windows File Manager is. File Manager displays the contents of each drive and directory in windows on-screen. You see not only file names, but also the icons for files; you can handle some operations simply by dragging files around or by double-clicking on a file name. File Manager makes it much easier to work with the files on your hard disk and floppy disks.

As with other applications, you can maximize the File Manager window to full-screen size, resize it and move it around, or minimize it to an icon to put it away temporarily. And, when you're finished working with File Manager, you should exit it to free up RAM (Random-Access Memory) for the other applications you're working in.

If you don't really need the steps in this task but do need help displaying files in File Manager, jump ahead to the next few tasks.

Begin Guided Tour Start File Manager

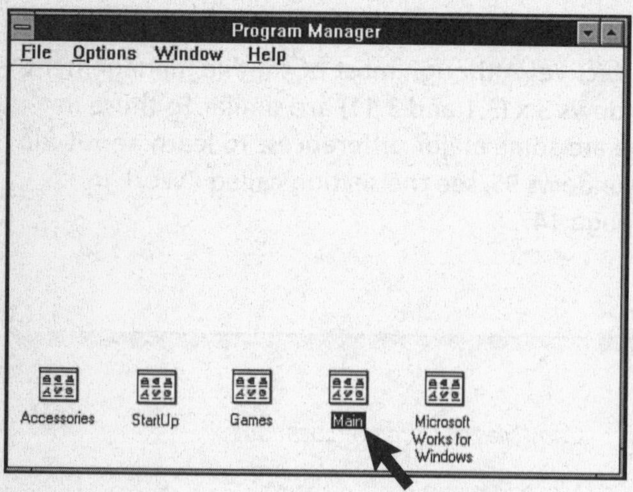

1 Double-click the **Main program group icon** to open its window.

2 Double-click the **File Manager icon** to start File Manager.

Guided Tour Start File Manager

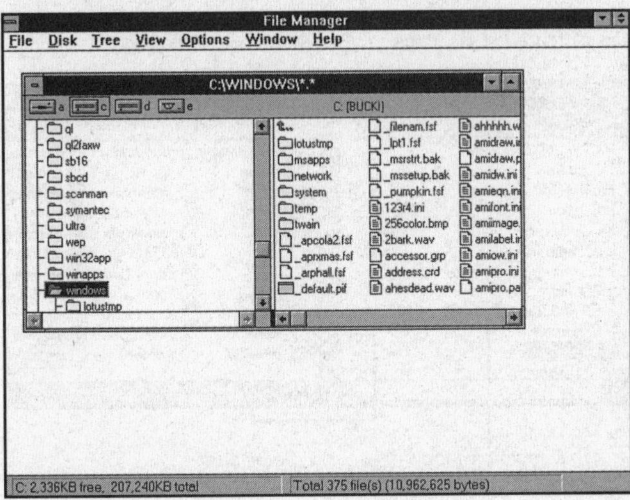

3 File Manager opens in its own window on-screen. You can work in File Manager, and resize or move its window as you see fit.

Begin Guided Tour Exit File Manager

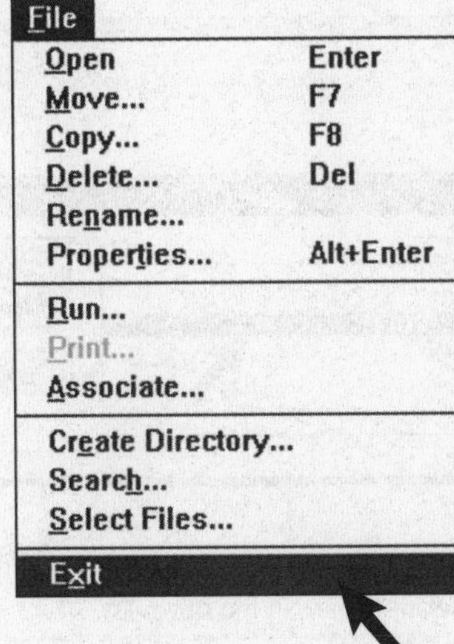

1 To exit File Manager, open the **File** menu and click **Exit**.

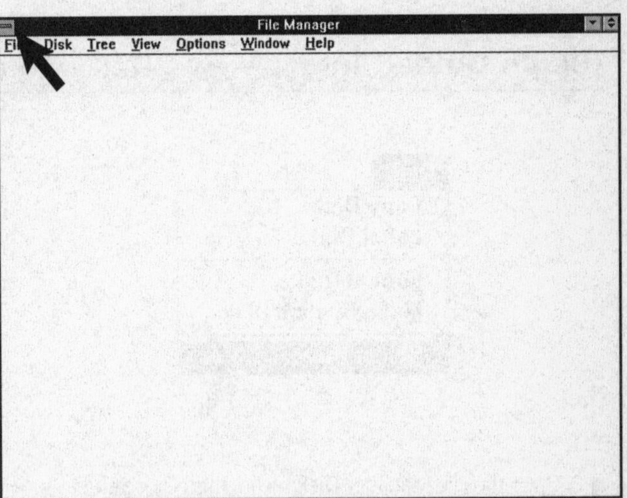

2 For a quick exit, you can double-click the File Manager's **Control-menu box** to close File Manager.

View Different Disks (Drives)

Most Windows application programs enable you to open many documents, each in its own window on-screen. File Manager works in a similar way, displaying the contents of each drive in a separate window. Each window is commonly called a *directory window*, because it shows what's in the directory you've selected on the current disk.

Normally File Manager divides each directory window into two parts. The left side shows the *directory tree* for the current disk, starting with the root directory. The right side of the window displays the *directory contents list* for the directory you've selected on the directory tree.

> This task just explains the basics of displaying directory windows. To learn more about working within a directory window, see "View Different Directories" on page 104.

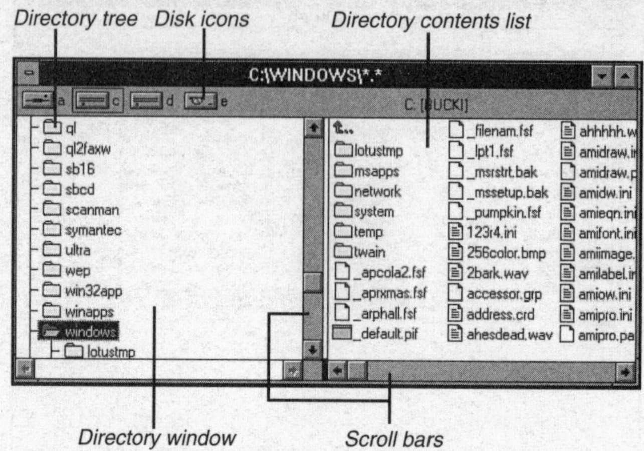

When you view the contents of a different disk drive, File Manager changes what's being displayed in the current directory window. (A later task, "Open More Directory (Drive) Windows" on page 109, covers moving between open windows.) There are three ways to get this done: use a menu command, the mouse, or the keyboard.

Begin Guided Tour View a Disk with the Menu

1. Open the File Manager **Disk** menu, then click **Select Drive**.

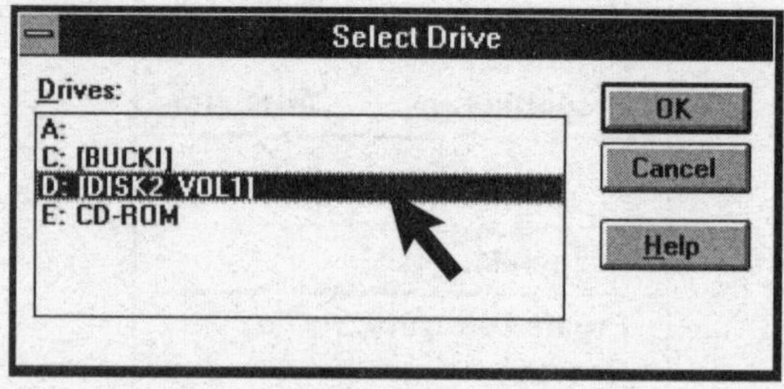

2. In the **Select Drive** dialog box, click the drive holding the disk you want to view in the Drives list.
3. Click **OK** or press **Enter** to close the Select Drive box and display the contents of the drive you selected in the current directory window.

Begin Guided Tour View a Disk with the Mouse or Keyboard

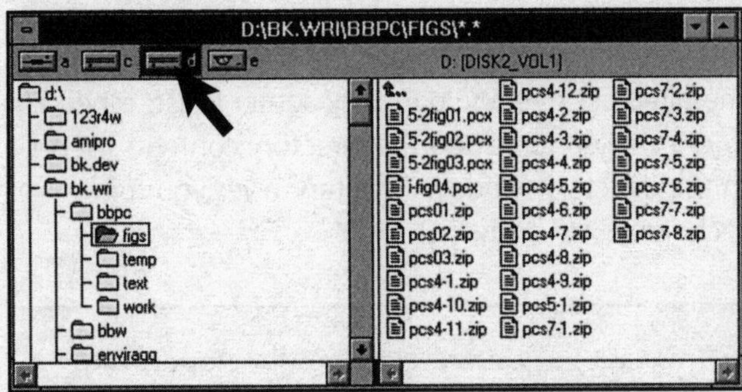

- To display another disk in the current directory window, click another disk icon at the top of the directory window.

- To do the same thing with the keyboard, press **Tab** or **F6** to move to the disk icons, use an **arrow** key to move the dotted outline to another disk icon, then press the **Spacebar**.

View Different Directories

Unlike DOS, the File Manager makes it easy to browse around to look at the contents of a disk. With simple pointing and clicking on, you can select any directory on the disk shown in the current directory window. Selecting a different directory changes the directory contents list so it displays the files and subdirectories contained in that directory. You also must select a directory to move, copy, or delete it.

You can move around directories in both the directory tree and directory contents list areas of the directory window. The directory tree gives a more graphical picture of which directories contain subdirectories. A line connects directories on the same level; subdirectories are indented below the directory that contains them, with a separate line branching off to connect those subdirectories. File Manager lets you move around using either the mouse or keyboard, although you'll probably find the mouse much more convenient.

The directory tree display starts from the root directory, which appears at the top of the directory tree window (but may not be visible in the file list). You can scroll through the list (using the scroll bars), and then select a directory to move *down* a level in the tree, displaying its subdirectories (in both the directory tree and directory contents list) and files (in the directory contents list only). If you choose, you can hide the display of subdirectories in the directory tree.

File Manager displays icons to represent directories and subdirectories in the directory tree. You'll see these two icons:

The open file icon indicates the currently-selected directory; its contents appear in the directory contents list.

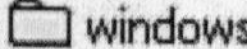

Closed file icons represent other directories and subdirectories; subdirectories are indented under the directory that holds them.

It pays to know how to navigate directories both in the directory tree and directory contents list, especially if you choose to display the directory contents list only in the directory window. This task gives you the techniques for both.

This task keys in on selecting directories. To learn more about selecting files in the file list, see "Select Files" on page 112.

Use the Tree Menu

The File Manager's Tree menu enables you to expand (display) and collapse (hide) directories and subdirectories in the directory tree. The Tree commands work on one or more *branches* in the directory tree. A branch includes a directory and all the subdirectories it contains, no matter how many levels of subdirectories there are. To use the commands on the Tree menu, select the directory that you want to work with in the tree. Open the **Tree** menu, and then select one of the following commands:

- **Expand One Level** displays the first level of subdirectories within the current directory.
- **Expand Branch** displays all subdirectories on all levels within the current directory.
- **Expand All** shows all subdirectories within all directories in the directory window.
- **Collapse Branch** hides all subdirectories of the current directory.

Change the Tree Icons

File Manager can provide greater detail about whether a directory contains any subdirectories. If you open the **Tree** menu and select **Indicate Expandable**

Branches, File Manager changes the directory tree icons as follows:

windows — File icons with a minus can be collapsed.

winword6 — File icons with a plus contain subdirectories that you can display (expand).

temp — File icons with no sign contain only files; they cannot be expanded or collapsed.

Begin Guided Tour   Select Directories in the Directory Tree

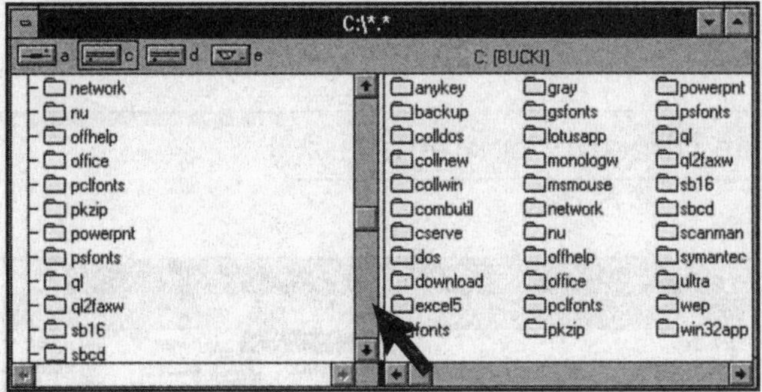

1 Use the scroll bar to display the directory you want in the directory tree.

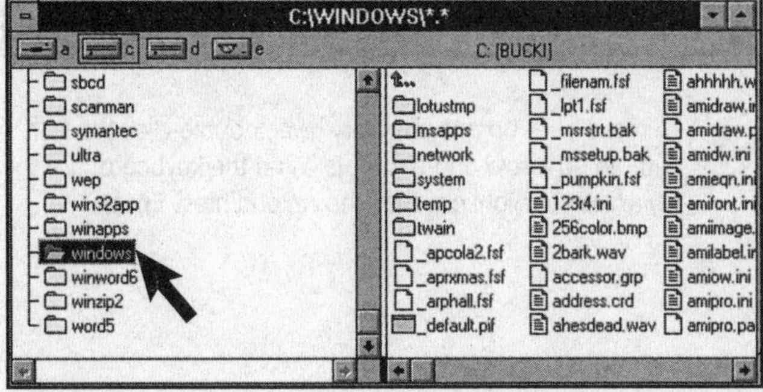

2 Click a directory to select it. To select with the keyboard, press **Tab** to move the highlight to the directory tree, and then use the **up** and **down arrow** keys to select a directory.

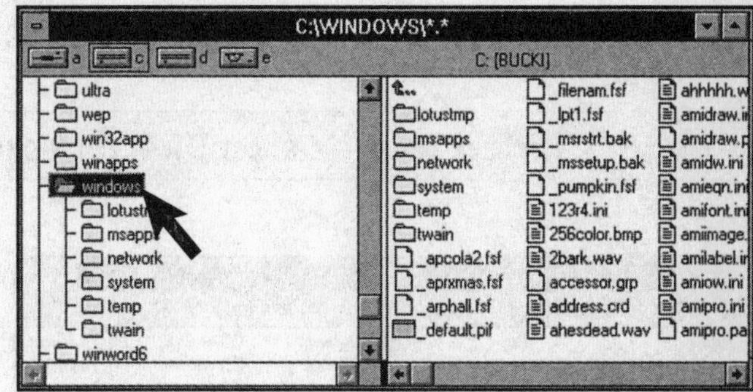

3 To display (or hide) a directory's subdirectories in the tree, double-click the directory name. With the keyboard: select the directory with the **arrow keys**, and then press **Enter**.

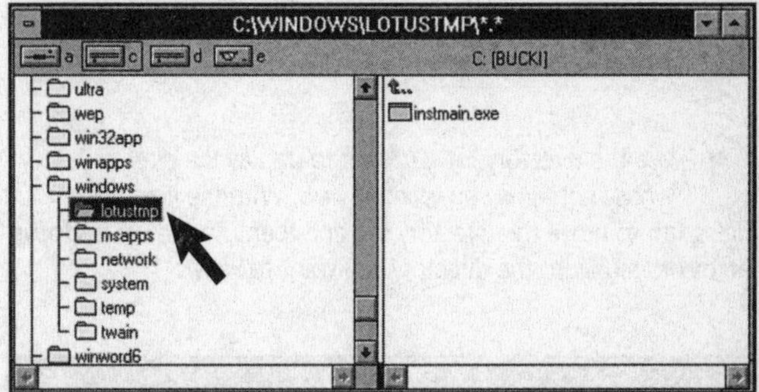

4 To move to the first subdirectory in a directory, click it or press the **right arrow** key.

5 Use the **up** and **down arrow** keys or click to move among the subdirectories.

6 Use the **left arrow** key or click to move up one directory level.

(continues)

Guided Tour Select Directories in the Directory Tree

(continued)

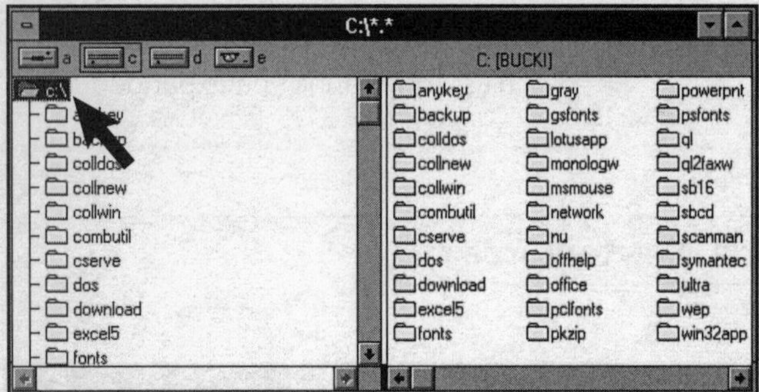

7 To return to the root directory, scroll up to display it, and then click it. With the keyboard: press **** (backslash).

Begin Guided Tour Select Directories in the Directory Contents List

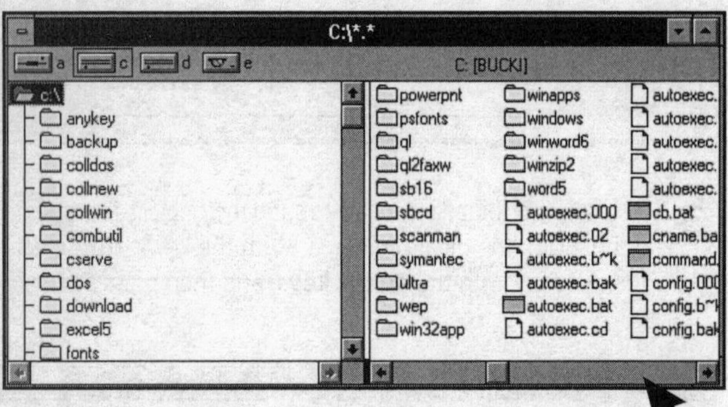

1 Use the directory list scroll bar to display the directory whose contents you want to view. With the keyboard: press **Tab** to move the directory list, and then use the **up** or **down arrow** to highlight the directory you want to view.

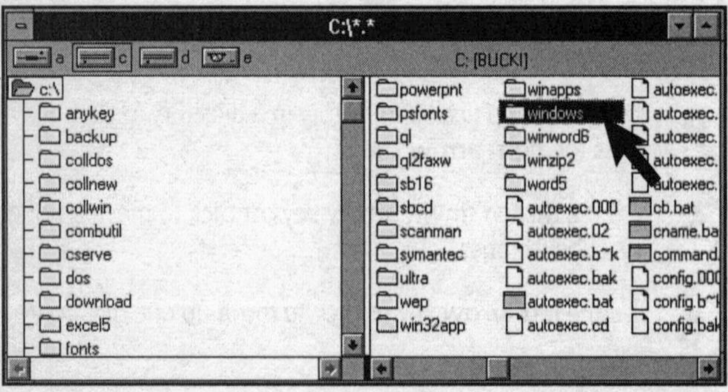

2 Double-click the directory to list its contents. With the keyboard: if you've highlighted the file name press **Enter** to display its contents. Repeat this step to display a subdirectory's contents.

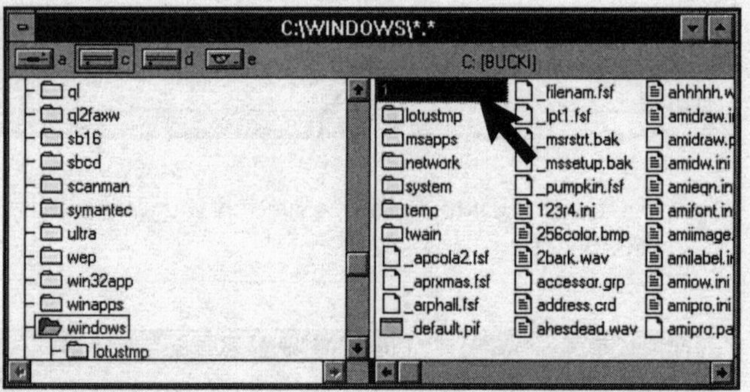

3 To move back up one directory level, double-click the icon with an up arrow and two dots. With the keyboard: use the **up arrow** to highlight that choice, and press **Enter**.

Change the Directory Window View

Being farsighted used to be a real hassle. You needed one pair of glasses (or no glasses) for normal activities, and a second pair of glasses for up-close detail activities like reading or tinkering with machinery. Bifocals eliminated this hassle by incorporating two types of correction in each lens; you wear one pair of glasses (bifocals), and simply look through the area of the lens that's suited to what you're doing.

Normally each of a disk's directory windows works like a bifocal lens; the directory tree is on one side, the contents list for the directory is on the other. In most cases, you use the part of the window that's suited for the current task, working with either directories or files. At times, you'll use both sides of the window (for example, when you move a file from one directory to another).

The File Manager View menu enables you to change the display of a directory window to show only what you need to see for the current operation. For example, you could choose

> **Tree Only** if you want to delete, move, or copy a directory.
>
> **Directory Only** if you want to see only the directory contents list for a directory window, especially if the disk is a floppy that has files but no directories.
>
> **Tree and Directory** to return to viewing the directory tree on the left and directory contents list on the right.

The *Guided Tour* explains how to change from the default view (Tree and Directory), to one of the other two views. You can use the same steps to return to Tree and Directory view by selecting it (rather than one of the other choices) from the View menu.

> The View menu changes apply to the current directory window only. To learn how to select another directory window to change its view, see "Open More Directory (Drive) Windows" on page 109.

Change the Split View

Ever mindful that you want to be efficient, Windows' creators always give you the option of arranging your window space the way you like. In Directory and Tree view, this means you can decide just how much space the directory tree and the directory contents list will take up in each directory window.

Most often, you'll want to make the directory tree's portion narrower so you'll be able to see more of the directory's contents. This eliminates a lot of white space that otherwise appears with the directory list. Whether you use the mouse or the keyboard to change the split, you'll use the *split bar* (the vertical bar that appears just to the right of the scroll bar) for the directory tree.

1. In Tree and Directory view, click in the directory window you want to change the split for.
2. Point to the split bar with the mouse until you see the split pointer, which has left- and right-pointing arrows (or open the **View** menu and select **Split**).
3. Press and hold the left mouse button; drag the split bar. (If you used the Split command: use the **left** and **right arrow** keys to move the split bar, and then press **Enter**.)

Begin Guided Tour View the Tree Only

1 Click in the directory window you want to change.

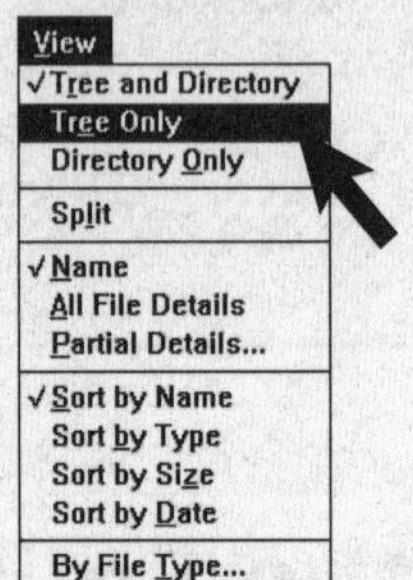

2 Open the **View** menu, and click **Tree Only**.

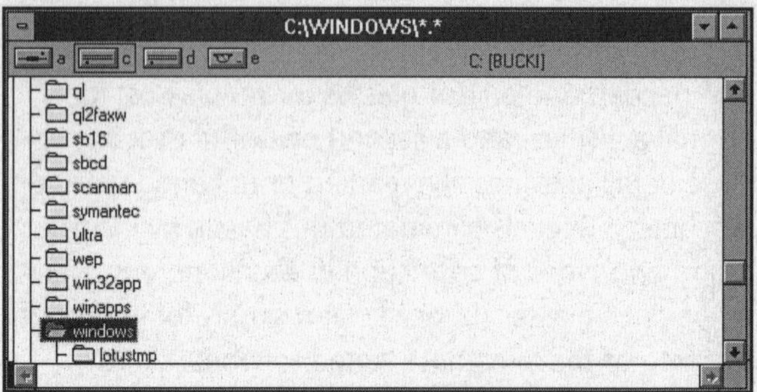

3 File Manager eliminates the display of the directory contents list, so the whole window shows only the directory tree.

Begin Guided Tour View the Directory Only

1 Click in the directory window you want to change.

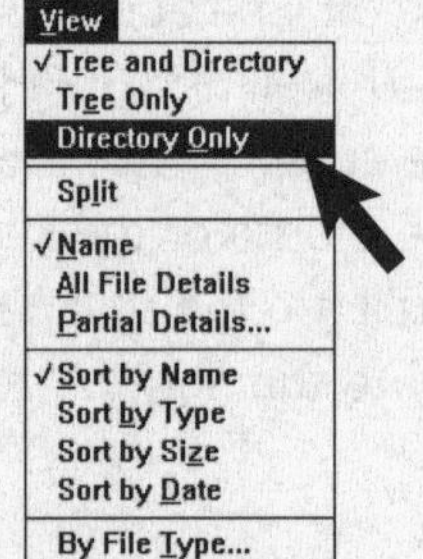

2 Open the **View** menu, and click **Directory Only**.

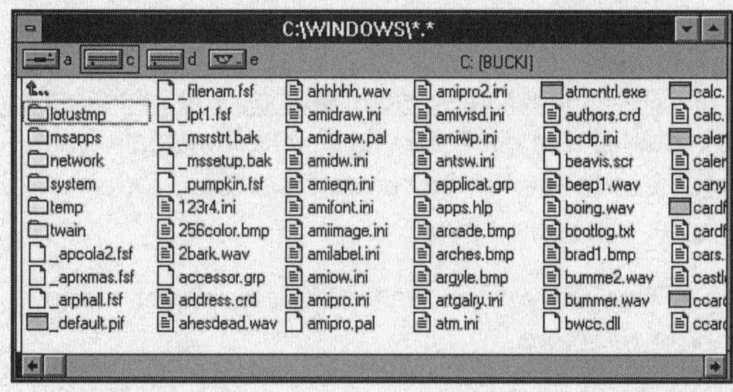

3 File Manager eliminates the display of the directory tree, so the whole window shows only the directory contents list.

Open More Directory (Drive) Windows

File Manager was designed to make it easier to work with files in different directories or on different drives. It follows that you'll need to display those other directories or drives—in additional directory windows—in File Manager; you'll also need to manipulate those windows and move between them. Each directory window can only display what's on one directory of one disk. To view other directories simultaneously, you have to open more windows.

This Task gets you working with the directory windows in File Manager. It covers a lot of ground, including:

- Opening another directory window, either for a different disk or the same one you're currently viewing. You'll need to do this when you're looking for files, or want to copy (or move) files from one directory to another.
- Selecting an open directory window, which you'll need to do to view its contents or to select a different View menu option.
- Refreshing a directory window, which updates the window's contents to reflect recent changes.
- Arranging and closing windows, to adjust how they're arranged on-screen or to remove them from view when you're done with them.

The *Guided Tour* for this task explains how to open another directory window.

> **If you want to see what's on another disk in another drive, but don't necessarily want to open a new window, File Manager can deal with it. For more, see "View Different Disks (Drives)" on page 102.**

Select an Open Directory Window

To perform certain operations in a directory window—like selecting files in the directory contents list—you must first select the directory window you want to work in; selecting it makes it the *current window*. File Manager offers a few different ways to select a new directory window:

- If you can see the title bar (or any other part) of the window you want to view, click it.
- Open the **Window** menu; at the bottom of the menu, click the name of the window you want to view.
- To move through the open directory windows, press **Ctrl+F6** or **Ctrl+Tab** until the one you want to display appears.

Open a Second Window for a Disk

Let's say a directory on your hard disk has filled up, and you want to move some of its files to a new directory you've created on the same disk. You *could* do this without opening a new window, but that requires remembering and typing in the new directory name. Why bother with that? Instead, you can open another window to display another directory on the same disk—and move or copy files to it by dragging them. See the *Guided Tour* in this task to learn how to get a second look at the disk shown in the current directory window.

When you open another directory window for a disk, initially it'll use the same view as the first window.

If you're showing just the tree in the first window (for example), you'll see just the tree in the second window. Once the second window is open, however, you can use it any way you want—change its view options, select a different directory in the directory list, or select a different file in the directory contents list.

> In some cases, the changes you make to a directory window don't appear there immediately. This happens, in particular, when you save, copy, or move files to that directory. When you make a change that should show up in a directory—but it doesn't—just *refresh* the contents of that window. Open the **Window** menu and click **Refresh**, or simply press **F5**.

Arrange and Close Directory Windows

You can move and resize directory windows to your heart's content. Here are all the options you have:

- To move a window, click its **title bar** and drag it to a new location. You can resize it by dragging its borders.
- To arrange all open directory windows for easy viewing, open the **Window** menu and select **Cascade** (which sizes the windows identically and stacks them like cards, showing the contents of only the top window).
- To see them side by side, select **Tile** (which sizes windows identically and places them so you can see at least some contents of all the windows). Press **Shift** and select **Window**, **Tile** to arrange directory windows side to side rather than top to bottom.
- Each directory window has its own Control menu so you can resize, maximize, or minimize the window. Double-click the **Control-menu box** to close the window.

Begin Guided Tour Open a Window to View Another Directory

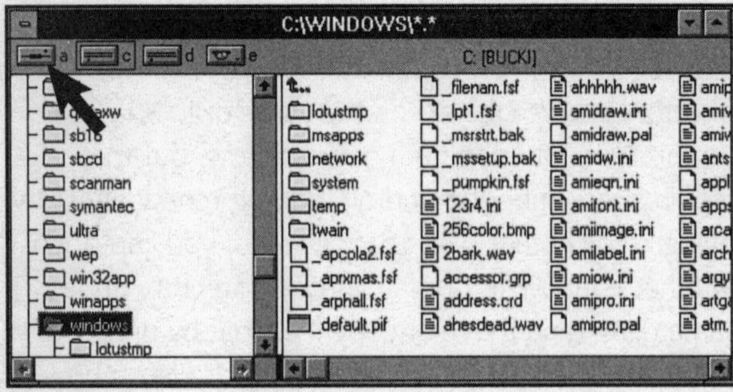

1 Double-click the **drive icon** for the disk you want to view in the current directory window.

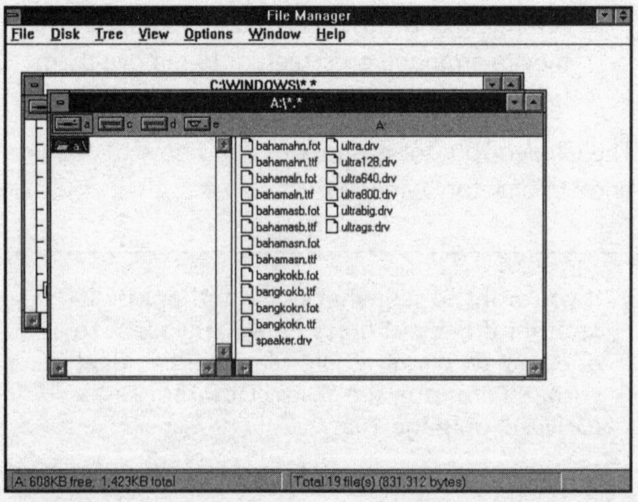

2 File Manager opens a directory window for the drive you selected, making it active on-screen.

Begin Guided Tour Open Another Window for the Current Directory

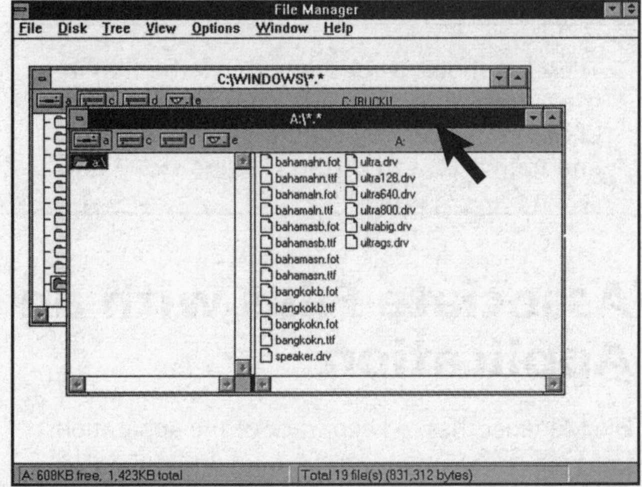

1 Select the drive for which you want to open a window, and then select a directory window for it.

2 Double-click the **drive icon** for the same disk. Or open the **Window** menu and click **New Window**.

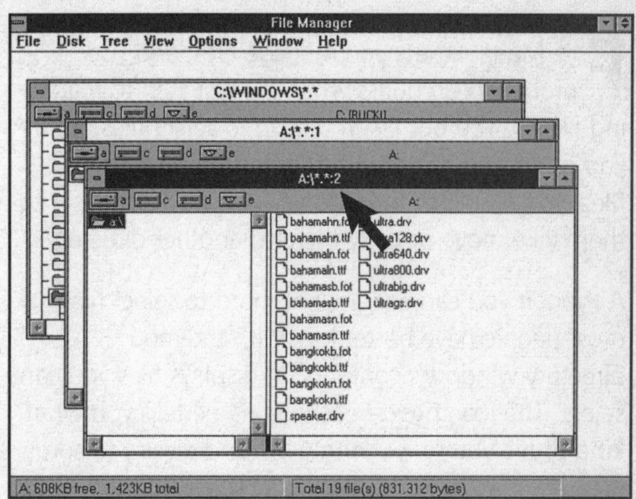

3 File Manager opens another window for the disk, adding a colon plus a numeral to the names in the title bars of the open windows for the same disk, so you know which is which.

Select Files

File Manager lets you manage files, and you probably can guess what the first step to managing files is. You got it—you have to *select* files before you can do anything with them. When you select files, you highlight them so you can do something to them (like move or copy them to another directory).

Although you can use the keyboard to select files, most people have better luck with the mouse. A directory window's contents list displays files you can select. The icon beside each file name tells you what kind of file you're working with, and gives you some idea of what you can do with it. These icons identify the file types in the directory contents list:

System or hidden files—Normally these don't appear on-screen, so you can't delete them by mistake.

Program files—These files start a program or routine. They have .EXE, .COM, .PIF, and .BAT extensions.

Document files—You create these in applications; File Manager lets you associate them with the application that created them.

Other files—These can include files that hold data a program might need to operate, or they can be backup files for documents.

You don't need step-by-step instructions for selecting a single file. Just find the file you want in the directory contents list, and click it to highlight it. With the keyboard, press **Tab** to move the highlight to the directory contents list, and then use the **arrow keys** to move the highlight to the file you want. To undo any selection, press **Ctrl+**; (or open the **File** menu, select **Select Files**, and click **Deselect**).

To learn how to select more than one file at a time, see the *Guided Tour* for this task.

> There's a shortcut for selecting all the files in the current directory of the directory window. Click in the directory contents list or **Tab** to it, and then press **Ctrl+/** (the forward slash).

Associate Files with an Application

File Manager tries to keep track of the applications used to create document files (and other files that aren't system or program files). It tracks the association between file name extensions (which indicate a particular kind of file) and the applications that can create or open files of that type. Why would File Manager care what application created a particular file? Because if a file is associated with that application, you can open the file in File Manager; doing so starts the application and opens the file in it. More on this next.

File Manager sets up automatic associations between Windows applications and the files they create. For example, File Manager assumes any files with the .WRI extension were created in the Windows Write accessory program. So, if you open a file with the .WRI extension from File Manager, Windows opens the Write application, then opens the .WRI file.

You can change any existing association in File Manager, or create a new association. You might need to do this is if (for example) an application program comes with a READ.ME file that tells you about the program. To open and read this file from File Manager, you could associate the **.ME** file name extension with the Windows Notepad accessory program. Note, however, that you should only associate a file type with an application that *can* open files of that type, or it won't work the way you expect it to.

See the *Guided Tour* to learn how to set up or change a file association in File Manager.

Open or Start Files

You highlight a file when you select it in the directory contents list; then you can move it, copy it, and so on. Opening (starting) a file in File Manager runs a program file, or opens a data file. The result of opening a file depends on the kind of file you open, as follows:

- Opening an executable file with an .EXE, .COM., .PIF, or .BAT extension runs the program that the file is supposed to start. If you opened a file called **msworks.exe**, for example, File Manager would run Microsoft Works for Windows.
- Opening a document file associated with an application starts the application on-screen, and then loads the document file.

File Manager offers a few different ways to open a file in the directory contents list of a directory window:

- Double-click the file.
- Press **Tab** to move the highlight to the directory contents list. Use the **arrow keys** to highlight the file you want to open, and then press **Enter**.
- When you see the file you want to open in the directory contents list, select (highlight) it. Then click the **File** menu, and **Open**.

If you want to open an application and load a particular file in it, you can do it in File Manager: drag the document's file name and drop it on top of the executable file's name in the directory contents list. If, for example, you dragged a file named **notes.wri** until it was over the file **write.exe**, you'd start Windows Write and load **notes.wri**.

Begin Guided Tour Select Adjacent Files

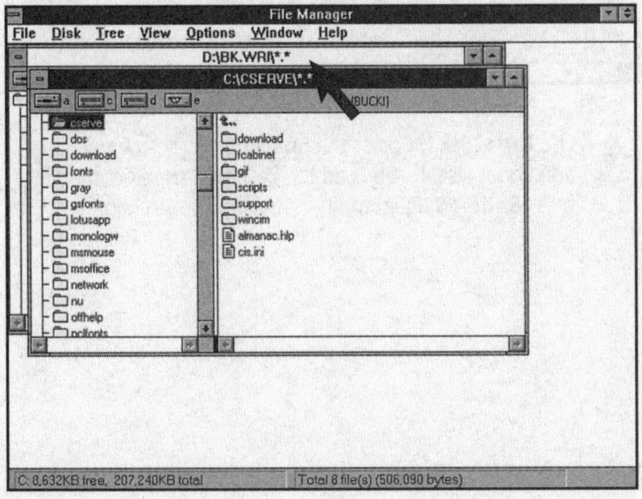

1 Select the directory window holding the files you want to select; doing so makes it the active window.

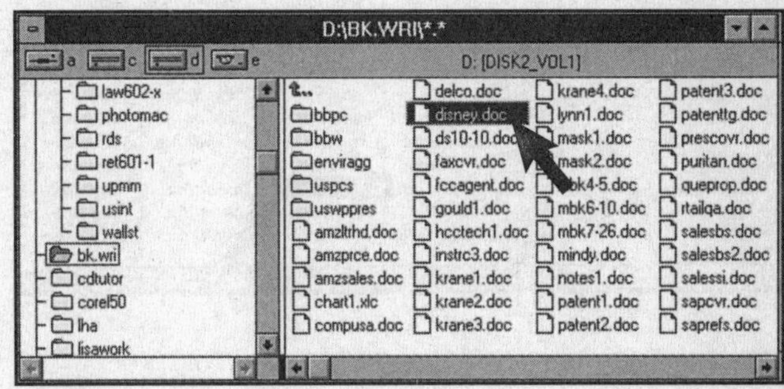

2 Click the first (top) file in the group you want to select.

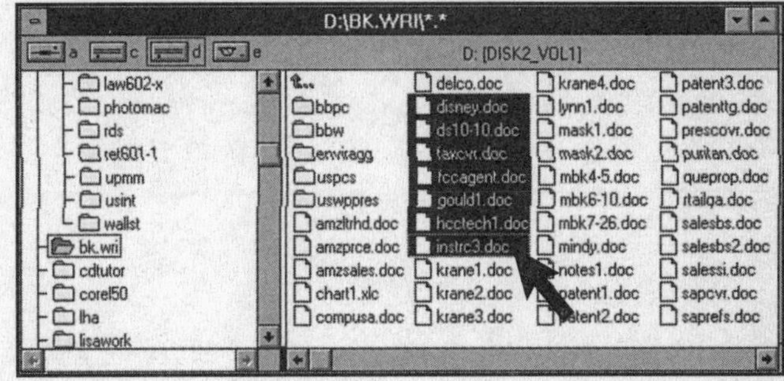

3 Press and hold **Shift**, and then click the last file in the group you want to select.

Begin Guided Tour Select Nonadjacent Files

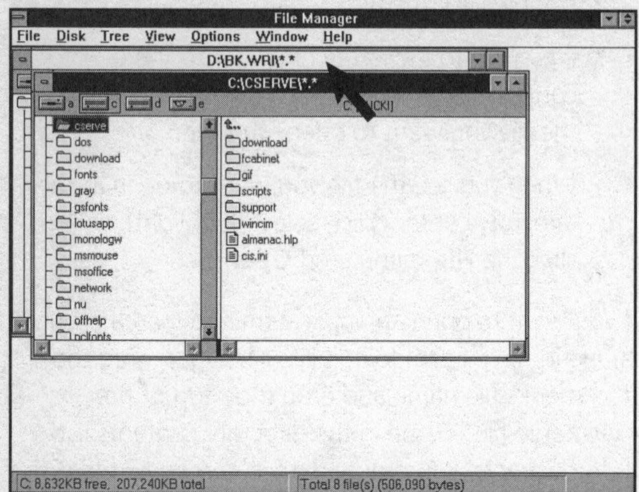

1 Select the directory window holding the files you want to select; doing so makes it the active window.

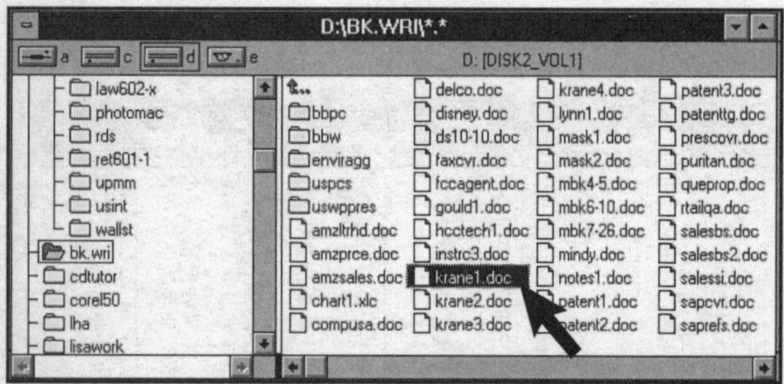

2 Click the first file in the group you want to select.

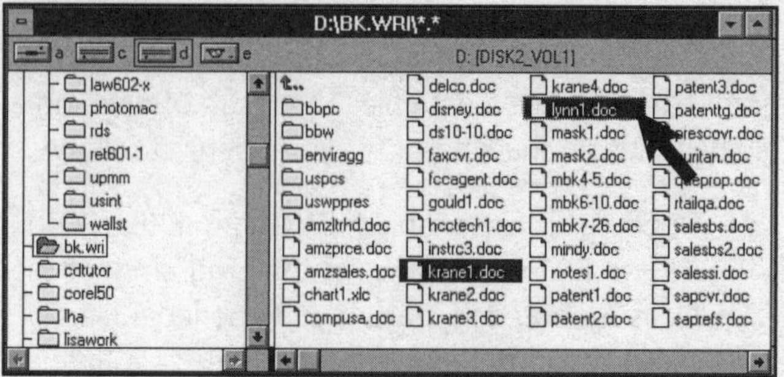

3 Press and hold **Ctrl**, and then click the next file you want to select. With the keyboard, press **Shift+F8**, move to the next file, and press the **Spacebar**.

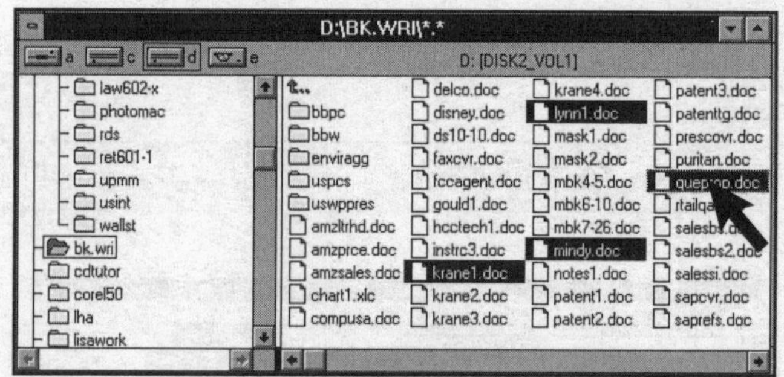

4 Use **Ctrl+click** (or press the **Spacebar**) to select any additional files. If you used the keyboard to select the files, press **Shift+F8** again to finish making the selection.

Begin Guided Tour Select Files with Similar Names or Extensions

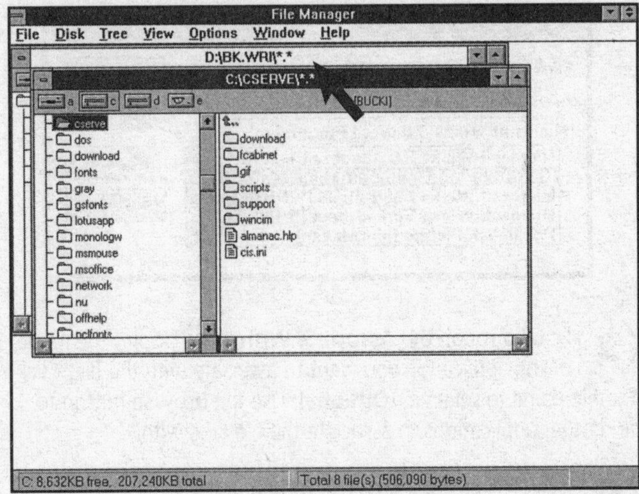

1 Select the directory window that holds the files you want to select; it becomes the active window.

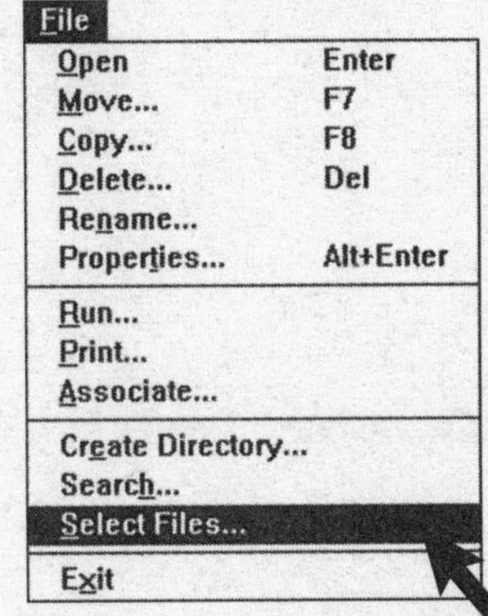

2 Open the **File** menu and click **Select Files**.

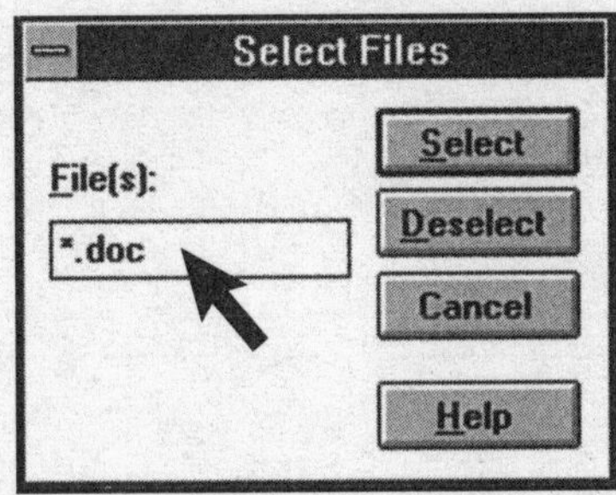

3 In the File(s) text box, use wild cards to indicate the files you want to select. For example, ***.doc** selects all files with the .doc extension. Entering **s*.*** selects all files starting with the letter S.

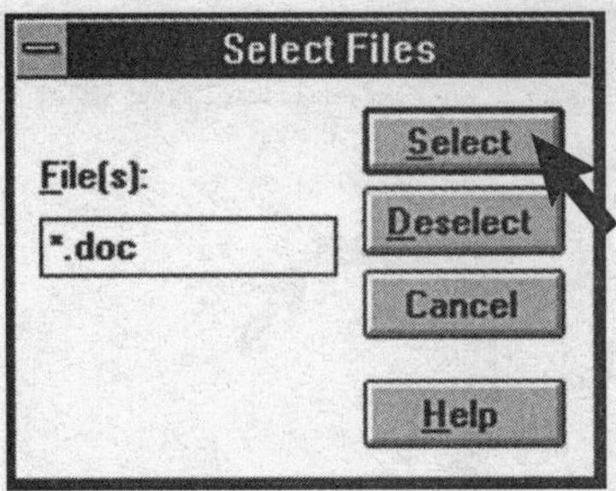

4 Click the **Select** button.

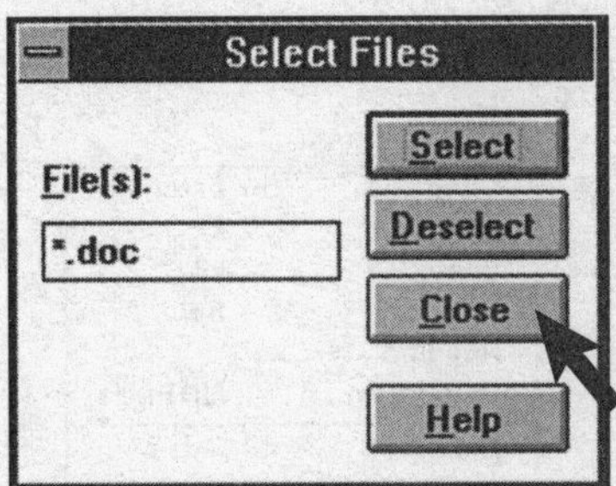

5 Click the **Close** button.

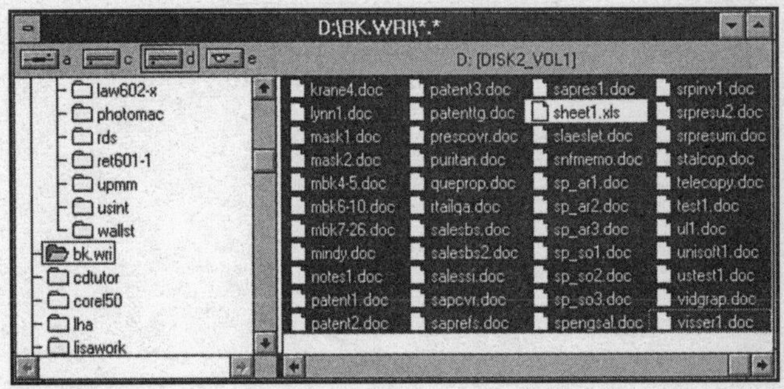

6 File Manager selects all the files matching the entry you specified, as shown here. Now you can perform the operation you need—copying, moving, or deleting.

Begin Guided Tour   Associate a File Type with an Application

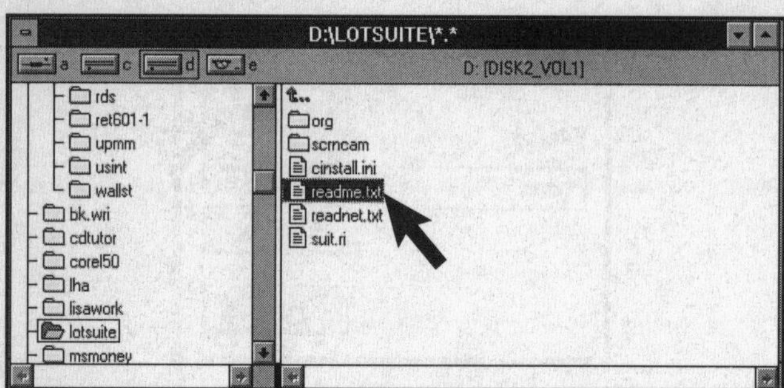

1 Select a file that has the extension you want to newly associate with a particular application (or change the association for).

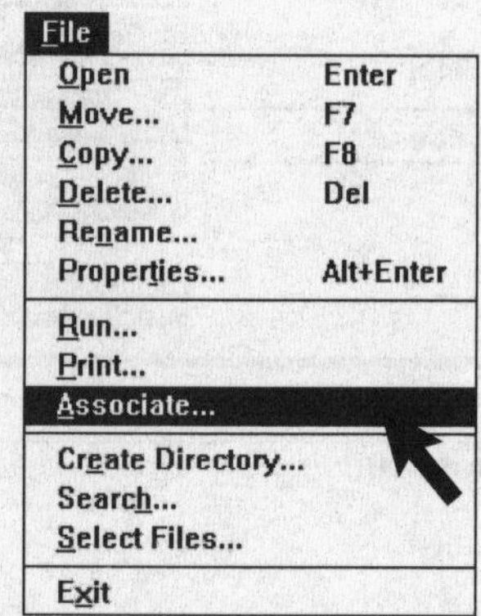

2 Open the **File** menu and click **Associate**.

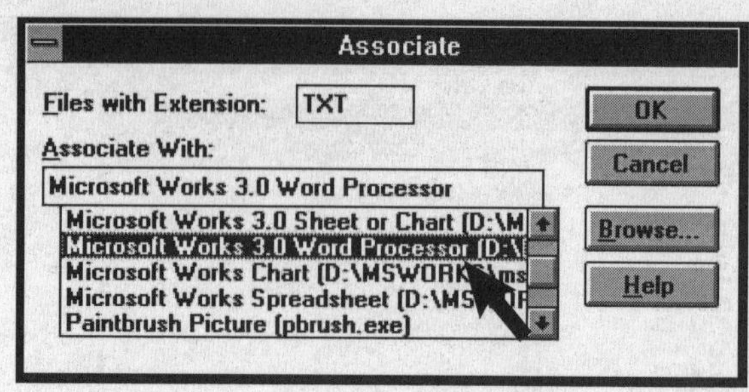

3 Scroll through the **Associate With** list to display the name of the application you want to associate with the file. Click the file name to select it. (**Optional:** Use the **Browse** button to find other applications to associate the file type with.)

4 Click **OK** or press **Enter** to complete the association.

Copy Files to Different Locations

Copying a file creates an exact copy of the file's contents, and places it in the directory on the disk you specify, leaving the original intact. Copying is one of the computer's great convenience features. Not only does it save you work, but it enables you to move your work from one computer to another (or share it) when those computers aren't connected together. For example, you might copy files if you

- Wrote a great recruiting letter to a prospective school volunteer, and you want to reuse most of the letter's contents for additional letters.
- Created an effective monthly budget spreadsheet, and you want to use a copy of it for the current month.
- Slaved all day on a report without finishing it, and you want to take a copy of it home to wrap it up over the weekend on your home computer.
- Have filled up your computer's hard drive, and you want to move some files to floppy disks by copying them to the floppies first, and then deleting them from the hard disk.

If you're a mouse fan, you're in luck when copying files. Rather than going through complicated typing routines, you can copy a file to a new location simply by dragging it into the directory you want to copy it to.

There are some tricks to doing this, depending on whether you're copying a file to another disk, or to a directory on the same disk as the original file. The *Guided Tour* here leads you through the details.

To copy files, you need to understand how to select directory windows, directories, and files. See these earlier tasks: "View Different Disks (Drives)" on page 102, "View Different Directories" on page 104, and "Select Files" on page 112.

Begin Guided Tour Drag to Copy to a Directory on Another Disk

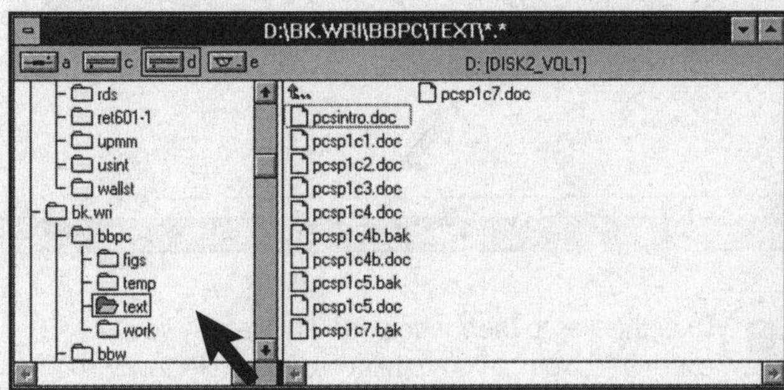

1 Open the directory window for the disk that holds the file(s) you want to copy. Select the directory that holds the files so they appear in the directory contents list.

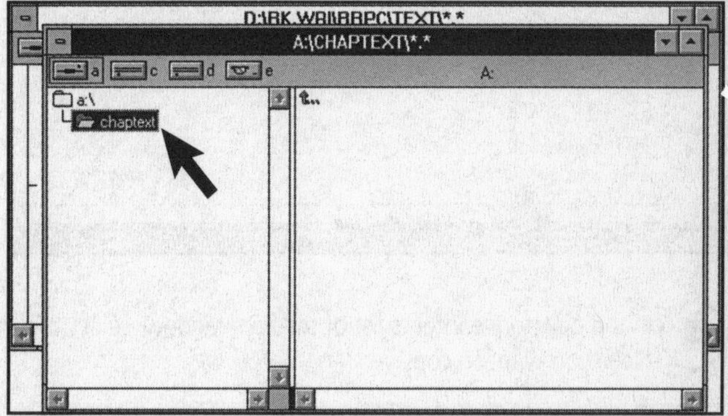

2 Open a directory window for the directory you want to copy the file(s) to, which selects that directory.

(continues)

Guided Tour Drag to Copy to a Directory on Another Disk

(continued)

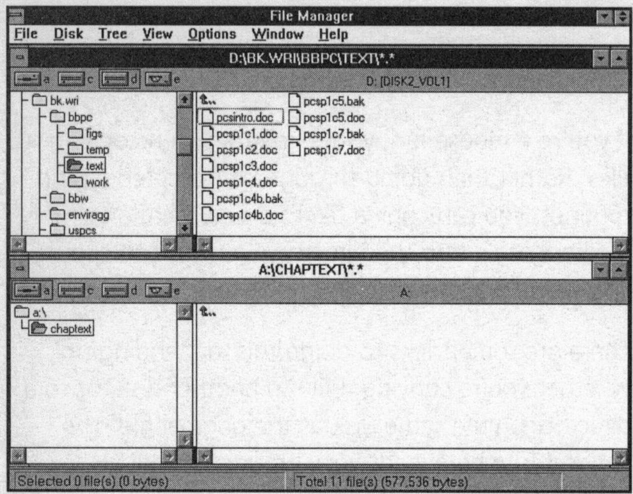

3 Arrange the two windows. You must be able to see the directory contents list of the directory you're copying from, and at least the directory tree of the directory you're copying to. Tiling the windows is a good choice.

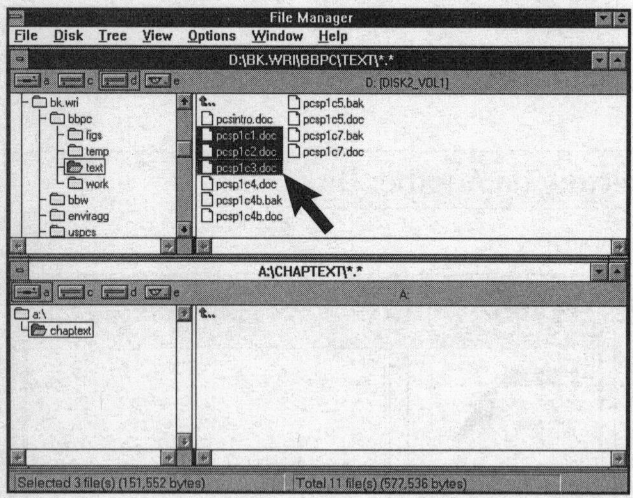

4 In the directory contents list of the first window, select the file(s) you want to copy.

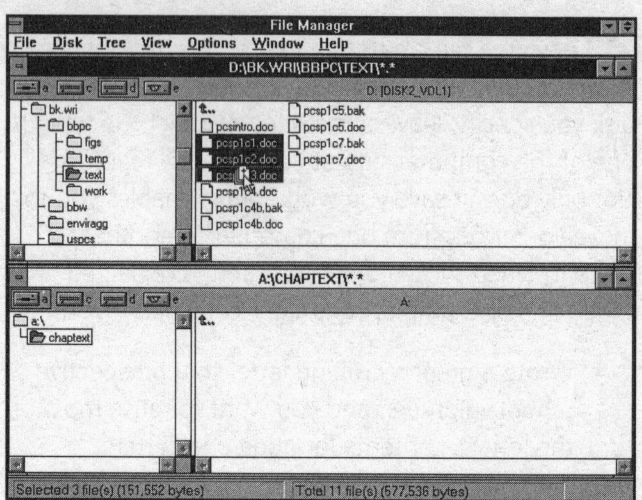

5 Point to the selected file(s); press and hold the left mouse button. Begin dragging. The pointer becomes a stack of papers with a **+** (plus sign).

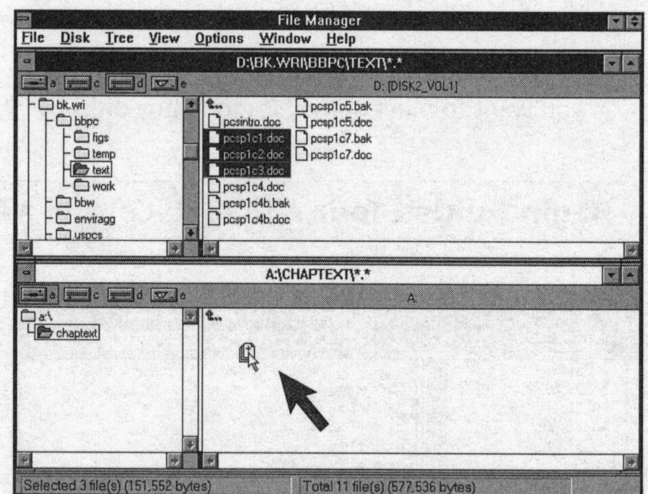

6 Drag the files to the window for the directory you're copying to. You can drag them over that directory's icon, in the tree or in the directory contents list. Release the mouse button.

Guided Tour Drag to Copy to a Directory on Another Disk

7. A dialog box appears, asking you to confirm the mouse operation. Click **Yes**.

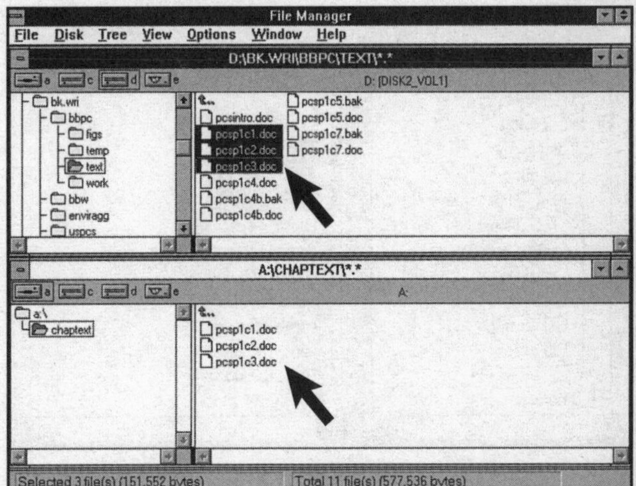

8. File Manager tells you it's copying the files. When it's finished, the file copies appear in the directory contents list for the directory you copied them to.

Begin Guided Tour Drag to Copy to a Directory on the Same Disk

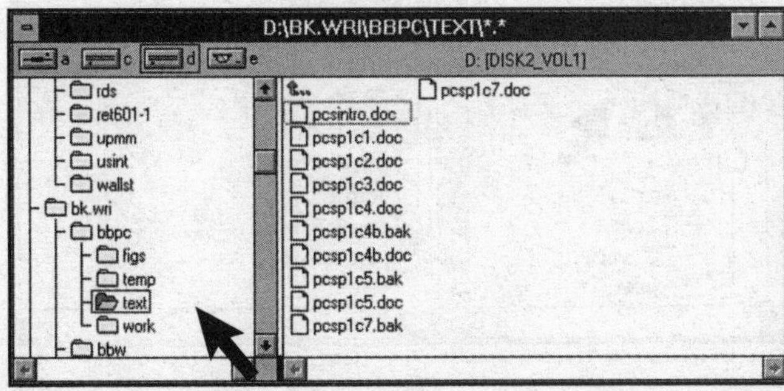

1. Open the directory window for the disk that holds the file(s) you want to copy.

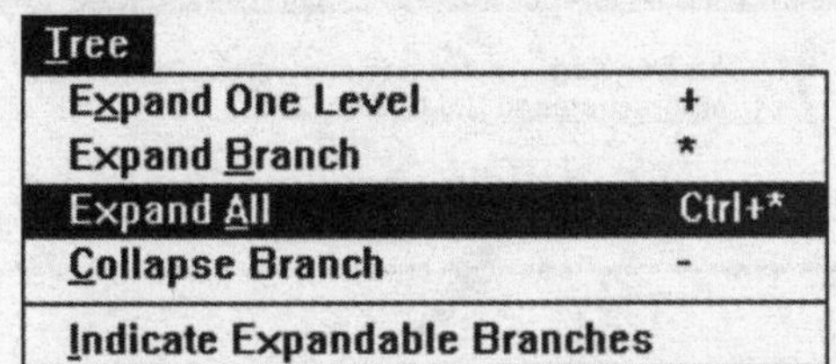

2. Select **Expand All** from the **Tree** menu to ensure the directory you want to copy to will be visible in the directory tree.

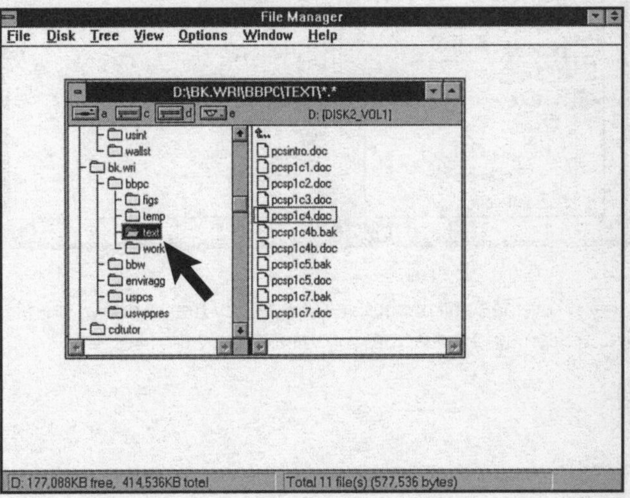

3. Select the directory that holds the file(s) you want to copy so the file(s) appear in the directory contents list.

(continues)

Guided Tour Drag to Copy to a Directory on the Same Disk

(continued)

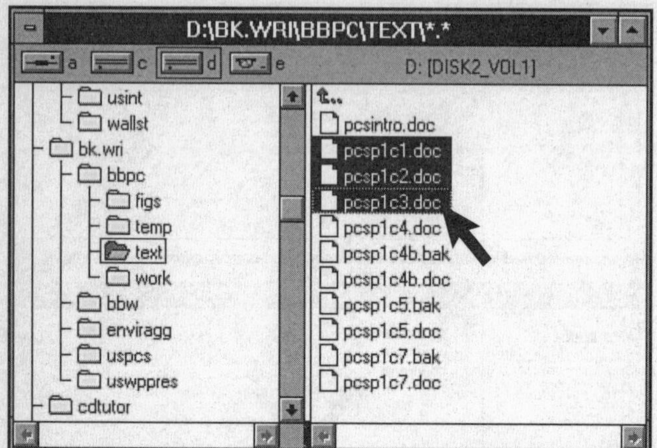

4 In the directory contents list, select the file(s) you want to copy.

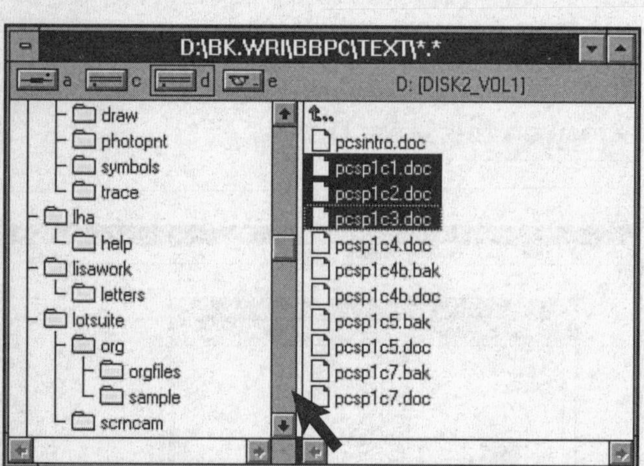

5 Use the scroll bar beside the directory tree to display the file icon for the directory you want to copy the file(s) to.

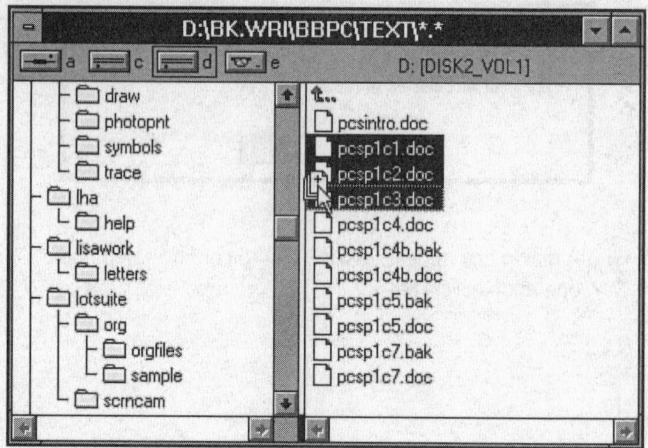

6 Point to the selected file(s). Press and hold **Ctrl**, and press and hold the left mouse button. Begin dragging. The pointer becomes a stack of papers with a **+** (plus sign).

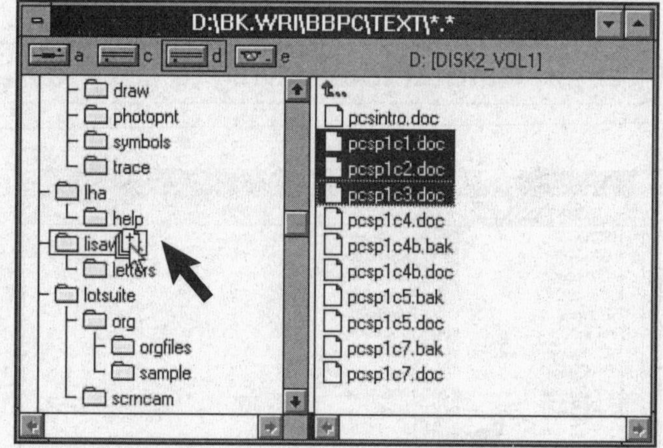

7 In the directory tree, drag the file(s) to the file icon for the directory you're copying to. Release the mouse button.

8 A dialog box appears, asking you to confirm the mouse operation. Click **Yes**.

Begin Guided Tour Copy Using File Copy

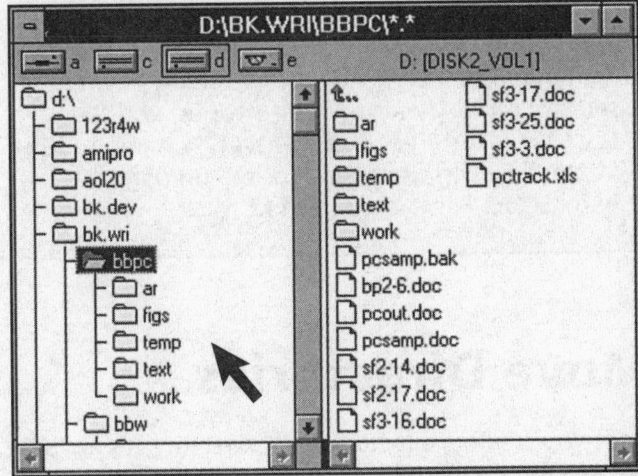

1 Open the directory window for the disk that holds the file(s) you want to copy. Select the directory that holds the file(s) so they appear in the directory contents list.

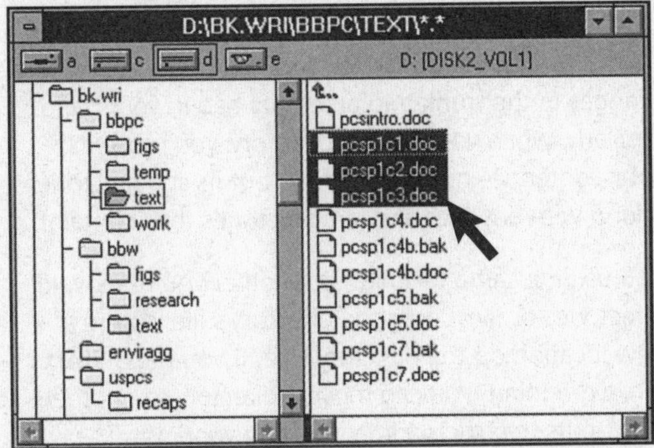

2 In the directory contents list, select the file(s) you want to copy.

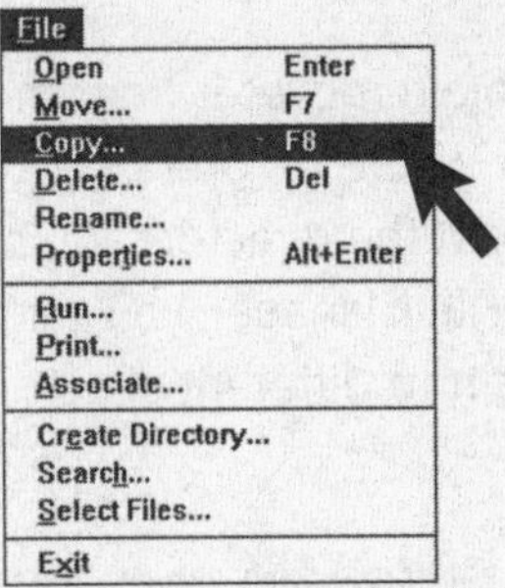

3 Open the **File** menu and click **Copy**, or press **F8**. The Copy dialog box appears.

4 In the **To** text box, type the path to the directory you want to copy to; include a drive letter, colon, and final backslash if you're copying to another disk. If you want to specify a new name for a single file you're copying, add the new name to the path.

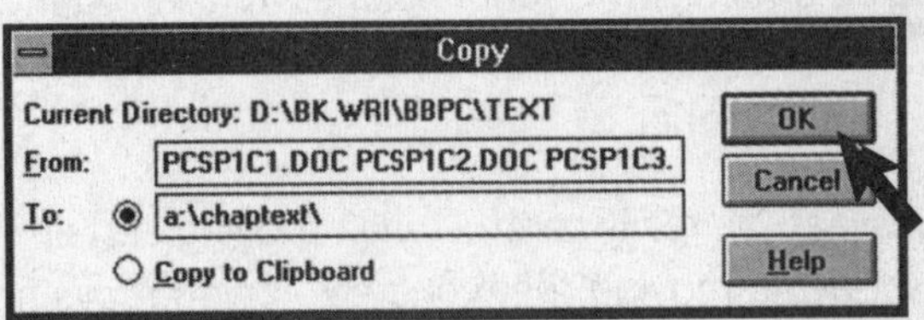

5 Click **OK** or press **Enter**.

6 A dialog box appears, asking you to confirm the copy. Click **Yes** or press **Enter**.

Move Files

Moving a file removes it from the disk and directory where it's presently stored, and places it on a new disk in the directory you specify. As with copying files in File Manager, you can move most files by dragging them to different directory windows with the mouse.

Knowing how to move files gives you a lot of control over the contents of your hard disk. It's also a more efficient method of repositioning a file than copying and then deleting the original. When might you consider moving a file? When

- You haven't opened a file or any of a group of files in six months or more. Files like these needlessly clutter your hard disk. Move them to floppy disks and store them in a cool, dry place.
- You brought a file home to work on it, and you don't really need to keep a copy on your home computer. Move it back to a floppy, and take it back to work.
- You had a directory that got really cluttered, so you added some subdirectories in it to organize its files. Move the files to the appropriate subdirectories.

One caveat: be really careful when moving certain files (or avoid moving them entirely). If you move a file that a program needs—such as a specialized data file, a template or style sheet file, or the startup file—you'll get error messages when the program tries to access the file and can't find it where it's supposed to be.

To move files, you need to understand how to select directory windows, directories, and files. See "View Different Disks (Drives)" on page 102, "View Different Directories" on page 104, and "Select Files" on page 112.

Move Directories

Once you create a directory or subdirectory, it's not set in stone on the directory tree. You can move it to a new location. You can even move a directory so it's contained within another directory, *demoting* the original directory to a subdirectory.

When you move a bag of groceries from your car trunk to your kitchen, all the contents travel with the bag. (You don't end up with your ice cream and oranges in the trunk and an empty bag in your hand.) Similarly, when you move a directory, you move its total contents—not only its files, but its subdirectories (along with any files and subdirectories they contain).

You use the same techniques whether you're moving directories or files: drag the directory's file icon to a new location on the directory tree. If you press **Shift** while dragging, you can move a directory to another disk (to its tree shown in a directory window). The *Guided Tour* describes this process in detail.

Begin Guided Tour Drag to Move Files to Another Disk

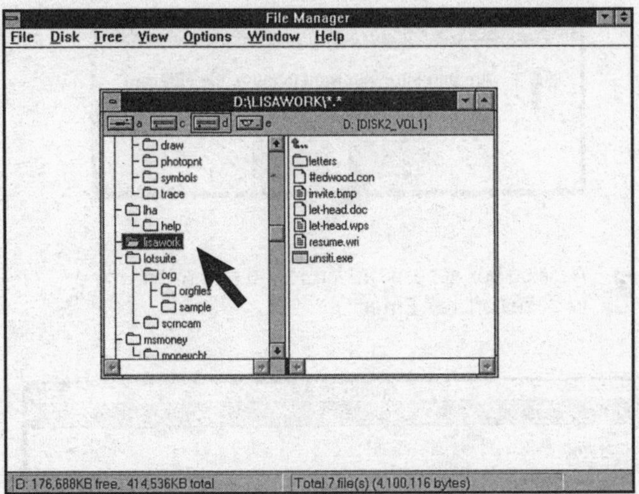

1 Open the directory window for the disk that holds the file(s) you want to move. Select the directory that holds the files so they appear in the directory contents list.

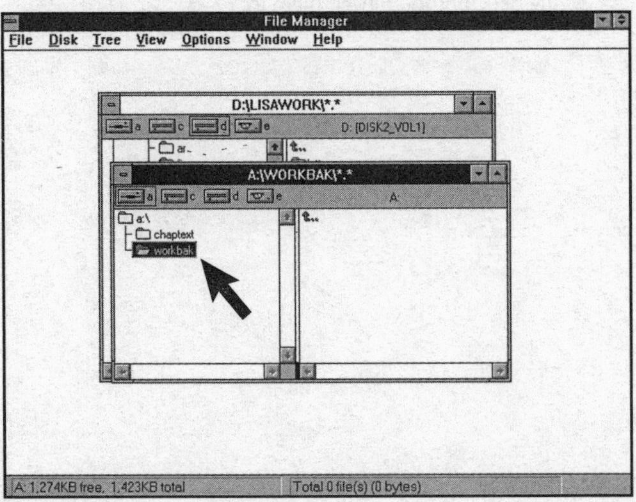

2 Open a directory window for the directory you want to move the file to; select that directory.

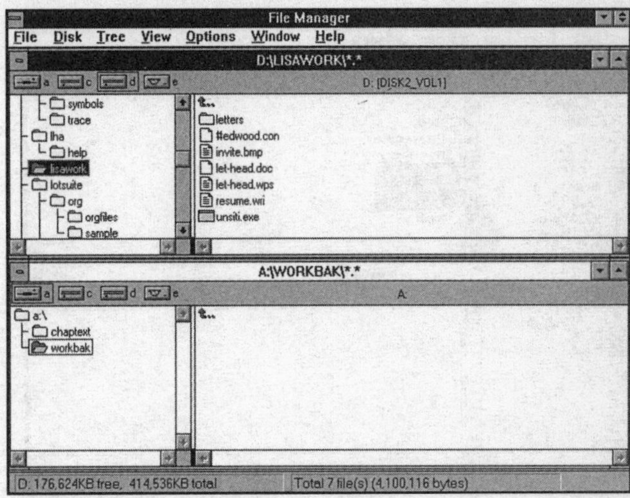

3 Arrange the two windows; tiling them is a good choice. You must be able to see the contents list of the directory you're moving from, and at least the tree of the directory you're moving to.

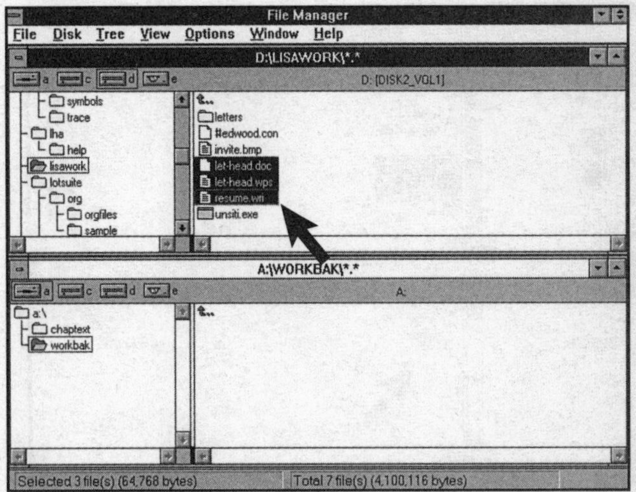

4 In the directory contents list of the first window, select the file(s) you want to move .

(continues)

Guided Tour Drag to Move Files to Another Disk

(continued)

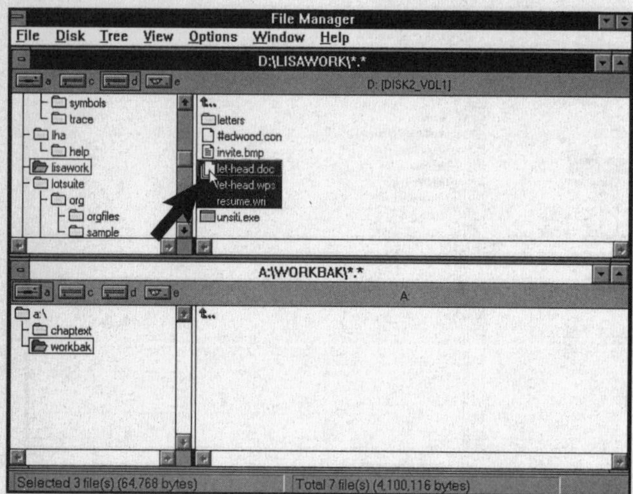

5 Point to the selected files (or the last file selected) in the group you want to move. Press and hold **Shift**. Then press and hold the left mouse button. Drag; the pointer becomes a stack of papers.

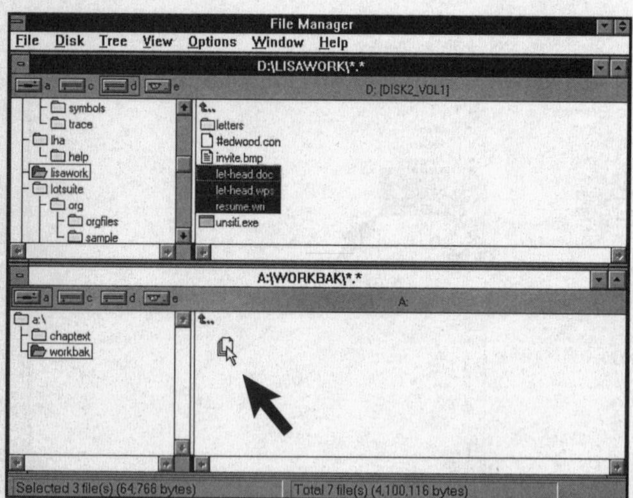

6 Drag the files to the window for the directory you're moving them to. You can drag them over its icon in either the tree or the directory contents list. Release the mouse button.

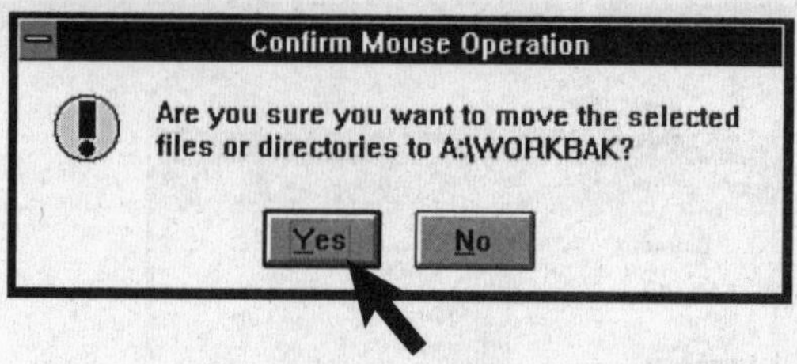

7 A dialog box appears, asking you to confirm the move. Click **Yes** or press **Enter**.

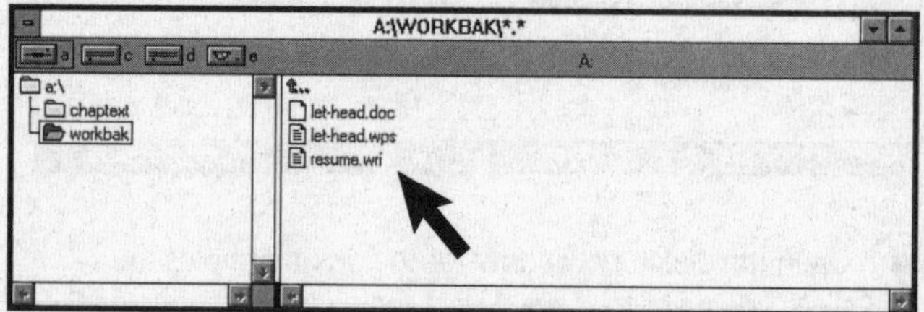

8 When you've finished, the files appear in the contents list of the directory you moved them to.

Begin Guided Tour Drag to Move Files on the Same Disk

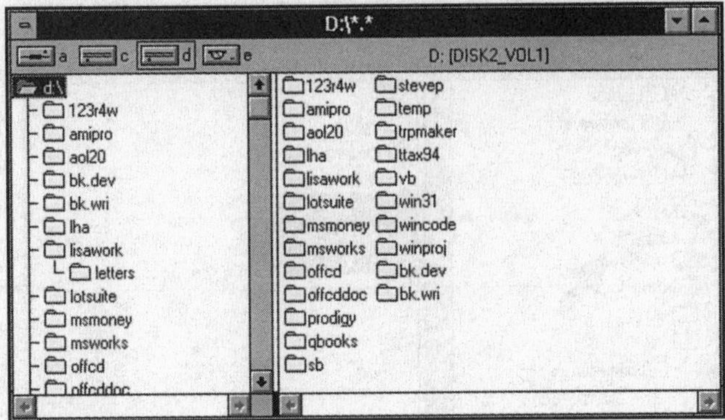

1 Open the directory window for the disk that holds the file(s) you want to move.

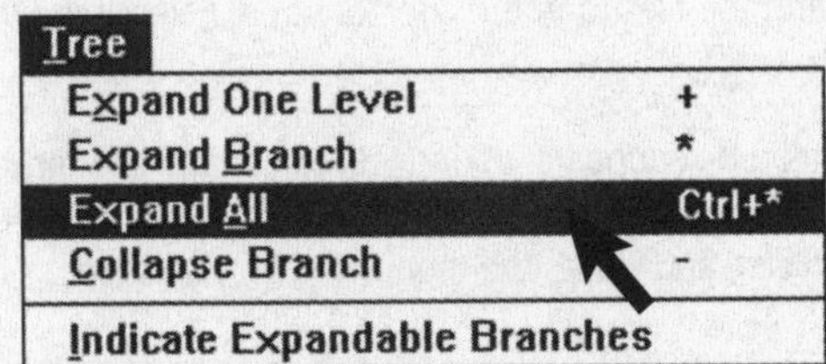

2 To ensure that the directory you want to move the files to will show in the directory tree, select **Expand All** from the **Tree** menu.

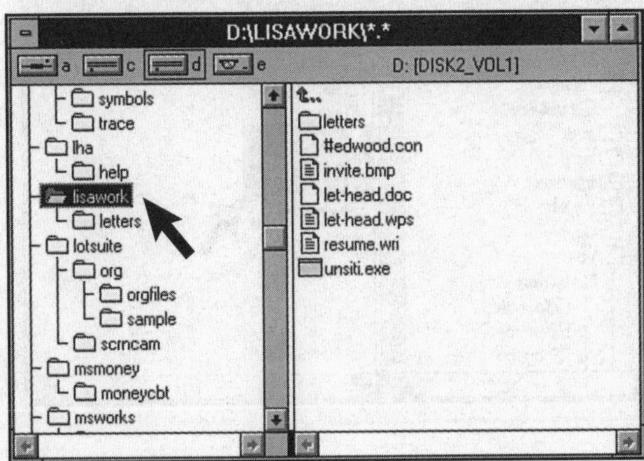

3 Select the directory that holds the file(s) you want to move; scroll till the file(s) appear in its contents list.

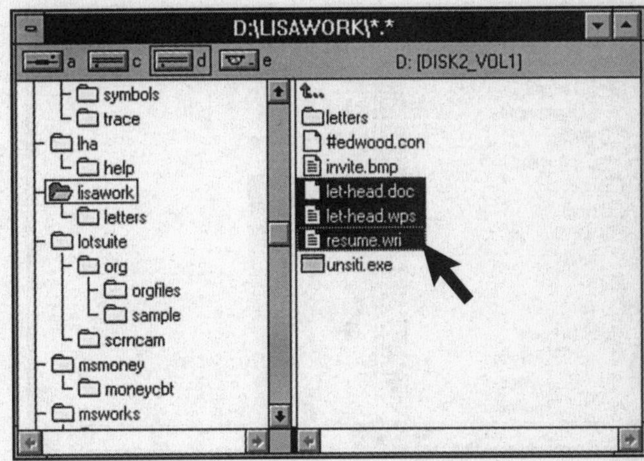

4 In the directory contents list, select the file(s) you want to move.

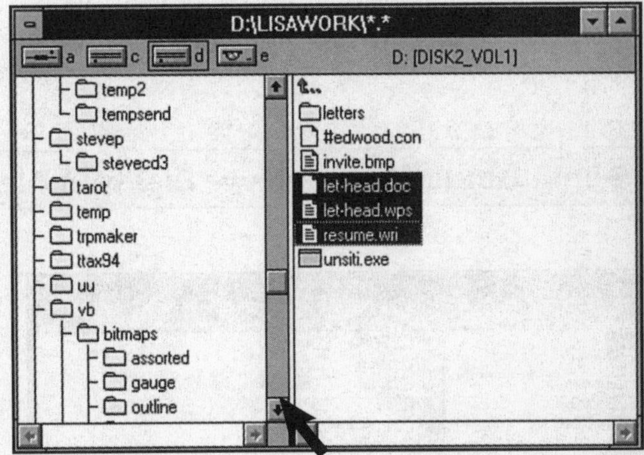

5 Use the scroll bar beside the tree to display the file icon for the directory you want to move the file(s) to.

(continues)

Guided Tour Drag to Move Files on the Same Disk

(continued)

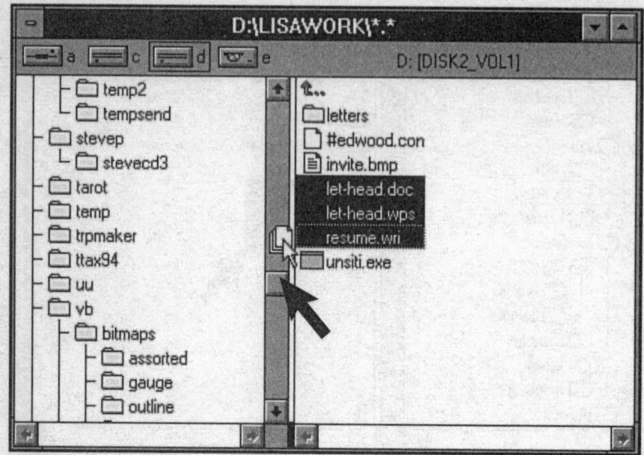

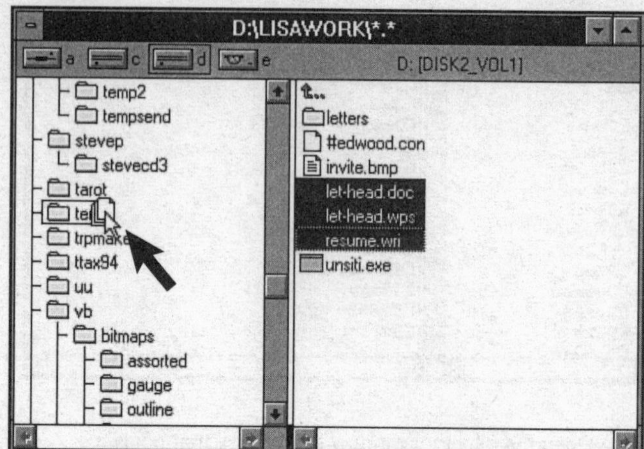

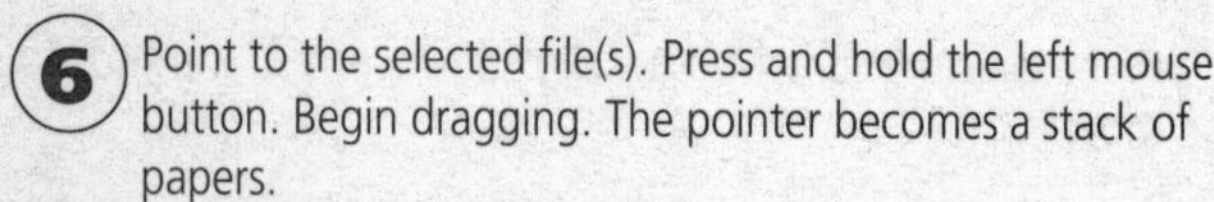

6 Point to the selected file(s). Press and hold the left mouse button. Begin dragging. The pointer becomes a stack of papers.

7 Drag the file(s) to the file icon for the directory you're moving the files to in the directory tree. Release the mouse button.

8 A dialog box appears, asking you to confirm the move. Click **Yes** or press **Enter**. File Manager tells you it's moving the file(s), and closes the menu when it's finished.

Begin Guided Tour Move Files with File Move

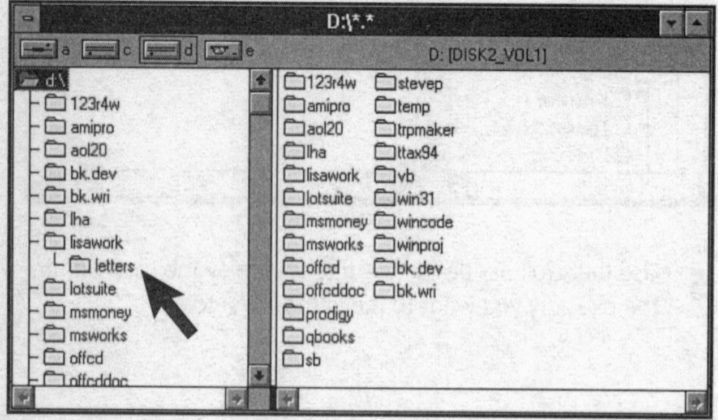

1 Open the directory window for the disk that holds the file(s) you want to move. Select the directory that holds the file(s) so they appear in the directory contents list.

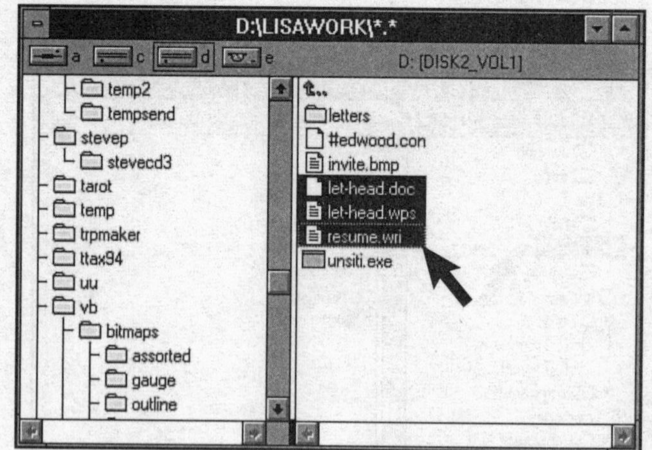

2 In the directory contents list, select the file(s) you want to move.

Guided Tour Move Files with File Move

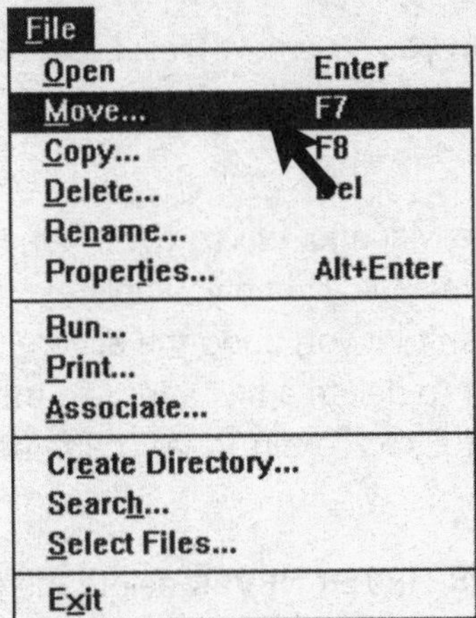

3 Open the **File** menu and click **Move**, or press **F7**. The Move dialog box appears.

4 In the **To** text box, type the path to the directory you want to move the file(s) to; include a drive letter, colon, and final backslash if you're moving them to another disk. If you're moving just one file, you can specify a new name for it. Click **OK**.

5 A dialog box appears, asking you to confirm the move. Click **Yes** or press **Enter**.

Delete Files

It's true: there's no such thing as a big enough hard drive, and every once in a while, you'll have to "clean house." Most hard disks seem infested with tiny pixies who go around at night copying files until every nook and cranny on the disk is completely full. Here are just a few instances when you'll need to delete files:

- The information in the files is so hopelessly outdated you'll never need it again. For example, you may not need to keep a complaint letter from 1985 on disk.
- Your system's accumulated a lot of .TMP files (files Windows temporarily creates for data files) in the \WINDOWS\TEMP directory, or in a program directory. Your system normally deletes these files when you shut it down, but if your system locks up and you have to reboot, these files may not be deleted as needed.
- An application has created a lot of .BAK files (document backup files) you don't think you need.
- You are literally out of space on your hard disk, and something has to go!

Deleting a file doesn't remove it from a disk right away, as explained in the "Understand Files" task on page 51 earlier in the book. File Manager simply neglects to display the file name in the directory window, and then tells DOS to make the space available when you save new files. Eventually, new parts of new files will fill up the disk space left by deleted files.

By default, File Manager warns you when you're about to delete a file. When you delete a file, File Manager doesn't let you undo the action. So, be sure you want to delete a file, and read the deletion message carefully to confirm that you're deleting the *right* file.

NEVER NEVER NEVER NEVER delete the following files from your hard disk: COMMAND.COM, AUTOEXEC.BAT, CONFIG.SYS. If you get rid of these files, you won't be able to boot your computer—*at all*! Also, avoid deleting files with .BAT, .EXE, .COM, .PIF, .DLL, .DAT, and .INI file name extensions, unless you're really sure of what you're doing. These files execute programs or give them more instructions to work properly. Without one of these files, your application may be kaput!

> For a clearer picture of what happens on disk when you delete files or directories, see "Understand How the Computer Stores Files" on page 45. "Delete Directories" on page 134 explains how to remove a directory and its contents from a disk.

Begin Guided Tour Delete Files

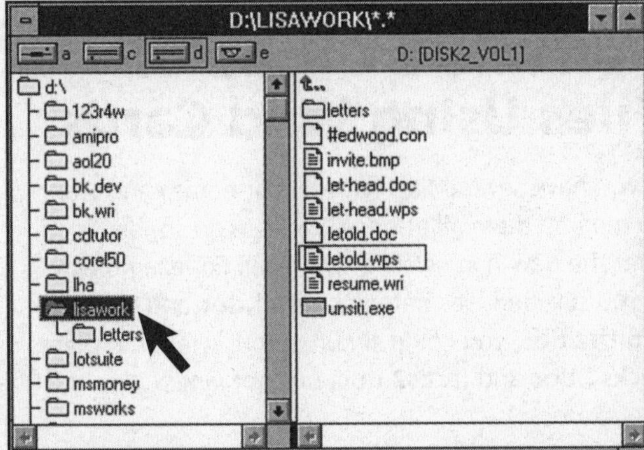

1 Open the directory window for the disk that holds the file(s) you want to delete. Select the directory that holds the files; scroll until they appear in the directory contents list.

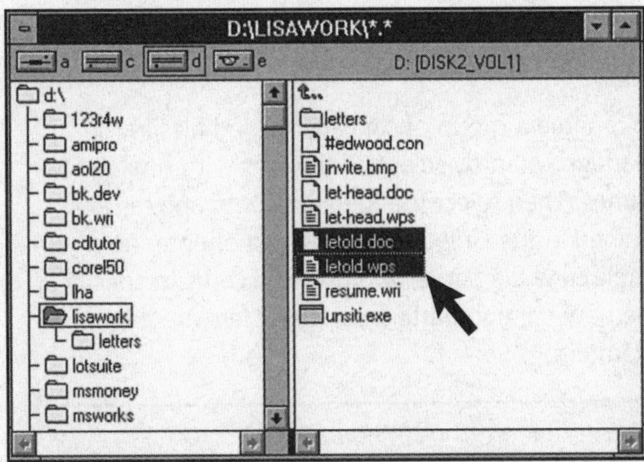

2 Select the file(s) you want to delete in the directory contents list of the directory window.

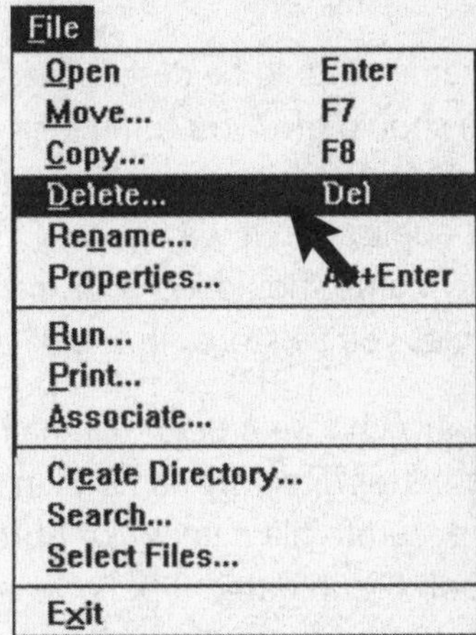

3 Open the **File** menu and click **Delete**. With the keyboard: press the **Del** key.

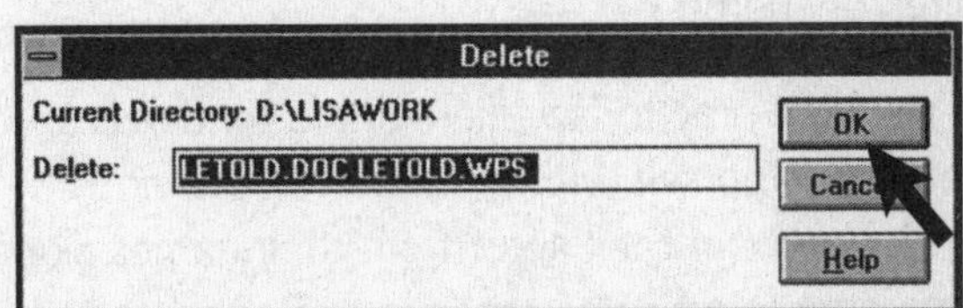

4 The Delete dialog box appears, listing the names of the file(s) you selected for deletion. Click **OK** to continue the deletion.

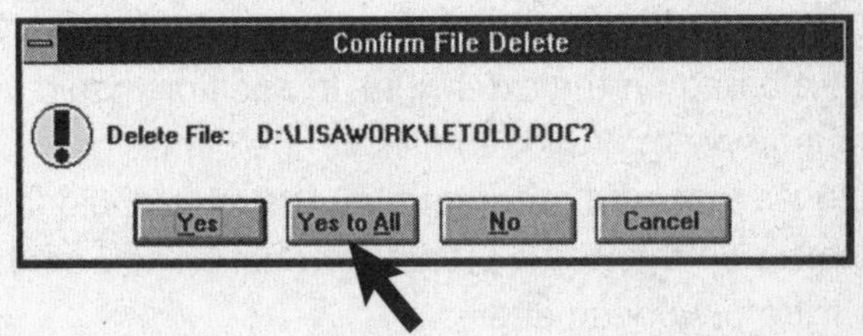

5 The Confirm File Delete dialog box appears. To delete a single file (or delete only the first file of a group), click **Yes** or press **Enter**. To continue deleting a group of files, click **Yes to All**.

Rename Files and Directories

Good file names should be descriptive. The name of the file should give you some idea of its contents, and the three-letter extension indicates the type of file (or what application it was created in). Similarly, a good directory name should jog your memory about what kinds of files you've stored in the directory.

You could certainly choose a better file name than **stuff.doc**, or a better directory name than **files**. You should choose accurate file names like **bbltr9-9.doc** for a letter to Bob Braun dated 9-9. For directories, go with something like **braun-pr** for a directory that holds all your correspondence files with Bob Braun. (By the way, it's a little-known secret that you can add a period—plus an extension of up to three letters—to any directory name.)

If you've fallen prey to lazy file-naming tendencies, you may find yourself with a disk full of files and directories you can't tell apart from their names alone. Take the time to do some renaming; use the upcoming *Guided Tour*.

As a rule, when you rename a file, you should change the base name only and keep the extension intact; doing so makes it easier to open the file in your application (or keep its File Manager association, which is based on the extension). In addition, avoid renaming system or hidden files, or the names of directories that hold program files. Doing so could (at best) mess up the way a program works or (at worst) keep it from working at all.

Note that you can only rename one directory or subdirectory at a time (because, coincidentally, you can only select one at a time). You can rename multiple files, but special rules apply.

When you rename a file at the DOS prompt, DOS lets you move the file to a new drive or directory if you type the path, too. File Manager doesn't let you do this. You can only rename the file, not move it while you're renaming.

Rename a Group of Files Using Wild Cards

If you have several files with similar names and want to rename them all at once, you can do so, provided that the new names are also similar. For example, if you selected files named **smith1.doc** and **smith2.doc**, you could simultaneously rename them **jacks1.doc** and **jacks2.doc**, but not *janes1.doc* and *jacks2.doc*.

As when you perform other file operations, File Manager lets you use wild card characters to rename groups of files with similar names. The ***** (asterisk) wild card takes the place of a group of contiguous characters, such as the three-letter file name extension. The **?** (question-mark) wild card stands for a single character.

To rename a group of similarly named files in File Manager, start by selecting the files with similar names. Then select the Rename command, as explained in the *Guided Tour*. Instead of entering a single new file name, you use wild cards to specify the new naming pattern for files. Here are a few examples:

Original names	*Naming pattern you type in the "To" text box*	*New names*
1992.xls		1992.wks
1993.xls		1993.wks
1994.xls	*.wks	1994.wks
1982.xls		1992.xls
1983.xls		1993.xls
1984.xls	??9?.*	1994.xls
smith1.doc		jones1.doc
smith2.doc	jones?.doc	jones2.doc

In that last example, you'd need to use a matching number of replacement characters leading up to the **?** wild card. If you used too few (as in j?.doc), the command wouldn't work. If you try to avoid this by using the j*.doc pattern, the command will work, but the new file names will be jmith1.doc and jmith2.doc. File Manager will overwrite only the first character, and keep the rest of the characters from the original file name intact.

Begin Guided Tour How to Rename

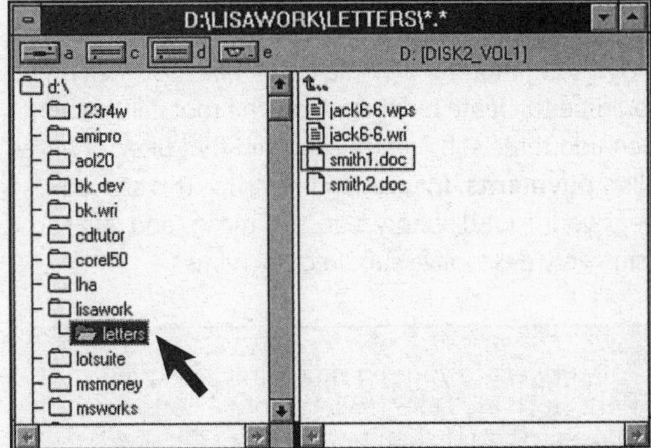

1 Open the directory window for the disk that holds the file or directory you want to rename. If you're renaming a directory, display it in the tree. If you're renaming a file, select the directory that holds the file; the file should appear in the contents list.

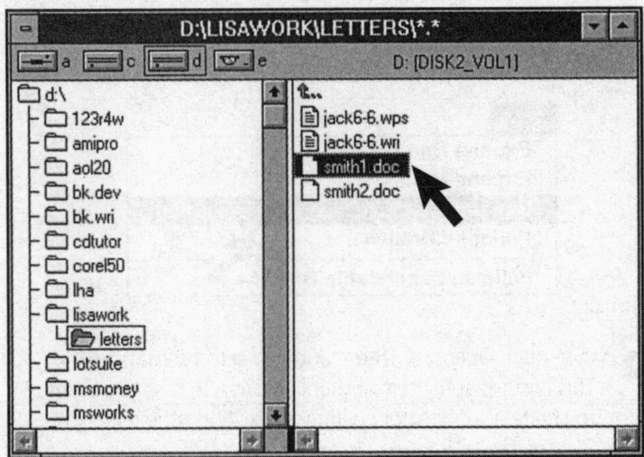

2 Select the file (in the contents list of the directory window), or the directory (in the tree) you want to rename.

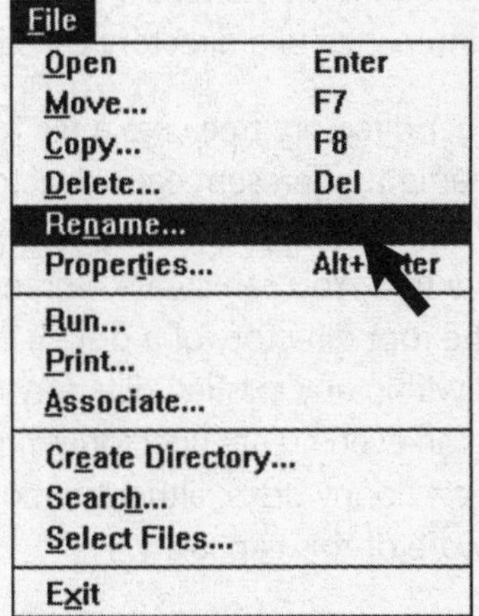

3 Open the **File** menu and click **Rename**.

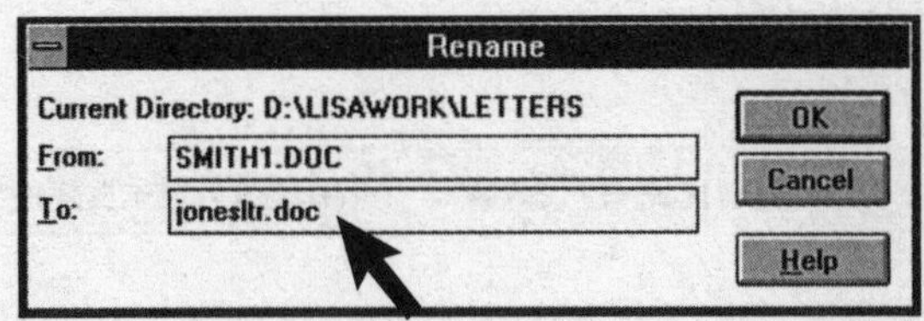

4 The Rename dialog box appears, listing the names of the file or directory to be renamed. Type a new name in the **To** text box. You can use wild cards if you want. Make sure you type an appropriate file name extension.

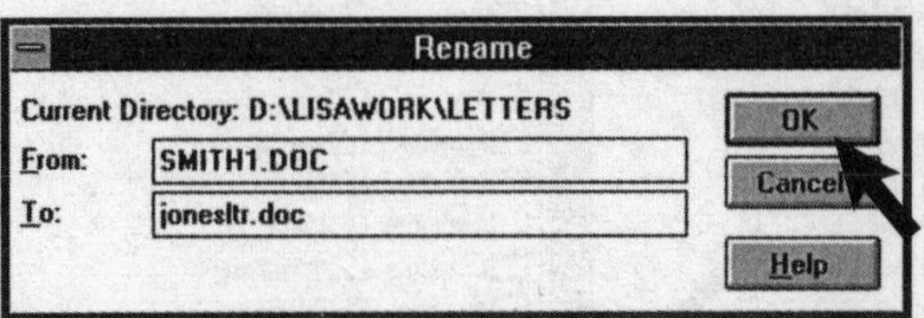

5 Click **OK** or press **Enter** to finish the renaming process.

Create Directories

An empty directory is like a blank canvass. You name it and fill it with what you want. Directories and subdirectories are the equivalent of file folders on a disk. You use them to organize your documents. For example, you might want to keep all the data files related to home repair, your mortgage, and home maintenance in a directory called \HOME.

The File Manager directory tree uses a file folder icon along with a name to represent each directory. File Manager lets you create a new directory anywhere on the directory tree. You can create a brand new directory off the root directory of a disk, \, or create a subdirectory within any existing directory or subdirectory. You can even create directories and subdirectories on floppy disks, although most users aren't aware of this capability.

When you create a new directory, you not only specify where on the disk it should be located, but also assign it a name of up to eight characters. You can even include a period and an extension of up to three letters in a directory name.

As when you name files, make sure you give descriptive names to your new directories. Also, don't hesitate to use subdirectories to create a "deep" directory tree. A common beginner mistake is to just add directory after directory under the root directory. For example, someone might create three directories named **carpymt**, **carins**, and **carrep** from the root to track information for a single car. A better strategy would be to create a directory off the root called **car**. Then add three subdirectories within that directory called **payments**, **insure**, and **repairs**. This strategy keeps your root directory lean and mean, and lets you assign very descriptive subdirectory names.

For answers to your burning directory questions (such as "Does having more directories make me better than my neighbor?"), see "Understand How the Computer Stores Files" on page 45.

Begin Guided Tour Make Directories

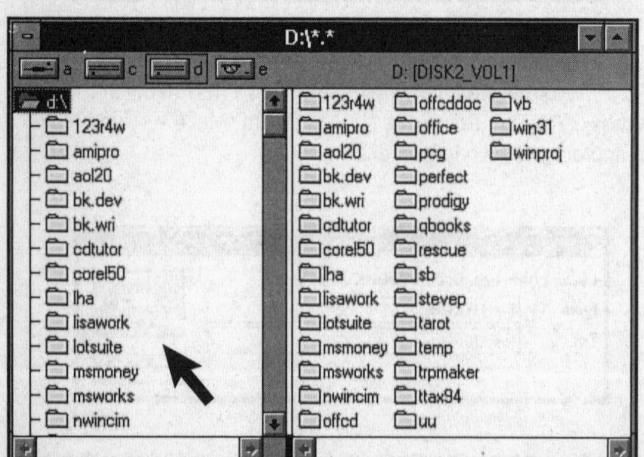

1 Open the directory window for the disk you want to create a directory on.

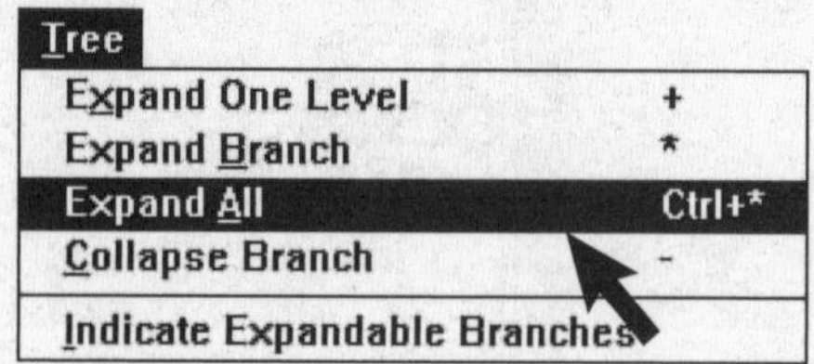

2 (Optional) Open the **Tree** menu and select **Expand All**. This ensures you'll see all subdirectories, in case you want to create a subdirectory within an existing subdirectory.

Guided Tour Make Directories

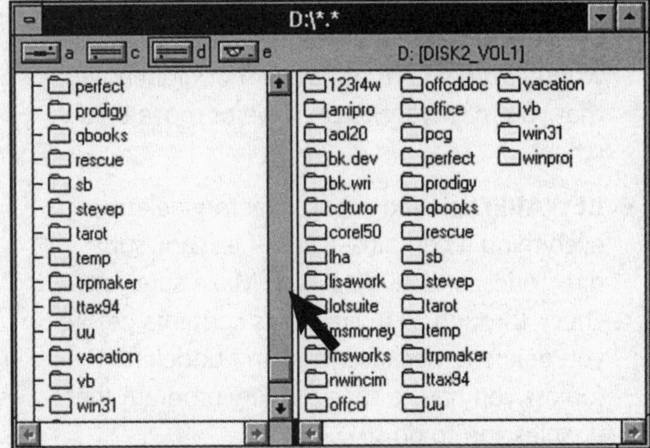

3 If necessary, use the scroll bar beside the directory tree to display the directory you want to create a subdirectory in.

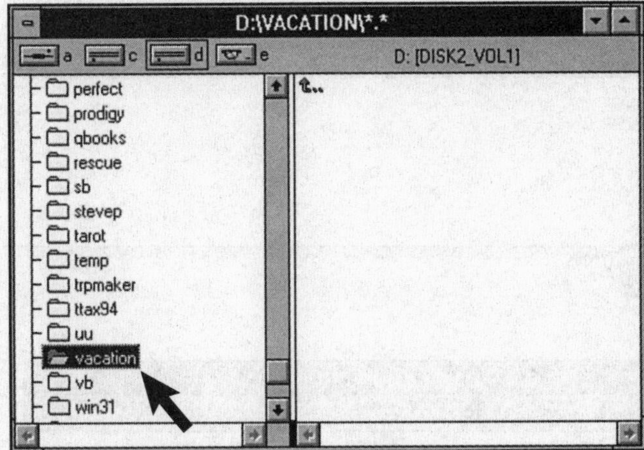

4 Click the directory to select it.

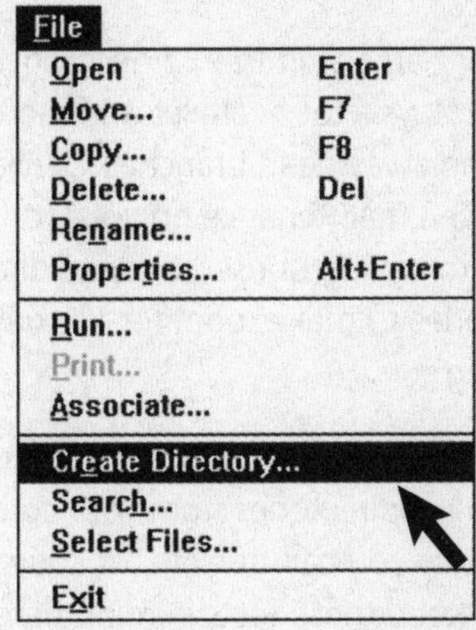

5 Open the **File** menu and select **Create Directory**.

6 In the Create Directory dialog box, type a name for the new (sub)directory in the **Name** text box; click **OK**.

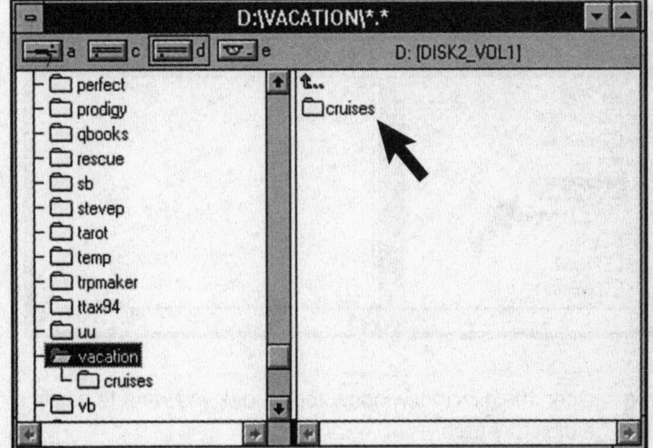

7 File Manager creates the new directory, and adds a branch for it to the directory tree in the current directory window.

Delete Directories

If you've ever had a fruit tree or decorative bush, you know it stays a lot healthier and more attractive if you prune away dead branches. Similarly, you should do routine maintenance on your computer's directory tree, removing unused or dead directories and subdirectories to make room for the new ones you'll be adding.

File Manager gives you the capability of deleting directories and subdirectories from your computer. The only directory you can't delete, of course, is the root directory. Keep these facts in mind before you start rampantly deleting files:

- Avoid deleting program directories or subdirectories, unless you're really sure of what you're doing and want to delete the program altogether.
- You can only delete one directory at a time, because File Manager only lets you select one directory at a time.
- Before you delete a directory, check to see whether it contains any system or hidden files that you may want to preserve or move elsewhere.
- **BEWARE:** deleting a (sub)directory deletes everything it contains—all its files, any subdirectories, and all *their* files. Make sure you check through all a directory's contents before you delete it, because you can't undelete it (unless you have a special utility program that enables you to do so).

If you don't want to delete all the files in a (sub)directory, move those files out first. For guidance on moving files, see "Move Files" on page 122.

Begin Guided Tour Get Rid of Directories

1 Open the directory window for the disk you want to delete a directory from.

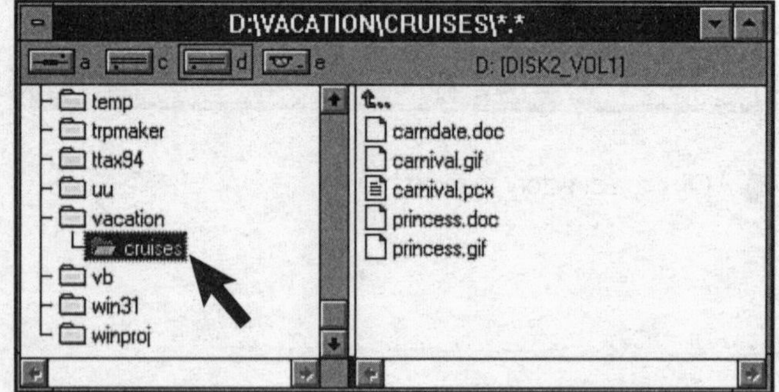

2 In the directory tree, select the (sub)directory you want to delete. Check the directory contents list quickly to ensure it doesn't contain any files you want to keep intact.

Guided Tour Get Rid of Directories

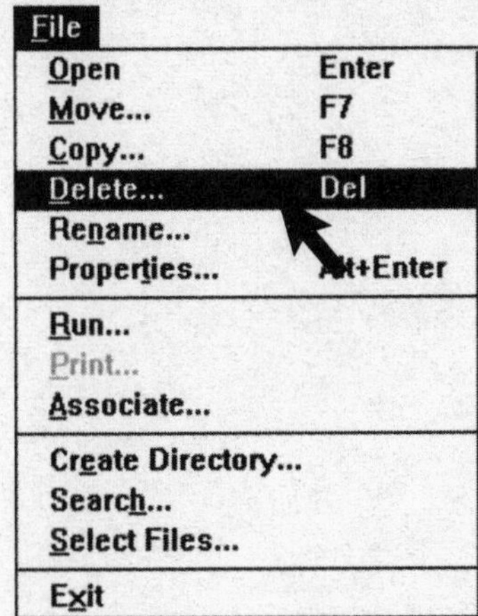

3 Open the **File** menu and click **Delete**, or press the **Delete** key.

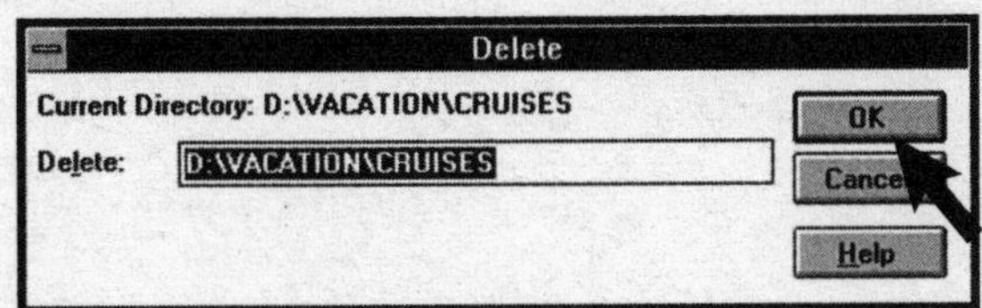

4 In the Delete dialog box, check the **Delete** text box to ensure it's displaying the correct (sub)directory to delete. Click **OK** or press **Enter**.

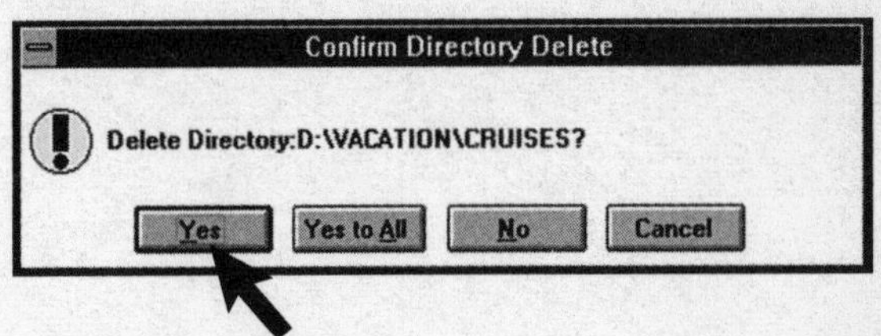

5 Click **Yes** to close the Confirm Directory Delete dialog box and continue the deletion.

6 At the Confirm File Delete dialog box, click **Yes to All** to delete all the directory's files. (Use **Yes** if you want to confirm the deletion for each file.)

HOW TO...

Find and Show Files and More with Windows 3.11

One benefit Windows' File Manager offers is a lot of flexibility when you work with your files. If you have too many files in a particular directory and want to narrow the list, File Manager can get it done. If you want to see certain details about a file, File Manager can oblige. File Manager can even help you find lost files, or format a floppy disk to make it ready to store your work.

This section explains how to customize File Manager so it suits your working style, as well as how to use handy features like searching and disk formatting.

What You Will Find in This Section

Rearrange the List of Files 138

Show Only Certain Files 140

Show File Details 142

Search for Files 144

Format Disks 146

Rearrange the List of Files

Individual users feel most comfortable with a filing system tailored to their needs. While one person may be content to throw all household receipts and paperwork in a box, another may prefer to have a separate folder for each kind of bill or receipt, with the folder contents organized by date or dollar value.

While File Manager starts out with one filing system for the directory contents list, you can refile (sort) information in any order that you prefer. By default, File Manager first lists directories alphabetically by name, and then lists files alphabetically by the file's base name (the part before the period and extension). This arrangement applies to all directory windows you open.

You can, however, select a directory window and change how it lists directories and files. This new *sort order* applies only to the current directory window, and to directory windows you open later. You can choose four different sort orders, and display different orders in different windows. Selecting one of the following options displays files of a particular type; deselecting the option hides those files.

Sort by Name	Lists directories in alphabetical order, and then arranges the file names alphabetically by their base names.
Sort by Size	Lists directories first, and then lists files in order of size, from largest to smallest.
Sort by Type	Lists directories first, and then lists files in alphabetical order by three-letter file name extension; this order makes it easier to find files of a certain type (such as executable files).
Sort by Date	Lists directories first, sorted by creation date (from most to least recent); then lists files sorted by last modification date (from most to least recent). This option helps when you're trying to determine the file you saved most recently, which is likely to have the most updated information.

You can only choose one sort order at a time. File Manager uses the order you specify when you sort any (sub)directory you've selected in the current directory window. If you close that directory window and then reopen it (as when you close the directory window for a floppy disk), the newly opened window adopts the sort order of the last window you've worked in, not the sort order it had before you closed it.

To learn more about working with different directory windows in File Manager, see "Open More Directory (Drive) Windows" on page 109.

Begin Guided Tour Rearrange Files

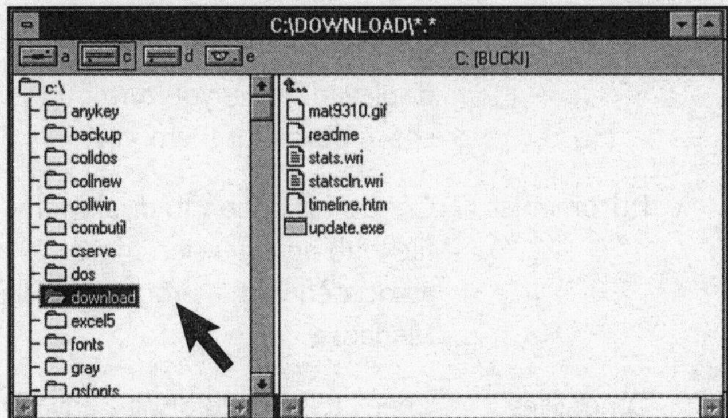

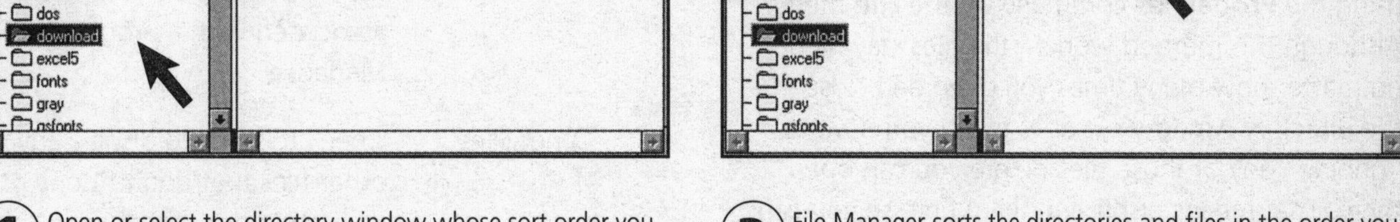

1 Open or select the directory window whose sort order you want to change.

3 File Manager sorts the directories and files in the order you specified, and updates the directory contents list accordingly.

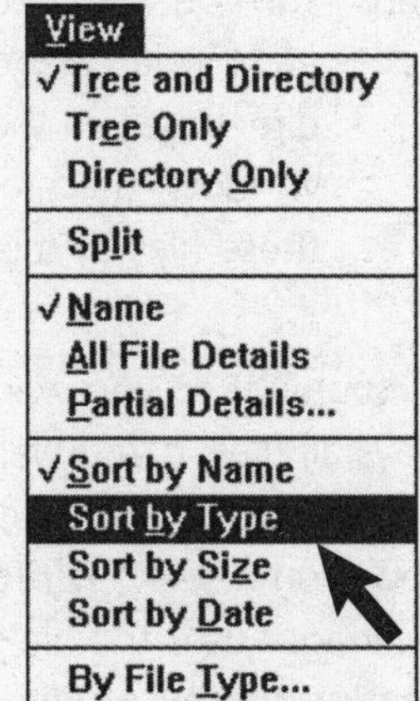

2 Open the **View** menu and click one of the four sorting options, such as **Sort by Type**.

Show Only Certain Files

Normally File Manager displays all the files and directories it finds—except for hidden and system files—in every directory window you open. If you want to unclutter the view, you could assign the **Hidden** attribute to these files and directories by using the **Properties** command on the **File** menu. Although this method works—the files stay hidden, no matter how many times you open and close the directory window—it does mean you have to "unhide" any of those files before you can open them. That means displaying them first, so you can remove the Hidden attribute. What a pain.

File Manager offers an easier way to hide certain files temporarily. You can display different kinds of files, and in different windows. (Of course, these new display settings apply only to the current directory window and to any directory windows you open after that, until you change them.) You can select these file listing options:

Name	You can use wild cards in this text box to display only the files that have certain naming attributes. For example, **a*.*** displays all files that begin with the letter **a**, and ***.doc** displays all files that end with **.DOC**. (This setting overrides all the other file display settings, which are listed next.)
Directories	Turning on this check box displays all directories, including subdirectories.
Programs	Selecting this check box shows only executable files with the .EXE, .COM, .PIF, and .BAT extensions; no other files are displayed unless you turn on the check boxes for them, too.
Documents	Check this option to display any file with an extension that's associated with a program in File Manager.
Other Files	Check this box to display any other files that don't fit one of the categories described in this list.
Show Hidden/ System Files	Turn on this check box to show any hidden or system files (or directories) in the directory window; be careful not to delete these files by mistake.

You can use any combination you want. Selecting all the options displays all files. If you want to list (for example) only the directories and executable files in a directory window, you'd select **Directories** and **Programs**. File Manager uses the file display options you specify, no matter which (sub)directory you've selected in the current directory window. If you close that window and reopen it (as when you close a directory window for a floppy disk), the newly opened window adopts the file display options of the last window you worked in, not the options it used before you closed it.

To learn how to create associations in File Manager, see "Select Files" on page 112.

Begin Guided Tour Display Specific Types of Files

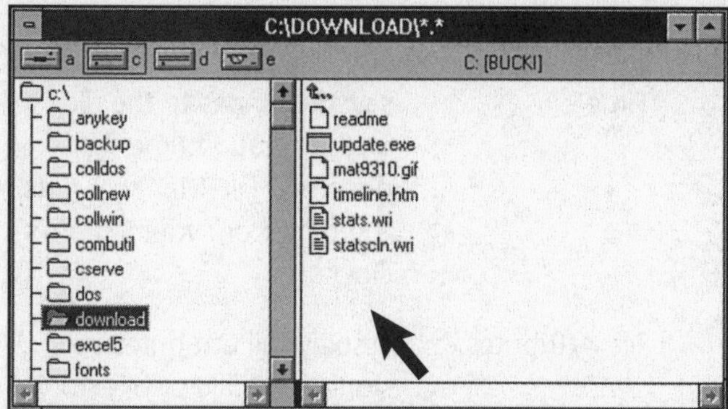

1 Open or select the directory window whose display options you want to change.

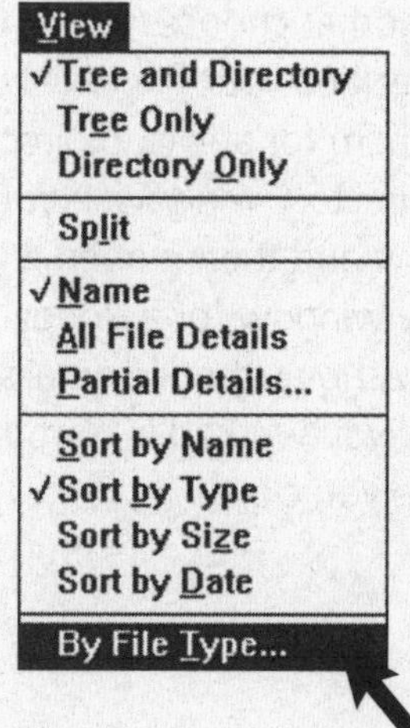

2 Open the **View** menu and click **By File Type**.

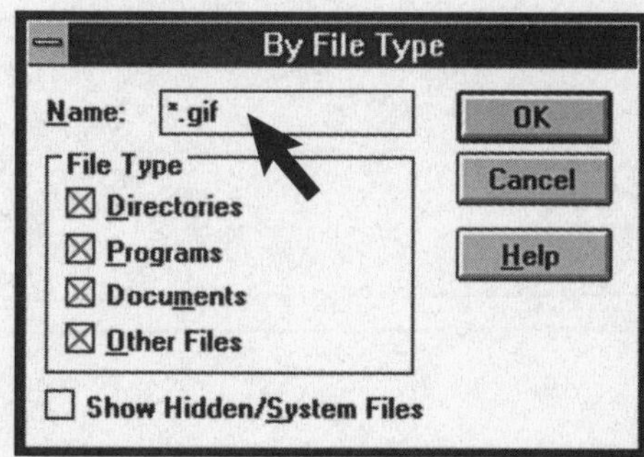

3 **(Optional)** In the By File Type dialog box, start by entering a file specification—using wild cards, if you like—in the **Name** text box. In this example, ***.gif**, displays all files with the .GIF extension. Jump to step 5.

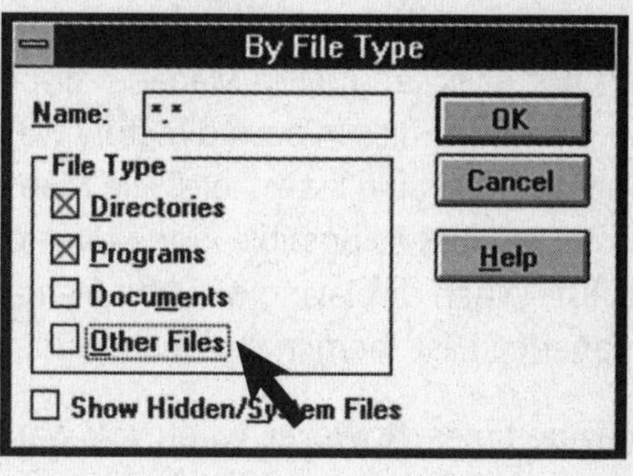

4 To limit the file display, turn additional options on and off by clicking on them. (In this example, we've turned off the display of document files and non-program files.) When you're done making selections, click **OK**.

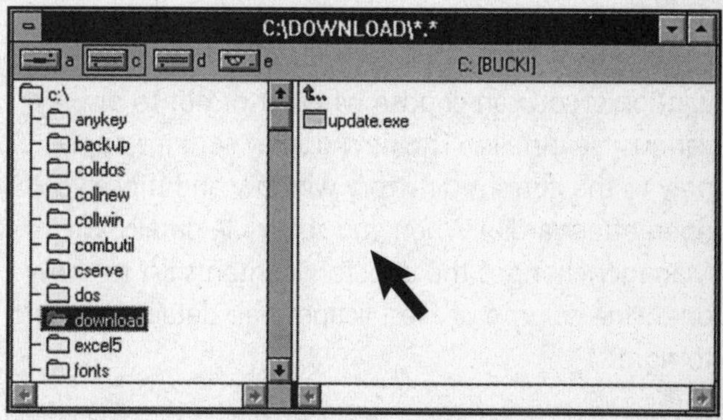

5 File Manager updates the directory contents list displayed in the current directory window.

Show File Details

As it's normally set up, File Manager displays only the names for files in each directory window you open. This clean, simple list enables File Manager to display as many files as possible in the directory contents list. When displaying only the file names, File Manager can list them in multiple columns.

There may be times, however, when you want to know more about a particular file. Is it more recent than another one with a similar name? Is it small enough to fit in the space you have left on a floppy disk?

File Manager does let you display more details about the files listed in the current directory window. You can display different levels of file details in different windows; you can choose whether or not to display various file details. (The new display settings apply only to the current directory window and those you open afterwards.) When you show file details, File Manager changes the directory contents list to show one wide column of files, listing their details from left to right:

Size	Gives the size of each file in bytes. No sizes are listed for directories.
Last Modification Date	Lists the date you last saved changes to the file, or the creation date for a directory; File Manager gets the date from your system's clock.
Last Modification Time	Lists the time of day you last saved changes to the file, or the creation time for a directory; File Manager gets the time from your system's clock.
File Attributes	Displays all attributes assigned to a file or directory.

You can use the display options in any combination you want. You'll need, however, to use one of two commands from the View menu: one displays all the details, and the other chooses which details to display. Once you've specified your file detail options, File Manager uses them for any (sub)directory you select in the current directory window. If you close that directory window and then reopen it (as when you close a directory window for a floppy disk), the newly opened window shows the file details specified for the last window you worked in, not the details it displayed before you closed it.

Begin Guided Tour Display All File Details

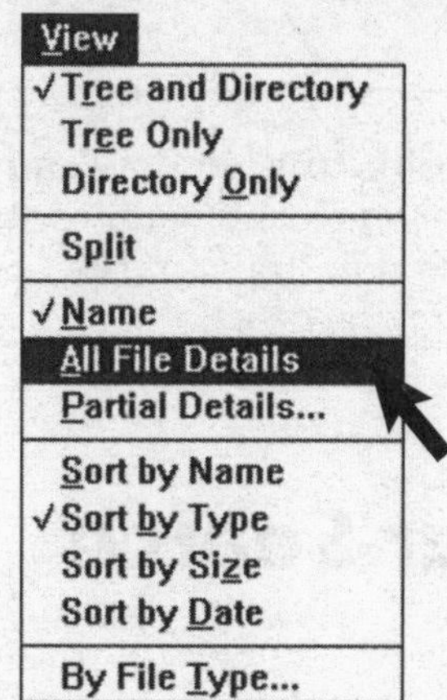

1 Open or select the directory window whose display of file details you want to change. Open the **View** menu and click **All File Details**.

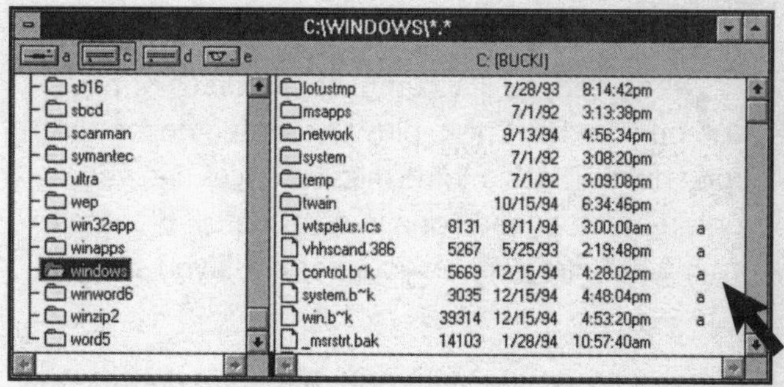

2 File Manager lists the files in one long column, with the size, last modification date, last modification time, and attributes listed to the right of each file name.

Begin Guided Tour Select the Details to Show

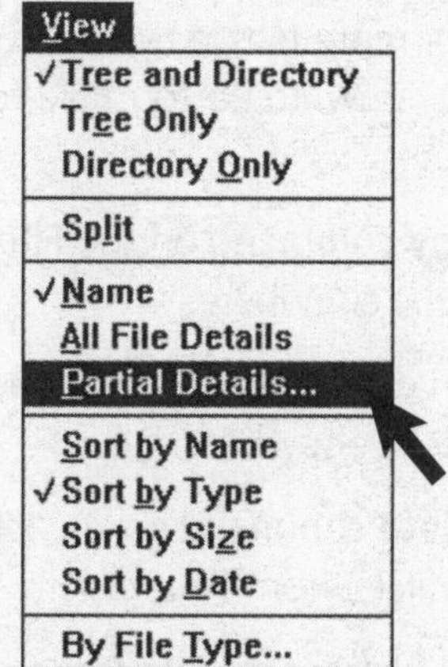

1 Open or select the directory window whose display of file details you want to change. Open the **View** menu and click **Partial Details**.

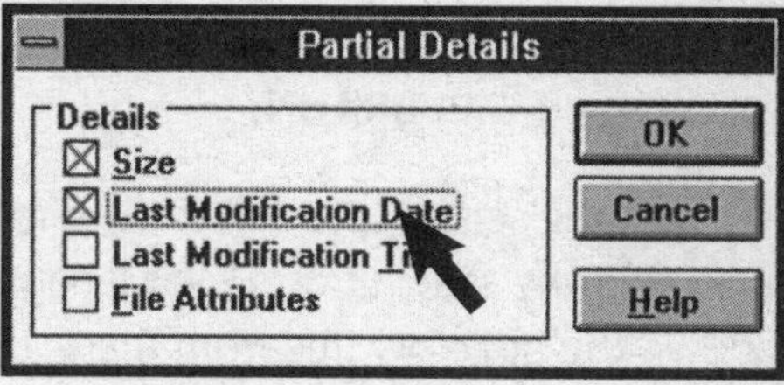

2 Click the check boxes for the details you want to display (if necessary, deselect the others). In this case, File Manager will show only each file's size and last modification date. When you're done making selections, click **OK**.

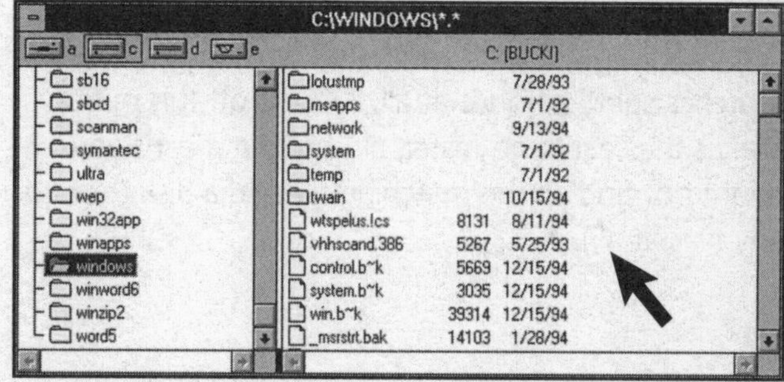

3 File Manager adjusts the display as you specified, displaying only the details you wanted; they appear to the right of each file's name.

Search for Files

Over time, you'll accumulate hundreds of files on your hard disk, plus uncounted dozens on floppy disks. That's a lot of files; chances are, you won't remember each one in great detail. It's easy to forget what directory on your hard disk you saved a file to.

File Manager releases you from the burden of remembering where every file is; it enables you to search for files. You can use File Manager's search capability to:

- **Search for a directory.** To do so, you specify the directory's name.
- **Search for a single file.** In this case, you specify the exact file name.
- **Search for files with similar name characteristics.** Using wild card characters, you can have File Manager find files with similar names. For example, enter ***.txt** to find all files with the **.TXT** file name extension, or **braun*.*** to find all files beginning with **BRAUN**.

Before you start the search, you select the directory you want to start the search from; File Manager searches down the directory tree from there. If you want to search an entire disk, for example, start the search from the root directory. If you start the search from another directory, such as \WINDOWS, File Manager searches only the \WINDOWS directory and its subdirectories, ignoring what's on the rest of the hard disk.

Also, you can determine whether or not File Manager searches subdirectories at all. Turning off this option makes the search go faster, although it means you might not find all the matching files on a disk (or find any files at all).

If you open a directory window and select the directory from which you want to start your search, you can skip step 4 of the *Guided Tour*.

Use Your Search Results

After you perform a search, File Manager displays a Search Results window, which lists the file(s) matching the criteria for your search. This window isn't just for show. You can perform certain file operations within it, which could make it unnecessary to open a new directory window for a file that's been found. Here are the things you can do with file(s) in the Search Results window:

- Select one or more files, as you would in any other window, to perform file-related operations.
- Use the **Copy** command on the **File** menu to copy the file(s) elsewhere.
- Use the **Move** command on the **File** menu to move the file(s) elsewhere.
- Use the **Delete** command on the **File** menu to remove the file(s) from your disk.
- Rename the file(s) using **File Rename**.
- View file details using the **...Details** commands on the **View** menu.

Begin Guided Tour Look for Files

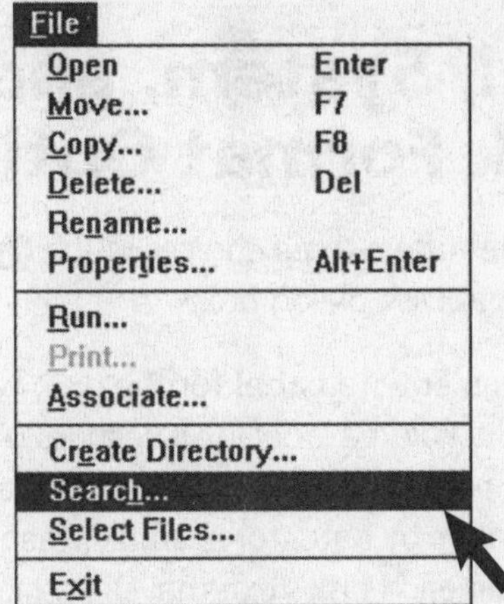

1 In File Manager, open the **File** menu and click **Search**.

2 In the **Search For** text box, enter the name of the file or directory (or the file specification with wild cards for a group of files) you want to search for.

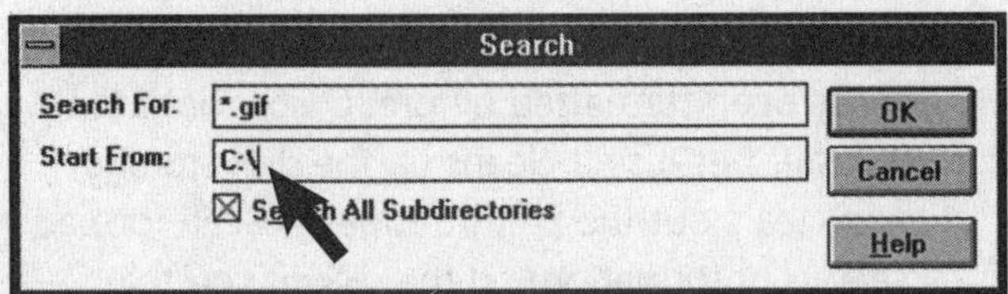

3 Edit the **Start From** text box to indicate what directory to start the search from. Usually you'll want to enter a drive letter plus a colon, and then a backslash, to select a disk's root directory.

4 **(Optional)** If you want to prevent a subdirectory search (which speeds up the search), deselect the **Search All Subdirectories** check box.

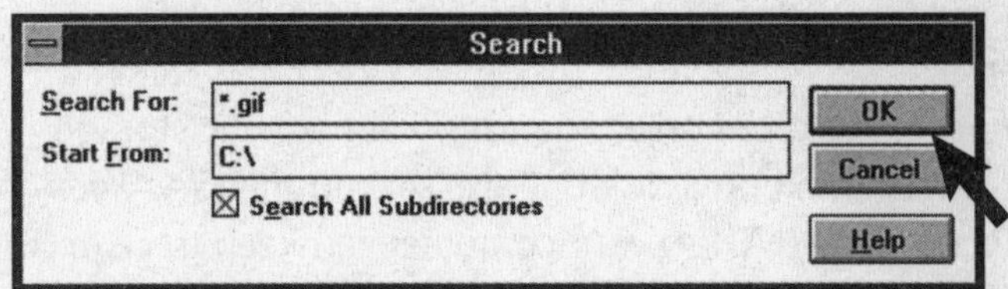

5 Click **OK** to start the search.

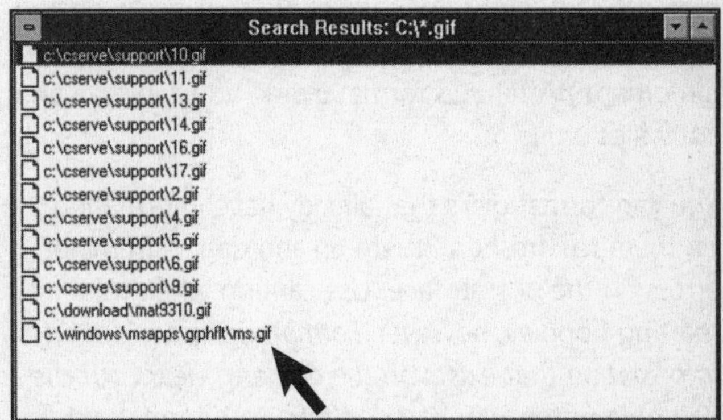

6 File Manager searches the disk from the directory you specified, displaying the Search Results in a new window. You can work with the files from this window, and then close it when you want.

Format Disks

You'll recall from the task called "Understand Disks and Drives" (on page 46) that all disks are covered with a magnetic material. Your computer's disk drive gives an "on" or "off" state to tiny pieces of this material to create readable characters of information. To enable your drive to handle such a delicate operation, the magnetic material needs to be precisely arranged on the disk surface. *Formatting* is the process of arranging the magnetic material on the disk so it can receive information.

Formatting not only organizes the magnetic storage information on a disk but also sets up the *File Allocation Table* (FAT) so your computer can keep track of what parts of what files are stored on specific parts of the disk. (For more on the FAT, see "Understand Files" on page 51.) Each disk has a specific capacity of storage space based on the density of the magnetic material. Different floppy drives are specifically geared to handle disks of a particular density. (More on this in a moment.) After you format a disk, you can save and copy files on it.

You can format disks that already have information on them to "freshen" them up and deal with minor errors on the disk surface. Use caution when reformatting floppies, however. *Formatting wipes out any information that exists on the disk and clears out the contents of the FAT*. You don't want to format a disk that holds data you need.

File Manager lets you format any floppy disk that matches the size and capacity of your floppy disk drive. It also enables you to set a few other disk options.

Because formatting is a tedious operation, you can buy preformatted disks. If you don't want to spend a few extra cents for this convenience, you can format your own disks.

Label, System, and Quick Format Options

File Manager offers three choices in the **Options** area of the Format Disk dialog box.

You can enter a **Label** for the disk, which is also called a *volume label* in DOS lingo. (A label is just a name for the disk. You may want to label your disks by date, for example, then add the date on each disk's external sticky label to keep them organized. Some backup programs automatically label your backup disks so the backup program knows when it's getting the disk it needs.) Your label can have up to 11 characters, and may *not* include Tabs or these characters:

* / \ | . , ; : + = [ ] ( ) & ^ < > "

You can select **Make System Disk** so File Manager formats the disk and copies system startup files to the disk, making it a *bootable* floppy disk. That is, if you insert the disk in drive A and start your computer, it reads the floppy for startup information.

You can perform a **Quick Format** on a disk that's been formatted before. Quick formatting is faster because it cleans up the disk storage and clears out the FAT, but doesn't scan for bad sectors (information) on the disk. If you think a disk has bad sectors, perform a full format.

If you've already formatted a floppy disk and just want to label it or copy system files to it, insert the disk in drive A, and then select **Label Disk** or **Make System Disk** from the **Disk** menu.

Name That Capacity

You may have noticed that your floppy disks or disk labels have "HD" or "DD" or something similar on them. These hieroglyphics refer to the disk's *density* (capacity), which is as important as the floppy's size. Disks of differing capacity and size combinations hold differing amounts of data. (See "Insert and Remove Floppy Disks" on page 31 to learn more about different floppy disk capacities.)

The disk's capacity depends on how efficient its magnetic storage material is. High-density (HD) disks hold more data than double-density (DD) disks of the same size. Older disk drives can only work with DD disks. Computers built in the last few years have high-density floppy disk drives which can work with both HD and DD disks of the right size. If your computer can't read a high-density floppy, it may have a double-density floppy disk drive. Check the box your disks came in to ensure your drive can handle them.

One caution—unless you tell File Manager otherwise, it will try to format a DD disk as high-density. If you format a disk this way, it might work OK for a while, but eventually it'll cause you to lose data. The moral is to pay attention and format DD disks as DD disks, and HD disks as HD disks.

Formatting a DD disk as HD slows down the formatting process drastically toward the end, which may clue you in that you've specified the wrong disk capacity for formatting.

Floppy Disk Capacities

Disk Size	*Type*	*Capacity*
3.5-inch	DSDD, double-sided double-density	720K
3.5-inch	DSHD, double-sided high-density	1.44M
5.25-inch	DSDD, double-sided double-density	360K
5.25-inch	DSHD, double-sided high-density	1.2M

Begin Guided Tour Format a Disk in Windows

1 If you're formatting a disk you've used before, double-check to make sure you've copied any files you might need from that disk. Insert the floppy disk in the appropriate drive.

2 In File Manager, open the **Disk** menu and click **Format Disk**.

3 In the Format Disk dialog box, use the **Disk In** choice to specify the drive you're using to format your floppy.

(continues)

Guided Tour Format a Disk in Windows

(continued)

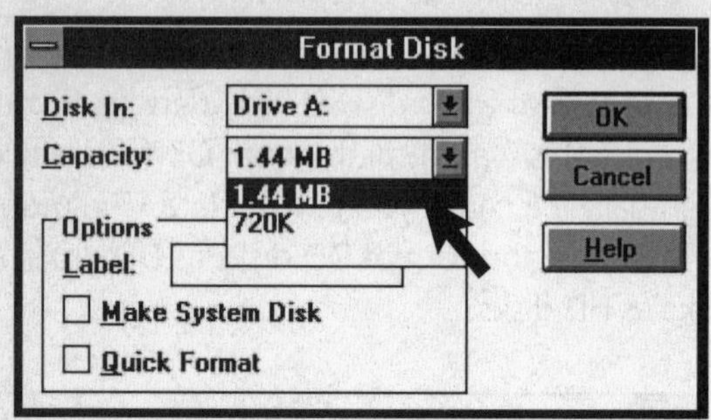

4 Use the **Capacity** list to specify the correct capacity of the floppy disk you're formatting.

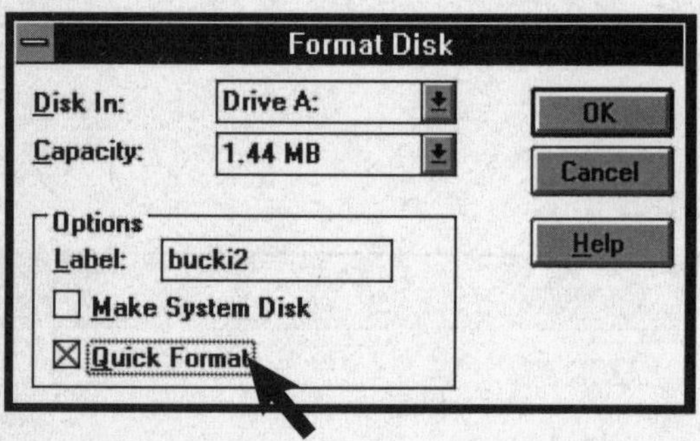

5 Specify any formatting options you desire, and then click **OK** to begin the format.

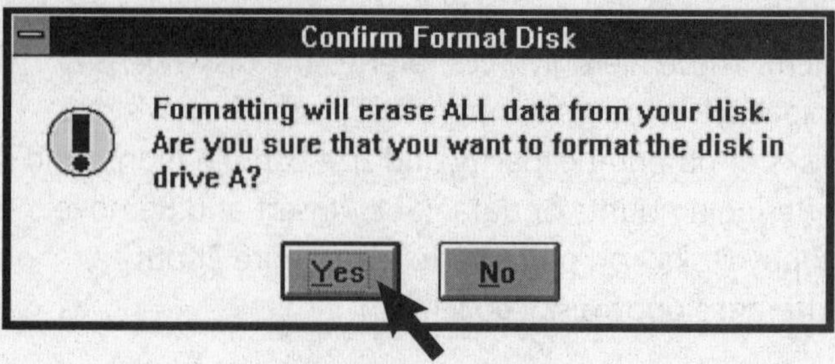

6 Click **Yes** when File Manager asks you to confirm the format.

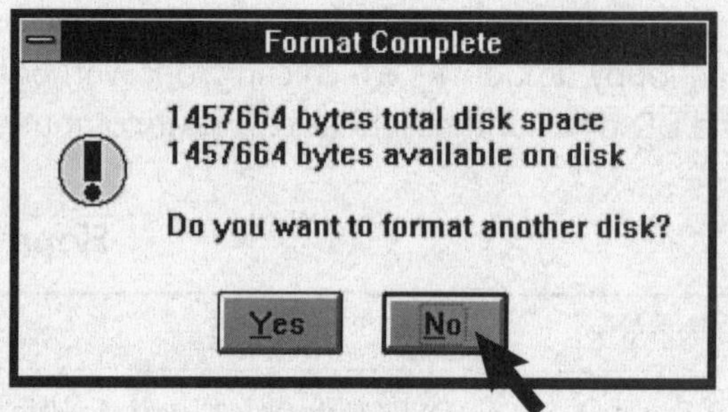

7 When it's finished formatting the disk, File Manager displays the Format Complete dialog box. If you want to format another, click **Yes**, remove the disk you've just formatted from the drive, and repeat steps 1–6. Otherwise, click **No**.

HOW TO...

Work in Windows 95

In an attempt to make your PC as easy to use (yet more powerful) than a Macintosh, Microsoft Corporation has recently developed a new version of Windows. Named Windows 95, this new and improved Windows is ushering in a new era of computing that makes it easier to run programs, manage your PC, and do your work.

Windows 95 hasn't completely displaced the Windows 3.1 and 3.11 features that made those operating systems easy to use. The Windows 95 screen still makes use of windows, icons, and your mouse to help you point and click your way to success. However, Windows 95 has improved on those basic features and has added several new features that can help you take control of your computer and improve its efficiency.

What You Will Find in This Section

Start and Shut Down Windows 95 150

Understand the New Look of Windows 154

Start Programs with the Start Button 157

Switch Between Running Programs 159

Enter Commands in Windows 95 161

Get On-Screen Help 163

Install New Programs 168

Go to the DOS Prompt 172

Manage Disks, Folders, and Files 173

Select Files and Folders 177

Copy or Move Files and Folders 179

Delete and Restore Files and Folders 182

Rename Files or Folders 185

Create New Folders 187

Save Time with Shortcuts 188

Change an Object's Properties 190

Use Built-in Windows Programs 192

Control Your Printer 195

Change the Video Display Properties 201

Take Control of Your Keyboard and Mouse 207

Start and Shut Down Windows 95

Before you can do anything in Windows 95, you have to turn on your computer. Unlike Windows 3.11, Windows 95 does not require that you enter the WIN command, because Windows 95 takes complete control of your PC. When you turn on your computer, Windows 95 starts automatically and displays the Windows Desktop, which you can use to run programs and manage your disks, folders (directories), and files.

And when you're done working in Windows 95, you don't have to exit to the ugly DOS prompt before shutting down your PC. You simply click the **Start** button, click **Shut Down**, confirm by clicking on **Yes**, and then wait until Windows says you can now safely shut down your PC.

By completely hiding DOS behind the scenes, Windows 95 is making the statement that your PC is no longer separate from the work you're trying to accomplish. You turn on your computer and start working.

This chapter assumes that you know how to use a mouse and perform basic Windows 3.11 operations. To learn more about basic mouse moves, how to open and close menus, and enter commands in dialog boxes, see "Get Around in Windows 3.11 Programs," page 57.

Start Windows 95 in Safe Mode

If you install a new program or a hardware device (such as a new video card), and you have problems starting Windows 95, you can start it in *safe mode*. When Windows starts in safe mode, it runs with a plain-vanilla setup that's almost sure to prod Windows into action. In safe mode, Windows 95 will not load any fancy display programs, and you won't be able to use your CD-ROM drive or printer. The purpose of safe mode is to get Windows up and running so you can correct any problems that are preventing it from starting in its usual way. Here's what you do to start Windows 95 in safe mode:

1. Turn on your monitor and then your system unit.
2. Wait until you see the message "Starting Windows 95," and then press and release the **F8** key. A list of startup options appears.
3. Press **3** to select safe mode, and then press **Enter**. Windows starts in safe mode, and a dialog box appears telling you that.
4. Click the **OK** button to close the dialog box. The Welcome to Windows 95 screen appears.

To *restart* Windows in safe mode, select **Shut Down** from the **Start** menu, click **Restart the computer?**, and click **Yes**. When you see the Starting Windows 95 message, press and release the **F8** key.

Begin Guided Tour Start Windows 95

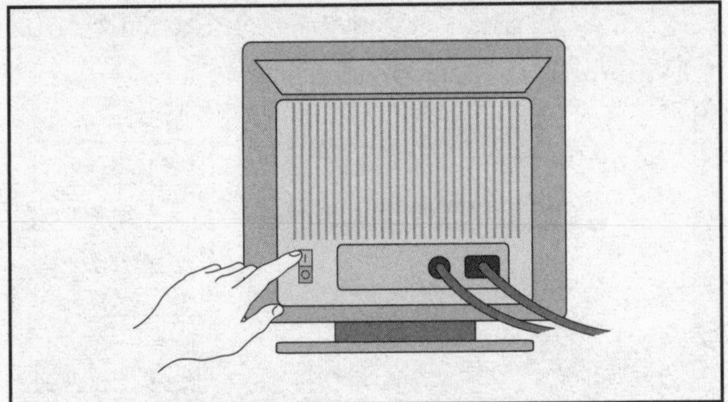

1 Flip the power switch on your monitor or press the power button to turn it on. (By turning the monitor on first, you prevent any electrical surges from the monitor startup from shooting through your system unit.)

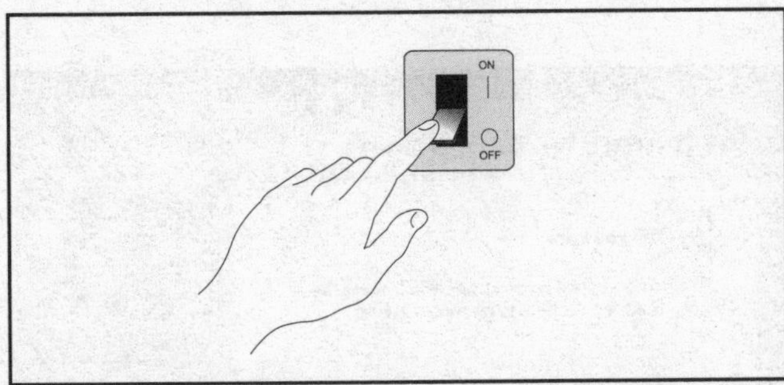

2 Flip the power switch or press the power button on your system unit to turn it on.

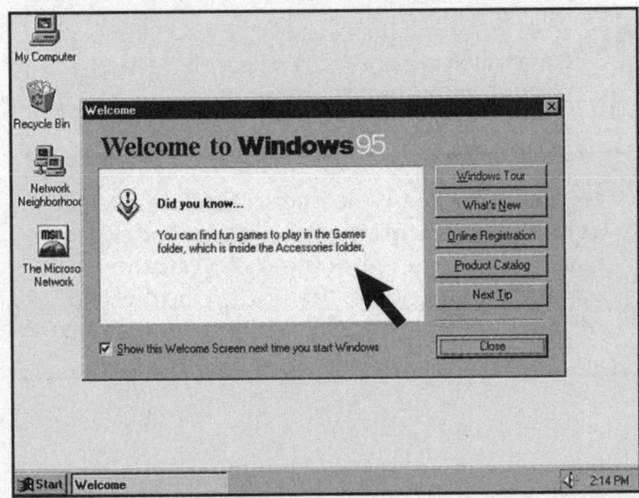

3 Your monitor displays some startup commands, and then the Welcome to Windows 95 dialog box appears, displaying the Tip of the Day. Read the tip.

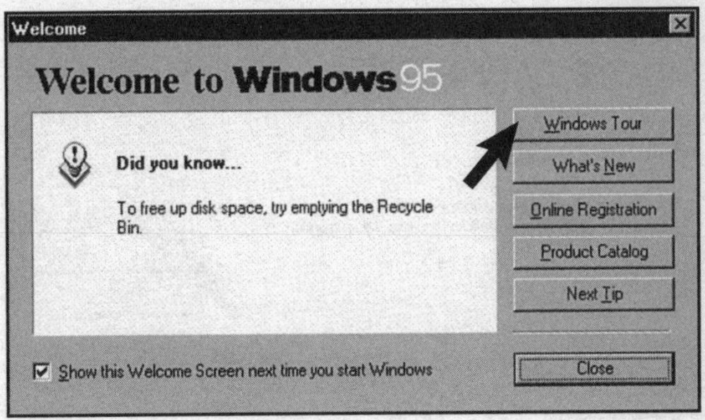

4 The **Windows Tour** option lets you view an interactive demonstration of how to use Windows 95. If this is your first encounter with Windows 95, click this button for a quick overview.

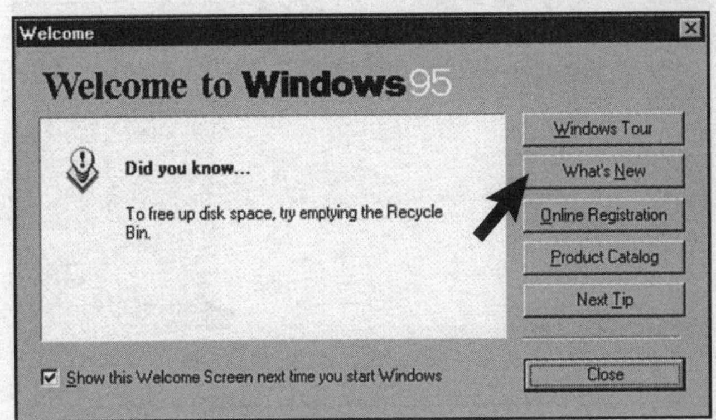

5 The **What's New** option gives you a quick peek at what has changed since Windows 3.11. Click this button to help with the transition from Windows 3.11 to Windows 95.

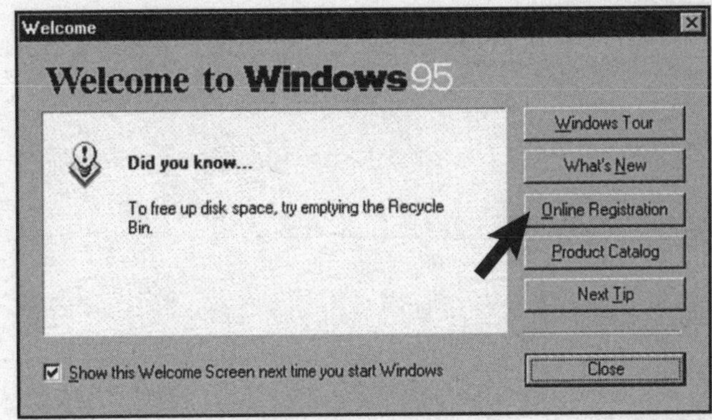

6 If you have a modem, click **Line Registration** to register your copy of Windows 95 over the phone, rather than by mail.

(continues)

Guided Tour Start Windows 95

(continued)

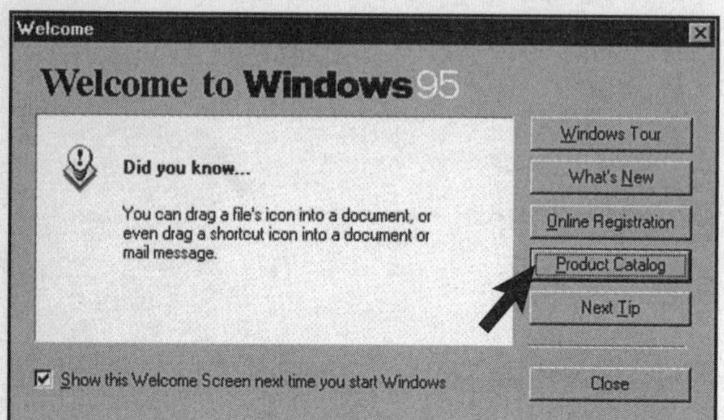

7 If you're interested in other Microsoft software designed especially for use in Windows 95, click the **Product Catalog** button.

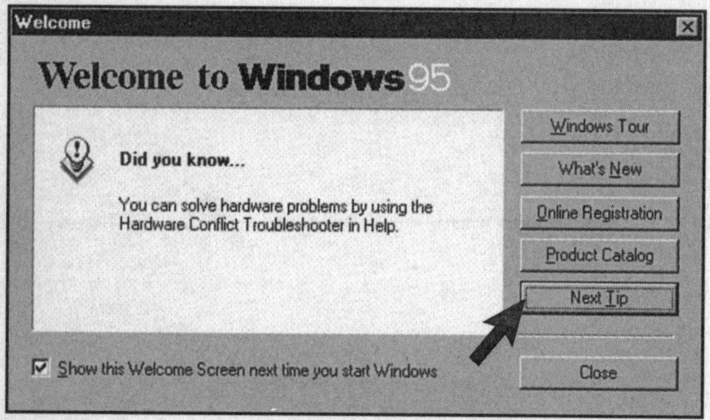

8 The **Next Tip** button displays another **Tip of the Day**. If you're looking for ways to save time with Windows 95, keep clicking and reading for additional tips.

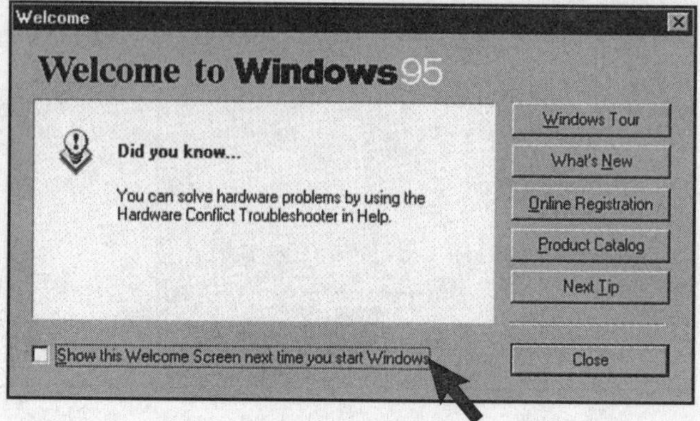

9 The **Show this Welcome Screen next time you start Windows** option displays this dialog box each time you start Windows. To prevent this dialog box from appearing, click this option to turn it off (a check mark appears in the box).

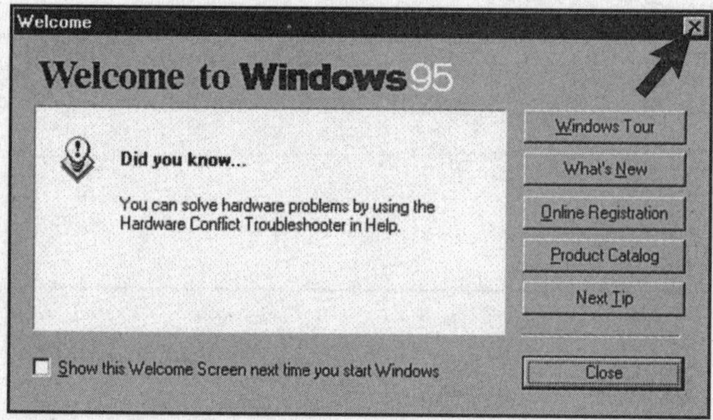

10 When you're ready to start using Windows 95, click the **Close** button to move this dialog box off the screen and start working on the Windows desktop.

You can view the Welcome screen later: select **Help** from the **Start** menu, click the **Index** tab, type **Welcome**, and double-click **Welcome Screen, viewing**. Click the button in the Help window to display the Welcome screen again.

Begin Guided Tour Shut Down Windows 95

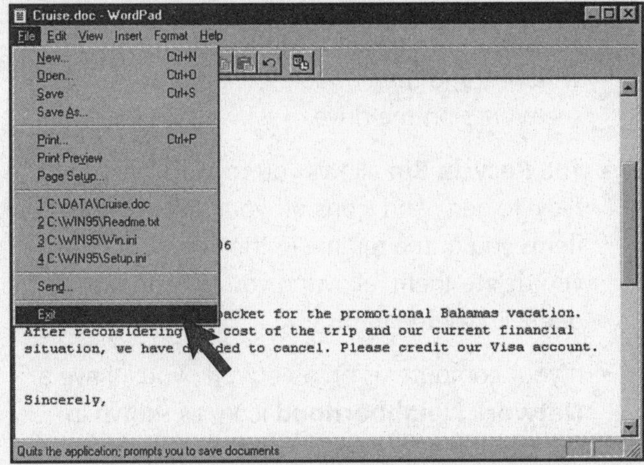

1 When you're done working and you want to turn off your computer, first save any work you've done in your programs, and then exit those programs.

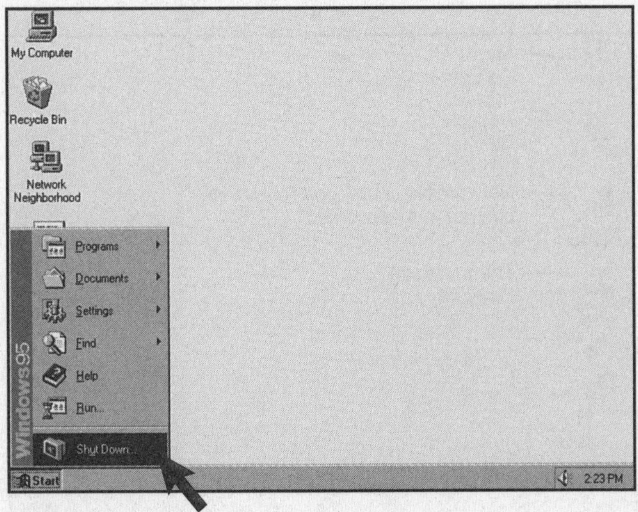

2 Click the **Start** button in the lower left corner of the screen, and then click the **Shut Down** command.

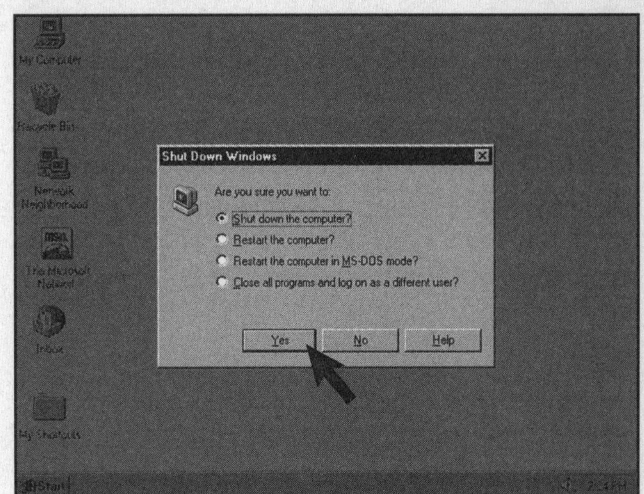

3 The Shut Down Windows dialog box appears, asking you to confirm that you really want to shut down. Make sure **Shut down the computer?** is selected, and then click the **Yes** button.

4 Wait a few seconds until you see the message saying that you can now safely turn off your computer. Then, turn off your computer, as explained in "Shut Down at the End of the Day" on page 30.

Understand the New Look of Windows

If you read the section on Windows 3.11 called "Get Around in Windows 3.11 Programs" on page 57 (or even just flipped through and looked at the pictures), you can see that Windows 95 is a whole new creature. Instead of displaying windows packed with tiny icons, the new Windows desktop contains a few icons, a Start button, a bar at the bottom, and a great expanse of open space.

Before you start running programs and getting into the inner workings of Windows 95, glance around at the desktop and take a look at the various elements that make up this simple screen. Then, take the Guided Tour for some hands-on experience.

- The **desktop** is the "great expanse of space" mentioned earlier. Whenever you run a program, it opens in a window on the desktop. In addition, you can place icons on the desktop for quick access to the programs you use most often.
- The **Start** button opens a menu that lets you run your Windows programs, shut down your computer, go out to the DOS prompt, and use the many programs that come with Windows 95.
- The **taskbar** where the Start button is located shows the names of all the programs you're running. You can quickly switch to a program by clicking on its name in the taskbar.
- **My Computer** is a *shortcut* icon that opens a window showing all the disk drives on your computer. Double-click this icon to open its window, and then double-click a drive icon to see what's on the drive.
- The **Recycle Bin** allows you to quickly dump files, folders, and icons off your system. The items you dump remain in the Recycle Bin until you delete them, allowing you to restore accidentally deleted items.
- If your computer is on a network, you'll have a **Network Neighborhood** icon, as shown in the picture. If, during installation, you chose to connect to Microsoft's new online service, you'll have the Microsoft Network icon. However, your desktop may not have these icons.

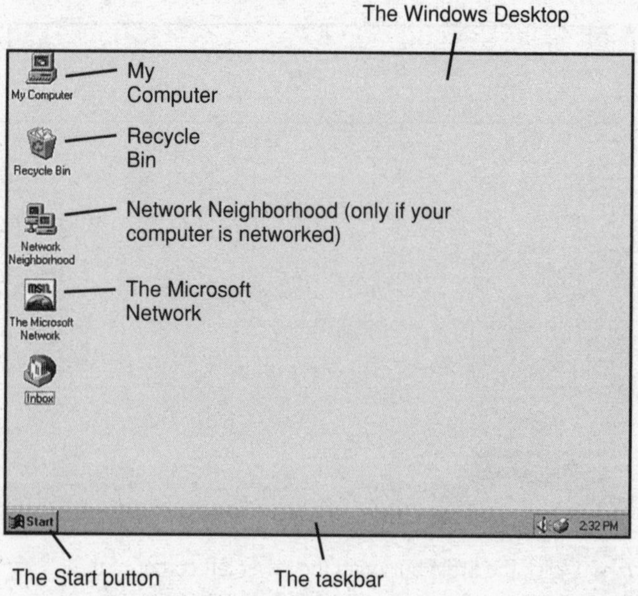

Begin Guided Tour Tour Windows 95

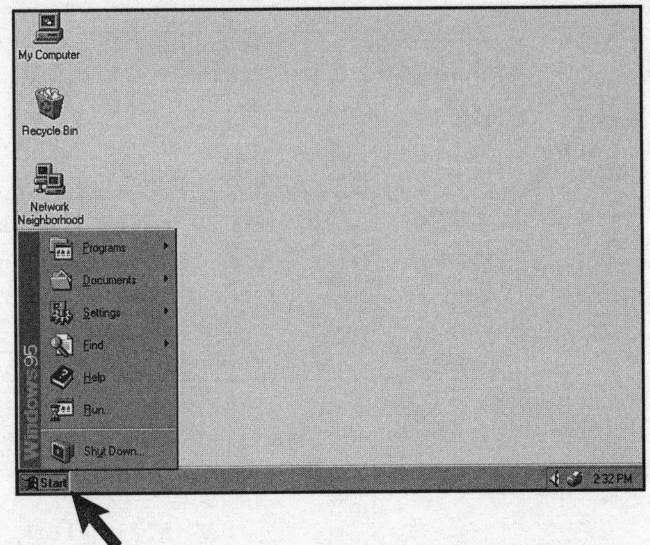

1 In the lower left corner of the Windows screen is a Start button. Click the button for a menu of all the programs you can run.

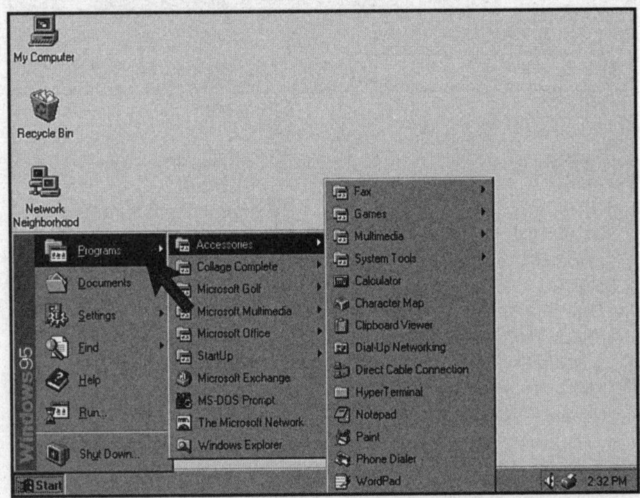

2 Some of the options on the Start menu are followed by an arrow. If you rest the mouse pointer on one of these items, a submenu opens, showing additional items. When you see the program you want, click it to run the program. To learn more about running programs, see "Start Programs with the Start Button" on page 157.

3 When you run a program, it appears in a Window. Its name also appears on the taskbar at the bottom of the screen. You can click the program's name at any time to go to it. See "Switch Between Running Programs" on page 159 for details.

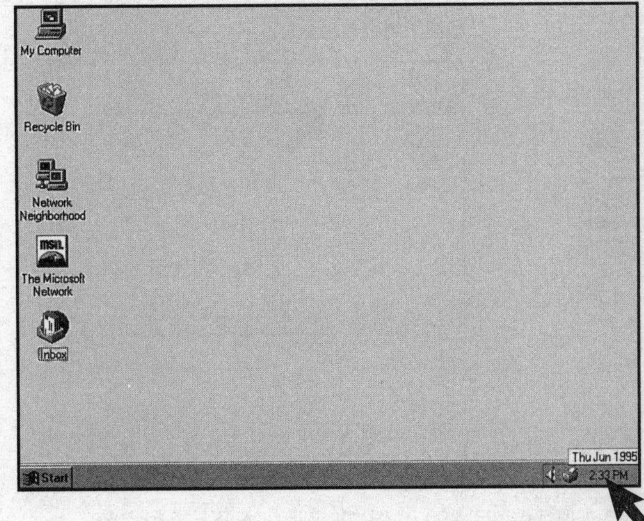

4 On the right end of the taskbar, the time appears. To see today's date, rest the mouse pointer on the time.

(continues)

Guided Tour Tour Windows 95

(continued)

5 In the upper left corner of the Windows desktop is the My Computer icon. Double-click the icon to view a window that shows icons for all the disk drives on your computer. For specifics on using My Computer, see "Manage Disks, Folders, and Files" on page 173.

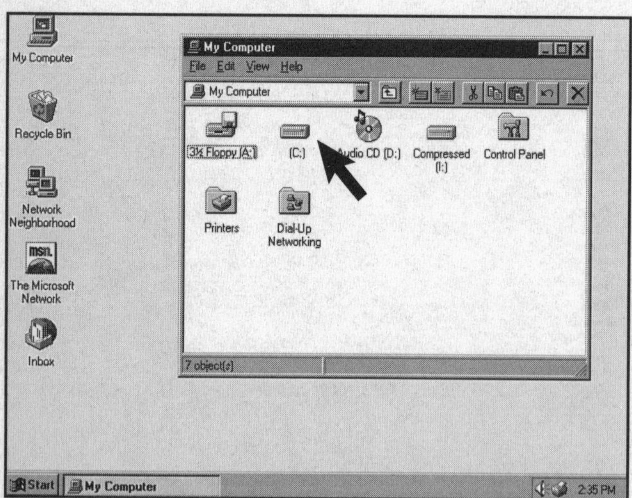

6 To see what's on a disk, double-click its icon to open another window. Each Window shows the files and folders (directories) on the disk.

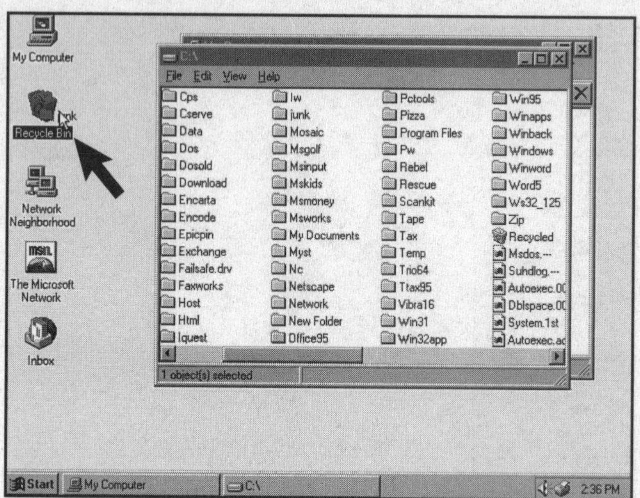

7 The Recycle Bin icon allows you to quickly remove a file, folder, or icon from your computer. Simply drag the icon that you want to remove over the **Recycle Bin** icon, and release the mouse button.

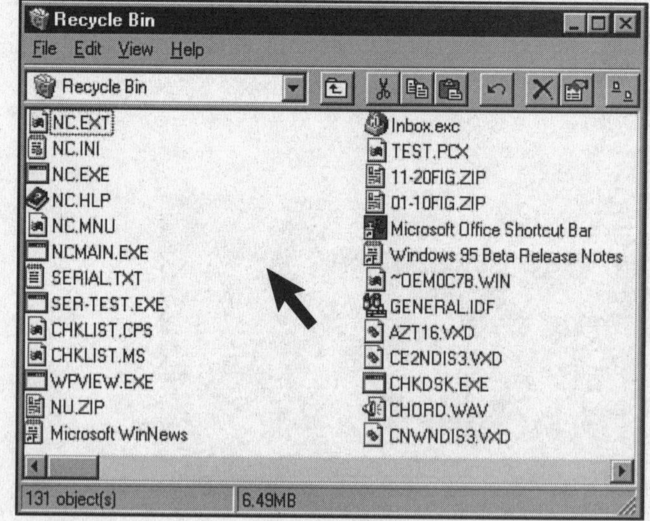

8 To see what's in the Recycle Bin, double-click its icon. A window opens, showing the Recycle Bin's contents and allowing you to restore the items or delete them. See "Delete and Restore Files and Folders" on page 182 for complete instructions.

Start Programs with the Start Button

Unlike Windows 3.11, Windows 95 does not clutter your screen with the Program Manager and with program group windows and program icons. All programs are neatly tucked away in the Start button. To start any program, you click the Start button and then weave your way through a series of menus and submenus by moving your mouse pointer over their names. When you see the program you want, you draw a bead on it with the mouse, and fire (click). The program starts, and you're ready to work.

How do programs get their names listed on the Start menu? Well, assuming you installed the new version of Windows over your old version, or your computer came with Windows 95 installed, the installation program added the program names automatically. Also whenever you install a new program (see "Install New Programs" on page 168), Windows adds the program name to the Start menu or one of its submenus. In addition, all the programs that come as a part of Windows 95 are listed on one of the Start menu's submenus.

To start a program in Windows 95, take the *Guided Tour*. This tour gives you some hands-on experience with using the Start menu to run your programs.

Resize Program Windows

Program and document windows behave nearly the same way in both Windows 3.11 and Windows 95. You can drag a window border to resize the window, or drag its title bar to move it. (See "Size and Arrange Windows" on page 80 for details.) However, you may notice that Windows 95 windows look a little different. Here's a quick rundown of the differences you'll see:

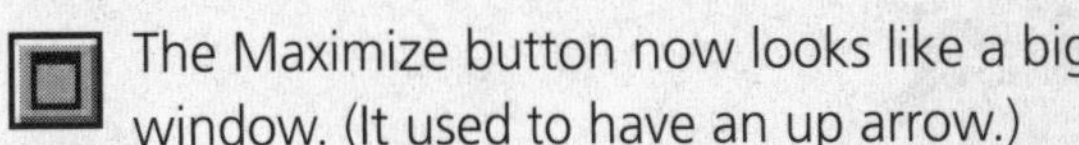

The Maximize button now looks like a big window. (It used to have an up arrow.)

The Minimize button (which used to look like a down arrow) now looks like a pancake, showing that the window will be flattened. Actually, it will disappear, but you'll still see its name in the taskbar.

The Restore button (which used to have a double-headed arrow on it) now has two overlapping windows on it.

The Close button (the button with the X on it) has no counterpart in Windows 3.11. You can now quickly close a window and exit the program by clicking on this button.

The Control-menu box now takes on various forms depending on the program you're running. You can still click this button (in the upper left corner of a window) to display a menu for sizing, moving, and closing the window.

In the lower right corner of each window is a resize area which you can drag to quickly change the size and dimensions of a window.

If the program you want to run is not on the Programs menu or a submenu, you can still run it. Click the **Start** button, and click **Run**. Type the command required to start the program, and then click **OK**.

Begin Guided Tour Start Programs

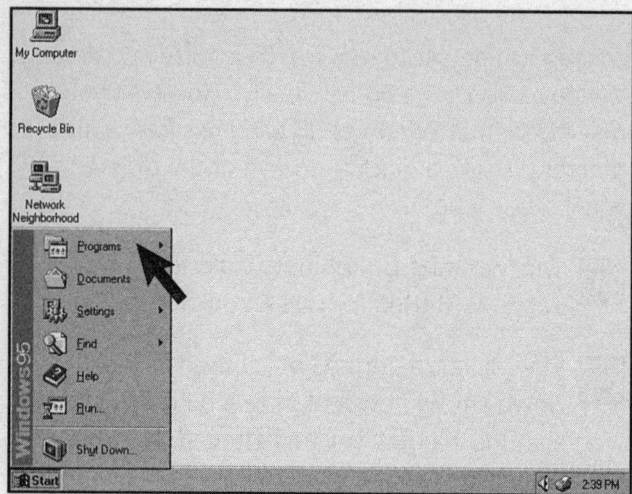

1 Click the **Start** button in the lower left corner of the screen. The Start menu pops up out of the taskbar, providing options for shutting down your computer, changing settings, and more. To run a program, rest the mouse pointer on **Programs** at the top of the Start menu.

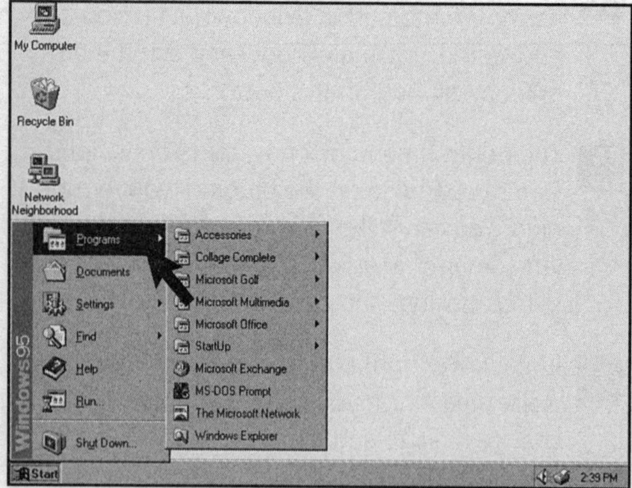

2 The **Programs** submenu shoots out from the Start menu. The items at the bottom of the list are programs you can run. At the top of the list are program groups (you can tell this because each item is followed by an arrow). If you move the mouse pointer over a program group, a submenu appears showing the names of the programs in that group.

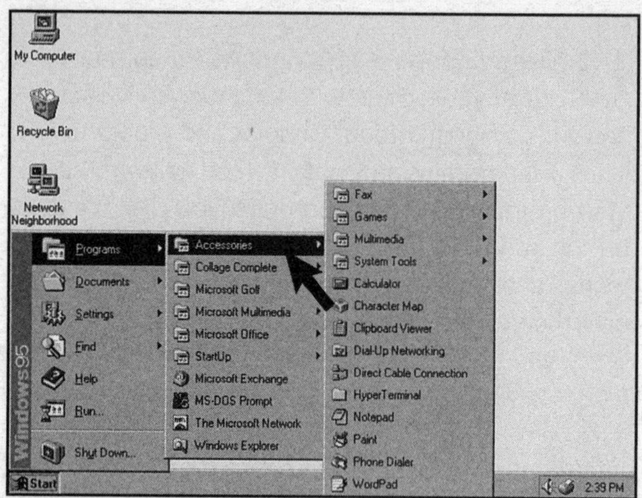

3 Rest the mouse pointer on one of the program groups at the top of the list. Each program group name is followed by an arrow, which indicates that this item opens a submenu. In this figure, the Accessories group is opened, showing the names of the programs that come with Windows 95.

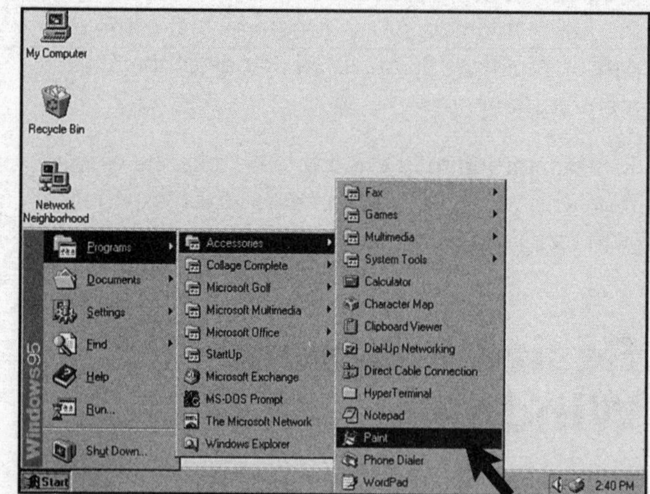

4 To run a program, click it. The program opens in its own window, just as in Windows 3.11, although the window has a slightly different look.

Switch Between Running Programs

As you run programs and open documents, the Windows desktop becomes so cluttered that you can never find what you need. Windows 95 introduces a taskbar to help you quickly dig your way out of the deepest stack of program windows.

Whenever you run a program in Windows 95, its name is added to the taskbar at the bottom of the screen. Whenever you want to return to a program, click the program's name in the taskbar, and the program immediately jumps to the front of the stack.

Other Taskbar Tricks

Notice that the right end of the taskbar displays the current time and a small icon of a speaker (if you have a sound card). If you start printing a document, this area will also include a printer icon. When you see an icon or item in this area of the taskbar, take one of the following steps to control it:

- Rest the mouse pointer on the time display to view the current date.
- Double-click the time to view a dialog box that lets you set the time and date on your computer.
- Double-click the speaker icon to change the volume and balance for your sound card, microphone, and CD-ROM drive.
- If you see a printer icon, you are currently printing one or more documents. To see which documents are printing, double-click the printer icon. For more details, see page 195.

Begin Guided Tour Switch Between Programs

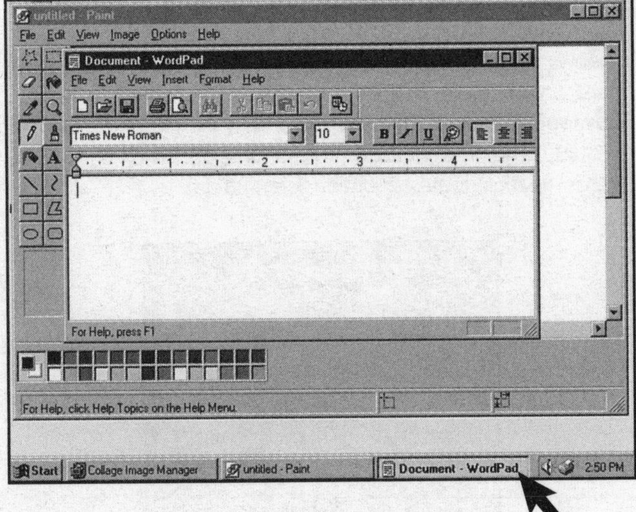

1 Run the programs you want to use. As you run programs, their names are added to the taskbar.

2 To switch to a program, click its name in the taskbar. Whether the program window was minimized or behind a stack of other windows, it is moved to the front of the stack and activated.

(continues)

Guided Tour Switch Between Programs

(continued)

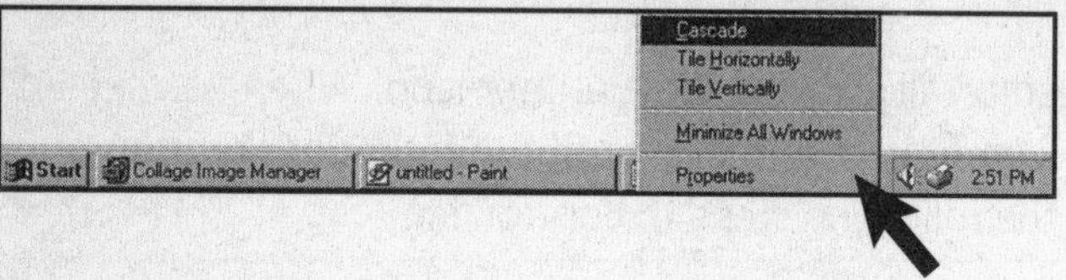

3 You can use the taskbar to quickly arrange open program windows. Right-click a blank area of the taskbar and click **Cascade**, **Tile Horizontally**, **Tile Vertically**, or **Minimize All Windows**.

4 You can move the taskbar to a different place on the desktop. Point to a blank space on the taskbar (not to a program name or the time), hold down the left mouse button, and drag the taskbar to the left, top, right, or bottom of the desktop.

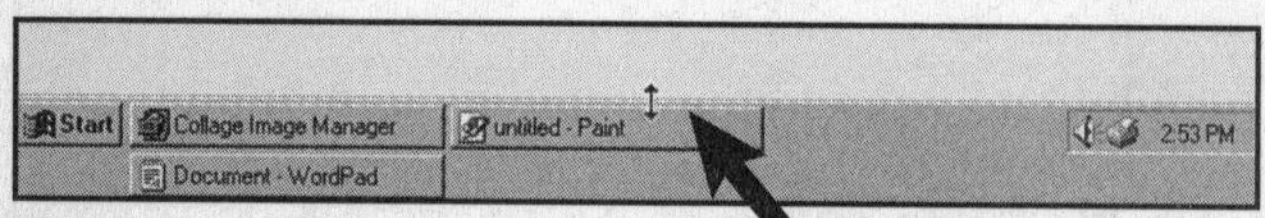

5 You can resize the taskbar to give more room to the program names. Drag an edge of the taskbar up or down to make it fatter or skinnier.

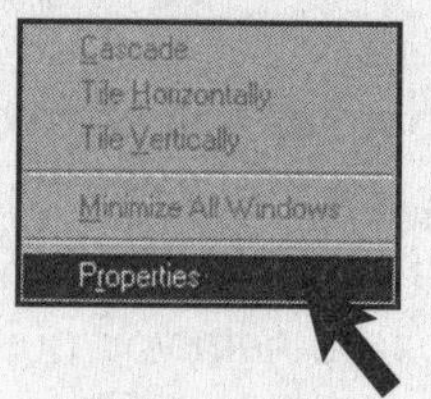

6 You can change other properties of the taskbar, such as hiding the time and keeping the taskbar on top. Right-click a blank area of the taskbar, and click **Properties**.

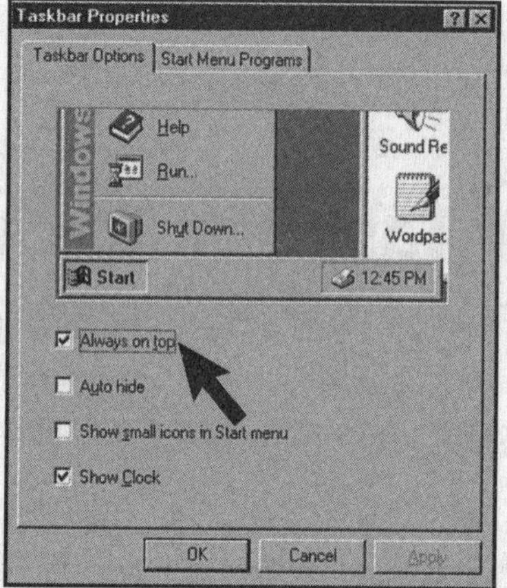

7 You can now change the way the taskbar is displayed. **Always on top** keeps the taskbar in the front of all windows. **Auto hide** shrinks the taskbar, so you have to move the mouse pointer to the bottom of the screen to bring it into view. **Show small icons in Start menu** controls the size of icons on the Start menu. **Show Clock** turns the time display on or off. (A check mark indicates an option is turned on).

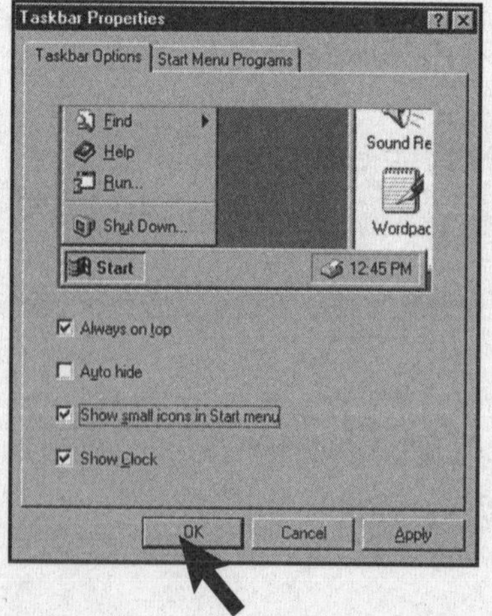

8 Enter your preferences, and click the **OK** button.

Enter Commands in Windows 95

Windows 95 has retained many of the same tools used in Windows 3.11 for entering commands. You'll find the standard menu bars at the top of each window. If you click a command that's followed by a series of dots (...), you'll get a dialog box asking for additional input. And most Windows programs contain toolbars containing buttons that let you bypass the menus.

You will find one new command feature in Windows 95—shortcut menus. If you right-click any object (and even a blank space on the Windows desktop), a menu pops up displaying the options available for the item you selected. You can then click the desired option to view a dialog box that asks for additional input. So, if you ever have a question as to what you can do with a particular object, simply right-click it; you don't have to scan all the menus to find out what's available.

Get Help in Dialog Boxes

Windows 95 dialog boxes don't differ much from the dialog boxes you meet in Windows 3.11. Most dialog boxes have tabs that display sets of related options, and you'll see list boxes, check boxes, option buttons, command buttons, and other standard dialog box features.

However, the new dialog boxes look a little more like windows. In the upper right corner of most dialog boxes, you'll see a Close button (with an X through it) and a question mark button. The question mark button is an ingenious tool for providing information about the options you have. When you click the question mark button, the mouse pointer grows a question mark. When you click an option, a small box appears explaining what the option does.

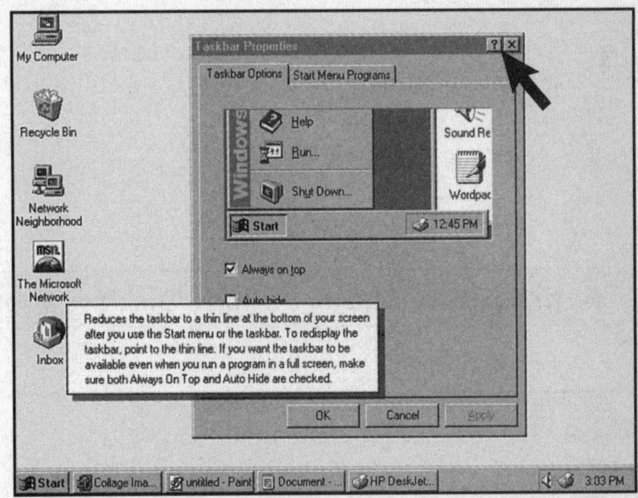

Another way to view information about a dialog box option is to right-click the option and then click **What's This?**.

Begin Guided Tour Enter a Menu Command from a Pull-Down Menu

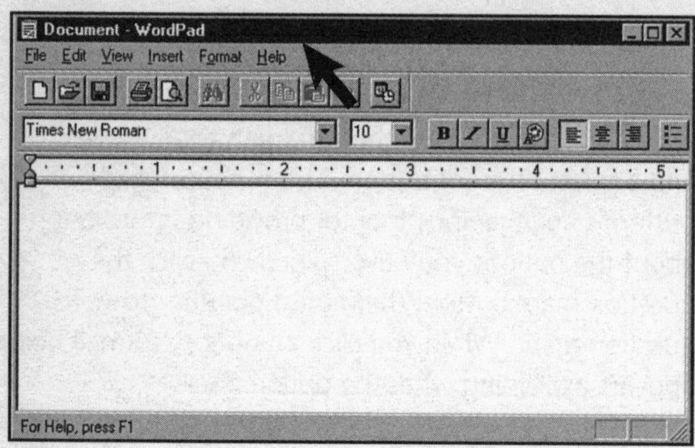

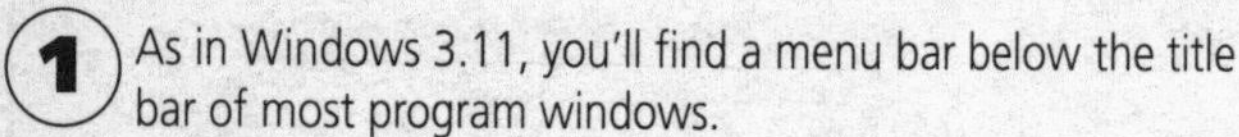

1 As in Windows 3.11, you'll find a menu bar below the title bar of most program windows.

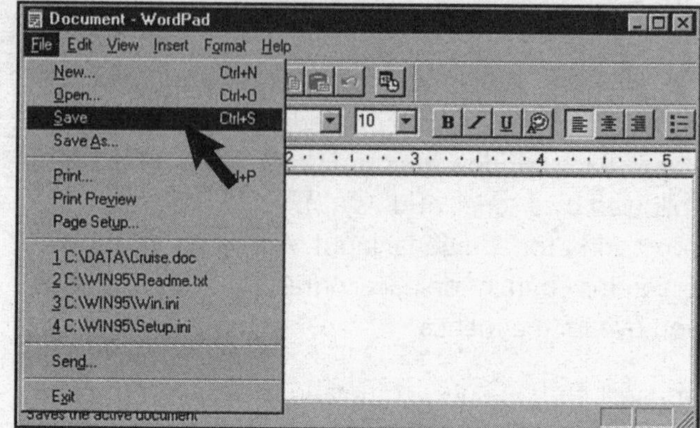

2 Click the name of a menu to open it. As you move the mouse pointer up or down over an option on the menu, the option appears highlighted.

3 To enter a command, click the menu option.

Begin Guided Tour Right-Click for Shortcut Menus

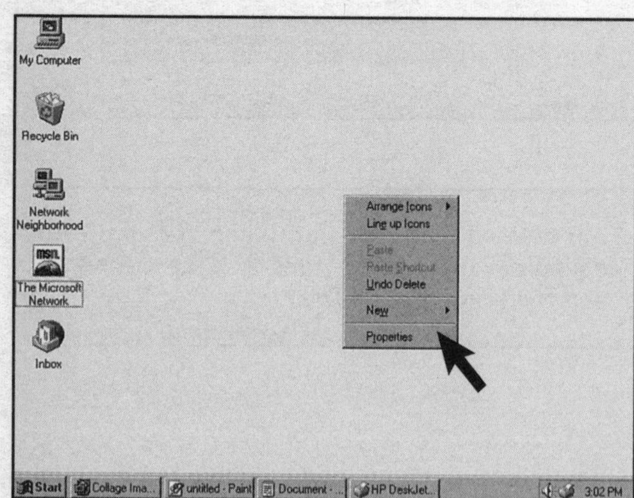

1 To enter a command for an icon, an area of the screen, or any other object, right-click the object. The shortcut menu shown here appears if you right-click a blank area of the Windows desktop.

2 Click the command you want to enter. What happens next depends on the command you selected.

Get On-Screen Help

Have you ever wished you had an experienced Windows tutor sitting next to you, offering helpful comments, tips, and explanations? Windows 95 offers such an aide in the form of its help system. The Windows 95 help system includes step-by-step instructions and animations of the basic tasks you must perform.

You simply open the **Start** menu and click **Help**. A Help window appears, showing a tabs for table of contents of Help topics, a searchable index, and a find feature for searching out specific Help topics. The Contents tab is useful for finding out how to perform a specific task, such as run a program or maintain your computer. Think of Contents as an on-screen book. The Index tab shows an alphabetical listing of topics, tasks, and anything else you might find in a typical index. The index is good if you know what you're looking for. The Find tab gives you a tool for searching for specific information when you're not quite sure what information you need.

Select the type of information you want, and then double-click a topic to learn how to perform any task in Windows. The *Guided Tour* leads you through the process of taking a Windows 95 tour and searching for specific help.

Begin Guided Tour Have Windows Show You How to Perform a Task

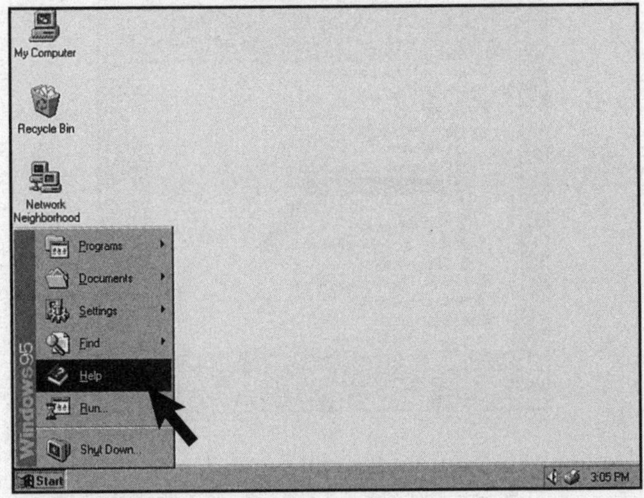

1 No matter which type of help you need, you must open the help system by clicking on the **Start** button and then clicking on **Help**.

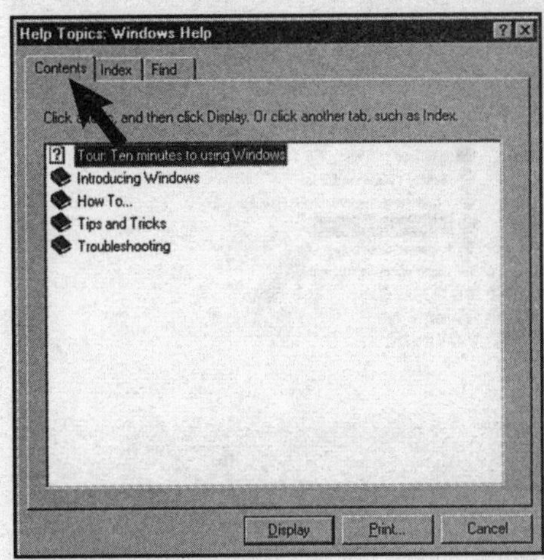

2 Windows displays a dialog box that provides a table of contents list, a searchable index tab, and a tab for finding help topics. If the Contents tab is not in front, click it.

(continues)

Guided Tour Have Windows Show You How to Perform a Task

(continued)

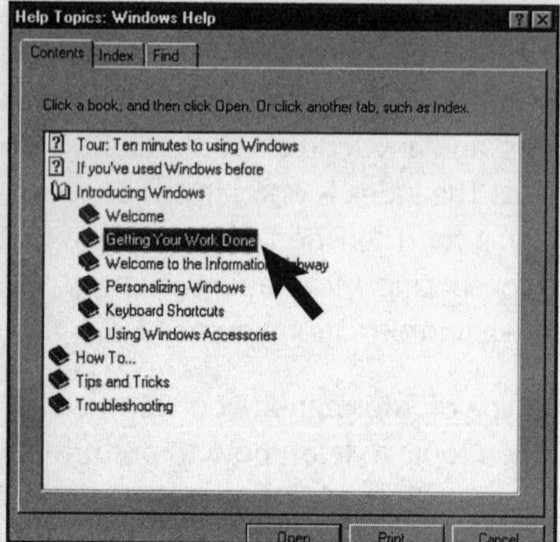

3 The Contents tab lists several "books" full of help topics. You can double-click a book to view the topics in it. In the figure above, I double-clicked on **Introducing Windows** and then on **Getting Your Work Done**.

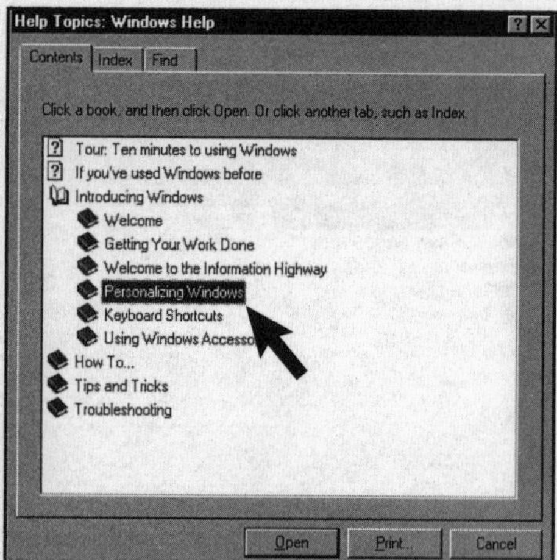

4 When you finally double-click an actual help topic (instead of a book), you usually get a screen that explains the task on the left and shows an animation on the right. Click the Play button at the bottom of the animation screen to start playing it.

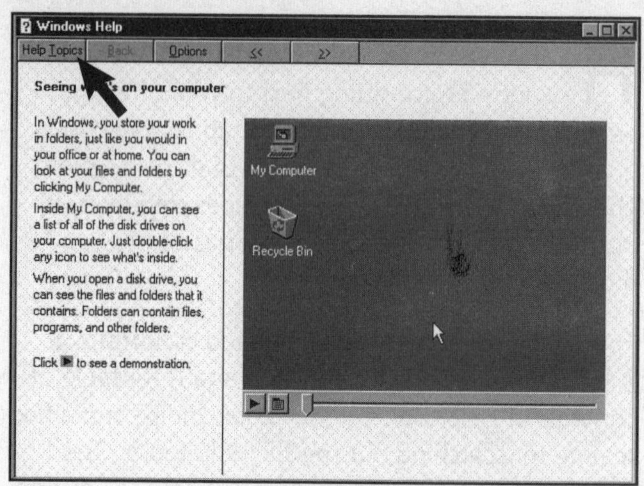

5 When the animation is done playing, it remains on-screen. You can go back to the list of help topics by clicking on the **Help Topics** button at the top of the help window.

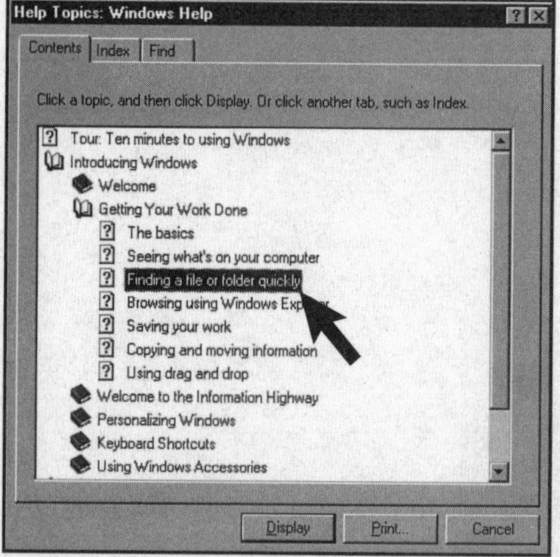

6 You are back at the Contents list. You can now double-click another topic, double-click an open book to close it, or double-click a closed book to see the topics in that book.

Guided Tour Have Windows Show You How to Perform a Task

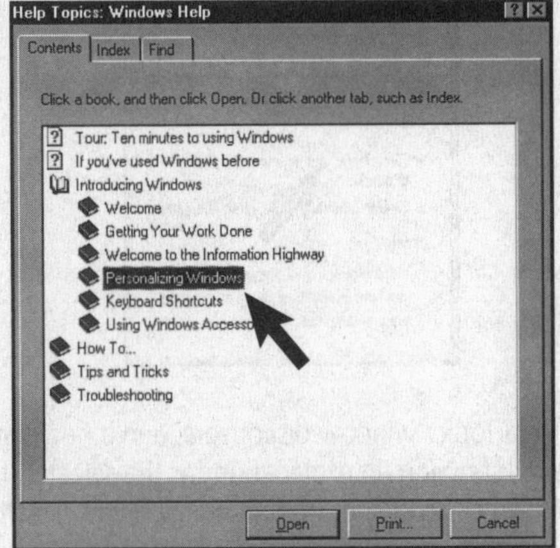

At the top of the Contents list is an icon labeled **Tour: Ten minutes to using Windows.** Double-click this icon to view a multimedia tour that explains the Windows 95 basics. If you do not see this icon, you may not have installed the complete Windows 95 help system.

7 When you are done with the help system, click the Close button (the button with the X) in the upper right corner of the window.

Begin Guided Tour Search the Index for Specific Help

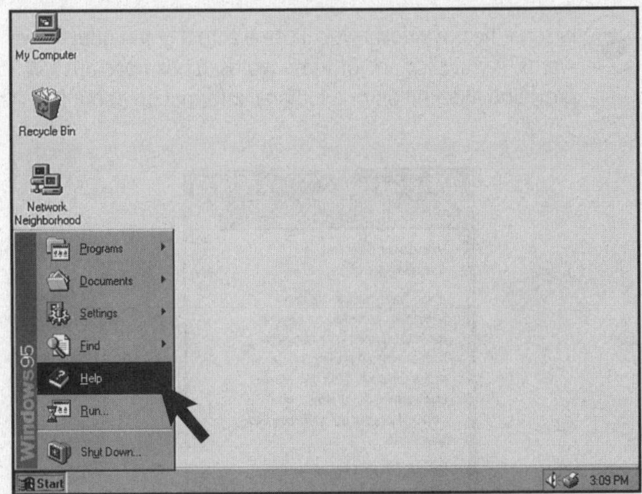

1 To get into the Windows help system, click the **Start** button and click **Help**.

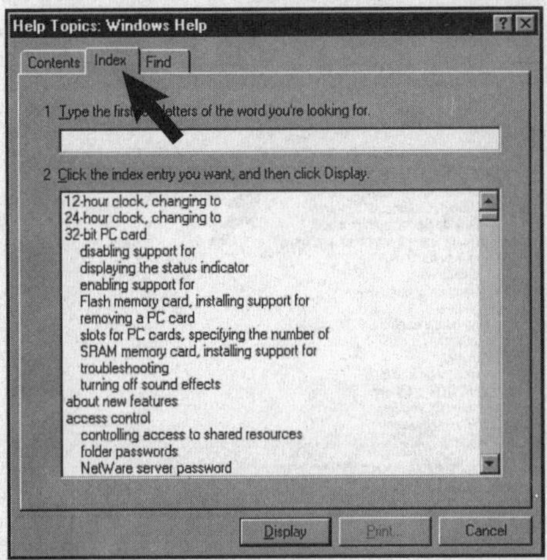

2 Unless you clicked on a different tab, the Contents tab is up front. Click the **Index** tab to display a complete index of entries in the help system.

(continues)

Guided Tour Search the Index for Specific Help

(continued)

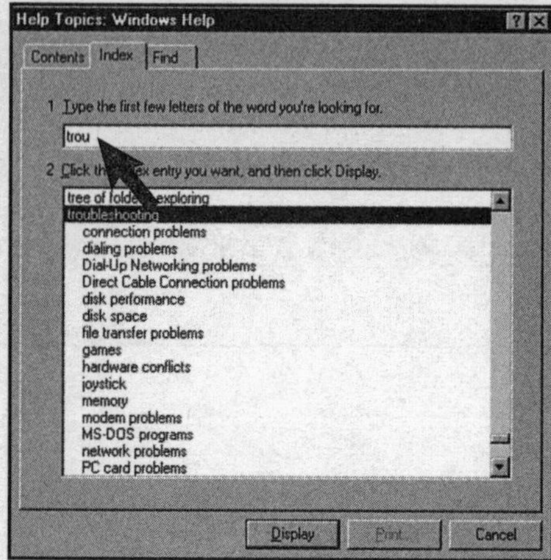

3 The index is set up like the index of a book. You can drag the scroll box to view additional entries, and then click the desired entry, or you can start typing the entry in the text box. As you type, Windows highlights the first index entry that matches what you typed.

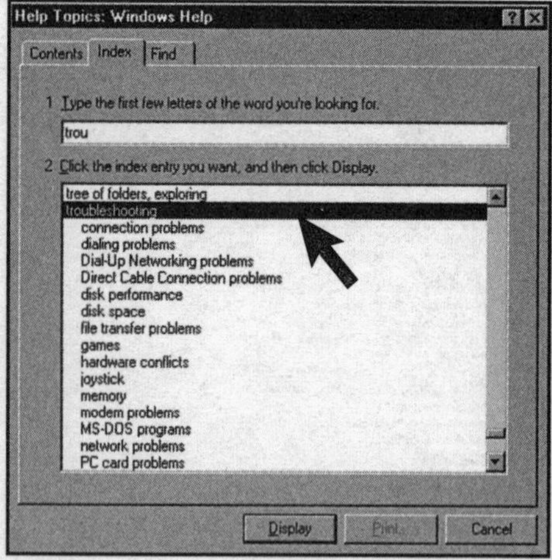

4 Once the desired index entry is highlighted, double-click it, or click the **Display** button at the bottom of the window.

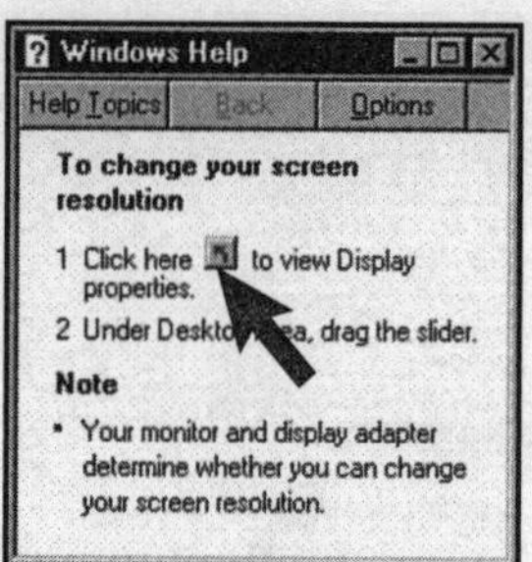

5 The Help Topics window disappears, and a new window appears, showing an explanation for the selected topic. If you see a button like the one shown here, you can click it to start performing the task.

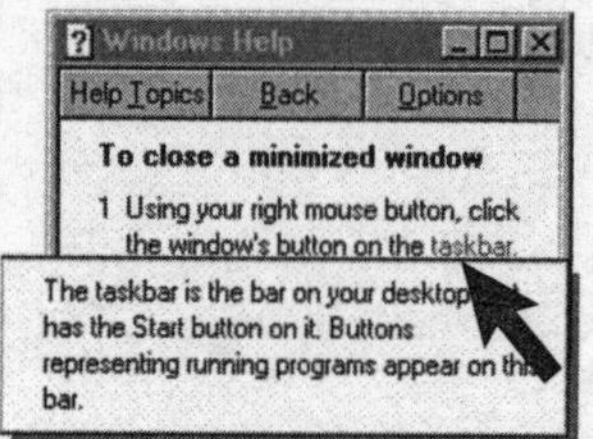

6 In some help windows, you'll come across green underlined words. If you click one of these words, a box pops up providing a definition or additional information about it.

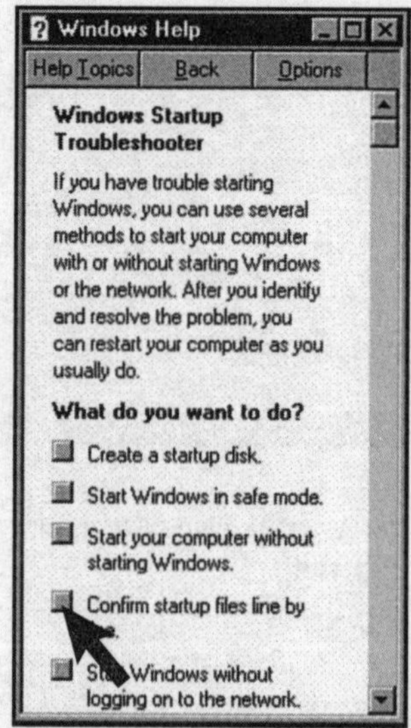

7 At the bottom of many help windows are buttons for obtaining additional help. Click a button to view more information about a topic.

Guided Tour Search the Index for Specific Help

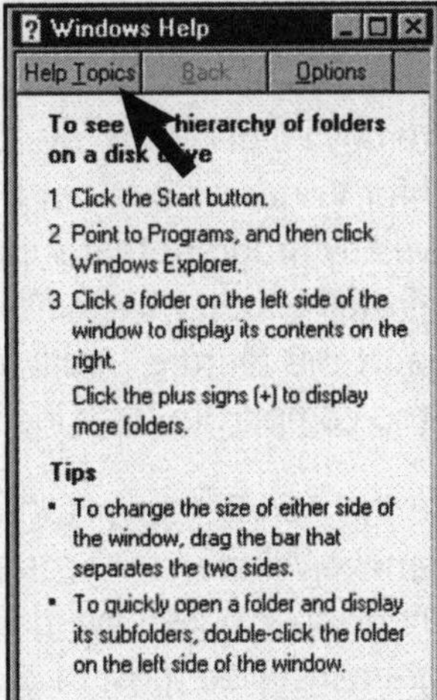

8 You can always get back to the index by clicking on **Help Topics**. To exit the help system, click the Close button in the upper right corner of the window.

The Find tab is similar to the Index tab, though more complex. It allows you to perform a thorough search of help topics. (I've had more luck finding information in the Index.)

Install New Programs

You come home from your local computer store with shopping bags full of new programs and CD-ROM discs, and a desire to get all your new acquisitions up and running in a hurry. In the old days, you usually had to sit down and flip through the documentation to figure out what command you had to enter to start installing the program, and whether you had to enter the command in DOS or Windows.

With Windows 95's Install New Program Wizard, all those concerns are over. You click an icon to add a new program to Windows, and then follow the on-screen instructions. The Wizard leads you step-by-step through the installation process, telling you to insert the necessary disks (or disc), giving you a list of install commands to choose from, and starting the installation program for you.

In addition to helping you install new programs, Windows Add/Remove Programs dialog box lets you remove some Windows 95 programs from your hard disk. It will not remove older Windows programs (those designed for Windows 3.11) or DOS programs, but it will remove any program that supports the Windows 95 uninstall feature. To uninstall programs that do not support this feature, you'll have to use other methods too complex to describe here.

You can also use the Add/Remove Programs dialog box to add or remove Windows 95 components to your system. When you installed Windows 95, the installation program installed most of the commonly used components for you, but to save disk space, it may not have installed some of the more advanced features or features that would consume a lot of disk space. You can remove components that you don't plan on using, or install components that you want to use (assuming you have sufficient space). The *Guided Tour* shows all.

Begin Guided Tour Install a Program

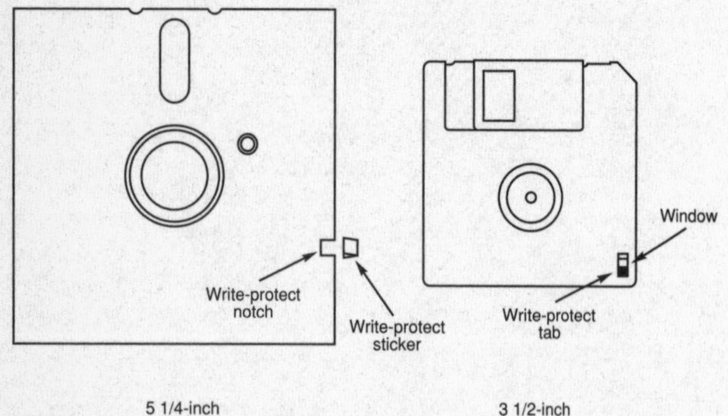

1 To install any new program that comes on floppy disks, first make sure the disks are write-protected. On 3.5-inch disks, you should be able to see through the write-protect hole. On 5.25-inch disks, apply a sticker over the write-protect notch on the side of the disk.

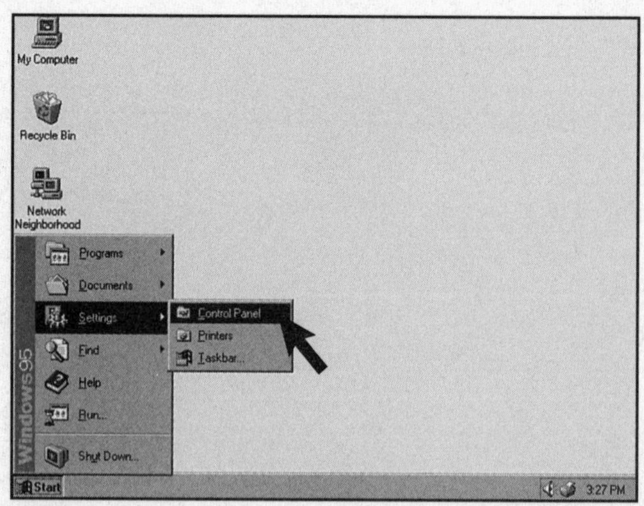

2 You use the Windows Control panel to install new programs. Click the **Start** button, move the mouse over **Settings**, and click **Control Panel**.

Guided Tour Install a Program

3 The Control Panel has icons that allow you to set up your system and enter your preferences. Double-click the **Add/ Remove Programs** icon to install a program.

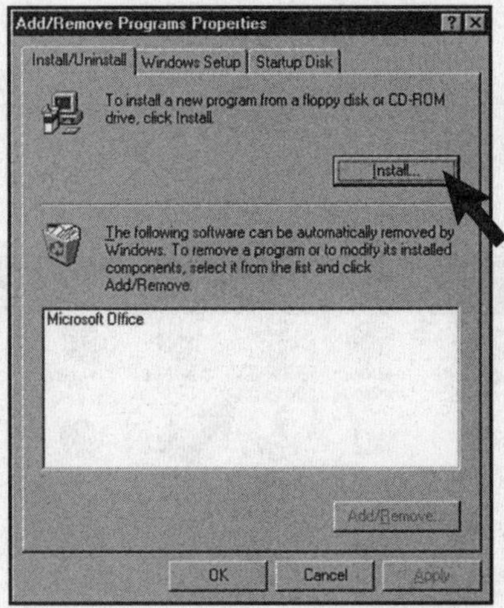

4 This dialog box is your key to installing programs. Click the **Install** button to begin.

5 You're told to insert the first floppy disk or the CD-ROM that stores the program into one of the drives. Do what you're told, and then click the **Next** button.

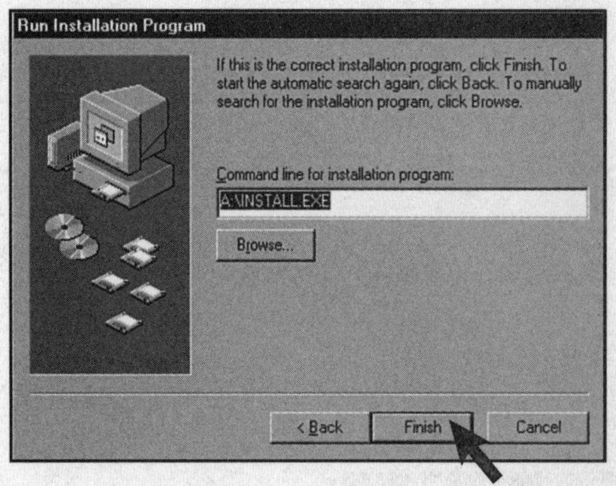

6 The Wizard searches the disk for an install or setup file it can run, and then displays the file's name. Click the **Finish** button to start the program's own installation program.

(continues)

Guided Tour Install a Program

(continued)

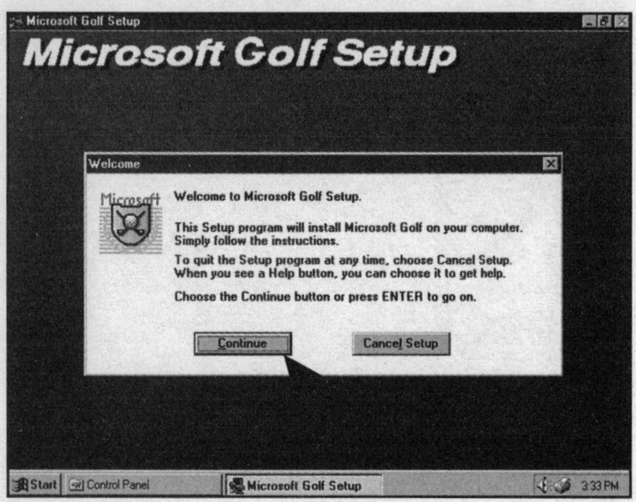

7 Each program has its own way of installing files. Most programs will lead you step-by-step through the installation. Follow the on-screen instructions.

If the installation program asks a question or allows you to make a choice, and you're not sure of the answer, just click **Yes** or **OK**. Installation programs are meant to be easy, and they usually default to the most common or safest answer.

Begin Guided Tour Uninstall Windows 95 Programs

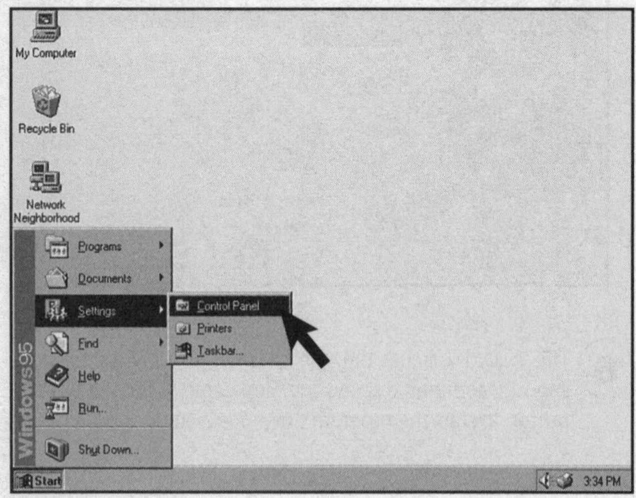

1 Windows lets you uninstall some Windows 95 programs, but not old Windows or DOS programs. Click the **Start** button, rest the mouse pointer on **Settings**, and click **Control Panel**.

2 You use **Add/Remove Programs** to uninstall Windows 95 programs. Double-click the icon now.

Guided Tour Uninstall Windows 95 Programs

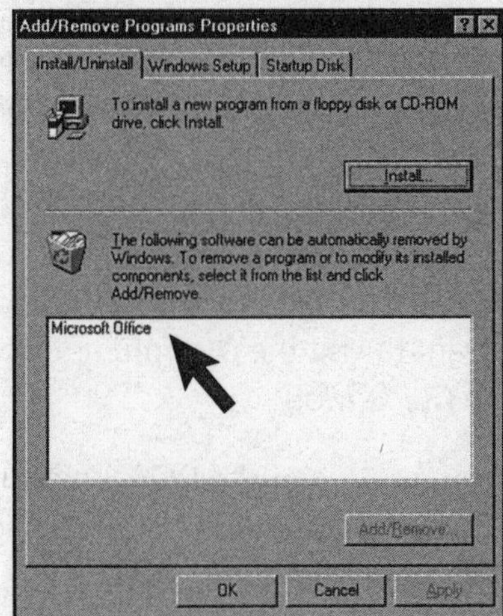

3 At the bottom of the Add/Remove Programs Properties dialog box is a list of all the programs you can remove from your system. If you don't see the program you want to remove, you can't use this procedure to remove it. Just click the **Cancel** button.

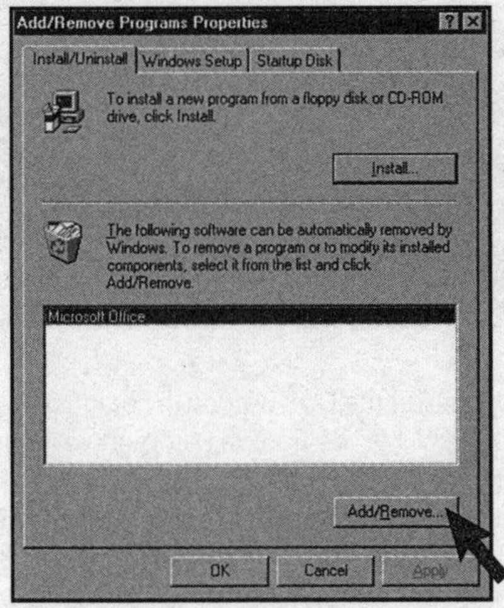

4 If you see the program you want to remove, click it in the list, and click the **Add/Remove** button.

5 Windows runs the program's setup utility, which varies from program to program. In this case, you can click the Remove All button to remove all files that pertain to this program. Follow the on-screen instructions to complete the task.

> If you choose to remove a component that another component requires in order to work right, Windows will warn you by displaying a dialog box asking for your confirmation.

Go to the DOS Prompt

If you still have a soft spot in your heart for DOS, or you just prefer running your DOS programs from the prompt, you can visit the *DOS prompt*. DOS (which rhymes with "gloss" and stands for Disk Operating System) is a set of computer instructions that works in the background to help your computer do its job. For details about DOS, see "Work with DOS" on page 211.

The DOS prompt is a symbol (or what techies call a command prompt) on the screen, which looks like C:\> and tells you that you can type a command to run a program or do some work in DOS. In Windows 95, you should be able to avoid the DOS prompt altogether. If you need to run a DOS program, you can use Windows Explorer or My Computer (see "Manage Disks, Folders, and Files" on page 173) to display the program's icon and then double-click it. If you don't want to visit the DOS prompt, you can safely skip the *Guided Tour*.

However, if you must go to the DOS prompt for any reason, the *Guided Tour* shows you how... and how to get back to Windows.

Begin Guided Tour Exit to DOS

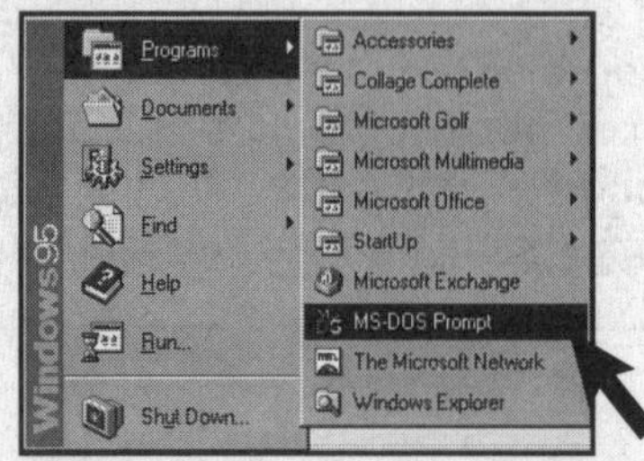

1 You can display the DOS screen in its own window at any time. Click the **Start** button, rest the mouse pointer on **Programs**, and click **MS-DOS Prompt** (the MS stands for Microsoft).

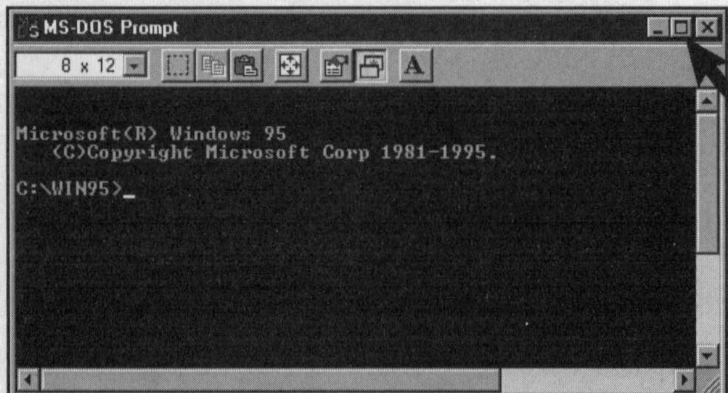

2 You now see the DOS prompt. To make the window bigger, click the **Maximize** button. Enter your commands at the DOS prompt as you normally would (see "Work with DOS" on page 211). You can exit the DOS window at any time by clicking on the **Close** button, or by entering **exit** at the DOS prompt.

3 You can't resize the DOS window by dragging its borders. To resize it, pick a size from the drop-down list in the toolbar, or click the **Full Screen** button. (If the toolbar is not displayed, right-click inside the title bar, and then click **Toolbar**.)

> You can quickly change the DOS display from full screen to a window by pressing **Alt+Enter**. DOS uses less memory in full screen view.

Manage Disks, Folders, and Files

If you read about Windows File Manager in earlier sections, you'll have to erase your memory. Windows 95 has replaced File Manager with two new folder and file management tools: Windows Explorer and My Computer.

Windows Explorer is considered to be File Manager's replacement. Like File Manager, it includes a directory tree on the left and a file list on the right. You can still copy and move files from one folder to another by dragging them, as you may have done in File Manager. My Computer takes a slightly different, more Macintosh, approach to file management. Each My Computer window contains icons that represent folders and files.

The *Guided Tour* shows you how to run both Windows Explorer and My Computer. Later tours in this chapter explain how to select files; copy, move, and delete selected files; create new folders; rename folders and files; and so on.

Arrange Icons in a Window

As you work with your files and folders, you may find that the folder and file names are not arranged efficiently. For example, you might want to view a list of the files arranged by date, so you can see which files you changed most recently, or by type, so you can select all your document files.

In addition, you might want to change the size of the icons, or display more information about each file and folder. To do this, you open the **View** menu and select any of the following options:

- **Large Icons** displays horsey looking icons that take up a lot of screen space.
- **Small Icons** display tiny icons that you may not be able to see clearly, but more of them fit inside the window.
- **List** displays the folders and files in alphabetical order using small icons.
- **Details** displays more information about each file and folder, including their sizes and the dates on which they were most recently changed.
- **Arrange Icons** opens a submenu that lets you arrange folders and files by **Name**, **Type**, **Size**, or **Date**, or have Windows arrange the icons automatically.
- **Line up Icons** arranges icons on an invisible grid, so they don't overlap, but usually does not arrange them to make the best use of screen space.

Icons: What They Stand for

As you look at the icons and file names in a list, you'll notice that the old filename extensions are no longer used. For example, you won't see .DOC for documents or .EXE for executable program files. Instead, Windows 95 relies heavily on each icon's appearance to convey the function of the file. As you look at the file lists in Explorer or My Computer, use the following guide to identify file types:

DOS program icons look like tiny windows. You can usually double-click one of these icons to run a DOS program.

Windows program icons are usually colorful and look like pictures that represent the programs.

Arrow.pcx

Document icons usually look like a piece of paper with one corner folded over. You can't "run" documents, but if you double-click a document icon that's *associated* with a program, Windows will run the program and open the document in it.

Argyle.bmp

Many document icons include a piece of paper in the background, with a picture of the program that opens the document in the foreground. This usually shows that the document is associated with a specific program.

> If you want to see the filename extensions for your files, open the **View** menu and select **Options**. Click the **View** tab, and then **Hide MS-DOS file extensions for file types that are registered**. This removes the check mark from the box. Click the **OK** button to put the change into effect.

Begin Guided Tour Run Windows Explorer

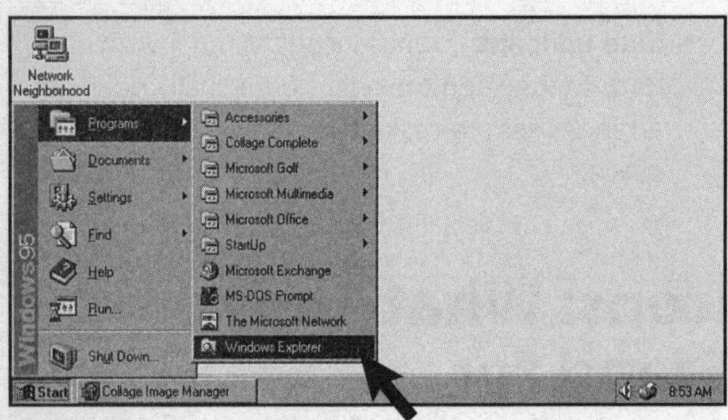

1 Windows Explorer lets you copy, move, and delete files and folders. To start it, click the **Start** button, rest the mouse pointer on **Programs**, and click **Windows Explorer**.

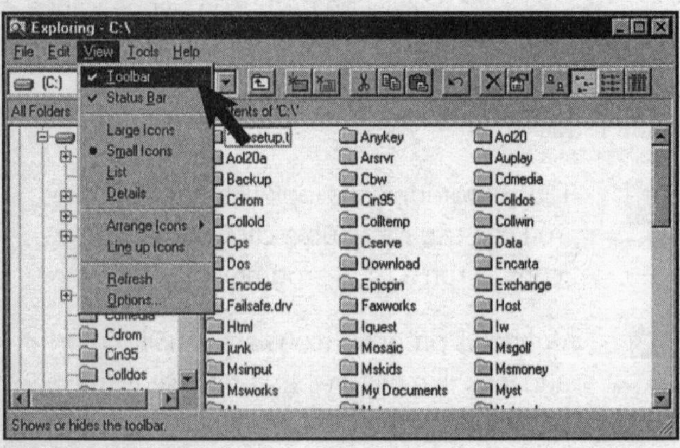

2 The toolbar at the top of the screen is very helpful. If it is not displayed on your screen, open the **View** menu and select **Toolbar**.

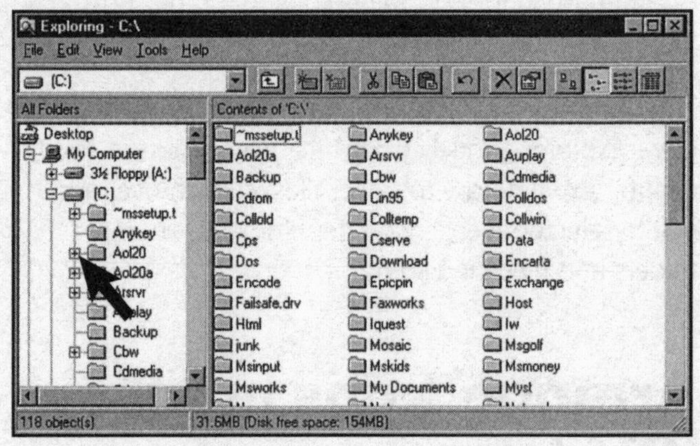

3 The list on the left shows the names of all the drives and folders. A plus sign next to a drive or folder means that there are more items inside. Click the plus sign to see those items.

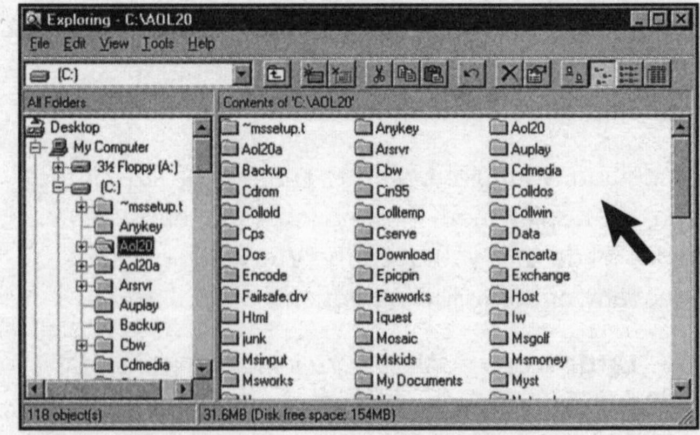

4 The file list on the right shows the names of the folders and files that are in the folder you selected on the left. Click a folder in the tree, or double-click a folder in the file list, to see its contents.

Guided Tour Run Windows Explorer

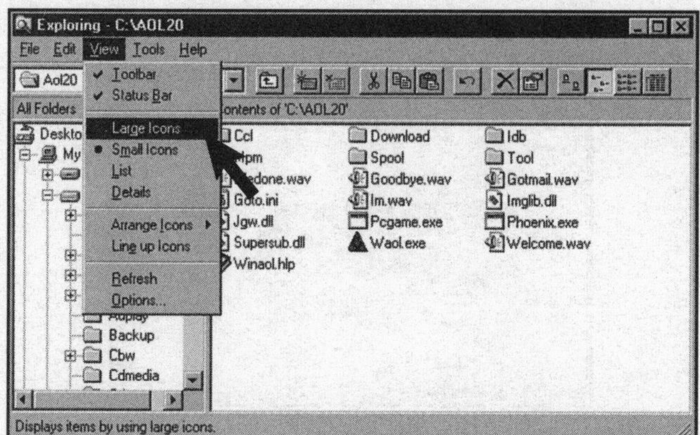

5 The View menu lets you change the size of the icons and how those icons are arranged. See "Arrange Icons in a Window" on page 173 for details.

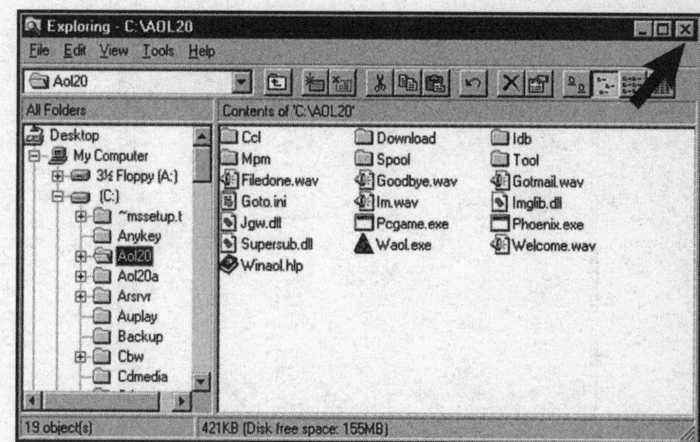

6 When you are finished with Windows Explorer, you can exit by clicking on the **Close** button.

If you see a program icon in Explorer or My Computer, you can double-click it to run the program.

Begin Guided Tour Run My Computer

1 My Computer takes a different approach to file and folder management. To run it, double-click the My Computer icon on the Windows desktop.

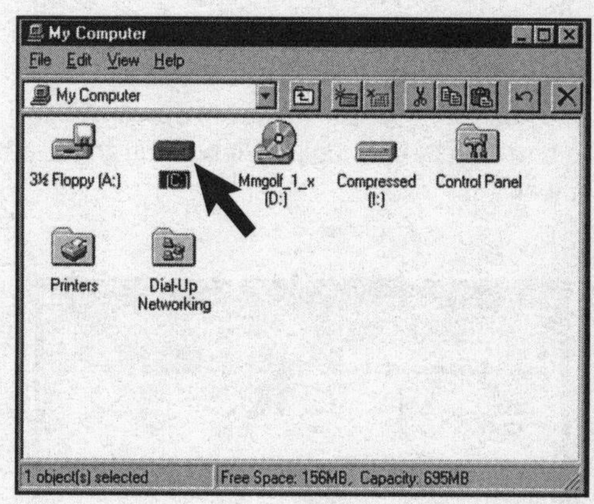

2 My Computer initially shows you icons for all your drives, for the Control Panel, and for your printers. Double-click a drive icon to view its contents.

(continues)

Guided Tour Run My Computer

(continued)

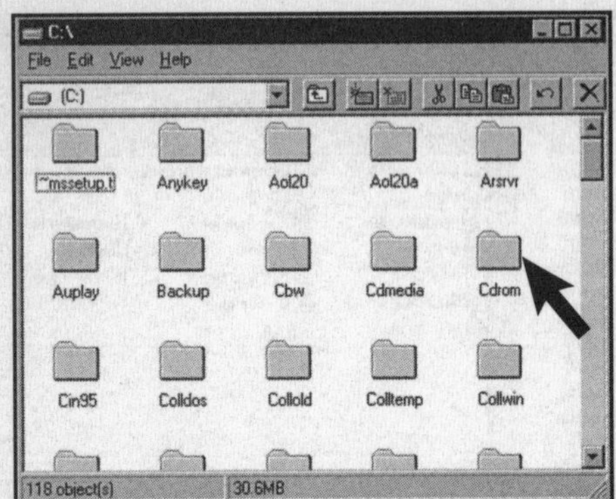

3 You can see the contents of a folder by double-clicking on it. This opens a new window that shows the folder's files and subfolders (if any).

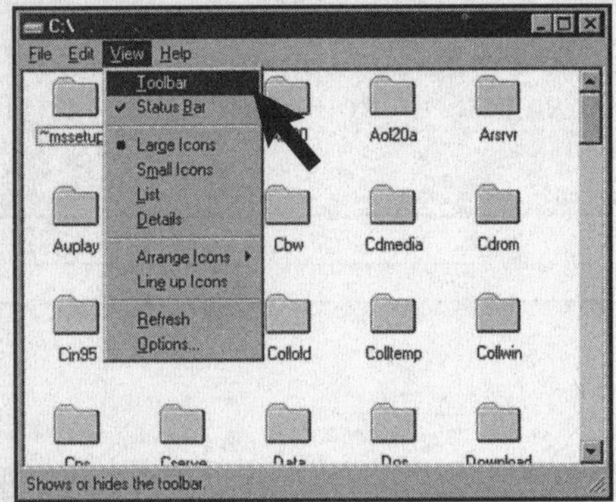

4 If you don't see a toolbar at the top of your window, you can turn it on by opening the **View** menu and selecting **Toolbar**.

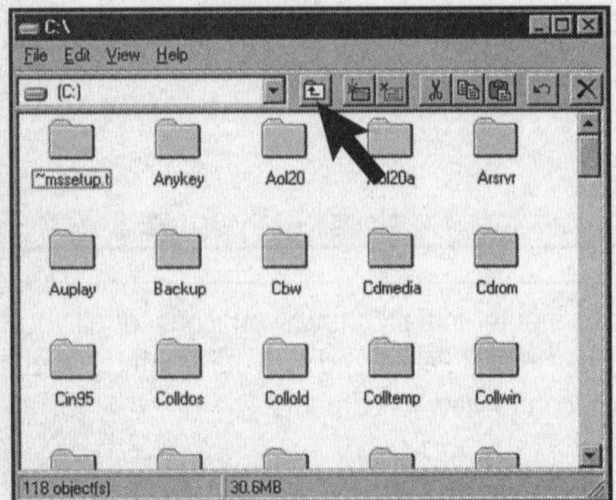

5 The **Up One Level** button is especially useful. You can click it to move to a higher level folder (or to the previous window). (You can do the same thing with the Backspace key.)

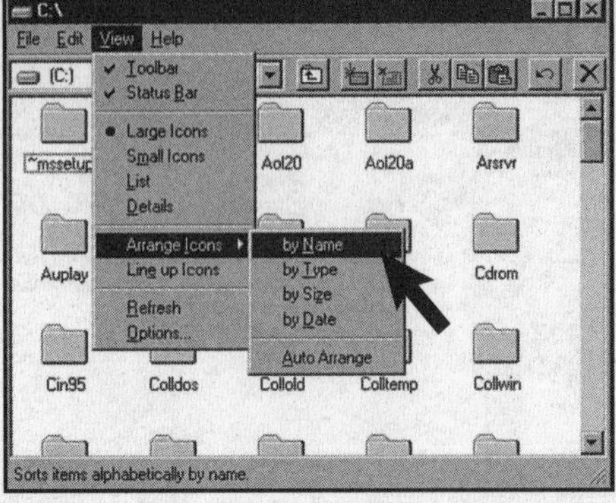

6 The View menu lets you change the size of the icons and how those icons are arranged. See "Arrange Icons in a Window" on page 173 for details.

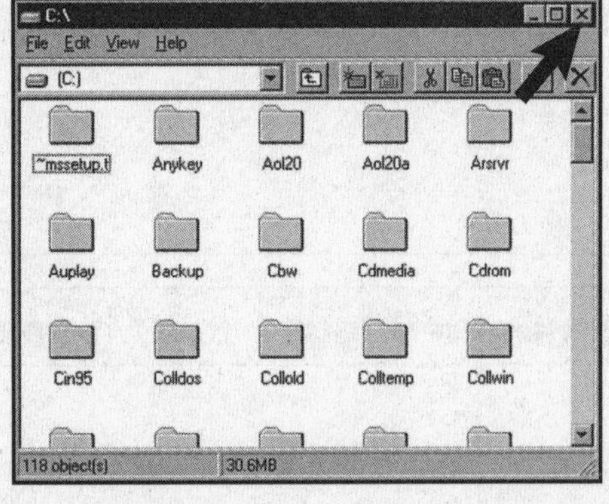

7 If your screen becomes too cluttered, you can close any part of the My Computer window by clicking on its Close button.

My Computer opens a window for each drive or folder you double-click. If you want to use only one window, whose contents change with each selection, open the **View** menu and select **Options**. Click **Browse folders by using a single window** that changes as you open each folder, and then click **OK**.

Select Files and Folders

The whole purpose of My Computer and Windows Explorer is to give you some way to organize the files and folders on your disks. You might need to delete files to free up disk space, copy files to share with others, or move files and folders to rearrange your work.

Whatever the case, you first have to select the folders and files you want to copy, move, or delete. Selecting a single file or folder is easy; you click it. If you click a folder, all of the subfolders and files in that folder are selected. If you click a file, only that file is selected.

However, working with individual files and folders may not always be the most efficient means of copying, moving, and deleting items. Sometimes, you'll need to work with groups of files and folders. The *Guided Tour* shows you the various methods of selecting multiple files and folders with the mouse. The steps in the *Guided Tour* work for both My Computer and Windows Explorer.

Begin Guided Tour Select Files and Folders

1 The easiest way to select a group of neighboring files or folders is to drag a box around them. (Move the mouse pointer to the upper left of the first file you want to select, and then hold down the left mouse button while you move the pointer to the down and to the right.) As you drag, all the items inside the box appear highlighted.

2 To select non-neighboring items, click the first item you want to select, and then hold down the Ctrl key while clicking on each additional item.

(continues)

Guided Tour Select Files and Folders

(continued)

3 Another way to select a group of neighboring items is to click the first item you want to select, and then hold down the Shift key while clicking on the last item.

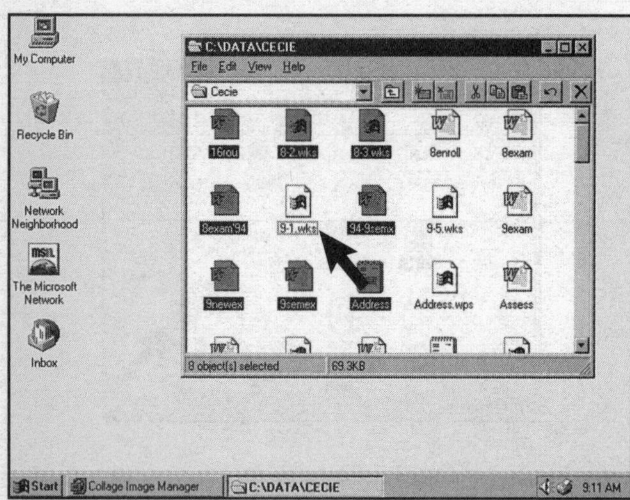

4 You can deselect a selected item by holding down the Ctrl key while clicking on it.

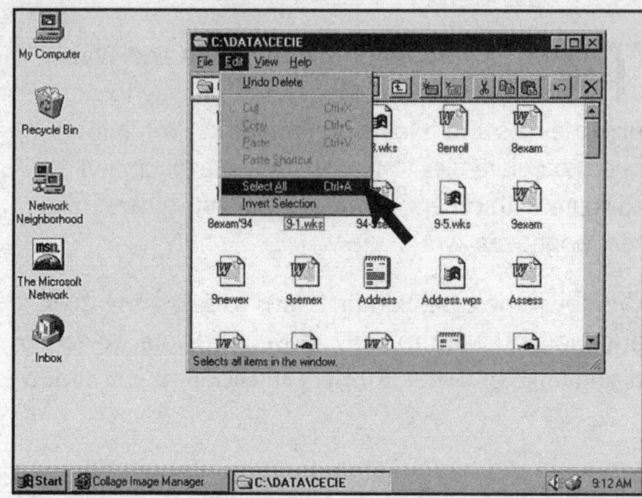

5 To select all the items in the list, open the **Edit** menu and click **Select All**.

To find out how many files you selected and how much space they consume, look at the bottom of the window. This information is often useful if you plan on copying files to a floppy disk, and you're not sure whether the files will take up too much space.

Copy or Move Files and Folders

Although your hard disk is hermetically sealed, you need some way to move or copy data from it. For example, you might want to rearrange the files you've created, copy a file to a floppy disk to send to a colleague, or transfer a file you received on a floppy disk to a folder on your hard disk.

Both Windows Explorer and My Computer provide the tools you need to move files back and forth from one disk or folder to another. You simply select the files you want to copy or move, and then drag them to another disk or folder window or over a disk or folder icon, and drop them in place. The *Guided Tour* shows just what you need to do.

Displaying the Destination for Copied or Moved Files

To copy or move files and folders, you drag the selected items from their original location to a *destination*. The destination can be a drive icon, a folder icon, or a window that displays a list of files. The only tricky part of copying and moving items is in displaying both the selected files and the destination icon or window.

In Windows Explorer, you should first select the drive or folder that has the items you want to copy or move. This displays the names of the files. After selecting the files, use the folder list on the left to bring the destination folder or drive icon into view. However, DO NOT select the drive or folder icon, because if you do, you won't be able to see the files you want to move.

In My Computer, the process is even more difficult, because the window that contains the files can become buried under the window that contains the destination icon. You'll have to drag windows around until you can see both the selected files and the destination icon or window.

Begin Guided Tour Copy Files or Folders

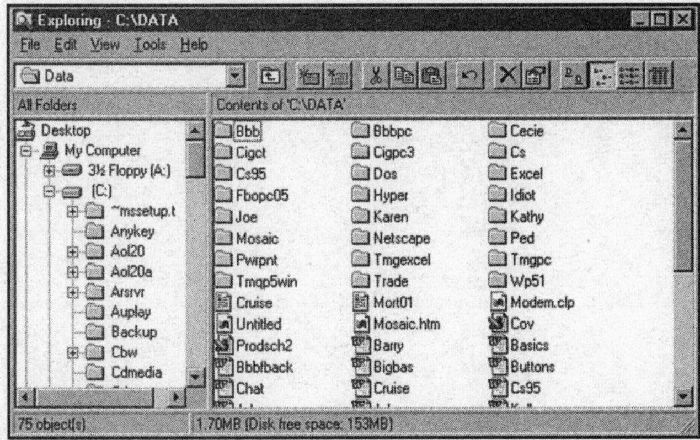

1 You copy files by dragging them from one window into another window or over another disk or folder icon. First, make sure you can see the files you want to copy and the icon for the drive or folder to which you want them copied.

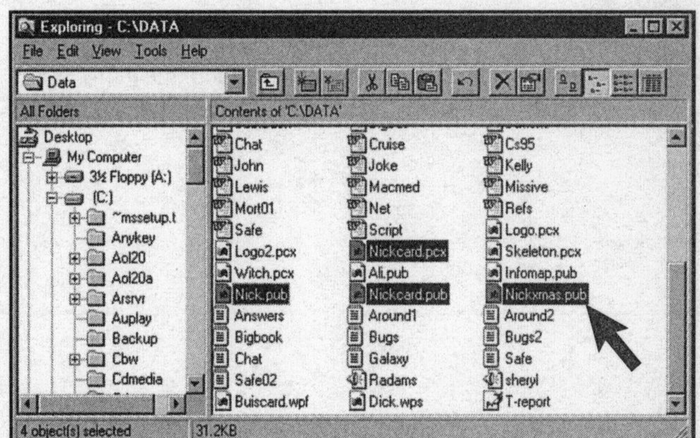

2 Select the files or folders you want to copy. See "Select Files and Folders" on page 177 for instructions.

(continues)

Guided Tour Copy Files and Folders

(continued)

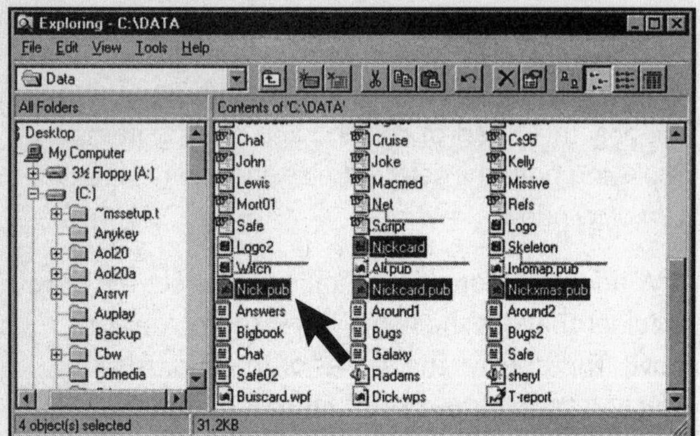

3 Move the mouse pointer over any one of the selected files, hold down the Ctrl key and the left mouse button, and drag the pointer over the disk or folder icon (or into the window) where you want the files or folders placed.

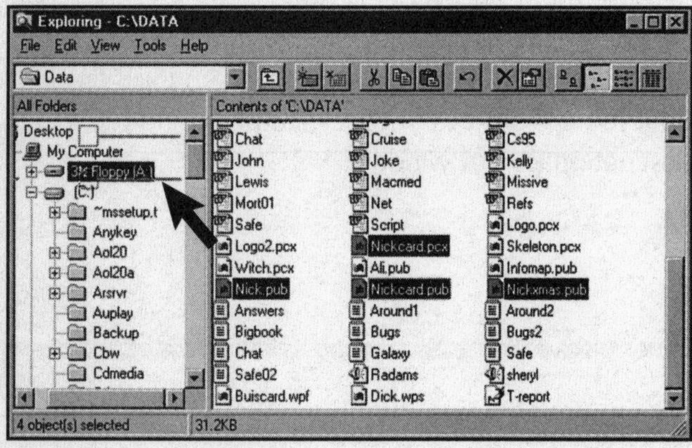

4 As you drag, a plus sign appears next to the mouse pointer to show that you are copying (not moving) the items. When you are over the destination icon, it appears highlighted.

5 Release the mouse button. When you release the mouse button, Windows shows the copy operation in progress.

If you are copying files to a different disk, you do not have to hold down the Ctrl key. Windows assumes that you want to copy (not move) the files.

Begin Guided Tour Move Files or Folders

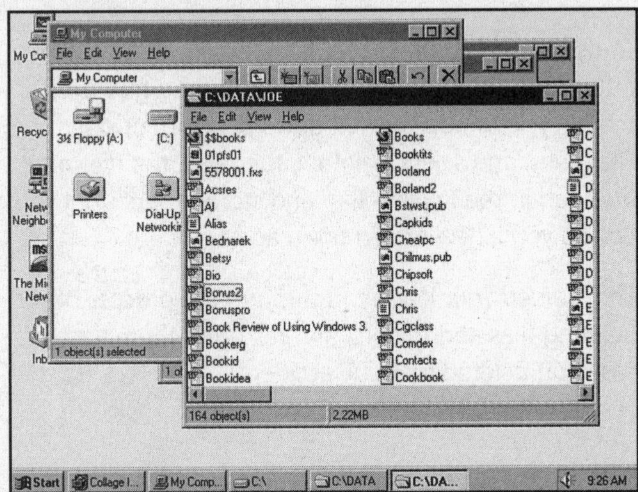

1 You move files by dragging them from one disk or folder to another. First, make sure you can see the files you want to move and the icon for the drive or folder to which you want them copied. In the picture, files will be moved from C:\DATA\JOE to drive A.

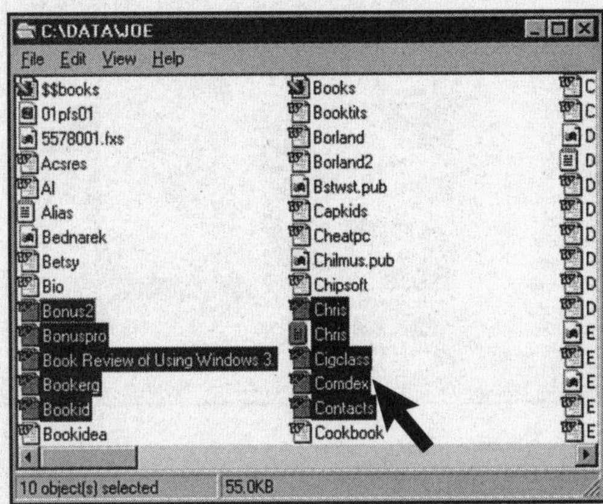

2 Select the files or folders you want to move. See "Select Files and Folders" on page 177 for instructions.

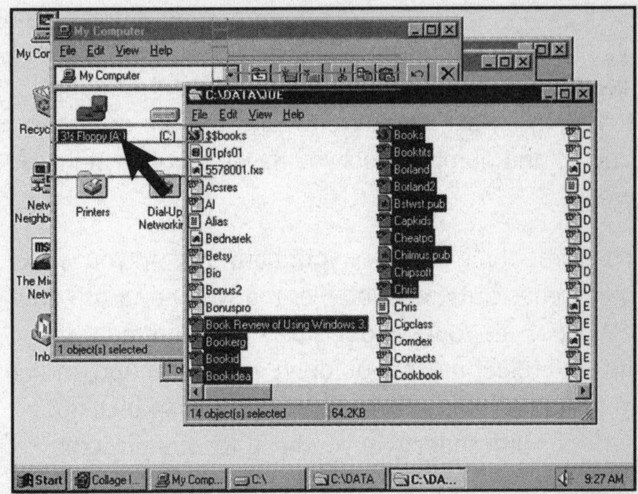

3 Move the mouse pointer over any one of the selected files, and hold down the Shift key while dragging the pointer over the disk or folder icon (or into the window) where you want the files or folders placed. (To move files to a different folder on the same disk, you do not have to hold down the Shift key.)

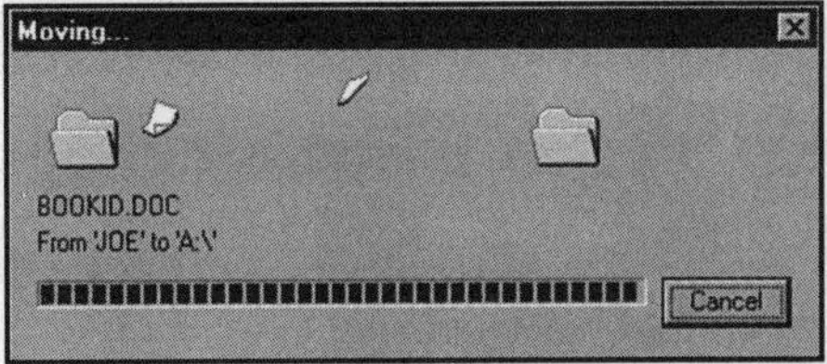

4 When you release the mouse button, Windows shows you the progress of the move. (To undo the move, you can open the Edit menu and select Undo Move.)

If you drag files using the right mouse button, a shortcut menu appears when you release the button, asking whether you want to move or copy the files or folders.

Delete and Restore Files and Folders

Every so often, your office will get so cluttered and disorganized that you just can't stand working there any longer. You have to take an hour or two to tidy up and dump papers you haven't looked at in weeks.

The same thing is true of your hard disk. As you work, it becomes cluttered with files that you never use or even look at. Your windows become cluttered with file and folder names you don't recognize. And, more importantly, these files and folders start to take up precious disk space that you need for storing some more useful items.

To delete useless items, you can use either My Computer or Windows Explorer. You can drag files over the Recycle Bin on the Windows desktop, or open the File menu and select Delete. Either way, the files are dumped in the Recycle Bin, and stored there until you decide you'll never need them again.

The *Guided Tour* leads you through the process of deleting files and folders, and restoring them (just in case you deleted them by accident).

Begin Guided Tour Delete Files and Folders

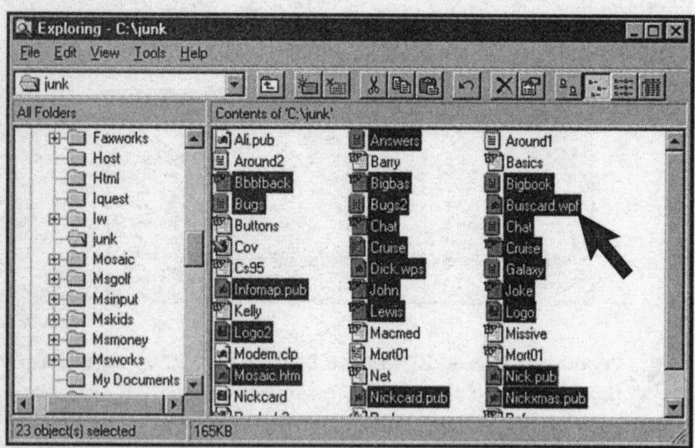

1 Before you can delete files and folders, you must select the ones you want to delete. See "Select Files and Folders" on page 177 for instructions.

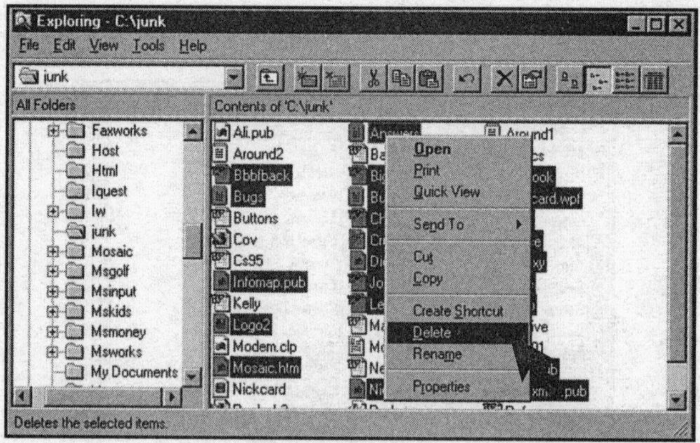

2 You have several options for deleting selected files. You can right-click a selected file, and then click **Delete**; or open the **File** menu and select **Delete**.

Guided Tour Delete Files and Folders

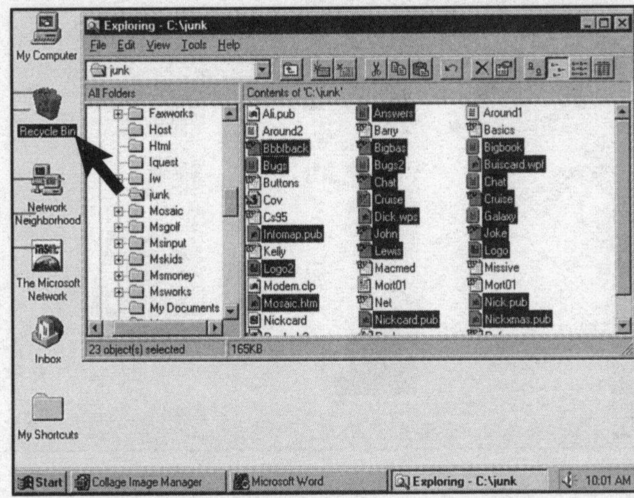

3 Another way to delete files is to drag any one of the selected files over the **Recycle Bin** icon on the desktop, and then release the mouse button.

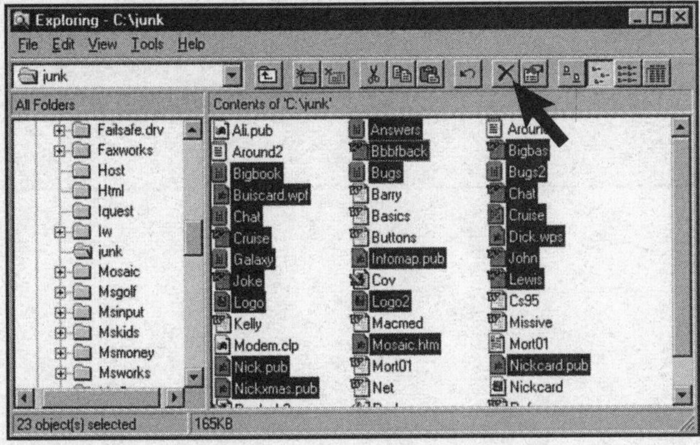

4 If the toolbar is displayed in My Computer or Windows Explorer, you can click the X button to quickly delete the selected files.

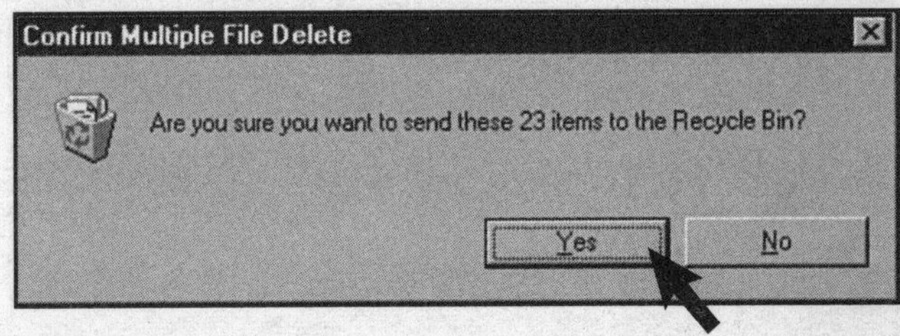

5 Regardless of which deletion method you choose, a dialog box appears, asking you to confirm. Click **Yes**.

Don't delete a file unless you know what kind of file it is, and you are sure you want to delete it. Although Windows has built-in safeguards to prevent you from deleting program and system files, you should still be careful.

Begin Guided Tour Restore Accidentally Deleted Items

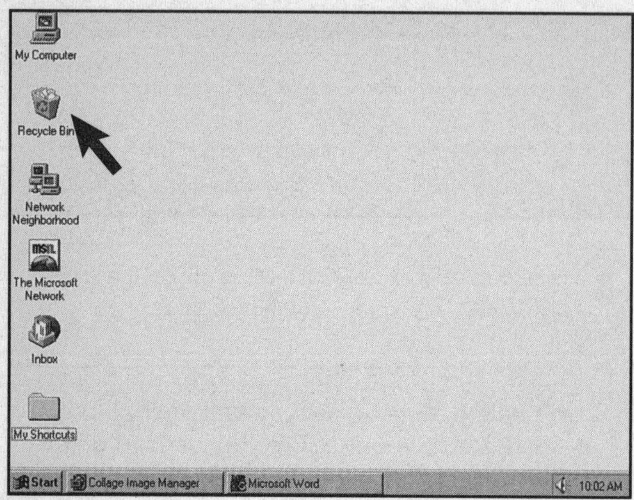

1 Whenever you delete a file or folder, it is stored in the Recycle Bin, until you choose to empty the bin. To display the contents of the Recycle Bin, double-click its icon.

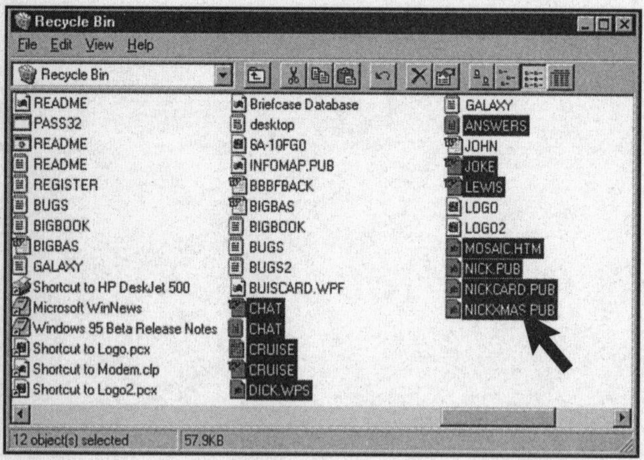

2 The Recycle Bin shows the names of all the items you deleted. To restore one or more items to their original locations, select the items just as you would in My Computer or Windows Explorer.

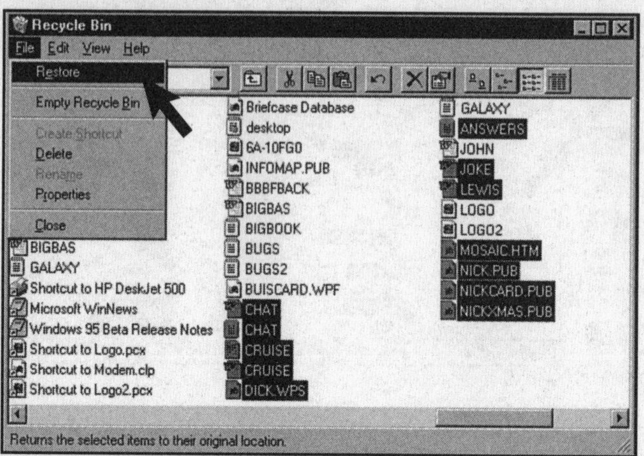

3 Open the **File** menu and select **Restore**. Files are moved from the Recycle Bin to their original folders.

The Recycle Bin stores deleted items on your hard disk, consuming valuable space. You should check the Bin regularly and then empty it if it contains no items you want to undelete. Open the **File** menu and select **Empty Recycle Bin**.

Rename Files or Folders

If you keep all your personal and business records in manila folders, you probably are used to the idea of pasting one label over another to rename the folder or use it for some other records. You can do the same thing more easily in Windows 95. And because Windows 95 allows for long filenames (up to 255 characters), you can even give some of your old data files more descriptive names. Just keep in mind that you cannot use any of the following characters:

\ ? : * ? " < > |

In Windows 3.11, there was little reason to rename files or folders, and the process was somewhat tedious. You had to enter the File Rename command and then use the dialog box that appeared to rename the file or directory. Windows 95 makes it much easier. You simply edit the file or folder name in the file list. The *Guided Tour* shows you just what to do.

Although Windows 95 lets you use long file names, your old DOS and Windows 3.11 programs won't be able to recognize these long filenames (they simply crop off any characters beyond the standard 8). If you continue to use old programs, you might want to keep the original file names you gave to your data files when you created them.

Begin Guided Tour Rename Files and Folders

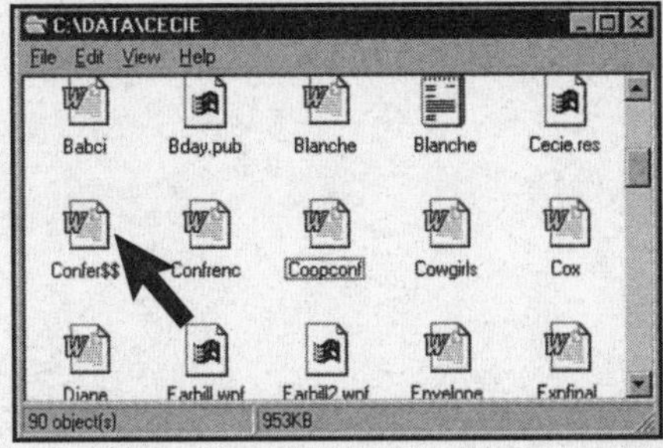

1 To rename a file or folder, it must be displayed in My Computer or Windows Explorer. Click the name or icon of the file or folder you want to rename.

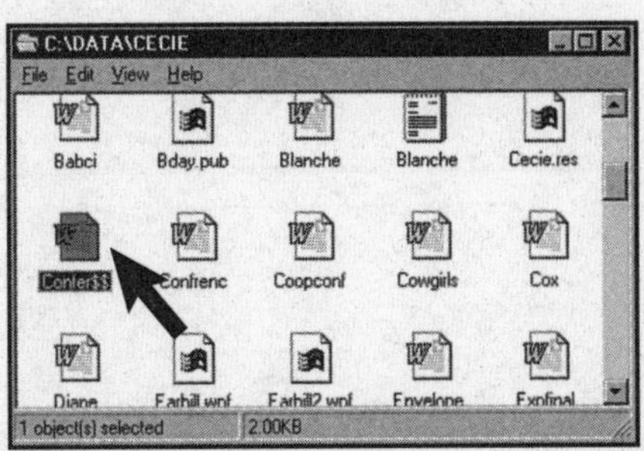

2 When you click a file or folder icon, it appears highlighted. Click the name of the file or folder again.

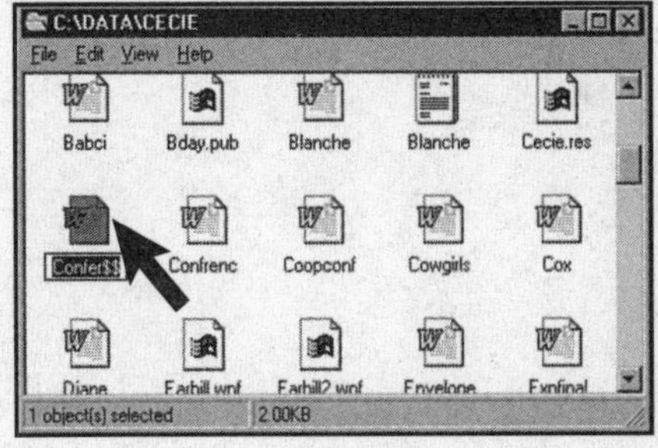

3 The name appears highlighted in a box. You can now type a new name for the file or folder, or click the name again to edit it.

(continues)

Guided Tour Rename Files and Folders

(continued)

4 If you clicked on the name again, an insertion point appears inside the name box. You can use the arrow keys to move the insertion point, and Backspace or Delete to delete characters. You can then type your change.

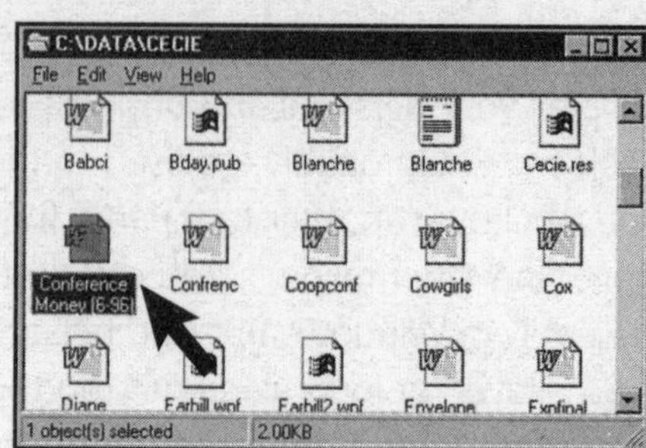

5 Click anywhere outside the file or folder icon to make your change permanent. Or press the Enter key.

> Rename only the files and folders you created. DO NOT rename any Windows 95 files or program files or folders.

Create New Folders

As you rearrange files and folders on your hard disk, you will occasionally need to create new folders in which to stick files and other folders. Windows 95 allows you to create folders on any disk or inside any folder that's displayed.

When creating folders inside folders, try not to embed folders any more than three deep. For example, you don't want a Data folder containing a Letters folder, containing a My Letters folder, containing a My Letters in 1996 folder, containing a My Letters in June folder, containing… well, you get the idea. If you go too deep, you'll have to open all those folders each time you want to load one of your files. Just a word of advice.

A quick way to create a folder is to right-click a blank area inside the window in which you want the new folder to appear. Rest the mouse pointer on **New**, and then click **Folder**. A folder icon appears named **New Folder**; you can type a new name for the folder.

Begin Guided Tour Add a New Folder

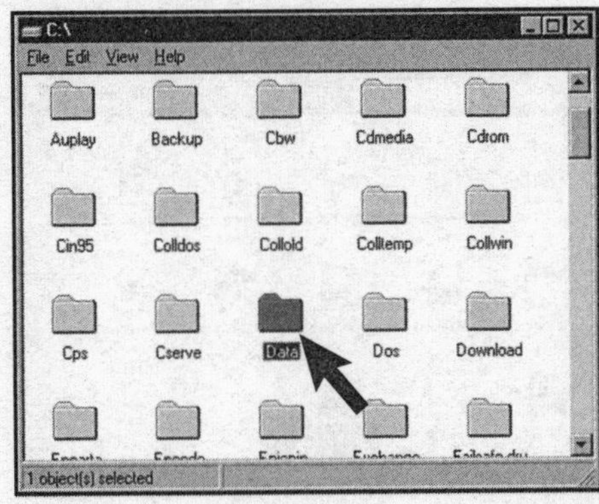

1 Any folder you create will be placed inside the active folder. Double-click the folder in which you want the new folder placed.

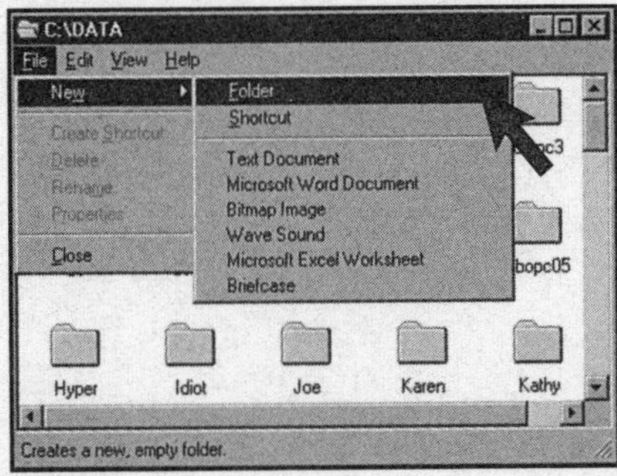

2 Open the **File** menu, rest the mouse pointer on **New**, and then click **Folder**.

3 Windows plops a new folder, cleverly called New Folder at the end of the file list.

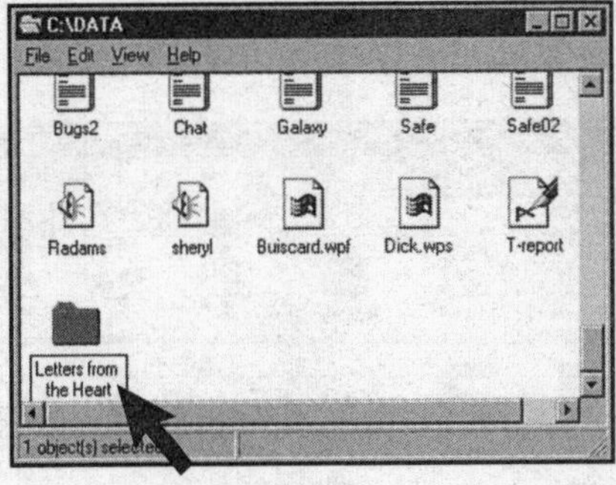

4 Type a new, more descriptive name for the folder, and then press **Enter**. When you start typing "New Folder" is replaced by the name you type.

Save Time with Shortcuts

Windows 95 is like a brand new desk. The top is free of clutter, offering only a few icons for running My Computer, the Recycle Bin, and perhaps a few other Windows utilities. And you have already seen how these icons provide quick access for getting at some of Windows more common features.

Wouldn't it be nice if you could add some icons for the programs you use most often, so you don't have to weave your way through the Start/Programs menu? Well, you can, by adding shortcuts to the desktop. *Shortcuts* are icons that point to specific programs and documents. Whenever you double-click the icon, windows runs the corresponding program or opens the document.

Windows provides two ways to add shortcuts to the desktop. The easiest way is to drag an icon from My Computer or Windows Explorer onto the desktop. Another way is to right-click the desktop, select New, select Shortcut, and then follow the on-screen instructions to complete the task. The *Guided Tour* shows the easier of the two methods.

Begin Guided Tour Create a Shortcut

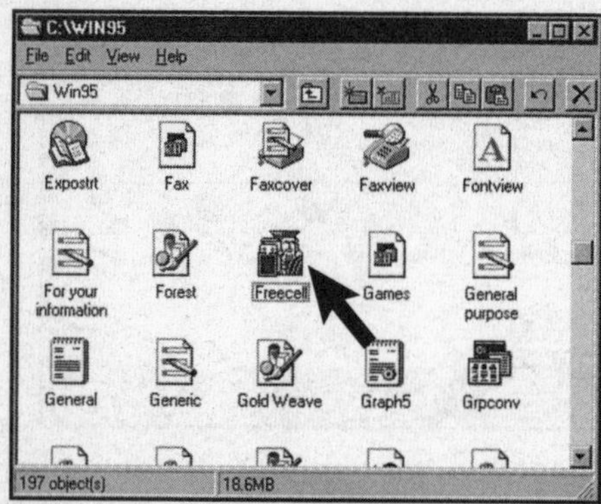

1 You can create shortcuts for quick access to files and programs. First, run Explorer or My Computer, and display the icon for which you want to create a shortcut.

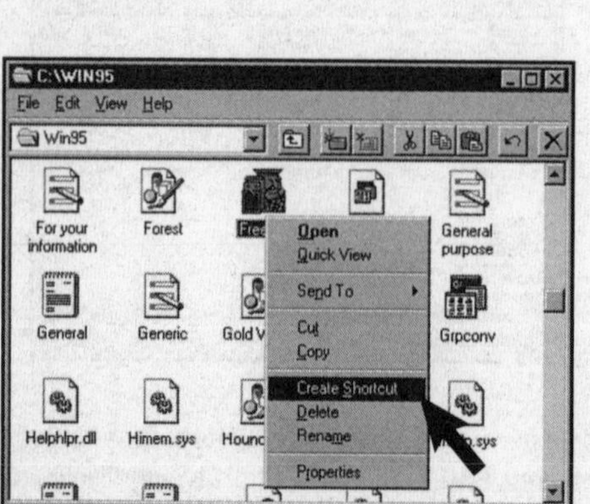

2 Right-click the icon for which you want to create a shortcut, and then click **Create Shortcut**.

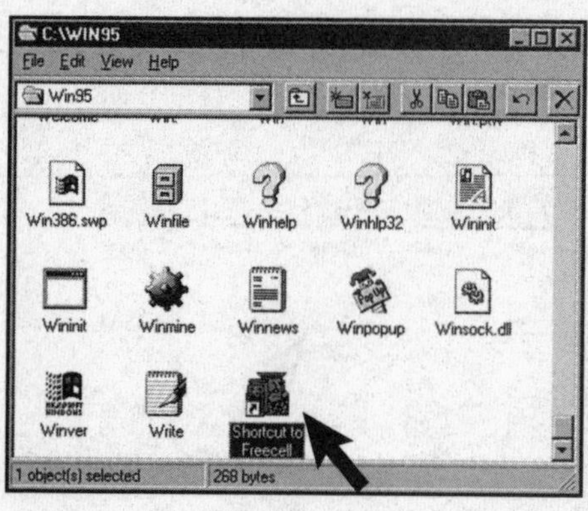

3 Windows creates a clone of the selected icon, and places it in the same window that contains the original icon. Drag the shortcut icon onto the Windows desktop to move it there.

Guided Tour Create a Shortcut

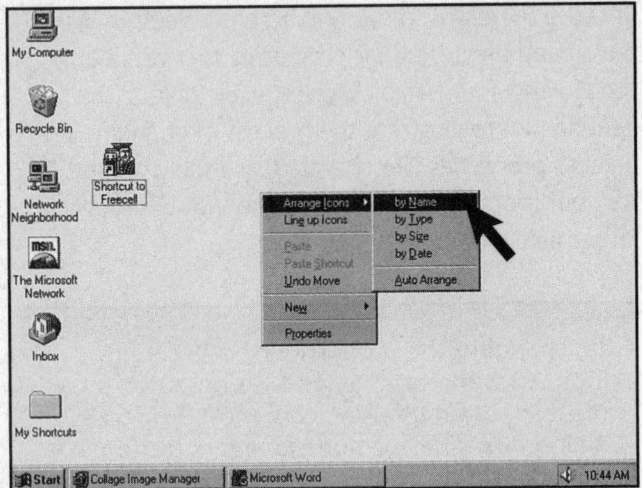

4 You can have Windows rearrange the shortcut icons on the desktop. Right-click a blank area of the desktop, move the mouse pointer over Arrange icons, and click the desired arrangement.

An even quicker way to create a shortcut on the desktop is to hold down the Ctrl key while dragging the original icon from Explorer or My Computer onto the desktop.

Change an Object's Properties

Your desktop consists of a collection of *objects*, each of which is controlled by its own settings. The taskbar is one object, file and folder icons are objects, each window is an object, and even the desktop itself is treated as an object. You can control these objects by changing their *properties*. For example, you can change the display properties to turn on a screen saver program or adjust the color of the Windows background.

The procedure for changing an object's properties is fairly simple. You right-click the object to view its shortcut menu, and then you click **Properties**. This brings up a dialog box that allows you to change the object's properties. This dialog box varies according to the object you selected. You enter your preferences, and then click **OK**.

Because there are so many different objects in Windows, and because their properties vary so greatly, the Guided Tour has picked a specific object (the Recycle Bin) to illustrate the process of changing an object's properties. (To change the display properties for your monitor, see "Change the Video Display Properties" on page 201.)

Try changing the properties of other items. Right-click the taskbar, on My Computer, on a file icon, or on a folder icon. Most Properties dialog boxes have a question mark button in the upper right corner, which you can click for help with specific options.

Begin Guided Tour Change Properties

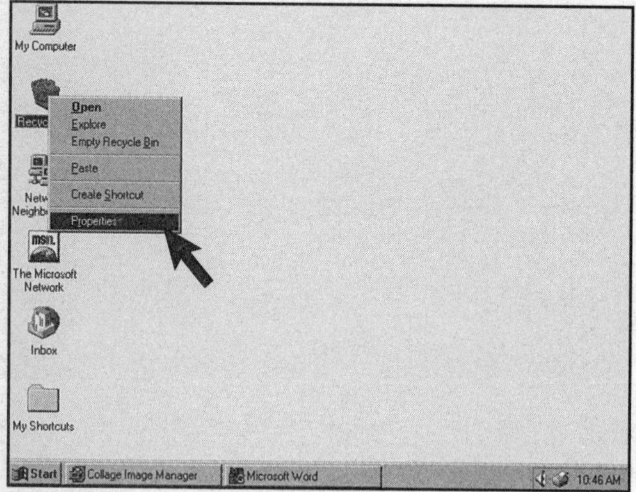

1 You can change the properties of almost any object in Windows. Right-click the object whose properties you want to change, and click **Properties**.

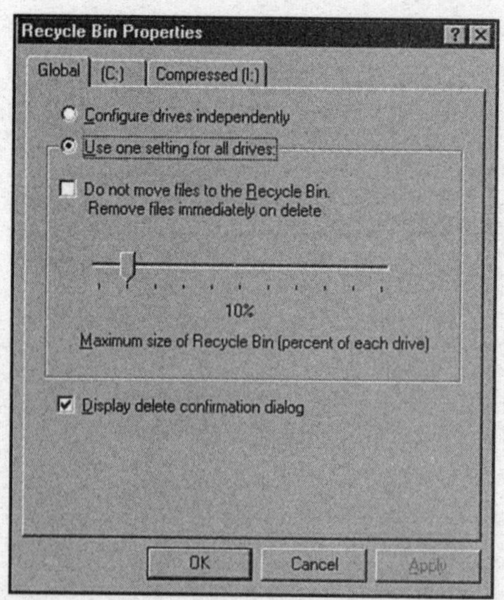

2 If, for example, you choose to change the properties of the Recycle Bin, Windows shows you the Recycle Bin Properties dialog box.

Guided Tour Change Properties

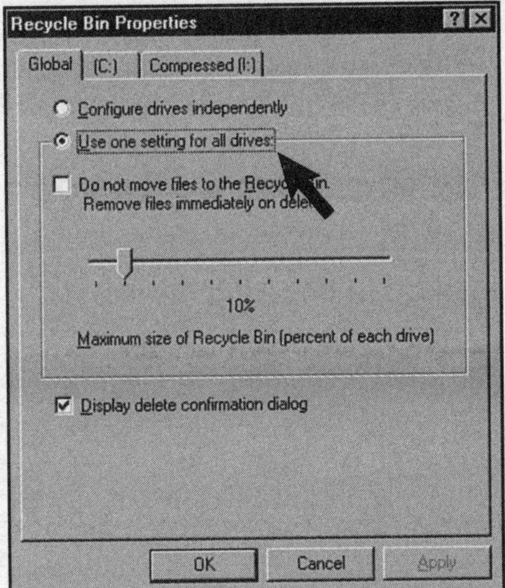

3 You can change the Recycle Bin properties for each hard drive, or use the same settings on all the drives on your system. For now, select **Use one setting for all drives**.

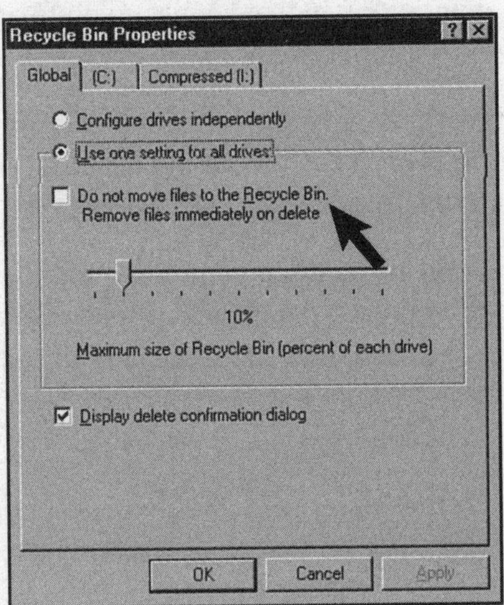

4 The Recycle Bin is used as a buffer to help you restore accidentally deleted files. If you want to turn this buffer off (a dangerous thing to do), click **Do not move files to the Recycle Bin**. Turning this option on tells Windows to immediately remove files from your hard disk when you delete them. I *strongly* recommend that you not do this.

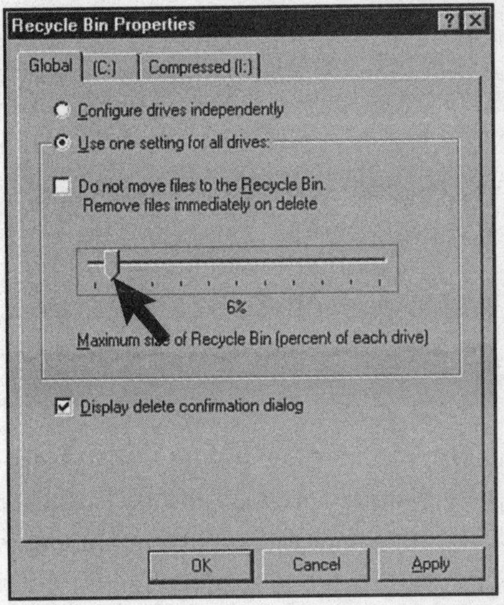

5 The Recycle Bin is set up to use 10% of your disk space for storing deleted files. Once the 10% is used up, Recycle Bin automatically deletes older files. You can drag the slider to the left or right to use more or less space for Recycle Bin.

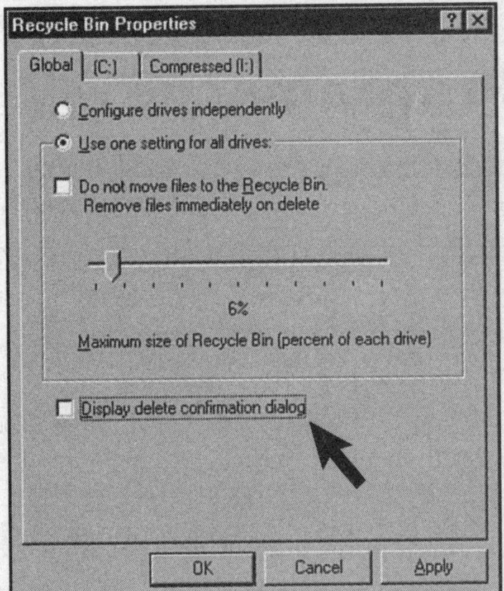

6 Whenever you delete a file, a dialog box appears asking if you're sure. To prevent this dialog box from appearing, click **Display delete confirmation dialog** to remove the check from the box.

7 Click the **OK** button to save your changes.

Use Built-in Windows Programs

Windows comes with a host of free programs, commonly called *applets* (small application programs), which you can use to do real work in Windows. Although these programs are not state-of-the-art, and won't provide you with the advanced options you'll find in other commercial programs, they do give you the power to do basic jobs in Windows, such as writing letters, drawing pictures, and dialing your phone.

Windows also includes a set of *utilities* to help you properly maintain your computer. For instance, ScanDisk can help restore data from damaged disks, and Disk Defragmenter can reduce file fragmentation and speed up your hard disk.

The *Guided Tour* shows you where to look for and how to run these Windows applets.

A List of the Windows 95 Programs

Detailed instructions on how to use all the Windows 95 applets could easily consume another 600 page book. So, instead of doing that, here's a list of the most commonly used applets and utilities and a brief description of each. As you run these applets, keep in mind that the Windows help system is close at hand. For instructions on how to use any of these applets, simply open the Help menu and click a topic.

Calc

Calculator is just like a hand-held calculator.

Charmap

Character Map lets you copy and insert special characters that do not appear on your keyboard.

Clipbd

Clipboard Viewer displays the contents of the data that you cut or copy from a document. (The Clipboard stores data temporarily, so you can paste it into another document.)

Dial-Up Networking

Dial-Up Networking is a **remote-computing** program, which lets you connect two computers (for example, your home and office computers) over the phone line. Each computer must have a modem.

Directcc

Direct Cable Connection lets you connect two computers with a cable and transfer files between the two computers. This is especially useful if you have to transfer files between a laptop and desktop computer.

Hypertrm

HyperTerminal is a modem communications program that connects you to another computer or to online services.

Notepad

Notepad lets you create and edit plain text files which can be opened in almost any program.

Mspaint

Paint offers a complete set of tools for drawing and painting pictures on your screen. You can also use Paint to create your own background designs for the Windows desktop.

Dialer

Phone Dialer is a programmable phone keyboard. You can use it (along with a modem) to dial phone numbers for you. After Dialer places the call, you can pick up the receiver and start talking.

Wordpad

WordPad is a more sophisticated word-processing program than Notepad. It allows you to style the text to make your documents more attractive.

Fax is a new program that can transform your computer (equipped with a fax modem) into a fax machine. You can then receive faxes, and send the documents you type to another fax machine.

Games is a group of computer games including FreeCell, Hearts, Minesweeper, PartyLine, and Solitaire. Most of these games are very addictive, but they do help hone your mouse skills.

Multimedia consists of several programs that control your sound card and CD-ROM drive. CD Player lets you play audio CDs. Media player plays computerized movie clips and sound recordings. Sound Recorder lets you plug a microphone into your sound card and record voices and other sounds. And Volume Control allows you to crank up the volume of your sound card or CD player.

Backup is a utility that copies the files on your hard disk, compresses them (so they take up less space), and places the compressed files on a set of floppy disks or a backup tape. If anything happens to your files, you can use Backup to restore the backed up files to your hard disk.

Disk Defragmenter rearranges the parts of each file on your hard disk, so your disk drive doesn't have to hunt all over for them. This increases the speed of your drive and the overall speed of your computer. Run this monthly.

DriveSpace compresses files on your hard disk, so they take up less space, and decompresses the files automatically when you need them. If you're running out of hard disk space, back up all your files, and then run DriveSpace.

ScanDisk looks for lost pieces of files on a disk and for bad spots on the disk itself. It can help you recover lost data, repair floppy disks, and reduce future data loss by preventing Windows from storing data on any bad areas of the disk.

Microsoft Exchange is a one-stop electronic mailbox for all your network e-mail and e-mail that you receive from online services.

The Microsoft Network is an online service offered by Microsoft Corporation. If you have a modem, you can subscribe to the service, and use it to connect to other computer users, do research, shop, send and receive mail, and much more.

Begin Guided Tour Use Windows Programs

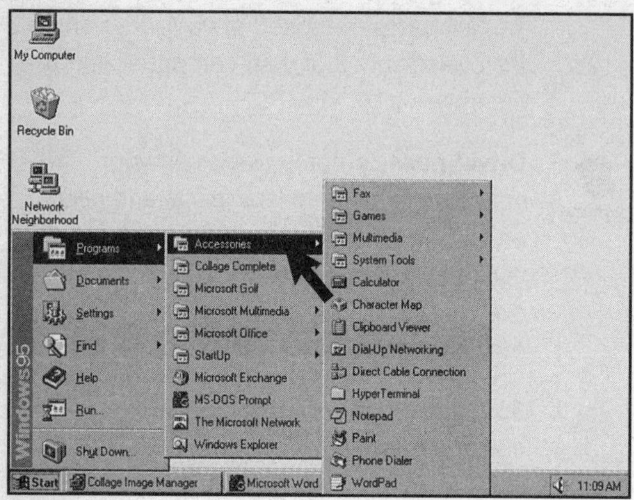

1 You can get to all Windows applets via the Start button. Click the **Start** button, rest the mouse pointer on **Programs**, and then on **Accessories**.

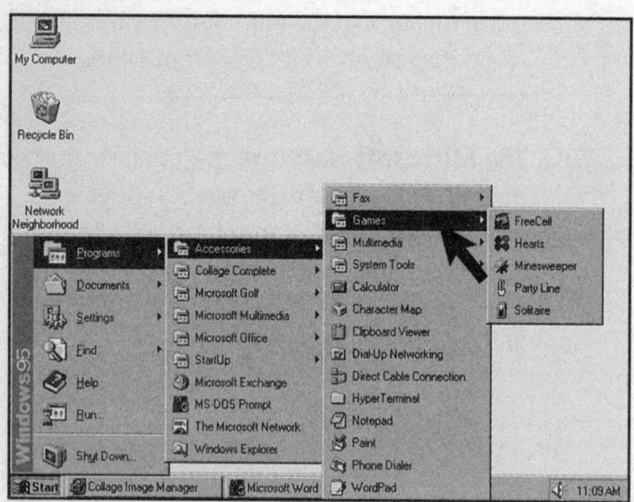

2 At the bottom of the Programs menu are a couple of applets, but the Accessories menu is the place where most applets hang out. At the top of the Accessories menu are the names of additional submenus. Move the mouse pointer over a submenu name to display its applets.

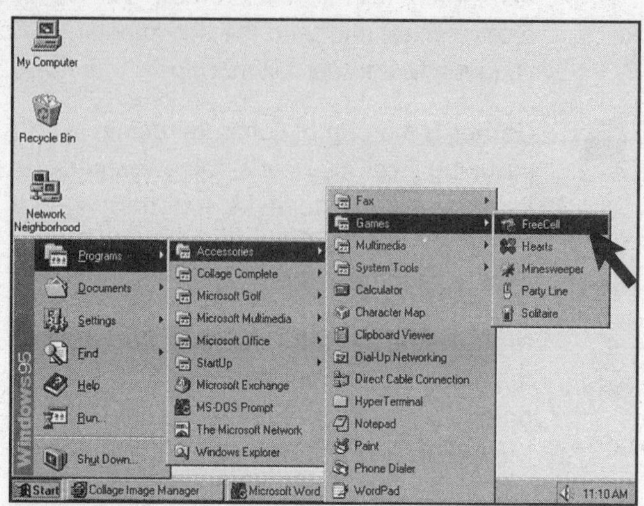

3 When you see the name of the applet you want to run, click it.

4 Windows runs the applet and automatically closes the Start menu. The applet displays its own window, complete with title bar and menu bar, so you can start performing a task.

Control Your Printer

Unless you've made a complete transition to paperless publishing, chances are that you have some sort of printer connected to your computer. If you already set it up to work in Windows 95, and the printer is working flawlessly, you can safely skip this section and move onto more interesting material.

However, if you haven't set up your printer yet, if the printer is printing strange symbols, or if you simply can't get the printer to start (or stop) printing, then the *Guided Tour* can help.

The first part of the *Guided Tour* leads you through the process of setting up your printer for the first time in Windows 95. If you just connected a new printer, or if you picked the wrong printer during the Windows installation, this section will help you get started.

How Windows 95 Prints

Windows allows you to print documents (from Windows programs) in the background while you are working in other programs. Windows does this by printing the documents to a temporary file on your hard disk and then *spooling* the documents to your printer. When you print a document from a Windows program, windows stores the document in a *queue* (a waiting line), and then feeds the document to the printer.

The second part of the *Guided Tour* explains how to manage the documents that Windows is in the process of printing. You'll learn how to start and stop your printer (in the event of a mishap), how to resume after you've corrected a problem, and how to cancel printing altogether.

Change Print Quality and Other Settings

Most printers are set up to print on 8.5-by-11-inch paper in portrait orientation (rather than sideways), using a certain print quality for text and graphics. Windows gives you a great deal of control over these settings, even more control than you can take by pressing the little buttons on your printer. To change the print settings in Windows, take the following steps:

1. Double-click **My Computer**, and double-click the **Printers** icon.
2. Right-click the icon for the printer whose settings you want to change, and click **Properties**. The Properties dialog box for the selected printer appears. Each tab lets you control a different aspect of printing.

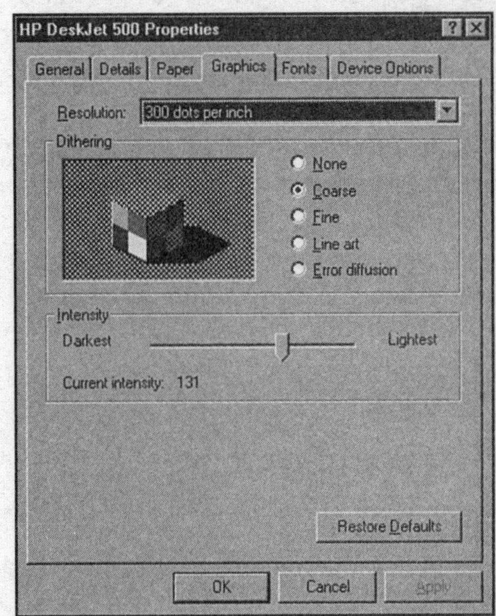

3. Click the General tab and change any of the following options:

> Comment: If you share this printer with other users, you can type a comment here to let other users know of printer settings or problems.

To insert a page between documents (so you know where a document begins and ends), select an option from the Separator page drop-down list.

4. Click the **Details** tab, and select any of the following options:

If you installed a printer, and it doesn't respond, try selecting a different port from the **Print to the following port** drop-down list. (LPT1 is the most common port setting.)

You can choose a different printer driver for this printer from the **Print using the following driver** drop-down list, but you're better off installing the new driver as explained earlier in this chapter.

The **Capture Printer Port** and **End Capture** buttons allow you to map the printer port to a network drive (if your computer is on a network), and disconnect the printer from the network drive.

The **Timeout** settings specify how long Windows should wait before reporting a printer error (for example, you forgot to turn on the printer, or it ran out of paper). If you have trouble printing large documents, you might want to increase the time in the **Transmission retry** text box to 90.

The **Spool Settings** button opens a dialog box that allows you to turn on print spooling (for faster printing) or print directly to the printer. You should usually use print spooling unless you have trouble with a particular print job.

The **Port Settings** button lets you turn print spooling for DOS programs on or off.

5. Click the **Paper** tab, and do any of the following:

In the **Paper size** list, click the desired paper or envelope size you want to print on.

Under **Orientation**, select **Portrait** to print text across the page, as in a personal or business letter, or click **Landscape** to print text sideways on a page (so the page is wider than it is tall).

Open the **Paper source** drop-down list, and click the type of paper feed you intend to use. For example, if you have a printer with two or more paper trays, you can select a specific tray.

6. Click the **Graphics** tab to change the following options for printing pictures:

From the **Resolution** drop-down list, select the desired print quality for pictures. Print quality is measured in dots per inch. The more dots, the higher the quality, but it takes longer to print. This does not affect text quality unless you choose to print text as graphics.

Under **Dithering**, select None for black-and-white graphics (no gray shading), Coarse if you selected a resolution of 300 dots per inch or more, Fine if you selected a resolution of 200 dots per inch or less, or Line art if you want clearly defined lines to appear between shaded areas. Error diffusion makes the picture look fuzzy.

Drag the **Intensity** slider to control the lightness or darkness of graphic images.

7. If you purchased a font cartridge for your printer, you can click the **Fonts** tab to install the cartridge.

8. Click the Device Options tab to change the following options:

Print quality lets you specify the print quality for text. If you select a high quality, the print will look nice, but the printer will use more ink and take more time to print a document.

Printer memory lets you select the amount of memory installed in the printer. Some printers let you plug in a cartridge or add memory chips to increase the amount of information the printer can process. Don't change this setting unless you added memory to your printer.

9. Click the **OK** button to save your changes.

If you have a question about any option in the dialog box, right-click the option's name, and then click **What's This?**.

Begin Guided Tour Set Up a Printer for Windows

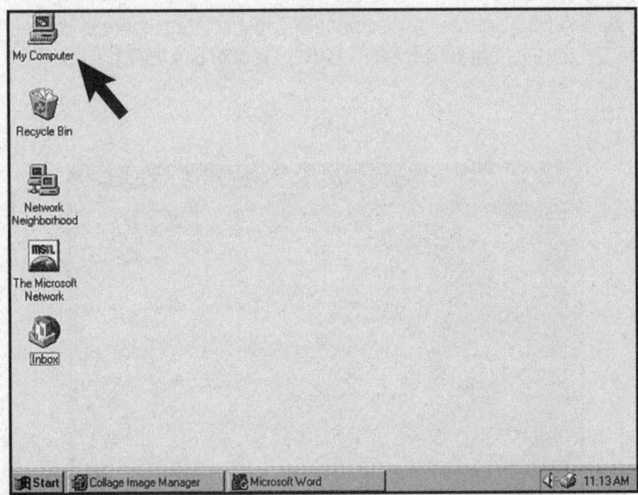

1 In addition to providing access to your disk drives, My Computer lets you manage your printers. Double-click **My Computer**.

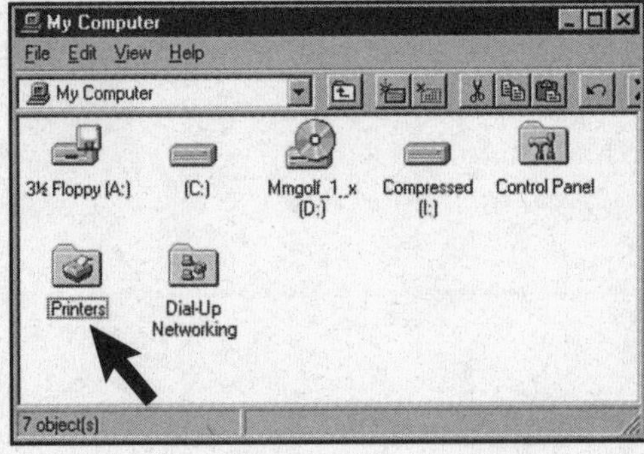

2 Double-click the **Printers** icon.

3 The Printers windows appears, showing icons for all the printers installed on your computer. Double-click the **Add Printer** button.

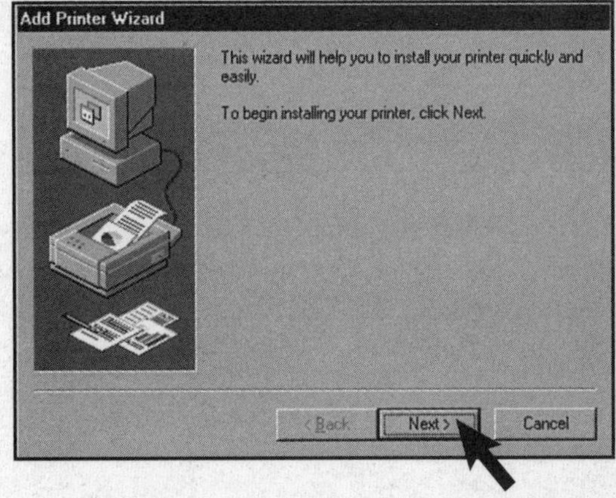

4 The Add Printer Wizard appears, which will lead you through the process of installing a printer driver. Click the **Next** button.

(continues)

Guided Tour Set Up a Printer for Windows

(continued)

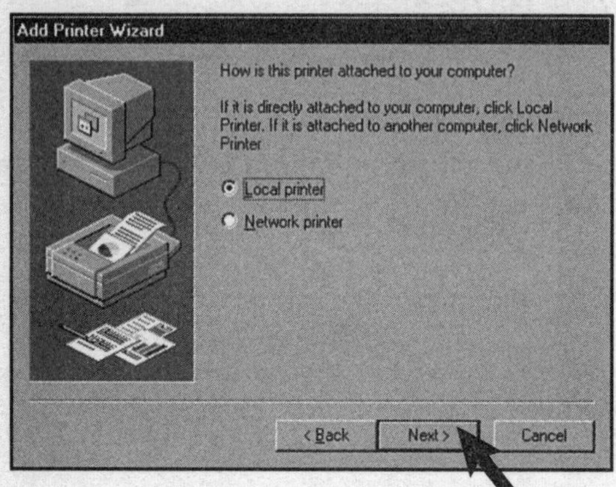

5 The Wizard asks if you want to install a local printer (connected directly to your system) or a network printer (which will be available to other computers on the network). Make sure **Local printer** is selected, and then click the **Next** button.

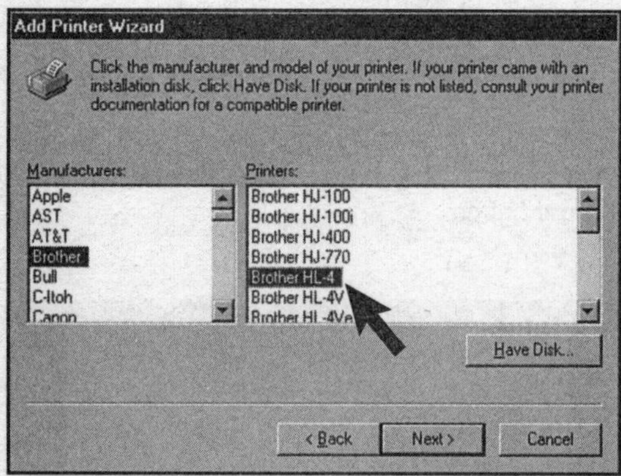

6 The Wizard now asks you to specify the manufacturer and model of your printer. Click the brand name of the printer in the **Manufacturers** list, and then click the make and model of your printer in the **Printers** list. Click the **Next** button.

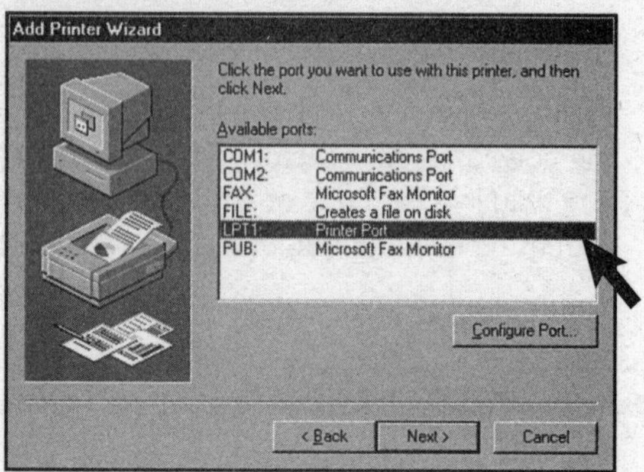

7 A list of printer ports appears. Most printers connect to the parallel printer port (LPT1). If in doubt, pick **LPT1**. Click the **Next** button.

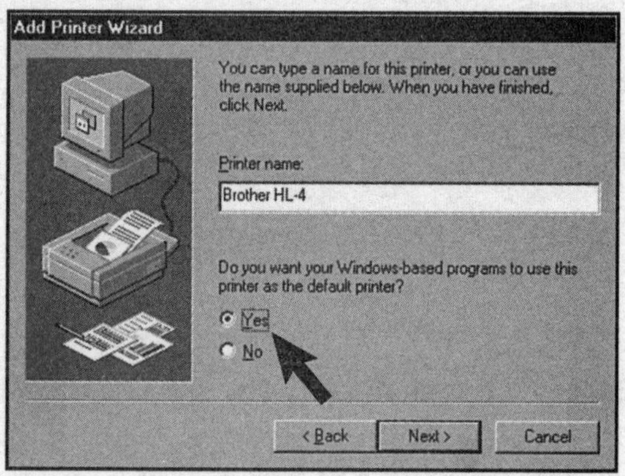

8 The Wizard asks if you want to use this printer as the default printer for your Windows programs. To have this printer act as your full-time printer for all your Windows programs, click **Yes**, and then click the **Next** button. If you select **No**, you'll have to select this printer in your program's printer setup in order to use it.

Guided Tour Set Up a Printer for Windows

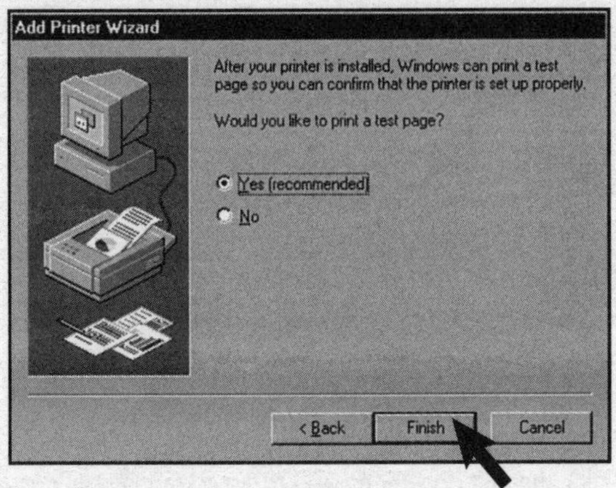

9. Click the **Finish** button. If the files for the selected printer are on your hard disk, the Wizard installs the printer and adds an icon for it in the Printers window. If the files are not available, the Wizard prompts you to insert a Windows disk or the manufacturer's disk.

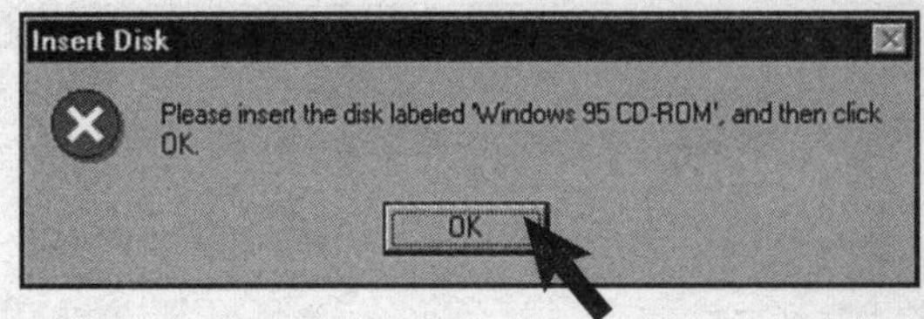

10. If prompted to insert a disk, insert the disk, and click the **OK** button.

To pick a different printer as the default, right-click its icon, and then click **Set As Default**.

Begin Guided Tour Pause, Cancel, and Resume Printing

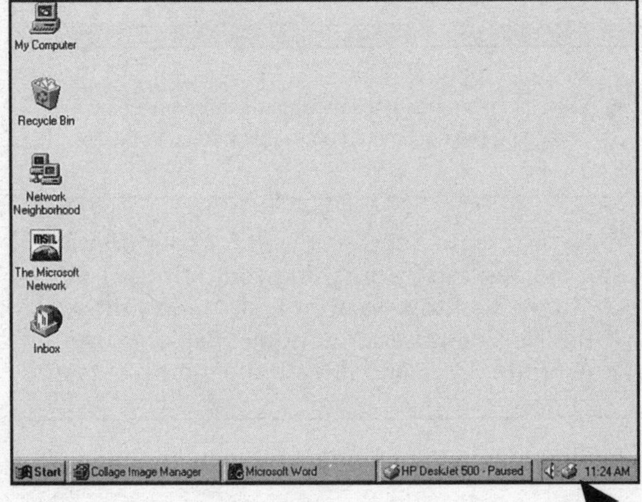

1. When you start printing, a printer icon appears next to the time in the taskbar. Double-click printer icon to view a list of documents in the print queue.

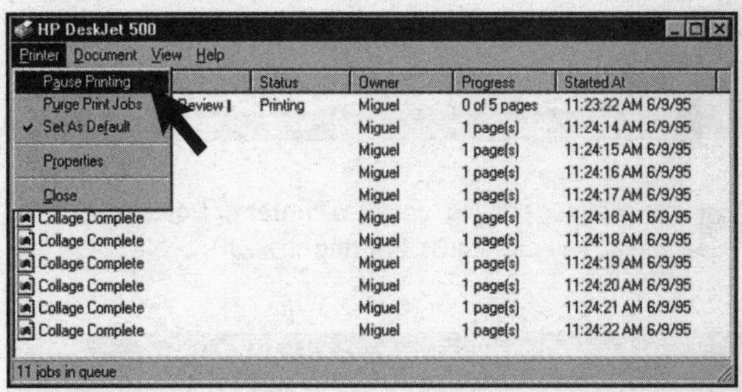

2. The print queue window appears, showing the status of the documents in the print queue. You can stop all printing by opening the **Printer** menu and clicking on **Pause Printing**.

(continues)

Guided Tour Pause, Cancel, and Resume Printing

(continued)

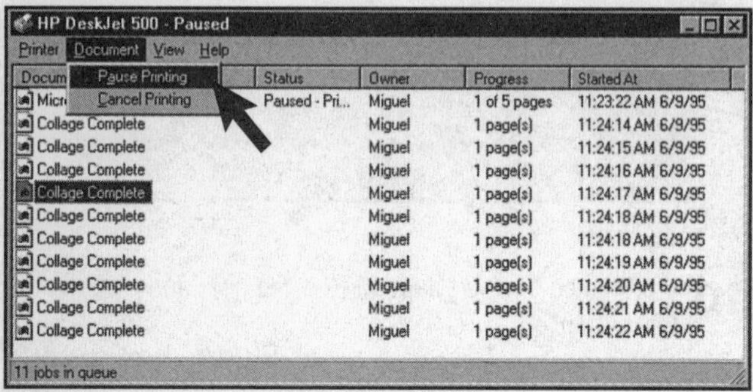

3 To pause the printing of a single document select the document, open the **Document** menu, and click **Pause Printing**. (Your printer may continue printing one or two pages, because Windows cannot control what is stored in your printer's memory.)

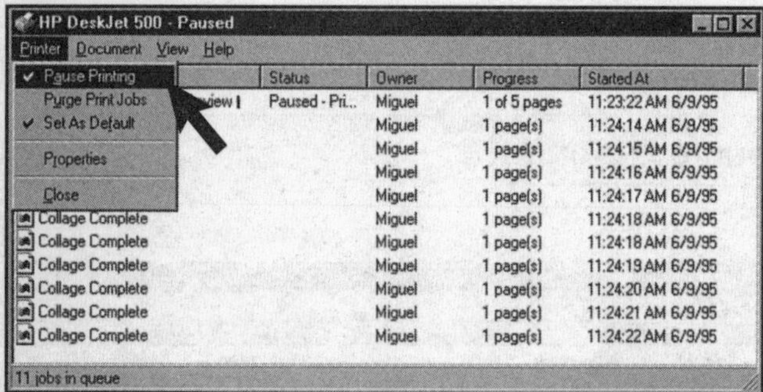

4 To continue printing, open the **Printer** or **Document** menu, and click **Pause Printing** again.

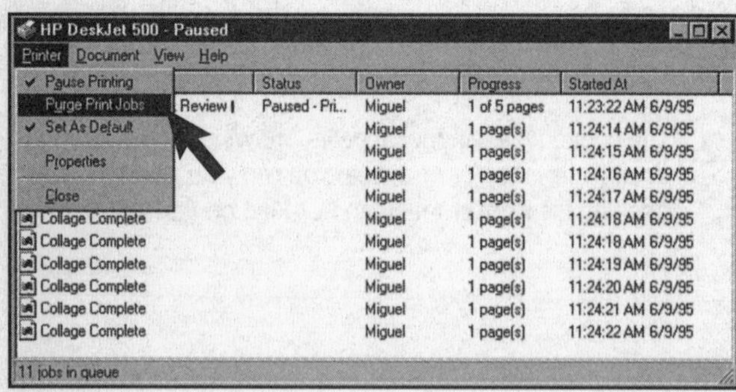

5 You can cancel all print jobs (and stop printing) by opening the **Printer** menu and selecting **Purge Print Jobs**. This removes all documents from the print queue.

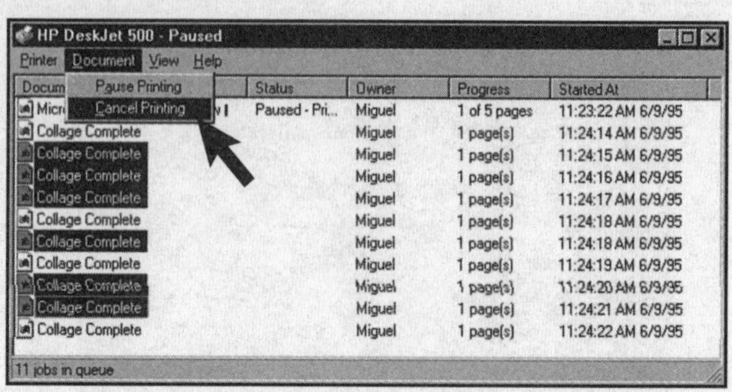

6 To remove one or more documents from the print queue, click the first document, and Ctrl+click additional documents. Open the **Document** menu and select **Cancel Printing**.

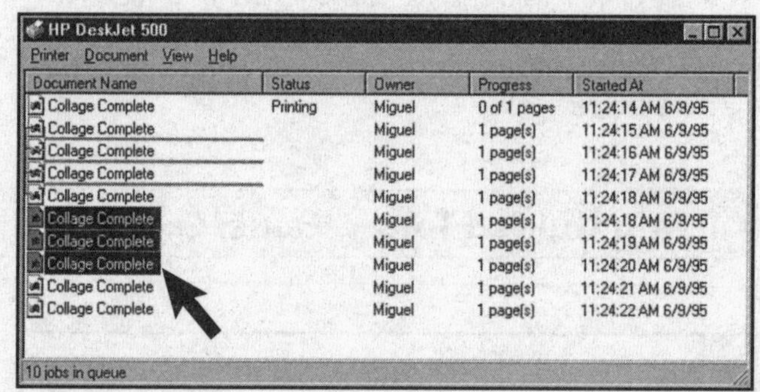

7 You can rearrange documents in the print queue by dragging the document names up or down in the list.

> You can create a shortcut icon for your printer on the desktop by dragging your printer icon onto the desktop. To print a file, simply drag it from My Computer or Windows Explorer over the printer icon, and release the mouse button.

Change the Video Display Properties

If you work in a large office, you probably walk past computers every day and see some sort of funky color scheme or design on the monitor. Maybe you've wondered how your colleague has managed to decorate her screen so expertly, and you have a secret desire to give your monitor a custom look.

Windows 95 provides an easy way for you to change the look of your Windows desktop. You can change the color of the desktop, add a design, change the resolution (so more information is displayed), and even turn on a screensaver, which displays moving pictures on the screen. The *Guided Tour* shows just how easy it is to customize your desktop.

Begin Guided Tour Change the Background Color and Design

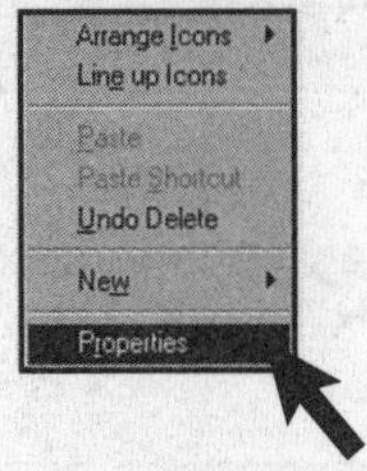

1 To change any of the display properties, right-click a blank area of the Windows desktop, and click **Properties**. (Another way to change display properties is to click the **Start** button, point to **Settings**, and click **Control Panel**; then, double-click the **Display** icon.)

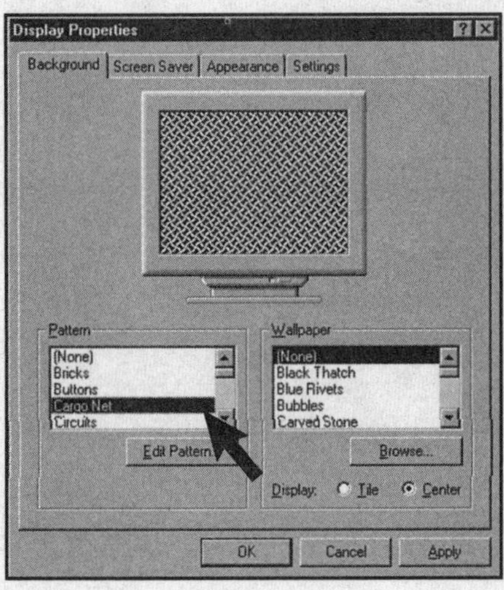

2 The Background tab appears up front. From the **Pattern** list, click the desired background pattern. A pattern gives some texture to the background, such as bricks or pillars.

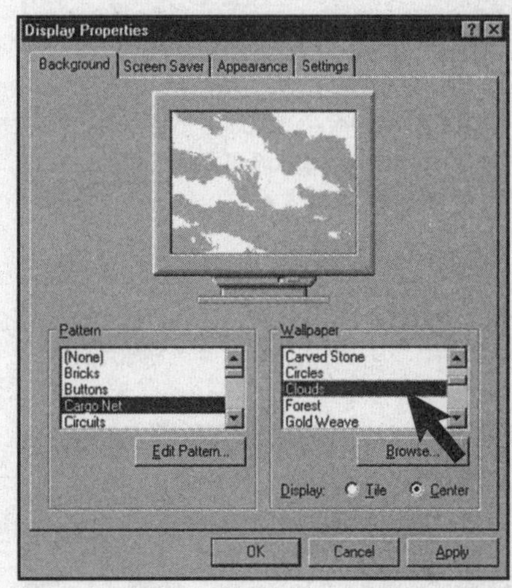

3 From the **Wallpaper** list, click the desired wallpaper design. Wallpaper is any graphic that lays on top of the desktop; Windows comes with several wallpaper designs from which you can select.

> You can create your own wallpaper by using the Paint program that comes with Windows (Start, Programs, Accessories, Paint). After creating your picture, open the File menu and select one of the Set as Wallpaper options.

(continues)

Guided Tour Change the Background Color and Design

(continued)

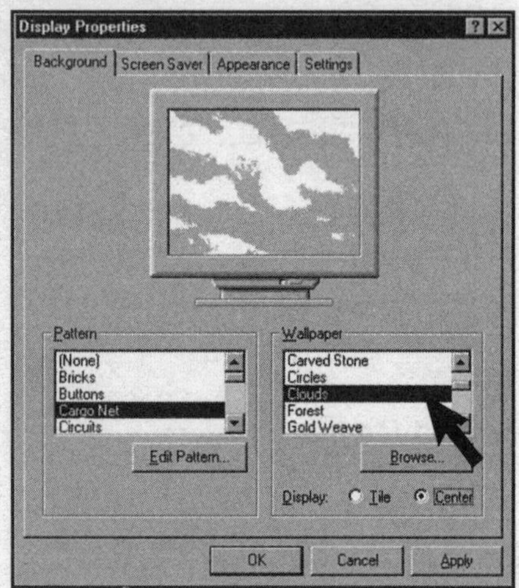

4 Select **Tile** to have the wallpaper design fill the screen or **Center** to have one section of the design placed in the middle of the screen.

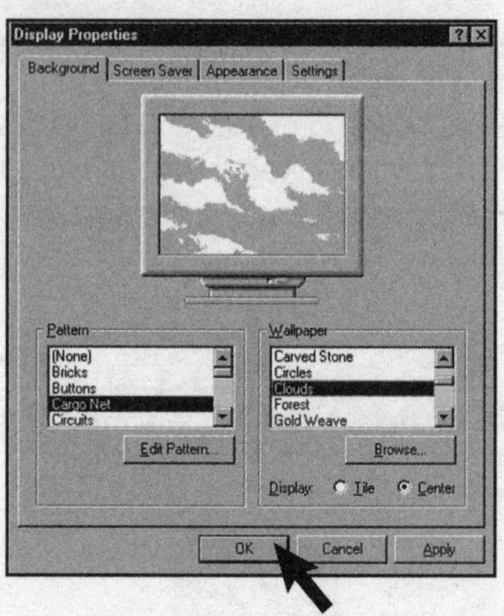

5 The preview area shows how the screen will look with the new settings. Click the **OK** button to save your changes.

Begin Guided Tour Turn on a Screen Saver

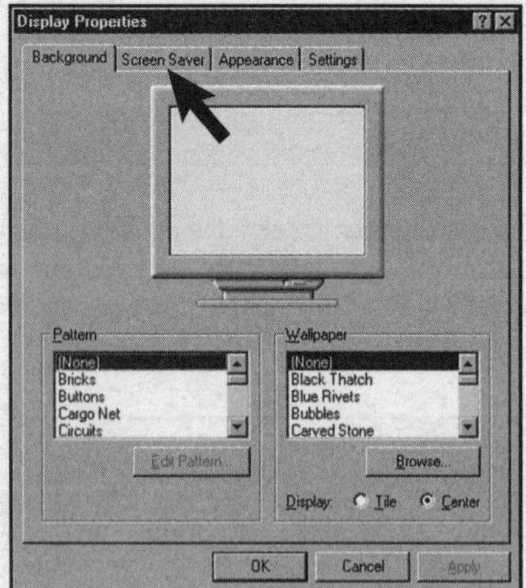

1 A screen saver displays moving pictures that can prevent a stagnant image from burning into your screen. To turn on a Windows screen saver, right-click a blank area of the Windows desktop, and click **Properties**. Click the **Screen Saver** tab to display its options. If you have a monitor that offers power saving features, such as reduced power use, you can enter the power saving settings here.

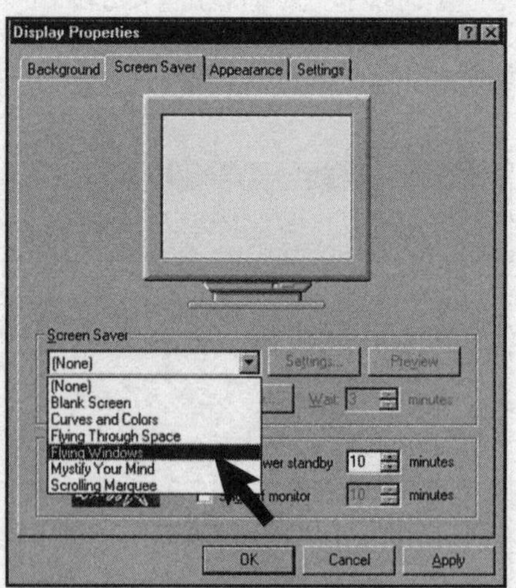

2 Windows comes with several basic screen savers. Open the **Screen Saver** drop-down list, and click the desired screen saver.

Guided Tour Turn on a Screen Saver

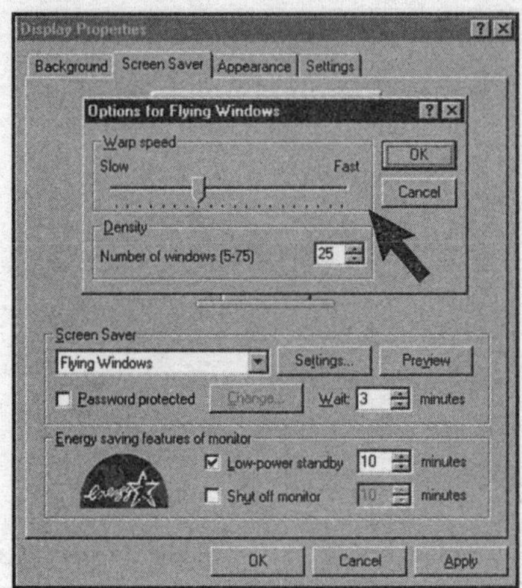

3 To change the settings for the selected screen saver, click the **Settings** button, enter your preferences, and click **OK**. (Preferences vary depending on the screen saver; for example, if you turn on Flying Windows, you can specify the number of flying windows and the speed at which they fly.)

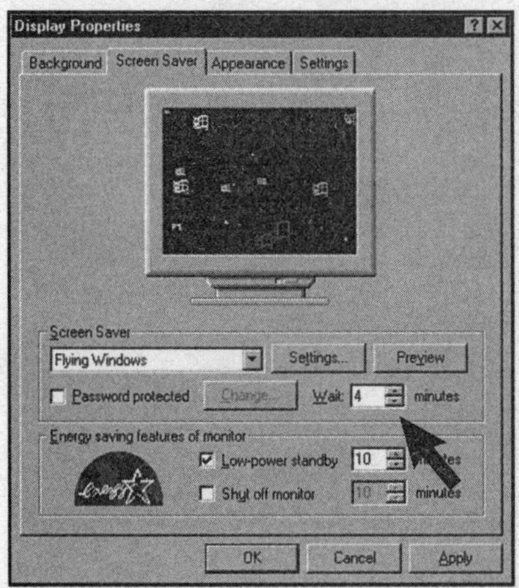

4 Click the arrows next to the **Wait ____ minutes** spin box to specify how long your computer should be inactive before the screen saver kicks in.

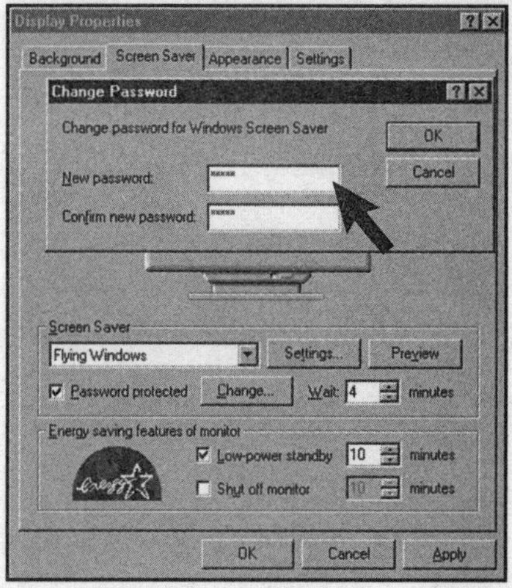

5 To use the screen saver to protect your computer from unauthorized use, click the **Password protected** option. Then, click the **Change** button, type your password in the **New password** and **Confirm new password** text boxes, and click **OK**. (Whatever you type appears as asterisks, so nobody can read the password as you type it.)

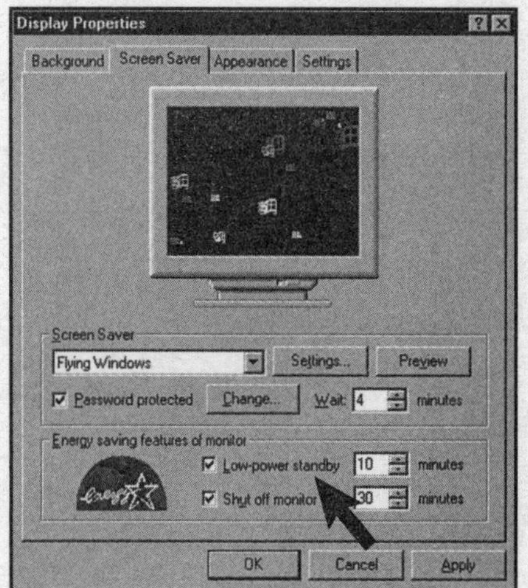

6 If you have an energy smart monitor, you can pick one of the following options to have Windows power down the monitor during periods of inactivity: **Low-power standby** triggers the monitor's power saving feature. The monitor remains on. Use the **minutes** spin box to specify how long the computer must remain inactive before the power saver kicks in. **Shut off monitor** turns the monitor off after a specified number of minutes (use the **minutes** spin box).

7 Click the **OK** button to save your changes.

Begin Guided Tour Change the Appearance of Windows

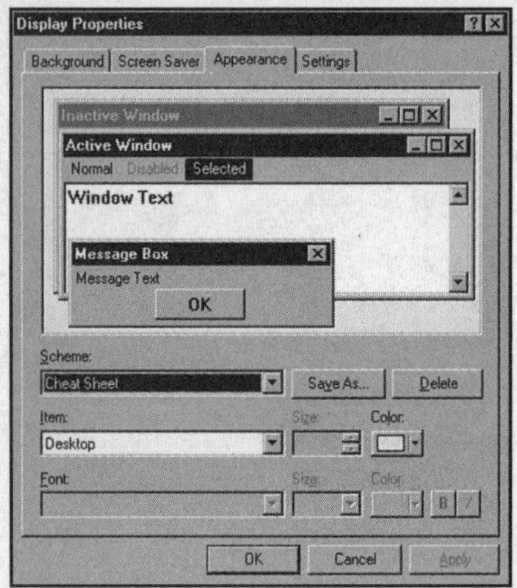

1 You can change the color of title bars, the thickness of window borders, and the size of text. Right-click a blank area of the Windows desktop, and click **Properties**. To change the look of your windows, click the **Appearance** tab.

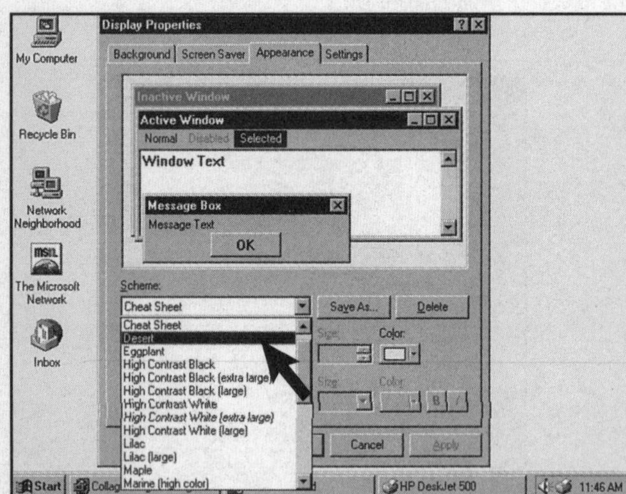

2 Windows comes with several predesigned color schemes. To use one of these schemes, open the **Scheme** drop-down list, and click the desired color scheme.

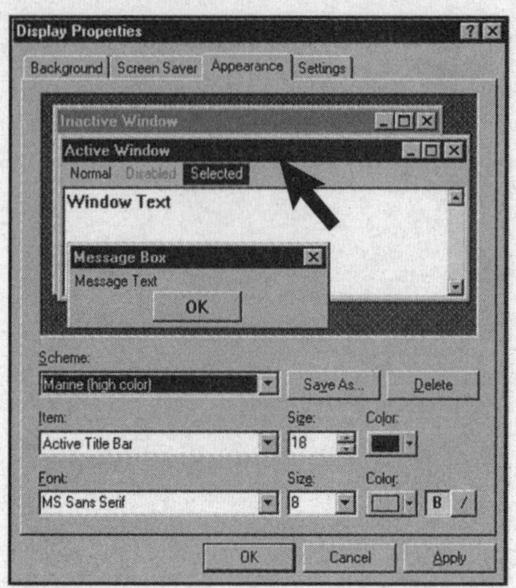

3 You can also change the look of individual objects. Click the object in the preview area. The **Item** drop-down list shows the name of the selected item, allowing you to change its look.

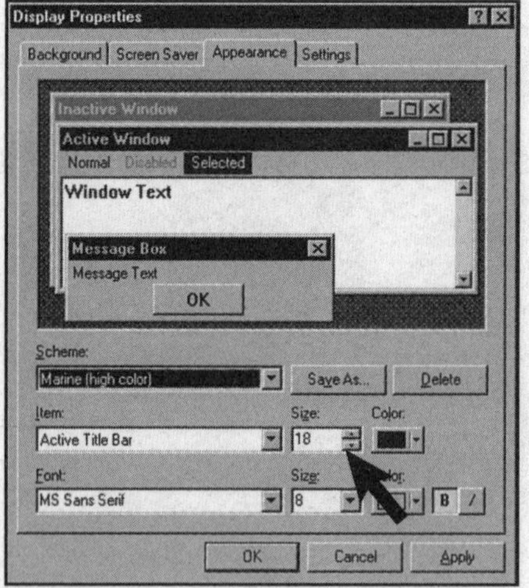

4 To change the size of the selected item, click the arrows to the right of the **Size** spin box.

Guided Tour Change the Appearance of Windows

5 To change the color of the selected item, open the **Color** drop-down list, and click the desired color.

6 If the selected item has text in it (as in a title bar or menu), you can use the **Font**, **Size**, and **Color** drop-down lists to control the appearance of the text.

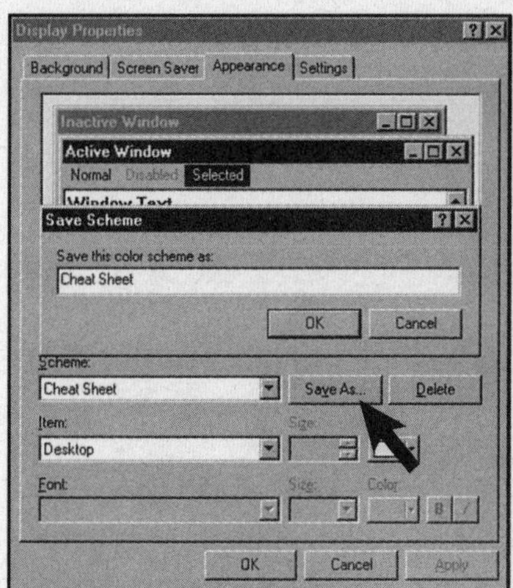

7 To save your settings as a new color scheme, click the **Save As** button, type a name for the new color scheme, and click **OK**.

8 Click the **OK** button to put your changes into effect.

Begin Guided Tour Change the Display Resolution

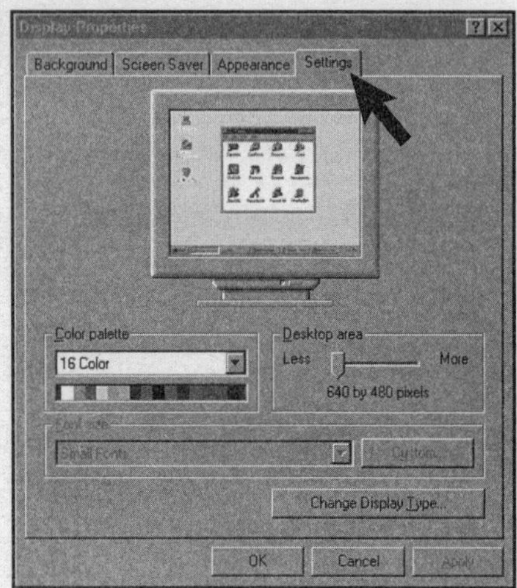

1 Display resolution controls the quality of the display. Right-click a blank area of the Windows desktop, and click **Properties**. Click the **Settings** tab to view the current resolution settings. You can set the number of colors used in the display, and the amount of information displayed on the desktop.

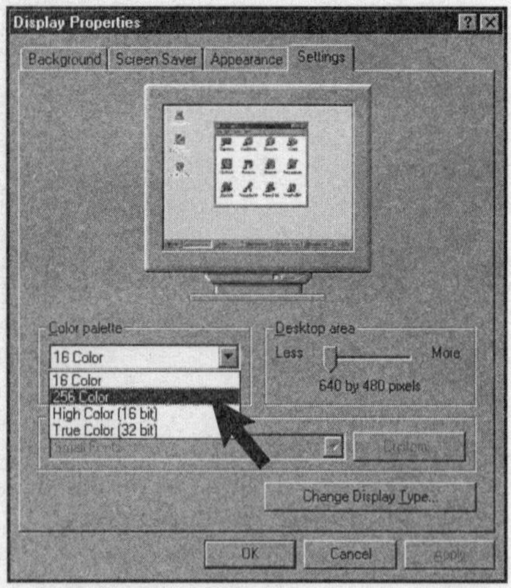

2 Open the **Color palette** drop-down list, and select the number of colors you want your monitor to display. (If you plan on playing video clips and viewing pictures, pick at least 256 colors.) If you pick more colors, more memory is required to display those colors.

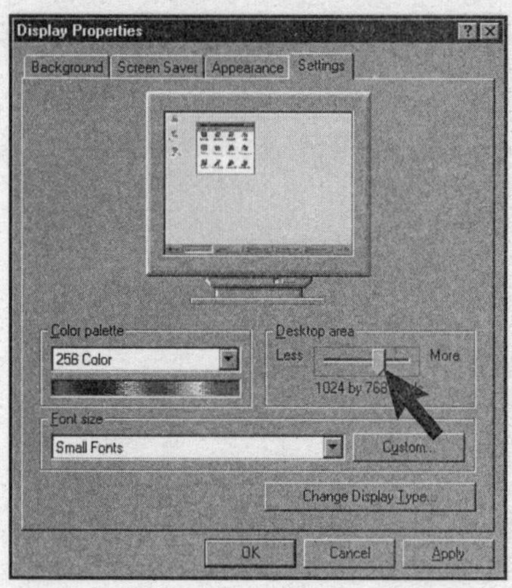

3 Drag the slider under **Desktop area** to the right, to increase the screen resolution, or to the left to decrease it. Higher resolutions (for example, 1024-by-768) display more information on the screen, but display smaller objects than lower resolutions (such as 640-by-480).

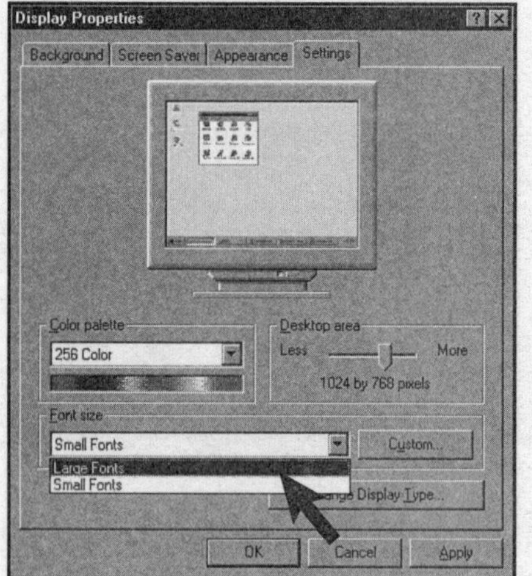

4 If you picked a higher resolution, you can use the **Font size** drop-down list to select a large or small font for the display. (You might want to pick a larger font size, so you can read the type.) Or, click the **Custom** button and pick a scaling percentage for the fonts.

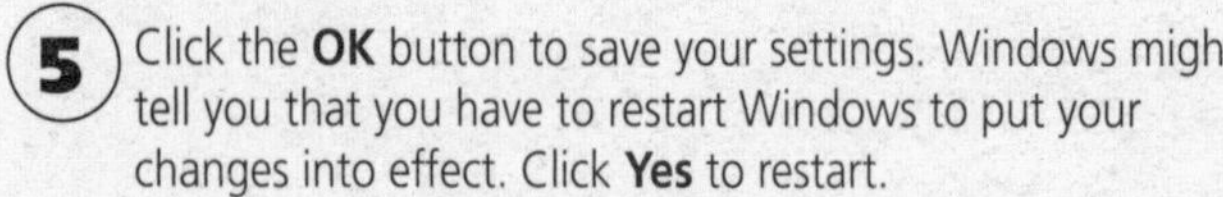

5 Click the **OK** button to save your settings. Windows might tell you that you have to restart Windows to put your changes into effect. Click **Yes** to restart.

Take Control of Your Keyboard and Mouse

Chances are that your keyboard and mouse behave pretty much as you want them to. The mouse pointer looks okay, it travels across the screen at a good clip, and (if you're right-handed) you don't have trouble left- and right-clicking. Likewise with the keyboard: if you hold down a key, it starts to repeat, and it repeats at a rate that is comfortable.

However, Windows does let you control the behavior of the keyboard and mouse. You can change the look of the mouse pointer, change the speed at which it travels across the screen, and even flip the left and right mouse buttons for all you lefties. You can also change the length of time you have to hold down a key before it starts to repeat, and the speed at which the key repeats. The *Guided Tour* leads you through these configuration options.

Begin Guided Tour Change Your Mouse Settings

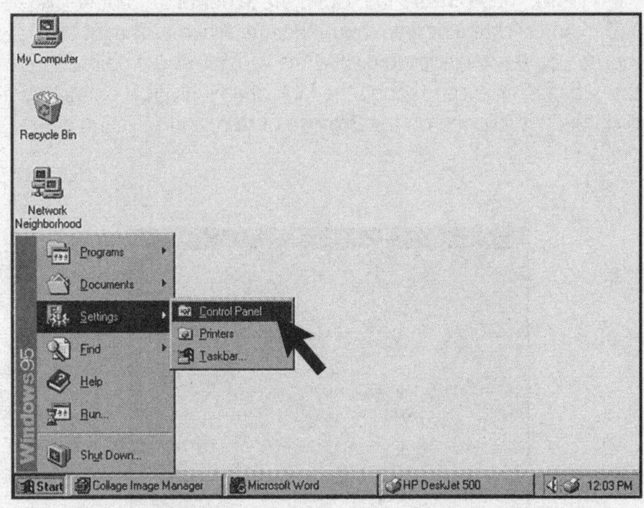

1 You change your mouse settings by using an icon in the Control Panel. To display the Control Panel, click the **Start** button, rest the mouse pointer on **Settings**, and click **Control Panel**.

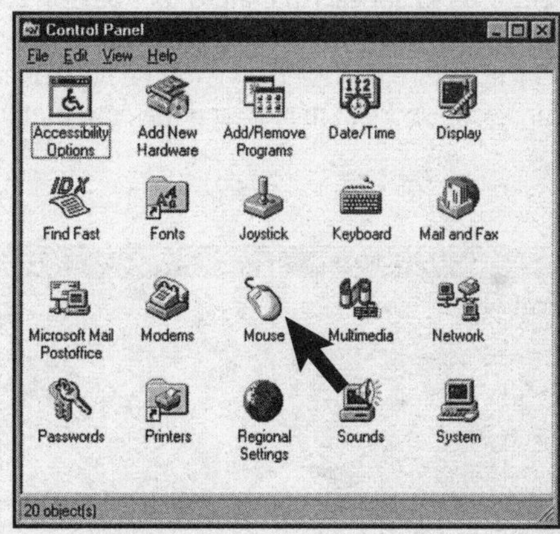

2 Double-click the **Mouse** icon.

(continues)

Guided Tour Change Your Mouse Settings

(continued)

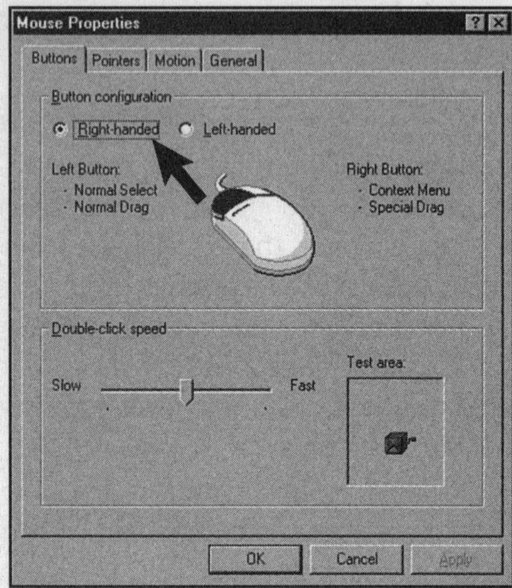

3 The Buttons tab appears in front. Under **Button configuration**, click **Right-handed** or **Left-handed**. Left-handed swaps the functions of the left and right mouse buttons, so the left button brings up shortcut menus, and the right button selects items.

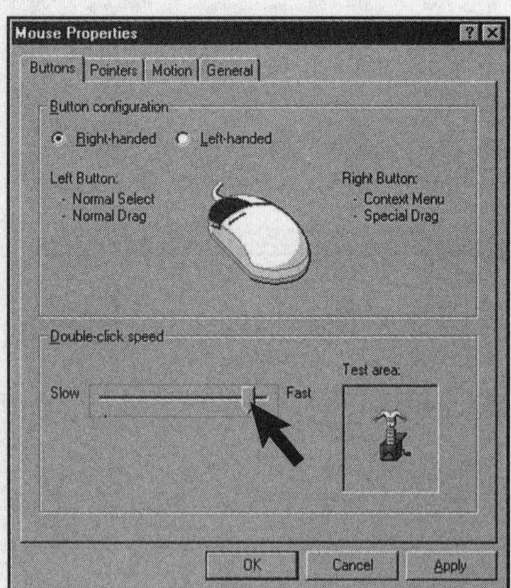

4 To change the speed at which you must click twice for Windows to acknowledge a double-click, drag the **Double-click speed** slider to the left or right. (You can double-click the jack-in-the box animation to test the speed.)

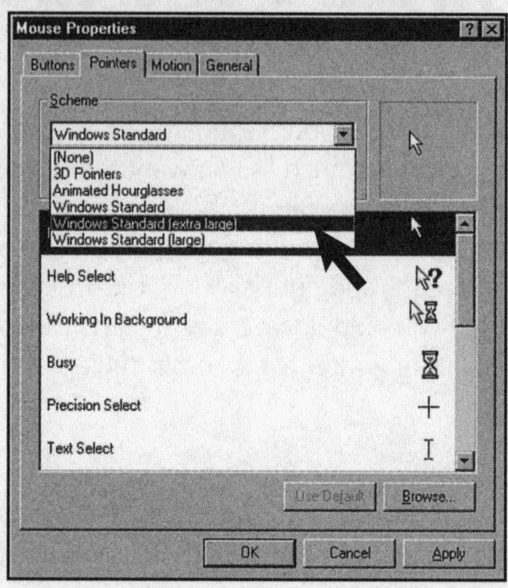

5 Click the **Pointers** tab. Open the **Scheme** drop-down list, and click the desired mouse pointer scheme. The list of mouse pointers changes to display the various mouse pointers in this scheme. (You can change the look of an individual pointer by clicking on it, clicking on the **Browse** button, and selecting a pointer.)

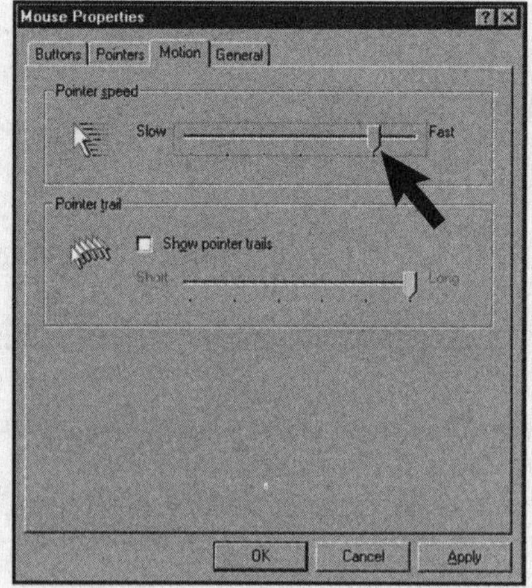

6 Click the **Motion** tab to set the speed at which the mouse pointer travels across the screen. Drag the **Pointer speed** slider to the left or right to change the speed of the pointer.

Guided Tour Change Your Mouse Settings

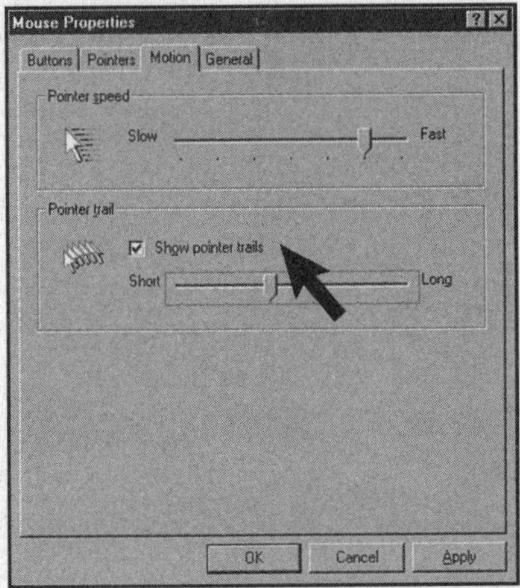

7 To have the mouse leave a trail as it travels across the screen, click **Show pointer trails**, and then use the slider to set the length of the pointer tail. (Roll your mouse around to test the effects of your change.)

8 Click the **OK** button to save your new mouse settings.

The General tab lets you pick a different mouse driver (the program that tells Windows how to control the mouse). If your mouse is working okay, avoid this option. If your mouse seems to freeze your computer, try selecting a different mouse driver.

Begin Guided Tour Change Your Keyboard Settings

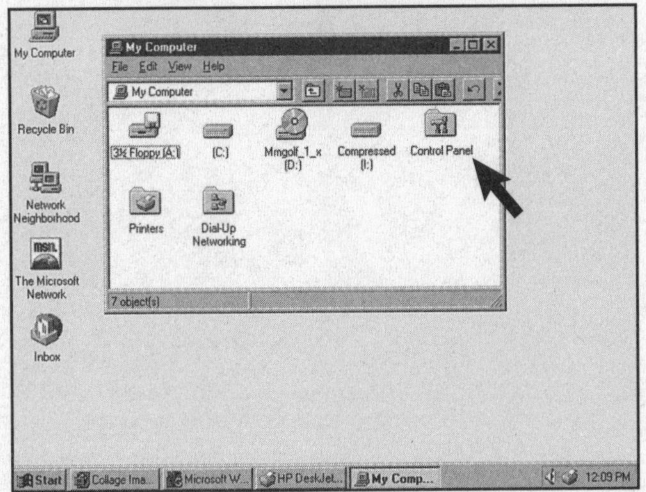

1 You change your keyboard settings by using an icon in the Control Panel. To display the Control Panel, double-click **My Computer**, and then double-click the **Control Panel** icon.

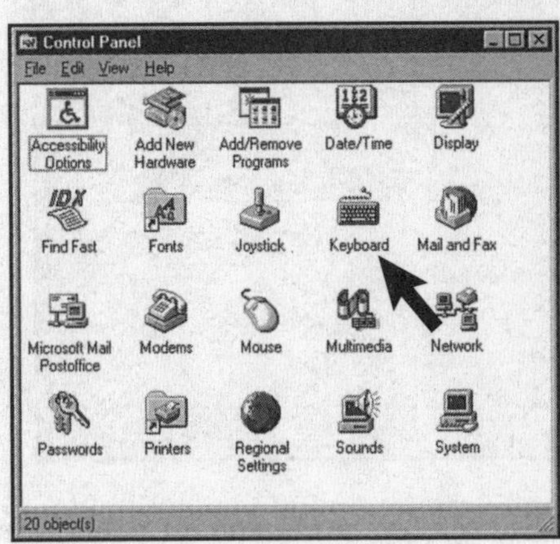

2 Double-click the **Keyboard** icon.

(continues)

Guided Tour Change Your Keyboard Settings

(continued)

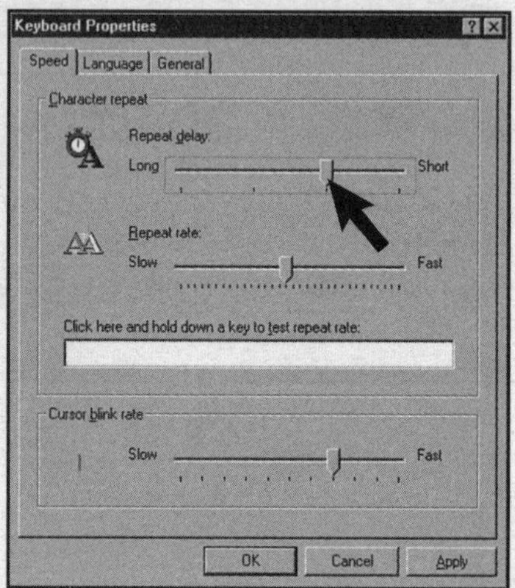

3 To change how long you have to hold down a key before it starts repeating, drag the **Repeat delay** slider to the left (so you have to hold down the key longer) or to the right (so the character will start repeating right away).

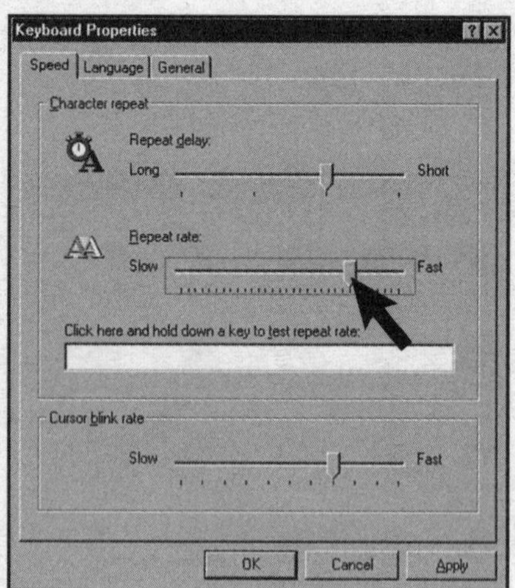

4 To change how fast the character repeats when it starts repeating, drag the **Repeat rate** slider to the left (to repeat slowly) or to the right (for a quicker pace).

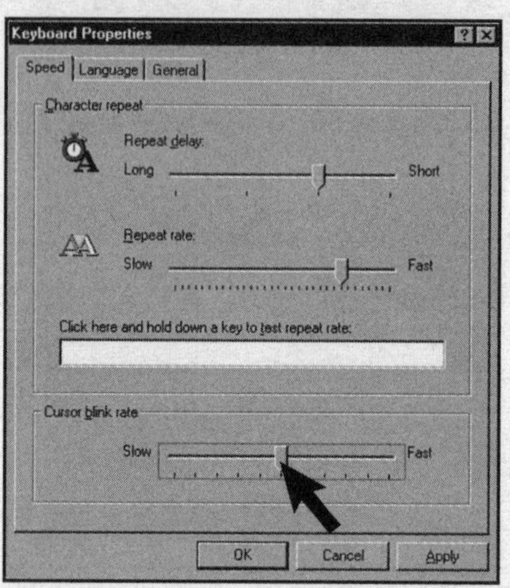

5 To change the speed at which the insertion point blinks, drag the **Cursor blink rate** slider to the left or right.

6 Click the **OK** button. Your changes are saved, and your keyboard will start acting as instructed.

HOW TO...
Work with DOS

Even though DOS has taken a bad rap over time as "user-unfriendly"—and you may prefer to avoid it like the plague—it pays to know basic DOS survival skills. You never know when you may need them.

For example, you may encounter a DOS application program (most likely a game program) that may be so cool you'll even brave the world of DOS to try it out.

This section teaches you the least you need to know about DOS. Here, you'll learn how to enter DOS commands, navigate through directories from the DOS prompt, work with DOS programs, and more.

What You Will Find in This Section

Enter Commands in DOS 212

Change Which Drive Is Active 215

Change Which Directory Is Active 217

Create and Remove a Directory 219

List Directory Contents 221

Use DOS to Format Disks 224

Start a DOS Program from the DOS Prompt 225

Work with Menus in a DOS Program 227

Work in a Dialog Box 229

Open a New or Existing File in a DOS Program 231

Save a File in a DOS Program 232

Exit a DOS Program 233

Enter Commands in DOS

Computers have to be told exactly what to do. They're smart, but they're ultra-obedient and they lack initiative. For example, when you start your computer, it boots up and then sits there and waits for your instructions. It displays a *prompt*, letting you know it's ready for your command. The prompt usually looks like **C:\>**.

This prompt comes from DOS, your computer's *disk operating system*, which loads automatically when you start your computer. DOS runs your computer, and lets you communicate with your computer by giving it specific commands. Without DOS (or a similar operating system), your computer can't run.

In DOS, you type a command at the prompt, then press **Enter** to run the command. This sounds simple enough, but it can be a headache, especially for newer users. You see, DOS speaks a unique, highly specialized language. The commands you type in have to be entered absolutely correctly; when you use a file name in a command line, you generally need to include the full *path* (disk drive letter, directory, and name) for a file. Otherwise, DOS won't understand what you mean and will flash the message **Bad command or file name**.

DOS calls the rules for entering commands its command *syntax*. There are specific parts to a DOS command; they must be entered in the right order and typed correctly. The DOS command plus the parts you enter make up a *command line*; here are the parts:

Start by typing the *command* itself. It must be spelled correctly. For example, you use the COPY command to copy files. Some commands, like *copy*, consist of an entire word. Other commands are abbreviations (*mem*) or acronyms (*md*).

Add parameters. *Parameters* tell DOS what file or other object to perform the command on (some commands require them, some don't). To delete a file, for example, you have to type the exact file name, including the directory path and three-letter file name extension.

Add delimiters, if they're needed. *Delimiters* include special characters you add, like the backslash (****), forward slash (**/**), and colon (**:**). These "punctuate" the command line for DOS. For example, you need to use the **** and **:** characters correctly in the path statement for a file, like **c:\work\file1.txt**. Delimiters usually appear within parameters.

Add *switches* to the end of command lines to fine-tune how the command works. (Some commands let you use switches, others don't.) You can add a **/p** switch to a DOS **del** (delete) command, for example, so that DOS will prompt you to verify that you want to delete the file. Available switches vary, and you can use more than one switch at a time. Some switches even can be fine-tuned by adding a colon and a parameter. For example, to display a list of files in a directory and sort the files by their three-letter extension, you would use the command and add the **:e** parameter to the **/o** switch. The full command with switch and parameter would be **dir /o:e**.

Be careful when you type in your DOS commands; DOS doesn't offer an "undo" feature. The *Guided Tour* that follows shows you how to enter a command (in this case, the one that copies a file from the hard disk to a floppy disk).

You can type commands in uppercase or lowercase letters in DOS. The one thing DOS doesn't care about is what case you use.

Identify Commands, Switches, and Parameters

You don't have to be a memory expert to use DOS commands and remember all the parameters and switches. You can ask DOS for help about commands, their switches, and their parameters. This is useful if you can't remember an exact command name or what to type with it. There are three different ways to get this help:

- At the DOS prompt, type **help** and press **Enter**. This displays a listing of available commands, giving a brief description of what each does.
- You can get help with a single command (such as finding out what switches you can use with it), if you know its name. At the DOS prompt, type **help**, press the **Spacebar**, then type the name of a command. Press **Enter**, and DOS displays a description of the command and information about the parameters and switches you can and/or should use with the command.

```
C:\>help del
Deletes one or more files.

DEL [drive:][path]filename [/P]
ERASE [drive:][path]filename [/P]

  [drive:][path]filename  Specifies the file(s) to delete.  Specify multiple
                          files by using wildcards.
  /P                      Prompts for confirmation before deleting each file.

C:\>
```

- DOS can simply tell you what parameters and switches to use with a command, if you already know what the command does. At the DOS prompt, type the command name, press the **Spacebar**, then type **/?**. Press **Enter**, and DOS displays information about the parameters and switches available with the command.

Change Your DOS Prompt

You've seen the familiar old DOS prompt, **C:\>**. If you're like me, "familiar" might be the same as "boring." Fortunately, you can use the prompt command to jazz up your DOS prompt. Just type the **prompt** command, then a space, then enter the combination of text and special characters you want your prompt to display. (Typing **prompt** without specifying any text or characters resets the prompt to the usual C:\>. Here's what you type to display special characters in a prompt:

Type this…	*To display this in the prompt…*
$Q	=
$$	$
$T	current system time
$D	current system date
$P	current drive and path
$V	DOS version
$N	Current drive
$G	>
$L	<
$B	|

For example, type this prompt command and press **Enter**: **prompt It's $T. Do you know where your computer is?$G** Your prompt will then look like this:

```
C:\>prompt It's $T. Do you know where your computer is?$G
It's 10:33:22.34. Do you know where your computer is?>
```

I use the command **prompt PG** so that DOS displays the full path (drive letter and directories) that I'm currently logged on to. This makes it much easier to navigate in DOS, because the prompt will always tell you where you're working. I've added this prompt command to one of my DOS startup files so that my prompt always works this way.

To change your prompt for every DOS work session, you need to add the prompt command line into your AUTOEXEC.BAT startup file. To learn how to edit this file, see "Modify Your Startup Files in Windows 3.11 and DOS" on page 412.

Begin Guided Tour Enter DOS Commands

```
C:\>copy
```

1 At the DOS prompt, type **copy** (the command). Then press the **Spacebar**.

```
C:\>copy c:\word\letter.doc
```

2 Type the name of the file you want to copy, including the drive, directory, and full file name with three-letter extension. This is a parameter required for the command, and it includes delimiters. In this case, you would type **c:\word\letter.doc**. Press the **Spacebar**.

```
C:\>copy c:\word\letter.doc a:
```

3 This command requires a second parameter: the drive letter of the disk you want to copy to, including the directory you want to copy to (if any). To copy to drive A, for example, type **a:** and press the **Spacebar**. (Make sure you have a formatted floppy disk in the drive you want to copy to.)

```
C:\>copy c:\word\letter.doc a: /v_
```

4 After you've entered the command and its parameters, you enter any switches you want to use with the command. In this case, type **/v** so DOS will prompt you to verify the copy operation.

5 Press **Enter** to run the command.

6 If a prompt appears and asks you for additional information before it can run a command (such as verifying the file copy in this case), respond to the prompt to finish the operation.

To cancel a DOS command that's already running, press and hold the **Ctrl** key, then press C and release both keys.

Change Which Drive Is Active

To perform work with the files on the disk in a particular drive, you need to *change to* that drive or *log on* to it. (This is also called activating the disk drive.) If you don't log on to the appropriate disk drive before trying to perform a DOS command on a file on that disk, DOS displays a **File not found** error message after you press Enter to execute the command.

These are just a few examples of when you would need to log on to another disk drive:

- You want to copy a file from a floppy disk to your hard disk. In this case, you could start the process by logging on to the floppy drive holding the disk with the file you want to copy.
- You want to see what files are saved on a floppy disk or stored on a CD-ROM. In this case, you could start the process by logging on to the floppy disk drive or CD-ROM drive holding the disk or disc you want to view the contents for.
- You've finished working with the files on a floppy disk, and you want to work with files on the hard disk. In this case, you would log back on to the hard disk.

As you learned in the task called "Understand Disks and Drives" on page 46 earlier in this book, most computers have three disk drives. The floppy drives are named *a* and *b*, and the hard disk drive is usually named *c*. If your computer has a CD-ROM drive or a second hard disk drive, it will be named *d*. You can log on to any drive that's connected to your system.

Do This In Case of Error

When you log on to a disk drive, it must contain a disk, and the disk must be formatted. Logging on to a hard disk drive isn't a problem, because the drive always contains a disk and that disk is formatted when you buy your computer. (In fact, you should never try to format your hard disk; doing so will wipe out all the data and programs on the drive.)

You can encounter problems, however, when you try to log on to a floppy drive or CD-ROM drive. Let's say you try to log on to drive A:, and get an error that reads

```
Not ready reading drive A

Abort, Retry, Fail?
```

This message means you can't log on because there is no disk in the drive. In this case, you can insert a disk in the drive and press **R** for Retry. To quit, you can press **F** for Fail, as shown here, which gives you a message telling you the drive isn't active; type the name of another drive plus a colon, and press **Enter**:

```
C:\>a:

Not ready reading drive A
Abort, Retry, Fail?f
Current drive is no longer valid>c:

C:\>
```

You'll also get an error message if you put a floppy disk that isn't formatted in the drive and try to log on to it. (You can pay a little more to buy *preformatted* disks at any computer store.) You'll get the same error message if the floppy disk or CD-ROM you've put in the drive is formatted for Macintosh computers (a PC can't read it). Let's say you try to log on to drive A:, and get an error that reads

```
General failure error reading drive A

Abort, Retry, Fail?
```

This message means the disk in the drive you're trying to log on to isn't formatted, or is in Macintosh format. In this case, you can insert a disk with the correct format in the drive and press **R** for Retry. To quit, you can press **F** for Fail, as shown here, which gives you a message telling you that drive isn't active; type the name of another drive plus a colon, and press **Enter**:

```
C:\>a:

General failure reading drive A
Abort, Retry, Fail?f
Current drive is no longer valid>c:

C:\>
```

To find out how to format a floppy disk with Windows 3.11, see "Format Disks" on page 146.

When You Don't Need to Log On to a Drive

Suppose you want to work with a file on a disk in some drive other than the one DOS is currently logged on to. You would simply specify the full path name, including drive letter. For example, let's say you have a floppy disk that you insert in drive A:, and the disk holds a file called MEMO.TXT that you want to delete. You can use this shortcut method to delete the file:

- At the DOS prompt, type **del a:\memo.txt** and press **Enter**. DOS removes the file from the disk in drive A:. You don't need to log back on to drive C:.

You can use this faster technique with other DOS commands like COPY and DIR. Don't worry if this confuses you. As you become comfortable working in DOS, it'll all become second nature. If not, you can work in the Windows File Manager if that's more comfortable.

Begin Guided Tour Change Drives

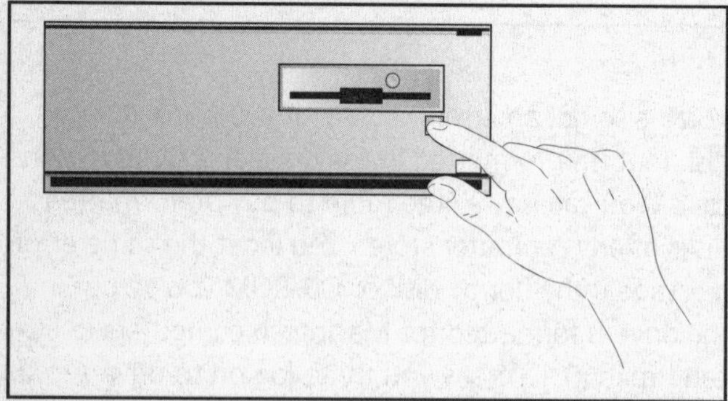

1 If you want to log on to a floppy disk drive or CD-ROM drive, insert a floppy disk or CD-ROM in that drive with the files you want to work with.

```
C:\>a:
```

2 At the DOS prompt, type the drive letter, followed by a colon. For example, to log on to floppy drive A:, type **a:**.

```
C:\>a:
A:\>
```

3 Press **Enter**. The computer logs on to that drive, and redisplays the prompt, indicating that it has logged on to the new drive.

Change Which Directory Is Active

In "Understand Directories" on page 55 earlier in this book, you learned that the directory structure of your hard disk resembles a tree. The *root directory* (signified by a backslash, ****) contains your system's startup files and directories.

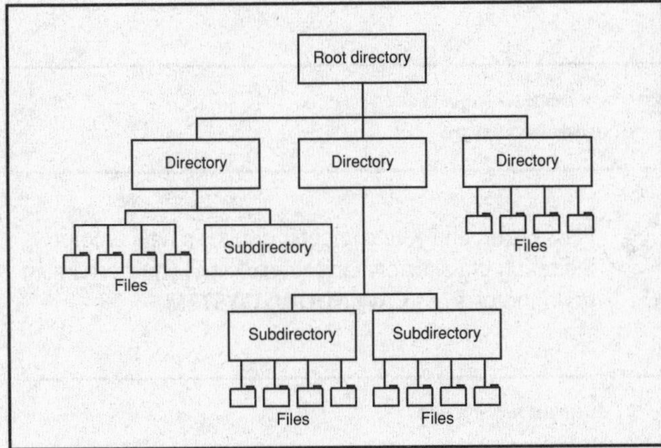

All *directories* branch from the root directory and hold files. You can create directories with the names you want, such as a **\WORK** directory to hold memos you create. The Install programs for applications create directories to hold the files for the programs. For example, the directory that holds the DOS program files is called **\DOS**.

Directories can hold *subdirectories*, which are also called child directories. These help group specialized files. For example, the directory holding your word processing program, \WINWORD, might hold a subdirectory to hold clip-art graphics files. This subdirectory might be called \WINWORD\CLIPART.

Just as you need to log on to the drive with the disk holding the files you want to work with, you need to change to the directory where your files are located before you can work with them in DOS.

When you work with files, you usually need to specify the *path* or *pathname* of the file. The full path includes the drive letter for the disk holding the file plus a colon, a backslash for the root directory, any directory and subdirectory names (separated by backslashes), the file name, and the extension. For example, C:\MSWORKS\CLIPART\STAR.WMF is the full pathname for the STAR.WMF clip-art file in Microsoft Works for Windows.

Moving Among Directory Levels

Quick quiz…Let's say you've changed to the directory called C:\WINDOWS. If you want to change to the C:\DOS directory, what command would you type?

If you answered "cd dos," you'd be wrong. Most books don't explain very well how the directory levels work. The root directory is the top level. The directories within the root directory are sometimes called *first-level* directories; they're one level "below" the root. (Subdirectories are one level "below" the directories that contain them.)

Why do you care? Because you can move up and down through the directory tree, but you *can't* really move "sideways" from one branch to another. To get to another branch (directory), you'd have to tell DOS to go back up a level, move over, then go down a level.

If you type **cd..** and press **Enter**, DOS moves up one level in the directory tree. If you type **cd ** and press **Enter**, DOS returns you all the way to the root directory, even if you're starting from a subdirectory two or more levels down the directory tree.

So, there are two correct answers to our quick quiz question:

- Starting from the C:\WINDOWS> prompt, you could type **cd..** and press **Enter** to move back to the root directory. Then, you could type **cd dos** and press **Enter**. You'd change to the \DOS directory, and the prompt would look like this: C:\DOS>.
- Starting from the C:\WINDOWS> prompt, you could type **cd \dos** and press **Enter**. The **** preceding **dos** tells DOS to move back to the root directory, then change to the DOS directory. The prompt would look like this: C:\DOS>.

Begin Guided Tour Change Directories

```
C:\>cd
```

1 You need to move to the directory where your files are located. At the prompt for the root directory in DOS, type **cd** (short for "change directory"). Then press the **Spacebar**.

```
C:\>cd windows
```

2 Type the name of the directory to change to, such as **windows**. (If you pressed **Enter** now, you would change to the C:\WINDOWS directory).

```
C:\>cd windows\system
```

3 **(Optional)** If you're changing to a subdirectory as well, type a **** then the name of the subdirectory. For example, you could add **\system** to your command line.

```
C:\>cd windows\system
C:\WINDOWS\SYSTEM>_
```

4 Press **Enter**, and your computer displays a new prompt indicating the directory (and subdirectory) you've changed to. In this case, it's **C:\WINDOWS\SYSTEM**.

```
C:\WINDOWS>cd system
C:\WINDOWS\SYSTEM>
```

5 Use a similar process to move from a directory to one of its subdirectories. Type **cd**, space, then the name of the subdirectory (for example **cd system**); press **Enter**.

Create and Remove a Directory

You don't have to create the root directory; it's set up for you automatically on any formatted disk. Beyond that, you do have total flexibility to make a new directory in the root, or within any directory or subdirectory. In fact, you can create several directory levels. For example, say you made a subdirectory named \PROJECTS under the \MSWORKS directory. You add a lot of files to C:\MSWORKS\PROJECTS, so you decide you need to better organize the files in that subdirectory. You decide to create two new subdirectories within that subdirectory: \HOME and \OFFICE.

To create one of these subdirectories (or any other directory or subdirectory), use the MD command and the *Guided Tour*.

Remove a Directory

If you no longer use a particular directory or subdirectory (or the files in it), that's wasted disk space; you may want to remove it from the disk. If you need more hard disk space, you could copy all those files to a floppy drive for storage, delete the originals, and then remove the directory from the hard disk.

Remember, however, that you have to delete all the files in a directory before you can remove it from a disk. Fortunately, there is a shortcut; the following example walks you through the process for removing a directory. Let's say you had a subdirectory on your computer called C:\MSWORKS\PROJECTS\WORK. Here are the steps for removing that subdirectory (or any other):

1. Change to the directory or subdirectory that holds the directory you want to delete. For example, change to the **C:\MSWORKS\PROJECTS** subdirectory if you want to remove its \WORK subdirectory.

2. To delete all the files in the directory or subdirectory you're removing, type **del**, space, then the name of the directory or subdirectory you want to remove (**del work**). Press **Enter**; DOS asks you to confirm whether you want to delete all the files in the directory. Type **y** and press **Enter**.

3. Now that the directory or subdirectory is empty, you can remove it. Type **rd** (for remove directory), space, then the name of the directory you want to remove (**rd work**). Press **Enter**; DOS deletes the directory, and you can no longer change to it.

Begin Guided Tour Add a Directory

```
C:\>d:
D:\>
```

1 Log on to the drive holding the disk you want to create a directory or subdirectory on. Type the drive letter and a **:** (as in **D:**), then press **Enter**. (Yes, you can create directories and subdirectories on floppy disks.)

```
C:\>d:
D:\>cd msworks\projects
D:\MSWORKS\PROJECTS>
```

2 Change to whichever directory or subdirectory will hold your new directory. In this example, you would change to **C:\MSWORKS\PROJECTS**.

```
C:\>d:
D:\>cd msworks\projects
D:\MSWORKS\PROJECTS>md home
```

3 At the DOS prompt, type **md**, press the **Spacebar**, then type the name of the new directory or subdirectory. In this case, for example, you would type **md home**.

```
C:\>d:
D:\>cd msworks\projects
D:\MSWORKS\PROJECTS>md home
D:\MSWORKS\PROJECTS>
```

4 Press **Enter** to create the directory or subdirectory.

5 Repeat steps 3 and 4 to create additional directories or subdirectories.

List Directory Contents

Over time, you accumulate a lot of files on your hard disk. You're likely to create hundreds of document files before you know it; sometimes it's hard to remember where you've saved one.

To know whether a directory or subdirectory holds the file(s) you want to work on, you have to be able to look at what's stored there. You might also want to see what subdirectories are in there. In DOS, you can do either of these with the DIR (short for "directory") command.

You can use the DIR command to view the contents of hard or floppy disks, as well as CD-ROMs.

> The DIR command offers a lot of switches, some of which will be described later in this task. Use **dir /?** to see what options DOS offers with this command. For more on using this technique for help about commands, see the task called "Enter Commands in DOS" on page 212.

Change the List Display

As you saw in the preceding example, if a directory or subdirectory contains a lot of files, some of them will scroll off the top of the screen when you use the dir command. This whole operation doesn't do you much good if you can't see everything in the list, right?

Fortunately, DOS provides several switches that enable you to control the appearance of the directory listing. Several of them are covered here. (Keep in mind that you can use more than one switch at a time. For example, you could combine the first two switches described here to display a list, pause it, and use the wide-list display.)

List Selected Files

If you remember an exact file name and want to see whether it's in the current directory, you can use the DIR command to find out. Type **dir**, press the **Spacebar**, then type the name of the file, including its three-letter extension, if any. For example, you could type **dir wacky.doc**. After you press **Enter** to execute the command, DOS lists the file if it is stored within the directory. If not, DOS displays **File not found**, and you'll need to look elsewhere to find the file.

You can use wild card characters with the DIR command to list only files with similar names. The * (asterisk) wild card takes the place of a group of contiguous characters, such as the three-letter file name extension. The **?** (question-mark) wild card stands for a single character. Here are a few ways to use wild card characters with the DIR command:

dir s*.* Lists all files in the current directory whose names start with S.

dir client??.xls Lists all files in the current directory whose names start with **client**, have two or more characters, and the **.xls** extension; all files of the type indicated by the extension match.

dir *.doc Lists all files in the current directory with the **.doc** extension, regardless of the name (which can have one to eight characters).

Begin Guided Tour List Contents of a Directory

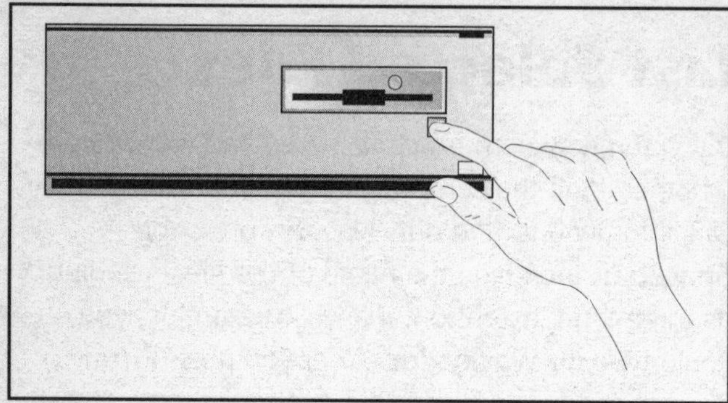

1 If you want to list files and directories that are on a floppy disk or CD-ROM, insert it into the appropriate drive.

```
C:\>d:
D:\>
```

2 Log on to the drive holding the disk whose contents you want to see. Type the drive letter and a **:** (as in **d:**). Press **Enter**.

```
D:\>cd msworks
D:\MSWORKS>
```

3 Change to the directory or subdirectory that holds what you want to list on-screen (files, directories, or subdirectories). Type **cd**, space, then the path you want to change to (in this case **cd msworks**); press **Enter**. (If you don't use these steps, this command shows you what's in the root directory.)

```
D:\MSWORKS>dir
```

4 Type **dir** and press **Enter**.

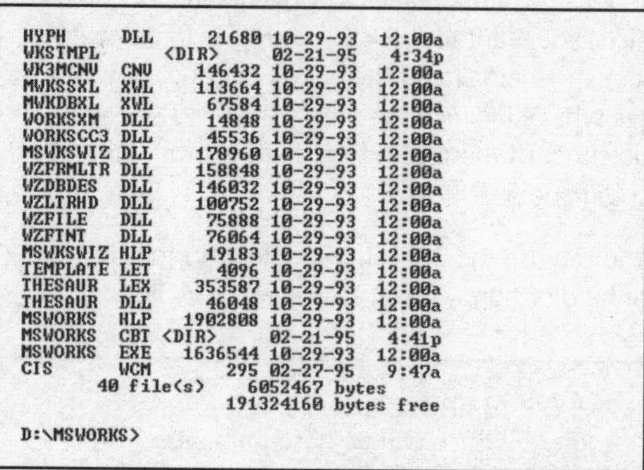

```
HYPH     DLL       21680 10-29-93  12:00a
WKSTMPL      <DIR>       02-21-95   4:34p
WK3MCNV  CNV      146432 10-29-93  12:00a
MWKSSXL  XWL      113664 10-29-93  12:00a
MWKDBXL  XWL       67584 10-29-93  12:00a
WORKSXM  DLL       14848 10-29-93  12:00a
WORKSCC3 DLL       45536 10-29-93  12:00a
MSWKSWIZ DLL      178960 10-29-93  12:00a
WZFRMLTR DLL      158848 10-29-93  12:00a
WZDBDES  DLL      146032 10-29-93  12:00a
WZLTRHD  DLL      100752 10-29-93  12:00a
WZFILE   DLL       75888 10-29-93  12:00a
WZFINT   DLL       76064 10-29-93  12:00a
MSWKSWIZ HLP       19183 10-29-93  12:00a
TEMPLATE LET        4096 10-29-93  12:00a
THESAUR  LEX      353587 10-29-93  12:00a
THESAUR  DLL       46048 10-29-93  12:00a
MSWORKS  HLP     1902808 10-29-93  12:00a
MSWORKS  CBT <DIR>       02-21-95   4:41p
MSWORKS  EXE     1636544 10-29-93  12:00a
CIS      WCM         295 02-27-95   9:47a
        40 file(s)     6052467 bytes
                     191324160 bytes free

D:\MSWORKS>
```

5 The list of subdirectories and files in the current directory scrolls onto the screen in one long column. If the list is too long to be shown on-screen, part of it will scroll off the top of the screen.

Begin Guided Tour Change the List Display

```
Volume in drive D is DISK2_VOL1
Volume Serial Number is 718F-63AE
Directory of D:\MSWORKS

.            <DIR>       02-21-95   4:33p
..           <DIR>       02-21-95   4:33p
SETUP        <DIR>       02-21-95   4:33p
WKSLANG  DLL     271872 10-29-93  12:00a
ZMODEM   FTD      33472 10-29-93  12:00a
VT220    TRD      28496 10-29-93  12:00a
KERMIT   FTD      23104 10-29-93  12:00a
YMODEM   FTD      27776 10-29-93  12:00a
XMODEM   FTD      25008 10-29-93  12:00a
VT100    TRD      15632 10-29-93  12:00a
ANSI     TRD      11296 10-29-93  12:00a
VT52     TRD       7024 10-29-93  12:00a
MSWORKS3 REG       4414 10-29-93  12:00a
MSWORKS3 TXT       5060 10-29-93  12:00a
SAMPLES      <DIR>       02-21-95   4:33p
CLIPART      <DIR>       02-21-95   4:34p
WORKSCC2 DLL     256336 10-29-93  12:00a
WORKSCC1 DLL     188560 10-29-93  12:00a
HY_EN    LEX      45568 10-29-93  12:00a
Press any key to continue . . .
```

1 Use **dir /p** to pause after each screen of files. As shown here, DOS will tell you to press a key to display the next screen of files. Subdirectory names appear in brackets like this: **<>**.

```
D:\MSWORKS>dir /w

 Volume in drive D is DISK2_VOL1
 Volume Serial Number is 718F-63AE
 Directory of D:\MSWORKS

[.]              [..]             [SETUP]          WKSLANG.DLL      ZMODEM.FTD
VT220.TRD        KERMIT.FTD       YMODEM.FTD       XMODEM.FTD       VT100.TRD
ANSI.TRD         VT52.TRD         MSWORKS3.REG     MSWORKS3.TXT     [SAMPLES]
[CLIPART]        WORKSCC2.DLL     WORKSCC1.DLL     HY_EN.LEX        HYPH.DLL
[WKSTMPL]        WK3MCNV.CNV      MWKSSXL.XWL      MWKDBXL.XWL      WORKSXM.DLL
WORKSCC3.DLL     MSWKSWIZ.DLL     WZFRMLTR.DLL     WZDBDES.DLL      WZLTRHD.DLL
WZFILE.DLL       WZFINT.DLL       MSWKSWIZ.HLP     TEMPLATE.LET     THESAUR.LEX
THESAUR.DLL      MSWORKS.HLP      [MSWORKS.CBT]    MSWORKS.EXE      CIS.WCM
        40 file(s)     6052467 bytes
                     191225856 bytes free

D:\MSWORKS>
```

2 Use **dir /w** to specify wide display, which lists the directory contents in several columns rather than one. In this list, subdirectory names appear in square brackets: **[]**.

```
D:\MSWORKS>dir /a:d

 Volume in drive D is DISK2_VOL1
 Volume Serial Number is 718F-63AE
 Directory of D:\MSWORKS

.            <DIR>       02-21-95   4:33p
..           <DIR>       02-21-95   4:33p
SETUP        <DIR>       02-21-95   4:33p
SAMPLES      <DIR>       02-21-95   4:33p
CLIPART      <DIR>       02-21-95   4:34p
WKSTMPL      <DIR>       02-21-95   4:34p
MSWORKS  CBT <DIR>       02-21-95   4:41p
        7 file(s)              0 bytes
                     191176704 bytes free

D:\MSWORKS>
```

3 Use **dir /a:d** to display only the subdirectories within the current directory.

```
MWKSSXL  XWL     113664 10-29-93  12:00a
TEMPLATE LET       4096 10-29-93  12:00a
THESAUR  DLL      46048 10-29-93  12:00a
THESAUR  LEX     353587 10-29-93  12:00a
VT100    TRD      15632 10-29-93  12:00a
VT220    TRD      28496 10-29-93  12:00a
VT52     TRD       7024 10-29-93  12:00a
WK3MCNV  CNV     146432 10-29-93  12:00a
WKSLANG  DLL     271872 10-29-93  12:00a
WORKSCC1 DLL     188560 10-29-93  12:00a
WORKSCC2 DLL     256336 10-29-93  12:00a
WORKSCC3 DLL      45536 10-29-93  12:00a
WORKSXM  DLL      14848 10-29-93  12:00a
WZDBDES  DLL     146032 10-29-93  12:00a
WZFILE   DLL      75888 10-29-93  12:00a
WZFRMLTR DLL     158848 10-29-93  12:00a
WZFINT   DLL      76064 10-29-93  12:00a
WZLTRHD  DLL     100752 10-29-93  12:00a
XMODEM   FTD      25008 10-29-93  12:00a
YMODEM   FTD      27776 10-29-93  12:00a
ZMODEM   FTD      33472 10-29-93  12:00a
        40 file(s)     6052467 bytes
                     191143936 bytes free

D:\MSWORKS>
```

4 Use **dir /o** to display the files and subdirectories, sorted in alphabetical order, with directories first. The files are alphabetized by the first letters of their file names (**dir /o:e** sorts file names by their three-letter extensions).

```
D:\MSWORKS\PROJECTS>dir /s

 Volume in drive D is DISK2_VOL1
 Volume Serial Number is 718F-63AE

Directory of D:\MSWORKS\PROJECTS

.            <DIR>       04-14-95   3:01p
..           <DIR>       04-14-95   3:01p
HOME         <DIR>       04-14-95   3:05p
        3 file(s)              0 bytes

Directory of D:\MSWORKS\PROJECTS\HOME

.            <DIR>       04-14-95   3:05p
..           <DIR>       04-14-95   3:05p
        2 file(s)              0 bytes

Total files listed:
        5 file(s)              0 bytes
                     145367040 bytes free

D:\MSWORKS\PROJECTS>
```

5 **Dir /s** lists not only the files in the current directory, but also the files in each subdirectory it contains.

```
WORKSCC1.DLL
HY_EN.LEX
HYPH.DLL
WKSTMPL
WK3MCNV.CNV
MWKSSXL.XWL
MWKDBXL.XWL
WORKSXM.DLL
WORKSCC3.DLL
MSWKSWIZ.DLL
WZFRMLTR.DLL
WZDBDES.DLL
WZLTRHD.DLL
WZFILE.DLL
WZFINT.DLL
MSWKSWIZ.HLP
TEMPLATE.LET
THESAUR.LEX
THESAUR.DLL
MSWORKS.HLP
MSWORKS.CBT
MSWORKS.EXE
CIS.WCM

D:\MSWORKS>
```

6 To list the file names only, use **dir /b**.

Use DOS to Format Disks

As you may recall from "Enter Commands in DOS" on page 212, you can format floppies in DOS by entering a simple DOS command, **format**. For more details about disk formatting and disk capacities, see "Format Disks" on page 146.

DOS requires that you pay extra attention to the floppy disk capacity. If you're using a high-capacity (HD) drive to format low-capacity (DD) disks, you need to use special switches when you enter the format command:

To format a 360K (5.25-inch DD) disk in a 1.2M (5.25-inch HD) drive, add the **/f:360** switch to the format command, as in **format a: /f:360**.

To format a 720K (3.5-inch DD) disk in a 1.44M (3.5-inch HD) drive, add the **/f:720** switch to the format command, as in **format a: /f:720**.

DOS also requires you to use switches to perform a quick format or make the formatted floppy a bootable system disk. Add the **/q** switch to perform a quick format, or the **/s** switch to create a system disk. For example, **format a: /f:720 /s** formats a 3.5-inch DD disk and copies the system files to it.

NEVER format your hard disk, even though DOS lets you do so. You'll lose all the data on the disk, and even an expert won't be able to recover it. Be careful. Early versions of DOS don't even warn you if you're inadvertently reformatting drive C.

Begin Guided Tour Format a Disk in DOS

1 If you're formatting a disk you've used before, double-check to make sure you've copied any files you might need from that disk. Insert the floppy disk in the appropriate drive.

```
C:\>format a: /s
```

2 Type **format** and press the **Spacebar**. Then type the letter of the drive holding the floppy disk plus a colon, as in **a:**. Press the **Spacebar** again, and add any switches you want to use.

3 Press **Enter**.

```
C:\>format a: /s
Insert new diskette for drive A:
and press ENTER when ready...
```

4 If you haven't already inserted your floppy in the drive, do so now and press **Enter**.

```
C:\>format a: /s
Insert new diskette for drive A:
and press ENTER when ready...

Checking existing disk format.
Saving UNFORMAT information.
Verifying 1.44M
Format complete.
System transferred

Volume label (11 characters, ENTER for none)? bucki2
```

5 DOS formats the disk, and then prompts you for a volume label. Type one if you want, and then press **Enter**.

```
C:\>format a: /s
Insert new diskette for drive A:
and press ENTER when ready...

Checking existing disk format.
Saving UNFORMAT information.
Verifying 1.44M
Format complete.
System transferred

Volume label (11 characters, ENTER for none)? bucki2

   1457664 bytes total disk space
    119808 bytes used by system
   1337856 bytes available on disk

       512 bytes in each allocation unit.
      2613 allocation units available on disk.

Volume Serial Number is 0414-1800

Format another (Y/N)?N
```

6 DOS asks whether you want to format another disk. If you do, remove the disk you've just formatted, type **Y**, press **Enter**, and repeat steps 2–5. Otherwise type **N** and press **Enter** to finish.

Start a DOS Program from the DOS Prompt

An earlier task in this book explained how to start Windows applications by double-clicking on icons. DOS is more mysterious; rather than using icons to start DOS applications, you need to know the right startup command and enter it at the DOS prompt.

If you have installed a DOS application on your hard disk, you need to start it to load it into RAM (your computer's random-access memory). You can run some DOS programs directly from a floppy disk or a CD-ROM; you would start them from the disk in a drive.

To start a DOS application, you log on to the drive that contains the program files. Then you type the startup command and press **Enter**. Here is a list of some common startup commands for DOS applications:

To run this DOS program...	*Use this command...*
America Online	aol
Carmen Sandiego	carmen
dBASE	dbase
DOS 4.1 or 5.0 Shell	dosshell
Harvard Graphics	hg
Lotus 1-2-3	123
Microsoft Word for DOS	word
Microsoft Works for DOS	works
The Norton Utilities	norton
Paradox for DOS	paradox
PC Tools	pctools
PFS: First Choice	first
PFS: First Publisher	fp
PRODIGY	prodigy
Q&A for DOS	qa
Quattro Pro for DOS	qp
Quicken for DOS	q
TurboTax	ttax
WordPerfect for DOS	wp
WordStar	ws

Some DOS programs have setup programs, others don't. A chapter on page 363 of this book, "Install New Programs," explains how to install a DOS program on your computer—whether it has a setup program or not.

Find the Startup Command

The startup command for most DOS programs really is the name of a program file called an *executable file*. Executable files contain instructions that your computer can read, such as program instructions. Executable files have the .EXE, .BAT, or .COM file name extensions. Find that executable file in a program's directory, and bingo, you've found your startup file.

The name for the executable file usually resembles the program's name; so does the name of the directory that holds the program's files; sometimes these names are abbreviations of the program's name. Following are just a few examples:

Program name	Directory name	Startup file name
Quicken	\quicken	quicken.exe or q.bat
The Norton Utilities	\nu	norton.exe
QuickLink Fax	\ql	qlmain.exe
Word for DOS	\word5	word.exe
Doom	\doom	doom.exe

Once you've identified the directory holding your program files and have changed to that directory, use **dir *.exe** (or ***.bat** or ***.com**) to list files that might be the startup file. Then try running the file with the name that most resembles the program name.

Find the Switches

As with regular DOS commands, the startup commands for some applications offer switches you can use to customize the way the program runs. You find the available switches by typing the startup command, followed by a space and **/?**, and pressing **Enter**. For The Norton Utilities 6.0, for example, typing **norton /?** and pressing **Enter** displays this list of switches:

```
C:\NU>norton /?
Norton Utilities, Norton Utilities 6.0, Copyright 1991 by Symantec Corporation

Run the Norton Utilities (and other programs) from a menu.

NORTON [/BW|/LCD] [/G0|/G1|/G2] [/NOZOOM]

  /BW       Forces the use of the Black and White color set.
  /LCD      For laptop displays.  Forces the use of the LCD color set.
  /G0       Disable font redefinitions and graphic mouse.
  /G1       Disable the graphic mouse (EGA/VGA only).
  /G2       Disable graphic dialogs (EGA/VGA only).
  /NOZOOM   Disables dialog box zooming.

C:\NU>
```

Begin Guided Tour Start a DOS Program

```
C:\>cd word5
C:\WORD5>
```

1 Log on to the disk drive that has the files for the program you want to run. Change to the directory that holds the files for the program (if you need to). If you have Microsoft Word 5.5 for DOS in a directory called WORD5, for example, change to the directory holding the program: type **cd word5** and press **Enter**.

```
C:\>cd word5
C:\WORD5>word
```

2 Type the startup command for the application, then press **Enter**. To start Word for DOS, for example, you would type **word** and press **Enter**.

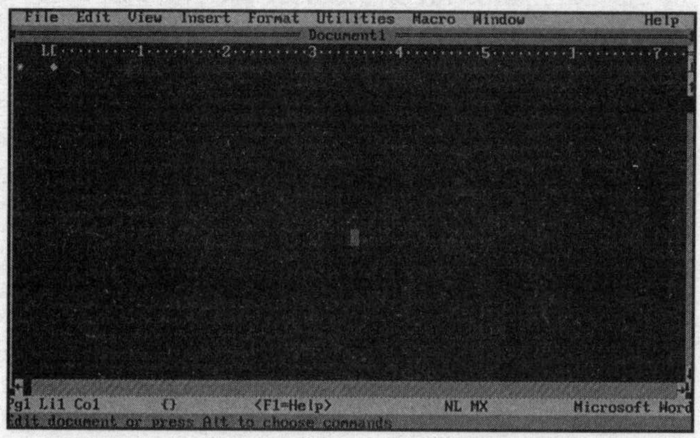

3 The application appears on-screen, usually with a brand new document open (as shown here).

Work with Menus in a DOS Program

Working in a DOS application can be even more mind-boggling than working in a Windows application, because many DOS programs are less mouse-savvy than Windows programs. That is, the DOS programs aren't as well-suited to work with the mouse as their Windows counterparts are. Some DOS applications don't even let you use a mouse to work in them (they're rare these days), or require you to use the keyboard when you're performing certain operations (like creating a macro). In DOS applications, getting around with the keyboard can be at least as important as navigating with the mouse. It helps to know both.

Choose a Command from a Menu in a DOS Program

Many DOS applications have *menu bars* near the top of the screen that list the names of available pull-down menus. Each pull-down menu offers a group of related commands. To tell your application what to do, open a pull-down menu and choose a command.

DOS applications give you more ways to activate the menu bar and choose a menu with the keyboard. Generally, you can use the **Alt** key or the **F10** key.

Other applications, like Quicken, also offer a Main menu that looks like a dialog box with a list of commands; each has a selection number or letter beside it. This type of menu lets you jump to different modules of the program (usually these offer their own pull-down menus), or exit the program. You can work with these *menu boxes* using either the mouse or keyboard. Click the command you want, or press its selection number/letter.

To close a menu without selecting a command from it, press **Esc** or click outside the menu. (If selecting a menu command displays a pop-up menu or submenu, use the same techniques presented in the *Guided Tour* to choose commands from it.)

Begin Guided Tour Choose Menu Commands with the Mouse

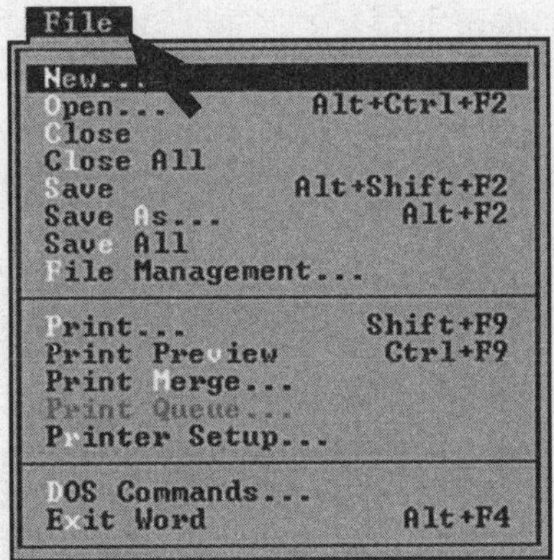

1. Click the name of the menu you want in the application's title bar; the program will display the pull-down menu.

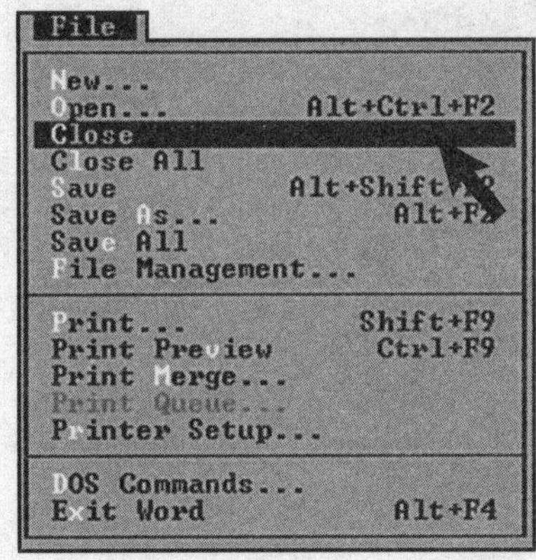

2. Click the command you want to select.

(continues)

Guided Tour Choose Menu Commands with the Mouse

(continued)

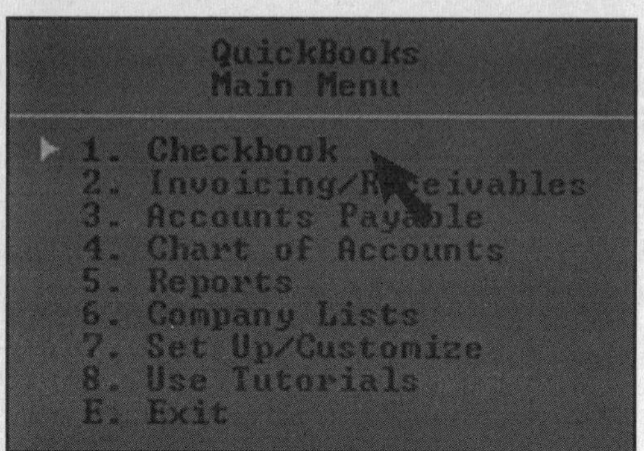

3 For Main menu boxes or similar menu lists, simply click the name of the command you want.

Begin Guided Tour Choose a Command with the Keyboard

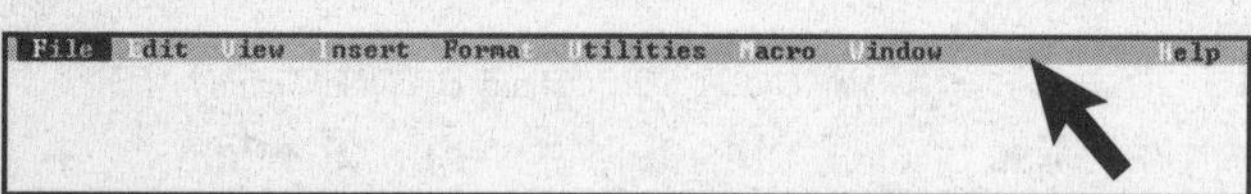

1 Activate the menu bar by pressing **Alt** or **F10**. This usually highlights the far left menu name on the menu bar.

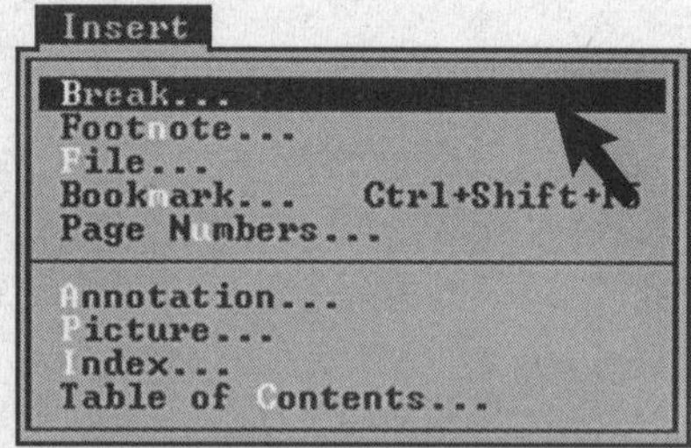

2 To display the pull-down menu of your choice, press the highlighted selection letter in its name (or use the **left** and **right arrow** keys to highlight the name of the menu you want, and press **Enter**).

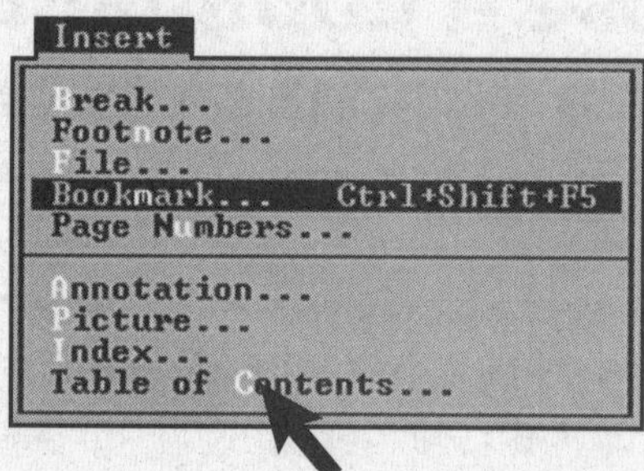

3 To choose a command, press the highlighted selection letter in its name (or use the **down arrow** key to highlight the name of the command you want, and press **Enter**).

If the command has a shortcut key combination beside it, you can press that key combination to bypass all these steps.

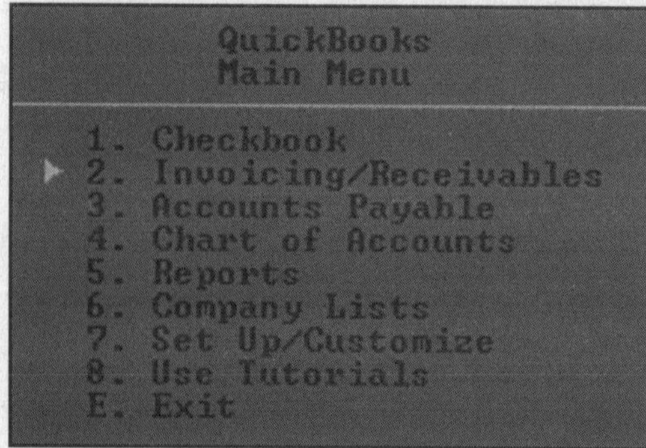

4 For Main menu boxes or similar menu lists, simply press the selection letter or number for the command you want (or use the **down arrow** key to highlight it, then press **Enter**).

Work in a Dialog Box

When you interact with an application, you may need to provide certain information or make certain choices for the application to perform the specific action you want. To make this quizzing easier, the program displays a *dialog box*, a special window that lets you "talk" with it and tell it exactly what to do. When you tell the program to proceed, it carries out all the instructions you gave it in the dialog box.

A dialog box will appear when you select a menu command that's followed by an ellipsis (**...**). Use this box to give the program precise instructions like these:

- Choose a file to open from a particular drive and directory.
- Specify whether text appears **bold**, in *italics*, or underlined.
- Ignore or change a word when the spell-checker finds a suspect spelling.

Dialog boxes offer different *controls* for choosing options. In some cases, you simply choose all the options that apply. In other cases, you have to select a single option from a group of several. Dialog boxes usually group related options in a box with a title. In a dialog box you use to format text, for example, you might find effects like bold, italics, and underlining grouped in an area called "Style." Many dialog boxes offer *preview* areas to show how your selected options would appear if you approved them.

The *Guided Tour* in this Task presents the different kinds of controls, and explains how to use each with both the mouse and the keyboard.

To move to a dialog box control with the keyboard, you can either press Tab repeatedly, or press Alt plus the highlighted selection letter in the control's name.

Begin Guided Tour Use Dialog Boxes

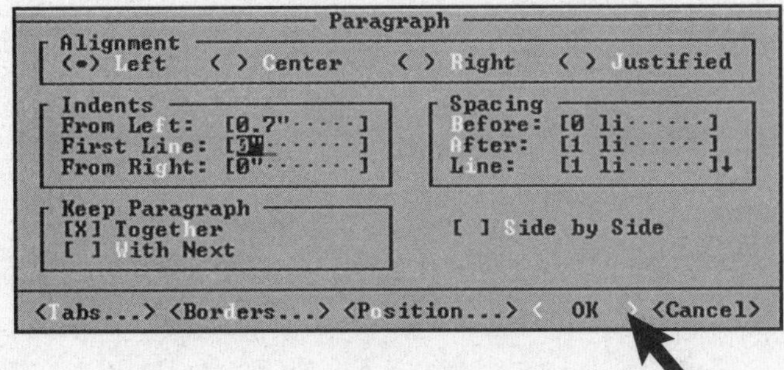

1 *Command buttons* carry out a command. Simply click a command button to select it. Most dialog boxes have the buttons shown here. Choosing **OK** accepts the selected options and closes the dialog box. **Cancel** closes the dialog box without executing the command that displayed it (or any of the options you selected).

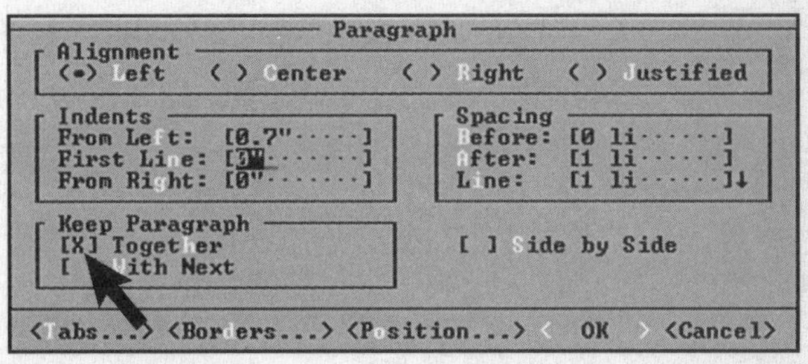

2 *Check boxes* let you toggle an option on (which makes an **X** appear in the box) and off. To select or deselect a check box, click it. Although check boxes may be grouped as shown here, you can select all the options in the group, none of them, or any combination.

(continues)

Guided Tour Use Dialog Boxes *(continued)*

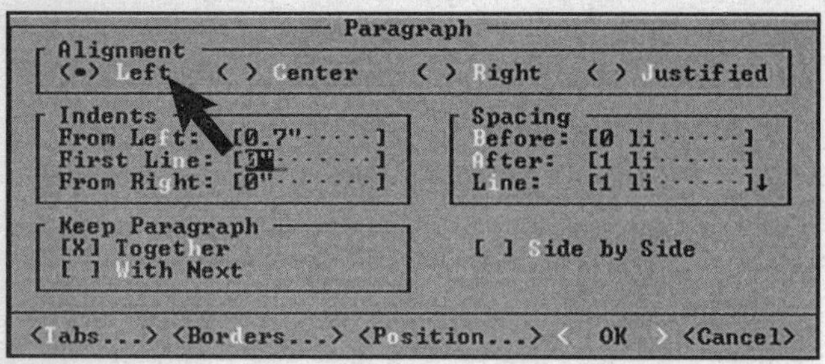

3 *Option buttons* always appear in groups because they are mutually exclusive; you can select only one option button at a time from each group. To select one, click it.

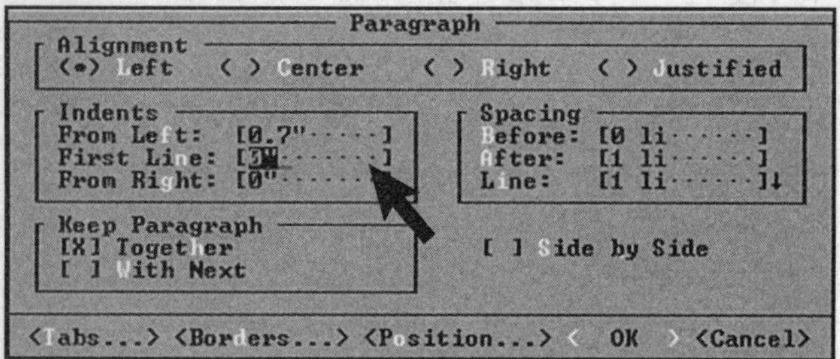

4 When you need to enter a value (such as the number of copies of a document to print), or a name (such as a new file name), you enter it in a *text box*. To use a text box, click it to place the insertion cursor in it, then type your selection.

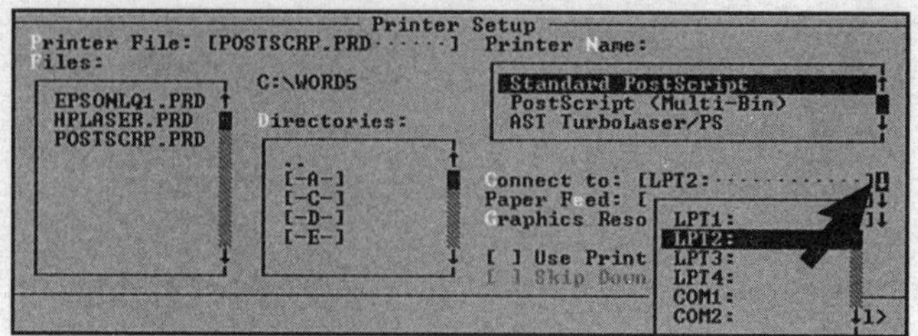

5 *List boxes* let you choose from a list of choices for an option. To make a choice, simply use the scroll bar to display it, then click it. In many cases, double-clicking on a choice in the list selects that choice and closes the dialog box, accepting any other options you've selected.

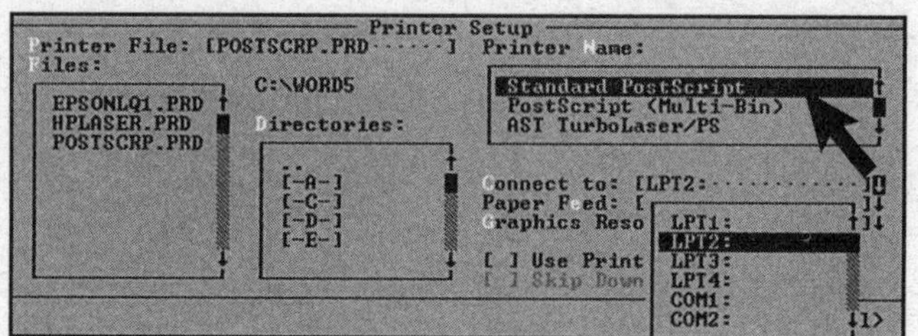

6 *Drop-down lists* hide all but the option you've selected until you display the list. Click the **down arrow** beside the list to display the choices, and then click the new choice.

Open a New or Existing File in a DOS Program

A *document* is a file you create in a program. Documents include spreadsheet, text, graphics, and database files, for example. When you start DOS applications, most programs open a new, blank document on the screen. You can work with this document, or open another file and work in it. Chances are, however, you won't create just one new document per work session. You might write a letter, then create a report, then put together a to-do list. Every time you want to start another document, you need to open a new file in the program.

In most programs, it only takes a simple menu command to start a new file. Open the **File** menu, and choose the **New** command. A new document appears on-screen.

To open a particular file that you've previously saved, you have to know which disk and directory it's stored on, and what the file's name is. These steps give an example of how the process might work in your application, and some steps you can try.

Begin Guided Tour Open a File

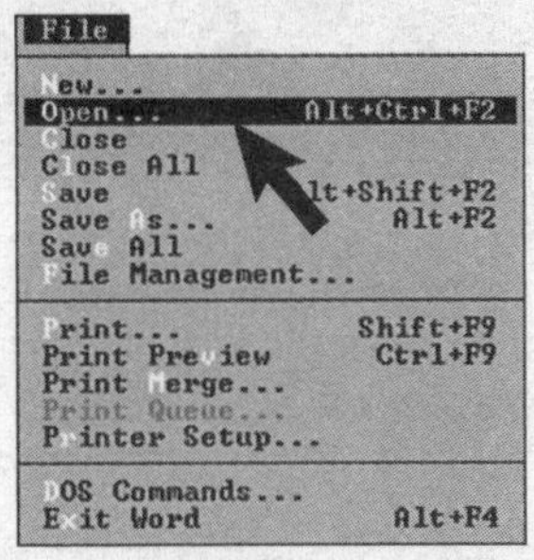

1 Open the **File** menu, then choose the **Open** command. (In some programs, the command might be different.)

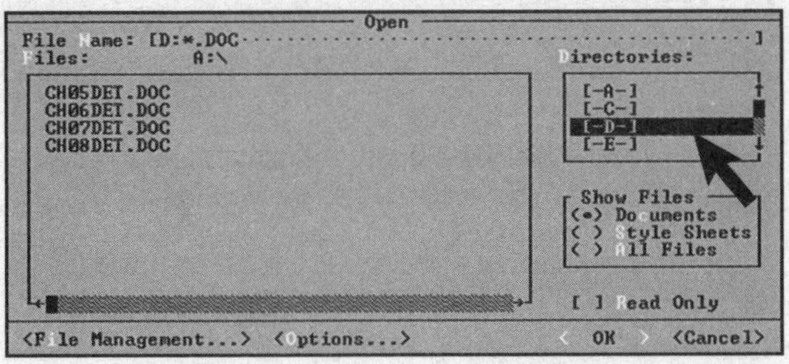

2 In the **Open** dialog box, display the **Drives** list, if there is one, then choose the drive letter for the disk that has the file you want to open. (In some programs, you choose the drive from the **Directories** list, where the drive name appears in square brackets.)

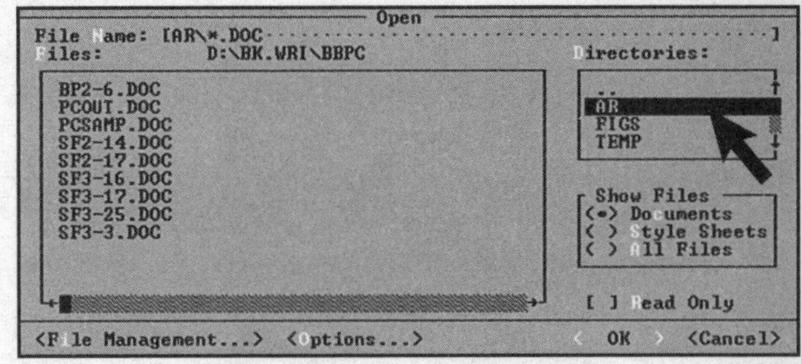

3 Select the **Directories** list, and scroll to display the name of the directory that holds your program files. Then highlight the directory's name to select it.

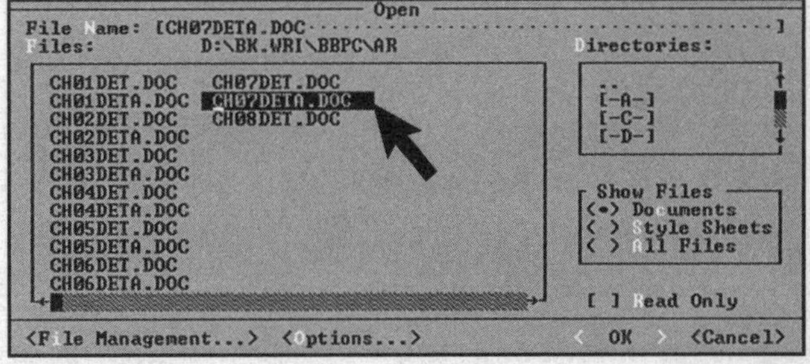

4 In the **File Name** list (or **Files** list), select the name of the file you want to open. Then click the **OK** button to close the dialog box (which opens the file), or simply double-click the file you want to open.

Save a File in a DOS Program

Saving your document in a file stores it on disk. The first time you save a file, you give the file a name and tell the computer what disk and directory to store it in. The program automatically adds a period and the appropriate extension to the file name. Subsequent saves update the file on disk; you don't have to specify the file's name again.

As a rule, you should try to save your work every five minutes or so to protect against data loss. Some programs even offer a **Save All** command on the **File** menu. Choosing it saves all open documents.

Make sure you choose memorable names for your files to make them easier to distinguish when you open them later. Sometimes it helps to date them for easy access. For example, you might call your resume file **res12-95.doc**. These steps give an example of how the process might work in your application and steps you can try.

Begin Guided Tour Save a File

1 Make the window that holds the document you want to save *active*: click it or select its name from the **Window** menu.

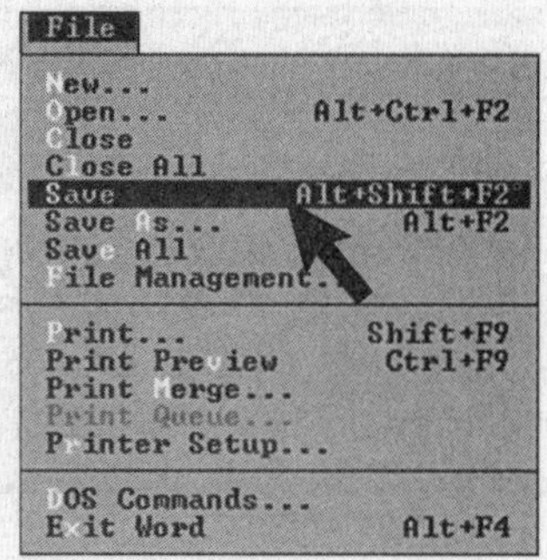

2 Open the **File** menu, and then choose the **Save** command.

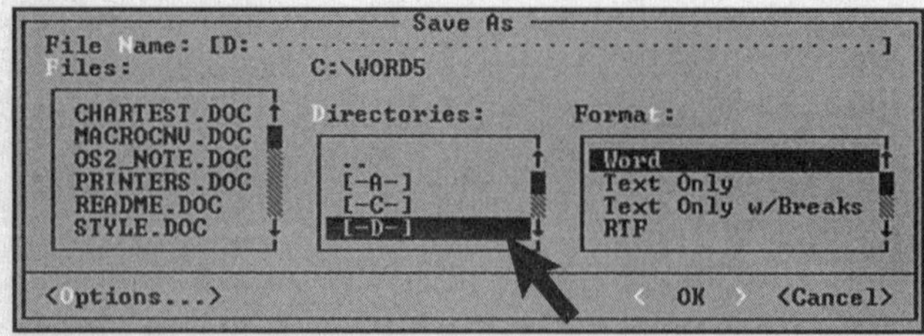

3 In the **Save As** dialog box, select the **Drives** list (if there is one) to display the list, then select the drive letter for the disk where you want to save the file. (In some applications, you select the drive from the **Directories** list, where drives appear in square brackets.)

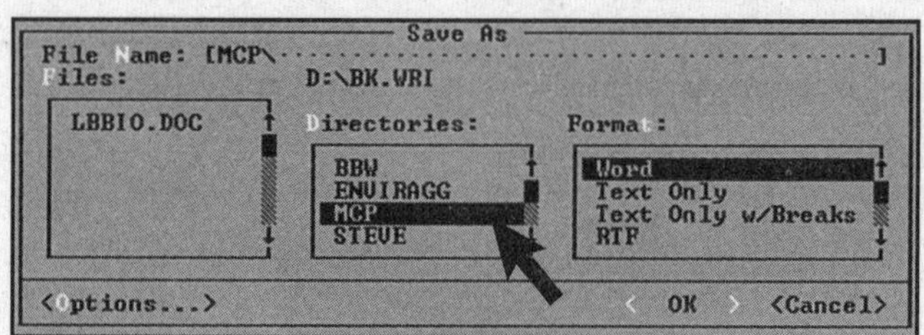

4 Select the **Directories** list and scroll it to display the name of the directory you want to save to. Highlight the directory's name to select it.

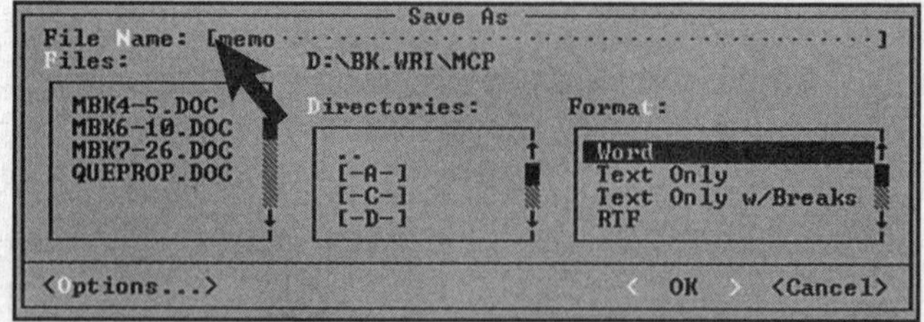

5 Choose the **File Name** box to highlight its contents. Type a name (up to eight characters) for the new file. You don't have to add the extension.

6 Click the **OK** button or press **Enter**. The program saves your file and closes the Save As dialog box.

Exit a DOS Program

Exiting a DOS application closes any open files in the program and removes them from RAM (random access memory). Then the program itself closes (is removed from RAM); you're returned to the DOS prompt.

Before you exit from any program, you should save your work. This prevents data loss and gets you out faster. If you haven't saved your work, the program will prompt you to do so. Click **Yes** to save if you've saved an open file before. If you haven't saved the open file, the Save As dialog box will appear, letting you name the file and specify a location for it.

> If you continue working on the file, be sure to save it again before you close it or exit the program. Open the File menu and choose Save again. The program saves your file; it doesn't display a dialog box or ask you for a file name again.

Shell Out to DOS Instead of Exiting

If you're working in a DOS application and need to perform one or two simple operations (like using DOS to delete a file or two), you don't have to shut down the DOS program to perform the operation. You can temporarily "shell out" to DOS rather than exiting. Here's how it works:

1. Click the application's **File** menu.
2. Look for a command like **Shell to DOS** or **DOS Commands**; click it.
3. Perform the DOS operations you want.
4. When you're finished working in DOS, type **exit** and press **Enter** to return to your DOS application.

Begin Guided Tour Exit a Program

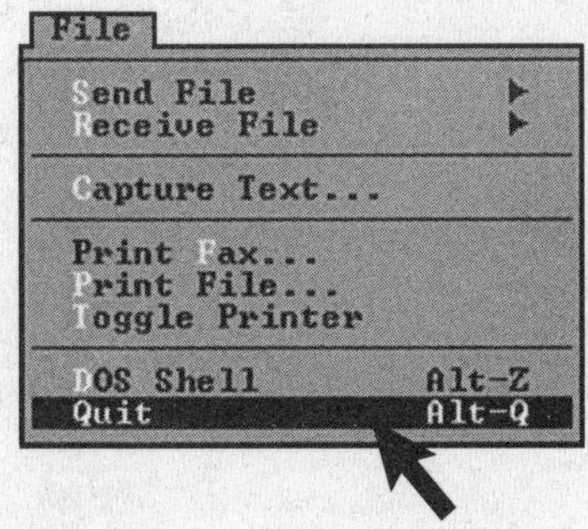

1 Open the program's **File** menu by clicking it. Then click **Quit** or **Exit**.

Press the exit shortcut-key combination, usually found beside the Exit or Quit command on the File menu. This combination may be **Alt+Q**, **Alt+X**, or **Alt+F4**.

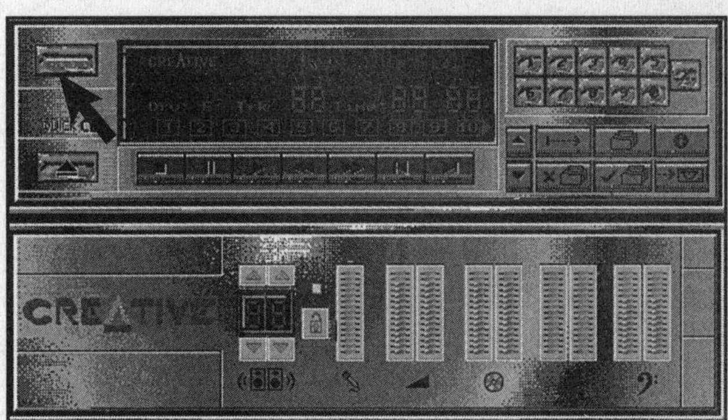

2 Some DOS applications have a *Close box* or special icon you can double-click to exit. Close boxes are usually found in the upper left corner of the application.

(continues)

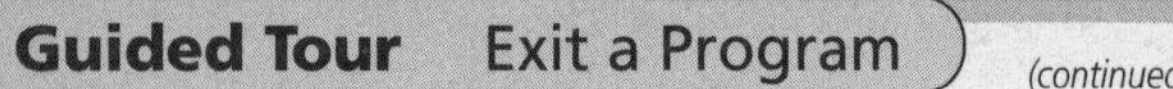

(continued)

3 Some programs (like this one) offer a **Quit!** option on the menu bar. To choose it and exit the program, click it.

QuickBooks
Main Menu

1. Checkbook
2. Invoicing/Receivables
3. Accounts Payable
4. Chart of Accounts
5. Reports
6. Company Lists
7. Set Up/Customize
8. Use Tutorials
E. Exit

4 Other DOS programs offer a Main menu screen, which generally offers an Exit command.

HOW TO...

Connect with the Outside World Using Online Services

No person is an island. Although you can use your computer in isolation if you prefer, adding a modem to your system enables you to connect with other users. In the last few years, millions of people have jumped online for the first time to search for information and graphics, get up-to-date reports on the news and stocks, buy and sell things, and chat or exchange messages with other users. This section introduces you to the three most popular online services (PRODIGY, America Online, CompuServe) and The Microsoft Network.

What You Will Find in This Section

Understand Online Communication 236

Connect to PRODIGY 239

Send Mail on PRODIGY 243

Find and Read Information on PRODIGY 247

Post on PRODIGY Bulletin Boards 250

Connect to America Online 255

Send Mail on America Online 258

Read Articles on America Online 262

Post in America Online Message Boards 266

Download Files from America Online 269

Connect to CompuServe 271

Send CompuServe Mail 274

Read Articles on CompuServe 278

Post Messages in CompuServe Forums 282

Download Files from CompuServe 285

Connect to The Microsoft Network with Windows 95 288

Get Up and Running on The Microsoft Network 293

Browse The Microsoft Network 295

Exchange E-Mail on The Microsoft Network 299

Converse with Other Microsoft Network Members 303

Understand Online Communication

You may have heard a lot of buzz lately about "going online" or "the Information Superhighway." If your computer has a modem (and you have a telephone line you can connect it to), then the amazing world of electronic online communication is wide open to you. You can join an online service or a bulletin-board system (BBS) to share files and messages with other users.

Think of each online service as a "library" of information from various sources. Not every library offers the same lineup of books and magazines. For example, while your neighborhood library may offer a lot to you, it may not have the Standard & Poor's stock information you need. You may have to go to another, larger library to find that information.

Similarly, each online service or BBS offers a unique set of information; joining the service or BBS only gives you access to its unique collection of information. Each online service also offers its own, unique connection software (this isn't always true of BBSs and the Internet).

This section introduces you to the three most popular online services, and gives you a crash course in connecting with BBSs and the Internet (a network connecting thousands of computers around the world). Although you can connect to any of these services with DOS or a Macintosh, this section focuses on using Windows to perform basic operations like connecting, sending mail, and reading news.

Begin Guided Tour Things to Do Online

1 *Read news.* Most services offer hourly updates about current events, as well as specialized areas for business, weather, sports, and other information.

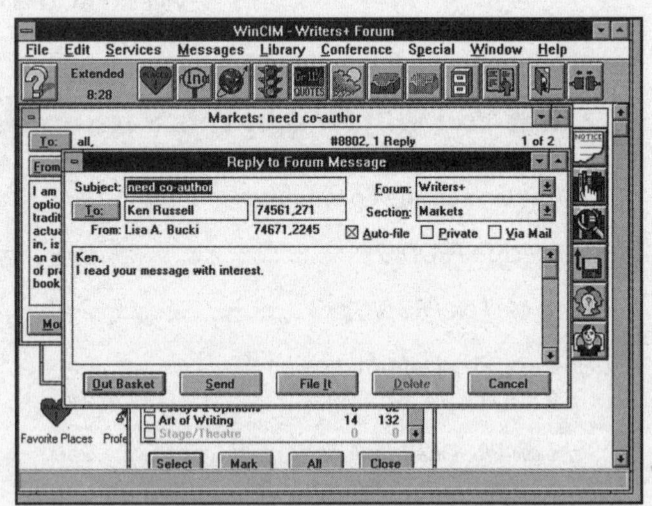

2 *Read and post general messages.* You can find these in *forums* or *departments*, online areas where users go to share information about special topics like having a home business. You can read or post messages.

Guided Tour Things to Do Online

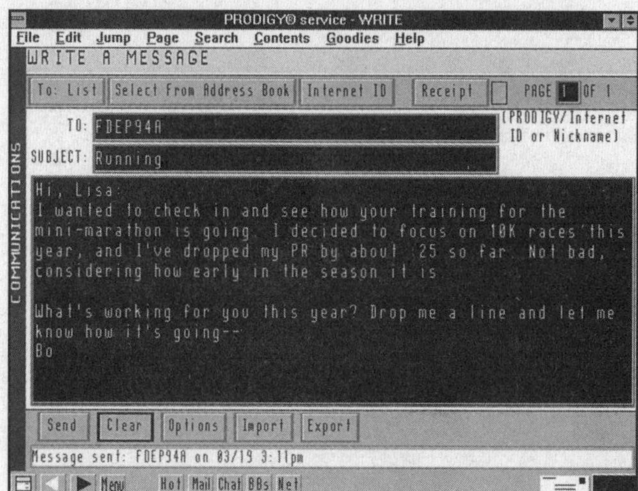

3 *Exchange private electronic mail.* Send a private letter to one or more users, without licking a single stamp.

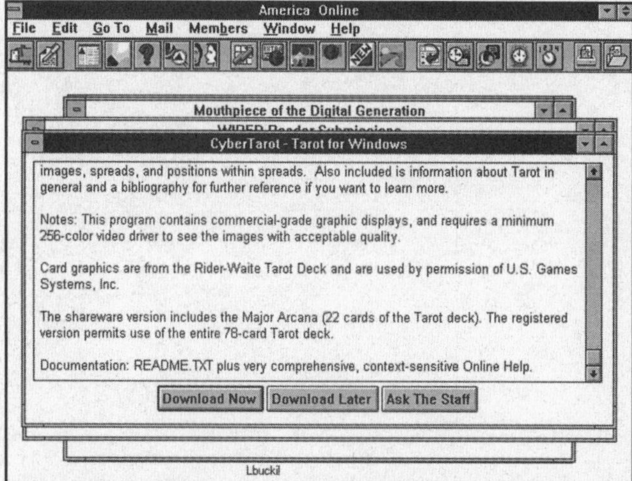

4 *Exchange files.* You can *upload* files (send them to another computer) for other users, or *download* files (get them from another computer) that you want. You may swap original documents, shareware or freeware programs, graphic files, sound files, and more in this way.

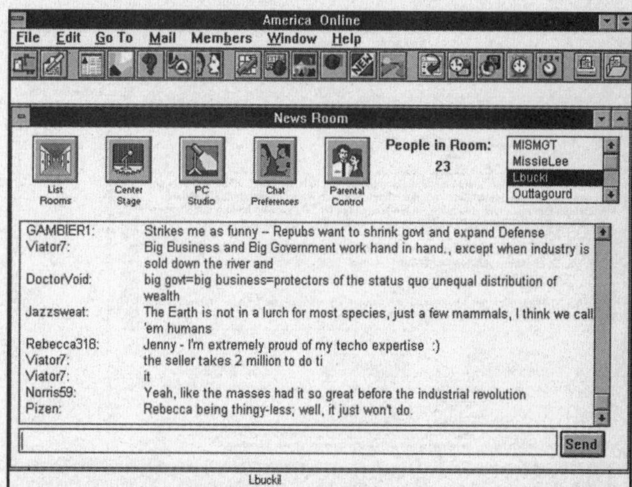

5 *Talk live online with other users.* Most services offer live *chat areas* where users can go to meet others from around the world to talk about a specific topic. Type in your message, and it appears instantly for all the other users in the chat area, who can reply immediately.

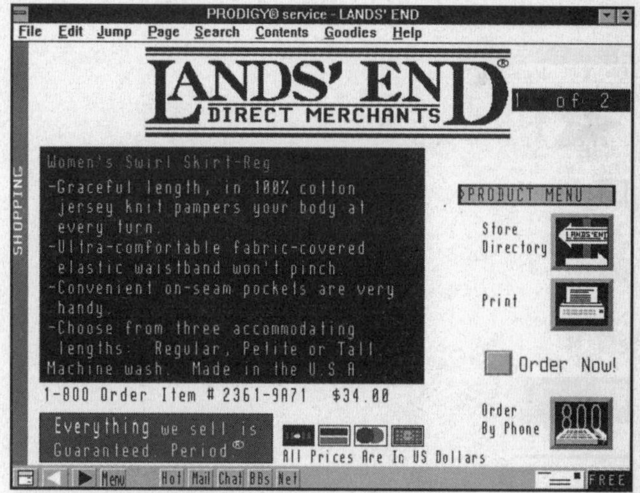

6 *Buy stuff, and more.* Visit a variety of online stores and spend, spend, spend. You can also make your travel reservations or purchase other services online.

(continues)

Guided Tour Things to Do Online

(continued)

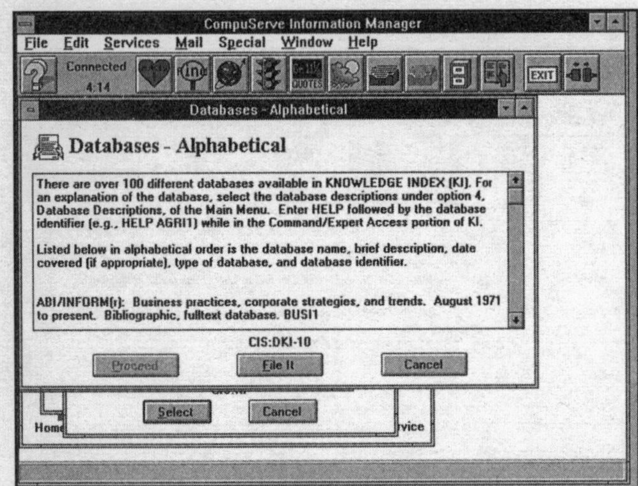

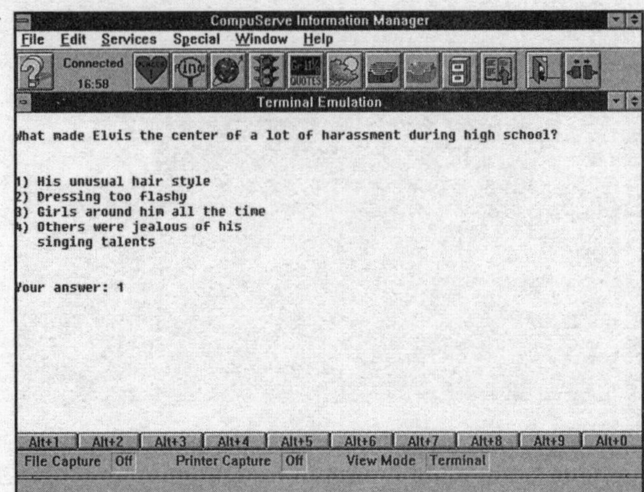

7 *Work smarter, not harder.* You can find a variety of databases and reference books online so you can find facts when you need them—whether for a school project, for a client proposal, or to settle a bet.

8 *Play a little.* Most online services offer game areas where you can play online by yourself or against online opponents, win contests, and download games for your personal use.

Connect to PRODIGY

PRODIGY, one of the most popular and fast-growing online services, was the first one that specifically targeted home and family users—especially those who aren't computer geeks. PRODIGY appeals to its audience by offering a lot of graphics, simple commands and screens, and even advertisements online. Although PRODIGY does offer plenty of "serious" information about news, weather, business, and financial markets, its forte is home, family, and consumer information.

PRODIGY offers e-mail, shopping, and chatting. Mostly, however, you may be working with *services* and *bulletin boards (BBs)* in PRODIGY. Services are areas offering icons you click to get information and articles, such as news or weather items. Bulletin boards are areas where users gather to read and post messages about topics of interest; right now, PRODIGY offers more than 70 bulletin boards (BBs).

This task explains how to log on and off of PRODIGY and how to set up the Autologon feature so you don't have to type your ID and password every time you get on PRODIGY. In addition, you'll find the basics for moving around in PRODIGY.

PRODIGY's Windows software has some features that are normal for Windows, such as a menu bar with pull-down menus and a lot of icons you can click to move around. Whereas the colorful icons in the main part of the screen vary as you move around in PRODIGY, the tool bar at the bottom of the PRODIGY screen offers a consistent set of icons you can click to navigate.

If the PRODIGY software didn't come installed on your computer or come with your modem, you can get it by calling 1-800-PRODIGY.

Click this command icon...	*To...*
	Return to the opening Highlights screen.
	Return to the previous screen.
	Proceed to the next screen.
Menu	Return to the menu list or screen.
Hot	Display your PersonalPath list of jump areas you like to visit often.
Mail	Use the Mail service.
Chat	Use the PRODIGY Chat service to talk online with other PRODIGY users.
BBs	Access more than 70 PRODIGY BBs, where you can read and post public messages.
Net	Access Internet Usenet Newsgroups.
	Find out whether you have mail.

Jump to Your Next Destination

In PRODIGY, you can move directly from feature to feature by using a *jump command*. To enter a jump command, open the **Jump** menu and click **Jump To**, or press **Ctrl+J**. In the Jump dialog box, type the Jump word you want, and then press **Enter** or click the **OK** button.

Begin Guided Tour Log On

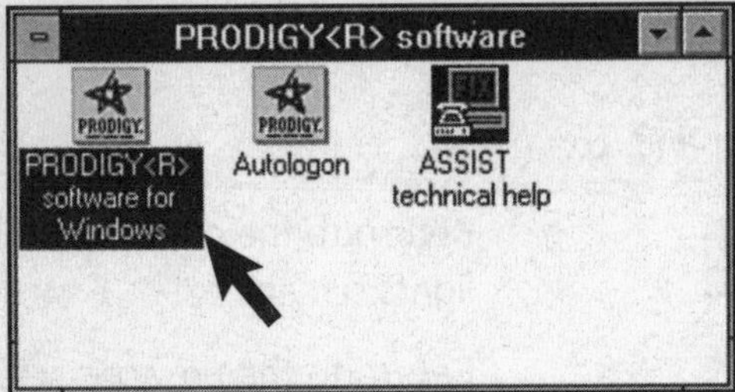

1 In Program Manager, double-click the **PRODIGY** software group icon to open its group window, and then double-click the **PRODIGY** program-item icon.

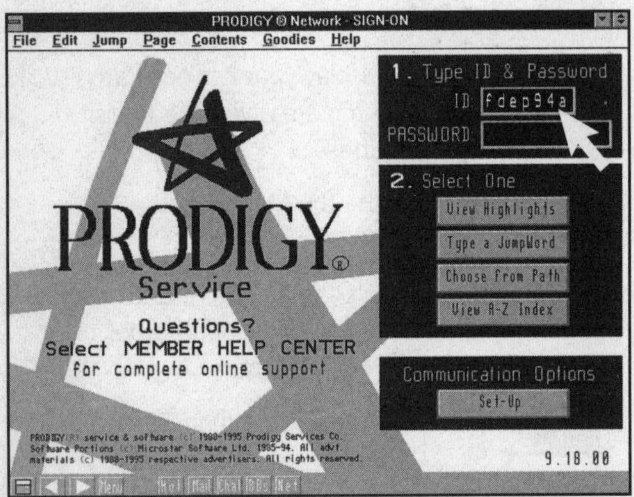

2 In the right side of the Sign-On screen, type your PRODIGY ID number. Press **Enter** or click in the **Password** text box.

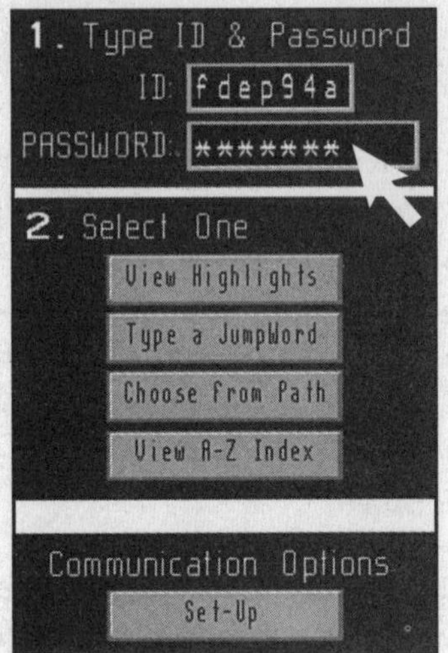

3 Type your PRODIGY password (you'll see asterisks for security).

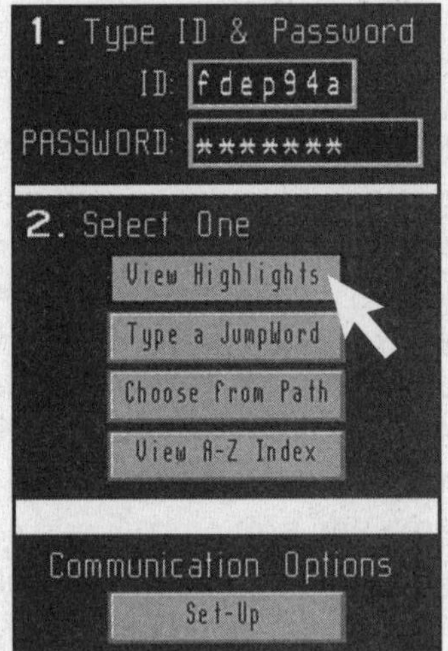

4 From the choices under **Select One**, choose where you want to go in PRODIGY by clicking on a button. PRODIGY signs you on and displays the screen you specified.

Begin Guided Tour Set Up Autologon

1 Log on to PRODIGY using the ID and password you want to create the autologon routine for.

2 Open the **Jump** menu and click **Jump To**, or press **Ctrl+J**.

3 In the Jump dialog box, type **autologon**, and then click the **OK** button.

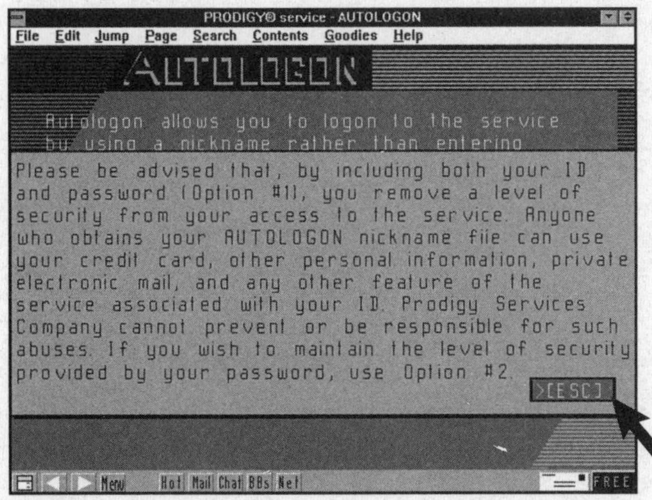

4 A warning screen appears. Read it carefully, and then click the **Esc** button.

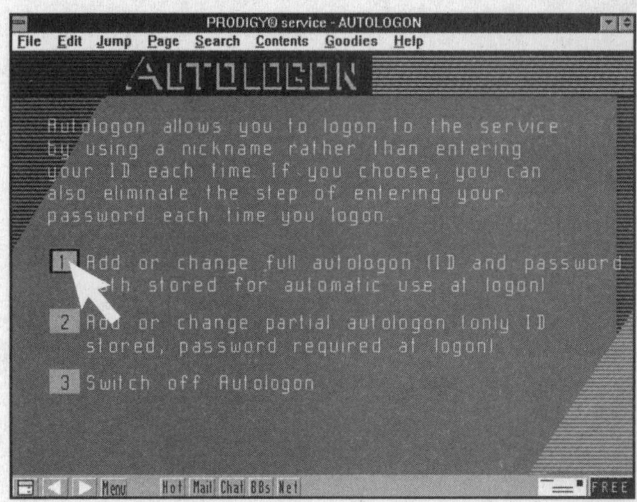

5 To store both the ID and password for autologon, click the **1** button for the first choice.

6 Type your password when prompted, and then click the **Esc** button.

7 Type a nickname to use for logon when prompted, and then click the **Esc** button.

(continues)

Guided Tour Set Up Autologon

(continued)

Your autologon has been activated. It will only work on this PC and in the current directory from which you are running the PRODIGY software. To logon in the future, select the PRODIGY Autologon icon from your PRODIGY program group.

To continue now, select ESC.

>[ESC]

8 A screen appears, telling you the Autologon setup is complete. Click the **Esc** button or press **Enter**.

9 The next time you log on to PRODIGY, double-click the **Autologon** icon.

Begin Guided Tour Log Off

1 Open the **File** menu and click **Exit**.

2 Click button **1** for **End This Session**, or press **Enter**.

Send Mail on PRODIGY

You probably have a basic idea about how the U.S. Postal Service works. A carrier picks up your letter. The local post office sorts letters according to destination, and sends them out on trucks and planes. At the destination city, the letters are again sorted according to postal carrier route, and then a carrier delivers your letter to the recipient's door.

Similarly, PRODIGY takes your private electronic mail (*e-mail*) messages, routes them along according to the address you give, and delivers them to your recipient's mailbox. Unlike U.S. mail, however, e-mail exists only in electronic format, and is transported via phone lines and computer networks rather than by plane or truck. You can exchange mail with any other PRODIGY user, as well as to users of many other online services and the Internet. All you need to know is the recipient's electronic address. More on these topics in a moment.

You can work online to compose, send, read, and manage your mail on PRODIGY. Of course, when you do so, you'll be charged for your online time. If you plan to send and receive a lot of e-mail on PRODIGY, consider downloading the Mail Manager, an add-in program that lets you deal with mail when you're not logged on to PRODIGY.

The Name Game

To send e-mail to another PRODIGY user, you address it to that user's ID number; if my PRODIGY ID is **fdep94b**, that's also my e-mail address. PRODIGY connects to all other users via the Internet, so it treats all other e-mail addresses as Internet addresses. The Internet address is generally a combination of the recipient's user name or ID and a suffix that's specific to the service provider; you need to know both parts of the puzzle.

Note that the Internet is picky about capitalization and punctuation. You need to type everything in lowercase characters, and put all periods and @ symbols in their correct positions. Here's how to address e-mail when you're sending it to users of other online services:

- *CompuServe addresses* consist of the user ID number with a period (rather than a comma), followed by **@compuserve.com**. So, to send e-mail from PRODIGY to the CompuServe user whose ID is 12345,123, you would address the mail to **12345.123@compuserve.com**.
- *America Online addresses* consist of the user's screen name in all lowercase letters and no spaces, followed by **@aol.com**. So the e-mail address for and AOL user with the screen name of BJ Poland would be **bjpoland@aol.com**.
- *Delphi addresses* are similar to AOL addresses, as in ***username*@delphi.com**.
- *Addresses for people with accounts directly on the Internet* have a unique form: a user name, followed by the **@** symbol and the name of the Internet site where that person's account is located. The catch is that there are thousands, if not millions, of Internet sites. Let's say you're addressing e-mail to someone whose user name

is **sjones**, and that person's account is located at **indiana.cica.edu**. The user's full e-mail address would be **sjones@indiana.cica.edu**, and you'd have to type it exactly.

Bet you didn't know that you have an Internet address! Take your PRODIGY ID number, typed in lowercase letters, and add **@prodigy.com** to create your Internet address, as in **fdep94b@prodigy.com**.

Begin Guided Tour   Create and Send Mail

1 Click the **Communications** button, or open the **Contents** menu and click **Communications**.

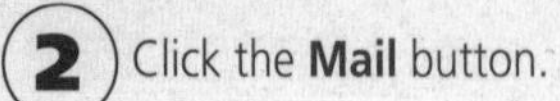

2 Click the **Mail** button.

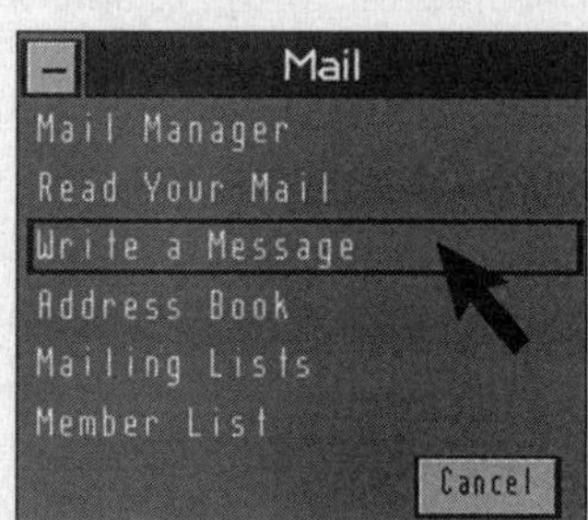

3 Click **Write a Message**.

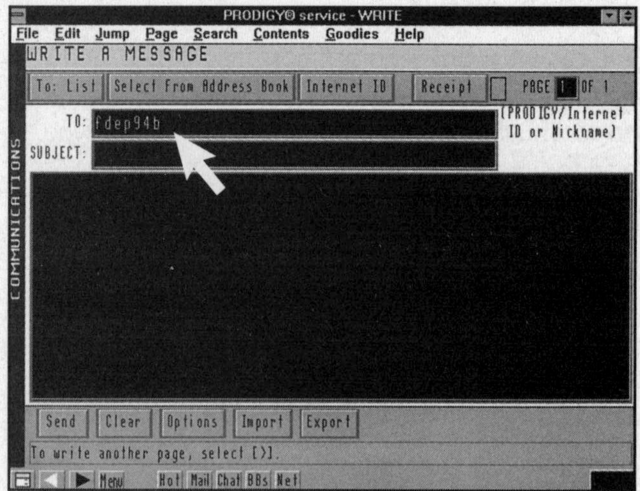

4 Enter the e-mail address to send the message to. **(Optional)** Use the **To:List** button to send the message to multiple recipients, and the Internet ID button to enter addresses longer than 40 characters.

Guided Tour Create and Send Mail

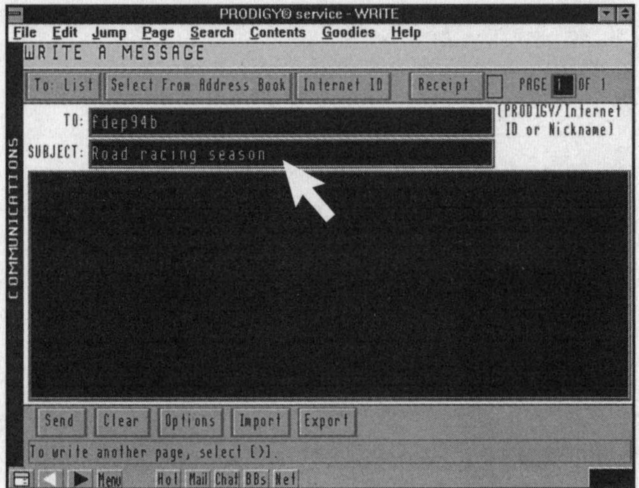

5 Click in the **SUBJECT** line and enter a topic for your message.

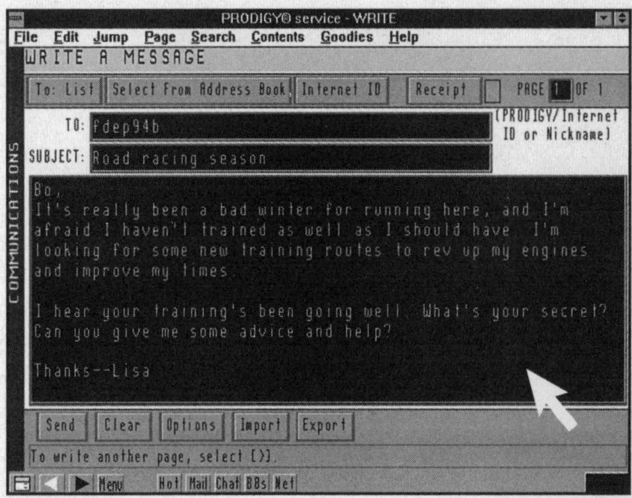

6 Press **Enter** to move to the message area, and type your message.

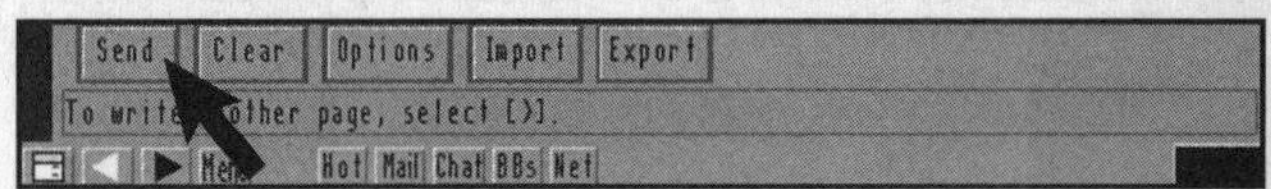

7 Click the **Send** button at the bottom of the screen to send your message. Click the **Clear** button to start a new message, and then repeat steps 1–7.

Begin Guided Tour Read Mail

1 Click the **Communications** button, or open the **Contents** menu and click **Communications**. (Two other methods: you can click the **Mail** button on the tool bar, or open the **Jump** menu and click **Read Mail**. Then skip to step 4.)

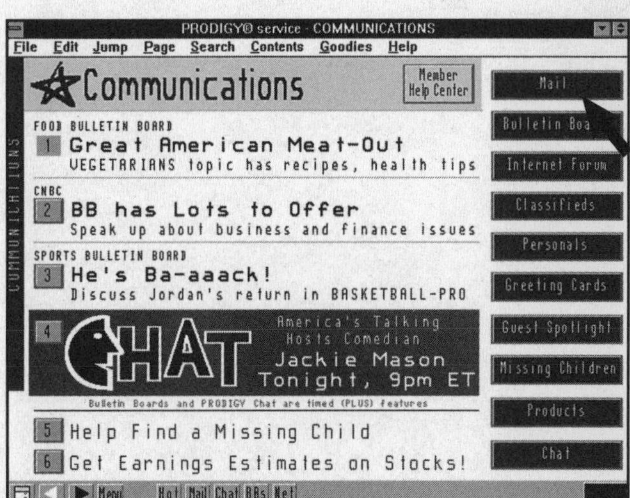

2 Click the **Mail** button.

(continues)

Guided Tour Read Mail

(continued)

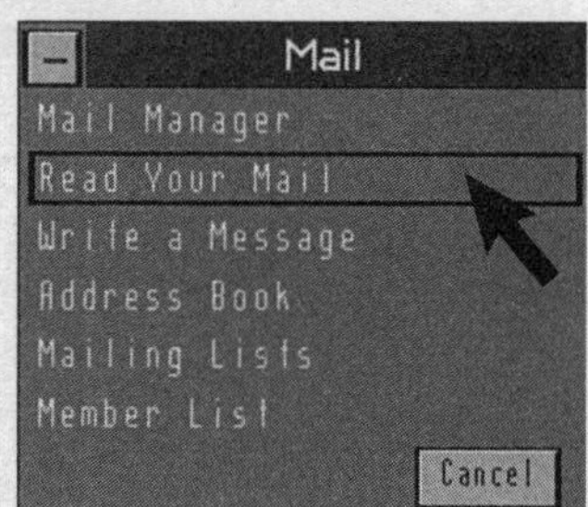

3 Click **Read Your Mail**.

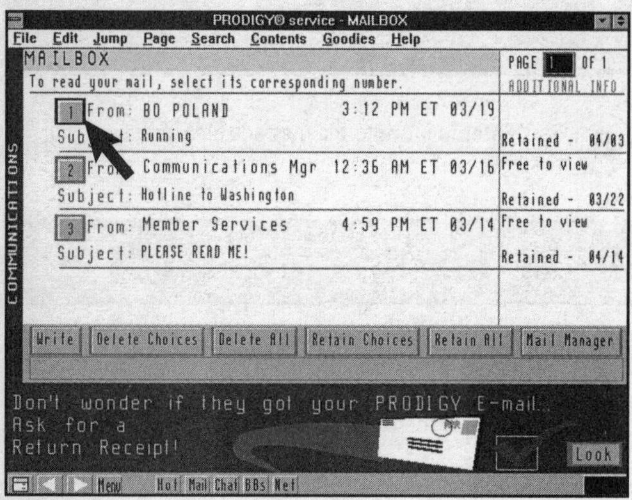

4 Click the numbered button next to the message you want to read.

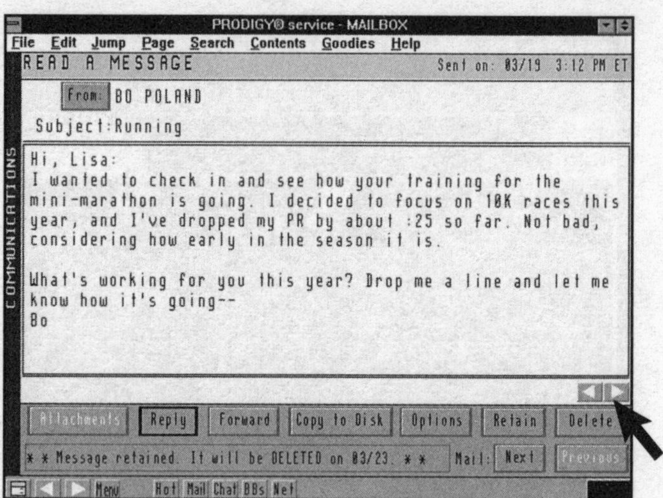

5 Read the message. If it has another page to read, click the **right arrow** button at the bottom right corner of the message window.

6 **(Optional)** Click the **From** button beside the sender's name, and then click **Add to Address Book** to save the sender's e-mail address.

7 Click a button to deal with the message. You can **Reply** to or **Forward** a message, click **Copy to Disk** to save it, or **Retain** it, or **Delete** it.

8 Use the **Next** or **Previous** buttons to read other messages as needed. Then use a jump command or the **Menu** button to go elsewhere in PRODIGY.

Find and Read Information on PRODIGY

PRODIGY divides much of its online information by *service* or *feature*, to make it easy for you to find the online resources you're interested in. The PRODIGY services include News/Weather, Business/Finance, Sports-ESPNET, Communications, Entertainment, Reference, Shopping, Computers, Travel, and Home/Family/Kids.

While the *articles* or *topics* listed within each service might change from day to day, PRODIGY always lists the services in the same locations. You can enter a service by clicking one of the buttons along the right side of PRODIGY's Highlights screen. To access a service from any screen, open the **Contents** menu and choose a service's name.

You have a few different options for moving around in a service and finding the articles you want to read:

- You can select on-screen buttons to move through a service and display the articles you want to read. This path you travel may vary a bit from service to service. To select a button, you can click it, or use **Tab** (or an **arrow** key) to highlight the button, and then press **Enter**.
- You can search for a particular article so you don't have to browse around through different services to find it.

See "Connect to PRODIGY" on page 239 to learn how to search for jump words for particular PRODIGY services.

Begin Guided Tour Browse and Read Information

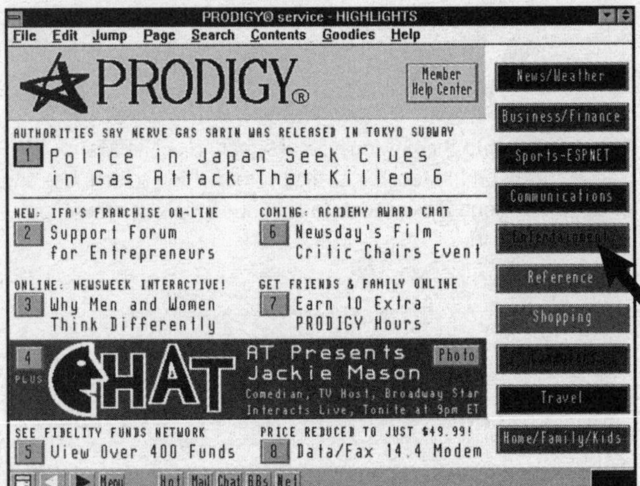

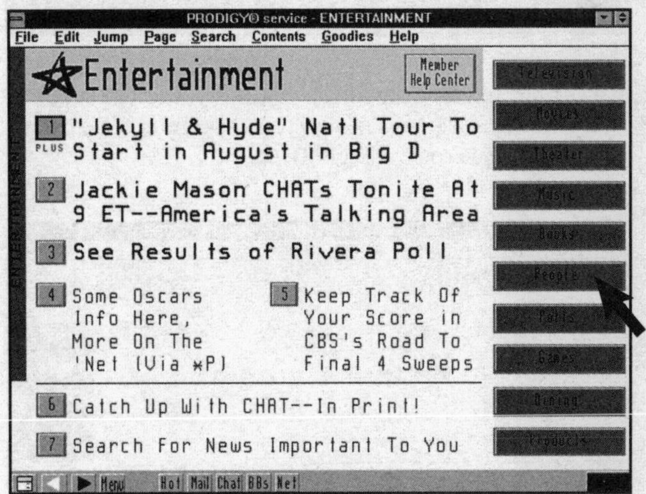

1. Click the button for a service at the right side of the screen, or open the **Contents** menu and click the service's name. For example, click the **Entertainment** button.

2. Click a button at the right side of the screen to look for particular topics within a service. In this case, for example, you could click **People**.

(continues)

Guided Tour Browse and Read Information

(continued)

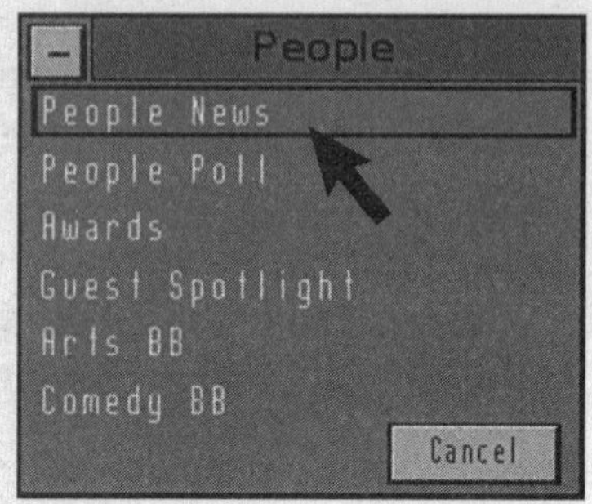

3 In the dialog box of choices that appears, click the choice you want. In this case, you could click **People News**.

4 When you see a topic that interests you, select its button (which usually has a number on it) by clicking it. From this screen, you could select **PHOTOS**.

5 If you see additional choices, select the one you want.

6 When an information window appears, you can read its contents. It may include a graphic. To close the information window, click its **Close box** in the upper left corner to put it away.

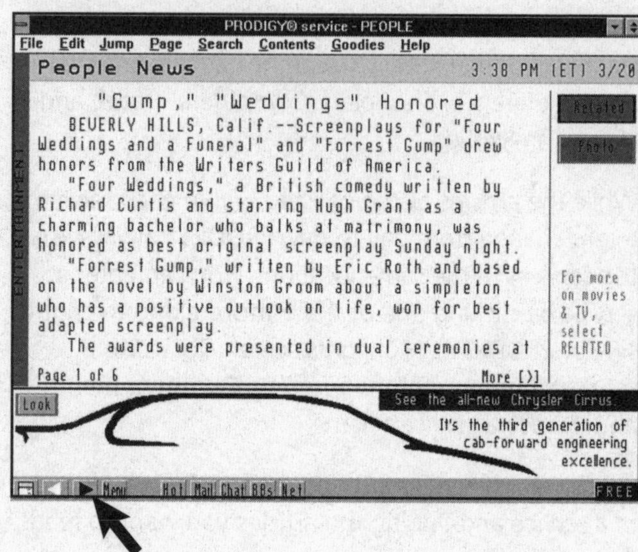

7 If an article you're viewing offers multiple pages, as shown here, click the next screen button on the tool bar. If a screen shows a **Related** button, select it to view a list of articles that also may interest you.

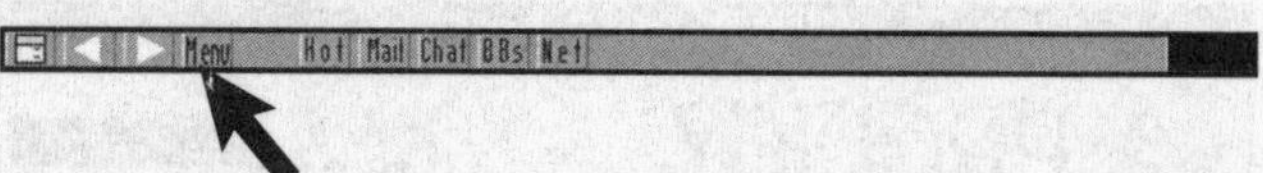

8 To move to the previous menu screen, click the **Menu** button on the tool bar at the bottom of the screen. Use any of steps 1 through 8 as needed to continue browsing around on PRODIGY.

Begin Guided Tour Search for an Article

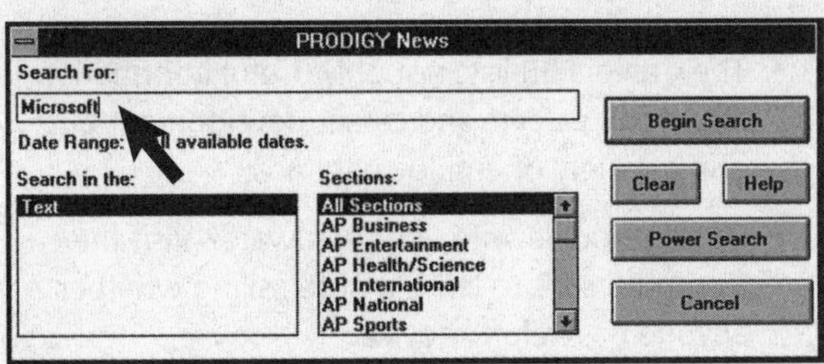

1. Open the **Search** menu and select **Quick Search**. Type the word or phrase you want to find an article about in the **Search For** text box.

2. **(Optional)** To narrow your search and make it faster, select a single service from the **Sections** list.

3. Click the **Begin Search** button.

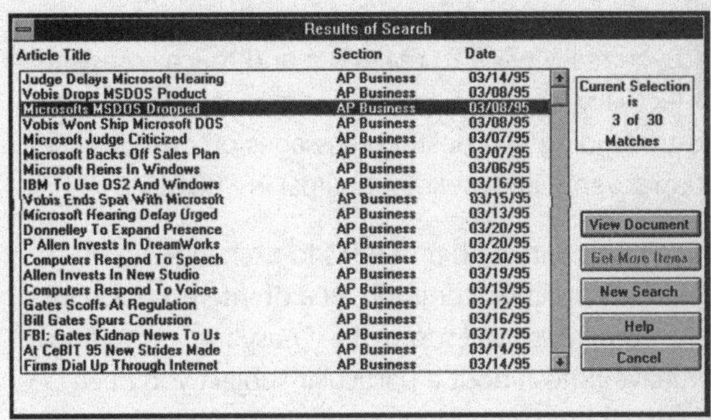

4. PRODIGY displays a list of articles containing the text you searched for. To read an article, scroll to it in the list and double-click it.

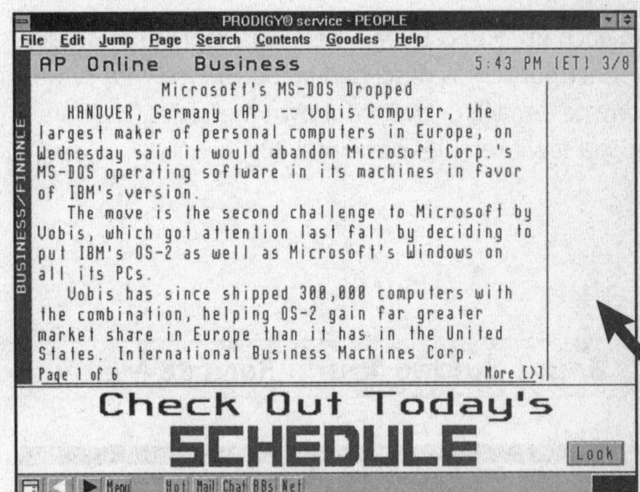

5. You can read the article just as you would read one you found by browsing.

Post on PRODIGY Bulletin Boards

If you really want to reach out and touch someone (actually, about two million someones), you ought to try reading and posting messages on one of more than seventy BBs (bulletin boards) in PRODIGY.

PRODIGY users gather in BBSs to exchange *notes* about a particular common area of interest. Each BB lists numerous topics to make it easy for you to find or leave notes about a particular subject you need help with. In fact, at last count, users were discussing over 2,000 specific topics on the various PRODIGY BBs. Even better, celebrity and expert guests join the BB discussions on occasion so you can go right to the top for the answers you need.

In each BB, you can read messages, reply to messages (either publicly as described in the *Guided Tour* or via private e-mail), or post your own messages. Here are just a few examples of helpful BBs:

- The Careers BB lists not only useful information about hot careers and career development but also a variety of employment ads.
- Having trouble with your hardware? Visit the Computers BB to leave a note asking whether anyone has helpful advice.
- So many movies.... So little time.... To check out which movies are worth seeing, check here.

You can find BBs as you're browsing around through the various PRODIGY services. Related BBs appear in the list of topics for the service. Another way: jump directly to the full listing of PRODIGY BBs and choose the one you want, as described here.

Always use good online manners in BBs. The PRODIGY message police look for people who break the rules (those who post notes that are obscene, threatening, and the like), and will bounce those notes back to the original owner.

Begin Guided Tour Read BB Messages

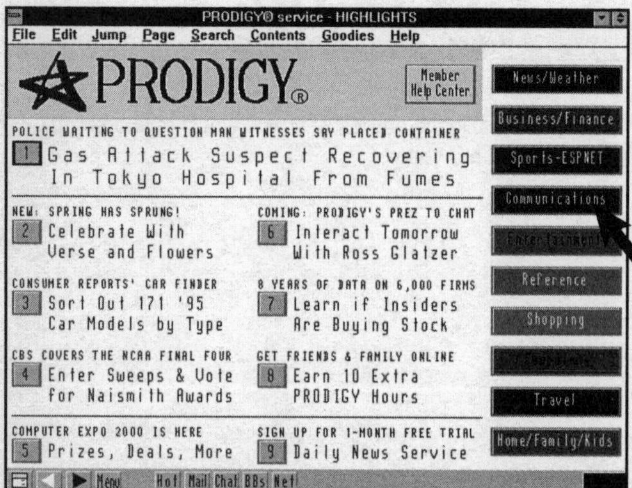

1 From the main Highlights screen, click the **Communications** button, or open the **Contents** menu and select **Communications**.

2 Click the **Bulletin Boards** button. (Instead of step 1, you can click the **BBs** button on the toolbar.)

Guided Tour Read BB Messages

3 Click the **Boards A-Z** button. This displays a list of all the PRODIGY BBs so you can choose one to visit. Use the **Page Down** and **Page Up** keys to scroll through the list of BBs.

4 To view a BB, click the **GO TO** button beside it. In this case, you could click to go to the **Health** BB.

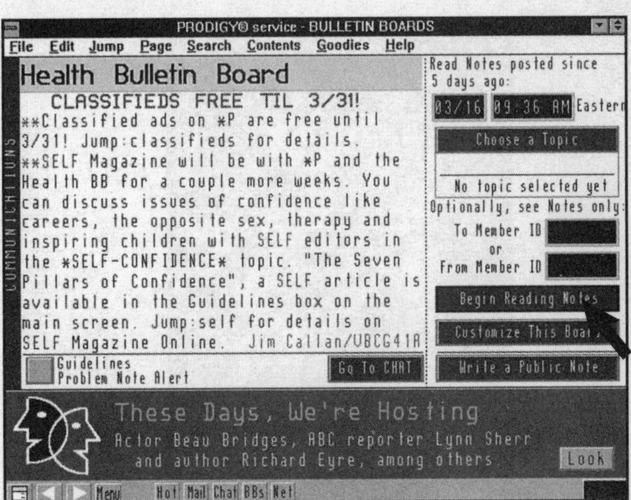

5 Click the **Begin Reading Notes** button.

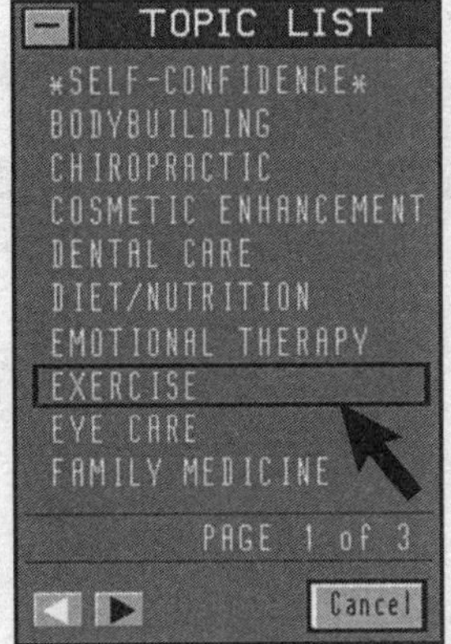

6 In the **Topics** list, use the **Page Down** key or **arrow** buttons to display all the topics for discussion. To select a topic, click it.

(continues)

Guided Tour Read BB Messages

(continued)

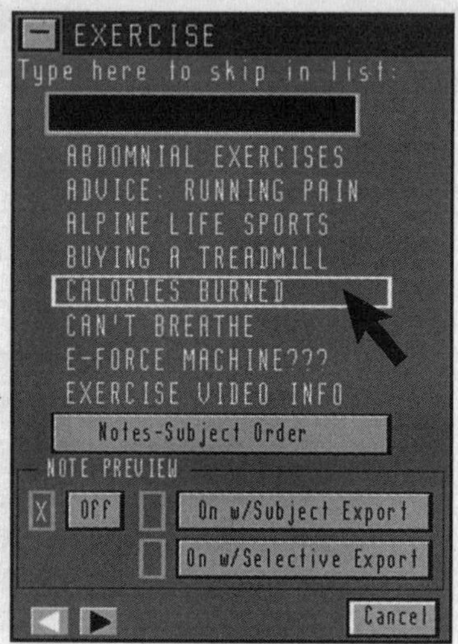

7 In the notes list, use the **Page Down** key or **arrow buttons** to display all the posted notes. To select a note, click it (or highlight it with an **arrow** key) and press **Enter**.

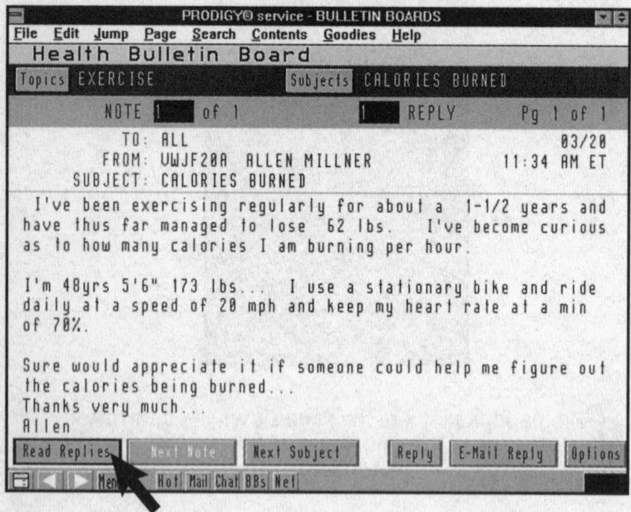

8 **(Optional)** Click (or press **Enter**) to select the **Read Replies** button.

9 **(Optional)** After viewing a reply, use the **Next Subject** or **Original Note** buttons if you want to move around.

10 Click the **Topics** or **Subjects** buttons at the top of the note to redisplay the list of BB topics or the subjects of notes within a topic, respectively.

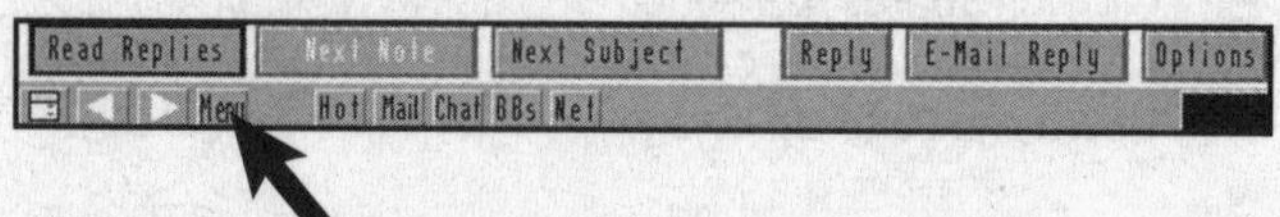

11 Use the **Menu** button on the tool bar as needed to move back to the list of BBs or to explore other activities in PRODIGY.

Begin Guided Tour Reply to a Message

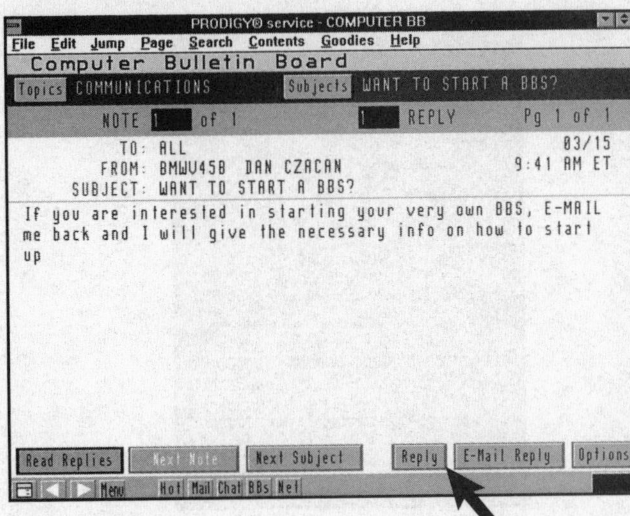

1 Find a BB message that interests you, and that you want to respond to. Click the **Reply** button to send a public message that anyone visiting the BB can read.

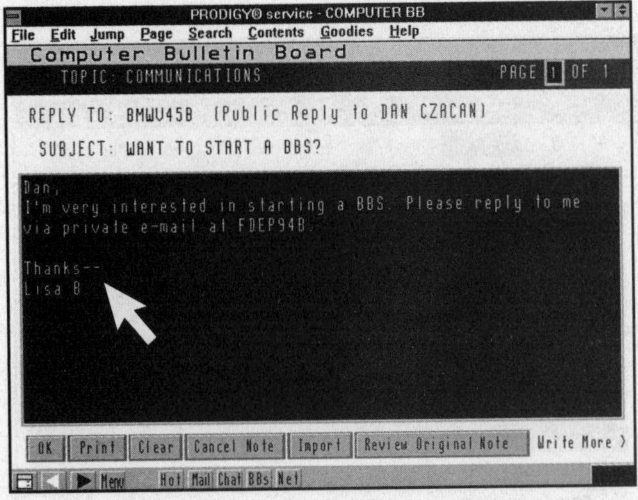

2 Type the text for your reply. **(Optional)** Click the **Print** button to create a copy of the reply you're sending. Click the **OK** button to send off the reply.

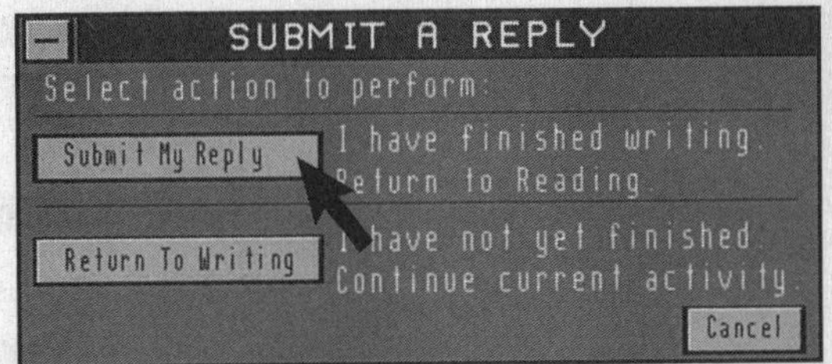

3 Click the **Submit My Reply** button.

Begin Guided Tour Post Your Own Message

1 Go to the board you want to post a note in. Select the **Write a Public Note** button.

2 If this is the first time you've visited the BB, you'll need to pick a topic to post to. Click **e**. Otherwise, PRODIGY posts your note with those in the topic you last visited.

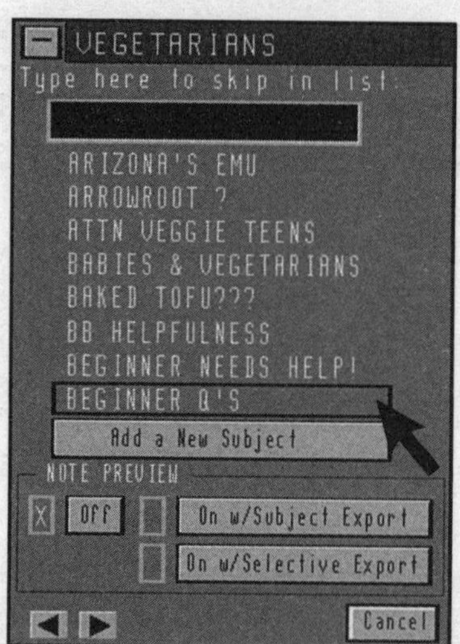

3 Click to select a subject for your note. (Or select **Add a New Subject** if you need to.)

4 **(Optional)** Type an ID to address the note to a particular user of the BB.

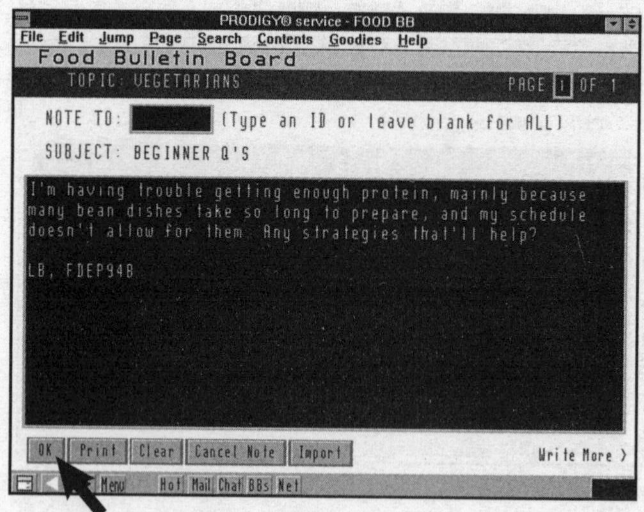

5 Type the text of your message and click the **OK** button to post it.

6 To write a note in a subject while you're reading other notes there, click the **Options** button in the lower right corner of the screen. Then click **Write a new Note in this Subject**.

Connect to America Online

America Online (AOL) provides its information to millions of users in a very friendly way. On its plus side, it offers the most graphical user interface of the three most popular online services, making it easy to get where you need to go by clicking. On the downside, the first time you visit a particular *department*, you have to wait while AOL downloads the graphics files for display on your system.

AOL presently offers 14 different departments: Personal Finance, Clubs & Interests, Travel, Computing, Today's News, Marketplace, People Connection, Newsstand, Education, Reference Desk, Internet Connection, Sports, Kids Only, and Entertainment. The Main Menu screen in AOL lets you enter any of the departments by clicking on an icon.

The window for each department offers an alphabetical listing of each of the *services* found in that department. Double-click the name of a service to go to it. Popular department features appear as icons at the left side of the window; click an icon to enter the service it represents. The Main Menu button lets you jump back to the Main Menu to enter another department. If you need help, click the **Member Services** button from any department window; to get an alphabetical list of that department's services, click the **Index** button.

What you can do depends on the service you're in. You can read and leave messages in *forums*, browse to find information, download files from *libraries*, and even chat with other users.

The icons along the top of the AOL Windows software let you jump to specific services or perform specific actions. Here's a rundown of what each icon does:

Click the icon…	*To…*
	Read new mail.
	Compose a mail message.
	Display the Main Menu.
	Display the Spotlight highlights window.
	Go to the Free Help service.
	View the Directory of Services list.
	Enter the Chat service.
	Enter the Quotes & Portfolios stock service.
	Read Today's News.
	Visit the Center Stage interactive meeting.
	Go to the Internet Connection department.
	See New Features & Services.
	Go to the Discover America Online service.
	Display the Keyword dialog box.
	Go to the Download Manager.
	Search for a File.

(continues)

Click the icon...	*To...*
	Display how long you've been connected to AOL.
	Change your Personal Choices settings.
	Print the displayed text or graphic.
	Save the displayed text or graphic.

If the AOL software didn't come installed on your computer or come with your modem, you can get it by calling 1-800-827-6364. If you need to install the software, follow the instructions on the disk label to start the installation process, and then respond to the on-screen prompts.

Use a Keyword to Move Around

You can jump directly to a service rather than moving to it by choosing a department. To go directly to a service, you use its *keyword*. Here's how to go to a service using its keyword, whether you know the keyword or not:

1. Open the **Go To** menu and click **Keyword** (or press **Ctrl+K** or click the keyword icon at the top of the screen).
2. If you know the keyword for the service you want to go to, type it in the **Enter word(s)** text box, and click **Go** or press **Enter**. Otherwise, proceed with the rest of the steps.
3. Type a topic to search for in the **Enter word(s)** text box. Click the **Search** button.
4. The Search Results window appears, listing areas dealing with the topic you searched for. Double-click one of the matching entries to see a description of it (or highlight it with an **arrow** key and click **View Description**).
5. The service description appears, including its keyword. Click the **Go** button or press **Enter** to jump to that service.

Begin Guided Tour Sign On

1 In Program Manager, double-click the **America Online** group icon to open its group window. Double-click the **America Online** program-item icon.

2 In the Welcome dialog box, open the **Screen Name** list and choose your screen name.

Guided Tour Sign On

3 Type your Password, and then click the **Sign On** button. Your computer dials into AOL, and you see the AOL Welcome screen.

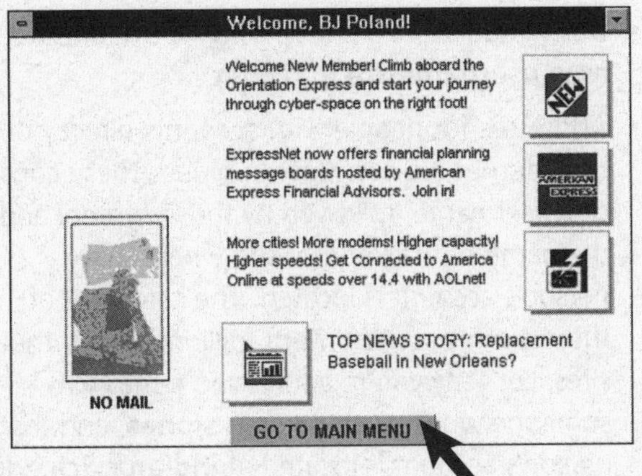

4 Click an icon to go to a service, or click the **GO TO MAIN MENU** button to start using AOL.

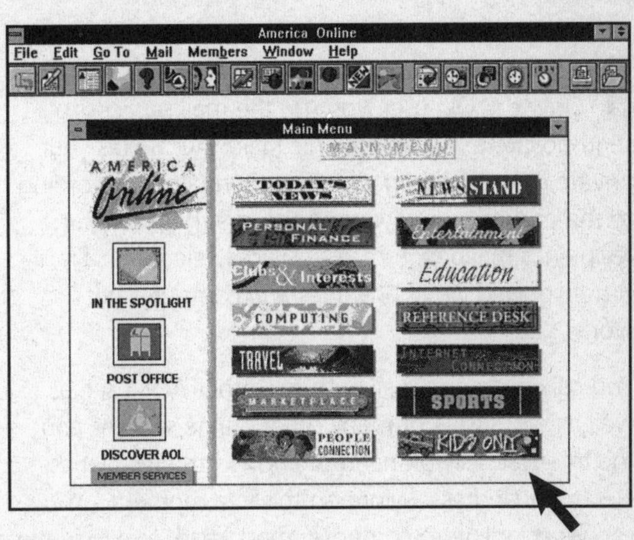

5 From the Main menu, you can click a button to start using a service.

Begin Guided Tour Sign Off

1 Open the **File** menu and click **Exit**.

2 In the confirmation dialog box, click **Yes**.

3 At the Goodbye dialog box, another user can sign on (or you can press **Alt+F4** to leave AOL).

Send Mail on America Online

To have private contact with another America Online (AOL) user, you use the mail services to send private e-mail (electronic mail). AOL takes your private e-mail messages, routes them along according to the address you give, and delivers them to your recipient's mailbox. E-mail exists only electronically; it is transported via phone lines and computer networks.

You can exchange mail with any other AOL user, as well as with users of many other online services and the Internet. All you need to know is the recipient's electronic address. (More on this in a moment.) You can work online to compose, send, read, and manage your mail in AOL. Of course, when you do so, you'll be charged for your online time. (AOL also lets you create mail offline and send it later. To learn more about this, see the **FlashSessions** choice on the **Mail** menu.)

E-Mail Recipient Names

To send e-mail to another AOL user, you address it to that user's screen name; if my screen name is **Lbucki**, that's also my e-mail address. Use the correct capitalization when you type another person's screen name to address mail; you must capitalize all the right letters, and use spaces when they're called for.

AOL connects to all other users via the Internet, so it treats all other e-mail addresses as Internet addresses. The Internet address is generally a combination of the recipient's user name or ID and a suffix that's specific to the service provider; you need to know both parts of the puzzle.

Note that the Internet is picky about capitalization and punctuation. You need to type everything in lowercase characters, and correctly position all periods and @ symbols. Here's how to address e-mail when you're sending it to users of other online services:

- CompuServe addresses consist of the user ID number with a period rather than a comma, followed by **@compuserve.com**. To send e-mail from AOL to the CompuServe user whose ID is **12345,123**, you would address the mail to **12345.123@compuserve.com**.
- PRODIGY addresses consist of the user's ID in all lowercase characters, followed by **@prodigy.com**. So, the e-mail address for a PRODIGY user with the ID of **FDEP94B** would be **fdep94b@prodigy.com**.
- Delphi addresses are similar to AOL addresses, as in ***username*@delphi.com**.
- Addresses for people with accounts directly on the Internet are even more unique. These consist of a user name, followed by the **@** symbol and the name of the Internet site where that person's account is located. The catch is that there are thousands, if not millions, of Internet sites. Let's say you're addressing e-mail to someone whose user name is **sjones**, and that person's account is located at **indiana.cica.edu**. The user's full e-mail address would be **sjones@indiana.cica.edu**, and you'd have to type it exactly.

Bet you didn't know that you have an Internet address! Take your screen name, typed in lowercase letters and with no spaces, and add **@aol.com** to create your Internet address, as in **bjpoland@aol.com**.

Begin Guided Tour Create and Send Mail

1 Open the **Mail** menu and select **Compose Mail**. Another way: you can press **Ctrl+M**, or click the **Compose Mail** icon (the second from the left at the top of the screen).

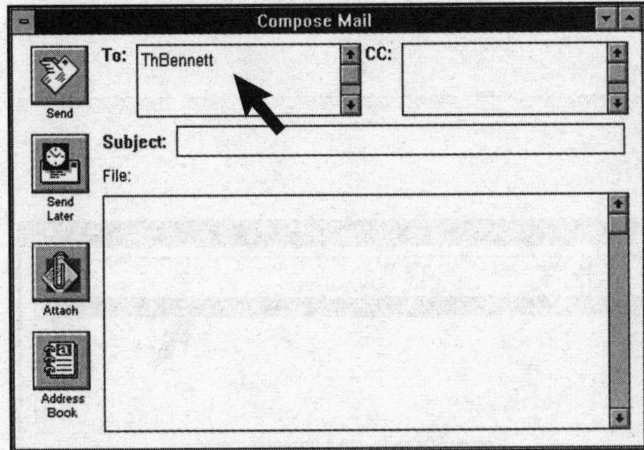

2 In the **To** list, type one or more e-mail addresses to send the message to. These addresses may include AOL addresses and addresses for other services.

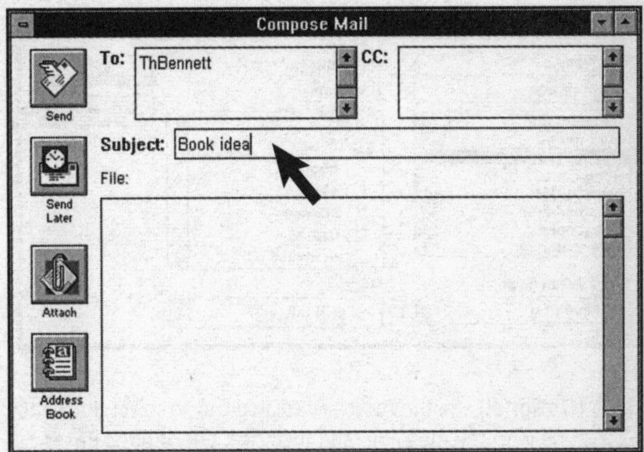

3 Click in the **Subject** line and type the subject for your message; then click in the blank text area of the **Compose Mail** window, and type the text of your message.

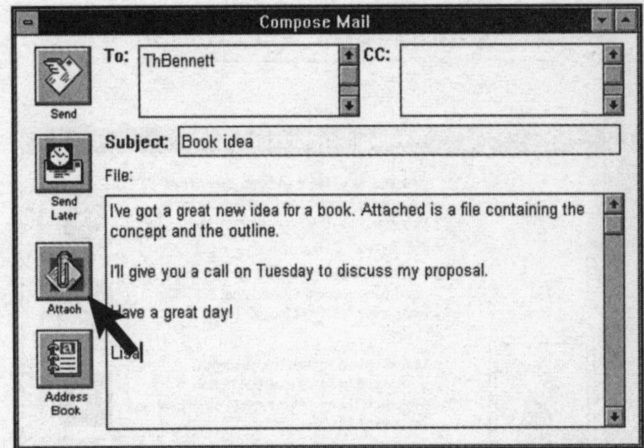

4 **(Optional)** If you want to send a file along with your message, click the **Attach** button.

(continues)

Guided Tour Create and Send Mail

(continued)

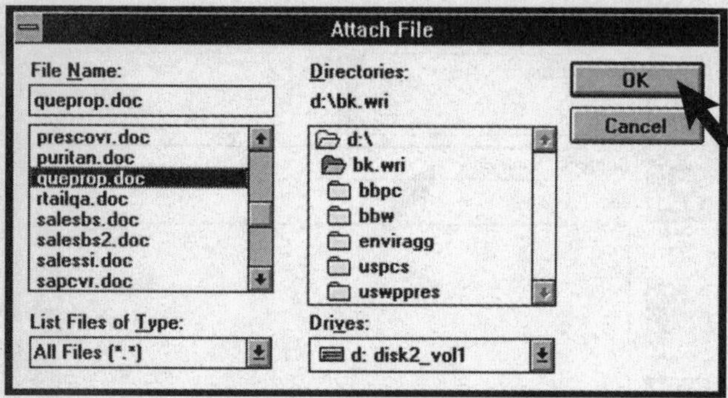

5 **(Optional)** Use the Attach File dialog box to select the file to send with the message, and then click **OK** or press **Enter**.

6 Click the **Send** button to send your message immediately. At the window informing you your mail has been sent, click **OK** or press **Enter**.

Begin Guided Tour Read Mail

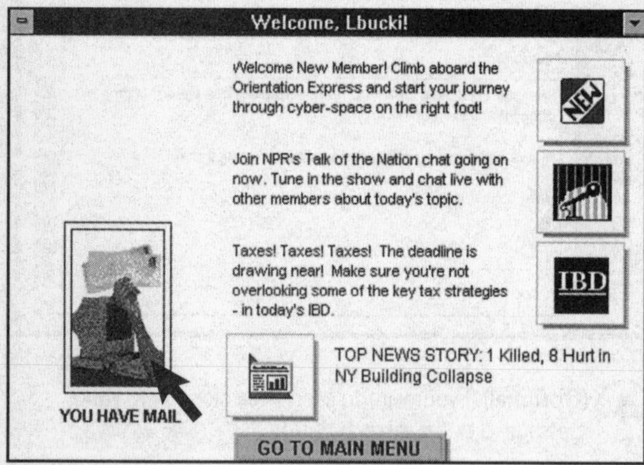

1 In the initial Spotlight window, click **You Have Mail**. Open the **Mail** menu and select **Read New Mail** or click the **Read Mail** icon (the far left one at the top of the screen).

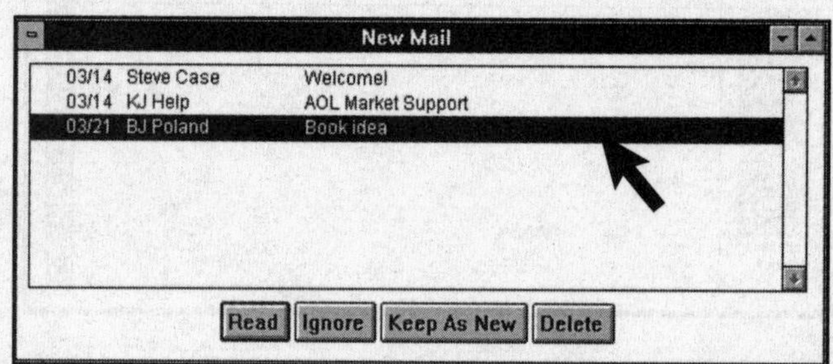

2 Either double-click the message you want to read, or use the **down arrow** key to highlight it, and then click **Read**.

Guided Tour Read Mail

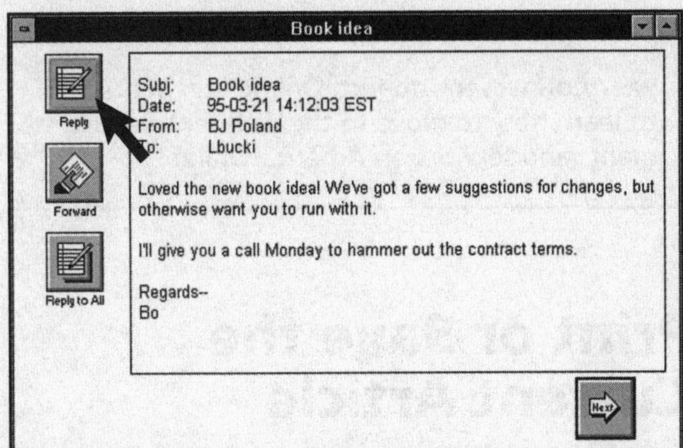

3 **(Optional)** Click the **Reply** button if you want to respond to a message.

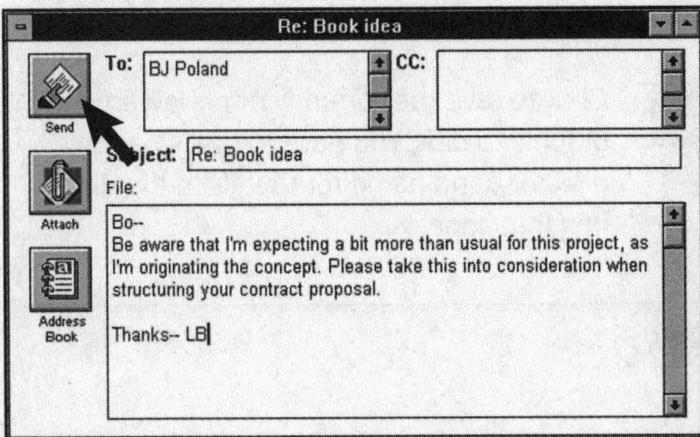

4 **(Optional)** Type your reply text, and then click the **Send** button. Double-click the **Control-menu box** to close your message window and the Reply window.

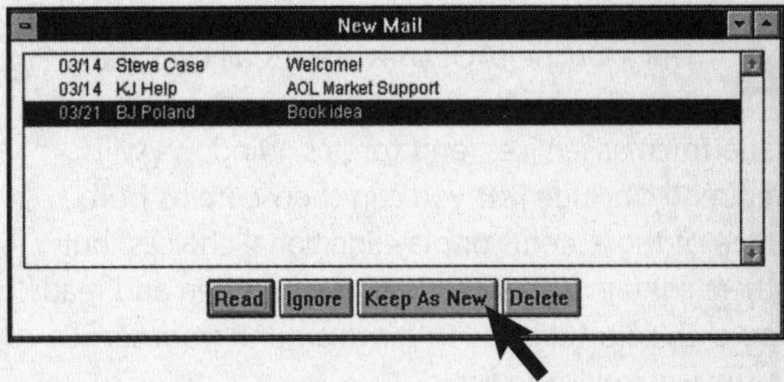

5 Select either the **Keep As New** or **Delete** button to determine what you want to do with the message you just read.

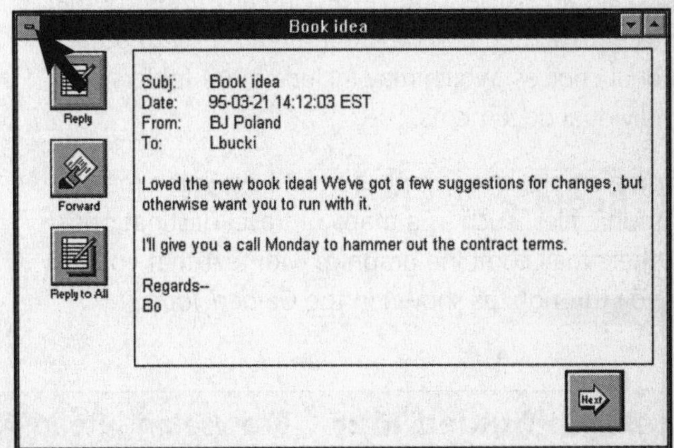

6 Read other messages, or close the mail windows to work elsewhere in AOL.

Read Articles on America Online

America Online (AOL) has articles all over the place. As you move around through various departments, services, and forums, windows will frequently include lists you can choose items from. Some of those items display additional choices, but others contain an article that you can open and read. You click colorful icons to move around from service to service and list to list.

When you're viewing a list of choices in AOL, look for items that have a document icon beside them. The document icon indicates that choosing that item displays an article. Double-clicking any list entry that has a file-folder icon beside it reveals a list of additional choices, which may include more folders or individual documents.

Some articles may simply be text files; some may be graphic files, such as a maps of travel destinations. Others may combine graphics with text that you can scroll through, as shown in the *Guided Tour*.

See "Connect to America Online" on page 255 to learn how to move to the different departments and services on America Online.

Print or Save the Current Article

Once you display an article or a graphic image, you may save it to disk by using one of the icons at the far right side of the toolbar on-screen:

Click to send the currently displayed article or graphic directly to your printer.

Click to save the currently displayed article or graphic to disk; you have to specify a disk, directory, and name for the file in the dialog box that appears.

Begin Guided Tour Browse and Read Articles

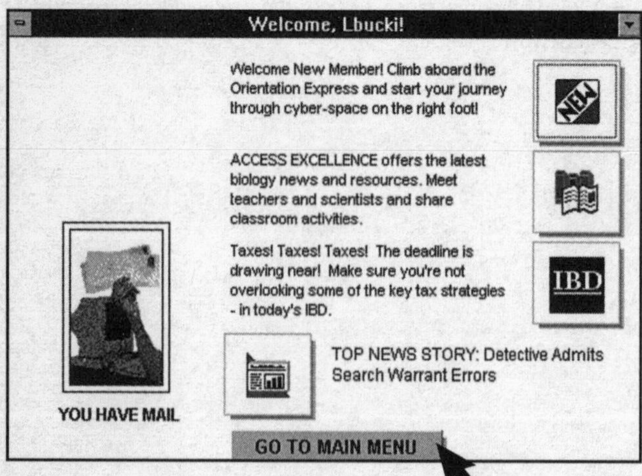

1 At the opening Spotlight screen, click the **GO TO MAIN MENU** button.

2 From the **Main Menu**, click a department to select it. For example, you can click the icon for the **Travel** department.

Guided Tour Browse and Read Articles

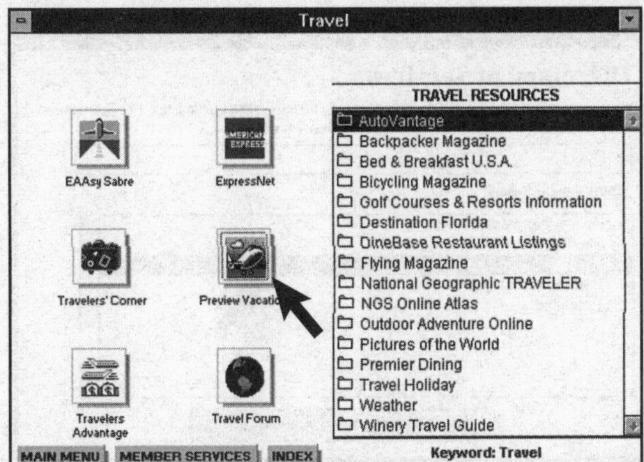

3 From the department window that opens, you can either double-click a folder in the list at the right to go to that particular service, or click an icon for a popular service at the left. For example, you could click **Preview Vacations**.

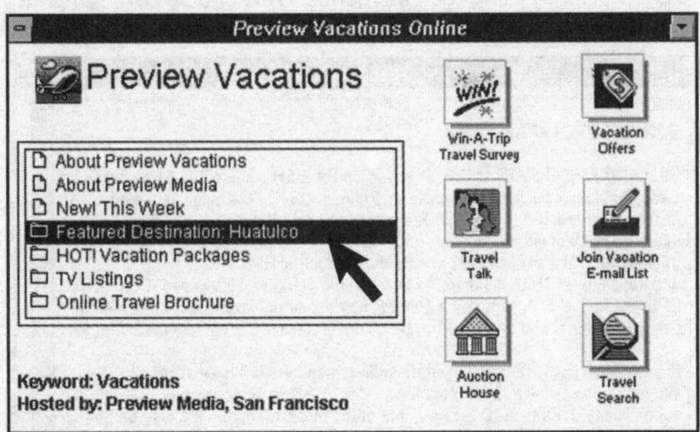

4 In the list of choices for the opening service window, double-click a folder for a topic to open it. If necessary, double-click folders in the subsequent windows that appear until you see a document listed that you want to read.

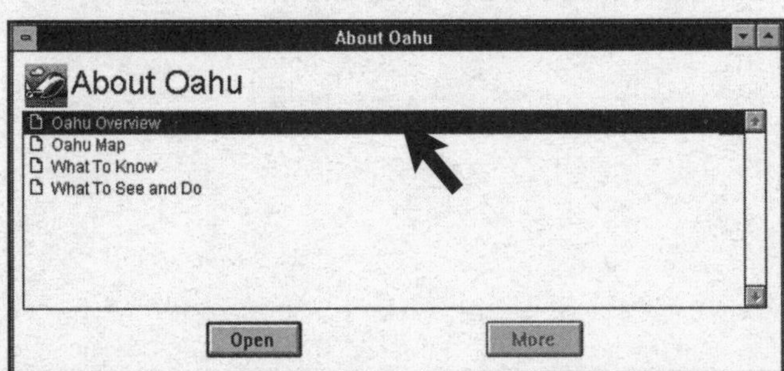

5 To open an article to read it, double-click it in the list, or highlight it with an **arrow** key, after which you can press **Enter** or click **Open**.

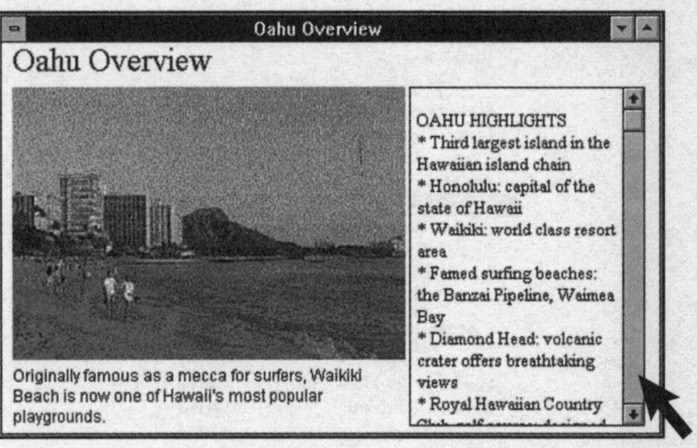

6 If the article holds more text than you can see at one time, use the scroll bar that appears to view more of the article. Save or print the article as desired. (You can start these processes using the **File** menu's **Print** and **Save** commands.)

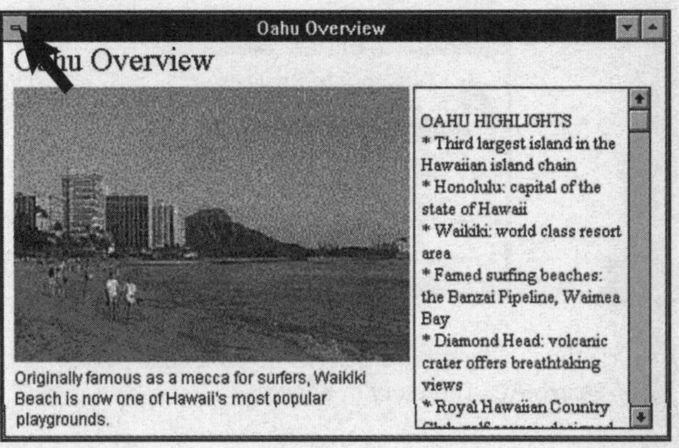

7 Double-click the **Control-menu box** for an article window to close it.

8 Continue browsing for articles by moving to new lists and selecting additional folders.

Begin Guided Tour Search for an Article

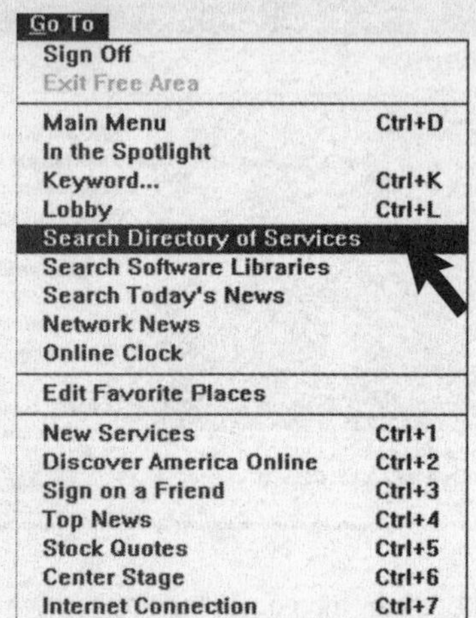

1 Open the **Go To** menu and select **Search Directory of Services**.

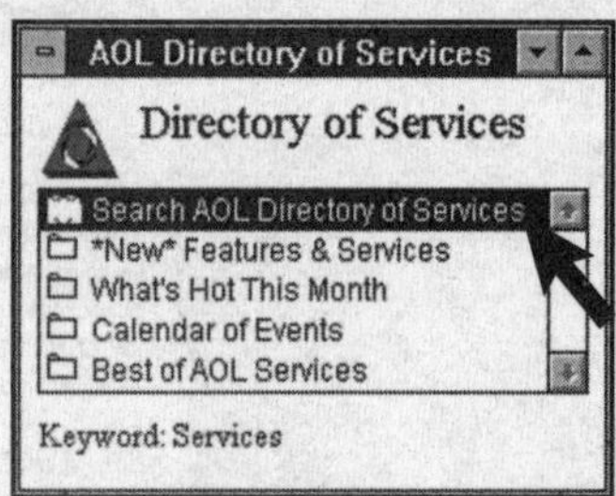

2 In the AOL Directory of Services window, double-click **Search AOL Directory of Services**.

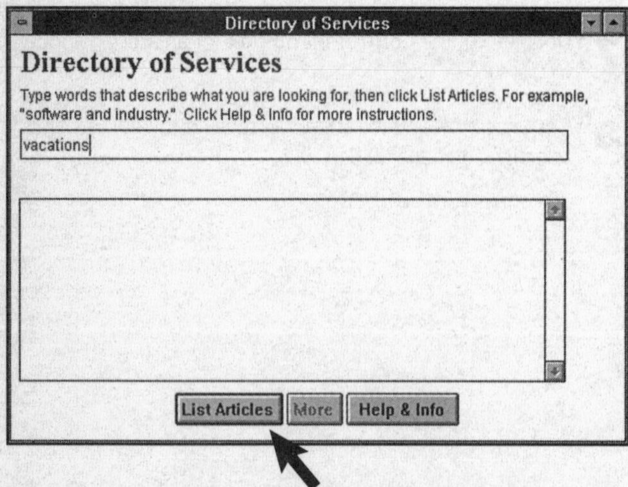

3 In the top text box of the Directory of Services dialog box, type the subject you want to search for. For example, enter vacations and then click List Articles.

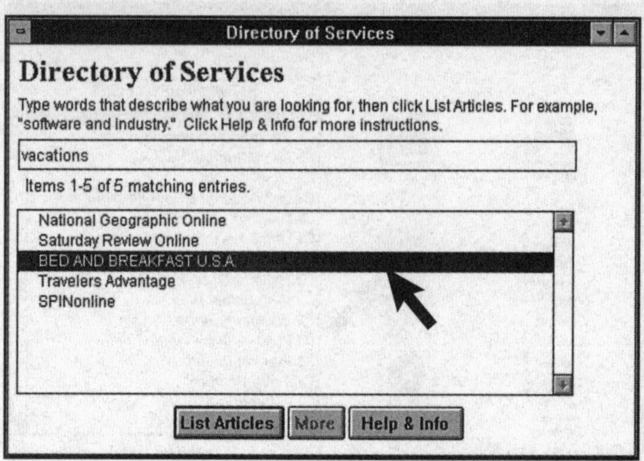

4 To preview an article from the list that appears, double-click an article. (If available, use the More button to see additional articles.)

5 Save or print the article, if you want. (You can start these processes using the **File** menu's **Print** and **Save** commands.)

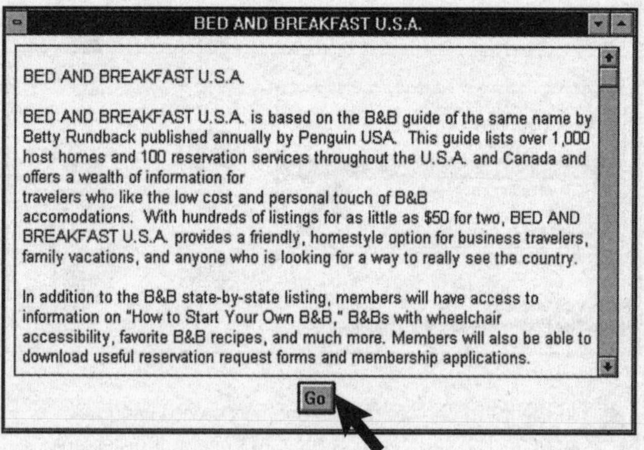

6 To go to the AOL service that holds the article and other related ones, click **Go** or press **Enter**.

Guided Tour Search for an Article

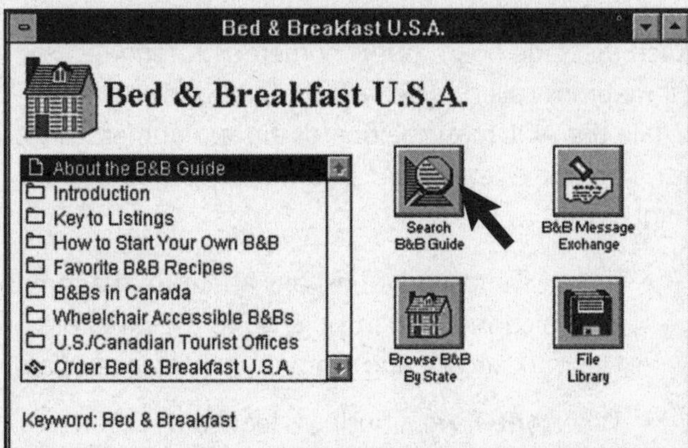

7 To search for an article within a service, click the **Search** icon if the service offers one.

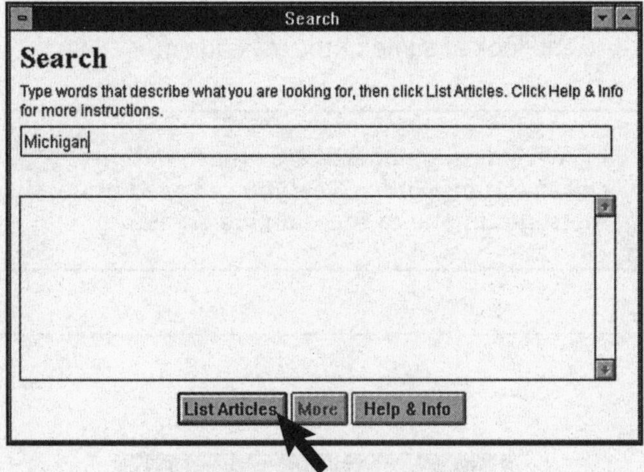

8 In the top text box of the Search dialog box, type the topic you want to search for; click **List Articles**.

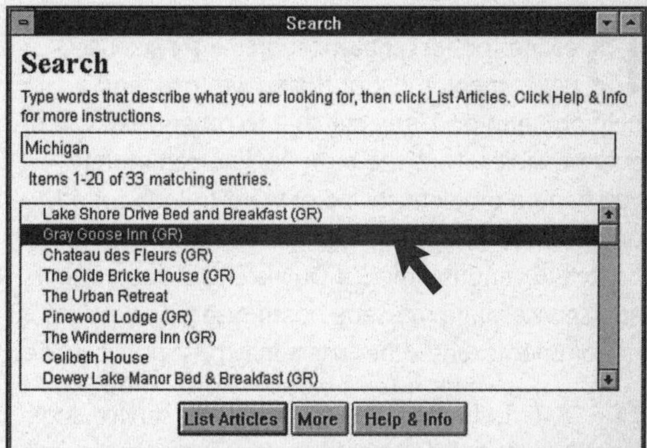

9 To preview an article from the list that appears, double-click an article. (If it's available, use the **More** button to see additional articles.)

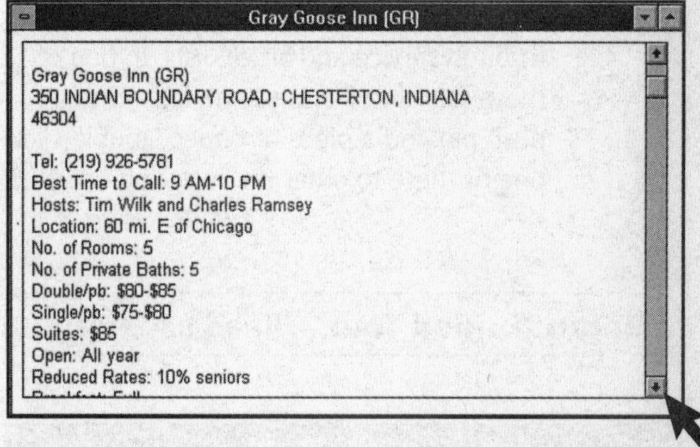

10 Use the scroll bar to read the rest of the article, if necessary.

Post in America Online Message Boards

Despite the fact that most online service users never meet, most of them love to extend a helping hand or a little chitchat to other users whenever possible. (Thus the term "online community.") If you need a problem solved or want to look for advice or ideas from other users, check out the *message boards* in various America Online (AOL) departments and services. In a message board, users post questions or comments, and other users may post public replies.

To find a message board in a service, look for a button with a picture of a push pin and piece of paper. The button title will usually include **message boards**, **messaging**, or **talk**. Click a button like this to enter the message board.

You also can enter message boards through service and article lists. In one of these lists, you'll also see an icon with a push pin and a piece of paper. Double-click one of these to enter the message board.

Each message board offers numerous *categories* (sometimes called *folders*) and topics of discussion. While the AOL message boards are too numerous to list, here are a few instances of message boards you might visit:

- If you want to ask questions about mutual funds you're considering buying, go to the Investor's Network service and jump on its message board.
- When you have a business legal question, visit the message board for the Small Business Center.
- If you're losing sleep at night about whether you've got the most popular Grateful Dead bumper sticker, go to the Grateful Dead Forum and look at some of the messaging.

In AOL, message boards are also sometimes called *forums*. Either way, you can read or post messages in one of these online areas.

Begin Guided Tour Read a Message

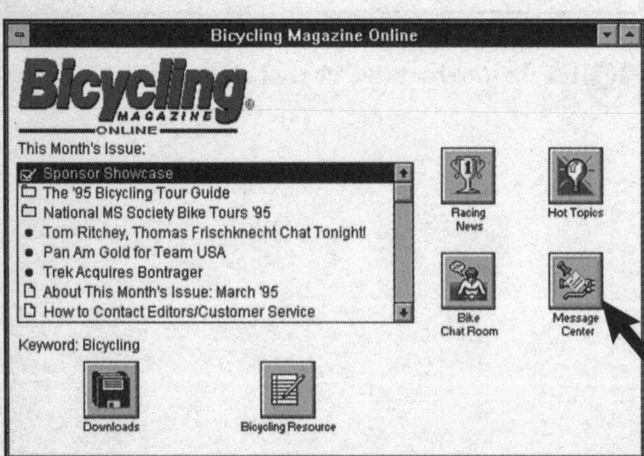

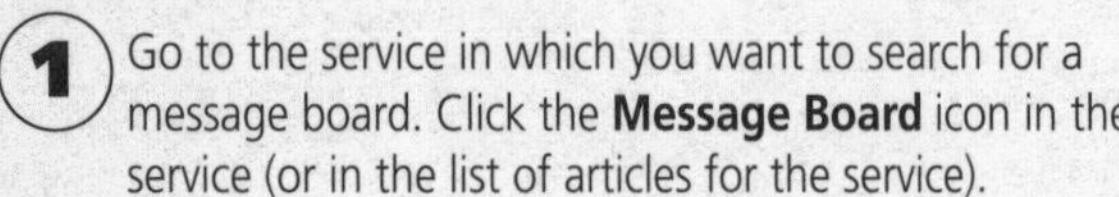

1 Go to the service in which you want to search for a message board. Click the **Message Board** icon in the service (or in the list of articles for the service).

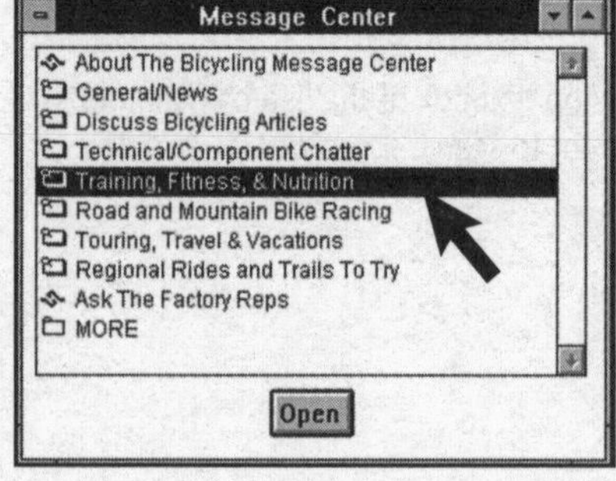

2 If you see another list of different message boards, select the one you want by double-clicking it.

Guided Tour Read a Message

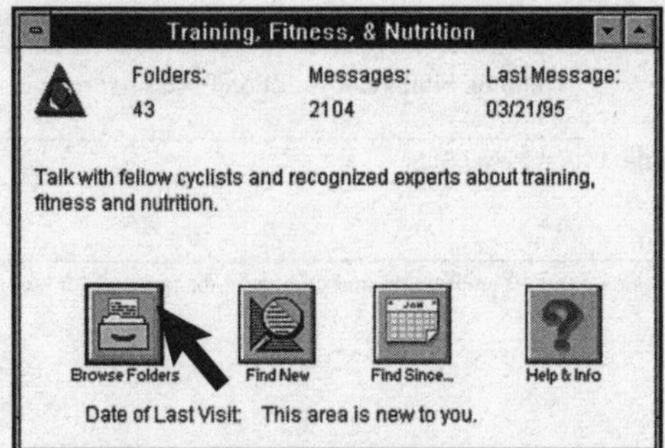

3 Click the **Browse Folders** button.

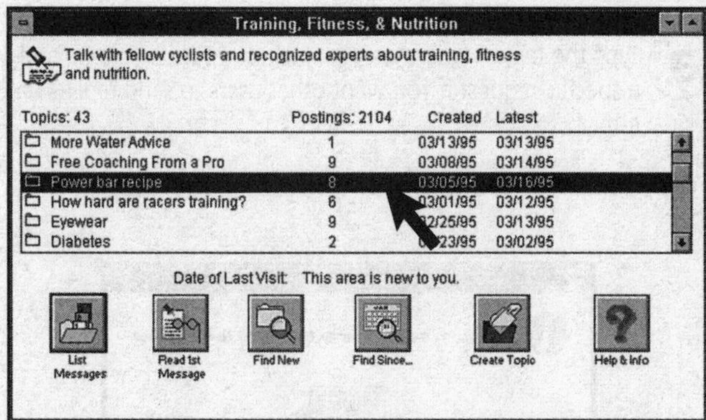

4 Use the **down arrow** key or **scroll bar** to move down through the list of folders (categories). When you want to read the messages in one of them, double-click it.

5 Use the **down arrow** key or **scroll bar** to move down through the list of messages. Note that the messages are listed from oldest to newest, so you need to scroll down through the list to get to the newer postings.

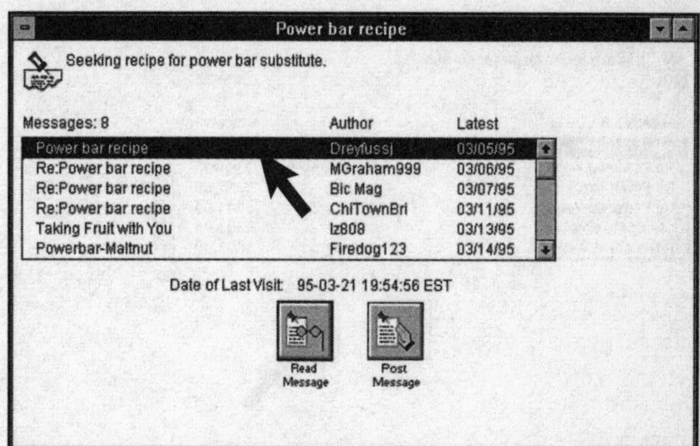

6 When you find a message you want to read, double-click it.

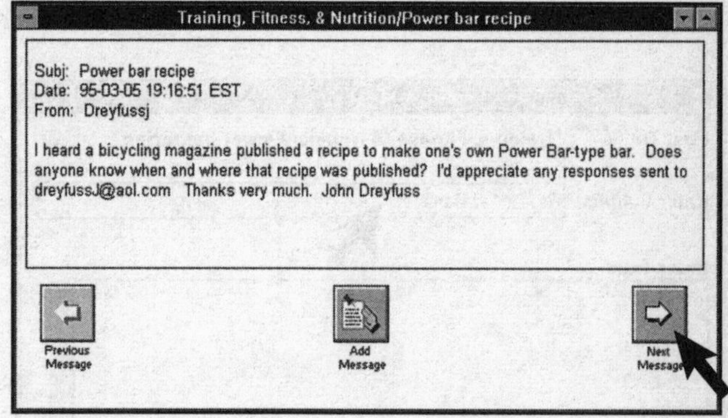

7 Use the **Next Message** and **Previous Message** buttons to view other messages in the folder.

Begin Guided Tour Post a Message

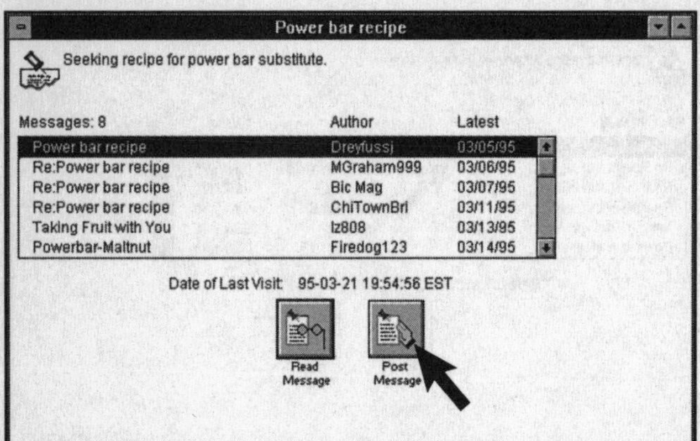

1 Go to a message board. Choose a category, and if you want, display a message you want to reply to. From the message list, click the **Post Message** button. Another way: from an open message, click the **Add Message** button.

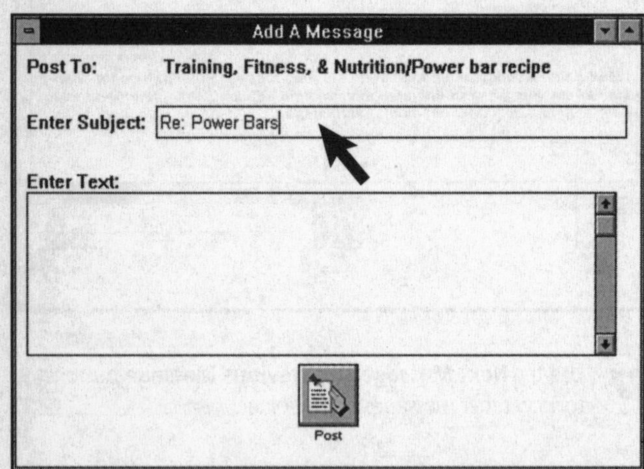

2 If necessary, type a topic for the message in the **Enter Subject** text box.

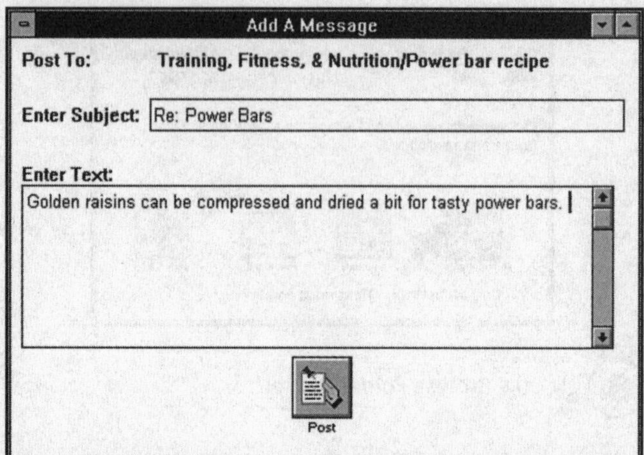

3 Type the text of your message. Include your user name and a specific request if you want other users to send replies via e-mail.

4 Click the **Post** button to select it.

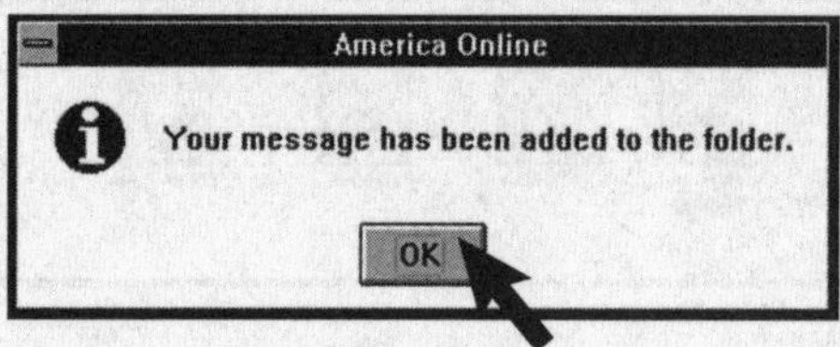

5 AOL displays a dialog box telling you your message has been added to the folder. Click **OK**. Your newly posted message appears at the bottom of the list of messages in the folder.

Download Files from America Online

Online services offer fantastic resources: material you can view on-screen *and* material you can transfer to your own computer over the phone lines. The process of transferring the files to your computer is called *downloading*.

America Online (AOL) offers document files, graphic files, program files, and more for download. Although there's no extra charge for downloading, you need to observe all copyright rules and other special rules when you reuse information. Generally, you can't reprint downloaded material for profit or plagiarize it; you need to get permission from the person who uploaded the information to reprint it. Most of the software programs you download will be *shareware* (as opposed to *freeware*). Although you're welcome to test the shareware, if you plan to use it regularly, you need to register it with its online publisher, which usually requires a fee.

AOL uses icons to clue you in about areas where you can find downloadable files, and to identify which files you can download:

Buttons similar to this one, with a stack of floppy disks on it, identify areas within services where you can find files to download.

In lists of files and folders, look for icons like this, which identify both areas with files to download, and individual files to download.

Begin Guided Tour Download a File

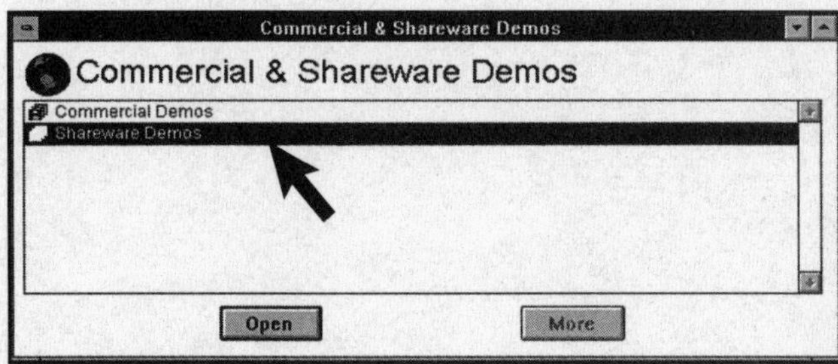

1 Display a file list that contains a file you want to download. You may have to go through several lists ("layers") by double-clicking on different categories or topics in lists to get a list with a file you want.

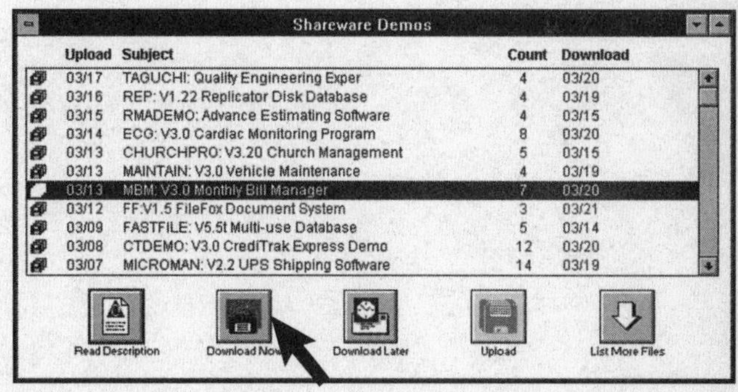

2 Scroll through the list. When you find a file you want to download, highlight it and click the **Download Now** button.

(continues)

Guided Tour Download a File

(continued)

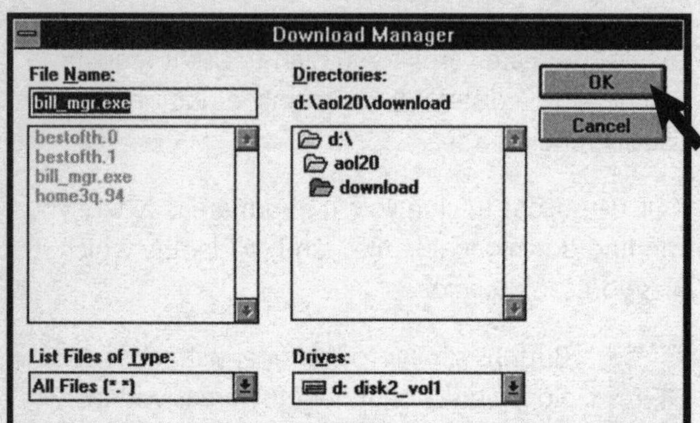

3 In the Download Manager dialog box, change the Drives, Directories, and File Name settings if you want. Then click **OK** or press **Enter**.

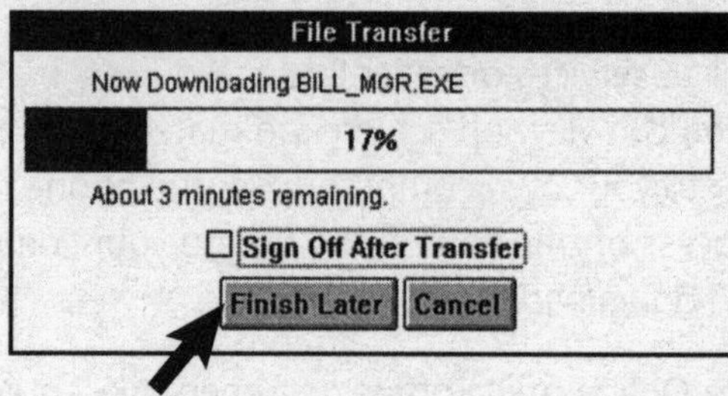

4 **(Optional)** You can turn on the **Sign Off After Transfer** check box while the file downloads, or click to **Finish Later** rather than download the file now.

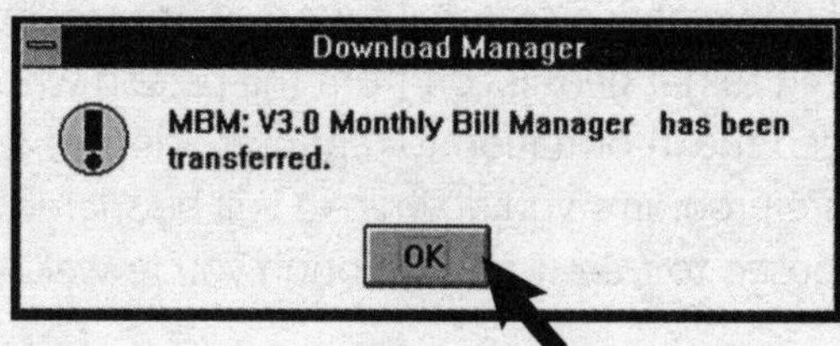

5 When the Download Manager finishes transferring the file, it displays a dialog box. Click **OK** to continue.

Connect to CompuServe

CompuServe is one of the oldest and best-known online services. It has traditionally catered to business users, offering extensive online data resources like the IQuest information databases, stock and company information, and Associated Press news (updated hourly). To use CompuServe, you can dial in with any communications software and navigate via text-based menus.

As of a couple of years ago, you could navigate with CompuServe Information Manager (*CIM*) for Mac, DOS, or Windows—more graphical software from CompuServe. In fact, WinCIM (the Windows version) is much more like Windows than the software from some other online services. Perhaps WinCIM is the easiest interface to use.

CompuServe offers a wide variety of *services* (where you can browse for articles and files), *databases* (where you can search for articles and abstracts), and *forums* (where you can exchange messages and files with other users). WinCIM gives you access to them all. The Services screen in WinCIM enables you to jump to some of the most popular areas in CompuServe.

To move around, generally you click icons (or double-click a choice in a list) to display related choices. Depending on the service you're in, you can perform different activities. You can read and leave messages in *forums*, browse to find information, download files from *libraries*, and even chat with other users.

Clicking one of the icons along the top of the WinCIM window performs a specific action. Here's a rundown of what each icon does:

Click the icon...	*To...*
	Get Help about the present activity.
	Display your list of Favorite Places to choose a place to go or to update the list.
	Perform a search to find a service or forum.
	Display the list of basic services.
	Display a dialog box so you can jump to a service or forum with a Go command.
	Display current quotes for stocks you select.
	Get the current weather.
	Manage the mail in your personal in box.
	Open your out box to send or manage messages in it.
	Open your personal filing cabinet to manage messages and articles stored there.
	Open your personal address book.
	Exit WinCIM.
	Disconnect from CompuServe without closing WinCIM.
	Get new mail, when this icon is present.

WinCIM really makes it easy to log on, as you'll see in the *Guided Tour*. Once you set up your system settings, including your password, all you have to do is start up WinCIM and choose where to go. WinCIM issues all the right commands to log on, including your password. The downside is that anyone can walk up to your computer and log on to your account.

Another nice feature of WinCIM is that it lets you do a lot of work offline. You can create and read mail messages, read and print stuff stored in your filing cabinet, and more.

Use a Go Command to Move Around

You can jump directly to a service or forum rather than moving to it by browsing around. To go directly to a service, you use its *Go command*. Here's how to go to a service using its Go command:

1. Open the **Services** menu and click **Go**. Another way: press **Ctrl+G** or click the **Go** icon (which looks like a traffic light) at the top of the screen.

2. Type the **Go command** in the **Service** text box and click **OK** or press **Enter**.

To find a list of Go commands, open the Go dialog box and use the Go command **quick**. At the screen that appears, type **2** and press **Enter** to list all the available Go commands. The Go command for a service appears to the right of the description for it. Press **Enter** to display more choices, or type **/exit** and press **Enter** to finish looking for Go commands.

Begin Guided Tour Log On and Go to a Service

1 In Program Manager, double-click the CompuServe group icon to open its group window. Double-click the CompuServe Information Manager program-item icon.

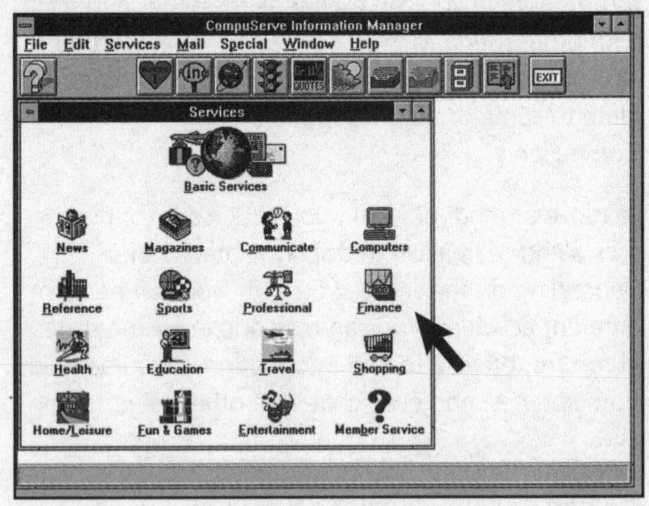

2 You can click any icon or select a menu command to perform an online activity, such as **Get New Mail** on the **Mail** menu. Making one of these choices starts the logon procedure.

Guided Tour Log On and Go to a Service

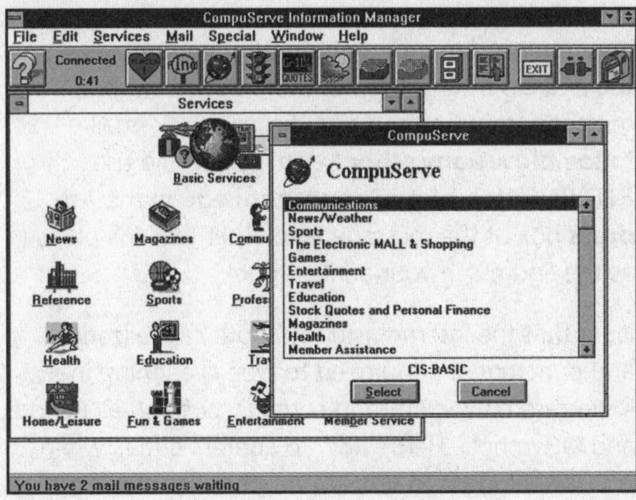

3 WinCIM logs you on to CompuServe, and takes you directly to the service or forum you specified.

Begin Guided Tour Log Off

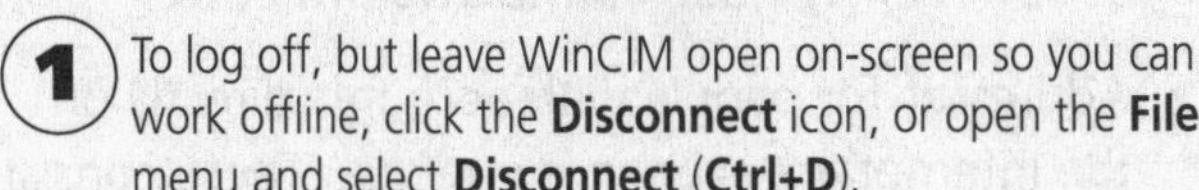

1 To log off, but leave WinCIM open on-screen so you can work offline, click the **Disconnect** icon, or open the **File** menu and select **Disconnect** (**Ctrl+D**).

2 To disconnect from CompuServe and leave WinCIM, click the **Exit** icon, or open the **File** menu and select **Exit** (**Alt+F4**).

Send CompuServe Mail

E-mail (electronic mail) between CompuServe users is private, as on other online services. CompuServe takes your private electronic mail (e-mail) messages, routes them along according to the address you give, and delivers them to your recipient's mailbox.

You can exchange mail with any other CompuServe user, as well as with users of many other online services and the Internet. You can work online to compose, send, read, and manage your mail in CompuServe. With the Basic membership, you can send up to $9 worth of e-mail messages each month—roughly equivalent to 90 three-page, text-only messages.

You can find e-mail addresses for other users while you're working in forums. CompuServe also enables you to search for addresses if you know the name of the person you want to find the address for. Having that person's city, state, and country helps, too.

E-Mail to Other Services

To send e-mail to another CompuServe user, you address it to that user's CompuServe ID number; if my ID number is **12345,0000**, that's also my e-mail address. CompuServe connects to all other users via the Internet, so it treats all other e-mail addresses as Internet addresses. The Internet address is generally a combination of the recipient's user name or ID and a suffix that's specific to the service provider; you need to know both parts of the puzzle.

You also need to include INTERNET: before the address of any Internet user to send them a message from CompuServe. So, to send e-mail to **joe.blow@any.school.edu**, you would use **INTERNET:joe.blow@any.school.edu** in the **Address** box of the message, and enter that full phrase as the address in your address book.

Note that the Internet is picky about capitalization and punctuation. You need to type everything in lowercase characters, and correctly position all periods and @ symbols. Here's how to address e-mail when you're sending it to users of other online services:

- America Online addresses consist of the user name followed by **@aol.com**. So, to send e-mail from CompuServe to the AOL user whose user name is **JBlow**, you would address the mail to **INTERNET:jblow@aol.com**.
- PRODIGY addresses consist of the user's ID in all lowercase characters, followed by **@prodigy.com**. So, the e-mail address for a PRODIGY user with the ID of **FDEP94B** would be **INTERNET:fdep94b@prodigy.com**.
- Delphi addresses are similar to AOL addresses, as in **INTERNET:username@delphi.com**.
- Addresses for people with accounts directly on the Internet are even more unique. These consist of a user name, followed by the **@** symbol and the name of the Internet site where that person's account is located. The catch is that there are thousands, if not millions, of Internet sites. Let's say you're addressing e-mail to someone whose user name is **sjones**, and that person's account is located at **indiana.cica.edu**. The user's full e-mail address would be **INTERNET:sjones@indiana.cica.edu**, and you'd have to type it exactly.

Bet you didn't know that you have an Internet address! Take your CompuServe ID, substitute a period for the comma, and add **@compuserve.com** to create your Internet address, as in **12345.0000@aol.com.**

Work Offline

WinCIM lets you compose and read mail offline, though there's no room to cover this in-depth here. As a brief example, open WinCIM but don't log on. Use the **Create Mail** command on the **Mail** menu. Compose a message, and then click the **Out-Basket** button. Create other messages this way. Then use the **Out-Basket** command on the **Mail** menu or click the **Out-Basket** icon. In the Out-Basket window, click **Send All**. WinCIM logs you on to CompuServe, and sends all your messages at once.

Use the Filing Cabinet

When you have a new mail message open in a window, you'll notice a button that reads *File It*. Clicking on this button enables you to save the message in your personal Filing Cabinet, so you can read it and print it offline, saving your precious online time for more urgent work like searching for information. Similarly, you can store found articles in your Filing Cabinet. You even can create custom *folders* in the Filing Cabinet to group messages and articles about a particular topic or client, for example. Here are some basics for using the Filing Cabinet:

- Click the **File It** button from a message or article window to display the filing cabinet. Click the folder you want to save to, and then click **Store**.
- To create a new folder, click the **New** button, type a name for the folder, and then click **OK**. You can then store messages and articles in it.
- To read files offline or delete or change folders, open the **Mail** menu and select **Filing Cabinet** (**Ctrl+F**), or click the icon at the top of the screen that looks like a file cabinet. Double-click a folder to open it. Double-click a file or article to view it.

Begin Guided Tour Create and Send Mail

1 Open the **Mail** menu and select **Create Mail**.

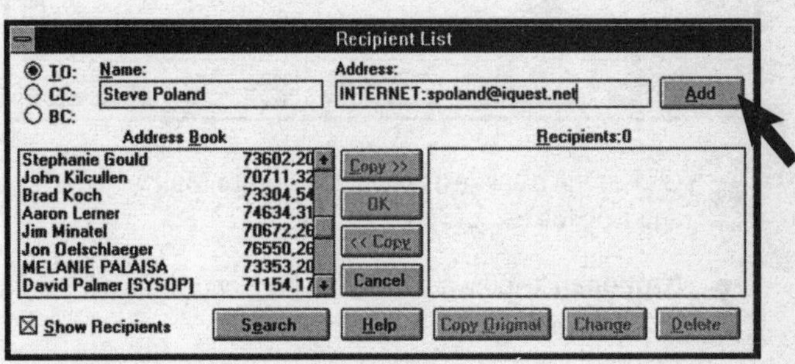

2 Type a Name, press **Tab**, and then type an address. Click **Add** to place it in the recipient list. Another way: double-click an entry from the Address Book list. You can use **<<Copy** to copy a new address from the recipient list to the address book.

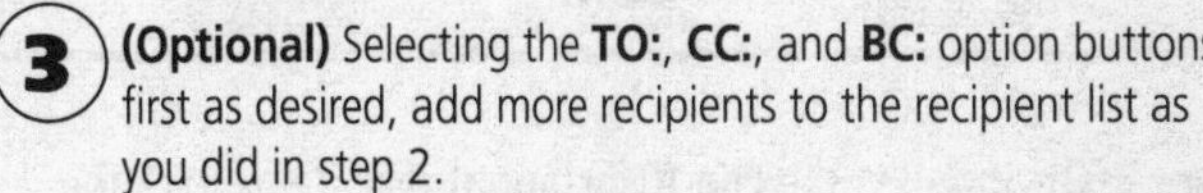

3 **(Optional)** Selecting the **TO:**, **CC:**, and **BC:** option buttons first as desired, add more recipients to the recipient list as you did in step 2.

(continues)

Guided Tour Create and Send Mail

(continued)

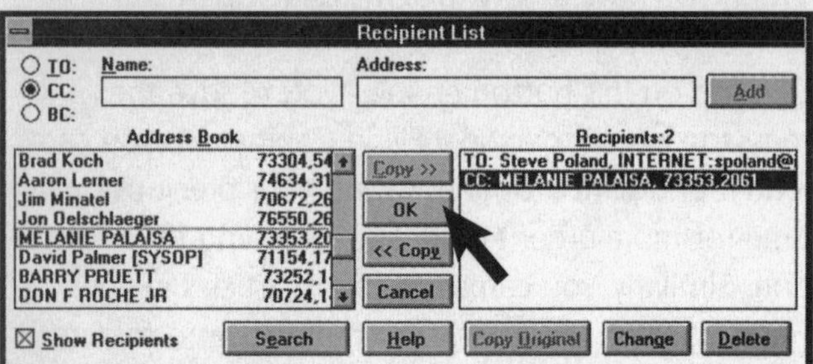

4. Click **OK** to finish the addressing and close the Recipient List dialog box.

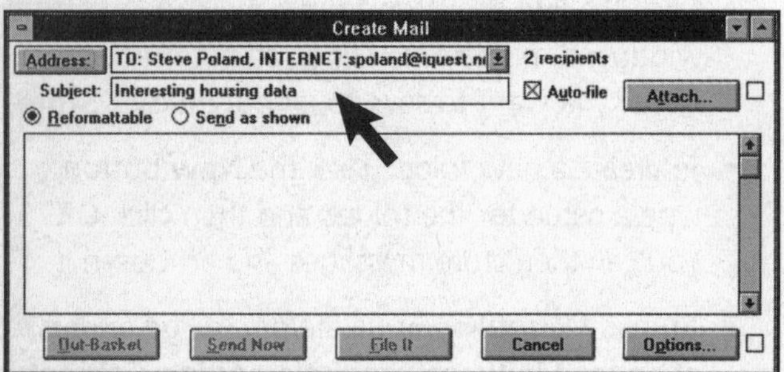

5. Type a Subject for the message.

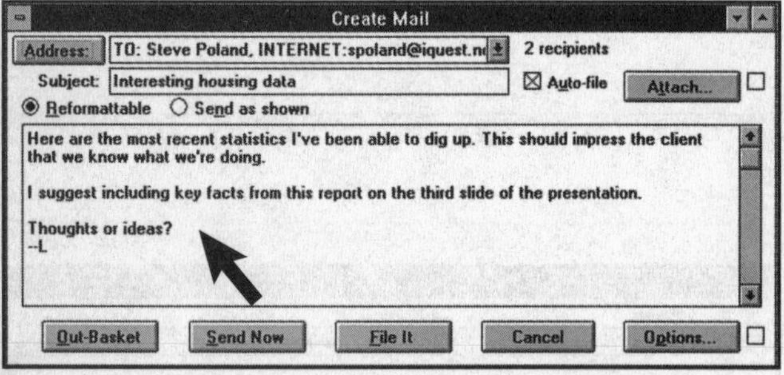

6. Click in the blank text area of the **Create Mail** window, and type the text of your message.

7. **(Optional)** If you want to send a file along with your message, click the **Attach** button.

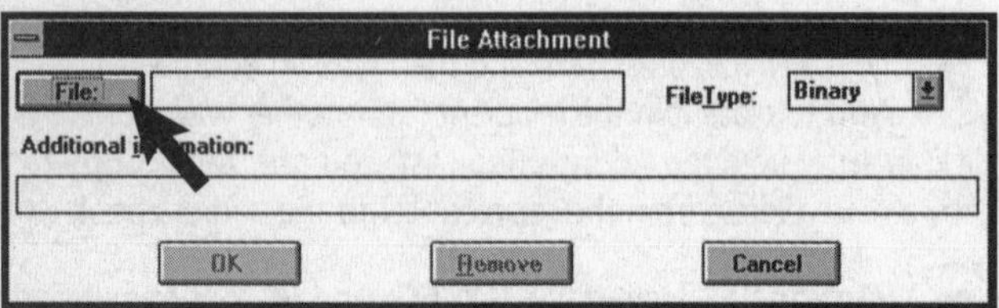

8. **(Optional)** In the **File Attachment** dialog box, click the **File** button.

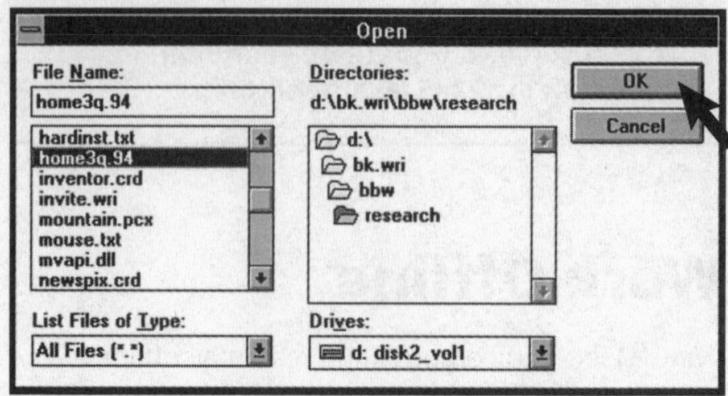

9. **(Optional)** In the **Open** dialog box, select the file to send with the message. If you're sending to an Internet address, you can only send a text file. Click **OK**.

10. **(Optional)** Type additional information about the file, and then click **OK**.

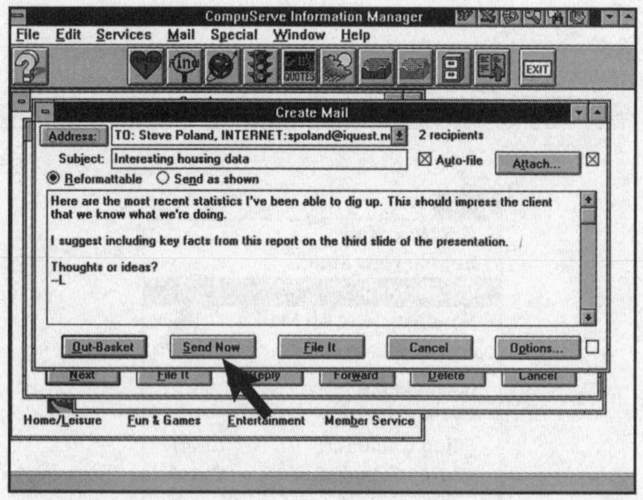

11. Click the **Send Now** button to send your message immediately. CompuServe closes the Create Mail window, sends the message, and displays a message in the status bar at the bottom of the WinCIM screen to tell you the message has been sent.

Begin Guided Tour Read Mail

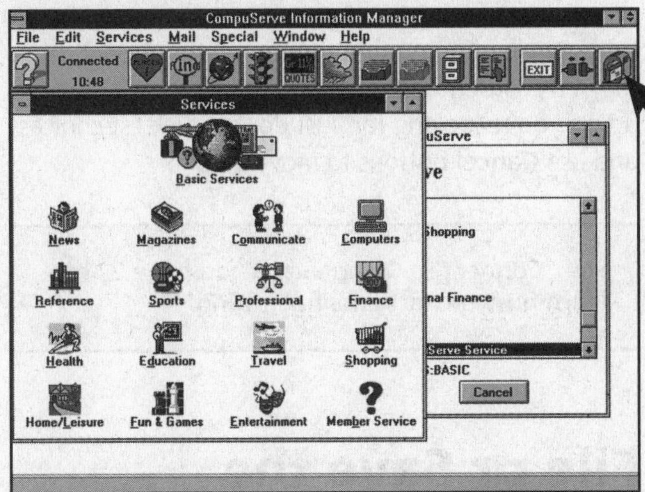

1 If the Mail icon appears at the far right side of the tool bar, click it. Or open the **Mail** menu and select **Get New Mail**.

2 In the **Get New Mail** list, either double-click the message you want to read, or use the **down arrow** key to highlight it, and then click **Get**.

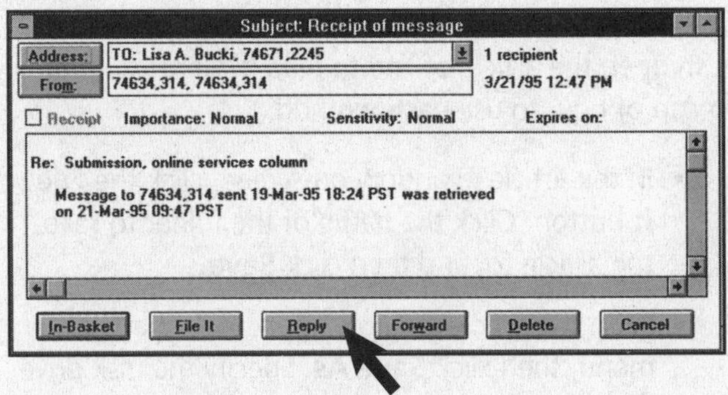

3 **(Optional)** Click the **Reply** button if you want to respond to a message.

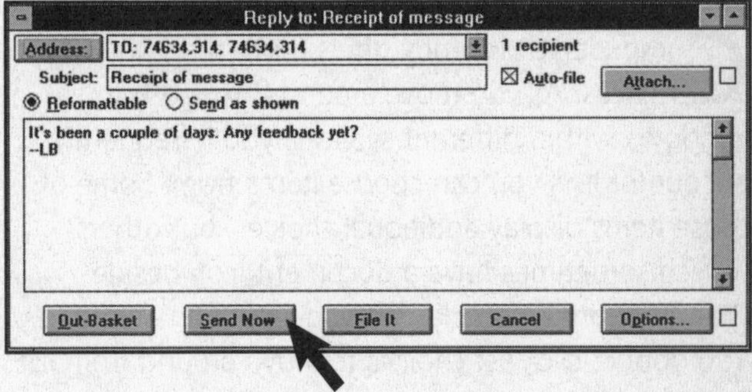

4 **(Optional)** Type your reply text, and then click the **Send Now** button.

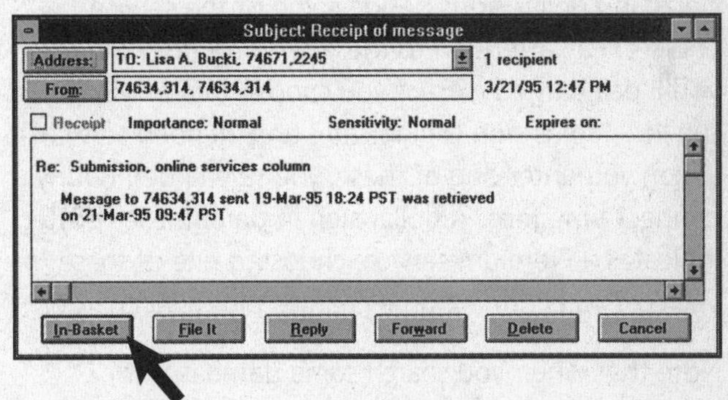

5 Select either the **In-Basket, File It,** or **Delete** button to determine what you want to do with the message you just read. The first two choices store the message in the In-Basket or Filing Cabinet for later reading.

6 Read other messages, or close the Get New Mail window so you can work elsewhere in CompuServe (click **Close**).

Read Articles on CompuServe

CompuServe currently offers more than 100 services. As you move around through the windows within different services, you'll frequently encounter lists you can choose items from. Some of those items display additional choices, but others (which sometimes have a document icon beside them) denote an article that you can open and read. You double-click list choices to move around from list to list or to display the text of an article.

When you're browsing around in CompuServe, looking for articles and forums, you may notice plus signs and dollar signs beside some of the service choices. Pay attention to these symbols; they indicate you'll be charged extra if you choose that service from the list. A plus sign (**+**) indicates an Extended service. When you enter one of these, you're charged hourly connect time fees. A dollar sign in parentheses [**($)**] indicates a Premium service; choosing one of these will cost you connect time charges plus a surcharge.

Note that when you search some databases for articles, you also incur additional charges for each search, and for each article you retrieve. CompuServe lets you know when there are additional charges so you can decide how much you're willing to pay for an article. (Also note that even though this task shows a sample search, you'll use other techniques to perform a search, depending on the service you're searching.)

When you select an article, it appears in its own window on-screen. Some articles may simply be text files; some may be graphic files, such as maps of travel destinations. The *Guided Tour* for this task gives an example of going to a specific article. Your steps may vary slightly depending on the location of the article you're looking for. Just double-click list choices and use **Cancel** buttons to move around.

See "Connect to CompuServe" on page 271 to learn how to start moving around.

File or Save the Current Article

Once you display an article, you may save it to disk or file it in your Filing Cabinet. Consider making this a habit, especially if you're paying a premium to view or search for an article in a database. If you save it to disk as a plain text (.TXT) file, you can view and print it like any other file. If you use the Filing Cabinet, you can open the article offline to read it. Here's a brief recap of how to use each method:

- In the article's window on-screen, click the **File It** button. Click the name of the folder to save the article to, and then click **Save**.
- With the article window open, click the **File** menu, then click **Save As**. Specify the disk drive and directory to save to in the Save As dialog box, as well as a name for the file. Click **OK** or press **Enter**.

Begin Guided Tour Browse for and Read Articles

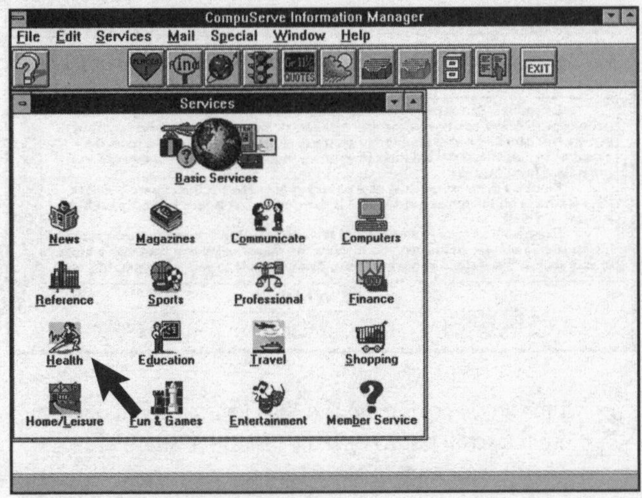

1 Log on to CompuServe by clicking one of the icons for a group of services. For example, you could click the **Health** icon.

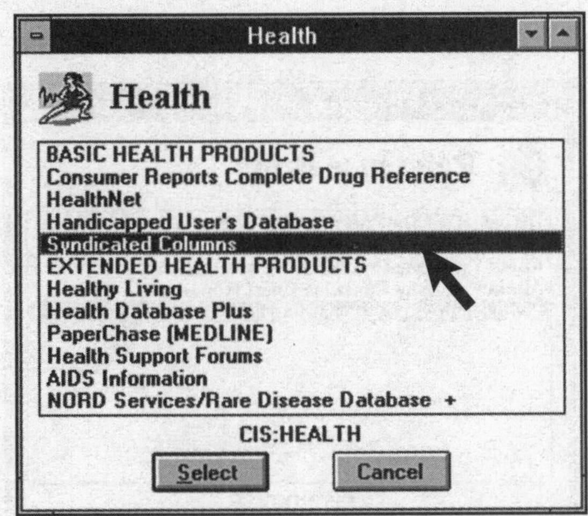

2 Double-click a specific service to go to it. In this case, double-click **Syndicated Columns**.

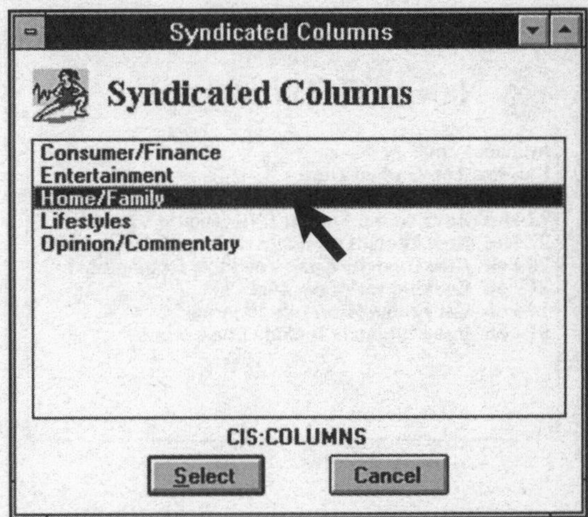

3 In the list that appears, double-click a specific choice to go to it. In this case, double-click **Home/Family**.

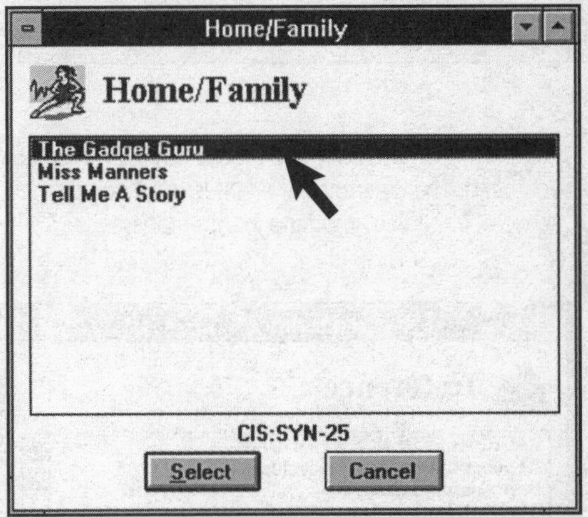

4 If yet another list appears, as it does here, double-click a specific choice to display the articles in it. In this case, double-click **The Gadget Guru**.

(continues)

Guided Tour Browse for and Read Articles

(continued)

5 Double-click an article in the list to open it in its own window. In this case, double-click **Computer Gadgets...**.

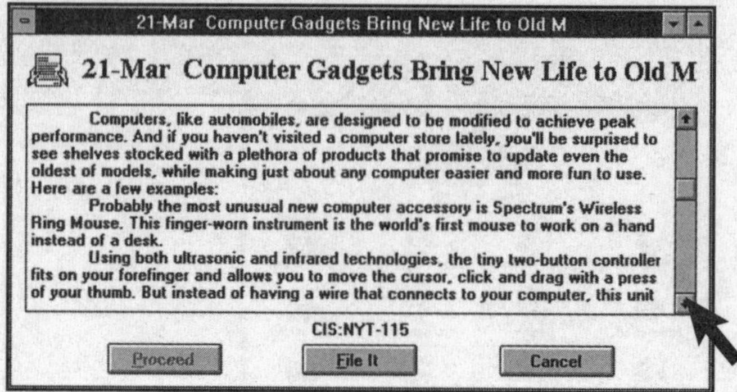

6 If the article holds more text than you can see at one time, use the **scroll bar** to view the rest of the article to see whether you want to file or save it.

Begin Guided Tour Search a Database

1 Log on to CompuServe, and browse to find the database you need. The Reference and Professional groups of services, in particular, offer a lot of databases.

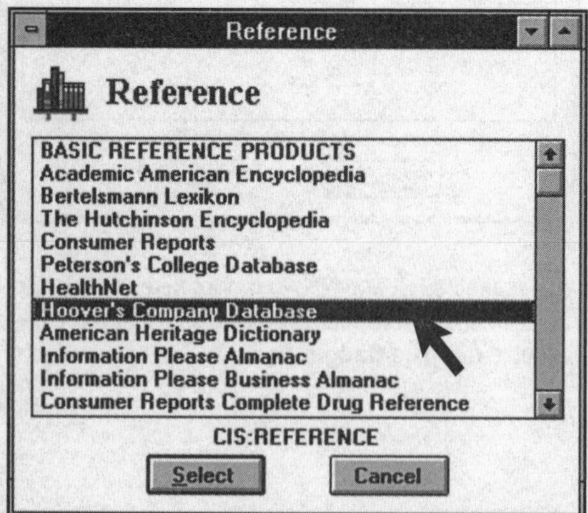

2 When you find a database you want to search, double-click it. In this case, you could double-click **Hoover's Company Database**.

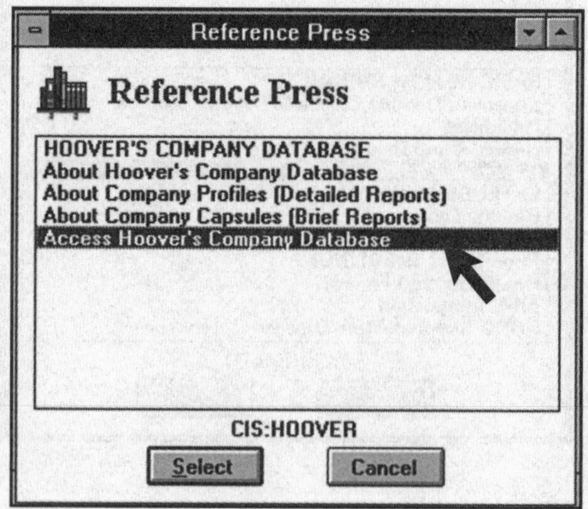

3 In the list of choices that appears, double-click the choice for accessing the database. In this case, you could double-click **Access Hoover's Company Database**.

Guided Tour Search a Database

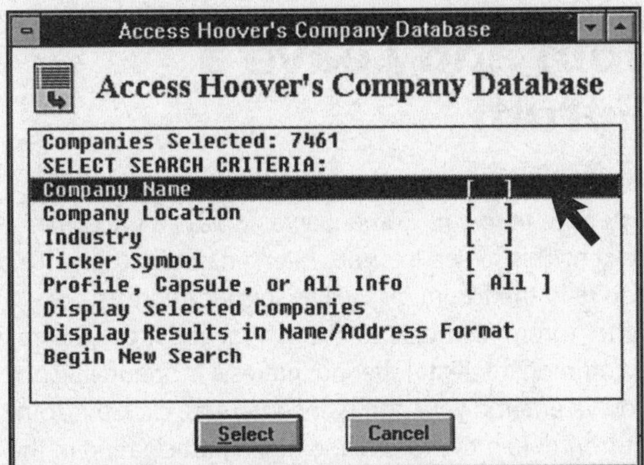

4 To enter the criteria you want the article to search for, double-click the name of the criterion. For example, double-click **Company Name**.

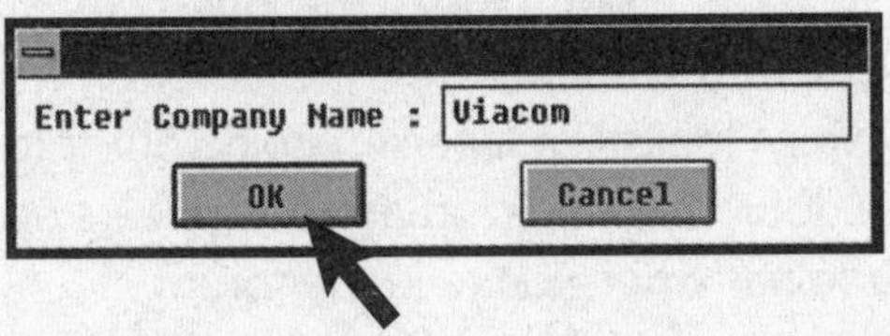

5 In the dialog box that appears, type the criteria you want to search for (for instance, a name such as **Viacom**) and click **OK**.

6 If necessary, repeat steps 4 and 5 to enter additional criteria for the names of different criteria to narrow the search. CompuServe tells you the number of matching articles at the top of the dialog box.

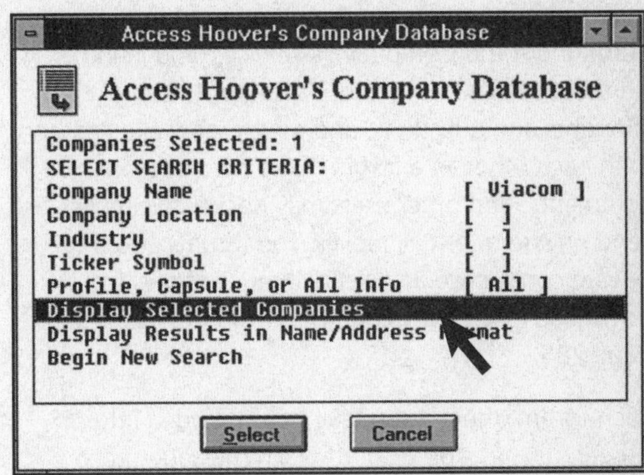

7 To see the matching article or articles, double-click the **Display Selected...** choice.

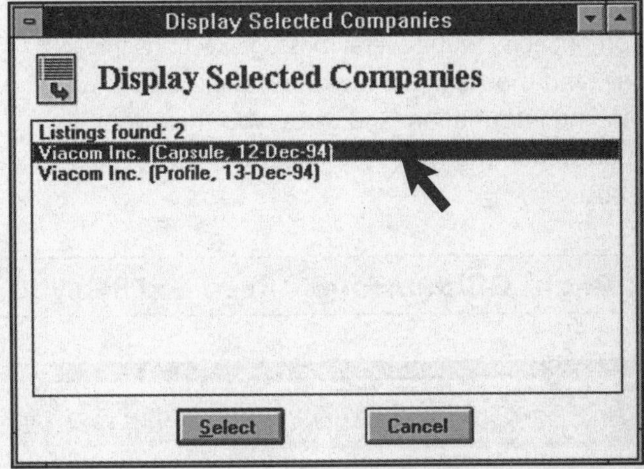

8 In the list of matching articles, double-click the one you want to read to open it. If the article holds more text than you can see at one time, use the **scroll bar** to view the rest of the article to see whether you want to file or save it.

9 Click **Cancel** to close the article.

Post Messages in CompuServe Forums

Throughout the CompuServe services, you'll find numerous forums where users gather to share thoughts and questions, and otherwise make contact with each other. In a forum, users post questions or comments, and other users may post public replies or send private or e-mail replies. The forums also offer private conference areas and libraries of files to download (see "Download Files from CompuServe," page 285).

Each forum offers a message board divided into numerous *message sections*. Each message section offers several topics of discussion. You can choose a topic of discussion, and then read the *thread* of related messages.

At last count, there were well over 300 forums in CompuServe, with several message sections in each one, and thousands of topics being discussed. You can find information (and users who share your interest) about anything from pet care to building a business.

Join and Leave a Forum

The first time you try to go to a CompuServe forum, you have to *join* it. CompuServe displays a Welcome screen. This screen lets you enter a name to use while you're in the forum, as well as specific interests, so other forum members can search for you if they share a common interest. Entering interests is optional. Once you've entered your name and interests, click the **Join** button to join the forum and begin participating in the messaging areas.

After you've done what you want to do in a forum, you have to leave it before you can go elsewhere in CompuServe and do other things. To leave a forum, open the **File** menu and click **Leave** (**Ctrl+L**), or click the leave forum icon, which looks like a person going out through a door. The leave forum icon appears on the toolbar when you're in the forum.

Begin Guided Tour Read and Reply to a Message

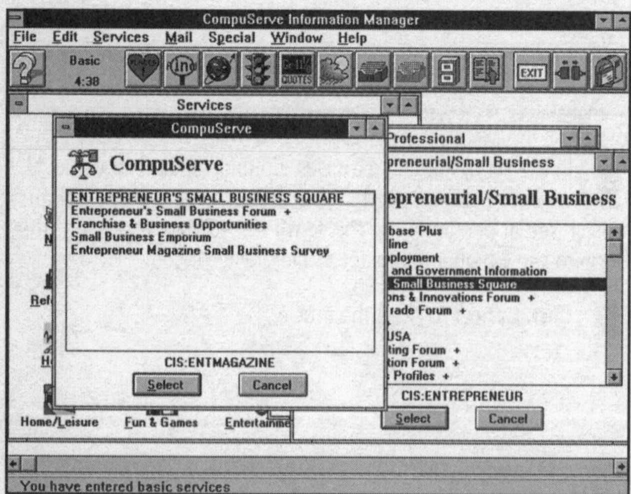

1 Browse around to find a window that lists the forum you want as a choice. Forums usually have **Forum** in the choice title.

2 Double-click the forum name, or highlight it with the **down arrow** and press **Enter**. For example, double-click **Entrepreneur's Small Business Forum**.

3 If you haven't been to the forum before, you must join it. Specify a name to use in the forum, list your interests, and then click **Join**.

Guided Tour Read and Reply to a Message

4 To display the list of message sections, click the **Messages** icon in the palette at the right side of the WinCIM screen, or open the **Messages** menu and click **Browse**.

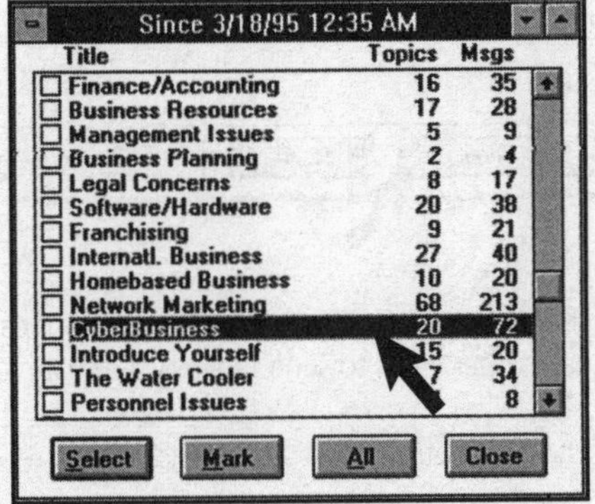

5 Scroll down through the list to look for an interesting message section. When you find one to browse, double-click it.

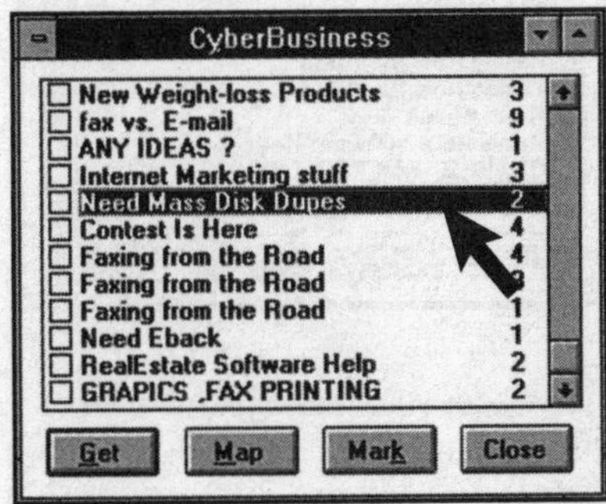

6 Scroll down through the list to look for an interesting topic. When you find one to browse, double-click it.

7 **(Optional)** The message appears on-screen. If you want to view replies to the message, click the **right-pointing arrow**. Click the **left-pointing arrow** to go back to the original message to reply to it.

8 To reply to the message, click the **Reply** button.

9 Type the text of your message. Click the **Send** button to complete your reply.

10 **(Optional)** If you want to send the message as a private message or as e-mail, click the **Private** or **Via Mail** check box at the upper right corner of the message window.

Begin Guided Tour Post a Message About a New Topic

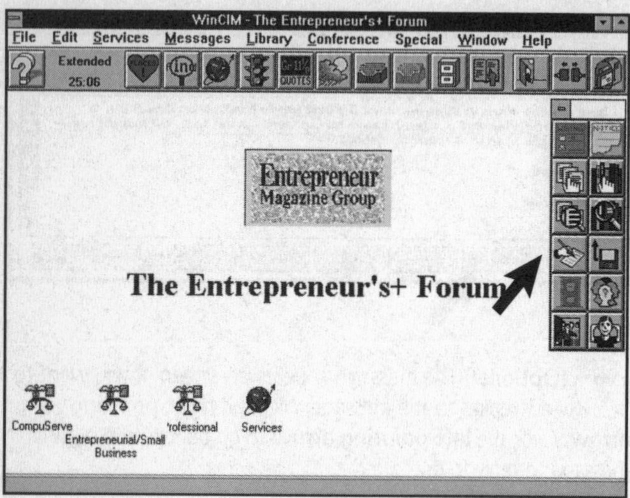

1 Go to a forum and select a **Message Section**. To post a message about a new topic, click the **New Message** icon in the palette at the right side of the WinCIM screen, or open the **Messages** menu and click **Create Message**.

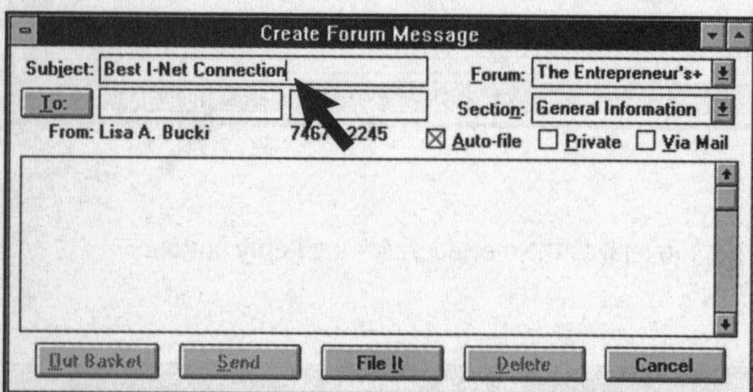

2 Type a topic for the posting in the **Subject** text box.

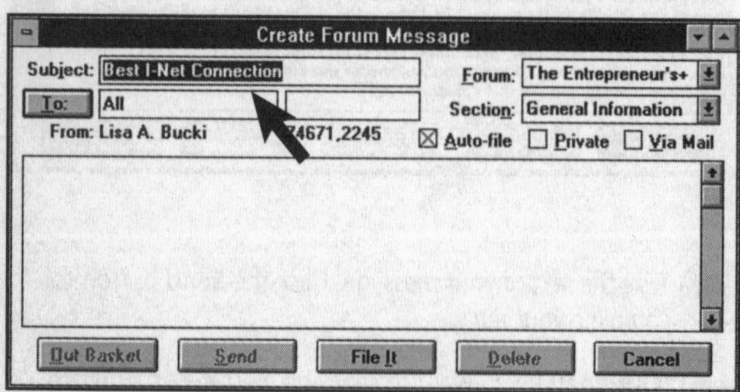

3 To address the message, use the **To** button to select an address book entry, or simply type **All** as shown here.

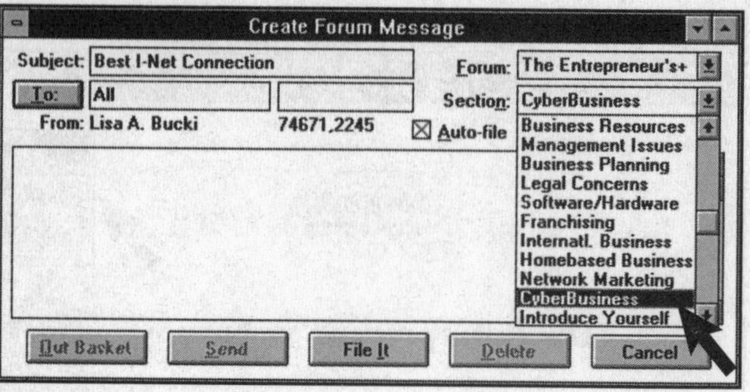

4 Open the **Section** list and select the message section you want to post your message to.

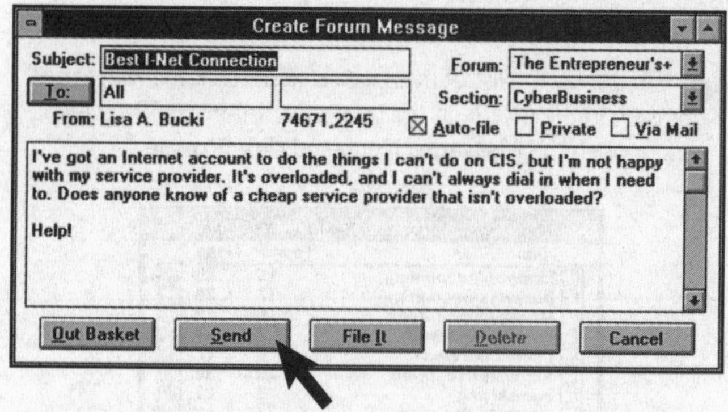

5 Type the text of your message. Include a specific request if you want other users to send replies via e-mail.

6 Click the **Send** button to post the message.

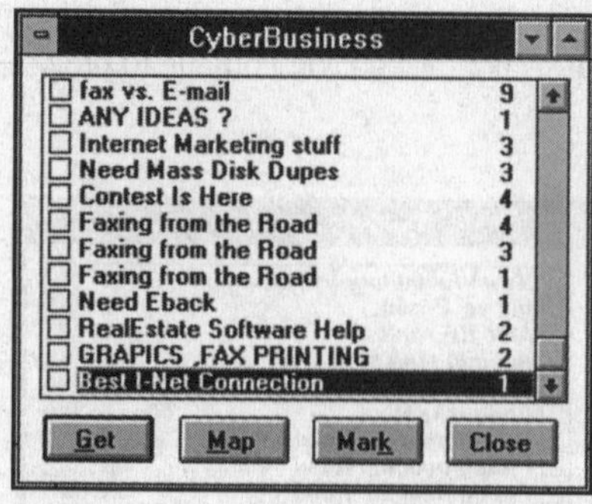

7 CompuServe adds your message to the list of messages in that message section.

Download Files from CompuServe

Every forum service in CompuServe also offers a *library* where users can find helpful and useful files. Each library divides the files into *library sections*, groups of related files. The forum libraries offer document files, graphic files, program files, and more that you can transfer to your computer over the phone lines and store on a hard or floppy disk. The process of transferring the files to your computer is called *downloading*.

Although there's no extra charge for downloading, you need to observe all copyright rules and other special rules when you reuse information. Generally, you can't reprint downloaded material for profit, or plagiarize it; to reprint information, you need to get permission from the person who uploaded it. Most software programs you download will be *shareware* (as opposed to *freeware*); you're welcome to test the shareware, but if you plan to use it regularly, you'll need to register it with its online publisher and pay a fee.

At last count, there were well over 300 forums in CompuServe, with thousands of files available. You can find files of all types, from helpful programs to manage your checkbook to photos of your favorite celebrities.

Begin Guided Tour Download a File Now

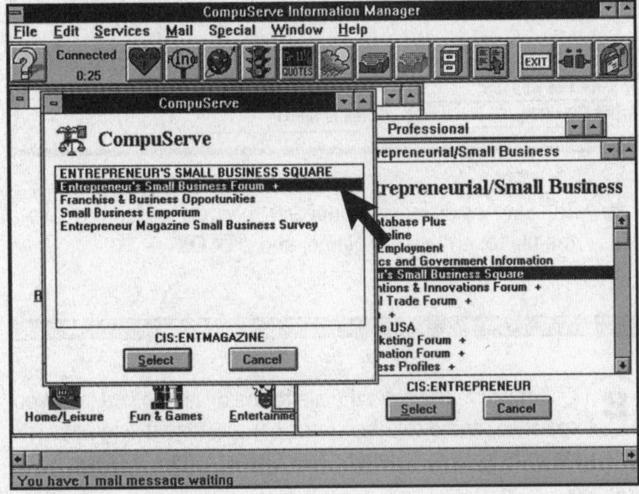

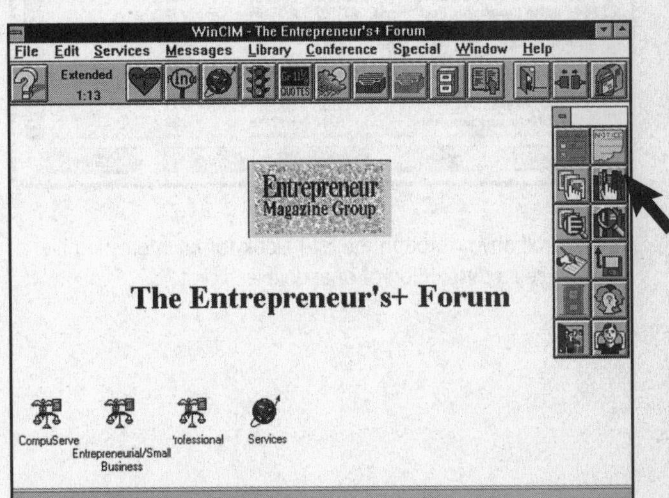

1 Browse around to find a window that lists the forum you want to choose. Forums usually have **Forum** in the choice title. Double-click the forum name. For example, double-click **Entrepreneur's Small Business Forum**.

2 If you haven't been to the forum before, you must join it. Specify a name to use in the forum, list your interests, and then click **Join**.

3 To display the list of library sections, click the Libraries icon in the palette at the right side of the WinCIM screen, or open the **Library** menu and click **Browse**.

(continues)

Guided Tour Download a File Now

(continued)

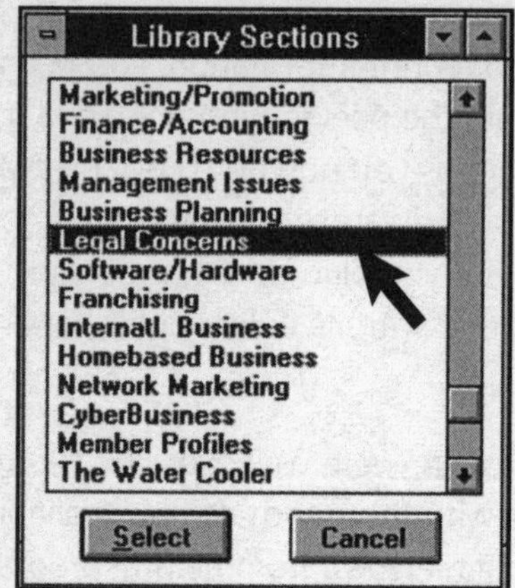

4 Scroll down through the list to look for an interesting library section. When you find one to browse, double-click it.

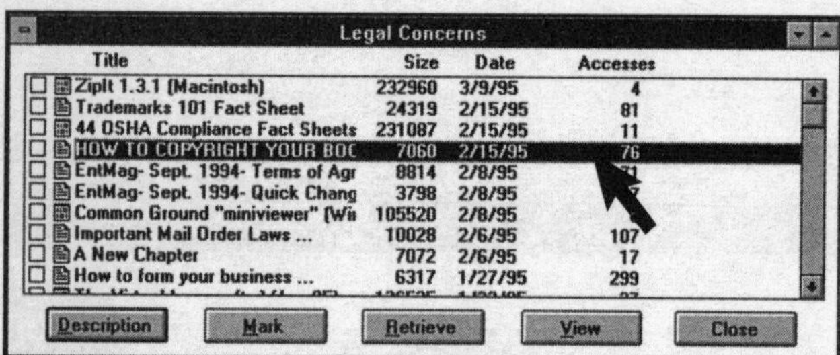

5 Scroll down through the list to look for an interesting file. To see a description of one, double-click it.

6 If you're satisfied that the file is one you want based on its description, click the **Retrieve** button. (You can select **Retrieve** from the previous window, as well.)

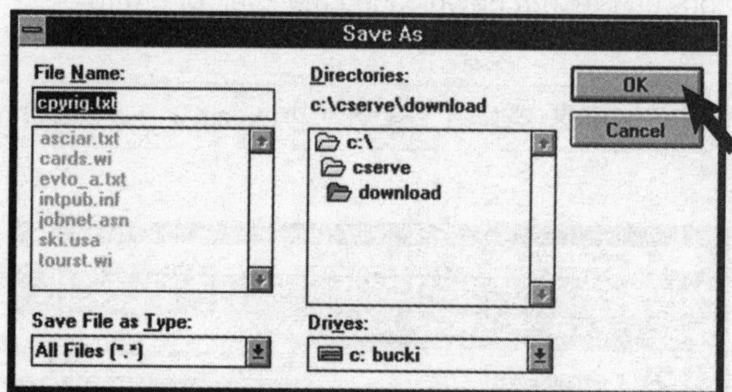

7 The Save As dialog box appears. Specify a location to save the file to, enter a File Name, and click **OK**.

C:\CSERVE\DOWNLOAD\CPYRIG.TXT Transferred Successfully

8 CompuServe transfers the file to the drive and directory you specified, and displays a status-bar message telling you when the transfer is completed. Click **Close** to close the file window.

Begin Guided Tour Search for a File

1 Go to the forum and click the **Search** icon in the pallet at the right side of the screen (or open the **Library** menu and select **Search**).

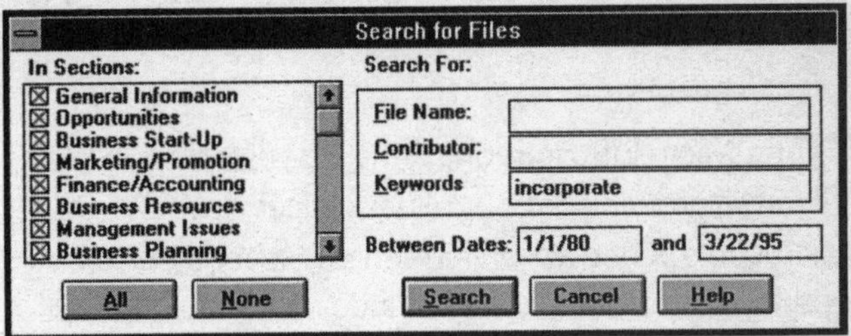

2 Type a File Name (you can use wild cards), Contributor (CompuServe ID), or Keywords to search for. Click **Search** or press **Enter**.

3 The matching files appear in the Library Search dialog box. You can select whether to see a **Description** of or **Retrieve** a file from the list.

Connect to The Microsoft Network with Windows 95

The Microsoft Network is the newest entry in the ever-growing list of online services. It is Microsoft's very own online service, scheduled to be opened for business when Windows 95 hits the market.

This new online service looks and acts very much like the veteran online services, offering the standard fare of e-mail, bulletin boards, special interest groups, information databases, and chat rooms. Sporting a look that combines the best of America Online and CompuServe, The Microsoft Network promises to be a strong contender in the world of global communications.

What gives The Microsoft Network its real marketing edge, however, is that the software comes as an integrated part of Windows 95. When you start Windows 95, The Microsoft Network icon appears on your desktop, allowing you to quickly connect and start using the service in a matter of minutes. Get your credit card ready, and follow the *Guided Tour* to open your account with The Microsoft Network.

Begin Guided Tour Start a Microsoft Network Account

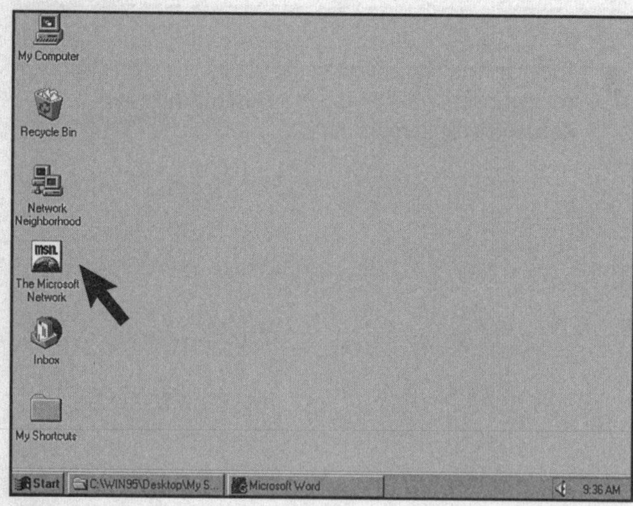

1 Before you can use The Microsoft Network, you must open an account. Double-click **The Microsoft Network** icon on your desktop.

2 A dialog box appears, offering to lead you through the sign-up procedure. Click the **OK** button to continue.

Guided Tour Start a Microsoft Network Account

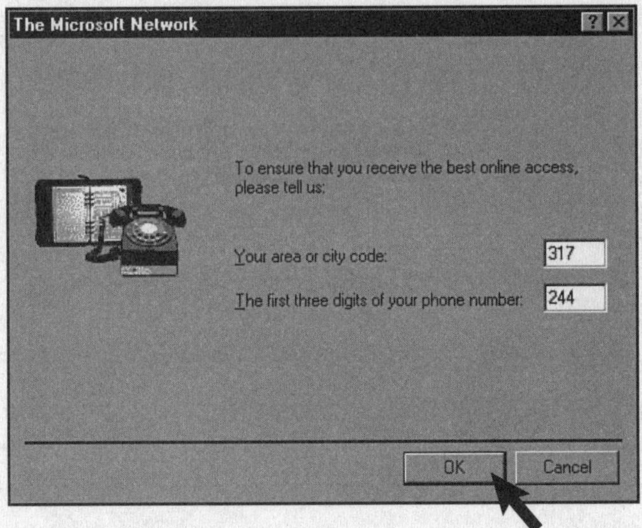

3 The next dialog box asks for your area code and first three digits of your phone number. Type the requested information in the text boxes, and click **OK**. (This information is used to determine a local number you can dial to connect.)

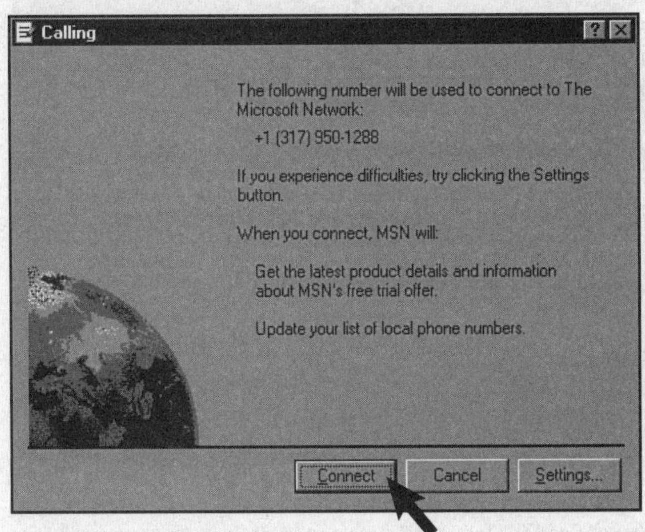

4 Your modem will now dial a local number to obtain a list of local connect numbers. Click the **Connect** button.

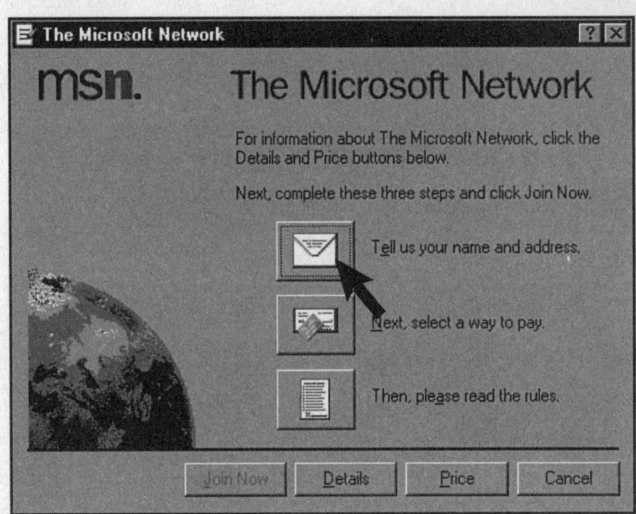

5 After obtaining the local phone numbers, a dialog box asks for some personal information. Click the **Tell us your name and address** button.

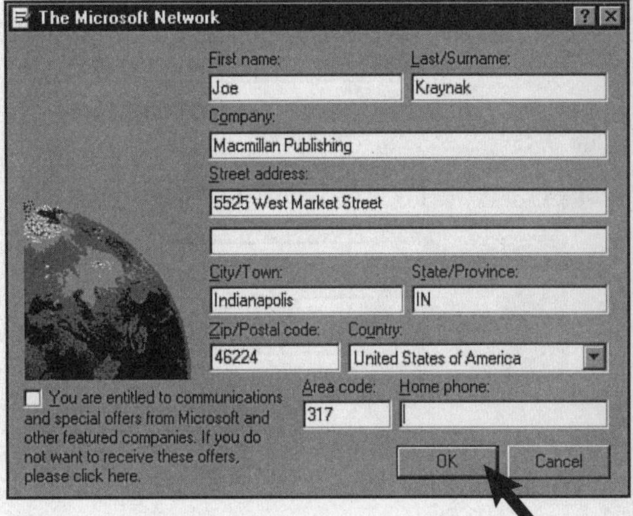

6 Type the requested information in each text box. You can move to the next text box by clicking inside it or pressing the **Tab** key. Click **OK** when you're done.

(continues)

Guided Tour Start a Microsoft Network Account

(continued)

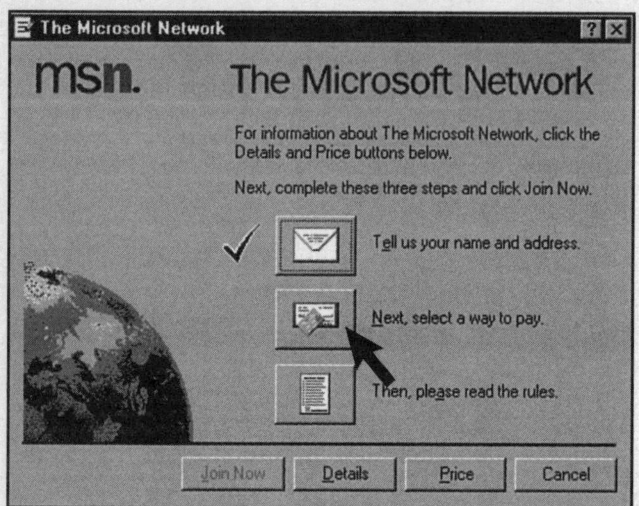

7 You return to the previous text box, and a check mark appears next to the first button. Click the **Next, select a way to pay** button to enter your credit card information.

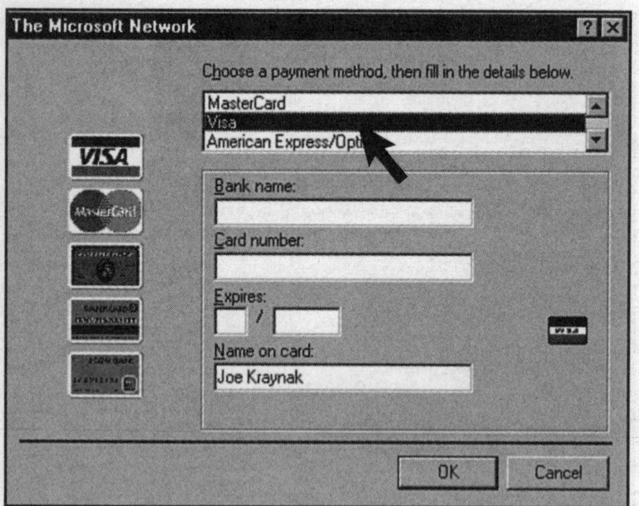

8 Choose the type of credit card you're using from the **Choose a payment method** list, and then enter the required credit card information. Click the **OK** button.

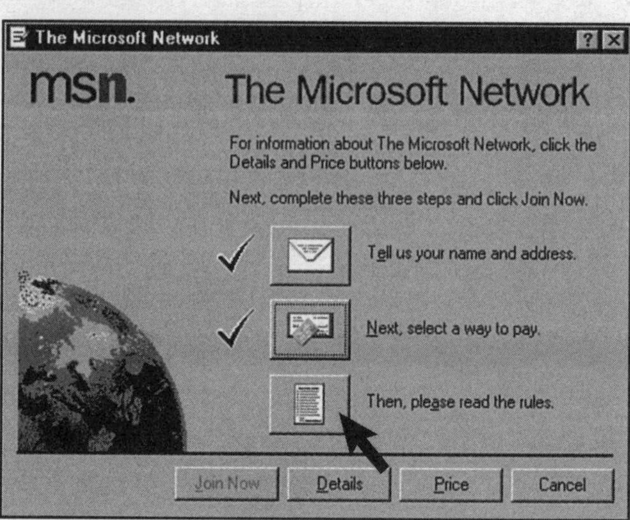

9 Next, you should read the legal contract, explaining the rules and regulations of the service. Click the **Then, please read the rules** button.

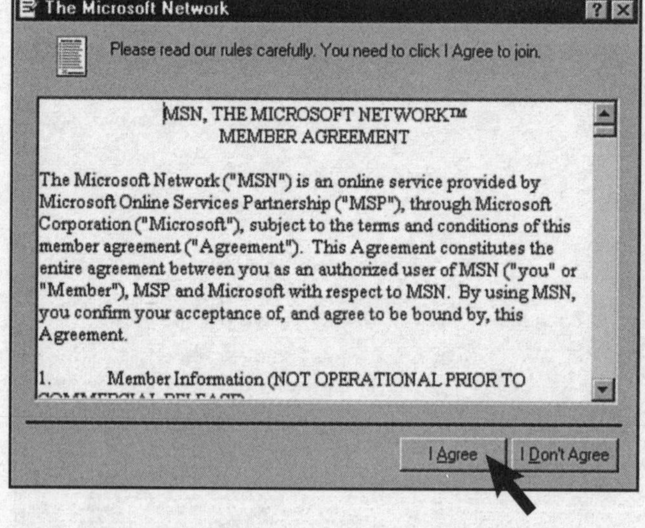

10 Read the long legal statement explaining your responsibilities as a user and Microsoft's responsibilities as a provider, and click the **I Agree** button.

Guided Tour Start a Microsoft Network Account

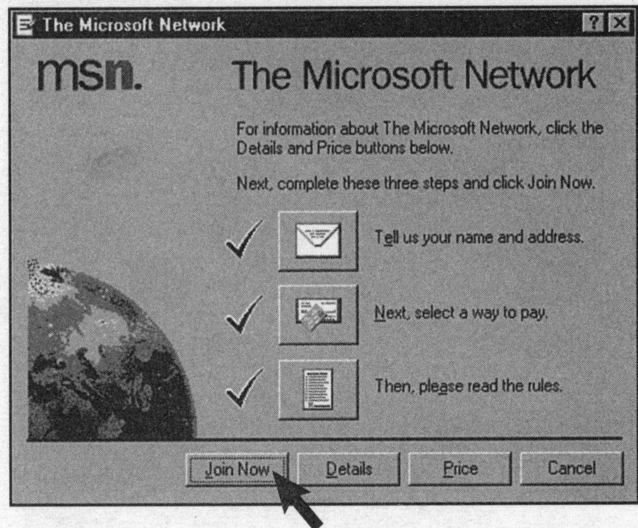

11 To view details about the service and pricing information, click the **Details** or **Price** button. Then, when you're ready to sign on, click the **Join Now** button.

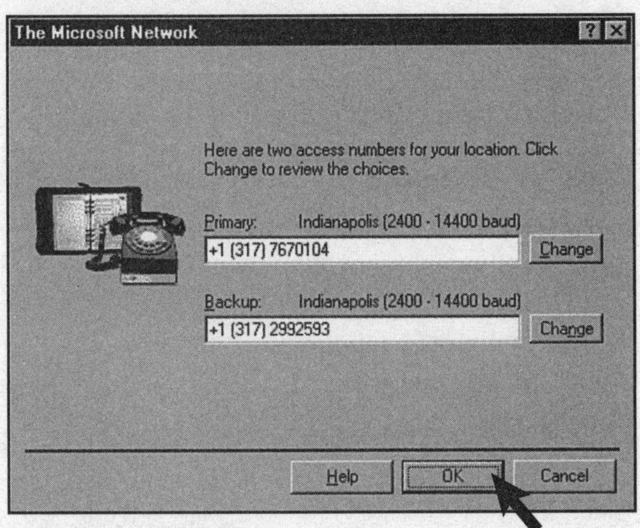

12 A dialog box appears, showing the primary and secondary local connect phone numbers. Click the **OK** button.

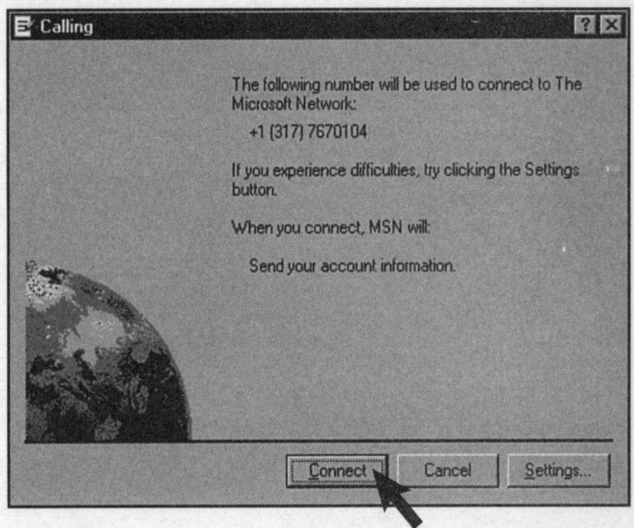

13 Another dialog box appears, showing the number that will be dialed. Click the **Connect** button.

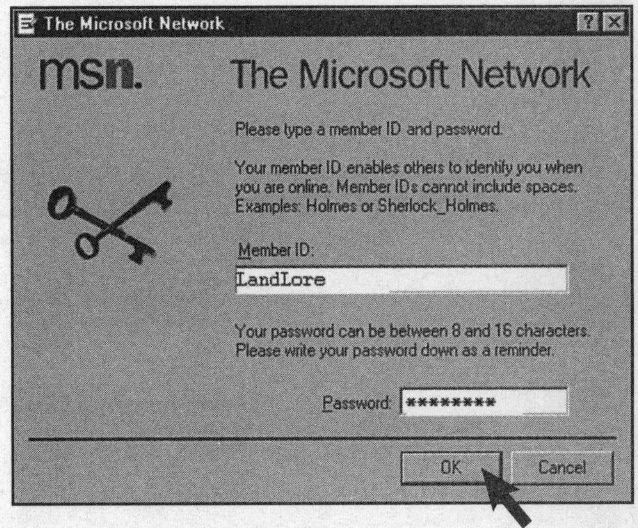

14 You're now asked to enter the name you want to use for the account (Member ID) and a password. The name you enter acts as your "handle." Type the requested information, and then click **OK**.

(continues)

Guided Tour Start a Microsoft Network Account

(continued)

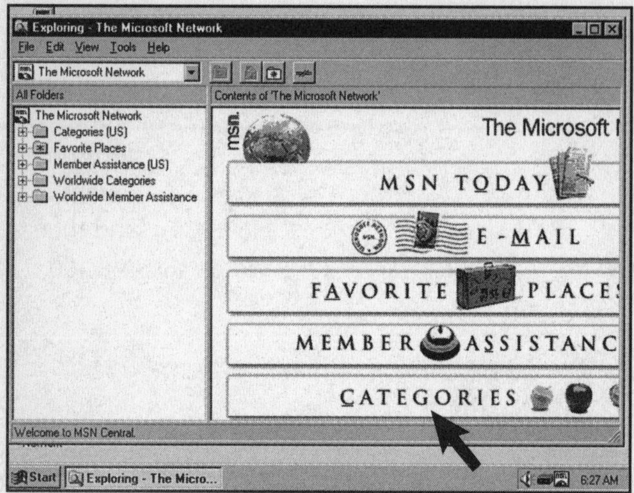

15 Your modem dials the local connect number and connects to The Microsoft Network. You can click an on-screen button to start using the service right away.

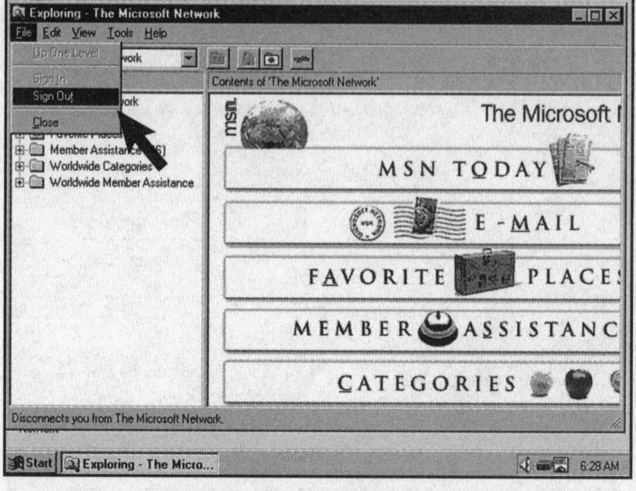

16 You can sign off at any time by opening the **File** menu and selecting **Sign Out**.

You can create another account for a member of your family or for a colleague by running the Sign Up program again. In My Computer or Explorer, go to the **Program Files/Microsoft Network** folder, and double-click the **Signup** icon. Follow the same steps given here to create another account.

Get Up and Running on The Microsoft Network

Now that you've set up your very own Microsoft Network account, you can dial into it and start tapping its many resources. The process is fairly simple, and is similar to that used for most online services. You double-click The Microsoft Network icon, type your user name and password, and then click the Connect button. The Microsoft Network program does the rest, dialing the phone number, establishing a connection with The Microsoft Network, and then entering your user name and password for you.

Once you're connected to The Microsoft Network, you'll see a screen with a bunch of huge buttons on it that represent the various Microsoft Network areas. To use the service, you simply click a button and then wait while the service transports you to the selected area.

But we're getting ahead of ourselves here. The first thing you have to do is connect to the service. The *Guided Tour* shows you just what to do.

Begin Guided Tour Sign On to The Microsoft Network

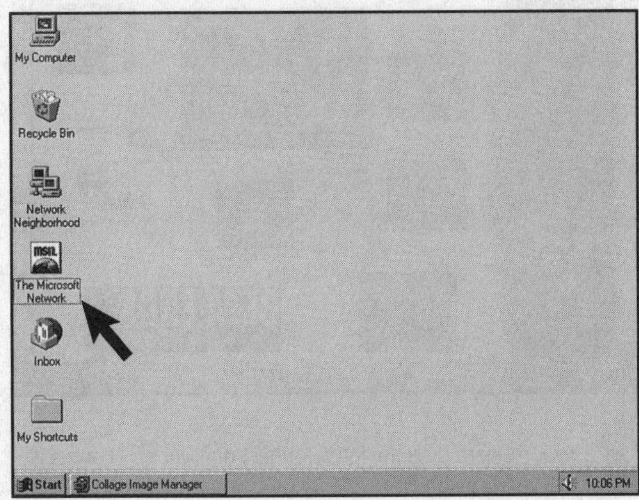

1 Once you've set up an account, signing on to The Microsoft Network is easy. Double-click **The Microsoft Network** icon on the desktop.

2 The Sign In dialog box asks you to type your member ID and password. If the supplied member ID is incorrect, drag over it and type the correct member ID.

(continues)

Guided Tour Sign On to The Microsoft Network

(continued)

3 Tab to the **Password** text box, and type your password. As you type, the password appears as a series of asterisks, so nobody can read it as you type.

4 You can click the **Remember my password** option, so you won't have to type your user ID or password the next time you sign in.

5 Click the **Connect** button.

6 Your modem dials the local connect number and connects to The Microsoft Network. To keep you informed of any new areas and features of The Microsoft Network, the service initially displays The MSN Today window. You can click the **Close** button if you want to get at The Microsoft Network main screen.

Browse The Microsoft Network

As of the writing of this book, The Microsoft Network is just being born, and does not have the wide offerings of some of the other services. That will undoubtedly change very quickly, as more companies and organizations join the Network.

Currently, when you connect to the Network, you encounter five on-screen buttons: MSN Today, E-Mail, Favorite Places, Member Assistance, and Categories. MSN Today explains the offerings and plans of the service. E-Mail runs Microsoft Exchange, which allows you to send and receive mail electronically. Favorite Places allows you to create a list of the sites you most commonly visit. Member Assistance provides answers to your questions. And Categories displays icons for all the areas on the service that you can visit.

To go to an area in The Microsoft Network, you click one of the Categories buttons. The Microsoft Network then takes on the appearance of a My Computer window, showing a collection of folder icons. The toolbar provides buttons that allow you to arrange the icons on-screen, move up to the previous folder level, sign out, and display a list of your favorite places. The *Guided Tour* shows you how to use The Microsoft Network screen to wander the service.

Begin Guided Tour Wander The Microsoft Network

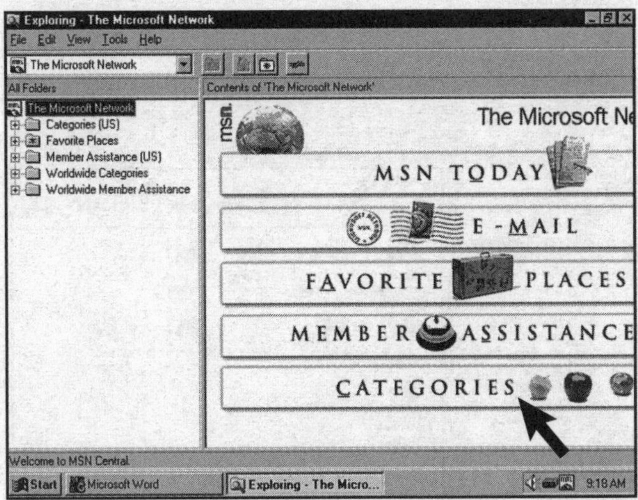

1 When you connect to The Microsoft Network, you're presented a series of buttons you can click. Click the **Categories** button to see what The Microsoft Network offers.

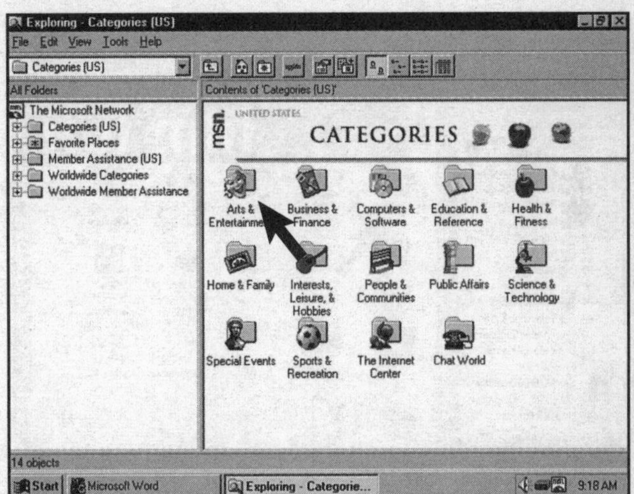

2 The folders represent the various areas on The Microsoft Network. To open a folder, double-click it.

(continues)

Guided Tour Wander The Microsoft Network

(continued)

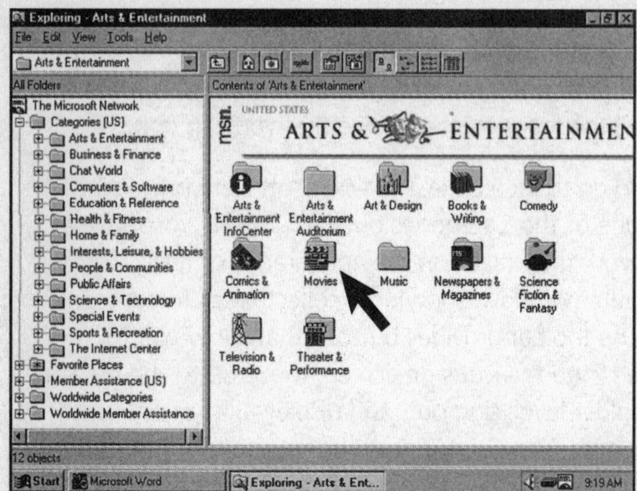

3 When you open a folder, you see icons for additional subfolders and for specific areas on the service. Double-click an icon to open the subfolder or go to that area.

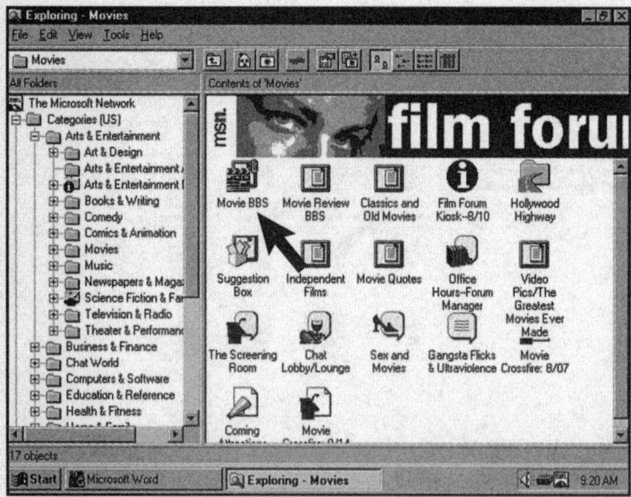

4 If you double-click an icon for a specific area, you are transported to that area, where you can obtain the information you want or exchange information with other users who share your interests.

5 To return to the previous screen, click the **Up One Level** button. You can also return to a place you've visited by selecting it from the drop-down list to the left of the Up One Level button. (You can also select an area from the **All Folders** list in the left pane.)

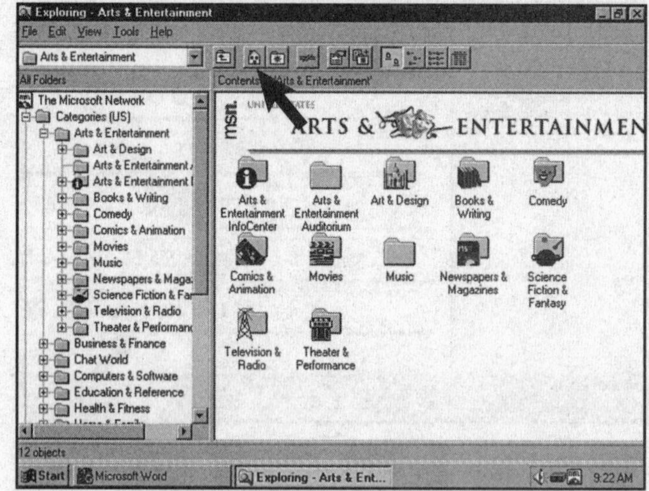

6 To return to the opening screen, click the **Go to MSN Central** button. You can then start wandering from the beginning. The MSN Central window also removes the All Folders pane, giving you more room on your screen.

Guided Tour Wander The Microsoft Network

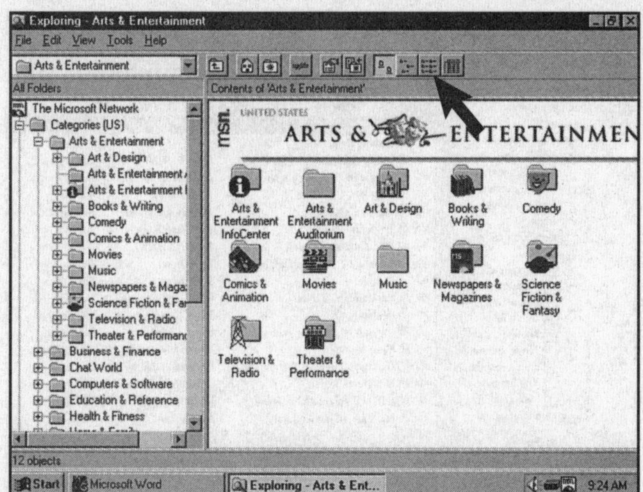

7 The four buttons on the far right of the toolbar should look familiar. These are the same buttons you find in My Computer, which allow you to pick an icon arrangement.

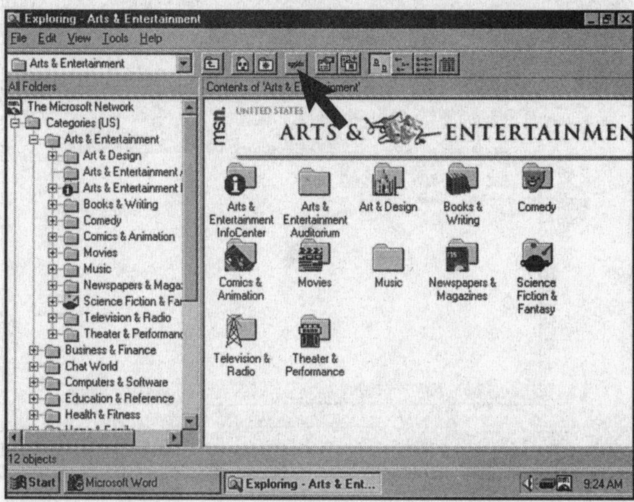

8 You can disconnect from the service at any time by clicking on the **Sign Out** button, or by selecting **Sign Out** from the **File** menu.

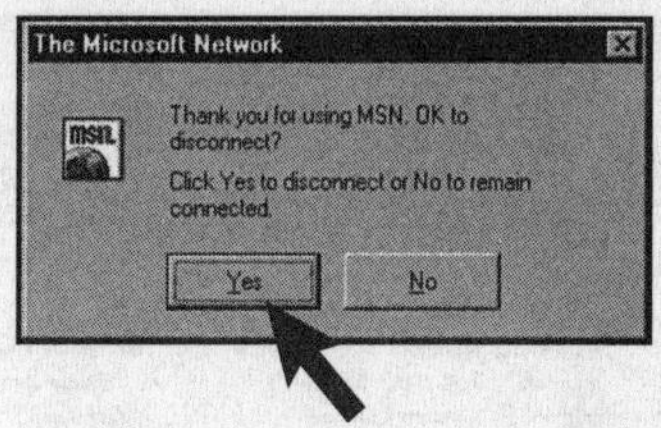

9 When you choose to sign out, a dialog box appears, asking for your confirmation. Click **Yes**.

If The Microsoft Network senses that you haven't done anything for several minutes, it automatically disconnects you from the service. This prevents you from racking up huge online costs just because you forgot to sign out.

Begin Guided Tour Create a List of Favorite Places

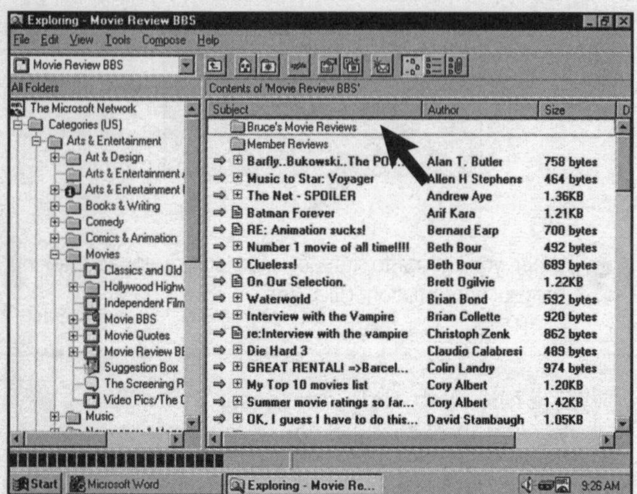

1. You can create icons for your favorite areas on The Microsoft Network. First, go to the area you want to add to your list of favorite places.

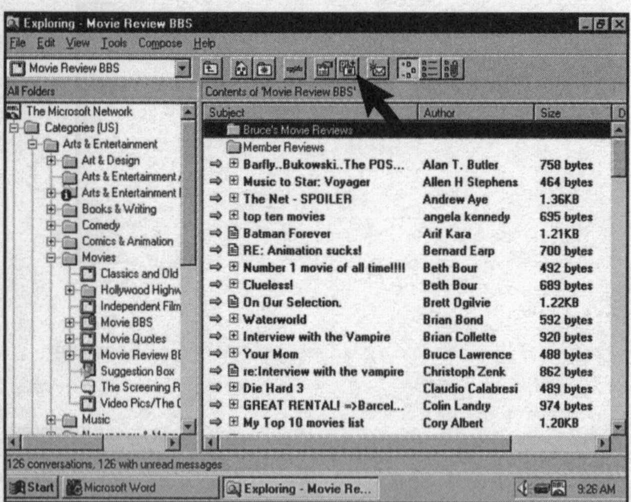

2. Click the **Add to Favorite Places** button, or open the **File** menu and select **Add to Favorite Places**.

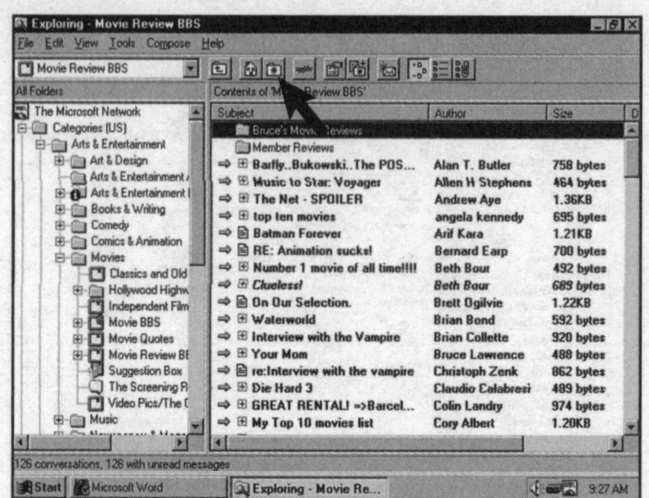

3. To go to a favorite place on the list, click the **Go to Favorite Places** button.

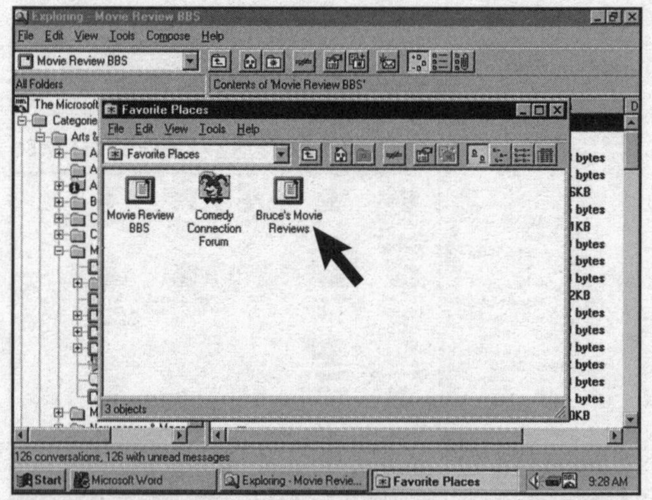

4. A window opens, showing icons for all the areas you added as favorite places. Double-click the desired icon to shoot to your favorite place.

Exchange E-Mail on The Microsoft Network

Like all the major online services, The Microsoft Network allows you to send mail to and receive mail from other users of the service and anyone who has an Internet e-mail address. To send a message, you simply provide the person's e-mail address, type a message, and then send it on its way. The message is stored in the person's electronic mailbox until he or she retrieves it. In a matter of minutes (sometimes seconds), your friends, colleagues, and relatives can read your latest missives.

There's no trick to sending and receiving e-mail on The Microsoft Network. The procedure is similar to that for any of the major online services. However, The Microsoft Network uses another Windows 95 program for managing e-mail: Microsoft Exchange. Whenever you choose to send or receive messages in The Microsoft Network, Windows automatically runs Microsoft Exchange.

The *Guided Tour* shows you how to send and receive mail on The Microsoft Network.

Begin Guided Tour Send Mail

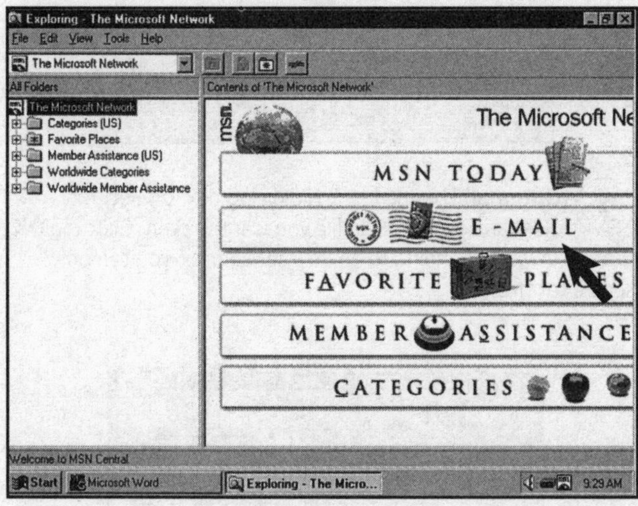

1 Sign in to The Microsoft Network, and then click the **E-Mail** button.

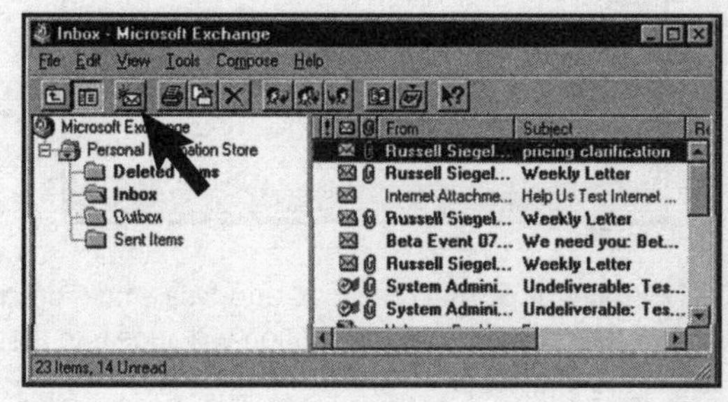

2 Windows runs Microsoft Exchange, its built-in e-mail manager. Click the **New Message** button, or open the **Compose** menu and click **New Message**.

(continues)

Guided Tour Send Mail *(continued)*

3 The New Message dialog box appears. In the **To** text box, type the recipient's member ID. (You can add recipient names by separating each member ID with a semicolon.)

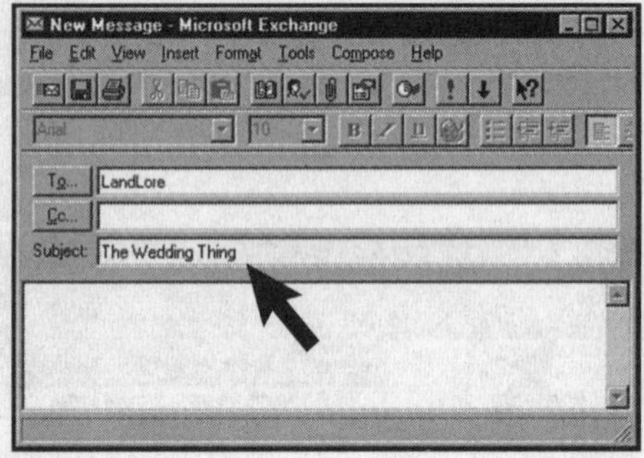

4 Click inside the **Subject** text box, and type a brief description of the message. This description will appear in the recipient's e-mail box.

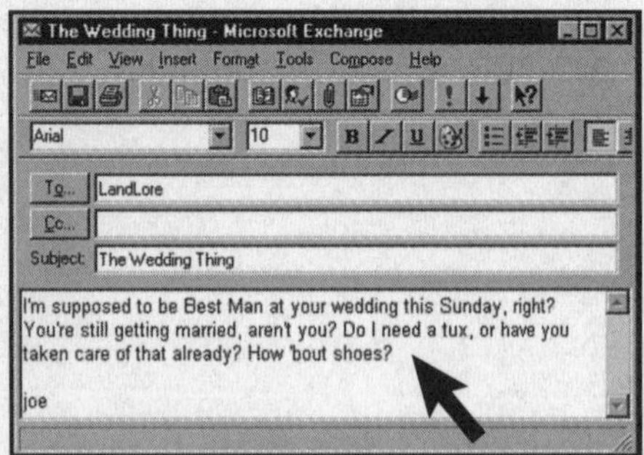

5 Click inside the message area near the bottom of the dialog box, and type your message.

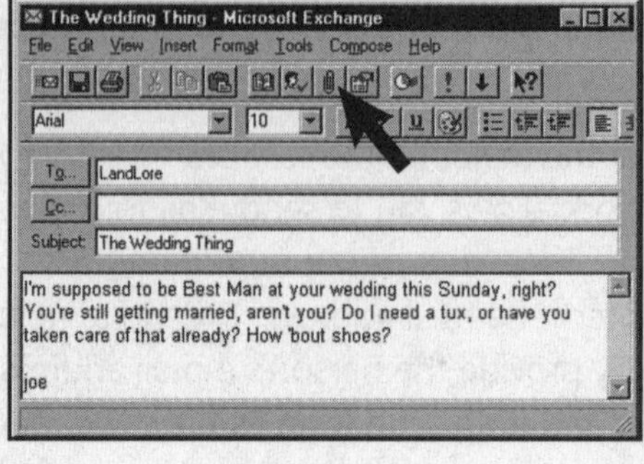

6 **(Optional)** If you want to send a file along with your message, click the **Insert File** button (or open the **Insert** menu and select **File**).

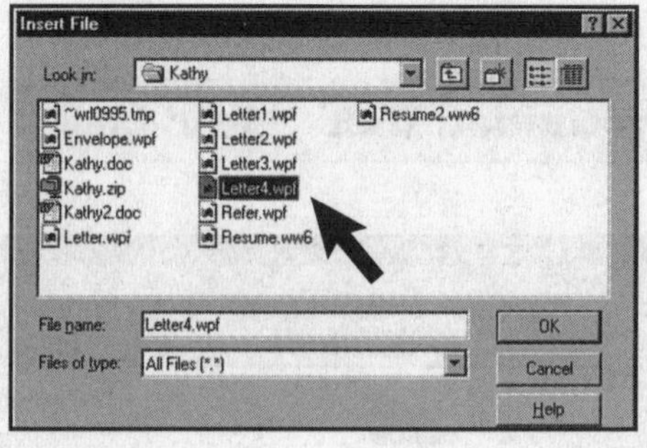

7 **(Optional)** Use the Insert File dialog box to select the folder and name of the file you want to send. Click the **OK** button. (If you're sending to an Internet address, you can only send a text file.)

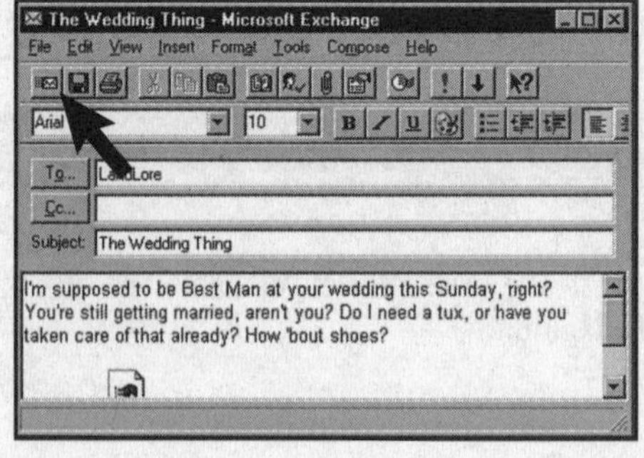

8 Click the **Send** button, or open the **File** menu and select **Send**. Microsoft Exchange sends the message and any files you attached.

Begin Guided Tour Read Incoming Messages

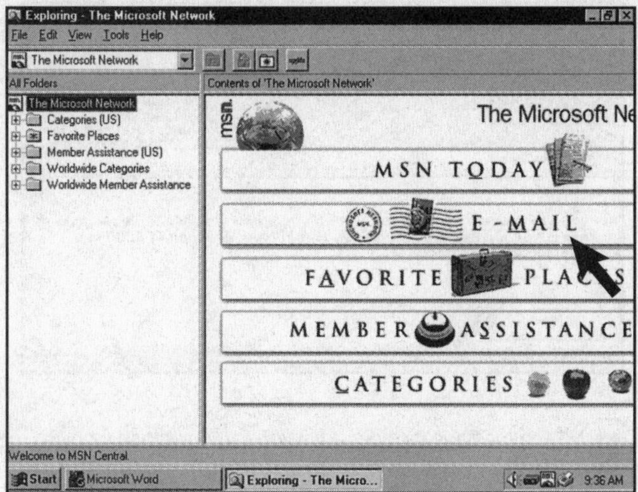

1. To read your e-mail messages, you have to connect to The Microsoft Network. Click the **E-Mail** button.

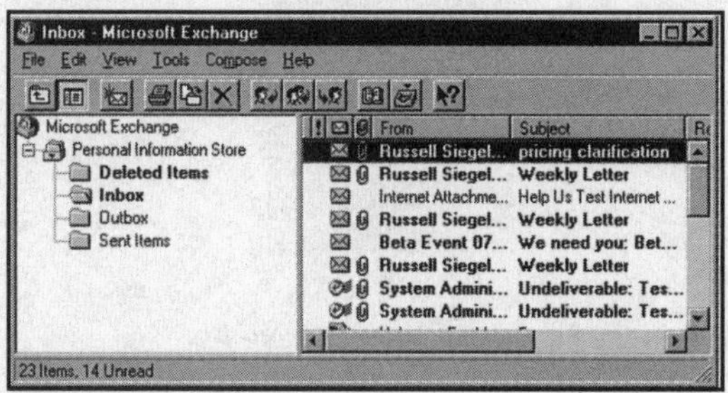

2. Windows automatically runs Microsoft Exchange, which checks for any new e-mail messages.

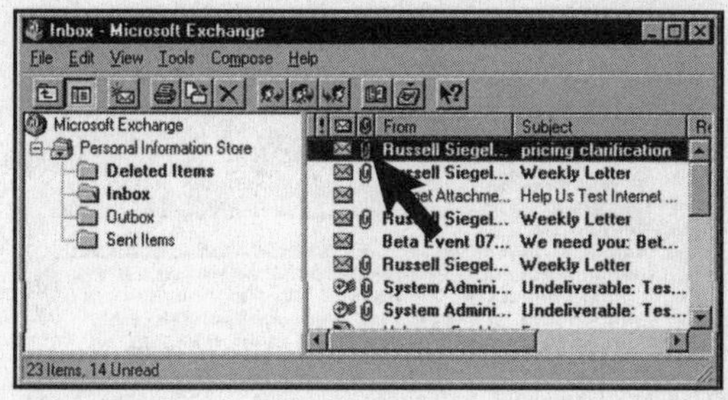

3. If you have new e-mail messages, a description of each message appears in the In Box. The paper clip next to the message description indicates that this message has a file attached to it. Double-click a message to read it.

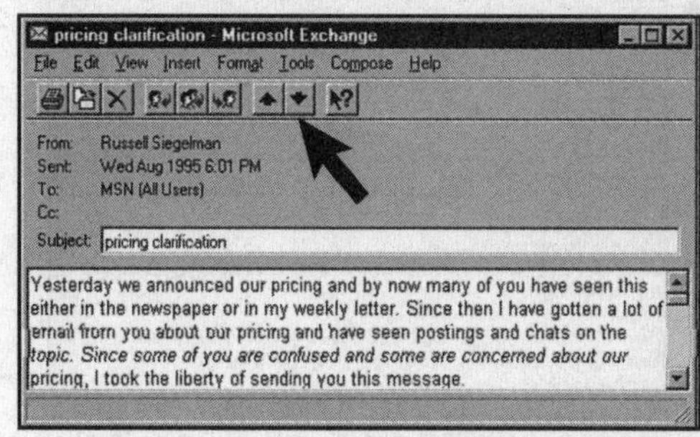

4. When the message is displayed, you can click the **Next** or **Previous** button to read additional e-mail messages.

(continues)

Guided Tour Read Incoming Messages

(continued)

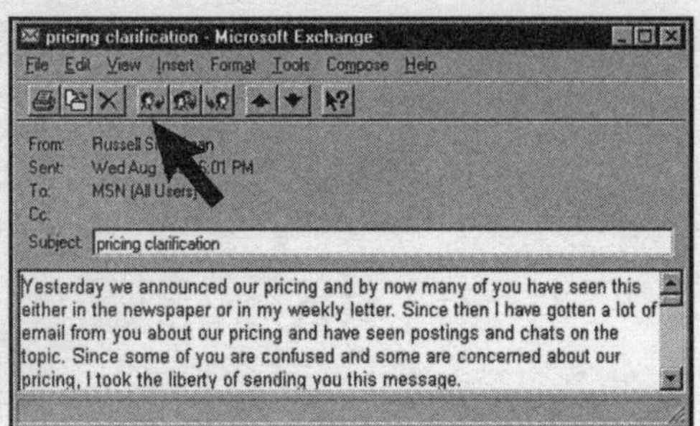

5 To reply to an e-mail message, click the **Reply to Sender** button.

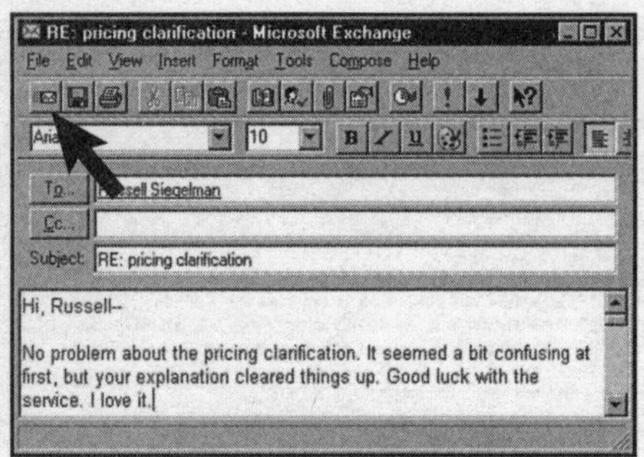

6 If you chose to reply, a dialog box appears, allowing you to send a message to the sender. Type your response, and then click the **Send** button.

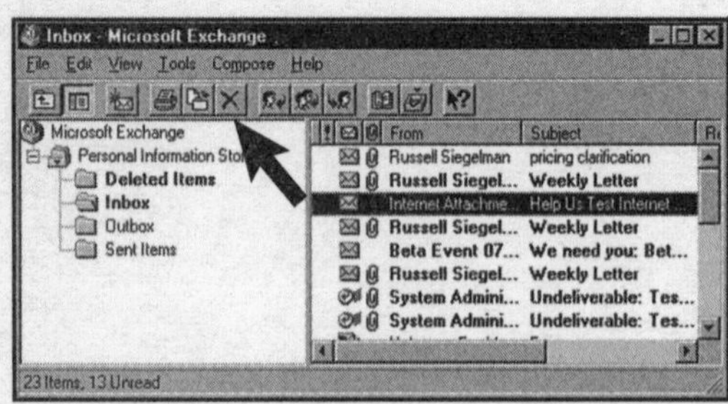

7 You can delete the message by clicking on its description and then clicking on the **Delete** button. However, after deleting a message, you won't be able to read it again.

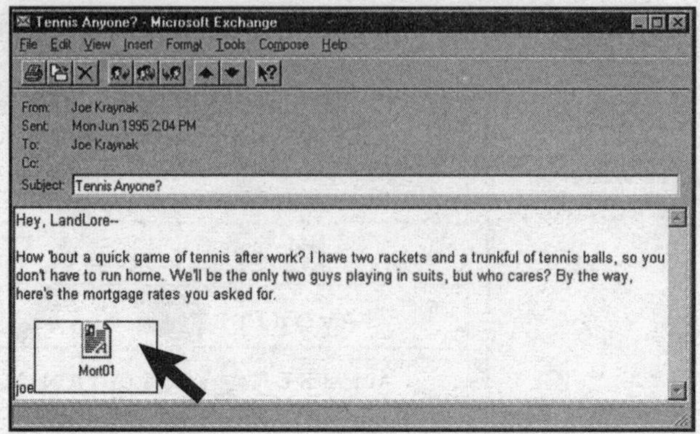

8 If the message includes a file you can download (copy to your computer), an icon appears at the bottom of the message area. Click the icon.

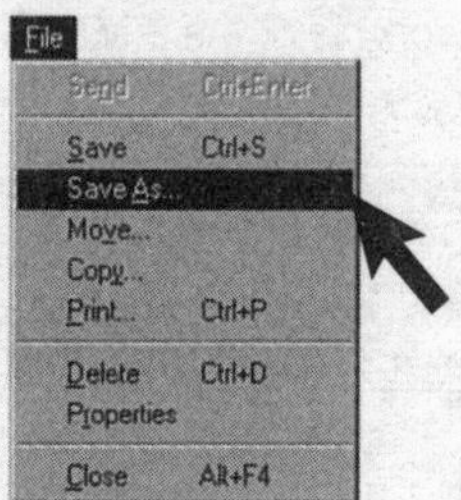

9 Open the **File** menu and click **Save As**.

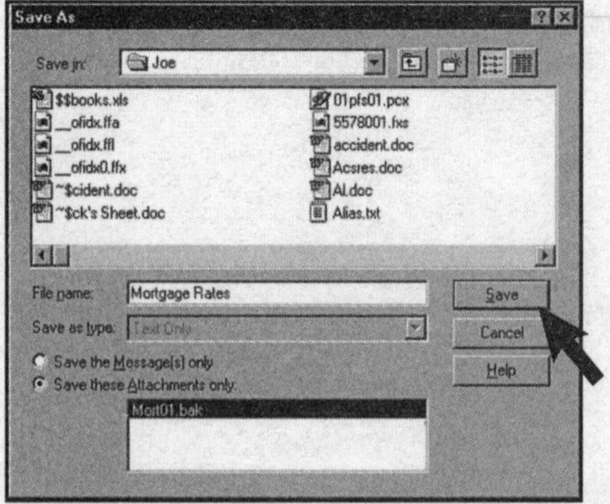

10 Select the drive and folder in which you want to save the file, and then click the **Save** button.

Converse with Other Microsoft Network Members

Online services wouldn't be much more than electronic libraries if it weren't for the people who populate these electronic cities. But because of those people, you can interact with actual human beings from around the world who share your personal and business interests, your concerns, and your joys. With such connections, you can obtain and give help, satisfy your curiosities, contribute your creations, and just have a good time.

In addition to e-mail, The Microsoft Network provides two means for communicating with other members. You can chat in any of several computerized meeting places, or post and read messages on electronic bulletin boards. The Microsoft Network offers bulletin boards for everything from gardening and cooking to personal finances and computers. You simply post a message and wait for replies, or read the questions and answers posted by other people.

In the chat rooms, you can carry on live conversations with other users. (You can think of chatting as a way of carrying on a telephone conversation by using your keyboard.) People from all over the world join in chat rooms to tell jokes, share stories and small talk, and create lasting (and not-so-lasting) relationships with people they have never seen (and usually will never see).

To tap into these two intriguing resources, take the *Guided Tour*. This tour will show you how to read and post bulletin board messages, and where to go for real-time conversations.

Begin Guided Tour Chat with Other Members

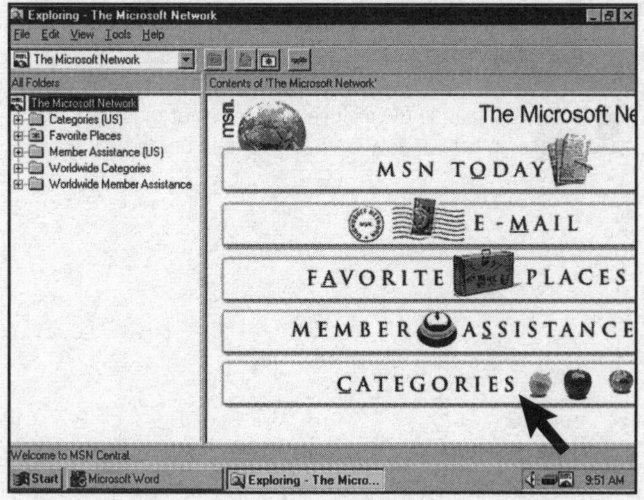

1 To converse with other users, first connect to The Microsoft Network, and then click the **Categories** button.

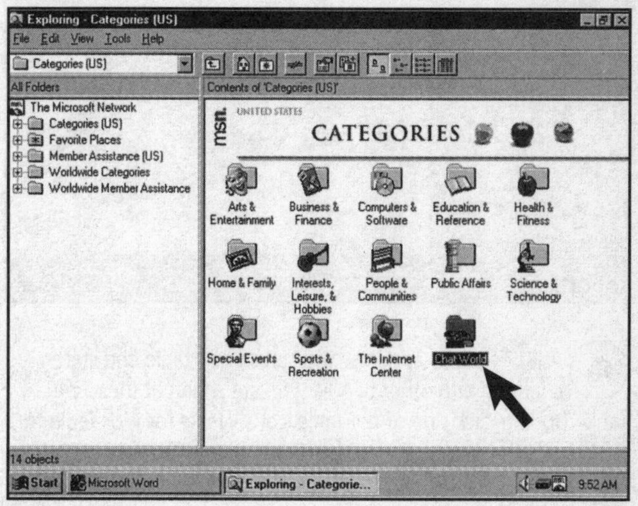

2 Double-click the **Chat World** icon to view a collection of icons for the various chat areas.

(continues)

Guided Tour Chat with Other Members

(continued)

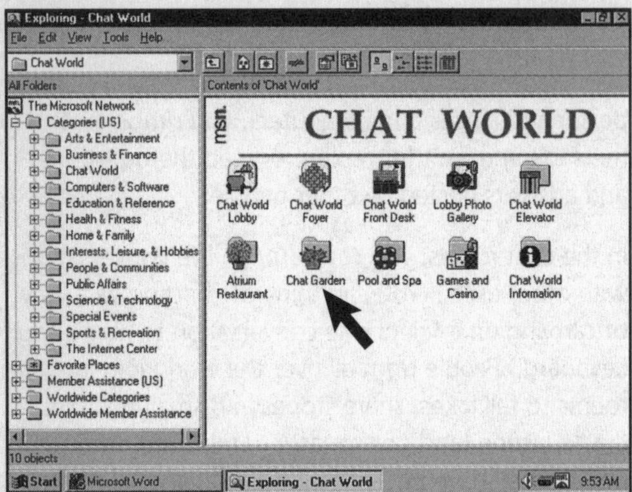

3 Another collection of icons appears. For now, double-click **Chat Garden**.

4 A list of tables appears. You can sit at a table and start chatting with other people who are sitting at the same table. Double-click one of the table icons. (Table for 4 or Table for 5 indicates the maximum number of people who can sit at the table.)

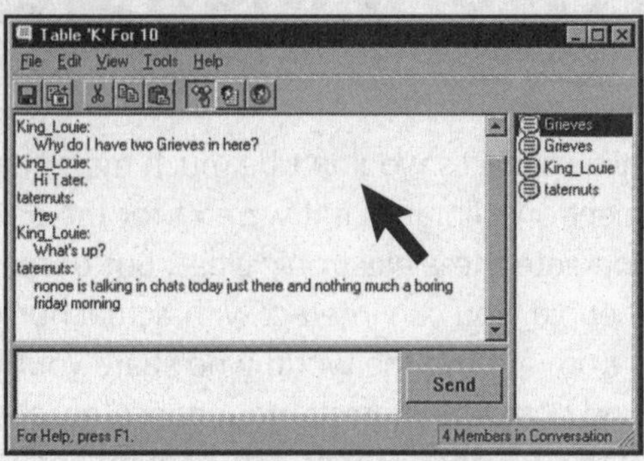

5 You've now pulled up a chair at the table. The member IDs of the people sitting at the table are listed on the right. The main conversation takes place in the big window in the middle.

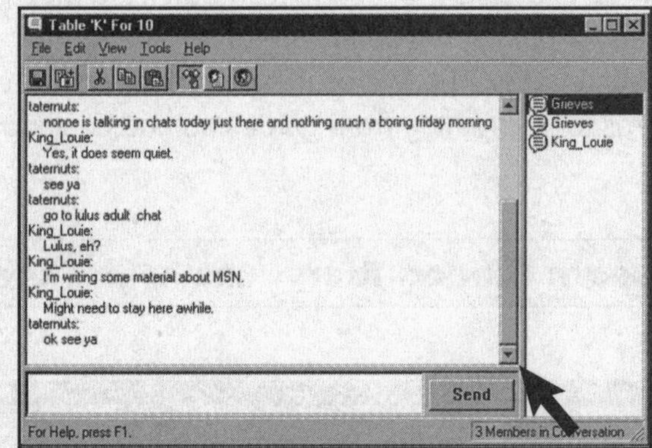

6 You can change the relative dimensions of the panes that make up the window by dragging their borders.

Guided Tour Chat with Other Members

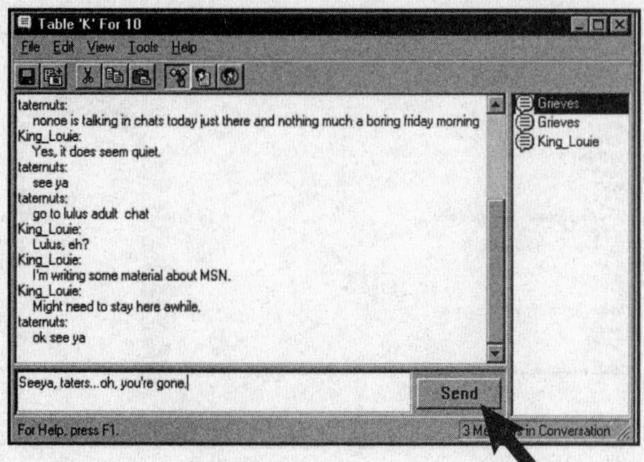

7 To contribute your own witty comments to the conversation, type in the message area, and then click the **Send** button.

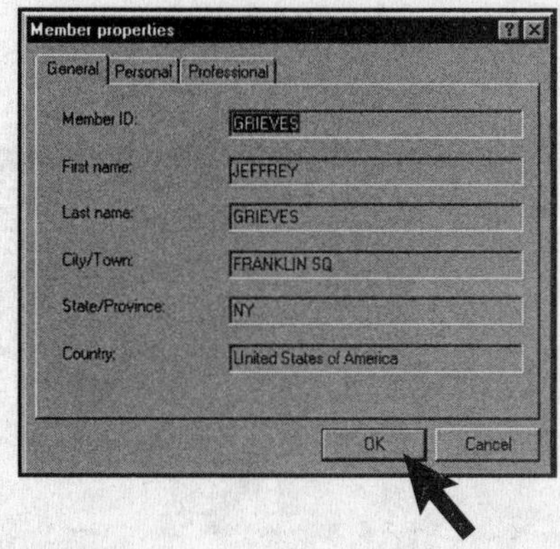

8 You can view personal and professional information about a person by double-clicking his or her member ID. Read the information, and then click the **OK** button.

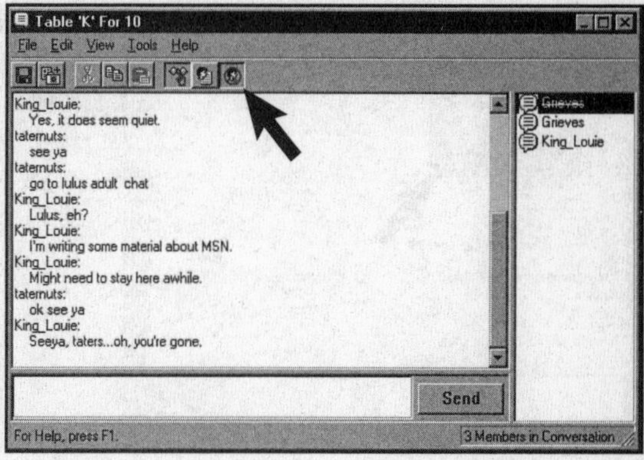

9 You can prevent a particular person's messages from appearing on your screen by clicking on the person's member ID, and then clicking on the **Ignore** button. A line appears through the member's ID.

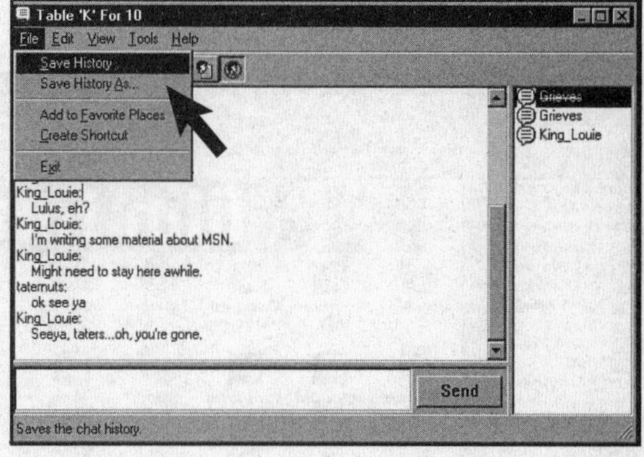

10 You can save a conversation as a text file to review later. Open the **File** menu, and select **Save History**. Type a name for the file, and click **Save**.

(continues)

Guided Tour Chat with Other Members

(continued)

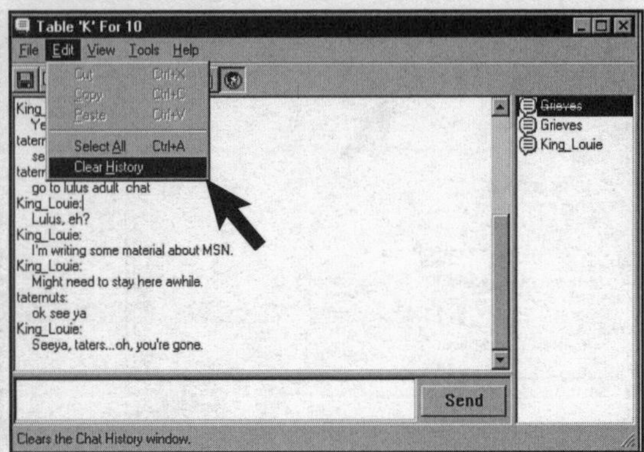

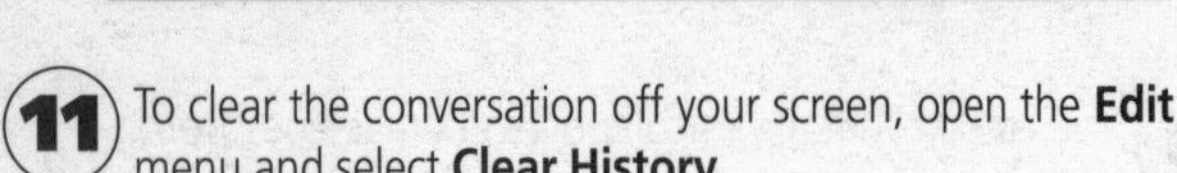

11 To clear the conversation off your screen, open the **Edit** menu and select **Clear History**.

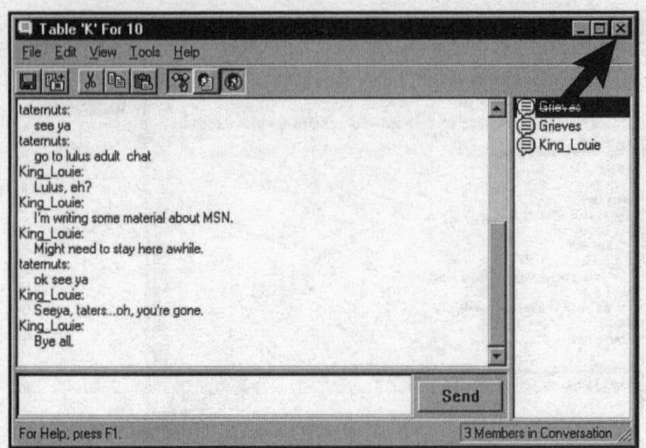

12 To leave a chat table, say your good-byes, and then click the **Close** button.

Begin Guided Tour Read and Respond to Bulletin Board Messages

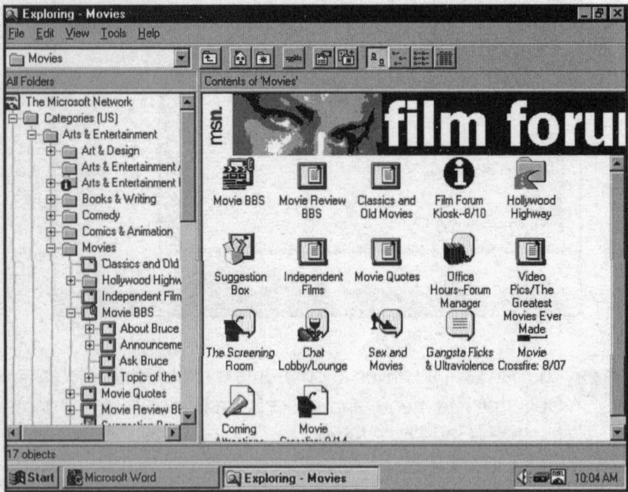

1 Several areas in The Microsoft Network have message boards where you can read and post messages. Connect to The Microsoft Network, and go to the area in which you're interested.

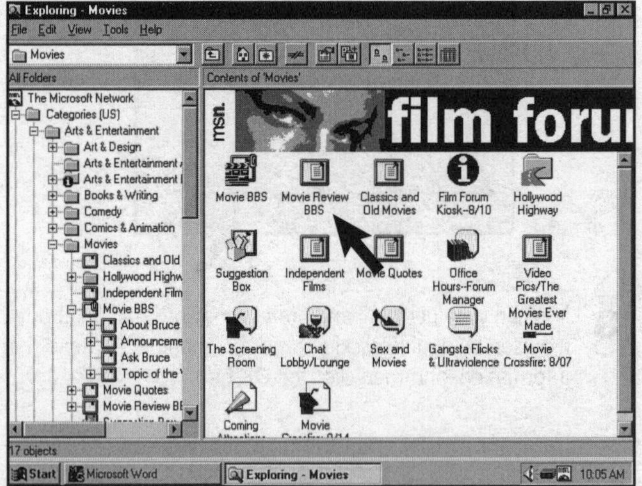

2 The icon for any area in which you can read and post messages looks like a piece of paper with a thumbtack stuck in it. Double-click the icon to view a list of recent messages.

Guided Tour Read and Respond to Bulletin Board Messages

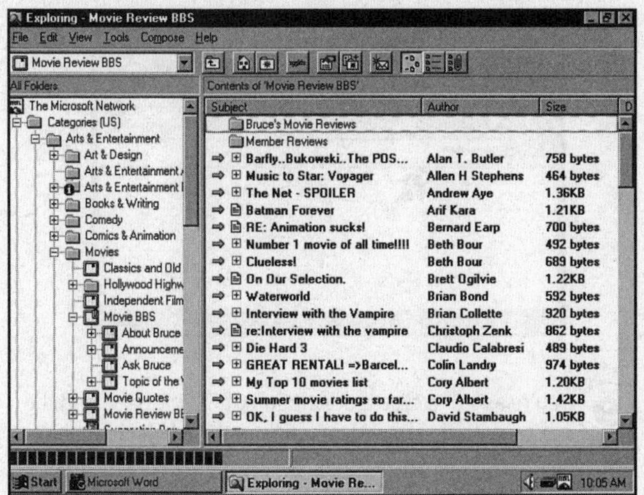

3 A list of the most recent postings appears. If this is your first visit to the area, the list will be long. If you visited recently, the list may be short, because it displays the names of only new messages.

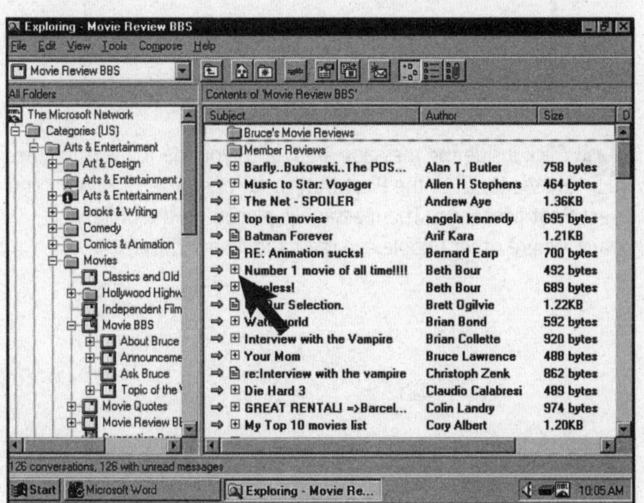

4 Next to most messages is a plus sign indicating that other people have responded to the initial posting. Click the plus sign to view a list of responses.

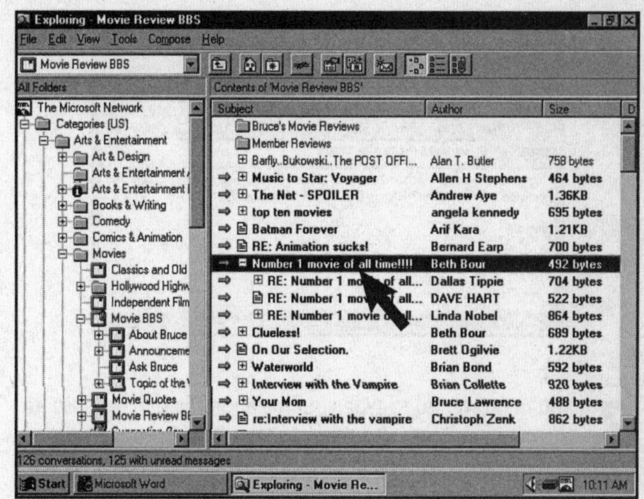

5 If you see a description of a message that piques your interest, you can double-click the description to read the entire message.

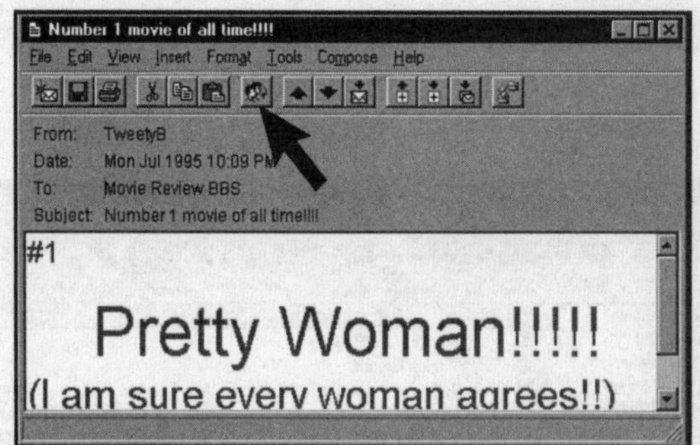

6 You can easily respond to a message. Click the **Reply to BBS** button.

(continues)

Guided Tour Read and Respond to Bulletin Board Messages

(continued)

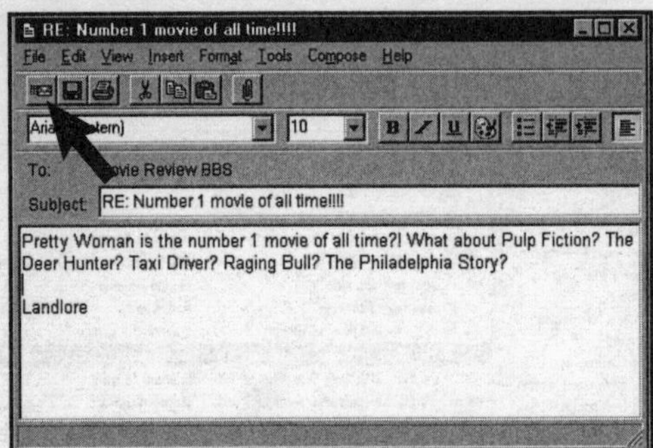

7 You're prompted to type your message. Type a response in the message area, and then click the **Post** button. The message is placed on the bulletin board, where it can be read by all.

You can reply privately to a BB message by opening the **Compose** menu and selecting **Reply by E-mail.** Only the person you respond to will be able to read the message.

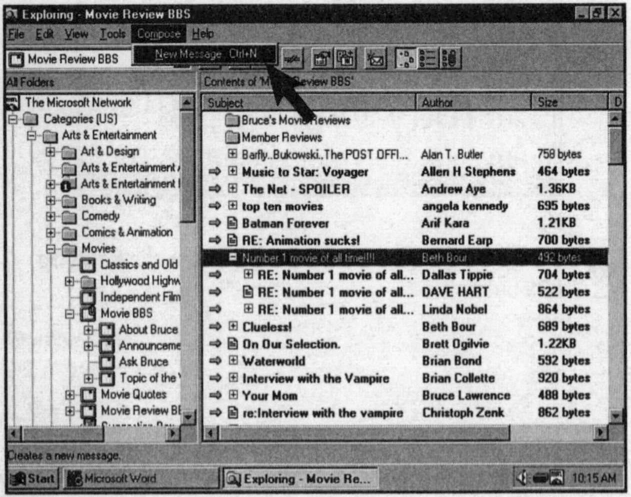

8 To start your own conversation on a message board, open the **Compose** menu and select **New Message**.

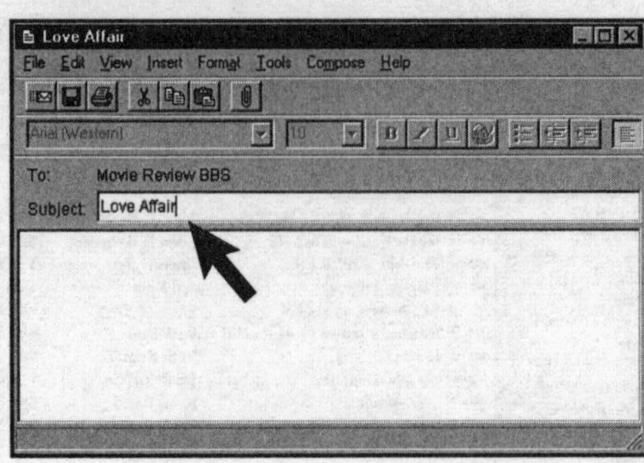

9 You're asked to type a description of the message and the message itself. Type a description in the **Subject** text box.

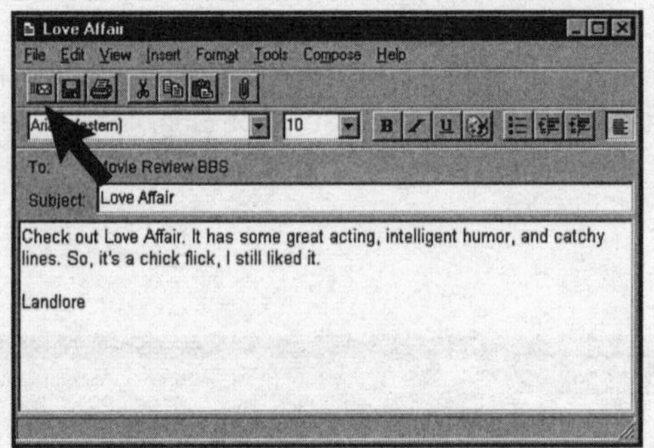

10 Click inside the message area, and type the full text for the message. Click the **Post** button, or open the **File** menu and select **Post Message**. The message is placed on the bulletin board, where other people can read and respond to it.

HOW TO...

Connect with the Outside World Using BBSs and the Internet

In this section, you'll discover how to connect to and exchange information with other users using Bulletin Board Systems (BBSs), and jump on the information superhighway with the Internet (a global network of computers).

The tasks in this section are akin to dipping your toe into water (a *large* body of water). You're not going to learn everything you'll need to know to be proficient on BBSs and the Internet. They are both such large topics that an entire *Big Basics Book* could be devoted to these topics alone. What you will find in this section, however, are the basics of getting connected and moving around—whether you're cruising BBSs or the Internet.

What You Will Find in This Section

Connect to a BBS with Windows 3.11 Terminal 310

Download and Upload Files with Terminal 313

Connect to the Internet: An Overview 316

Connect to an Internet Server Through Windows 3.11 Terminal 318

Get Wired with Windows 95 Dial-Up Networking 322

Connect to a BBS with Windows 3.11 Terminal

Using your general communications software or the Windows Terminal Accessory program, you can join and take advantage of any one of thousands of public Bulletin Board Systems (BBSs) in the world. Individuals and organizations run BBSs to provide electronic gathering places for users with common interests, or to provide information and support about products and services. For example, NASA has a BBS with information about space missions and the like. The people who run and maintain BBSs are called *sysops*—short for SYStem OPeratorS.

There are several different ways to find BBSs to join. You can read computer magazines to learn about different BBSs; one magazine, *BoardWatch*, focuses specifically on BBSs—and each month publishes a list of ones you can join. You can keep your eye peeled when you're using an online service for descriptions of BBSs; you can call a service called User Group Locator at 914/876-6678 to find out whether there's a computer user group near you that offers a BBS. The Yellow Pages in some areas even have entries for local BBSs. Look for these under "Computer Bulletin Boards."

When you join a BBS, usually you have to answer a list of questions to register. If there's a fee for joining the BBS (no, they're not all free), you may need to give a credit card number as well. The costs for joining BBSs vary wildly. Some are free. Some charge an annual fee. Some, like the one called ECHO (East Coast Hang Out), charge a monthly fee. Monthly fees generally range from $10 to $20.

Also, if the phone number for the BBS is a long distance call for you, don't forget that you'll have long distance charges for the time you're logged on to the BBS. These can add up quickly.

If you find a BBS you want to dial into, it's a process that takes a couple of steps. First, you have to start Windows Terminal and set up its communication settings so they'll work with the BBS. (This can be a trial and error thing—different BBSs may use different communications settings.) Then you set up the phone number, dial into the BBS and log on, as explained in the *Guided Tour*.

To set up Terminal to communicate with a BBS, open the **Settings** menu and select **Communications**. Although the setting you need will vary from BBS to BBS, you should start by choosing **9600** baud for speed. Also select **8** data bits, **None** for Parity, and **1** for Stop Bits (this is **8-N-1** in shorthand). If these settings don't work for a BBS and you get garbled screens while you're in it, try a slower modem speed like **2400** or **4800** and change the other settings to **7-E-2**, another common combination.

Also, Windows Terminal usually has trouble displaying the ANSI or RIP graphics in some BBSs. If you log on to a BBS and have some trouble with it, choose a BBS display mode that doesn't use color or graphics.

Some BBSs require special software to run (especially if it's a Windows-based BBS). When you try to sign on, the BBS will tell you that you need the software, and may ask whether you want to download it to your system. To learn more about doing so, see "Download and Upload Files with Terminal" on page 313.

Begin Guided Tour Log On to a BBS with Terminal

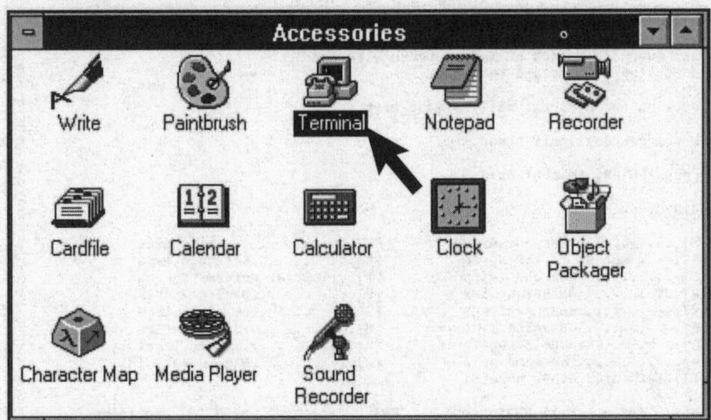

1 Double-click the **Accessories** program group icon to open its group window. Double-click the **Terminal** program-item icon.

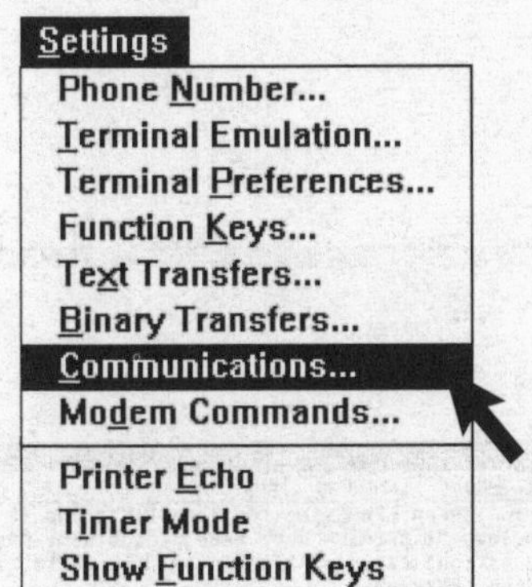

2 If you've already saved the dialing information for the BBS, open that file, and skip to step 6 (or else open the **Settings** menu and click **Communications**).

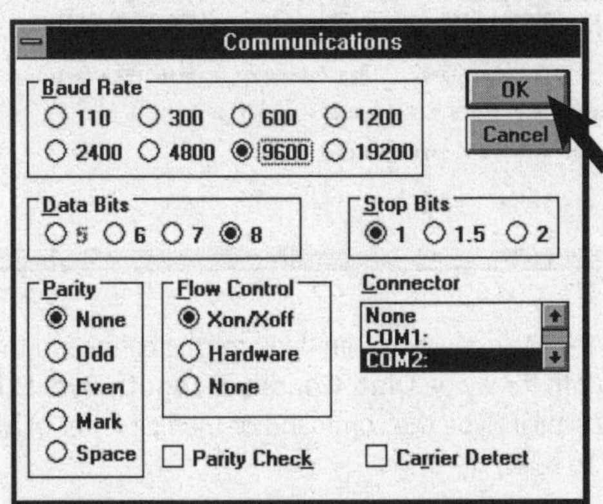

3 Adjust the Communication settings as needed. The settings shown here are quite typical. Then click **OK**.

4 Open the **Settings** menu and select **Phone Number**.

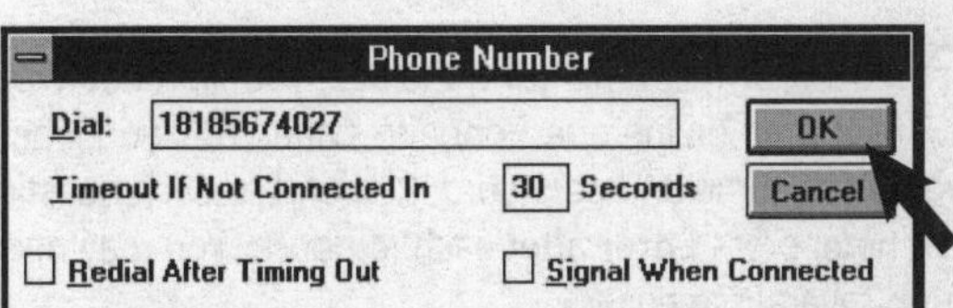

5 In the **Dial** text box of the Phone Number dialog box, enter the phone number for the BBS, including **1** and an area code if necessary. Click **OK**.

6 Open the **Phone** menu and select **Dial**. Terminal dials the phone and connects to the BBS.

(continues)

Guided Tour Log On to a BBS with Terminal

(continued)

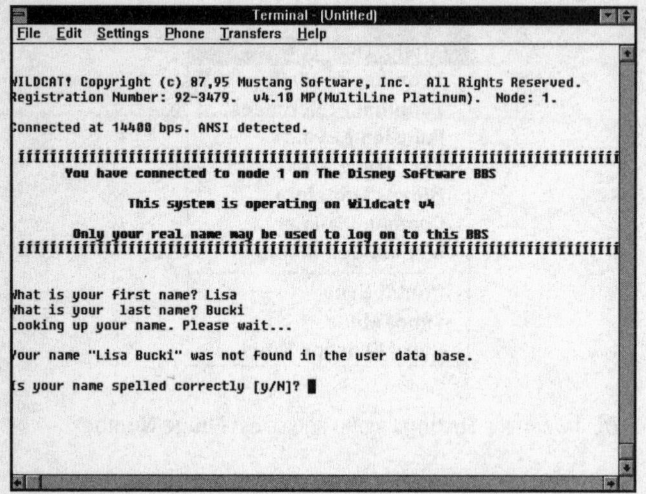


```
Terminal - (Untitled)
File  Edit  Settings  Phone  Transfers  Help
'and every last inch of me's covered with hair!"
  -Gaston  - Beauty & the Beast

Checking for personal mail, please wait.

No new personal mail found.

Press [ENTER] to continue?

Main menu:

[M].............Message menu        [F].................File menu
[C]....Comments to the sysop        [B]............Bulletin menu
[P]...........Page the sysop        [I]...Initial welcome screen
[Q]............Questionnaire        [V]............Verify a user
[Y]............Your settings        [S]........System statistics
[U]............Userlog list         [N]................Newsletter
[G].........Goodbye & Logoff        [H]................Help level
[*]..............Command help       [W]............Who is online
[T]..Talk with other node(s)

Conf: "[0] - E-Mail Conference    BBS", time on 1, with 105 remaining.

Main menu: [M F C B P I Q 0 Y S U N G H * W T] ?
```

7 If it's your first time using the BBS, you'll probably have to fill out an online questionnaire. Otherwise, you'll be asked for your user name and password. Respond to each question as shown here; press **Enter** after each response. You may need to go through several screens.

8 The Main menu screen for the BBS appears.

Begin Guided Tour Quit the BBS

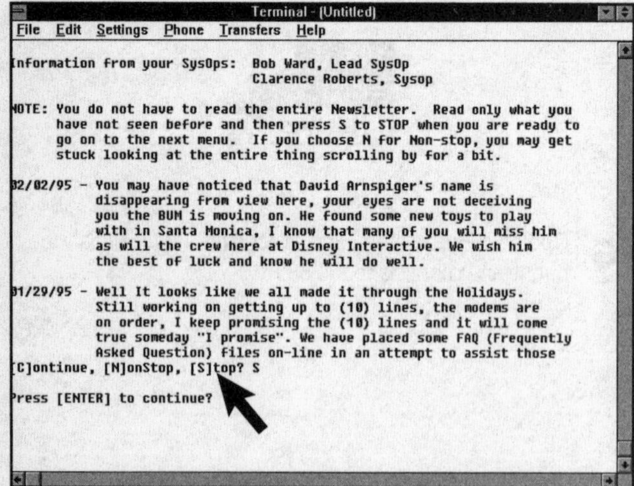


```
Terminal - (Untitled)
File  Edit  Settings  Phone  Transfers  Help
          on order, I keep promising the (10) lines and it will come
          true someday "I promise". We have placed some FAQ (Frequently
          Asked Question) files on-line in an attempt to assist those
[C]ontinue, [N]onStop, [S]top? S

Press [ENTER] to continue?

Main menu:

[M].............Message menu        [F].................File menu
[C]....Comments to the sysop        [B]............Bulletin menu
[P]...........Page the sysop        [I]...Initial welcome screen
[Q]............Questionnaire        [V]............Verify a user
[Y]............Your settings        [S]........System statistics
[U]............Userlog list         [N]................Newsletter
[G].........Goodbye & Logoff        [H]................Help level
[*]..............Command help       [W]............Who is online
[T]..Talk with other node(s)

Conf: "[0] - E-Mail Conference    BBS", time on 5, with 102 remaining.

Main menu: [M F C B P I Q 0 Y S U N G H * W T] ? G

Are you sure you wish to logoff [Y/n]?
```

1 From wherever you are in the BBS, select the commands that return you to the Main menu. In this case, for example, you press **S** for Stop, and then press **Enter**.

2 On the Main menu screen, look for the command that logs you off. It may be **Quit**, **Goodbye**, **Logoff**, **Bye**, **Exit**, or something similar. Type the command or the first letter of the command to select it.

3 If you're asked to confirm logging off, press **Y** or type **yes** and press **Enter**. If necessary, open the **Phone** menu in Terminal and select **Hangup** to make sure you have cleared the line for other BBS calls.

Download and Upload Files with Terminal

You can use the Windows Terminal accessory program to dial into BBSs, some online services (like CompuServe), an Internet account, or another user's computer system. When you're connected to another computer, you can exchange files using basic Terminal procedures.

If you're browsing the contents of a BBS or an area on the Internet and you find a file you want to transfer to your system, you can *download* it to your disk. If you're browsing around on the system you're connected to and you find an area that accepts files contributed by individual users, you can *upload* a file—that is, transfer it from your disk to the other system.

The commands on the Transfers menu enable you to download and upload files. When you're transferring a file with Terminal, you need to make sure you know what kind of file you're transferring—text or binary. Text files are plain ASCII, and usually have a .TXT or .ASC file name extension. In general, you can treat all other files as binary.

You must be in a file area of a BBS to transfer files. You can't just do it randomly from any location. Initiate the file transfer first in the BBS, usually by choosing a command to download or upload a file. Then select the appropriate **Receive** (download) or **Send** (upload) command from Terminal's **Transfers** menu. The *Guided Tour* here walks you through the process.

Begin Guided Tour Download a File

```
Terminal - WBBS.TRM
File  Edit  Settings  Phone  Transfers  Help

MAIN Library
  File Name      Size  Date      Description
- ------------- ----- --------- ----------------------------------------
A ACZAR210.ZIP   320K 05/17/94 ACZAR 2.10 Archive Shell <ASP>
B BBSGRP.ZIP      17K 02/26/95 A Listing of INTERNET Newsgroups available
C CH1ADULT.TXT  1.9K 09/22/94 WBBS Channel 1 - Adult Files access registration
D CMP141.ZIP    1.5M 02/02/95 CMPQwk 1.4 QWK Reader for Win3.1.
E CMP14PAT.ZIP   75K 02/02/95 Patch for CMP141.ZIP
F CS44.ZIP      162K 01/26/94 Cs44 -  is an on-line GIF viewer. It
G CTSSPU21.ZIP  147K 12/13/94 CTS Serial Port Utilities v2.1: Test, fix & cont
H DAT212.ZIP    196K 10/21/94 DAT file for VirusScan, version 2.1.2
I DCTERM.ZIP    1.2M 09/24/94 DC Term for DOS - Image viewing terminal with
J DCTERMW.ZIP   879K 09/24/94 DC Term for Windows - Image viewing terminal wit
K FASTT4W.ZIP   304K 07/30/94 Fasttag For Windows: Offline tagger for TFLE
L FASTTSYS.ZIP  1.6K 07/30/94 Fasttag For Windows: Sysop Documentation
M FORUMREG.TXT  2.8K 09/23/94 Registrtaion form to create a Forum on WBBS
N FOXX26.ZIP    801K 11/21/94 Foxpro v2.6 runtime. This program will be needed
O IAGOWM10.ZIP   70K 02/17/95 Iagos war manual for tradewars game...
P IRABBS.ZIP    361K 04/12/94  FREE! A Tutorial about BBSING
Q NODELIST.TXT   35K 12/08/94 List of all Forums on MajorNet

Enter letter of file or file name to select from this page,
? for help, R to redraw page, X to exit, or RETURN for next page: B
```

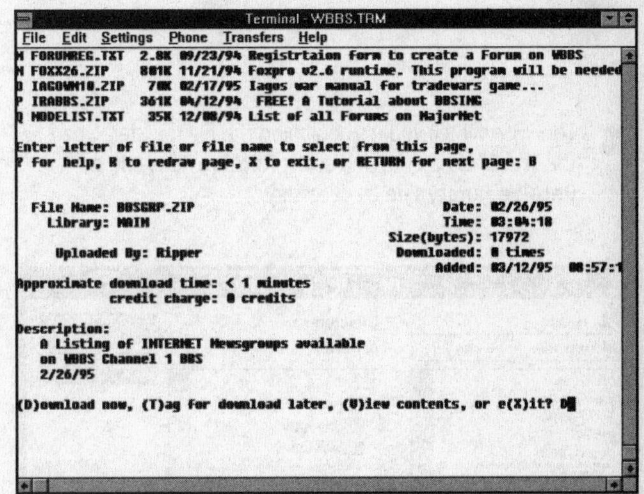

1 Start Terminal, and log on to your chosen BBS or service, and go to an area that offers files to download. Select the file to download. In this case, you must press the letter to the left of the file to select it, and then press **Enter**.

2 After you select a file, the BBS will usually ask whether you want to download it. Select that command. Here you would type **D** and press **Enter**.

(continues)

Guided Tour Download a File *(continued)*

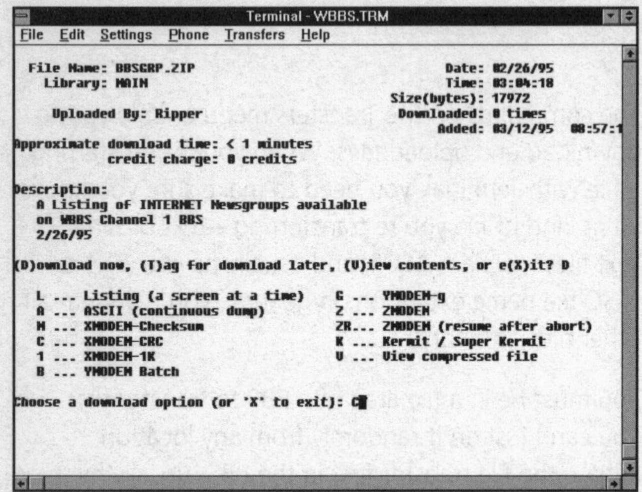

3 The BBS will ask you what download protocol you want to use to ensure a smooth transfer. Select **XMODEM-CRC**, the default for Terminal; in this case, type **C** and press **Enter**.

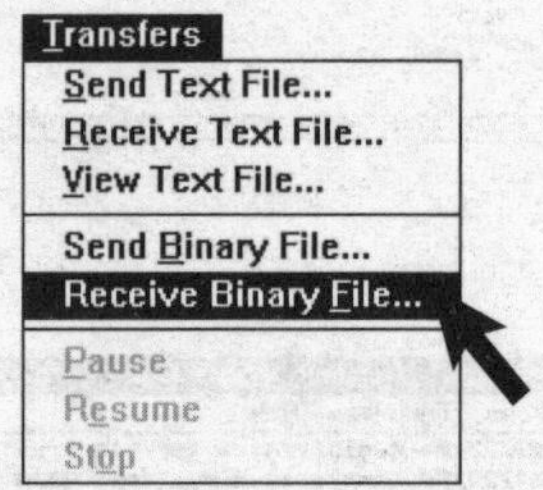

4 The BBS will tell you it's beginning the file transfer. Open the **Transfers** menu, and select **Receive Text File** or **Receive Binary File** as necessary.

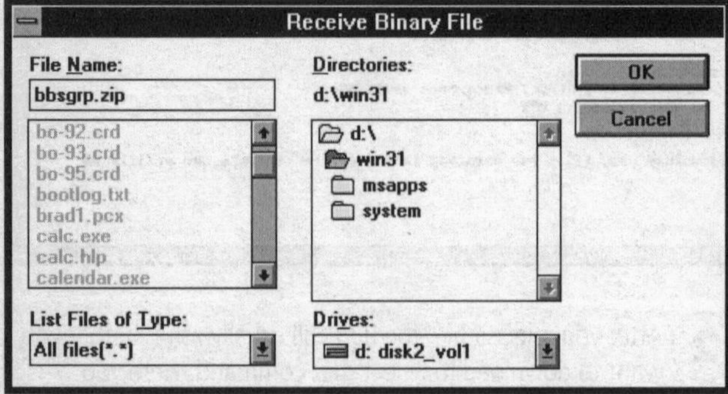

5 In the Receive... File dialog box, specify where you want to save the file and the name you want to save it under. Click **OK** or press **Enter**.

6 The file transfer begins, indicated by the status bar that appears at the bottom of the Terminal window. When the transfer is finished, the status bar disappears.

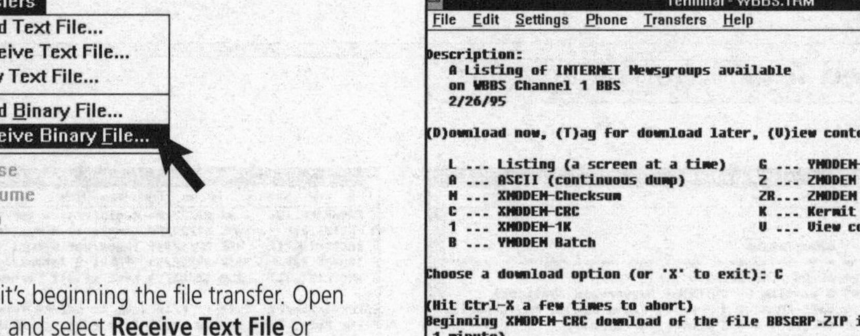

7 Press **Enter** to display the next command line prompt, and then select the command you want to continue working in the BBS or service.

Begin Guided Tour Upload a File

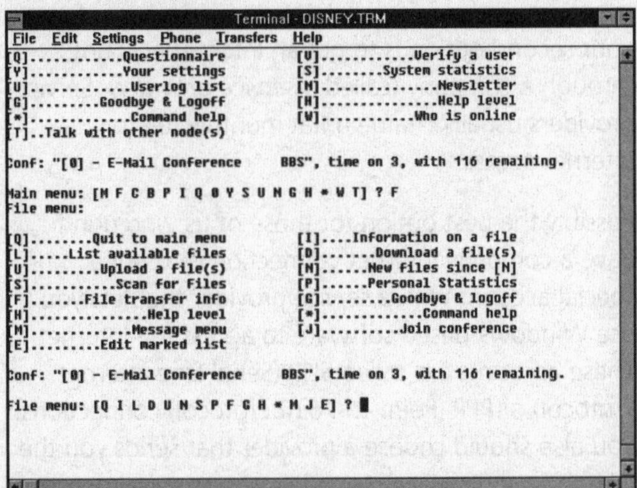

1 Log on to your BBS or service, and then go to the library or area to upload a file to. (You'll usually see an option for uploading.) Select the command for uploading. In this case, select **Upload a File** by pressing **U**.

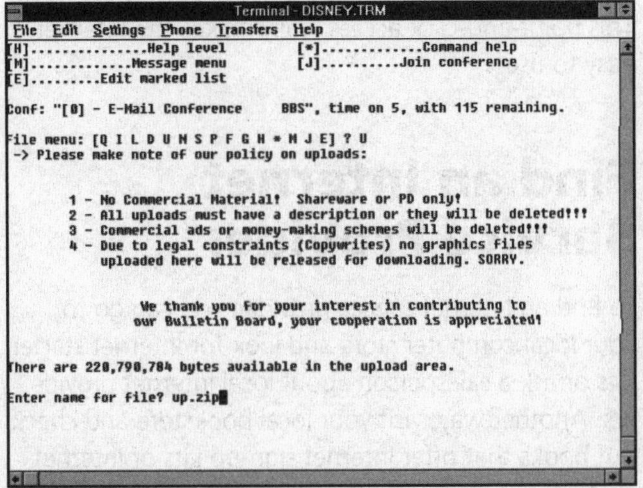

2 Read the upload policy if one appears, and then follow the on-screen prompts to enter information about the file. In this case, type the file name first, and then press **Enter**.

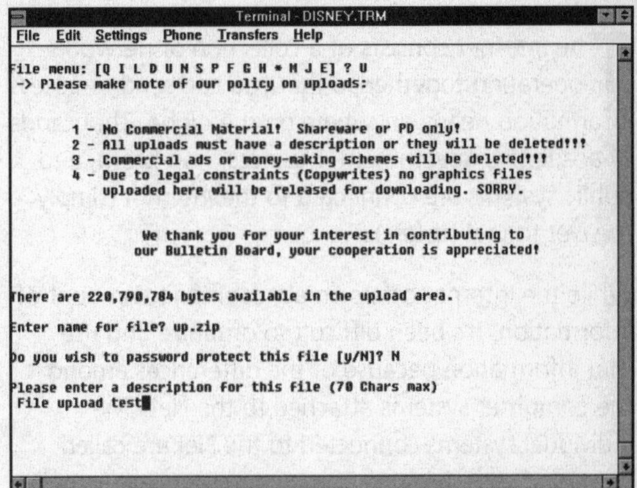

3 Continue responding to the questions, pressing **Enter** after each response.

4 When prompted to start the upload, open the **Transfers** menu and select **Send Text File** or **Send Binary File**.

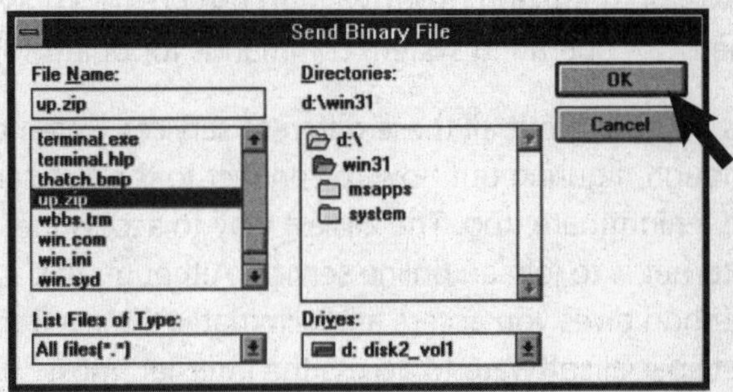

5 In the Send... File dialog box, specify the file you want to upload, and then press **Enter** or click **OK**.

6 Terminal sends the file. Once it's sent, press **Enter** to display the next command line prompt, and then select the command you want to continue working in the BBS or service.

Connect to the Internet: An Overview

The Internet consists of a collection of networks operating together so that you can send or access information nearly anywhere on the globe. Thousands of academic, government, business, non-profit, and public systems are connected to the Internet (simply *the Net* to real surfers).

While the Internet offers an almost infinite amount of information, it's been difficult to organize and use that information because of the differences among the computer systems attached to the Net. The individual systems connected to the Net are called *servers* or *sites*, because these computers are actually servers for local networks. Over time, several different server types and services have evolved as standards on the Internet.

E-mail, Internet Relay Chat (IRC), and Newsgroups are services users can access to exchange private, instant, and public messages, respectively. Archie, Gopher, File Transfer Protocol (FTP), and World Wide Web (WWW) are different sites (servers) on the Internet that are repositories for many different kinds of information (files and resources)—and each uses a different method for storage, organization, and access of that information. For example, to access information on an FTP server, you need to have Internet FTP access and have the right kind of software to use FTP (or know the UNIX operating system commands for doing so).

As if figuring out all these different services weren't enough, figuring out how to connect to the Net can be a nightmare, too. The easiest way to access the Internet is to join an online service. Although this method gives you access and eliminates the need to get special software to access the Internet, most online services don't offer access to all types of Net services and sites. For example, your online service may not offer WWW access.

Your second option is to get an Internet account through a company (called a *service provider*). Service providers usually charge a flat monthly fee for Internet access.

Possibly the best option for those of us who don't have a company Internet connection is to get a special account with a service provider that lets you use Windows-based software to access the Internet. These accounts are called SLIP (Serial Line Internet Protocol) or PPP (Point-to-Point Protocol) connections. You also should choose a provider that sends you the Windows software you need to access your Internet connection. Another option to get connected is to buy an Internet startup kit (like Internet-in-a-Box from Spry) from your local computer store. You can install the software and set it up to work with your account; some packages let you use your modem to dial in and set up your account with a particular service provider. This point-and-click access really makes the Internet easy to use.

Find an Internet Service Provider

To find an Internet service provider, you can go to your local computer store and look for Internet starter kits or ask a salesperson about local Internet providers. Another way: visit your local bookstore and check out books that offer Internet sign-up kits or Internet magazines (which are littered with ads and offers from companies that want to get you connected). If you travel a lot, you'll want a provider that has access numbers all over the country; if you want a full-blown graphical connection, look for a provider that provides already-configured software for every account. Here are a few of the more well-known Internet service providers:

- Portal Information Network, 408/973-9111
- PSI, 800/827-7482

- Pipeline USA, 212/267-3636
- Netcom, 800/501-8649
- Delphi, 800/544-4005

The list that follows shows the icons for one Windows-based collection of programs that provides Internet access. The program icons for other software from kits (or other service providers) may look slightly different, but you should have icons for each of the programs mentioned here.

> A site's address gives you a clue about the kind of site it is, so you'll know how to connect to it. To identify the site, look for **www** (World Wide Web sites), **ftp** (FTP sites), or **gopher** (Gopher sites) in the address.

E-mail. You can send mail to anyone on the Internet or any online service, provided you have his or her e-mail address.

Read news and public messages. The Internet offers thousands of newsgroups focusing on different topics, from the serious and academic to the obscure and obscene. You *subscribe* to the newsgroups that interest you so you can post an article, or read articles posted there by others.

Search for information through Archie. When you access an Archie site, you can search for files to find where they're located on the Internet.

View and retrieve what's in the directories of an FTP site. When you connect to an FTP site through your Internet connection, you can view what's stored in the directories of the FTP server, view the files, and copy them to your computer.

Browse for information by selecting links on World Wide Web sites. Web sites are graphical, letting you click highlighted words and icons to jump around, get files, preview sounds and video, and more.

Find information on Gopher sites by working through a system of organized menus. This can be an easy way to get to the topic you want, because it resembles working in many other online services.

Chat live online with other users on an Internet Relay Chat (IRC) channel.

Connect to an Internet Server Through Windows 3.11 Terminal

Using your general communications software or the Windows Terminal Accessory program, you can usually log on to your Internet account with a service provider. The interface you get depends on your service provider, and on the type of connection you have. (If you only have access in this way, most likely you have a *dial-in terminal* account.) The problem is that using a dial-in terminal account is clunky at best and difficult at worst.

You may get an opening menu system, from which you choose commands by typing a *hot key* (a highlighted letter in a menu command) and pressing **Enter**. Other service providers provide a UNIX command-line interface only. In this type of system (as with DOS), you have to type a cryptic command at a prompt and press **Enter** to move around. Even if your provider offers a menuing system, you'll probably have to use the command line for some activities (such as FTP). If you hate DOS, then this kind of account probably isn't for you.

When you join your service provider, you get a *username* (also called a *login name*) and a password. The service should also tell you what your e-mail ID is; usually, you combine your username, an **@** symbol, and the *domain name* (address) for the service provider. For example, an e-mail address might look like **jblow@bubba.net**. You need to know your exact username and password to log in through Terminal.

You also need to know the phone number to connect with. If the phone number is a long distance call for you, don't forget that you'll have long distance charges for the time you're logged on to the Internet, and you'll have to include **1** and the area code when you specify the phone number in Terminal.

> There's quite a variety in how service providers and other UNIX connections are organized. Your steps may not completely match those listed here. If you have problems logging on or getting around, contact the company or organization for the host you're connecting to.

To set up Terminal to communicate with your host, open the **Settings** menu and choose **Communications** as noted in the numbered steps that follow. Although the settings you need will vary among service providers, you should start by choosing (under **Baud Rate**) the fastest speed your modem and the service provider's modem can support. (Choose the next higher number if your modem's speed isn't listed.)

Your service provider should have told you what to choose for the rest of the settings. Common choices are **8** data bits, **None** for Parity, and **1** for Stop Bits (this is **8-N-1** in shorthand).

To dial into your Internet account with Terminal, follow these initial steps:

Begin Guided Tour Connect to the Internet

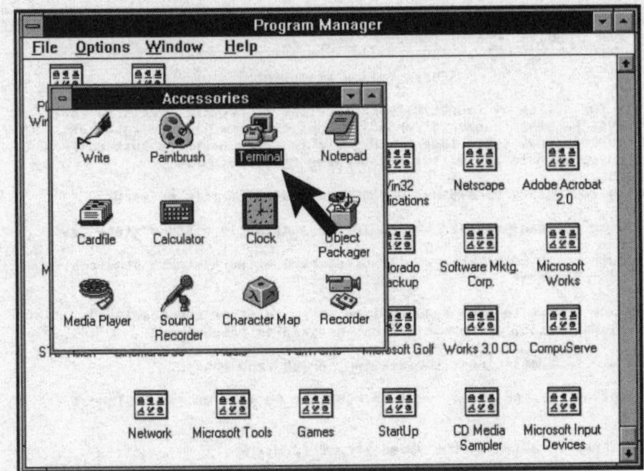

1 Double-click the **Accessories** program-group icon to open its group window. Double-click the **Terminal** program-item icon.

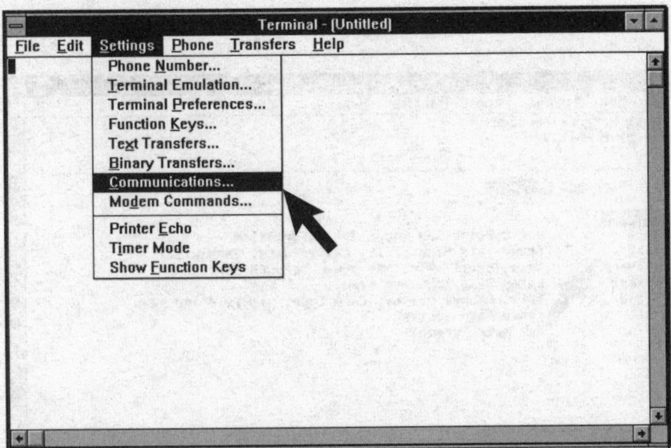

2 Open the **Settings** menu and select **Communications**.

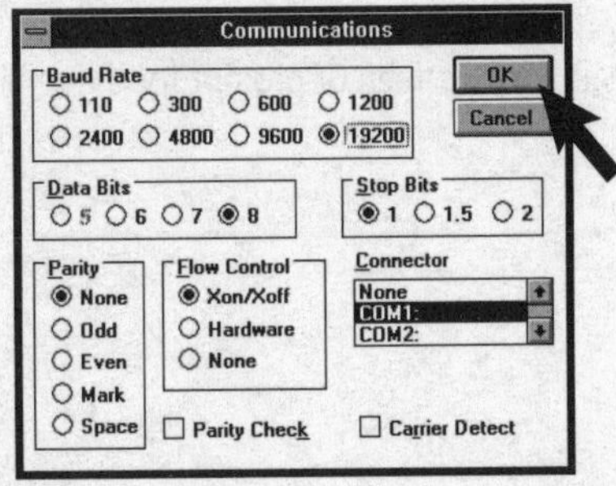

3 Adjust the communications settings as needed. (Your service provider can tell you which settings you need.) Then click **OK** or press **Enter**.

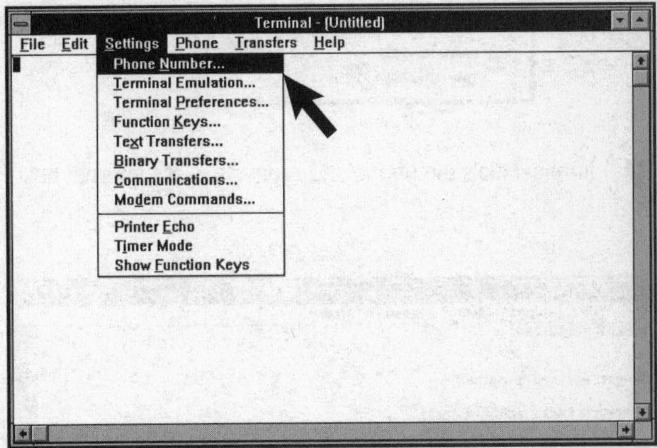

4 Open the **Settings** menu and choose **Phone Number**.

5 In the **Dial** text box of the Phone Number dialog box, enter the phone number for your Internet host (including **1** and the area code if necessary). Press **Enter** or click **OK**.

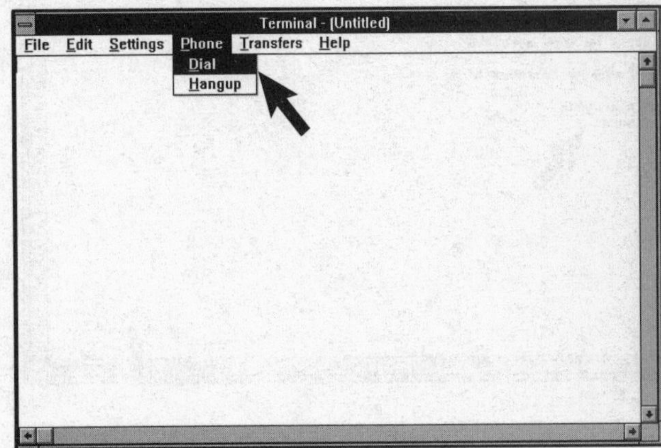

6 Open the **Phone** menu and choose **Dial**.

(continues)

Guided Tour Connect to the Internet

(continued)

Terminal
Dialing:555-5555
Time Remaining: 24
Cancel

7 Terminal dials the phone and connects to the Internet host.

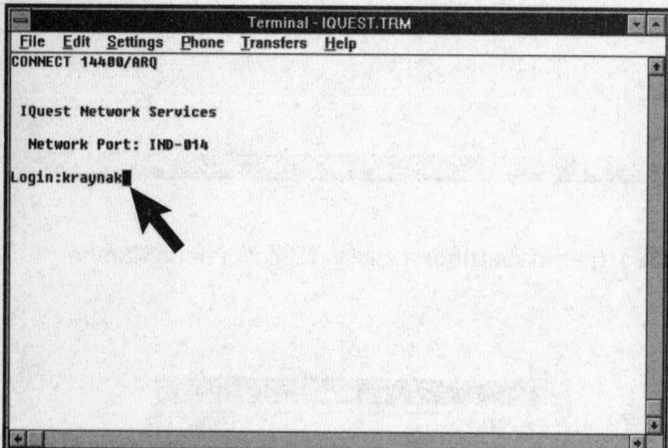

8 The host asks you for your username or login name. Type it at the prompt and press **Enter**.

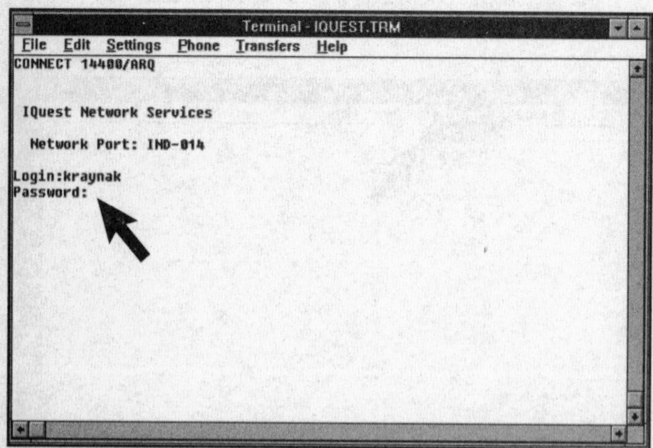

9 The host asks you for your password. Type it at the prompt (you may not see anything, or you may just see asterisks), and then press **Enter**.

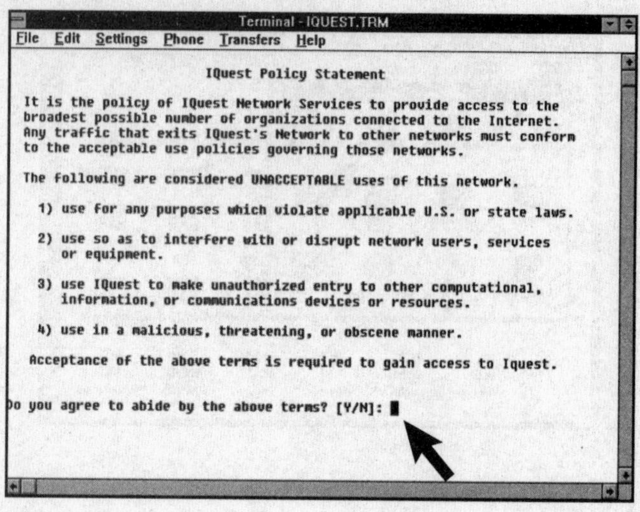

10 You may have to respond to a policy statement or other opening screens. Continue as prompted.

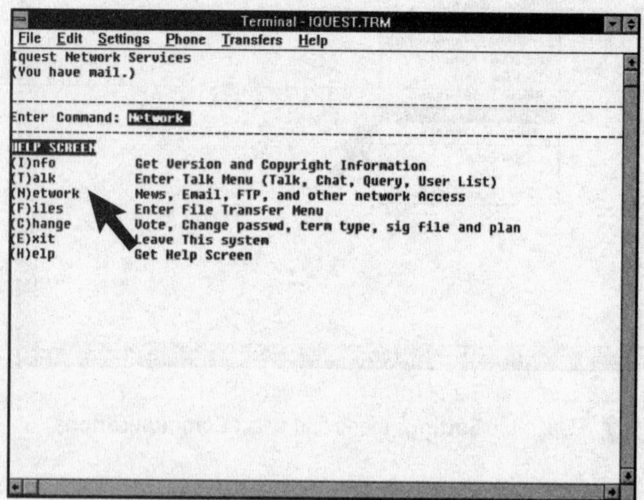

11 The Main menu screen or prompt for the service appears.

Guided Tour Connect to the Internet

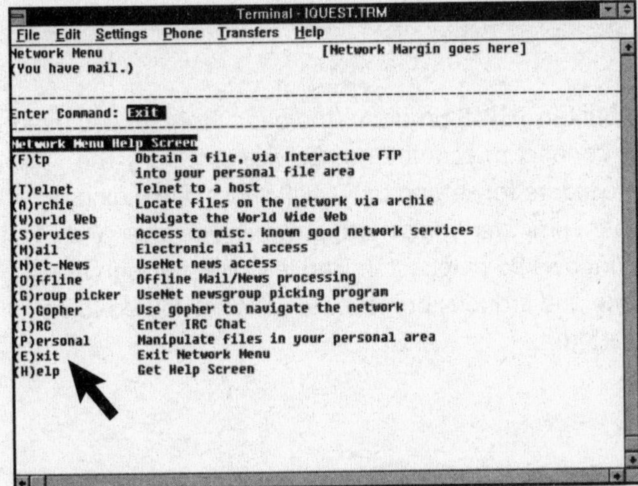

12 Do your work online. Exit from each service as you use it by giving the Quit (**q**) or Exit command.

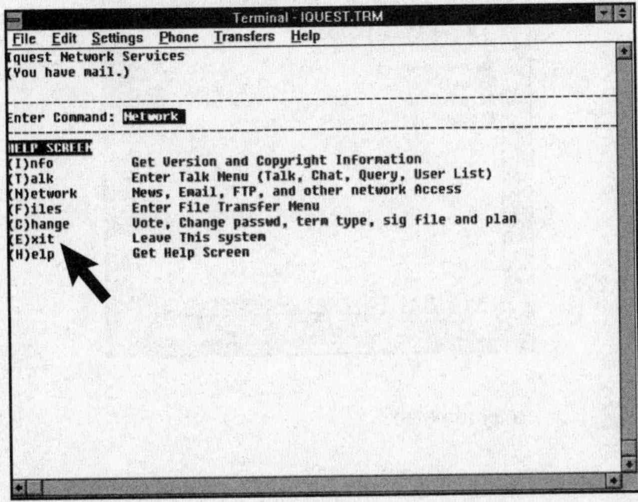

13 To close your Internet connection, return to the Main menu. Choose the **Exit** command. For example, type **E** and press **Enter**. You may see a message such as "Goodbye!" on-screen.

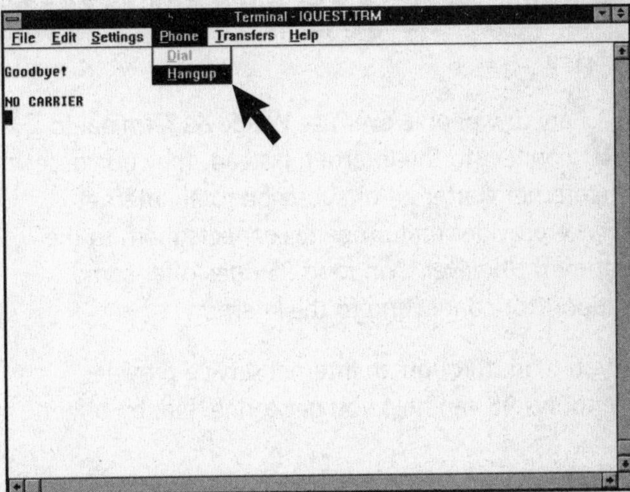

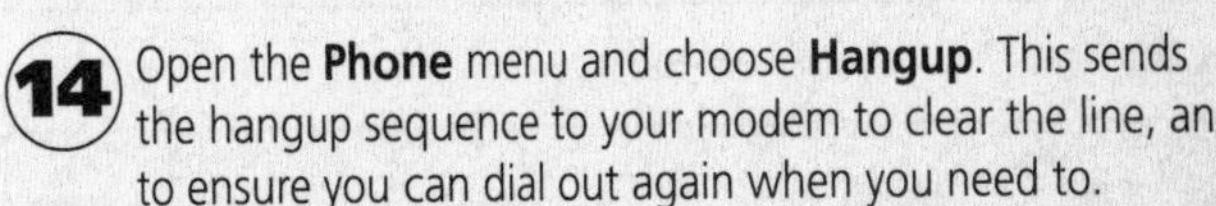
14 Open the **Phone** menu and choose **Hangup**. This sends the hangup sequence to your modem to clear the line, and to ensure you can dial out again when you need to.

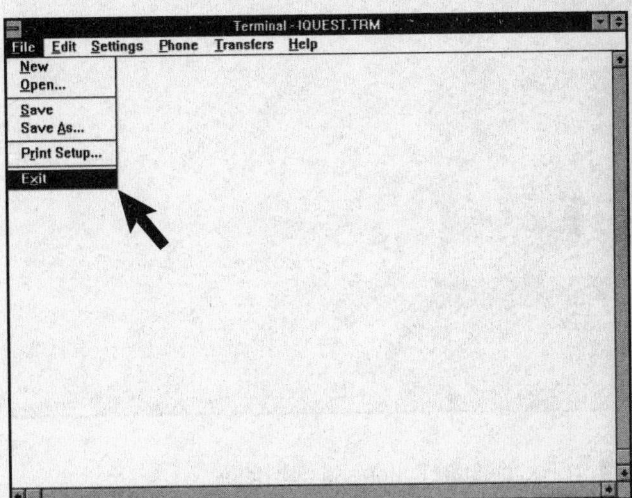

15 Open the **File** menu and choose **Exit** to close Terminal.

Get Wired with Windows 95 Dial-Up Networking

Very few people ever use Windows Terminal to connect to the Internet. Instead, they purchase an Internet starter kit or subscribe to an Internet service provider that properly connects them to the Internet. However, Windows 95 does offer some support for connecting to the Internet.

If you work through an Internet service provider, Windows 95 can help you get connected, by offering a built-in TCP/IP program (the basic program you need to connect to your Internet service provider). The procedure for setting up TCP/IP varies depending on your computer and service provider. However, the Windows 95 help system can lead you through the long and arduous process. Here's what you do to get started:

Begin Guided Tour Connect with Windows 95

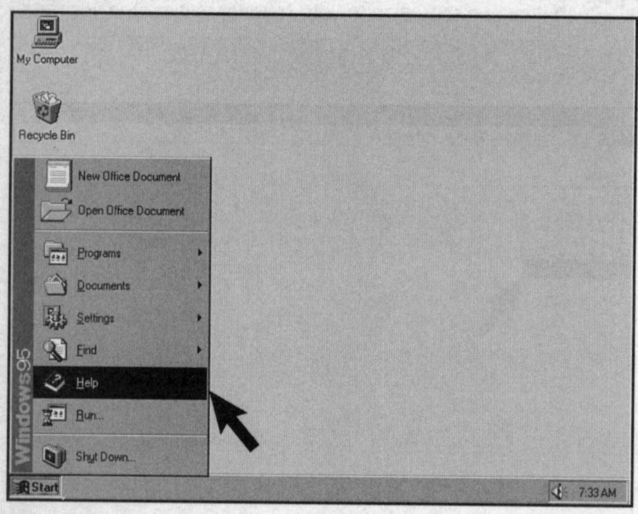

1 Click the **Start** button and click **Help**.

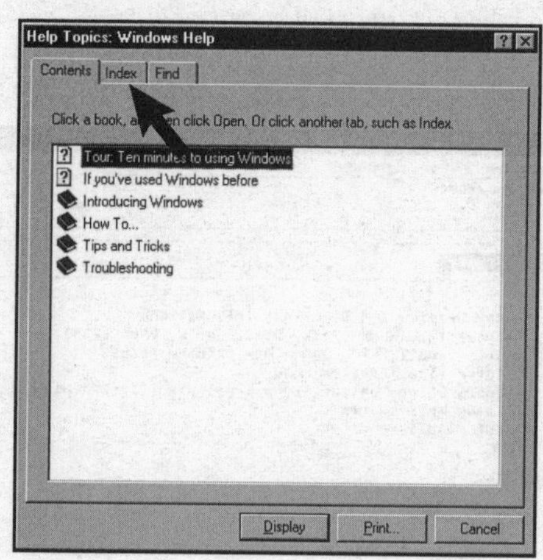

2 Click the **Index** tab.

Guided Tour Connect with Windows 95

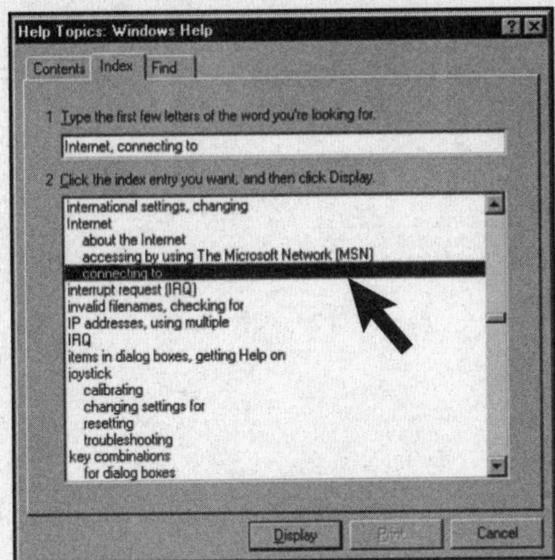

3 In the text box at the top of the index, type **Internet**, and then double-click the **connecting to** entry. The Help window appears, telling you how you can connect to the Internet.

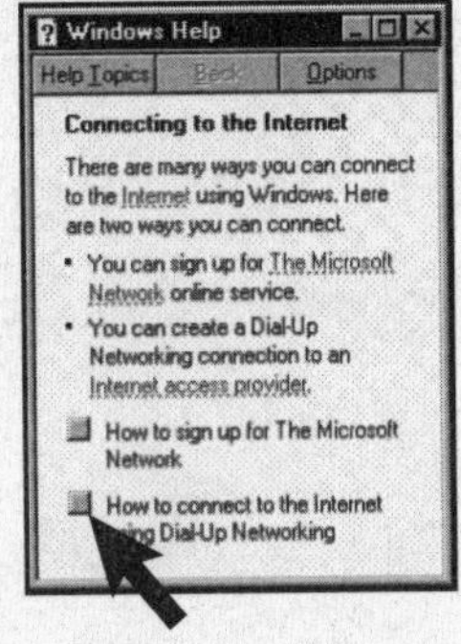

4 Click the button next to **How to connect to the Internet using Dial-Up Networking**. The Help system displays the first of seven steps in the process: finding an Internet service provider.

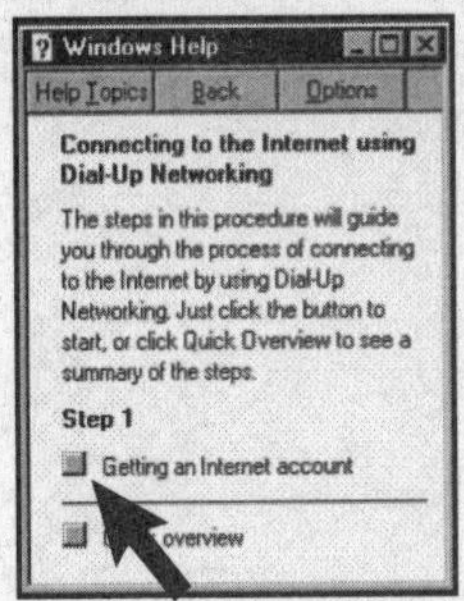

5 Follow the instructions on the screen to connect to your Internet service provider.

PART 2

Do It Yourself...

Say you've had your PC for a few months. You're familiar with Windows now, and you're feeling comfortable behind the keyboard. You've written a few letters, played a few games, maybe even jumped on the information superhighway. However, until now, you relied on someone with a little more computer savvy to help you with the advanced stuff. You haven't felt confident enough to try to install new hardware, clean the inside of your computer, defragment your hard drive, or some of the other advanced but necessary tasks PC owners should be familiar with.

You don't need to rely on anyone else any more. In this part, you will expand your PC knowledge by learning how to do some fundamental (but sometimes scary) PC tasks. By the end of this section, you'll realize that some of those things you were asking friends to do for you really aren't hard at all, and you can do them yourself.

What You Will Find in This Part

Keep Your Computer Clean and Healthy 327

Install New Programs 363

Make Your Computer Work Faster and Better 387

Install New Hardware 415

Keep Your Data Safe 443

DO IT YOURSELF

Keep Your Computer Clean and Healthy

One of the basic requirements of owning a PC is that you keep it clean so it functions properly. If your PC's fan is full of lint, your keyboard is sticky from soda spills and chocolate-smudged fingers, and your monitor is coated with dust, you won't get maximum performance from your PC.

How often you clean your computer depends on where you use it and how much you use it: a PC used eighteen hours a day in an un-air-conditioned construction office will need lots more regular cleaning than a computer used part-time in a fancy, climate-controlled high-rise or your air-conditioned home. Of course, some parts of your PC will need to be cleaned more than others. For example, your keyboard and monitor will probably need to be cleaned more often than the inside of your system unit. When it's time to clean a part of your PC, check with the appropriate task in this section.

What You Will Find in This Section

Clean Your Computer 328

Clean the Monitor 331

Clean Your Printer 333

Clean the Keyboard 336

Clean the Mouse 338

Clean the Disk Drives 341

Clean a CD-ROM Drive 344

Clean a Tape Backup Drive 347

Clean Inside Your Computer 349

Select and Install a Surge Protector 353

First Aid: Spilled Liquid on Keyboard or Mouse 355

First Aid: Unstick a Jammed Disk 360

Clean Your Computer

Computers are a lot like cars: keep your PC in good shape and it'll last a long, long time. Okay, so you don't need to change the oil in your computer or rotate its tires. But it's still a good idea to keep your computer free of dirt and grime by giving it a bath every so often.

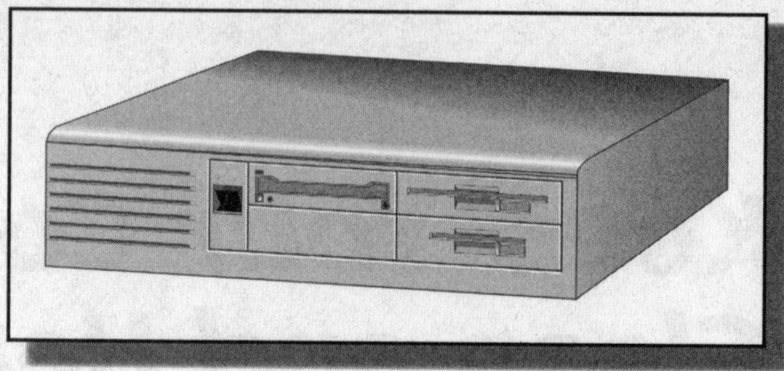

This task talks about general computer cleaning. See the other parts of this section for specifics on cleaning the monitor, keyboard, mouse, disk drives, and other important parts of your computer.

Why bother keeping your computer clean?

- A build-up of dust around the computer can choke off air circulation inside the machine. That makes the PC run hotter, and it won't last as long.
- The same dust can get inside the PC and cover its delicate parts (like the disk drives). This dust can cause premature failure and your computer may just stop working someday or result in lost data.
- Dust and dirt around the drive slots can muck up the disks as you insert and remove them. This might cause you to lose valuable data.
- Dirty connections on the back of your computer can make the accessories you've connected to it (like a printer) malfunction.
- A clean computer is just nicer to use and look at, and safer to use for your valuable data.

You don't need special tools or cleaners to give your computer a good wash. All you need is a regular mild household cleaner (Fantastik and Formula 409 work well), and some paper towels or soft cotton cloths. If you use cloths, be sure they're white; otherwise the color can bleed from the cloth onto your computer!

For a professional, top-notch job, you also need an upright or canister vacuum cleaner with a soft-brush hose attachment. Change the bag before you start, to ensure that the vacuum has good suction. The better the suction, the more thorough the cleaning. By the way, forget those miniature battery-powered vacuums they advertise for cleaning computers. They aren't strong enough.

Begin Do It Yourself Clean the Computer

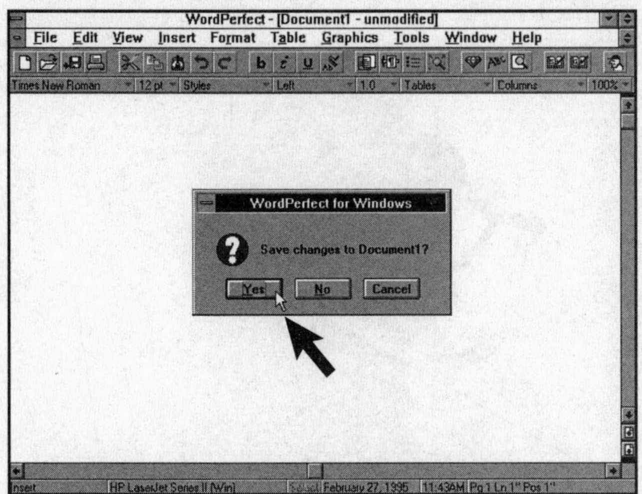

1 If the computer is on, save your work (if necessary), exit any programs that are running, and remove any diskettes in the disk drives. **Turn the PC off** (very important). For added protection, unplug the computer.

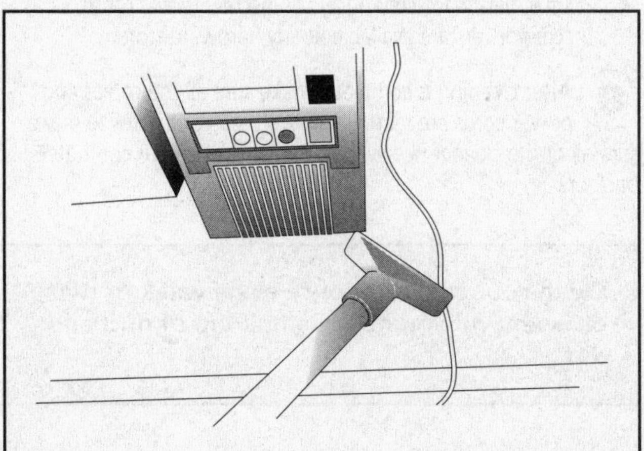

2 Use the soft-brush attachment of a good vacuum to clean around the computer. If the PC is a floor-standing model, it's really important to clean the carpet or floor around the computer thoroughly, as this is a primary source of dust. Your computer is no cleaner than the bed it lies in!

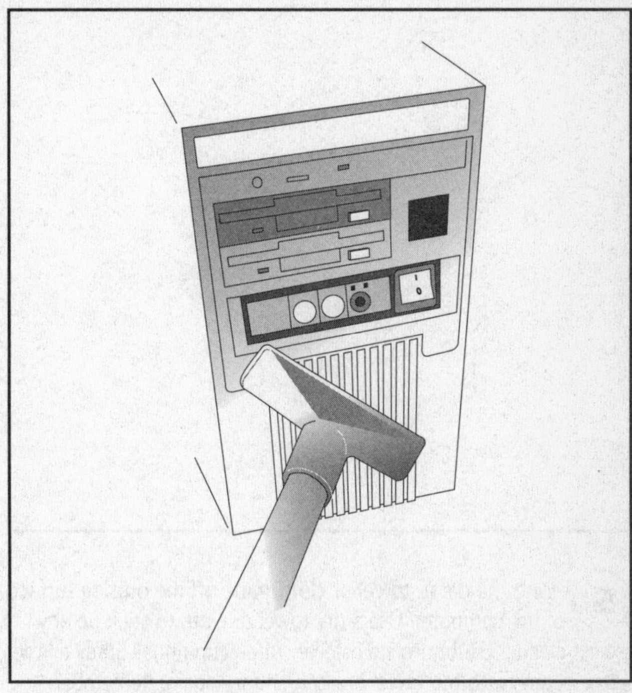

3 Again, using the soft-brush attachment of the vacuum, remove all loose dust inside the ventilation slots, the disk drive openings, and other nooks and crannies.

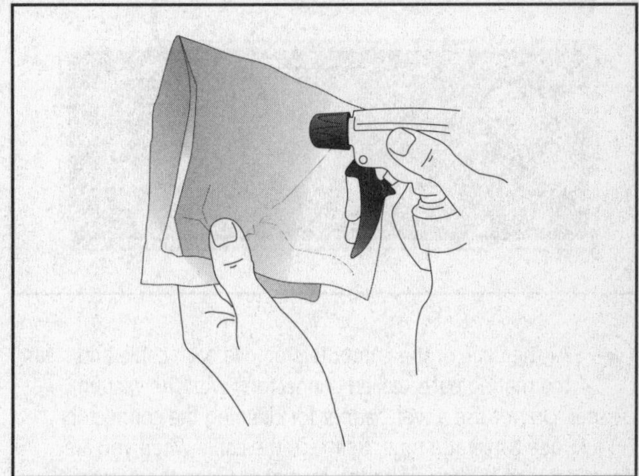

4 Moisten a paper towel or soft cloth with regular household cleaner, like Formula 409 or Fantastik (don't use soaps or detergents, since they leave a residue). *Never spray the cleaner directly on the computer!* Especially don't spray on or in any openings. Don't overwet the towel or cloth.

(continues)

Do It Yourself Clean the Computer

(continued)

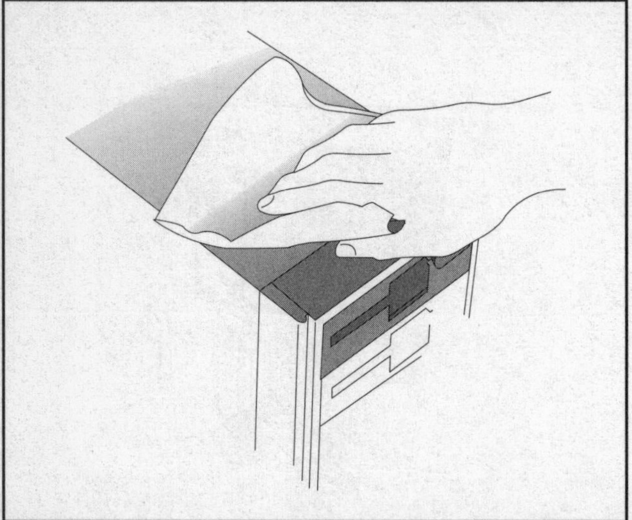

5 Using the damp towel or cloth, wipe off the outside surface of the computer. Use a dry towel or cloth to soak up any excess cleaner. Stubborn stains, like coffee cup rings? Spray a little extra cleaner into the towel or cloth and try again. Remember: don't spray cleaner right on your computer, or else the liquid could drip inside.

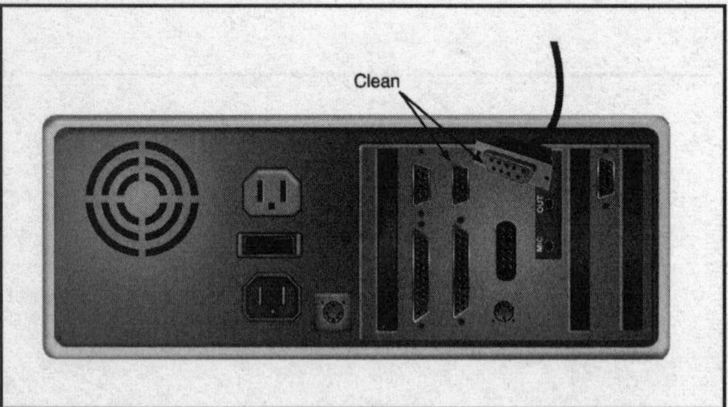

6 At the back of the computer, remove each cable and clean the mating parts (called connectors) with the vacuum cleaner. *Do not use a wet cleaner* for cleaning the connectors. Do just one cable at a time. Reattach the cable when you are done cleaning it, then go to the next one. Clean the power cord, too.

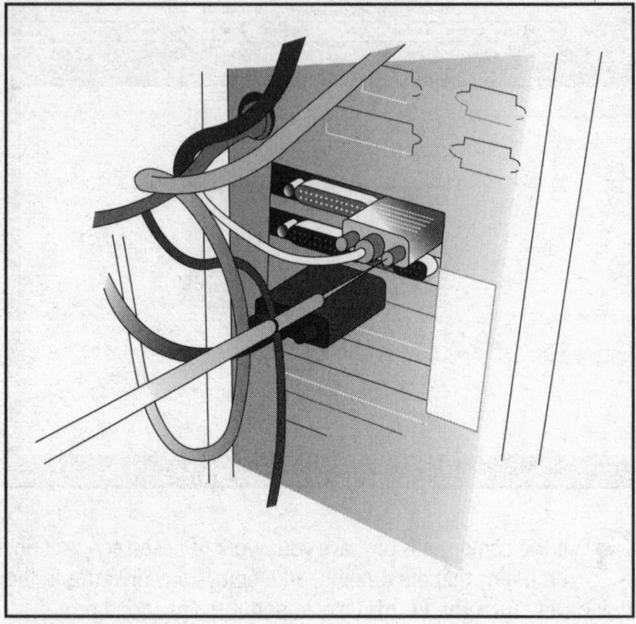

7 If any of the connectors are screwed on, you will need a small flat-head screwdriver to unscrew them. These screwdrivers are available at any hardware store.

8 After cleaning is complete, make sure all the cables and power cords are reattached. Wait a few minutes to make sure all of the cleaner has evaporated, and turn your computer back on.

Clean your computer once every week or two, or whenever you notice a buildup of dust and dirt.

Clean the Monitor

Imagine you have a giant picture window that overlooks the Pacific Ocean. Every night you're treated to beautiful orange-and-red sunsets over a cool blue sea. Now imagine the picture window covered with a thick film of dirt and grease. Hardly the inspiration for romantic sunset dinners.

You'd never think of marring the beauty of nature by letting the picture window stay dirty. Same with your computer monitor. Don't let its sharp, colorful pictures be diminished by a layer of dirt and grime on the screen. Cleaning your computer monitor is one of the simplest jobs you'll do in keeping your computer in top-notch shape, so there's no reason you shouldn't do it on a regular basis.

While keeping your monitor clean is no difficult task, you have to exercise some degree of care to prevent damage. Certain kinds of cleaners can be hazardous to the surfaces of your monitor. Here's what you need in your monitor-cleaning toolkit:

- A soft, white, cotton cloth (a good-quality paper towel is okay, too).
- Household non-residue spray cleaner, like Formula 409 or Fantastik. Stay away from soaps or detergents, as these leave residue. *Don't* use furniture cleaner, because many brands contain an ingredient that can actually attract dust.
- Some cotton swabs (otherwise known as Q-Tips).

- For a really good job, a special anti-static cloth. This cloth, available at almost any photographic supply store, is specially prepared with an anti-static "coating." Wiping something with the cloth helps reduce static that can attract dust.

Because your computer's monitor is your porthole into what your PC is doing, you ought to clean it every week or so, or whenever you notice build-up of dust. You'll notice that the more you use your computer, the more the screen will attract dust. Why? When the monitor is on, the screen creates an electrostatic field, which attracts dust.

Begin Do It Yourself Clean Your Monitor

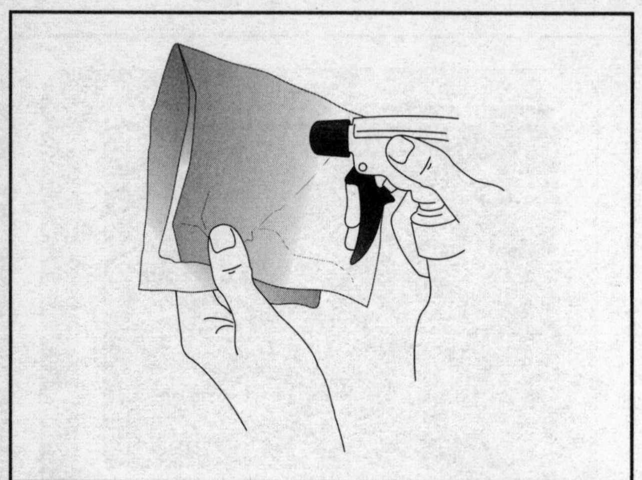

1 With the monitor off, spray some household cleaner onto the cloth. Don't spray too much; you just want the cloth damp, not soaking.

2 Use the cloth to wipe clean the cabinet of the monitor. If the monitor hasn't been cleaned for a while, it will probably have caked-on grime that will need some extra cleaner. Instead of applying lots of cleaner to the trouble spots (the excess cleaner may seep inside the monitor), use the regular amount and just go over the same area a few more times.

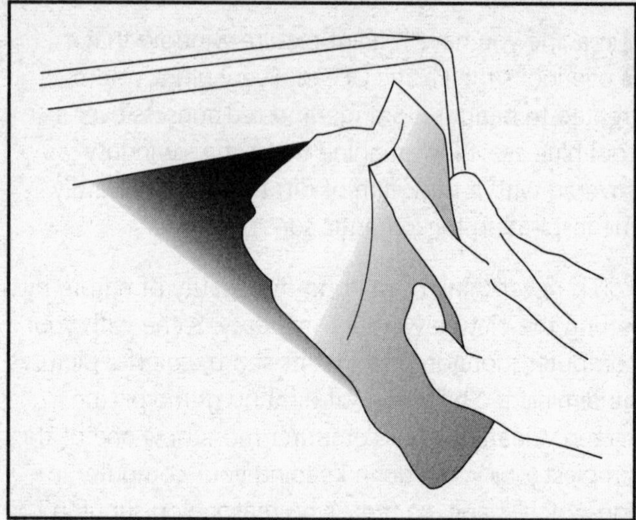

3 If there's any dust or dirt caught in the ventilation slots or other nooks-and-crannies of the monitor, dampen some cotton-tipped swabs with cleaner, then use the swabs to clean the hard-to-reach places. Remember: not too much cleaner. Use a dry cloth to wipe off any remaining cleaner.

4 Wet another cloth with plain water, and use it to clean off the monitor screen. Window cleaner is generally not recommended unless it is specifically designed for both glass and plastic surfaces. Regular window cleaner might harm the plastic coating used on some anti-glare screens.

5 If you opted for the anti-static cloth, let the screen dry. Then use the cloth to wipe off the surface. Keep the cloth handy and use it on a weekly (or even daily) basis to keep dust off the monitor screen.

Clean Your Printer

Just about everyone's least favorite *Peanuts* cartoon strip character is Pigpen, a slovenly youth who always leaves a trial of grit behind him. Pigpen doesn't take care of himself, and his appearance shows it. No one wants to be around Pigpen's dust cloud, and he has few friends because of it.

Would you believe that Pigpen serves as an excellent example of how appearances mean everything? No, you wouldn't believe that? In that case, we'll just come right out and say it: A dirty printer makes for dirty documents. Because no one sees your fancy Armani suit when they read a letter you sent them, their opinion of you is formed almost completely from the document they hold in their hands. Though the logic is sometimes strange, it's true: a dirty or smudged document must mean the person who prepared it is a Pigpen. And therefore has no friends.

If you want to win friends and influence people, a great way to start is making sure your printer is producing the fine, high-quality pages it's designed to produce. A minute spent cleaning the outside (and sometimes the inside) every now and then can help guarantee your documents come out crisp and sharp. And, regular cleaning helps keep your printer running in tip-top shape, and might even help prevent premature failure.

Most folks have one of three types of printers: laser, inkjet, or dot-matrix. Cleaning the outside of these three types is generally the same; cleaning the innards differs, because they all use different printing technologies. In the "Do It Yourself" section that follows, we provide instructions for general printer cleaning. (For deep-down inside cleaning, you will want to refer to the manual that came with the printer; the manufacturer may want you to perform some very specific cleaning steps required for the exact model you are using.)

What do you need to clean your printer? Not much. Here's a short list:

- Paper towels.
- Ordinary household cleaner, like Fantastik or 409.
- A medium-sized (half-inch-wide or so) soft artists brush.
- Some cotton-tipped swabs (otherwise known as Q-Tips).
- Printer cleaner paper.

The printer cleaner paper described here is available at most any computer store. Different versions are available for different printer types (and some printer models), so make sure you buy the right kind. The cleaner paper is designed to feed through your printer like regular paper; in doing so, it picks up excess gunk that is otherwise hard to reach by hand. Most printer paper can be reused, though usually not more than five to ten times. The cleaning paper represents the easiest and safest way of cleaning the internal parts of your computer.

For heavy deposits of grime, put the cleaner paper through the printer several times, then throw the gross thing away when you're done.

Begin Do It Yourself Clean the Printer

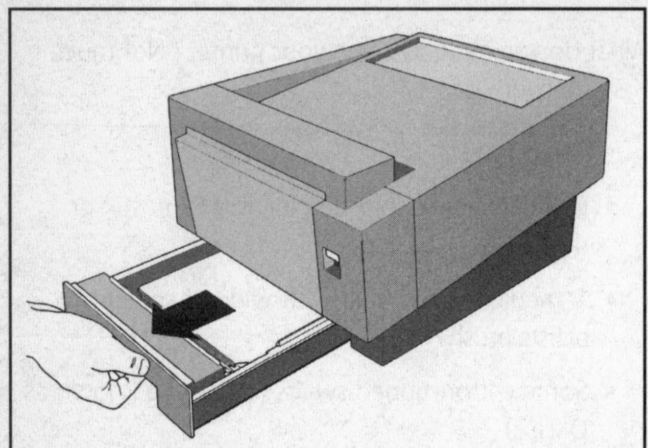

1 Remove all paper from the printer. If you're using a laser or inkjet printer, remove the paper tray.

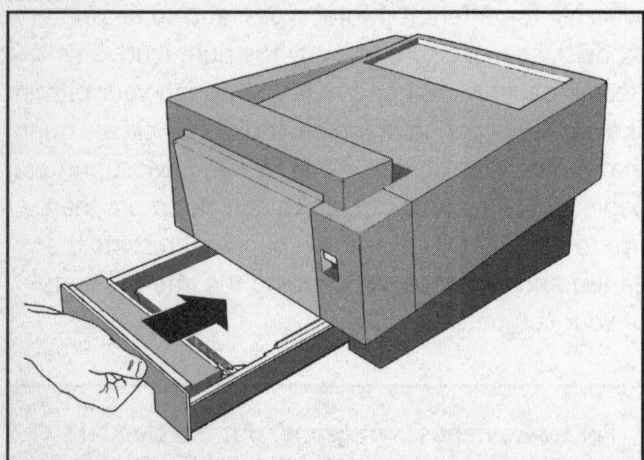

2 If you're using a paper tray, take all the paper out of the tray; set it aside. Clean out the empty tray by wiping it with a dry paper towel. Be sure to get all the dirt and paper dust out. Put the paper back in when you're finished.

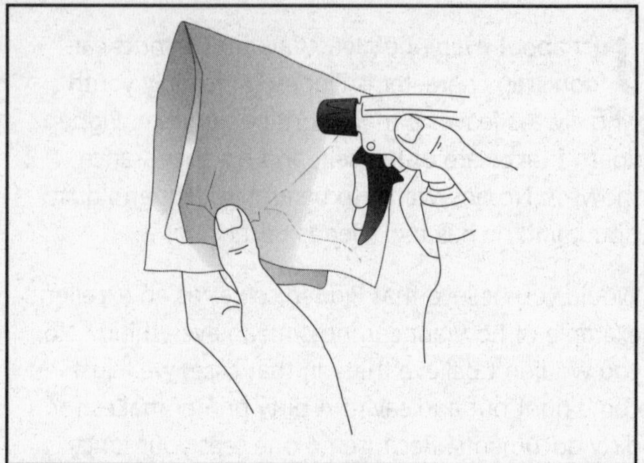

3 With the printer turned off, clean the outside of it, using the household spray and paper towels. Lightly spray the household cleaner into a towel, and use the damp towel to remove any dust and dirt on the printer.

4 For laser printers, press the **Release** button to open the printer so you can access the insides. Use the soft brush to gently wipe away any dirt and paper dust that may have accumulated. Close the printer when you're done.

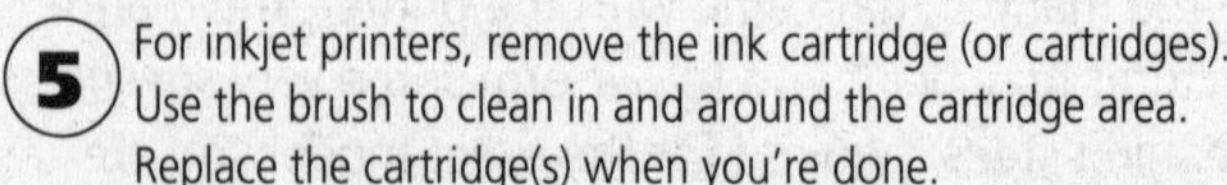

5 For inkjet printers, remove the ink cartridge (or cartridges). Use the brush to clean in and around the cartridge area. Replace the cartridge(s) when you're done.

6 For dot-matrix printers, use the brush to clean any loose dirt or paper dust that has accumulated around the paper platen, as well as around the print head.

Do It Yourself Clean the Printer

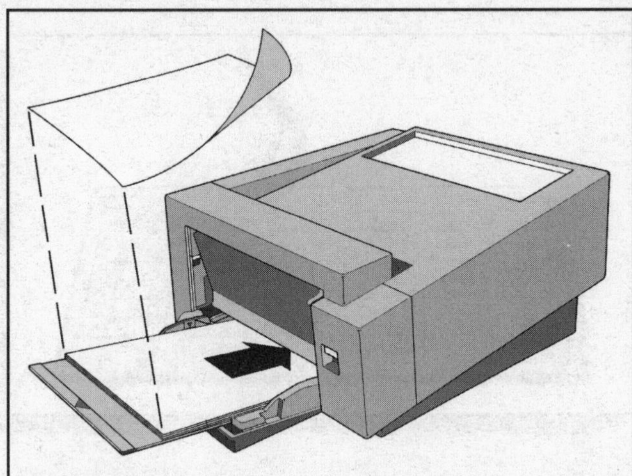

7 Load a sheet of cleaner paper into the printer. (When using a laser or ink jet printer, load the cleaner paper on top of the regular paper; when using a dot-matrix printer, simply load the paper into the platen.) Be sure to observe proper orientation, as the cleaner paper is usually designed to go in one way. The paper may jam in the printer if you put it in backwards or upside-down.

8 Turn the printer on; if necessary, let it warm up.

9 Print a blank page using a word processor or text editor. (When using Windows, for example, start the Windows Notepad program.) In the blank (empty) document screen of Notepad, choose **File**, **Print**. Printing starts immediately. After the cleaning paper is pushed through the printer, remove it completely and store it for future use.

Clean the Keyboard

No other part of your computer gets as grimy and yucky as the keyboard. And no wonder: you spend the day pounding on the keys and getting them all dirty. The little slots and openings between the keys seem to trap airborne dust willies, not to mention crumbs from those Cheetos you've been eating. And—sorry, this part is pretty gross—junk from your hair (and your beard if you have one of those) can fall into the keyboard, scuzzing up the works even more.

Okay, so now you know the bad news. The good news is that cleaning your keyboard is a simple job you can do any time. And it makes for great excuses. Like maybe when your boss calls you to an important meeting ("not now, I'm cleaning my keyboard"), or your mom phones you long distance from Des Moines ("gotta run, Mom, my 'S' key is sticking").

Here are the things you need to clean a keyboard:

- Some high-quality paper towels.
- Household non-residue spray cleaner, like Formula 409 or Fantastik. Don't use soaps, detergents, or furniture cleaner.
- A soft artist's brush, about a half- to three-quarters of an inch wide.

Begin Do It Yourself Clean Your Keyboard

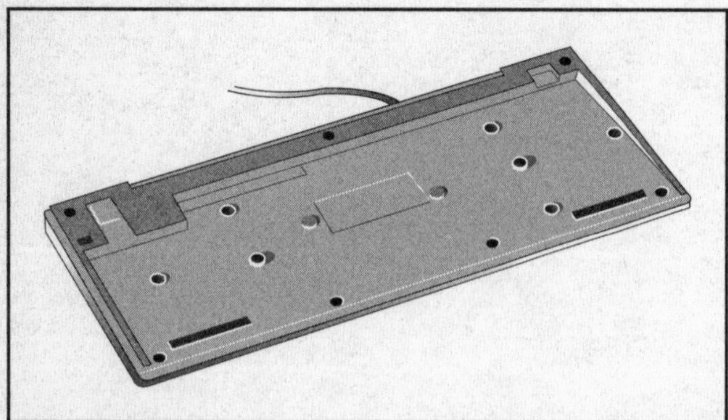

1. With the computer off, lay several paper towels on the desk. Turn the keyboard over and gently shake out the excess gunk. If there's an accumulation of dirt inside, gently tap on the back side of the keyboard to dislodge the excess.

2. Turn the keyboard back over. Use the brush to whisk out any remaining dirt, furballs, and other foreign matter from in between the keys.

Do It Yourself Clean Your Keyboard

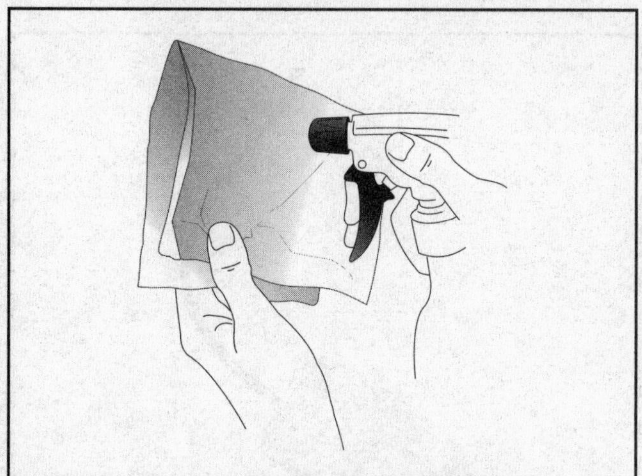

3 Spray some household cleaner onto the cloth. Don't spray too much; you just want the cloth damp, not soaking.

4 Use the cloth to wipe clean the tops of the keys. If the keyboard hasn't been cleaned for a while, it will probably have caked on grime that will need some extra cleaner. Instead of applying lots of cleaner to the trouble spots (the excess cleaner may seep inside the monitor), though, use the regular amount and just go over the same area a few more times.

5 With a dry cloth, wipe off any excess cleaner from the keys, especially if any cleaner has seeped between the keys. Wait ten minutes for all the cleaner to evaporate before turning the computer back on.

Tip of the day: You get best results when you clean the keyboard often. A build up of muck can cause the keyboard to malfunction, requiring that it be replaced. Most computer keyboards are fairly inexpensive, and they can be replaced for under $50. But there's no sense in spending that money if you don't need to. Keep your keyboard in shipshape and it'll last longer.

Clean the Mouse

Thanks to Microsoft Windows, most computers—whether they are used in the office or at home—have a mouse. This little contraption lets you move an on-screen pointer by pushing a small box around the desk. The mouse works by rolling action: as you push the mouse, a ball underneath the thing turns, which controls the pointer on the computer's screen.

No matter how good a housekeeper you are, in time the ball (and the delicate insides of the mouse) will get gritty and dirty. Periodic cleaning keeps the mouse in top shape, and prevents premature wear. It also helps prevent these annoying side effects:

- The pointer "skips" and drags when you push the mouse. That is, instead of moving in a smooth motion, the pointer freezes then zooms whenever you push the mouse.
- The pointer doesn't move at all when you push the mouse. Although this problem can also be caused by such things as a mouse that isn't plugged in, it's also a sign that the mouse is dirty, especially if the pointer moves in one direction—like up and down—but not in the other direction.
- You hear crunching noises when you roll the mouse.

All of these are good indications that the mouse is dirty, and should be cleaned. You're better off, however, if you don't wait for signs like these to happen before cleaning your mouse. It can be very difficult to remove months and months (or years and years) of dirty build-up inside the mouse. And dirty insides can wear down the rubber ball in the underbelly of the mouse. When the ball gets pitted and worn because of dirt, the mouse has to be replaced. They don't often sell replacement mouse balls, so you have to fork out for a whole new mouse, not just the ball.

You don't need anything special to clean the mouse. Often, just a facial tissue (a.k.a. Kleenex) is all that's

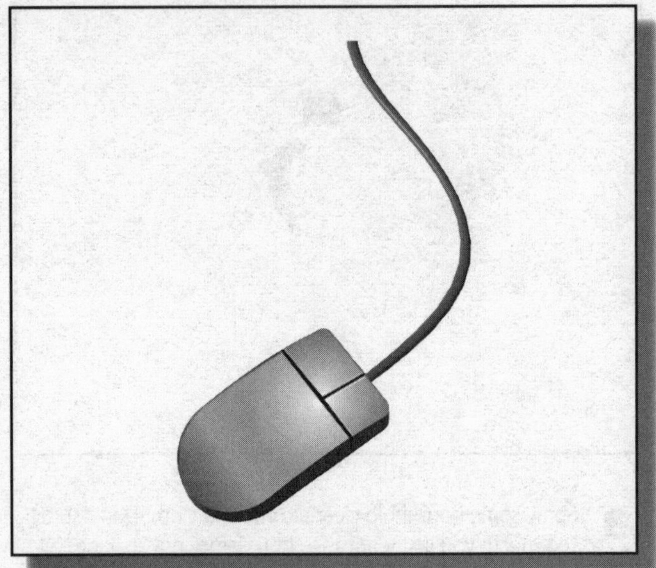

required. But if the mouse suffers from a severe case of the grungies, you should add the following items to your cleaning repertoire:

- A pencil with an eraser. Just an ordinary eraser on an ordinary pencil will do. But the eraser should be clean.
- A couple of round toothpicks. Better yet, an "orange stick" from a manicuring set.
- A small (quarter-inch-wide) artist's brush.

You can purchase a mouse cleaner kit from most computer stores. About the only ingredient of the kit that's really worth the purchase price is the special cleaner engineered for use on the rubber mouse ball. This is the only cleaner you should use with the mouse ball. Do not use household cleaners, soaps, detergents, alcohol, or anything else (in a pinch, you can use a little bit of water to remove excess crud from the ball).

Remember: Don't use cleaning fluid on the mouse ball. The fluid might dry out the rubber.

Begin Do It Yourself Clean Your Mouse

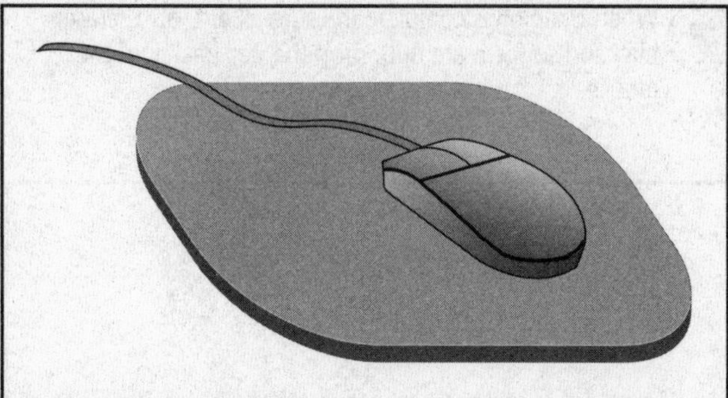

1 Inspect the mouse pad, if you use one. A mouse pad that is old, worn out, or visibly dirty should be replaced. They're cheap these days, and depending on how often you use your computer, you may want to consider replacing the mouse pad every six to twelve months. Don't use a mouse pad? You should. It'll provide a better surface for your mouse, and will actually help clean the mouse while you use it. When buying a new pad, choose only the cloth-covered ones, not the cheap plastic ones.

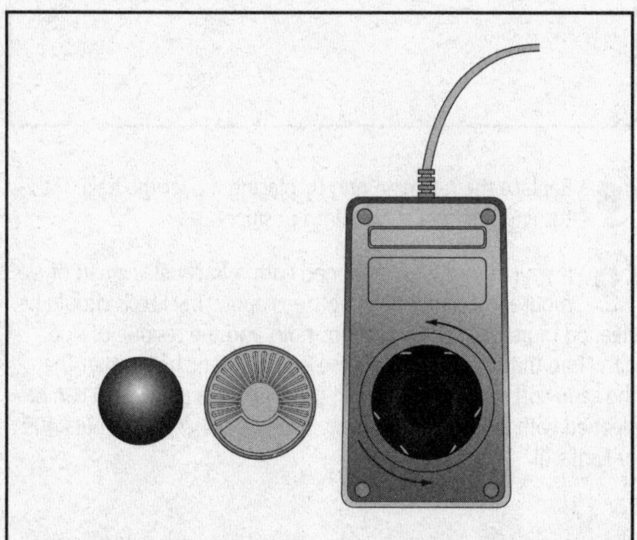

2 With the computer off, turn the mouse over and carefully remove the ball. On many brands of mice, this is done by twisting a plastic retaining ring a quarter or a half turn. If you're not sure how to remove the retaining ring, and find no instructions printed on the bottom of the mouse, consult the manual that came with the mouse. Forcing the ring can break it, and you'll end up having to replace the entire mouse.

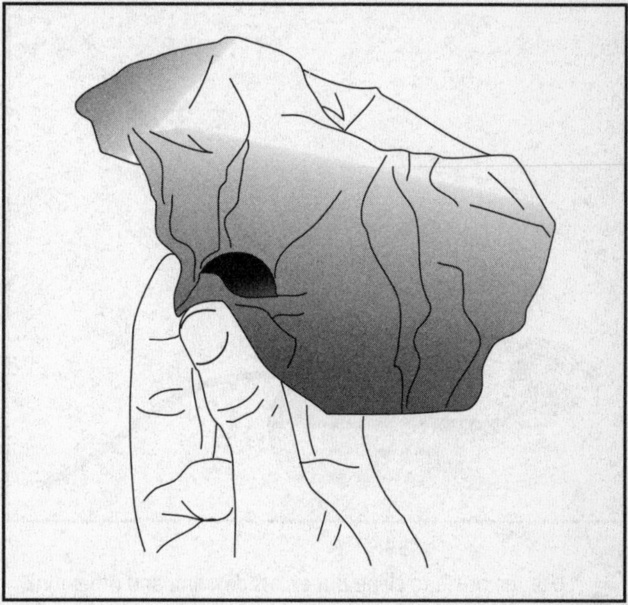

3 With the ring removed, empty the ball into your hand. Be careful not to drop it. The mouse ball is made of a special kind of rubber that can be permanently deformed if it's allowed to drop on a hard surface.

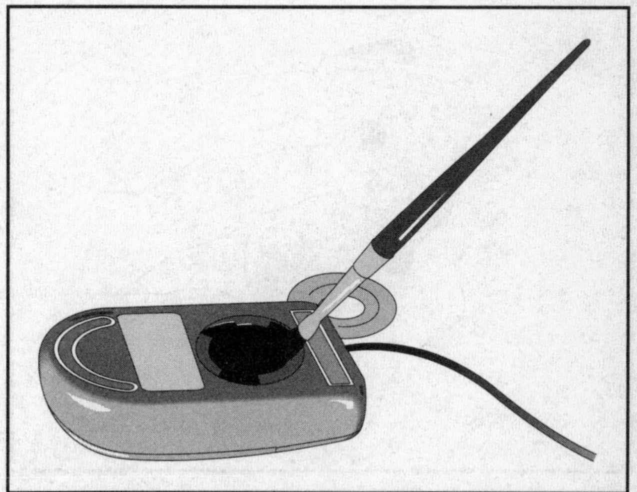

4 Use the facial tissue to wipe off the ball. If the mouse is extra dirty, use a small amount of water to help clean it off. If you're using a mouse cleaning kit, you can use the special cleaner that comes with the kit. Do not use any other kind of cleaner, especially ***not*** a cleaner containing alcohol. The alcohol can dry out the rubber of the ball, and ruin it.

(continues)

Do It Yourself Clean Your Mouse

(continued)

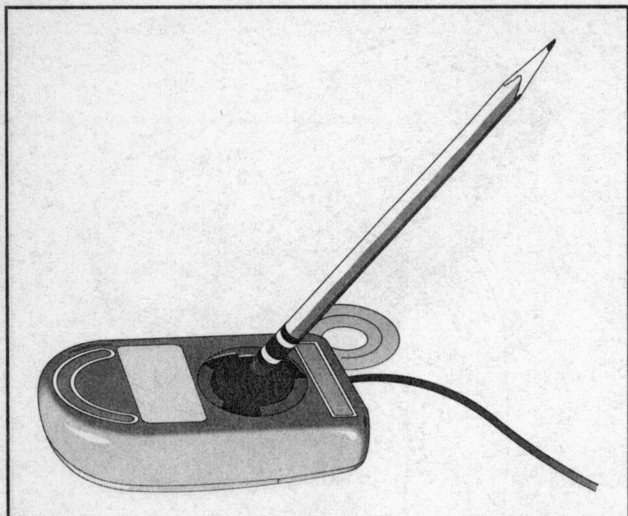

5 Use the brush to clean out excess dirt, lint, and other junk from the inside of the mouse. Avoid trying to blow out the gunk, with either your own breath or a can of compressed air. All this usually does is force the dirt deeper into the mouse.

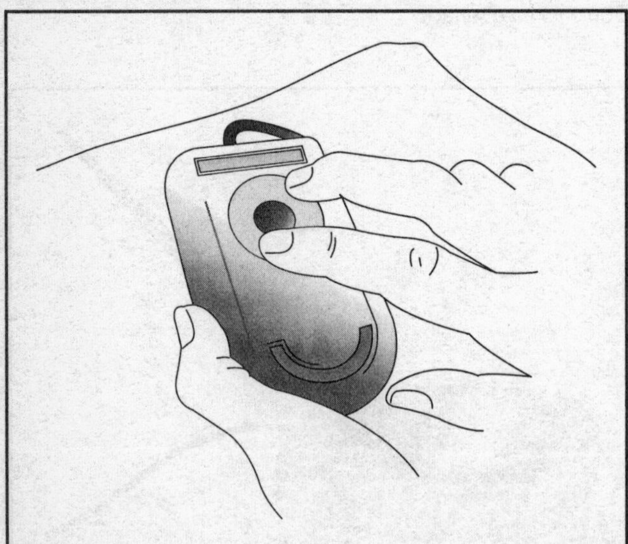

6 Rollers inside the mouse transmit the rolling of the ball as a signal to the computer; often dirt gets caked on these. This dirt is best removed with toothpicks and a pencil eraser. If you use the eraser, be sure errant eraser bits don't get trapped inside the mouse. Wipe out the insides of the mouse frequently when you are cleaning the rollers. For best results, the rollers should be completely free of caked-on grime. Any foreign matter will interfere with the smooth operation of the mouse.

When cleaning is complete (be sure all dirt, dust, eraser bits, and so forth are out), drop the ball back into the mouse.

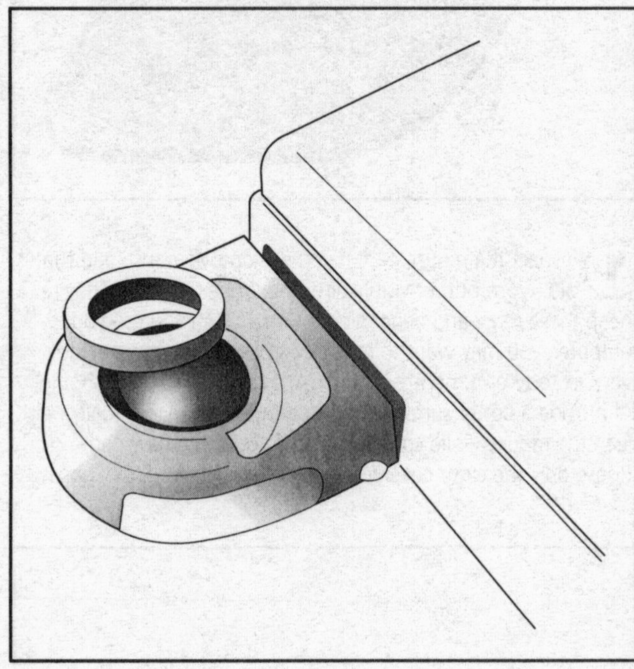

8 Replace the retaining ring by placing it over the ball, and turning it to lock it back into position.

9 If your computer is equipped with a trackball instead of a mouse, the same cleaning steps apply. Trackballs should be cleaned more frequently to remove dirt and the residue of skin oils. Note that most trackballs use a hard plastic ball, rather then the semi-soft rubber ball used in a mouse. This plastic ball can be cleaned with an ordinary household cleaner, such as Formula 409 or Fantastik.

Clean the Disk Drives

There's nothing more critical to the operation of your PC than the cleanliness of the floppy disk drives. Everyone uses the floppy disk drives of their computer at least every once in a while, even if the PC is equipped with a hard disk drive. The floppy drives are used to install new programs, share data with others, and make backups of the hard disk drive.

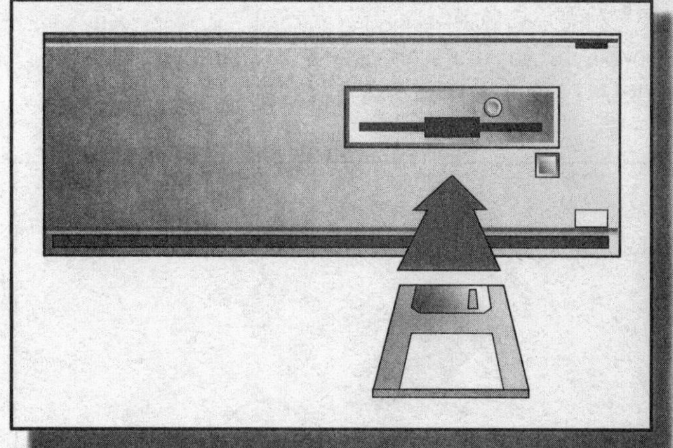

Floppy disk drives get dirty in three ways:

- The magnetic coating used to store data rubs off the floppy disk and collects on the magnetic heads used by the drive to read the data from the disk.
- Dust and grime from the outside gets inside the drive when you insert a dirty disk.
- Dust naturally settles inside the floppy disk drive over time.

Any amount of dust and dirt can prove injurious to the data on a disk, and can even damage a floppy disk drive. Dirt is gritty, and this grit can shorten the life of your disks and disk drives. In addition, a heavy layer of dirt makes electronic components run hotter, which can shorten their life expectancy.

If you clean nothing else on your computer you should clean the floppy disk drives. If you don't, you run an increased risk of someday losing some valuable data. Unless your computer is used in a very dusty environment, you can adequately clean the floppy disk drives with a commercial disk-drive-cleaning kit, available at most any computer store. The cleaning kit is designed to remove the buildup of the magnetic coating (as well as dirt) that can collect on the magnetic heads inside the drive. Using the kit every couple of months can help prevent data loss, and can actually prolong the life of your disks and disk drives. As an added precaution against dirty disk drives, store your floppy disks in a box or disk caddy, to prevent the disks from getting dusty.

The "Do It Yourself" that follows assumes you're using a kit designed for cleaning floppy disk drives. These directions are generic and the pictures show cleaning 5 1/4-inch disk drives (kits are also available for 3 1/2-inch drives); for specifics, read the instructions that come with the cleaning kit.

Are your disk drives really dirty inside? You should remove the cover of the PC and clean inside, including the disk drives, as explained in "Clean Inside Your Computer" on page 349.

Begin Do It Yourself Clean the Drives

1 Leaving the computer turned on, remove any disks from the disk drives. (Removing any disks may seem pretty obvious, but you'd be surprised how many times people have tried to clean the floppy drives with a disk still inside!)

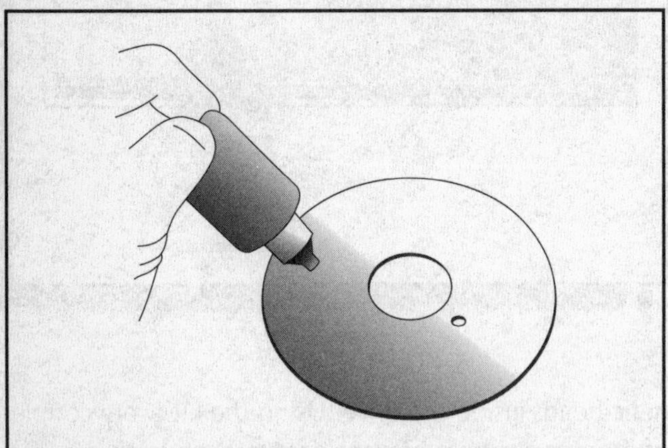

2 Use the cleaning spray included with the cleaning kit; liberally coat the cleaning-pad disk. Spray both sides of the disk; there are two magnetic heads inside the floppy disk drive: one for the top of the disk, one for the bottom.

3 Insert the cleaning-pad disk into its carrier. Make sure it fits all the way in.

4 Insert the cleaning-pad disk and carrier into the floppy disk drive, just as if it were a regular floppy disk; make sure the opening of the carrier goes in first.

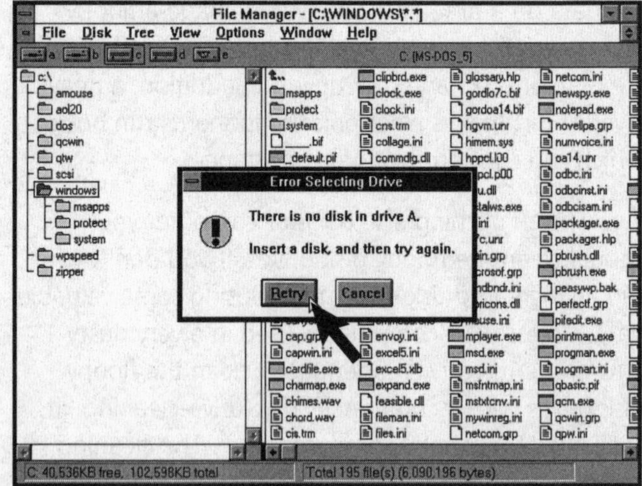

5 If you are using Windows 3.11, activate the disk drive by starting the **File Manager**. Click the icon for the disk drive containing the cleaning pad disk, either **A** or **B**. File Manager will indicate an error, that the disk is unreadable. Click **Retry** several times to reactivate the drive. (Activation turns the pad, which cleans the magnetic heads in the disk drive.) If your cleaning kit comes with a program disk, use that program to activate the disk drives.

Do It Yourself Clean the Drives

```
C:\>A:

Not ready reading drive A
Abort, Retry, Fail?
```

6 If you are using DOS, at the DOS prompt type the letter of the drive that contains the cleaning disk, followed by a colon, such as **A:** or **B:**. Then press **Enter** to activate the disk drive. After a moment, an error message appears, telling you the disk could not be read. Choose **Retry** a few times to reactivate the drive.

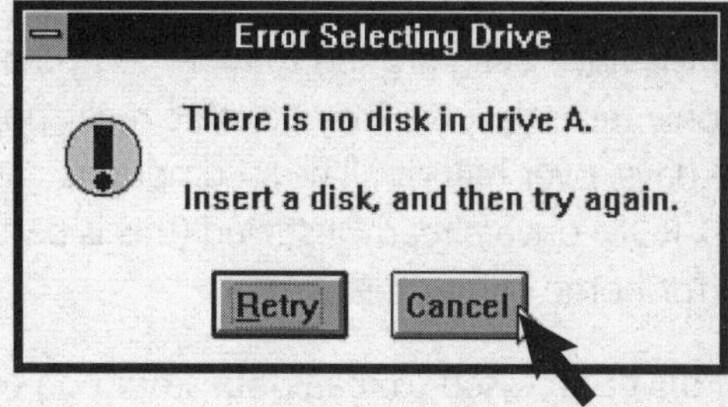

7 When you are done cleaning, remove the cleaning disk. If using the Windows Program Manager, choose **Cancel** to stop reading the floppy disk. If using DOS, choose **Fail** to tell the computer you no longer wish to access the disk drive (you may have to choose **Fail** more than once).

8 Repeats steps 3 through 7 to clean the other floppy disk drive, if your computer is so equipped. IMPORTANT: After cleaning, wait at least five minutes (ten minutes is even better) for all the cleaning solution that remains in the floppy disk drives to evaporate. This is an important step; trying to use a regular disk with wet read/write heads may cause even more build-up of magnetic coating on the heads inside the drive.

Clean a CD-ROM Drive

CD-ROMs have been around for over ten years, but only recently have they become really popular. These days, over half of all new computers come with a CD-ROM drive already installed (this is particularly true for home computers).

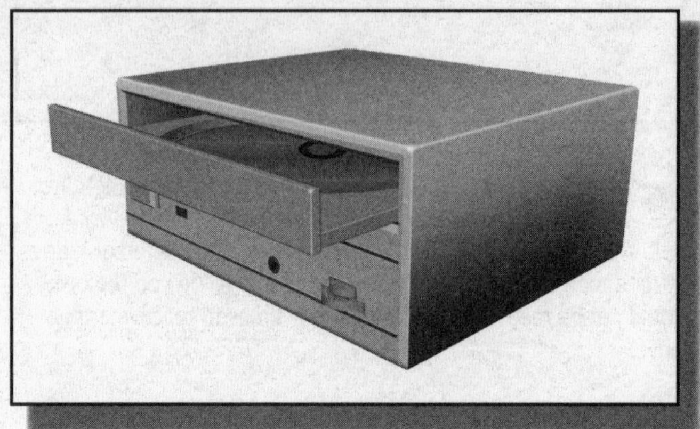

CD-ROM drives are used to read data stored on five-inch plastic discs. The discs look just like audio CDs. In fact, they are exactly the same, except that a CD-ROM is designed to hold computer data instead of music. The big advantage of CD-ROM is that one disc can store about 600 million bytes of information. That's equivalent to roughly 500 high-density floppy disks!

Just like everything else in your computer, CD-ROM drives are prone to get dirty—especially the optical lens through which the disc is read. And when they get dirty, they don't work as well. The most common symptom of a dirty CD-ROM drive is something called *random read errors*. This simply means that the drive fails to read data, and does so on a more-or-less random basis. The software that controls the CD-ROM in your computer compensates for a lot of these random read errors (the disk just re-reads the bad part), but it can't compensate for lots of errors. The result is a cryptic error message that says something like **Drive X not ready**, or worse, a malfunctioning program.

Fortunately, CD-ROM drives don't often get as dirty as other parts of your computer, and cleaning them is a rather straightforward task. For best results, use a commercial CD cleaning kit to keep your CD-ROM drive in tip-top shape. Since the basic mechanism of a CD-ROM is identical to that of a home audio CD player, you can use a regular audio CD cleaning kit, which is essentially designed to clean the lens (you should not attempt to clean the lens manually, as this could damage the fragile mounting of the lens). There's no need to spend extra for an overpriced "CD-ROM cleaning kit."

The do-it-yourself that follows assumes you're using a CD cleaning kit, most of which consists of a cleaning disk and cleaning solution. These directions are generic; read the instructions that come with the cleaning kit you use for specifics.

Begin Do It Yourself Clean a CD-ROM Drive

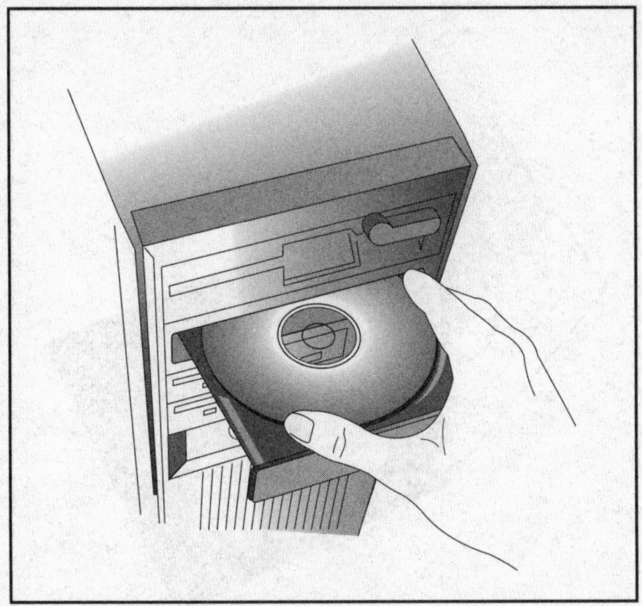

1 With your computer on, remove any discs in your CD-ROM drive. If your CD-ROM drive is the kind that uses disc caddies, have an empty caddy ready.

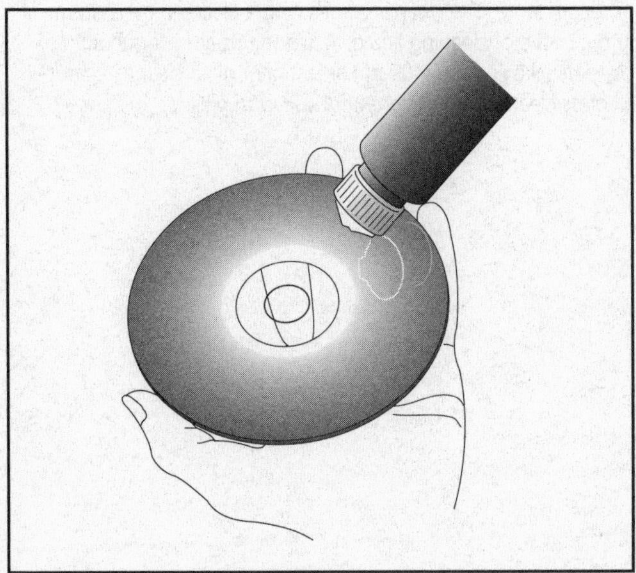

2 Use the cleaner that comes with the kit to coat the cleaning disk. Don't apply too much cleaner.

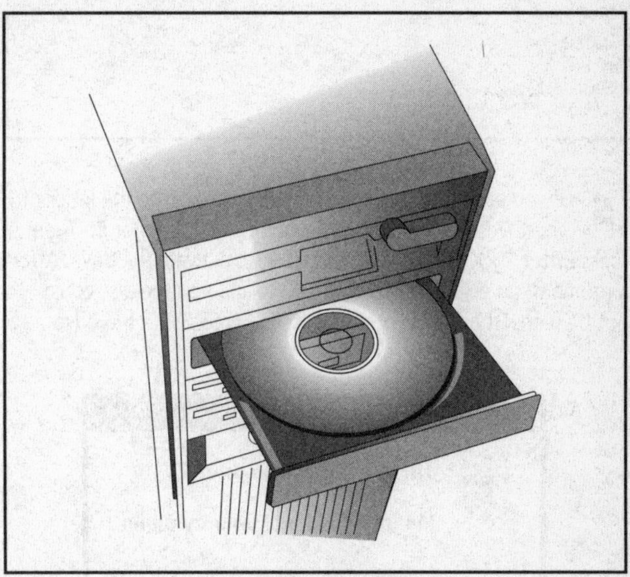

3 Insert the cleaning disk into the CD-ROM drive (put the cleaning disk in a caddy if your drive requires a caddy).

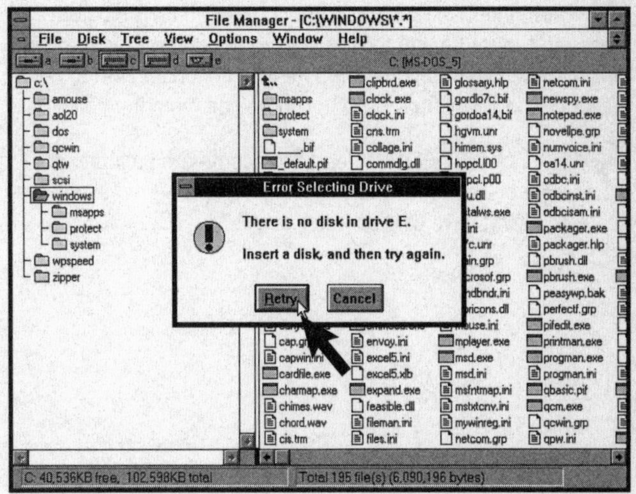

4 If you are using Windows 3.11, activate the CD-ROM drive by starting the **File Manager** (if using Windows 95, open the **Explorer**). Click the icon for the CD-ROM, such as **D** or **E**. File Manager will indicate an error, that the disk is unreadable. Click **Retry** several times to reactivate the drive. (Activation turns the pad, which cleans the CD-ROM drive.) If your cleaning kit comes with a program disk, use that program to activate the disk drives.

(continues)

Do It Yourself Clean a CD-ROM Drive

(continued)

```
C:\>A:

Not ready reading drive A
Abort, Retry, Fail?
```

5 If you are using DOS, at the DOS prompt type the letter of the CD-ROM, followed by a colon, such as **D:** or **E:**. Then press **Enter**. Type **DIR**, and press **Enter**, to activate the drive. After a moment, an error message appears telling you the disc could not be read. Choose **Retry** a few times to reactivate the drive.

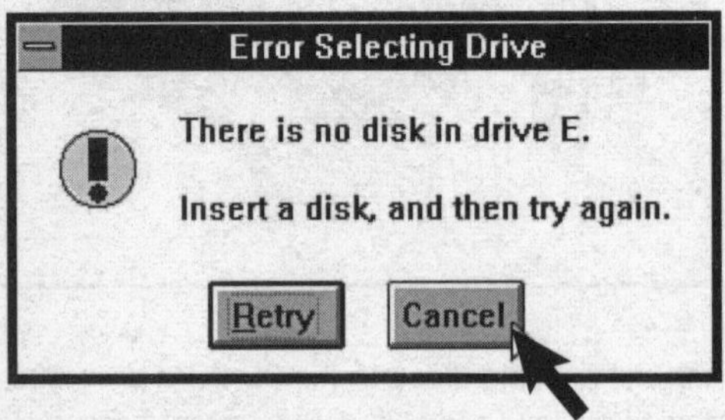

6 When you are done cleaning, remove the cleaning disc from the CD-ROM drive. If using the Windows Program Manager, choose **Cancel** to stop reading the floppy disk. If using DOS, choose **Fail** to tell the computer you no longer wish to access the drive (you may have to choose **Fail** more than once).

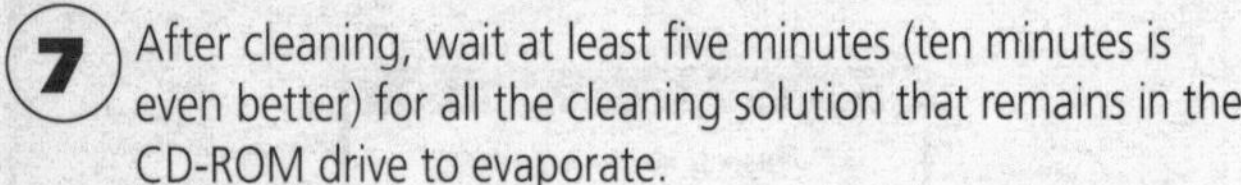

7 After cleaning, wait at least five minutes (ten minutes is even better) for all the cleaning solution that remains in the CD-ROM drive to evaporate.

8 CD-ROMs can get dirty, too, and these should be cleaned if you notice any dirt and smudges on them. CD-ROM discs can be cleaned with a CD disc cleaner, available at most any music or record store. The cleaner comes with a cleaning mechanism and a bottle of cleaning liquid. *Avoid* the use of household cleaners (like Formula 409 or Fantastik) or glass cleaner, as not all glass cleaners are designed for use with plastic.

Clean a Tape Backup Drive

If you're serious about the data on your computer's hard disk drive, you probably have a *tape backup drive* installed on your PC. The tape drive stores megabytes of data on a special high-quality cassette. Each cassette can hold between several hundred megabytes of data from your hard disk drive. If something should happen to the hard disk drive, you have the copy of the data on the tape as a backup. Hence the name.

Tape backup drives are little more than fancy audio cassette players—well, at least the general idea is the same. The drive uses a magnetic head to read and write pieces of information on a long length of tape. The tape is shuttled back and forth past the head, the way it is in an audio cassette player.

The magnetic heads used in a tape backup drive get dirty over time. They also pick up residual magnetic coating from the tape. This dirt and magnetic coating can interfere with the proper operation of the tape backup drive, and can conceivably cause data loss. Obviously, since the purpose of a tape backup drive is to *prevent* data loss, anything that jeopardizes your data should be avoided.

You know the tape backup drive needs to be cleaned if you get errors when trying to back up or restore data. You should not wait until you get these errors to clean the drive. Depending on how often you use the tape backup drive, you may want to make cleaning it a regular job. For example, you might clean the drive twice a year (or pick any other dates you think you'll remember). If you can't remember, write it down on a calendar.

As with floppy disk drives, you can purchase a cleaning kit especially designed for tape backup drives. Such a kit may even have been included with the drive when you bought it.

The "Do It Yourself" steps that follow assume you're using a commercially available cleaning kit for tape backup drives; most of these consist of a cleaning tape and cleaning solution. These directions are generic; for specifics, read the instructions that come with the cleaning kit.

Tape backup drives uses tapes of several different sizes. Be sure to get the cleaning kit for your kind of drive.

Begin Do It Yourself Clean a Tape Drive

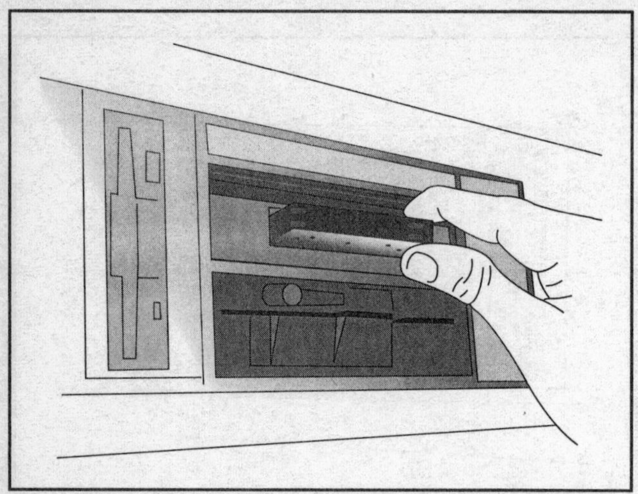

1 With the computer on, remove any tapes in your tape backup drive.

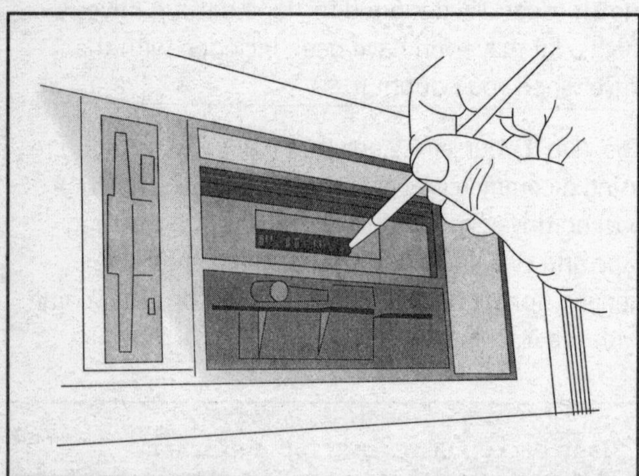

2 Use a small (quarter-inch-wide) artist's brush to whisk out any excess dust from the inside of the drive slot. To access this slot you will need to use your finger to open the protective door on the front of the drive.

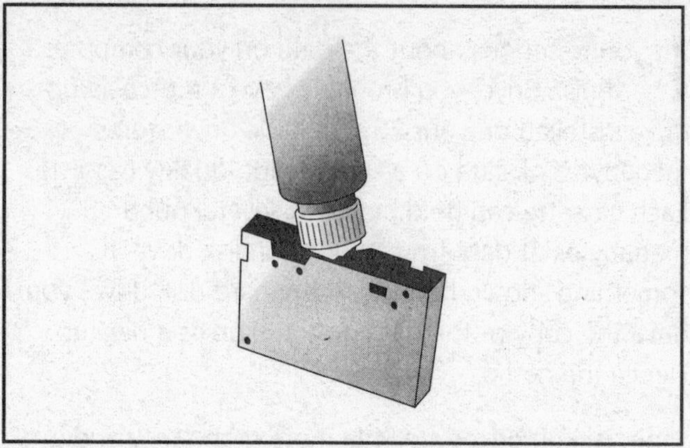

3 Use the cleaner that comes with the cleaning tape to dampen it. Don't apply too much cleaner.

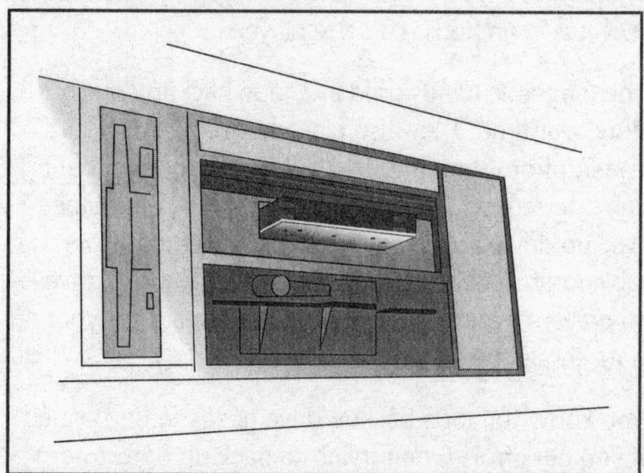

4 Insert the cleaning tape into the tape drive. Make sure you insert the cleaning tape the right way!

5 Use the software that comes with the cleaning kit to activate the tape backup drive. If no software is included, activate the drive by running your regular tape-backup software. When you are done cleaning, exit the cleaning program that came with the cleaning kit. Remove the cleaning tape from the backup drive.

6 IMPORTANT: After cleaning, wait at least five minutes (ten minutes is even better) for all the cleaning solution that remains in the tape backup drives to evaporate. This is an important step; trying to use a backup tape with wet read/write heads may cause even more build-up of magnetic coating on the heads inside the drive.

Clean Inside Your Computer

Maybe you do this at you own house: once a year, around springtime when the weather is clear, you go through the joint and give it a thorough cleaning. Upstairs, downstairs, attic, basement; you name it, it gets cleaned. This so-called spring cleaning is designed to give a much-needed facelift to your house, which has been closed up and collecting dust the past winter.

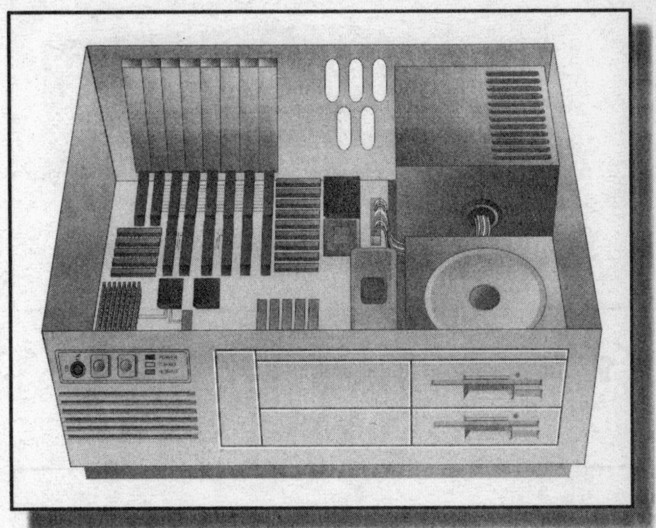

Now imagine a spring cleaning for your PC. Don't laugh. Every once in a while, your computer can really use a thorough inside-out cleaning. Not only do you give the computer a bath on the outside (see "Clean Your Computer" on page 328), but you open 'er up and get all the accumulated dust and other junk out of the inside.

Why clean the inside of your computer? You'd be surprised how much dust can collect inside that beast, even if you use your computer in a relatively clean environment like an air-conditioned office. PCs use fans to suck in air, so the innards of the computer are kept cool. Along with the air comes—you guessed it—dust.

There's no effective way to keep this dust out of your computer. It's a fact of life that after a year or two, most computers (assuming they are used daily) collect a thick layer of muck that can impede the operation of the machine.

Dust is like a blanket: the more dust, the hotter the components get. And hot electronics is something you want to avoid. Heat damages electronic equipment. More than once has dust been the reason for a computer "meltdown"; one or more parts inside the computer fail under the heat, and the PC gives out. This can be expensive to fix.

In order to clean inside your computer, you have to remove its cover or case. This is not dangerous, and as long as you are careful, there is little risk of damaging anything. If you are comfortable with a screwdriver, you can safely clean the inside of your computer.

What you need for the job:

- A #1 Phillips-head screwdriver. This screwdriver fits the screws used by most computers to fasten the case. A few brands of computers (like certain models made by Compaq) use "Torx" screws that require a special tool, available at most hardware stores.
- A small flat-head screwdriver, for removing cables screwed onto the back of the computer.
- An artist's brush (about one-inch wide will do it).
- A can of compressed air. You can buy these at most any photographic, automotive, or computer-supply store.
- A bottle of "technical-grade" isopropyl alcohol, available at many pharmacies. Technical-grade has less water than regular rubbing alcohol, and is preferred.
- A bunch of cotton-tipped swabs.

Clean the inside of the computer about once every year or two, or more if the PC shows signs of heavy dust buildup.

Begin Do It Yourself Clean Your Computer

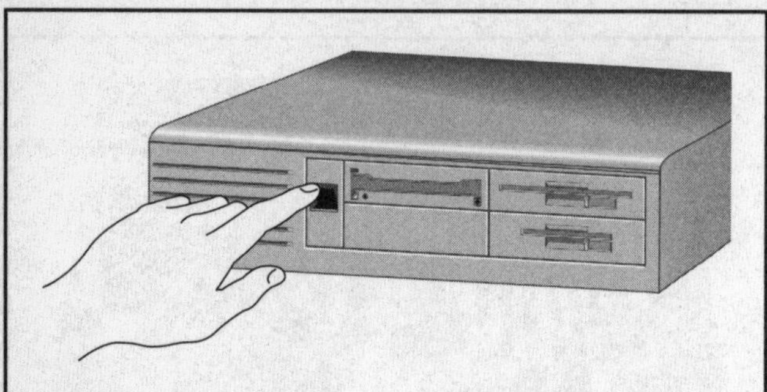

1 Turn your computer off and unplug it.

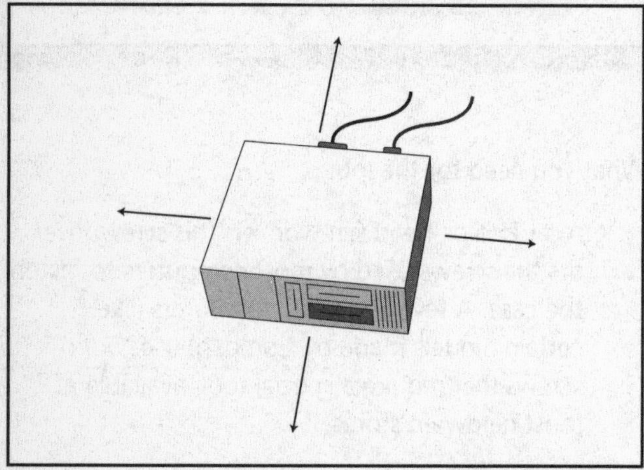

2 If your computer is a desktop model, remove the monitor (if it's sitting on top) and clear off your desk so you can access the top, sides, and back. If your computer is the floor-standing model, clear out an area so you can work on the computer.

3 For now, leave all cables attached to your computer, unless they interfere with opening it up. If you must remove a cable from the front or back of the computer, note the connector the cable attaches to. Use the small flat-head screwdriver to loosen the connector, if necessary.

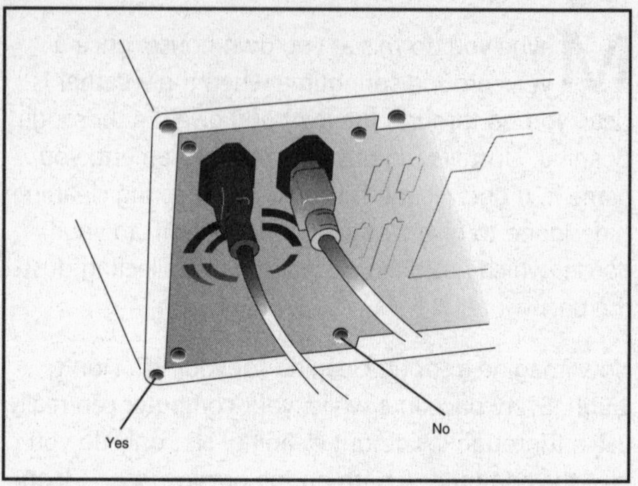

4 Locate the screws used to secure the top or case to the computer. (You may need to refer to the manual that came with your computer to locate all the screws). Whatever you do, ***don't*** just loosen a screw because you see it. This is especially true of screws on the back of the computer, away from the case. These screws are often used to secure parts (like the power supply and hard disk drive) inside the computer, and there is no reason to remove them. In fact, doing so may damage your computer.

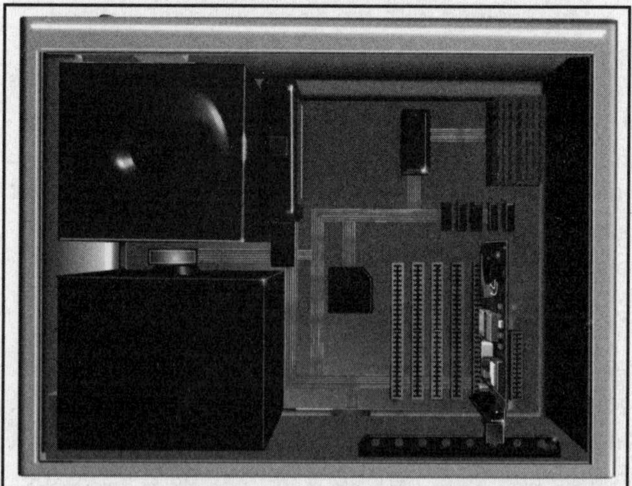

5 With all the appropriate screws removed, carefully lift the top or case and pull it away from the computer. The inside of your computer should now be visible.

6 As a precaution, touch a metal object like a doorknob. This discharges excess static from your body. Static electricity can damage your computer's electronics.

Do It Yourself Clean Your Computer

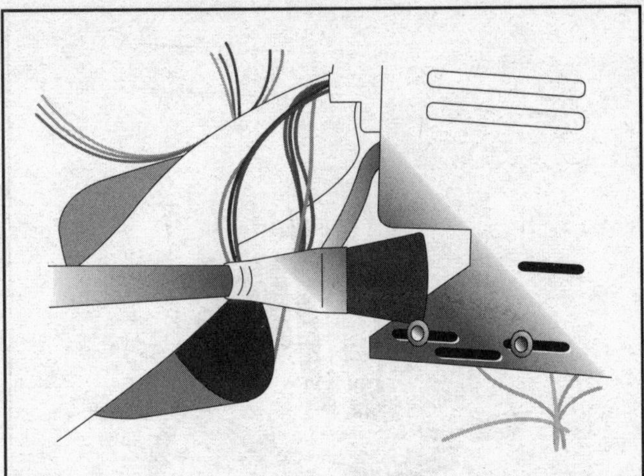

7 Use the artist's brush to whisk out the sediment of dust that has collected inside the computer. Periodically use the can of compressed air to expel the dust from the insides of the PC. If the dust is heavy, you may even want to wear a dust mask during this step, especially if you are sensitive to dust.

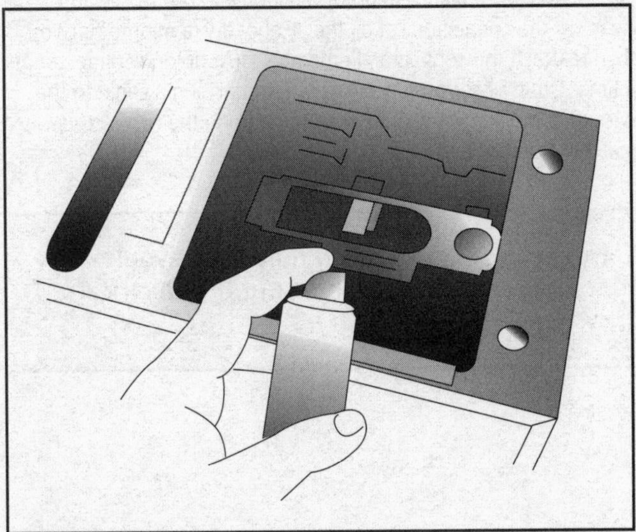

8 For hard-to-reach spots, use the can of compressed air to blast dust out of the crevices inside the computer. Try to aim the nozzle of the air can so that the dust is blown out of the computer, not further inside.

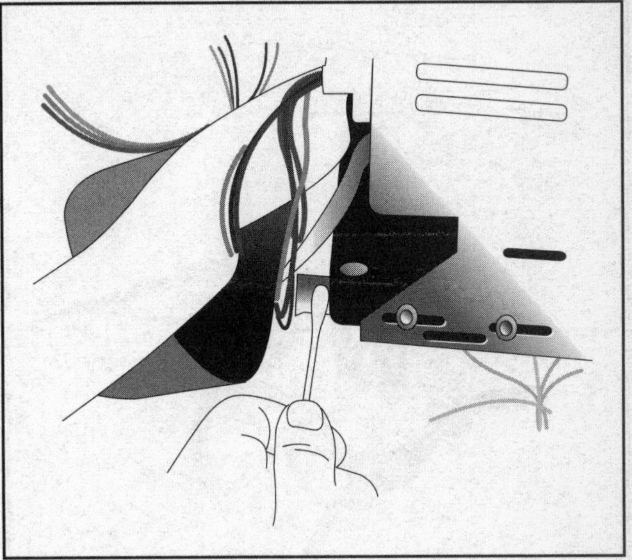

9 For out-of-the-way areas that are too dirty for the compressed air, use the cotton-tipped swabs to wipe off excess dust. Don't be miserly with the swabs. When the tip gets dirty, use the other end. When both ends get dirty, throw it away and use another swab. For the average computer, you may use a dozen or two swabs.

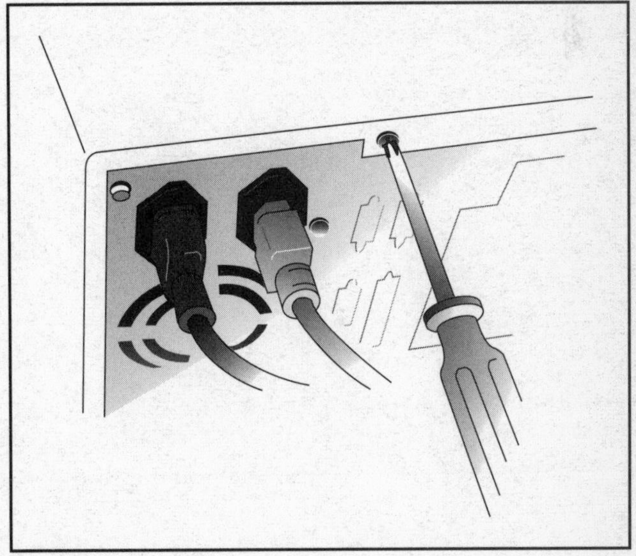

10 When all is clean inside, replace the cover, being sure that it fits snugly, the way it was when you removed it. Replace the screws. Don't overtighten.

(continues)

Do It Yourself Clean Your Computer

(continued)

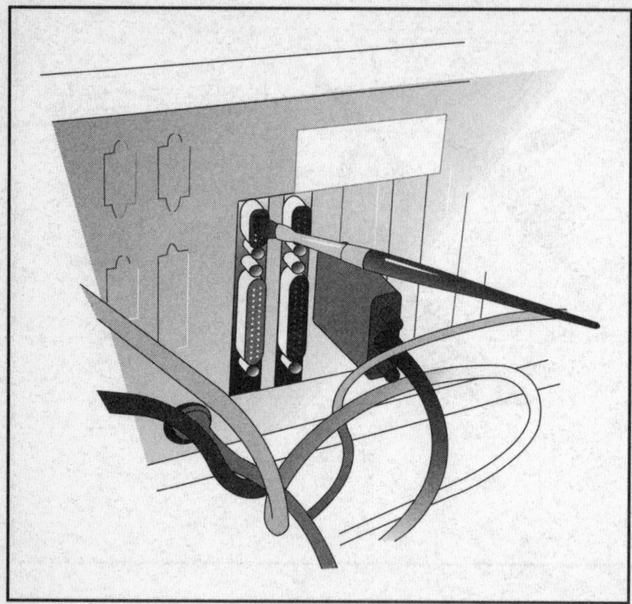

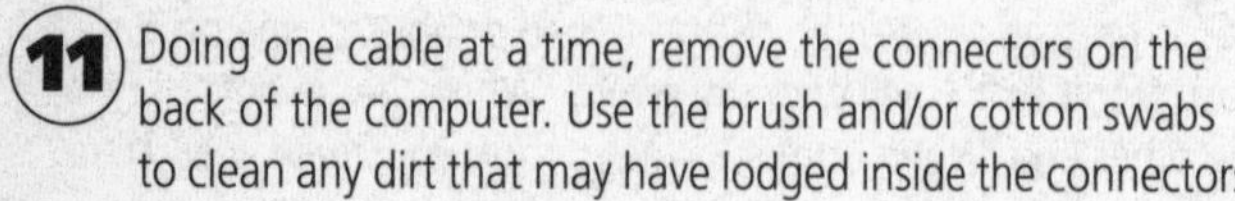

11 Doing one cable at a time, remove the connectors on the back of the computer. Use the brush and/or cotton swabs to clean any dirt that may have lodged inside the connectors.

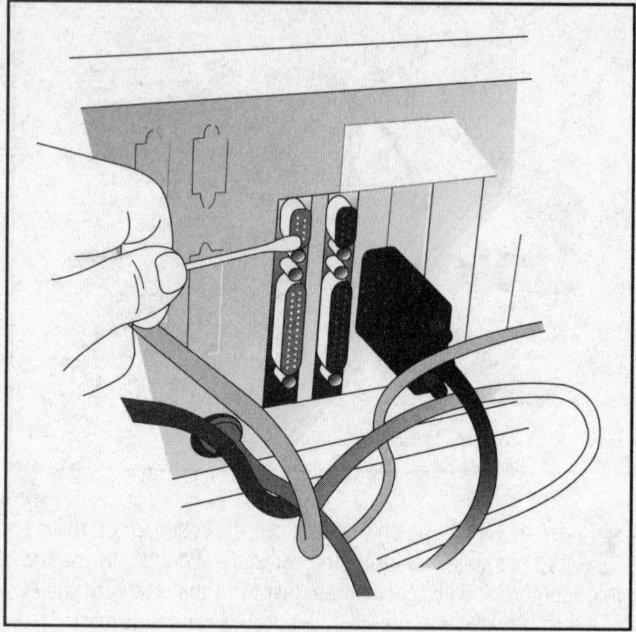

12 If the dirt buildup on the connector is heavy, wet a cotton swab with technical-grade alcohol, and use the swab to clean off the connector. Let all the alcohol dry (a minute or two), then reattach the connector. Remember: Just do one connector at a time. Otherwise, you run the risk of reattaching a cable to the wrong connector. When you're done cleaning the connectors, reattach them before using your computer.

Never, *ever* use cleaning fluid inside your computer. You could short out the electrical system and your PC.

Select and Install a Surge Protector

Snap! Crackle! Pop!! No, it's not breakfast cereal talking to you, it's the sound of various electrical denizens that lurk inside the wiring at your home or office.

A little background. The juice at the electrical outlet is far from pure. The outlets in your home or office are supposed to deliver about 117 volts of electricity. But along with this 117 volts of regular electricity are short-lived jolts of much higher voltage—sometimes exceeding several hundred volts! The power supply inside your computer is designed to handle minor variations in excessive electricity, but it can't handle them all.

The problem is worse when there's an electrical storm. The charge of lightning nearby can get into the high tension lines nearby, and some of that voltage can enter your computer by way of the power cord. A large enough bolt can permanently damage your computer, even if it's not turned on when the lightning strikes.

When there's a jolt of too much electricity in the power lines, it's called a *spike* or a *surge*. You can (and should) protect your computer investment by purchasing a surge protector, available at most any computer store. They're also available—usually for less money—at Radio Shack and many home-improvement or hardware stores.

The typical surge suppressor looks like an electrical outlet strip. There are sockets for plugging in five or six electrical devices, like your computer, monitor, printer, external modem, and other goodies you have connected to your PC. Each outlet on the strip is protected against surges—those instantaneous spikes of too-high voltages. The strip is designed to filter out these surges, and in some cases, self-destruct if the voltage is way too high. It's cheaper to replace the surge protector than all your computer gear.

Keep these points in mind when selecting a surge protector:

- Some power systems are inherently "dirtier" than others. In this case, "dirt" means lots of surges that can disrupt the operation of the computer. Many modern high-rise buildings have big and expensive power conditioners in their basements that help filter out most of the surges.
- The most powerful surges come from lightning strikes. If you live in an area prone to thunderstorms—Florida, for example—you should definitely consider a surge protector for every electronic device in your house or office.
- Not all surges come from the outside like a lightning strike. Some are caused by appliances inside, such as a refrigerator or an air conditioner. In fact, surges like these are generally the most common.
- Many surges are not strong enough to do actual damage to your computer, but they can be troublesome just the same. For example, the surge from an electrical appliance (like a refrigerator) may not be strong enough to cause damage, but the spike could cause your computer to suffer momentary power overload. This can cause your computer to "freeze" in mid-track, which means you lose any data you were working on.

- Not all surge protectors are the same. Some do a better job at eliminating or reducing surges. You can gauge the quality of a surge suppressor by its specifications, but these specs are highly technical; they mean nothing to the average person.
- Your best bet is to buy a quality name-brand surge protector from a reputable dealer. You can certainly pay too much for a surge protector, but for the most part, the ones that retail for under $10 generally don't provide enough protection. Watch magazines like *Consumer Reports* for objective tests of surge suppressors.
- For best results, purchase a surge protector with a built-in circuit breaker. A circuit breaker rated at 15 to 20 amps is sufficient for computer use. You need the higher amperage if you use a laser printer.
- Surge suppressors can wear out. If your surge suppressor lacks an indicator that shows you it is no longer effectively blocking voltage spikes, you should replace the suppressor as a matter of course every 24 to 36 months (replace more often if you live in an area prone to lots of lightning strikes).

Begin Do It Yourself Connect a Surge Protector

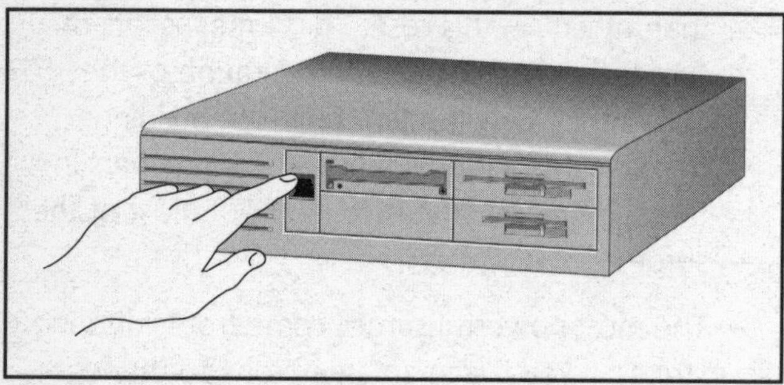

1 Turn off your computer and all other equipment connected to it (printer, monitor, external modem, etc.).

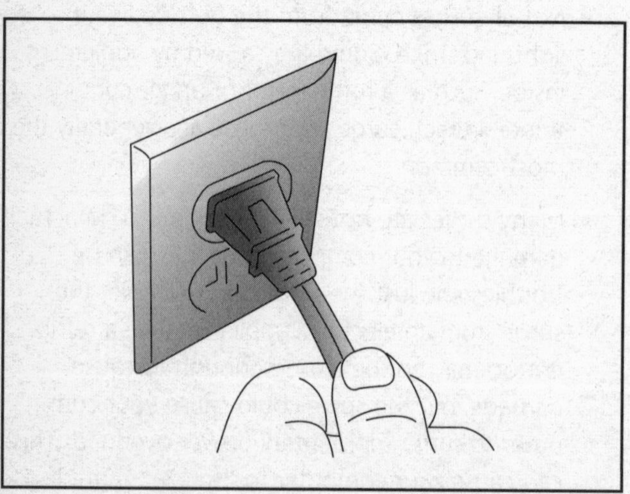

2 Unplug the power cords for your computer and peripherals from the wall.

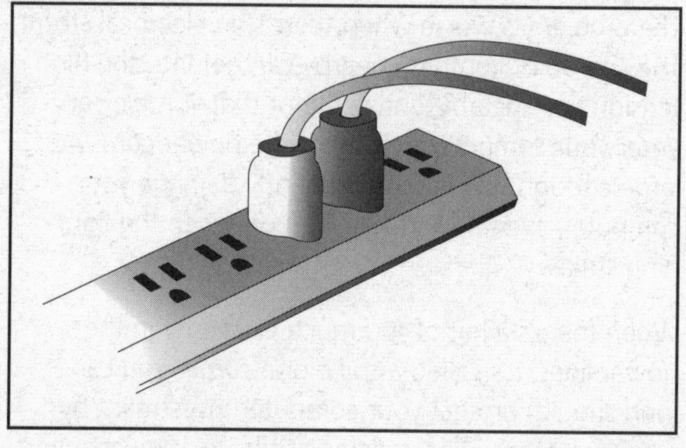

3 Plug in the surge protector. Then plug all the power cords into the surge protector.

If you have more power cords than surge-protector outlets, purchase a second surge protector. Do not plug extension cords into the surge suppressor. Plugging in too many electrical devices diminishes the effectiveness of the surge protector.

First Aid: Spilled Liquid on Keyboard or Mouse

Yikes! Even though you've been warned against it, you placed your coffee mug beside your computer. And now, being all thumbs, you knocked the coffee mug over and the liquid spilled inside the keyboard and mouse. What now?

Odds are, you can save both keyboard and mouse, but you have to act quickly. The most important step is *turning off your computer*. The faster you turn the computer off, the less likely a short circuit will damage the keyboard, mouse, or computer. If your computer is on when the spill occurs, try to quickly save any work in progress, then hit the power button.

With the computer safely turned off, you can go about trying to undo the damage you did. Preferably before the boss comes back from lunch.

The steps that follow involve disassembling the mouse or keyboard. There's a certain risk in damaging the mouse or keyboard even further by taking them apart, but consider this: most mice and keyboards cost under $50. You don't risk much by trying to fix things yourself. And, since a new mouse or keyboard doesn't cost very much, there's no sense taking either one to the repair shop. The average repair bill there runs $75 for labor alone.

Of course, all this doesn't apply to laptop computers, specialty keyboards, or mice—which may cost much more than $40. Use your own discretion in trying to fix these yourself.

These first-aid directions are generic, though they do apply to the majority of keyboard and mouse designs now available. Some designs are different, and you'll have to accommodate them.

Your success at reviving a keyboard or mouse that's suffered a liquid spill depends on the liquid that was spilled. Liquids that are hard to get out (because they leave a residue):

- Coffee
- Tea
- Drinks with sugar
- Juice

Liquids that are easier to get out:

- Water
- Diet sodas (the clear kind is preferable)

Begin Do It Yourself Liquid in Keyboard

1. Unplug the keyboard from the computer. This is a precautionary measure to prevent further damage to your computer.

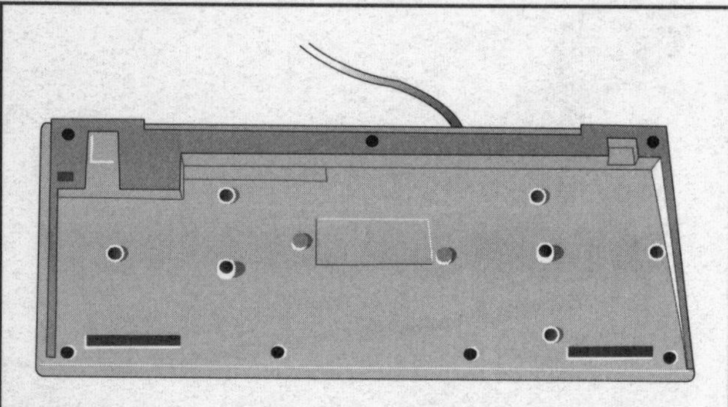

2. Spread out some paper towels on your desk. Turn the keyboard over and let the excess fluid seep out.

3. Using a small, Phillips-head screwdriver, remove the screws on the bottom of the keyboard. Save the screws in a small cup (one without coffee!) Note: The screws are hidden on some keyboards, such as under stickers. Peel back the stickers to reveal all the screws,

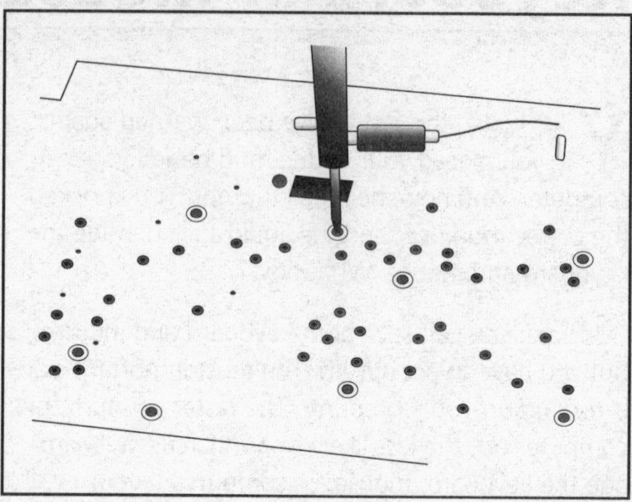

4. Carefully separate the two halves of the keyboard casing.

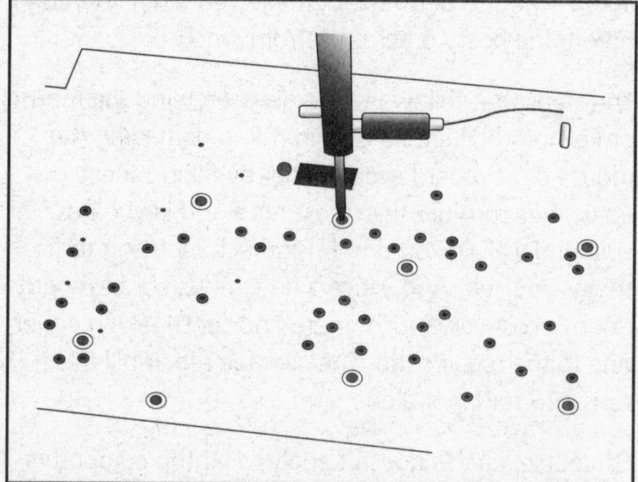

5. Using a jeweler's Phillips-head screwdriver (available at Radio Shack and many hobby stores), remove all the screws you see on the back side of the main printed circuit board inside the keyboard. Be sure to save all of these screws, too. The keyboard may not work right if you are missing just one of these screws when you put the thing back together.

Do It Yourself Liquid in Keyboard

6 Carefully lift off the printed circuit board. Inside are the foam "cushions" attached to the back side of the keys. (Not all keyboards use this design, but many do. Your keyboard may use a rubber membrane, but the cleaning steps are generally the same.). These foam cushions are made with a piece of metalized plastic, so that when you press down on a key, electrical contact is made on the circuit board. Carefully inspect the foam cushions. If any are loose, use Super Glue to glue them back. If any are soaked with liquid, the keyboard is most likely totaled, and you should get a new one.

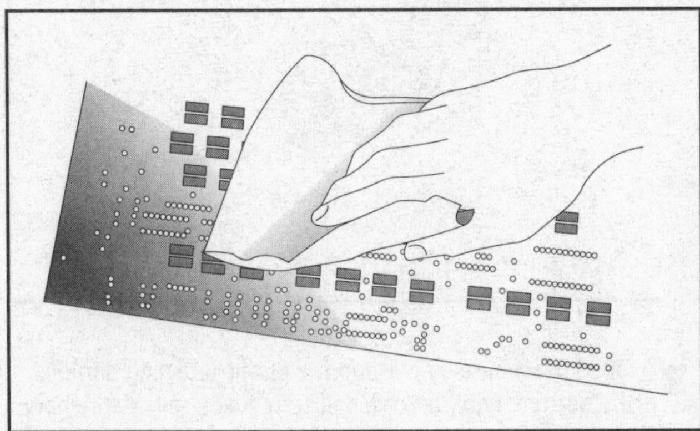

7 With a paper towel, clean off the contact surface of the keyboard's printed circuit board.

8 With another paper towel, or with a cotton-tipped swab, gently clean off the metalized foil on the back side of the key contacts. Don't wipe too vigorously or you'll pull the cushion off the key.

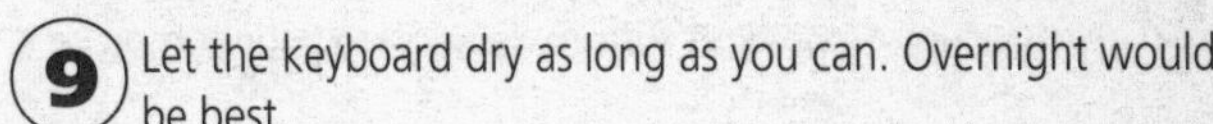

9 Let the keyboard dry as long as you can. Overnight would be best.

10 When it's dry, replace the keyboard circuit board, being careful to line up the screw holes. Replace the screws and tighten, but don't overtighten. Remember: You need to replace all the screws, or the keyboard probably won't work right.

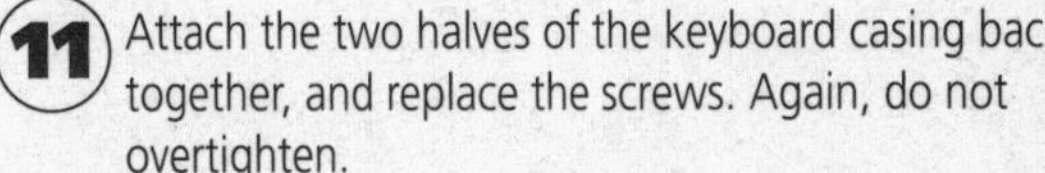

11 Attach the two halves of the keyboard casing back together, and replace the screws. Again, do not overtighten.

(continues)

Do It Yourself Liquid in Keyboard

(continued)

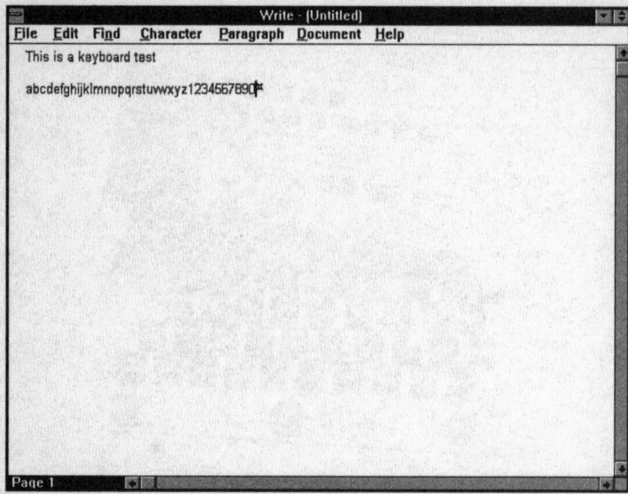

12 Test the keyboard by plugging it back into the computer. Turn the computer on. If the computer doesn't indicate a "stuck key failure" or other error message, try pressing each key to make sure it works. Be sure you test all the keys, including editing keys and function keys. Use one of your application programs, like a word processor, to test the full operation of the keyboard.

Begin Do It Yourself Liquid in Mouse

1 Unplug the mouse from the computer. This is a precautionary measure, to prevent further damage to your computer.

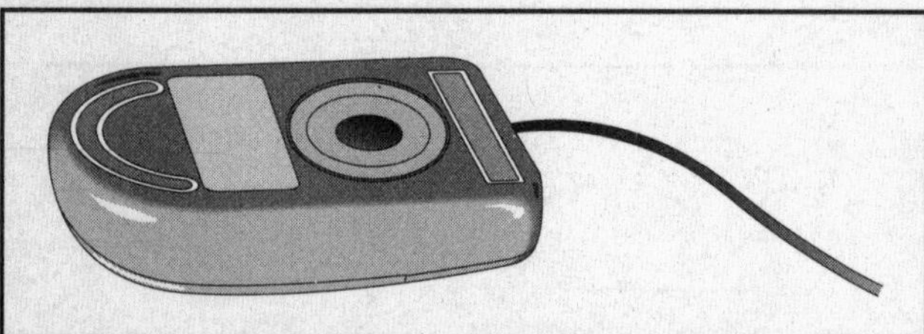

2 Spread out some paper towels on your desk. Place the mouse on it to let the excess liquid ooze out.

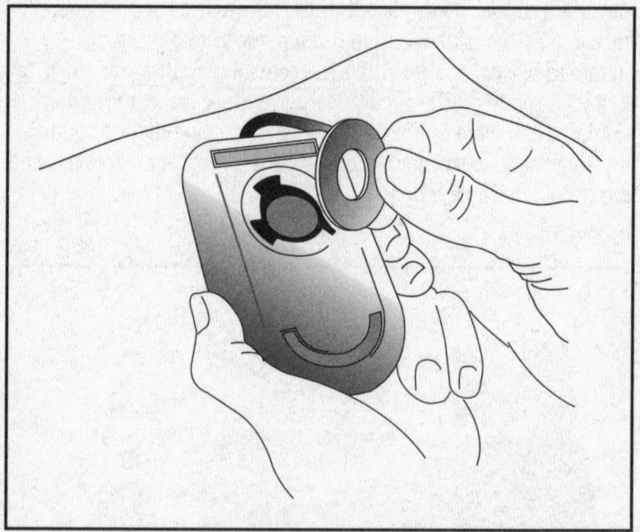

3 Open the mouse by twisting the plastic retaining ring on the bottom a quarter or a half turn. If you're not sure how to remove the retaining ring, and no instructions are printed on the bottom of the mouse, consult the manual that came with the mouse. Forcing the ring can break it, and you'll end up having to replace the entire mouse.

Do It Yourself Liquid in Mouse

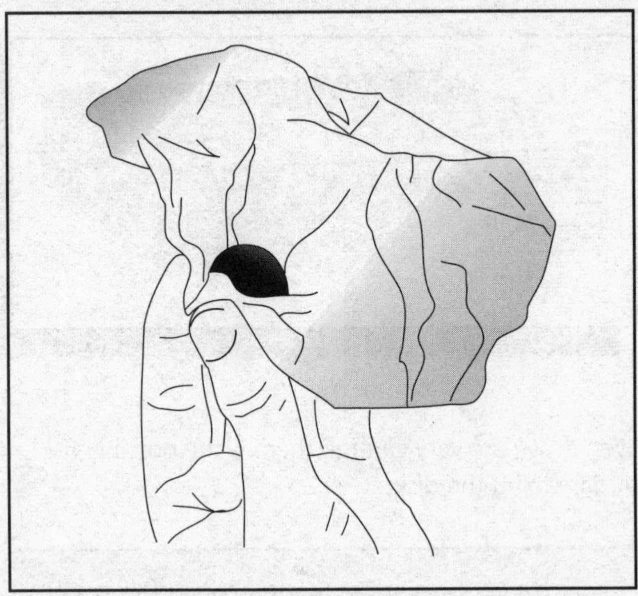

4 Remove the roller ball; clean it with plain water and a facial tissue.

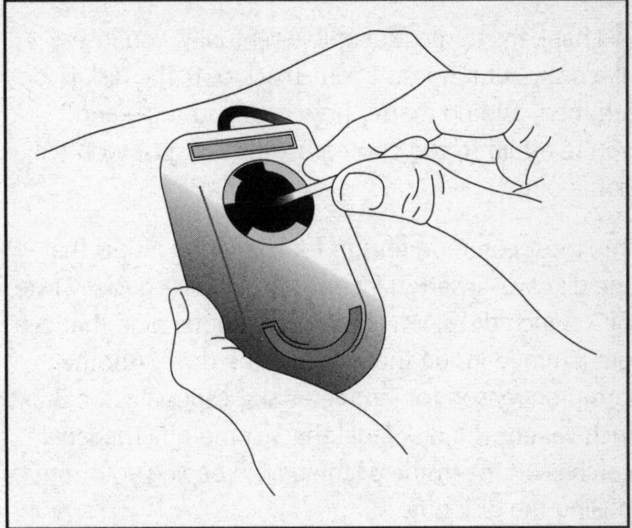

5 Use a cotton-tipped swab to remove the liquid inside the mouse. Let the mouse dry as long as you can. Overnight would be best.

6 When the mouse is dry, replace the ball and retaining ring.

7 Test the mouse by plugging it back into the computer. Turn the computer on. If the computer doesn't indicate an error message, try using the mouse by moving it on your table. Click all the buttons on the mouse to determine whether they work.

First Aid: Unstick a Jammed Disk

It happens to most people, eventually. You insert a disk, but it doesn't come back out. The disk is jammed, and no matter how hard you tug—and you're afraid to tug ***too*** hard—the disk just won't come out.

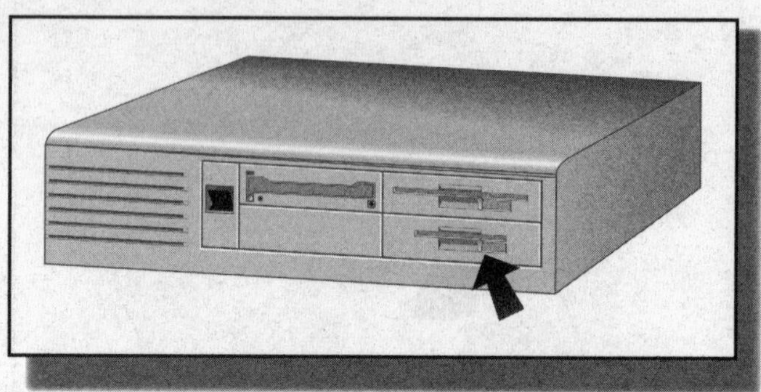

The most common reason for a jammed disk is that the disk was inserted incorrectly. This is especially true of 3.5-inch disks, which contain a metal slide that can get jammed inside the works of the drive. Another common reason for jammed disks, especially the 3.5-inch variety, is a disk label that's come off. The label catches on the inside of the drive, keeping you from pulling the disk out.

If you are the victim of a stuck disk, follow these steps to extract it from your computer disk drive. **Warning:** Even if you are very careful, there is the possible risk of damaging the disk.

For a *really* stuck disk, you may need to take your computer into the repair shop

Begin Do It Yourself Unstick a Disk

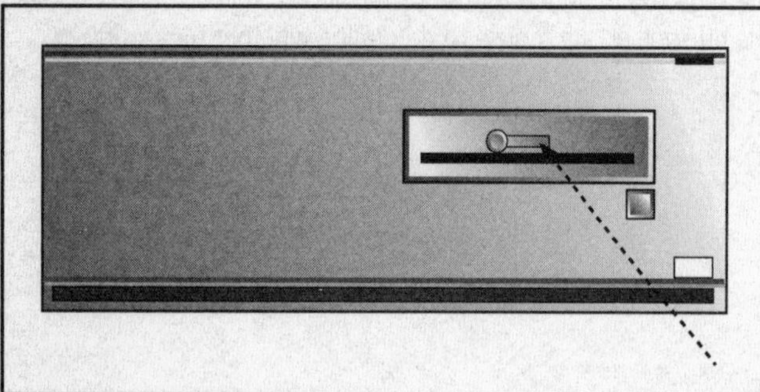

1. If the drive is the 5.25-inch variety, open the latch and try to wiggle the disk free. Sometimes, you can help extricate the disk by repeatedly opening and closing the latch.

2. If the drive is the 3.5-inch variety, push the release button all the way in and try to grab the disk with your fingers. If the disk doesn't come out far enough, try gently grasping it with a small pair of pliers. Don't pull so hard that you damage the drive or disk.

3. If the disk still won't budge, you may need to disassemble the computer in order to reach the disk drives inside. (See "Clean Inside Your Computer" on page 349 for details on taking your computer apart.) Once the computer is apart, you may be able to manually free the obstruction that's keeping the disk from coming out.

Do It Yourself Unstick a Disk

4 On 3.5-inch disks: If the metal slide was caught in the drive, more than likely it is now bent or damaged. DO NOT reinsert this disk into the drive, or it will get stuck again. The disk is not totally ruined, however. Carefully pry the metal slide from the disk. It is only there to protect the disk, and is not absolutely required. Be careful not to touch the exposed disk or you may lose your data.

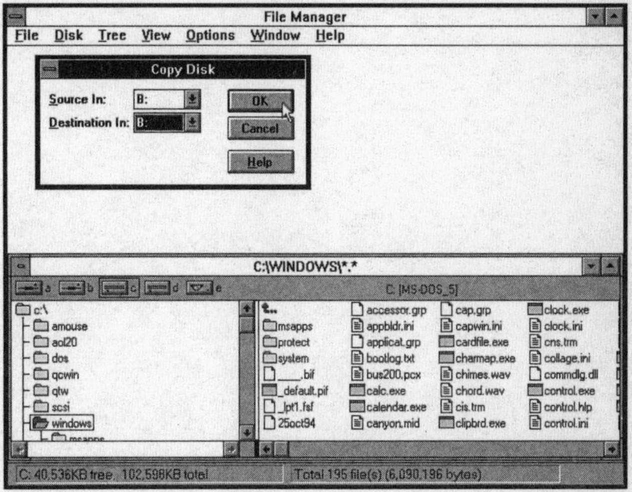

5 Once the slide is off the disk, use it to make a copy on a new, undamaged disk. Verify that the copy is good, and throw away the damaged disk.

DO IT YOURSELF

Install New Programs

Installing new programs isn't as hard as it sounds. Most programs nowadays come with special setup utilities that install the program for you. However, every program's setup utility is different, so you need to know how to handle the different types. In this section, you'll learn how to install programs in DOS, Windows 3.11, and Windows 95. You'll also learn how to uninstall (remove) programs when you no longer need them on your system.

What You Will Find in This Section

Install a DOS Program That Has a Setup Utility 364

Install a Windows 3.11 Program That Has a Setup Utility 366

Install a Window 3.11 Program That Has No Installation Utility 369

Install a Program in Windows 95 372

Install a Program from a "ZIP" File 374

Uninstall a DOS Program 378

Uninstall a Windows 3.11 Program 381

Uninstall a Program in Windows 95 384

Install a DOS Program That Has a Setup Utility

Despite the popularity of Windows, there are still plenty of DOS-based programs you might buy and use on your computer. Typical DOS-based programs include games, certain kinds of personal enhancement software like diet and eating programs, and even mainstream applications like WordPerfect for DOS.

Because there are few standards in the world of DOS-based programs, installing them differs greatly from one software package to the next. The better DOS-based software comes with a separate program just for installing it on your computer. This installation program helps you copy the program files to your computer's hard disk drive (most programs these days require a hard disk drive), and sets up the software automatically so you can use it right away.

For this task, we'll refer to the program that helps you install a DOS-based program on your computer as a *SETUP utility*. This is just a generic name. The name of the actual program that does the installation may not be SETUP. It may be INSTALL, or SBINST, QSETUP, or another such name. If you're not sure of the program's name (common names are SETUP and INSTALL), you have to check the documentation for the program to find out.

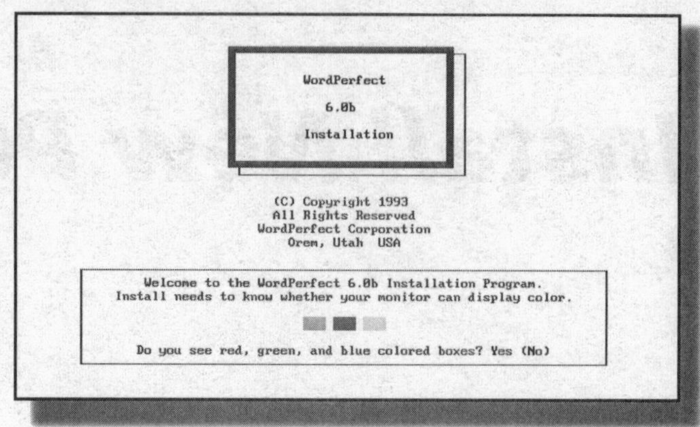

SETUP utilities are most often executable programs with .EXE filename extensions (such as SETUP.EXE)—but not always. Other possibilities include .COM and .BAT. The file-name extension doesn't really matter, because you refer to the SETUP utility just by the main part of the name. So don't worry if you have a SETUP.BAT rather than a SETUP.EXE.

Don't be afraid to read the manual that comes with the software you are installing. It may provide useful tips and hints for installing the program on your computer.

Begin Do It Yourself Install a DOS Program

1 Before installing any new software, make copies of your important system configuration files (AUTOEXEC.BAT, CONFIG.SYS, WIN.INI, and SYSTEM.INI). "Make a Backup of Important System Files" on page 444 will tell you how to do this.

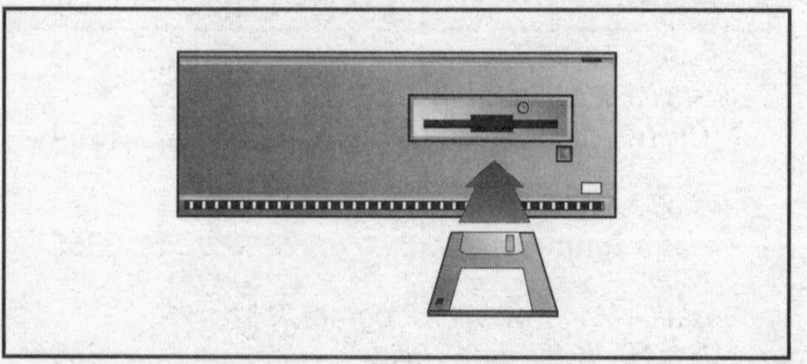

2 Open the software package and find the disk that contains the SETUP utility. This disk is often marked SETUP or INSTALL (or with some other descriptive name). Start your computer if it's not on already, and put the disk in your computer's disk drive.

Do It Yourself Install a DOS Program

```
C:\>A:
```

3 At the DOS prompt, type **A:** or **B:**, depending on the floppy disk drive that contains the SETUP disk, and press the **Enter** key. (If you are installing the software from a CD-ROM, type the drive letter that corresponds to the CD-ROM drive, such as **D:** or **E:**).

```
C:\>A:

A:\>setup
```

4 Type **SETUP** (or the unique name of the installation program, if it's not SETUP), and press the **Enter** key. The SETUP utility starts.

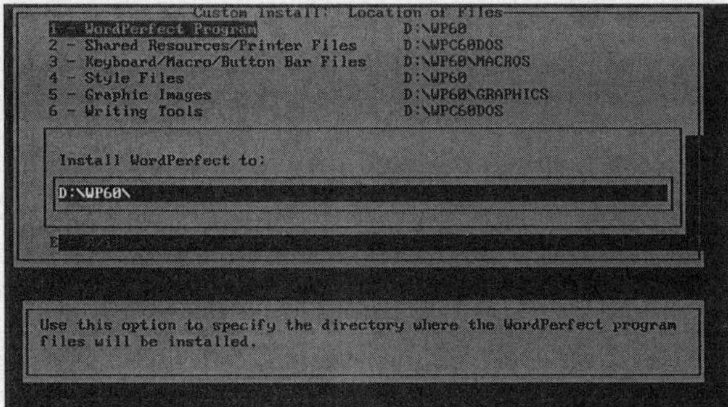

5 Most SETUP utilities are *prompt-based*; a series of prompts will ask you how you want the program installed on your computer. When you are done answering the prompts, the SETUP utility copies the appropriate files until the installation process is complete. What you are asked depends entirely on the specific program you are installing. During the installation process you may be asked to remove the current installation disk and replace it with another.

6 If the program you just installed requires that you restart the computer before you run the software (most do), restart your computer now by pressing the **Ctrl**, **Alt**, and **Del** keys simultaneously.

```
D:\>cd \wp60
```

7 With the computer running, working at the DOS prompt, change to the drive/directory that contains the program you just installed (if the program is in the WP60 directory, for example, type **CD \WP60**) and press **Enter**. Then change to the appropriate directory with the **CD** command.

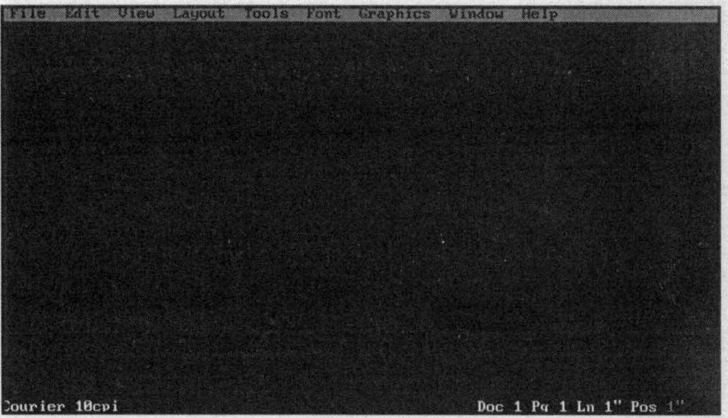

8 Start the program by typing its name (such as **WP** for WordPerfect), and pressing the **Enter** key.

Install a Windows 3.11 Program That Has a Setup Utility

With few exceptions, special installation programs come with software for Windows 3.11. These programs make it easier to install the software on your computer's hard disk drive.

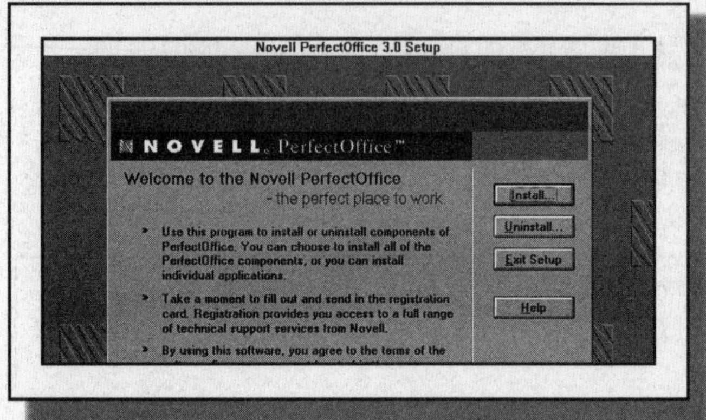

For the most part, this installation program—we'll call it a "SETUP utility"—is automatic. After you start the SETUP utility, the installation process more or less runs by itself. All the right files are copied to your hard drive, and the software is set up for you so that you only have to double-click its icon in the Windows 3.11 Program Manager.

Depending on the software, you may need to answer some questions about how you want the programs installed. For example, you may need to tell the SETUP utility where on your computer's hard disk drive you want the program files copied to. You may also need to indicate the options of the software you wish to use. The SETUP utility uses this information to copy only the needed files from the program disks to your computer's hard drive.

As it was in the task on installing a program from the DOS prompt, the name "SETUP utility" is generic here. The name of the actual program that does the installation may not be called SETUP. Although SETUP is by far the most common, the installation utility may be named INSTALL or something else. If you're not sure of the program's name, check the documentation.

Don't be afraid to read the manual that comes with the Windows 3.11 software you are installing. It may provide useful tips and hints for installing the program on your computer.

Before installing any new software, make copies of your important system configuration files (AUTOEXEC.BAT, CONFIG.SYS, WIN.INI, and SYSTEM.INI). Refer to "Make a Backup of Important System Files" on page 444 for more on how to do this.

Begin Do It Yourself Install a Windows 3.11 Program

1 After opening the software package, find the disk that contains the SETUP utility. This disk is often marked SETUP or INSTALL (or with some other descriptive name).

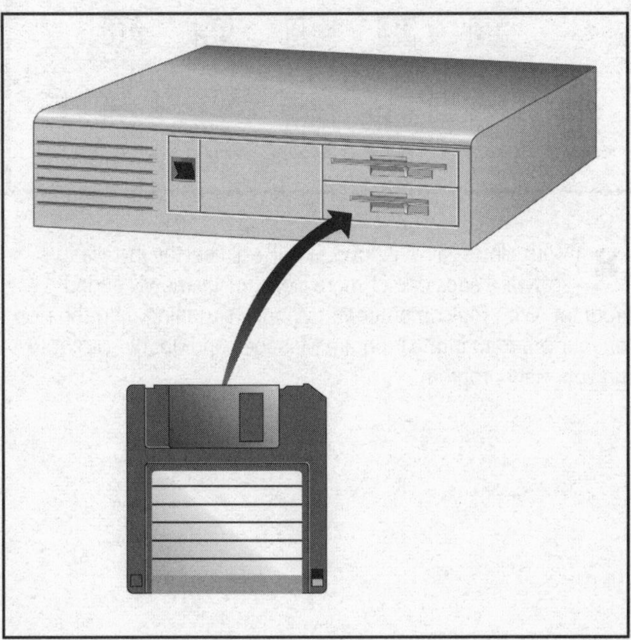

2 Start your computer if it's not already on. Run Windows 3.11 (if it's not already running) by typing **WIN** at the DOS prompt. Put the disk in your computer's disk drive.

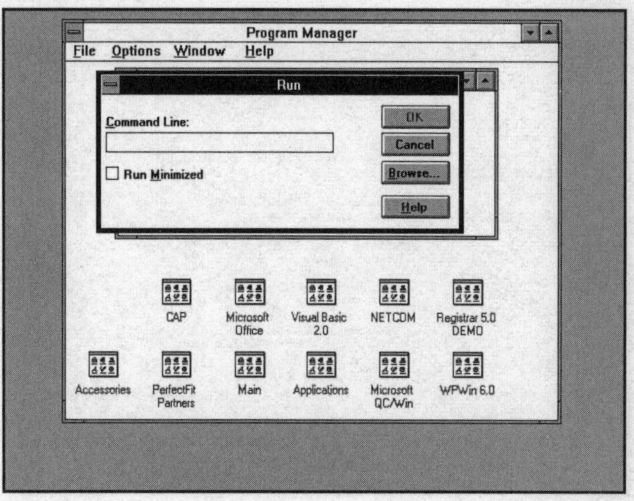

3 From the Windows Program Manager, select **File**, **Run**. The Run dialog box appears.

4 At the Run dialog box, type **A:\SETUP** or **B:\SETUP**, depending on the floppy disk drive that contains the SETUP disk, and click the **OK** button. (If you are installing the software from a CD-ROM, use instead the drive letter that corresponds to the CD-ROM drive, such as **D:** or **E:**). The SETUP utility starts (the one shown in the picture is just an example).

(continues)

Do It Yourself Install a Windows 3.11 Program

(continued)

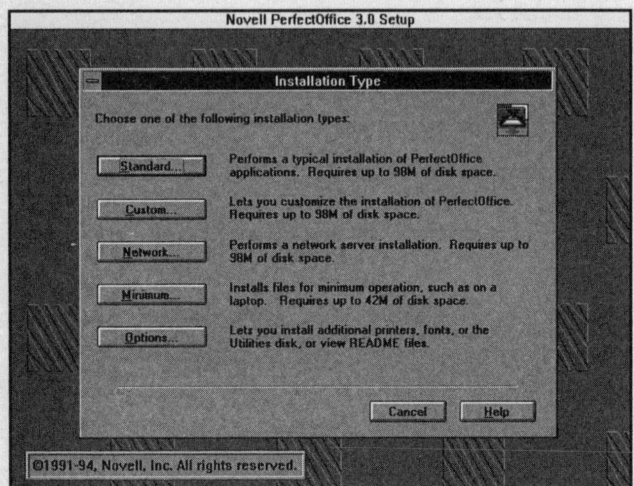

5 Most SETUP utilities are *prompt-based*—a series of prompts will ask how you want the program installed on your computer. What you are asked depends entirely on the specific program you are installing. During the installation process you may be asked to remove the current installation disk and replace it with another.

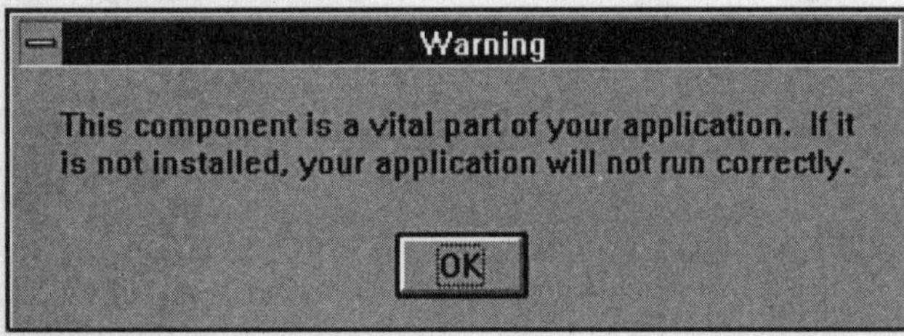

6 When you are done answering the prompts, the SETUP utility copies the appropriate files until the installation process is complete.

7 If your newly installed program requires that you restart the computer before you run the software (most do), restart your computer now by first exiting Windows 3.11 (select **File, Exit Windows**, and then click **OK**). At the DOS prompt, press the **Ctrl**, **Alt**, and **Del** keys simultaneously.

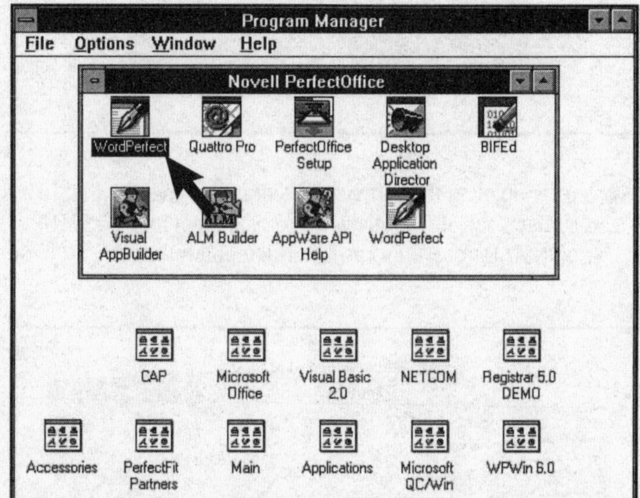

8 With almost all Windows SETUP utilities, the installation software adds one or more icons for the newly added program. With the computer and Windows running, find the icon for your program in the Program Manager, and double-click it to run your new program.

Install a Windows 3.11 Program That Has No Installation Utility

Not all programs—whether for DOS or Windows 3.11—come with a utility that helps install the program on your computer's hard disk drive. Although installation utilities are the norm with commercial software, some shareware, freeware, and "underground" software is distributed without an installation program.

You might obtain this kind of software through an online service like CompuServe or America Online, or even on the Internet. In addition, a number of computer stores sell packages of low-cost "try-it-before-you-buy-it" shareware disks. The low cost of the software prohibits the publisher from spending lots of time and money creating a full-blown installation utility.

Programs that lack an installation program are generally easy to install, but you have to do all the work yourself. It also means you have to know a little more about your computer, including how subdirectories work. (See "Organize Files and Directories with Windows 3.11" on page 99 if you are unfamiliar with the file structure of your personal computer.)

Before installing any new software, make copies of your important system configuration files (AUTOEXEC.BAT, CONFIG.SYS, WIN.INI, and SYSTEM.INI). (Refer to "Make a Backup of Important System Files" on page 444.)

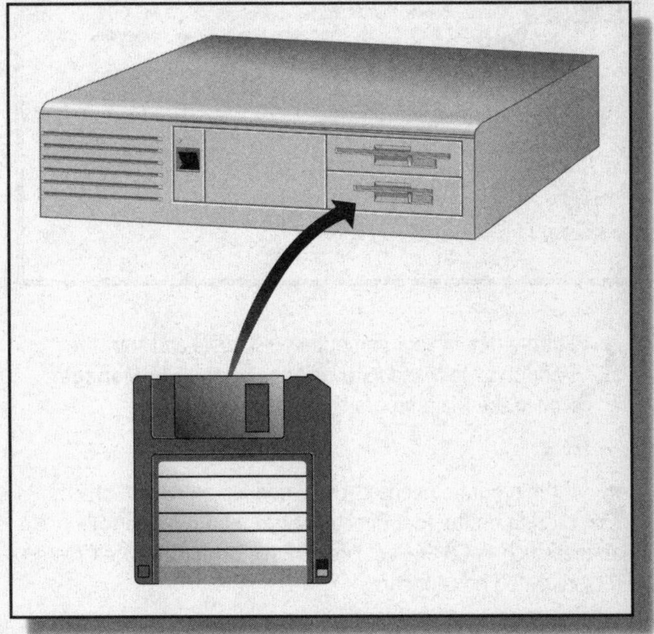

Note: The steps here assume the program you want to install comes on a disk.

Many programs come with "readme" files—short, simple instructions on how to install and use the software. Look for a file named README (or something similar) and use the DOS EDIT program or the Windows Notepad, to view the file.

Begin Do It Yourself Install a Program Using Windows 3.11

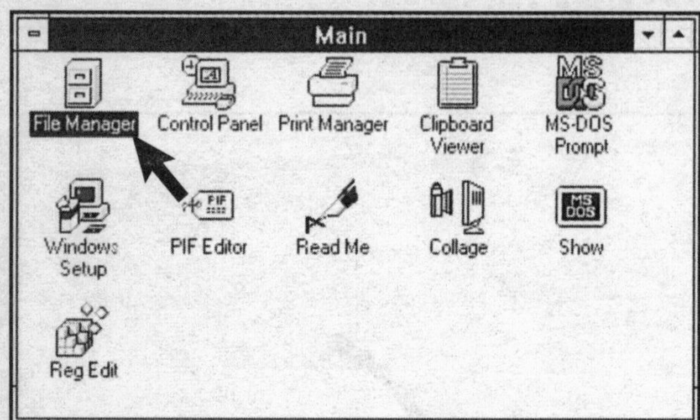

1 Put the disk in your computer's disk drive and start the Windows File Manager by clicking on the **File Manager** icon in the Main program group.

2 If the program needs its own subdirectory, create one by clicking on the root directory of your hard drive in File Manager (such as **C:**). Select **File**, **Create Directory**. The Create Directory dialog box appears.

3 In the Create Directory dialog box, type the name for the new subdirectory, such as **NEWDIR**. Click **OK** when you are done.

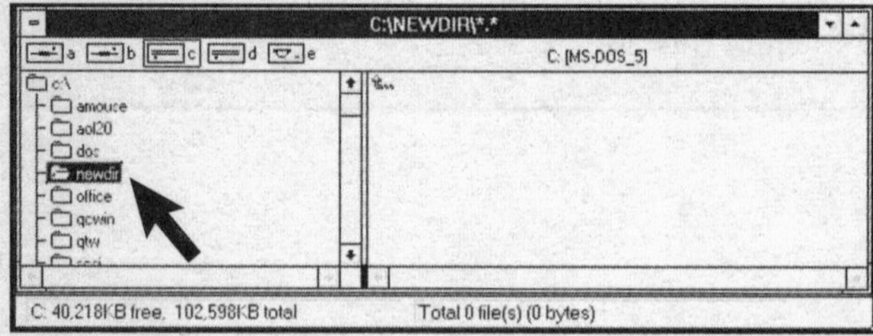

4 Change to the newly-created directory: find it in the File Manager directory list and click it. The directory is empty (it has no files) because you just made it.

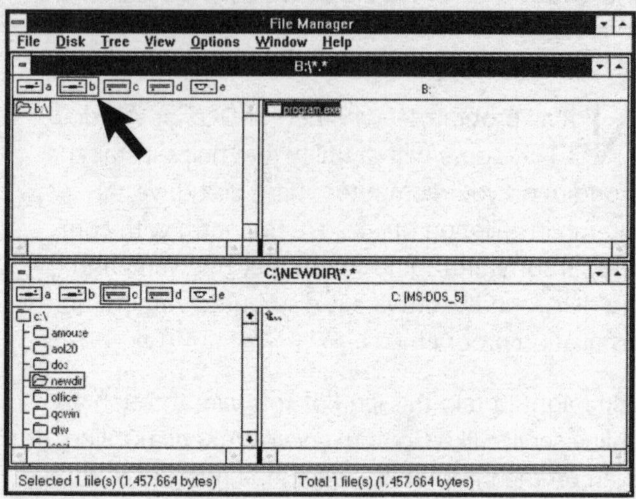

5 Double-click the drive button that contains the program disk (such as A: or B:). A second drive window (for the floppy disk) opens. Arrange the windows so you can see the contents of both: click the **Window** menu and then on **Tile**.

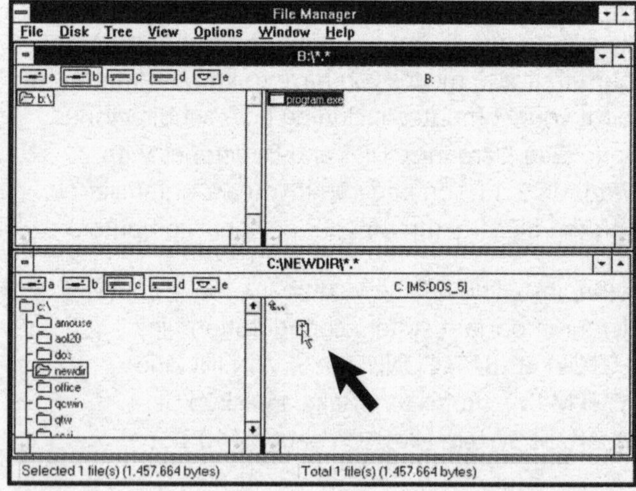

6 Use the mouse to drag the file(s) from the floppy disk to the newly created directory.

7 Exit File Manager when File Manager is done copying the files by choosing **File, Exit**.

Do It Yourself Install a Program Using Windows 3.11

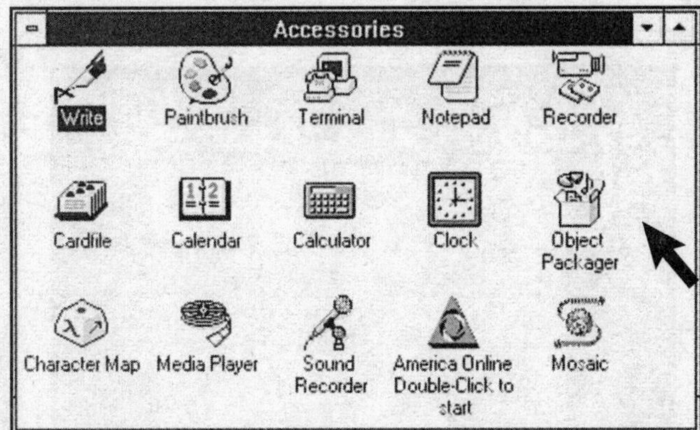

8 In Program Manager, create a program icon so you can easily start the program in Windows 3.11. Use a program group you already have (like **Accessories**). Open the program group by double-clicking on it.

9 In Program Manager, select **File**, **New**. The New Program Object dialog box appears.

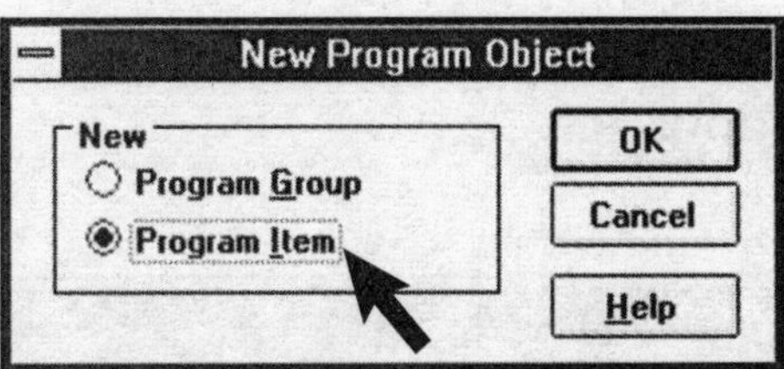

10 In the New Program Object dialog box, make sure the **Program Item** option is selected, and click **OK**. The Program Item Properties dialog box appears.

11 In the Program Item Properties dialog box, type a description of the file, along with the path and file name for the program just installed. Click **OK** when you're done.

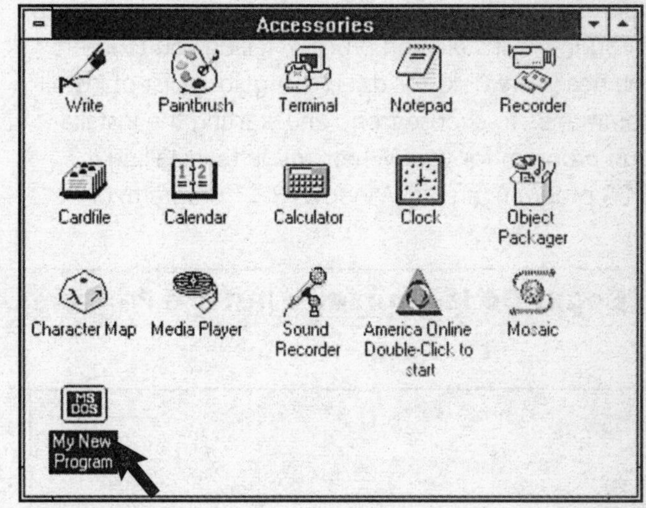

12 To start the program, double-click its newly created icon in Program Manager.

Install a Program in Windows 95

You come home from your local computer store with shopping bags full of new programs and CD-ROMs, and a desire to get all your new acquisitions up and running in a hurry. In the old days, you usually had to sit down and flip through the documentation to figure out what command you had to enter to start installing the program, and whether you had to enter the command in DOS or Windows 3.11.

With Windows 95's Install New Program Wizard, all those concerns are over. You click an icon to add a new program to Windows, and then follow the on-screen instructions. The Wizard leads you step-by-step through the installation process, telling you to insert the necessary disks (or disc), giving you a list of install commands to choose from, and starting the installation program for you. Whether you're installing a DOS program, an old Windows 3.11 program, or a program designed especially for Windows 95, the New Program Wizard can help you get started.

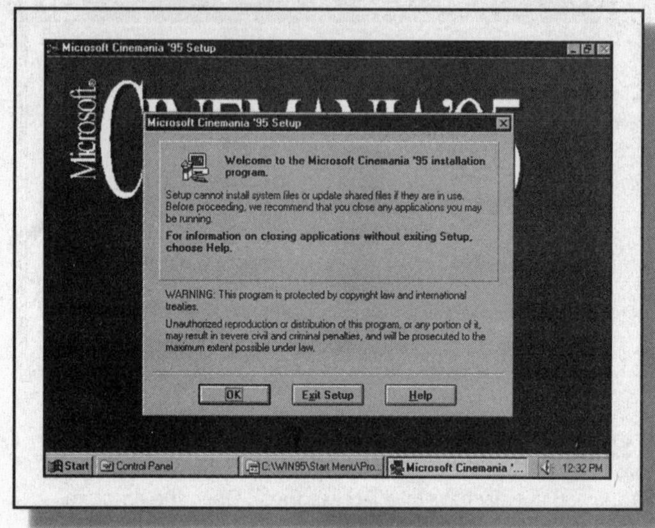

Begin Do It Yourself Install a Program Using Windows 95

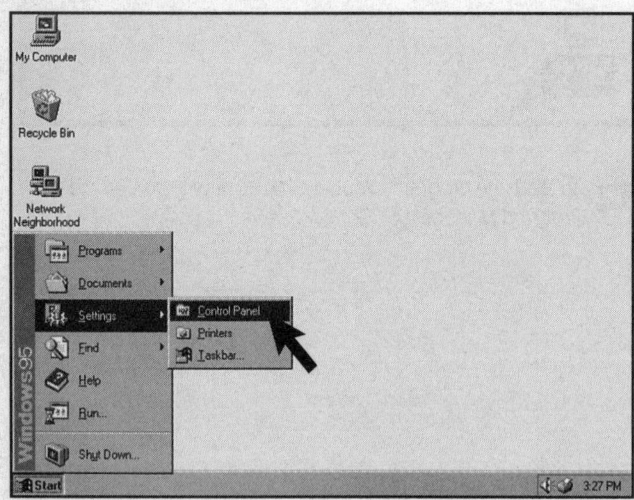

1 You use the Windows 95 Control Panel to install new programs. Click the **Start** button, move the mouse over **Settings**, and click **Control Panel**.

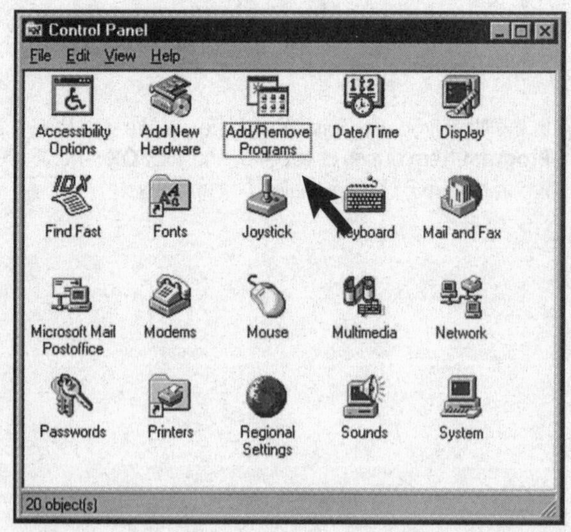

2 The Control Panel has icons that allow you to set up your system and enter your preferences. Double-click the **Add/ Remove Programs** icon to install a program.

Do It Yourself Install a Program Using Windows 95

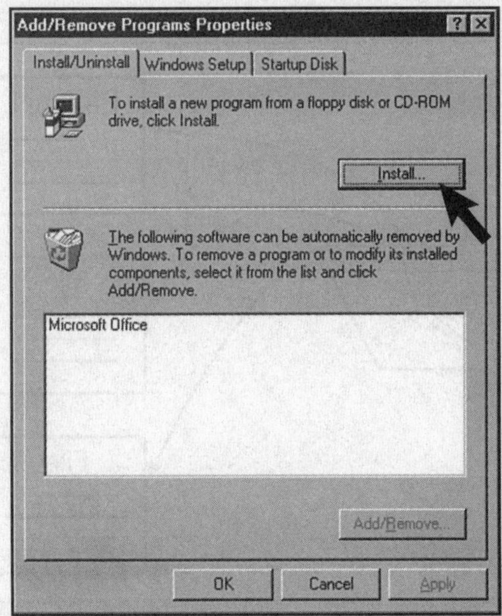

3 This dialog box is your key to installing programs. Click the **Install** button to begin.

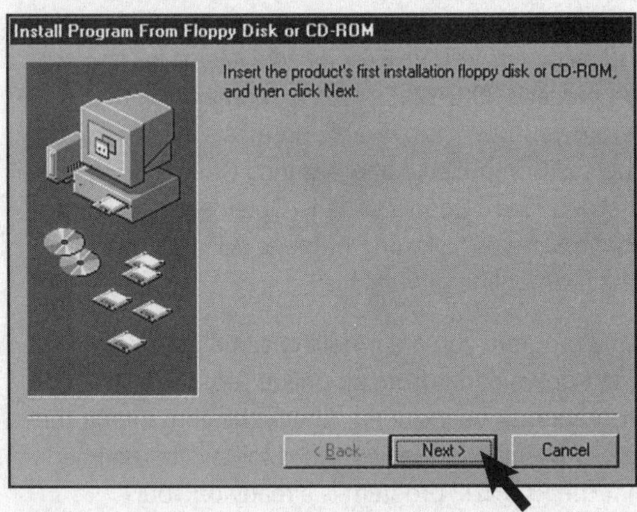

4 You're told to insert the first floppy disk or the CD that stores the program into one of the drives. Do as you're instructed, and then click the **Next** button.

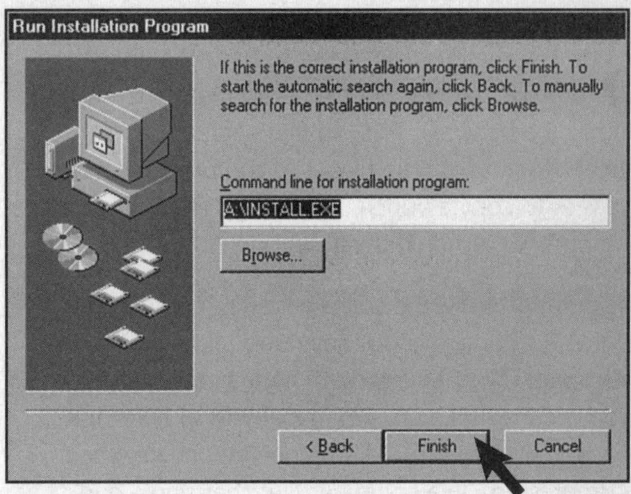

5 The Wizard searches the disk for an install or setup file it can run, and then displays the file's name. Click the **Finish** button to start the program's own installation program.

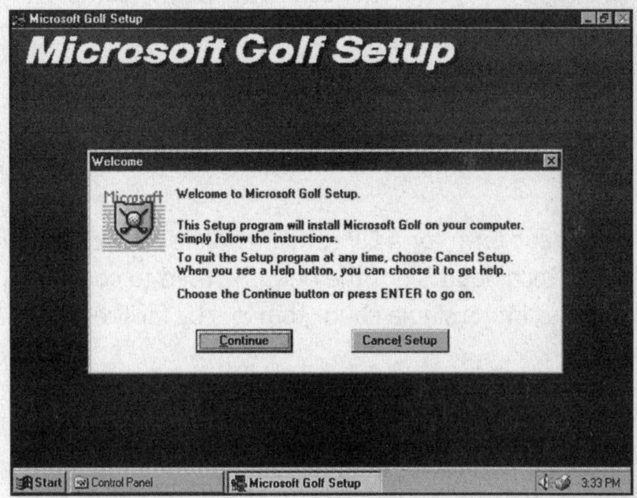

6 Each program has its own way of installing files. Most programs will lead you step-by-step through the installation. Follow the on-screen instructions.

If the installation program asks a question or allows you to make a choice, and you're not sure of the answer, just click **Yes** or **OK**. Installation programs are meant to be easy, and they usually default to the most common or safest answer.

Install a Program from a "ZIP" File

Some commercial software comes on a disk that contains just one big file (as do many shareware and free programs). This big file is actually a "container" for lots of little files. The *container file* makes it easier to copy a bunch of little files to your computer's hard disk drive.

Most importantly, the container also "compresses" all the individual files so they don't take up as much disk space. That way, even though all the files for a program may take up two megabytes of hard disk space, they may only take up one megabyte when "compressed" in a container file. That single one-megabyte file can fit on a standard floppy disk; two one-megabyte files would not.

The container file is most often referred to as a "ZIP" or "ZIPped" file, after the technique used to compress the individual files into a single compact one. Such files are generally easy to identify; their names have .ZIP extensions. If you see a file named PROGRAM.ZIP, for example, you can be pretty sure it is a ZIP container file.

The generic term for a ZIP container file is an *archive*. The ZIP technique is not the only one used to compress files into a single chunk, but it is by far the most common.

Before you can use the files in a ZIP archive, you must *decompress* (or "unpack") them. This requires a decompression program. The most common program for decompressing ZIP files is PKUNZIP, provided as shareware by the company who pioneered the ZIP file format. A number of ZIP-compatible programs are available; some cost money, others are free.

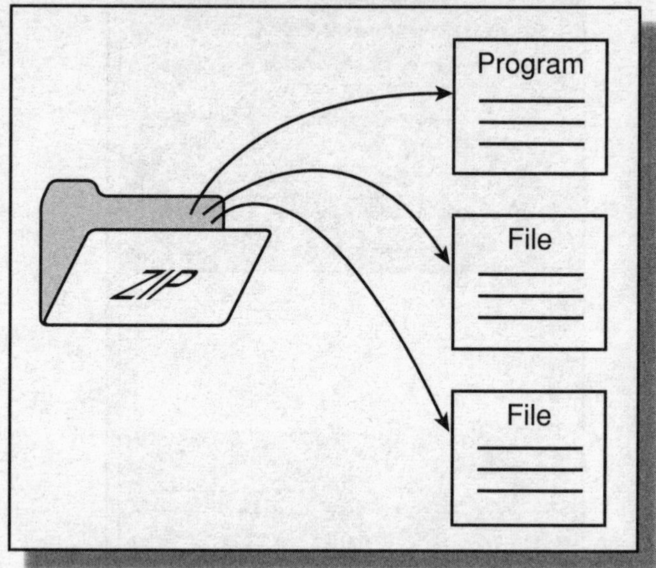

You need a separate program to unpack a ZIP file. If you get a ZIP file but don't have the required decompression software, you're out of luck. You will need to find a copy of PKUNZIP (or its equivalent) before you can proceed. PKUNZIP, which is shareware ("try-before-you-buy") is available on most online services (such as CompuServe and America Online) or on the Internet. (See "Connect to the Outside World Using Online Services," starting on page 235, for more details on online services.)

If the program you are installing came on a disk (you didn't download it from an online service), a PKUNZIP program may be included. Check the contents of the disk to be sure. In the steps that follow, it's assumed that the PKUNZIP program is already on your computer's hard disk drive. If it's not, see "Do It Yourself—Copy the PKUNZIP Program to Your Computer," later in this task.

Begin Do It Yourself Decompress a ZIP File

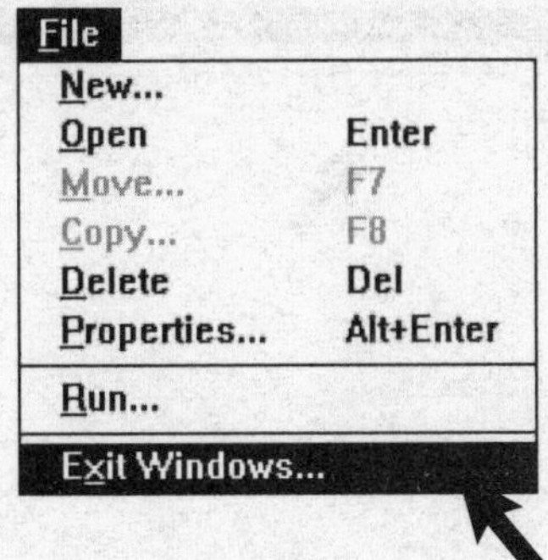

1 If you are running Windows 3.11, return to the DOS prompt by choosing **File, Exit Windows**, and then **OK**, in the Program Manager.

2 Use the DOS **CD** command to change to the directory that contains the ZIP file you want to decompress. Type **CD \MYDIR**, for example, if the directory you want is MYDIR.

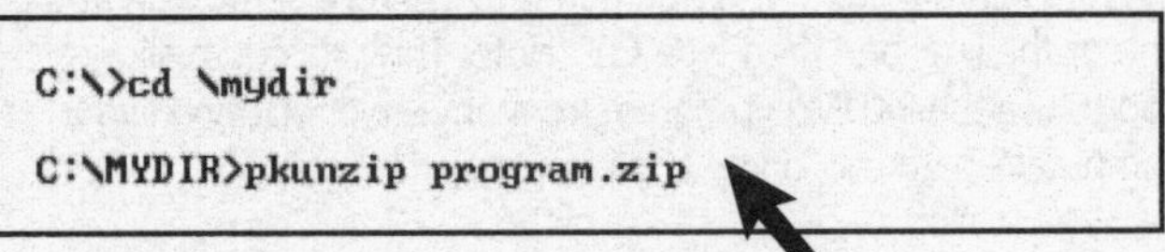

3 Type **PKUNZIP**, a space, and then the disk drive letter where the archive file resides, followed by a colon. Finally, type the name of the ZIP file. If the ZIP filename is PROGRAM.ZIP, for example, type **PKUNZIP A:PROGRAM.ZIP**.

```
C:\>cd \mydir

C:\MYDIR>pkunzip program.zip

PKUNZIP (R)    FAST!    Extract  ti
Copr. 1989-1993 PKWARE Inc. All Rig
PKUNZIP Reg. U.S. Pat. and Tm. Off.

■ 80486 CPU detected.
■ EMS version 4.00 detected.
■ XMS version 2.00 detected.
■ DPMI version 0.90 detected.

Searching ZIP: PROGRAM.ZIP
  Exploding: TAPCIS.EXE
  Exploding: MAIL.SAV
  Exploding: WPSGA.SAV
  Exploding: CEVIDEO.SAV
  Exploding: MSBASIC.SAV
  Exploding: WRITER.SAV

C:\MYDIR>
```

4 Some ZIPped files contain messages. Read the messages and follow any prompts that may appear. The process of decompressing the files contained in a ZIP file is usually automatic. You need only sit back and wait for the DOS prompt to reappear.

5 If the program is supposed to run under DOS, type the name of the program and press **Enter** to start it. If the program is supposed to run under Windows 3.11, start Windows, and create a Program Manager icon for the program, following steps 11 through 14 in "Install a Windows 3.11 Program That Has No Installation Utility" on page 369).

Begin Do It Yourself Copy the PKUNZIP Program to Your Computer

1 See "Install a Windows 3.11 Program That Has No Installation Utility" on page 369 to review how to copy a program (in this case, PKUNZIP) from a disk to your computer's hard disk drive. Instead of putting the PKUNZIP program in its own directory, however, put it in your C:\ root directory instead (the program's full file name is PKUNZIP.EXE).

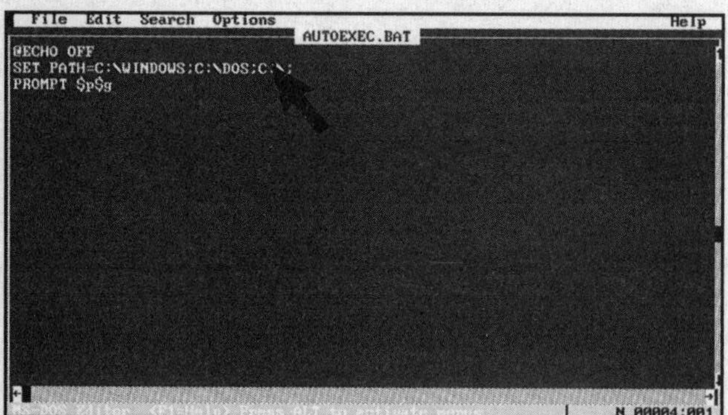

2 If you are using DOS, at the DOS prompt, type **EDIT \AUTOEXEC.BAT**. This starts the DOS EDIT program and opens the AUTOEXEC.BAT file automatically for editing.

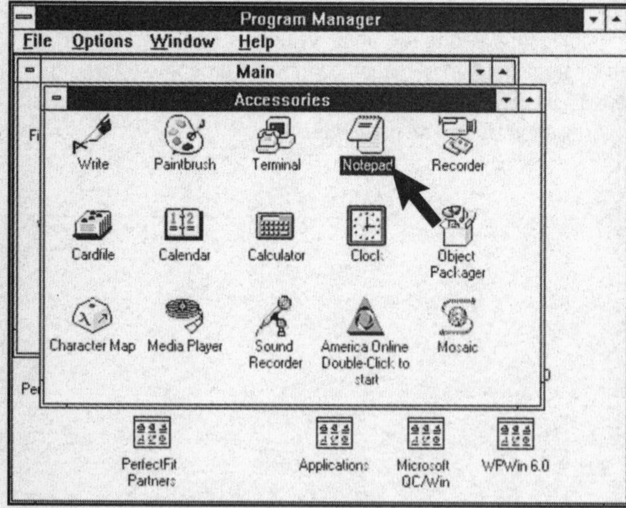

3 If you are using Windows 3.11, start the **Notepad** program by double-clicking on it (normally you'll find it in the Accessories program group). In Notepad, select **File, Open**, type **\AUTOEXEC.BAT**, and click **OK**. This loads the AUTOEXEC.BAT file into the Notepad program.

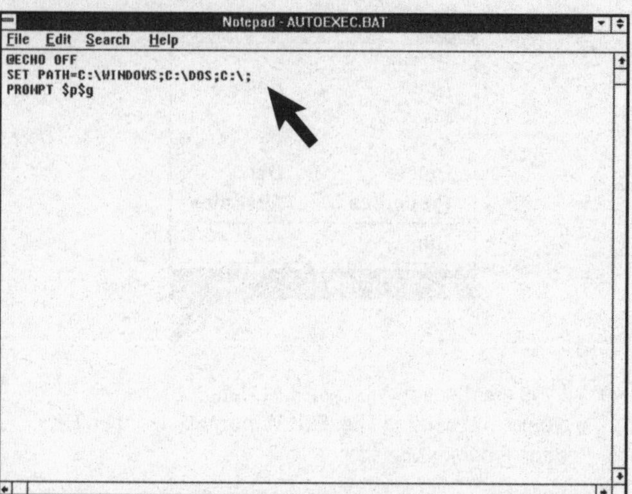

4 Look at the PATH= command. It contains all the directories that you want DOS to always look in for files. At the very least, it should say **PATH=C:**. Additional subdirectories, if any, may be specified as well. These are shown with a semicolon, such as

PATH=C:\;C:DOS;C:\WP60

Look carefully to make sure the C:\ root directory is specified in the PATH command. If it is not, add it by typing a semicolon at the end of the line, and then type **C:**. (Note: This procedure allows you to use the PKUNZIP program from any subdirectory on your computer's hard disk drive. This is an important step.)

5 Save the edited AUTOEXEC.BAT file by choosing **File, Save** (both EDIT and Notepad programs), and then exit by choosing **File, Exit**.

Do It Yourself Copy the PKUNZIP Program to Your Computer

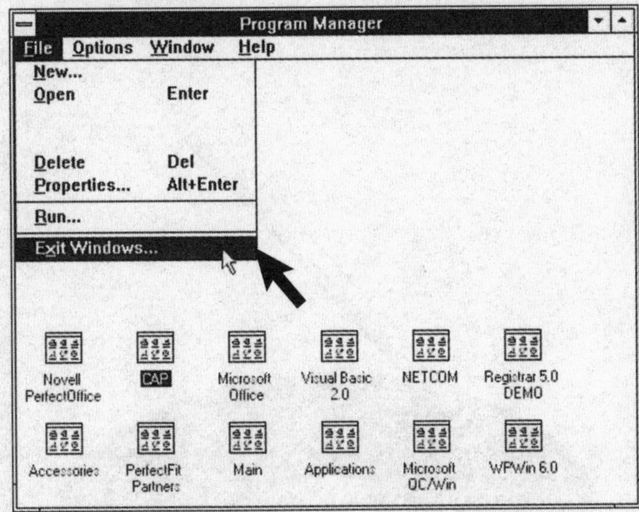

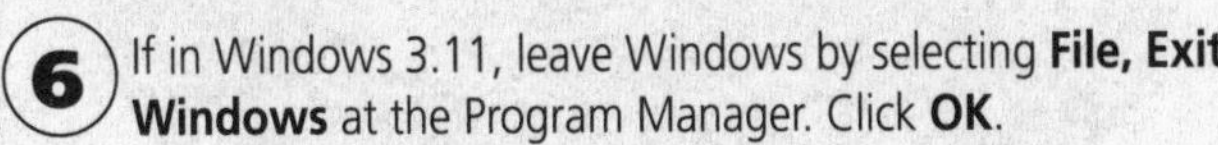

6 If in Windows 3.11, leave Windows by selecting **File, Exit Windows** at the Program Manager. Click **OK**.

7 Restart your computer by pressing the **Ctrl**, **Alt**, and **Del** keys simultaneously. Once your computer is restarted, you can follow the "Do It Yourself" steps (earlier in this task) for decompressing a ZIP file.

Uninstall a DOS Program

A few years ago, you swore by your ABC word processor, with its state-of-the-art features. Now, you swear *at* it. You've switched to another word processing program, and the ABC word processor is just eating up space on your computer's hard disk drive.

Uninstalling is the act of removing a program you no longer need (or want) from your computer system. Many of the latest software programs—especially those designed for use with Microsoft Windows—come with an "uninstaller" utility that makes this process easy. Not all programs offer this utility; some leave the job of file uninstalling up to you.

The task of uninstalling software manually is easiest if the program is designed to be used under DOS, rather than Microsoft Windows. The reason: When they are installed, DOS programs typically make fewer changes to your system; often program files are added to just one or two subdirectories on your computer's hard disk drive.

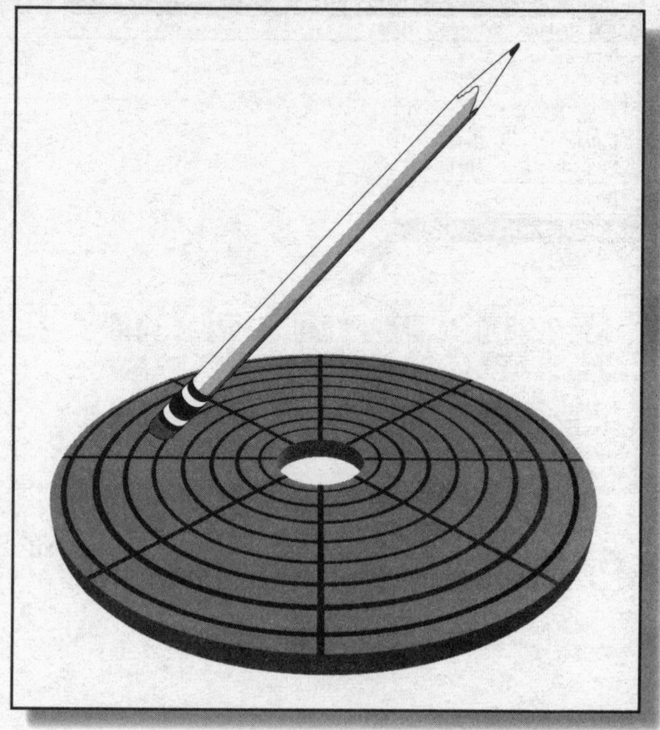

A number of "installation/deinstallation" utilities (another name for "uninstaller") are available to help you remove unwanted programs. They work by watching the files and changes made to your computer when you install new software. Then, when you want to remove the software, the utility knows which files and disk subdirectories to remove, and what changes to undo.

Prior to uninstalling any software, make a backup of your entire computer's hard disk drive, as explained in "Back Up the Contents of Your Hard Disk Drive with Microsoft Backup" on page 458. This is to ensure the integrity of your system in case you accidentally remove a file the computer needs. Make "protection" copies of the computer's AUTOEXEC.BAT and CONFIG.SYS files by copying these files to a blank disk.

If the program you want to delete consists of just one file, you can simply delete it from the computer's hard disk drive by typing ERASE *PROGRAM*.EXE, where *PROGRAM.EXE* is the name of the program file you want to remove.

Begin Do It Yourself Delete a DOS Program

Note: As a precaution, make sure you are using the Mirror or Undelete features of DOS (Mirror is found in DOS 5.0; Undelete in DOS 6.x). These utilities help track deleted files, making it easier to reclaim them if you delete the wrong one. See "Set Up Undelete to Maximize Your Undeletion Success" on page 452 for more information on using these utilities.

```
C:\>cd \mydir
```

1 Identify the subdirectory (or subdirectories) that contain the files for the program you want to delete. Type **CD \ MYDIR** and press **Enter**, where MYDIR is the name of the subdirectory that contains the program files.

```
C:\>cd \mydir

C:\MYDIR>dir *.*

 Volume in drive C is MS-DOS_5
 Volume Serial Number is 18A1-5E0C
 Directory of C:\MYDIR

.            <DIR>      03-16-95  10:01a
..           <DIR>      03-16-95  10:01a
TAPTRY   EXE    336656 08-21-94   9:37a
MAIL     SAV     57780 03-16-95   8:33a
WPSGA    SAV     68495 03-14-95   4:03p
CEVIDEO  SAV    104967 03-01-95   8:19p
MSBASIC  SAV     12821 01-11-95  12:50p
WRITER   SAV      1492 03-11-95   8:51p
        8 file(s)     582211 bytes
                    40466432 bytes free

C:\MYDIR>
```

2 Type **DIR *.***, and press **Enter**, to display a directory of files in the current subdirectory. Verify that the files you see are the ones you want to remove.

```
C:\>cd \mydir

C:\MYDIR>dir *.*

 Volume in drive C is MS-DOS_5
 Volume Serial Number is 18A1-5E0C
 Directory of C:\MYDIR

.            <DIR>      03-16-95  10:01a
..           <DIR>      03-16-95  10:01a
TAPTRY   EXE    336656 08-21-94   9:37a
MAIL     SAV     57780 03-16-95   8:33a
WPSGA    SAV     68495 03-14-95   4:03p
CEVIDEO  SAV    104967 03-01-95   8:19p
MSBASIC  SAV     12821 01-11-95  12:50p
WRITER   SAV      1492 03-11-95   8:51p
        8 file(s)     582211 bytes
                    40466432 bytes free

C:\MYDIR>
C:\MYDIR>copy *.sav A:
```

3 If the subdirectory contains any data files you want to keep, copy these to a floppy disk drive (or another subdirectory of your computer's hard disk drive).

```
C:\MYDIR>erase *.*
All files in directory will be deleted!
Are you sure (Y/N)?
```

4 To erase the files, type **DEL *.***, and press **Enter**. DOS asks whether you're sure you want to delete all the files in the current directory. To delete, type **Y** at the prompt.

```
C:\MYDIR>dir

 Volume in drive C is MS-DOS_5
 Volume Serial Number is 18A1-5E0C
 Directory of C:\MYDIR

.            <DIR>      03-16-95  10:01a
..           <DIR>      03-16-95  10:01a
        2 file(s)          0 bytes
                    41000960 bytes free

C:\MYDIR>
```

5 To verify that the files are deleted, type **DIR *.***, and press **Enter**. If a file remains, someone probably "locked" it against deletion by turning on the "read-only" attribute of the file. See your DOS manual for more information on using the DOS ATTRIB command (and the read-only attribute) so you can delete the stubborn file.

(continues)

Do It Yourself Delete a DOS Program

(continued)

6 Repeat steps 1 through 5 for every subdirectory that contains files for the program you want to delete.

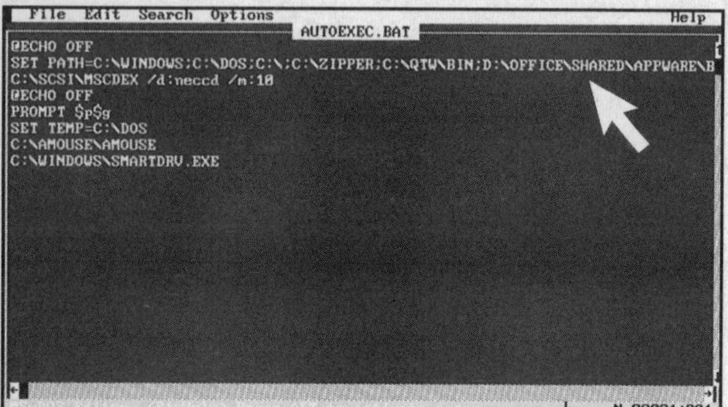

```
File  Edit  Search  Options                                              Help
                               AUTOEXEC.BAT
@ECHO OFF
SET PATH=C:\WINDOWS;C:\DOS;C:\;C:\ZIPPER;C:\QTW\BIN;D:\OFFICE\SHARED\APPWARE\B
C:\SCSI\MSCDEX /d:neccd /m:10
@ECHO OFF
PROMPT $p$g
SET TEMP=C:\DOS
C:\AMOUSE\AMOUSE
C:\WINDOWS\SMARTDRV.EXE
                                                              N 00001:001
```

7 Some DOS programs modify the AUTOEXEC.BAT and CONFIG.SYS files. When installed, a program may (for example) add its subdirectory path to the PATH= statement in the AUTOEXEC.BAT file. (See "Modify Your Startup Files in Windows 3.11 and DOS" on page 412 for more information.)

```
File  Edit  Search  Options                                              Help
                               CONFIG.SYS
DEVICE=C:\DOS\SETVER.EXE
DEVICE=C:\WINDOWS\HIMEM.SYS
DEVICE=C:\SCSI\MA13B.SYS
DEVICE=C:\SCSI\NECCDR.SYS /d:neccd
BREAK=ON
FILES=60
BUFFERS = 10
STACKS=9,256
SHELL=C:\DOS\COMMAND.COM C:\DOS\ /E:1024 /p
DEVICE=C:\WINDOWS\EMM386.EXE 2048 RAM
DOS=HIGH,UMB
Lastdrive=Z
                                                              N 00001:001
```

8 Repeat step 7 to edit the CONFIG.SYS file. Type **EDIT CONFIG.SYS** at the DOS prompt and press **Enter**. Look for references to the deleted program file and/or subdirectory, and remove them. When you're done, select **File, Save**, and then **File, Exit**.

9 Restart your computer by pressing **Ctrl+Alt+Del**. Note any discrepancies if your computer does not start normally. Use your computer and other software for several minutes to ensure that all is working correctly.

```
C:\MYDIR>cd \

C:\>rd \mydir
```

10 If everything is running well, you can delete the subdirectory (or subdirectories) that used to house the program files. Type **RD *MYDIR*** (where \MYDIR is the name of the directory you want to delete) and press **Enter**. (Note: Do not delete subdirectories until you are sure the computer is working properly.)

```
C:\MYDIR>undelete

Directory: C:\MYDIR
File Specifications: *.*

    Deletion-tracking file contains   12 deleted files.
    Of those,   12 files have all clusters available,
                 0 files have some clusters available,
                 0 files have no clusters available.

    MS-DOS directory contains    6 deleted files.
    Of those,    6 files may be recovered.

Using the deletion-tracking file.

     WRITER   SAV    1492  3-11-95  8:51p  ...A  Deleted:  3-16-95 10:20a
All of the clusters for this file are available. Undelete (Y/N)?
```

11 If all is NOT working satisfactorily, it may be because you accidentally deleted a file you should have kept. You can use the Undelete command in DOS 5.0 or later to restore files you previously deleted. See "Restore an Accidentally Deleted File with Undelete" on page 448 for more information. If you edited the computer's CONFIG.SYS and AUTOEXEC.BAT files, you can restore these to their original condition by copying the versions you saved on the disk back to your computer's hard disk.

Uninstall a Windows 3.11 Program

Have a Windows 3.11 program you no longer need? Odds are, it's taking up a lot of space on your computer's hard disk, and you should delete it to clear room for another program. This is called "uninstalling"—removing a program you no longer need (or want) from your computer system.

A number of the latest top-notch Windows software come with an "uninstaller" utility that makes this process easy. You just run the uninstaller for that program, and it removes all the files that were originally installed on your system. Just as importantly, it undoes a lot of changes many programs make to the Windows 3.11 environment when they are installed. The uninstaller utility is by far the safest way to remove an old program you no longer need.

A number of "installation/deinstallation" (another name for "uninstaller") utilities are available to help you remove unwanted programs from a computer. They work by watching the files and changes made to your computer when you install new software. When you want to remove the software, the utility knows which files and disk subdirectories to remove, and what changes to undo.

Uninstalling Windows 3.11 programs does have some risks. If you do not use the uninstaller utility that came with the program you want to remove (or a separate installation/deinstallation utility), proceed with caution. Attempting to delete files and alter Windows configuration settings can render your computer unusable. Always, *always* make a backup of your computer's hard disk drive before uninstalling Windows software.

Prior to uninstalling any software, make a backup of your entire computer's hard disk drive, as explained in "Back Up the Contents of Your Hard Disk Drive with Microsoft Backup" on page 458. This is to ensure the integrity of your system in case you accidentally remove a file the computer needs.

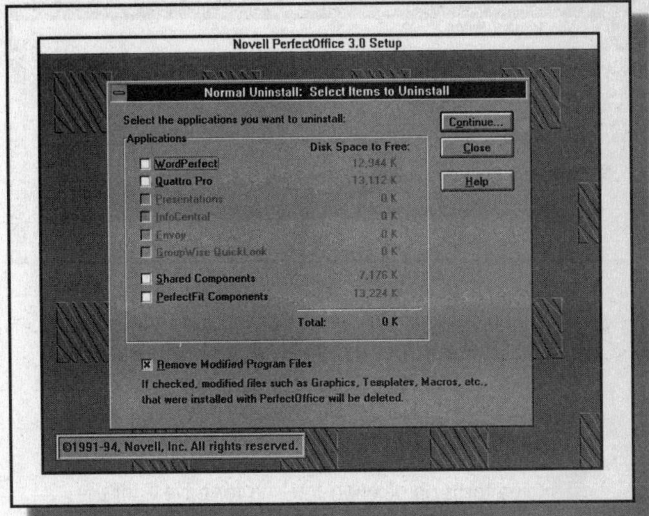

Make "protection" copies of the computer's AUTOEXEC.BAT, CONFIG.SYS, WIN.INI, and SYSTEM.INI files by copying these files to a blank disk. The AUTOEXEC.BAT and CONFIG.SYS files are located in the root directory of the computer's hard disk drive. The WIN.INI and SYSTEM.INI files are typically located in the \WINDOWS directory.

If the program you want to delete consists of just one file, you can simply delete it from the computer's hard disk drive by deleting the program file from the Windows 3.11 File Manager.

Begin Do It Yourself Delete a Windows 3.11 Program

1 If you do not already use the deletion-tracking feature in DOS 5 or 6, see "Set Up Undelete to Maximize Your Undeletion Success" on page 452.

MIRROR /tc

This line turns on deletion-tracking for drive C: (if the program you want to delete is on another drive, substitute that drive's name for *c*— for example, **MIRROR /td** for the D: drive). Exit Windows 3.11 and restart your computer to enable the Mirror program. The Mirror program scans your computer's hard disk drive for deletions. With this program activated, you can reclaim erased files.

2 Identify the subdirectory (or subdirectories) that contain the files for the program you want to delete.

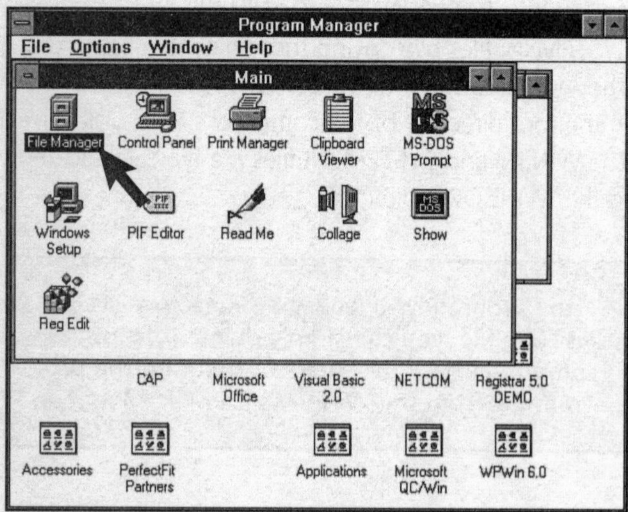

3 Start the Windows 3.11 **File Manager** by double-clicking on its icon in the Windows Program Manager. In the directory list of File Manager, click the directory that contains the program files you want to delete.

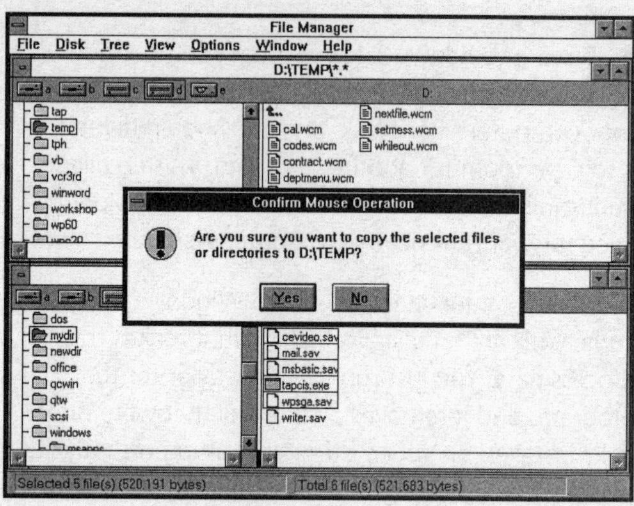

4 If the subdirectory contains any data files you want to keep, copy these to a floppy disk drive or another subdirectory of your computer's hard disk drive.

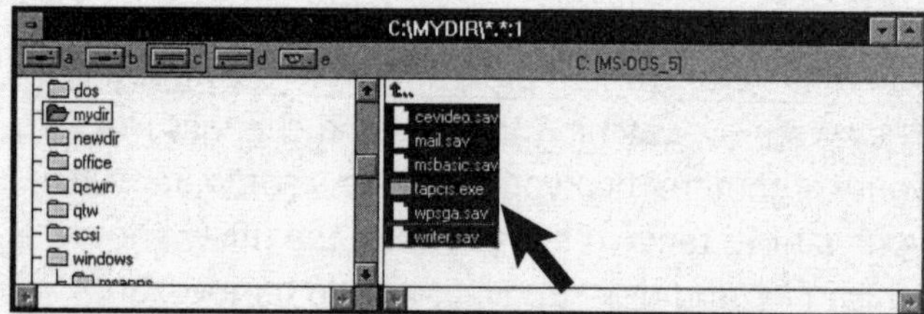

5 Select all the files: in the file list, click the first file in the subdirectory, hold down the **Shift** key, and click the last file of the subdirectory.

6 To erase the files, select **File, Delete**, and click **OK** (or press the **Delete** key as a shortcut).

Do It Yourself Delete a Windows 3.11 Program

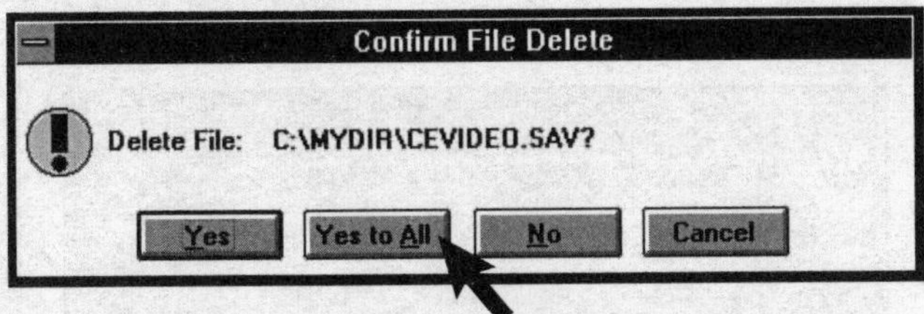

7 If the Confirm File Deletion dialog box appears (it may not, depending on the options you've selected for File Manager), select **Yes to All**. Repeat steps 4 through 6 for every subdirectory that contains files for the program you want to delete. When you're done, close File Manager: select **File, Exit Windows**.

8 Exit Windows by choosing **File, Exit** Windows at the Program Manager, and then clicking on **OK**.

9 At the DOS prompt, press **Ctrl+Alt+Del** to reset your computer. Note any discrepancies if your computer does not start normally. Use your computer, Windows, and other software for several minutes to ensure that all is working correctly.

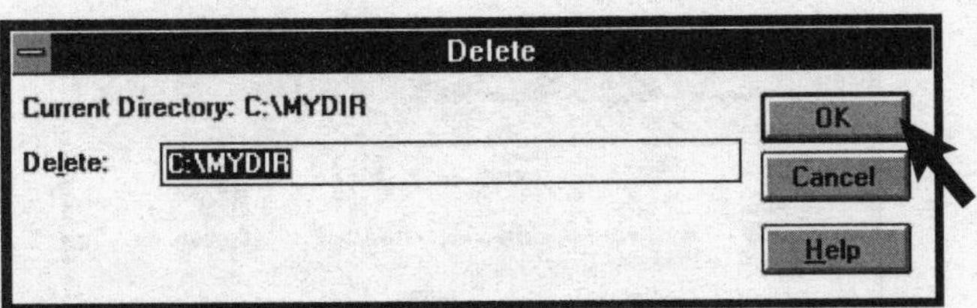

10 If all is working satisfactorily, you can delete the subdirectory (or subdirectories) that used to house the program files. Run File Manager; click the subdirectory you want to delete. Press the **Delete** key, and click **OK**.

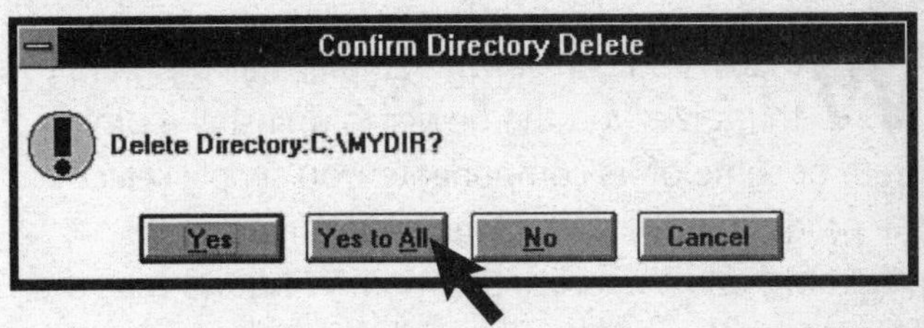

11 If the Confirm Directory Deletion dialog box appears, select **Yes to All**. Repeat the previous steps for every subdirectory previously used by the deleted program. (Note: Do not delete subdirectories until you are sure the computer is working properly. You cannot reclaim a deleted file if its subdirectory is also deleted.)

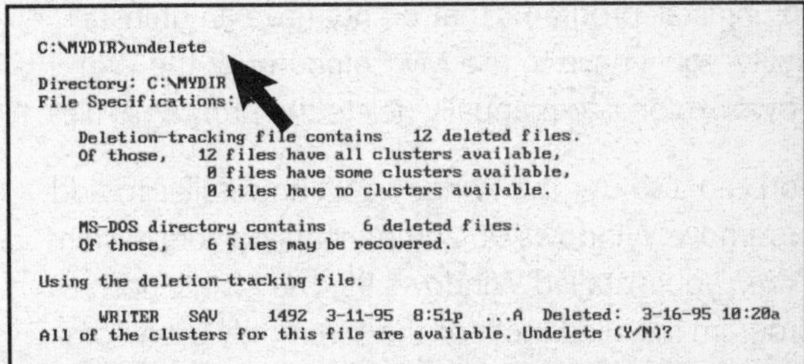

12 If all is NOT working satisfactorily, it may be because you accidentally deleted a file you should have kept. You can use the Undelete command (in DOS 5.0 or later) to restore files you previously deleted. See "Restore an Accidentally Deleted File with Undelete" on page 448 for more information.

Many programs alter the WIN.INI and SYSTEM.INI files when they are installed. You can use the Notepad program to edit these files, removing unwanted references to the deleted file. You should only do so, however, if you know precisely what you are doing. Refer to the manual that came with your program, or consult a knowledgeable friend.

Uninstall a Program in Windows 95

Windows 95 comes with an uninstall program that gives you the power to uninstall a program or some of its components. You simply select the program from a list of installed Windows 95 programs, and then click a button. Windows runs the program's setup utility, which allows you to remove or add some or all of the program's components.

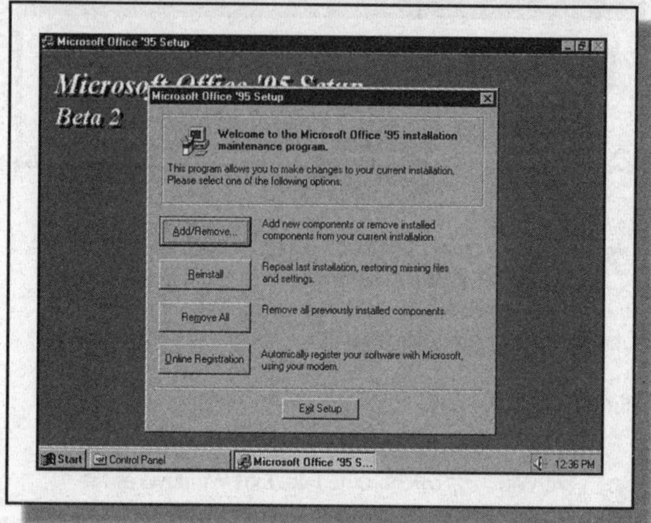

Windows 95 itself does not uninstall the programs. It simply runs the program's setup utility. Most Windows 95 programs will come with such a utility, but older Windows programs and DOS programs do not. To uninstall programs that do not have an uninstall utility, you'll have to use My Computer or the Windows Explorer to manually delete the program's files.

You can also use the Windows 95 uninstaller to add or remove Windows 95 components on your system. When you installed Windows 95, the installation program installed most of the commonly used components for you, but to save disk space, it may not have installed some of the more advanced features or features that would consume a lot of disk space. You can remove components that you don't plan on using, or install components that you want to use (assuming you have sufficient disk space).

Begin Do It Yourself Uninstall Windows 95 Programs

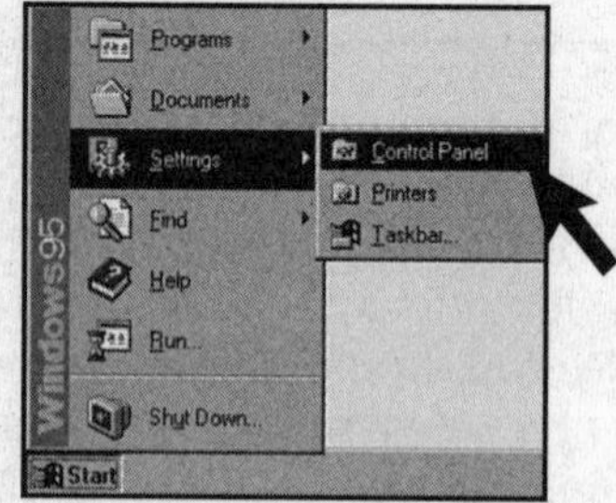

1 Windows lets you uninstall some Windows 95 programs, but not old Windows or DOS programs. Click the **Start** button, rest the mouse pointer on **Settings**, and then click **Control Panel**.

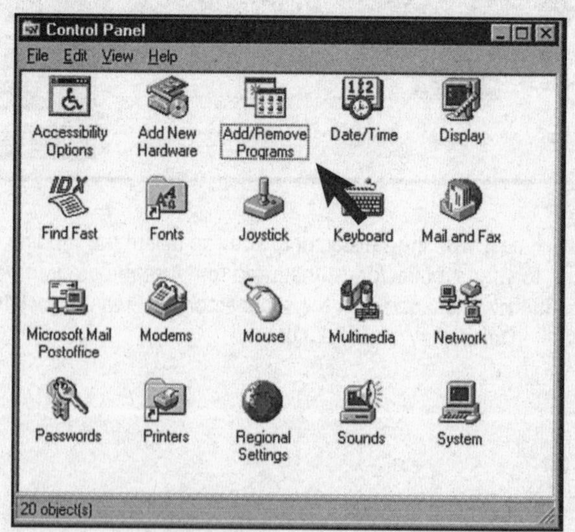

2 You use **Add/Remove Programs** to uninstall Windows 95 programs. Double-click the icon now.

Do It Yourself Uninstall Windows 95 Programs

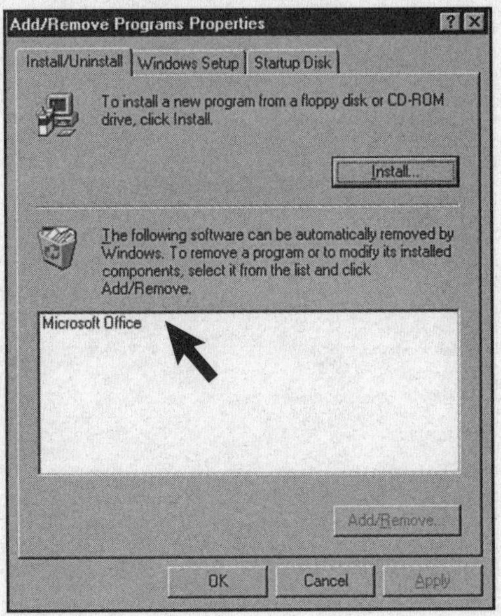

3 At the bottom of the Add/Remove Programs Properties dialog box is a list of all the programs you can remove from your system. If you don't see the program you want to remove, you can't use this procedure to remove it.

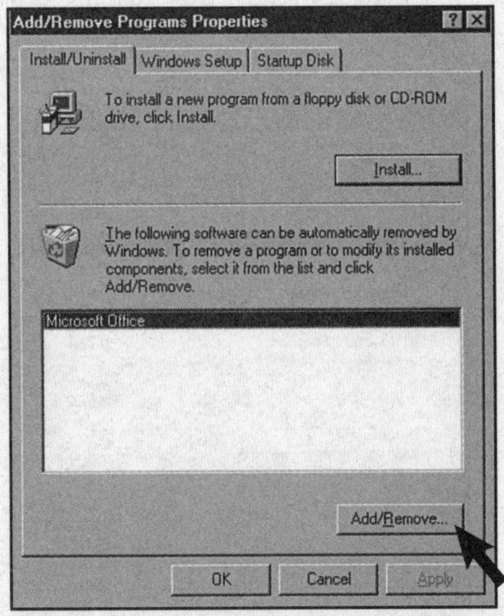

4 If you see the program you want to remove, click it in the list, and then click the **Add/Remove** button.

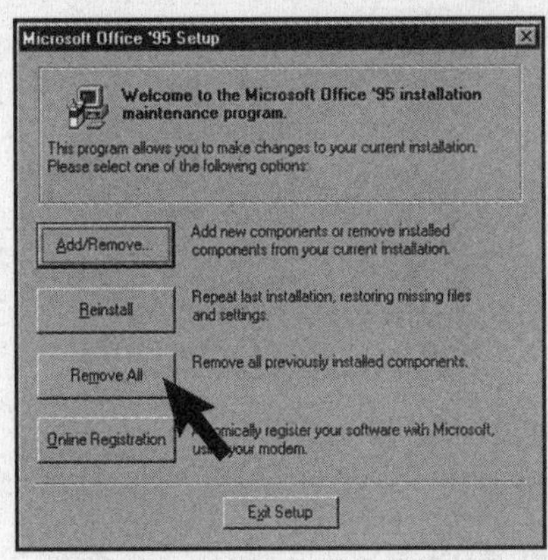

5 Windows runs the program's setup utility, which varies from program to program. In this case, you can click the **Remove All** button to remove all files that pertain to this program. Follow the on-screen instructions to complete the task.

Begin Do It Yourself Remove Windows 95 Components

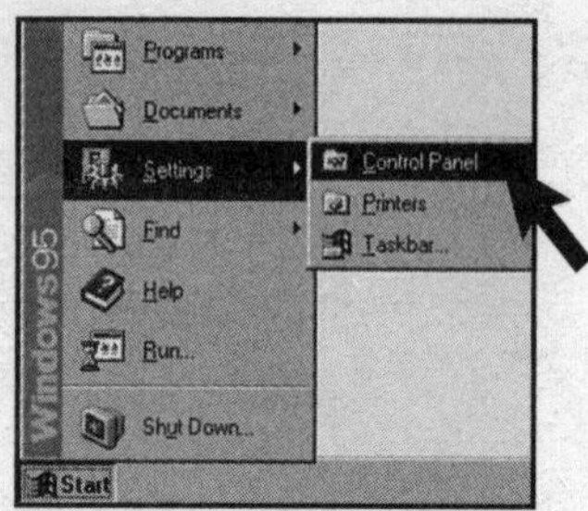

1 When you installed Windows 95, it may have installed components you never use, or failed to install components you want. Click the **Start** button, rest the mouse pointer on **Settings**, and click **Control Panel**.

2 Use the Add/Remove Programs icon to install or uninstall Windows components. Make sure you have your Windows installation disks handy, and then double-click the **Add/Remove Programs** icon.

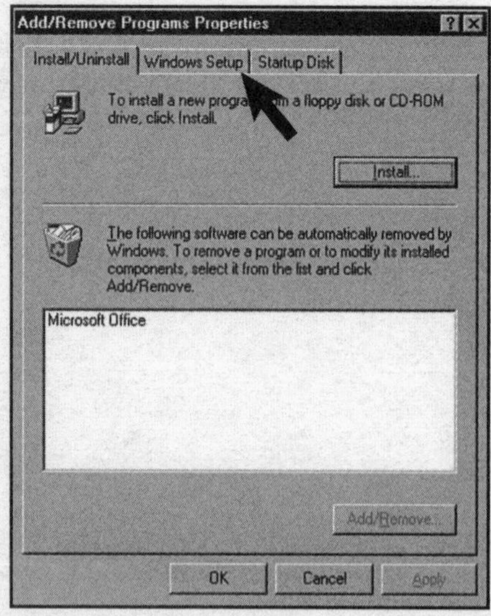

3 Click the **Windows Setup** tab to display a list of the Windows components installed on your computer. A white box with no check mark means the component is not installed. A gray box indicates some parts of the component are installed. A white box with a check means all parts are installed.

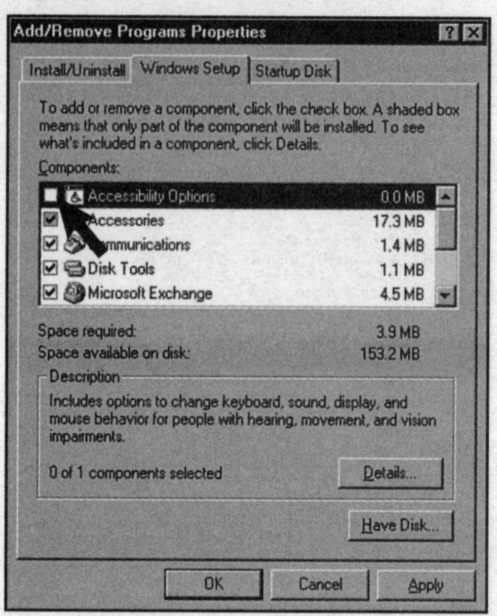

4 To install all elements of a component, click its check box until the check box appears white with a check mark in it. To uninstall all parts of a component, remove the check mark.

5 To install selected elements of a component, click the component, and then click the **Details** button.

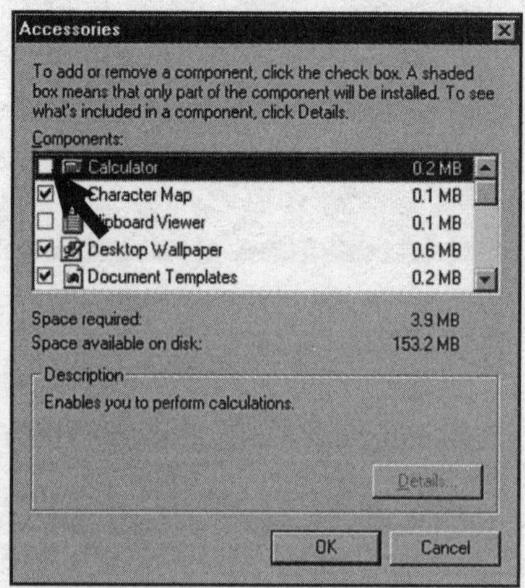

6 You see all the parts that make up the selected component. Click a check box to add or remove a check mark. Then, click the **OK** button.

7 Repeat steps 4-6 for each component on the list. Then, click the **OK** button.

DO IT YOURSELF

Make Your Computer Work Faster and Better

No one likes to wait in line. You hate it at the grocery store, and you hate it sitting behind your computer, waiting for it to finish the job you gave it. But don't blame your computer. As software becomes more and more complex, your computer has more work to do. What used to take just a few computational steps using yesterday's software may now take dozens.

This doesn't mean you have to sit twiddling your thumbs as your computer grinds away at your letter to Aunt Martha. There are a number of simple steps you can do to increase the performance of your computer, and this section describes the most important ones. Even if your computer is reasonably fast and has sufficient memory, you may want to try one or two of the techniques in the following pages, because in reality no computer is "too fast."

What You Will Find in This Section

Delete Old Files to Make More Room 388

Copy Old Files to a Disk 391

Make a "Startup" Disk 394

Optimize a Disk with Defrag 398

Increase Available Memory with MemMaker 402

Compress a Drive with DriveSpace 406

Modify Your Startup Files in Windows 3.11 and DOS 412

Delete Old Files to Make More Room

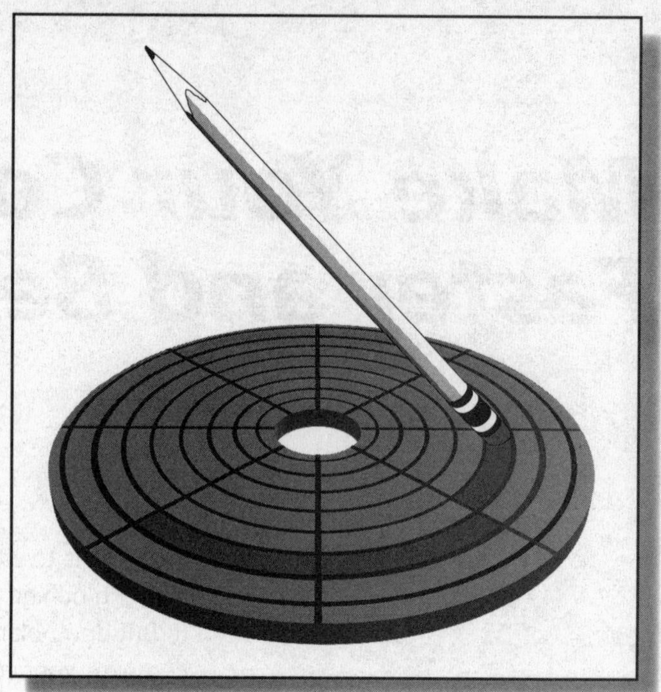

The microprocessor or "brain" of a computer largely determines how fast it works. A faster brain means a faster computer. Also important is the computer's hard disk drive, the main place to store your programs and valuable data. A slow disk drive can make using your computer a nightmare, because even simple jobs can take a long time.

Apart from replacing your computer's hard disk drive with a new, faster model, there are ways to improve the efficiency of the hard drive, which can improve the overall speed of your computer.

The simplest and most economical way to speed up a hard disk drive is—surprise!—remove files you no longer need. As a rule, the more space your files take up on the computer's hard drive, the slower the hard drive gets when retrieving and storing data. Any hard disk drive that is more than 50 percent full is a good candidate for pruning, especially if you've noticed a general slowdown of your computer.

Getting rid of files you no longer need also helps you improve your own efficiency with your computer. With fewer files to contend with, you can better find the files you want among the ones that remain.

You'll find two general types of files on a computer: program files and data files. *Program files* are the ones that came with the programs installed on your computer. If you are no longer using a certain program, you should consider removing its files. This will give you more space, which will help the hard drive operate faster. (See "Uninstall a DOS Program" on page 378 and "Uninstall a Windows 3.11 Program" on page 381 for more information on removing programs you no longer use.)

Data files are the ones you create by *using* the programs on your computer. A typical data file is a document you write (like a letter or a school report) with a word processor such as Microsoft Word or WordPerfect. On most computer systems, data files don't take up as much room as program files (especially if the programs are designed to be used with Microsoft Windows), but you should still be in the habit of removing unnecessary data files to make extra room. After a typical pruning of outdated data files, you may find you have 10 or 15 percent more hard disk space.

You can delete files in Windows 95 by using the Windows Explorer or My Computer. Select the files you want to delete and then drag them to the Recycle Bin, as explained in "Delete and Restore Files and Folders" on page 182. Be sure to empty the Recycle Bin, because it temporarily stores deleted files on your hard disk, consuming valuable disk space.

Begin Do It Yourself Delete Old Files Using Windows 3.11

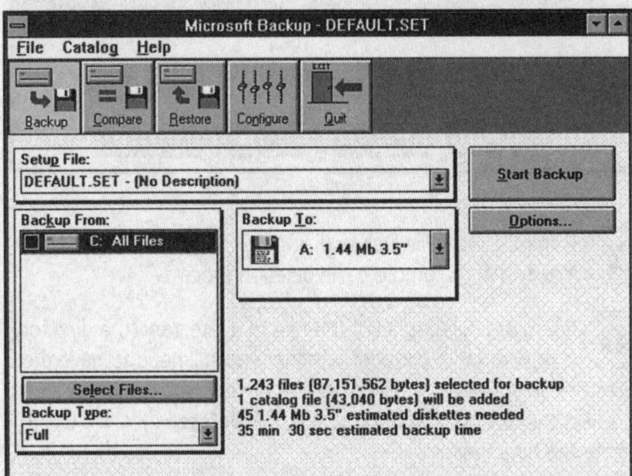

1 Before deleting files from your computer's hard disk drive, make a complete backup of the hard disk drive. See "Back Up the Contents of Your Hard Disk Drive with Microsoft Backup" on page 458 for more information on making backups. You can restore files from the backup in case you delete a file by mistake.

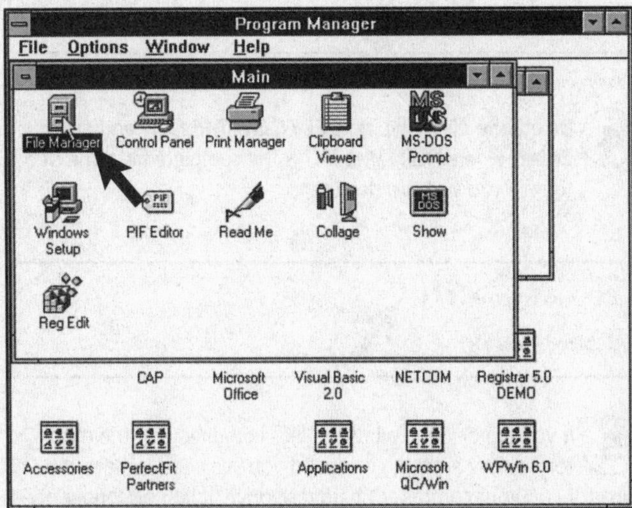

2 In Windows, double-click the **File Manager** icon in the Main program group.

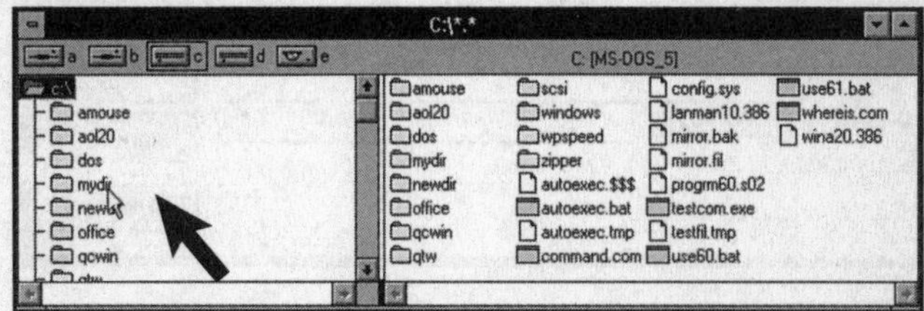

3 In File Manager, click the directory that contains the file(s) you want to delete.

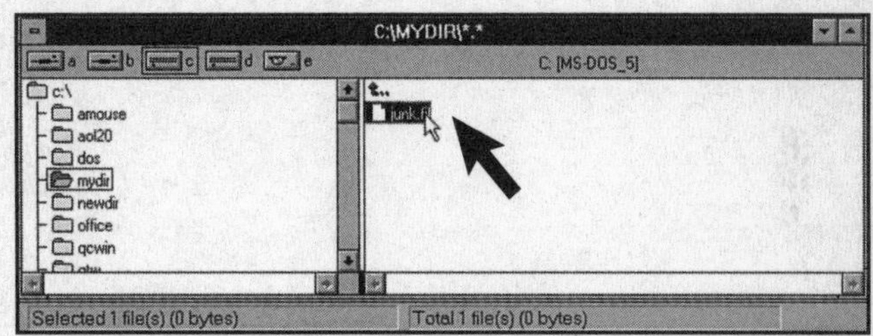

4 Locate the file(s) you want to delete, and select it in the file list (if you are deleting more than one file, press and hold the **Shift** or **Ctrl** key to select multiple files).

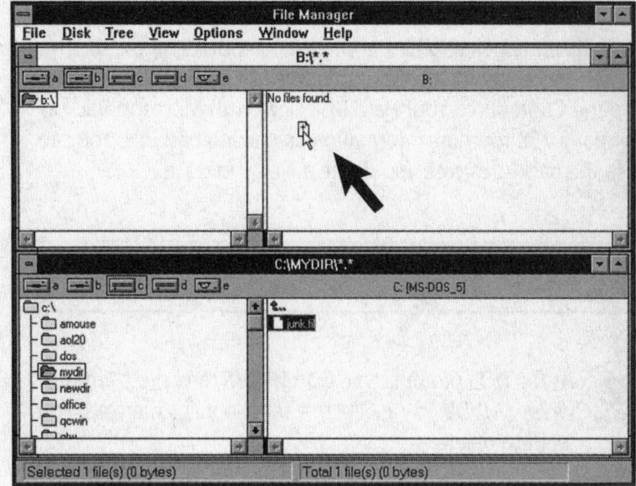

5 If you think you may need the file at some later date, but don't want to keep it on your computer's hard disk drive, copy the file to a disk (see "Copy Old Files to a Disk" on page 391 for more information). You can use this disk to keep an "archive" of the file, in case it's ever needed again.

(continues)

Do It Yourself Delete Old Files Using Windows 3.11

(continued)

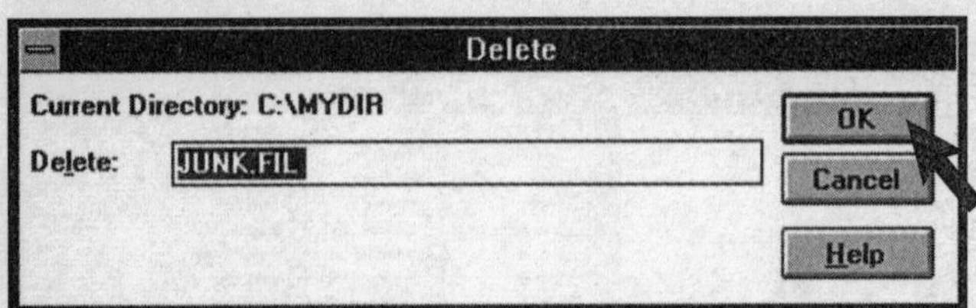

6 With the file(s) to delete still selected, press the **Delete** key. Click **OK** in the Delete dialog box.

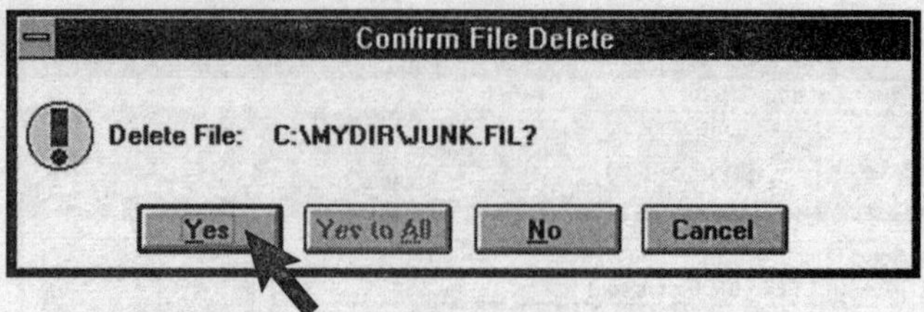

7 If the Confirm File Delete dialog box appears, click **Yes** or **Yes to All** to complete the deletion process.

8 If you are deleting all of the files in a directory (the directory is now empty), consider whether you still need to have the directory on your computer's hard disk drive. If you no longer need it, select the directory, and then press the **Delete** key. Click **OK** to delete the directory.

9 If the Confirm Directory Delete dialog box appears, click **Yes** to complete the deletion process.

Begin Do It Yourself Delete Old Files Using DOS

```
C:\WINDOWS>backup C: A:
```

1 Before deleting files from your computer's hard disk drive, make a complete backup of the hard disk drive. See "Back Up the Contents of Your Hard Disk Drive with Microsoft Backup" on page 458 for more information on making backups. You can use the backup in case you delete a file by mistake.

```
C:\>CD \PATH
```

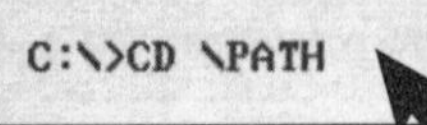

2 At the DOS prompt, type **CD *MYDIR***, and press **Enter**, where *\MYDIR* is the directory that contains the file(s) you want to delete.

```
C:\>copy junk.fil B:
```

3 If you think you may need the file at some later date, but don't want to keep it on your computer's hard disk drive, copy the file to a floppy disk (as explained in "Copy Old Files to a Disk" on page 391). Use this disk to keep an "archive" of the file, in case it's ever needed again.

```
C:\>del junk.fil
```

4 Delete the file by typing **DEL *FILENAME.EXT***, and press **Enter**, where *FILENAME.EXT* is the complete filename of the file you want to delete.

```
C:\>del junk.fil

C:\>rd \path
```

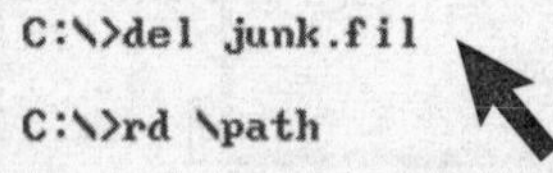

5 If you are deleting all of the files in a directory (the directory is now empty), consider if you still need to have the directory on your computer's hard disk drive. If you no longer need it, type **CD ** to return to the root directory of the hard drive. Then type **RD *MYDIR***, where *\MYDIR* is the name of the directory you want to delete.

Copy Old Files to a Disk

The previous task detailed deleting files you no longer need from your computer's hard disk drive (specifically "data" files, the files you create with your programs). You might find that most of your old files are ready for the trash heap anyway, but there may be some you want to keep a little longer.

If you want to keep a file, but no longer use it actively, consider copying it to a floppy disk for long-term storage. Then, if you ever find that you do need the file, you can dig up the floppy disk and retrieve the file from it.

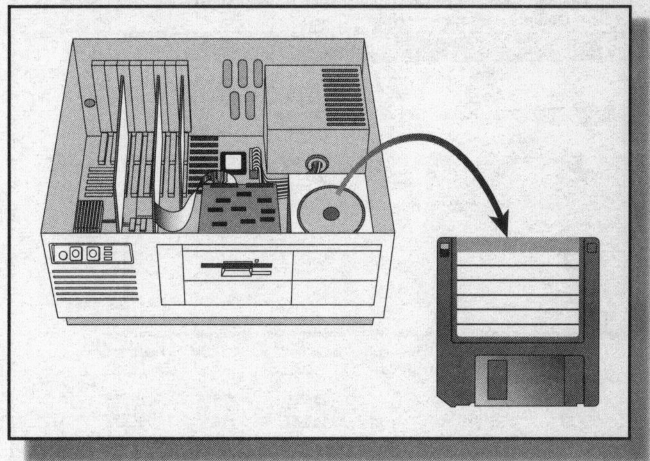

There is a limit to the size and number of files you can store on a floppy disk. Obviously, you cannot copy more files than will fit on one disk. If you use 3.5-inch high-density floppy disk drives, you can store up to 1.44 megabytes of files (or 224 files, whichever comes first) before running out of space; 5.25-inch high-density disk drives can store only 1.2 megabytes of files, or no more than 224 files.

Most data files are smaller than 1.44 or 1.2 megabytes, but not all are. You might create a complex picture in a graphics program, for example, and the resulting file may be bigger than 1.44 megabytes. If it is, the file will not fit on a standard floppy disk.

Yet there are ways to copy this file to a floppy disk, thereby freeing up space on your computer's hard disk drive. One way is to use a "compression" program, such as PKZIP. You can usually find and download these compression programs from online services. See "Connect with the Outside World Using Online Services" on page 235 for more information on where to get this program. Closer to home, you can use the disk-compression utility included in DOS (called DoubleSpace in versions 5.0 and 6.0, DriveSpace in versions 6.2 and higher). This feature can effectively double the storage capacity of your hard disk and floppy disks. See your DOS manual for more information.

Be sure to label each disk you use to store old files. If possible, keep like files together on one disk, to make it easier to find them later on.

Begin Do It Yourself Copy Old Files Using Windows 3.11

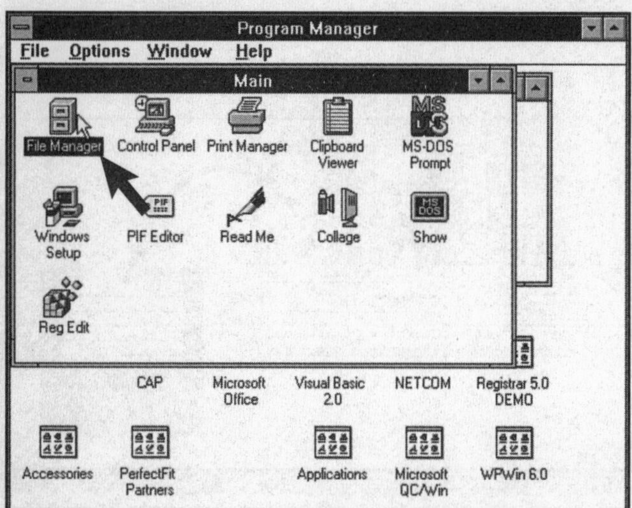

1 In Windows, double-click the **File Manager** icon in the Main program group.

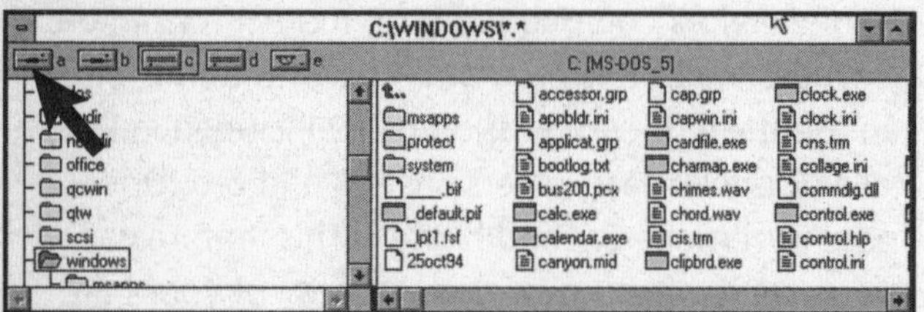

2 Insert a blank formatted disk into the disk drive and double-click (don't single-click) on the drive icon (**A:** or **B:**) to display the window for the floppy disk drive.

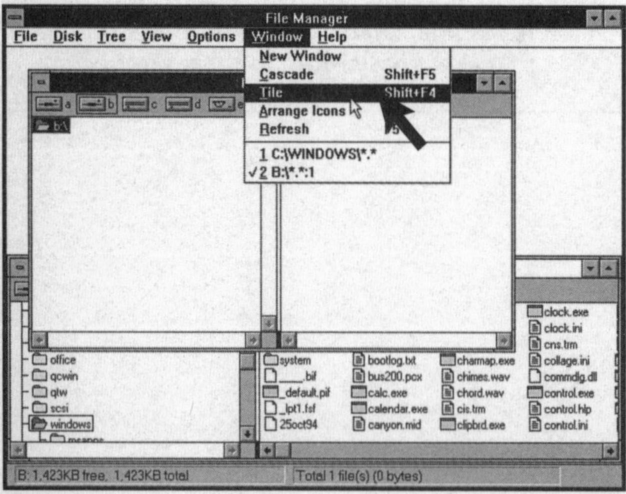

3 Arrange the windows so you can see both the hard disk drive contents and the floppy disk drive contents at the same time (the **Window**, **Tile** command makes this easy).

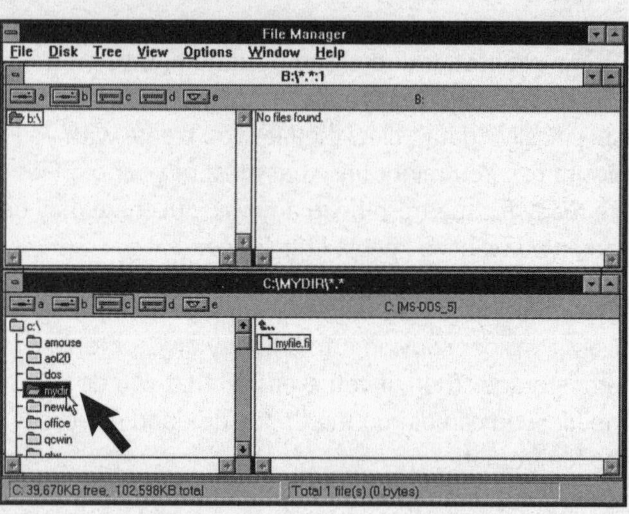

4 In the hard disk drive window, click the directory that contains the file you want to copy.

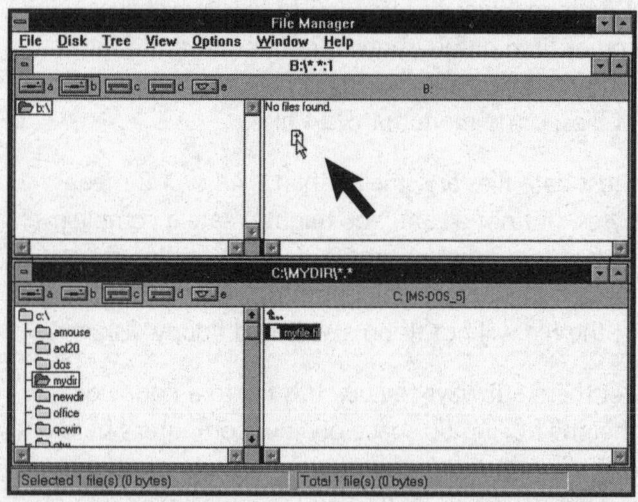

5 In the hard disk drive window, click the file you want to copy; drag the file into the floppy disk drive window.

Do It Yourself Copy Old Files Using Windows 3.11

6 If prompted to confirm the copy, click the **Yes** button. Repeat steps 4 through 6 for each additional file you want to copy.

The steps for copying files in Windows 95 are similar. You run My Computer or Windows Explorer, and then drag files from their folders to the floppy disk drive icon. For details, see "Copy or Move Files and Folders" on page 179.

Begin Do It Yourself Copy Old Files Using DOS

1 Insert a blank, formatted disk into the disk drive; type **CD *MYDIR***, and press **Enter**, where *\MYDIR* is the directory that contains the file you want to copy.

```
C:\>cd \mydir

C:\MYDIR>copy filename.exe A:
```

2 Type **COPY *FILENAME.EXE* A:** or **COPY *FILENAME.EXE* B:** and press **Enter**, where *FILENAME.EXE* is the exact filename of the file you want to copy (use **A:** or **B:** to indicate the drive that contains the disk you want to copy to). Repeat these steps for each file you want to copy.

Make a "Startup" Disk

When you turn on your computer, it goes through a number of steps to start and display the **C:** prompt or the Windows Program Manager. Shortly after turning on your computer, it refers to several important files on the computer's hard disk drive for instructions on how it should start. If something should happen to these files on your computer's hard disk drive, your computer is often rendered completely unusable, until the files on the hard drive can be replaced or repaired. An ugly catch-22 situation can occur, however: you need to access the hard drive to replace the system files, but you *can't* access the hard drive because the computer won't start without the system files!

Nine times out of ten, you can access your computer's hard disk drive even if the system files on it are damaged—or somehow got erased. To work this magic, you create something called a *startup* or *boot disk*. The idea is simple: the disk contains only the basic system files your computer needs to start. Once you've started the computer with this disk, you can usually access the computer's hard disk drive (though not always, for some highly technical reasons).

Why create a startup disk in the first place? As you develop schemes and methods for improving the speed and efficiency of your computer, there is a greater chance of damaging or erasing an important file accidentally. Creating a startup disk just in case something happens to the system files is simply good

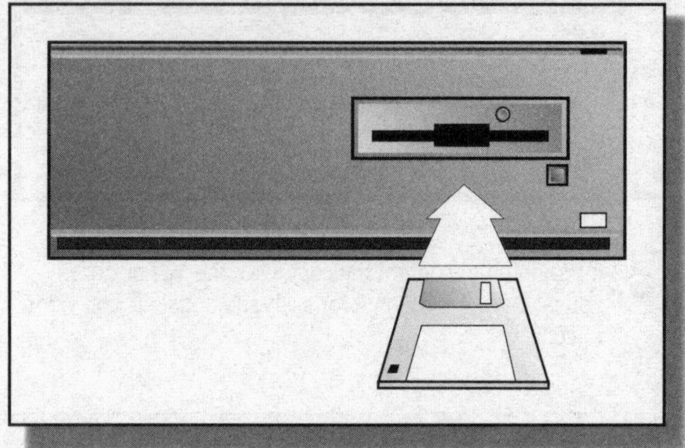

(and cheap) insurance. You should create a startup disk before performing any other "optimization" procedures outlined in the remaining tasks of this chapter.

To create a startup disk you need a new, blank disk for the A: drive of your computer. That is, if the A: drive is a 5.25-inch disk drive, that should be the size you use to create the startup disk. If the A: drive is a 3.5-inch disk drive, then that should be the size you use.

From time to time, make a new startup disk to ensure that the operating system files are the latest versions.

Begin Do It Yourself Create a Startup Disk in Windows 3.11

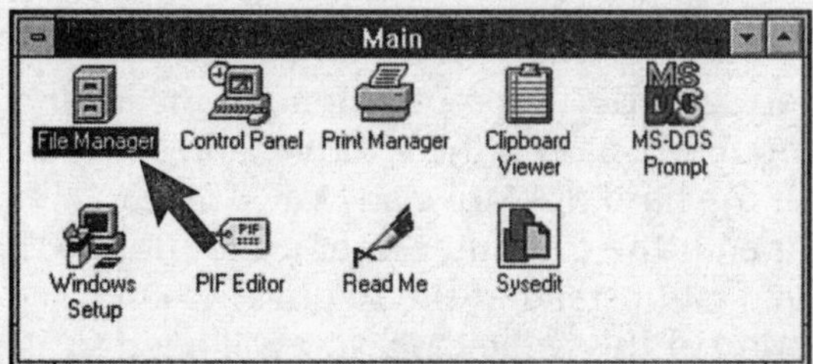

1 Even if the disk you use for the startup disk is formatted, you should format it again. This is most easily done using the Windows File Manager. Start the **File Manager** by double-clicking on its icon in Program Manager.

2 Insert the disk you want to format in drive A, and then (in File Manager) choose **Disk**, **Format Disk**.

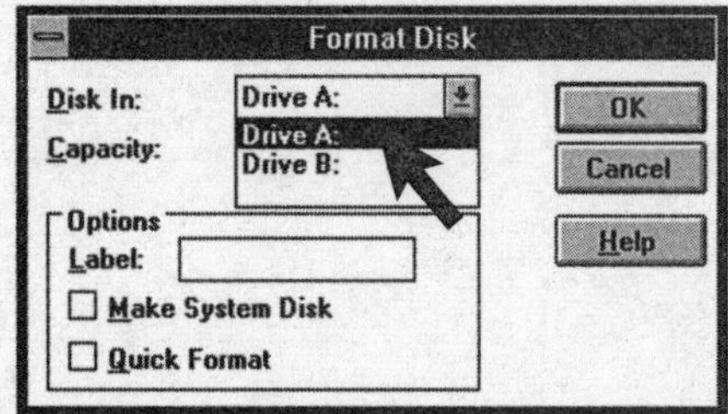

3 Choose **Drive A** in the **Disk In** box, if it is not already selected. Choose the capacity of the disk you are using (either standard or high-density; high-density is preferred).

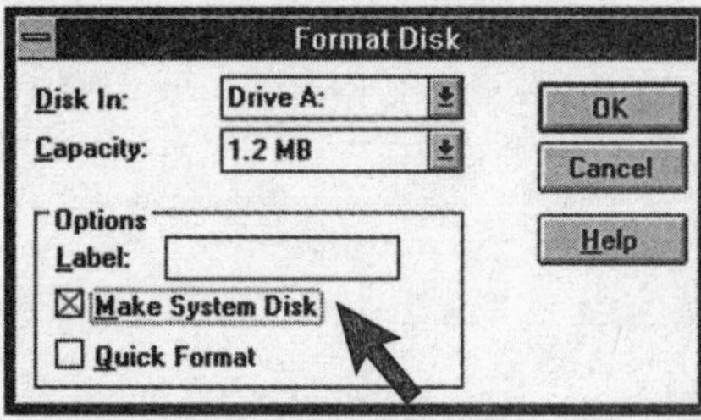

4 Choose the **Make System Disk** option, then choose **OK**. This adds the special system files to the disk so that the computer can start when using that disk.

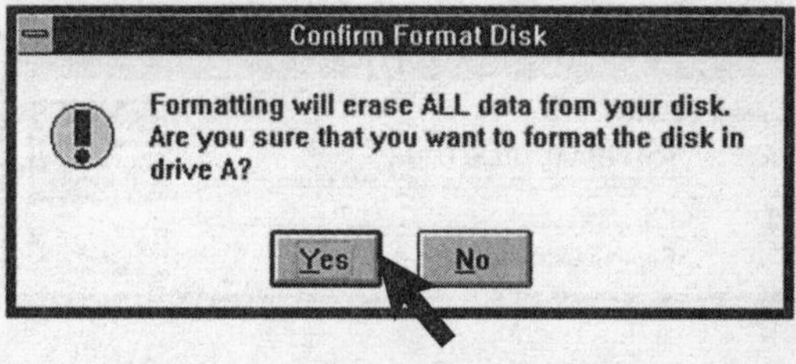

5 Answer **Yes** to the **Confirm Format Disk** dialog box that appears. Formatting commences. When it is done, answer **No** to the prompt that asks if you wish to format another disk.

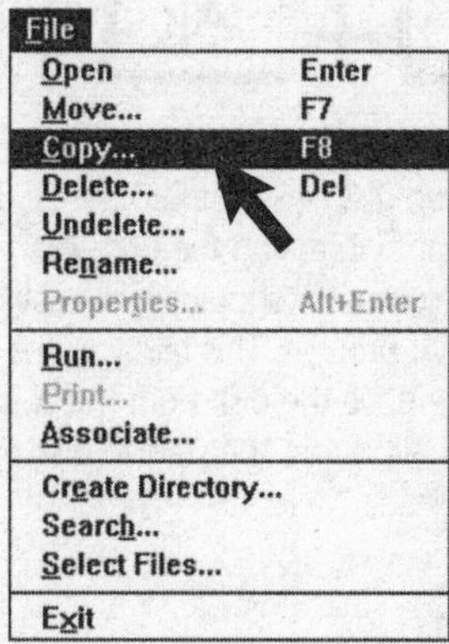

6 Choose **File**, **Copy**. The Copy dialog box appears.

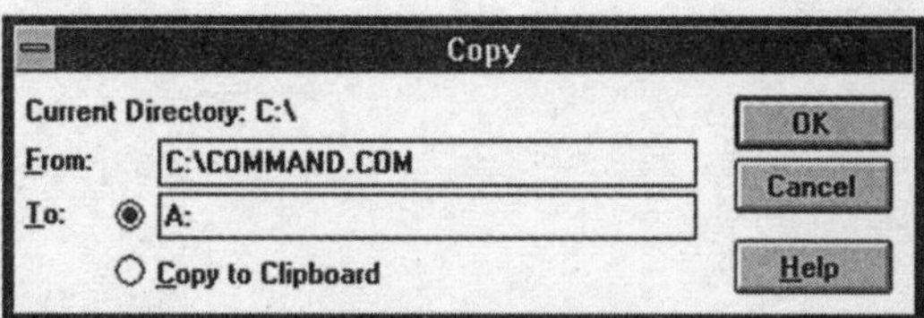

7 Type **C:\COMMAND.COM** in the **From** box, type **A:** in the **To** box, and then choose **OK**.

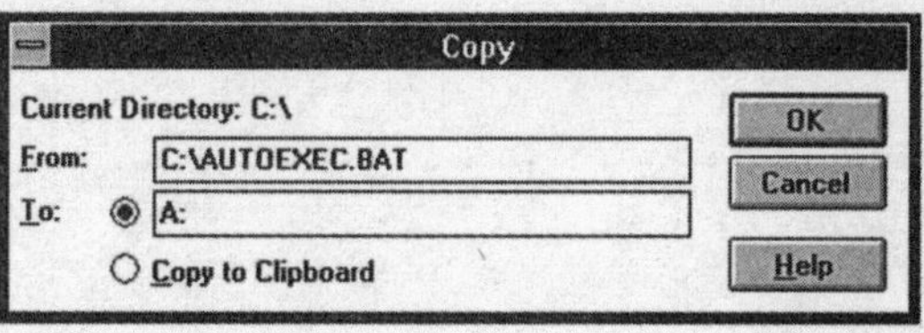

8 Repeat steps 6 and 7, but type **C:\AUTOEXEC.BAT** in the **From** box instead.

(continues)

Do It Yourself Create a Startup Disk in Windows 3.11

(continued)

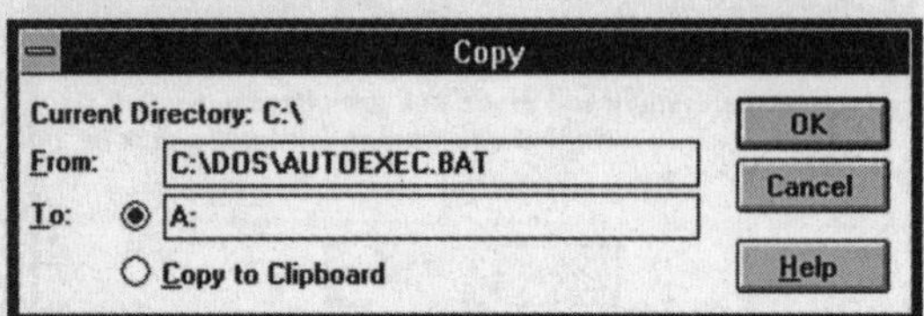

9 Repeat steps 6 and 7, but type **C:\DOS\AUTOEXEC.BAT** on the **From** box instead.

10 Test the startup disk: insert it into the A: drive, and reset your computer by pressing the **Ctrl**, **Alt**, and **Del** keys at the same time. The computer should start—using the disk in drive A—and display the **A:** prompt. This tells you the startup disk is working correctly. Remove the disk from the A: drive, and restart your computer normally. Store the startup disk in a safe place.

If you see the C: prompt instead, it means the computer bypassed the A: drive, and started with the hard disk drive anyway. This can happen if the computer is set up to use the C: drive first (instead of the A: drive) when starting. If this is the case, you will need to consult with the manual that came with your computer to change its setup parameters so it will load from a disk in the A: drive before using the C: drive.

Begin Do It Yourself Create a Startup Disk in Windows 95

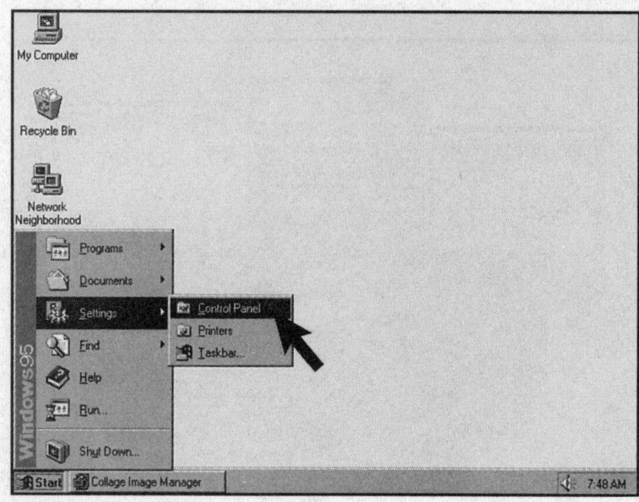

1 You use the Control Panel to create a startup disk. To display it, click the **Start** button, move the pointer over **Settings**, and click **Control Panel**.

2 The Control Panel window appears. Double-click the **Add/ Remove Programs** icon.

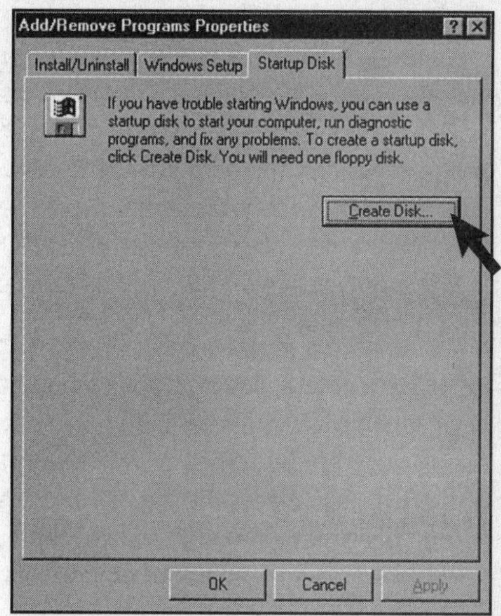

3 Click the **Startup Disk** tab, and then click **Create Disk**.

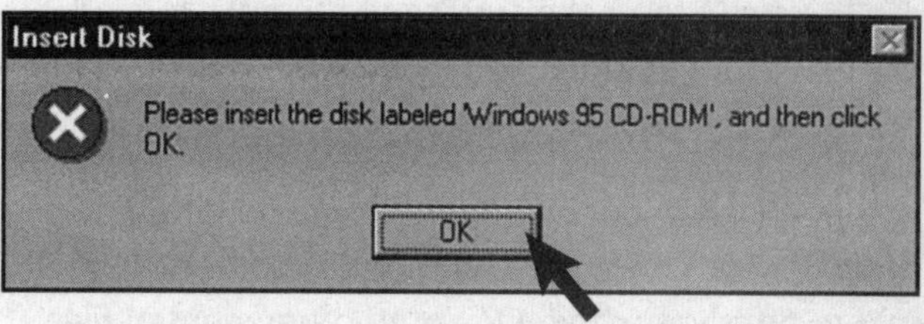

4 Windows will copy the startup files from the installation disks. Insert your Windows 95 CD or floppy Disk 1 into the drive, and click **OK**.

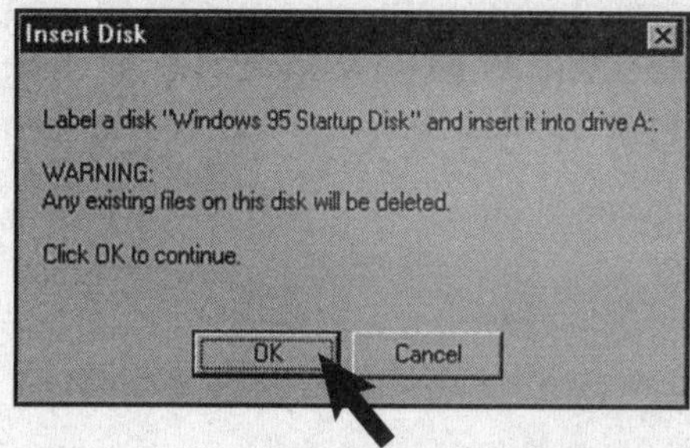

5 Windows copies the required files, and then prompts you to insert a labeled disk into drive A. Label a blank floppy disk "Windows Startup," and stick it in floppy drive A. Click **OK**.

6 Windows formats the floppy disk, and copies the startup files to it. Remove the new startup disk from your floppy disk drive, and store it in a secure place.

Optimize a Disk with Defrag

Your computer's hard disk is a lot like a record (remember those, before audio compact discs?). Your programs and files are recorded in concentric circles on the surface of the hard drive. The disk operating system (DOS) controls where these files go when you copy them to your hard disk drive. DOS finds the first empty space on the hard drive, and starts filling it with your files.

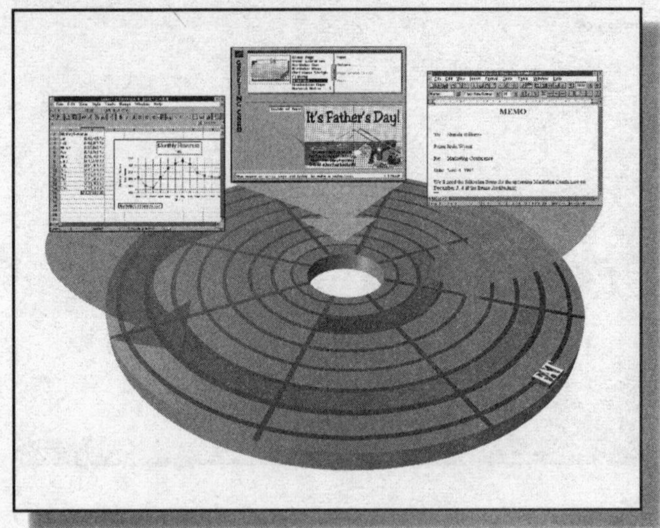

Now suppose you delete files from the computer's hard disk drive. This leaves "holes"—empty spaces where the files used to be. When new files are stored on the disk drive, DOS places the file in these empty places. If the hole isn't big enough to hold the file, the file is chopped up and separated among lots of holes.

You can imagine what can happen to the files on your computer's hard disk drive after a while. Large files can be strewn over the surface of the disk. To read the file, your computer has to jump all over the hard disk drive and pick up all its pieces.

When a file is chopped up and stored on different spots of your computer's hard disk drive, the file is said to be fragmented. One or two fragmented files are usually no problem. But lots of fragmented files can seriously degrade the performance of your computer. Each time the file is chopped apart, the computer must work that much harder to read the file from the hard drive. In many cases, all this jumping around slows down the computer's performance.

DOS (version 6.0 and later) and Windows 95 come with a handy utility program called Defrag (in DOS) and Disk Defragmenter (in Windows 95). (Windows 3.1 does not come with such a program.) The name "Defrag" comes from the job it does: the utility *defragments* fragmented files. Despite its complex-sounding name, the Defrag utility is actually easy to use. It guides you step-by-step through the defragmenting process (which you'll hear called "optimization"). Defrag even suggests the method of optimization your hard drive needs to be more efficient.

Use the Defrag utility once a month or so, to keep your computer in tip-top shape.

Begin Do It Yourself Use Defrag in DOS

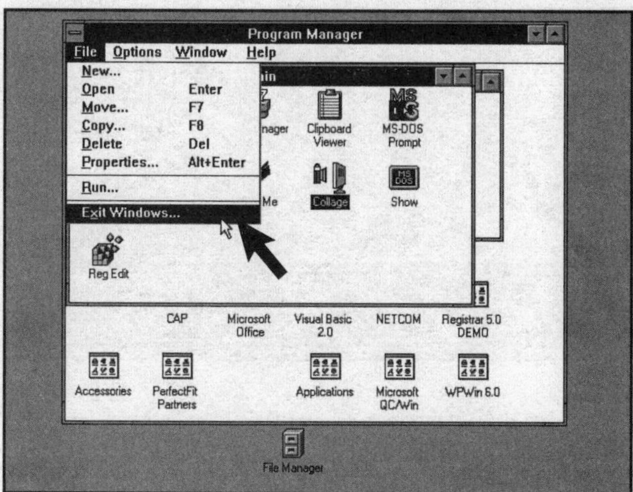

1 Exit all programs, including Windows. The Defrag utility will not run if you're in Windows.

2 At the DOS prompt, type **SCANDISK**, and press **Enter** to run the ScanDisk utility. This utility checks the integrity of all the files, and optionally, the surface of your computer's hard disk drive, and is highly recommended before using the Defrag utility. If the ScanDisk utility detects an error, it guides you through the process of fixing it. See "Check a Disk for Errors with ScanDisk" on page 454.

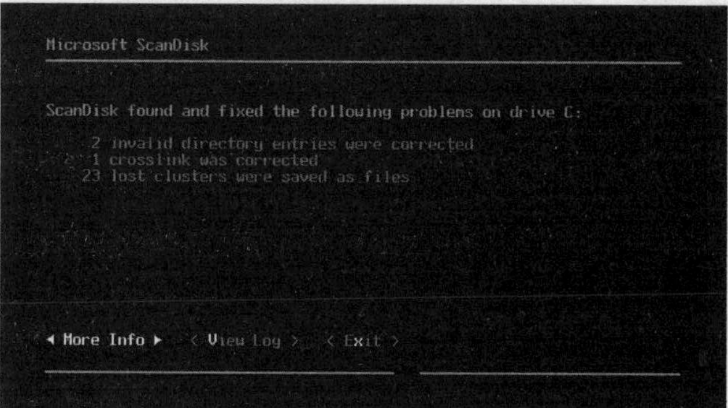

3 If all checks out okay in the ScanDisk utility, choose **Exit** at the final screen to return to the DOS prompt. If there are errors, you will need to use the ScanDisk utility to correct them. See "Check a Disk for Errors with ScanDisk" on page 454.

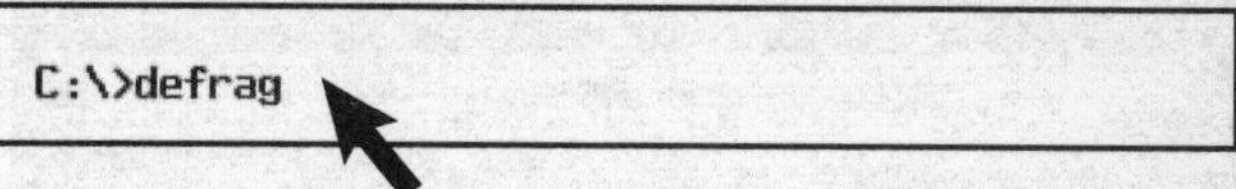

4 At the DOS prompt, type **DEFRAG** and press **Enter**. The Defrag utility starts and does some preliminary testing.

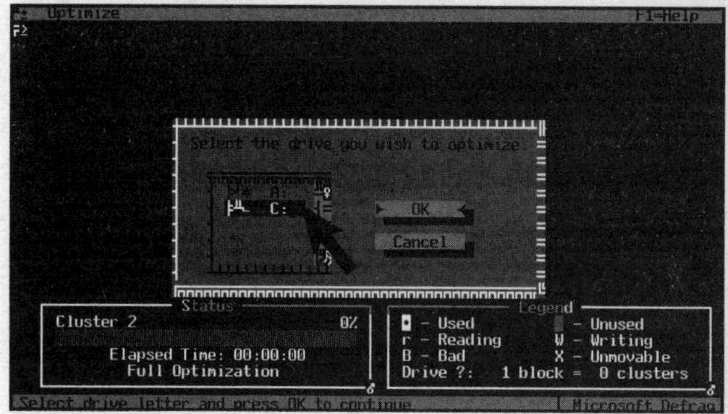

5 Defrag detects the disk drives you have installed in your computer, including the ones for floppy disks. To optimize the hard disk drive, choose **C:** (or whatever letter represents the hard disk drive you want to optimize). Choose **OK**.

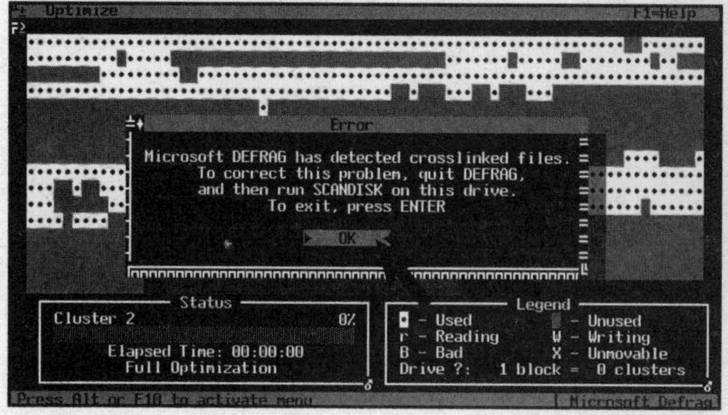

6 If the Defrag utility detects an error in the files, it displays a message indicating a problem, and asks you to run the ScanDisk utility. Choose **OK** to hide the message. You are returned to the DOS prompt, and you should begin at Step 2 (see, now you know why you should run ScanDisk first!).

(continues)

Do It Yourself Use Defrag in DOS

(continued)

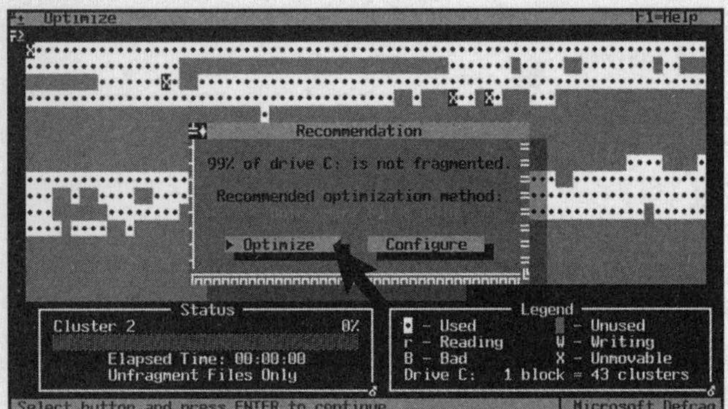

7 If it finds no errors, the Defrag utility indicates the percentage of the drive that is fragmented, and recommends either of two optimization methods: files and full disk. The *file* method is faster, and is usually recommended when the disk is not heavily fragmented. The *full disk* method is slower, and is recommended when the disk is heavily fragmented. Choose **Optimize** to proceed with the optimization process (and skip to step 10), or choose **Configure** to select a different optimization scheme.

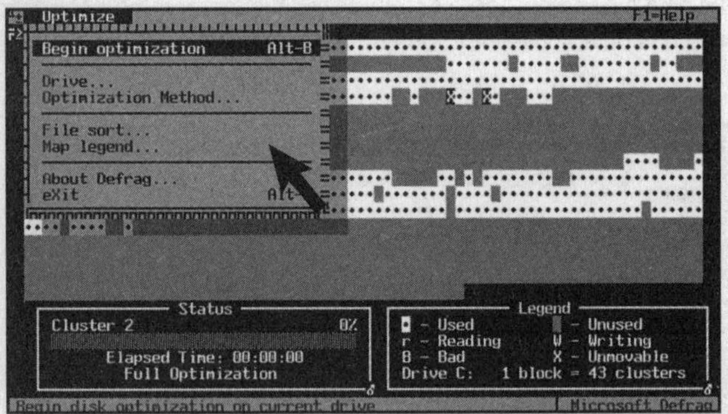

8 If you choose **Configure**, the Optimize menu appears, where you can configure the settings. Choose **Optimization Method** to choose a different optimization method.

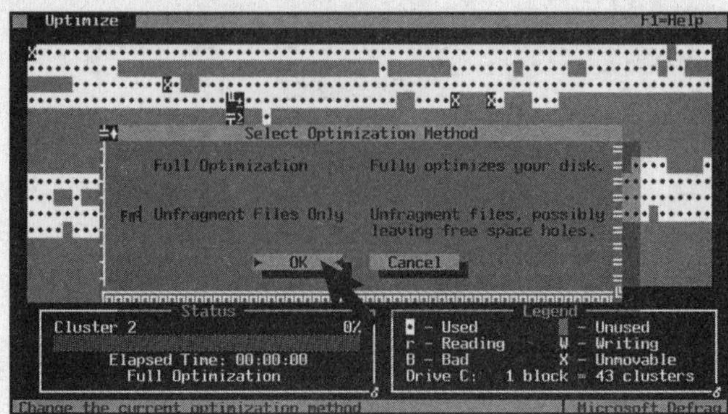

9 Select the optimization scheme you want in the dialog box (either **full** or **files only**), and choose **OK**.

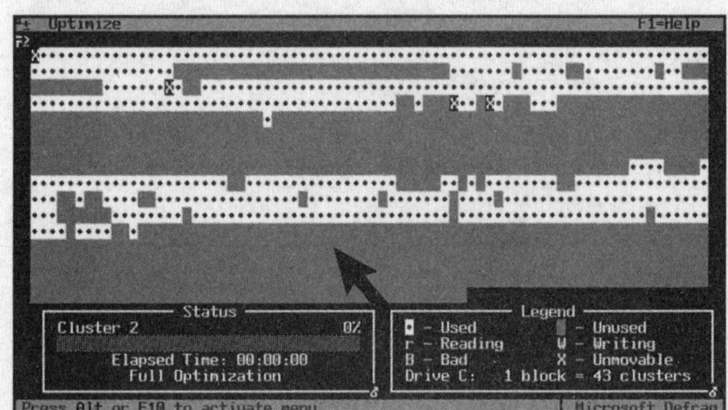

10 Optimization begins. While the disk is being optimized, you can press the **Esc** key to safely cancel optimization. DO NOT TURN YOUR COMPUTER OFF during optimization, or data loss could result. If you do stop the optimization process by pressing **Esc**, select **Cancel** to cancel optimization, or **Resume** to keep going.

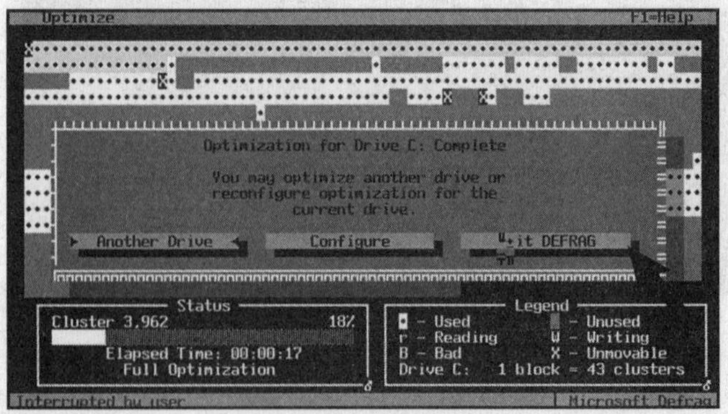

11 The Defrag utility displays a message when the process is complete. To exit the Defrag utility, choose **Exit Defrag**.

Begin Do It Yourself Use Disk Defragmenter in Windows 95

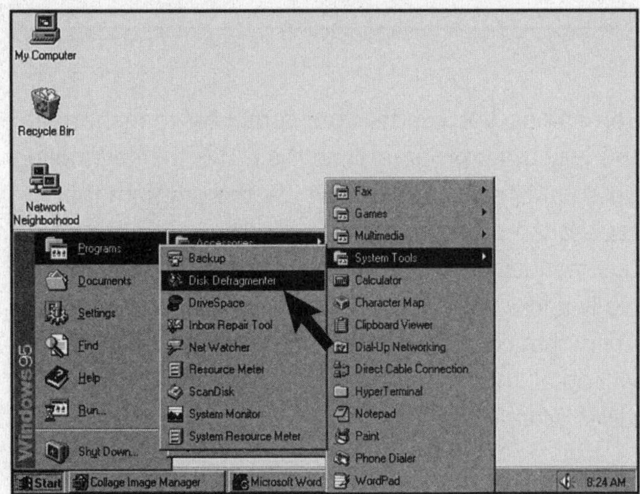

1 Windows 95 comes with a disk defragmenter that you can safely run from Windows (even when other programs are running). Click the **Start** button, rest the mouse pointer on **Programs**, and then on **Accessories**. Move the mouse pointer over **System Tools**, and then click **Disk Defragmenter**.

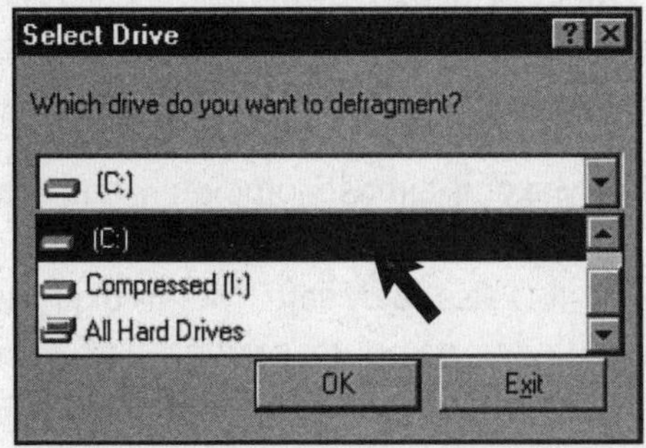

2 A dialog box appears, asking which disk drive you want to defragment. Open the **Which drive do you want to defragment?** drop-down list, and click the desired drive. You can defragment all your disks by clicking on **All Hard Drives**.

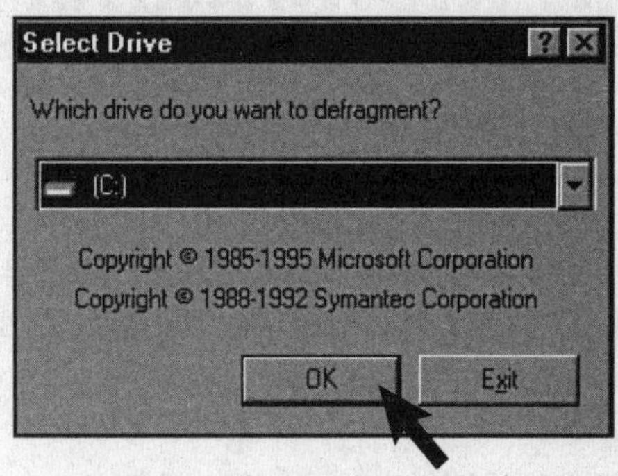

3 Click the **OK** button. Another dialog box appears, indicating the percent of file fragmentation on the disk, and telling you whether or not you need to defragment the disk.

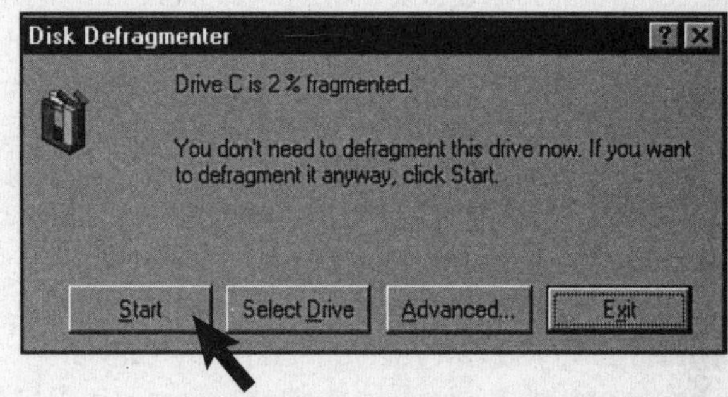

4 Click the **Start** button. Defragmenter starts to defragment the files on the disk.

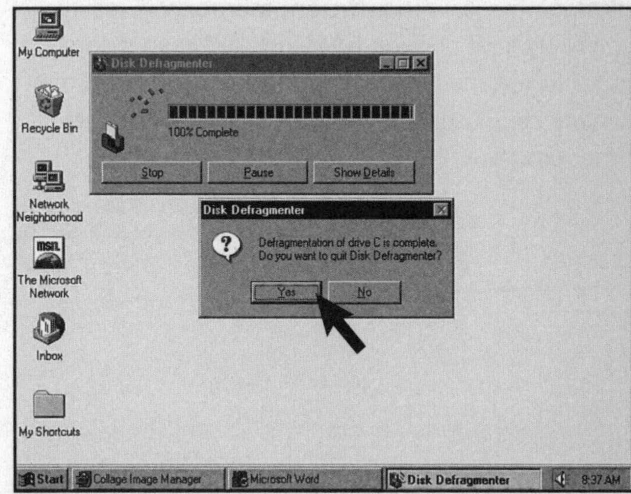

5 Wait until the defragmentation is complete. Click **Yes** to quit Defragmenter.

Increase Available Memory with MemMaker

Your computer has two basic kinds of memory. The hard disk drive inside your computer is the long-term memory for storing programs and data. This kind of memory is magnetic, because it uses a magnetic medium to permanently store information ("permanent" is in the eye of the beholder: you can always erase magnetic data if you need to).

Your computer also has a completely temporary memory: *random-access memory*, or *RAM*. The RAM is used to store programs and data while you're using your computer. Compared to the wide open spaces of your computer's hard disk drive, RAM space is a fairly scarce commodity. You don't have oodles and oodles of it to play around with, so it's always a good idea to conserve the RAM space you do have, so your programs run better.

You don't really have to worry about how your computer is using RAM space unless you want to. For the most part, you can use your computer day after day and never give a second thought to how its RAM is being used. There may come a time, however, when you try to use a program (particularly a DOS-based program) and it refuses to run. You may see a message that says **Insufficient memory**. In reality, you likely have enough RAM installed in your computer to run the program, but some of the RAM may already be in use, and therefore unavailable to any other program.

Sometimes, you can tell your computer to rearrange the way other programs use the RAM, thereby freeing up enough space so you can use the program that caused the no-more-memory message. You can do this manually—which is not recommended unless you really know what you're doing—or you can use a utility that comes with DOS version 6.0 and later that will do all the technical work for you. This utility is called *MemMaker*.

The object of MemMaker is to make as much space in the "conventional" part of the RAM area of your computer as possible. This so-called conventional area is the first 640K of RAM installed in your computer. It does this by moving certain kinds of program files—called "drivers"—to other areas of the RAM (for you technical types, these areas are the upper-memory and high-memory areas). By moving these drivers out of conventional RAM, there's more space available for your other programs to run.

Using MemMaker is almost completely automatic. You just answer a series of prompts as they appear on your screen. It is also fairly safe; MemMaker makes "backups" of your computer's critical files automatically, to protect them in case it makes a change that causes trouble.

If you have Windows 95, you don't need to worry about running MemMaker, because Windows 95 optimizes your computer's memory automatically for you.

Begin Do It Yourself Run MemMaker

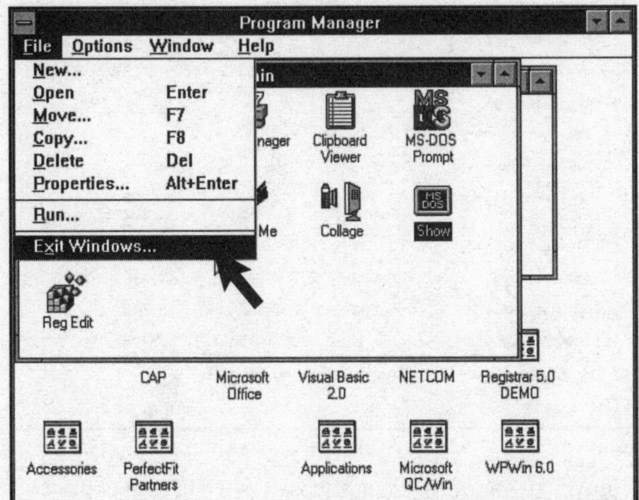

1 Exit all programs, including Windows. (If you have Windows 95, you don't need to run MemMaker; Windows 95 does it for you.) The MemMaker utility will not work if you're in Windows. Remove all disks from your computer's floppy disk drives.

2 At the DOS prompt, type **MEMMAKER**, and press **Enter** to run the MemMaker utility. The MemMaker utility starts and displays the opening screen. Press **Enter** to continue. Another way: press **F3** to return to the DOS prompt.

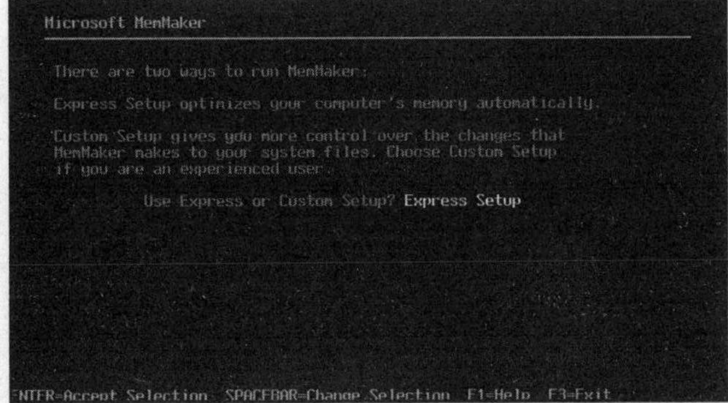

3 MemMaker has two modes: Custom Setup and Express Setup. Unless you are an experienced user and know a lot about how your computer works and the way it manages RAM, use **Express Setup**, by pressing the **Enter** key. The remaining steps assume you're using Express Setup.

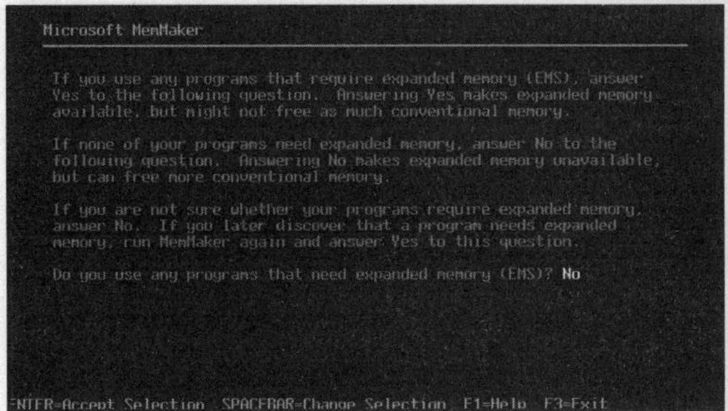

4 Indicate if any of your DOS programs use *expanded memory* (*EMS*). Not many DOS programs—especially those that are less than four or five years old—use EMS memory, so you are usually safe answering **No** (press **Enter**). If you're not sure whether any of your DOS programs use EMS memory, still answer **No**, then test the program. If you later discover that a program needs expanded memory you can run the MemMaker utility again, and answer Yes to this question.

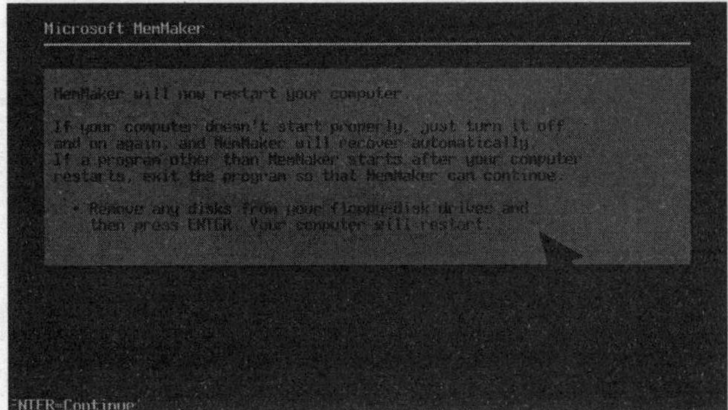

5 MemMaker analyzes your computer and makes tentative changes to its setup files. When prompted, restart your computer by pressing the **Enter** key. This process repeats twice. While your computer is restarting the second time, note any error messages or unusual behavior.

6 After the computer starts, MemMaker will run automatically; it will ask you whether there was a problem. Answering **Yes** to the **Does your system appear to be working properly** question keeps the changes MemMaker made. Answering **No** undoes the changes, and your computer's old configuration is returned. When you are done using MemMaker, press **F3** to return to the DOS prompt.

Begin Do It Yourself Display How Much Memory Is Being Used

1 You can ask for a report of how your computer's memory is used with the MEM program, which also comes with DOS 5.0 and later. At the DOS prompt, type **MEM /C | MORE**, and press the **Enter** key.

```
Modules using memory below 1 MB:

  Name          Total       =   Conventional    +   Upper Memory
  --------  ----------------   ----------------   ----------------
  MSDOS       15,501   (15K)     15,501   (15K)         0    (0K)
  HIMEM        1,168    (1K)      1,168    (1K)         0    (0K)
  EMM386       6,064    (6K)      6,064    (6K)         0    (0K)
  CNFIGNAM       448    (0K)        448    (0K)         0    (0K)
  PCMSS        7,280    (7K)      7,280    (7K)         0    (0K)
  PCMCS       37,504   (37K)     37,504   (37K)         0    (0K)
  PCMSCD      20,176   (20K)     20,176   (20K)         0    (0K)
  COMMAND      2,928    (3K)      2,928    (3K)         0    (0K)
  SNAP       105,952  (103K)    105,952  (103K)         0    (0K)
  SETVER         592    (1K)          0    (0K)       592    (1K)
  POWER        4,688    (5K)          0    (0K)     4,688    (5K)
  MOUSE       24,560   (24K)          0    (0K)    24,560   (24K)
  SMARTDRV    29,024   (28K)          0    (0K)    29,024   (28K)
  ULTRA        6,144    (6K)          0    (0K)     6,144    (6K)
  Free       523,040  (511K)    458,208  (447K)    64,832   (63K)

Memory Summary:

-- More --
```

2 In one or more screens, MEM displays the amount of memory your computer is using. Listed are any device drivers, as well as programs you have run. Three columns are provided to show you how much memory each program takes up, and what kind (conventional or "upper memory") is used.

```
  MOUSE       24,560   (24K)          0    (0K)    24,560   (24K)
  SMARTDRV    29,024   (28K)          0    (0K)    29,024   (28K)
  ULTRA        6,144    (6K)          0    (0K)     6,144    (6K)
  Free       523,040  (511K)    458,208  (447K)    64,832   (63K)

Memory Summary:

-- More --

  Type of Memory       Total   =     Used    +     Free
  ----------------  ----------   ----------   ----------
  Conventional         655,360      197,152      458,208
  Upper                129,840       65,008       64,832
  Reserved             131,072      131,072            0
  Extended (XMS)     7,472,336    2,327,760    5,144,576
  ----------------  ----------   ----------   ----------
  Total memory       8,388,608    2,720,992    5,667,616

  Total under 1 MB     785,200      262,160      523,040

  Largest executable program size        458,112   (447K)
  Largest free upper memory block         61,984    (61K)
  MS-DOS is resident in the high memory area.

C:\>
```

3 If the **—More—** prompt appears at the bottom of the screen, press the **Enter** key to see more of the list.

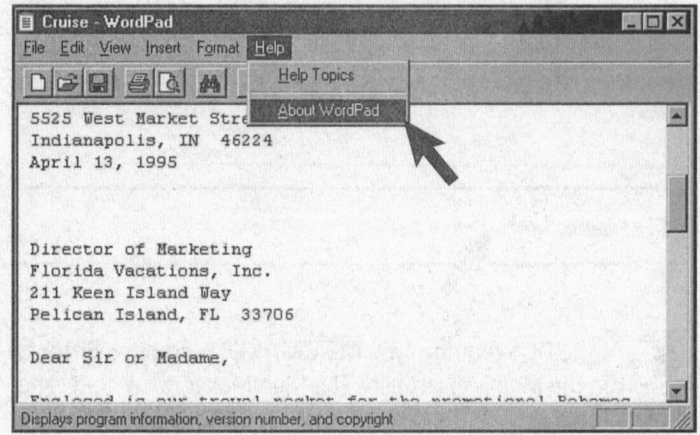

4 In Windows 3.11 or Windows 95, you can quickly check how much memory is available by opening any program's **Help** menu and selecting the **About** command.

Do It Yourself Display How Much Memory Is Being Used

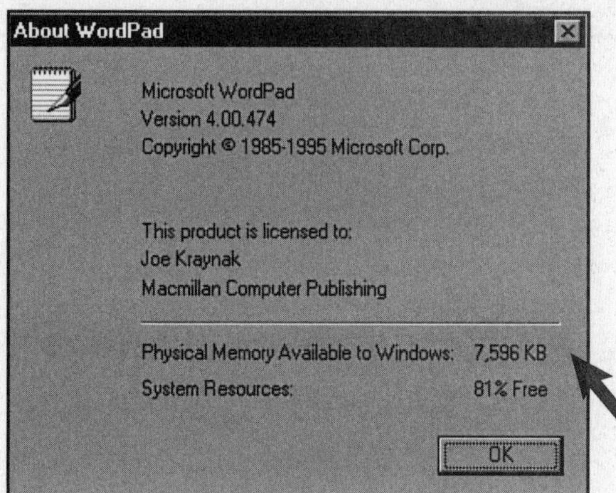

5 This dialog box appears, showing the amount of unused memory and the percentage of system resources that are available.

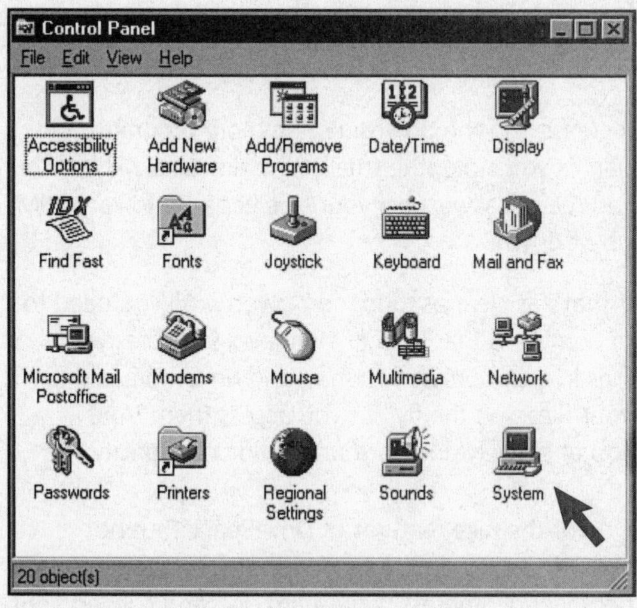

6 In Windows 95, you can check the amount of RAM installed on your computer. Display the Control Panel (select **Start**, **Settings**, **Control Panel**). Then, double-click the **System** icon.

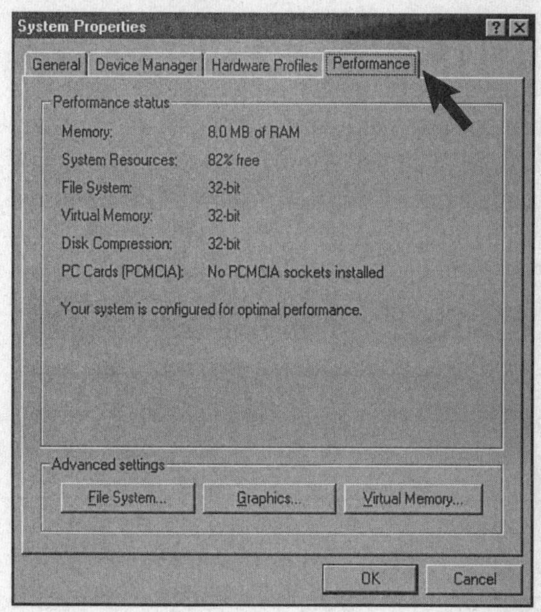

7 Click the **Performance** tab. The total RAM installed on your computer is displayed at the top of the dialog box. Click **OK** when you're done.

Compress a Drive with DriveSpace

Hard disk space is just like closet space—you never seem to have quite enough. This isn't surprising, with all the disk-hogging programs available for DOS and Windows. That 120M hard disk that seemed so huge a few years back is now brimming with files, leaving you no extra room. Fortunately, DOS and Windows 95 have a built-in utility to solve your storage problems.

Versions of DOS earlier than 6.0 do not include DriveSpace or any other compression utilities.

DriveSpace (called DoubleSpace in versions 6.0 through 6.2 of MS-DOS) gives you the ability to store more data on the same hard disk. If you're lucky, you can effectively double the capacity of your hard disk. Obviously, the disk doesn't physically change—rather, the method of file storage changes. Here's how it works.

A specific portion of your hard disk is set aside as a huge hidden file. Assuming you compress your entire hard disk, which might be 120M in size, this file consumes perhaps 115M of that as the *compressed volume*. DOS (or Windows 95) then performs some acrobatics and renames the few megabytes—5M in our case—as drive H: (or something similar), all the while referring to the newly compressed volume as drive C:. As far as you and your programs are concerned, everything works normally—and you now have approximately 230M of disk space (115M × 2). DOS intercepts all files coming and going to that compressed volume, and makes sure they are compressed into less space.

Of course, some files compress more than others, so that new disk size is an estimate. If you store lots of word processing or database files, that amount might increase. On the downside, the more programs and games you store, the smaller the disk size will be. You can realistically expect your true capacity to vary 50M, up or down.

If that's as clear as mud, don't worry. All you need to remember is that DOS or Windows 95 stores your files in a compressed format, and uncompresses your files "on the fly" as you access them. And you effectively double your hard disk's capacity.

One of the nice features of DriveSpace (but not possible with DoubleSpace) is that you can permanently "uncompress" your hard disk and convert your files back to their original state. Say you scrape up a few bucks and buy another hard drive. Well, with all that extra room, you certainly will have no need for DriveSpace anymore. But you must uncompress the files on that 120M hard disk. How do you do that? Just choose Uncompress and follow the instructions on the screen.

Begin Do It Yourself Compress a Drive in DOS

1 Before you compress files on your drive, perform a backup (refer to "Back Up the Contents of Your Hard Disk Drive with Microsoft Backup" on page 458, for details).

Note: If you have Windows 95, DO NOT run the DOS version of DriveSpace. It cannot handle long filenames allowed in Windows 95 and can render some files inaccessible.

2 Exit all programs, including Windows, and type **DRVSPACE** at the DOS prompt. (If you have DOS 6.0 or 6.2, type **DBLSPACE** instead.)

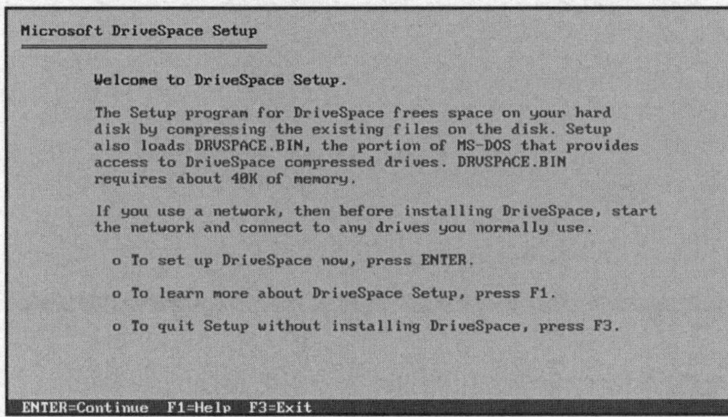

3 Read the instructions on the screen about DriveSpace, then press **Enter**.

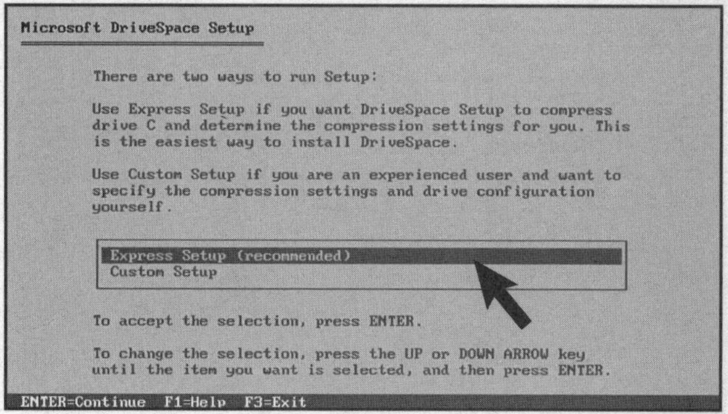

4 The easiest way to compress your drive is to choose **Express Setup**. Press **Enter** to accept this option. If you want to set aside some already-empty space on your disk as a compressed drive, choose **Custom Setup**. (These steps assume you've selected Express Setup.)

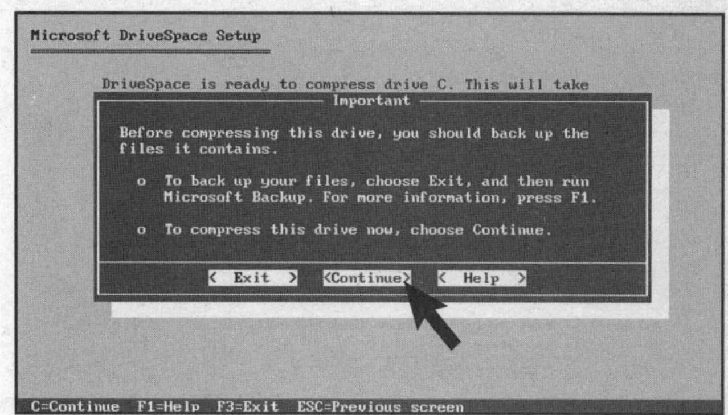

5 A warning appears, reminding you to back up your files—but you've already done that in step 1, right? Press **Tab** to select **Continue** and press **Enter**.

(continues)

Do It Yourself Compress a Drive in DOS

(continued)

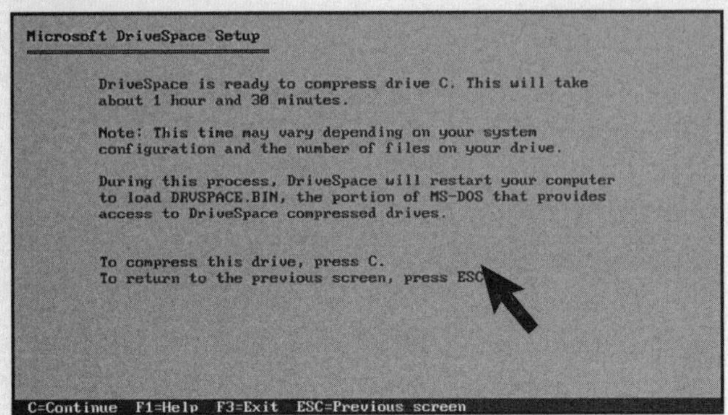

6 DriveSpace Setup estimates and displays the time it will take to compress your drive. Depending on your hard disk's size and present number of files, drive compression can take anywhere from 30 minutes to over 3 hours. Press **C** to compress the drive.

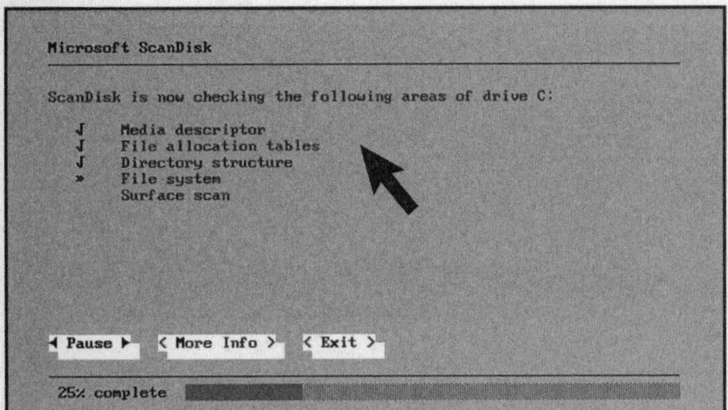

7 To begin the compression process, ScanDisk checks your disk for any potential problems and corrects them.

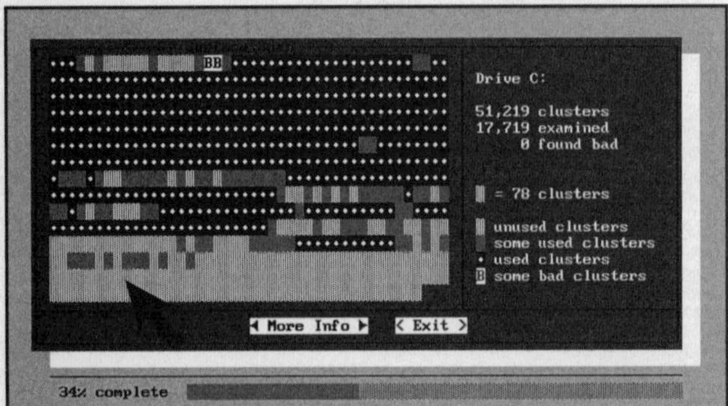

8 ScanDisk also double-checks your drive's reliability by performing a surface scan.

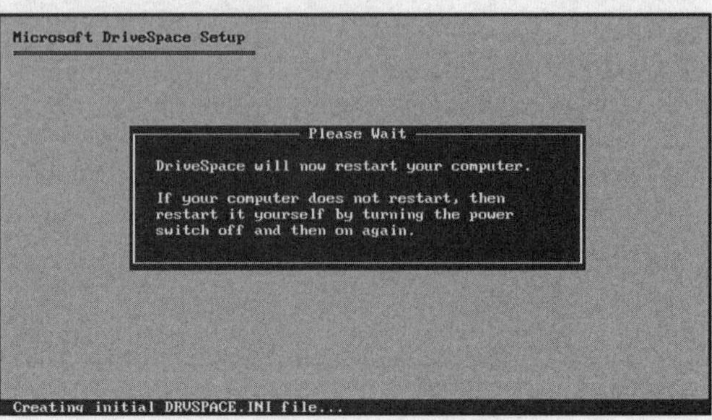

9 When the surface scan is complete, DriveSpace restarts your computer to enable its new settings.

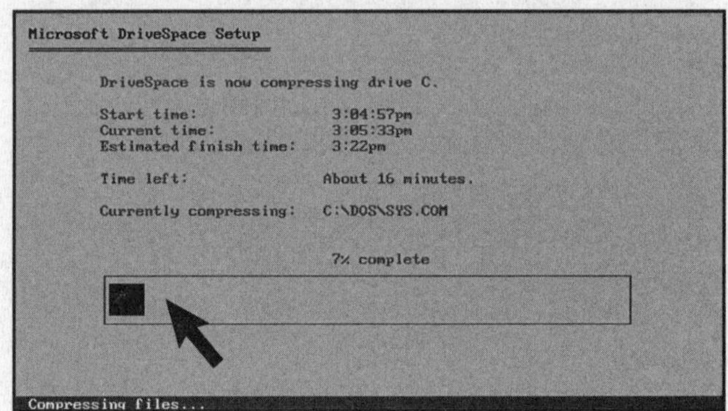

10 After restarting, DriveSpace proceeds to compress and defragment the files on your hard disk.

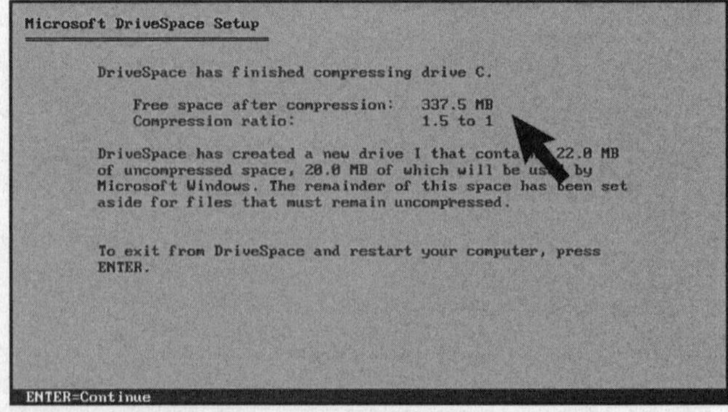

11 Finally, DriveSpace displays the results of the drive compression, showing approximately how much free space is available and the compression ratio. Press **Enter** to allow your computer to restart.

Begin Do It Yourself Uncompress a Drive in DOS

1 Before you uncompress your drive, perform a backup (refer to "Back Up the Contents of Your Hard Disk Drive with Microsoft Backup" on page 458, for details).

2 Exit all programs, including Windows, and type **DRVSPACE** at the DOS prompt.

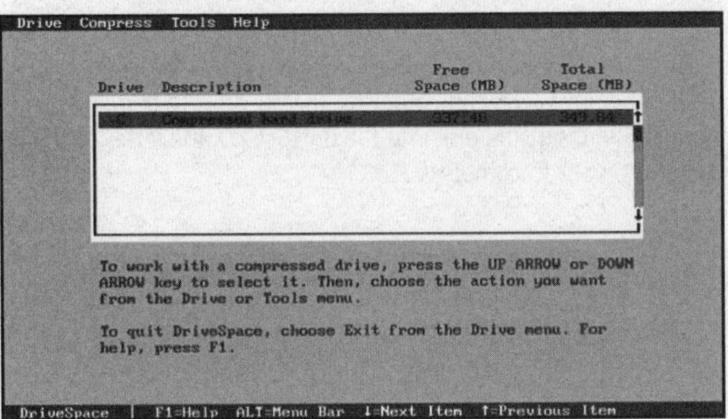

3 DriveSpace displays a screen that shows the compressed drive(s) you have on your computer. You can select from several menu options when working with DriveSpace.

4 Choose **Uncompress** from the **Tools** menu. You can do this by pressing **Alt+T** then moving down to **Uncompress**.

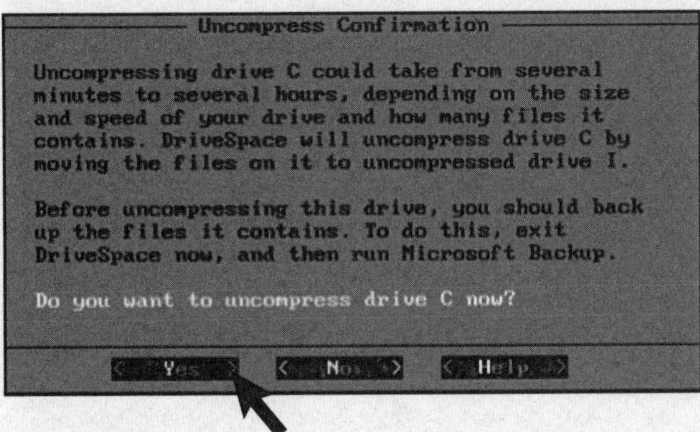

5 Confirm your choice to uncompress the drive by pressing **Y** for Yes.

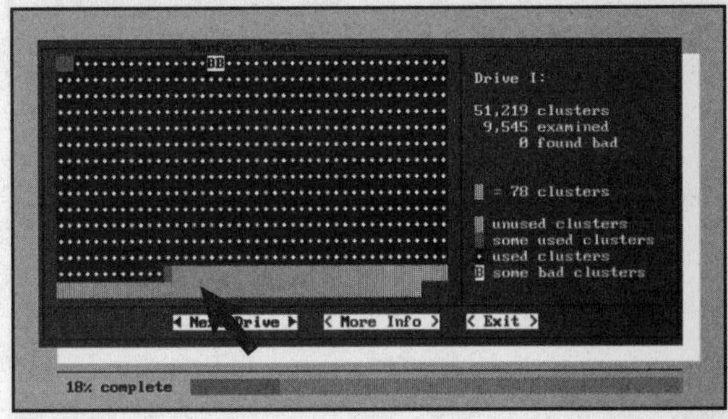

6 ScanDisk checks your disk for any potential problems, and follows up with a thorough surface scan.

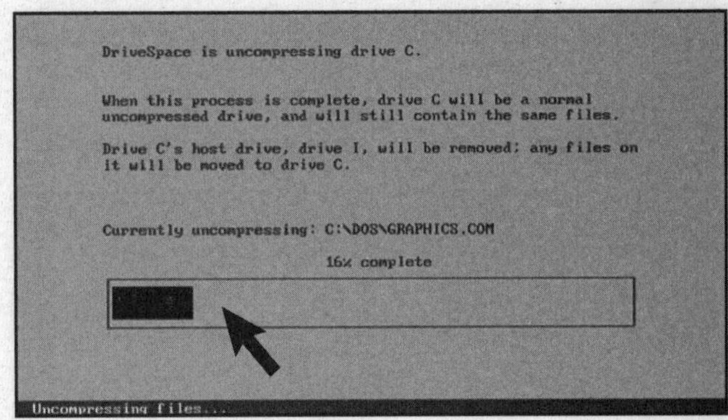

7 The files are then uncompressed and returned to their original state on the C: drive.

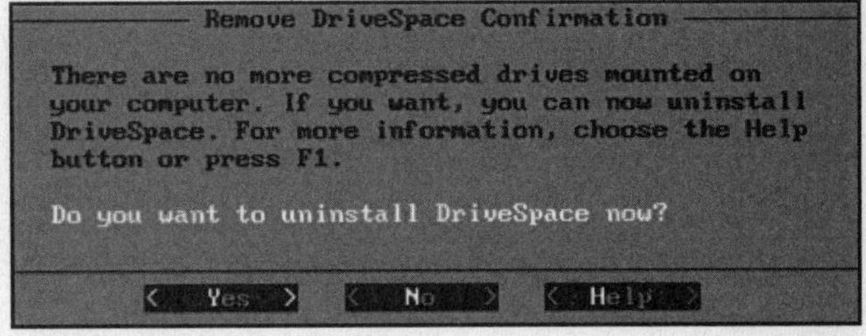

8 If no other compressed drives are detected on your computer, DriveSpace asks whether you want to remove the special drivers from your startup files. Press **Y** to confirm. After you've pressed Y, your computer restarts; your drive will appear as it did before you compressed it.

Begin Do It Yourself Run Windows 95's DriveSpace

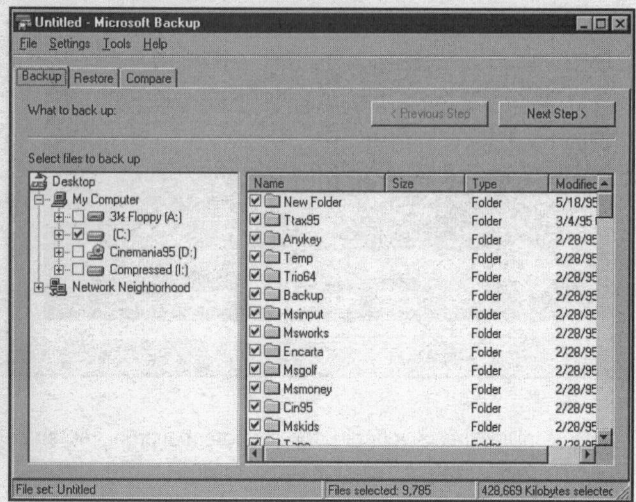

1 Before you compress files on your drive, perform a backup (refer to "Back Up the Contents of Your Hard Disk Drive with Microsoft Backup" on page 458, for details).

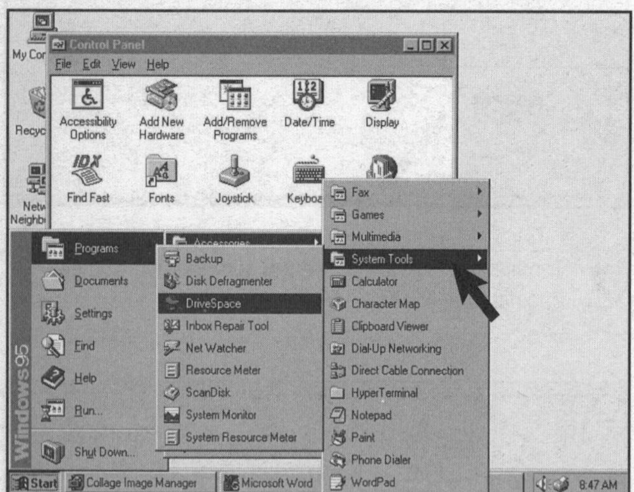

2 Click the **Start** button, move the mouse pointer over **Programs**, and then over **Accessories**. Move the mouse pointer over **System Tools**, and then click **DriveSpace**.

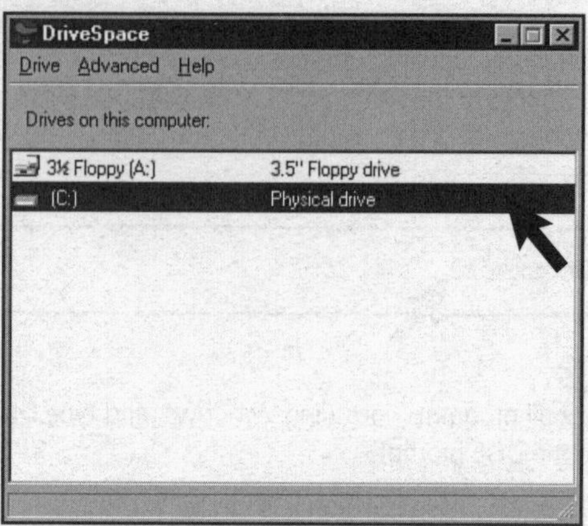

3 The DriveSpace dialog box appears, showing you a list of the drives you can compress. (If you want to compress a floppy disk, insert the disk into the drive.) Click the letter of the drive you want to compress.

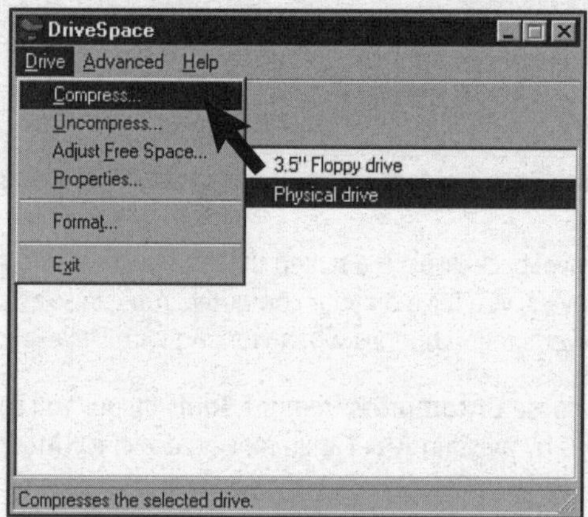

4 Open the **Drive** menu and select **Compress**.

Do It Yourself Run Windows 95's DriveSpace

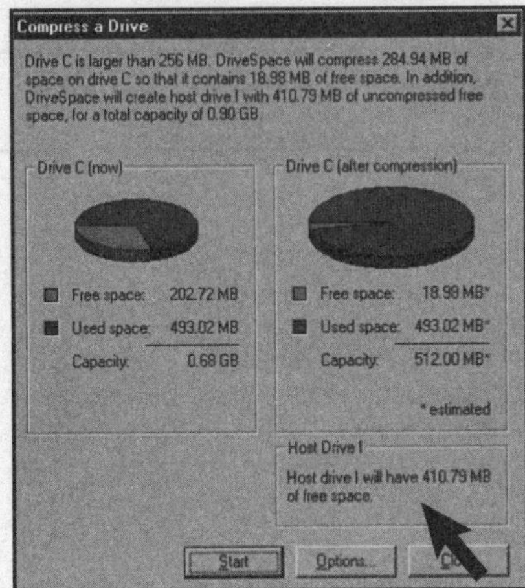

5 These graphs show you how much free space the drive currently has, and how much space it will have after compression. If you are compressing a large hard disk, the graphs are confusing, as shown here. From the graphs, you'd think you're going to lose disk space, but if you look in the lower right corner of the dialog box, you'll see that after compression you will gain a new uncompressed drive that more than makes up for the free space you're about to lose.

6 Click the **Start** button. A dialog box appears, cautioning you to back up your files before compressing them. Assuming you already did this, or you're feeling very lucky, move on to step 7.

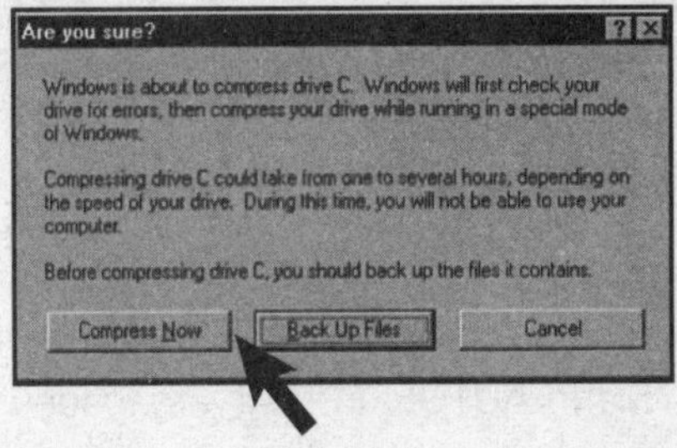

7 Click the **Compress Now** button, and wait until the compression is complete. Depending on the size of the compressed drive and the amount of data that needs to be compressed, this can take from several minutes to several hours.

Caution! NEVER run an old version of DriveSpace after installing Windows 95. Older versions of DriveSpace can't handle the long filenames that Windows 95 allows. You'll end up losing your data.

Modify Your Startup Files in Windows 3.11 and DOS

Out of the hundreds, possibly thousands, of files on your computer, only a handful specifically instruct it on how to operate. Two files in particular, CONFIG.SYS and AUTOEXEC.BAT, are loaded after you turn on your computer. These contain commands to load drivers, define settings, and generally prepare your computer for everyday use. Sometimes you may need to modify these *startup files* to make your system run more efficiently.

When properly configured, these files tell your computer how to operate at peak performance. If you notice that your system runs more slowly than usual, your startup files may be due for a tune-up. Properly configuring these files can be like tuning up your car—overwhelming unless you know exactly what to look for. Editing the files is the easy part, but knowing the correct settings is where things get tricky. So unless you really need to change them, don't modify your startup files.

There is no hard-and-fast rule to dictate what should be in these files. Individual users have different needs; the files will vary accordingly. The contents of sample CONFIG.SYS and AUTOEXEC.BAT files are shown in this section. These samples give you a good idea of the basic items in your startup files, but you can modify them to suit your own needs. Also, depending on the version of DOS you use, some commands may not be available.

As you can see, these are simple text files; you can use the EDIT program, included with DOS 5.0 and higher, to modify (edit) these files. This task explains how to open, modify, and save changes to the configuration files, should it ever be necessary.

```
DEVICE=C:\DOS\HIMEM.SYS
DEVICE=C:\DOS\EMM386.EXE
DOS=UMB
DOS=HIGH
DEVICE=C:\DOS\SETVER.EXE
DEVICE=C:\DOS\ANSI.SYS
SHELL=C:\DOS\COMMAND.COM C:\DOS\ /E:256 /p

echo off
prompt $p$g
C:\DOS\SMARTDRV.EXE
PATH C:\WINDOWS;C:\DOS
```

The startup CONFIG.SYS and AUTOEXEC.BAT files reside in the root directory of your computer's hard disk drive. You may have many files named CONFIG and AUTOEXEC, but the extension (SYS and BAT, respectively) may be different. For example, you may see AUTOEXEC.BAK or CONFIG.OLD. These additional files are typically stored on your computer's hard disk drive as "protection backups" made by software installation programs. This way, if any changes in the startup files cause problems, you can rename the most recent AUTOEXEC.BAK to AUTOEXEC.BAT or CONFIG.OLD to CONFIG.SYS—which will restore your computer to the way it ran before you made the changes.

If you use Windows, two additional configuration files are important. These files are WIN.INI and SYSTEM.INI, stored in the \WINDOWS directory. These files are used exclusively by Windows; their contents are typically set by Windows and Windows applications. These files can also be manually edited, however, should the need arise. Although you can edit these files with the EDIT program from DOS, it is handier to use the System Configuration Editor, or SYSEDIT. Typically you will never need to manually edit the WIN.INI or SYSTEM.INI, since the same modifications can be made via the Control Panel.

Prior to making any changes to any configuration file, be sure to make backups of it on a separate floppy disk. (See "Back Up the Contents of Your Hard Disk Drive with Microsoft Backup" on page 458 for more information.) Neither the EDIT or SYSEDIT programs make backup copies of your startup files, so you may want to create a "startup disk" (see "Make a "Startup" Disk" on page 394).

Begin Do It Yourself Modify Your Startup Files Using DOS

1. At the DOS prompt, type **EDIT \AUTOEXEC.BAT**, and press the **Enter** key. This starts the EDIT program and displays your AUTOEXEC.BAT file.

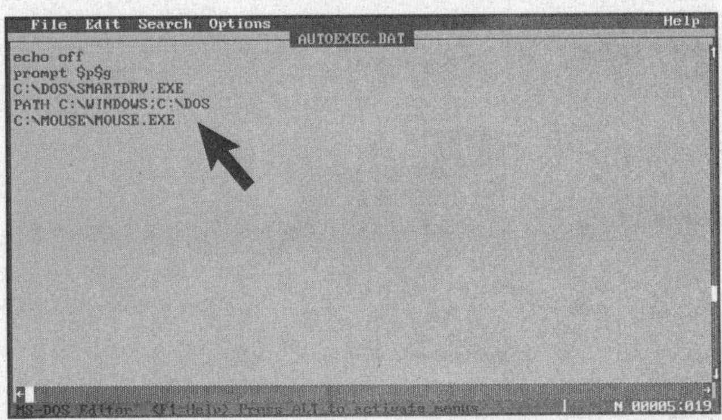

2. Make appropriate changes to the file, such as adding the command **C:\MOUSE\MOUSE.EXE**. Typically you will add a command after the last line in the file.

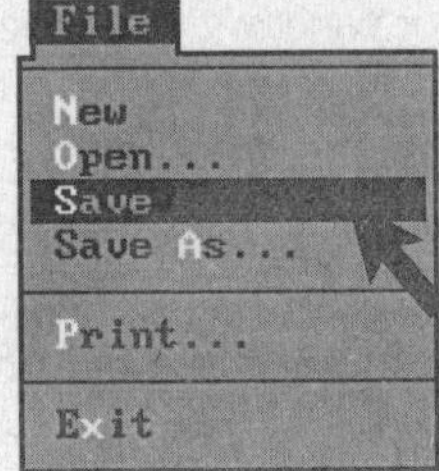

3. When you are finished, choose **Save** from the **File** menu.

4. To exit the EDIT program, choose **Exit** from the **File** menu.

5. If you need to modify the CONFIG.SYS file, type **EDIT \CONFIG.SYS** at the DOS prompt.

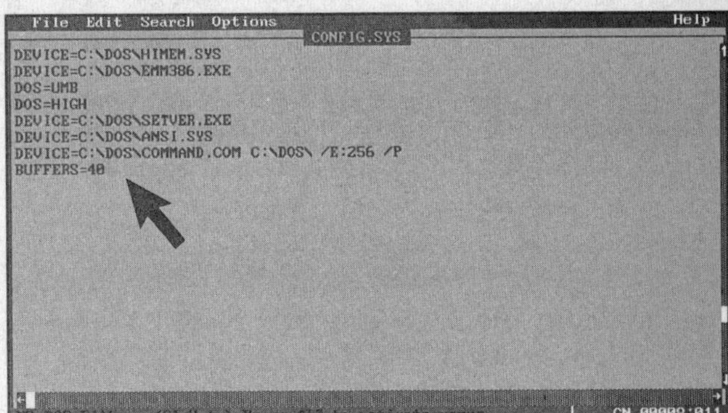

6. Make appropriate changes to the file, such as adding the command **BUFFERS=40**.

7. When you are finished, choose **Save** from the **File** menu.

8. Choose **Exit** from the **File** menu to leave the EDIT program. Any changes you make to the startup files won't take effect until you restart your computer.

Begin Do It Yourself Modify Your Startup Files Using Windows 3.11

1 From the Program Manager, choose **Run** from the **File** menu. Type **SYSEDIT** in the Run dialog box and click **OK**.

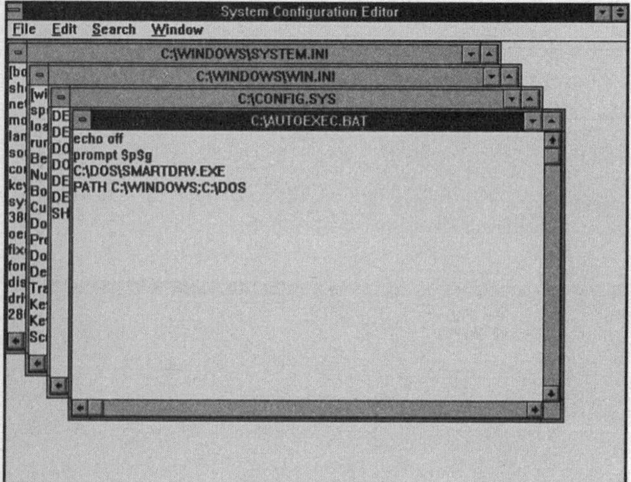

2 Immediately, the System Configuration Editor loads and displays several files: SYSTEM.INI, WIN.INI, CONFIG.SYS, and AUTOEXEC.BAT.

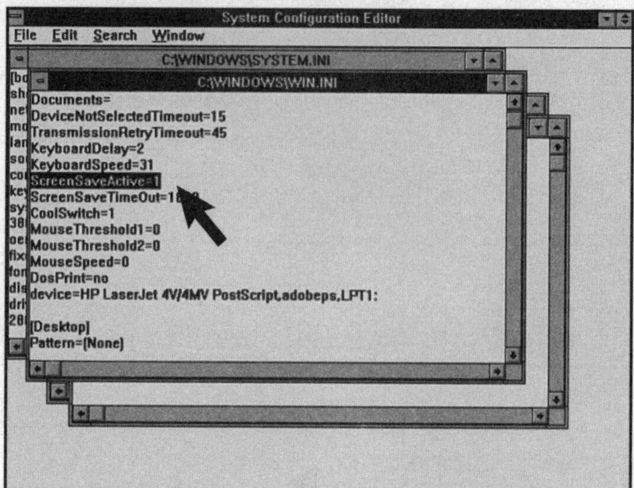

3 Although four or more files are displayed, you don't need to edit each one. Simply edit the file(s) you want. If you want to make the screen saver inactive, for example, click the **WIN.INI** window and scroll down until you see **ScreenSaveActive=1**.

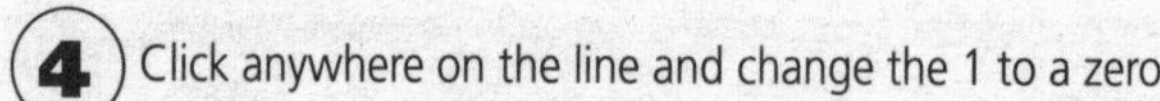

4 Click anywhere on the line and change the 1 to a zero.

5 To save the file, choose **Save** from the **File** menu.

6 To exit SYSEDIT, or System Configuration Editor, choose **Exit** from the **File** menu. Any changes you make to the startup or Windows configuration files won't take effect until you restart your computer or Windows, respectively.

In Windows 95, you can run the System Editor by double-clicking on its icon in My Computer or Windows Explorer. The SysEdit icon is in the WINDOWS\SYSTEM folder. You can create a shortcut for this icon by dragging it onto the Windows desktop.

DO IT YOURSELF

Install New Hardware

A computer is a "work in progress"—it's never really "complete" because you can continue to add stuff to it as your needs change. You might be satisfied with your computer today, but tomorrow you may want to add a new printer, or get on the online bandwagon by installing a modem and joining all your friends on the Internet.

This chapter discusses things you can add to your computer. We've limited it to general accessories, such as a printer, joystick, or modem. Other accessories may be available for your specific computer (especially if you own a laptop); refer to the user's guide that came with your computer for more details on adding gear to it.

While reading this section, bear in mind that of all things related to your computer, hardware differs the most. For example, a sound card from one manufacturer may look, act, and even smell different from the sound card made by someone else. So, use this section as a guide only—to help you understand the basic procedures of installing accessories. When you install any hardware, always have the instruction manual for both your computer and the accessory available.

What You Will Find in This Section

Install a Printer 416

Install a Joystick 420

Install a Mouse 421

Install an External Modem 425

Attach Speakers to a Sound Card 430

Install an Adapter Card Inside Your Computer 432

Install a CD-ROM Drive 435

Install Hardware in Windows 95 439

Install a Printer

By itself, a computer is a marvelous thing. But it has this habit of keeping things to itself—that is, unless you connect a printer to it so you can make paper copies of the work you do on your PC or to share with others.

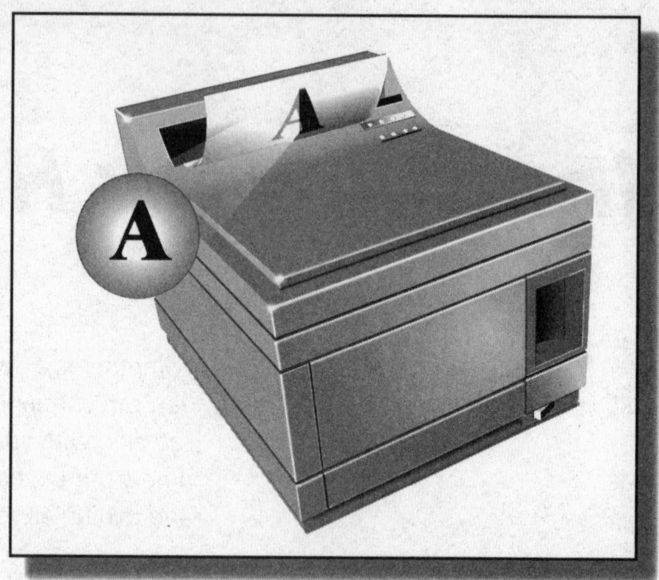

Printers come in all sorts of shapes and sizes, and they use different technologies to produce a finished page. The popular printer types are dot-matrix, inkjet, and laser. *Dot-matrix* printers cost the least but produce the fuzziest results. *Laser* printers—which actually use a pencil-point laser beam to create the page—are the most expensive, but their print quality is unrivaled. As you might have guessed, the output quality of *inkjet* printers is somewhere between that of dot-matrix and laser printers.

Most printers can print both text and graphics, either separately or on the page at the same time. The majority of printers print only in black, but some more costly models print in color (these tend to use the inkjet technology). Color printers are often used with graphics programs, to print pictures and artwork.

Fortunately, the type of printer—and whether it prints in color or just black—doesn't matter much when you're connecting the thing to your computer. Printers hook up to computers with a single cable, and the installation is typically simple and straightforward: plug one end of the cable to the printer, and the other end to the computer.

That said, you may run into complications when you try to get your computer to communicate with your printer. Different printers respond to different instructions; in fact, printers use a unique language, and they require your computer to speak that language as well.

Differences in language are handled not by your applications (word processor, electronic spreadsheet, and so forth), but by a small program known as a *printer driver*. There is a printer driver for every model of printer on the market. When you install a new printer, hooking the thing up to your computer is only one part of the job; the other part is installing the printer driver and getting your software to recognize the new printer you have installed.

In the world of DOS programs, software installation of a new printer varies between programs; you have to read up on the steps in the manual for each DOS program you own. In the world of Windows programs, however, software installation of a new printer is the same procedure, no matter what program you use. In this task, we'll describe the steps for installing a new printer in Windows.

We'll look at connecting a printer using one of your computer's *parallel* connections—by far the most common (and on many printers, the only) way of attaching a printer to a computer. If your printer uses a *serial* connection, the task of attaching the printer to the computer is considerably more difficult. You will need to consult the manual that comes with the printer to find out what kind of connection you need. You may also need to ask a knowledgeable friend or associate for help.

You will need your original Windows disks to install a new printer.

Begin Do It Yourself Set Up a Printer

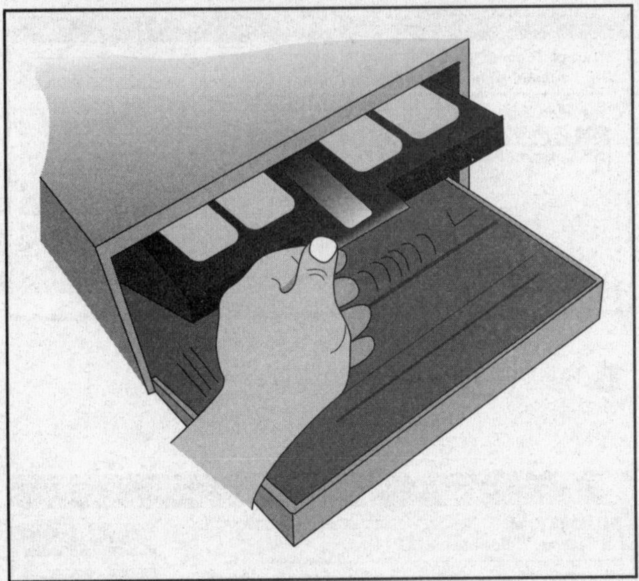

1 Unpack the printer from the box and remove all shipping materials. Insert the ribbon, ink cartridge, or toner cartridge (depending on the type of printer you have), according to the instructions packed with the printer.

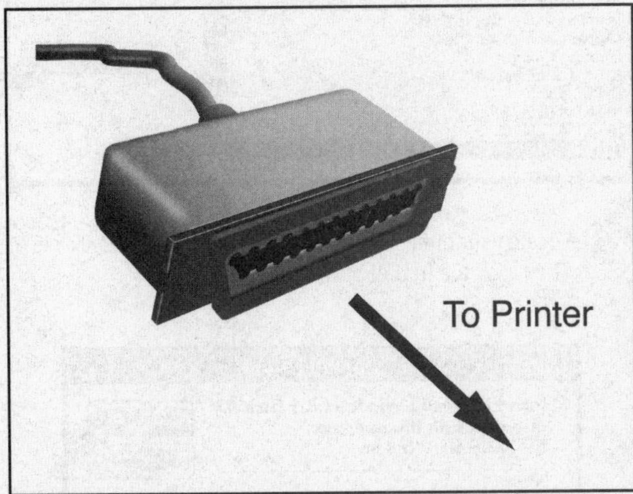

2 Find the printer cable. Connect one end to the printer. The printer cable uses different connectors on each end; only one of these will attach to the printer.

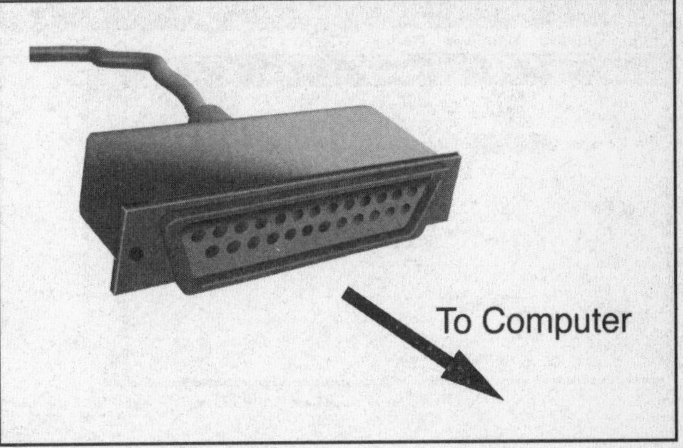

3 With your computer off, connect the other end of the printer cable to the computer. Most likely, your computer will have only one connector of the correct size and shape to accept the printer cable. Use this connector.

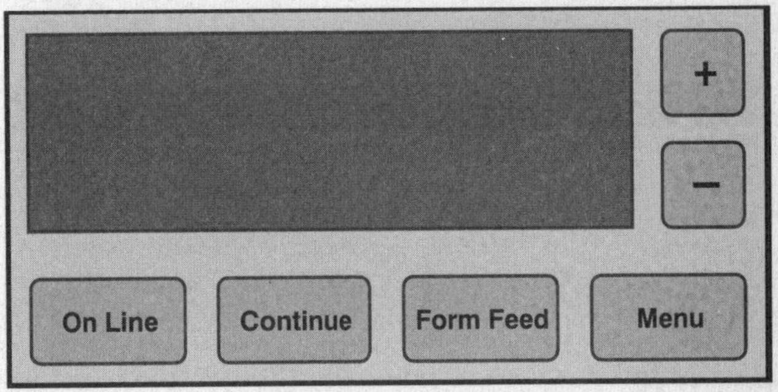

4 Most printers have a built-in self-test, often activated by pressing and holding one of the control buttons on the front panel of the printer (usually the **On-line** button) while turning the printer on; check the manual that came with the printer for more information. Insert some paper into the printer and perform the self-test now.

5 Turn on your computer and start Windows by typing **win** at the DOS prompt (if Windows doesn't start automatically).

(continues)

Do It Yourself Set Up a Printer

(continued)

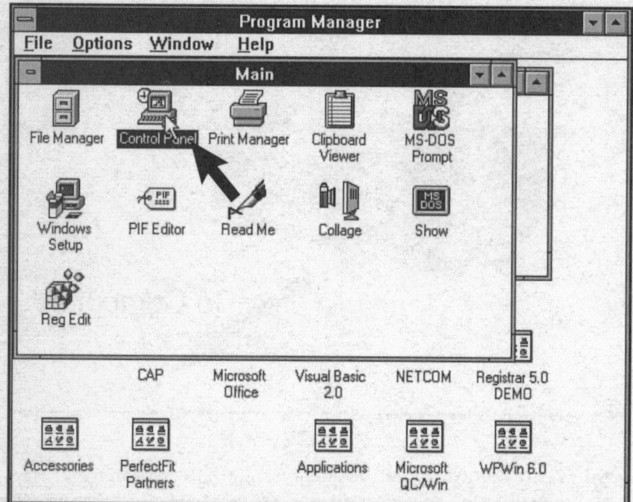

6 In Windows Program Manager, double-click the **Main** program-group icon. Then double-click on the **Control Panel** icon.

7 In the **Control Panel** window, find the **Printers** icon, and double-click it to open the Printers window.

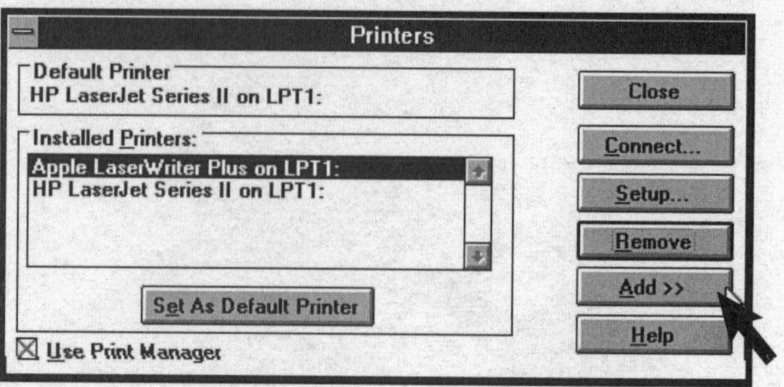

8 Click the **Add>>** button to add a new printer.

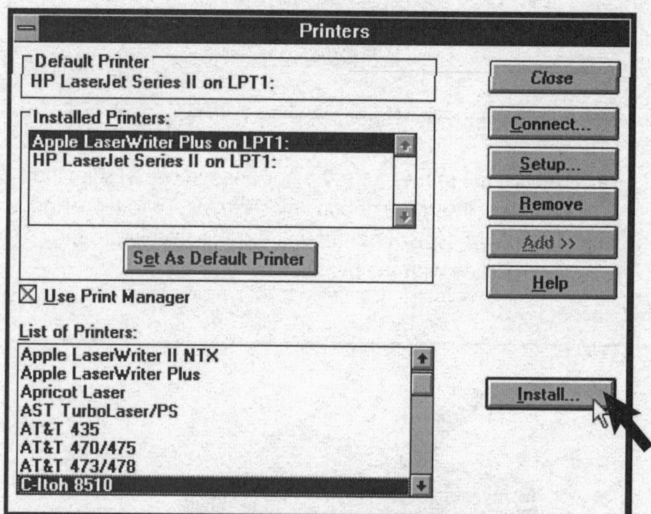

9 Locate your printer in the **List of Printers** list and click it. Then click the **Install** button.

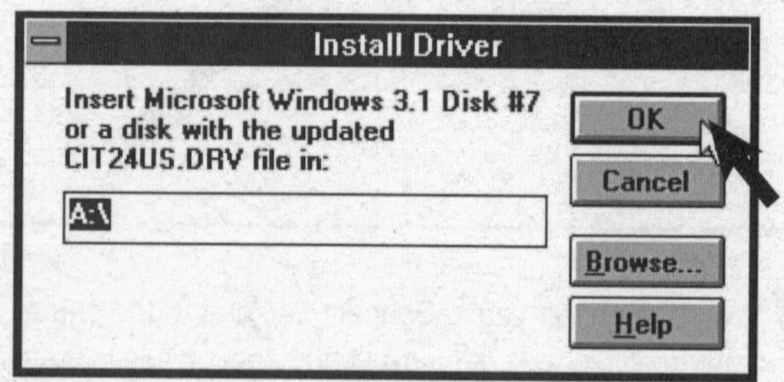

10 Insert the numbered Windows disk (that comes with your package of Windows) into the appropriate disk drive as instructed, and then select **OK**.

Do It Yourself Set Up a Printer

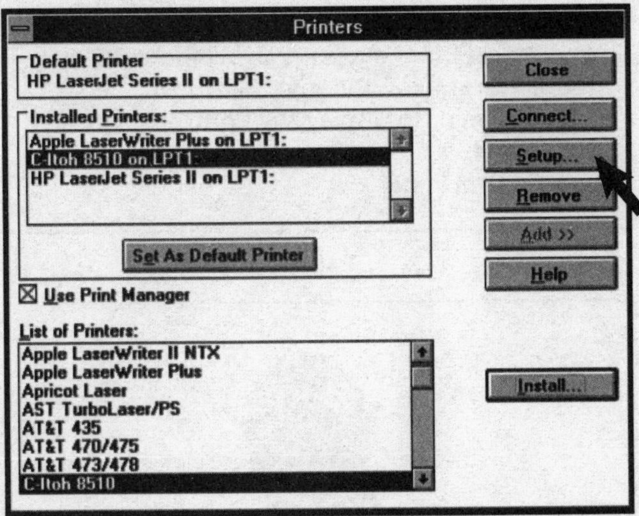

11 In the **Installed Printers** list, click the just-installed printer, and then click the **Setup** button.

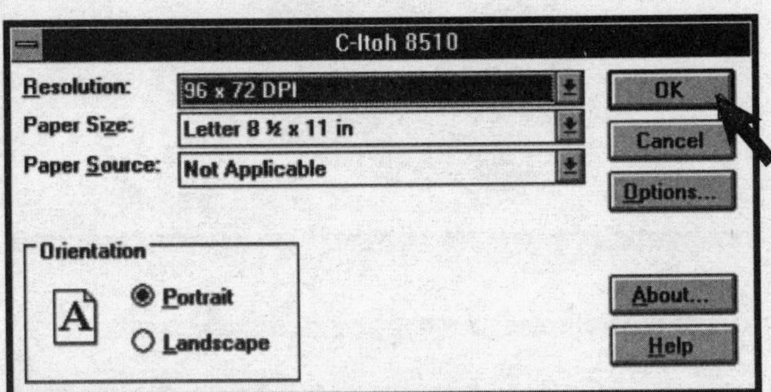

12 In the Setup dialog box, select the setup options for your printer. This dialog box looks different depending on the specific printer you use. You probably won't need to make any changes (in which case, just click **Cancel**). But if you do make changes, select the options you want; click **OK** when you're done.

13 With the printer still selected in the **Installed Printers** list, click the **Set As Default Printer** button, then click the **Close** button to close the Printers window.

Install a Joystick

Many computer games—especially the "shoot 'em up" action type—need or prefer a joystick for controlling the on-screen action. A *joystick* is a calculator-sized box with a handle-like stick going into it. To control your on-screen tank, gun, airplane, or whatever, you merely move the stick around. It's called a "joystick" after the name given by early fighter pilots for the control yoke in airplanes. Although joysticks work the same, some are fancier than others.

Installing a joystick is easy, but it requires that your computer already be equipped with an adapter card that has a *game port* on it. If your computer lacks an adapter card with a game port, you will need to add one. See "Install an Adapter Card Inside Your Computer" on page 432 for more information.

Many sound cards come with a game port. If your computer has a sound card, look on it to see if you can find the distinctive game port. If you're lucky, it will be labeled for you.

You can calibrate a joystick in Windows 95 by double-clicking on the **Joystick** icon in the Control Panel. To display the Control Panel, click the **Start** button, point to **Settings**, and click **Control Panel**.

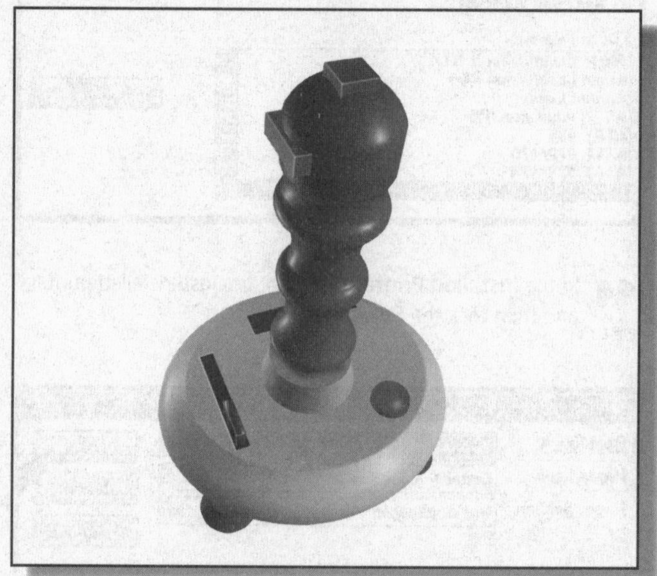

Begin Do It Yourself Plug In a Joystick

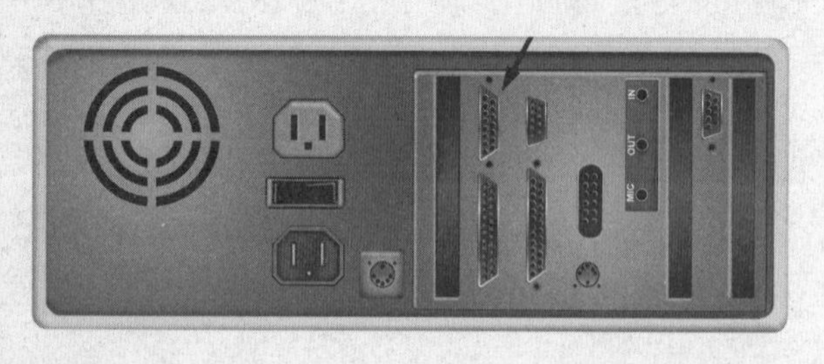

1 With your computer turned off, locate the game port on the back of your computer. It is shaped like a "D" and has 15 pins on it.

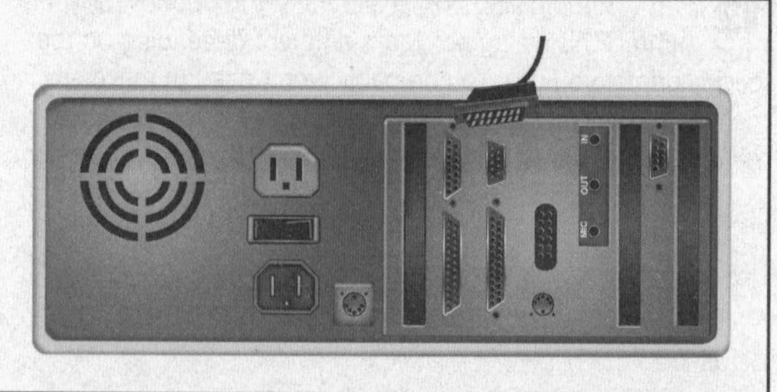

2 Plug the end of the joystick cable into the game port. Then turn on your computer and run your game software.

3 When using your game software, you will likely be asked to "calibrate" the joystick. This is easy, and usually entails moving the stick to the upper left, then to the lower right. Once it's calibrated, you can start playing!

Install a Mouse

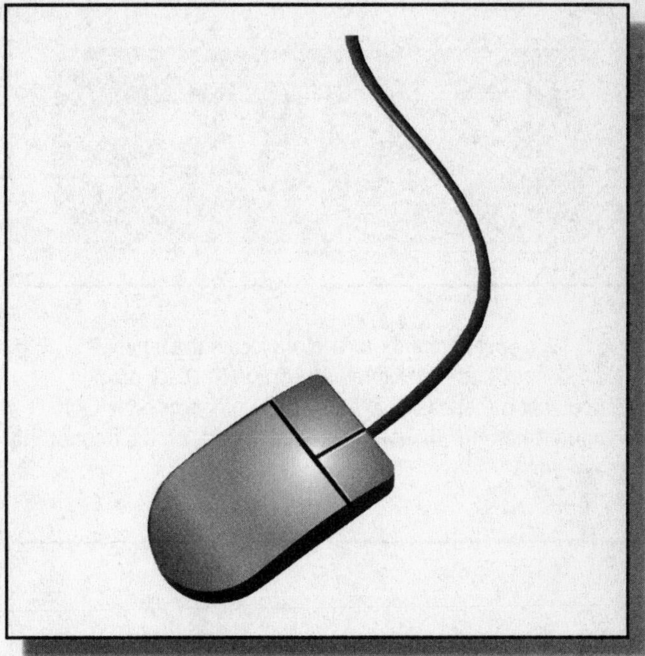

Before the Macintosh was introduced in 1984, few computer users ever heard of a *mouse*, let alone saw one. The kind of mouse used with a computer doesn't have ears or a tendency to make elephants scramble. Instead, a computer mouse is a device (roughly palm-sized) that moves an on-screen pointer when you roll it around. The computer interprets the action of the mouse pointer as a user pointing at something on-screen and saying, *I want this*.

Today the computer mouse is common. Nearly all new computers are sold with mice, and a growing number of programs require them (Microsoft Windows, for example, is nearly useless without a mouse).

If your computer is not yet equipped with a mouse, you can add one with relative ease. Though you can spend a lot of money on a mouse, typical no-name models cost under $20. For the most part, and for most jobs, they function just as well as the more expensive models.

The typical *after-market* mouse (one you have to install because the computer didn't come with one) uses one of your PC's *serial ports* to attach to your computer. It's called a "serial" port because the data goes in and out of the connector one bit at a time—in serial (one after the other) fashion. Since the mouse hooks up to your computer by way of a serial port, your computer must have one available, and it must be the correct size to accept the connector on the end of the mouse cable.

More than likely, unless you have attached an external modem to your computer, the proper serial port on your PC is available and waiting to be hooked up to a mouse. In the event that a serial port is not available, you'll have to add one. This entails opening your computer and installing an additional adapter card that has one or more serial ports on it. Opening your computer is the easy part; getting the serial port adapter card to "talk" to your computer is the hard part, and is beyond the scope of this book (if you do it wrong, your computer may lock up and refuse to operate). If you need to install an additional serial port, have your dealer do it, or enlist the help of a knowledgeable friend.

In addition to installing the mouse hardware, you will need to tell your computer that you're using a mouse. This entails installed special mouse software that comes with the mouse you buy. Software installation is usually automatic, but you will want to consult with the manual that comes with your mouse for specifics.

The cable of the typical serial mouse is equipped with a 9-pin "D" connector. If the serial port on your PC is a 25-pin "D" connector, you will need an adapter, available from your dealer. If you have a BUS mouse, it has a round plug that you insert into a special mouse port on your computer. The outlet should be clearly marked; if it's not marked, look for it near the outlet for your keyboard.

Begin Do It Yourself Install a Mouse in Windows 3.11

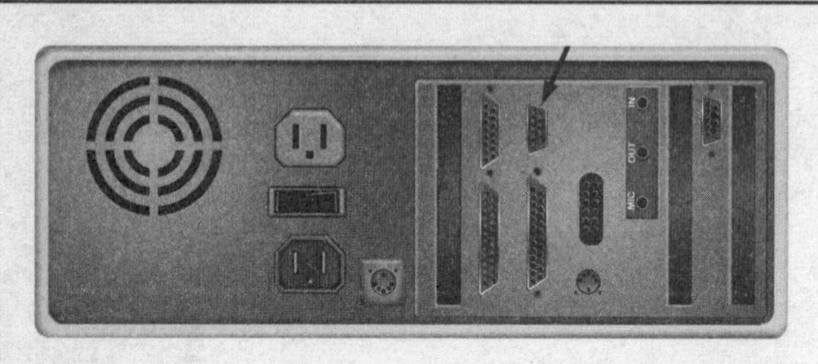

1 With your computer turned off, locate the 9-pin "D" connector or circular mouse port on the back of your computer. It is shaped like a "D" and has nine pins on it. (Some computers have the mouse and keyboard ports on the front of the system unit.)

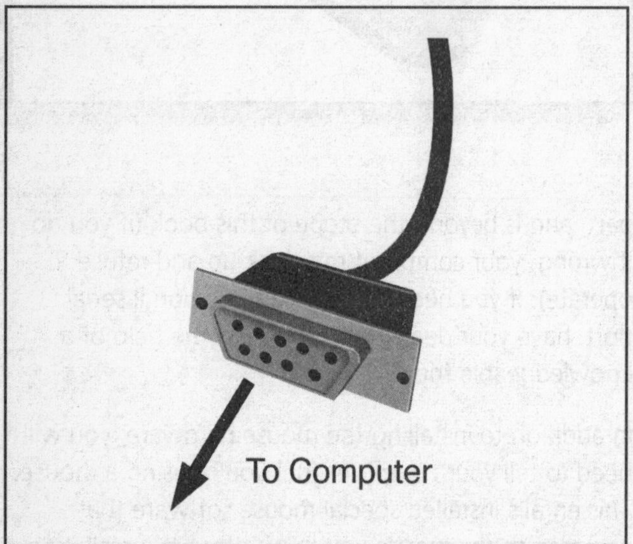

2 Plug the end of the mouse cable into the serial or mouse port on the back of the computer.

3 Turn on your computer. If Windows loads automatically, leave Windows by choosing **File**, **Exit** in the Program Manager.

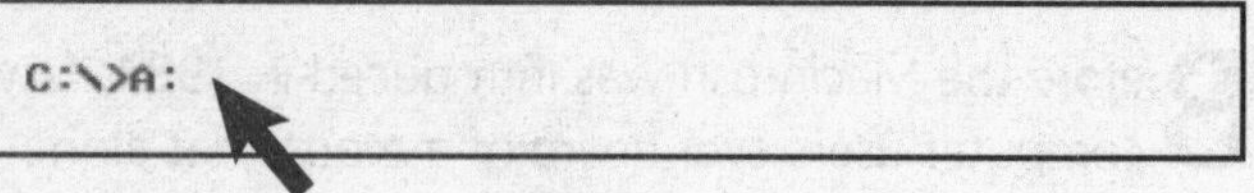

4 Insert the disk that came with the mouse in your computer's floppy disk drive. Type **A:** (or **B:** if the disk is in drive B) and press **Enter**.

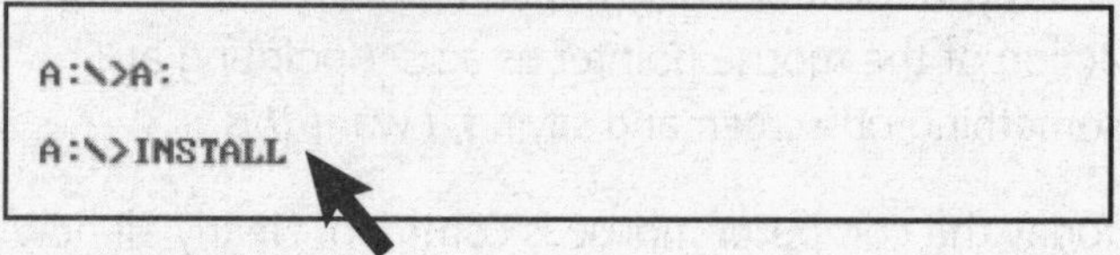

5 Your mouse comes with an installation disk and an automated program that installs the mouse software on your computer, making some necessary changes to your computer's configuration files. Type the name of the mouse software installation program (such as **INSTALL** or **SETUP**), and press **Enter**. Follow the on-screen prompts (if any) to complete the installation of the mouse.

6 When the software installation is complete, restart your computer by pressing the **Ctrl**, **Alt**, and **Del** keys at the same time. When your computer restarts, you will be able to use your mouse with your programs.

Begin Do It Yourself Install a Mouse in Windows 95

1. With your computer turned off, locate the 9-pin "D" connector or circular mouse port on the back of your computer. It is shaped like a "D" and has nine pins on it. (Some computers have the mouse and keyboard ports on the front of the system unit.)

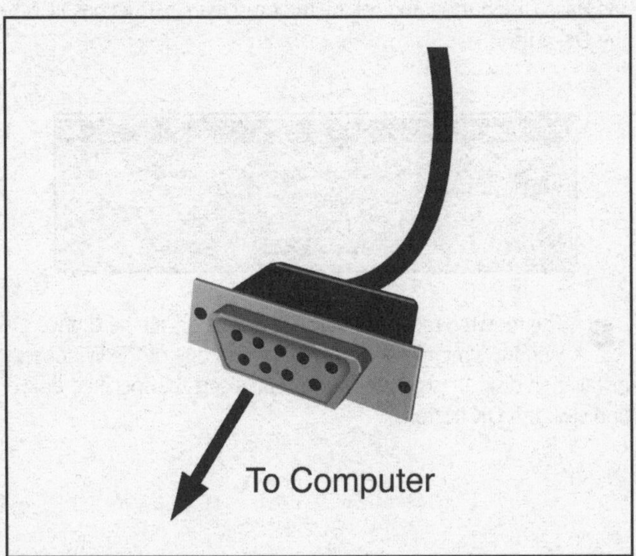

2. Plug the end of the mouse cable into the serial or mouse port on the back of the computer.

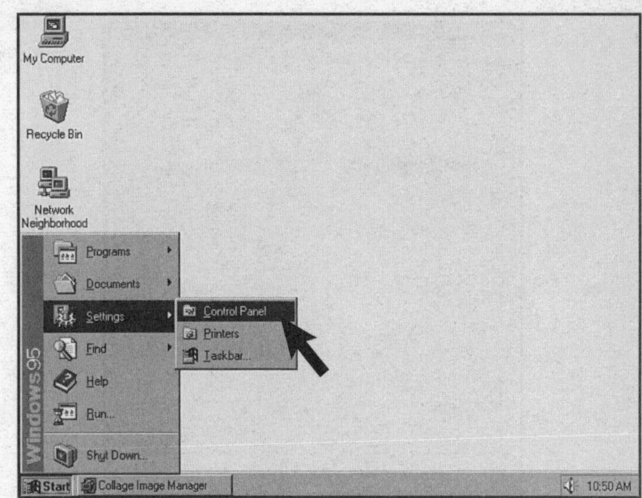

3. Turn on your computer. Windows 95 loads automatically on startup. If the Welcome dialog box appears, click the **Close** button. Click the **Start** button, move the mouse pointer over **Settings**, and click **Control Panel**.

4. The Control Panel has a Mouse icon. Double-click the **Mouse** icon to view the current mouse settings.

(continues)

Do It Yourself Install a Mouse in Windows 95

(continued)

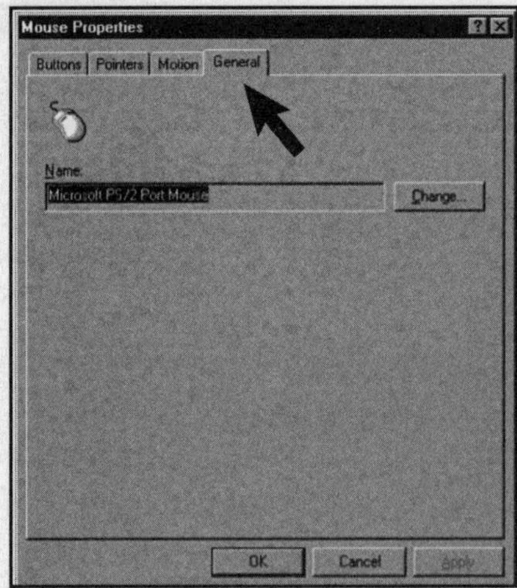

5 The Mouse Properties dialog box shows the current settings for the mouse. Click the **General** tab to specify the type of mouse you have.

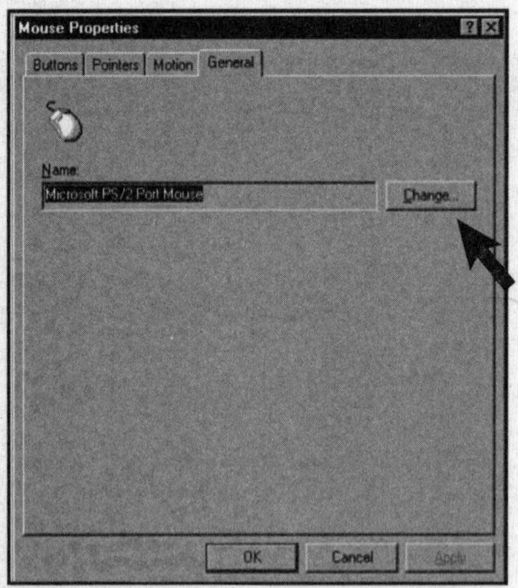

6 The Name text box displays the type of mouse Windows thinks is installed. Click the **Change** button to pick a mouse type.

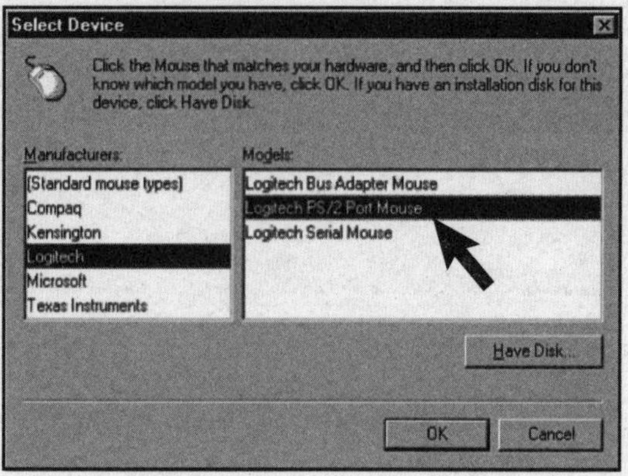

7 The Select Device dialog box lets you pick a mouse type. Click the manufacturer's name and the model. (If the mouse came with a disk that has its own Windows 95 driver, click the Have Disk button and follow the on-screen instructions.) Click the **OK** button.

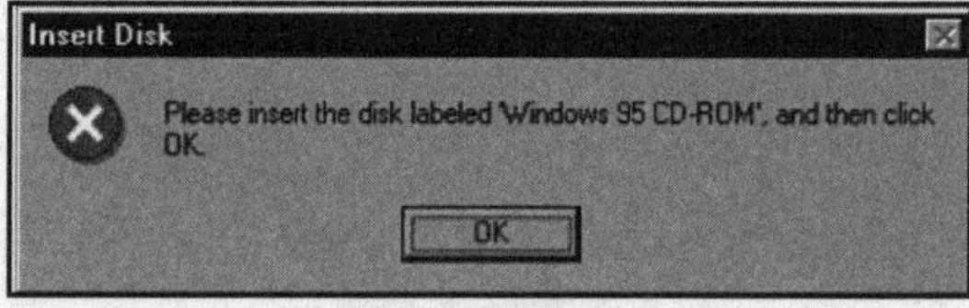

8 The required mouse driver may not be on the hard drive. Windows might need to copy it from one of the Windows installation disks. If prompted for a disk, insert the specified disk, and click the **OK** button.

Install an External Modem

Modems are used to allow your computer to talk to other computers over the telephone. Computers "talk" in a strange, high-pitched squeal that's unintelligible to us. But modems understand this gibberish, and that's all that matters.

Talking to other computers has its benefits. For example, you might call up the computers at one of the online services like CompuServe, America Online, or PRODIGY (see "Connecting with the Outside World Using Online Services" on page 235 for more information on online services). Once there, you can use your computer to browse through their vast reservoir of files. You might do a report for school, or locate the month's fluctuation in prices of your favorite stocks. You can even leave messages or chat with other computer users from around the world.

A modem is also a necessary ingredient if you want to jump onto the Internet bandwagon. Like the online services just mentioned, the Internet is really a collection of computer networks. Your computer can "chat" with the Internet computers as long as you have a modem and the appropriate software.

Modems come in two general flavors: internal and external. The *internal* kind fits inside your computer. There's no cable or connection to worry about. At its simplest level, all you do is plug the modem into an empty expansion slot inside your computer. The *external* modem is in its own case outside your computer, and connects to your PC through a cable. External modems can be easier to install (depending on the modem and computer), but they tend to be a little more expensive.

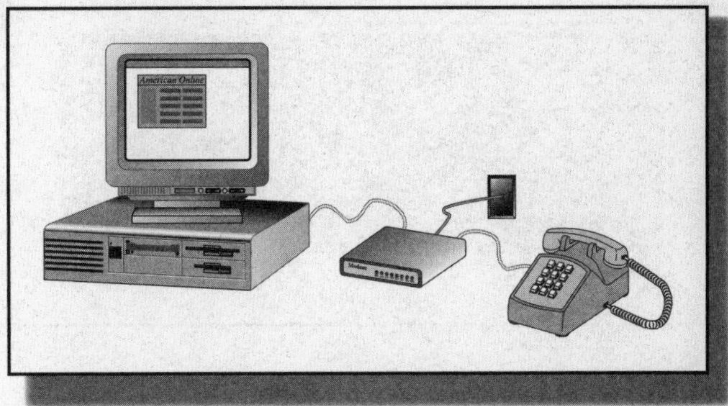

These days, most modems also include a fax capability, letting you send and receive faxes. Software that runs on your computer controls the modem so it sends out the right kind of squeals (they are different for other modems, and for fax machines).

This task describes installing an external modem to your computer. (For instructions on installing an internal modem, see "Install an Adapter Card Inside Your Computer" on page 432.) For the external modem, your computer must have a serial port available. If there is no such serial port, you'll need to add one. This entails opening your computer and installing an additional adapter card that has one or more serial ports on it. Adding more serial ports can be a highly complicated issue. If you need to install an additional serial port, have your dealer do it, or get help from a knowledgeable friend.

In addition to installing the modem itself, you'll need to install the software that runs it; this software comes with the modem. If your modem serves double duty—as modem and fax—it will have two programs: one for using it as a modem, and one for using it as a fax.

Begin Do It Yourself Install a Modem in DOS or Windows 3.11

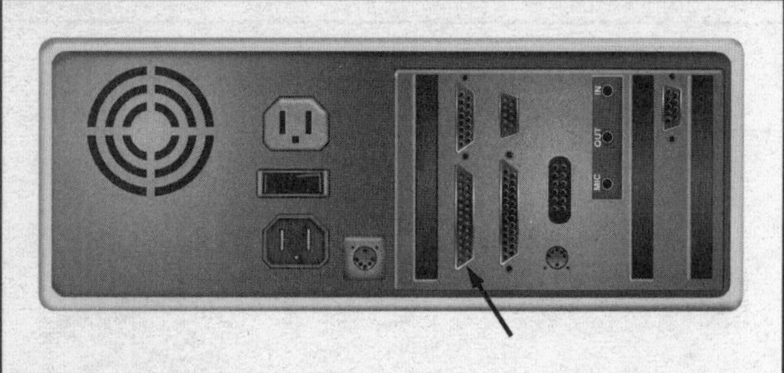

1 With your computer turned off, locate the serial 9-pin or 25-pin "D" connector on the back of your computer. It is shaped like a "D" and has nine pins on it.

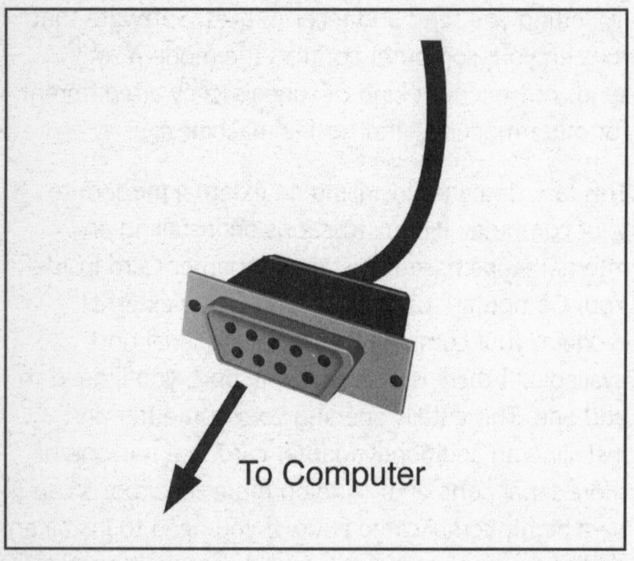

2 Plug one end of the modem cable into the serial port. If the cable doesn't match your connector, you'll need to get an adapter (9-pin-to-25-pin, or vice versa), available at your computer dealer.

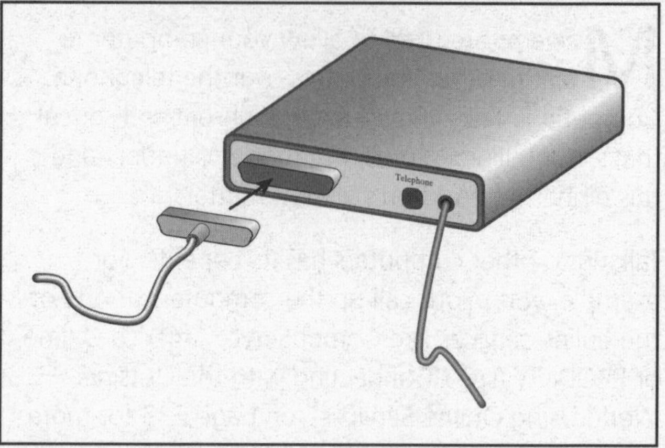

3 Plug the other end of the modem cable into the 9- (or 25-) pin connector on back of the modem.

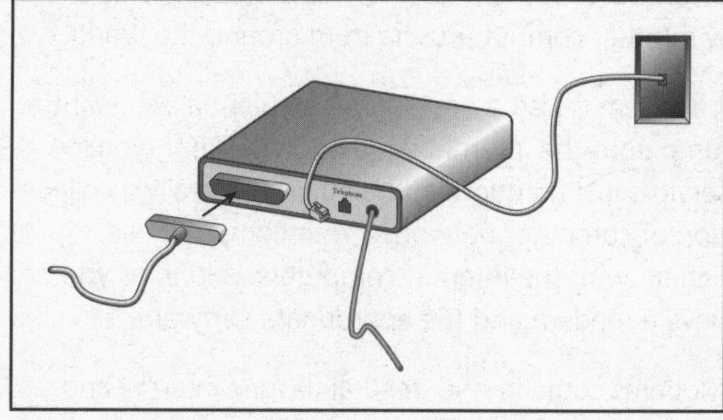

4 Plug one end of the phone wire into the modem, and the other end into a nearby telephone outlet.

5 Turn on your computer. Determine whether the installation software that comes with your modem is supposed to be used under DOS or Windows. If it's for Windows, start Windows (by typing **WIN** at the DOS prompt) if it's not already started.

Do It Yourself Install a Modem in DOS or Windows 3.11

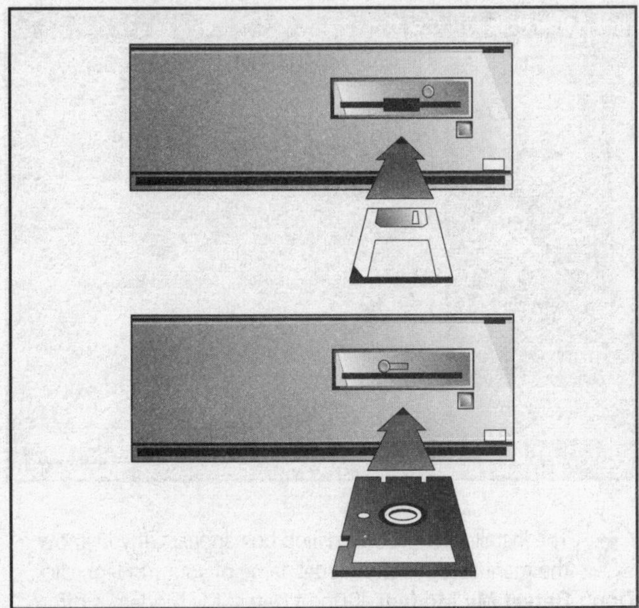

6 Insert the disk that came with the modem in your computer's floppy disk drive.

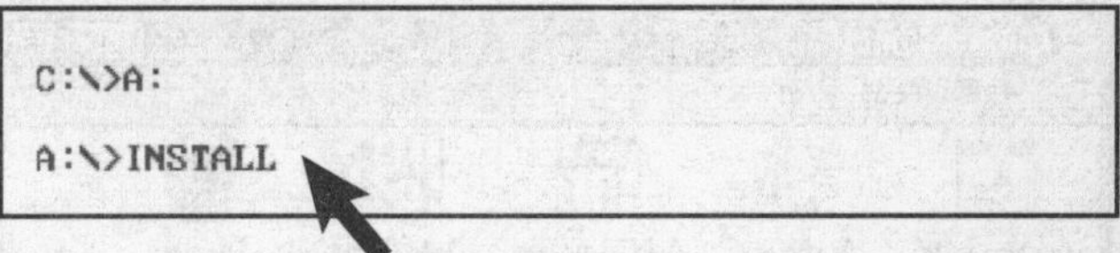

7 If you're using DOS, type **A:** (or **B:** if the disk is in drive B) and press **Enter**. Type the name of the modem software's installation program (such as **INSTALL** or **SETUP**), and press **Enter**. Follow the on-screen prompts to complete the installation.

8 If you're using Windows 3.11, select **File**, **Run** in the Windows Program Manager. In the Run dialog box, type **A:INSTALL** or **B:INSTALL**, depending on the drive and the name of the installation program. Click **OK**. Follow the on-screen prompts to complete the modem software installation.

Begin Do It Yourself Install a Modem in Windows 95

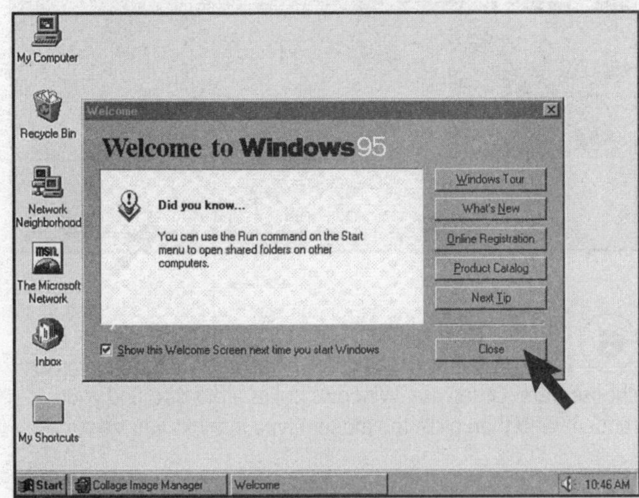

1 Connect your modem as explained in steps 1-4 above. Then, turn on your computer to start Windows 95. If the Welcome to Windows 95 dialog box appears, click the **Close** button.

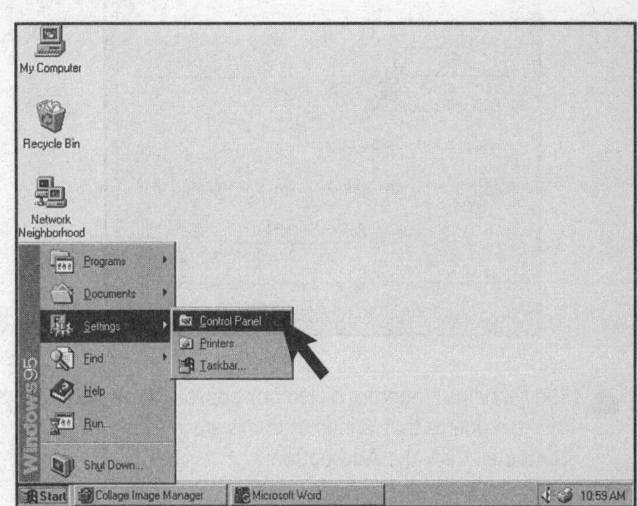

2 Click the **Start** button, point to **Settings**, and click **Control Panel**.

(continues)

Do It Yourself Install a Modem in Windows 95

(continued)

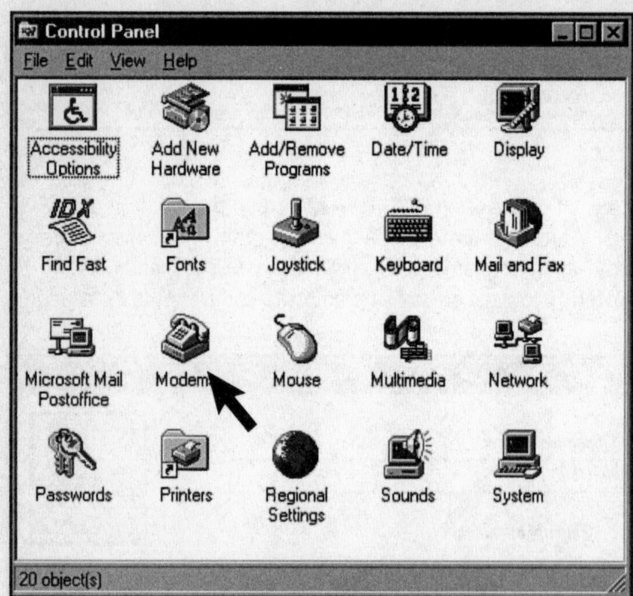

3 Double-click the **Modems** icon.

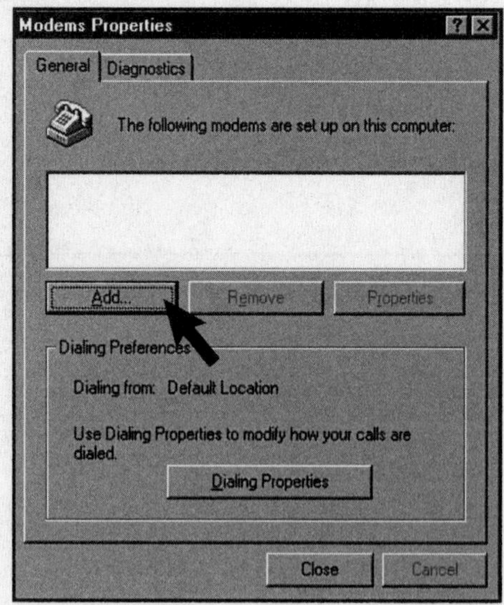

4 The Modems Properties dialog box appears, showing a list of the modems that Windows thinks are installed on your computer. Click the **Add** button.

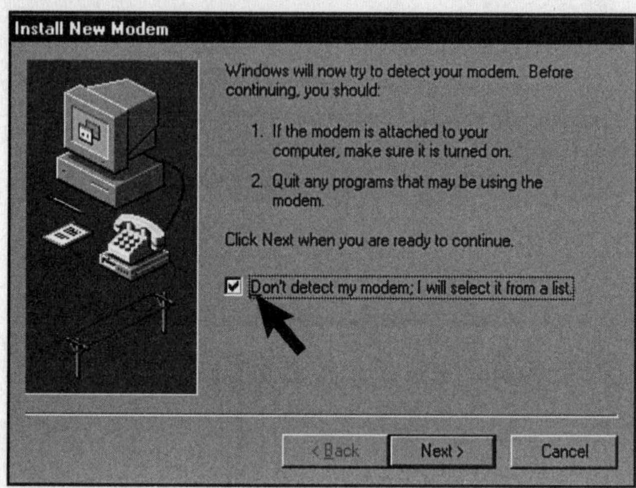

5 The Install New Modem dialog box appears. If you know the manufacturer and model name of your modem, click **Don't Detect My Modem**. If Don't Detect My Modem is off, you'll have to wait while Windows tries to determine the modem type.

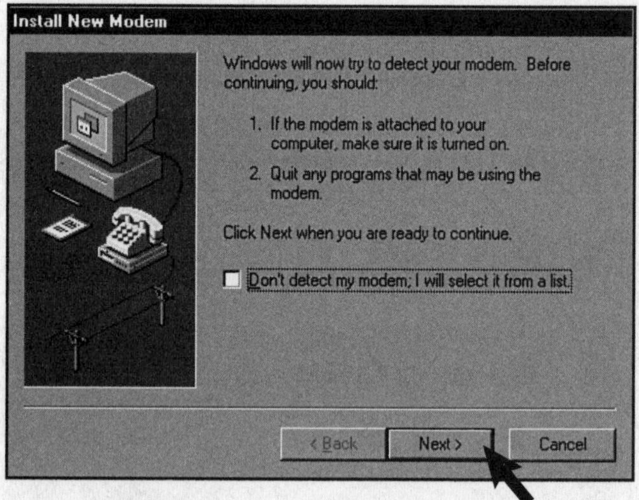

6 Click the **Next** button. If you clicked on Don't Detect My Modem, the next dialog box presents a list of modems to choose from. Otherwise, Windows pokes around to find your modem, and then picks the modem type it thinks you have.

Do It Yourself Install a Modem in Windows 95

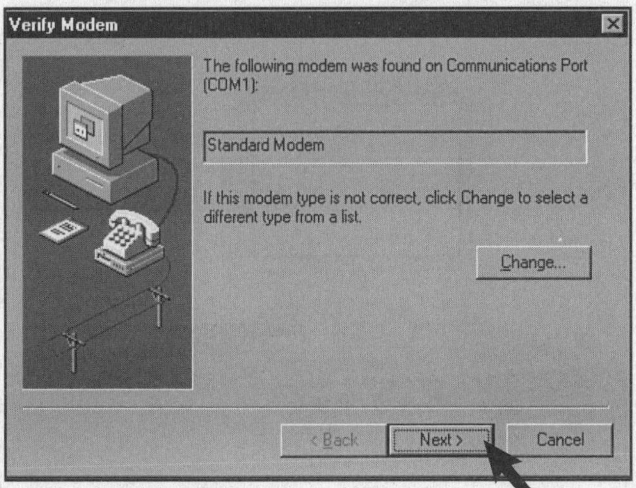

7 Take one of the following steps:

If Windows picked a modem type, and you agree with it, click the **Next** button, and then click the **Finish** button. You're done.

If Windows picked a modem type that does not match your modem (or if it picked Standard), click the **Change** button and proceed to step 8.

If you chose to pick a modem type from a list, proceed to step 8.

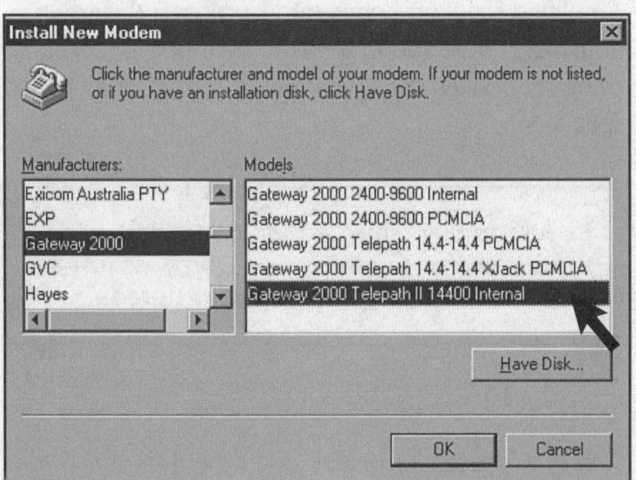

8 Click the brand name of the modem in the **Manufacturers** list, and click the model in the **Models** list. (If the precise model is not listed, pick a model that looks close. If the modem came with a disk, insert the disk, click **Have Disk**, and follow the instructions.)

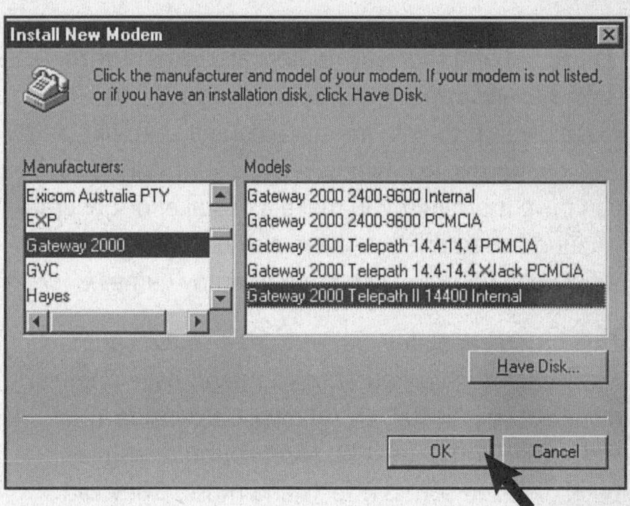

9 Click the **OK** button.

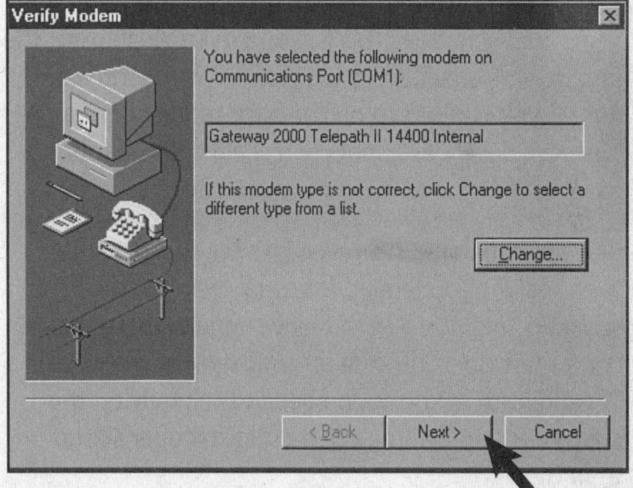

10 You're returned to the Verify Modem dialog box, where the name of the selected modem is displayed. Click the **Next** button. Windows indicates that it is about to complete the installation.

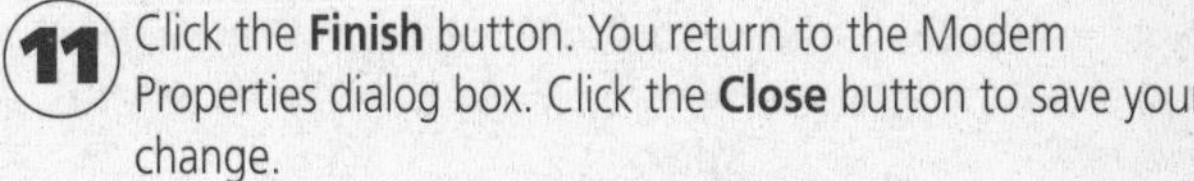

11 Click the **Finish** button. You return to the Modem Properties dialog box. Click the **Close** button to save your change.

Attach Speakers to a Sound Card

More and more computers are coming with sound capability. The sounds your computer makes are up to you. You can make it chirp like a *Star Trek* communicator whenever you start Windows. You can have it groan if you make a mistake, or generate exciting sound effects—even play background music—when you're playing one of many games.

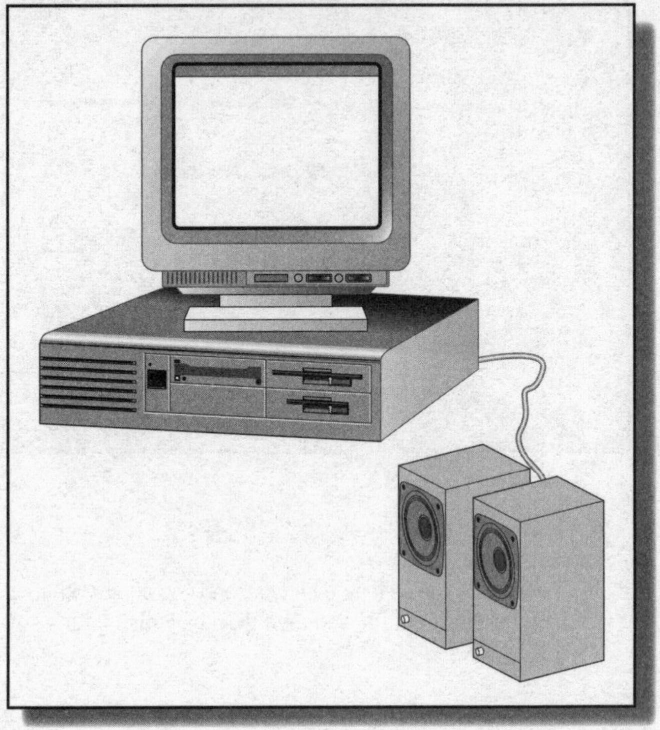

This sound capability comes from a *sound card* installed in the computer (if you don't have one installed, see "Install an Adapter Card Inside Your Computer" on page 432. Most sound cards play back digitized sound effects and music. They can also record sound, so you can make your own effects (or share voice-annotated documents with friends and associates).

For a sound card to make sound, you have to attach some speakers to it. This is a simple job: just insert the plug for the speakers into a jack on the sound card (which you can get to on the back of your computer). This task describes connecting speakers to a sound card; we'll help you plug them into the correct jack!

Before continuing, however, let's pause to consider the speakers you'll need for computer sound. The speakers that come with many sound-card-equipped computers don't provide amplification of their own. The strength of the sound depends entirely on the sound card, and some cards put out louder sound than others.

If you find the sound isn't loud enough for your tastes, first try to turn up the volume on the sound card (many sound cards have volume controls) or the "master volume" control on the sound software running on your computer. If these steps don't improve the sound volume, you may want to consider replacing the speakers with better, amplified types. Amplified speakers come with (surprise!) their own amplifiers. Their sound tends to be much louder (and of better quality) than what you get from unamplified speakers.

Be sure to buy "shielded" speakers designed specifically for computer use. Don't use just any old speaker like the ones on your stereo.

Begin Do It Yourself Connect Speakers to a Sound Card

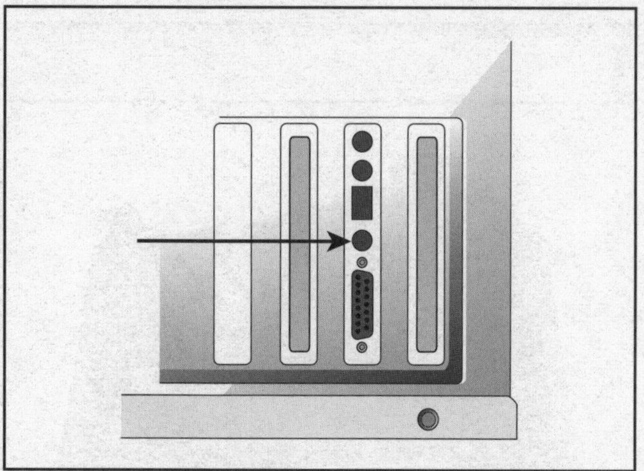

1 With your computer turned off, locate the Speaker jack on the sound card in the back of your computer. Most sound cards have several jacks that look alike, and you can damage the speakers and/or sound card if you plug the speakers into the wrong jack.

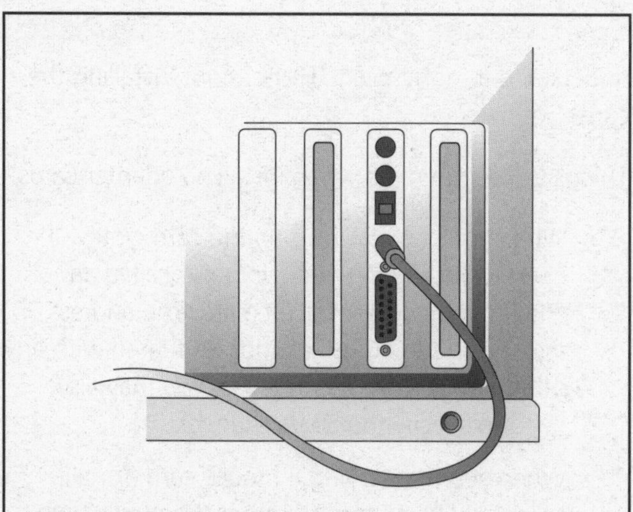

2 Plug the speaker plug into the speaker jack on the sound card.

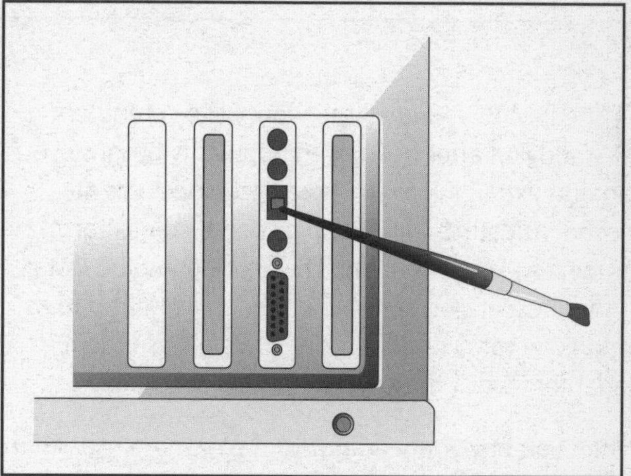

3 If your sound card has a volume control on it, set the control initially to about half to three quarters (if the control is numbered, set it between 5 and 7).

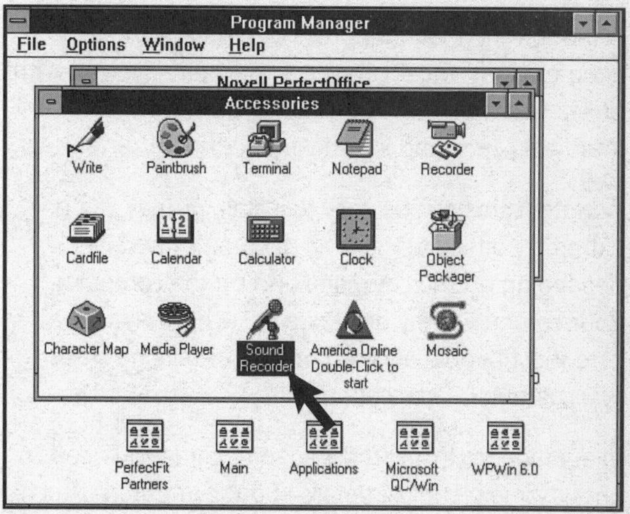

4 Turn on your computer and start your sound software (if you're using Windows, start Windows, then use the **Sound Recorder** program—usually found in the Accessories group—to play back sound). While listening to sounds adjust the volume control (if applicable) on the sound card.

Install an Adapter Card Inside Your Computer

The IBM PC—and all the work-alike computers modeled after it—gained popularity because you can add extra junk to it. These accessories are attached inside the computer, in special connectors known as *expansion slots*. The accessories you install in these expansion slots are commonly referred to as *expansion cards* or *adapter cards*. We'll use the term "adapter cards" throughout this task.

When you buy your computer, one or more expansion slots are probably already taken up by adapter cards. So-called *base unit* adapter cards are typically used for the disk drives in your computer, as well as for the parallel, serial, and game connectors at the back of your computer.

Although there are hundreds of different kinds of adapter cards, most computer users are involved with only a handful. These are sound cards, CD-ROM interface cards, and internal modems.

Adapter cards can be easy to install, or they can be extremely difficult. The level of complexity varies depending on the card, and also on the computer. Your computer may be set up in such a way that a card most people have no trouble installing causes you splitting headaches.

In addition, to install most adapter cards you need to know some technical details about computers—such as how to tell a serial port from a parallel port, how ports are named, and what technicians mean by *interrupts*, *port addresses*, and a strange thing known as *DMA channels*. If these subjects are alien to you, you're better off having someone who knows computers install your adapter cards for you.

This task only summarizes the technical setup of adapter cards. Each card is different; you **MUST** have the manual for your card by your side when installing it. If you don't have a manual handy, or if you don't understand it, don't even THINK about installing the card. Get help.

Things to keep in mind when installing adapter cards:

- When you're installing a sound card, you will need to specify the *interrupt* (also called an "IRQ") and *address* for the card. The address and interrupt you use cannot be shared with any other device in your computer. You may also need to specify the DMA channel.
- When you're installing a mouse card (for a so-called "port" mouse rather than for a serial mouse), you will need to specify the interrupt. The interrupt you use cannot be shared with any other device in your computer.
- When installing an internal modem (with or without a fax capability), you will need to specify the interrupt and serial port designator (such as COM1 or COM2) used for the card. Normally the interrupt and serial port designator you use cannot be shared with any other device in your computer.

Begin Do It Yourself Install an Adapter Card

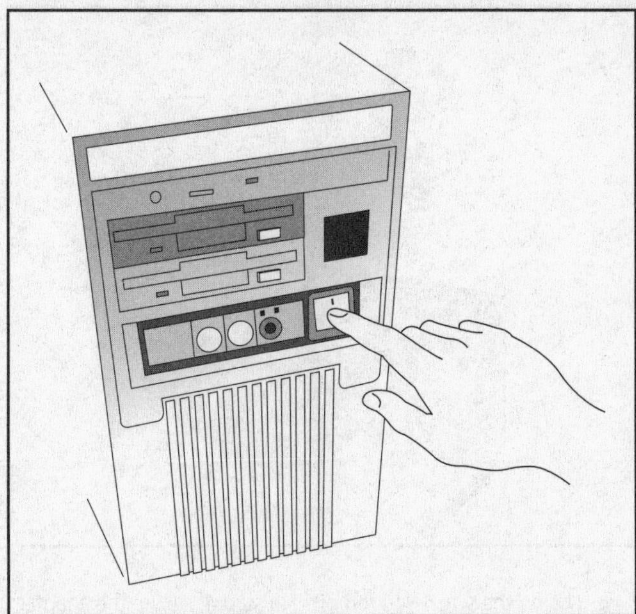

1 Turn your computer off, and unplug it.

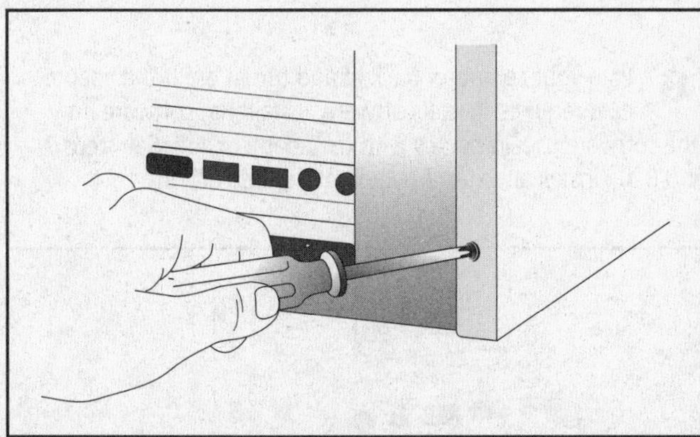

2 Open the computer by removing the cabinet screws. (You can find specifics on how this is done in "Clean Inside Your Computer" on page 349.)

Windows 95 comes with a special hardware installation tool that can help you set up new adapter cards. It even includes a utility for tracking down and resolving any conflicts that may render an adapter card unusable. For details, refer to "Install Hardware in Windows 95" on page 439.

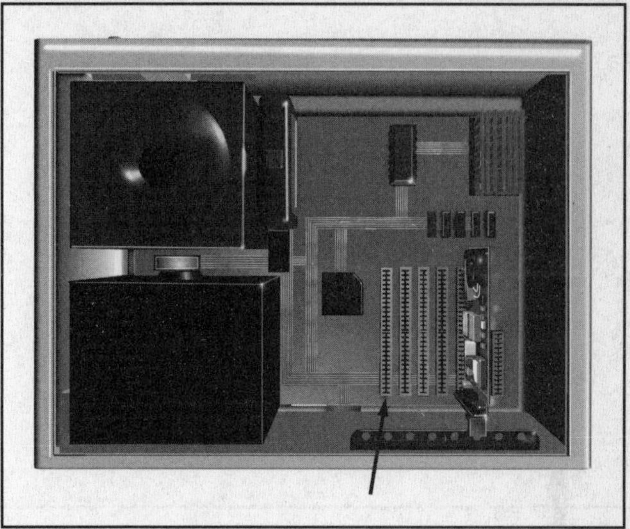

3 Locate an empty expansion slot inside your computer. On most PCs, some slots have two connectors, and others have one. Look at the mating connector at the bottom of the adapter card, and use an expansion slot that matches the connector on the card. (In a pinch, you can install an adapter card that needs only one connector in an expansion slot with two connectors.)

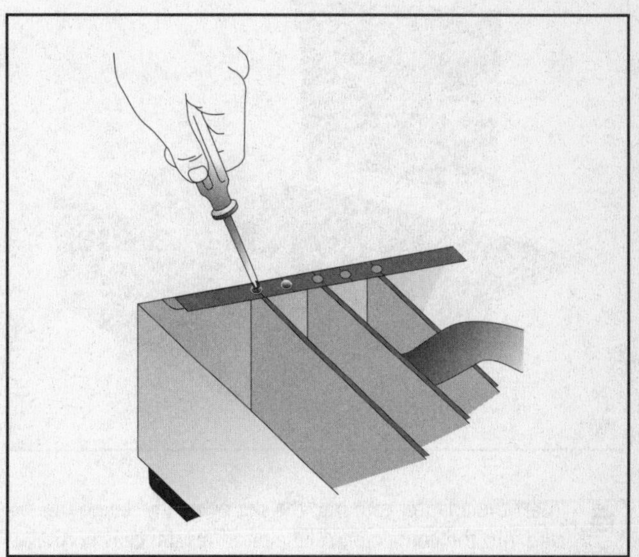

4 Using a #1 Phillips screwdriver, remove the back plate on the back of the computer for the expansion slot you want to use. Store the removed plate in a safe place. Keep the screw handy because you'll need it in a bit.

(continues)

Do It Yourself Install an Adapter Card

(continued)

5 Before installing the adapter card, set any DIP or jumper switches on the card that are required to use the card with your computer. (This is where the technical mumbo-jumbo, like interrupts and address ports, comes in. Be sure to refer to the manual that comes with the card for specific details.)

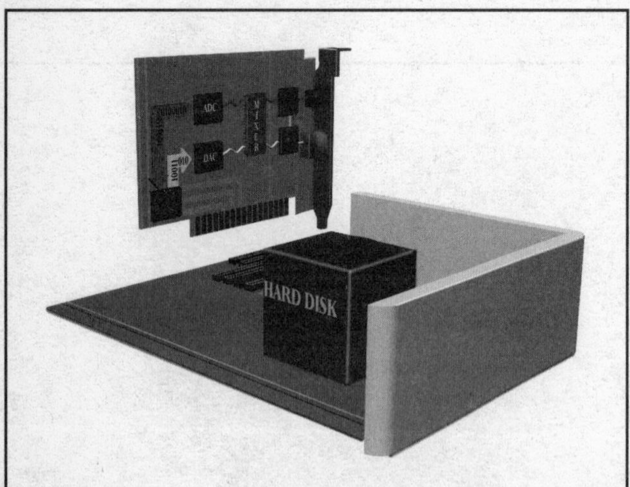

6 Insert the adapter card into the slot by gently sliding the card into the connector. A little bit of resistance is normal, but don't apply too much pressure, or you may break something.

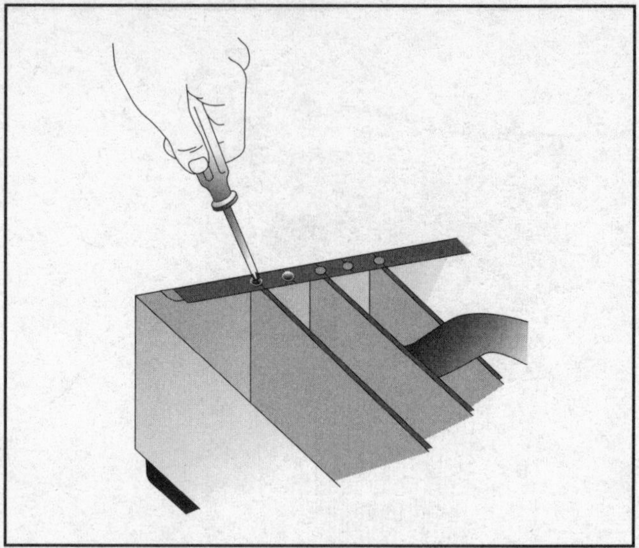

7 Using the screw you removed in step 4, secure the adapter card to the computer's case. Don't over-tighten. Before replacing the cabinet and closing the computer, you should test the operation of the adapter card. If the card connects to some external accessories (like a mouse, modem, or speakers), attach them now.

8 Plug your computer back in and turn it on. If the adapter card requires special software, install that software now (the software usually comes with the adapter card). See steps 7 and 8 in "Install an External Modem" for instructions.

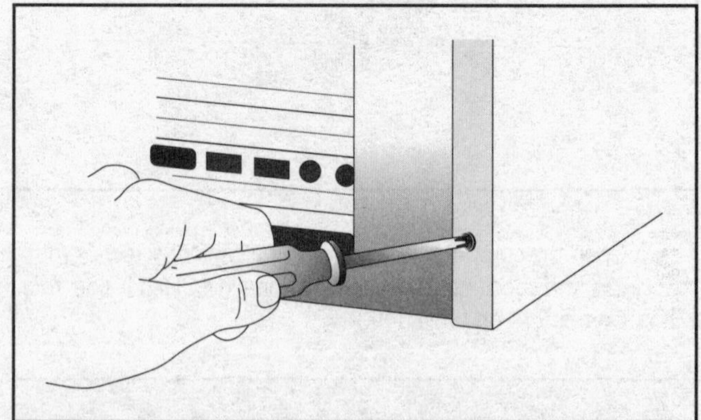

9 If the operation of the adapter card checks out, turn your computer back off. Put the computer back together by replacing the cabinet and cabinet screws. Your computer is now ready for regular use.

Install a CD-ROM Drive

CD-ROM (Compact Disc Read-Only Memory) is the trendy thing in computers these days. A CD-ROM looks identical to an audio compact disc, but is designed to hold computer data—over 600 megabytes of it—rather than music. Because of the vast amounts of data that can be economically stored on a single disc, CD-ROMs are fast becoming a popular way to distribute large amounts of information. This information might be an encyclopedia, or it might be the complete works of William Shakespeare.

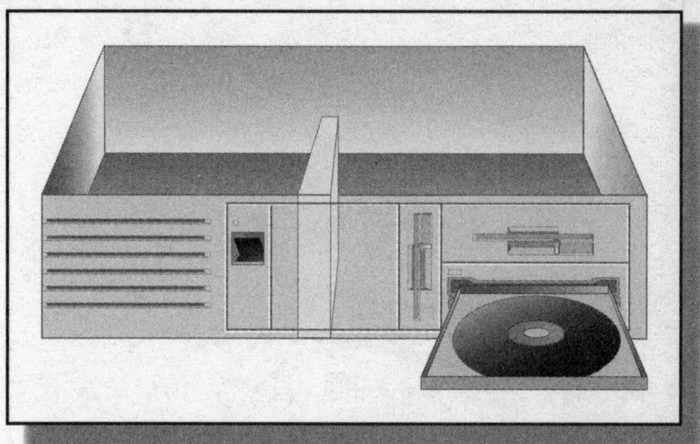

Over half of all new computers destined for the home market come with CD-ROM drives. Presently about 10 percent of all business computers have CD-ROM drives. As CD-ROMs become increasingly popular, more and more computer users are installing CD-ROM drives in their PCs.

Installing a CD-ROM drive entails two discrete steps: installing the drive itself (if it's an internal model; external models are also available, but are generally more expensive), and installing the *interface card* used as the actual link between the CD-ROM drive and your computer.

There is nothing particularly difficult about installing a CD-ROM drive in your computer, but complications can and do occur. The problem is the interaction between the CD-ROM interface card and your computer. If the card is not set up just right, your computer may balk and refuse to let you use the CD-ROM. Worse, your computer may refuse to work altogether. Though not common, it's not unheard of to install a CD-ROM, only to have a computer "play dead" when you turn it on! Should your CD-ROM installation prove challenging, your best bet is to enlist the help of your dealer or a knowledgeable friend.

This task describes installing an internal CD-ROM, and briefly discusses the technical issues you may have to resolve to get the drive to work. To be successful, you need to know some of the technical details about computers, including interrupts and port addresses. If you are unfamiliar with these subjects have your dealer or a knowledgeable friend install the CD-ROM drive for you.

You'll need an empty *disk drive bay* (the "bay" is the opening where the floppy disk drive mechanism fits in your computer) to install an internal CD-ROM. If you don't have a free disk drive bay, you won't be able to install a CD-ROM without removing a floppy disk drive. If you decide to do this, you're best off taking your computer to a dealer; this could get complicated.

Begin Do It Yourself Install a CD-ROM Drive

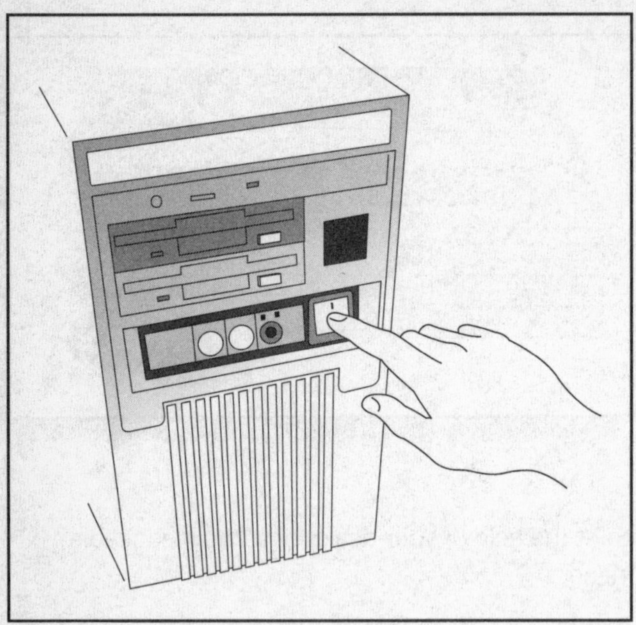

1 Turn your computer off, and unplug it.

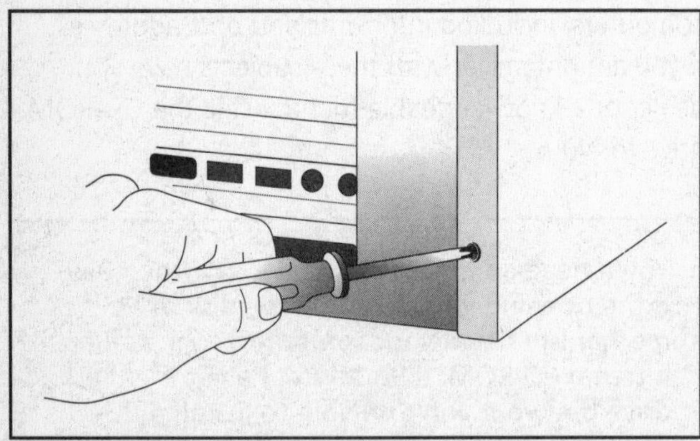

2 Open the computer by removing the cabinet screws. You can find specifics on how this is done in "Clean Inside Your Computer" on page 349.

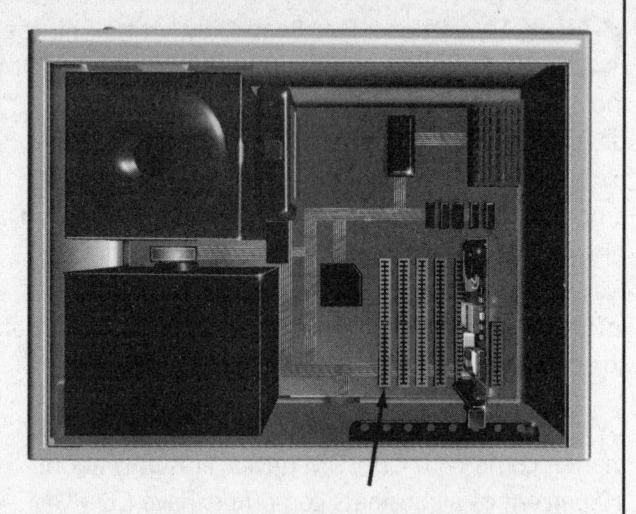

3 Locate an empty expansion slot inside your computer. On most PCs, some slots have two connectors; some have one. Look at the mating connector at the bottom of the interface card that comes with the CD-ROM drive. Match the connector on this card to the connector in your computer. (In a pinch, you can install an adapter card that needs only one connector in an expansion slot that has two connectors.)

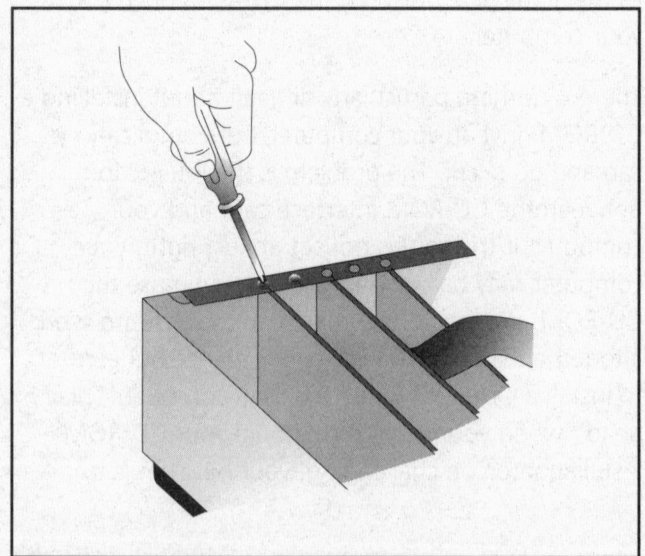

4 Using a #1 Phillips screwdriver, remove the back plate on the back of the computer for the expansion slot you want to use. Store the removed plate in a safe place. Keep the screw handy.

Do It Yourself Install a CD-ROM Drive

5 Before installing the CD-ROM interface adapter, set any DIP or jumper switches on the card that are required to use the card with your computer. Most cards come factory set for the most common installations, but you may need to reset the card to accommodate your specific computer. Be sure to refer to the manual that comes with the card for specific details.

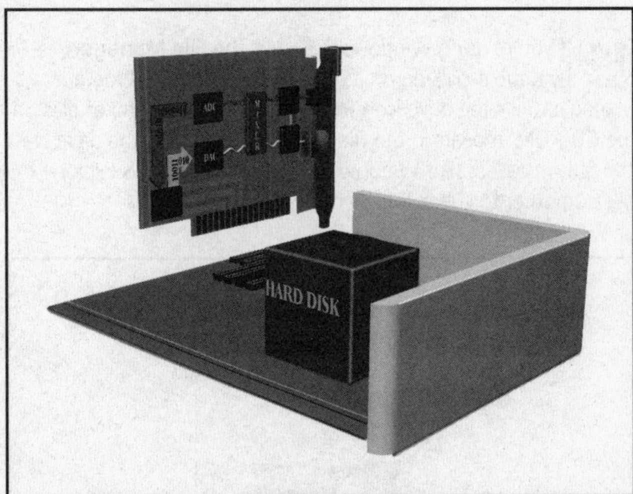

6 Insert the CD-ROM interface card into the slot by gently sliding the card into the connector. A little bit of resistance is normal, but don't apply too much pressure, or you may break something.

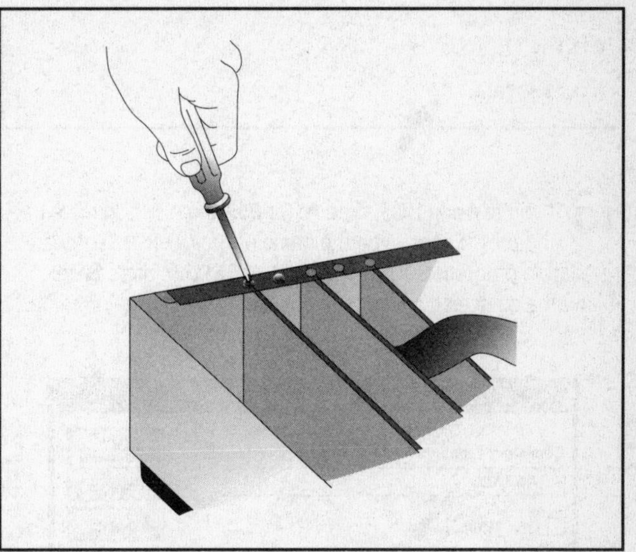

7 Using the screw you removed in step 4, secure the adapter card to the computer's case. Don't over-tighten.

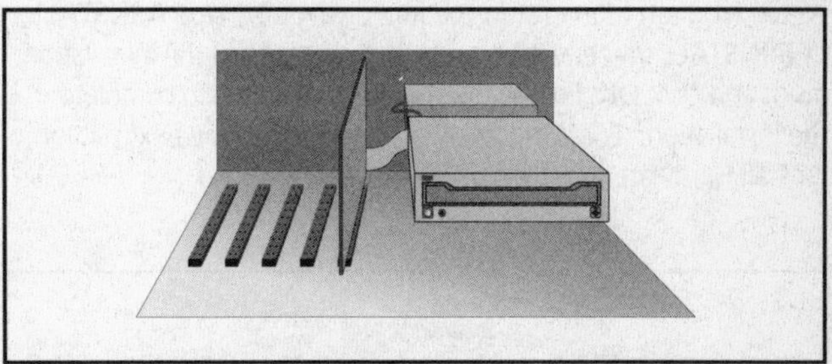

8 Remove the plastic cover for the disk drive bay you want to use. Insert the CD-ROM drive into the bay, and attach it to your computer using the screws supplied with the CD-ROM drive. Connect the CD-ROM drive to the interface card you installed in step 6. Be sure to orient the cable properly. Connect the power cable (included with the drive) between the CD-ROM drive and the computer's power supply.

9 Plug in your computer and turn it on. Before you can use your CD-ROM drive, you must tell your computer it now has one. Determine if the installation software that comes with your CD-ROM drive is supposed to be used under DOS or Windows. If it's for Windows, start Windows (if it's not already started). Insert the floppy disk that came with the CD-ROM drive into your computer's floppy disk drive.

(continues)

Do It Yourself Install a CD-ROM Drive

(continued)

10 If you're using DOS, type **A:** (or **B:** if the disk is in drive B) and press **Enter**. Type the name of the CD-ROM software installation program (such as **INSTALL** or **SETUP**); press **Enter**. Follow the on-screen prompts to complete the installation.

11 If you're using Windows, select **File**, **Run** in the Windows Program Manager. In the Run dialog box, type **A:INSTALL** or **B:INSTALL** (depending on which drive contains the installation disk), and click **OK**. Follow the on-screen prompts to complete the installation. (For Windows 95, skip ahead to the next section, "Install Hardware in Windows 95.")

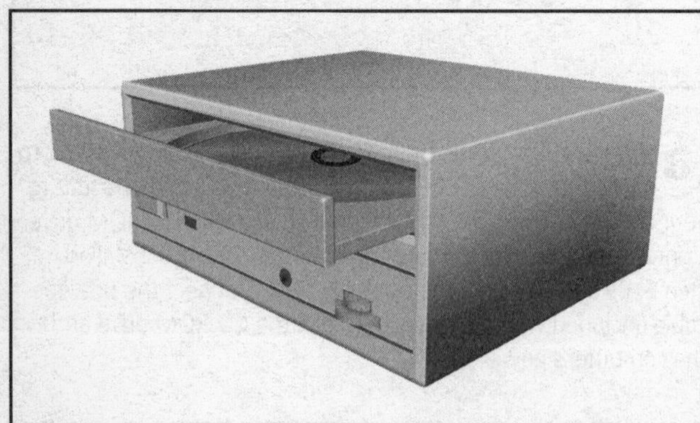

12 After installation is complete, test the operation of the CD-ROM drive by inserting a data disc into the drive.

13 If you're using DOS, type **D:** and press **Enter** (this assumes the CD-ROM is drive D). Type **DIR** to see a listing of the files on the CD-ROM. If you see this listing, the CD-ROM was installed correctly.

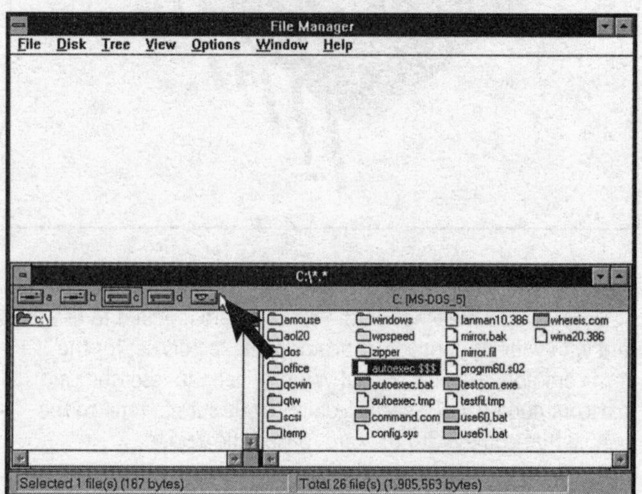

14 If you're using Windows 3.1, start the **File Manager** by double-clicking on its icon in the Windows Program Manager. Click the drive icon for the CD-ROM. A listing of files on the CD-ROM appears in the File Manager window if the drive was correctly installed. (For Windows 95, use the Windows Explorer or My Computer to check for the drive.)

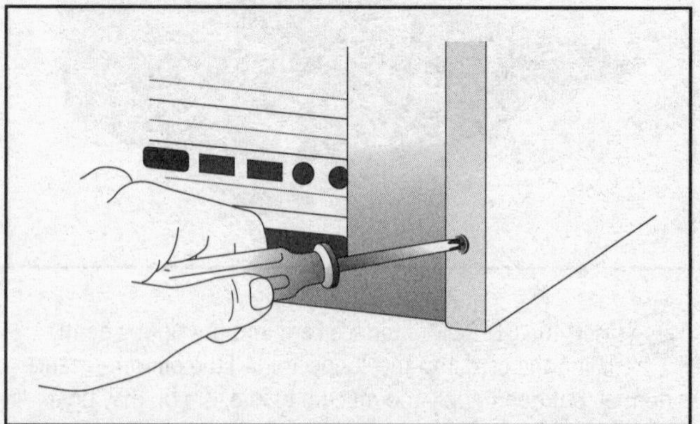

15 If the operation of the CD-ROM drive checks out, turn your computer back off. Put the computer back together by replacing the cabinet and cabinet screws. Your computer is now ready for regular use.

Install Hardware in Windows 95

When you installed Windows 95, the setup program searched for hardware devices (sound card, modem, printer, mouse, and so on) on your computer, and set up these devices to work in Windows. However, if you add a sound card, game card, or other device to your system, you must run through the hardware setup again.

Fortunately, Windows 95 offers a Wizard that can lead you through the process of installing a new device and help you resolve any problems that might occur. Just follow the steps to run the Add New Hardware Wizard, and then follow the on-screen instructions.

Plug-and-Play Hardware in Windows 95

Windows 95 is ushering in the era of plug-and-play hardware. With plug-and-play devices, you no longer have to worry about setting up the device to get along with all your other devices. You simply turn off the computer, connect the device, turn on your computer, and you're ready to roll.

But in order for plug-and-play to work, your system (and the device you want to install) must meet the following requirements:

- Your computer must have PCI or VLB expansion slots (or some other type of expansion slot that is capable of handling plug-and-play expansion boards).
- Your computer must have a BIOS (a set of instructions that tells the various computer components how to work together) that supports plug-and-play.
- Your operating system (Windows 95, in this case) must support plug-and-play standards, which it does.
- The device you are connecting to your computer must be plug-and-play compatible.

If your system (or new device) does not meet all of the requirements on the list, you can't take advantage of plug-and-play technology. However, even without plug-and-play, the Add New Hardware Wizard makes it much easier to install new devices on your computer.

Begin Do It Yourself Install Hardware in Windows 95

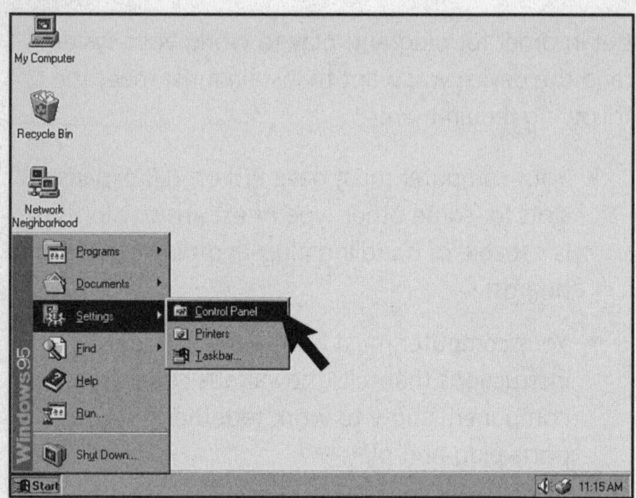

1 Exit all running programs. This prevents you from losing any data in case Windows locks up during the process. Click the **Start** button, move the mouse pointer over **Settings**, and then click **Control Panel**.

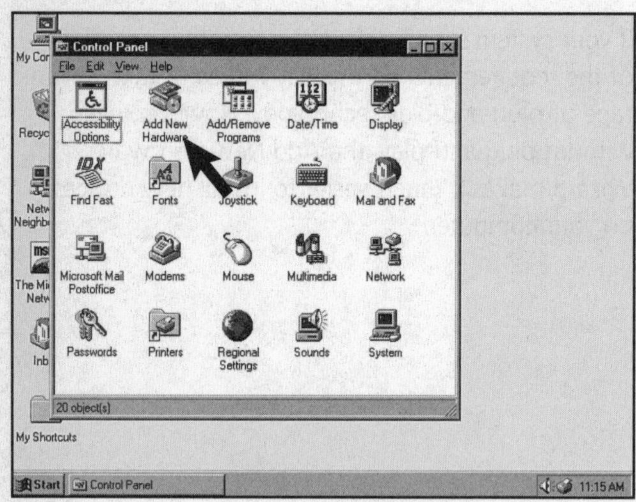

2 Double-click the **Add New Hardware** icon.

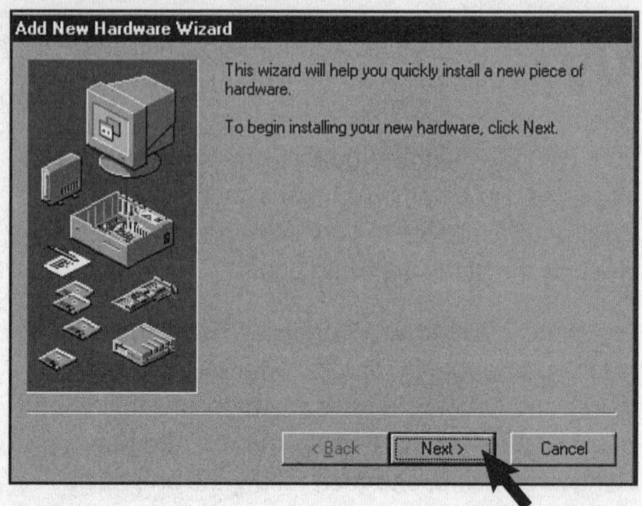

3 The Add New Hardware Wizard appears, informing you about what the Wizard will do. Click the **Next** button.

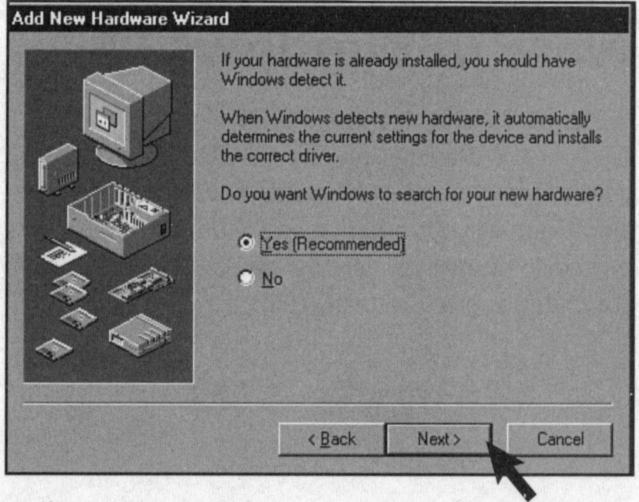

4 The Wizard asks if you want it to search for new hardware on your system. Make sure **Yes (Recommended)** is selected, and then click the **Next** button.

Do It Yourself Install Hardware in Windows 95

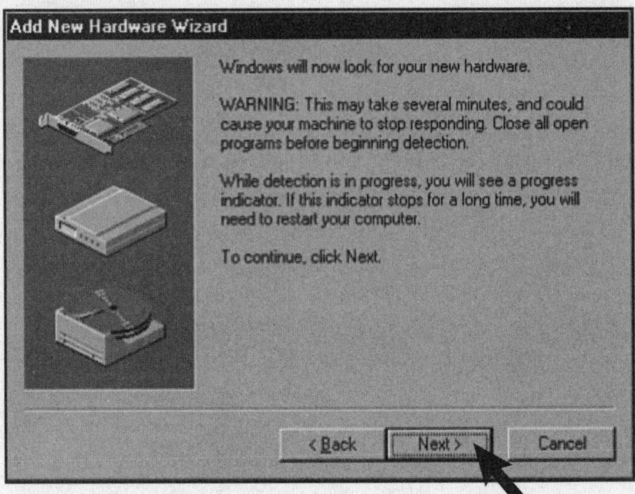

5 The Wizard indicates that it is now about to search your system for any new devices. Click the **Next** button.

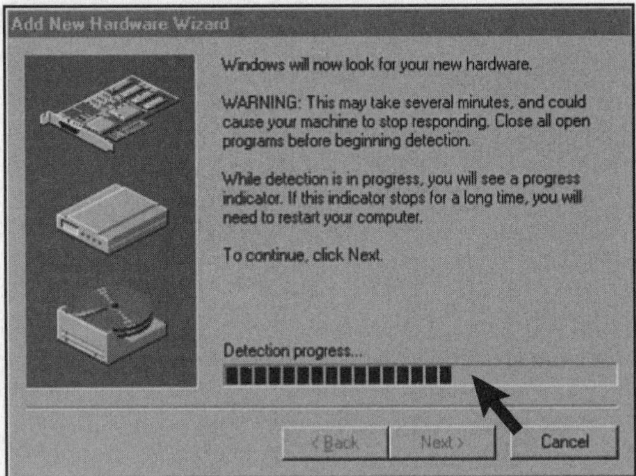

6 Wizard searches your computer for any new hardware that's installed. This can take several minutes; wait patiently.

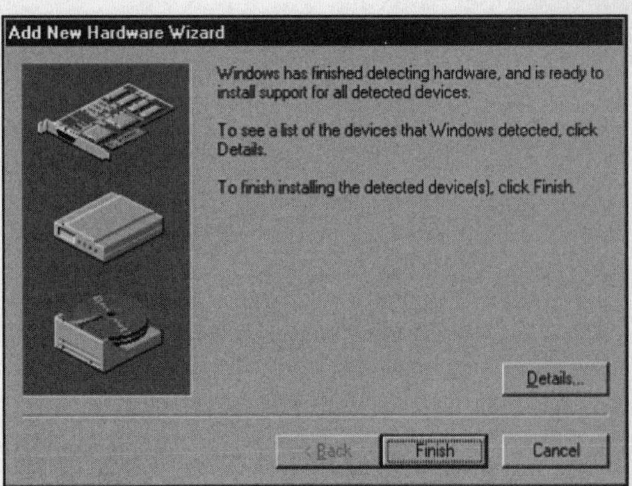

7 Wait until the detection process is complete (several minutes), and then click the **Finish** button. The Wizard installs the new device.

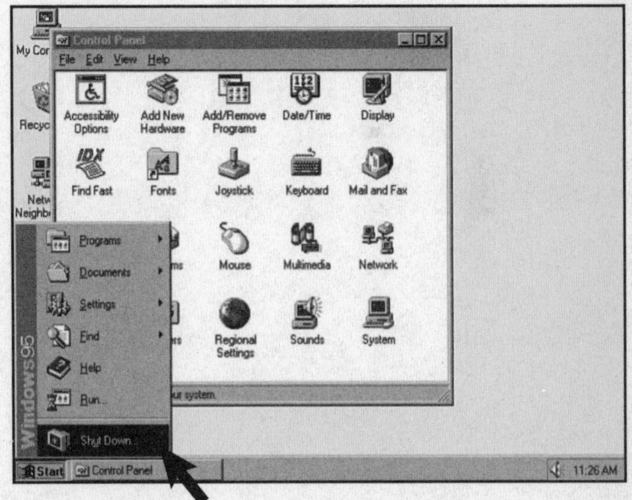

8 Click the **Start** button, click **Shut Down**, and follow the on-screen instructions to shut down and restart your computer.

DO IT YOURSELF

Keep Your Data Safe

People are too trusting of their computers. It's not uncommon for someone to spend hours—even days—working on a document, only to lose the document somewhere in the bowels of the computer. How the data is lost is not important (often it's some momentary glitch that no one can explain); what is important is that your work is forever gone. History. Deep-sixed.

Most computer users, especially novice users, are simply unaware of the potential for losing important work. Computers are the wonder of the twentieth century, they think, so they must be infallible.

Don't be lulled into a false sense of security when using your computer. While catastrophes don't happen every day, you should remember that bad things can and do happen with the precious data you toil and sweat over. Fortunately, there are a number of simple techniques you can use to help protect that data. Why, with a little bit of luck, you can even reclaim files you've accidentally deleted yourself.

This section describes a number of ways you can help prevent the loss of important data. You'll also read about ways to check the integrity of your disk drive and files, how to make protection copies of important files in case anything happens to the originals, and more.

What You Will Find in This Section

Make a Backup of Important System Files 444

Restore an Accidentally Deleted File with Undelete 448

Set Up Undelete to Maximize Your Undeletion Success 452

Check a Disk for Errors with ScanDisk 454

Back Up the Contents of Your Hard Disk Drive with Microsoft Backup 458

Restore the Contents of Your Hard Disk with Microsoft Backup 464

Check for Viruses with Microsoft AntiVirus 469

Make a Backup of Important System Files

Before you install any new software, the first order of business is to make "protection" copies of the critical files that customize the way your computer works. These files go by the cryptic names of CONFIG.SYS, AUTOEXEC.BAT, WIN.INI, and SYSTEM.INI. Note that not all computers have all four files. Which of these *customization files* you have depends on whether you have Windows installed on your PC (Windows needs WIN.INI and SYSTEM.INI), and on the version of Windows you are using. More about this later.

The customization files tell your computer exactly how you want it to behave. The files contain settings that are unique to your computer. If something should happen to the files when you install a new program, you can't just copy the same files from a friend's computer and expect your computer to work properly. You have to use your own customization files. You can see why it makes sense to make copies of these files before you install any new software. You keep a copy in case anything happens to the original—and believe me, many unexpected things can. Often the problem has nothing to do with what you do day-to-day on your computer. Beware: the loss of these important files can render your computer useless, and if they're corrupted, it's almost as bad.

What could happen to your customization files? Plenty. During their installation process, many programs alter one or more customization files, and something in this alteration may not agree with your computer. Should your computer fail to operate after you've installed a new program, you can rely on your copies of the original customization files to put your system back to the way it was, where you can better determine what to do next.

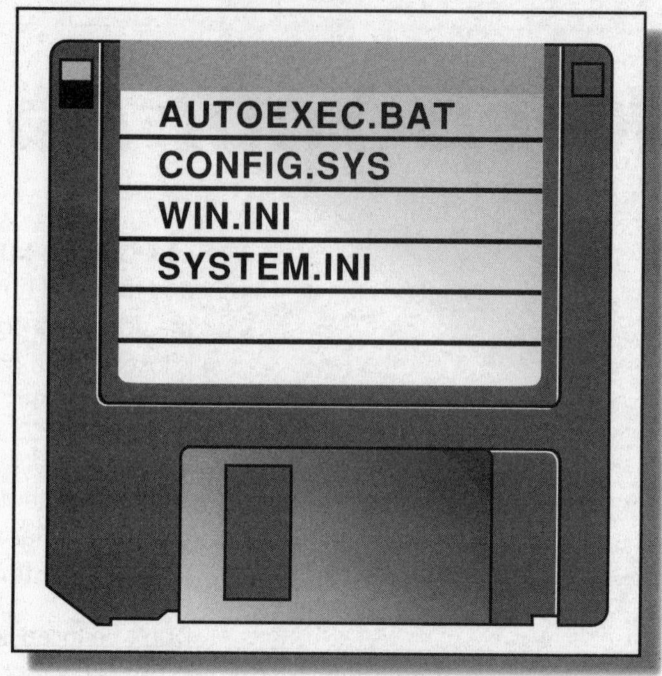

What exactly do the four customization files do?

- **CONFIG.SYS** tells your computer you want to run special programs, called drivers, whenever the PC is first started. Most drivers let you use special hardware—like a CD-ROM drive or a sound card—with your computer. If you have Windows 95 on your computer, it may not have a CONFIG.SYS file.
- **AUTOEXEC.BAT** is a collection of commands you want your computer to run every time it starts. You might (for example) include commands in the AUTOEXEC.BAT file that tell your computer to load a memory manager program when it starts up, and then to run Windows automatically. (Note: If you have Windows 95 on your computer, it may not have an AUTOEXEC.BAT file.)
- **WIN.INI** is used with Windows (if you don't have Windows, you won't have this file). It contains basic settings for using Windows.

- **SYSTEM.INI** is used with Windows (if you don't have Windows, you won't have this file). It contains important system information so Windows knows how to interact with your computer.

The CONFIG.SYS and AUTOEXEC.BAT files are typically located in the "root" directory of your hard drive (for example, C:\). The root directory is the main directory, and all other directories—like DOS or WINDOWS—branch from it. Therefore, to copy these files, look in the root directory for them.

The WIN.INI and SYSTEM.INI files are typically located in the WINDOWS directory of your hard drive (for example, C:\WINDOWS\). Look in this directory for these files.

> If you find your computer does not work properly following the installation of a new program, use the copies of the customization files on the disk to return your system configuration choices to the way they were. If possible, you may first want to make a copy of the altered customization files on a separate disk, in case you want to compare the old and new versions of the files.

Begin Do It Yourself Make a Backup Using Windows 3.11

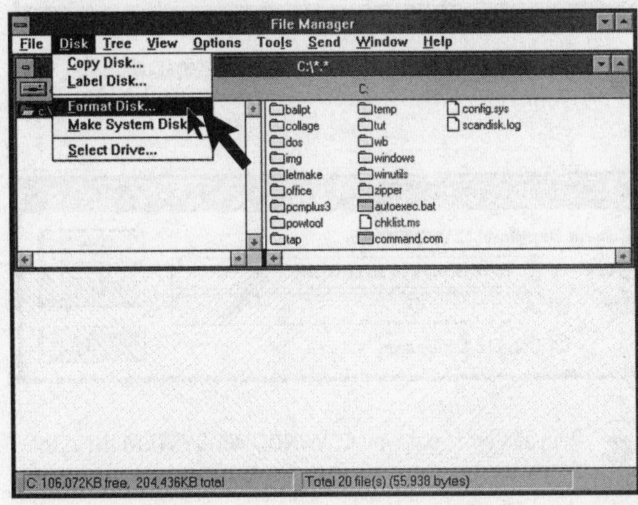

1 Use a blank, formatted disk to hold the copies of your customization files. If you don't have a blank, formatted disk handy, create one now. See "Format Disks" on page 146 for more information.

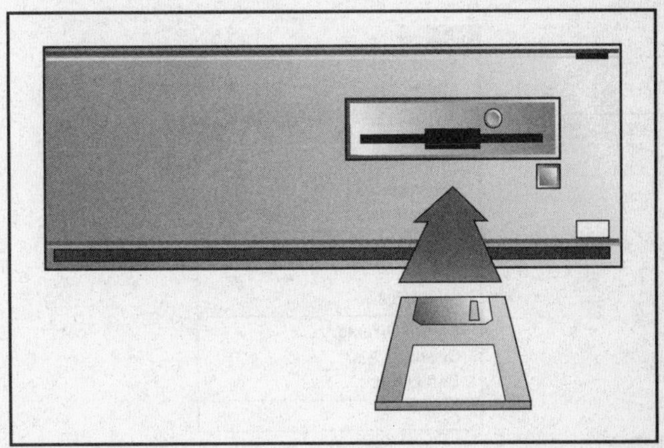

2 Insert the disk into the floppy drive.

(continues)

Do It Yourself Make a Backup Using Windows 3.11

(continued)

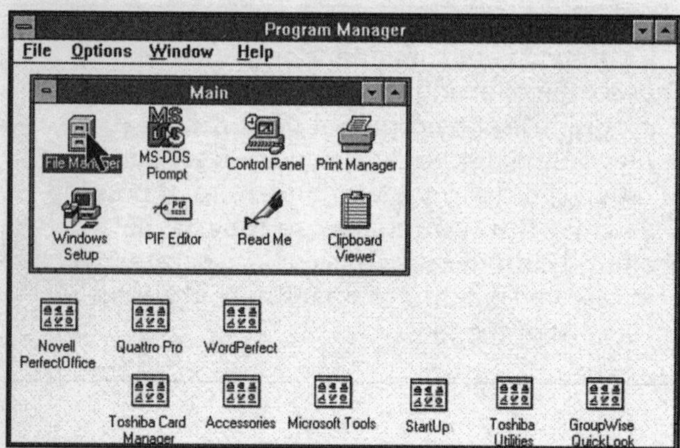

3 At the Windows Program Manager, double-click the **Main** program group and then double-click the **File Manager** icon.

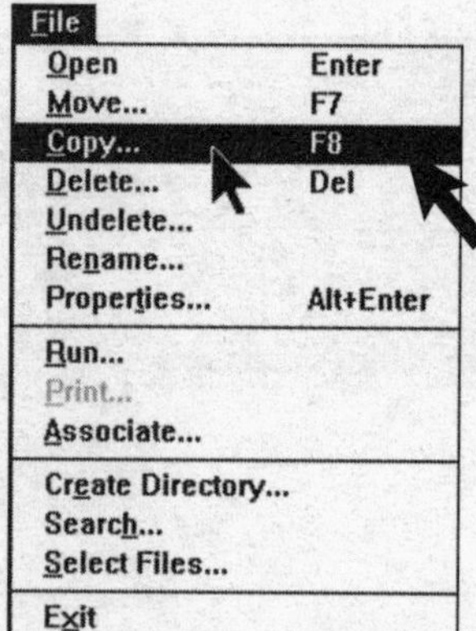

4 Click **File**, **Copy**. The Copy dialog box appears.

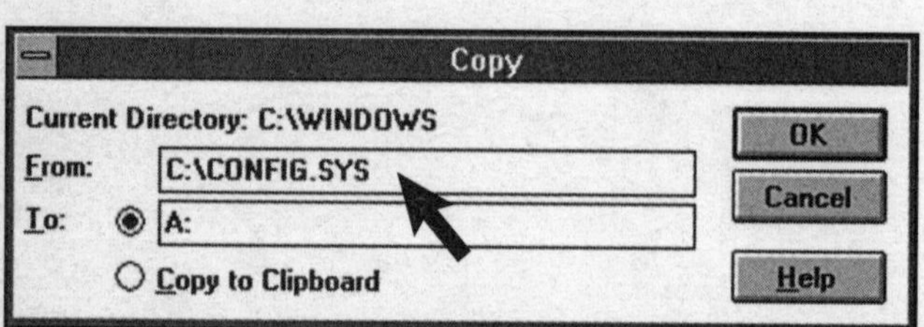

5 In the **From:** box, type **C:\CONFIG.SYS**. In the **To:** box, type **A:** (or B: if the disk you are using is in drive B). Click **OK** when you're done. The file is copied.

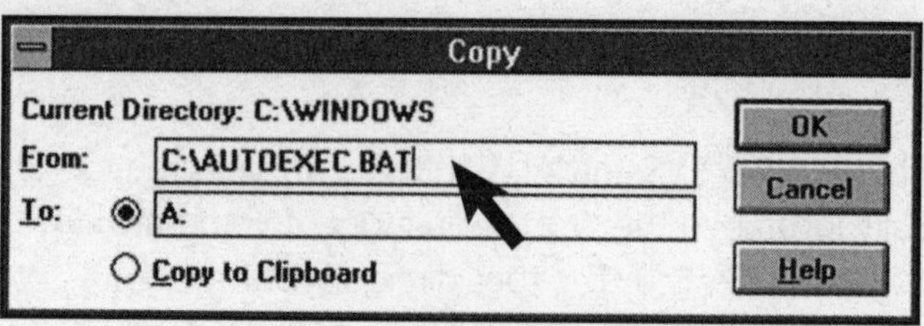

6 Repeat step 5, but type **C:\AUTOEXEC.BAT** in the **From:** box.

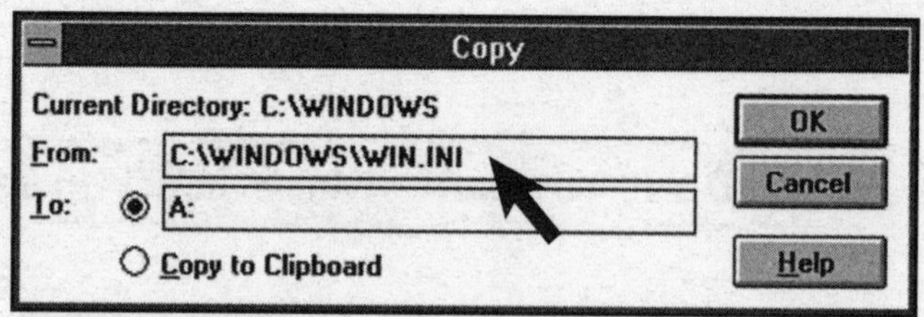

7 Repeat step 5, but type **C:\WINDOWS\WIN.INI** in the **From:** box.

8 Repeat step 5, but type **C:\WINDOWS\SYSTEM.INI** in the **From:** box.

Do It Yourself Make a Backup Using Windows 3.11

In Windows 95, you can copy the system files using Windows Explorer or My Computer. Simply drag CONFIG.SYS and AUTOEXEC.BAT from the root directory of drive C to the floppy disk drive icon. Drag SYSTEM.INI and WIN.INI from C:\WINDOWS to the floppy drive icon. For details on how to copy files in Windows 95, see "Copy or Move Files and Folders" on page 179.

9 Remove the disk from the drive, label it, and store it in a safe place. You may now install your new program.

Begin Do It Yourself Make a Backup Using DOS

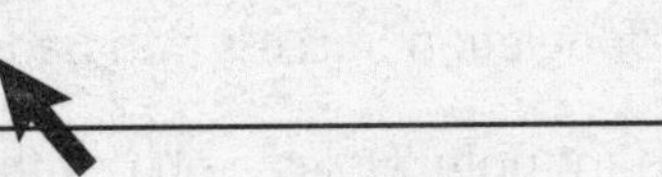

1 Use a blank, formatted disk to hold the copies of your customization files. If you don't have a blank, formatted disk handy, create one now. (See "Format Disks" on page 146 for more information.)

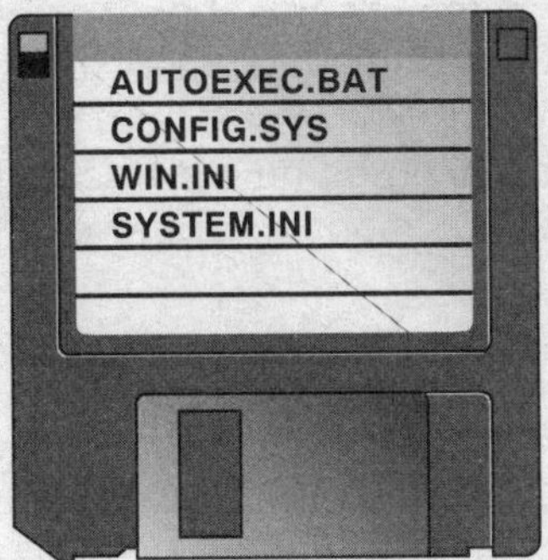

2 Insert the disk into the floppy drive (for example, the A: drive).

C:\DOS>COPY C:\CONFIG.SYS A:

3 Type the following commands at the DOS prompt. The commands assume your customization files are in the normal directories, and the disk you are copying the files to are in drive A:.

COPY C:\CONFIG.SYS A: [Enter]
COPY C:\AUTOEXEC.BAT A: [Enter]
COPY C:\WINDOWS\WIN.INI A: [Enter]
COPY C:\WINDOWS\SYSTEM.INI A: [Enter]

4 Remove the disk from the drive, label it, and store it in a safe place. You may now install your new program.

Restore an Accidentally Deleted File with Undelete

If you accidently deleted a file, no need to panic. Windows 3.1 (and MS-DOS 5.0 and later) come with a nifty little program called Undelete that will revive files that have been inadvertently deleted. The Undelete program works because the MS-DOS operating system (which is also used with Windows) doesn't really erase a file when you press the Delete key. What it actually does is remove the index entry of the file, leaving the data of the file intact. The operating system marks the space previously taken by the file as available, so that another file can take its place.

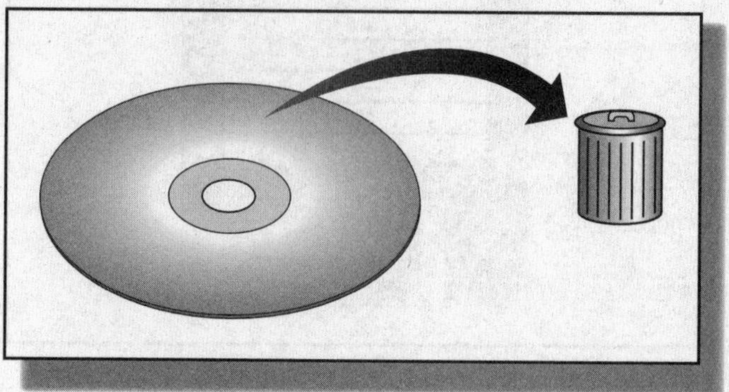

As long as you reclaim the file quickly, before doing much more work on your computer, there is a very good chance that you will be completely successful raising from the "dead." The longer you wait, the more chance that the data from another file will overwrite the spot occupied by the deleted file. When this happens, you may be able to revive only part of the file, or you may not be able to get it back at all.

The Undelete command has two basic levels of operation. The first level, called *standard*, does its magic by using the quirk of MS-DOS just described. It's the method the Undelete command uses if you have not specified that you want to use the delete-tracking system. This delete-tracking system is the second level: it stores information about deleted files in a special hidden registry, and gives you a better chance of reclaiming lost files.

In this task, you will learn how to use the Undelete programs that come with Windows and MS-DOS to reclaim a deleted file. These are separate programs, so they are used differently. The process is nearly the same whether the delete-tracking system is used or not. For an explanation of how to set up the delete-tracking system, see "Set Up Undelete to Maximize Your Undeletion Success" on page 452.

Important note: Unless you use the delete-tracking method, if you delete a directory, you will not be able to revive any of the files it contained that were deleted along with it.

MS-DOS (version 6.x and above) offers an additional delete-protection system called Delete Sentry. It is similar in function to the more commonly used delete-tracking method. See the MS-DOS manual for more info on Delete Sentry.

Begin Do It Yourself Restore a File Using Windows 3.11

1 As soon as you realize you've deleted a file by mistake, run the Windows Undelete program. The usual spot for the **Undelete** program icon is the **Tools** group in Microsoft Windows.

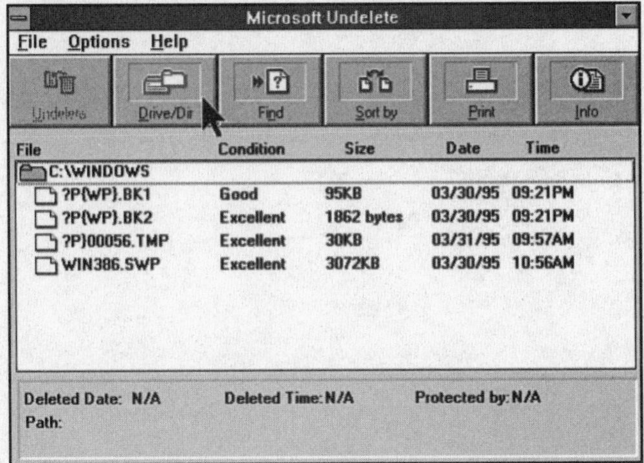

2 In the Microsoft Undelete window, click the **Drive/Dir** button.

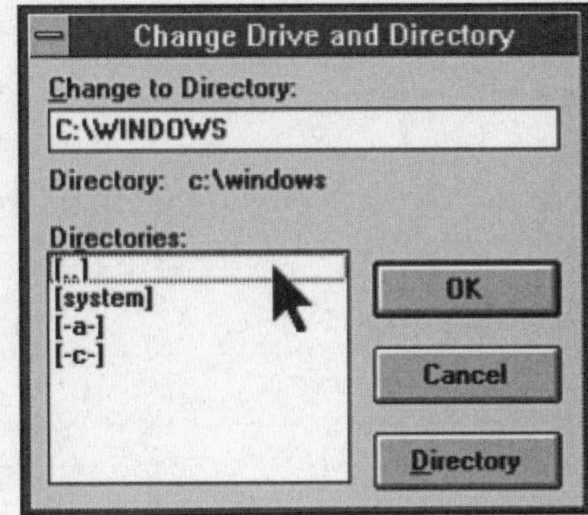

3 Specify the directory that contains the erased file, and click **OK**.

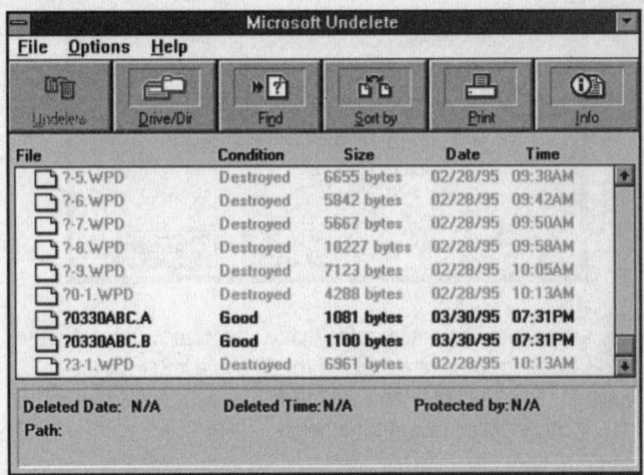

4 The Microsoft Undelete window displays all recently deleted files, their names, and the condition they're in. Click once on the file you want to undelete. (File names that start with a question mark mean MS-DOS didn't track them, and doesn't know the full file name; files with complete names were tracked.)

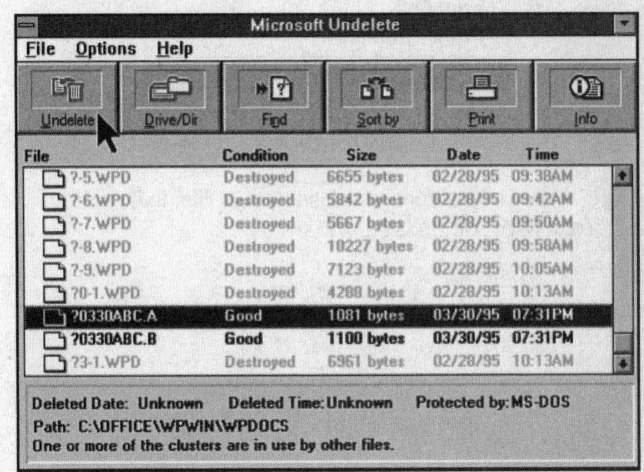

5 Click the **Undelete** button. The Undelete program attempts to undelete the file.

(continues)

Do It Yourself Restore a File Using Windows 3.11

(continued)

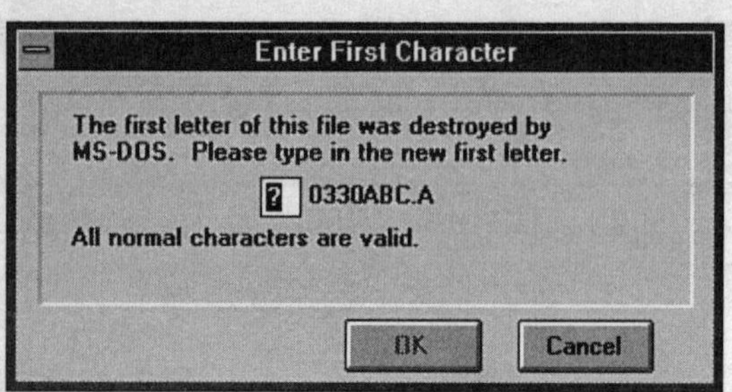

6 If you are undeleting a file that was erased without delete-tracking, you are asked to provide a first letter for the filename. Type the letter, and select **OK**. Repeat steps 3 through 6 for any other file you want to undelete.

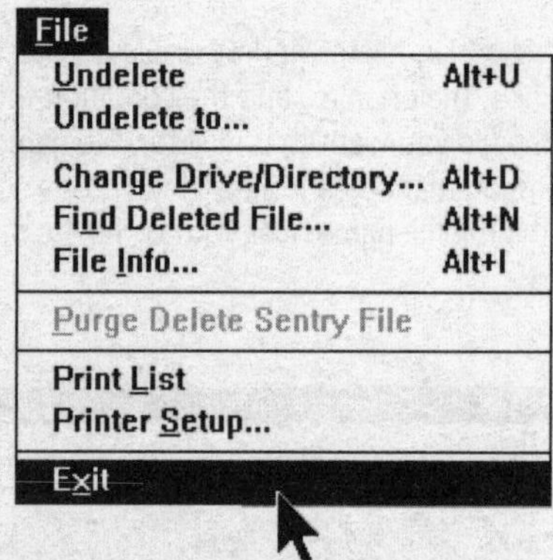

7 When you are done undeleting, select **File**, **Exit** to close the Microsoft Undelete window.

Windows 95 makes it even easier to undelete files. You simply double-click the **Recycle Bin** icon, Ctrl+click the names of the files you want to undelete, and then open the **File** menu and select **Restore**. See "Delete and Restore Files and Folders" on page 182 for details.

Begin Do It Yourself Restore a File Using DOS

```
C:\>CD \DOS
```

1 As soon as you realize you've deleted a file by mistake, run the DOS Undelete program; first change to the directory that contains the deleted file. If the deleted file is in the C:\DOS directory, for example, type **CD \DOS** and press **Enter**.

```
C:\>CD \DOS
C:\DOS>UNDELETE
```

2 Run the Undelete program by typing **UNDELETE** and pressing **Enter**.

```
C:\>CD \DOS
C:\DOS>UNDELETE
UNDELETE - A delete protection facility
Copyright (C) 1987-1993 Central Point Software, Inc.
All rights reserved.
Directory: C:\DOS
File Specifications: *.*
    Delete Sentry control file not found.
    Deletion-tracking file contains    2 deleted files.
    Of those,    2 files have all clusters available,
                 0 files have some clusters available,
                 0 files have no clusters available.
    MS-DOS directory contains   32 deleted files.
    Of those,   15 files may be recovered.
Using the Deletion-tracking method.
      FILETEST TXT    47988  3-30-95 11:32a  ...A  Deleted:  3-30-95 11:39a
All of the clusters for this file are available. Undelete (Y/N)?
```

3 When the Undelete program runs, it finds all recently deleted files in the current directory. Then it tells you which, if any, can be undeleted.

4 You are prompted to decide whether to undelete each deleted file. If you don't want to undelete a file, press the **N** key. If you want to undelete a file, press the **Y** key.

```
    Delete Sentry control file not found.
    Deletion-tracking file contains    2 deleted files.
    Of those,    2 files have all clusters available,
                 0 files have some clusters available,
                 0 files have no clusters available.
    MS-DOS directory contains   31 deleted files.
    Of those,   14 files may be recovered.
Using the MS-DOS directory method.
      ?UWR1739 TMP        0  3-30-95  9:02p  ...A  Undelete (Y/N)?n
   ** ?WT1112  TMP     1280  1-25-95  7:15p  ...A
Starting cluster is unavailable. This file cannot be recovered
with the UNDELETE command.  Press any key to continue.
      ?WT3F16  TMP     1280  1-28-95 10:35p  ...A  Undelete (Y/N)?y
      Please type the first character for ?WT3F16 .TMP: T
File successfully undeleted.
      ?WT1F4C  TMP        0  2-28-95  9:47a  ...A  Undelete (Y/N)?y
      Please type the first character for ?WT1F4C .TMP:
```

If you are undeleting a file that was erased without delete-tracking, you are asked to provide a first letter for the file name. Type the letter at the prompt.

If you are using the delete-tracking option, the Undelete command will only display those files tracked with delete-tracking. If you want to undelete a file that was erased without delete-tracking, start the Undelete program by typing **UNDELETE /DOS**.

Set Up Undelete to Maximize Your Undeletion Success

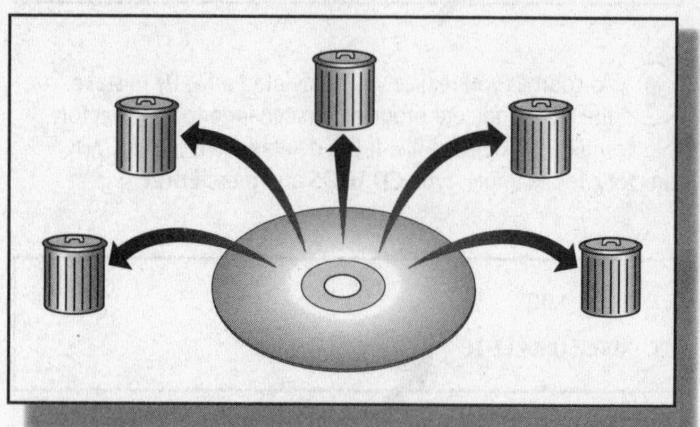

Never fear (well, fear a little) if you accidentally delete a file you meant to keep. As does MS-DOS version 5.0 and later, Windows 3.11 comes with a handy utility program called Undelete that will revive many files that have been accidentally deleted. You can read more about the Undelete program and how to use it (in both Windows and DOS) in "Restore an Accidentally Deleted File with Undelete" on page 448.

By itself, the MS-DOS operating system offers a rather crude means to revive dead files. Depending on how your computer was used since the file was deleted, the Undelete command may or may not bring back the file you deleted. The file may either be completely gone, or it may have chunks—called *clusters*—missing from it. When you undelete the file, you could get only scraps and pieces.

If you have MS-DOS 5.0 or later, you can use a feature called "delete-tracking" to give you better results when undeleting files. The delete-tracking feature stores important aspects about all deleted files; the Undelete program can use this information to guarantee better success at restoring lost files.

The delete-tracking system is turned on and off at the DOS prompt, when Windows is not running. For it to be most effective, you should tell your computer you want to use the delete-tracking system every time the PC starts up, so you don't have to instruct it yourself. This is done by typing the commands to trigger the delete-tracking feature in the startup file (AUTOEXEC.BAT) your computer uses to load itself with what it needs whenever it cranks up. (See "Modify Your Startup Files in Windows 3.11 and DOS" on page 412 for more information on modifying startup files.)

> MS-DOS versions 6 and later offer an additional option called Delete Sentry. You can use this option instead of, or in addition to, delete-tracking. See the MS-DOS manual for more info on Delete Sentry.

Begin Do It Yourself DOS Undelete

```
C:\DOS>UNDELETE /STATUS
```

1 Before making any changes, determine whether the delete-tracking system is already in use. Do this by typing **UNDELETE /STATUS** at the DOS prompt. A message will tell you whether delete-tracking is active. If it is, you can skip this task.

```
C:\DOS>EDIT \AUTOEXEC.BAT
```

2 At the DOS prompt, type **EDIT \AUTOEXEC.BAT** and press **Enter**. This starts the DOS Edit program, and loads the AUTOEXEC.BAT startup file.

Do It Yourself DOS Undelete

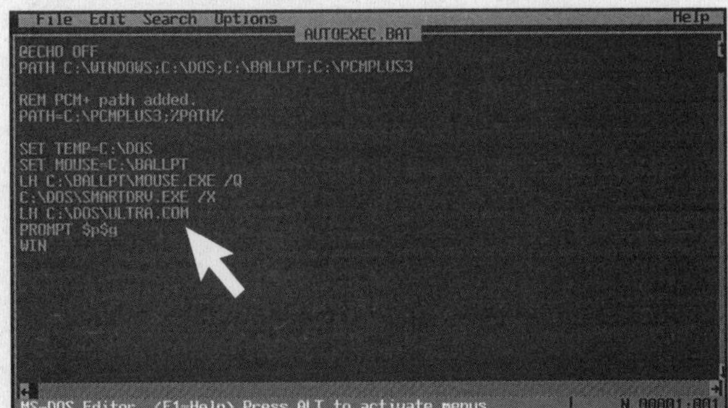

3 If you don't use Windows (there is no WIN command line at the bottom of the AUTOEXEC.BAT file), move to the end of the text and insert a new line by pressing **Enter**. If you are using windows (a WIN command is at the bottom of the file), insert a new blank line immediately before the WIN command.

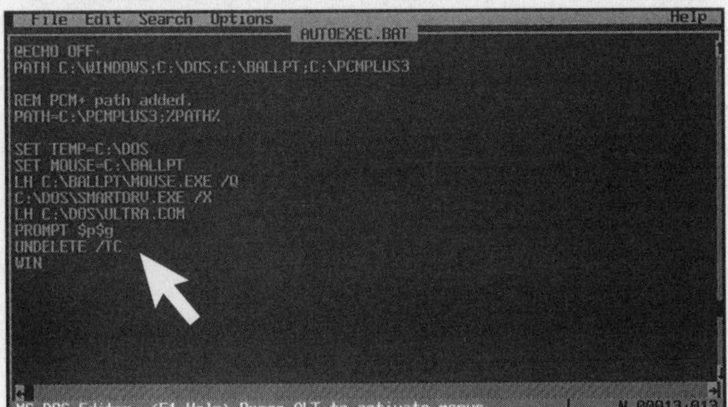

4 If you are using MS-DOS 6.x or later, type **UNDELETE /TC** to enable the delete-tracking feature for the C: drive.

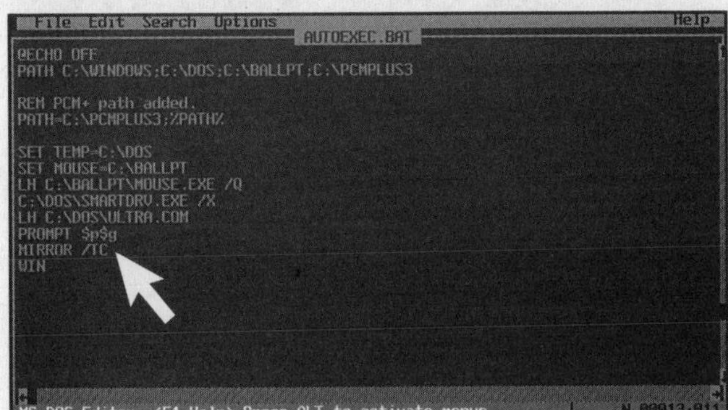

5 If you are using MS-DOS 5.0, type **MIRROR /TC** to enable the delete-tracking feature for the C: drive.

6 Select **File**, **Save** to save the modified AUTOEXEC.BAT file.

7 Select **File**, **Exit** to leave the Edit program.

8 Restart your computer (so the changes in the AUTOEXEC.BAT file can take effect) by pressing **Ctrl+Alt+Del**.

In Windows 95, you can change the properties of the Recycle Bin by right-clicking on its icon and selecting **Properties.** Use the dialog box that appears to change the amount of disk space used for the Recycle Bin and to enter file delete preferences.

Check a Disk for Errors with ScanDisk

If you are using MS-DOS 6.x or later (or Windows 95) on your computer, you have a powerful ally available: the ScanDisk program. This handy little program checks the integrity of your hard disk drive (and floppy disks too, though this isn't done as often), as well as all the files on it.

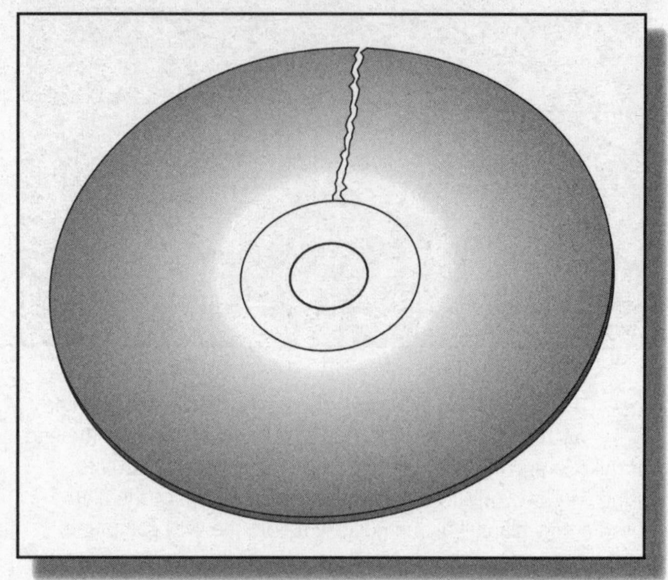

In addition (unlike the CHKDSK utility program detailed in the previous task), ScanDisk can optionally survey the entire surface of your computer's hard disk drive, looking for trouble spots. If there's a glitch on the surface of the hard drive—whether or not data is there—ScanDisk can spot it. The ScanDisk program can then "mark" the bad spot so that it will never be used to store data. And if the bad spot does store some data, ScanDisk can often recover it and move it to an undamaged area, to prevent data loss.

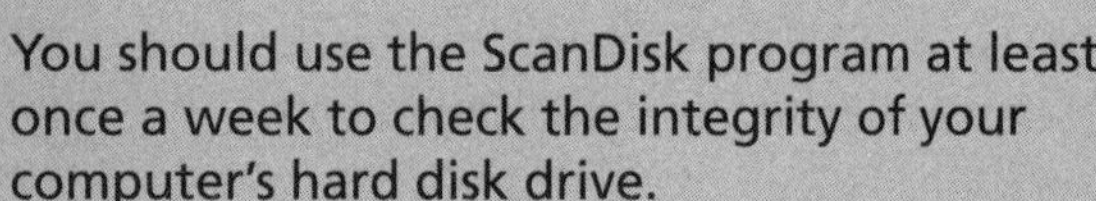

You should use the ScanDisk program at least once a week to check the integrity of your computer's hard disk drive.

Begin Do It Yourself Check a Disk from the DOS Prompt

```
C:\>scandisk
```

1 Exit all programs, including Windows by choosing **File**, **Exit**. At the DOS prompt, type **SCANDISK** and press **Enter**. The ScanDisk utility program starts, and immediately reviews your computer's hard disk drive.

```
Problem Found

One or more files on drive C are stored incorrectly, and are
overwriting each other's data. Some of these files probably
contain invalid data. To find out which files are involved,
choose More Info.

Choose Fix It to have ScanDisk correct the way the files are
stored so that they no longer overwrite each other's data.
Because the data is already scrambled, some or all of the
files will probably still contain invalid data. However, the
files will no longer share that data.

< Fix It >   < Don't Fix It >   < More Info >
```

2 If ScanDisk finds a problem, it displays a message and asks whether you want to fix it, or not fix it. Usually you'll want to select **Fix It** to correct the problem.

Do It Yourself Check a Disk from the DOS Prompt

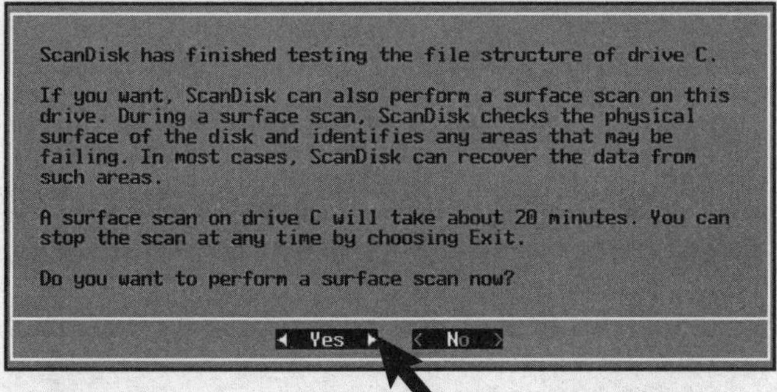

3 After scanning the disk drive and fixing problems (if any), ScanDisk offers to scan the entire surface of the hard disk drive. Choosing **Yes** starts the scan (which can take from five minutes to over an hour, depending on the size of the hard disk drive). Choosing **No** bypasses the surface scan test.

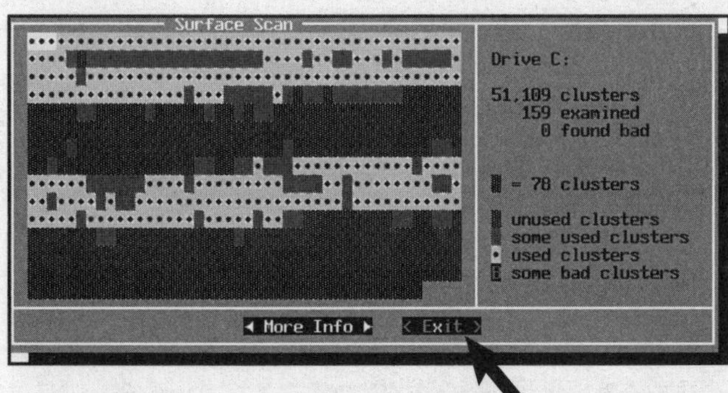

4 If you do elect to perform a surface scan, you can stop the process any time by choosing **Exit**.

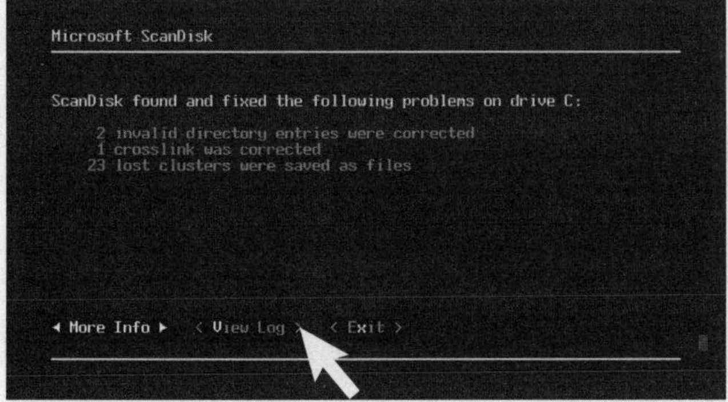

5 Once the surface scan is complete, ScanDisk displays a report indicating what, if any, problems were found, and the remedies taken. You can choose to view the complete log by selecting **View Log**.

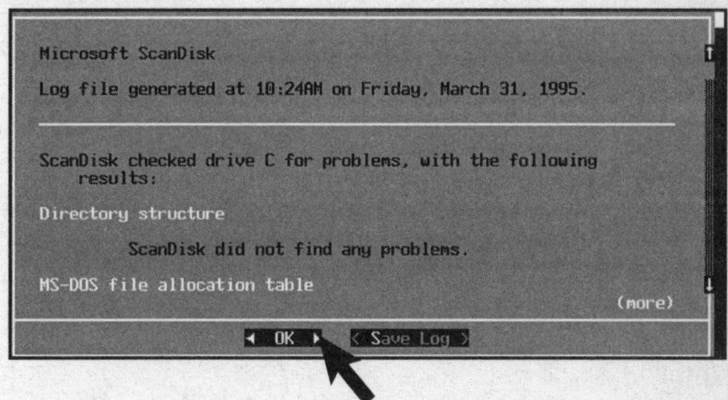

6 The View Log screen displays a categorized report of the scanning process. Select **OK** when you're done reading the log, or select **Save Log** to save the log in a text file (the file is named SCANDISK.LOG).

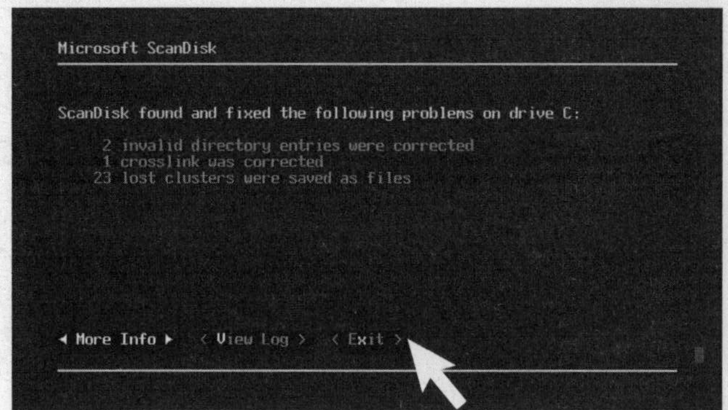

7 Select **Exit** when you are done using ScanDisk.

Begin Do It Yourself Check a Disk in Windows 95

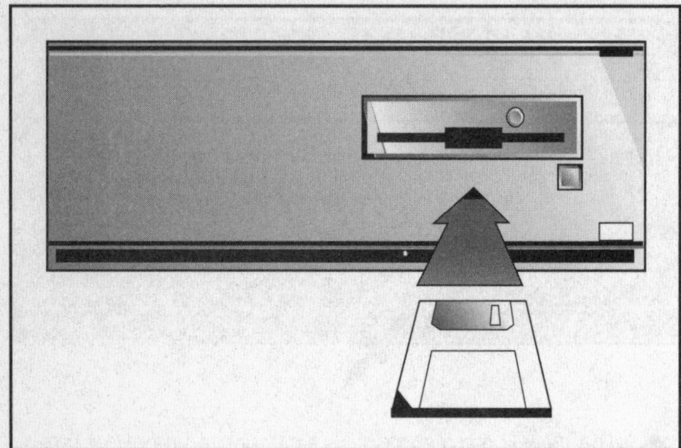

1 To fix a floppy disk, insert the disk into one of the floppy disk drives, and close the door, if necessary.

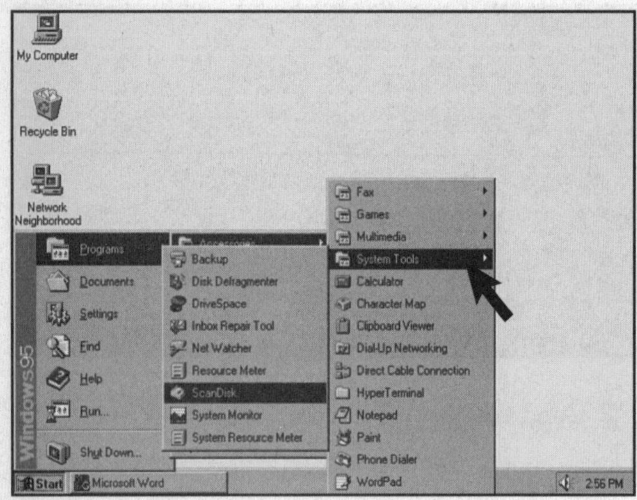

2 Click the **Start** button, move the mouse pointer over **Programs**, and then over **Accessories**. Rest the mouse pointer on **System Tools**, and then click **ScanDisk**.

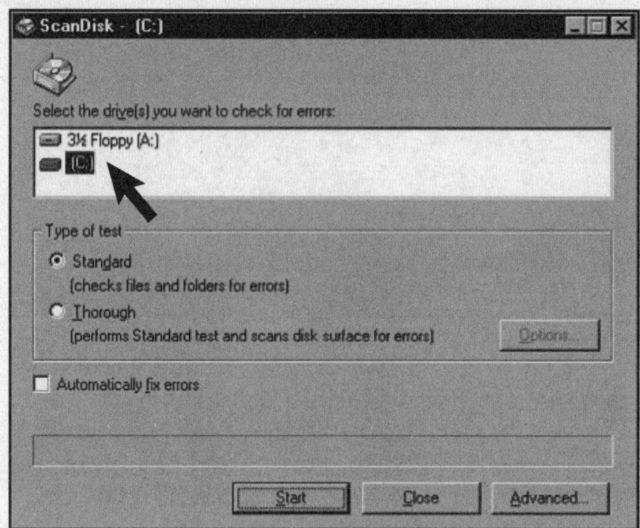

3 A dialog box appears, asking you to pick a disk to check. Click the letter of the drive you want to check.

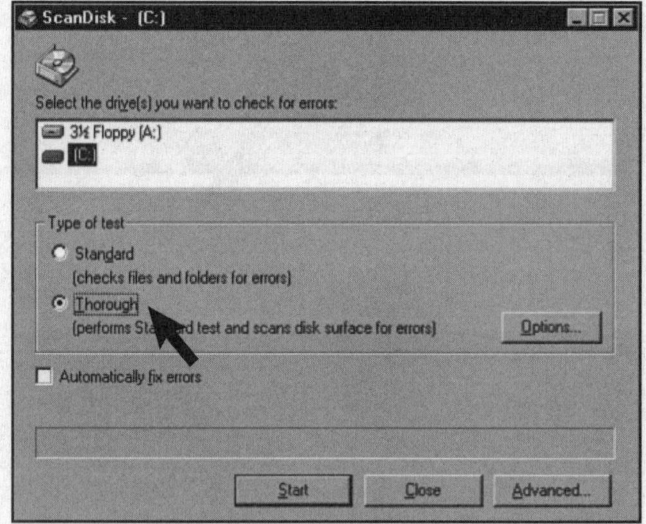

4 To have ScanDisk check for and repair only file and folder problems, click **Standard**. If you want ScanDisk to also check for bad places on the disk, click **Thorough**.

Do It Yourself Check a Disk in Windows 95

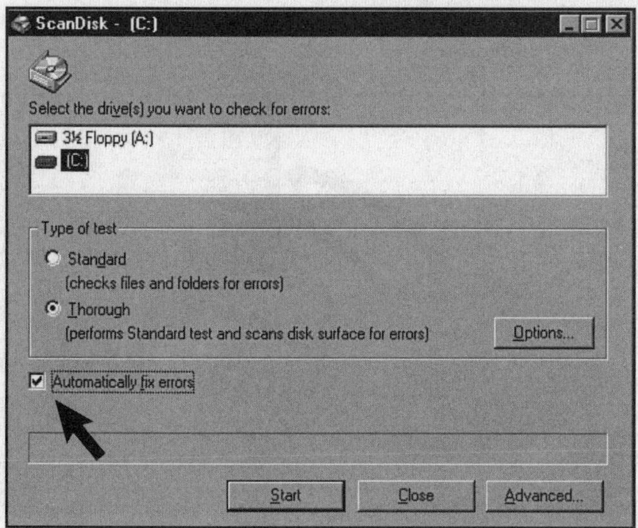

5 To have ScanDisk repair errors without asking for confirmation, click **Automatically fix errors**. (If you leave this unchecked, ScanDisk will let you choose how to repair the error. For example, if ScanDisk finds a lost file cluster, it lets you delete the cluster or save it.)

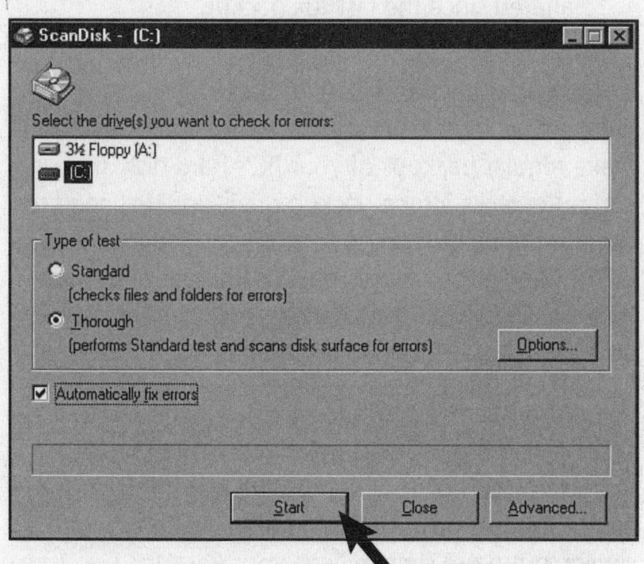

6 Click the **Start** button. ScanDisk starts checking the disk. If ScanDisk finds a problem, it either corrects the problem or displays a prompt asking you how you want to correct the problem. Follow the on-screen instructions until the operation is complete.

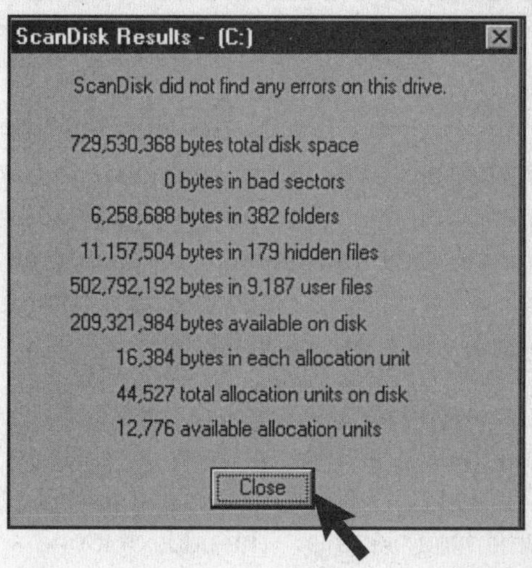

7 When ScanDisk is done, it displays a log of all the problems it found and corrections it made. Click the **Close** button, and then click **Close** again, to quit.

Back Up the Contents of Your Hard Disk Drive with Microsoft Backup

Computers can be finicky. Though a finicky personality suits cats, it's not an endearing trait in a computer. You might use your computer to keep track of important information; you want to be able to trust that the data you feed into your computer will be there when you need it.

Unfortunately, there are no guarantees in life. Murphy is alive and well and living inside your computer, and has a whole set of Murphy's Laws just for PCs. One goes something like this: "The odds of losing a file are directly proportional to the importance of the file." It always seems that the more you need some scrap of data stored on your computer, the likelier it is that the computer gremlins just had that scrap for lunch.

To ward off such a catastrophe, make regular *backup copies* of the data and program files stored on your computer's hard disk drive. That way, if anything happens to these files, you can repair the damage using the copy you made. Of course, you only use the backup copy if something awful happens to the original file. If nothing ever happens to the original, the backup is never used; it's just there for your peace of mind.

You don't always have to back up your entire hard drive every time you want to create a backup. You have other incremental backup options you can perform. Using the steps in the *Guided Tour*, you will be asked what type of backup you would like to perform (step 7). You have the following three options:

Full backs up all files, even if they haven't been altered since the last backup.

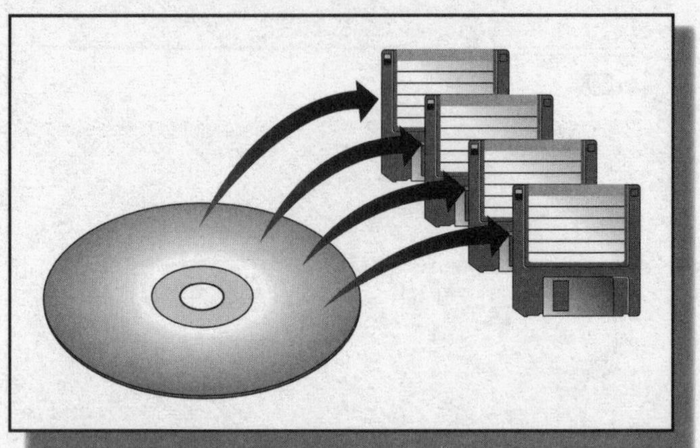

Incremental backs up only those files that have been altered since the last backup (full or incremental).

Differential backs up those files that have been altered since the last full backup.

If your computer has a *tape backup* drive, you will want to use it (and the software that comes with it) to make regular backups of your PC's hard disk. If your computer lacks a tape backup drive, you will need to use the floppy disk drives to store your backup files. Using floppy disks makes backups harder and more time-consuming, but such is the cost of doing business with a cold-blooded and finicky computer.

If you use Microsoft Windows 3.1, it comes with a utility called Backup that helps you make that all-important copy of your computer's hard disk drive—all of it, or just parts of it. Windows 95 comes with a similar, but more simple, version of Backup.

Do note that the more data there is on your computer's hard disk drive, the more floppy disks it takes to back it up. It is not uncommon to need 30 or 40 disks to store the complete contents of a 250-megabyte hard drive. Because so many floppy disks are needed for a full backup of the entire hard drive, you might want to back up only certain files (such as data files) or folders. If something happens to your program files, you can reinstall your programs.

> The following tasks discuss the Windows (3.1 and 3.11) and Windows 95 versions of Backup. MS-DOS also comes with a backup program; check the MS-DOS manual for more information.

Begin Do It Yourself Back Up in Windows 3.11

1 In Windows, locate the **Backup** program icon and double-click it to start the Backup program. The normal spot for the Backup program icon is the **Microsoft Tools** group in Program Manager.

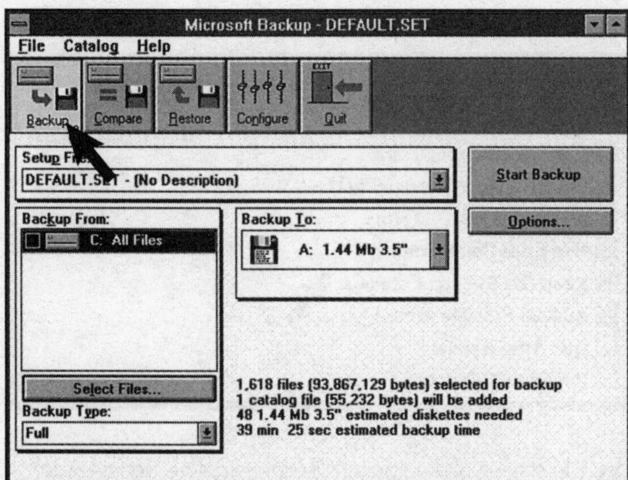

2 In the Microsoft Backup window, click the **Backup** button. If your computer has more than one hard drive, and that drive is not already selected, select the hard disk drive you want to **Backup From**.

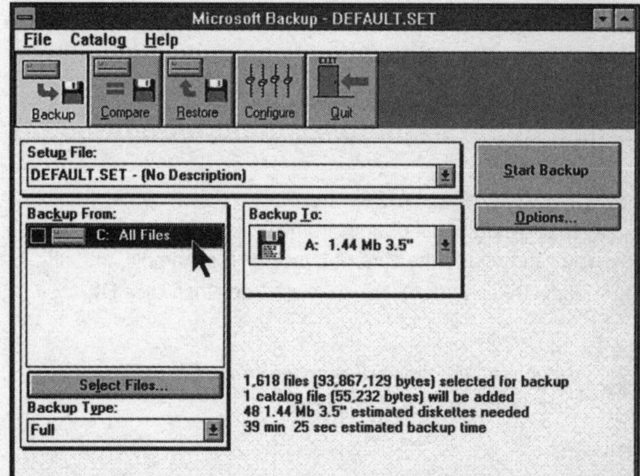

3 If you want to specify files to back up, double-click the hard disk drive in **Backup From**, turn off the **All Files** option. Finally, click **Selected Files**. If you don't want to select files (you want to back up the entire hard disk drive), skip to step 7.

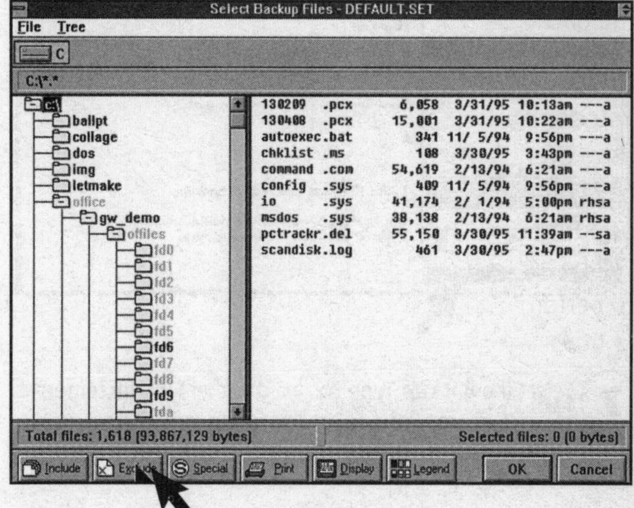

4 If you choose to back up only selected files, specify the directory and/or files you want to back up in the Select Backup Files dialog box. You do this by clicking a directory or file, and then clicking **Include** or **Exclude** to choose whether or not to back up each directory or file.

(continues)

Do It Yourself Back Up in Windows 3.11

(continued)

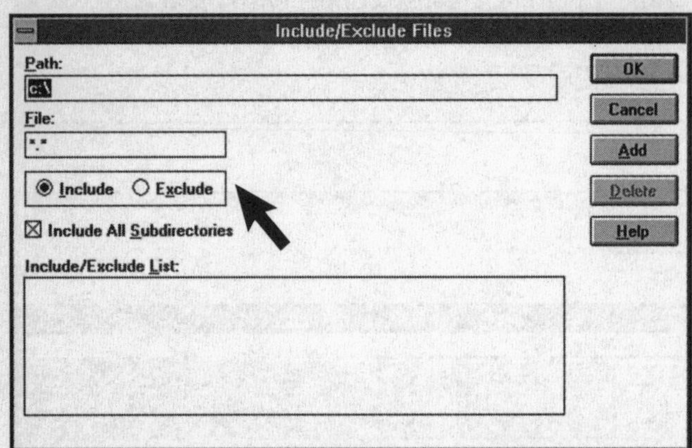

5 If you choose to include or exclude a directory/file, you can specify additional options in the Include/Exclude Files dialog box. You can exclude the current directory, for example, and all the subdirectories underneath it. Select **Add**, then click **OK**.

6 When you are done selecting files, click **OK** to close the Select Backup Files dialog box.

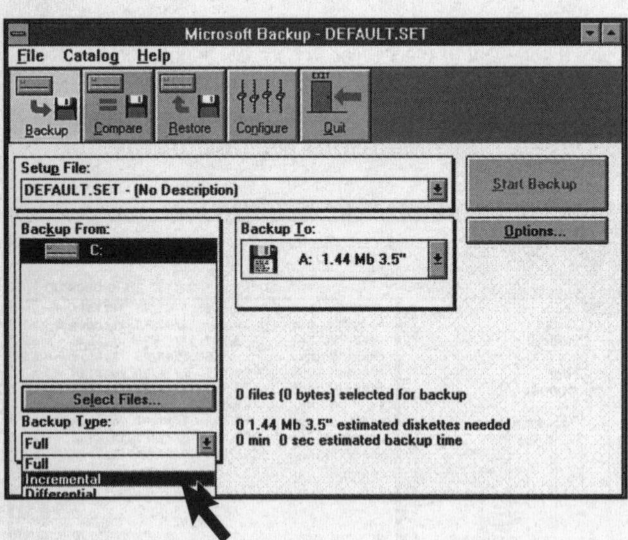

7 Select the **Backup Type** you want: either **Full**, **Incremental**, or **Differential**. See the text in this task for an explanation of each type.

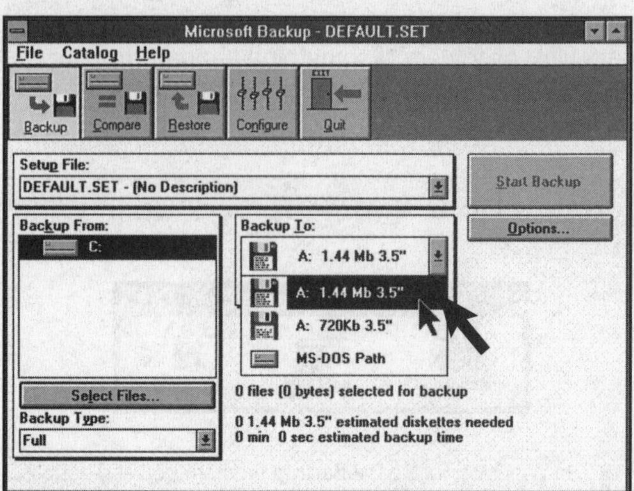

8 Select the floppy drive you want to **Backup To**.

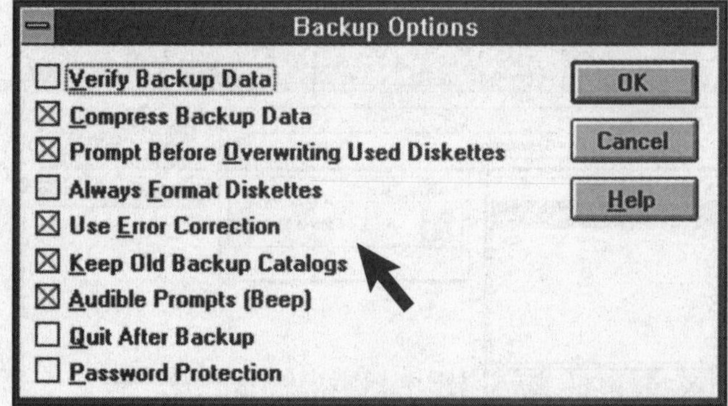

9 To change backup options (such as whether you want to compress the backup data on the floppy disk), select **Options**. In the Backup Options dialog box, you can select the options you want to use. When you're done setting your options, select **OK**.

Do It Yourself Back Up in Windows 3.11

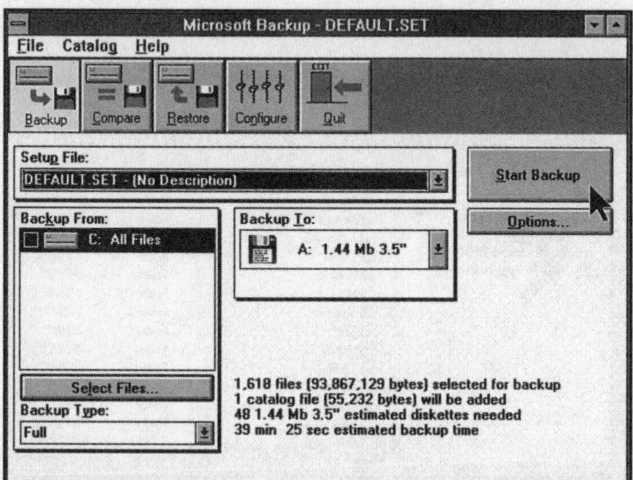

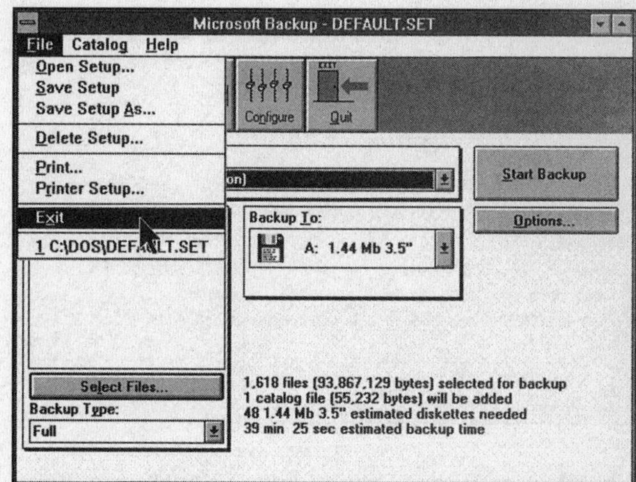

10 Select **Start Backup** to start the backup process. While it's going on, have your disks ready; insert them one by one into the floppy disk drive as prompted. *Number the disks as you use them, so you can keep track of them.*

11 When the backup is complete, put your new backup disks in a safe place; select **File, Exit** to leave the Backup program. If asked to save any changes you've made to the backup settings, select to save the settings in **DEFAULT.SET**, and select **OK**.

Begin Do It Yourself Back Up in Windows 95

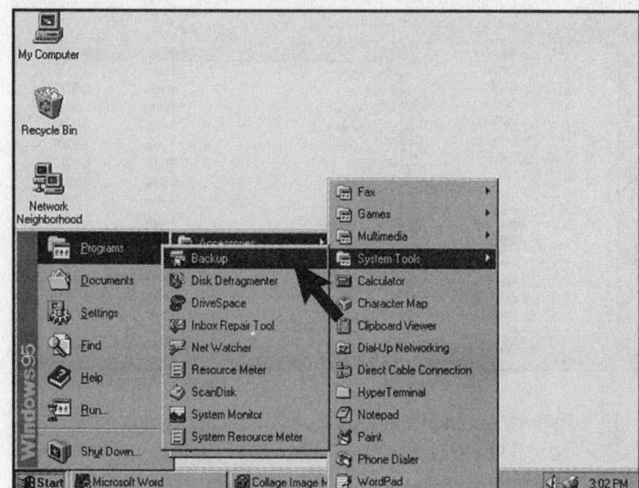

1 Click the **Start** button, point to **Programs**, **Accessories**, and **System Tools**, and then click **Backup**.

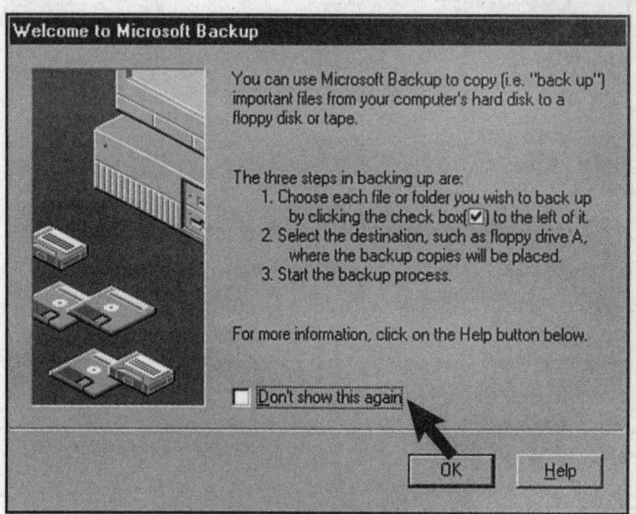

2 The first time you run Backup, a dialog box appears, providing an overview of the process. Read the information, and then click **Don't show this again** (so it won't come up next time). Click the **OK** button.

(continues)

Do It Yourself Back Up in Windows 95

(continued)

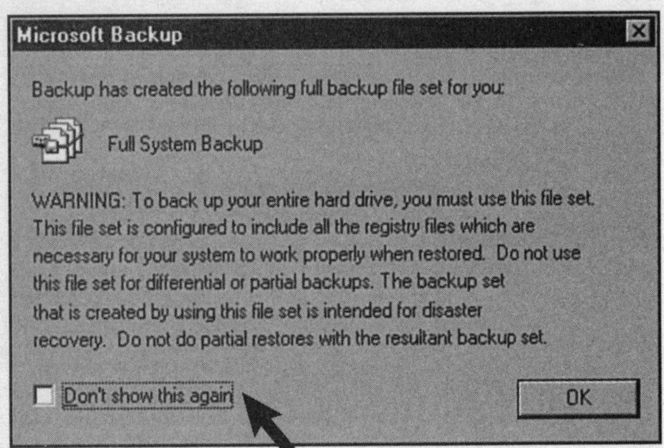

3 Another dialog box appears, indicating that Backup created a file set for backing up all your system files. Read the message, click **Don't show this again**, and click the **OK** button.

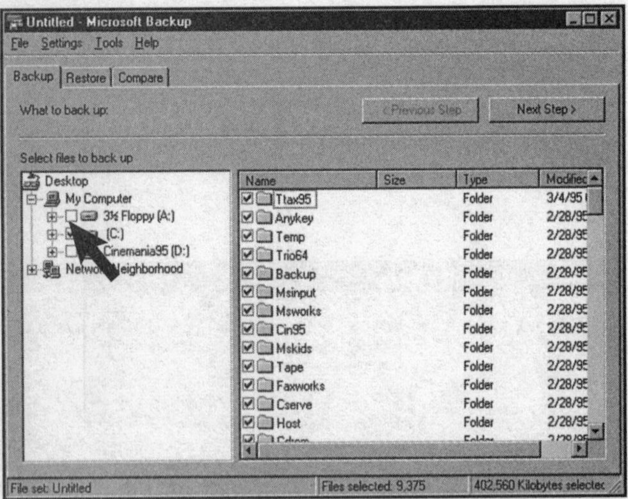

4 The Backup screen appears, allowing you to start backing up files. You can back up all the files on a drive by clicking inside the check box next to the drive letter. To back up selected files and folders, skip to step 5.

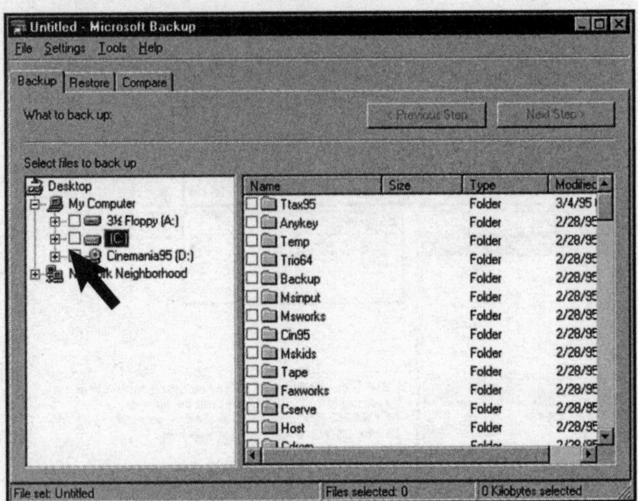

5 Click the plus sign next to the icon for the drive that contains the folders and files you want to back up. The tree expands to show the first layer of folders on the selected drive.

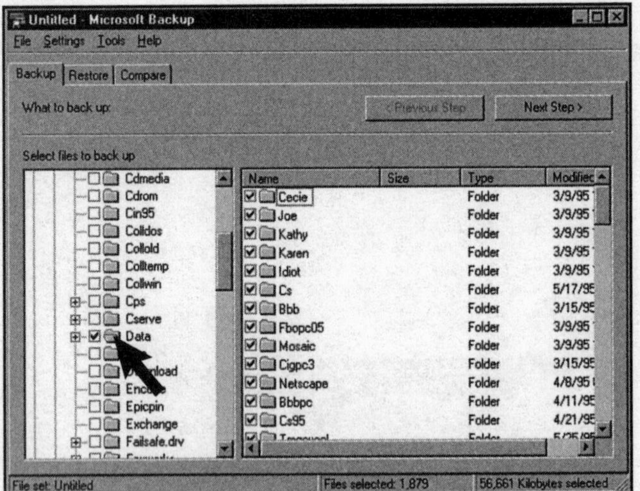

6 To back up an entire folder, click the check box next to its icon. If you click the check box next to a folder that has subfolders, all its subfolders and files are selected.

Do It Yourself Back Up in Windows 95

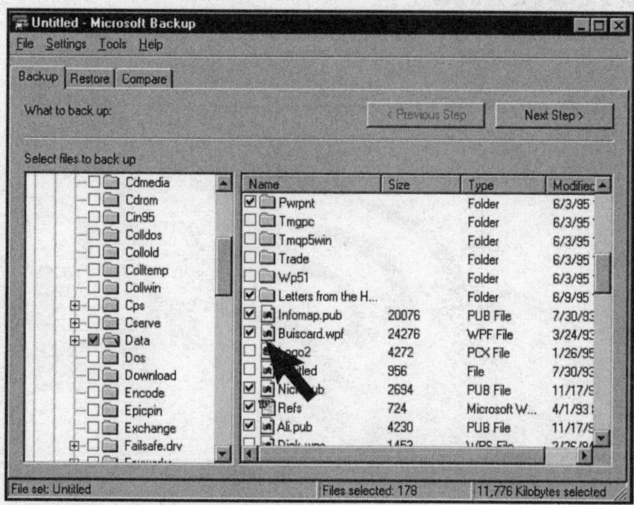

7 To back up only some files in a folder, click the folder's icon in the tree list, and then click the check box next to each file and subfolder you want to back up in the file list.

8 Click the **Next Step** button.

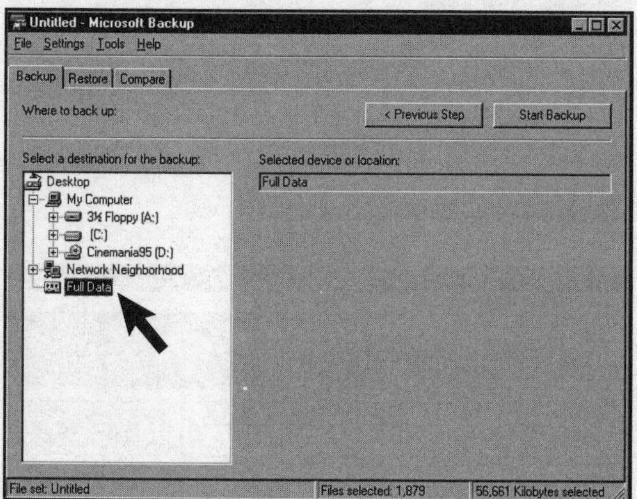

9 Backup asks which drive you want to use to store the backup files. Click the icon for the drive you want to use to store the backup files. This can be a floppy drive, tape backup drive, network drive, or another hard disk drive.

10 If you're backing up to a floppy drive or a tape backup unit, make sure you have a disk or tape in the drive. Click the **Start Backup** button.

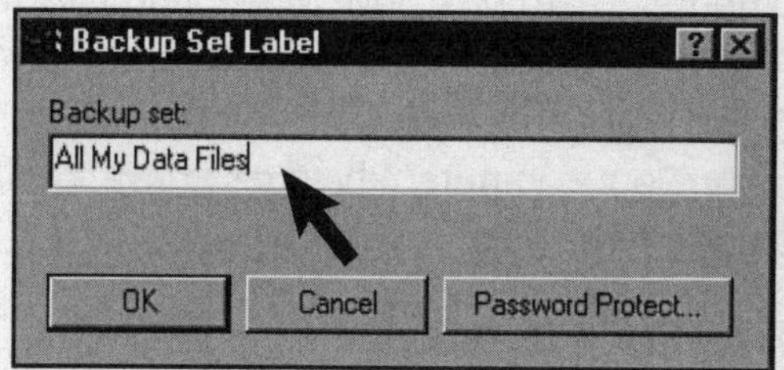

11 A dialog box appears, prompting you to type a name for the backup set. A record of the backup will be stored under this name, allowing you to quickly restore files later. Type a name for the backup set, and then click the **OK** button.

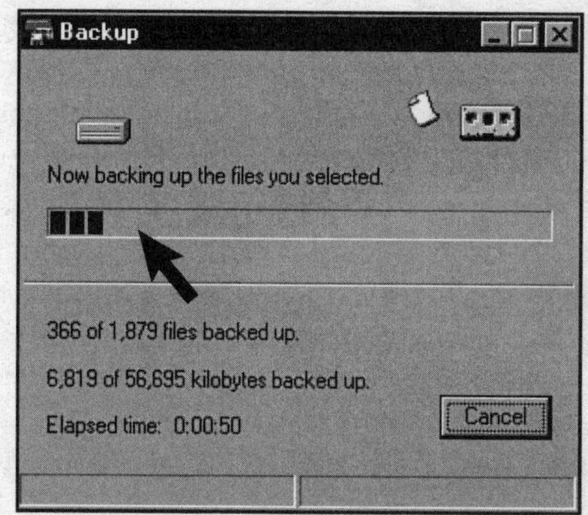

12 Backup starts the backup operation, and displays on-screen instructions to help you complete the process. Follow the on-screen instructions until the backup operation is finished. Store your backup tape or disks in a clean, dry, safe area.

Restore the Contents of Your Hard Disk with Microsoft Backup

The inverse of backing up the files on your computer's hard disk drive is restoring files that were lost of damaged. The Backup program, described in the previous task, is useful not only for backing up your computer's hard disk drive, but also for restoring files.

The restoration process is a bit simpler than the backup process, and it doesn't take as long. Normally you'll want to restore only one or two files that were erased (or otherwise met an untimely end).

Do note that the success of restoring a file to your computer's hard disk drive depends entirely on how "fresh" the file is. If you've deleted a file that you alter from time to time—it's the text of the book you're writing, for example—you will only be able to restore the file to the way it was the last time you backed it up. If you haven't backed up the file in two months, then the restored copy will be two months old; you'll have lost two months' work. This is why making regular backups is so important.

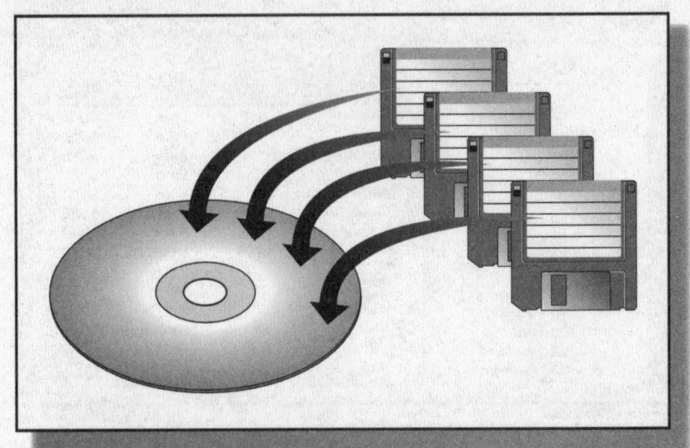

Before you start to restore a file, make sure you have all your backup disks ready. During the restoration process, you will be prompted to insert specific numbered disks into the computer.

Begin Do It Yourself Restore in Windows 3.11

1 In Windows, locate the **Backup** program icon and double-click it to start the Backup program. The normal spot for the Backup program icon is the **Microsoft Tools** group in Program Manager.

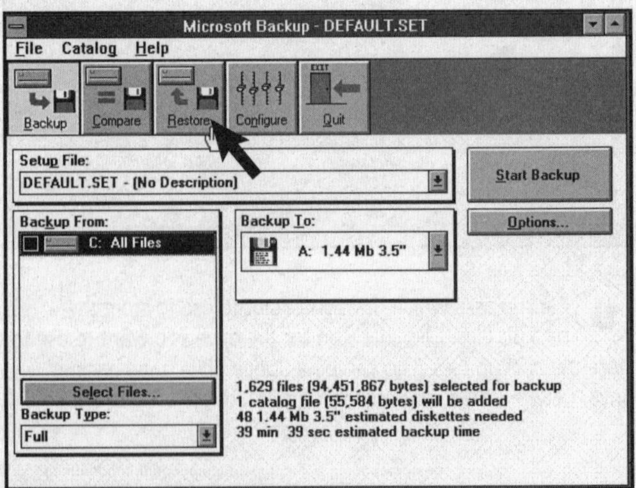

2 In the Microsoft Backup window, click the **Restore** button.

Do It Yourself — Restore in Windows 3.11

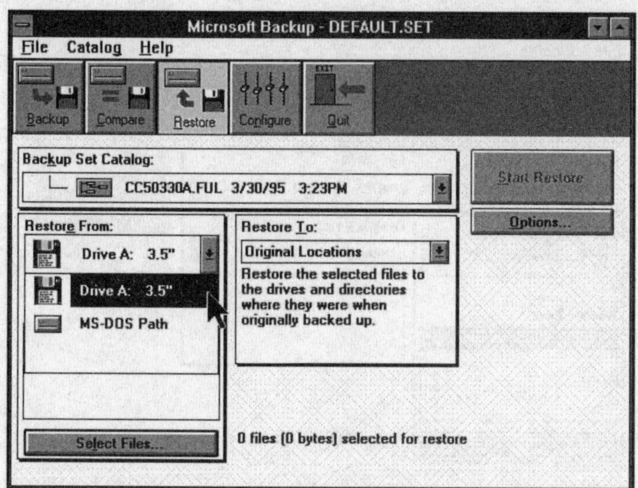

3 Select the disk drive you want to **Restore From**.

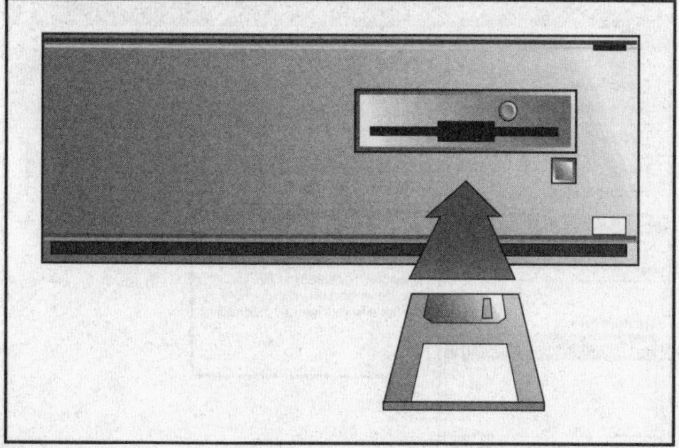

4 Put the first disk in your set of backup disks into the drive.

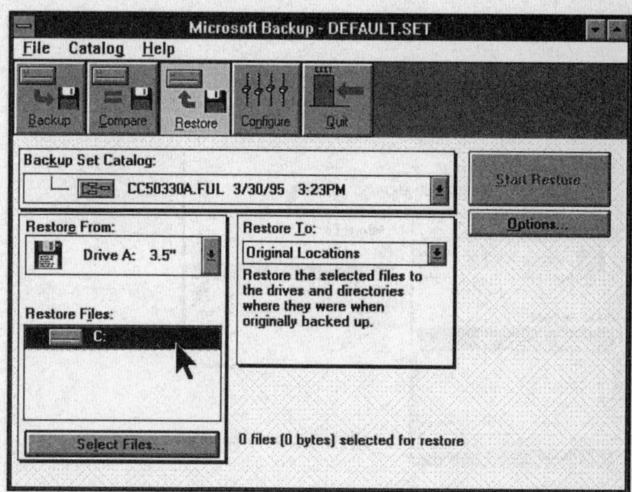

5 Select the hard disk drive you want to **Restore Files To**.

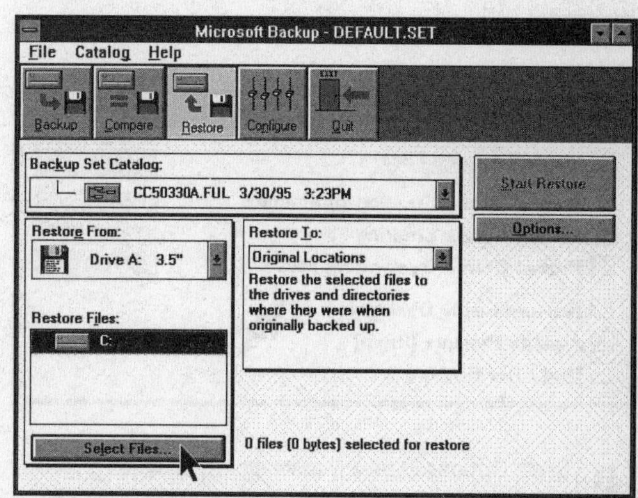

6 If you want to select certain files to restore, click **Select Files**. In the Select Restore Files dialog box, double-click those files you want to restore. (If you want to select multiple files, press and hold the **Shift** key and drag the mouse pointer over those files you want to select.) When you are done selecting files, click **OK**.

(continues)

Do It Yourself Restore in Windows 3.11

(continued)

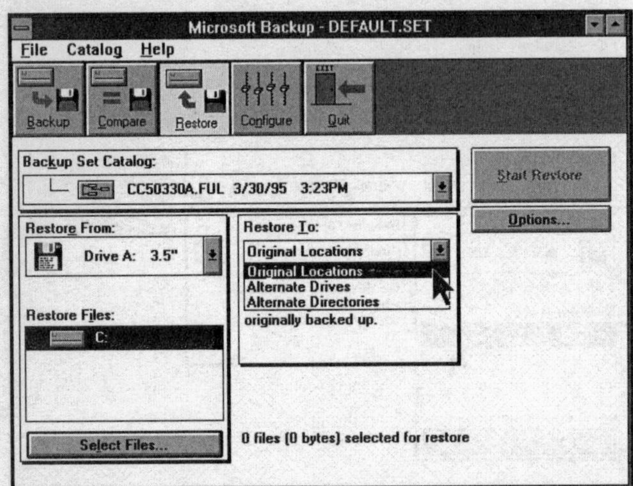

7 In the **Restore To** list, select where you want the files restored to. Your available options are **Original Locations** (the usual choice), **Alternate Drives**, and **Alternate Directories**.

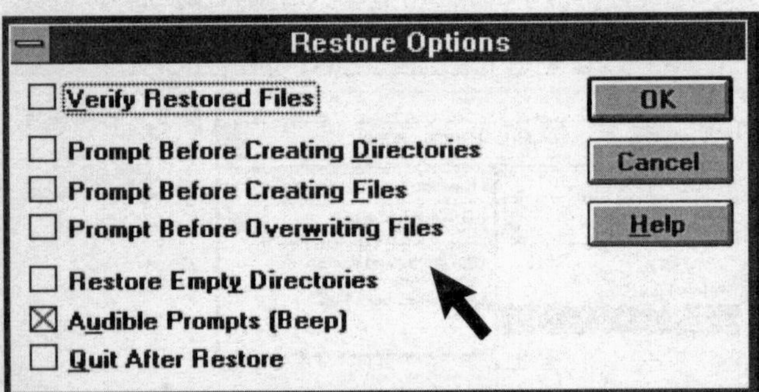

8 Select **Options** to set any restoration options, like prompting before creating directories and files. Click **OK** in the Restore Options dialog box when you are done selecting options.

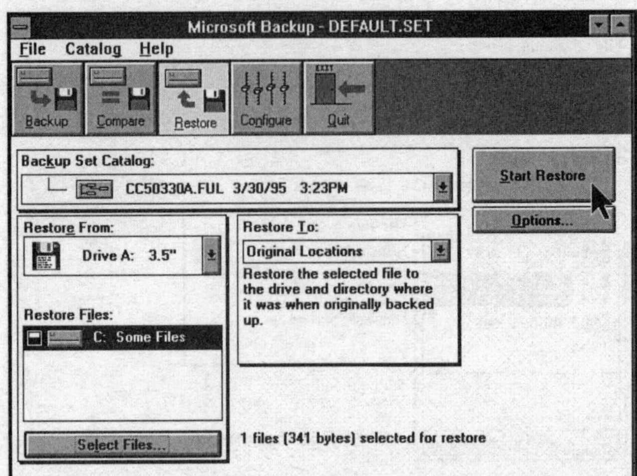

9 Select **Start Restore** to begin the restoration process.

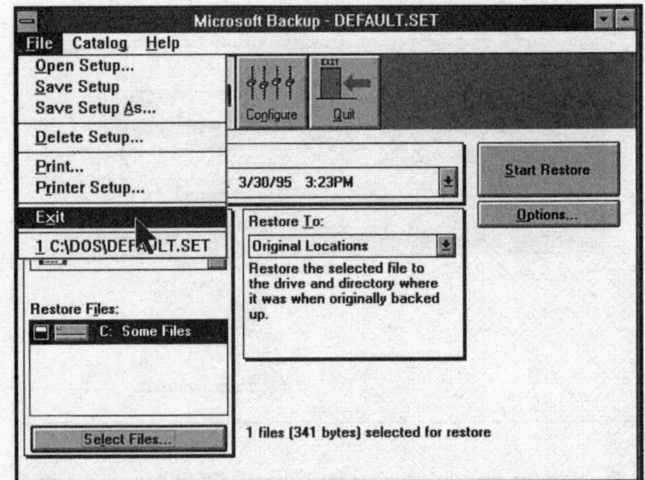

10 When the restoration is complete, put the backup disks in a safe place; select **File**, **Exit** to leave the Backup program. If asked to save any changes you made to the Restore settings, choose to save the settings in **DEFAULT.SET**, and click **OK**.

Begin Do It Yourself Restore in Windows 95

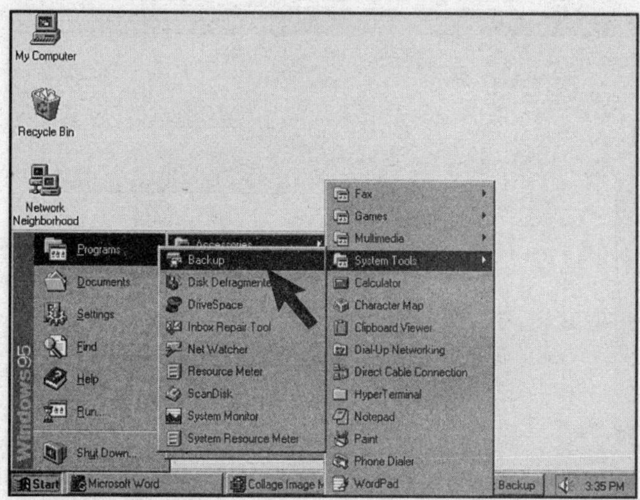

1 With Windows 95 running, click the **Start** button, point to **Programs**, **Accessories**, and **System Tools**, and then click **Backup**.

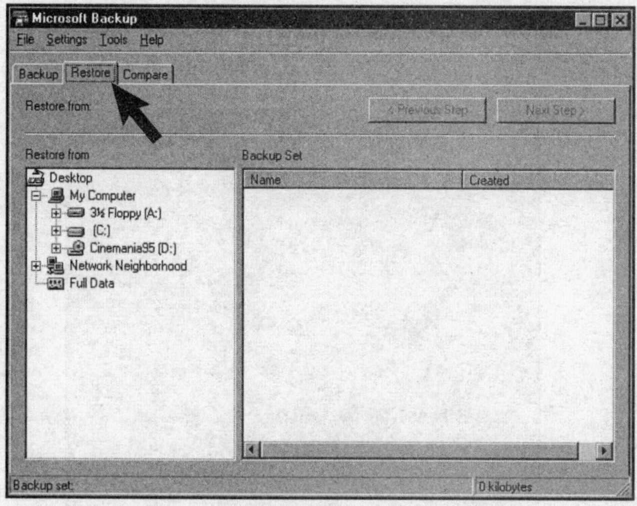

2 Microsoft Backup starts as if you intended to back up files. Click the **Restore** tab.

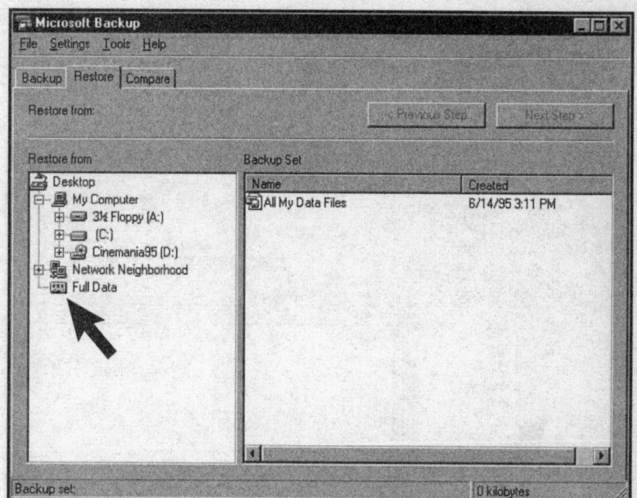

3 A list of the drives you might have used for the backup appears. Insert your backup tape or the last floppy disk of the backup set into the drive. In the **Restore from** list, click the drive that contains the backup disk or tape.

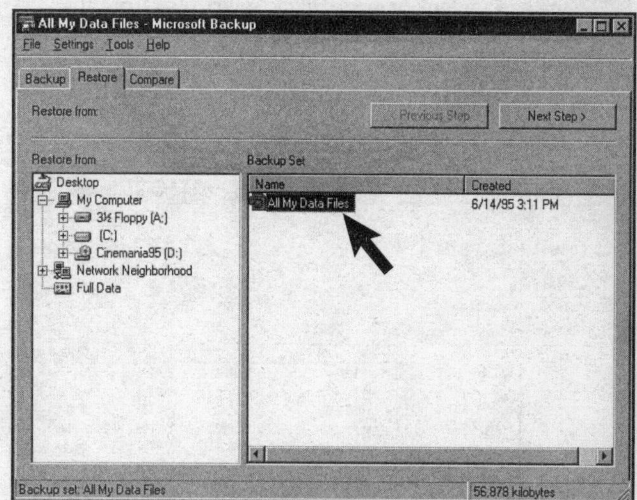

4 In the **Backup Set** list, if there is more than one backup set name, click the name of the backup set you want to restore. (You entered a backup set name when you performed the backup.)

(continues)

Do It Yourself Restore in Windows 95

(continued)

5 Click the **Next Step** button.

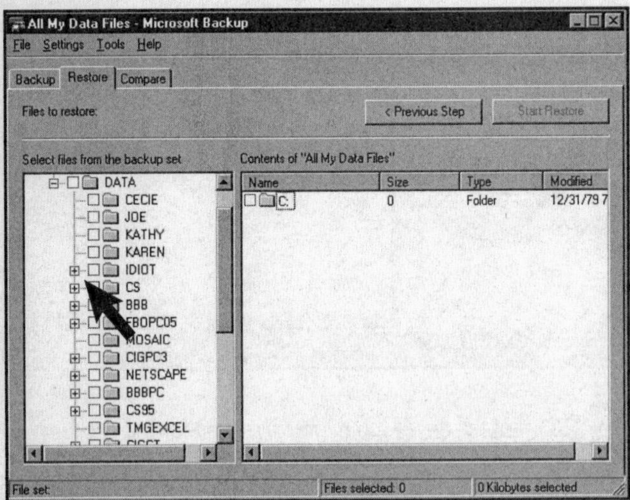

6 A list appears, showing all the folders and files that are on the backup tape or disks. Under **Select files from the backup set**, click each plus sign to display all the folders and subfolders that were backed up. With all folder and subfolder names displayed, you can select individual folders to restore.

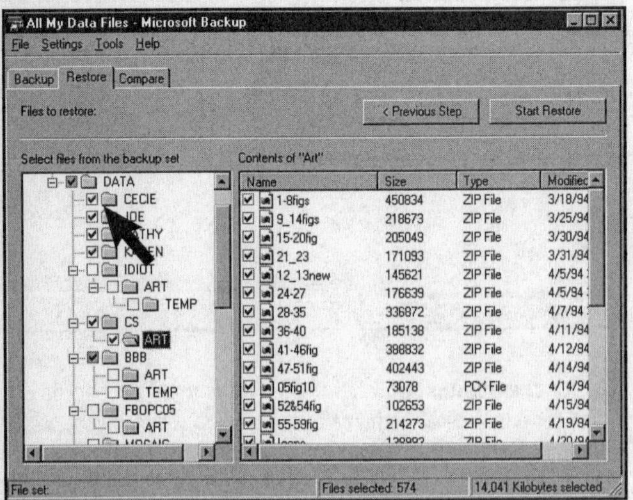

7 To restore the contents of an entire folder, click its check box under **Select files from the backup set**.

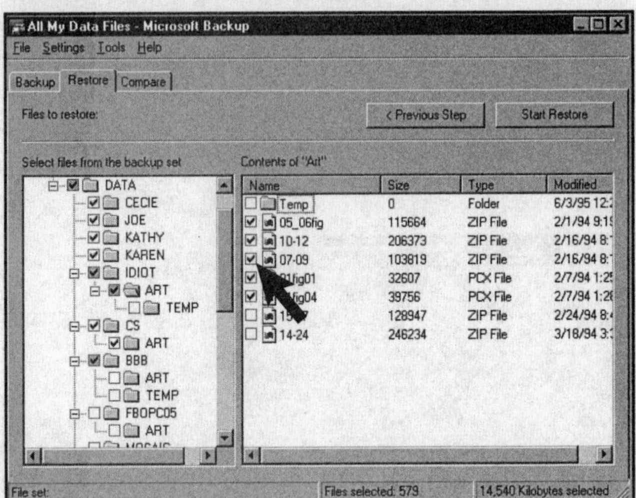

8 To restore selected files in a folder, click the folder under **Select files from the backup set**, and then click the check box next to each file you want to restore in the **Contents of** list.

9 Click the **Start Restore** button.

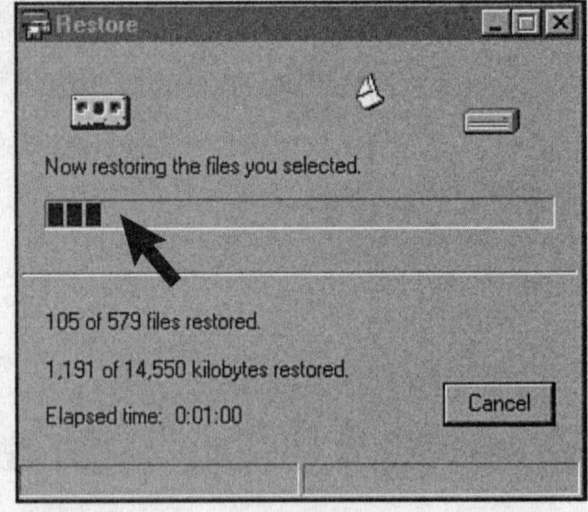

10 If you are restoring from floppy disks, a dialog box appears, telling you which disk to insert. Follow the on-screen instructions until the restore operation is complete.

Check for Viruses with Microsoft AntiVirus

We live in strange times. Not only can people get sick with a virus, computers can, too. With computers, however, a virus is not a living microbe, but a program specifically designed by some bored programmer to cause damage to the data in your computer. No one really knows why people make the effort to create a computer virus (few ever admit doing so), but we computer users have to live with the fact there are now several hundred known computer viruses out there, and any one could cause trouble.

Viruses invade a personal computer in a number of ways. The most common happens when you use an "infected" program. You may obtain this program from a friend or download it from an online service like CompuServe. It might accidentally come from a commercial program you bought and installed on your computer.

Realistically (and fortunately), commercial software is seldom infected by a computer virus, and the same is true of programs available through online services like CompuServe, America Online, and PRODIGY (but not the Internet!). Programs that might affect the reputation of a service or a company are checked before they are made publicly available. It is far more likely your computer will get infected by a program you get from a friend or associate.

Also, fortunately, there are programs available designed to ferret out viruses—and if possible, destroy them. In fact, Windows 3.11 comes with such a program; it's called Microsoft AntiVirus. It's extremely easy to use, so you should get into the habit of running it at least once a month, or more often if you regularly install new software on your computer, or share disks with others.

Begin Do It Yourself Check for Virus in Windows 3.11

1 In Windows, locate the **AntiVirus** program icon and double-click it to start the AntiVirus program. The normal spot for the AntiVirus program icon is the **Microsoft Tools** group in Program Manager.

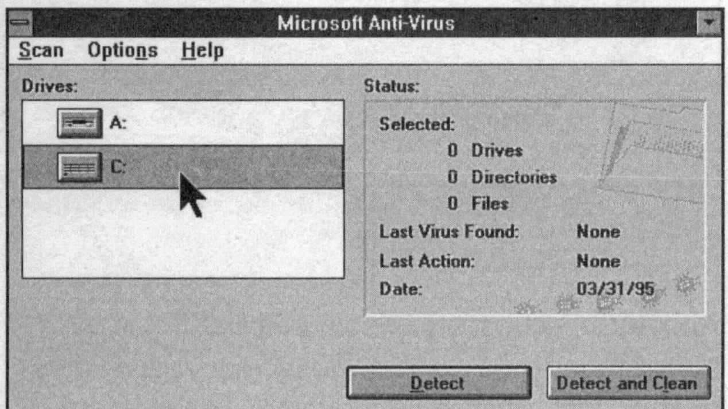

2 The AntiVirus program starts, and does some preliminary testing. When you're ready to scan for viruses, select the drive you want to check, such as drive C: for your computer's hard disk drive.

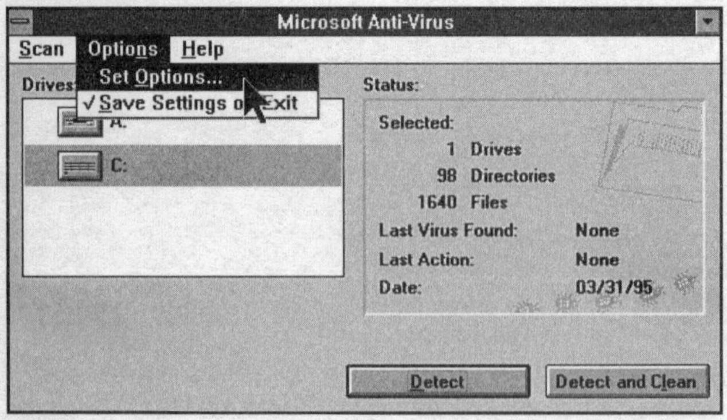

3 Select **Options**, **Set Options** to set any options you want to use. Many of these options are of a special nature. You will want to refer to the online help that comes with the AntiVirus program (select **Help**, **Index**) for more information.

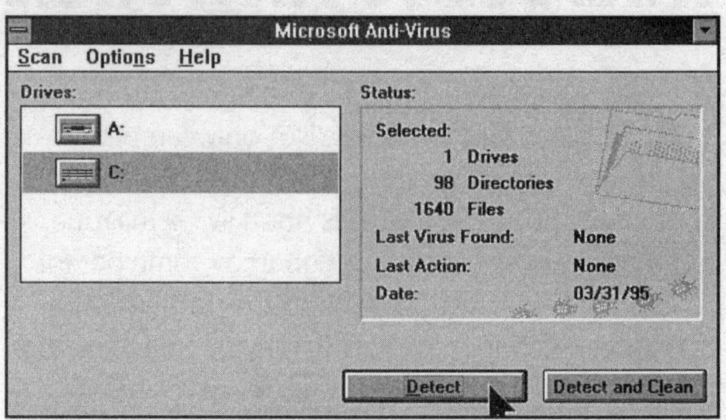

4 Select **Detect** to look for viruses, or **Detect and Clean** to not only look for viruses, but to attempt to get rid of them.

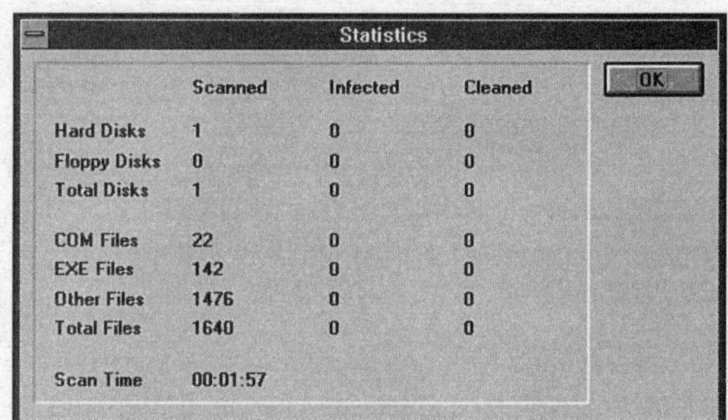

5 After scanning your computer's disk drive, the program displays a Statistics report, indicating the number and type of files it checked, and whether any were infected and/or cleaned. Click **OK** after reviewing the report.

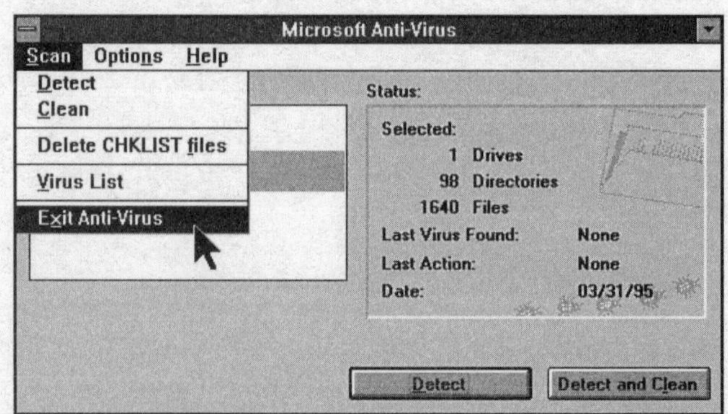

6 When you're done, select **Scan**, **Exit Anti-Virus** to leave the AntiVirus program.

PART 3

101 Quick Fixes

If you're lucky, you'll be able to run your computer and programs without encountering a single problem. However, most people are not so fortunate. One day, you'll turn on your computer and encounter a blank screen, or your printer won't print, or you'll get an error message telling you that a file you've worked on for a month has gone south.

Whatever the problem is, you'll need help, and you'll want that help quick. In this section, 101 of the most common problems and their solutions are listed. In this basket of solutions, you'll find answers to hardware problems, software problems, and problems with DOS, Windows (versions 3.1 and 3.11), and Windows 95, intermixed—because it's not always clear which particular part of your computer is causing the problem. In each solution, however, you'll find out just where to look to find the root cause.

If you're completely lost, turn to the Quick Finder table at the beginning of this section for help. There, you'll find a statement of the problem and some places in this section where you can locate the answer.

QUICK FIXES

Quick Finder Table

When your computer locks up, your screen blacks out, or an error message pops up on your screen (phrased in the form of a question), you need help, and you need it quick. This *Quick Finder Table* is designed to get you the help you need in a hurry. The table lists the problems by category (Startup problems, Sound card problems, etc.), gives you the number of the Quick Fix that'll breathe life back into your PC, and gives you the appropriate page number so you can fix the problem now instead of digging through pages to search for a solution.

Startup Problems

Problem	*Quick Fix Number*	*Page*
Additional RAM caused computer to lock up.	5	487
`Bad or missing command interpreter` message.	6	487
Beeping during startup, no display.	3	486
Blank screen, but computer seemed to start okay.	2	485
Boot error message.	4	486
Causes of startup problems—finding the cause.	7	487
`CMOS RAM` error message.	5	487
`Command interpreter is bad` message.	6	487
Computer emits strange beeps at startup, no display.	3	486
Computer refuses to start, and displays `Bad or missing command interpreter` message.	6	487
DOS 6.0 startup options.	7	487
DOS error message appears: `Non-system disk or disk error`.	4	486
Floppy disk left in drive during startup.	4	486

Startup Problems *Continued*

Problem	*Quick Fix Number*	*Page*
Installed RAM, now computer won't start right.	5	487
Loud beeping, no display.	3	486
Monitor blank at startup.	1	485
Monitor displays `Non-system disk or disk error` message.	4	486
No display at startup.	1, 2	485
No lights or sounds during startup.	1	485
No startup after installing RAM.	5	487
`Non-system disk or disk error` message.	4	486
Power on—monitor blank.	1	485
Power on—strange computer beeps.	3	486
Startup commands run too fast.	7	487
Step through the startup commands.	7	487
Tracing a startup problem.	7	487

Disk Problems

Problem	*Quick Fix Number*	*Page*
Bad areas on a disk.	12	489
Bad disk.	9	488
`Cannot write to disk` message.	8	488
Can't save a file to a floppy disk.	8, 9, 11	488-489
Can't save a file—disk is full.	11	489
Can't save or open file—message says `Sector not found`.	12	489
Can't save or open files.	9	488
Can't use drives compressed with DriveSpace or DoubleSpace.	14	490
Compressed drives are slow.	14	490
Computer is slower than usual.	13	490
`Disk full` message.	11	489
DoubleSpace problems.	14	490
DriveSpace problems.	14	490
Error message says my drive is invalid.	10	489
`Error writing to or reading from disk in drive` message.	9	488
File opens slowly.	13	490
Files trashed after installing DriveSpace or DoubleSpace.	14	490
Floppy drive grinds unnaturally.	9	488
Floppy drive is "invalid."	10	489
Floppy drive won't read the disk.	9	488

Problem	*Quick Fix Number*	*Page*
`Insufficient disk space` message.	11	489
`Invalid drive` message.	10	489
Lost data on a disk.	12	489
Making a bad disk usable.	12	489
More disk space needed.	11	489
Problems with DriveSpace or DoubleSpace.	14	490
Recovering lost data on a disk.	12	489
Saving files—floppy disk doesn't work.	8	488
`Sector not found` message.	12	489
Speeding up a computer.	13	490
Write-protected disks.	8	488

File Problems

Problem	*Quick Fix Number*	*Page*
Can't insert picture in document.	18	493
Codes appear in file.	18	493
Copied a file from another computer—can't use the file.	19	493
Deleted file accidentally.	15	491
Document disappeared.	17	493
Documents created in other applications.	18	493
Downloaded files—using.	19	493
File disappeared.	17	493
File format problems.	18	493
Files—using downloaded files.	19	493
Finding lost files.	16, 17	492-493
Forgot to save the file.	17	493
Graphics—can't use in document.	18	493
Graphics—inserting into documents.	18	493
Inserting pictures in documents.	18	493
Lost files—finding.	16, 17	492-493
Power outage before saving file.	17	493
Recover accidentally deleted files.	15	491
Searching for lost files.	16, 17	492-493
Symbols in file—where did they come from?	18	493

(continues)

File Problems *Continued*

Problem	*Quick Fix Number*	*Page*
Unzipping compressed files.	19	493
Using copied files.	19	493
Where was a file saved?	16, 17	492-493
Window that contained document is hidden under another window.	16	492

Memory Problems

Problem	*Quick Fix Number*	*Page*
Aggressively scanning with MemMaker.	22	497
Computer locks up after running MemMaker.	22	497
Conventional memory too low.	20	495
Freeing up memory.	20	495
`Insufficient memory` message in Windows.	21	496
MemMaker's Custom setup— problems with.	22	497
MemMaker—problems after running MemMaker.	22	497
MemMaker—running MemMaker for more memory.	20	495
Memory problems in Windows.	21	496
Memory—checking available memory.	20	495
Memory—freeing memory for use by other programs.	20	495
Memory—using disk space as memory in Windows.	21	496
More memory with DOS 6.0's MemMaker.	20	495
`Out of memory` message.	20	495
Program won't run because there's not enough conventional memory.	20	495
Running more applications in Windows.	21	496
Virtual memory in Windows.	21	496
Windows memory—getting more memory in Windows.	21	496

Video Problems

Problem	*Quick Fix Number*	*Page*
Bad graphics.	25	499
Blank screen in Windows.	26	499
Blank screen in DOS or Windows.	23	498
Dead monitor.	23	498
Flickering monitor.	27	500
Fuzzy pictures.	25	499

Problem	Quick Fix Number	Page
Game screens look bad.	25	499
Garbage on the screen.	28	500
Graphics and movies look bad.	25	499
Headaches from monitor.	27, 30	500-501
Installed new display card, now monitor whines loudly.	24	498
Monitor is black.	23	498
Monitor whines more loudly than usual when turned on.	24	498
Monitor—strange patterns on the screen.	28	500
No picture on monitor.	23	498
Screen saver problems.	23	498
Small pictures and movie clips.	29	501
Windows won't start after changing display driver.	26	499

Sound Card Problems

Problem	Quick Fix Number	Page
CD-ROM drive—using sound card with CD-ROM drive.	43	508
Conflict with another device.	31, 33, 35	502-504
Control volume.	32	503
Drivers for sound cards—installing.	31	502
Installed sound card, but it doesn't work.	31	502
Loading sound card drivers in Windows.	36	504
Microphone doesn't work.	38	505
MIDI port setting in Windows.	36	504
Missing command lines in Windows startup files.	36	504
Mouse and sound card won't work together.	33, 35	503, 504
No sound after returning to Windows from DOS application.	34	504
Only one speaker works.	37	505
`Out of environmental space` message.	31	502
Recording sounds—can't record.	38	505
Sound card doesn't work in Windows.	34, 36	504
Sound card never worked.	31	502
Speaker problems.	31, 37	502, 505
Stereo sound doesn't work.	37	505
Turn volume up or down.	32	503
Upgraded with sound card, but mouse or other device doesn't work.	35	504
Volume control.	32	503

(continues)

CD-ROM Problems

Problem	*Quick Fix Number*	*Page*
Application on CD locks up system.	41	507
Audio CD problems.	39, 43	506, 508
CD speakers—how to connect.	42	507
CD-ROM drive and sound board—connecting.	42	507
CD-ROM drive in sideways system unit.	45	509
CD-ROM drive locks up the system.	41	507
CD-ROM never worked.	39	506
Device conflict with CD-ROM drive.	39, 41	506-507
Disc—CD-ROM drive can't read disc.	40	506
Disc caching with CD-ROM drives.	44	509
Drivers—installing for CD-ROM drive.	39, 40	506
External CD-ROM drive doesn't work.	39	506
Files—CD-ROM drive can't read files on the disc.	40	506
Freezes—System freezes when running CD application.	41	506
MemMaker—after running MemMaker, CD-ROM drive won't work.	22, 40	497, 506
Music CDs—playing.	43	508
Playing audio and music CDs.	43	508
Plugging speakers into CD-ROM drive.	42	507
Slow movie clips.	44	509
Sound board—using with CD-ROM drive.	42	507
Speeding up a CD-ROM drive.	44	509
System locks up when running application from CD.	41	507
System unit standing on end with CD-ROM drive.	45	509

Printing Problems

Problem	*Quick Fix Number*	*Page*
Entered multiple print commands, still no printing.	47	511
Feed adjustment knob on form-feed printers.	50	513
Half-page printouts.	49	512
Memory problems in laser printers.	49, 53	512, 514
Misaligned print.	50	513
Non-printable region.	50	513
On-line light is blinking.	46	510
On-line light is lit, but printer still won't print.	47	511
Paper jam.	52	514

Problem	Quick Fix Number	Page
Paper tray is too full.	52	514
Partial pages printed.	49	512
Port—wrong printer port.	46	510
Print chopped off at left or right.	50	513
Print doesn't match what's on the screen.	51	513
Print driver—installing.	46	510
Print queue—documents backed up in queue.	47	511
Print queue—starting and restarting print jobs.	47	511
Print too close to left or right edge of page.	50	513
Print too close to the top or bottom of page.	50	513
Printer fonts—using to speed up printing.	53	514
Printer prints half pages.	49	512
Printer won't print.	46	510
Printer—selecting in Windows.	48	512
Printing in the background.	47	511
Printout looks like garbage.	48	5612
Screen and printer text looks different.	51	513
Screen fonts—installing.	51	513
Slow printing.	53	514
Speeding up printing in Windows.	53	514
Spooler—understanding and using.	47	511
Strange codes in printed copy.	48	512
Symbols appear in printed document.	48	512
Testing printer.	46	510
Tractor feed printer problems.	46	510
TrueType fonts—using in Windows to speed printing.	53	514
Windows Print Manager problems.	47	511
Wrong printer port selected.	46	510

Mouse Problems

Problem	Quick Fix Number	Page
Application can't use a mouse.	54	515
Dirty mouse.	55	516
DOS applications run from Windows have no mouse pointer.	58	518
Fast (too fast) mouse pointer.	59	520
Installing mouse driver.	54	515

(continues)

Mouse Problems *Continued*

Problem	*Quick Fix Number*	*Page*
Jumpy mouse pointer.	55	516
Lost mouse after installing modem.	54, 56	515, 517
Modem installation incapacitated the mouse.	54, 56	515, 517
Mouse doesn't work.	54	515
Mouse driver in Windows—selecting.	57	518
Mouse pointer disappears in DOS applications run from Windows.	58	518
Mouse pointer not visible.	54	515
Mouse set up to use wrong COM port.	54	515
No mouse after installing.	54	515
Skipping mouse pointer.	55	516
Slow mouse.	59	520
Slowing down the mouse pointer.	59	520
Speeding up the mouse pointer.	59	520
Windows mouse problems.	57	518
Wrong Windows mouse driver.	57	518

Keyboard Problems

Problem	*Quick Fix Number*	*Page*
Beeps sound during typing or entering commands.	65	522
Computer beeps when I type.	65	522
Computer locked.	60	520
Error message says `Keyboard not found`.	61	521
Keyboard cable became disconnected.	60	520
Keyboard doesn't work—computer beeps.	65	522
Keyboard locked.	60	520
`Keyboard not found` message.	60, 61	520-521
Keyboard stopped working after running MemMaker.	60	520
MemMaker incapacitated the keyboard.	60	520
New text replaces old text.	63	522
Pressing keys causes computer to beep.	65	522
Type appears in all UPPERCASE LETTERS.	62	521
Typing replaces existing text.	63	522
UPPERCASE LETTERS appear for everything typed.	62	521

Modem Problems

Problem	Quick Fix Number	Page
Baud rate problems.	70	524
Busy signal.	68	524
Call waiting—problems with.	71	525
Phone jack—check with telephone.	66	522
COM port setting—wrong COM port for modem.	66	522
Communications settings—match to remote computer.	70	524
Dialing—modem won't dial.	66	522
Disable call waiting.	71	525
Disabling the modem speaker.	72	525
Disconnect—modem disconnects when someone calls.	71	525
Disconnects—modem disconnects before entering Hangup command.	67, 70	523-524
Hearing voices from the modem.	69	524
Local echo—turning off.	74	526
Local echo—turning on.	73	526
Modem dials but doesn't connect.	67, 70	523-524
Modem disconnects when someone calls.	71	525
Modem doesn't respond.	66	522
Modem initialization string—entering.	70	524
Modem jacks—wrong jack in use.	67	523
Modem lights don't come on.	66	522
Modem setup in communications application.	70	524
Muting the modem.	72	525
NO CARRIER.	70	524
No sound from modem.	66	522
Premature disconnect.	67, 70	523-524
Screen doesn't respond during typing.	73	526
Terminal emulation—picking the right one.	70	524
Text does not appear on-screen.	73	526
Turning off the modem speaker.	72	525
Typing appears double on-screen.	74	526
Typing doesn't appear on screen.	73	526
Voices from modem.	69	524
Wrong baud rate.	70	524
Wrong numbers.	69	524

(continues)

Problems with DOS

Problem	*Quick Fix Number*	*Page*
`Abort, Retry, Fail?` message.	75	526
Application—try to run, but get `Bad command or filename` message.	76	526
Applications run slowly from DOS.	80	528
`Bad command or filename` message.	76	526
Can't copy file to a drive or directory.	77	527
Changing drives—receive `Abort, Retry, Fail?` message.	75	526
Commands—learning more about DOS commands.	81	528
Computer can't read disk in floppy drive.	79	527
Computer won't let me copy a file.	77	527
Copy file—DOS displays `File not found` message.	78	527
Copy file—DOS won't let me copy a file.	77	527
Delete file—DOS displays `File not found` message.	78	527
Disk cannot be read.	79	527
DOS can't find the specified file.	78	527
DOS can't use the disk in the floppy drive.	79	527
DOS is slower than normal.	80	528
`File cannot be copied onto itself` message.	77	527
`File not found` message.	78	527
Floppy disk problems.	75	526
Floppy drive can't read disk.	79	527
`General failure reading drive` message.	79	527
Learning more about DOS commands.	81	528
No disk in drive.	75, 79	526-527
`Not ready reading drive A` message.	79	527
Program—try to run, but get `Bad command or filename` message.	76	526
Running application from wrong directory.	76	526
Slow DOS.	80	528
Speeding up DOS with Defrag.	80	528

Problems with DOS Applications

Problem	*Quick Fix Number*	*Page*
Anti-virus program interferes with installation.	82	529
Application won't run.	83	529
Computer freezes when running application.	84	529
Entered command to run application, but it won't run.	83	529

Problem	Quick Fix Number	Page
Installed new device, now program freezes computer.	36, 84	504, 529
Installing application—need to disable anti-virus program.	82	529
Monitor blanks when running application.	85	530
Mouse freezes computer.	84	529
Prevent anti-virus program from running at startup.	82	529
Program conflicts with other program.	84	529
Program won't run.	83	529
Screen doesn't look right.	85	530

Microsoft Windows Woes

Problem	Quick Fix Number	Page
Accidentally deleted a program group.	90	534
Application freezes Windows.	87, 92	532, 535
Applications seem slow in Windows.	88	532
Associated files in File Manager.	91	534
`Bad command or filename` appears when `WIN` command entered.	86	530
Can't print from applications to printer.	89	534
Can't run Windows.	86	530
Deleting unused fonts and Windows files.	93	537
DOS applications—running from Windows.	94	539
Entered WIN command, but Windows won't start.	86	530
Exit Windows—can't exit Windows.	87	532
Fax application—printing problems.	89	534
File associations—creating in Windows File Manager.	91	534
File Manager can't open file.	91	534
Fonts—deleting fonts you don't use.	93	537
`General Protection Fault` message.	92	535
Installing DOS applications—creating icons for Windows.	94	539
MemMaker—after running MemMaker, can't run Windows.	87	532
Modes—running Windows in different modes.	87	532
Permanent swap file—creating to speed up Windows.	88	532
PIFs—using PIFs to run DOS applications.	94	539
Printer—can't use printer after installing fax program.	89	534
Program group—rebuilding after deleting.	90	534
Quit Windows—can't quit Windows.	87	532
Rebooting from Windows.	88	532

(continues)

Microsoft Windows Woes *Continued*

Problem	*Quick Fix Number*	*Page*
Recovering deleted program groups.	90	534
Screen colors—picking a simple scheme to speed up Windows.	88	532
Speeding up Windows.	88	532
Startup—Windows won't run.	86	530
System locked up.	92	535
Too many fonts in use.	88	532
Too many Windows applications running.	88	532
Unused fonts and files—deleting.	93	537
Useless Windows files—deleting.	93	537
Windows froze and displayed `General Protection Fault` message.	92	535
Windows is locked up.	87	532
Windows Setup—installing DOS applications to run in Windows.	94	539
Windows won't start.	86	530

Problems with Windows Applications

Problem	*Quick Fix Number*	*Page*
Application's documentation says to edit Windows system files.	99	541
Application freezes Windows.	96	540
Application won't run; Windows says file is missing.	97	540
Can't run DOS utilities from Windows.	98	541
Defrag won't run in Windows.	98	541
Documentation says to edit WIN.INI or SYSTEM.INI.	99	541
DOS utilities won't run from Windows.	98	541
Edit SYSTEM.INI and WIN.INI.	99	541
Group window—where did it go?	95	540
Lost icon for installed Windows application.	95	540
Missing application file.	97	540
Program won't run.	97	540
ScanDisk won't run in Windows.	98	541
Startup files—editing.	99	541
Windows freezes when application is run.	96	540
Windows startup files—editing.	99	541

Miscellaneous Problems

Problem	*Quick Fix Number*	*Page*
Date wrong on computer.	100	542
Microsoft Backup won't run.	101	543
Setting time on the computer.	100	542
Wrong date on computer.	100	542
Wrong time on computer.	100	542

Startup Problems

1: I have no lights, no sounds, nothing.

If you flip the power switch or press the button on your computer, and you don't hear some grinding or see any lights come on, the PC isn't getting juice. Make sure the power cord is securely plugged into a wall outlet and into the back of the PC. If you plug your PC into a power strip, make sure the power strip is plugged in and turned on.

If all the connections are okay, unplug your computer from the wall outlet and plug in a device (such as a lamp) that you know works. If the lamp doesn't work in that outlet, you may have tripped a circuit breaker or blown a fuse; fix that problem, and your computer should start. If the lamp works but the computer doesn't, your computer may have a faulty power cord or power supply; seek professional help.

2: I see the lights and hear the sounds, but there's still no display.

Your computer is probably starting all right, but something is wrong with the monitor or one of its connections. Try the following solutions:

- Make sure the monitor is plugged into a wall outlet or power strip, and that it is on (see the previous solution for more information). Your monitor should have a power indicator that lights when the power is on.
- If the power is on but you still have no picture, crank up the brightness control *on your monitor*. Then readjust the brightness once you get a picture.
- Turn everything off and check the connection between the monitor and the system unit. (This connection wiggles free at times.)

3: Why is my computer beeping?

If you hear a series of loud beeps you haven't heard before, this is usually a sign that your video card has become disconnected or has died. Because a dead video card can't announce its death on video, the computer beeps to give you an audio announcement.

If you know all the safety tips about plugging in expansion cards, turn off the computer and monitor, open your system unit, and make sure the video card is plugged securely into its slot. If that doesn't solve the problem, turn the computer and monitor off and call the manufacturer.

4: My monitor displays "Non-system disk or disk error."

You usually get this message if you happened to leave a non-bootable floppy disk in drive A. Take the disk out of drive A, and press any key to boot from your hard disk. If you have an old computer and you boot it from a floppy disk, this message is telling you to insert a bootable floppy disk into drive A and press any key.

If you don't have a bootable disk handy, you'll have to get one from a friend or colleague unless you followed the instructions outlined in "Make a 'Startup' Disk" on page 394 in Part 2. After you have your computer up and running, you can create a bootable floppy disk by using the DOS FORMAT command:

1. Insert a new floppy disk into drive A. (You have to use drive A; DOS won't boot from a disk in drive B.)
2. At the DOS prompt, type **format a: /s** and press **Enter**. DOS formats the disk and copies the files needed to boot your computer to the disk.

You can also create a bootable floppy disk using Windows 3.11 File Manager (see "Format Disks" on page 146). If you have a formatted floppy disk on hand (for drive A), you can quickly turn it into a system disk. Insert the disk into drive A, open the File Manager's **Disk** menu, and select **Make System Disk**.

Windows 95 has a special feature for creating a startup disk. Take the following steps:

1. Click the **Start** button and move the mouse pointer over Settings.
2. Click **Control Panel**. The Control Panel window appears.
3. Double-click the **Add/Remove Programs** icon to display the Add/Remove Programs Properties dialog box.
4. Click the **Startup Disk** tab, and then click **Create Disk**. A dialog box appears, prompting you to insert Windows Disk 1 in one of the drives.
5. Follow the on-screen instructions to complete the operation.
6. Remove the new startup disk from your floppy disk drive, and label it. Store the disk in a clean, dry place away from any magnets.

5: My monitor displays "CMOS RAM error."

Something's wrong with your computer setup. At this point, you can usually press the F1 key to access your computer's setup options. Check the options, and change any settings you know are wrong; don't mess with any you are unsure of. Save the settings and try to reboot. In most newer computers (manufactured in the last three years), you can simply access the setup options and then save (without changing anything). This makes the computer recheck its memory and fix any memory problems automatically.

If you keep getting this message, it may be a sign that the battery that keeps your CMOS alive is losing its charge. Seek professional help at this point to replace the CMOS battery. (*CMOS*, pronounced "SEA-moss," is a battery-powered device that stores important information—including the date and time, the number of disk drives the computer has, the type of hard disk it's using, and how much memory is installed.)

6: What is a bad or missing command interpreter?

If you start your computer and you get a message that says you have a **Bad or missing command interpreter**, your DOS *command interpreter* (a file called COMMAND.COM) is either missing or messed up. The command interpreter is the DOS workhorse; it loads when you boot your computer, it allows you to enter DOS commands, and it translates DOS-related commands (such as **File**, **Copy**) from your other applications. If COMMAND.COM doesn't load on startup, you can't use your computer.

To fix the problem, first you have to boot your computer from a floppy disk. If you don't have a bootable floppy disk, get one from a friend or colleague, or create one on another computer, as explained in "My monitor displays 'Non-system disk or disk error." on page 472. Once you have your computer running, find the DOS disks that you used to install DOS on your computer (or the DOS disks that came with your computer). Copy COMMAND.COM from the first DOS disk to the root directory of drive C (C:\); COMMAND.COM must be in the root directory, or it won't load on startup.

One last warning: Make sure the COMMAND.COM file you copy is for the same version of DOS you have on your hard drive—otherwise you'll keep getting this message. To test which DOS version you're using, type **ver** at the DOS prompt, and press **Enter**.

7: Can I slow down the startup to see what's happening?

Whenever you boot your computer, the startup commands scroll by too fast for you to read them. If you have DOS 6.0 or later, you can slow down and step through the commands. When you turn on the computer, wait until you see the **Starting MS-DOS...** message; when you see it, press and release the **F8** key. DOS runs the startup commands one at a time, asking you to confirm each line (you can skip the commands you think are causing problems).

To bypass all the startup commands, wait for the **Starting MS-DOS...** message, and then hold down the **F5** or the **Shift** key. If the computer starts okay, you know that one of the commands in CONFIG.SYS or AUTOEXEC.BAT is causing the problem. For details on how to edit these files, see "Modify Your Startup Files in Windows 3.11 and DOS" on page 412.

If you have an older version of DOS (5.0 or earlier), you can't step through the commands. You can bypass *all* the commands in AUTOEXEC.BAT and CONFIG.SYS by renaming those files (try AUTOEXEC.OLD and CONFIG.OLD). To isolate a problem command line in one of the startup files, you have to engage in some serious trial-and-error. Copy CONFIG.SYS and AUTOEXEC.BAT to another disk or directory (so you can safely edit the original files); then try preventing any problem command lines from running. You do this by typing **REM** and a space before the command line you want your computer to ignore. (For details on how to edit CONFIG.SYS and AUTOEXEC.BAT, see "Modify Your Startup Files in Windows 3.11 and DOS" on page 412.)

In Windows 95, you can also step through the startup commands. When you see the message **Starting Windows 95**, press the **F8** key. You'll see a menu of startup options. Type the number next to the desired option.

Disk Problems

8: My computer says it cannot write to the disk.

The disk you're trying to save to is *write-protected*. Don't remove the write-protection just yet; most disks are write-protected for a reason. For example, most application disks come write-protected, so you can't hurt the disk when installing the application, or you might write-protect a disk that contains important files.

When you're sure you want to write to this disk, go ahead and remove the write-protection. For 3.5-inch disks, slide the write-protect tab so you can no longer see through the hole in the disk. For 5.25-inch disks, remove the sticker that covers the notch on the side of the disk.

9: I get error messages saying "Error writing to or reading from disk in drive."

This error message usually pops up after you hear your floppy disk drive grinding unnaturally. The drive is trying its best to use the floppy disk, but it's not having any luck. The disk is probably bad, and you'll have to throw it away. Before you fling the disk in the nearest trash can, try to recover any files it may have:

- Try copying the files from the damaged floppy disk to your hard disk or to another floppy disk.
- If you have DOS 6.2 or later, go to the DOS prompt, type **scandisk a:** or **scandisk b:**, and press **Enter**. Follow the on-screen instructions to recover your files.

- If you have a version of DOS that's earlier than 6.2, go to the DOS prompt, type **chkdsk a: /f** or **chkdsk b: /f**, and press **Enter**.
- If you have Windows 95, click the **Start** button; point to **Programs**, **Accessories**, and **System Tools**; and then click **ScanDisk**. For details on how to use ScanDisk, see "Check a Disk for Errors with ScanDisk" on page 454.

10: What d'ya mean my drive's not valid?!

You probably forgot to insert a disk in the floppy drive before trying to save a file to it, or you typed the wrong drive letter. Check your typing, and make sure there's a formatted disk in the drive you're trying to use.

11: I get an error message saying that my disk is full.

Your disk *is* full. Use a different disk, or delete files from the disk before you try to save additional files. On a hard disk, it is good practice to use no more than 90 percent of the total space. Your computer needs some space for temporary files, and if you don't provide this space, you might encounter serious problems.

If you get this message while trying to save a file to your hard disk, you might have to save the file to a formatted floppy disk for the time being. Then, move some data files (files you create) off the hard disk to floppy disks to free up some space. See "Make Your Computer Work Faster and Better" on page 387 for details.

For a permanent solution to an overcrowded hard drive, consider having a newer, bigger hard drive installed. Most applications nowadays gobble up hard drive space; there never seems to be enough. Another option is to run a *disk compression* utility, such as Stacker or the DOS utility known as DoubleSpace or DriveSpace (which comes with DOS 6.0 and later and Windows 95). These utilities compress the files on your disk so they take up less space when not in use. When you run or open the file, the utility automatically decompresses the file. Although this slows down your computer a little, it is much less costly than installing a new hard drive.

For instructions on how to run DriveSpace from the DOS prompt or from Windows 95, see "Compress a Drive with DriveSpace" on page 406. You should not run DriveSpace from Windows 3.1 or 3.11; exit Windows first, and then run DriveSpace.

> Caution! If you have Windows 95, be sure to use its DriveSpace program and not the one that comes with DOS. The DOS DriveSpace utility does not handle the long file names that Windows 95 allows.

12: What does "Sector not found" mean?

The disk has a bad spot on it. (Hey, it happens.) The bad sector isn't a big problem unless there's some data saved to that sector, in which case you might lose the data. You may be able to recover the data using DOS 6.2's ScanDisk or a utility program, such as The Norton Utilities or PC Tools. To use ScanDisk, go to the DOS prompt, type **scandisk *c:*** (where *c:* represents the letter of the disk drive that has the bad sector), and press **Enter**. Follow the on-screen instructions to recover your data.

If the error occurred on a floppy disk, try to recover any data from the disk (using ScanDisk), and then throw the disk away. On floppy disks, if one sector goes bad, it's likely that additional neighboring sectors will follow suit sometime soon. Rather than risk losing data, discard the disk.

Hard disks are too expensive to throw away (and bad sectors usually are not a sign of the demise of neighboring sectors), so the best thing to do is use ScanDisk (or one of the utility programs specified earlier) to scan the hard disk. These utility programs lock out any bad sectors, so DOS won't try to use them again. To prevent a bigger disaster, back up your work often and run ScanDisk regularly. For details, see "Check a Disk for Errors with ScanDisk" on page 454.

13: My disk seems slower than usual.

Run a defragmentation program. If you have DOS 6.0 or later, type **defrag *c:*** (where *c:* is the letter of the drive you want to defragment) and press **Enter**. Follow the on-screen instructions to continue. Defragmenter pulls all the pieces of each file together, placing them on neighboring areas of the disk. This makes it easier (and faster) for your computer to read the files. For details on how to use Defrag (or Disk Defragmenter in Windows 95), see "Optimize a Disk with Defrag" on page 398. (You should not run Defrag from Windows 3.1 or 3.11; exit Windows, and then run Defrag from the DOS prompt.)

Running CHKDSK or ScanDisk can also help with a sluggish drive. At the DOS prompt, type **chkdsk *c:*** or **scandisk *c:*** (where *c:* is the letter of the sluggish drive) and press **Enter**. To use ScanDisk in DOS or Windows 95, see "Check a Disk for Errors with ScanDisk" on page 454. (You should not run ScanDisk from Windows 3.1 or 3.11; exit Windows first, and then run ScanDisk from the DOS prompt.)

14: I've had trouble ever since I installed DoubleSpace (or DriveSpace).

These DOS file-compression programs can double your disk space, but they may cause occasional problems. Here are the three most common problems and their solutions:

- **Trashed files.** This is usually caused by a computer crash. You can try to recover your data by using ScanDisk, but you probably won't have much luck.

- **Can't access compressed disk.** Try remounting the disk. Run DoubleSpace (enter **dblspace**) or DriveSpace (enter **drvspace**) at the DOS prompt. Select the drive letter from the list of drives, and then open the **Drive** menu and select **Mount** (in Windows 95, open the **Advanced** menu and select **Mount**). To have DriveSpace automatically mount compressed drives, open the **Tools** menu and select **Options** (in Windows 95, select **Settings** from the **Advanced** menu); then select **Enable automounting**.

- **Doublespaced drives are slow.** One of the drawbacks of data compression is that it takes time to compress and decompress files. You may be able to increase the speed by running DoubleSpace or DriveSpace and choosing the **Defragment** option from the **Tools** menu. In Windows 95, run Disk Defragmenter (see "Optimize a Disk with Defrag" on page 398) and click the compressed drive to defragment it.

File Problems

15: Oops! I deleted a file; can I get it back?

Maybe. DOS 6.0 comes with a program called Undelete that can help you recover deleted files. If, when you installed DOS 6, you chose to install the Windows 3.1 (or 3.11) versions of the utilities, you have Microsoft Undelete for Windows on your computer. Open the **Microsoft Tools** group and double-click the **Undelete** icon. Click the **Drive/Dir** button; when a dialog box appears, use it to change to the directory containing the file that was accidentally deleted. Click the file's name, and then click the **Undelete** button. You may have to type the first character of the file's name. If you can't remember it, type anything; you can always rename the file later.

If you have Windows 95, undeleting files is even easier. The Windows 95 Recycle Bin temporarily stores all deleted files. Double-click the **Recycle Bin** icon, and click the file you want to undelete (Ctrl+click to choose additional files). Now, open the **File** menu and select **Restore**. The Recycle Bin restores all selected files to their original folders and disks.

> If you delete a file accidentally, don't copy any files to the disk that contains the deleted file—and don't install any applications on the disk. If you write anything to the disk, you might destroy parts of the deleted file, making it unrecoverable.

To undelete at the DOS prompt, change to the C:\DOS directory, and enter **undelete *c:\dirname*** (where *c:\dirname* is the drive and directory that contain the deleted file). For more information about Undelete, see "Keep Your Data Safe" on page 443.

If you don't have DOS 6.0 or later, run out to the store and buy it, but *don't* install it. Installing the program can destroy the deleted file completely. You can run Undelete from one of the DOS disks. Another option is to invest in a utility program, such as The Norton Utilities or PC Tools. Don't install these programs right now; run the program's Undelete utility from one of the floppy disks. After undeleting the file, you can safely install your new program.

16: I know the file's here, but where is it?

If you use Windows 3.1 (or 3.11), the File Manager can help you find misplaced files:

1. Open the **Main** group window in Windows, and double-click the **File Manager** icon.
2. Open the **File** menu and select **Search**. The Search dialog box appears.
3. Type the name of the file you're looking for, or type a wildcard entry (for example, type ***.doc** to find all files whose names end in .DOC).
4. Press the **Tab** key to move to the **Start From** text box.
5. Type the letter of the drive you want to search, followed by a colon and backslash (for example, type **c:**). To search all the directories on the drive, make sure there is an **X** in the **Search All Subdirectories** check box.
6. Click the **OK** button. File Manager searches the disk, and then displays a list of all the files that match your search entry. You can now select files from this list.

If you misplace a file in Windows 95, click the **Start** button, point to **Find**, and click **Files or Folders**. A dialog box appears, asking you to type the name of the lost file or folder. Type a name in the **Named** text box, pick the disk you want to search from the **Look in** drop-down list, and then click the **Find Now** button. Windows searches the selected drive for the specified file or folder and displays a list of items that match your search instructions.

If the file you're looking for has no extension (or you can't remember it), insert an asterisk at the end of the search file name. For example, type **myfile.*** to search for all files that start with MYFILE and end in any extension. You can also use the question mark (**?**) wild-card character to search for files. For example, **M????.*** finds all files whose name starts with M, has five or fewer characters, and ends in any extension.

If you don't have Windows, you can search for files at the DOS prompt. Type **dir *filename.ext* /s** (where *filename.ext* is the name of the file you're looking for) and press **Enter**. If you have the DOS Shell (the DOS equivalent of Windows 3.11 File Manager), you can use it to search for files. To run DOS Shell, change to the **C:\DOS** directory, type **dosshell**, and press **Enter**. Click the letter of the drive that contains the misplaced file. Open the **File** menu and select **Search**. Type the name of the file (or type a wildcard entry) and then click the **OK** button.

One trick I often use to find misplaced files is to run the application I used when I created or saved the file. Then I open the **File** menu and select **Save**. The application usually displays a dialog box showing the name of the directory where the application saves its files. Nine times out of ten, my lost file is in that directory.

If you're looking for a document file in Windows 95, you can find recently opened documents on the Documents menu. Click the **Start** button and point to **Documents**. Windows shows a list of files you've recently worked on. Click the file to run the program used to edit the file, and open the file in that program.

17: The file I was working on is gone!

Often people "lose" files by closing (or minimizing) the window that the file is in, or by opening another window on top of it. If the program you're working in has a **Window** menu, open it; chances are the file's name will appear at the bottom of the menu. You can display the file by clicking its name.

If you turned off your computer without exiting the program first—or if your computer crashed or suffered a power outage—then the file probably *is* gone. You may be able to salvage the file (or parts of it) by running **DOS CHKDSK /F** or **SCANDISK** and telling the program to save the parts of the files it finds. You can then open those files in a text editor (such as Windows Notepad) to see what they contain. Look for these files in the root directory of the drive you checked. Recovered files are named *FILEnnnn*.CHK (where *nnnn* is a number from 0001 to 9999).

Some applications back up your documents automatically as you work. When you run the application after a system crash, the application gives you the option of recovering your lost file. But even if your application doesn't offer this valuable feature, most applications create backup files for each file you save. You may be able to recover your work by opening the backup file. (Backup files commonly have the same name as the original file, but they use the .BAK extension.)

To avoid losing files, always exit a program before shutting down your computer. Most programs have a safety feature that asks if you want to save your work before exiting. If you shut down your computer when your program is running, you bypass this important safety net.

18: Why can't I insert this graphic in my document?

Your document might not like that particular graphic. Most applications allow you to use graphics that are saved in a specific *format* (or file type). For example, an application may be able to handle only those graphics that were created with PC Paintbrush (files that end in .PCX). If the file is saved as a Windows Metafile (.WMF), the application may not accept it (or be able to read it).

If you're having trouble with a particular graphic, open it in the program you used to create it, and then try to save the graphic in a different format. (Simply changing the file's extension doesn't change the file type; you must select a file type, usually from the **Save As** list in the Save As dialog box.) If you did not create the graphic (for example, if it is a piece of clip art), you may be out of luck.

19: I just downloaded a file—how do I use it?

Downloading consists of copying a file (usually from an online service or the Internet) to your computer. Many files are in a form you can use as-is. Other files might be *compressed* so they'll take up less disk space and travel faster over phone lines or a network connection. So the answer to the question of what to do with a downloaded file depends on what kind of file you downloaded.

If you obtained a graphic image or movie clip, you need a *viewer application* that can display the image or clip. Usually, you can find the viewer in the same place you downloaded the other files (assuming you got it on the Internet or through an online service, such as CompuServe or America Online).

If you downloaded a text file (one that ends in .TXT), you can open the file in any word processing or text-editing application and read it.

Most other downloaded files are compressed; you can't use the file until you decompress it. If you're lucky, you got hold of a *self-extracting* file (the file's name ends in .EXE). Move the file to a separate directory, and then run the file from the DOS prompt or from File Manager. You can then delete the .EXE file you downloaded, if you want to free up some disk space.

Most other compressed files end in .ZIP. To decompress a ZIP file, you need a program called PKZIP. Download this file from your online service or from the Internet site where you downloaded the ZIP file. The PKZIP file is typically compressed as a self-extracting file. Here's what you do to unzip the PKZIP file and use it to decompress files:

1. Make a directory called ZIP for the PKZIP file you downloaded, and move the file to this directory.
2. Change to the **ZIP** directory, type the name of the compressed PKZIP file (without the extension), and press **Enter**. The PKZIP file decompresses itself.
3. To unzip a file that has the ZIP extension, change to the **ZIP** directory.
4. Type **pkunzip c:*dirname**filename*.zip c:*dirname*** (where *c* is the letter of the drive where the zipped file is stored, *dirname* is the directory that contains the file, and *filename*.zip is the name of the compressed file; the second *dirname* is the same as the first).
5. Press **Enter**. PKZIP unzips the file and stores the unzipped version in the same directory where the ZIP file is stored.

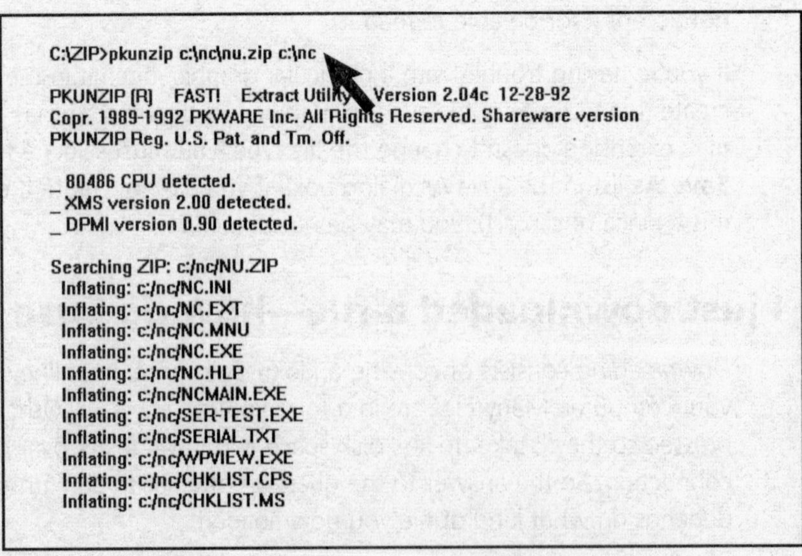

```
C:\ZIP>pkunzip c:\nc\nu.zip c:\nc

PKUNZIP (R)   FAST!   Extract Utility   Version 2.04c  12-28-92
Copr. 1989-1992 PKWARE Inc. All Rights Reserved. Shareware version
PKUNZIP Reg. U.S. Pat. and Tm. Off.

 80486 CPU detected.
 XMS version 2.00 detected.
 DPMI version 0.90 detected.

Searching ZIP: c:/nc/NU.ZIP
  Inflating: c:/nc/NC.INI
  Inflating: c:/nc/NC.EXT
  Inflating: c:/nc/NC.MNU
  Inflating: c:/nc/NC.EXE
  Inflating: c:/nc/NC.HLP
  Inflating: c:/nc/NCMAIN.EXE
  Inflating: c:/nc/SER-TEST.EXE
  Inflating: c:/nc/SERIAL.TXT
  Inflating: c:/nc/WPVIEW.EXE
  Inflating: c:/nc/CHKLIST.CPS
  Inflating: c:/nc/CHKLIST.MS
```

For more information about PKZIP, refer to "Install New Programs" on page 363. If the file's name ends in .HQX or .SEA, you downloaded a Macintosh file—and unless you have a Mac, you can't do anything with this file.

Memory Problems

20: I keep getting "Out of memory" messages in DOS.

The first step is to find out how much memory the program you are trying to run needs—and how much free memory your computer has. Check the program's documentation to find out how much memory is required. To find out how much free memory your system has, type **mem** at the DOS prompt and press **Enter**. You'll see a bunch of numbers; the number you need is the **Free Conventional**. If this number is lower than the amount of memory required by the application, you need to free up some memory.

In DOS 6.0 and later, memory is usually expressed by a three-digit number, such as 589K (kilobytes). In earlier versions of DOS, look for the words "Largest executable program size" instead of "Free Conventional." Also, in early versions of DOS, memory is shown as a six-digit number (for example, 603,050) representing bytes instead of kilobytes. Just divide the number by 1024 to determine the number of kilobytes.

The easiest way to reclaim memory is to run MemMaker (it comes with DOS versions 6.0 and later). At the DOS prompt, enter **memmaker**, and then follow the on-screen instructions. Refer to "Make Your Computer Work Faster and Better" on page 387 for details.

If you still can't run the program, you may have memory resident programs that are running on startup. To prevent these programs from running, reboot your computer, wait until you see the **Loading MS-DOS...** message, and then press and release the **F8** key. DOS lets you step through the startup commands, and you can skip any you think might be causing problems (for example, a command that loads an antivirus program or screen saver can cause problems). When you're done, enter the **MEM** command again to see how much memory you've reclaimed. You can skip all the commands in AUTOEXEC.BAT and CONFIG.SYS by pressing the **F5** or **Shift** key when you see **Loading MS-DOS...**.

If a particular startup command is causing problems, you can prevent it from loading by adding **REM** before the command line in AUTOEXEC.BAT or CONFIG.SYS. See "Make Your Computer Work Faster and Better" on page 387 for details. The following figure shows how to skip commands with REM.

One more thing… If the program you're trying to run can use *expanded memory* (and you have a couple megabytes of extended memory and DOS 5.0 or later), you can make a portion of your computer's *extended* memory act as if it were expanded memory. Here's what you do:

1. Open your CONFIG.SYS file and look for a line like **DEVICE=C:\DOS\EMM386.EXE**.
2. Make sure there's a command line such as **DEVICE=C:\DOS\HIMEM.SYS** before the EMM386.EXE line; add the HIMEM.SYS line if it is missing.
3. If the EMM386.EXE line has **NOEMS** in it, delete NOEMS and type **256 RAM** (to use a quarter megabyte of RAM) or **512 RAM** (to use a half megabyte of extended memory as expanded).
4. Save the CONFIG.SYS file and then reboot your computer. This expanded memory is now available for your program to use.

Warning: This is not the best option for most programs. It disables most of what MemMaker does to free up conventional memory, and it reduces the amount of extended memory available for Windows applications.

21: Can I make the "Insufficient memory" messages in Windows go away?

If your computer has four megabytes or less of RAM, you're probably going to encounter the "Insufficient memory" message on a regular basis. The good news is that you can do something about it:

- Install more RAM. I consider 8 megabytes the *absolute* minimum amount of RAM you should have on your system.
- Quit all the applications except the one you want to use. (Don't just minimize the windows; exit the applications.)

- Run Windows 3.1 or 3.11 in Enhanced mode. (If you have Windows for Workgroups or Windows 95, you have no choice; it always runs in Enhanced mode.) To find out which mode Windows is running in, open the Program Manager's **Help** menu and select **About Program Manager**. If you're running in Standard mode, quit Windows and then restart with the **win /3** command.
- Turn off any fancy options, such as screen savers, wallpaper, or Windows color schemes.
- In Windows 3.1 or 3.11, increase the size of the swap file used as *virtual memory* (disk space that acts like RAM). (A swap file is a temporary file that Windows uses to transfer data back and forth between RAM and the disk.) To increase the swap file size, open the **Main** group window, double-click the **Control Panel** icon, double-click the **386 Enhanced** icon, and click the **Virtual Memory** button. Click the **Change** button, and type a bigger number in the **New Size** text box. (Enter a number that's close to the number given in the **Recommended Size** box.)
- In Windows 95, low-memory messages usually indicate that the combined total of RAM and virtual memory (disk space) is insufficient. If you have less than 4M of RAM, install an additional 4M. If you have at least 8M of RAM, try clearing some disk space, so Windows can use the free space as virtual memory. Windows 95 does a good job of managing virtual memory, so you should not have to change any settings.

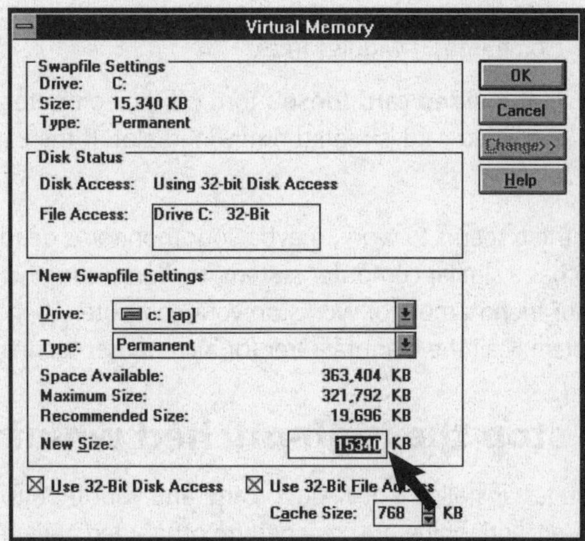

22: I ran MemMaker, and now I can't run anything!

If you can't even boot your computer, boot with the recovery disk you created in "Keep Your Data Safe" on page 443. (You *did* create a recovery disk, didn't you?) Now, change to the **C:\DOS** directory, and enter **memmaker /undo**. This returns your system to the way it was before you ran MemMaker.

MemMaker rarely causes problems if you run the Express setup. If you ran the Custom setup and set the **Scan the upper memory area aggressively?** option to Yes, MemMaker might have gone a little too far. You can run MemMaker again with this option turned off. Another Custom option that causes problems is the one for using the *monochrome* region (an area of memory reserved for black-and-white display adaptors). Try running MemMaker with this option turned off, too.

Video Problems

23: My monitor is dead!

Don't panic. The monitor may only appear to be dead. First, check the obvious:

- **Are you running a screen blanker?** Some screen saver programs blank the screen instead of displaying pretty pictures. Usually, the press of a key or a mouse move will snap your screen right out of it.
- **Is the monitor plugged in and turned on?** Your monitor should have a power indicator that lights when the power is on. Could the outlet be bad? If so, test the monitor in an outlet that you know is good.
- **Crank up the brightness control.** The brightness control is usually on the front or side of the monitor, making it easy to turn it way down by mistake.
- **Maybe it's the connection between the monitor and the system unit.** Turn everything off and check the connection between the monitor and the system unit (sometimes it wiggles free).
- **Is the video card loose?** Turn off the computer, open the case, and make sure the video card is seated firmly in its slot. If the card is loose, gently rock it back into place.

If nothing seems to work, maybe your monitor *is* dead. If you have a friend or colleague who has a similar computer system, try connecting his or her monitor to your computer. If your friend's monitor works on your computer, then you know that the monitor is the problem. Call the manufacturer (or a computer technician).

24: Can I stop the high-pitched whining noise?

If you just installed a new video card, and your monitor starts to cry out in an unusually high-pitched whine, turn everything off *immediately*. The card may be set to a higher resolution than the monitor can handle. Check the manual that came with the video card and the one that came with your monitor. Make sure the card is set to display at the same resolution as the monitor. If you can't stop the whining, turn the computer off and call a qualified computer technician.

If the monitor has always whined, maybe you just purchased a whiny monitor. Earplugs may be the only solution.

25: Why are the pictures so fuzzy?

You either have a low-resolution monitor, or your monitor is using a low-resolution video driver. If you have a VGA monitor (640-by-480 dpi, 16 colors) you can expect any pictures or movie clips to look pretty fuzzy. If you have an SVGA monitor capable of displaying at least 256 colors, pictures should look pretty clear, even at the lower resolution (640-by-480 dpi).

A monitor usually comes with its own *video driver* (a program on a floppy disk or on the hard disk, if the monitor came with the computer package). You have to run a setup program from Windows to install the drivers and use them. If the drivers don't have their own installation program, use the Windows Setup utility (for Windows 3.1 or 3.11). If you run into problems after selecting a Windows video driver, skip to the next solution to recover.

Windows 95 makes it easy to pick a different video driver and resolution. Simply right-click on a blank area of the Windows desktop, click **Properties**, and click the **Settings** tab. Change the options as desired. Settings of 256 colors and 640-by-480 are usually sufficient for displaying images clearly. For more details, see "Change the Video Display Properties" on page 201.

26: I changed my Windows display driver, and now Windows won't display anything!

You picked the wrong Windows video driver for your display adapter. Trouble is, you can't get into Windows to fix the problem. And if your computer is set up to start Windows automatically, you're in a real bind.

If you have Windows 3.1 or 3.11 on your computer, the first step is to reboot. If your computer is set up to start Windows automatically (and you have DOS 6.0 or later), wait for the **Starting MS-DOS...** message to appear, and then press and release the **F8** key. Step through the commands one by one, and answer **No** to the **WIN** command. While you're at it, watch for a command line that runs the video driver; you might need this information when you select a video driver for Windows. (If you don't have DOS 6.0 or later, start your computer with a bootable floppy disk.) Now you're ready to pick a Windows video driver. Here's what you do to pick a video driver in Windows 3.1 or 3.11:

1. Change to the **WINDOWS** directory. For example, at the **C:\>** prompt, type **cd \windows**, and press **Enter**.
2. Type **setup** and press **Enter**. The Setup screen appears, allowing you to change video drivers and other options.
3. Use the **up arrow** key to move to the **Display** option, and press **Enter**. At the bottom of the screen, Setup displays a list of video drivers.
4. Highlight your monitor's video driver and press **Enter**, or select **VGA** (this sets the display back to the Windows-standard VGA, which works for all VGA and SVGA monitors).
5. Restart Windows, and it should come up now.

```
Windows Setup

    If your computer or network appears on the Hardware Compatibility List
    with an asterisk next to it, press F1 before continuing.

    System Information
       Computer:            MS-DOS System
       Display:             VGA
       Mouse:               Microsoft, or IBM PS/2
       Keyboard:            Enhanced 101 or 102 key US and Non US keyboards
       Keyboard Layout:     US
       Language:            English (American)
       Codepage:            English (437)
       Network:             No Network Installed

       Complete Changes: Accept the configuration shown above.

    To change a system setting, press the UP or DOWN ARROW key to
    move the highlight to the setting you want to change. Then press
    ENTER to see alternatives for that item. When you have finished
    changing your settings, select the "Complete Changes" option
    to quit Setup.
```

In Windows 95, turn off your computer, wait a minute, and then turn it back on. When you see the message **Starting Windows 95**, press the **F8** key. A menu appears, showing a list of startup options. Select the **Safe Mode** option by typing the number next to it. In safe mode, Windows uses a basic video driver. You can now pick a different video driver or continue working with the basic driver. To pick a different video driver in Windows 95, see "Change the Video Display Properties" on page 201.

27: That flickering is driving me crazy!

Either the cord that connects your monitor to the system unit is loose, your monitor is too close to a source of electrical interference, or you have an old interlaced monitor. To check the connection, turn off the system unit and the monitor. Now, make sure the monitor cord is securely plugged into the back of the system unit; tighten the screws (if the cord has them).

If you still see a flicker, try moving the monitor a couple feet away from the wall, or from another device that may be causing interference—a TV set, for example. Sometimes another electrical energy source can make the screen flicker.

If the screen still flickers, you probably have an old *interlaced* monitor. These monitors have an almost imperceptible flicker (like that of fluorescent lights). As the monitor ages, the flicker may become more noticeable. Sometimes you can solve the problem by selecting a lower resolution setting, but then your graphics will look lousy.

28: My screen has all sorts of weird patterns.

You picked the wrong video driver again. If you encounter the problem in Windows 3.1 or 3.11, see your Windows documentation. If the problem occurred in Windows 95, see "Change the Video Display Properties" on page 201. If the problem happened in a DOS application, run the application's setup program again, and pick a different video driver.

If you can't find a video driver that works, contact the manufacturer of the video card and find out if you have the most up-to-date driver. The *driver* (the program that tells the video card how to display text and pictures) commonly undergoes revisions to fix any bugs; new versions keep coming out. By installing the latest driver, you reduce the likelihood that you'll encounter display problems with new applications.

While you're talking to the manufacturer, ask if anyone else has experienced similar problems with the video card, video driver, or monitor. In some cases, a poorly designed video card or monitor might be the cause of the problem.

29: Why are the pictures so tiny?!

When you hear all the hype about multimedia, you expect your monitor to display full-screen pictures like a TV set. In the real world, however, this rarely happens. Instead, you get these dinky pictures surrounded by a sea of black; you expect to see a disclaimer that reads, "This picture had been formatted to fit your screen."

The trouble is that the technology of graphic files hasn't quite caught up with display technology. A full-screen graphic image or movie clip takes up an enormous amount of storage space, and would require Herculean computer power to display. What you end up with are dinky pictures. Don't worry—it's normal.

If the picture is way too small, you might try changing to a lower resolution display setting. For example, if you selected 1024-by-768, try changing to 640-by-480, 256 colors. Although your pictures won't look as sharp, you will be able to see them full-size.

30: My monitor gives me headaches.

Mine does, too. I'm going to get complaints from ergonomics specialists for saying this, but I've found that if I look up slightly at my monitor (about 10 degrees), I get fewer headaches than if I look straight ahead or down slightly. I also do neck rolls every 15 to 20 minutes to make sure I still have a neck.

Then again, it might not be all the monitor's fault. Your work area may be poorly lit, or may use fluorescent lights. For that matter, one of your light sources (a lamp or window) might be bouncing light off your monitor, creating screen glare. Try positioning the monitor at a 90-degree angle to any light source. If you have an old, interlaced monitor, it might have an imperceptible flicker that may be causing the problem. Go out and buy a non-interlaced monitor; the additional expense will pay off in health benefits.

Also, take frequent breaks—walk, talk, live a little. Although the news is ripe with stories about the computer age, don't forget that *you* are a person. You can't stare at a monitor all day and expect to feel limber and energized when you come home.

Sound Card Problems

31: I just installed the sound card, and it doesn't work.

This is a tough one, because the solution can range from something simple like cranking up the volume to something complex, like fooling around with switches on the card. Here are some solutions to try:

- **Look for simple solutions.** Are your speakers plugged into the right jack, the output jack? (It's easy to plug the speakers into the microphone or input jack by mistake.) If you have amplified speakers, are they plugged into the power supply and turned on (or do they need batteries)? Is the volume cranked up (most sound cards have a volume control like on a radio)? Are you running a program that plays sounds and that is compatible with your sound card? Is sound turned on (and turned up) in the program?
- **Did you install the drivers?** The sound card should come with one or more disks containing the sound card drivers. You must run the installation program to set up your computer to use the sound card.
- **Did you get the "Out of environmental space" message?** Try adding the following line to the end of your CONFIG.SYS file:

  shell=c:\command.com /e:512 /p

  For details on how to edit CONFIG.SYS, see "Make Your Computer Work Faster and Better" on page 387. Reboot your computer after making the change.
- Is the sound card in conflict with another device? Each device has its own *Input/Output address* and *interrupt* settings (IRQs). (The address tells the computer where the device is, and the interrupt provides a way for the device to demand attention.) If two devices try to use the same settings, one or both devices won't work.

  Check the documentation that came with each card that's installed in your computer. If you find a setting that matches a setting on your sound card, change the setting on the sound card (usually by using jumpers or flipping tiny DIP switches). You'll also have to run the sound card's setup program again. (Resolving hardware conflicts is usually a very tedious process.) Common interrupts are 7, 9, 10, and 11.
- To resolve a device conflict in Windows 95, you can use the Hardware Conflict Troubleshooter. To run it, click the **Start** button, click **Help**, click the **Contents** tab and double-click **Troubleshooting**. Double-click **If you have a hardware conflict**, and then follow the on-screen instructions. The Hardware Conflict Troubleshooter asks a series of questions to help you determine the cause of the problem and correct it.

For more details about installing sound cards and other hardware, see "Install New Hardware" on page 415.

32: How do I turn it down (or up)?

You'd think there would be one master volume control, but there are usually at least three. Most sound cards have a volume control (on the back of the card) that allows you to adjust the strength of the signal coming out of the card. The speakers also have a volume control—and most programs that use sound also have a volume setting.

To get the right loudness, I usually set each control at midrange and then adjust from there. You'll have to experiment with the controls to get the right combination.

In Windows 95, you can quickly display the volume controls by double-clicking the speaker icon in the taskbar (just to the left of the time display). This displays volume and balance controls for the sound card, CD-ROM drive, microphone, and other devices.

33: The sound card worked before, but then I installed ________.

If you installed a new hardware device, chances are the device is using the same Input/Output address or interrupt setting as your sound card. You'll have to change the conflicting setting on one of the cards, and then run its installation or configuration program again. For details, see "Install New Hardware" on page 415.

If you installed a new application or game that's messing up your sound card, check your CONFIG.SYS and AUTOEXEC.BAT files to make sure the application installation didn't change your sound card settings. See "Modify Your Startup Files in Windows 3.11 and DOS" on page 412, for details on how to view and change CONFIG.SYS and AUTOEXEC.BAT.

If you have Windows 95, you can view the current settings for your sound card by using the Device Manager. Open the Control Panel (**Start**, **Settings**, **Control Panel**), and then double-click the **System** icon. Click the **Device Manager** tab. Click the sound card in the list of hardware, and then click **Properties**. Click the **Resources** tab to view the interrupt, DMA channel, and I/O settings for the card. At the bottom of this dialog box is a list showing any devices with which your sound card may be in conflict.

To resolve a device conflict in Windows 95, you can use the Hardware Conflict Troubleshooter. To run it, click the **Start** button, click **Help**, click the **Contents** tab and double-click **Troubleshooting**. Double-click **If you have a hardware conflict**, and then follow the on-screen instructions. The Hardware Conflict Troubleshooter asks a series of questions to help you determine the cause of the problem and correct it.

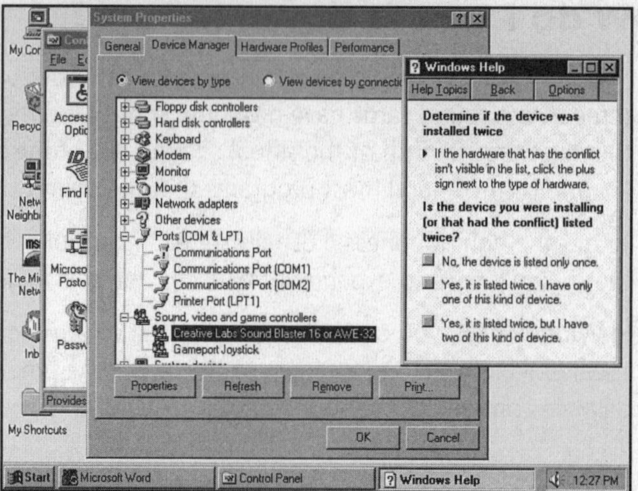

34: I run a DOS application from Windows, and when I return, my Windows applications won't play sounds.

Learn to live with it. When you go from any version of Windows to DOS, the DOS sound drivers take control of the sound card. They don't relinquish control when you return to Windows. The best way to deal with this problem is to exit Windows completely before running any DOS applications or games that cause this problem.

35: The sound card upgrade *degraded* my system.

If you install a sound card and lose your mouse or CD-ROM drive in the process, you can usually trace the problem back to a hardware conflict. The sound card is using the same input/output address or interrupt setting as the device you lost. You'll have to change the address or interrupt on the sound card, and then run the sound card's installation or configuration program again. For details, see "Install New Hardware" on page 415.

36: I can't get my sound card to work in Windows.

If you're working in Windows 3.1 or 3.11, you probably need to manually enter some command lines in WIN.INI and SYSTEM.INI. (These files contain important commands that Windows carries out on startup.) Usually, when you install the sound card drivers, the installation program edits these files for you—but sometimes the installation program fails.

Check the documentation that came with your sound card. It should include a list of the commands you need to add to your Windows system files and directions on where you need to add them. For information on how to edit WIN.INI and SYSTEM.INI, see "Modify Your Startup Files in Windows 3.11 and DOS" on page 412.

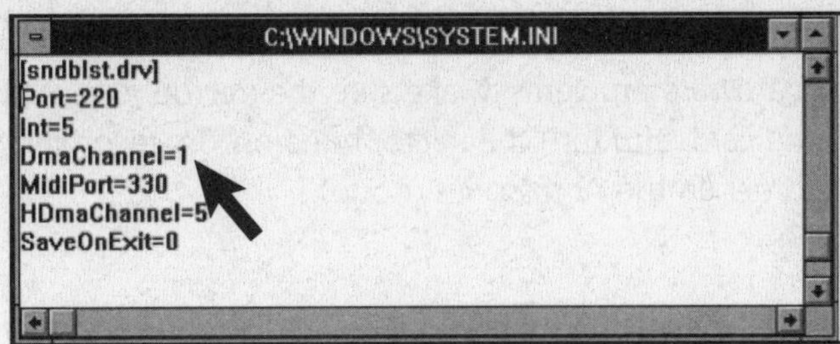

One more thing… If you get a message about the MIDI Port Setting in Windows 3.1 or 3.11, there's probably *nothing wrong with* the MIDI Port Setting. To solve the problem, exit Windows, turn off your computer, wait about 30 seconds, and restart your computer.

If you have problems with your sound card in Windows 95, try reinstalling the sound card using the Add New Hardware wizard. For details, see "Install Hardware in Windows 95" on page 439.

37: It's supposed to be in stereo!

If this problem just cropped up, chances are you turned off one of the speakers by mistake, or one speaker disconnected from the power source. (I had a pair of cheap speakers that constantly disconnected from the power source.)

If the problem has been present from day one, you probably selected the wrong output setting for the card. Run the sound card's setup or configuration utility again; make sure you've selected **stereo** (rather than mono) output. Also, if the sound card program (device driver) has a balance control, make sure it is set in the middle.

38: My microphone doesn't work.

If you have a Soundblaster (or compatible) card, and you're working in Windows, run the **SB16Mixer** utility (it's in the Soundblaster 16 group window). Crank up the **Mic** setting. Now open the **Options** menu, make sure **Save Settings on Exit** has a check mark next to it, and then exit the SB16 Mixer utility.

If you have a different type of card, or if adjusting the Mic setting doesn't help, check for hardware problems. Make sure the microphone is plugged into the Mic jack on the sound card, and turn the microphone on. Try recording with the Windows Sound Recorder (in the Accessories group).

CD-ROM Problems

39: The CD-ROM drive doesn't work.

Whenever something doesn't work (no lights, no sound, no sign of life), check the obvious first:

- Do you have an external CD-ROM drive? If so, make sure it is plugged in, connected to your system unit, and turned on.
- Make sure the drive has a *computer* CD-ROM in it (not an audio CD), and that the disc is inserted properly in the drive (writing-side-up).
- Did you install the drivers that came with the CD-ROM drive? Without a driver (instructions that tell your computer how to use a device), your CD-ROM drive won't respond.
- If you just installed the CD-ROM drive, check for hardware conflicts. Each device has a specific input/output address and interrupt assigned to it. If the address and interrupt conflict with another device, your CD-ROM drive won't work. Check the documentation that came with your CD-ROM drive and the other drives that are installed on your system.
- If you're having trouble in Windows 95, try running the Add New Hardware wizard. For details, see "Install Hardware in Windows 95" on page 439.

40: The drive seems to work all right, but I can't get at the files on the disc.

If you know that the CD-ROM drive has power—and that it's spinning the disc all right—you probably did not install the driver for the CD-ROM drive, or you installed the wrong driver. Try the following fixes:

- Make sure the correct driver is loading. There should be a command in your CONFIG.SYS file that loads the driver. You should see a command something like this:

  DEVICEHIGH=C:\CDROM\MTMCDAI.SYS /D:MTMIDE01 /P:170,15

  Check your CD-ROM documentation to find out the exact command to type. Also, make sure the driver specified in CONFIG.SYS is on your disk in the specified directory.

- Check AUTOEXEC.BAT for a line that has **MSCDEX.EXE** in it. Without this line, your computer won't recognize the CD-ROM drive. If the line is missing, add a line like **C:\DOS\MSCDEX.EXE /D:MTMIDE01 /M:10** to your AUTOEXEC.BAT file. Again, check your documentation to find out the exact command to enter.
- If the driver or MSCDEX.EXE is set up to load into the high memory area (with commands like LOADHIGH or DEVICEHIGH), remove the LOADHIGH (or LH) command and change DEVICEHIGH to **DEVICE**. This loads the drivers into conventional memory instead. For details on how to edit CONFIG.SYS and AUTOEXEC.BAT, see "Modify Your Startup Files in Windows 3.11 and DOS" on page 412.
- If you're having trouble in Windows 95, try running the Add New Hardware wizard. For details, see "Install Hardware in Windows 95" on page 439.

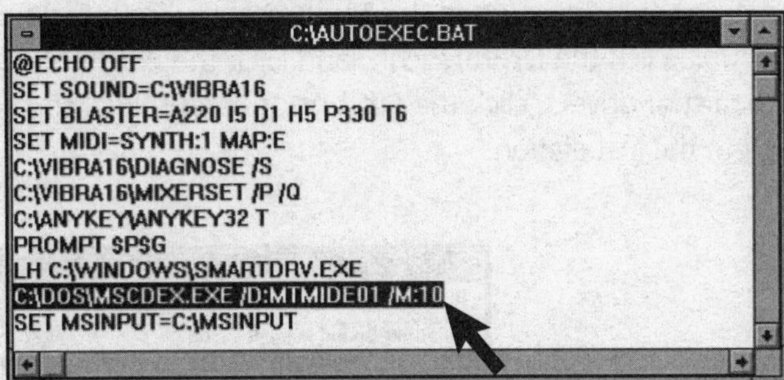

41: The CD-ROM drive locks up my system.

Don't jump to conclusions. Is it the CD-ROM drive or the application you're running from the disc? If your computer freezes up when you run a particular application, it's the application's fault. Check the documentation that came with the application to determine whether there's a fix for the problem. If you can't find anything, call the developer's technical support line.

If every CD-ROM application you try to run freezes your system, you probably have a hardware conflict. One of your other devices (maybe a sound board or the mouse) is in conflict with your CD-ROM drive. You'll have to check the documentation to find out which settings are conflicting, and then change the settings on one of the devices. Refer to "Install New Hardware" on page 415 for more information on how to resolve hardware conflicts.

42: Where's the sound supposed to come from?

Most CD-ROM drives have two sound output jacks: one on the front and one (or two for stereo output) on the back. The front jack is for a set of earphones. Plug the earphones in, and you can jam while you're playing DOOM.

The jack on the back allows you to connect the drive to a set of amplified speakers or to a sound card. If you have a sound card, you'll probably want to connect the CD-ROM sound output jacks to the sound card's input jacks. Then, connect the sound card's output jacks to your speakers. You end up with a ball of tangled wire behind your computer, but the sound quality is pretty good.

43: What about music CDs?

Most newer CD-ROM players can play audio CDs, but you need a special program to play them. Most sound cards and CD-ROM players come with the program you need. For example, Soundblaster 16 comes with a program called QuickCD that enables you to play audio CDs in DOS or Windows.

Windows 3.1 requires a special driver, as well—it's called the MCI Audio driver. To activate this driver, open the **Main** group window, double-click the **Control Panel** icon, double-click the **Drivers** icon, and click the **Add** button. Select **[MCI] CD Audio** from the list of drivers, click the **OK** button, and follow the on-screen instructions to complete the installation.

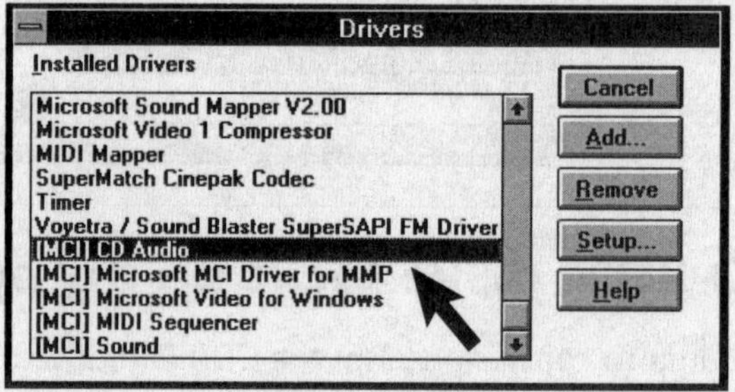

If [MCI] CD Audio is not on the list of drivers, look for a file on your Windows installation disks named **MCICDA.DR_**. Insert the disk in the floppy drive (A or B). Then, go to the DOS prompt, change to the WINDOWS directory, and type

```
expand a:mcicda.dr_ c:\windows\system\mcicda.drv
```

or

```
expand b:mcicda.dr_ c:\windows\system\mcicda.drv
```

Press **Enter**. You can now perform the steps given in the previous paragraph to activate the driver.

If you have Windows 95, playing audio CDs is a no-brainer. You simply load the audio CD into the CD-ROM drive and close the drawer. Windows 95 starts playing the CD automatically.

44: The movie clips are s-l-o-w.

Buy a computer with a 100MHz Pentium chip and a 4X ("quad-speed") CD-ROM drive. My point is that movie clips require a pretty fast computer. If you have a 486SX 25MHz computer with 4 megabytes of RAM, you can expect the movies to crawl.

The only way you can really speed up a CD-ROM drive is to use a *disk caching* program (such as SmartDrive). Check your CONFIG.SYS and AUTOEXEC.BAT files to make sure one of the files has a command line that loads SmartDrive. If neither file has the command, add the following command to AUTOEXEC.BAT (add the command before the command that loads MSCDEX):

```
c:\dos\smartdrv.exe
```

In Windows 95, you can increase the speed of the CD-ROM drive simply by telling Windows the speed of your CD-ROM drive. To do this, double-click the **System** icon in the Control Panel. Click the **Performance** tab, and then click the **File System** button. From the **Optimize access pattern for** drop-down list, click the speed of your CD-ROM drive (the speed is usually etched into the front of the drive). You can drag the **Supplemental cache size** slider to the right to increase the cache size for the drive, but this uses additional memory. Increase the cache size only if you use the CD-ROM drive frequently.

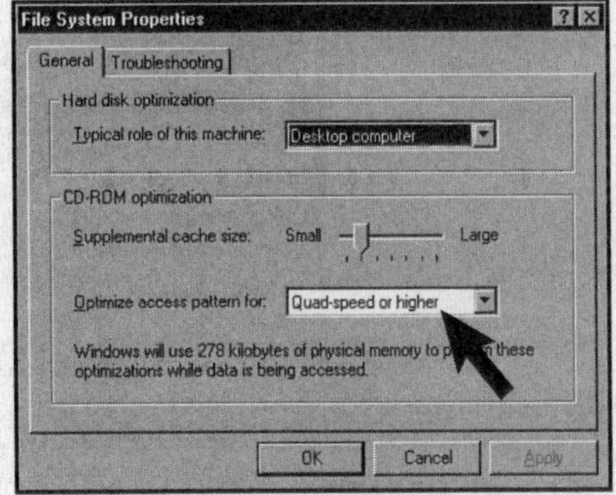

45: I stood my system unit on end, and now the CD-ROM drive is slow.

Never set a system unit that's equipped with a CD-ROM drive on its side. Besides the fact that you'll have a hard time inserting the disk, CD-ROM drives aren't built to spin vertically.

Printing Problems

46: My printer won't print.

Make sure the printer has paper, is plugged in and turned on, and that the **On Line** light is lit (not blinking). You can usually make this light come on by filling the printer with paper, and then pressing the **On Line** button, the **Reset** button, or the **Load** button... what the heck, press all the buttons (just kidding).

If everything checks out, and the printer still won't print, look for the following:

- If you have a tractor-feed mechanism on the printer, make sure the sheet feeder switch is in the proper position: for single-sheets or continuous forms.
- Check your printer setup in the application you're printing from to make sure it's sending the data to the right printer port (usually **LPT1**). In Windows, do the following to check the printer port: open the **Main** group window, double-click the **Control Panel** icon, double-click **Printers**, and click the **Connect** button. Pick the correct printer port, and then click the **OK** button.

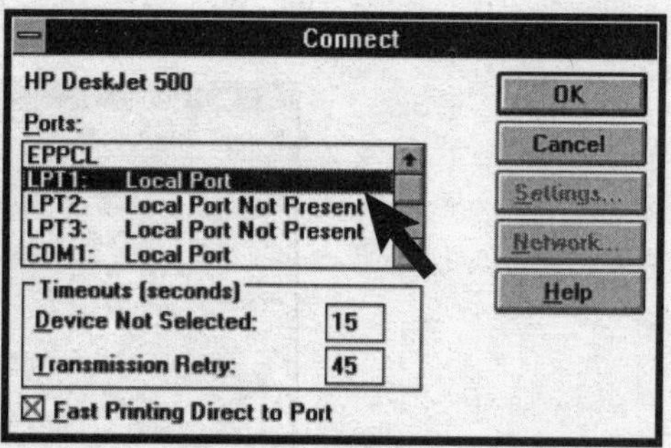

- Are you having problems in only one application? If you can print from other applications, the problem is with the printer setup in the problem application.
- Is it a printer problem? To determine whether the printer has a problem, type **dir > lpt1** at the DOS prompt and press **Enter**. This prints the current directory list. If it prints okay, the problem is in the Windows printer setup—or the application's setup. If the directory does not print (or prints incorrectly), the problem is probably with the printer. Most printers have a self-test; check the documentation to figure out how to run the test for your printer.

If you've tried everything and the printer still isn't responding, your printed documents might be "stuck in traffic" in the *print queue*. Skip to the next topic to learn how to proceed.

47: I tried three times to print this thing, and I haven't gotten even one copy!

Your printed documents are in the *print queue*—a waiting line. Applications commonly send printed documents to disk, and then feed them from disk to the printer. If something goes wrong, the document has to stand in line until the printer is ready. If you keep entering the print command over and over, you end up with a long line of documents.

In Microsoft Windows 3.1 and 3.11, a program called Print Manager handles the printing for all your applications. To view the Print Manager's queue, here's what you do:

1. Press **Ctrl+Esc**. The Task List appears, showing the names of all the applications. If documents are waiting in the queue, Print Manager should appear in the list.
2. Click **Print Manager**.
3. Click **Switch To**. The Print Manager window appears, showing a list of files waiting in the print queue.
4. Click the printer you're using. It should be marked **[Stalled]**.
5. Click the **Resume** button. Printing should start.

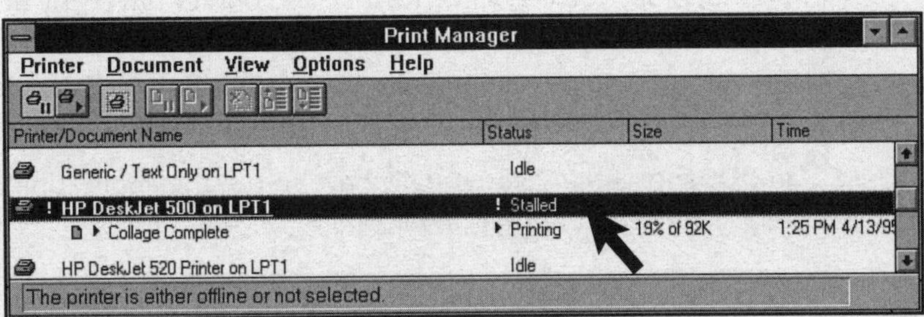

If you're working with a DOS application, it probably has its own print queue (or *spooler*) that handles background printing. Check the documentation to find out what the application calls its queue, and where it stores the command to get to it.

> In Windows 95, you can quickly view the print queue by double-clicking the printer icon in the taskbar. Whenever you start printing, the printer icon appears on the right side of the taskbar, next to the time display.

48: It prints all right, but the print looks like garbage.

If you get a bunch of foreign-looking symbols, you selected the wrong printer driver. In Windows 3.1 or 3.11, do the following to check the printer driver:

1. Open the **Main** group window, and double-click the **Control Panel** icon.
2. Double-click **Printers**. The Installed Printers list appears, showing the names of the printers that Windows is set up to use.
3. Click the printer you're using, and then click the **Set As Default Printer** button.
4. Click the **Close** button to save your changes.

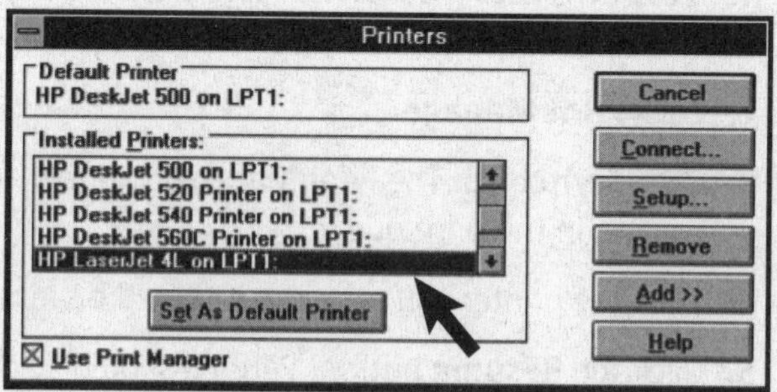

In Windows 95, you can view the installed printer drivers by double-clicking the **My Computer** icon and then double-clicking the **Printers** icon. Right-click on the printer driver you want to use as the default, and click **Set As Default**.

> In DOS applications, you usually have to run the application's setup utility again to select a different printer driver.

If you have an off-brand printer, you can probably set it up to *emulate* (act like) a brand-name printer. In most cases, you have to pry open a panel on the printer and flip some DIP switches to turn on the emulation. The printer documentation tells you how to get to the switches, which ones you need to flip, and what position each one has to be in. You then select the printer driver for the brand-name printer.

If by "the print looks like garbage" you mean that the print is too light or streaky, you may have to change the print cartridge or ribbon (or clean it). Before cleaning an inkjet cartridge, read the instructions. I once destroyed a $20 cartridge by swabbing the wrong area with alcohol.

49: It prints only half of a page!

Laser printers (and some inkjets) are weird; they print an entire page at one time, storing the entire page in memory. If the page has a big, complex graphic image (or lots of fonts), the printer may be able to store only a portion of the page. The best fix is to get more memory for your printer.

The quickest fix is to use fewer fonts on the page and try using a less complex graphic image. You might also try printing the document at a lower resolution. In most applications (and in Windows), you can choose a lower resolution through the printer setup.

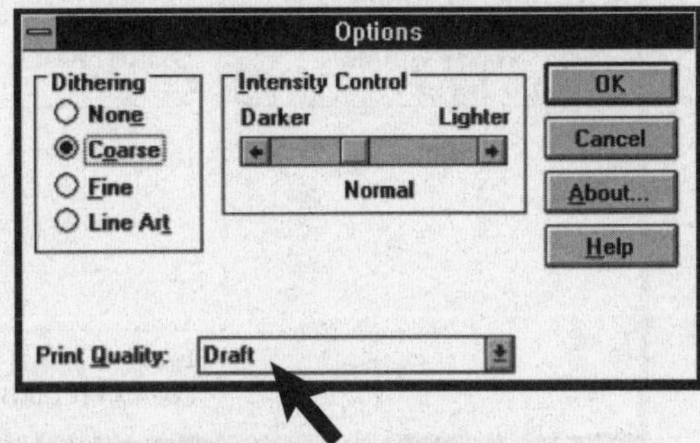

50: I can't get the type lined up right.

If the print is too close to the top or bottom of the page, you can usually make adjustments using the printer's controls. Most dot-matrix printers have a *feed adjustment button* that allows you to move the page up or down a short distance for minor problems. With inkjet and laser printers, the feed is controlled internally, and you usually don't have a problem with aligning text at the top or bottom of the page.

If the print is too close to the left or right edge of the page, you might be able to adjust how the paper feeds into the printer. If you can't make adjustments on the printer itself, try changing your margins in your document. If the entire document is out of whack, be sure to select the entire document before changing margins.

Most inkjet and dot-matrix printers have a *non-printable* region around the page. If you set the margins too narrow, you might end up having text chopped off the left or right side of the page. Try increasing (widening) the margins to move the text back into the printable region of the paper.

51: The print on-screen doesn't match the page.

Fonts typically come in pairs—one font for the printer and one for the screen. If the *printer font* has no matching *screen font*, the application takes liberties and selects a screen font it thinks looks like the printer font.

To correct this problem, make sure you install both the screen and printer font for every font you use. If you're using fonts in Windows, keep in mind that TrueType fonts (displayed with a **TT** on Windows menus) consist of one font that controls both the screen and the printer. By using TrueType fonts only, you're sure to get in print what you see on the screen.

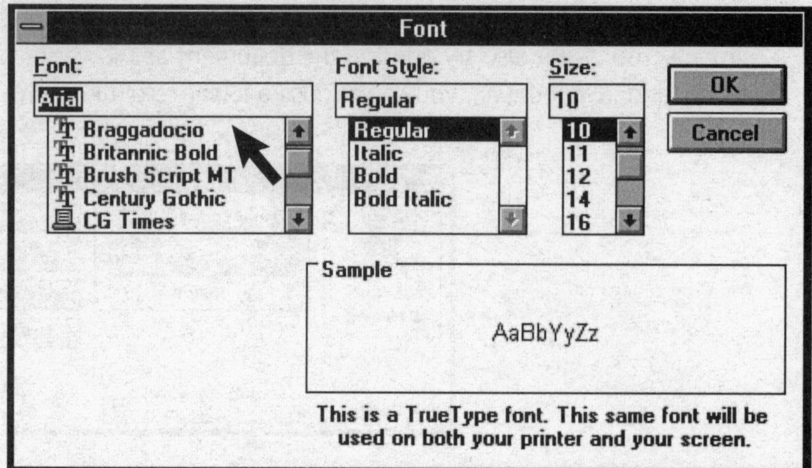

52: I hate these paper jams.

You can prevent most paper jams by loading the paper properly into the printer. With laser and inkjet printers, be sure not to fill the paper trays too full. Also, use the recommended weight and type of paper.

53: Is it always this slow?

Yes—printing is one of the slowest operations a computer performs, especially if you're printing complex color graphics. There are, however, a few things you can do to speed up printing:

- Don't do anything else while you're printing. If you work in another application while you're printing, you use computer resources that might otherwise be used solely for printing.
- Add memory to your printer. This shifts the work load from your computer to your printer.
- In Windows 3.1 or 3.11, run the Print Manager (from the Main window), open the **Options** menu, and select **High Priority**. Windows allocates more computing power to your print jobs, and less to any other tasks you're trying to perform.
- Use the latest printer driver. New, improved printer drivers usually print faster. Contact the printer manufacturer to find out whether they've created any new drivers for your printer. (A driver is a program that tells Windows or an application how to communicate with the printer.)
- In Windows (all versions), use TrueType fonts (fonts marked **TT**).
- Use only the built-in printer fonts. Most printers have about a dozen built-in fonts that aren't very fancy, but they do print fast. (In Windows applications, printer fonts have a printer icon next to them.)

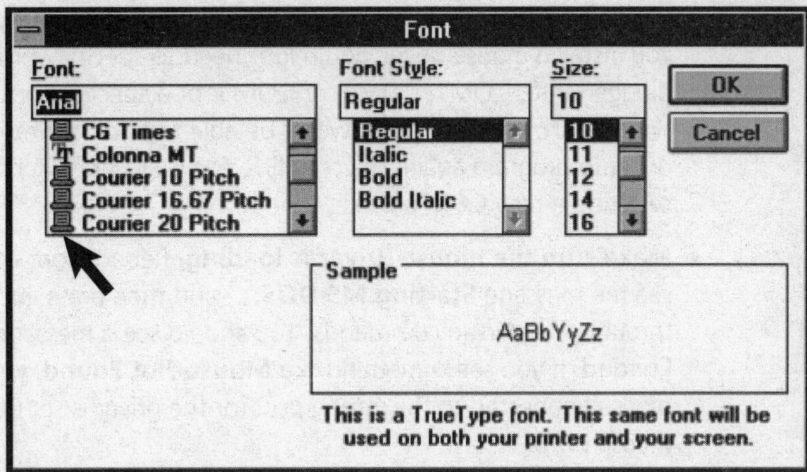

Mouse Problems

54: My mouse doesn't work, period.

If you don't even get a mouse pointer, make sure your mouse is plugged securely into the correct port, and then check the following:

- **When you connected the mouse, did you install a mouse driver?** Connecting a mouse to your computer is not enough. You must install a *mouse driver* that tells the computer how to use the mouse. If you have a mouse setup program, run it. If the mouse didn't come with a setup program, it should have a file called MOUSE.EXE or MOUSE.SYS. Make a directory called **MOUSE**, copy the mouse files to that directory, and then add the command **C:\MOUSE\MOUSE.EXE** to your AUTOEXEC.BAT file or **DEVICE=C:\MOUSE\MOUSE.SYS** to your CONFIG.SYS file. Then reboot your computer. (You should have a mouse command in *either* the AUTOEXEC.BAT or CONFIG.SYS FILE, *not both*. Running two mouse drivers is as bad as running no mouse driver.)

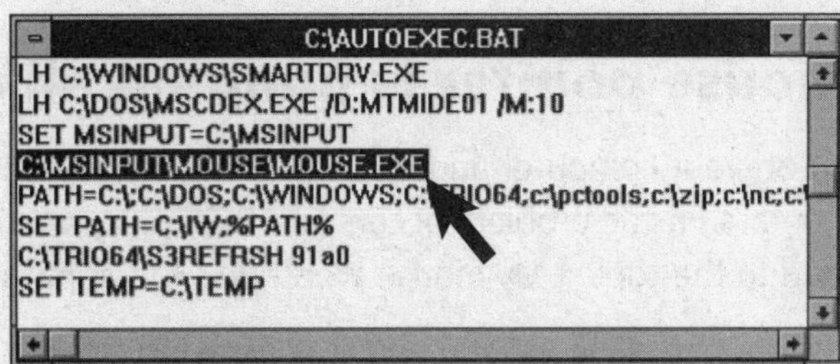

- **When you installed the mouse driver, did you specify a COM port?** When you install a mouse driver, you might need to specify which port the mouse is plugged into: COM1, COM2, or COM3, or a special mouse port. If you pick the wrong port, your computer won't be able to find your mouse. Run the installation or setup program again; select a different COM port. Reboot your computer after selecting a new COM port.
- **Make sure the mouse driver is loading.** Reboot your computer, wait until you see the message **Starting MS-DOS...**, and then press and release the F8 key. Step through the startup commands. You should see a message like **Mouse Driver Loaded**. If you see something like **Mouse Not Found**, you probably have the mouse connected to the wrong port (or the driver is set up to use the wrong mouse port).
- **Look for a README file in the MOUSE directory.** Some mice have strange quirks that are documented in a README.TXT file. Look for such a file in your MOUSE directory, open it, and read it. You can view a README file at the DOS prompt by changing to the directory that contains the file, and then entering **type readme.txt lmore**. The **lmore** switch tells DOS to display one screen at a time.
- **Is the mouse pointer hidden?** Mouse pointers like to hide in the corners or edges of your screen. Roll the mouse on your desktop to see if you can bring the pointer into view.
- **Are you in a program that uses a mouse?** Some programs don't *support* (aren't designed to run with) a mouse; you won't see the mouse pointer in these programs. For example, you won't see a mouse pointer at the DOS prompt, but you should see one in the DOS Shell. Run a program that you know uses a mouse to see whether it works there.
- Do you have the mouse problem in Windows 95? To change a mouse setting, press **Ctrl+Esc**, press **Esc**, and then press the **Tab** key until My Computer is highlighted. Press **Enter**. Use the arrow keys to highlight the Mouse icon, and press **Enter**. If you can't even get the mouse pointer to appear, press **Ctrl+PgDn** to select the General tab, and then press **Alt+C** to select the Change button. Use the down arrow key to select the mouse manufacturer. Press **Tab** and use the down arrow key to select the mouse model you have. Press **Enter** to save your change.

55: My mouse pointer is jumping all over the screen.

Turn off your computer and clean your mouse. (See "Clean the Mouse" on page 338 for details.) If the problem occurs in a DOS program running under Windows, skip ahead to the topic "My mouse won't do DOS applications from Windows."

If you clean the mouse and you're still having trouble, open your CONFIG.SYS and AUTOEXEC.BAT files; make sure you have only one mouse driver loading. If you find a mouse command line in both files, add **REM** plus a space before *one* of the commands. For details on how to edit CONFIG.SYS and AUTOEXEC.BAT, see "Modify Your Startup Files in Windows 3.11 and DOS" on page 412.

If you're having trouble with MOUSE.SYS, and you have a MOUSE.EXE (or MOUSE.COM) file, remove the MOUSE.SYS command from CONFIG.SYS, add the MOUSE.EXE (or MOUSE.COM) command to AUTOEXEC.BAT, and then reboot your computer.

If that doesn't work, call the mouse manufacturer and make sure you have the latest mouse driver (the program that tells your computer how to use the mouse). Microsoft, Logitech, and other mouse manufacturers constantly improve their mouse drivers to correct for bugs that crop up in the latest programs.

56: I installed a modem, and now the mouse doesn't work!

Mice and modems both use COM ports. Normally the mouse uses COM1 and the modem uses COM2. If your mouse and modem don't seem to get along, they're probably set to use the same COM port. Leave the mouse port setting as is, and try changing the setting for the modem. Here's what you do:

1. If you have an internal modem, look at the back of it for a set of tiny switches. These switches let you change the COM port setting for the card itself.
2. If you find the switches, write down their original positions, and then flip the switches to select a different COM port (try **COM2** or **COM4**). (If you don't see switches, you might have to go inside your computer to change jumpers on the modem card; consult the documentation.)
3. Once you've changed the COM port on the hardware, you must change it in the telecommunications program you're using. This can be a fax program, online service, Internet program, Windows Terminal, or whatever program you use with your modem. In America Online, for example, you click the **Setup** button, select **Setup Modem**, and then click the COM port setting, as shown here.

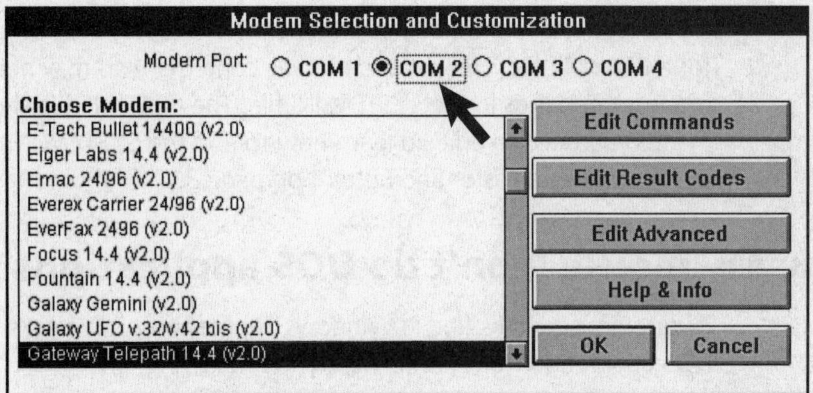

In Windows 95, you can change the modem's COM port setting by selecting the **Modems** icon in the Control Panel and selecting the **Diagnostics** tab (you can change tabs by pressing **Ctrl+PgDn**). Press **Alt+H** or click the **Help** button to run the Modem Troubleshooter. The Troubleshooter will ask you a series of questions to help you identify the problem and fix it.

57: My mouse won't do Windows.

First, make sure the mouse is set up on COM1 or COM2 (in Windows, the mouse won't work on COM3 or COM4). Then, make sure you have the correct mouse driver loaded in Windows 3.1 or 3.11:

1. Open the **Main** group window, and double-click the **Windows Setup** icon.
2. Open the **Options** menu, and select **Change System Settings**. The Change System Settings dialog box appears.
3. Open the **Mouse** drop-down list, and click the driver for your mouse. If you're unsure, select a **Microsoft** mouse driver (most mice are Microsoft-compatible).

In Windows 95, you can change all your mouse settings by double-clicking the **Mouse** icon in the Control Panel. But, if you can't use your mouse, you can't click. So, to pick a different mouse driver with your keyboard, press **Ctrl+Esc**, press **Esc**, and then press the **Tab** key until My Computer is highlighted. Press **Enter**. Use the arrow keys to highlight the Mouse icon, and press **Enter**. If you can't even get the mouse pointer to appear, press **Ctrl+PgDn** to select the General tab, and then press **Alt+C** to select the Change button. Use the down arrow key to select the mouse manufacturer. Press **Tab** and use the down arrow key to select the mouse model you have. Press **Enter** to save your change.

If you're still having trouble in Windows 3.1 or 3.11, look in your mouse driver directory for a README file. Open it and read its contents. You may need to edit some of the mouse commands in the SYSTEM.INI file. The README file should tell you which commands you need to edit. To learn how to edit the SYSTEM.INI file, see "Make Your Computer Work Faster and Better" on page 387.

58: My mouse won't do DOS applications from Windows.

If your mouse works fine in Windows applications, but freaks out when you try to run a DOS application from Windows, try the following fixes:

- **If the DOS application is in a window, press Alt+Enter to run it in full-screen mode.** If you can use the mouse in full-screen mode (in Windows 3.1 or 3.11), try adding the following command to the **[NonWindowsApp]** section of your SYSTEM.INI file:

  MouseInDosBox=1

1 means Yes (you do want the mouse pointer to appear in a DOS window).

In Windows 95, you can make a DOS application run in full-screen mode. Right-click on the program's icon, and select **Properties**. Click the **Screen** tab, and click **Full-screen**. Click **OK** to save your change.

- **Make sure the correct mouse is selected in Windows.** In Windows 3.1 or 3.11, open the **Main** group window, double-click the **Windows Setup** icon, open the **Options** menu, and select **Change System Settings**. Open the **Mouse** drop-down list, and select the mouse you're using.

  In Windows 95, double-click **My Computer**, double-click **Control Panel**, and then double-click the **Mouse** icon. Click the **General** tab. If the correct mouse driver is not displayed, click the **Change** button, and then select the correct manufacturer and model.

- **Make sure only one mouse driver is running.** If both AUTOEXEC.BAT and CONFIG.SYS contain a mouse command, use the **REM** command to disable the **DEVICE=MOUSE.SYS** command in **CONFIG.SYS**. Usually, MOUSE.COM (or MOUSE.EXE) works better.

- **Use the latest version of the mouse driver.** If you have an old mouse driver (pre-version-8.20), contact the mouse manufacturer and ask for an updated driver. If you upgrade to the latest DOS version, you might already have the driver you need. Check the **C:\DOS** directory for a file called **MOUSE.COM**. Add the command **C:\DOS\MOUSE.COM** to your AUTOEXEC.BAT file, and remove all other references to mouse drivers in AUTOEXEC.BAT and CONFIG.SYS.

- **Make sure there is only one MOUSE.INI file on your hard drive.** In Windows 3.1 or 3.11, use the File Manager's Search feature (select **File**, and then **Search**) to find the MOUSE.INI files. Delete all the MOUSE.INI files except the one in the \WINDOWS directory. Windows 95 doesn't use a MOUSE.INI file to control your mouse.

- **Use the VGA driver that came with Windows.** In Windows 3.1 or 3.11, open the **Main** group window, double-click the **Windows Setup** icon, open the **Options** menu, and select **Change System Settings**. Open the **Display** drop-down list, and select **VGA**. This tells Windows to use its standard VGA driver. (This might solve your DOS problem, but reduce the quality of the display in Windows applications. Check with the manufacturer of the display card you're using to see about a permanent fix.)

You can change video drivers in Windows 95 by right-clicking on a blank area of the Windows desktop and selecting **Properties**. Click the **Settings** tab, and then click **Change Display Type** to view the current video driver and change it, if desired.

59: My mouse pointer moves too fast or too slow.

You can usually change the mouse speed by running a mouse setup program at the DOS prompt or in Windows. Setup programs usually let you change the mouse speed, flip the mouse buttons (for left-hand use), and change the double-click interval (the speed at which you have to click twice when you enter a "double-click").

In DOS, find the directory that contains the mouse files, and then look for a SETUP or MSETUP program file. In Windows 3.1 or 3.11, take the following steps:

1. Open the **Main** group window, and double-click the **Control Panel** icon.
2. Double-click the **Mouse** icon. The Mouse dialog box appears.
3. Drag the box in the **Mouse Tracking Speed** control bar to the left to slow down the mouse pointer, or to the right to speed it up.
4. Click the **OK** button to save your changes.

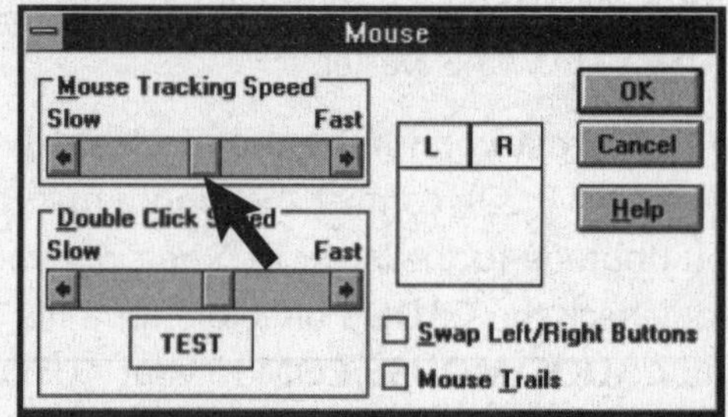

In Windows 95, double-click the **Mouse** icon in the Control Panel (**Start**, **Settings**, **Control Panel**) to change your mouse settings. Click the **Motion** tab in the Mouse Properties dialog box to change the speed at which the mouse pointer travels across the screen.

Keyboard Problems

60: My keyboard doesn't work at all.

Turn your computer off; make sure your keyboard is plugged securely into the keyboard port (usually at the back of the system unit). Also make sure the cord is connected securely to the keyboard; you might have to flip the keyboard over to do this. Then turn on your computer. (Never connect or disconnect a keyboard or any other device when the computer is on.) If the keyboard still doesn't work, check the following:

- Is the computer locked? Many computers come with a lock and key most people never use. If you keep the keys in the lock, however, someone might have turned the key for fun. After unlocking the computer, you usually have to press a special key to proceed with the boot operation.

- Turn off your computer, unplug the keyboard from the computer, and check to see whether any pins in the keyboard plug are bent or pushed in. (When my son was six, he tried plugging in the keyboard—and ended up jamming three of the pins.) You can usually repair the plug with a pair of long-nose pliers and a gentle touch. Be careful when plugging it back in.
- Did the keyboard stop working after you ran MemMaker? You probably ran MemMaker with the option to scan the upper memory area aggressively. MemMaker may have taken the memory area used by the keyboard. Enter **memmaker /undo** at the DOS prompt, and follow the on-screen instructions. If you choose to run MemMaker again, set the **Scan the upper memory area aggressively?** option to No.
- If the keyboard doesn't work in Windows 3.1 or 3.11, open the **Main** group Window, and double-click the **Windows Setup** icon. Open the **Options** menu and select **Change System Settings**. From the **Keyboard** drop-down list, select the keyboard that matches yours. If you're not sure, select the **Enhanced** option.

  In Windows 95, double-click the **Keyboard** icon in the Control Panel (you can display the Control Panel by double-clicking **My Computer** and then **Control Panel**). Click the **General** tab to see which keyboard Windows is set up to use. Click the **Change** button to change the keyboard type.

If you can't bring your keyboard back to life, maybe it's fried (or maybe the keyboard cord is damaged). If you have access to another keyboard, plug it into your computer and see if it works. If the other keyboard works, your keyboard is dead. If you're personally attached to your keyboard, you can take it to a repair shop, but it's probably cheaper to just buy a new one.

61: I get a "Keyboard not found" message.

Either your keyboard plug popped out of its socket, or your computer is locked. Check the lock first. If that doesn't solve your problem, turn off your computer and make sure the keyboard is plugged in. Some keyboards have a connector on the keyboard, too (the connector looks like a phone connector); check this connection while you're at it.

62: When I type, everything is in UPPERCASE LETTERS.

You pressed the Caps Lock key by mistake. Press it again to return your keyboard to normal. By the way, if you're "talking" to someone on an online service (conversing by typing), it's considered bad manners to type in all uppercase letters—it's the equivalent of shouting.

63: Everything I type replaces existing text.

You changed from Insert mode to Overtype mode. In Insert mode, all text is inserted at the cursor position, and surrounding text is adjusted to make room for the new text. In Overtype mode, everything you type replaces existing text. In most applications, you can switch back to Insert mode by pressing the **Ins** key. If that doesn't work, check the documentation or the application's Help system to determine how to change modes.

64: I press one key and it acts like a different one.

If you have a Gateway computer, you inadvertently remapped your keyboard. Some keyboards have a Remap feature that allows you to make one key act like another. Advanced users like to remap keys to customize the keyboard and make it a real time-saver. The rest of us dream about replacing our keyboard with one that has no Remap key.

If you happen to remap a few keys, you can bring them back to normal. Press the **Remap** key, and then press the key you remapped twice. This essentially maps the key to itself. On a Gateway AnyKey keyboard, you can return the entire keyboard to normal by pressing **Ctrl+Alt+Suspnd Macro**.

65: Each key I press beeps at me.

Could be that the *keyboard buffer* is full (the buffer holds approximately 15-20 keystrokes). Maybe the computer is busy performing some other task, and can't give the keyboard its full attention yet. Wait until the computer is finished with whatever task it's performing, and then try typing again.

If you waited and you're still getting beeps, maybe you're pressing the wrong keys. Some applications beep if you click an option or press a key that's not currently available. If you know you're pressing the right keys, exit the application, return to the DOS prompt, and reboot your computer.

If the problem persists, turn off your computer and check your keyboard connections. If the keyboard is securely connected, maybe the wiring inside the cable is damaged, or maybe your keyboard is on the blink.

Modem Problems

66: There's no sign of life—no dialing, no lights, no modem.

If nothing happens, or if your communications program displays a distress signal saying that it cannot find the modem, try the following to determine the cause:

- Run your communications program or **Windows Terminal** (in the **Accessories** group in all versions of Windows). Type **AT** and press **Enter**. If you get an **OK** message, your modem and COM port settings are okay. Check the settings in the application you're using to determine whether they're correct for your modem.
- Type **ATDT** followed by your phone number, and press **Enter**. The modem should dial, and you should get a message that says **Busy**. This tells you that your modem is capable of dialing out, and that the problem is probably with the modem setup in the application you're using. Check your setup to make sure you have the correct modem selected.
- If you have an external modem, make sure the power is turned on and the modem is plugged into the serial (COM) port on your computer. Then make sure the correct COM port is selected in the application (usually **COM 2**).
- Keep trying to dial with different COM port settings until the modem dials or you run out of COM port settings to try. Most internal modems have tiny switches on the back that you can flip to give the modem a different COM port setting. Make sure the COM port setting in your communications program matches the COM port setting on your modem.
- In most cases, your mouse is set up to use COM1, and your modem is on COM2. If your modem is set up to use COM3, the mouse on COM1 might conflict with it. Try changing the modem to **COM2** or **COM4**.
- Plug a regular phone into the phone jack and make sure you get a dial tone. Also, check the phone plug connection on the modem and phone jack. (I once encountered a brand-new modem that was missing one of the copper contacts inside the modem jack.) Make sure all the contacts are there, and that the cable you're using is in good shape.

In Windows 95, you can use the Modem Troubleshooter to fix any modem problems. First, display the Control Panel (click **Start**, point to **Settings**, and click **Control Panel**). Double-click the **Modems** icon, and then click the **Diagnostics** tab. Click the **Help** button. The Modem Troubleshooter screen appears. Answer the questions to determine the cause of the problem and fix it.

67: My modem dials, but never connects.

Well, your modem is working, but you may have a problem with the number you're dialing or with the phone line. Check the following:

- Is the Line jack connected to the phone jack on the wall? Most modems have two jacks: one marked **Phone** and one marked **Line**. Make sure you connect the line jack to the wall jack.
- Did you set up your application correctly for *pulse* or *tone* dialing? Pick up your phone, and dial a couple numbers. If you hear tones of various pitches, you have tone service. If you hear clicks, you have rotary (or pulse) service. Select the type of

service in your application's Modem Setup dialog box, or use **ATDT** to make a tone call or **ATDP** for rotary (pulse) service.

- Do you need to dial a special number to get an outside line? If you work in an office, you may have to dial a 9 or some other number to get an outside line. Add this number, followed by a comma, before the phone number you want to dial. The comma tells the modem to pause before dialing the rest of the number, to wait for a dial tone.

68: I keep getting a busy signal.

You may not hear it, but if a message appears on-screen saying the line is busy, the computer you're calling is all tied up with incoming calls. Enter the **Hangup** command, and try again later. Also, check the number you're dialing.

69: I hear voices from the modem.

You dialed the wrong number. If your phone is plugged into your modem, lift the receiver and apologize for dialing the wrong number. (If your phone isn't connected, you'll notice that the voice keeps getting more and more angry, and then the person hangs up.) Check the phone number you entered, and pray that this guy doesn't have Caller ID.

70: My modem dials and then immediately disconnects or displays a NO CARRIER message.

Look at the bright side; at least your modem is working. You probably have a problem with your telecommunications settings or with your login entries:

- If you're trying to call a bulletin board or online service that requires you to enter a name and password, maybe your name and password entries are wrong (or you didn't pay your bills).
- Make sure you have the correct modem selected. In most applications, you can select the type of modem from a list. If your modem isn't listed, check the documentation to find out its *modem initialization string*; enter this manually. (The modem initialization string sets preferences for how the modem operates. For example, **ATM0** mutes the modem, so it makes no sound as it dials.)
- Try setting the baud rate (the speed at which modems transfer data) to a slower speed. Maybe the service or BBS you're calling can handle only 2400 bps. (Most newer modems have an *automatic fallback* feature that enables the modem to pick a slower baud rate automatically if necessary.)
- Check the *terminal emulation*. The terminal emulation setting tells your computer how to act when connecting to another computer. This is usually **DEC VT-100**, but if that doesn't work, try a different emulation.

- Check the following communications settings: data bits, parity, and stop bits. Most computers are set up to use **8** data bits, **No** parity, and **1** stop bit. Try to reconnect using these standard settings. The figure that follows shows the dialog box used to enter communications settings for Windows Terminal.

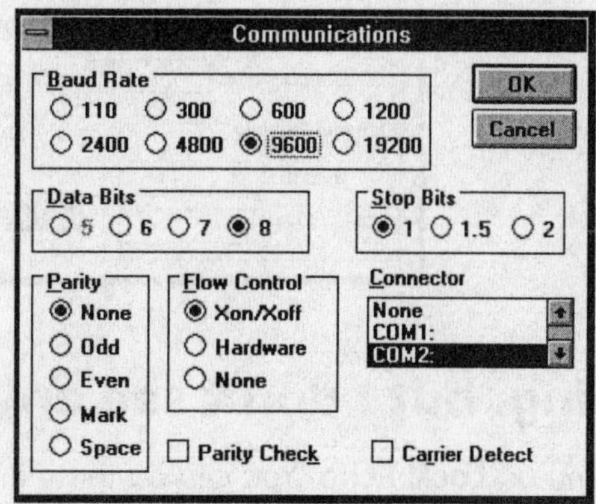

71: I have call waiting; whenever I get a call, I lose my modem.

Any interference on the phone line can disconnect the modem. To disable call waiting, pick up the receiver and dial ***70** (or ***1170** if you have pulse or rotary service). This disables call waiting for your next call. When you disconnect, call waiting is re-enabled automatically.

Windows 95 comes with a special option that can disable call waiting for you. Display the Modems Properties dialog box (by double-clicking the **Modems** icon in the Control Panel). Then, click the **Dialing Properties** button. Click **This location has call waiting** and then pick the number you would have to dial to disable it from the **To disable it, dial** drop-down list. Click the **OK** button to save your change.

72: Do I *have to* listen while my modem dials?

No. You can silence your modem speaker by entering the command **ATM0** (that's "A-T-M-Zero") in your telecommunications program (or by adding it to your modem initialization screen). This tells your modem to set the speaker volume at zero. To turn the speaker volume back on, type **ATM1**.

Some online services (CompuServe, for example) allow you to turn the modem speaker off in the modem setup dialog box. In other services, you have to add the **ATM0** code to the modem initialization string.

In Windows 95, you can set the modem speaker volume through the Modems Properties dialog box. To display the dialog box, double-click the **Modems** icon in the Control Panel. Click the **Properties** button. Under **Speaker Volume**, drag the slider to the left to lower the volume or to the right to crank it up. Click **OK** to save your change.

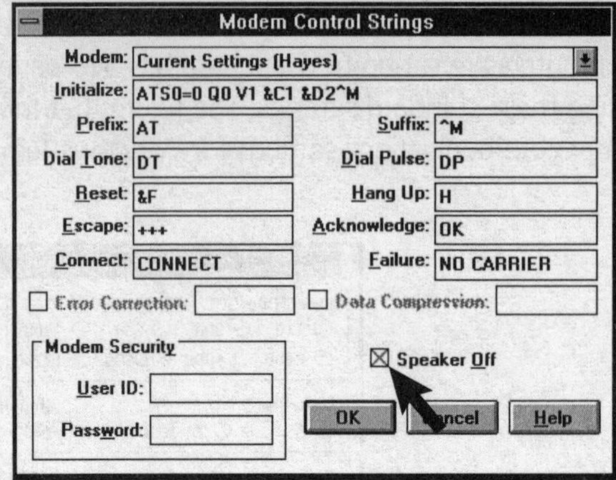

73: I'm typing, but I don't see anything.

Try turning on **Local Echo**. You can do this manually in a telecommunications program by entering **ATE1**.

74: Everything I type comes up double.

Change the **Duplex** setting to **Full** and the **Local Echo** setting to **Off**. Full Duplex means the computer can send and receive data at the same time. Local Echo makes everything you type appear on your screen. If the remote computer is also echoing everything you type, you get a double echo.

Problems with DOS

75: My screen displays "Abort, Retry, Fail?". Which should I pick?

This message usually follows another message that states the nature of the problem. Read that message first. If there's anything you can do to correct the problem (such as inserting a disk into drive A), correct the problem and type **R** for Retry. Otherwise type **A** for Abort. If Abort doesn't work, type **F** for Fail.

76: I try to run my program, and I keep getting a "Bad command or file name" message.

First, make sure you're typing the command correctly; check the program's documentation. Also, try changing to the directory that contains the program's files. Usually the installation program places the program's files in a separate directory on your hard disk. In order to run the program, first you have to change to its directory. Here's what you do:

1. To find out the names of the directories on your hard disk, type **cd** and press **Enter**. This changes to the beginning (root) directory of the current drive.
2. Type **dir /a:d /w** and press **Enter**. DOS displays the names of all the directories that branch off from the root directory.
3. To change to one of the listed directories, type **cd *dirname*** (where *dirname* is the name of the directory) and press **Enter**. CD stands for "change directory."
4. Type **dir /w** and press **Enter** to view a list of files in the directory. Any files that end in .BAT, .COM, or .EXE are *executable*—files that might run the program.
5. Type the file's name (without the .BAT, .COM, or .EXE extension) and press **Enter**.

77: When I try to copy a file, DOS tells me that the file cannot be copied onto itself.

You're trying to copy a file to a drive and directory that contain a file of the same name. You have two options: copy the file to a different drive or directory, or give the copy a new name. To rename a file as you copy it, enter **copy *name1.ext* c:*dirname**name2.ext*** (where *name1* is the file's current name, *ext* is the extension, *dirname* is the name of the destination directory, and *name2* is the name of the copy).

78: When I try to copy or delete a file, DOS displays the "File not found" message.

You're either mistyping the file's name, or the file is not where you think it is. To find out whether the file is where you think it is, change to the drive and directory where you think the file is stored, and use the **DIR** command to view a list of files (or change to the drive and directory in File Manager). If the file isn't there, you can use the DIR command to search for the file. Type **dir *filename.ext* /s** at the DOS prompt (where *filename* is the name of the file you're looking for, and *ext* is its extension), and press **Enter**. The **/s** switch tells DOS to rifle through all the directories.

79: What does "Not ready reading drive A" mean?

You activated drive A before inserting a disk (or, if the drive has a door, you forgot to close the door). Insert a disk, close the door if there is one, and press **R** for Retry. If the problem persists, turn your computer off, and check under the hood (inside the system unit) for a disconnected or damaged floppy drive cable. If the cable's disconnected, plug it back in. If it's damaged, get help from a qualified service technician.

If you get a **General failure reading drive A** message, you inserted a disk, but the disk was not formatted (or it has a flaw). Type **A** for Abort or **F** for Fail. If the disk is new, change back to drive **C**, and then enter the **format a:** or **format b:** command to format the floppy disk. If the floppy disk has data on it, DON'T format it. Instead, change back to drive **C**, type **scandisk a:** or **scandisk b:** and press **Enter**. If you don't have DOS 6.2 or later, use the CHKDSK command instead of SCANDISK.

80: Is DOS always this s-l-o-w?

Windows and some applications allow you to *shell out to DOS* (return to the DOS prompt without exiting the application). Because your computer is still running Windows or your application in the background, DOS commands may run a bit more slowly. To exit DOS and return to your application (don't forget to!), try entering **exit** at the DOS prompt.

If you're not shelled out to DOS, and it still appears slow, try running the DOS Defragmenter (DOS versions 6.0 and later). Type **defrag c:** at the DOS prompt and press **Enter**. This *optimizes* your hard disk (makes its storage more efficient) and makes it easier for DOS to read and write files to the disk.

81: I know most of the basic DOS commands, but how can I learn more about them?

If you're not sure which command to enter, type **help** at the DOS prompt and press **Enter**. This opens the DOS Help system. Use the **Page Up** and **Page Dn** keys to display the command you want help with. Use the **Tab** key to select a command, and then press **Enter** (or click the command with your mouse).

For help with a specific command, type **help *commandname*** and press **Enter**. This starts the Help system and displays the help screen for the specified command.

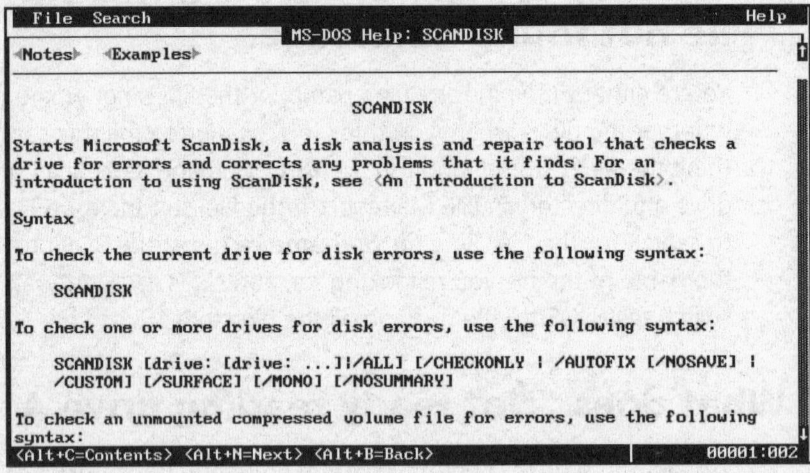

Problems with DOS Applications

82: When I install applications, my computer tells me to close any antivirus programs that are running.

Some installation programs edit your AUTOEXEC.BAT and CONFIG.SYS files to make sure your system can run the application—but antivirus programs don't like changes. As soon as the installation program starts to meddle with your system files, the antivirus program kicks in and says, "Whoa, bud, this is my computer," and it refuses to let the installation program continue. You have to disable the antivirus program if you hope to get anywhere.

Antivirus programs are commonly loaded on startup by a command in the AUTOEXEC.BAT file. You can open this file, add **REM** before the antivirus command line, save the file, and reboot. Another way is to reboot the computer, and then press and release the **F8** key when you see the **Starting MS-DOS...** message. Step through the startup commands; skip the command that runs the antivirus program. If you used REM to skip the anti-virus command, you can remove the REM after installing the application to have anti-virus run on startup again.

83: I entered the command, but the program won't run.

Change to the drive and directory where the program's files are stored, and try entering the startup command again. If that doesn't work, maybe you're not typing the right command. Check the documentation that came with the program, or type **dir /w** and press **Enter** to view a list of the program files. Any files that end in .BAT, .COM, or .EXE are *executable* (files that might run the program). Type the file's name without the extension and press **Enter**. See "I try to run my program, and I keep getting a 'Bad command or file name' message," earlier in this section, for details.

If you get an error message that says an essential file is missing, try reinstalling the program. Sometimes a file gets corrupted, and you have to replace it.

84: The program runs and then crashes.

The causes of system crashes are difficult to track, because any conflict between two applications or devices can cause the problem. Try the following fixes:

- If the program doesn't even show its face, you probably selected the wrong video driver when you installed the program. Run the setup program again; try a different video driver.
- Do you have other applications running? If you do, try closing them and then running your other application. Also, check your AUTOEXEC.BAT file to see if it is running any applications on startup (such as a screen saver or antivirus program).

These *memory-resident* programs often cause problems. Add the REM command before these commands to prevent them from running. Then reboot your computer.

- If the program freezes when you move the mouse, the mouse driver is usually at fault. Try reinstalling the mouse driver that came with your mouse.

  If you just installed another device (such as a sound card), it may have an interrupt setting (IRQ) that conflicts with the mouse interrupt. Try running the sound card's setup program again, choosing a different IRQ setting. For more information, see "I just installed the sound card, and it doesn't work," earlier in this section.

  If that doesn't fix the problem, call the mouse manufacturer and ask for an updated mouse driver.

- Try reinstalling the application. Sometimes a corrupted file can make an application crash. By replacing the corrupted file with a fresh copy, you might be able to prevent future crashes.
- At the DOS prompt, type **scandisk** or **chkdsk /f** and press **Enter**. Follow the messages as they appear. Sometimes *lost file clusters* (parts of files that get scattered over a disk) can cause strange problems. ScanDisk and CheckDisk sweep these clusters off the disk.

85: The display doesn't look quite right.

When you installed the program, you probably selected the wrong video driver. If the display is clear enough to allow you to work, you may be able to select a video display driver. Look for an **Options** menu or command; this should provide you with a list of video drivers. Select the driver that matches your monitor and driver type.

If you can't make out the screen, run the program's **Install** or **Setup** utility again. With most applications, you can change an installation setting without having to go through the entire installation process again. However, with other applications, you may not be so lucky.

Microsoft Windows Woes

86: I entered the WIN command, but Windows won't start.

You don't have to enter a command to start Windows 95, but you might have trouble when you enter the WIN command to start Windows 3.1 or 3.11. Try changing to the drive and directory that contains the Windows files (usually C:\WINDOWS). Then type **win** and press **Enter**. If that doesn't work, check the following:

- Is your system powerful enough to run Windows? You must have a 286 or better computer (386, 486, Pentium), and it must have at least 2 megabytes of RAM before Windows will even say hello.
- If you're running any other programs (such as a DOS screen saver, an antivirus program, or a menu program) exit those programs and unload them from memory before running Windows. You may have to remove the commands that start these programs from your AUTOEXEC.BAT file (or add the **REM** command before their command lines) and then reboot your computer.
- Try starting Windows in a different **mode**. Windows 3.1 can run in one of three *modes*: Enhanced, Standard, or Real. Windows starts in Enhanced mode on a 386 or better computer with 2 or more megabytes of RAM. In Enhanced mode, Windows allows you to *multitask* (perform operations in two applications at the same time), and use disk space as memory. On a 286 computer (or a 386 with less than 2 megabytes of RAM), Windows starts in Standard mode (which does not allow multitasking, and cannot use disk space as RAM). Real mode is for old computers that can't run Windows in Standard or Enhanced mode.

  If you have trouble running Windows 3.1, try starting it with the **WIN /S** or **WIN /R** command. If you have an older computer, it may not be able to run Windows in Enhanced mode. The **/S** switch starts Windows in Standard mode, and the **/R** switch starts it in Real mode.

  Windows for Workgroups starts in Enhanced mode. Although you can't use the /R switch to run it in Real mode, you can use WIN /S to run it in Standard mode.
- Make sure your CONFIG.SYS file has one of the following commands:

  DEVICE=C:\WINDOWS\HIMEM.SYS

  or

  DEVICE=C:\DOS\HIMEM.SYS

  Add the line if it is missing. This loads a memory-management driver that gives Windows access to additional memory. If your computer has a 286 processor—or less than 1 megabyte (1024K) of RAM—don't use HIMEM.SYS.
- Make sure the CONFIG.SYS file has a **BUFFERS=20** (or 30) command and **FILES=20** (or more) command. After editing and saving CONFIG.SYS, reboot your computer. Then try running Windows again. Your computer uses the buffers when reading and writing to disk.
- If you could run Windows in the past, but you couldn't run it after you installed MemMaker, you probably ran MemMaker with the aggressive memory option on. Type **memmaker /undo** and press **Enter** to return your system to normal. You can run MemMaker again, but stick with the default (safe) configuration.

If you have trouble running Windows 95, try using the startup disk you created during the installation process. Once you get Windows up and running from the floppy drive, try running ScanDisk on your hard drive (the drive that contains Windows 95). A crash may have damaged some of the Windows files.

87: I can't get out of Windows.

You probably have a DOS application running. Switch to that application by pressing **Ctrl+Esc** to view the Task List (in Windows 3.1 or 3.11) or by clicking the program's name in the taskbar (in Windows 95); then, exit the application as you normally would (usually by selecting **File** and then **Exit**). Now, try to exit Windows.

If one of your applications froze Windows, giving you no access to your mouse or keyboard, wait awhile. Sometimes Windows is busy printing or playing around with files in the background. It needs a few minutes to put its toys away before it will shift attention back to your mouse or keyboard.

If you've waited long enough, press **Ctrl+Alt+Del**. If all goes as planned, you get a screen telling you which application is causing the problem and giving you some options. The safest option is to press the **Enter** key. This closes the problem application and returns you to Windows. You should now exit Windows, reboot your computer, and restart. If your computer is still locked up, press **Ctrl+Alt+Del**, and then press that key combination again to reboot. It's not a good idea to reboot your computer when Windows is running, but sometimes it's the only option.

88: Is Windows always this s-l-o-w?

Yes, Windows is slow. The good news is that you can improve your system's performance without upgrading:

- **Bypass the advertising screen in Windows 3.1 or 3.11.** To start Windows, type **win :** and press **Enter**. The colon tells Windows not to display the Windows advertising screen at startup.
- **Run fewer applications.** The more applications you have running at once, the slower Windows performs. To find out which applications are running in Windows 3.1 or 3.11, press **Ctrl+Esc**. To quit an application, select it from the **Task List**, and click the **End Task** button. In Windows 95, you can quickly close down an application by right-clicking on its name in the taskbar, and then clicking **Close**.
- **Clean up your INI files in Windows 3.1 or 3.11.** When Windows starts, it reads each and every line in WIN.INI and SYSTEM.INI. By removing blank lines, you give Windows less to read. See "Make Your Computer Work Faster and Better" on page 387 to learn how to edit your system files. Windows 95 uses INI file commands sparingly, so editing these files in Windows 95 won't help much.
- **Create a permanent swap file in Windows 3.1 or 3.11.** A permanent swap file works faster than a temporary file. To create a permanent swap file, first run DOS's Defragment utility (enter **defrag** at the DOS prompt). Then, open the **Main** group window, double-click the **Control Panel** icon, and double-click the **386 Enhanced** icon. Click the **Virtual Memory** button and click **Change**. Open the **Type** drop-down list, and select **Permanent**. Keep clicking **OK** buttons till you're back in the Control Panel. When asked if you want to restart Windows, click the **Restart Windows** button. (In Windows 95, this is unnecessary.)

- **Reduce available fonts.** In Windows 3.1 and 3.11, each font has a line in the WIN.INI file, which Windows must read at startup. To remove fonts, open the **Main** group window, double-click the **Control Panel** icon, and double-click the **Fonts** icon. Select the fonts you want to remove, and click the **Remove** button. This removes the instructions from WIN.INI, but keeps the font files on disk so you can add them back in later. Do NOT remove the font called MS Sans Serif; Windows uses this easy-to-read font to display text in its menus, dialog boxes, and windows.

  You can also remove fonts in Windows 95. Double-click the Fonts icon in the Control Panel. Select the fonts you want to remove, and then open the File menu and select Delete.

- **Defragment your hard drive.** The temporary swap files that Windows uses require disk space. By *defragmenting* your hard disk, you free up sections of the disk to use for these temporary swap files. You can use the DOS 6 Defrag program, or a third-party program such as PC Tools or The Norton Utilities. To use DOS 6 Defrag, exit Windows, and then enter **defrag** at the DOS prompt. Then follow the on-screen instructions.

  Windows 95 comes with its own Disk Defragmenter that you can safely run from Windows. To run it, click the **Start** button, point to **Programs**, **Accessories**, and **System Tools**, and then click **Disk Defragmenter**.

- **Use solid colors.** In Windows 3.1 and 3.11, open the **Main** group window and double-click the **Control Panel** icon. If you're currently using a fancy color scheme, double-click the **Colors** icon, and use the dialog box that appears to select a simple color scheme for Windows. If you're using a screen saver or fancy wallpaper, double-click the **Desktop** icon in the Control Panel, and turn off the screen saver and fancy wallpaper.

- **Change your video driver to a lower resolution and fewer colors.** Although high-resolution graphics do look good, they also slow down your computer. If you have an icon for your video adapter, double-click it, and use the dialog box that appears to select a 640-by-480 resolution, 16-color driver. If you don't have an icon in Windows 3.1 or 3.11, open the **Main** group window, double-click the **Windows Setup** icon, open the **Options** menu, and select **Change System Settings**. Open the **Display** drop-down list and select **VGA**. Select **OK**. Click the **Restart Windows** to put your changes into effect.

You can change the resolution and colors in Windows 95 by right-clicking on a blank area of the Windows desktop and selecting **Properties**. Use the dialog box that appears to change the background color, turn off any screen savers and wallpaper, use solid window colors, and select a lower resolution and number of colors. See "Change the Video Display Properties" on page 201 for details.

89: I installed a fax program, and now I can't print.

Fax programs typically disguise themselves as printers. Whenever you enter the **Print** command in an application, the fax program kicks in, transforms your document into a graphic image that can be transmitted as a fax, and starts dialing your modem.

To prevent this from happening again in Windows 3.1 or 3.11, you must set up your printer to act as the *default printer*. Open the **Control Panel** and double-click the **Printers** icon. Click your printer in the **Installed Printers** list, and then click the **Set As Default Printer** button. Click the **Close** button to save your changes.

In Windows 95, fax programs are treated as printers. Double-click the **My Computer** icon, and then double-click the **Printers** icon. Right-click on the printer you want to use, and click **Set As Default**. Now, when you print, the information will be sent to this printer rather than to the fax program.

90: I just deleted a program group, and I want it back!

If you wiped out one of the standard program groups (in Windows 3.1)—StartUp, Main, Accessories, or Games—you can re-create these groups with the Windows Setup command. Open the File Manager's **File** menu and select **Run**. Type **setup /p** and press **Enter**. (This won't work in Windows for Workgroups.)

If you wiped out a program-group window that was created when you installed a Windows application, you have to rebuild the window. Open the Program Manager's **File** menu, select **New**, select **Program Group**, and click **OK**. Type a name for the group window, and click **OK**. You can now use the **File/New/Program Item** command to create program-item icon(s) for running the application(s). Use the dialog box that appears to name the icon, and to select a name and location for the executable program file.

If you deleted the program group in Windows 95, it might still be residing in the Recycle Bin (if you didn't empty it). Double-click the **Recycle Bin** icon and select all the files that were in the program group. Open the **File** menu and select **Restore**.

91: I double-clicked on a file icon in Windows, but it won't run.

You haven't *associated* the selected file with an application. File Manager (in Windows 3.1 and 3.11) and My Computer or Windows Explorer (in Windows 95) use file associations to figure out which program to run for each file type. If you double-click a file that ends in .PCX, for example, Windows runs Paintbrush and opens the selected .PCX file. If the file you selected is not associated with an application, Windows doesn't know which application to run.

To associate a file type with an application in Windows 3.1 or 3.11, click the document file you want to associate. Open the **File** menu and select **Associate**. From the **Associate With** list, select the application to which you want to associate this file type. If the application does not appear in the list, click the **Browse** button, and select the drive, directory, and name of the file that executes the program. Click the **OK** button. (Don't associate a file type with a DOS application unless you can run the application successfully from Windows.)

In Windows 95, whenever you double-click an unassociated file, a dialog box appears asking you to specify which program you want to run to open the file. If the program is listed, click it. If the program is not listed, click the **Other** button, and then use the dialog box that appears to select the desired program file. To create a permanent file association (so Windows will always run the selected program when you double-click this file type), make sure **Always use this program to open this file** has a check mark next to it. Then, click the **OK** button.

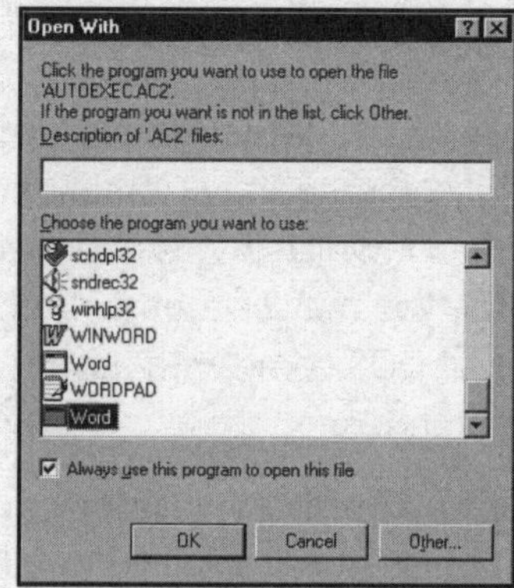

92: I got a General Protection Fault error—what does it mean?

If an application attempts to store some data in an address that's already being used, the application will lock up, and Windows will usually display a message indicating that a *general protection fault* (*GPF*) has occurred, or your system may simply lock up. If this happens to you, take the following steps:

1. Write down the GPF message (if there is one). This message usually indicates the name of the application that caused the fault, and the memory address where the fault occurred.
2. Write down exactly what you were doing when the fault occurred. Were you saving a file, printing, moving the mouse? Write down the names of the other applications you were running.
3. If no message is displayed, wait about a minute to see if your system will unlock itself. Sometimes (especially on slower computers), the system may just be busy, not locked—and it will return control to you if you just wait.
4. If no message appears and Windows is still locked, press **Ctrl+Alt+Del**. A message appears, indicating the name of the application causing problems and asking you to make a decision. This message may also indicate that the system is simply busy and you should wait longer.

5. Perform one of the following steps:

    Press **Esc** to cancel the reboot.

    Press **Enter** to quit the current application and return to Windows.

    Press **Ctrl+Alt+Del** to reboot. *Avoid taking this option.* When you reboot Windows, you risk losing anything you were working on, and you may end up with lots of .TMP files scattered all over your hard disk.

If you consistently encounter the same GPF in an application, try the following fixes:

- **Exit and restart Windows.** Sometimes a GPF will cause additional GPFs in the current work session. Exiting and restarting resets Windows and may prevent additional GPFs.
- **Upgrade to the latest version of DOS.** If you have a version of DOS written for a specific computer (say Compaq), run that DOS version only on the Compaq computer for which it was designed. If you run it on a different make or model of computer, you may encounter problems. Also, try using DOS 5 or DOS 6.x. Both versions of DOS come with advanced memory-management tools that may help eliminate problems.
- **Disable any memory-resident applications.** If you have any memory-resident applications that run from your AUTOEXEC.BAT file, use the **REM** command to disable them. Memory-resident programs include DOS screen savers and screen-capture programs. If you're not sure, copy CONFIG.SYS and AUTOEXEC.BAT (to CONFIG.OLD and AUTOEXEC.OLD), and then create the following "plain vanilla" versions to boot your computer:

  for AUTOEXEC.BAT:

  ```
  C:\WINDOWS\SMARTDRV.EXE
  PROMPT $P$G
  PATH C:\DOS;C:\;C:\WINDOWS
  SET TEMP=C:\TMP
  ```

  for CONFIG.SYS:

  ```
  DEVICE=C:\DOS\SETVER.EXE
  DEVICE=C:\WINDOWS\HIMEM.SYS
  DOS=HIGH
  BUFFERS=50
  FILES=30
  STACKS=9,256
  ```

- **Use SMARTDrive as your disk-caching program.** If you have a disk-caching program, such as QEMM or 386MAX, use the **REM** command in CONFIG.SYS and AUTOEXEC.BAT to remove any of its command lines, and then add the SMARTDrive command line to AUTOEXEC.BAT:

  C:\WINDOWS\SMARTDRV.EXE

- **Reinstall the application.** Sometimes reinstalling the application or device driver that is causing problems will correct the problem.
- **Call the manufacturer for an updated driver.** Sooner or later, manufacturers hear of problems that occur with their products. They may have the fix you need.

93: I don't use many of my fonts and some of my Windows files; can I get rid of them?

The best way to get rid of unneeded fonts and Windows files is to work through Windows. Don't just fire up File Manager and hack away; you might delete something important.

To get rid of fonts you don't use in Windows 3.1 and 3.11, open the **Main** group window, double-click the **Control Panel** icon, and double-click the **Fonts** icon. Select the fonts you want to remove (hold down the **Ctrl** key while clicking each font). DO NOT select any of the System fonts; Windows needs these for the display. Click the **Remove** button. A dialog box appears, asking for confirmation. To remove the font files from disk, click the **Delete Font File From Disk** option, and then click the **OK** button. (If you don't delete the file from the disk, Windows merely removes the font reference from the WIN.INI file.)

You can add and remove fonts in Windows 95 by double-clicking the **My Computer** icon, double-clicking **Control Panel**, and double-clicking the **Fonts** icon. The window that appears shows icons for all the fonts installed on your computer. To remove a font, simply drag it over the **Recycle Bin** icon. To install new fonts, open the **File** menu and select **Install New Font**.

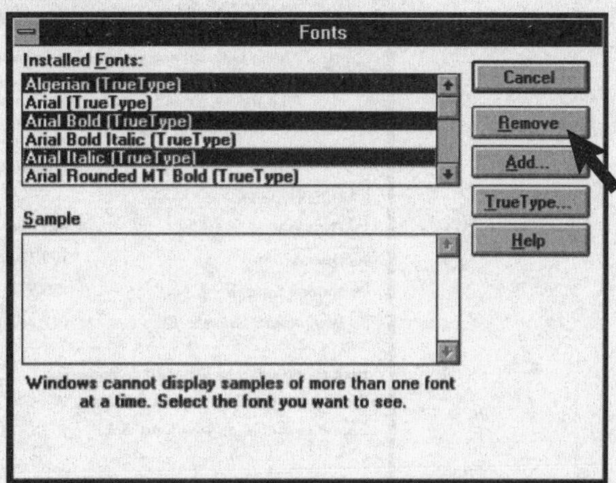

The easiest and safest way to delete inessential Windows 3.1 or 3.11 files is to use Windows Setup. Windows Setup lets you delete groups of files or individual files. (The procedure for Windows 95 is much different, see "Remove Windows 95 Components" on page 386 for details.)

1. Open the **Main** program group and double-click the **Windows Setup** icon.
2. Open the **Options** menu, and select **Add/Remove Windows Components**. The Windows Setup dialog box appears, showing the groups of inessential Windows files.
3. To delete an entire group of Windows files, click the group to remove the **X** from its check box. To remove individual files from a group, perform steps 4 through 7.
4. To delete individual files, click the **Files** (or **Select Files**) button for the group that contains the file(s) you want to delete.
5. Click each file you want to delete in the **Install these files on the hard disk** list. If you select a file by mistake, click it again to deselect it.
6. Click the **Remove** button. The selected files are moved to the **Do not install these files** list.
7. Click the **OK** button. You are returned to the Windows Setup dialog box, where you can choose to delete more files.
8. Repeat steps 5 through 8 to delete additional files.
9. Click the **OK** button. A dialog box appears, asking you to confirm the deletions.
10. Click **Yes** or **Yes to All**. The files are deleted.

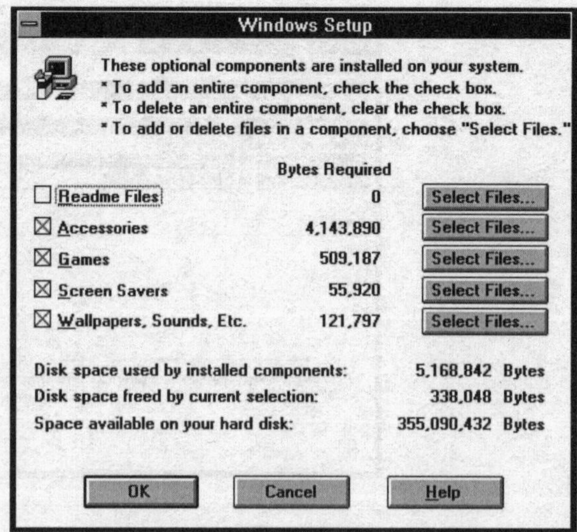

94: Can I run a DOS application from Windows?

Usually, yes. A quick way to run a DOS application in Windows 3.1 or 3.11 is to open Program Manager's **File** menu, select **Run**, and then enter the command required to run the application from the DOS prompt. (You may have to specify the drive letter and directory name, or use the Browse button to select it from a list.) In Windows 95, click the **Start** button and select **Run** to display the Run dialog box.

However, using the File/Run command isn't the best way to run a DOS application in Windows 3.1 or 3.11. It's better to use the Windows Setup utility to create an icon for the application. Windows Setup also creates a *program information file* (*PIF*) for the DOS application (or uses the PIF file included with the application), which tells Windows the best way to run it. Here's what you do:

1. If the DOS application is not installed, follow the installation instructions to install it from the DOS prompt.
2. Open the **Main** window and double-click the **Windows Setup** icon.
3. Open the **Options** menu and select **Set Up Applications**. The Setup Applications dialog box appears.
4. Click **Ask you to specify an application**, and click **OK**. A dialog box appears, asking you to specify the name of the file that runs the program and the name of the group window in which you want the icon to appear.
5. Click the **Browse** button, and then select the drive, directory, and name of the file that runs the program. If you see a file whose name ends in .PIF, that's the file you want; otherwise, pick one of the files that ends in .BAT, .COM, or .EXE.
6. Click the **OK** button.
7. From the **Add to Program Group** drop-down list, click the program group in which you want the icon to appear.
8. Click the **OK** button. If all goes as planned, Windows creates a program information file for the application, assigns it an icon, and places the icon in the Applications group.

If you get a message indicating that Setup cannot set up this application, you can create an icon using the Program Manager's **File/New** command.

You can edit PIF files by using the Windows PIF editor (its icon is in the Main group window). But this topic is beyond the scope of this book.

Windows 95 has replaced PIFs with Properties dialog boxes. If you right-click on the icon for a DOS program and select **Properties**, a dialog box appears, which allows you to enter the settings that control the operation of the DOS program. To learn what the options in this dialog box do, right-click on the option and click **What's This?**

Problems with Windows Applications

95: I installed the application, now where is it?

In Windows 3.1 and 3.11, most Windows applications plop a big group window on your screen, complete with one or two icons for running the application. Just double-click the icon to run the application.

Some applications, however, minimize the group window and hide it somewhere in the Program Manager. Maximize the Program Manager window. If you see a scroll bar at the bottom edge or right side of the Program Manager window, use it to bring additional icons into view. Double-click the group icon for the application, and you'll find the program-item icons you use to run the application.

In Windows 95, programs are typically added to the Start menu. Click the **Start** button, move the mouse pointer over **Programs**, and look for your new program. Some items on the Programs submenu display additional submenus; try pointing to these items. If you can't find the program there, try using My Computer to look in various folders for the program. You can also use the Find command on the Start menu to search for programs.

96: My application locks up Windows.

Join the club. Applications commonly lock up Windows for one reason or another. Wait a minute or two to see if Windows snaps out of it; sometimes Windows is busy doing other things like printing or putting files away.

If Windows remains frozen, press **Ctrl+Alt+Del**, and then press **Enter** to quit the application that's not responding. You should now exit Windows, reboot your computer, and restart. If that doesn't bring Windows out of its funk, press **Ctrl+Alt+Del** twice. And if *that* doesn't work, press your computer's **Reset** button.

If the same application repeatedly locks up Windows, refer to the "Microsoft Windows Woes" section under "I got a General Protection Fault error—what does it mean?" on page 521. This application may have a bug that prevents it from running smoothly on your system or with other applications.

97: When I try to run the application, it says I'm missing a file.

One of the files the application needs in order to run is missing, or the application doesn't know where to look for it. First, make sure your AUTOEXEC.BAT file has the **C:\WINDOWS** directory somewhere in the PATH statement. (The PATH statement tells DOS where to look for files.) If C:\WINDOWS is not in the PATH statement, go to the end of the PATH statement and type **;C:\WINDOWS**. Save the AUTOEXEC.BAT file, exit

Windows, and reboot your computer. (Skip ahead to the topic "The documentation says I have to edit my system files; how do I do that?" on this page to learn how to view and edit AUTOEXEC.BAT in Windows.)

If that doesn't solve the problem, try reinstalling the application. Sometimes essential files can get deleted when Windows crashes (or if you turn off your computer before exiting Windows). If the problem persists, call the technical support number for your program; you can usually find it in the documentation.

98: Why can't I run DOS utilities from Windows?

Some DOS utilities, such as ScanDisk and MemMaker, fiddle with your hardware and configuration settings... really important, complicated stuff. If Windows is running, it makes matters even more complicated. If one of the DOS utilities happens to conflict with Windows while doing its job, your system might crash and mess itself up. For example, if your system crashes while ScanDisk is rearranging all your data, you might lose a chunk or two—or make your entire hard drive inaccessible. To stay on the safe side, exit Windows, and *then* start the DOS utility from the prompt.

Fortunately, Windows 95 comes with its own set of utilities, making it unnecessary to jump out to the DOS prompt. You can find most of these utilities by clicking the **Start** button and then pointing to **Programs**, **Accessories**, and **System Tools**. Click the desired utility to run it.

99: The documentation says I have to edit my system files; how do I do that?

Whenever you install a Windows application, the setup utility adds commands to your WIN.INI and SYSTEM.INI files—and may modify AUTOEXEC.BAT or CONFIG.SYS. If the application doesn't run as it should, however, you may have to enter additional changes (as specified in the application's documentation or README file).

Fortunately, Windows comes with a program that opens—and lets you edit—all four of these important system files. Trouble is, you won't find the application in any of the group windows (in Windows 3.1 or 3.11) or on the Start menu in Windows 95. You have to create an icon for it yourself. Here's how you create an icon for the System Editor in Windows 3.1 or 3.11:

1. Display the **Windows Program Manager** window.
2. Open the group window in which you want the icon placed. The **Main** group window is a good one.
3. Open the Program Manager's **File** menu, and select **New**.
4. Click **OK**. The Program Item Properties dialog box appears.
5. Type **System Editor** in the **Description** text box.
6. Tab to the **Command Line** text box.

7. Type **c:\windows\system\sysedit.exe**.
8. Press **Enter**. Windows creates a program-item icon for the System Configuration Editor, which you can use to start the application.

In Windows 95, you can find the SysEdit icon in the WINDOWS\SYSTEM folder. You can double-click the icon to run SysEdit, or drag the icon to the Windows desktop to create a shortcut for the System Editor. However, Windows 95 does not give INI files a big role, so you usually don't have to worry about editing them.

To edit a system file, double-click the **System Editor** icon you just created, and then click the window that contains the file you want to edit. After entering your changes, open the **File** menu and select **Save**. To activate any changes in SYSTEM.INI or WIN.INI, you must restart Windows. To activate changes in AUTOEXEC.BAT or CONFIG.SYS, exit Windows and reboot your computer. See "Modify Your Startup Files" in "Make Your Computer Work Faster and Better" (starting on page 387), for details.

Miscellaneous Problems

100: My computer loses time.

If your computer is losing 15 seconds a day or more, you may have a cheap clock, or your computer's internal battery is going bad (a much more serious problem). This battery keeps juice flowing to the computer's CMOS (Complementary Metal-Oxide Semiconductor, pronounced *SEA-moss*), which stores some pretty important information—how much memory the computer has, where the hard drive is, and so on. If the CMOS "forgets," you won't be able to use your computer.

Your computer uses the internal battery only when the power is turned off, so the more you use your computer (or keep it on), the longer the battery lasts. Batteries typically last two to five years.

If your computer starts to lose time, don't panic—you may have a rechargeable battery. Leave your computer on for an entire day, and see if that corrects the problem. If the problem persists, replace the battery before it dies. (This usually requires opening the system unit, disconnecting the old battery, and plugging in the new one. You might want to have a service technician do this for you. If you're a do-it-yourselfer, call Ray-O-Vac for a booklet on how to choose and replace CMOS batteries: 1-800-CCB-CLOCK.)

To be on the safe side, you should get a utility program such as PC Tools or The Norton Utilities. These programs can help you create a *recovery diskette* that stores a copy of the CMOS information. If your battery dies, you can then have it replaced and use the recovery disk to rebuild the CMOS. These utility programs also allow you to check the CMOS battery—something that MSD (Microsoft Diagnostics) does not let you do. A less expensive way to copy this information is to run your computer's setup program and copy down all the settings. (You don't have to know what all these settings mean; just make sure you log them all.)

101: I just installed DOS 6.22 (or later), and when I try to run MS-Backup, I get a message saying I have the incorrect DOS version.

You can't use Microsoft Backup 6.0 or later to restore backup files created with an earlier version of Backup. To restore these files, use the **Restore** command. To learn how to use the Restore command, type **help restore** at the DOS prompt, and press **Enter**.

If you are trying to restore backups created with Microsoft Backup for DOS 6.2 or earlier, the problem is that Microsoft Backup 6.22 uses a different data-compression technology. If you have DoubleSpace (*not* DriveSpace) installed, you can proceed with the Restore operation. If you switched to DriveSpace when you upgraded to DOS 6.22, however, you'll have to reinstall the old Microsoft Backup files.

SOFTWARE BUYERS' GUIDE

By themselves, computers are mere big, dumb brutes that are only too happy to just sit there mindlessly, fans a-whirring, clocks a-ticking, hard drives a-spinning. Your hardware is, in fact, totally useless without some kind of software to bring the computer to life. Whether you want to write letters, keep track of your money, store addresses, or paint some digital masterpiece, you'll need to install the appropriate programs on your machine.

For most people, though, the hard part is choosing which software to buy. Whatever you're looking to do with your computer, there are probably several different software packages available, each with varying features and prices. How's a body to choose? Well, that's what this section is all about. I'll take you on a guided tour of dozens of software programs in all the most popular categories. You'll get basic data such as the manufacturer's name and address and the price of the program, and I'll also rate each program in terms of features, ease of use, and popularity.

What Software Categories Are Covered?

The Buyers' Guide is divided into a dozen sections that cover all the following categories:

- Communications
- Databases
- Desktop publishing
- Education
- Entertainment
- Graphics and drawing
- Home finance and accounting
- Integrated packages
- Personal organizers
- Presentation graphics
- Spreadsheets
- Word processing

Just so you know what's what, the next few sections give you a brief description of each category.

Communications

Communications programs (see page 550) enable you to connect to the outside world using a modem. You can use them to dial in to commercial online services such as CompuServe and America Online, bulletin board systems, or computers linked to the Internet. If you have a fax/modem, some programs even let you send faxes directly from your computer (and receive incoming faxes, as well).

Databases

A *database* is a collection of information that's organized so that retrieving and manipulating the information is relatively painless. A database can store info on anything from the CDs in your CD library and recipes to addresses and beer bottle collections. You use database software (see page 552) to create the various databases you need, input and edit the data, and perform tasks such as sorting, searching, and printing reports.

Most database programs come in one of two flavors:

- A *flat-file* database program uses independent databases to store information. Each entry is separated into multiple *fields*, where each field contains a specific piece of information. In an address database, for example, you'd likely have fields for first name, last name, street address, city, state, ZIP code, and so on. Each of these entries is called a *record*. Because flat-file database programs are simple to use and inexpensive, they're a good choice for home use.
- In a *relational* database program, each database is also organized by record with each record having multiple fields. The difference is that two or more databases can be related by data in a common field. For example, a database of customer information and a database of orders placed by customers could be related by a common "customer account number" field. Relational database programs are powerful, complex, and more expensive than their flat-file cousins, so they're mostly used in businesses.

Desktop Publishing

Desktop publishing (DTP, for short; see page 554) involves using your computer to create and print documents that combine text and graphics. Typical DTP projects include newsletters, pamphlets, ads, leaflets, brochures, and even books. Many high-end word processors include some powerful DTP features, but major DTP jobs require the specialized page layout and organization features that are found only in dedicated DTP programs. There are also programs that, while not strictly a part of the DTP family, perform a similar function by enabling you to create greeting cards, banners, and the like.

Education

Educational software is designed to teach some kind of skill or subject. Adult educational programs (see page 556) might teach you how to type, how to speak a foreign language, or how to play the piano. Educational programs (see page 558) for kids run the gamut from math and reading skills to adventure stories and animal facts. I've also included a separate table for reference software such as encyclopedias and dictionaries (see page 564).

Games

If, as they say, all work and no play creates dull boys (and, presumably, dull girls), then help is just around the corner in the form of the myriad games available for PCs (see page 566). There are fast-paced arcade games, shoot-em-up games with an emphasis on blood and gore, simulation games, adventure games, and lots more.

Graphics and Drawing

Artistic stumblebums who wouldn't dream of slapping around oils or watercolors on a real canvas usually find they have no trouble getting up to speed on the virtual canvas of a graphics or drawing program (see page 570). That's because most of these programs make drawing basic shapes and adding cool effects as easy as wiggling a mouse.

Integrated Packages

If you think you'll only be using the basic features of your software, it's a waste to plunk down the big bucks for a fancy-schmancy program that has all the bells and whistles. Instead, you might want to consider an integrated package (see page 570) that combines multiple programs (usually at least a word processor, spreadsheet, and database) into a single program. Sure, the individual modules lack many of the features found in dedicated programs, but you're paying a fraction of the cost.

Personal Finance and Accounting

This category (see page 572) includes low-end programs that are sophisticated, checkbook substitutes for home use and high-end packages that offer full-blown accounting features for small- and medium-sized businesses.

Personal Organizers

Personal organizers (or personal information managers, as they're often called; see page 574) are like the electronic version of a secretary or assistant. You can use them to store addresses and phone numbers, create to-do lists, schedule meetings and appointments, and more. Everything except fetching you coffee.

Spreadsheets

Spreadsheet programs (see page 576) are the software that took the "crunch" out of that familiar business pastime, "number-crunching." Use a spreadsheet to figure up your car payments or your financial future. These programs can do nearly anything from simple arithmetic to complex math, and can help you get a handle on loan payments, mortgages, or paying for your kids' college education.

Software Suites

Software suites (see page 578) are the latest trend in program packaging. A "suite" is a collection of applications bundled together and sold for a fraction of what the applications would cost separately. Unlike an *integrated* package (one big application that works like several small ones), the various programs in a suite can be run as *stand-alone* applications; they work fine by themselves, and have full features. Usually the manufacturers of a suite have designed these applications so you can transfer your work easily from one to another.

Word Processing

Word processing is the most popular of all the software categories. That's because writing—whether it's a letter to a loved one, a memo, or a book—is something most of us do every day, either at work or at home. You can use a word processing program (see page 578) not only to type your prose, but also to edit it, format it, print it, and (in some cases) check the spelling and grammar of your work.

What's in the Tables?

In each of the tables presented in the rest of this section, you'll find these fields to help you make informed decisions when you buy software:

Program The name of the software program.

Manufacturer The name, address, and phone number of the company that manufactures the program.

Price The list price of the program and the upgrade price, if applicable. Note, however, that you'll rarely have to pay list price for a program these days. Most software stores should be selling programs at anywhere from 25% to 50% off the list price.

Platforms The types of operating systems the program needs—DOS by itself or Windows (that is, DOS-plus-Windows, which means you'll need a version of DOS that can run Windows).

System Requirements The equipment and features needed on your computer to run the program. For both PC platforms (Windows and DOS), I've created a "Minimum System" that you need for basic tasks. The "System Requirements" field will tell you what you need over and above these minimums (if anything). Here are the Minimum Systems for each platform:

Minimum Windows 95 System: 386 25MHz processor; VGA graphics adapter; 4M RAM; 30M hard disk space; mouse; DOS 3.1; 1.2M or 1.44M floppy disk drive or CD-ROM drive.

Minimum Windows 3.x System: 286 processor; EGA graphics adapter; 2M RAM; DOS 3.1; Windows 3.1; mouse; hard disk.

Minimum DOS System: 8088 processor; CGA graphics adapter; 640K RAM; DOS 2.0; hard disk.

If you need help reading and understanding the system requirements on a software package, refer to "Look at Software Requirements" on page 7 in Part 1 of this book.

Hard Disk Usage The number of kilobytes or megabytes the program takes up on your hard disk. For programs that enable you to install subsets, I'll give both the minimum and maximum amounts of space the program will use.

Full-Featured Rates the program on whether it has enough features to do a good job for you. I use these ratings:

★★★★ Excellent

★★★ Very good

★★ Adequate

★ Caution when buying

Ease of Use Rates the program on how easy it is to use. "Ease of use" encompasses whether the program is easy to install and well organized, has a well-designed interface, offers a useful help system, and makes everyday tasks easier to do. I use the same rating scale.

Popularity Rates the program on recent sales and the total number of users. In the software industry, the cream usually rises to the top, so you're pretty safe correlating strong sales with good quality. (The popular stuff is also easier to find.)

Features A summary of the program's main features.

With the onslaught of new programs designed especially for Windows 95, read the software packages carefully. If you have Windows 3.1 or 3.11 applications, they will run under Windows 95, but Windows 95 programs will *not* run under Windows 3.1 or 3.11. Also, programs designed especially for Windows 95 will typically run better under Windows 95 than will older programs designed for Windows 3.1 or 3.11. Just make sure you purchase the right program for the operating system you have by reading the system requirements on the software box carefully.

Communications Programs

Program	*Manufacturer*	*Price*	*Platforms*	*System Requirements*
Crosstalk	Digital Communications Associates, Inc. 1000 Alderman Drive Alpharetta, GA 30202 (800) 348-3221 (404) 442-4930	List price: $179 ($195 with Crossfax)	Windows, DOS	Windows—Minimum System plus: 4M RAM DOS—Minimum System plus: 286 or better processor.
HyperACCESS	Hilgraeve, Inc. Genesis Centre 111 Conant Avenue, Suite A Monroe, MI 48161 (800) 826-2760 (303) 243-0576	List price: $149	Windows	Windows—Minimum System.
PROCOMM PLUS	DataStorm Technologies, Inc. P.O. Box 1471 Columbia, MO 65205 (800) 315-3282 (314) 443-3282	List price: $179 Upgrade price: $69	Windows, DOS	Windows—Minimum System plus: 4M RAM. DOS—Minimum System.
QmodemPro	Mustang Software, Inc. 6200 Lake Ming Road Bakersfield, CA 93306 (800) 999-9619 (805) 873-2500	List price: $99 Upgrade price: $50	Windows, DOS	Windows—Minimum System plus: 386 processor, 4M RAM DOS—Minimum System
Smartcom	Hayes Microcomputer Products, Inc. P.O. Box 105203 Atlanta, GA 30348 (800) 874-2937 (404) 441-1617	List price: $79 ($149 for Smartcom Data/Fax Pro)	Windows, DOS	Windows—Minimum System. DOS—Minimum System
WinComm PRO	Delrina Corp. 6320 San Ignacio Ave. San Jose, CA 95119 (800) 268-6082 (408) 363-2345	List price: $129 Upgrade price: $19.95	Windows	Windows—Minimum System plus: 386 or better processor, 4M RAM.
WinFax PRO	Delrina Corp. 6320 San Ignacio Ave. San Jose, CA 95119 (800) 268-6082 (408) 363-2345	List price: $129 Upgrade price: $19.95	Windows	Windows—Minimum System plus: 4M RAM.

Hard Disk Usage	Full-Featured	Ease of Use	Popularity	Features
4.5M	★★★	★★	★★★	Phone book (unlimited entries); QuickPads (customizable button bars); large number of file transfer protocols; scripting language.
1.5M	★★★★	★★★★	★	Phone book (unlimited entries); large number of file transfer protocols; built-in text editor; automatic virus detection; Internet e-mail access; many prewritten login scripts; scripting language.
4M	★★★★	★★★★	★★★★	Phone book (unlimited entries); supports many file transfer protocols; large number of prewritten login scripts; fax support; automatic modem detection; scripting language.
5M	★★★	★★★	★	Phone book (limited to 4,096 entries); multiple file transfer protocols; prewritten login scripts; fax support; scripting language.
3M	★★★	★★★	★★	Phone book (unlimited entries); multiple file transfer protocols; built-in text editor; a few prewritten login scripts; scripting language.
4M–7M	★★★★	★★★★	★★★	Phone book (unlimited entries); support for many file transfer protocols; a few prewritten login scripts; automatic virus detection; Internet e-mail access; shares a COM port with WinFax PRO; scripting language.
5.5M–10M	★★★★	★★★★	★★★★	Phone book (unlimited entries); 101 predesigned fax cover pages; fax annotation; optical character recognition.

Database Programs

Program	Manufacturer	Price	Platforms	System Requirements
Access	Microsoft Corp. One Microsoft Way Redmond, WA 98052 (800) 426-9400 (206) 882-8080	List price: $495 Upgrade price: $129	Windows	Windows—Minimum System plus: 386 or better processor, 6M RAM.
Alpha Five	Alpha Software Corp. 168 Middlesex Tpk. Burlington, MA 01803 (800) 451-1018 (617) 229-2924	List price: $129	Windows, DOS	Windows—Minimum System plus: 8M RAM. DOS—Minimum System plus: 286 or better processor, DOS 3.1 or later.
Approach	Lotus Development Corp. 55 Cambridge Pkwy. Cambridge, MA 02142 (800) 635-6887 (617) 577-8500	List price: $495 Upgrade price: $79	Windows	Windows—Minimum System plus: 386 or better processor, 6M RAM.
dBASE 5	Borland International, Inc. 100 Borland Way Scotts Valley, CA 95066 (800) 682-9299 (408) 431-1000	List price: $795 Upgrade price: $149	Windows, DOS	Windows—Minimum System plus: 6M RAM. DOS—Minimum System plus: 286 or better processor, DOS 3.1 or later.
FoxPro	Microsoft Corp. One Microsoft Way Redmond, WA 98052 (800) 426-9400 (206) 882-8080	List price: $695 Upgrade price: $129	Windows, DOS	Windows—Minimum System plus: 386 or better processor, 4M RAM. DOS—Minimum System plus: 286 or better processor, DOS 3.1 or later.
Paradox	Borland International, Inc. 100 Borland Way Scotts Valley, CA 95066 (800) 682-9299 (408) 431-1000	List price: $495 Upgrade price: $129	Windows, DOS	Windows—Minimum System plus: 386 or better processor, 4M RAM. DOS—Minimum System plus: 286 or better processor, DOS 3.1 or later.
Q&A	Symantec Corp. 10201 Torre Ave. Cupertino, CA 95014 (800) 441-7234 (408) 253-9600	List price: $249.95	Windows, DOS	Windows—Minimum System plus: 386 or better processor, 4M RAM, DOS 3.3 or later, VGA graphics adapter. DOS—Minimum System.

Hard Disk Usage	Full-Featured	Ease of Use	Popularity	Features
6M–23M	★★★★	★★★	★★★★	Relational; Wizards for automating table creation, queries, and more; Cue Cards; automatic form and report generation; query-by-example; Quick Sort; OLE support; Access Basic programming language.
15M	★★★	★★★★	★	Relational; Genies for automating table creation, queries, and more; data dictionary; OLE support; Report Editor.
12M	★★★	★★★	★★	Relational; Assistants for automating table creation, queries, and more; tabbed notebook interface; automatic form and report generation; Fast Format; macro programming language.
10M-32M	★★★★	★★★	★★★★	Relational; Experts for automating table creation, queries, and more; Crystal Reports; built-in text editor; Expression Builder; OLE support; dBASE programming language.
10M	★★★	★★★	★★★	Relational; Screen Builder; report generator; dBASE compatibility; Rushmore technology; FoxPro programming language.
20M	★★★★	★★★★	★★★★	Relational; Experts for automating table creation, queries, and more; query-by-example; Visual Form Designer; Report Designer; PAL programming language.
15M	★★	★★★★	★★★	Flat-file; built-in word processor; DAVE (Do Anything Very Easily) intelligent query assistant; natural language query interface; macro language.

Desktop Publishing Programs

Program	*Manufacturer*	*Price*	*Platforms*	*System Requirements*
Corel Ventura	Corel Corp. 1600 Carling Avenue Ottawa, ON K1Z 8R7 (800) 772-6735 (613) 728-8200	List price: $495.00 (CD-ROM), $595 (floppy disk)	Windows	Windows—Minimum System plus: 386 or better processor, 8M RAM, VGA graphics adapter.
FrameMaker	Frame Technology Corp. 1010 Rincon Circle San Jose, CA 95131 (800) 843-7263 (408) 433-3311	List price: $895.00	Windows	Windows—Minimum System plus: 386 or better processor, 8M RAM, VGA graphics adapter.
MyAdvancedBrochures	MySoftware Co. Menlo Park, CA (800) 325-3508 (415) 473-3600	List price: $99.95	Windows	Windows—Minimum System plus: 4M RAM.
PageMaker	Aldus Corp. 411 First Ave. South Seattle, WA 98104 (800) 333-2538 (206) 622-5500	List price: $895.00	Windows	Windows—Minimum System plus: 386 or better processor, 4M RAM, VGA graphics adapter.
PFS: Publisher	SoftKey International, Inc. 201 Broadway Cambridge, MA 02139 (800) 826-0706 (617) 494-1200	List price: $119.95	Windows	Windows—Minimum System.
Print Shop Deluxe	Broderbund Software 500 Redwood Blvd. Novato, CA 94948 (800) 521-6263 (415) 382-4400	List price: $49.95	Windows, DOS	Windows—Minimum System plus: 4M RAM, VGA graphics adapter. DOS—Minimum System plus: 386 or better processor, DOS 3.0 or later, IBM RAM, VGA graphics adapter.
Publisher	Microsoft Corp. One Microsoft Way Redmond, WA 98052 (800) 426-9400 (206) 882-8080	List price: $139	Windows	Windows—Minimum System plus: 4M RAM, VGA graphics adapter.
QuarkXPress	Quark, Inc. 1800 Grant St. Denver, CO 80203 (800) 788-7835	List price: $895.00	Windows	Windows—Minimum System plus: 386 or better processor, 4M RAM, VGA graphics adapter.

Hard Disk Usage	*Full-Featured*	*Ease of Use*	*Popularity*	*Features*
14M	★★★★	★★★	★★	Quick Format; Type Assist; Copy Editor; Publication Manager.
10M	★★★★	★	★★	Support for headers, footers, footnotes; Page Layout palette; global styles.
8M	★★	★★	★	Creates brochures, mailers, postcards, flyers.
8M–15M	★★★	★★	★★★★	Pasteboard metaphor; drag-and-drop; spell-checker; multiple document interface; support for Pantone, Munsell, Trumatch, and other color systems; scripting language.
4M	★★	★★★	★★	Word processor; spell checker; thesaurus; templates.
5M–10M	★★	★★★★	★★★★	Creates greeting cards, banners, signs, calendars; large graphics library; dozens of template designs.
6M–13M	★★★	★★★★	★★★	PageWizards automate page layout; Cue Cards; WordArt; spell checker; drawing tools; OLE support; Print Troubleshooter; Layout Checker.
10M	★★★★	★★★★	★★★★	Spell checker; thesaurus; four-color separation; support for all major color systems (Pantone, etc.); precise control of rotation and kerning.

Educational Programs—Adult

Program	*Manufacturer*	*Price*	*Platforms*	*System Requirements*
Ancient Lands	Microsoft Corp. One Microsoft Way Redmond, WA 98052 (800) 426-9400 (206) 882-8080	List price: $79.95	Windows	Windows—Minimum System plus: 386 or better processor, VGA graphics adapter, CD-ROM, sound card.
Bodyworks	Software Marketing Corp. 9830 South 51st St. Building A-131 Phoenix, AZ 85044 (602) 893-3377	List price: $69.95	Windows	Windows—Minimum System plus: 386 or better processor, VGA graphics adapter, CD-ROM.
Cinemania	Microsoft Corp. One Microsoft Way Redmond, WA 98052 (800) 426-9400 (206) 882-8080	List price: $79.95	Windows	Windows—Minimum System plus: 386 or better processor, VGA graphics adapter, CD-ROM, sound card.
French Assistant	MicroTac Software, Inc. 4375 Jutland Drive, Suite 110 San Diego, CA 921174M RAM (800) 366-4170	List price: $99.95	Windows	Windows—Minimum System plus: 386 or better processor,
Mavis Beacon Teaches Typing	Mindscape 60 Leveroni Court Novato, CA 94949 (415) 883-3000	List price: $49.95	Windows	Windows—Minimum System plus: 386 or better processor, 4M RAM, VGA graphics adapter.
Microsoft Complete Baseball	Microsoft Corp. One Microsoft Way Redmond, WA 98052 (800) 426-9400 (206) 882-8080	List price: $79.95	Windows	Windows—Minimum System plus: 386 or better processor, 4M RAM, CD-ROM, sound card.
Microsoft Musical Instruments	Microsoft Corp. One Microsoft Way Redmond, WA 98052 (800) 426-9400 (206) 882-8080	List price: $79.95	Windows	Windows—Minimum System plus: 386 or better processor, VGA graphics adapter, CD-ROM, sound card.
Miracle Piano Teaching System	Mindscape 60 Leveroni Court Novato, CA 94949 (415) 883-3000	List price: $480	DOS	DOS—Minimum System plus: DOS 3.1 or later.
PharmAssist	Software Marketing Corp. 9830 South 51st St. Building A-131 Phoenix, AZ 85044 (602) 893-3377	List price: $69.95	Windows	Windows—Minimum System plus: 386 or better processor, VGA graphics adapter.

Hard Disk Usage	*Full-Featured*	*Ease of Use*	*Popularity*	*Features*
2M	★★★	★★★★	★★	Multimedia coverage of ancient Greece, Rome, Egypt; 5 hours of narration, music, sound effect; 21 animations and video clips.
3M	★★★★	★★★★	★★★	Comprehensive anatomy reference; 140 color diagrams; 14 3-D models; 37 video clips and animations.
1M	★★★	★★★★	★★★★	19,000 movie reviews; biographies of 3,000 film personalities; Academy Award winners; movie industry articles.
4M	★★★	★★★★	★★	100,000-word dictionary; automatic and interactive translating; over 3,000 verb conjugations; grammar help.
6M	★★★★	★★★★	★★★★	Artificial intelligence simulates typing teacher; on-the-fly custom lessons; games.
2M	★★★	★★★	★★★	History; player biographies; almanac; statistics; multimedia.
2M	★★★	★★★★	★★★★	200 instruments; 1,500 sound samples.
5M	★★★★	★★★★	★★★	Miracle Keyboard (plugs into serial port); interactive lessons; 40 songs; practice games.
2M	★★★	★★★	★★	Drug descriptions; how different drugs interact; color illustrations.

(continues)

Educational Programs—Adult Continued

Program	Manufacturer	Price	Platforms	System Requirements
Spanish Assistant	MicroTac Software, Inc. 4375 Jutland Drive, Suite 110 San Diego, CA 92117 (800) 366-4170	List price: $99.95	Windows	Windows—Minimum System plus: 386 or better processor, 4M RAM.
Sportsworks	Software Marketing Corp. 9830 South 51st St. Building A-131 Phoenix, AZ 85044 (602) 893-3377	List price: $69.95	DOS	DOS—Minimum System plus: DOS 3.3 or later, VGA graphics adapter.
Typing Tutor	Que Software 201 W. 103rd St. Indianapolis, IN 46290 (800) 992-0244	List price: $49.95	Windows, DOS	Windows—Minimum System. DOS—Minimum System plus: 286 or better processor, DOS 4.0 or later.
Your Personal Trainer for the SAT	Davidson & Associates, Inc. P.O. Box 2961 Torrance, CA 90509 (800) 556-6141	List price: $59.95	Windows	Windows—Minimum System plus: 3M RAM, VGA graphics adapter.

Educational Programs—Kids

Program	Manufacturer	Price	Platforms	System Requirements
3-D Dinosaur Adventure	Knowledge Adventure, Inc. 4502 Dyer St. La Crescenta, CA 91214 (800) 542-4240 (818) 542-4200	List price: $69.95	DOS	DOS—Minimum System plus: 286 or better processor, DOS 3.1 or later, VGA graphics adapter, CD-ROM, sound card.
Arthur Teacher's Trouble	Broderbund Software 500 Redwood Blvd. Novato, CA 94948 (800) 521-6263 (415) 382-4400	List price: $39.95	Windows	Windows—Minimum System plus: 386 or better processor, 4M RAM, Super VGA graphics adapter, CD-ROM, sound card.
Bug Adventure	Knowledge Adventure, Inc. 4502 Dyer St. La Crescenta, CA 91214 (800) 542-4240 (818) 542-4200	List price: $69.95	DOS	DOS—Minimum System plus: 286 or better processor, DOS 3.1 or later, VGA graphics adapter, CD-ROM, sound card.
Creative Writer	Microsoft Corp. One Microsoft Way Redmond, WA 98052 (800) 426-9400 (206) 882-8080	List price: $64.95	Windows	Windows—Minimum System plus: 386 or better processor, VGA graphics adapter.

Hard Disk Usage	Full-Featured	Ease of Use	Popularity	Features
4M	★★★	★★★★	★★	100,000-word dictionary; automatic and interactive translating; over 3,000 verb conjugations; grammar help.
2M	★★	★★	★★	Describes 150 sports in 12 categories; on-line quizzes; bookmarks.
2M	★★★	★★★★	★★★★	Lessons; games (Mouse Invaders, Keyrobics, Mouserobics); graphs; reports.
3M	★★★	★★★★	★★	Sample SAT questions; test booklets in SAT format; training schedule; graphs; SAT game.

Hard Disk Usage	Full-Featured	Ease of Use	Popularity	Features
1M	★★★	★★	★★	Ages 3+; film clips; 3-D screens and movies (with 3-D glasses); games; storybook.
1M	★★	★★★★	★★★	Ages 6-10; interactive text; animations.
1M	★★★	★★	★★	Ages 5+; 3-D photos; movies; games; readings; music.
3M	★★★★	★★★	★★★	Ages 8-14; Writing Studio; Idea Workshop; Splot Machine (generates random phrases); Projects department (newspaper, greeting card, etc.); Library stores documents.

(continues)

Educational Programs—Kids Continued

Program	*Manufacturer*	*Price*	*Platforms*	*System Requirements*
Dinosaurs	Microsoft Corp. One Microsoft Way Redmond, WA 98052 (800) 426-9400 (206) 882-8080	List price: $79.95	Windows	Windows—Minimum System plus: 386 or better processor, 4M RAM, VGA graphics adapter, CD-ROM, sound card.
Fine Artist	Microsoft Corp. One Microsoft Way Redmond, WA 98052 (800) 426-9400 (206) 882-8080	List price: $64.95	Windows	Windows—Minimum System plus: 386 or better processor, VGA graphics adapter.
Just Grandma and Me	Broderbund Software 500 Redwood Blvd. Novato, CA 94948 (800) 521-6263 (415) 382-4400	List price: $39.95	Windows	Windows—Minimum System plus: 386 or better processor, 4M RAM, Super VGA graphics adapter, CD-ROM, sound card.
Kid's Zoo	Knowledge Adventure, Inc. 4502 Dyer St. La Crescenta, CA 91214 (800) 542-4240 (818) 542-4200	List price: $69.95	DOS	DOS—Minimum System plus: 286 or better processor, DOS 3.1 or later, VGA graphics adapter, CD-ROM, sound card.
Kid Works 2	Davidson & Associates, Inc. P.O. Box 2961 Torrance, CA 90509 (800) 556-6141	List price: $59.95	Windows, DOS	Windows—Minimum System plus: 4M RAM, VGA graphics adapter. DOS—Minimum System plus: 286 or better processor, DOS 3.3 or later, VGA graphics adapter.
Math Ace	Magic Quest 125 University Ave. Palo Alto, CA 94301 (415) 321-5838	List price: $35	DOS	DOS—Minimum System plus: 286 or better processor, VGA graphics adapter, sound card.
Math Blaster: In Search of Spot	Davidson & Associates, Inc. P.O. Box 2961 Torrance, CA 90509 (800) 556-6141	List price: $59.95	Windows, DOS	Windows—Minimum System plus: 386 or better processor, 4M RAM, VGA graphics adapter, CD-ROM. DOS—Minimum System plus: 286 or better processor, DOS 3.3 or later, VGA graphics adapter, CD-ROM.

Hard Disk Usage	Full-Featured	Ease of Use	Popularity	Features
2M	★★★	★★★★	★★★	Ages 8+; six movies; Timeline; Families; Atlas; pronunciations.
5M	★★★★	★★★	★★★	Ages 8-14; Painting Studio; Gallery; Drawing Tricks; Project Workshop; painting tools; drawing tools; effects; sound generator.
1M	★★	★★★★	★★★★	Ages 3-8; interactive text; animations.
1M	★★★	★★	★★	Ages 3-6; film clips; 3-D images; movies; games; storybook.
5M	★★★	★★	★★	Ages 4-12; Story Writer; Story Illustrator; Story Player (reads created stories aloud).
1M	★★★	★★★	★★	Ages 4-8; four math teaching games: Math Ace, Bubble Gum Machine, Hide and Seek, Function Shoot; Smart Lab.
2M	★★★	★★★	★★★★	Ages 6-12; four math teaching games: Math Blaster, Trash Zapper, Number Recycler, and Cave Runner; six difficulty levels.

(continues)

Educational Programs—Kids Continued

Program	*Manufacturer*	*Price*	*Platforms*	*System Requirements*
Prehistoria	Grolier Electronic Publishing, Inc. Sherman Turnpike Danbury, CT 06816 (800) 285-4534	List price: $69.95	Windows	Windows—Minimum System plus: 386 or better processor, 4M RAM, VGA graphics adapter, CD-ROM.
Reader Rabbit	The Learning Company 6493 Kaiser Drive Fremont, CA 94555 (800) 852-2255	List price: $42	Windows, DOS	Windows—Minimum System plus: 386 or better processor, 4M RAM, VGA graphics adapter, sound card. DOS—Minimum System plus: 286 or better processor, DOS 3.3 or later, VGA graphics adapter.
The New Kid on the Block	Broderbund Software 500 Redwood Blvd. Novato, CA 94948 (800) 521-6263 (415) 382-4400	List price: $39.95	Windows	Windows—Minimum System plus: 386 or better processor, 4M RAM, Super VGA graphics adapter, CD-ROM, sound card.
The Tortoise and the Hare	Broderbund Software 500 Redwood Blvd. Novato, CA 94948 (800) 521-6263 (415) 382-4400	List price: $39.95	Windows	Windows—Minimum System plus: 386 or better processor, 4M RAM, Super VGA graphics adapter, CD-ROM, sound card.
Undersea Adventure	Knowledge Adventure, Inc. 4502 Dyer St. La Crescenta, CA 91214 (800) 542-4240 (818) 542-4200	List price: $69.95	DOS	DOS—Minimum System plus: 286 or better processor, DOS 3.1 or later, VGA graphics adapter, CD-ROM, sound card.
Where in the World is Carmen Sandiego?	Broderbund Software 500 Redwood Blvd. Novato, CA 94948 (800) 521-6263 (415) 382-4400	List price: $60	DOS	DOS—Minimum System plus: 286 or better processor, DOS 3.3 or later, VGA graphics adapter, CD-ROM.

Hard Disk Usage	Full-Featured	Ease of Use	Popularity	Features
2M	★★★	★★★	★★	Ages 10+; Gallery; Creature Show; Time Tracker; Classifications; Grolier Museum.
1M	★★	★	★★★	Ages 5-8; Word Mine; Match Pond; Vowel Pond; Alphabet Dance.
1M	★★	★★★★	★★★	Ages 6-12; interactive text; animations.
1M	★★	★★★★	★★★	Ages 3-8; interactive text; animations.
1M	★★★	★★	★★	Ages 5+; 3-D photos; movies; games; readings; music; 3-D museum.
1M	★★★	★★	★★★★	Ages 8+; geography lessons via photos, video, sound.

Educational Programs—Reference

Program	*Manufacturer*	*Price*	*Platforms*	*System Requirements*
American Heritage Talking Dictionary	SoftKey International, Inc. 201 Broadway Cambridge, MA 01239 (800) 227-5609 (617) 494-1200	List price: $59.95	Windows	Windows—Minimum System plus: 386 or better processor, 4M RAM, CD-ROM, sound card.
Bookshelf	Microsoft Corp. One Microsoft Way Redmond, WA 98052 (800) 426-9400 (206) 882-8080	List price: $99	Windows	Windows—Minimum System plus: 386 or better processor, 4M RAM, VGA graphics adapter, CD-ROM, sound card.
Columbia Electronic Dictionary of Quotations	AApex Software Corp. 952 Greg St., Suite 101 Sparks, NV 89431 (800) 728-7650	List price: $89.95	Windows	Windows—Minimum System.
Compton's Interactive Encyclopedia	Compton's New Media 2320 Camino Vida Roble Carlsbad, CA 92009 (800) 862-2206	List price: $149.95	Windows	Windows—Minimum System plus: 386 or better processor, 4M RAM, VGA graphics adapter, CD-ROM, sound card.
Encarta	Microsoft Corp. One Microsoft Way Redmond, WA 98052 (800) 426-9400 (206) 882-8080	List price: $139	Windows	Windows—Minimum System plus: 386 or better processor, 4M RAM, VGA graphics adapter, CD-ROM, sound card.
New Grolier Multimedia Encyclopedia	Grolier Electronic Publishing, Inc. Sherman Turnpike Danbury, CT 06816 (800) 285-4534	List price: $100	Windows, DOS	Windows—Minimum System plus: 386 or better processor, 4M RAM, VGA graphics adapter, CD-ROM, sound card. DOS—Minimum System plus: 39 or better processor, DPS 3.1 or later, VGA graphics adapter, CD-ROM, sound card.
Random House Unabridged Dictionary	Random House Reference and Electronic Publishing 201 E. 50th St. New York, NY 10022 (800) 733-3000	List price: $100	Windows, DOS	Windows—Minimum System plus: 4M RAM, CD-ROM. DOS—Minimum System plus: 286 or better processor, 2M RAM, CD-ROM.

Hard Disk Usage	Full-Featured	Ease of Use	Popularity	Features
2M	★★★★	★★★	★★★	200,000 definitions; pronunciations; WordHunter; thesaurus; anagram construction tool.
1M	★★★	★★★	★★★★	American Heritage Dictionary; Columbia Dictionary of Quotations; Concise Columbia Encyclopedia; Hammond International World Atlas; People's Chronology; Roget's Thesaurus; World Almanac and Book of Facts.
5.5M	★★	★★	★★	18,000 quotations; 3,500 authors; 1,500 subjects; search engine.
1M	★★★	★★★★	★★★	Encyclopedia: 32,000 articles; 7,000 images; 12 animations; 800 maps.
2M	★★★★	★★★	★★★★	Encyclopedia: 26,000 articles; 7,000 images; 100 animations and video clips; 800 maps.
1M	★★	★★★	★★	Encyclopedia: 23,000 articles; 3,000 images; 87 animations and videos; 250 maps.
1M	★★	★★	★★	315,000 definitions; search engine; anagram construction tool.

(continues)

Educational Programs—Reference Continued

Program	Manufacturer	Price	Platforms	System Requirements
Software Toolworks World Atlas	Mindscape 60 Leveroni Court Novato, CA 94949 (415) 883-3000	List price: $100	Windows, DOS	Windows—Minimum System plus: 386 or better processor, 4M RAM, VGA graphics adapter, CD-ROM, sound card. DOS—Minimum System plus: Minimum System plus: 286 or better processor, 2M RAM, CD-ROM, sound card.

Games

Program	Manufacturer	Price	Platforms	System Requirements
Chessmaster 4000	Mindscape 60 Leveroni Court Novato, CA 94949 (415) 883-3000	List price: $59.95	Windows	Windows—Minimum System plus: 386 or better processor, 4M RAM, 256-color VGA graphics adapter, CD-ROM.
Doom	ID Software c/o Starpak Software P.O. Box 1230 Greeley, CO 80632 (800) 434-2637	List price: $40	DOS	DOS—Minimum System plus: 386 or better processor, 4M RAM, VGA graphics adapter.
King's Quest VII: The Prince-less Bride	Sierra On-Line, Inc. P.O. Box 3404 Salinas, CA 93912 (800) 757-7707	List price: $79.95	Windows	Windows—Minimum System plus: 386 or better processor, 4M RAM, VGA graphics adapter, CD-ROM, sound card.
Links 386 Pro	Access Software 4910 W. Amelia Earhart Drive Salt Lake City, UT 84116 (800) 800-4880	List price: $69.95	DOS	DOS—Minimum System plus: 386 or better processor, DOS 3.3 or later, 2M RAM, Super VGA graphics adapter.
Microsoft Arcade	Microsoft Corp. One Microsoft Way Redmond, WA 98052 (800) 426-9400 (206) 882-8080	List price: $30	Windows	Windows—Minimum System plus: 386 or better processor, VGA graphics adapter.

Hard Disk Usage	Full-Featured	Ease of Use	Popularity	Features
1M	★★	★★★	★★	200 maps; 1,000 photos; 150 video clips.

Hard Disk Usage	Full-Featured	Ease of Use	Popularity	Features
2M	N/A	★★	★★★	Strategy game; multiple views; different chess sets; chess advice; chess tutorial.
5M	N/A	★★★	★★★★	Arcade game; kill every alien in sight as you battle your way through a Martian building.
2M	N/A	★★★	★★★★	Adventure game; help Princess Rosella of Daventry find her prince and safeguard the future of Daventry.
8M	N/A	★★	★★★★	Sports game; play golf from different points of view; includes replays, saved shots.
3M	N/A	★★★	★★	Arcade games; Asteroids; Battlezone; Centipede; Missile Command; Tempest.

(continues)

Games Continued

Program	*Manufacturer*	*Price*	*Platforms*	*System Requirements*
Microsoft Golf	Microsoft Corp. One Microsoft Way Redmond, WA 98052 (800) 426-9400 (206) 882-8080	List price: $64.95	Windows	Windows—Minimum System plus: 386 or better processor, 4M RAM, Super VGA graphics adapter.
Myst	Broderbund Software 500 Redwood Blvd. Novato, CA 94948 (800) 521-6263 (415) 382-4400	List price: $60	Windows	Windows—Minimum System plus: 386 or better processor, 4M RAM, Super VGA graphics adapter, CD-ROM, sound card.
Return to Zork	Activision 11601 Wilshire Blvd., Suite 100 Los Angeles, CA 90025 (800) 477-3650 (310) 473-9200	List price: $79.95	DOS	DOS—Minimum System plus: 386 or better processor, 4M RAM, VGA graphics adapter, CD-ROM, sound card.
SimCity 2000	Maxis 2 Theater Square Orinda, CA 94563 (510) 254-9700	List price: $54.95	DOS	DOS—Minimum System plus: 386 or better processor, DOS 3.3 or later, 4M RAM, Super VGA graphics adapter.
Strike Commander	Origin 110 Wild Basin Rd., Suite 230 Austin, TX 78746 (800) 245-4525 (512) 328-0282	List price: $39.95	DOS	DOS—Minimum System plus: 486 or better processor, DOS 5.0 or later, 4M RAM, 256-color VGA graphics adapter.
The Seventh Guest	Virgin Games, Inc. 18061 Fitch, Suite C Irvine, CA 92714 (714) 833-1999	List price: $79.95	Windows, DOS	DOS—Minimum System plus: 386 or better processor, DOS 5.0 or later, 2M RAM, Super VGA graphics adapter, CD-ROM, sound card.
Ultima VIII: Pagan	Origin 110 Wild Basin Rd., Suite 230 Austin, TX 78746 (800) 245-4525 (512) 328-0282	List price: $79.95	DOS	DOS—Minimum System plus: 386 or better processor, DOS 3.3 or later, 2M RAM, 256-color VGA graphics adapter.
X-Wing	LucasArts P.O. Box 10307 San Rafael, CA 94912 (800) 782-7927 (415) 721-3300	List price: $55.95	DOS	DOS—Minimum System plus: 386 or better processor, 256-color VGA graphics adapter.

Hard Disk Usage	Full-Featured	Ease of Use	Popularity	Features
7M	N/A	★★	★★★	Sports game; digitized images of real golf holes; full-motion video fly-overs of each hole.
2M	N/A	★★★★	★★★★	Adventure game; explore a mysterious island and discover why all the inhabitants are missing.
3M	N/A	★★★★	★★★	Adventure game; save the underground Empire of Zork from the evil IT&L Corporation.
5M	N/A	★★★	★★★	Simulation game; plan and build a city at the close of the 20th century.
3M	N/A	★★	★★	Flight simulation game; in 2011, pilot an F-16 for a band of mercenaries called the Wildcats.
2M	N/A	★★	★★★	Adventure game; you're a reporter in a Gothic mansion where six guests have been murdered and you have to find out what happened to the seventh guest.
4M	N/A	★★★	★★★	Fantasy role-playing game; fight your way off the island Pagan and back to Brittania.
3M	N/A	★	★★★	Flight simulation game; lead a Rebel assault on the Death Star.

Graphics and Drawing

Program	*Manufacturer*	*Price*	*Platforms*	*System Requirements*
Adobe Illustrator	Adobe Systems, Inc. 1585 Charleston Rd. Mountain View, CA 94039 (800) 833-6687	List price: $469	Windows	Windows—Minimum System plus: 386 or better processor, 4M RAM, DOS 3.3 or later, VGA graphics adapter.
CorelDRAW	Corel Corp. 1600 Carling Avenue Ottawa, ON K1Z 8R7 (800) 772-6735 (613) 728-8200	List price: $595	Windows	Windows—Minimum System plus: 386 or better processor, 8M RAM, VGA graphics adapter.
Fractal Design Painter	Fractal Design Corp. 335 Spreckels Dr., Suite F Aptos, CA 95003 (800) 297-2665 (408) 688-5300	List price: $499 Upgrade price: $149	Windows	Windows—Minimum System plus: 386 or better processor, 8M RAM, SVGA graphics adapter.
PC Paintbrush	SoftKey International, Inc. 201 Broadway Cambridge, MA 01239 (800) 227-5609 (617) 494-1200	List price: $60	Windows	Windows—Minimum System plus: VGA graphics adapter.
Visio	Shapeware Corp. 1601 Fifth Ave., Suite 800 Seattle, WA 98101 (800) 446-3335 (206) 521-4500	List price: $199	Windows	Windows—Minimum System plus: 386 or better processor, 4M RAM, VGA graphics adapter.

Integrated Packages

Program	*Manufacturer*	*Price*	*Platforms*	*System Requirements*
ClarisWorks	Claris Corp. 5201 Patrick Henry Dr. Santa Clara, CA 95052 (800) 325-2747 (408) 987-8227	List price: $249 Upgrade price: $49	Windows	Windows—Minimum System plus: 386 or better processor, 4M RAM, VGA graphics adapter.
Microsoft Works	Microsoft Corp. One Microsoft Way Redmond, WA 98052 (800) 426-9400 (206) 882-8080	List price: $139	Windows, DOS	Windows—Minimum System plus: VGA graphics adapter. DOS—Minimum System plus: DOS 3.0.
PFS:WindowWorks	SoftKey International, Inc. 201 Broadway Cambridge, MA 02139 (800) 826-0706 (617) 494-1200	List price: $149	Windows	Windows—Minimum System plus: 386 or better processor, 4M RAM, DOS 5.0 or later, VGA graphics adapter.

Hard Disk Usage	Full-Featured	Ease of Use	Popularity	Features
12M	★★★★	★★	★★★	Drawing tools; text layout tools; page layout tools; clip art; supports major color matching systems (Pantone, Trumatch, etc.); Adobe Type Manager; Separator; Streamline; TypeAlign.
37M–75M	★★★★	★★	★★★★	Drawing tools; text layout tools; page layout tools; clip art; templates; supports major color matching systems (Pantone, Trumatch, etc.); PowerLines; CorelMOVE; CorelPHOTO-PAINT; CorelSHOW; CorelCHART; CorelTRACE.
10M	★★★	★★★	★★★★	Drawing tools; brushes; special effects; natural paint tools and textures; TWAIN support; macro recorder.
5M	★★★	★★★	★★	Drawing tools; text layout tools; natural paint tools; special effects; brushes.
11M	★★★	★★★★	★★★★	Drawing tools; text layout tools; SmartShapes (job-specific stencils); used for maps, flowcharts, org charts, space plans, schematics, etc.

Hard Disk Usage	Full-Featured	Ease of Use	Popularity	Features
3M–8M	★★	★★★	★★	Includes: word processor, spreadsheet, database, graphics. Assistants automate routine tasks such as creating tables.
4M–14M	★★★★	★★★★	★★★★	Includes: word processor, spreadsheet, database, communication; Wizards automate routine tasks; Microsoft Draw; WordArt, clip art; spell checker; thesaurus; OLE support.
6M–11M	★★★	★★★	★★	Includes: word processor, spreadsheet, database, communications, charting, address book, label maker, WinFax Lite; spell checker; supports OLE

(continues)

Integrated Packages Continued

Program	Manufacturer	Price	Platforms	System Requirements
WordPerfect Works	WordPerfect, the Novell Applications Group 1555 North Technology Way Orem, UT 84057 (800) 451-5151 (801) 225-5000	List price: $109	Windows	Windows—Minimum System plus: 4M RAM.

Personal Finance and Accounting

Program	Manufacturer	Price	Platforms	System Requirements
CA-Simply Accounting	Computer Associates International, Inc. One Computer Associates Plaza Islandia, NY 11788 (800) 773-5445 (516) 342-2000	List price: $89	Windows, DOS	Windows—Minimum System. DOS—Minimum System plus: DOS 3.0 or later.
Kiplinger's Simply Money	Computer Associates International, Inc. One Computer Associates Plaza Islandia, NY 11788 (800) 773-5445 (516) 342-2000	List price: $69.99	Windows	Windows—Minimum System plus: 386 or better processor, 4M RAM, VGA graphics adapter.
DacEasy	DacEasy Inc. 17950 Preston Rd., Suite 200 Dallas, TX 75252 (800) 322-3279 (214) 248-0305	List price: $149.95	Windows, DOS	Windows—Minimum System plus: 4M RAM. DOS—Minimum System plus: DOS 3.0.
M.Y.O.B.	Teleware, Inc. 300 Roundhill Drive Rockaway, NJ 07866 (800) 322-6962 (201) 586-2200	List price: $199.95	Windows, DOS	Windows—Minimum System plus: 386 or better processor, DOS 5.0 or later, 4M RAM.
Managing Your Money	Block Financial Software, Inc. 55 Walls Dr. P.O. Box 912 Fairfield, CT 06430 (800) 537-9993 (203) 256-5000	List price: $79.95	Windows, DOS	Windows—Minimum System plus: 386 or better processor, VGA graphics. DOS—Minimum System plus: DOS 3.0 or later, EGA or better graphics.
Money	Microsoft Corp. One Microsoft Way Redmond, WA 98052 (800) 426-9400 (206) 882-8080	List price: $24.95	Windows	Windows—Minimum System.

Hard Disk Usage	Full-Featured	Ease of Use	Popularity	Features
7M	★★★	★★	★★★	Includes: word processor, spreadsheet, database, drawing, paint; spell checker.

Hard Disk Usage	Full-Featured	Ease of Use	Popularity	Features
5M	★★	★★★	★★	Icon interface; predefined charts of accounts; A/R; A/P; G/L; payroll; inventory; preset reports (balance sheet, income statement, etc.); audit trail.
5M	★★	★★	★★	Icon interface; link to CheckFree; financial advice.
20M	★★★	★★★★	★★★	Predefined charts of accounts; A/R; A/P; G/L; payroll; inventory; Personal Assistant; audit trail; interactive tutorial; DacAdvisor; contact manager.
6M	★★★	★★★	★★	Predefined charts of accounts; A/R; A/P; G/L; payroll; checkbook; drill-down; predefined reports; contact manager.
20M	★★★★	★★★	★★★	SmartDesk natural interface; link to CheckFree; Report Gallery; Chart Gallery; tax forms.
2M	★★★	★★★	★★★	Financial Wizards; Transaction Cue Cards; Pay On-Line; predefined financial reports; charting; tax forms; investment tracking.

(continues)

Personal Finance and Accounting Continued

Program	Manufacturer	Price	Platforms	System Requirements
PeachTree Accounting	PeachTree Software, Inc. 1505-C Pavilion Pl. Norcross, GA 30093 (800) 288-0068 (404) 564-5800	List price: $169	Windows, DOS	Windows—Minimum System. DOS—Minimum System plus: DOS 3.3 or later.
Profit	Microsoft Corp. One Microsoft Way Redmond, WA 98052 (800) 426-9400 (206) 882-8080	List price: $199	Windows	Windows—Minimum System plus: 386 or better processor, 4M RAM.
QuickBooks	Intuit, Inc. 155 Linfield Avenue P.O. Box 3014 Menlo Park, CA 94026 (800) 624-8742 (415) 322-0573	List price: $149.95 Upgrade price: $34.95	Windows, DOS	Windows—Minimum System plus: VGA graphics adapter. DOS—Minimum System plus: DOS 3.0 or later.
Quicken	Intuit, Inc. 155 Linfield Avenue P.O. Box 3014 Menlo Park, CA 94026 (800) 624-8742 (415) 322-0573	List price: $69.95 Upgrade price: $29.95	Windows, DOS	Windows—Minimum System plus: 4M RAM DOS—Minimum System plus: DOS 3.0 or later.

Personal Organizer Programs

Program	Manufacturer	Price	Platforms	System Requirements
Ascend	Franklin Quest Co. 2550 S. Decker Lake Blvd. Salt Lake City, UT 84119 (800) 877-1814 (801) 975-9992	List price: $199	Windows	Windows—Minimum System.
Commence	Jenson-Jones, Inc. Parkway 109 Office Center 328 Newman Spring Road Red Bank, NJ 07701 (800) 688-7080 (908) 530-4666	List price: $395.00	Windows	Windows—Minimum System plus: 3M RAM.
DeskTop Set	Okna Corp. 12 Rt. 17 North, #212 Paramus, NJ 07652 (800) 438-6562 (201) 909-8600	List price: $89	Windows	Windows—Minimum System plus: 4M RAM
ECCO Professional	Arabesque Software, Inc. 2340 130th NE Bellevue, WA 98005 (800) 457-4243 (206) 869-9600	List price: $395.00	Windows	Windows—Minimum System plus: 386 or better processor; VGA graphics adapter.

Hard Disk Usage	Full-Featured	Ease of Use	Popularity	Features
5M	★★★	★★★	★★★	Predefined charts of accounts; A/R; A/P; G/L; payroll; inventory; SmartGuide help text; Custom Forms Designer; many predefined reports; Cash Manager.
9M	★★	★★★	★★	Wizards automate accounting tasks; Profit Signs; predefined reports.
10M	★★★★	★★★	★★★★	Predefined charts of accounts; A/R; A/P; G/L; inventory; audit trail.
8M	★★★★	★★★★	★★★★	Checkbook metaphor; predefined accounts; charting; predefined reports; tax planner; Snapshot; investment tracking; link to CheckFree.

Hard Disk Usage	Full-Featured	Ease of Use	Popularity	Features
2M	★★★	★★★	★★	Phone book; phone dialer; appointment scheduler; hierarchic to-do lists; daily journal; quotations database; flat-file database; notepads; global search.
6M	★★★★	★★	★★	Address book; phone dialer; appointment scheduler; to-do lists; calendar; notepads; global search; Agent function automates regular tasks.
3M	★★★★	★★★★	★★★	Address book; phone dialer; calendar; appointment scheduler; to-do lists; Caller ID; phonetic search.
8M	★★★★	★★	★★★★	Phone book; calendar; phone dialer; appointment scheduler; to-do lists; notepads; global search.

(continues)

Personal Organizer Programs Continued

Program	*Manufacturer*	*Price*	*Platforms*	*System Requirements*
Organizer	Lotus Development Corp. 55 Cambridge Pkwy. Cambridge, MA 02142 (800) 635-6887 (617) 577-8500	List price: $99 Upgrade price: $49	Windows	Windows—Minimum System plus: 4M RAM, VGA graphics adapter.
PackRat	Polaris Software, Inc. 15175 Innovation Dr. San Diego, CA 92128 (800) 722-5728 (619) 592-7400	List price: $395	Windows	Windows—Minimum System plus: 386 or better processor, VGA graphics adapter.
Sharkware	CogniTech Corp. 500 Sugar Mill Rd., #240-A Atlanta, GA 30350 (800) 947-5075 (404) 518-4577	List price: $189.95	Windows	Windows—Minimum System plus: 386 or better processor, 4M RAM, VGA graphics adapter.
SideKick	Starfish Software 1700 Green Hills Rd. Scotts Valley, CA 95066 (800) 370-8963 (408) 439-0942	List price: $29.95	Windows	Windows—Minimum System plus: 386 or better processor, 4M RAM.

Spreadsheet Programs

Program	*Manufacturer*	*Price*	*Platforms*	*System Requirements*
Microsoft Excel	Microsoft Corp. One Microsoft Way Redmond, WA 98052 (800) 426-9400 (206) 882-8080	List price: $495 Upgrade price: $129	Windows	Windows—Minimum System plus: 4M RAM.
Lotus 1-2-3	Lotus Development Corp. 55 Cambridge Pkwy. Cambridge, MA 02142 (800) 635-6887 (617) 577-8500	List price: $495 Upgrade price: $129	Windows, DOS	Windows—Minimum System plus: DOS 3.3 or later, VGA graphics adapter. DOS—Minimum System plus: 1M RAM, DOS 3.0 or later.
Quattro Pro	WordPerfect, the Novell Applications Group 1555 North Technology Way Orem, UT 84057 (800) 451-5151 (801) 225-5000	List price: $395 Upgrade price: $99	Windows, DOS	Windows—Minimum System plus: 4M RAM. DOS—Minimum System.

Hard Disk Usage	Full-Featured	Ease of Use	Popularity	Features
8M	★★★★	★★★★	★★★★	Address book; phone dialer; calendar; appointment scheduler; to-do lists; daily planner; notepad; anniversary notification.
8M	★★★★	★★★	★★★	Phone book; phone dialer; appointment scheduler; to-do list; notepad; recurring-events scheduler; macro language.
7M	★★★	★★★★	★★	Contacts manager; phone dialer; appointment scheduler; to-do list; notepads.
3M	★★★	★★★	★★★★	Address book; phone dialer; calendar; appointment scheduler; to-do lists; daily planner; notepad.

Hard Disk Usage	Full-Featured	Ease of Use	Popularity	Features
8M–28M	★★★★	★★★★	★★★★	Wizards automate routine tasks (charting, functions, etc.); in-cell editing; spell checker; Microsoft Query; pivot tables; Analysis Toolpack; Solver; Scenario Manager; auditor; Visual Basic for Applications macro language.
8M–14M	★★★★	★★★	★★★	Assistants automate routine tasks; Version Manager (multi-user scenario manager); in-cell editing; SmartMaster templates; mapping; links to Lotus Approach; macro language.
24M	★★★★	★★★★	★★	Experts automate routine tasks; Interactive Tutors; Data Modeling Desktop; consolidator; scenario manager; auditor; spell checker; macro language.

Software Suites

Program	Manufacturer	Price	Platforms	System Requirements
Lotus SmartSuite Professional Edition	Lotus Development Corp. 55 Cambridge Pkwy. Cambridge, MA 02142 (800) 635-6887 (617) 577-8500	List price: $659 Upgrade price: $239	Windows	Windows—Minimum System plus: 386 or better processor, 8M RAM, VGA graphics.
Microsoft Office Professional	Microsoft Corp. One Microsoft Way Redmond, WA 98052 (800) 426-9400 (206) 882-8080	List price: $639 Upgrade price: $399	Windows	Windows—Minimum System plus: 4M RAM.
PerfectOffice	WordPerfect, the Novell Applications Group 1555 North Technology Way Orem, UT 84057 (800) 451-5151 (801) 225-5000	List price: $659 Upgrade price: $239	Windows	Windows—Minimum System plus: 4M RAM.

Word Processing

Program	Manufacturer	Price	Platforms	System Requirements
Ami Pro or Word Pro	Lotus Development Corp. 55 Cambridge Pkwy. Cambridge, MA 02142 (800) 635-6887 (617) 577-8500	List price: $495 Upgrade price: $129	Windows	Windows—Minimum System.
Microsoft Word	Microsoft Corp. One Microsoft Way Redmond, WA 98052 (800) 426-9400 (206) 882-8080	List price: $495 Upgrade price: $129	Windows, DOS, Mac	Windows—Minimum System plus: 4M RAM. DOS—Minimum System plus 4M RAM, 286 or better processor. Mac—Minimum System.
WordPerfect	WordPerfect, the Novell Applications Group 1555 North Technology Way Orem, UT 84057 (800) 451-5151 (801) 225-5000	List price: $395 Upgrade price: $95	Windows, DOS, Mac	Windows—Minimum System plus: 386 or better processor, 6M RAM, VGA graphics. DOS—Minimum System plus: 286 or better processor. Mac—Minimum System plus: 4.5M RAM on Power Mac.

Hard Disk Usage	Full-Featured	Ease of Use	Popularity	Features
40M–84M	★★★★	★★★★	★★	Ami Pro; Lotus 1-2-3; Lotus Approach; Freelance Graphics; Lotus Organizer; ScreenCam.
29M–82M	★★★★	★★★★	★★★★	Microsoft Word; Microsoft Excel; Microsoft Access; Microsoft Mail; Microsoft PowerPoint.
40M–114M	★★★★	★★★	★★★	WordPerfect; Quattro Pro; Paradox; Envoy; GroupWise; InfoCentral; Visual AppBuilder; WordPerfect Presentations.

Hard Disk Usage	Full-Featured	Ease of Use	Popularity	Features
5M–20M	★★★	★★★★	★★	Spell checker; grammar checker; thesaurus; drawing module; charting module; tables; templates; macro language.
5M–25M	★★★★	★★★★	★★★★	Spell checker; grammar checker; thesaurus; AutoCorrect; AutoText; multiple levels of Undo; Wizards automate routine tasks; tables; templates; WordArt; Microsoft Draw; WordBasic macro language.
10M-32M	★★★★	★★★	★★★	Spell checker; grammar checker; thesaurus; QuickCorrect; QuickFormat; QuickFinder; QuickList; File Manager; tables; templates; TextArt; WordPerfect Draw; macro language.

Index

Symbols

* (asterisk) wild card character, 90, 130
? (question mark) wild card character, 90, 130
\ (backslash) in filenames, 55
| (vertical hash mark)
  as pointer, 38
  power switch symbol, 29
... (ellipsis) beside menu commands, 72-73
3-D Dinosaur Adventure (childrens program), 558
3.5-inch floppy disks, 11
  inserting/removing, 31-32
5.25-inch floppy disks, 11
  described, 31
  inserting/removing, 32
386 Enhanced mode (startup mode), 58
  /3 switch, 58

A

Access (database program), 552
access time (CD-ROM drives), defined, 11, 48
accounting software, 547
accounts
  PPP (Point-to-Point Protocol), 316
  SLIP (Serial Line Internet Protocol), 316
acronyms (as DOS commands), 212
activating DOS disk drives, 215-216
adapter cards, installing, 432-434
Add New Hardware Wizard (Windows 95), 439-441
Add Printer Wizard (Windows 95), 197
Add/Remove Programs dialog box (Windows 95), deleting programs from hard disk, 168-171
addresses of Internet sites (servers), 317
Adobe Illustrator (drawing program), 570
adult educational software, 556-558
All File Details command (View menu), 143
Alpha Five (database program), 552
America Online (online service)
  articles, printing/reading/saving, 262-265
  bulletin boards, 266
    posting messages to, 266-268
  connecting to, 255-257
  customer support telephone number, 256
  downloading files from, 269-270
  forums, defined, 266
  mail
    adding names to Address Book, 261
    addresses, 274
    reading, 260
    sending, 258-261, 274-277
  services (departments), 255-256
    jumping to (with keywords), 256-258
  toolbar icons, 255
American Heritage Talking Dictionary program, 564
Ami Pro (word processing program), 578
Ancient Lands program, 556
anti-glare screens, 37
AntiVirus (Microsoft AntiVirus), 469-470
applets
  defined, 192
  DiskDefragmenter, 192
  ScanDisk, 192
  Windows 95
    list of, 192-194
    starting, 194
applications
  Windows 3.1, starting with mouse, 38
  Windows 95, starting with mouse, 38
  see also programs; software
Approach (database program), 552
Arcade program (Microsoft Arcade), 566
Arrange Icons command (View menu), 173
arranging windows, 80-83
arrows (as pointer), 38

Arthur Teacher's Trouble (childrens program), 558
Ascend (personal organizer program), 574
assembling components, 23-25
Associate command (File menu), 116
associations (files), 112
asterisk (*) wild card character, 90, 130
AUTOEXEC.BAT file (startup file)
- backups, 444-447
- defined, 60, 444
- deleting, 128
- editing, 412-414

B

background printing (Windows 95), 195
backslash character (\) in filenames, 55
Backup program (Windows 95), 193
backups (files)
- hard drives, 458-463
  - *restoring files, 464-468*
- system files, 444-447

bays (drives), defined, 435
BBS (Bulletin Board Systems), 236-238
- connecting to
  - *fees, 310*
  - *with Windows Terminal, 310-312*
- Microsoft Network, 303
  - *posting/reading messages, 307-308*
- PRODIGY
  - *defined, 239*
  - *posting messages in, 250-254*
- sysops (SYStem OPerators), 310

bits, defined, 46-47
BoardWatch (magazine), 310
Bodyworks program, 556
Bookshelf program (reference), 564
boot disk (startup disk), designing, 394-397
booting (startup), 28-29
- cold-boot (restarting), 43
- rebooting (warm-boot) , 41-42
  - *Windows 95 in safe mode, 150*

brownout, defined, 13
bubblejet printers, 12
Bug Adventure (childrens program), 558
bus types
- defined, 14
- system requirements, 12

buttons
- Help window, 84
- in dialog boxes, 77
- Maximize button, 63, 157
- Minimize button, 63, 157
- Windows 95
  - *Close button, 157*
  - *Restore button, 157*
  - *Start button, 154*

buying decisions
- financing, 18
- manufacturers, 17-18
- pricing, 18
- selecting computer, 15-18
  - *laptops, 10*
- services, 18
- software
  - *packages with purchase, 17-18*
  - *requirements, 7-9*
  - *types of, 4-6*
- warranties, 18

By File Type command (View menu), 141
By File Type dialog box, 141
bytes, defined, 46-47

C

CA-Simply Accounting (accounting program), 572
caddies (CD-ROMs), 34
Calculator program (Windows 95), 192
Cancel Printing command (Document menu), 200
cancelling
- DOS commands, 214
- print jobs (Windows 95), 201

capacity of disks, 147
Carmen Sandiego (Where in the World Is Carmen Sandiego?) program, 562
- starting, 225

carry-in service (warranties), 18
cascading
- menus, displaying, 73
- windows, 80, 83
  - *directory windows, 110-112*
  - *Windows 95, 160*

Categories (Microsoft Network), 295
CD Player program (Windows 95), 193
CD-ROM drives
- balance, adjusting (Windows 95), 159
- cleaning, 344-346
- closing, 34-35
- defined, 14
- drive D, 48
- installing, 435-438
- Multimedia PC 2 standard, 16
- opening, 34-35
- system requirements, 11
- volume, adjusting (Windows 95), 159

CD-ROMs (Compact Disc Read-Only Memory), 10-11
- disk caddy, 34
- eject icons, 34
- handling, 35
- inserting/removing, 34-35

central processing unit, *see* CPU
CGA (Color Graphics Adapter) monitor, 8, 11
Character Map program (Windows 95), described, 192
characters in filenames, 53
chat rooms (Microsoft Network), 303-306
check boxes in dialog boxes, 75-76
- DOS, 229

Chessmaster 4000 program (game), 566
child directories (subdirectories), 56, 217
- displaying, 105

childrens educational software, 558-562
CIM (CompuServe Information Manager), 271
Cinemania program, 556
circuit boards, 11
ClarisWorks (integrated software package), 570
cleaning computer, 328-330
clicking mouse, 40
Clipboard, defined, 192
Clipboard Viewer program (Windows 95), described, 192
Close button (Windows 95), 157
Close command (File menu), 92
closing
- CD-ROM drive, 34-35
- files, 92

program groups, 64
windows, 80, 83
directory windows, 110-112
clusters on disks, 51
cold-boot (restarting), 43
Collapse Branch command (Tree menu), 104
Color Graphics Adapter (CGA) monitor, 8, 11
Columbia Electronic Dictionary of Quotations program, 564
command buttons (dialog boxes), 75-76
DOS, 229
command line (DOS), parts of, 212
command prompt (DOS prompt), 172
COMMAND.COM file, deleting, 128
commands
... (ellipsis) beside, 72-73
Disk menu
Format Disk, 147
Select Drive, 102
Document menu
Cancel Printing, 200
Pause Printing, 200
DOS
cancelling, 214
COPY, 212
delimiters, 212
DIR, 221-223
entering in, 212-214
help (to identify parts of command line), 213
parameters, 212
parts of command line, 212
startup, 225-226
switches in, 212, 226
syntax (rules), 212
Edit menu
Copy, 39
Cut, 39
Select All, 178
entering in Windows 95, 161-162
File menu, 72
Associate, 116
Close, 92
Copy, 121
Create Directory, 133
Delete, 135, 182
Empty Recycle Bin, 184
Exit, 30, 98, 233
Move, 127
New, 231
Preview, 96
Print Preview, 96
Quit, 233
Rename, 130
Restore, 184
Run, 60, 69
Save, 30, 92
Save All, 232
Save As, 94
Search, 145
Select Files, 112, 115
Set as Wallpaper, 201
File menu, Delete, 129
grayed out, 73
Help menu, 72
Jump menu (PRODIGY), Jump To, 239
New menu, Folder, 187
Printer menu
Pause Printing, 200
Purge Print Jobs, 200
Search menu (PRODIGY), Quick Search, 249
selecting, 71-73
with mouse, 38
Services menu (CompuServe), Go, 272
Start menu, Help, 152
toggling on/off, 73
Tools menu, User Setup, 95
Transfers menu (Terminal)
Receive, 313
Send, 313
Tree menu, 104
Expand All, 104, 125, 132
Expand Branch, 104
Expand One Level, 104
triangles beside, 73
View menu
All File Details, 143
Arrange Icons, 173
By File Type, 141
Details, 173
Directory Only, 107-108
Large Icons, 173
Line Up Icons, 173
List, 173
Small Icons, 173
Sort by Date, 138
Sort by Name, 138
Sort by Size, 138
Sort by Type, 138
Toolbar, 174
Tree and Directory, 107
Tree Only, 107-108
Window menu, 72
Commence (personal organizer program), 574
communications software, 546
list of, 550
compressed files, *see* ZIP files
compressing
hard disk drives, 406-411
Compton's Interactive Encyclopedia program, 564
CompuServe (online service)
connecting to, 271-273
databases, defined, 271
forums
defined, 271
downloading files from, 285-287
joining, 282
jumping to, 272-274
leaving, 282
posting messages to, 282-284
mail
addresses, 274
reading, 277
sending to other online services, 274
services
defined, 271
fees, 278
jumping to, 272-274
reading articles, 278-281
saving articles, 278
toolbar icons, 271
CompuServe Information Manager (CIM), 271
computer cover, removing, 350
CONFIG.SYS file (startup file)
backups, 444-447
defined, 444
deleting, 128
editing, 412-414
Confirm Directory Delete dialog box, 135
Confirm File Delete dialog box, 129, 135
confirmation dialog box, displaying/hiding, 191
container files, *see* ZIP files
Contents tab, Help (Windows 95), 163
Control menu, displaying, 74-77
Control-menu box, 63, 74
COPY command (DOS), 212
Copy command (Edit menu), 39
Copy command (File menu), 121
Copy dialog box, 121

copying
files, 117-121
old files (to free up space on hard drive), 391-393
to another disk, 117-121
to same disk, 119
Windows 95, 179-181
ZIP files (compressed files), 376
folders (Windows 95), 179-181
text with mouse, 39
Corel Ventura (desktop publishing program), 554
CorelDRAW! (drawing program), 570
CPU (Central Processing Unit)
defined, 7, 10, 13
Multimedia PC 2 standard, 16
Create Directory command (File menu), 133
Create Directory dialog box, 133
Creative Writer (childrens program), 558
crosshairs (as pointer), defined, 38
Crosstalk (communications program), 550
customizing desktop (Windows 95), 201-206
Cut command (Edit menu), 39
cutting
files, 122-127
text with mouse, 39

D

DacEasy (personal finance program), 572
data compression (modems), defined, 12
data files
defined, 51, 388
deleting to increase computer speed, 388-390
databases
defined, 546
flat-file databases, defined, 546
list of, 552
purchasing software decisions, 5
relational databases, defined, 546
software, 546-548, 574
software purchasing decisions, 4
see also spreadsheets
date display
in DOS prompt, 213
Windows 95 taskbar, setting, 159
dBASE 5 (database program), 552
starting, 225
decompression software (PKUNZIP), 374
defragmenting files (on hard disk drive), 398-401
Delete command (File menu), 129, 135, 182
Delete dialog box, 129, 135
deleting
directories, 134, 135
files, 128-129
defined, 52, 128
DOS, 216
old files (to increase computer speed), 388-390
startup files, 128
undeleting, 448-453
Windows 95, 182-184
folders, Windows 95, 182-184
icons, program-item icons, 67
programs from hard disk (Windows 95), 168-171
delimiters (in DOS command lines), 212
Delphi (service provider), 317
mail addresses, 274
density of disks, 147
designing
directories, 132-133
files, 87-88
icons
program-group icons, 65
shortcut icons (Windows 95), 188-189
program groups, 65-67
desktop
defined, 154
Windows 95, 154-156
customizing, 201-206
date display, 155
display resolution, 206
editing object properties, 190-191
My Computer icon, 154
Network Neighborhood icon, 154
patterns, 201
Recycle Bin, 154, 183
screen savers, 202
Start button, 154
taskbar, 154, 159
wallpaper, 201
desktop publishing software, 546
list of, 554
DeskTop Set (personal organizer program), 574
Details command (View menu), 173
Dial-Up Networking program (Windows 95), 322-323
described, 192
dialog boxes
Add/Remove (Windows 95), deleting program from hard disk, 168-171
By File Type, 141
check boxes in, 75-76
command buttons, 75-76
Confirm Directory Delete, 135
Confirm File Delete, 129, 135
confirmation, displaying/hiding, 191
Copy, 121
Create Directory, 133
defined, 75-77, 80
Delete, 129, 135
directory lists in, navigating, 78
DOS, 229-230
drop-down lists, 75-77
Format Disk, 147
options, 146
increment/spinner buttons, 76-77
Jump (PRODIGY), 239
list boxes in, 75-77
Move, 127
New Program Object, 65
option buttons in, 75-76
selecting with keyboard, 76
selecting with mouse, 38
Print, 96
Recycle Bin Properties, 190
Rename, 131
Run, 60
Save As, 92
scroll bars, 79
scrolling in, 79
Select Drive, 102
Shut Down Windows, 153
tabs in, 75, 77
text boxes, 75-76
User Setup, 95
Windows 95, 161-162
dictionary software (reference software), 546-547, 564-566

Digital Signal Processor (DSP), 12
Dinosaurs (childrens program), 560
DIR command (DOS), 221-223
Direct Cable Connection program (Windows 95), described, 192
directories
contents, viewing, 106
copying to disks, 119
defined, 55
deleting, 134-135
designing, 55-56, 132-133
directory tree, 55, 104
editing directory tree icons, 104
DOS
contents list, 221-223
deleting, 219-220
designing, 219-220
moving between levels, 217-218
switching, 217-218
moving, 122-127
naming (renaming), 130-131
navigating, 105
root directory (main directory), 55, 217
searching for Windows 3.11, 144-145
selecting, 105
structure of, 55
subdirectories, 56, 217
displaying, 105
viewing, 104-106
directory lists (dialog boxes), navigating, 78
Directory Only command (View menu), 107, 108
Directory view, switching, 107
directory windows
cascading, 110-112
closing, 110-112
defined, 102
displaying, 102-103
moving, 110
opening
several, 109-111
to view another directory, 110
selecting open windows, 109
tiling, 110-112
views, switching, 107-108
discs, *see* CD-ROMs
disk caddies (CD-ROMs), 34
DiskDefragmenter (DOS disk defragmenter), 192-193, 398-401
disk error message, 28
Disk menu commands
Format Disk, 147
Select Drive, 102
disks, 46
bits, defined, 46-47
bytes, defined, 46-47
defragmenting files on, 398-401
density, 147
error checking (with ScanDisk program), 454-457
floppy disks
inserting, 31-32
jammed, 360-361
protecting against damage, 33
storage capacity, 33
write-protecting, 33, 168
formatting, 146-148
defined, 47
in DOS, 224
quick formatting, 146
hard disks, 549
defined, 46
formatting, 224
labels, 146
read/write head, 48
removing, 31-32
sectors on
clusters of, 51
defined, 47, 51
startup disks, designing, 394-397
storage capacity, 46-47, 147
tracks on, defined, 47, 51
display resolution (Windows 95), 206
display, *see* desktop
displaying
dialog boxes (confirmation dialog boxes), 191
directories
simultaneously, 109
subdirectories, 105
DOS prompt (Windows 95), 172
files
attributes, 142-143
last modification date, 142-143
size, 142-143
temporarily, 140-141
menus
Control menu, 74-77
icon menus, 74
shortcut menus, 39
submenus, 73
modes, 58-59
toolbars (Windows 95), 174
dithering (printing), 196
document files, defined, 112
document icons (Windows 95), 174
Document menu commands
Cancel Printing, 200
Pause Printing, 200
documents
closing, 92
defined, 87, 231
printing, 96
and viewing (Windows 95), 159
previewing before, 96-97
Windows 95, 196-200
saving, 92-93
and renaming, 94
automatically, 95
starting, 87
DOOM program (game), 566
DOS (Disk Operating System)
command lines, 212-213
commands
cancelling, 214
COPY, 212
delimiters, 212
DIR, 221-223
entering, 212-214
help (to identify parts of command line), 213
parameters, 212
startup, 225-226
switches, 212, 226
syntax (rules), 212
defined, 172
dialog boxes in, 229-230
directories
contents list, 221-223
deleting, 219-220
designing, 219-220
moving between levels, 217-218
switching, 217-218
disk formatting, 224
drives
compressing, 407-408
defragmenting hard drive files, 398-401
logging on (activating), 215-216
uncompressing, 409
exiting/shutting down, 30
files
deleting, 216
designing, 231
editing startup files, 412-414
opening, 231
pathname, 217
saving, 232

installing
uninstalling, 378-380
with a Setup program, 364-365
program icons (Windows 95), 174
programs
exiting, 233-234
menus in, 227-228
ScanDisk (error checking), 454-457
shell out to DOS, 233-234
starting from DOS prompt, 225-226
system requirements, 7-8, 548
windows, resizing, 172
DOS 4.1 or 5.0 Shell program, starting, 225
DOS prompt
defined, 172
displaying (Windows 95), 172
editing, 213-214
dot pitch, defined, 11
dot-matrix printers, 12
cleaning, 334
installing, 416-419
dots-per-inch (monitors), 11
double-clicking
icons, 62
mouse, 40
double-density disks (DD), 147
double-sided floppy disks, defined, 33
downloading
files
from America Online, 269-270
from CompuServe, 285-287
with Terminal, 313-315
dragging with mouse, 40
dragging-and-dropping data, 39
drawing software, 547, 570
drives
bays, defined, 435
CD-ROM drive
balance adjustments, 159
cleaning, 344-346
closing, 34-35
defined, 14
drive D, 48
installing, 435-438
Multimedia PC 2 standard, 16
opening, 34-35
system requirements, 11
volume adjustments, 159
defined, 46
displaying in DOS prompt, 213
DOS, logging on (activating), 215-216
error checking (with ScanDisk program), 454-457
floppy disk drives
cleaning, 341-343
defined, 14
drive A, 48
drive B, 48
Multimedia PC 2 standard, 16
system requirements, 11
hard disk drives
compressing, 406-411
defined, 8, 11, 13, 46
drive C, 48
file backups, 458-463
space on, 391-393
speed, 388-390
Multimedia PC 2 standard, 16
restoring files, 464-468
system requirements, 11
list of
Explorer, 174
My Computer, 175
reading from disks, defined, 48-50
speed (access time), 48
tape backup drives
cleaning, 347-348
defined, 347
viewing in File Manager, 102-103
writing to disks, defined, 48-50
DriveSpace program (Windows 95)
compressing hard drives, 406-411
described, 193
running, 410-411
drop-down lists (dialog boxes), 75-77
DOS, 229
DSP (Digital Signal Processor), 12
DTP (desktop publishing software), 546
DX processors, 10
DX/2 processors, 10
DX/4 processors, 10

E

e-mail
addresses, online services, 274
reading, on America Online, 260
sending
on America Online, 258-261
on CompuServe, 274-277
on Microsoft Network, 299-308
on PRODIGY, 243-246
to other online services from CompuServe, 274
E-Mail (Microsoft Network category), 295
ECCO Professional (personal organizer program), 574
ECHO (East Coast Hang Out; BBS), 310
Edit menu commands
Copy, 39
Cut, 39
Select All, 178
editing
desktop objects (Windows 95), 190-191
DOS prompt, 213-214
files, startup files, 412-414
icons, directory tree, 104
program groups, 65-67
taskbar properties (Windows 95), 160
educational software, 546-547
adult, 556-558
childrens, 558-562
reference, 564-566
EGA (Enhanced Graphics Adapter) monitor, 8, 11
EISA bus (Enhanced Industry Standard Architecture), 12
ellipsis (...) beside menu commands, 73-72
Empty Recycle Bin command (File menu), 184
Encarta program (reference), 564
encyclopedia software (reference software), 546-547, 564-566
energy smart monitors, 203
Enhanced Graphics Adapter (EGA) monitor, 8, 11
entering commands in DOS, 212-214

equipment, *see* **hardware; software, requirements**
error correction (modems), defined, 12
error diffusion (print quality), 196
error messages
disk error, 28
logging on DOS disk drives, 215-216
Non-system disk, 28
errors (disk errors), checking with ScanDisk, 454-457
Excel (spreadsheet program), 576
Exchange (Microsoft Exchange), 299
described, 193
executable files, defined, 225
Exit command (File menu), 30, 98, 233
exiting
DOS, 30
Explorer (Windows 95), 175
File Manager, 100-101
Help, 85
Windows 95, 165
menus, 72
programs, 98
DOS, 233-234
shell out to DOS, 233-234
windows, 83
Windows 3.1, 30
Windows 95 (keep), 30, 150-153
Expand All command (Tree menu), 104, 125, 132
Expand Branch command (Tree menu), 104
Expand One Level command (Tree menu), 104
expansion cards, installing, 432-434
expansion slots, 14
system requirements, 11
Experts, defined, 87
Explorer (Windows 95)
defined, 173
drive list (plus sign next to drive), 174
exiting, 175
file lists, 173-174
files/folders
copying, 179-181
deleting, 182-184
designing, 187
restoring deletions, 182-184
selecting, 177-178
folder list (plus sign next to folder), 174
shortcut icons, designing, 188-189
starting, 174
exporting files, 89
eye-strain exercises, 36-37

F

FAT files (File Allocation Table), 51-52
Favorite Places (Microsoft Network category), 295
Fax program (Windows 95), described, 193
File Manager
directories, viewing, 104-106
directory windows (drives)
opening several, 109-111
switching views, 107-108
viewing, 102-103
exiting, 100-101
starting, 100-101
Tree menu, 104
View menu commands, 107
File menu commands, 72
Associate, 116
Close, 92
Copy, 121
Create Directory, 133
Delete, 129, 135, 182
Empty Recycle Bin, 184
Exit, 30, 98, 233
Move, 127
New, 231
Preview, 96
Print Preview, 96
Quit, 30, 233
Rename, 130
Restore, 184
Run, 60, 69
Save, 30, 92
Save All, 232
Save As, 94
Search, 145
Select Files, 112, 115
Set as Wallpaper, 201
files, 51
associations, 112
attributes, displaying in window, 142-143
AUTOEXEC.BAT file
defined, 60, 444
deleting, 128
closing, 92
COMMAND.COM file, deleting, 128
compressing on hard drive, 406-411
CONFIG.SYS file
defined, 444
deleting, 128
container files (ZIP files), 374-377
copying, 117-121
old files (to free up space on hard drive), 391-393
to another disk, 117-121
to same disk, 119
data files, defined, 51, 388
defragmenting, 398-401
deleting, 128-129
defined, 52, 128
old files (to increase computer speed), 388-390
undeleting, 448-453
designing, 87-88
display options, 142-143
document files, defined, 112
DOS (Disk Operating System)
deleting, 216
designing new, 231
directory list contents, 221-234
opening, 231
pathname, 217
saving, 232
downloading with Terminal, 313-315
executable files, defined, 225
Explorer, list of, 174
FAT file, 51-52
fragmented, 52
hard disk drives
backups, 458-463
restoring files, 464-468
hiding temporarily, 140-141
last modification date (displaying in window), 142-143
Microsoft Works for Windows, opening, 89
moving, 122-127
My Computer, list of, 175
naming, 53-54
backslash character (\), 55
components of filenames, 54
renaming, 130-131

- opening, 89, 113-116
  - *from another program, 89-91*
  - *shortcut, 91*
- paths, 54
- program files, defined, 51, 112, 388
- saving, 92-93
  - *and renaming, 94*
  - *automatically, 95*
- searching for
  - *Windows 3.11, 144-145*
  - *with wild card characters, 90*
- selecting, 112-116
  - *nonadjacent files, 114*
- size, displaying in window, 142-143
- starting, 113-116
- startup files, editing in DOS/Windows 3.11, 412-414
- system files
  - *backups, 444-447*
  - *defined, 112*
- SYSTEM.INI, 412, 445
- time, displaying in window, 142-143
- uploading with Terminal, 313-315
- WIN.INI files, defined, 412, 444
- Windows 3.11, sorting list of, 138-139
- Windows 95
  - *arranging icons for, 173*
  - *copying, 179-181*
  - *deleting, 182-184*
  - *designing, 187*
  - *extensions, 173*
  - *identifying file types, 173-176*
  - *long filenames, 185-186*
  - *renaming, 185-186*
  - *restoring deletions, 182-184*
  - *selecting, 177-178*
- ZIP files (container files)
  - *decompressing (with PKUNZIP), 375*
  - *installing programs from, 374-377*

financial software (personal finance), 547, 572-574

financing purchases, 18

Fine Artist (childrens program), 560

flat-file database programs, defined, 546

flatbed scanners, 13

floppy disk drives
- cleaning, 341-343
- defined, 11, 14
- drive A, 48
- drive B, 48
- Multimedia PC 2 standard, 16
- system requirements, 11

floppy disks
- formatting, 146-148
  - *defined, 47*
  - *in DOS, 224*
  - *quick formatting, 146*
- inserting/removing, 31-32
- jammed, 360-361
- protecting against damage, 33
- sectors
  - *defined, 47, 51*
  - *clusters of, 51*
- storage capacity, 33, 46-47, 147
- tracks on, defined, 47, 51
- write-protecting, 33, 168

Folder command (New menu), 187

folders
- Explorer, list of, 174
- My Computer, list of, 175
- Windows 95
  - *copying, 179-181*
  - *deleting, 182-184*
  - *designing, 187*
  - *renaming, 185-186*
  - *restoring deletions, 182-184*
  - *selecting, 177-178*

Format Disk command (Disk menu), 147

Format Disk dialog box, 146-147

formatting disks, 146-148
- defined, 47
- DOS, 224
- hard disks, 224
- quick formatting, 146

forums, CompuServe
- downloading files from, 285-287
- joining/leaving, 282
- posting messages to, 282-284
- *see also* America Online, bulletin boards

FoxPro (database program), 552

Fractal Design Painter (drawing program), 570

fragmented files, 52

FrameMaker (desktop publishing program), 554

French Assistant program, 556

G

game software, 547, 566-568

Games program (Windows 95), described, 193

general failure error reading drive A (error message), 215

Go command (Services menu; CompuServe), 272

Golf program (Microsoft Golf), 568

graphics software, 547, 570

GUIs (Graphical User Interfaces), Microsoft Windows, 8

H

hand-held scanners, 13

hard disk drives
- cleaning, 347-348
- compressing, 406-411
- defined, 8, 11, 13, 46
- drive C, 48
- error checking (with ScanDisk program), 454-457
- files
  - *backups, 458-463*
  - *restoring, 464-468*
- Multimedia PC 2 standard, 16
- space, increasing, 391-393
- speed, increasing, 388-390
- system requirements, 11

hard disk usage, defined, 549

hard disks
- defined, 46
- formatting, 146-148, 224
  - *defined, 47*
  - *quick formatting, 146*
- sectors on
  - *clusters of, 51*
  - *defined, 47, 51*
- storage capacity, 46-47, 147
- tracks on, defined, 47, 51

hardware
- connecting components, 23-25
- installing
  - *adapter cards, 432-434*
  - *CD-ROM drives, 435-438*
  - *in Windows 95, 439-441*
  - *joystick, 420*
  - *modems (external), 425-429*
  - *mouse, 421-424*
  - *printers, 416-419*

sound cards, 432-434
speakers (connecting to sound cards), 430-431
monitors, adjusting for viewing comfort, 36-37
plug-and-play hardware (Windows 95), 439
purchasing, 10-15
requirements, 10-12, 16
selecting location for, 20-21
system unit, defined, 10
unpacking, 22
Harvard Graphics program, starting, 225
HD (high-density) disks, 11
Help
contents, 85
exiting, 85
hypertext links, 84
topics, 85
moving between, 85
searching, 86
window buttons, 84
Windows 95, 163-167
dialog boxes, 161-162
exiting, 165
index, 166
Help command (Start menu), 152
Help menu commands, 72
hidden files, *see* system files
hiding
confirmation dialog boxes, 191
files temporarily, 140-141
high-density (HD) floppy disks, 11, 33, 147
horizontal printing (landscape orientation), 196
HyperACCESS (communications program), 550
HyperTerminal program (Windows 95), described, 192
hypertext links (Help), 84

I

IBM-compatible software requirements, 7-9
icons
directory tree icons, editing, 104
eject icons, 34
menus for, displaying, 74
program group icons
defined, 62
described, 68
double-clicking, 62
moving, 67
program-group icons, 64
designing, 65
program-item icons
defined, 62
deleting, 67
described, 68
double-clicking, 62
shortcut icons (Windows 95), printer, 200
toolbars
list of, 71
selecting, 71-73
Windows 95
arranging, 173
document icons, 174
DOS program icons, 174
identifying file types, 173-176
My Computer icon, 154
Network Neighborhood icon, 154
program icons, 174
shortcut icons, 188-189
Tour: Ten minutes to using Windows icon, 165
importing files, 89
increment buttons (dialog boxes), 76-77
indexes, Help (Windows 95), 166
information manager software (personal organizer software), 547
inkjet printers, 12
cleaning, 334
installing, 416-419
inserting
CD-ROMs (Compact Disc Read-Only Memory), 34-35
floppy disks, 31-43
Install New Program Wizard (Windows 95), 168, 372-373
installing
computers, common-sense guidelines, 20-21
DOS
uninstalling, 378-380
with a Setup programs, 364-365
hardware
adapter cards, 432-434
CD-ROM drives, 435-438
joystick, 420
modems (external), 425-429
mouse, 421-424
printers, 416-419
sound cards, 432-434
speakers (connecting to sound cards), 430-431
programs ZIP files (container files), 374-377
surge suppressors (protector), 353-354
Windows 3.11
uninstalling, 381-383
with a Setup program, 366-368
without a Setup program, 369-371
Windows 95, 372-373
hardware, 439-441
printers, 416-419
programs in, 168-171
uninstalling, 384, 386
integrated software packages, 547, 570-572
Internet
accounts, PPP/SLIP, 316
connecting to
overview, 316-317
with Dial-Up Networking (Windows 95), 322-323
online services, 316
service providers, 316
e-mail address, 318
list of, 317
user ID, 318
sites (servers), 316
addresses, 317
connecting to sites with Windows Terminal, 318-321
startup kit, 316
ISA bus (Industry Standard Architecture), 12

J

joysticks, 14
defined, 420
installing, 420
system requirements, 11
Jump dialog box (PRODIGY), 239
Jump menu commands (PRODIGY), Jump To , 239
Just Grandma and Me (childrens program), 560

K

K (kilobytes), defined, 33
keyboard, 14
  cleaning, 336-337
    spilled liquid on, 355-359
  configuring settings (Windows 95), 209-210
  connecting, 23-24
  system requirements, 11
Kid Works 2 (childrens program), 560
Kid's Zoo (childrens program), 560
King's Quest VII: The Prince-less Bride program, 566
Kiplinger's Simply Money (personal finance program), 572

L

labels (disk labels), 146
landscape orientation (horizontal), 196
laptops, defined, 10
Large Icons command (View menu), 173
laser printers, 12
  cleaning, 334
  installing, 416-419
Line Up Icons command (View menu), 173
Links 386 Pro program (game), 566
links in Help, 84
liquid spills on keyboard or mouse, cleaning, 355-359
list boxes (dialog boxes), 75-77
  DOS, 229
List command (View menu), 173
loading automatically at startup, 60-61
locked-up computer, rebooting, 41-42
logging on DOS disk drives, 215-216
Lotus 1-2-3 (spreadsheet program), 576
  starting, 225
Lotus SmartSuite, 578

M

M (megabytes), defined, 11, 33
M.Y.O.B. (personal finance program), 572
Macintosh software requirements, 7-9
maintenance (cleaning), 328-330
  CD-ROM drives, 344-346
  computer, 328-330
  floppy disk drives, 341-343
  hard disk drives
    compressing, 406-411
    defragmenting files on, 398-401
    space on, 391-393
    speed, 388-390
  inside computer, 349-352
  jammed disks, 360-361
  keyboard, 336-337
  memory, increasing available memory, 402-405
  monitors, 331-332
  mouse, 338-340
  printer, 333-335
  spilled liquid on keyboard or mouse, 355-359
  startup disks, 394-397
  startup files, editing, 412-414
  tape backup drives (for hard drives), 347-348
  virus checking (Microsoft AntiVirus), 469-470
Managing Your Money (personal finance program), 572
Math Ace (childrens program), 560
Math Blaster: In Search Of Spot (childrens program), 560
Mavis Beacon Teaches program, 556
Maximize button (Windows 95), 63, 157
maximizing windows, 63, 80-82
Media Player program (Windows 95), described, 193
megabytes (M), defined, 11, 33
Member Assistance (Microsoft Network category), 295
MemMaker, 402-405
memory
  hard disk drive, 402
  increasing available memory, 402-405
  RAM (Random-Access Memory), 402
menu bar, defined, 62
menus
  commands
    ... (ellipsis) beside, 72-73
    DOS, 212-214, 227-228
    grayed out, 73
    selecting, 71-73
    selecting in Windows 95, 161-162
    toggling on/off, 73
    triangles beside, 73
  Control menu, displaying, 74-77
  exiting, 72
  icon menus, displaying, 74
  pull-down menus, opening, 72
  selecting with mouse, 38
  shortcut menus (Windows 95), 161-162
    displaying, 39
  submenus, displaying, 73
microphones, 15
  adjusting balance and volume (Windows 95), 159
  connecting to sound card, 24-25
  system requirements, 12
  see also sound cards; speakers
Microsoft AntiVirus, 469-470
Microsoft Arcade program, 566
Microsoft Backup program, 458-468
Microsoft Complete program, 556
Microsoft Excel (spreadsheet program), 576
Microsoft Exchange program (Windows 95), 193, 299
Microsoft Golf program, 568
Microsoft Musical program, 556
Microsoft Network program (Windows 95)
  accounts for family members, 292
  bulletin boards, 303
    posting/reading messages, 307-308
  categories, browsing, 295-298
  chat rooms (real-time conversations), 303-306
  connecting to, 288-294

defined, 193
mail, sending, 299-308
Microsoft Office (software suite), 578
Microsoft Windows, *see* Windows 3.11; Windows 95
Microsoft Word (word processing program), 578
Microsoft Word for DOS, starting, 225
Microsoft Works for DOS, starting, 225
Microsoft Works for Windows (integrated software package), 570
files, opening, 89
Minimize button (Windows 95), 157
described, 63
minimizing windows, 63, 80-82
Miracle Piano Teaching program, 556
modems, 12, 15
connecting, 23-25
data compression, defined, 12
error correction, defined, 12
external, 425
installing, 425-429
hardware purchasing decisions, 5
internal, 425
system requirements, 12
modes, displaying, 58-59
Money (personal finance program), 572
monitors
adjusting for viewing comfort, 36-37
anti-glare screens, 37
brightness, adjusting, 28, 37
cleaning, 331-332
connecting, 23-25
contrast, adjusting, 37
defined, 11, 14
dot pitch, defined, 11
energy smart monitors, 203
eye-strain exercises, 36-37
H-phase (horizontal control), 37
Multimedia PC 2 standard, 16
non-interlaced, defined, 36
system requirements, 8, 11
turning on/off, 30
V-size (vertical control), 37
motherboard, defined, 14
mouse, 14
cleaning, 338-340
spilled liquid on, 355-359
clicking, 40
configuring settings (Windows 95), 207-210
connecting, 23-24
copying text with, 39
defined, 421
double-clicking, 40
dragging with, 40
dragging-and-dropping data, 39
drawing/painting with, 39
installing, 421-424
mouse pad, 38
moving text with, 39
pointer, 38
doesn't move, 338
drags/skips when moving, 338
mouse trails, 209
shapes of, 38
pointing, 40
right-clicking, 39-40
selecting with, 38-39
starting applications with, 38
system requirements, 8, 11
Move command (File menu), 127
Move dialog box, 127
moving
directories, 122-127
files, 122-127
Windows 95, 179-181
folders (Windows 95), 179-181
icons, program group icons, 67
in dialog boxes, 79
taskbar (Windows 95), 160
text with mouse, 39
windows, 62, 81
directory windows, 110
MPC2 standard, 16
MS-DOS, *see* DOS
MSN Today (Microsoft Network category), 295
Multimedia PC 2 standard, 16
Multimedia program (Windows 95), described, 193
multimedia-compliant computers, 16
My Computer (Windows 95)
defined, 173
drive list, viewing, 175
file list, 173
viewing, 175
files/folders
copying, 179-181
deleting, 182-184
designing, 187
renaming, 185-186
restoring deletions, 182-184
selecting, 177-178
folder list, viewing, 175
shortcut icons, designing, 188-189
starting, 175
windows, closing, 176
My Computer icon (Windows 95), 154
MyAdvancedBrochures (desktop publishing program), 554
Myst program (game), 568

N

naming
directories, renaming, 130-131
files, 53-54
backslash character (\), 55
components of filenames, 54
renaming, 130-131
when saving, 94
Windows 95, 185-186
folders, Windows 95, 185-186
navigating, 105
Help topics, 85
Net, *see* Internet
Netcom (service provider), 317
Network Neighborhood icon (Windows 95), 154
Network, *see* Microsoft Network
New command (File menu), 231
New Grolier Multimedia Encyclopedia program, 564
New Kid on the Block, The (childrens program), 562
New menu commands, Folder, 187
New Program Object dialog box, 65
non-interlaced monitors, defined, 36
Non-system disk error message, 28
Norton Utilities program, starting, 225
Not ready reading drive A (error message), 215
notebook computer, defined, 10
Notepad program (Windows 95), described, 192

O

objects, editing properties of (Windows 95), 190-191
Office (software suite), 578
on-site warranties, 18
online services, 236-238, 316
  America Online
    adding names to Address Book, 261
    articles, reading/printing/saving, 262-265
    connecting to, 255-257
    customer support telephone number, 256
    downloading files from, 269-270
    jumping services (with keywords), 256-258
    posting messages to bulletin boards, 266-268
    reading mail messages, 260
    sending mail, 258-261, 274-277
    services (departments), 255-256
    toolbar icons, 255
  CompuServe
    articles, reading/saving, 278-281
    connecting to, 271-273
    databases, 271
    downloading files from, 285-287
    forums, 271
    jumping to forums or services, 272-274
    posting messages to forums, 282-284
    reading mail, 277
    services, 271
    toolbar icons, 271
  Microsoft Network
    accounts for family members, 292
    bulletin boards, 303
    browsing categories, 295-298
    chat rooms (real-time conversations), 303-306
    connecting to, 288-294
    posting/reading BBS messages, 307-308
    sending mail, 299-308
  PRODIGY
    browsing services, 247-249
    bulletin boards, 239
    connecting to, 239-242
    customer support telephone number, 239
    jumping to new service, 239
    passwords, 240
    posting messages to bulletin boards, 250-254
    reading articles, 247-249
    reading mail, 245
    replying to bulletin board messages, 253
    sending mail, 243-246
    services, 239
    toolbars, 239
opening
  CD-ROM drive, 34-35
  directory windows, 109-111
  files, 89, 113-116
    DOS, 231
    from another program, 89-91
    Microsoft Works for Windows, 89
    shortcut, 91
  menus, 72
  program groups, 64
operating system, hardware requirements, 7-8
optimization, *see* defragmenting
option buttons (dialog boxes), 75-76
  DOS, 229
Organizer (personal organizer program), 576
orientations (landscape/ portrait), 196

P

packages of software (integrated), 547, 570, 572
packing slip, 22
PackRat (personal organizer program), 576
PageMaker (desktop publishing program), 554
Paint program (Windows 95), 192
Paradox (database program), 552
  starting, 225
parallel ports, defined, 12
parameters in DOS command lines, 212
passwords, PRODIGY, 240
paths (file paths), defined, 54, 217
patterns (desktop)
  defined, 201
  switching (Windows 95), 201
Pause Printing (Document menu), 200
Pause Printing (Printer menu), 200
pausing printing (Windows 95), 201
PC Paintbrush (drawing program), 570
PC Tools program, starting, 225
PeachTree Accounting (accounting program), 574
Pentium, processing power, 10
PerfectOffice (software suite), 578
personal organizer software, 574-576
  information managers, 547
PFS: Publisher (desktop publishing program), 22, 554
PFS:WindowWorks (integrated software packages), 570
PharmAssist program, 556
Phone Dialer program (Windows 95), 192
Pipeline USA (service provider), 317
PKUNZIP (decompressing ZIP files), 374-375
platforms, defined, 548
playing sound, *see* sound cards
plug-and-play hardware (Windows 95), 439
Point-to-Point Protocol (PPP), 316
pointer (mouse), 38
  doesn't move, 338
  drags/skips when moving, 338
  shapes of, 38
  Windows 95,
    mouse trails, 209
    speed, 207-210
pointing mouse, 40
Portal Information Network (service provider), 316
portrait orientation (vertical), 196
ports
  defined, 12, 14
  parallel ports, 12
  serial ports, 12, 421
  system requirements, 12

POST (Power-On-Self-Test), 28
posting messages, 236
power switch, 29
- cold booting with (restarting), 43

Power-On-Self-Test (POST), 28
PPP (Point-to-Point Protocol) connection, 316
Prehistoria (childrens program), 562
Preview command (File menu), 96
previewing documents before printing, 96
pricing computers, 18
Print dialog box, 96
Print Manager, 96
Print Preview command (File menu), 96
Print Shop Deluxe (desktop publishing program), 554
Printer menu commands
- Pause Printing, 200
- Purge Print Jobs, 200

printers
- bubblejet printers, 12
- cleaning, 333-335
- connecting, 23-25
- defined, 12, 15
- dot-matrix printers, 12
- inkjet printers, 12
- installing, 416-419
- laser printers, 12
- system requirements, 12
- turning on/off, 29-30
- Windows 95
  - *changing settings, 195-200*
  - *installing, 198*
  - *print quality, 196*
  - *shortcut icons, 200*

printing
- dithering, 196
- documents, 96
  - *and viewing (Windows 95), 159*
  - *previewing before, 96-97*
- error diffusion (print quality), 196
- orientations (landscape/horizontal), 196
- Windows 95
  - *background printing, 195*
  - *cancelling, 201*
  - *pausing, 200*
  - *resuming printing, 201*

processors, 7, 10
PROCOMM PLUS (communications program), 550
PRODIGY (online services)
- bulletin boards
  - *Careers, 250*
  - *Computers, 250*
  - *defined, 239*
  - *posting messages to, 250-254*
  - *reading articles, 247-249*
  - *replying to messages on, 253*
- connecting to, 239-242
- customer support telephone number, 239
- mail
  - *addresses, 274*
  - *reading, 245*
  - *sending, 243-246*
- passwords, 240
- services
  - *browsing, 247-249*
  - *defined, 239*
  - *jumping to new, 239*
- starting, 225
- toolbars, 239

Profit (accounting program), 574
program files
- defined, 51, 112, 388
- deleting to increase computer speed, 388-390

program groups
- defined, 64
- designing/editing, 65-67
- icons
  - *defined, 62, 64, 68*
  - *designing, 65*
  - *double-clicking, 62*
  - *moving, 67*
  - *Windows 95, 174*
- opening/closing, 64

Program Manager, 62-63
program windows, resizing (Windows 95), 157-158
program-item icons
- defined, 62, 68
- deleting, 67
- double-clicking, 62

programs
- 3-D Dinosaur Adventure, 558
- Access, 552
- accounting, 547, 572-574
- Adobe Illustrator, 570
- Alpha Five, 552
- American Heritage Talking Dictionary, 564
- Ami Pro, 578
- Ancient Lands, 556
- applets
  - *defined, 192*
  - *DiskDefragmenter, 192-193*
  - *ScanDisk, 192-193*
- Approach, 552
- Arthur Teacher's Trouble, 558
- Ascend, 574
- Backup, 193
- Bodyworks, 556
- Bookshelf, 564
- Bug Adventure, 558
- CA-Simply Accounting, 572
- Calculator, 192
- CD Player, 193
- Character Map, 192
- Chessmaster 4000, 566
- Cinemania, 556
- ClarisWorks, 570
- Clipboard Viewer, 192
- Columbia Electronic Dictionary of Quotations, 564
- Commence, 574
- communications, 546
  - *list of, 550*
- Compton's Interactive Encyclopedia, 564
- Corel Ventura, 554
- CorelDRAW!, 570
- Creative Writer, 558
- Crosstalk, 550
- DacEasy, 572
- database, 546
  - *list of, 552*
- dBASE 5, 552
- desktop publishing, 546
  - *list of, 554*
- DeskTop Set, 574
- Dial-Up Networking, 192
- Dinosaurs, 560
- Direct Cable Connection, 192
- DOOM, 566
- DOS
  - *exiting, 233-234*
  - *installing with a Setup program, 364-365*
  - *menus in, 227-228*
  - *shell out to DOS, 233-234*
  - *starting from DOS prompt, 225-226*
  - *uninstalling, 378-380*
- drawing/graphics, 547, 570
- DriveSpace, 193
- ECCO Professional, 574

educational, 546-547
adult, 556-558
childrens, 558-562
reference, 564-566
Encarta, 564
Excel, 576
exiting, 98
Fax, 193
financial (personal finance), 547, 572-574
Fine Artist, 560
FoxPro, 552
Fractal Design Painter, 570
FrameMaker, 554
French Assistant, 556
games, 547, 566-568
Games, 193
HyperACCESS, 550
HyperTerminal, 192
installing from a ZIP file (container file), 374-377
integrated packages, 547, 570-572
Just Grandma and Me, 560
Kid Works 2, 560
Kid's Zoo, 560
King's Quest VII: The Prince-less Bride, 566
Kiplinger's Simply Money, 572
Links 386 Pro, 566
Lotus 1-2-3, 576
Lotus SmartSuite, 578
M.Y.O.B., 572
Managing Your Money, 572
Math Ace, 560
Math Blaster: In Search Of Spot, 560
Mavis Beacon Teaches, 556
Media Player, 193
Microsoft Arcade, 566
Microsoft Complete, 556
Microsoft Exchange, 193
Microsoft Golf, 568
Microsoft Musical, 556
Microsoft Network, 193
Microsoft Office, 578
Microsoft Word, 578
Microsoft Works, 570
Miracle Piano Teaching, 556
Money, 572
Multimedia, 193
MyAdvancedBrochures, 554
Myst, 568
New Grolier Multimedia Encyclopedia, 564
New Kid on the Block, The, 562
Notepad, 192
Organizer, 576
PackRat, 576
PageMaker, 554
Paint, 192
Paradox, 552
PC Paintbrush, 570
PeachTree Accounting, 574
PerfectOffice, 578
personal organizers, 547, 574-576
PFS: Publisher, 554
PFS:WindowWorks, 570
PharmAssist, 556
Phone Dialer, 192
Prehistoria, 562
Print Shop Deluxe, 554
PROCOMM PLUS, 550
Profit, 574
Publisher, 554
Q&A, 552
QmodemPro, 550
QuarkXPress, 554
Quattro Pro, 576
QuickBooks, 574
Quicken, 574
Random House Unabridged Dictionary, 564
Reader Rabbit, 562
references, 546-547
Return to Zork, 568
Seventh Guest, The, 568
Sharkware, 576
SideKick, 576
SimCity 2000, 568
Smartcom, 550
Software Toolworks, 566
Sound Recorder, 193
Spanish Assistant, 558
Sportsworks, 558
spreadsheets, 547-548, 576
starting
by double-clicking program-item icons, 64
with Start button (Windows 95), 157-158
Strike Commander, 568
suites, 548, 578
switching between, 70
Tortoise and the Hare, The, 562
Typing Tutor, 558
Ultima VIII: Pagan, 568
Undersea Adventure, 562
Visio, 570
Volume Control, 193
Where in the World is Carmen Sandiego? (geography), 562
WinComm PRO, 550
Windows 3.11
installing with a Setup program, 366-373
starting, 38
uninstalling, 381-383
Windows 95
built-in programs list (applets), 192-194
deleting from hard disk, 168-171
installing, 168-171
uninstalling, 384-386
starting, 38, 194
Undelete, 448-453
uninstalling, 170
WinFax PRO, 550
word processing, 548-578
WordPad, 192
WordPerfect, 578
WordPerfect Works, 572
X-Wing, 568
Your Personal Trainer for the SAT, 558
providers, *see* service providers
PSI (service provider), 316
Publisher (desktop publishing program), 554
pull-down menus, opening, 72
Purge Print Jobs command (Printer menu), 200

Q&A (database program), 552
starting, 225
QmodemPro (communications program), 550
QuarkXPress (desktop publishing program), 554
Quattro Pro (spreadsheet program), 576
starting, 225
question mark (?), wild card character, 90, 130
queue (printing), defined, 195
Quick Search command (Search menu; PRODIGY), 249
QuickBooks (accounting program), 574

Quicken (accounting program), 574
  starting, 225
Quit command (File menu), 30, 233
quitting, *see* exiting

R

RAM (Random-Access Memory), 8
  defined, 10, 13, 402
  Multimedia PC 2 standard, 16
  system requirements, 10
Random House Unabridged Dictionary program, 564
Reader Rabbit program (childrens program), 562
reading from disks, defined, 48-50
rebooting (warm-boot), 41-42
  Windows 95 in safe mode, 150
Receive command (Transfer menu; Terminal), 313
recording sound, *see* sound cards
Recycle Bin (Windows 95), 154, 183
Recycle Bin Properties dialog box, 190
reference software, 546-547, 564-566
relational database programs, defined, 546
removing
  CD-ROMs (Compact Disc Read-Only Memory), 34-35
  computer cover, 350
  floppy disks, 31-43
  see also deleting
Rename command (File menu), 130
Rename dialog box, 131
renaming
  directories, 130-131
  files, 130-131
    Windows 95, 185-186
  folders, My Computer, 185-186
Reset button, cold booting with, 43
resizing windows, 63
Restore button (Windows 95), 157
Restore command (File menu), 184
restoring windows, 80-82
Return to Zork program (game), 568
right-clicking mouse, 39-40
root directory (main directory), 55, 217
Run command (File menu), 60, 69
Run dialog box, 60
running programs, *see* starting

S

/s switch (Standard mode), 58
safe mode (Windows 95), 150
Sandiego, Carmen (Where in the World Is Carmen Sandiego?) program, 562
Save command (File menu), 30, 92
Save All command (File menu), 232
Save As command (File menu), 94
Save As dialog box, 92
saving
  before shutting down, 30
  documents, 92-93
  files, 92-93
    and renaming, 94
    automatically, 95
    DOS, 232
ScanDisk program (Windows 95), 192-193
(error checking disks), 454-457
scanners, defined, 13, 15
screen display, *see* desktop
screen savers
  defined, 202
  switching (Windows 95), 202
screens, *see* monitors
scroll bars, 79
scrolling
  in dialog boxes, 79
  windows, 64
Search command (File menu), 145
Search menu commands (PRODIGY), Quick Search, 249
Search Results window, 144
searching
  for files
    Windows 3.11, 144-145
    with wild card characters, 90
  Help topics, 86
sectors on disks, 47
  clusters of, 51
Select All command (Edit menu), 178
Select Drive command (Disk menu), 102
Select Drive dialog box, 102
Select Files command (File menu), 112, 115
selecting, 39
  commands with mouse, 38
  dialog box items, 75
    with keyboard, 76
    with mouse, 38
  directories, 105
  directory windows (open), 109
  files, 112-116
    nonadjacent, 114
    Windows 95, 177-178
  folders, Windows 95, 177-178
  Help topics, 85
  location of computer, 20-21
  menus
    commands, 71-73
    with mouse, 38
  toolbar icons, 71-73
  windows, 80-83
Send command (Transfer menu; Terminal), 313
Serial Line Internet Protocol (SLIP), 316
serial ports, defined, 12, 421
servers, 316
  addresses, 317
  connecting to (Windows Terminal), 318-321
service providers, 318
  defined, 316
  e-mail address, 318
  list of, 317
  user ID, 318
services
  defined, 239
  Internet services, 316
  see also BBS (Bulletin Board System); online services
Services menu commands (CompuServe), Go, 272
Set as Wallpaper command (File menu), 201
setup instructions, 22-25
setup programs
  DOS, 364-365
  Windows 3.11, 366-368
Seventh Guest program, The (game), 568

shareware, defined, 269
Sharkware (personal organizer program), 576
shell out to DOS, 233-234
shortcut icons (Windows 95)
  designing, 188-189
  printer, designing, 200
shortcut menus (Windows 95), 161-162
  displaying, 39
shut down (Windows 95), 30, 150-153
Shut Down Windows dialog box, 153
SideKick (personal organizer program), 576
SimCity 2000 program (game), 568
sites (servers), 316
  addresses, 317
  connecting to (Windows Terminal), 318-321
sizing
  taskbar (Windows 95), 160
  windows, 80-83
    DOS, 172
    Windows 95, 157-158
slimline system units, 10
SLIP (Serial Line Internet Protocol) accounts, 316
slots (expansion slots), 11, 14
Small Icons command (View menu), 173
Smartcom (communications program), 550
software
  accounting software, 547, 572-574
  buying decisions, 4-6
  communications software, 546
    list of, 550
  database software, 546
    list of, 552
  desktop publishing software, 546
    list of, 554
  drawing/graphics software, 547, 570
  educational software, 546-547
    adult, 556-558
    childrens, 558-562
    reference, 564-566
  financial (personal finance) software, 547, 572, 574
  game software, 547, 566-568
  integrated packages, 17, 547, 570-572
  personal organizers (information managers), 547, 574-576
  reference software, 546-547
  shareware, defined, 269
  spreadsheet software, 547-548, 576
  suites, 548, 578
  word processing software, 548-578
  system requirements, 7-9
  see also programs
Software Toolworks program, 566
Sort by Date command (View menu), 138
Sort by Name command (View menu), 138
Sort by Size command (View menu), 138
Sort by Type command (View menu), 138
sorting files (Windows 3.11), 138-139
sound cards, 15
  balance, adjusting, 159
  installing, 432-434
  microphones, connecting, 24-25
  Multimedia PC 2 standard, 16
  speakers, 24-25, 430-431
  system requirements, 12
  volume, adjusting, 159
Sound Recorder program (Windows 95), 193
Spanish Assistant program, 558
speakers, 15
  connecting to sound card, 24-25, 430-431
  shielded, 430
  system requirements, 12
  volume, adjusting, 430
  see also microphones; sound cards
special characters, wild card characters, 90
  renaming files with, 130-131
spinner buttons (dialog boxes), 76-77
Sportsworks program, 558
spreadsheets, *see* databases
Standard mode (startup mode), 58
Start buttons (Windows 95), 154
  starting programs with, 157-158
Start menu commands, Help, 152
starting
  Explorer (Windows 95), 174
  File Manager, 100-101
  files, 87-88, 113-116
  Help (Windows 95), 163
  My Computer, 175
  programs
    by double-clicking program-item icons, 64
    DOS, 225-226
    with Start button (Windows 95), 157-158
  rebooting Windows 95 (warm boot), 150
  Windows 3.1, 58-59
    programs, 38
  Windows 95, 58-59, 150-153
    built-in programs (applets), 194
    programs, 38, 68-69
    rebooting (warm-boot), 41
startup, 28
  cold-boot (restarting), 43
  fixing problems, 28-29
  loading Windows automatically at, 60-61
  rebooting (warm-boot), 41-42
  startup disk, creating, 394-397
startup command (DOS), 225-226
startup files, editing in DOS/Windows 3.11, 412-414
startup modes, 58
Strike Commander program (game), 568
subdirectories, 56, 217
  displaying, 105
submenus, displaying, 73
suites (software suites), 548, 578
Super VGA (SVGA) monitor, 8, 11
surge suppressors (protector), 13, 15
  connecting all components to, 28
  installing, 353-354
  selecting, 353-354
  system requirements, 13
  turning on/off, 29-30
SVGA (Super VGA) monitor, 8, 11

switches
- defined, 58
- in DOS command lines, 212, 226

switching
- between programs, 70
- directory window views, 107-108

SX processors, 10
syntax (DOS commands), 212
sysops (SYStem OPerators), 310
system files
- backups, 444-447
- defined, 112
- undeleting, 448-453

system operators (sysops), 310
system requirements, 548
- bus types, 12
- CPU (Central Processing Unit), 10
- DOS (Disk Operating System), 548
- drives, 11
- hardware, 11-13
- Multimedia PC 2 standard (multimedia-compliant), 16
- RAM (Random-Access Memory), 10
- scanners, 13
- UPS (Uninterruptable Power Supply), 13
- Windows 3.1, 548
- Windows 95, 548

system unit, 13
- defined, 10
- plugging in to power source, 24
- turning on/off, 29-30

SYSTEM.INI files, 412, 445
- backups, 444-447

T

tabs
- in dialog boxes, 75, 77

tape backup drives
- cleaning, 347-348
- defined, 347

taskbar (Windows 95), 154, 159
- customizing, 160

Terminal
- connecting
  - *to a BBS, 310-312*
  - *to Internet sites (servers), 318-321*
- downloading/uploading files, 313-315

text, copying/moving, 39
text boxes (dialog boxes), 75-76
tiling windows, 80, 83
- directory windows, 110-112
- Windows 95, 160

time display
- in DOS prompt, 213
- Windows 95 taskbar, 159

title bar, defined, 62, 80
toggling commands, 73
Toolbar command (View menu), 174
toolbars
- icons
  - *list of, 71*
  - *selecting, 71-73*
- online services
  - *America Online, 255*
  - *CompuServe, 271*
  - *PRODIGY screen, 239*
- Windows 95, displaying, 174

Tools menu commands, User Setup, 95
Tortoise and the Hare, The (childrens program), 562
Tour: Ten minutes to using Windows icon (Windows 95), 165
tower system units, 10
tracks on disks, defined, 47, 51
transfer rate (CD-ROMs), 11
Transfers menu commands (Terminal)
- Receive, 313
- Send, 313

Tree and Directory command (View menu), 107
Tree menu commands, 104
- Expand All, 104, 125, 132
- Expand Branch, 104
- Expand One Level, 104

Tree Only command (View menu), 107, 108
Tree view, switching, 107
TurboTax program, starting, 225
Typing Tutor program, 558

U

Ultima VIII: Pagan program (game), 568
Undelete program (Windows 95), 448-453
undeleting files, 448-453
Undersea Adventure (childrens program), 562
uninstalling programs
- defined, 378
- DOS, 378-380
- in Windows 95, 384, 386
- Windows 3.11, 381-383

uploading files (Terminal), 313-315
UPS (Uninterruptable Power Supply), 13, 15
User Group Locator (finding BBSs), 310
User Setup command (Tools menu), 95
User Setup dialog box, 95

V

vertical hash mark (|), as pointer, 38
vertical printing (portrait orientation), 196
VGA (Video Graphics Array) monitor, 8, 11
video cards, Multimedia PC 2 standard, 16
View menu commands
- All File Details, 143
- Arrange Icons, 173
- By File Type, 141
- Details, 173
- Directory Only, 107-108
- Large Icons, 173
- Line Up Icons, 173
- List, 173
- Small Icons, 173
- Sort by Date, 138
- Sort by Name, 138
- Sort by Size, 138
- Sort by Type, 138
- Toolbar, 174
- Tree and Directory, 107
- Tree Only, 107-108

viewing
- directories, 104-106
- drives in File Manager, 102-103
- Windows 95
  - *documents while printing, 159*
  - *Welcome screen, 152*

viruses, checking for (Microsoft AntiVirus), 469-470
Visio (drawing program), 570
Volume Control program (Window 95), 193

W

wallpaper (Windows 95 desktop)
- customizing, 202
- defined, 202

warm-boot (rebooting), 41-42
- Windows 95 in safe mode, 150

warranties, 18

Welcome screen (Windows 95), viewing, 152

Where in the World is Carmen Sandiego? (childrens geography program), 562

wild card characters, 90
- renaming files with, 130-131

WIN.INI files, 412
- backups, 444-447
- defined, 444

WinCIM (CompuServe Information Manager for Windows), 271

WinComm PRO (communications program), 550

Window menu commands, 72

windows
- border, 80
- cascading, 80, 83
- closing, 80, 83
- directory windows
  - *cascading, 110-112*
  - *closing, 110-112*
  - *defined, 102*
  - *displaying, 102-103*
  - *moving, 110*
  - *opening, 109-111*
  - *selecting open window, 109*
  - *tiling, 110-112*
- DOS (Disk Operating System), resizing, 172
- maximizing, 63, 82
  - *defined, 80*
- minimizing, 63, 82
  - *defined, 80*
- moving, 62, 81
- My Computer, closing, 176
- resizing, 63, 80-82
- restoring, 80
- scrolling, 64
- Search Results window, 144
- selecting, 80-83
- sizing, 80-83
- tiling, 80, 83
- title bar, 80
- Windows 95
  - *cascading, 160*
  - *Close button, 157*
  - *Control-menu box, 157*
  - *customizing, 204*
  - *Maximize button, 157*
  - *Minimize button, 157*
  - *resizing, 157-158*
  - *Restore button, 157*
  - *tiling, 160*

Windows 3.1
- applications, starting, 38
- documents, printing, 96
- files, opening, 89-91
- Help, 84-86
- loading automatically at startup, 60-61
- program groups
  - *designing/editing, 65-67*
  - *opening/closing, 64*
- Program Manager, 62-63
- shutting down, 30
- starting, 58-59, 68-69
- system requirements, 548

Windows 3.11
- directories, searching for, 144-145
- disks, formatting, 146-148
- files
  - *display options, 142-143*
  - *editing startup files, 412-414*
  - *hiding temporarily, 140-141*
  - *searching for, 144-145*
  - *sorting list of, 138-139*
- installing
  - *uninstalling, 381-383*
  - *with a Setup program, 366-368*
  - *without a Setup program, 369-371*

Windows 95
- CD-ROM drive, adjusting balance and volume, 159
- commands, entering, 161-162
- desktop, 154
  - *customizing, 201-206*
  - *date display, 155*
  - *display resolution, 206*
  - *editing object properties, 190-191*
  - *My Computer icon, 154*
  - *Network Neighborhood icon, 154*
  - *patterns, 201*
  - *Recycle Bin, 154, 183*
  - *screen savers, 202*
  - *Start button, 154*
  - *taskbar, 154, 159*
  - *wallpaper, 201*
- Dial-Up Networking (Internet connections), 322-323
- dialog boxes, 161-162
- documents, printing, 96
- DOS prompt, displaying, 172
- DriveSpace program, running, 410-411
- exiting, 30, 150-153
- Explorer, 173
  - *drive list, 174*
  - *exiting, 175*
  - *file/folder list, 174*
  - *starting, 174*
- files/folders
  - *arranging icons for, 173*
  - *copying, 179-181*
  - *deleting, 182-184*
  - *designing, 187*
  - *extensions, 173*
  - *identifying file types, 173-176*
  - *long filenames, 185*
  - *moving, 179-181*
  - *naming, 53*
  - *opening, 89-91*
  - *renaming, 185-186*
  - *restoring deletions, 182-184*
  - *selecting, 177-178*
- hard disk drive, defragmenting files, 398-401
- hardware
  - *installing, 439-441*
  - *plug-and-play hardware, 439*
  - *removing, 386*
- Help, 84-86, 163-167
  - *exiting, 165*
  - *index, 166*
- icons
  - *arranging, 173*
  - *document icons, 174*
  - *DOS program icons, 174*
  - *program icons, 174*
  - *shortcut icons, 188-189*
  - *Tour: Ten minutes to using Windows icon, 165*
- keyboard, configuring settings, 209-210
- loading automatically at startup, 60-61
- microphone, adjusting balance and volume, 159
- mouse, configuring settings, 207-210
- My Computer, 173
  - *starting, 175*

printers
- *changing settings, 195-200*
- *installing, 198*
- *print quality, 196*

printing, cancelling/pausing/resuming, 201

program groups
- *designing/editing, 65-67*
- *opening/closing, 64*

programs
- *built-in programs list (applets), 192-194*
- *deleting from hard disk, 168-171*
- *installing, 168-171, 372-373*
- *ScanDisk (error checking), 454-457*
- *starting, 38, 157-158*
- *Undelete, 448-453*
- *uninstalling, 170, 384-386*

safe mode, 150

sound cards, adjusting balance and volume, 159

starting, 58-59, 68-69, 150-153
- *rebooting (warm-boot), 41*

system requirements, 548

taskbar, customizing, 160

toolbar, displaying, 174

windows
- *cascading, 160*
- *Close button, 157*
- *Control-menu box, 157*
- *customizing, 204*
- *Maximize button, 157*
- *Minimize button, 157*
- *resizing, 157-158*
- *Restore button, 157*
- *tiling, 160*

wizards
- *Add New Hardware Wizard, 439-441*
- *Add Printer Wizard, 197*
- *Install New Program Wizard, 168, 372-373*

Windows Explorer, *see* Explorer

Windows Terminal, *see* Terminal

WinFax PRO (communications program), 550

wizards, 87
- Windows 95
  - *Add New Hardware Wizard, 439-441*
  - *Add Printer Wizard, 197*
  - *Install New Program Wizard, 168, 372-373*

Word (word processing program), 578

word processing software, 548-578
- buying, 4

WordPad program (Windows 95), 192

WordPerfect (word processing program), 578
- starting, 225

WordPerfect Works (integrated software package), 570-572

WordStar program, starting, 225

write-protection (floppy disks), 33, 168

writing to disks, defined, 48-50

X-Y-Z

X-Wing program (game), 568

Your Personal Trainer for the SAT program, 558

ZIP files (container files)
- decompressing (with PKUNZIP), 375
- installing programs from, 374-377

Complete and Return this Card for a *FREE* Computer Book Catalog

Thank you for purchasing this book! You have purchased a superior computer book written expressly for your needs. To continue to provide the kind of up-to-date, pertinent coverage you've come to expect from us, we need to hear from you. Please take a minute to complete and return this self-addressed, postage-paid form. In return, we'll send you a free catalog of all our computer books on topics ranging from word processing to programming and the internet.

Mr. ☐ Mrs. ☐ Ms. ☐ Dr. ☐

Name (first) ☐☐☐☐☐☐☐☐☐☐☐ (M.I.) ☐ (last) ☐☐☐☐☐☐☐☐☐☐☐☐☐☐☐

Address ☐☐☐☐☐☐☐☐☐☐☐☐☐☐☐☐☐☐☐☐☐☐☐☐☐☐☐☐☐☐☐☐☐☐☐

City ☐☐☐☐☐☐☐☐☐☐☐☐☐☐☐ State ☐☐ Zip ☐☐☐☐☐ ☐☐☐☐

Phone ☐☐☐ ☐☐☐ ☐☐☐☐ Fax ☐☐☐ ☐☐☐ ☐☐☐☐

Company Name ☐☐☐☐☐☐☐☐☐☐☐☐☐☐☐☐☐☐☐☐☐☐☐☐☐☐☐☐☐☐☐☐☐

E-mail address ☐☐☐☐☐☐☐☐☐☐☐☐☐☐☐☐☐☐☐☐☐☐☐☐☐☐☐☐☐☐☐☐☐

1. Please check at least (3) influencing factors for purchasing this book.

Front or back cover information on book .... ☐
Special approach to the content .... ☐
Completeness of content .... ☐
Author's reputation .... ☐
Publisher's reputation .... ☐
Book cover design or layout .... ☐
Index or table of contents of book .... ☐
Price of book .... ☐
Special effects, graphics, illustrations .... ☐
Other (Please specify): ______________________ ☐

2. How did you first learn about this book?

Saw in Macmillan Computer Publishing catalog .... ☐
Recommended by store personnel .... ☐
Saw the book on bookshelf at store .... ☐
Recommended by a friend .... ☐
Received advertisement in the mail .... ☐
Saw an advertisement in: ______________________ ☐
Read book review in: ______________________ ☐
Other (Please specify): ______________________ ☐

3. How many computer books have you purchased in the last six months?

This book only .... ☐ 3 to 5 books .... ☐
2 books .... ☐ More than 5 .... ☐

4. Where did you purchase this book?

Bookstore .... ☐
Computer Store .... ☐
Consumer Electronics Store .... ☐
Department Store .... ☐
Office Club .... ☐
Warehouse Club .... ☐
Mail Order .... ☐
Direct from Publisher .... ☐
Internet site .... ☐
Other (Please specify): ______________________ ☐

5. How long have you been using a computer?

☐ Less than 6 months ☐ 6 months to a year
☐ 1 to 3 years ☐ More than 3 years

6. What is your level of experience with personal computers and with the subject of this book?

	With PCs	With subject of book
New	☐	☐
Casual	☐	☐
Accomplished	☐	☐
Expert	☐	☐

Source Code ISBN: 0-5676-1-624-0

7. Which of the following best describes your job title?

- Administrative Assistant ☐
- Coordinator ☐
- Manager/Supervisor ☐
- Director ☐
- Vice President ☐
- President/CEO/COO ☐
- Lawyer/Doctor/Medical Professional ☐
- Teacher/Educator/Trainer ☐
- Engineer/Technician ☐
- Consultant ☐
- Not employed/Student/Retired ☐
- Other (Please specify): ________ ☐

8. Which of the following best describes the area of the company your job title falls under?

- Accounting ☐
- Engineering ☐
- Manufacturing ☐
- Operations ☐
- Marketing ☐
- Sales ☐
- Other (Please specify): ________ ☐

9. What is your age?

- Under 20 ☐
- 21-29 ☐
- 30-39 ☐
- 40-49 ☐
- 50-59 ☐
- 60-over ☐

10. Are you:

- Male ☐
- Female ☐

11. Which computer publications do you read regularly? (Please list)

____

Comments: ________

Fold here and scotch-tape to mail.

NO POSTAGE NECESSARY IF MAILED IN THE UNITED STATES

BUSINESS REPLY MAIL

FIRST-CLASS MAIL PERMIT NO. 9918 INDIANAPOLIS IN

POSTAGE WILL BE PAID BY THE ADDRESSEE

ATTN MARKETING
MACMILLAN COMPUTER PUBLISHING
MACMILLAN PUBLISHING USA
201 W 103RD ST
INDIANAPOLIS IN 46209-9042